Principles of Computer Security

Fourth Edition

Principles of Computer Security

Fourth Edition

Wm. Arthur Conklin
Gregory White
Dwayne Williams
Roger Davis
Chuck Cothren

New York   Chicago   San Francisco
Athens   London   Madrid   Mexico City
Milan   New Delhi   Singapore   Sydney   Toronto

Cataloging-in-Publication Data is on file with the Library of Congress

Principles of Computer Security, Fourth Edition

1234567890   RMN RMN   1098765

ISBN: Book p/n 978-0-07-183598-5 and CD p/n 978-0-07-183599-2 of set 978-0-07-183597-8

MHID: Book p/n 0-07-183598-9 and CD p/n 0-07-183599-7 of set 0-07-183597-0

Sponsoring Editors
MEGHAN MANFRE, TIMOTHY GREEN

Editorial Supervisor
JODY McKENZIE

Project Editor
HOWARD SEVERSON, FORTUITOUS PUBLISHING

Acquisitions Coordinator
AMY STONEBRAKER

Technical Editor
BOBBY E. ROGERS

Copy Editor
BILL McMANUS

Proofreaders
PAUL TYLER, RICHARD CAMP

Indexer
JACK LEWIS

Production Supervisor
JAMES KUSSOW

Composition
CENVEO® PUBLISHING SERVICES

Art Director, Cover
JEFF WEEKS

About the Authors

Dr. Wm. Arthur Conklin is an associate professor and Director of the Center for Information Security Research and Education in the College of Technology at the University of Houston. He holds two terminal degrees, a Ph.D. in Business Administration (specializing in Information Security) from The University of Texas at San Antonio (UTSA) and the degree Electrical Engineer (specializing in Space Systems Engineering) from the Naval Postgraduate School in Monterey, CA. He holds CompTIA Security+, CISSP, CSSLP, CRISC, DFCP, GICSP, and CASP certifications. An ISSA Fellow, he is also a senior member of ASQ and a member of IEEE and ACM. His research interests include the use of systems theory to explore information security, specifically in cyber-physical systems. He has coauthored six security books and numerous academic articles associated with information security. He is active in the DHS-sponsored Industrial Control Systems Joint Working Group (ICSJWG) efforts associated with workforce development and cybersecurity aspects of industrial control systems. He has an extensive background in secure coding and is a former co-chair of the DHS/DoD Software Assurance Forum working group for workforce education, training, and development.

Dr. Gregory White has been involved in computer and network security since 1986. He spent 19 years on active duty with the U.S. Air Force and is currently in the Air Force Reserves assigned to the Pentagon. He obtained his Ph.D. in Computer Science from Texas A&M University in 1995. His dissertation topic was in the area of computer network intrusion detection, and he continues to conduct research in this area today. He is currently the Director for the Center for Infrastructure Assurance and Security and is an associate professor of computer science at The University of Texas at San Antonio. Dr. White has written and presented numerous articles and conference papers on security. He is also the coauthor for five textbooks on computer and network security and has written chapters for two other security books. Dr. White continues to be active in security research. His current research initiatives include efforts in high-speed intrusion detection, community infrastructure protection, and visualization of community and organization security postures.

Dwayne Williams is Associate Director, Special Projects for the Center for Infrastructure Assurance and Security (CIAS) at the University of Texas at San Antonio and has more than 22 years of experience in information systems and network security. Mr. Williams's experience includes six years of commissioned military service as a Communications-Computer Information Systems Officer in the U.S. Air Force, specializing in network security, corporate information protection, intrusion detection systems, incident response, and VPN technology. Prior to joining the CIAS, he served as Director of Consulting for SecureLogix Corporation, where he directed and provided security assessment and integration services to Fortune 100, government, public utility, oil and gas, financial, and technology clients. Mr. Williams graduated in 1993 from Baylor University with a Bachelor of Arts in Computer Science. Mr. Williams is a Certified Information Systems Security Professional (CISSP), CompTIA Advanced Security Practitioner (CASP), and coauthor of McGraw-Hill's *Voice and Data Security*, *CompTIA Security+ All-in-One Exam Guide*, and *CASP CompTIA Advanced Security Practitioner Certification Study Guide*.

Roger L. Davis, CISSP, CISM, CISA, is an Account Manager for Microsoft. He has served as president of the Utah chapter of the Information Systems Security Association (ISSA) and various board positions for the Utah chapter of the Information Systems Audit and Control Association (ISACA). He is a retired Air Force lieutenant colonel with 35 years of military and information systems/security experience. Mr. Davis served on the faculty of Brigham Young University and the Air Force Institute of Technology. He coauthored McGraw-Hill's *CompTIA Security+ All-in-One Exam Guide* and *Voice and Data Security*. He holds a Master's degree in Computer Science from George Washington University, a Bachelor's degree in Computer Science from Brigham Young University, and performed post-graduate studies in electrical engineering and computer science at the University of Colorado.

Chuck Cothren, CISSP, is a Principal Solutions Specialist at Symantec Corporation applying a wide array of network security experience, including performing controlled penetration testing, incident response, and security management to assist a wide variety of clients in the protection of their critical data. He has also analyzed security methodologies for Voice over Internet Protocol (VoIP) systems and supervisory control and data acquisition (SCADA) systems. He is coauthor of the books *Voice and Data Security*, and *CompTIA Security+ All-in-One Exam Guide*.

About the Technical Editor

Bobby E. Rogers is an Information Security Engineer working as a contractor for Department of Defense agencies, helping to secure, certify, and accredit their information systems. His duties include information system security engineering, risk management, and certification and accreditation efforts. He retired after 21 years in the United States Air Force, serving as a network security engineer and instructor, and has secured networks all over the world. Bobby has a Master's degree in Information Assurance (IA), and is pursuing a doctoral degree in Cybersecurity from Capitol Technology University, Maryland. His many certifications include CRISC, CISSP-ISSEP, C | EH, and MCSE: Security as well as the CompTIA A+, Network+, Security+, and Mobility+ certifications.

■ Acknowledgments

We, the authors of *Principles of Computer Security, Fourth Edition*, have many individuals who we need to acknowledge—individuals without whom this effort would not have been successful. This edition would not have been possible without Tim Green, whose support and faith in the authors made this edition possible. He brought together an all-star production team that made this book more than just a new edition, but a complete learning system.

The list needs to start with those folks at McGraw-Hill Education who worked tirelessly with the project's multiple authors and contributors and led us successfully through the minefield that is a book schedule and who took our rough chapters and drawings and turned them into a final, professional product we can be proud of. We thank all the good people from the Acquisitions team, Tim Green and Amy Stonebraker; from the Editorial Services team, Jody McKenzie and Howie Severson; from the Illustration and Production teams, James Kussow and Amarjeet Kumar and the composition team at Cenveo Publisher Services. We also thank the technical editor, Bobby Rogers; the copy editor, Bill McManus; the proofreader, Paul Tyler; and the indexer, Jack Lewis; for all their attention to detail that made this a finer work after they finished with it.

We also need to acknowledge our current employers who, to our great delight, have seen fit to pay us to work in a career field that we all find exciting and rewarding. There is never a dull moment in security, because it is constantly changing.

We would like to thank Art Conklin for herding the cats on this one.

Finally, we would each like to individually thank those people who—on a personal basis—have provided the core support for us individually. Without these special people in our lives, none of us could have put this work together.

—*The Author Team*

To Susan, your love and support is what enables me to do all the things I do.

—*Art Conklin, Ph.D.*

I would like to thank my wife, Charlan, for the tremendous support she has always given me. It doesn't matter how many times I have sworn that I'll never get involved with another book project only to return within months to yet another one; through it all, she has remained supportive.

I would also like to publicly thank the United States Air Force, which provided me numerous opportunities since 1986 to learn more about security than I ever knew existed.

To whoever it was who decided to send me as a young captain—fresh from completing my master's degree in artificial intelligence—to my first assignment in computer security: thank you, it has been a great adventure!

—*Gregory B. White, Ph.D.*

Josie, thank you for all the love and support. Macon, John, this is for you.

—*Chuck Cothren*

Geena, thanks for being my best friend and my greatest support. Anything I am is because of you. Love to my kids and grandkids!

—*Roger L. Davis*

To my wife and best friend, Leah, for your love, energy, and support—thank you for always being there. Here's to many more years together.

—*Dwayne Williams*

■ *This book is dedicated to the many security professionals who daily work to ensure the safety of our nation's critical infrastructures. We want to recognize the thousands of dedicated individuals who strive to protect our national assets but who seldom receive praise and often are only noticed when an incident occurs. To you, we say thank you for a job well done!*

ABOUT THIS BOOK

■ Important Technology Skills

Information technology (IT) offers many career paths, and information security is one of the fastest-growing tracks for IT professionals. This book provides coverage of the materials you need to begin your exploration of information security. In addition to covering all of the CompTIA Security+ exam objectives, additional material is included to help you build a solid introductory knowledge of information security.

Tech Tip *sidebars provide inside information from experienced IT professionals.*

Key Terms, *identified in red, point out important vocabulary and definitions that you need to know.*

Cross Check *questions develop reasoning skills: ask, compare, contrast, and explain.*

Engaging and Motivational— *Using a conversational style and proven instructional approach, the authors explain technical concepts in a clear, interesting way using real-world examples.*

Makes Learning Fun!— *Rich colorful text and enhanced illustrations bring technical subjects to life.*

Proven Learning Method Keeps You on Track

Designed for classroom use and written by instructors for use in their own classes, *Principles of Computer Security* is structured to give you comprehensive knowledge of information security. The textbook's active learning methodology guides you beyond mere recall and—through thought-provoking activities, labs, and sidebars—helps you develop critical-thinking, diagnostic, and communication skills.

Effective Learning Tools

This feature-rich textbook is designed to make learning easy and enjoyable and to help you develop the skills and critical-thinking abilities that will enable you to adapt to different job situations and to troubleshoot problems. Written by instructors with decades of combined information security experience, this book conveys even the most complex issues in an accessible, easy-to-understand format.

Try This! *exercises apply core skills in a new setting.*

Chapter Review *sections provide concept summaries, key terms lists, and lots of questions and projects.*

Notes, Tips, and **Warnings** *create a road map for success*

Key Terms List *presents the important terms identified in the chapter.*

Offers Practical Experience—
Tutorials and lab assignments develop essential hands-on skills and put concepts in real-world context.

Robust Learning Tools—
Summaries, key terms lists, quizzes, essay questions, and lab projects help you practice skills and measure progress.

Each chapter includes

- **Learning Objectives** that set measurable goals for chapter-by-chapter progress

- **Illustrations** that give you a clear picture of the concepts and technologies

- **Try This!, Cross Check,** and **Tech Tip** sidebars that encourage you to practice and apply concepts in real-world settings

- **Notes, Tips,** and **Warnings** that guide you, and **Exam Tips** that give you advice or provide information specifically related to preparing for the exam

- **Chapter Summaries** and **Key Terms Lists** that provide you with an easy way to review important concepts and vocabulary

- **Challenging End-of-Chapter Tests** that include vocabulary-building exercises, multiple-choice questions, essay questions, and on-the-job lab projects

■ It Pays to Get Certified

In a digital world, digital literacy is an essential survival skill. Certification demonstrates that you have the knowledge and skill to solve technical or business problems in virtually any business environment. CompTIA certifications are highly valued credentials that qualify you for jobs, increased compensation, and promotion.

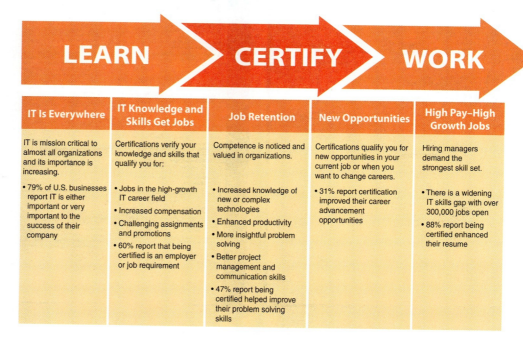

■ CompTIA Security+ Certification Helps Your Career

■ **Security is one of the highest demand job categories,** growing in importance as the frequency and severity of security threats continues to be a major concern for organizations around the world.

- **Jobs for security administrators are expected to increase by 18%**—the skill set required for these types of jobs maps to the CompTIA Security+ certification.

- **Network Security Administrators** can earn as much as $106,000 per year.

- **CompTIA Security+ is the first step** in starting your career as a Network Security Administrator or Systems Security Administrator.

- **More than 250,000** individuals worldwide are CompTIA Security+ certified.

- **CompTIA Security+ is regularly used in organizations** such as Hitachi Systems, Fuji Xerox, HP, Dell, and a variety of major U.S. government contractors.

- **Approved by the U.S. Department of Defense (DoD)** as one of the required certification options in the DoD 8570.01-M directive, for Information Assurance Technical Level II and Management Level I job roles.

■ Steps to Getting Certified and Staying Certified

1. **Review the exam objectives.** Review the certification objectives to make sure you know what is covered in the exam: http://certification.comptia.org/examobjectives.aspx

2. **Practice for the exam.** After you have studied for the certification exam, review and answer sample questions to get an idea of what type of questions might be on the exam: http://certification.comptia.org/samplequestions.aspx

3. **Purchase an exam voucher.** You can purchase exam vouchers on the CompTIA Marketplace, www.comptiastore.com.

4. **Take the test!** Go to the Pearson VUE website, www.pearsonvue.com /comptia/, and schedule a time to take your exam.

5. **Stay certified!** Effective January 1, 2011, new CompTIA Security+ certifications are valid for three years from the date of certification. There are a number of ways the certification can be renewed. For more information go to http://certification.comptia.org/ce.

■ For More Information

- **Visit CompTIA online**   Go to http://certification.comptia.org/home.aspx to learn more about getting CompTIA certified.
- **Contact CompTIA**   Please call 866-835-8020 and choose Option 2, or e-mail questions@comptia.org.
- **Connect with CompTIA**   Find CompTIA on Facebook, LinkedIn, Twitter, and YouTube.

■ Content Seal of Quality

This courseware bears the seal of CompTIA Approved Quality Content. This seal signifies this content covers 100 percent of the exam objectives and implements important instructional design principles. CompTIA recommends multiple learning tools to help increase coverage of the learning objectives.

■ CAQC Disclaimer

The logo of the CompTIA Approved Quality Content (CAQC) program and the status of this or other training material as "Approved" under the CompTIA Approved Quality Content program signifies that, in CompTIA's opinion, such training material covers the content of CompTIA's related certification exam.

The contents of this training material were created for the CompTIA Security+ exam covering CompTIA certification objectives that were current as of the date of publication.

CompTIA has not reviewed or approved the accuracy of the contents of this training material and specifically disclaims any warranties of merchantability or fitness for a particular purpose. CompTIA makes no guarantee concerning the success of persons using any such "Approved" or other training material in order to prepare for any CompTIA certification exam.

CONTENTS AT A GLANCE

CONTENTS

Chapter 8
■ Physical Security   190

Chapter 9
■ Network Fundamentals   220

Chapter 10
■ Infrastructure Security   252

Chapter 14
■ System Hardening and Baselines   408

Chapter 15
■ Types of Attacks and Malicious Software   464

FOREWORD

Selecting a book is tricky for me. If it is for personal reading, will I like reading it? If it is for my professional development, will it meet the need? If it is for my students, will it be clear and concise? This new edition of *Principles of Computer Security* passes all three tests with flying colors. I enjoyed reading it. If I needed to pass the CompTIA Security+ or other practitioner examination, it would prepare me. And finally, based on personal experience, students will like this book and find it to be valuable reading and study material. It even has practice exams for certification and has an e-book for my convenience.

For more than 40 years I have worked in some variety of computer security. When people ask me what defines my job, I respond with "I don't know until I read the morning newspaper because the security environment changes rapidly." If you want to get into the computer security industry, reading and understanding this book is a great introduction. Now in its fourth edition, the 25 chapters of *Principles of Computer Security* focus on a broad spectrum of important topics to prepare the reader to be a certified computer security practitioner. The real deal maker for me is the further endorsement of the contents: the book is based on CompTIA Approved Quality Content (CAQC) and serves as both an exam preparation guide and a useful reference.

Dr. Conklin and his team of coauthors ease the reader into the meat of the topic by reviewing both security trends and concepts. They then address security from two different perspectives. First they focus on the organization's need for security, and then focus on the important role of people. These two perspectives are intertwined; it is essential for a security practitioner to understand the security environment and how the people make it work.

Every practitioner needs to understand the underlying technology and tools of computer security. Some individuals have an idea about security topics but do not have the essential knowledge needed to address them in depth. The authors have provided nine masterful chapters introducing these key concepts. For example, in a single chapter they provide the basis for the reader to deal with security of networks. This chapter supports everything the reader needs to know to address standards and protocols, infrastructure security, remote access and authentication, as well as wireless. The authors integrate these concepts to support public key infrastructure (PKI) and intrusion detection systems for network security without forgetting the importance of physical security in protecting the information system as well as infrastructure.

One of the most debated topics in security is the importance of cryptography. Some would assert that almost all digital security can be accomplished with cryptography, that security and cryptography are inseparable, with cryptography being the cornerstone of securing data in both transmission and storage. However, if computer security were as easy as "encrypt everything," this would be a very short book. While cryptography is very important and a very complex security measure, it is not a panacea—but it does provide for lively discussions. The authors bring all these components together with a comprehensive chapter on intrusion detection and prevention.

Once the reader has mastered the basics, the authors address e-mail, malicious software, instant messaging, and web components in such a way that the reader can apply his or her knowledge of networks and security fundamentals. The reader will then be provided with an overview of secure software development. In 2015, both the U.S. Department of Homeland Security and CSO magazine concluded that poorly developed software is one of the biggest cyber threats—perhaps 90 percent of the threats come through poor software design.

In the final analysis, security is really all about risk management. What is your organization's appetite for risk and how is that risk managed? The chapters covering risk management lead the reader through these less technical issues to gain an understanding how these impact the organization. Baselines and change management are essential to understanding what assets are being secured and how they are being changed. A reader who learns these skills well will be able to work in incident response, disaster recovery, and business continuity. Understanding these processes and how they work with technical issues expands career opportunities.

The authors conclude their review of the principles of computer security with an examination of privacy, legal issues, and ethics. Although these topics appear at the end of the book, they are crucial issues in the modern world. Remember, as a computer security practitioner, you will have legal access to more data and information than any else in the organization.

Although not the last chapter in the book, I have decided to comment on forensics last. The authors have done a wonderful job of addressing this complex topic. But why mention it last? Because many times forensics is what one does after computer security fails. It makes a good epitaph for a wonderful book.

Tonight it is 15 degrees and snowing outside while I sit in my study—warm, dry, and comfortable; my home is my castle. Not bad for mid-winter in Idaho; however, I should not forget that one reason I am comfortable is because certified computer security practitioners are protecting my information and privacy as well as the critical infrastructure that supports it.

For Instructors

I have taught from prior editions of this book and have used its companion laboratory manual for several years. Both *Principles of Computer Security, Fourth Edition* and *Principles of Computer Security Lab Manual, Fourth Edition* have instructor materials on a companion Web site available to adopting instructors. Instructor manuals, including the answers to the end-of-chapter questions, PowerPoint slides, and the test bank of questions for use as quizzes or exams, make preparation a snap.

Corey D. Schou, PhD
Series Editor
University Professor of Informatics
Professor of Computer Science
Director of the National Information Assurance Training and Education Center
Idaho State University

PREFACE

Information and computer security has moved from the confines of academia to mainstream America in the 21st century. Data breaches, information disclosures, and high-profile hacks involving the theft of information and intellectual property seem to be a regular staple of the news. It has become increasingly obvious to everybody that something needs to be done to secure not only our nation's critical infrastructure but also the businesses we deal with on a daily basis. The question is, "Where do we begin?" What can the average information technology professional do to secure the systems that he or she is hired to maintain? One immediate answer is education and training. If we want to secure our computer systems and networks, we need to know how to do this and what security entails.

Our way of life, from commerce to messaging to business communications and even social media, depends on the proper functioning of our worldwide infrastructure. A common thread throughout all of these, however, is technology—especially technology related to computers and communication. Thus, an individual, organization, or nation who wanted to cause damage to this nation could attack it not just with traditional weapons but with computers through the Internet. Complacency is not an option in today's hostile network environment. The protection of our networks and systems is not the sole domain of the information security professional, but rather the responsibility of all who are involved in the design, development, deployment, and operation of the systems that are nearly ubiquitous in our daily lives. With virtually every system we depend upon daily at risk, the attack surface and corresponding risk profile is extremely large. Information security has matured from a series of technical issues to a comprehensive risk management problem, and this book provides the foundational material to engage in the field in a professional manner.

So, where do you, the IT professional seeking more knowledge on security, start your studies? This book offers a comprehensive review of the underlying foundations and technologies associated with securing our systems and networks. The IT world is overflowing with certifications that can be obtained by those attempting to learn more about their chosen profession. The information security sector is no different, and the CompTIA Security+ exam offers a basic level of certification for security. In the pages of this book you will find not only material that can help you prepare for taking the CompTIA Security+ exam but also the basic information that you will need in order to understand the issues involved in securing your computer systems and networks today. In no way is this book the final source for learning all about protecting your organization's systems, but it serves as a point from which to launch your security studies and career.

One thing is certainly true about this field of study—it never gets boring. It constantly changes as technology itself advances. Something else you will find as you progress in your security studies is that no matter how much technology advances and no matter how many new security devices are developed, at its most basic level, the human is still the weak link in the security chain. If you are looking for an exciting area to delve into, then you have certainly chosen wisely. Security offers a challenging blend of technology and people issues. And securing the systems of tomorrow will require everyone to work together, not just security, but developers, operators, and users alike. We, the authors of this book, wish you luck as you embark on an exciting and challenging career path.

Wm. Arthur Conklin, Ph.D.
Gregory B. White, Ph.D.

INTRODUCTION

Computer security is becoming increasingly important today as the number of security incidents steadily climbs. Many corporations are now spending significant portions of their budgets on security hardware, software, services, and personnel. They are spending this money not because it increases sales or enhances the product they provide, but because of the possible consequences should they not take protective actions. Security has become a comprehensive risk management exercise in firms that take the risks seriously.

Why Focus on Security?

Security is not something that we want to have to pay for; it would be nice if we didn't have to worry about protecting our data from disclosure, modification, or destruction from unauthorized individuals, but that is not the environment we find ourselves in today. Instead, we have seen the cost of recovering from security incidents steadily rise along with the rise in the number of incidents themselves. Since hackers have learned how to monetize hacks, the playing field has become significantly more dangerous. There are now incentives for a professional class of hacker with the intent of reaping benefits both long and short term. With the advent of advanced persistent threats, the rise of nation-state hacking, and the increase in criminal activity from botnets to ransomware, the IT playing field is now viewed as a contested environment, one where hacking can result in gains. Law enforcement is too overwhelmed and under-resourced to make a dent in the problem, and the result is a need for trained security practitioners in all business segments—and a further need for security-aware IT personnel in regular IT positions. Security has become a mainstream topic.

A Growing Need for Security Specialists

To protect our computer systems and networks, we will need a significant number of new security professionals trained in the many aspects of computer and network security. This is not an easy task, as the systems connected to the Internet become increasingly complex, with software whose lines of code number in the millions. Understanding why this is such a difficult problem to solve is not hard if you consider how many errors might be present in a piece of software that is several million lines long. When you add the additional factor of how fast software is being developed—from necessity as the market is constantly moving—understanding how errors occur is easy.

Not every "bug" in the software will result in a security hole, but it doesn't take many to affect the Internet community drastically. We can't just blame the vendors for this situation, because they are reacting to the demands of government and industry. Most vendors are fairly adept at developing patches for flaws found in their software, and patches are constantly issued to protect systems from bugs that may introduce security problems. This introduces a whole new problem for managers and administrators—patch management. How important this has become is easily illustrated by how many of the most recent security events have occurred as a result of a security bug for which a patch was available months prior to the security incident; members of the community had not correctly installed the patch, however, thus making the incident possible. One of the reasons this happens is that many of the individuals responsible for installing the patches are not trained to understand the security implications surrounding the hole or the ramifications of not installing the patch. Many of these individuals simply lack the necessary training.

Because of the need for an increasing number of security professionals who are trained to some minimum level of understanding, certifications such as the CompTIA Security+ have been developed. Prospective employers want to know that the individual they are considering hiring knows what to do in terms of security. The prospective employee, in turn, wants to have a way to demonstrate his or her level of understanding, which can enhance the candidate's chances of being hired. The community as a whole simply wants more trained security professionals.

Preparing Yourself for the CompTIA Security+ Exam

Principles of Computer Security, Fourth Edition is designed to help prepare you to take the CompTIA Security+ certification exam. When you pass it, you will demonstrate you have that basic understanding of security that employers are looking for. Passing this certification exam will not be an easy task, for you will need to learn many things to acquire that basic understanding of computer and network security.

How This Book Is Organized

The book is divided into chapters to correspond with the objectives of the exam itself. Some of the chapters are more technical than others—reflecting the nature of the security environment where you will be forced to deal with not only technical details but also other issues such as security policies and procedures as well as training and education. Although many individuals involved in computer and network security have advanced degrees in math, computer science, information systems, or computer or electrical engineering, you do not need this technical background to address security effectively in your organization. You do not need to develop your own cryptographic algorithm, for example; you simply need to be able to understand how cryptography is used, along with its strengths and weaknesses. As you progress in your studies, you will learn that many security problems are caused by the human element. The best technology in the world still ends up being placed in an environment where humans have the opportunity to foul things up—and all too often do.

Onward and Upward

At this point, we hope that you are now excited about the topic of security, even if you weren't in the first place. We wish you luck in your endeavors and welcome you to the exciting field of computer and network security.

For instructor resources, visit www.mhprofessional.com/PrinciplesSecurity4e. Adopting teachers can access the support materials identified below. Contact your McGraw-Hill Education sales representative for details on how to access the materials.

Instructor Materials

The *Principles of Computer Security* companion Web site (www.mhprofessional.com/PrinciplesSecurity4e) provides many resources for instructors:

- Answer keys to the end-of-chapter activities in the textbook
- Answer keys to the lab manual activities (lab manual available separately)
- Engaging PowerPoint slides on the lecture topics (including full-color artwork from the book)
- An Instructor Manual
- Access to test bank files and software that allows you to generate a wide array of paper- or network-based tests, and that features automatic grading
- Hundreds of practice questions and a wide variety of question types and difficulty levels, enabling you to customize each test to maximize student progress
- Blackboard cartridges and other formats may also be available upon request; contact your sales representative

Introduction and Security Trends

Security is mostly a superstition. It does not exist in nature, nor do the children of men as a whole experience it. Avoiding danger is no safer in the long run than outright exposure. Life is either a daring adventure or nothing.

—HELEN KELLER

In this chapter, you will learn how to

- **Define computer security**
- **Discuss common threats and recent computer crimes that have been committed**
- **List and discuss recent trends in computer security**
- **Describe common avenues of attacks**
- **Describe approaches to computer security**
- **Discuss the relevant ethical issues associated with computer security**

Why should we be concerned about computer and network security? All you have to do is turn on the television or read the newspaper to find out about a variety of security problems that affect our nation and the world today. The danger to computers and networks may seem to pale in comparison to the threat of terrorist strikes, but in fact the average citizen is much more likely to be the target of an attack on their own personal computer, or a computer they use at their place of work, than they are to be the direct victim of a terrorist attack. This chapter will introduce you to a number of issues involved in securing your computers and networks from a variety of threats that may utilize any of a number of different attacks.

■ The Computer Security Problem

Fifty years ago companies did not conduct business across the Internet. Online banking and shopping were only dreams in science fiction stories. Today, however, millions of people perform online transactions every day. Companies rely on the Internet to operate and conduct business. Vast amounts of money are transferred via networks, in the form of either bank transactions or simple credit card purchases. Wherever there are vast amounts of money, there are those who will try to take advantage of the environment to conduct fraud or theft. There are many different ways to attack computers and networks to take advantage of what has made shopping, banking, investment, and leisure pursuits a simple matter of "dragging and clicking" (or tapping) for many people. Identity theft is so common today that most everyone knows somebody who's been a victim of such a crime, if they haven't been a victim themselves. This is just one type of criminal activity that can be conducted using the Internet. There are many others and all are on the rise.

Definition of Computer Security

Computer security is not a simple concept to define, and has numerous complexities associated with it. If one is referring to a computer, then it can be considered secure when the computer does what it is supposed to do and only what it is supposed to do. But as was noted earlier, the security emphasis has shifted from the computer to the information being processed. Information security is defined by the information being protected from unauthorized access or alteration and yet is available to authorized individuals when required. When one begins considering the aspects of information, it is important to realize that information is stored, processed, and transferred between machines, and all of these different states require appropriate protection schemes. Information assurance is a term used to describe not just the protection of information, but a means of knowing the level of protection that has been accomplished.

Historical Security Incidents

By examining some of the computer-related crimes that have been committed over the last 30 or so years, we can better understand the threats and security issues that surround our computer systems and networks. Electronic crime can take a number of different forms, but the ones we will examine here fall into two basic categories: crimes in which the computer was the target, and incidents in which a computer was used to perpetrate the act (for example, there are many different ways to conduct bank fraud, one of which uses computers to access the records that banks process and maintain).

We will start our tour of computer crimes with the 1988 Internet worm (Morris worm), one of the first real Internet crime cases. Prior to 1988, criminal activity was chiefly centered on unauthorized access to computer systems and networks owned by the telephone company and companies that provided dial-up access for authorized users. Virus activity also existed prior to 1988, having started in the early 1980s.

Tech Tip

Historical Computer Security

Computer security is an ever-changing issue. Fifty years ago, computer security was mainly concerned with the physical devices that made up the computer. At the time, computers were the high-value items that organizations could not afford to lose. Today, computer equipment is inexpensive compared to the value of the data processed by the computer. Now the high-value item is not the machine, but the information that it stores and processes. This has fundamentally changed the focus of computer security from what it was in the early years. Today the data stored and processed by computers is almost always more valuable than the hardware.

Computer security and information security both refer to a state where the hardware and software perform only desired actions and the information is protected from unauthorized access or alteration and is available to authorized users when required.

The Morris Worm (November 1988)

Robert Morris, then a graduate student at Cornell University, released what has become known as the Internet worm (or the Morris worm). The worm infected roughly 10 percent of the machines then connected to the Internet (which amounted to approximately 6000 infected machines). The worm carried no malicious payload, the program being obviously a "work in progress," but it did wreak havoc because it continually re-infected computer systems until they could no longer run any programs.

Citibank and Vladimir Levin (June–October 1994)

Starting about June of 1994 and continuing until at least October of the same year, a number of bank transfers were made by Vladimir Levin of St. Petersburg, Russia. By the time he and his accomplices were caught, they had transferred an estimated $10 million. Eventually all but about $400,000 was recovered. Levin reportedly accomplished the break-ins by dialing into Citibank's cash management system. This system allowed clients to initiate their own fund transfers to other banks.

Kevin Mitnick (February 1995)

Kevin Mitnick's computer activities occurred over a number of years during the 1980s and 1990s. Arrested in 1995, he eventually pled guilty to four counts of wire fraud, two counts of computer fraud, and one count of illegally intercepting a wire communication and was sentenced to 46 months in jail. In the plea agreement, Mitnick admitted to having gained unauthorized access to a number of different computer systems belonging to companies such as Motorola, Novell, Fujitsu, and Sun Microsystems. He described using a number of different "tools" and techniques, including social engineering, sniffers, and cloned cellular telephones.

Omega Engineering and Timothy Lloyd (July 1996)

On July 30, 1996, a software "time bomb" went off at Omega Engineering, a New Jersey–based manufacturer of high-tech measurement and control instruments. Twenty days earlier, Timothy Lloyd, a computer network program designer, had been dismissed from the company after a period of growing tension between Lloyd and management at Omega. The program that ran on July 30 deleted all of the design and production programs for the company, severely damaging the small firm and forcing the layoff of 80 employees. The program was eventually traced back to Lloyd, who had left it in retaliation for his dismissal.

Worcester Airport and "Jester" (March 1997)

In March of 1997, telephone services to the FAA control tower as well as the emergency services at the Worcester Airport and the community of Rutland, Massachusetts, were cut off for a period of six hours. This disruption occurred as a result of an attack on the phone network by a teenage computer "hacker" who went by the name "Jester."

The Melissa Virus (March 1999)

Melissa is the best known of the early macro-type viruses that attach themselves to documents for programs that have limited macro programming

Tech Tip

Intellectual Curiosity

In the early days of computer crime, much of the criminal activity centered on gaining unauthorized access to computer systems. In many early cases, the perpetrator of the crime did not intend to cause any damage to the computer but was instead on a quest of "intellectual curiosity"—trying to learn more about computers and networks. Today the ubiquitous nature of computers and networks has eliminated the perceived need for individuals to break into computers to learn more about them. While there are still those who dabble in hacking for the intellectual challenge, it is more common today for the intellectual curiosity to be replaced by malicious intent. Whatever the reason, today it is considered unacceptable (and illegal) to gain unauthorized access to computer systems and networks.

capability. The virus, written and released by David Smith, infected about a million computers and caused an estimated $80 million in damages.

The Love Letter Virus (May 2000)

Also known as the "ILOVEYOU" worm and the "Love Bug," the Love Letter virus was written and released by a Philippine student named Onel de Guzman. The virus was spread via e-mail with the subject line of "ILOVEYOU." Estimates of the number of infected machines worldwide have been as high as 45 million, accompanied by a possible $10 billion in damages (it should be noted that figures like these are extremely hard to verify or calculate).

The Code Red Worm (2001)

On July 19, 2001, in a period of 14 hours, over 350,000 computers connected to the Internet were infected by the Code Red worm. The cost estimate for how much damage the worm caused (including variations of the worm released on later dates) exceeded $2.5 billion. The vulnerability was a buffer-overflow condition in Microsoft's IIS web servers, had been known for a month.

The Slammer Worm (2003)

On Saturday, January 25, 2003, the Slammer worm was released. It exploited a buffer-overflow vulnerability in computers running Microsoft SQL Server or SQL Server Desktop Engine. Like the vulnerability in Code Red, this weakness was not new and, in fact, had been discovered and a patch released in July of 2002. Within the first 24 hours of Slammer's release, the worm had infected at least 120,000 hosts and caused network outages and the disruption of airline flights, elections, and ATMs. At its peak, Slammer-infected hosts were generating a reported 1TB of worm-related traffic *every* second. The worm doubled its number of infected hosts every 8 seconds. It is estimated that it took less than 10 minutes to reach global proportions and infect 90 percent of the possible hosts it could infect.

Website Defacements (2006)

In May of 2006, a Turkish hacker using the handle iSKORPiTX successfully hacked over 21,000 websites in a single effort. The rationale for his actions was never determined, and over the next few years he hacked hundreds of thousands of websites, defacing their cover page with a statement of his hack. A nuisance to some, those affected had to clean up their systems, including repairing vulnerabilities, or he would strike again.

Cyberwar? (2007)

In May of 2007, the country of Estonia was crippled by a massive denial-of-service (DoS) cyberattack against all of its infrastructure, firms (banks), and government offices. This attack was traced to IP addresses in Russia, but was never clearly attributed to a government-sanctioned effort.

Operation Bot Roast (2007)

In 2007, the FBI announced that it had conducted Operation Bot Roast, identifying over 1 million botnet crime victims. In the process of dismantling the botnets, the FBI arrested several botnet operators across the United

Tech Tip

Speed of Virus Proliferation

The speed at which the Slammer worm spread served as a wakeup call to security professionals. It drove home the point that the Internet could be adversely impacted in a matter of minutes. This in turn caused a number of professionals to rethink how prepared they needed to be in order to respond to virus outbreaks in the future. A good first step is to apply patches to systems and software as soon as possible. This will often eliminate the vulnerabilities that the worms and viruses are designed to target.

States. Although seemingly a big success, this effort made only a small dent in the vast volume of botnets in operation.

Conficker (2008–2009)

In late 2008 and early 2009, security experts became alarmed when it was discovered that millions of systems attached to the Internet were infected with the Downadup worm. Also known as Conficker, the worm was believed to have originated in Ukraine. Infected systems were not initially damaged beyond having their antivirus solution updates blocked. What alarmed experts was the fact that infected systems could be used in a secondary attack on other systems or networks. Each of these infected systems was part of what is known as a *bot network* (or *botnet*) and could be used to cause a DoS attack on a target or be used for the forwarding of spam e-mail to millions of users.

U.S. Electric Power Grid (2009)

In April 2009, Homeland Security Secretary Janet Napolitano told reporters that the United States was aware of attempts by both Russia and China to break into the U.S. electric power grid, map it out, and plant destructive programs that could be activated at a later date. She indicated that these attacks were not new and had in fact been going on for years. One article in the *Kansas City Star*, for example, reported that in 1997 the local power company, Kansas City Power and Light, encountered perhaps 10,000 attacks for the entire year. By 2009 the company experienced 30–60 million attacks.

 Try This!

Software Patches

One of the most effective measures security professionals can take to address attacks on their computer systems and networks is to ensure that all software is up to date in terms of vendor-released patches. Many of the outbreaks of viruses and worms would have been much less severe if everybody had applied security updates and patches when they were released. For the operating system that you use, go to your favorite web browser to find what patches exist for the operating system and what vulnerabilities or issues the patches were created to address.

Fiber Cable Cut (2009)

On April 9, 2009, a widespread phone and Internet outage hit the San Jose area in California. This outage was not the result of a group of determined hackers gaining unauthorized access to the computers that operate these networks, but instead occurred as a result of several intentional cuts in the physical cables that carry the signals. The cuts resulted in a loss of all telephone, cell phone, and Internet service for thousands of users in the San Jose area. Emergency services such as 911 were also affected, which could have had severe consequences.

The Current Threat Environment

The threats of the past were smaller, targeted, and in many cases only a nuisance. As time has gone on, more organized elements of cybercrime have entered the picture along with nation-states. From 2009 and beyond, the cyberthreat landscape became considerably more dangerous, with new adversaries out to perform one of two functions: deny you the use of your computer systems, or use your systems for financial gain including theft of intellectual property or financial information including personally identifiable information.

Advanced Persistent Threats

Although there are numerous claims as to when advanced persistent threats (APTs) began and who first coined the term, the important issue is to note that APTs represent a new breed of attack pattern. Although specific definitions vary, the three words that comprise the term provide the key elements: advanced, persistent, and threat. *Advanced* refers to the use of advanced techniques, such as spear phishing, as a vector into a target. *Persistent* refers to the attacker's goal of establishing a long-term, hidden position on a system. Many APTs can go on for years without being noticed. *Threat* refers to the other objective: exploitation. If an adversary invests the resources to achieve an APT attack, they are doing it for some form of long-term advantage. APTs are not a specific type of attack, but rather the new means by which highly resourced adversaries target systems.

GhostNet (2009)

In 2009, the Dalai Lama's office contacted security experts to determine if it was being bugged. The investigation revealed it was, and the spy ring that was discovered was eventually shown to be spying on over 100 countries' sensitive missions worldwide. Researchers gave this APT-style spy network the name GhostNet, and although the effort was traced back to China, full attribution was never determined.

Operation Aurora (2009)

Operation Aurora was an APT attack first reported by Google, but also targeting Adobe, Yahoo, Juniper Networks, Rackspace, Symantec, and several major U.S. financial and industrial firms. Research analysis pointed to the People's Liberation Army (PLA) of China as the sponsor. The attack ran for most of 2009 and operated on a large scale, with the groups behind the attack consisting of hundreds of hackers working together against the victim firms.

Stuxnet, Duqu, and Flame (2009–2012)

Stuxnet, Duqu, and Flame represent examples of state-sponsored malware. Stuxnet was a malicious worm designed to infiltrate the Iranian uranium enrichment program, to modify the equipment and cause the systems to fail in order to achieve desired results and in some cases even destroy the equipment. Stuxnet was designed to attack a specific model of Siemens programmable logic controller (PLC), which was one of the clues pointing to its objective, the modification of the uranium centrifuges. Although neither the United States nor Israel has admitted to participating in the attack, both have been suggested to have had a role in it.

Duqu (2011) is a piece of malware that appears to be a follow-on of Stuxnet, and has many of the same targets, but rather than being destructive

y

in nature, Duqu is designed to steal information. The malware uses command and control servers across the globe to collect elements such as keystrokes and system information from machines and deliver them to unknown parties.

Flame (2012) is another piece of modular malware that may be a derivative of Stuxnet. Flame is an information collection threat, collecting keystrokes, screenshots, and network traffic. It can record Skype calls and audio signals on a machine. Flame is a large piece of malware with many specific modules, including a kill switch and a means of evading antivirus detection.

Because of the open nature of Stuxnet—its source code is widely available on the Internet—it is impossible to know who is behind Duqu and Flame. In fact, although Duqu and Flame were discovered after Stuxnet, there is growing evidence that they were present before Stuxnet and collected critical intelligence needed to conduct the later attack. The real story behind these malware items is that they demonstrate the power and capability of nation-state malware.

Sony (2011)

The hacker group LulzSec reportedly hacked Sony, stealing over 70 million user accounts. The resulting outage lasted 23 days, and cost Sony in excess of $170 million. One of the biggest issues related to the attack was Sony's poor response, taking more than a week to notify people of the initial attack, and then communicating poorly with its user base during the recovery period. Also notable was that although the credit card data was encrypted on Sony's servers, the rest of the data stolen was not, making it easy pickings for the disclosure of information.

Saudi Aramco (Shamoon) (2012)

In August of 2012, 30,000 computers were shut down in response to a malware attack (named Shamoon) at Saudi Aramco, an oil firm in Saudi Arabia. The attack hit three out of four machines in the firm, and the damage included data wiping of machines and the uploading of sensitive information to Pastebin. It took 10 days for the firm to clean up the infection and restart its business network.

Data Breaches (2013–present)

From the end of 2013 through to the time of this writing, data breaches have dominated the security landscape. Target Corporation announced its breach in mid-December, 2013, stating that the hack began as early as "Black Friday" (November 29) and continued through December 15. Data thieves captured names, addresses, and debit and credit card details, including numbers, expiration dates, and CVV codes. In the end a total of 70 million accounts were exposed. Following the Target breach, Home Depot suffered a breach of over 50 million debit and credit card numbers in 2014.

JP Morgan Chase also had a major data breach in 2014, announcing the loss of 77 million account holders' information. Unlike Target and Home Depot, JP Morgan Chase did not lose account numbers or other crucial data elements. JP Morgan Chase also mounted a major PR campaign touting its security program and spending in order to satisfy customers and regulators of its diligence.

At the end of 2014, Sony Pictures Entertainment announced that it had been hacked, with a massive release of internal data. At the time of this writing, hackers have claimed to have stolen as much as 100 terabytes of data, including e-mails, financial documents, intellectual property, personal data, HR information...in essence, almost everything. Additional reports indicate the destruction of data within Sony; although the extent of the damage is not known, at least one of the elements of malware associated with the attack is known for destroying the Master Boot Record (MBR) of drives. Attribution in the Sony attack is also tricky, as the U.S. government has accused North Korea, while other groups have claimed responsibility, and some investigators claim it was an inside job. It may take years to determine correct attribution, if it is even possible.

Nation-State Hacking (2013–present)

Nation-states have become a recognized issue in security, from the Great Firewall of China to modern malware attacks from a wide range of governments. Threat intelligence became more than a buzzword in 2014 as firms such as CrowdStrike exposed sophisticated hacking actors in China, Russia, and other countries. In 2014 CrowdStrike reported on 39 different threat actors, including criminals, hacktivists, state-sponsored groups, and nation-states. Learning how these adversaries act provides valuable clues to their detection in the enterprise. Groups such as China's Hurricane Panda represent a real security threat. Hurricane Panda focuses on aerospace firms and Internet service companies.

Not all threats are from China. Russia is credited with its own share of malware. Attribution is difficult, and sometimes the only hints are clues, such as the timelines of command and control servers for Energetic Bear, an attack on the energy industry in Europe from the Dragonfly group. The Regin platform, a complete malware platform, possibly in operation for over a decade, has been shown to attack telecom operators, financial institutions, government agencies, and political bodies. Regin is interesting because of its stealth, its complexity, and its ability to hide its command and control network from investigators. Although highly suspected to be deployed by a nation-state, its attribution remains unsolved.

In 2015, data breaches and nation-state hacking hit new highs with the loss of over 20 million sensitive personnel files from the computers at the U.S. Office of Personnel Management (OPM). This OPM loss, reportedly to China, was extremely damaging in that the data loss consisted of the complete background investigations on peoples who had submitted security clearances. These records detailed extensive personal information on the applicants and their family members, providing an adversary with detailed intelligence knowledge. In the same year it was reported that email systems in the Department of State, the Department of Defense, and the White House had been compromised, possibly by both Russia and China. The sensitive nuclear negotiations in Switzerland between the U.S., its allies, and Iran were also reported to have been subject to electronic eavesdropping by parties yet unknown.

Threats to Security

The incidents described in the previous sections provide a glimpse into the many different threats that face administrators as they attempt to protect

Operation Night Dragon was a name given to an intellectual property attack executed against oil, gas, and petrochemical companies in the United States. Using a set of global servers, attackers from China raided global energy companies for proprietary and highly confidential information such as bidding data for leases. The attack shed new light on what constitutes critical data and associated risks.

their computer systems and networks. There are, of course, the normal natural disasters that organizations have faced for years. In today's highly networked world, however, new threats have developed that we did not have to worry about 50 years ago.

There are a number of ways that we can break down the various threats. One way to categorize them is to separate threats that come from outside of the organization from those that are internal. Another is to look at the various levels of sophistication of the attacks, from those by "script kiddies" to those by "elite hackers." A third is to examine the level of organization of the various threats, from unstructured threats to highly structured threats. All of these are valid approaches, and they in fact overlap each other. The following sections examine threats from the perspective of where the attack comes from.

Viruses and Worms

While your organization may be exposed to viruses and worms as a result of employees not following certain practices or procedures, generally you will not have to worry about your employees writing or releasing viruses and worms. It is important to draw a distinction between the writers of malware and those who release malware. Debates over the ethics of writing viruses permeate the industry, but currently, simply writing them is not considered a criminal activity. A virus is like a baseball bat; the bat itself is not evil, but the inappropriate use of the bat (such as to smash a car's window) falls into the category of criminal activity. (Some may argue that this is not a very good analogy since a baseball bat has a useful purpose—to play ball—but viruses have no useful purpose. In general, this is true, but in some limited environments, such as in specialized computer science courses, the study and creation of viruses can be considered a useful learning experience.)

Cross Check

Malware

Viruses and worms are just two types of threats that fall under the general heading of malware. The term malware comes from "malicious software," which describes the overall purpose of code that falls into this category of threat. Malware is software that has a nefarious purpose, designed to cause problems to you as an individual (for example, identity theft) or your system. More information on the different types of malware is provided in Chapter 15.

By number, viruses and worms are the most common problem that an organization faces because literally thousands of them have been created and released. Fortunately, antivirus software and system patching can eliminate the largest portion of this threat. Viruses and worms generally are also nondiscriminating threats; they are released on the Internet in a general fashion and aren't targeted at a specific organization. They typically are also highly visible once released, so they aren't the best tool to use in highly structured attacks where secrecy is vital.

Intruders

The act of deliberately accessing computer systems and networks without authorization is generally referred to as **hacking**, with individuals who conduct this activity being referred to as **hackers**. The term hacking also applies to the act of exceeding one's authority in a system. This would include authorized users who attempt to gain access to files they aren't permitted to access or who attempt to obtain permissions that they have not been granted. While the act of breaking into computer systems and networks has been glorified in the media and movies, the physical act does not live up to the Hollywood hype. Intruders are, if nothing else, extremely patient, since the process to gain access to a system takes persistence and dogged determination. The attacker will conduct many pre-attack activities in order to obtain the information needed to determine which attack will most likely be successful. Typically, by the time an attack is launched, the attacker will have gathered enough information to be very confident that the attack will succeed.

Generally, attacks by an individual or even a small group of attackers fall into the **unstructured threat** category. Attacks at this level generally are conducted over short periods of time (lasting at most a few months), do not involve a large number of individuals, have little financial backing, and are accomplished by insiders or outsiders who do not seek collusion with insiders. Intruders, or those who are attempting to conduct an intrusion, definitely come in many different varieties and have varying degrees of sophistication (see Figure 1.1). At the low end technically are what are generally referred to as **script kiddies**, individuals who do not have the technical expertise to develop scripts or discover new vulnerabilities in software but who have just enough understanding of computer systems to be able to download and run scripts that others have developed. These individuals generally are not interested in attacking specific targets,

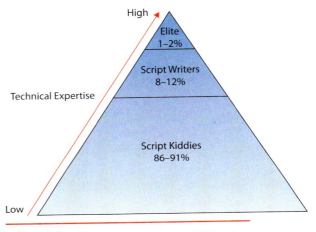

• **Figure 1.1**   Distribution of attacker skill levels

but instead simply want to find any organization that may not have patched a newly discovered vulnerability for which the script kiddie has located a script to exploit the vulnerability. It is hard to estimate how many of the individuals performing activities such as probing networks or scanning individual systems are part of this group, but it is undoubtedly the fastest growing group and the vast majority of the "unfriendly" activity occurring on the Internet is probably carried out by these individuals.

At the next level are those people who are capable of writing scripts to exploit known vulnerabilities. These individuals are much more technically competent than script kiddies and account for an estimated 8 to 12 percent of malicious Internet activity. At the top end of this spectrum are those highly technical individuals, often referred to as **elite hackers**, who not only have the ability to write scripts that exploit vulnerabilities but also are capable of discovering new vulnerabilities. This group is the smallest of the lot, however, and is responsible for, at most, only 1 to 2 percent of intrusive activity.

Insiders

It is generally acknowledged by security professionals that insiders are more dangerous in many respects than outside intruders. The reason for this is simple—insiders have the access and knowledge necessary to cause immediate damage to an organization. Most security is designed to protect against outside intruders and thus lies at the boundary between the organization and the rest of the world. Insiders may actually already have all the access they need to perpetrate criminal activity such as fraud. In addition to unprecedented access, insiders also frequently have knowledge of the security systems in place and are better able to avoid detection. Attacks by insiders are often the result of employees who have become disgruntled with their organization and are looking for ways to disrupt operations. It is also possible that an "attack" by an insider may be an accident and not intended as an attack at all. An example of this might be an employee who deletes a critical file without understanding its critical nature.

Employees are not the only insiders that organizations need to be concerned about. Often, numerous other individuals have physical access to company facilities. Custodial crews frequently have unescorted access throughout the facility, often when nobody else is around. Other individuals, such as contractors or partners, may have not only physical access to the organization's facilities but also access to computer systems and networks. A contractor involved in U.S. Intelligence computing, Edward Snowden, was charged with espionage in 2013 after he released a wide range of data illustrating the technical capabilities of U.S. intelligence surveillance systems. He is the ultimate insider with his name becoming synonymous with the insider threat issue.

Criminal Organizations

As businesses became increasingly reliant upon computer systems and networks, and as the amount of financial transactions conducted via the Internet increased, it was inevitable that criminal organizations would eventually turn to the electronic world as a new target to exploit. Criminal activity on the Internet at its most basic is no different from criminal activity in the physical world. Fraud, extortion, theft, embezzlement, and forgery all take place in the electronic environment.

One difference between criminal groups and the "average" hacker is the level of organization that criminal elements employ in their attack. Criminal groups typically have more money to spend on accomplishing the criminal activity and are willing to spend extra time accomplishing the task provided the level of reward at the conclusion is great enough. With the tremendous amount of money that is exchanged via the Internet on a daily basis, the level of reward for a successful attack is high enough to interest criminal elements. Attacks by criminal organizations usually fall into the **structured threat** category, which is characterized by a greater amount of planning, a longer period of time to conduct the activity, more financial backing to accomplish it, and possibly corruption of, or collusion with, insiders.

Nation-States, Terrorists, and Information Warfare

As nations have increasingly become dependent on computer systems and networks, the possibility that these essential elements of society might be targeted by organizations or nations determined to adversely affect another nation has become a reality. Many nations today have developed to some extent the capability to conduct **information warfare**. There are several definitions for information warfare, but a simple one is that it is warfare conducted against the information and information processing equipment used by an adversary. In practice, this is a much more complicated subject, because information not only may be the target of an adversary, but also may be used as a weapon. Whatever definition you use, information warfare falls into the **highly structured threat** category. This type of threat is characterized by a much longer period of preparation (years is not uncommon), tremendous financial backing, and a large and organized group of attackers. The threat may include attempts not only to subvert insiders but also to plant individuals inside of a potential target in advance of a planned attack.

An interesting aspect of information warfare is the list of possible targets available. We have grown accustomed to the idea that, during war, military forces will target opposing military forces but will generally attempt to destroy as little civilian infrastructure as possible. In information warfare, military forces are certainly still a key target, but much has been written about other targets, such as the various infrastructures that a nation relies on for its daily existence. Water, electricity, oil and gas refineries and distribution, banking and finance, telecommunications—all fall into the category of **critical infrastructures** for a nation. Critical infrastructures are those whose loss would have severe repercussions on the nation. With countries relying so heavily on these infrastructures, it is inevitable that they will be viewed as valid targets during conflict. Given how dependent these infrastructures are on computer systems and networks, it is also inevitable that these same computer systems and networks will be targeted for a cyberattack in an information war.

As demonstrated by the Stuxnet attacks, and the cyberattacks in Estonia, the risk of nation-state attacks is real. There have been numerous accusations of intellectual property theft being sponsored by, and in some cases even performed by, nation-state actors. In a world where information dominates government, business, and economies, the collection of information is the key to success, and with large rewards, the list of characters willing to spend significant resources is high.

Tech Tip

Information Warfare
Once only the concern of governments and the military, information warfare today can involve many other individuals. With the potential to attack the various civilian-controlled critical infrastructures, security professionals in nongovernmental sectors today must also be concerned about defending their systems against attack by agents of foreign governments.

Security Trends

The biggest change affecting computer security that has occurred over the last 30 years has been the transformation of the computing environment from large mainframes to a highly interconnected network of smaller systems. This interconnection of systems is the Internet and it now touches virtually all systems. What this has meant for security is a switch from a closed operating environment in which everything was fairly contained to one in which access to a computer can occur from almost anywhere on the planet. This has, for obvious reasons, greatly complicated the job of the security professional.

The type of individual who attacks a computer system or network has also evolved over the last 30 years. As illustrated by the sample of attacks listed previously, the attackers have become more focused on gain over notoriety. Today computer attacks are used to steal and commit fraud and other crimes in the pursuit of monetary enrichment. Computer crimes are big business today, not just because it is hard to catch the perpetrators, but also because the number of targets is large and the rewards greater than robbing local stores.

In the early days of computers, security was considered to be a binary condition in which your system was either secure or not secure. Security efforts were made to achieve a state of security, meaning that the system was secure. Today, the focus has changed. In light of the revelation that a pure state of security is not achievable in the binary sense, the focus has shifted to one of risk management. Today, the question is how much risk your system is exposed to, and from what sources.

The motive behind most computer attacks falls into one of two categories:
1. To deprive someone the use of their system.
2. To use someone else's system to enrich oneself.

In some cases, the use of a denial-of-service attack (item 1) precedes the actual heist (item 2).

Over the past several years a wide range of computer industry firms have begun issuing annual security reports. Among these firms is Verizon, which has issued its annual Data Breach Investigations Report (DBIR) since 2008 and is lauded because of its breadth and depth. The 2015 DBIR was based on over 2,100 data breaches and 79,790 security incidents in 61 countries. Perhaps the most valuable aspect of the DBIR is its identification of common details that result in a data breach. The Verizon DBIRs are available at www.verizonenterprise.com/DBIR/

■ Targets and Attacks

There are two general reasons a particular computer system is attacked: either it is specifically targeted by the attacker, or it is an opportunistic target.

Specific Target

In this case, the attacker has chosen the target not because of the hardware or software the organization is running but for another reason, perhaps a political reason. An example of this type of attack would be an individual in one country attacking a government system in another. Alternatively, the attacker may be targeting the organization as part of a **hacktivist** attack. For example, an attacker may deface the web site of a company that sells fur coats because the attacker feels that using animals in this way is unethical. Perpetrating some sort of electronic fraud is another reason a specific system might be targeted. Whatever the reason, an attack of this nature is decided upon before the attacker knows what hardware and software the organization has.

Opportunistic Target

The second type of attack, an attack against a target of opportunity, is conducted against a site that has software that is vulnerable to a specific exploit. The attackers, in this case, are not targeting the organization; instead, they have learned of a vulnerability and are simply looking for an organization with this vulnerability that they can exploit. This is not to say that an attacker might not be targeting a given sector and looking for a target of opportunity in that sector, however. For example, an attacker may desire to obtain credit card or other personal information and may search for any exploitable company with credit card information in order to carry out the attack.

Targeted attacks are more difficult and take more time than attacks on a target of opportunity. The latter simply relies on the fact that with any piece of widely distributed software, there will almost always be somebody who has not patched the system (or has not patched it properly) as they should have.

Minimizing Possible Avenues of Attack

Understanding the steps an attacker will take enables you to limit the exposure of your system and minimize those avenues an attacker might possibly exploit. There are multiple elements to a solid computer defense, but two of the key elements involve limiting an attacker's avenues of attack. The first step an administrator can take to reduce possible attacks is to ensure that all patches for the operating system and applications are installed. Many security problems that we read about, such as viruses and worms, exploit known vulnerabilities for which patches exist. The reason such malware caused so much damage in the past was that administrators did not take the appropriate actions to protect their systems.

The second step an administrator can take is system hardening, which involves limiting the services that are running on the system. Only using those services that are absolutely needed does two things: it limits the possible avenues of attack (those services with vulnerabilities that can be exploited), and it reduces the number of services the administrator has to worry about patching in the first place. This is one of the important first steps any administrator should take to secure a computer system. System hardening is covered in detail in Chapter 14.

While there are no iron-clad defenses against attack, or guarantees that an attack won't be successful, you can take steps to reduce the risk of loss. This is the basis for the change in strategy from a defense-based one to one based on risk management. Risk management is covered in detail in Chapter 20.

■ Approaches to Computer Security

While much of the discussion of computer security focuses on how systems are attacked, it is equally important to consider the structure of defenses. There are three major considerations when securing a system:

- **Correctness** Ensuring that a system is fully up to date, with all patches installed and proper security controls in place; this goes a long way toward minimizing risk. Correctness begins with a secure development lifecycle (covered in Chapter 18), continues through patching and hardening (Chapters 14 and 21), and culminates in operations (Chapters 3, 4, 19, and 20).

- **Isolation** Protecting a system from unauthorized use, by means of access control and physical security. Isolation begins with infrastructure (covered in Chapters 9 and 10), continues with access control (Chapters 8, 11, and 12), and includes the use of cryptography (Chapters 5, 6, and 7).

- **Obfuscation** Making it difficult for an adversary to know when they have succeeded. Whether accomplished by obscurity, randomization, or obfuscation, increasing the workload of an attacker makes it more difficult for them to succeed in their attack. Obfuscation occurs throughout all topics, as it is a built-in element, whether in the form of random numbers in crypto or address space randomizations, stack guards, or pointer encryption at the operating system level.

Each of these approaches has its inherent flaws, but taken together, they can provide a strong means of system defense.

■ Ethics

Any meaningful discussion about operational aspects of information security must include the topic of ethics. *Ethics* is commonly defined as a set of moral principles that guides an individual's or group's behavior. Because information security efforts frequently involve trusting people to keep secrets that could cause harm to the organization if revealed, trust is a foundational element in the people side of security. And trust is built upon a code of ethics, a norm that allows everyone to understand expectations and responsibilities. There are several different ethical frameworks that can be applied to making a decision, and these are covered in detail in Chapter 25.

Ethics is a difficult topic; separating right from wrong is easy in many cases, but in other cases it is more difficult. For example, writing a virus that damages a system is clearly bad behavior, but is writing a worm that goes out and patches systems, without the users' permission, right or wrong? Does the ends justify the means? Such questions are the basis of ethical discussions that define the challenges faced by security personnel on a regular basis.

■ Additional References

1. http://en.wikipedia.org/wiki/Timeline_of_computer_security_hacker_history
2. http://www.informationisbeautiful.net/visualizations/worlds-biggest-data-breaches-hacks/www.verizonenterprise.com/DBIR/

Chapter 1 Review

■ Chapter Summary

After reading this chapter and completing the quizzes, you should understand the following regarding security threats and trends.

Define computer security

- Computer security is defined by operating in a manner where the system does what it is supposed to do and only what it is supposed to do.
- Information security is defined by the information being protected from unauthorized access or alteration and yet is available to authorized individuals when required.

Discuss common threats and recent computer crimes that have been committed

- There are a number of different threats to security, including viruses and worms, intruders, insiders, criminal organizations, terrorists, and information warfare conducted by foreign countries.
- There are two general reasons a particular computer system is attacked: it is specifically targeted by the attacker, or it is a target of opportunity.
- Targeted attacks are more difficult and take more time than attacks on a target of opportunity.
- The different types of electronic crime fall into two main categories: crimes in which the computer was the target of the attack, and incidents in which the computer was a means of perpetrating a criminal act.
- One significant trend observed over the last several years has been the increase in the number of computer attacks and their effectiveness.

List and discuss recent trends in computer security

- There are many different ways to attack computers and networks to take advantage of what has made shopping, banking, investment, and leisure pursuits a simple matter of "dragging and clicking" for many people.
- The biggest change that has occurred in security over the last 30 years has been the transformation of the computing environment from large mainframes to a highly interconnected network of much smaller systems.

Describe common avenues of attacks

- An attacker can use a common technique against a wide range of targets in an opportunistic attack, only succeeding where the attack is viable.
- An attacker can employ a variety of techniques against a specific target when it is desired to obtain access to a specific system.

Describe approaches to computer security

- There are three main approaches an enterprise can employ, one based on correctness, one involving isolation, and one involving obfuscation. The ideal method is to employ all three together.

Discuss the relevant ethical issues associated with computer security

- Ethics is commonly defined as a set of moral principles that guides an individual's or group's behaviors.
- Because information security efforts frequently involve trusting people to keep secrets that could cause harm to the organization if revealed, trust is a foundational element in the people side of security.

■ Key Terms

computer security *(1)*
critical infrastructure *(11)*
elite hacker *(9)*
hacker *(9)*
hacking *(9)*
hacktivist *(12)*

highly structured threat *(11)*
information warfare *(10)*
script kiddie *(9)*
structured threat *(10)*
unstructured threat *(9)*

■ Key Terms Quiz

Use terms from the Key Terms list to complete the sentences that follow. Don't use the same term more than once. Not all terms will be used.

1. A(n) _____ is characterized by a greater amount of planning, a longer period of time to conduct the activity, more financial backing to accomplish it, and the possible corruption of, or collusion with, insiders.

2. A hacker whose activities are motivated by a personal cause or position is known as a(n) _____.

3. A(n) _____ is one whose loss would have a severe detrimental impact on the nation.

4. _____ is conducted against the information and information processing equipment used by an adversary.

5. Actors who deliberately access computer systems and networks without authorization are called _____ .

6. A(n) _____ generally is short-term in nature, does not involve a large group of individuals, does not have large financial backing, and does not include collusion with insiders.

7. A(n) _____ is a highly technically competent individual who conducts intrusive activity on the Internet and is capable of not only exploiting known vulnerabilities but also finding new vulnerabilities.

8. The act of deliberately accessing computer systems and networks without authorization is generally referred to as _____.

9. A(n) _____ is an individual who does not have the technical expertise to develop scripts or discover new vulnerabilities in software but who has just enough understanding of computer systems to be able to download and run scripts that others have developed.

10. A(n) _____ is characterized by a much longer period of preparation (years is not uncommon), tremendous financial backing, and a large and organized group of attackers.

■ Multiple-Choice Quiz

1. Which threats are characterized by possibly long periods of preparation (years is not uncommon), tremendous financial backing, a large and organized group of attackers, and attempts to subvert insiders or to plant individuals inside a potential target in advance of a planned attack?

   A. Unstructured threats

   B. Structured threats

   C. Highly structured threats

   D. Nation-state information warfare threats

2. In which of the following is an attacker looking for any organization vulnerable to a specific exploit rather than attempting to gain access to a specific organization?

   A. Target of opportunity attack

   B. Targeted attack

   C. Vulnerability scan attack

   D. Information warfare attack

3. The rise of which of the following has greatly increased the number of individuals who probe organizations looking for vulnerabilities to exploit?

   A. Virus writers

   B. Script kiddies

   C. Hackers

   D. Elite hackers

4. For what reason(s) do some security professionals consider insiders more dangerous than outside intruders?

   A. Employees (insiders) are easily corrupted by criminal and other organizations.

   B. Insiders have the access and knowledge necessary to cause immediate damage to the organization.

   C. Insiders have knowledge of the security systems in place and are better able to avoid detection.

   D. Both B and C

5. The act of deliberately accessing computer systems and networks without authorization is generally known as:

   A. Computer intrusion

   B. Hacking

   C. Cracking

   D. Probing

6. What is the most common problem/threat an organization faces?

   A. Viruses/worms

   B. Script kiddies

   C. Hackers

   D. Hacktivists

7. Warfare conducted against the information and information processing equipment used by an adversary is known as:

   A. Hacking

   B. Cyberterrorism

   C. Information warfare

   D. Network warfare

8. An attacker who feels that using animals to make fur coats is unethical and thus defaces the web site of a company that sells fur coats is an example of:

   A. Information warfare

   B. Hacktivisim

   C. Cyber crusading

   D. Elite hacking

9. Criminal organizations would normally be classified as what type of threat?

   A. Unstructured

   B. Unstructured but hostile

   C. Structured

   D. Highly structured

10. Which of the following individuals have the ability to not only write scripts that exploit vulnerabilities but also discover new vulnerabilities?

    A. Elite hackers

    B. Script kiddies

    C. Hacktivists

    D. Insiders

■ Essay Quiz

1. Reread the various examples of computer crimes at the beginning of this chapter. Categorize each as either a crime where the computer was the target of the criminal activity or a crime in which the computer was a tool in accomplishing the criminal activity.

2. A friend of yours has just been hired by an organization as its computer security officer. Your friend is a bit nervous about this new job and has come to you, knowing that you are taking a computer security class, to ask your advice on measures that can be taken that might help prevent an intrusion. What three things can you suggest that are simple but can tremendously help limit the possibility of an attack?

3. Discuss the major difference between a target of opportunity attack and a targeted attack. Which do you believe is the more common one?

Lab Project

• Lab Project 1.1

A number of different examples of computer crimes were discussed in this chapter. Similar activities seem to happen daily. Do a search on the Internet to see what other examples you can find. Try and obtain the most recent examples possible.

chapter 2

General Security Concepts

"A people that values its privileges above its principles soon loses both."
—Dwight D. Eisenhower

In this chapter, you will learn how to

- Define basic terms associated with computer and information security

- Identify the basic approaches to computer and information security

- Identify the basic principles of computer and information security

- Distinguish among various methods to implement access controls

- Describe methods used to verify the identity and authenticity of an individual

- Recognize some of the basic models used to implement security in operating systems

In Chapter 1, you learned about some of the various threats that we, as security professionals, face on a daily basis. In this chapter, you start exploring the field of computer security. Computer security has a series of fundamental concepts that support the discipline. In this chapter we will begin with an examination of security models and concepts and proceed to see how they are operationally employed.

Basic Security Terminology

The term **hacking** has been used frequently in the media. A *hacker* was once considered an individual who understood the technical aspects of computer operating systems and networks. Hackers were individuals you turned to when you had a problem and needed extreme technical expertise. Today, primarily as a result of the media, the term is used more often to refer to individuals who attempt to gain unauthorized access to computer systems or networks. While some would prefer to use the terms *cracker* and *cracking* when referring to this nefarious type of activity, the terminology generally accepted by the public is that of hacker and hacking. A related term that may sometimes be seen is **phreaking**, which refers to the "hacking" of the systems and computers used by a telephone company to operate its telephone network.

 The field of computer security constantly evolves, introducing new terms frequently, which are often coined by the media. Make sure to learn the meaning of terms such as *hacking*, *phreaking*, *vishing*, *phishing*, *pharming*, and *spear phishing*. Some of these have been around for many years, such as hacking, whereas others have appeared only in the last few years, such as spear phishing.

Security Basics

Computer security itself is a term that has many meanings and related terms. Computer security entails the methods used to ensure that a system is secure. Subjects such as authentication and access controls must be addressed in broad terms of computer security. Seldom in today's world are computers not connected to other computers in networks. This then introduces the term *network security* to refer to the protection of the multiple computers and other devices that are connected together. Related to these two terms are two others: *information security* and *information assurance,* which place the focus of the security process not on the hardware and software being used but on the data that is processed by them. Assurance also introduces another concept, that of the availability of the systems and information when we want them. The common press and many professionals have settled on *cybersecurity* as the term to describe the field. Still another term that may be heard in the security world is COMSEC, which stands for *communications security* and deals with the security of telecommunication systems.

Cybersecurity has become regular headline news these days, with reports of break-ins, data breaches, fraud, and a host of other calamities. The general public has become increasingly aware of its dependence on computers and networks and consequently has also become interested in the security of these same computers and networks. As a result of this increased attention by the public, several new terms have become commonplace in conversations and print. Terms such as *hacking, virus, TCP/IP, encryption,* and *firewalls* are now frequently encountered in mainstream news media and have found their way into casual conversations. What was once the purview of scientists and engineers is now part of our everyday life.

With our increased daily dependence on computers and networks to conduct everything from making purchases at our local grocery store, banking, trading stocks, and receiving medical treatment to driving our children to school, ensuring that computers and networks are secure has become of paramount importance. Computers and the information they manipulate has become a part of virtually every aspect of our lives.

The "CIA" of Security

Almost from its inception, the goal of computer security has been three-fold: confidentiality, integrity, and availability—the "CIA" of security. The purpose of **confidentiality** is to ensure that only those individuals who have the authority to view a piece of information may do so. No unauthorized individual should ever be able to view data they are not entitled to access. **Integrity** is a related concept but deals with the generation and modification of data. Only authorized individuals should ever be able to create or change (or delete) information. The goal of **availability** is to ensure that the data, or the system itself, is available for use when the authorized user wants it.

As a result of the increased use of networks for commerce, two additional security goals have been added to the original three in the CIA of security. **Authentication** attempts to ensure that an individual is who they claim to be. The need for this in an online transaction is obvious. Related to this is **nonrepudiation**, which deals with the ability to verify that a message has been sent and received and that the sender can be identified and verified. The requirement for this capability in online transactions should also be readily apparent. Recent emphasis on systems assurance has raised the potential inclusion of the term **auditability**, which refers to whether a control can be verified to be functioning properly. In security, it is imperative that we can track actions to ensure what has or has not been done.

The Operational Model of Computer Security

For many years, the focus of security was on prevention. If we could prevent everyone who did not have authorization from gaining access to our computer systems and networks, then we assumed that we had achieved security. Protection was thus equated with prevention. While the basic premise of this is true, it fails to acknowledge the realities of the networked environment our systems are part of. No matter how well we seem to do in prevention technology, somebody always seems to find a way around our safeguards. When this happens, our system is left unprotected. Thus, we need multiple prevention techniques and also technology to alert us when prevention has failed and to provide ways to address the problem. This results in a modification to our original security equation with the addition of two new elements—detection and response. Our security equation thus becomes:

$$\text{Protection} = \text{Prevention} + (\text{Detection} + \text{Response})$$

This is known as the **operational model of computer security**. Every security technique and technology falls into at least one of the three elements of the equation. Examples of the types of technology and techniques that represent each are depicted in Figure 2.1.

• **Figure 2.1**   Sample technologies in the operational model of computer security

Cybersecurity Framework Model

In 2013, President Obama signed an executive order directing the U.S. National Institute of Science and Technology (NIST) to work with industry and develop a cybersecurity framework. This was in response to several significant cybersecurity events where the victim companies appeared to be unprepared. The resulting framework, titled *Framework for Improving Critical Infrastructure Cybersecurity,* was created as a voluntary system, based on existing standards, guidelines, and practices, to facilitate adoption and acceptance across a wide array of industries.

The Cybersecurity Framework provides a common taxonomy and mechanism to assist in aligning management practices with existing standards, guidelines, and practices. Its purpose is to complement and enhance risk management efforts through

1. Determining their current cybersecurity posture

2. Documenting their desired target state with respect to cybersecurity

3. Determining and prioritizing improvement and corrective actions

4. Measuring and monitoring progress toward goals

5. Creating a communication mechanism for coordination among stakeholders

The framework is composed of five core functions, as illustrated in Figure 2.2. Two of these core functions, *Identify* and *Protect,* describe actions taken before an incident. *Detect* is the core function associated with intrusion detection or the beginning of an incident response. The last two, *Respond*

Tech Tip

Cybersecurity Framework

The NIST Cybersecurity Framework is a risk-based approach to implementation of cybersecurity activities in an enterprise. The framework provides a common taxonomy of standards, guidelines, and practices that can be employed to strengthen cybersecurity efforts. The framework can be obtained from NIST:

www.nist.gov/cyberframework/ upload/cybersecurity-framework-021214-final.pdf

• **Figure 2.2**   Cybersecurity Framework core functions

and *Recover,* detail actions that take place during the post-incident response. Examples of the items under each function are illustrated in the figure. In addition to the five functions, the framework has levels of implementations referred to as tiers. These tiers represent the organization's ability from Partial (Tier 1) to Adaptive (Tier 4).

Security Tenets

In addition to the CIA elements, there are additional tenets that form a basis for system security. The three operational tenets found in secure deployments are session management, exception management, and configuration management.

Session Management

Session management is the set of activities employed to establish a communication channel between two parties, identifying each in a manner that allows future activity without renewed authentication. Session management allows an application to authenticate once and have subsequent activities ascribed to the authenticated user. Sessions are frequently used in web applications to preserve state and user information between normally stateless clicks.

Sessions are typically identified by an ID that is known to both sides of the conversation. This ID can be used as a token for future identification. If confidentiality is required, then the channel should be secured by an appropriate level of cryptographic protection.

Session management includes all the activities necessary to manage the session, from establishment, during use, and at completion of the conversation. Because the session represents the continuity of a security condition established during authentication, the level of protection that should be afforded to the session ID should be commensurate with the level of security initially established.

Exception Management

Exceptions are the invocation of conditions that fall outside the normal sequence of operation. Whether by error or malicious action, exceptions are changes to normal processing and need to be managed. The special processing required by conditions that fall outside normal parameters can result in errors either locally or in follow-on processes in a system. The handling of exceptions, referred to as *exception handling,* is an important consideration during software development.

Exception management is more than just exception handling in software development. When the operation of a system encounters an exception, whether it is invoked by a person, process, technology, or combination, the system must effectively handle the condition. This can mean many different things, sometimes even operating outside normal policy limits. Exception management can also be nontechnical in nature: systems or environments that cannot follow organizational security policy, for example, must be documented, exceptions must be approved, and mitigations must be put in place to lower the risk associated with exceptions to policy. The bottom line is simple: either the system must handle the condition and

Tech Tip

Session Management Cheat Sheet

Session management is a common task for web applications, and the Open Web Application Security Project (OWASP) has a cheat sheet to assist in the correct implementation of session management. See https://www .owasp.org/index.php/Session_ Management_Cheat_Sheet.

recover, or it must fail and be recovered by separate action. Designing in exception handling makes a system more resilient, because exceptions will happen, and how they are handled is the only unknown outcome.

Configuration Management

Configuration management is key to the proper operation of IT systems. IT systems are first and foremost systems, groups of elements that work together to achieve a desired resultant process. The proper configuration and provisioning of all of the components in a system is essential to the proper operation of the system. The design and operation of the elements to ensure the proper functional environment of a system is referred to as configuration management. Configuration management is a key operation principle and is thoroughly covered in Chapter 21.

Security Approaches

There are multiple approaches an organization can take to address the protection of its networks: ignore security issues, provide host security, provide network-level security, or provide a combination of the latter two. The middle two, host security and network-level security, have prevention as well as detection and response components. Rather than view these two approaches as independent solutions, a mature organization uses both in a complementary fashion.

If an organization decides to ignore security, it has chosen to utilize the minimal amount of security that is provided with its workstations, servers, and devices. No additional security measures will be implemented. Each "out of the box" system has certain security settings that can be configured, and they should be. To actually protect an entire network, however, requires work in addition to the few protection mechanisms that come with systems by default.

Host Security

Host security takes a granular view of security by focusing on protecting each computer and device individually instead of addressing protection of the network as a whole. When host security is used, each computer is relied upon to protect itself. If an organization decides to implement only host security and does not include network security, there is a high probability of introducing or overlooking vulnerabilities. Most environments are filled with different operating systems (Windows, UNIX, Linux, OS X), different versions of those operating systems, and different types of installed applications. Each operating system has security configurations that differ from those of other systems, and different versions of the same operating system may in fact have configuration variations between them.

Host security is important and should always be addressed. Security, however, should not stop there, as host security is a complementary process to be combined with network security. If individual host computers have vulnerabilities embodied within them, then network security can provide another layer of protection that will, hopefully, stop any intruders who have gotten that far into the environment.

Tech Tip

Got Network?

A classic black T-shirt in the security industry says "got root?" It's a takeoff on the successful ad campaign "got milk?" and indicates the power of root privilege. Similar to "got root?" is "got network?", for if you truly "own" the network, then you have significant control over what passes across it and can result in information disclosure. To ensure a secure posture, both network and host access levels must be controlled.

A longtime discussion has centered on whether host- or network-based security is more important. Most security experts now generally agree that a combination of both is needed to adequately address the wide range of possible security threats. Certain attacks are more easily spotted and some attacks are more easily prevented using tools designed for one or the other of these approaches.

Chapter 2: General Security Concepts

Network Security

In some smaller environments, host security by itself may be an option, but as systems become connected into networks, security should include the actual network itself. In **network security**, an emphasis is placed on controlling access to internal computers from external entities. This control can be through devices such as routers, firewalls, authentication hardware and software, encryption, and intrusion detection systems (IDSs).

Network environments tend to be unique entities because usually no two networks have exactly the same number of computers, the same applications installed, the same number of users, the exact same configurations, or the same available servers. They will not perform the same functions or have the same overall architecture. Since networks have so many variations, there are many different ways in which they can be protected and configured. This chapter covers some foundational approaches to network and host security. Each approach may be implemented in a myriad of ways, but both network and host security need to be addressed for an effective total security program.

Security Principles

In the mid-1970s, two computer scientists from MIT, Jerome Saltzer and Michael Schroeder, published a paper on design principles for a secure computer system. The Saltzer and Schroeder paper, titled "The Protection of Information in Computer Systems," has been hailed as a seminal work in computer security, and the eight design principles are as relevant today as they were in 1970s. These principles are useful in secure system design and operation.

Least Privilege

One of the most fundamental principles in security is **least privilege**. This concept is applicable to many physical environments as well as network and host security. Least privilege means that a subject (which may be a user, application, or process) should have only the necessary rights and privileges to perform its task with no additional permissions. Limiting an object's privileges limits the amount of harm that can be caused, thus limiting an organization's exposure to damage. Users may have access to the files on their workstations and a select set of files on a file server, but no access to critical data that is held within the database. This rule helps an organization protect its most sensitive resources and helps ensure that whoever is interacting with these resources has a valid reason to do so.

 Try This!

Examples of the Least Privilege Principle

The security concept of least privilege is not unique to computer security. It has been practiced by organizations such as financial institutions and governments for centuries. Basically it simply means that individuals are given only the absolute minimum of privileges that are required to accomplish their assigned job. Examine the security policies that your organization has in place and see if you can identify examples of where the principle of least privilege has been used.

The concept of least privilege applies to more network security issues than just providing users with specific rights and permissions. When trust relationships are created, they should not be implemented in such a way that everyone trusts each other simply because it is easier. One domain should trust another for very specific reasons, and the implementers should have a full understanding of what the trust relationship allows between two domains. If one domain trusts another, do all of the users automatically become trusted, and can they thus easily access any and all resources on the other domain? Is this a good idea? Is there a more secure way of providing the same functionality? If a trusted relationship is implemented such that users in one group can access a plotter or printer that is available on only one domain, it might make sense to simply purchase another plotter so that other, more valuable or sensitive resources are not accessible by the entire group.

Another issue that falls under the least privilege concept is the security context in which an application runs. All applications, scripts, and batch files run in the security context of a specific user on an operating system. They execute with specific permissions as if they were a user. The application may be Microsoft Word and run in the space of a regular user, or it may be a diagnostic program that needs access to more sensitive system files and so must run under an administrative user account, or it may be a program that performs backups and so should operate within the security context of a backup operator. The crux of this issue is that a program should execute only in the security context that is needed for that program to perform its duties successfully. In many environments, people do not really understand how to make programs run under different security contexts, or it may just seem easier to have all programs run under the administrator account. If attackers can compromise a program or service running under the administrator account, they have effectively elevated their access level and have much more control over the system and many more ways to cause damage.

Try This!

Control of Resources

Being able to apply the appropriate security control to file and print resources is an important aspect of the least privilege security principle. How this is implemented varies depending on the operating system that the computer runs. Check how the operating system that you use provides for the ability to control file and print resources.

Separation of Privilege

Protection mechanisms can be employed to grant access based on a variety of factors. One of the key principles is to base decisions on more than a single piece of information. The principle of **separation of privilege** states that the protection mechanism should be constructed so that it uses more than one piece of information to make access decisions. Applying this principle to the people side of the security function results in the concept of **separation of duties**.

The principle of separation of privilege is applicable to physical environments as well as network and host security. When applied to people's actions, separation of duties specifies that for any given task, more than one individual needs to be involved. The task is broken into different duties, each of which is accomplished by a separate individual. By implementing a task in this manner, no single individual can abuse the system for his or her own gain. This principle has been implemented in the business world, especially financial institutions, for many years. A simple example is a system in which one individual is required to place an order and a separate person is needed to authorize the purchase.

While separation of duties provides a certain level of checks and balances, it is not without its own drawbacks. Chief among these is the cost required to accomplish the task. This cost is manifested in both time and money. More than one individual is required when a single person could accomplish the task, thus potentially increasing the cost of the task. In addition, with more than one individual involved, a certain delay can be expected because the task must proceed through its various steps.

Fail-Safe Defaults

Today, the Internet is no longer the friendly playground of researchers that it once was. This has resulted in different approaches that might at first seem less than friendly but that are required for security purposes. **Fail-safe defaults** is a concept that when something fails, it should do so to a safe state. One approach is that a protection mechanism should deny access by default, and grant access only when explicit permission exists. This is sometimes called **default deny**, and the common operational term for this approach is **implicit deny**.

Frequently in the network world, administrators make many decisions concerning network access. Often a series of rules will be used to determine whether or not to allow access (which is the purpose of a network firewall). If a particular situation is not covered by any of the other rules, the implicit deny approach states that access should not be granted. In other words, if no rule would allow access, then access should not be granted. Implicit deny applies to situations involving both authorization and access.

The alternative to implicit deny is to allow access unless a specific rule forbids it. Another example of these two approaches is in programs that monitor and block access to certain web sites. One approach is to provide a list of specific sites that a user is *not* allowed to access. Access to any site not on the list would be implicitly allowed. The opposite approach (the implicit deny approach) would block all access to sites that are not specifically identified as authorized. As you can imagine, depending on the specific application, one or the other approach will be more appropriate. Which approach you choose depends on the security objectives and policies of your organization.

Economy of Mechanism

The terms *security* and *complexity* are often at odds with each other, because the more complex something is, the harder it is to understand, and you cannot truly secure something if you do not understand it. Another reason complexity is a problem within security is that it usually allows too many opportunities for something to go wrong. If an application has 4000 lines

Implicit deny is another fundamental principle of security and students need to be sure that they understand this principle. Similar to least privilege, this principle states that if you haven't specifically been allowed access, then it should be denied.

of code, there are a lot fewer places for buffer overflows, for example, than in an application of two million lines of code. The principle of **economy of mechanism** is described as always using simple solutions when available.

An example of the principle concerns the number of services that you allow your system to run. Default installations of computer operating systems often leave many services running. The keep-it-simple principle tells us to eliminate or disable those services that we don't need. This is also a good idea from a security standpoint because it results in fewer applications that can be exploited and fewer services that the administrator is responsible for securing. The general rule of thumb is to eliminate or disable all nonessential services and protocols. This of course leads to the question, how do you determine whether a service or protocol is essential or not? Ideally, you should know what your computer system or network is being used for, and thus you should be able to identify and activate only those elements that are essential. For a variety of reasons, this is not as easy as it sounds. Alternatively, a stringent security approach that one can take is to assume that no service is necessary (which is obviously absurd) and activate services and ports only as they are requested. Whatever approach is taken, there is a never-ending struggle to try to strike a balance between providing functionality and maintaining security.

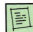 Keep it simple: Another method of looking at the principle of economy of mechanism is that the protection mechanism should be small and simple.

Complete Mediation

One of the fundamental tenets of a protection system is to check all access requests for permission. Each and every time a subject requests access to an object, the permission must be checked; otherwise an attacker might gain unauthorized access to an object. **Complete mediation** refers to the concept that each and every request should be verified. When permissions are verified the first time, and the result is cached for subsequent use, performance may be increased, but this also opens the door to permission errors. Should a permission change subsequent to the first use, this change would not be applied to the operations after the initial check.

Complete mediation also refers to ensuring that all operations go through the protection mechanism. When security controls are added after the fact, it is important to make certain that all process flows are covered by the controls, including exceptions and out-of-band requests. If an automated process is checked in one manner, but a manual paper backup process has a separate path, it is important to ensure all checks are still in place. When a system undergoes disaster recovery or business continuity processes, or backup and/or restore processes, these too require complete mediation.

Open Design

The principle of **open design** holds that the protection of an object should not rely upon secrecy of the protection mechanism itself. This principle has been long proven in cryptographic circles, where hiding the algorithm ultimately fails and the true protection relies upon the secrecy and complexity of the keys. The principle does not exclude the idea of using secrecy, but merely states that, on the face of it, secrecy of mechanism is not sufficient for protection.

Another concept in security that should be discussed in this context is the idea of **security through obscurity**. In this case, security is considered effective if the environment and protection mechanisms are confusing or thought to be not generally known. Security through obscurity uses the approach of protecting something by hiding it. Noncomputer examples of this concept include hiding your briefcase or purse if you leave it in the car so that it is not in plain view, hiding a house key under a doormat or in a planter, or pushing your favorite ice cream to the back of the freezer so that everyone else thinks it is all gone. The idea is that if something is out of sight, it is out of mind. This approach, however, does not provide actual protection of the object. Someone can still steal the purse by breaking into the car, lift the doormat and find the key, or dig through the items in the freezer to find your favorite ice cream. Security through obscurity may make someone work a little harder to accomplish a task, but it does not prevent anyone from eventually succeeding.

Similar approaches are seen in computer and network security when attempting to hide certain objects. A network administrator may, for instance, move a service from its default port to a different port so that others will not know how to access it as easily, or a firewall may be configured to hide specific information about the internal network in the hope that potential attackers will not obtain the information for use in an attack on the network.

In most security circles, security through obscurity is considered a poor approach, especially if it is the only approach to security. Security through obscurity simply attempts to hide an object; it doesn't implement a security control to protect it. An organization can use security through obscurity measures to try to hide critical assets, but other security measures should also be employed to provide a higher level of protection. For example, if an administrator moves a service from its default port to a more obscure port, an attacker can still actually find this service; thus a firewall should be used to restrict access to the service. Most people know that even if you do shove your ice cream to the back of the freezer, someone may eventually find it.

Least Common Mechanism

The principle of **least common mechanism** states that mechanisms used to access resources should be dedicated and not shared. Sharing of mechanisms allows a potential cross-over between channels resulting in a protection failure mode. For example, if there is a module that enables employees to check their payroll information, a separate module should be employed to change the information, lest a user gain access to change versus read access. Although sharing and reuse are good in one sense, they can represent a security risk in another.

Common examples of the least common mechanism and its isolation principle abound in ordinary systems. *Sandboxing* is a means of separating the operation of an application from the rest of the operating system. Virtual machines perform the same task between operating systems on a single piece of hardware. Instantiating shared libraries, in which separate instantiation of local classes enables separate but equal coding, is yet another. The key is to provide a means of isolation between processes so information cannot flow between separate users unless specifically designed to do so.

It often amazes security professionals how frequently individuals rely on security through obscurity as their main line of defense. Relying on some piece of information remaining secret is generally not a good idea. This is especially true in this age of reverse-engineering, where individuals analyze the binaries for programs to discover embedded passwords or cryptographic keys. The biggest problem with relying on security through obscurity is that if it fails and the secret becomes known, there often is no easy way to modify the secret to re-secure it.

Principles of Computer Security

Psychological Acceptability

Psychological acceptability refers to the users' acceptance of security measures. Users play a key role in the operation of a system, and if security measures are perceived to be an impediment to the work a user is responsible for, then a natural consequence may be that the user bypasses the control. Although a user may understand that this could result in a security problem, the perception that it does result in their performance failure will present pressure to bypass it.

Psychological acceptability is often overlooked by security professionals focused on technical issues and how they see the threat. They are focused on the threat, which is their professional responsibility, so the focus on security is natural and it aligns with their professional responsibilities. This alignment between security and professional work responsibilities does not always translate to other positions in an organization. Security professionals, particularly those designing the security systems, should not only be aware of this concept, but pay particular attention to how security controls will be viewed by workers in the context of their work responsibility, not with respect to security for its own sake.

Defense in Depth

Defense in depth is a principle that is characterized by the use of multiple, different defense mechanisms with a goal of improving the defensive response to an attack. Another term for defense in depth is layered security. Single points of failure represent just that, an opportunity to fail. By using multiple defenses that are different, with differing points of failure, a system becomes stronger. While one defense mechanism may not be 100 percent effective, the application of a second defense mechanism to the items that succeed in bypassing the first mechanism provides a stronger response. There are a couple of different mechanisms that can be employed in a defense-in-depth strategy: layered security and diversity of defense. Together these provide a defense-in-depth strategy that is stronger than any single layer of defense.

A bank does not protect the money that it stores only by using a vault. It has one or more security guards as a first defense to watch for suspicious activities and to secure the facility when the bank is closed. It may have monitoring systems that watch various activities that take place in the bank, whether involving customers or employees. The vault is usually located in the center of the facility, and thus there are layers of rooms or walls before arriving at the vault. There is access control, which ensures that the people entering the vault have to be given authorization beforehand. And the systems, including manual switches, are connected directly to the police station in case a determined bank robber successfully penetrates any one of these layers of protection.

Networks should utilize the same type of **layered security** architecture. There is no 100 percent secure system, and there is nothing that is foolproof, so a single specific protection mechanism should never be solely relied upon. It is important that every environment have multiple layers of security. These layers may employ a variety of methods, such as routers, firewalls, network segments, IDSs, encryption, authentication software, physical security, and traffic control. The layers need to work together in a coordinated manner so that one does not impede another's functionality and introduce a security hole.

As an example, consider the steps an intruder might have to take to access critical data held within a company's back-end database. The intruder first has to penetrate the firewall and use packets and methods that will not be identified and detected by the IDS (more information on these devices can be found in Chapter 13). The attacker next has to circumvent an internal router performing packet filtering, and then possibly penetrate another firewall used to separate one internal network from another (see Figure 2.3). From there, the intruder must break the access controls that are on the database, which means having to do a dictionary or brute-force attack to be able to authenticate to the database software. Once the intruder has gotten this far, the data still needs to be located within the database. This may in turn be complicated by the use of access control lists outlining who can actually view or modify the data. That is a lot of work.

• **Figure 2.3**   Layered security

This example illustrates the different layers of security many environments employ. It is important to implement several different layers because if intruders succeed at one layer, you want to be able to stop them at the next. The redundancy of different protection layers assures that there is no one single point of failure pertaining to security. If a network used only a firewall to protect its assets, an attacker able to penetrate this device successfully would find the rest of the network open and vulnerable.

An example of how different security methods can work against each other is exemplified when firewalls encounter encrypted network traffic. An organization may utilize encryption so that an outside customer communicating with a specific web server is assured that sensitive data being exchanged is protected. If this encrypted data is encapsulated within Secure Sockets Layer (SSL) or Transport Layer Security (TLS) packets and then sent through a firewall, the firewall may not be able to read the payload information in the individual packets.

The layers usually are depicted starting at the top, with more general types of protection, and progressing downward through each layer, with increasing granularity at each layer as you get closer to the actual resource, as you can see in Figure 2.4. This is because the top-layer protection mechanism is responsible for looking at an enormous amount of traffic, and it would be overwhelming and cause too much of a performance degradation if each aspect of the packet were inspected. Instead, each layer usually digs deeper into the packet and looks for specific items. Layers that are closer to the resource have to deal with only a fraction of the traffic that the top-layer security mechanism does, and thus looking deeper and at more granular aspects of the traffic will not cause as much of a performance hit.

• **Figure 2.4**   Various layers of security

Diversity of Defense

Diversity of defense is a concept that complements the idea of various layers of security. It involves making different layers of security dissimilar so that even if attackers know how to get through a system that comprises one layer, they may not know how to get through a different type of layer that employs a different system for security.

If an environment has two firewalls that form a demilitarized zone (DMZ), for example, one firewall may be placed at the perimeter of the Internet and the DMZ. This firewall analyzes the traffic that is entering through that specific access point and enforces certain types of restrictions. The other firewall may then be placed between the DMZ and the internal network. When applying the diversity-of-defense concept, you should set up these two firewalls to filter for different types of traffic and provide different types of restrictions. The first firewall, for example, may make sure that no FTP, SNMP, or Telnet traffic enters the network but allow SMTP, SSH, HTTP, and SSL traffic through. The second firewall may not allow SSL or SSH through and may interrogate SMTP and HTTP traffic to make sure that certain types of attacks are not part of that traffic.

Access Control

The term *access control* has been used to describe a variety of protection schemes. It sometimes refers to all security features used to prevent unauthorized access to a computer system or network. In this sense, it may be confused with authentication. More properly, **access control** is the ability to control whether a subject (such as an individual or a process running on a computer system) can interact with an object (such as a file or hardware device). Authentication, on the other hand, deals with verifying the identity of a subject. To help understand the difference, consider the example of an individual attempting to log into a computer system or network.

Authentication is the process used to verify to the computer system or network that the individual is who they claim to be. The most common method to do this is through the use of a user ID and password. Once the individual has verified their identity, access controls regulate what the individual can actually do on the system. Just because a person is granted entry to the system does not mean that they should have access to all data the system contains.

Authentication Mechanisms

Access controls define what actions a user can perform or what objects a user can have access to. These controls assume that the identity of the user has been verified. It is the job of authentication mechanisms to ensure that only valid users are admitted. Described another way, authentication is using some mechanism to prove that you are who you claim to be. There are three general factors commonly used in authentication. In order to verify your identity, you can provide

- Something you know (knowledge factor)
- Something you have (possession factor)
- Something about you (something that you are; inherent factor)

The most common authentication mechanism is to provide something that only you, the valid user, should know. The most frequently used example of this is the common user ID (or username) and password. In theory, since you are not supposed to share your password with anybody else, only you should know your password, and thus by providing it, you are proving to the system that you are who you claim to be. Another mechanism for authentication is to provide something that you have in your possession, such as a magnetic stripe card that contains identifying information. The third mechanism is to use something about you for identification purposes, such as your fingerprint or the geometry of your hand. Obviously, for the second and third mechanisms to work, additional hardware devices need to be used (to read the card, fingerprint, or hand geometry).

Access Control vs. Authentication

It may seem that access control and authentication are two ways to describe the same protection mechanism. This, however, is not the case. Authentication provides a way to verify to the computer who the user is. Once the user has been authenticated, the access controls decide what operations the user can perform. The two go hand-in-hand but they are not the same thing.

Authentication and Access Control Policies

Policies are statements of what the organization wants to accomplish. The organization needs to identify goals and intentions for many different aspects of security. Each aspect will have associated policies and procedures.

Group Policy

Operating systems such as Windows and Linux allow administrators to organize users into groups, to create categories of users for which similar access policies can be established. Using groups saves the administrator time, as adding a new user will not require the administrator to create a completely new user profile; instead, the administrator can determine to which group the new user belongs and then add the user to that group.

A group policy defines for the group things such as the applicable operating system and application settings and permissions. Examples of groups commonly found include administrator, user, and guest. Take care when creating groups and assigning users to them so that you do not provide more access than is absolutely required for members of that group. It would be simple to make everybody an administrator—it would cut down on the number of requests users make of beleaguered administrators—but this is not a wise choice, as it also enables users to modify the system in ways that could impact security. Establishing the rights levels of access for the various groups up front will save you time and eliminate potential problems that might be encountered later on. More on this subject will be covered in Chapter 14.

> **Tech Tip**
>
> **Group Policy**
> *The term* group policy *has different meanings in Linux and Windows systems. In Linux, group policies typically refer to group-level permissions associated with file systems. In Windows, group policies refer to Active Directory objects used to enforce configuration and permissions across a domain.*

Password Policy

Since passwords are the most common authentication mechanism, it is imperative that organizations have a policy that addresses them. The *password policy* should address the procedures used for selecting user passwords (specifying what is considered an acceptably complex password in the organization in terms of the character set and length), the frequency with which passwords must be changed, and how passwords will be distributed. Procedures for creating new passwords should an employee forget her old password also need to be addressed, as well as the acceptable handling of passwords (for example, they should not be shared with anybody else, they should not be written down, and so on). It might also be useful to have the policy address the issue of password cracking by administrators, to enable them to discover weak passwords selected by employees.

> A password policy is one of the most basic policies that an organization can have. Make sure you understand the basics of what constitutes a good password along with the other issues that surround password creation, expiration, sharing, and use.

Note that the developer of the password policy and associated procedures can go overboard and create an environment that negatively impacts employee productivity and leads to poorer security, not better. If, for example, the frequency with which passwords are changed is too great, users might write them down or forget them. Neither of these is a desirable outcome, as the former makes it possible for an intruder to find a password and gain access to the system, and the latter leads to too many people losing productivity as they wait for a new password to be created to allow them access again. More information on password policies can be found in Chapter 22.

■ Security Models

An important issue when designing the software that will operate and control secure computer systems and networks is the security model that the system or network will be based upon. The security model will implement the security policy that has been chosen and enforce those characteristics deemed most important by the system designers. For example, if confidentiality is considered paramount, the model should make certain no data is disclosed to unauthorized individuals. A model enforcing confidentiality may allow unauthorized individuals to modify or delete data, as this would not violate the tenets of the model because the true values for the data would still remain confidential. Of course, this model may not be appropriate for all environments. In some instances, the unauthorized modification of data may be considered a more serious issue than its unauthorized disclosure. In such cases, the model would be responsible for enforcing the integrity of the data instead of its confidentiality. Choosing the model to base the design on is critical if you want to ensure that the resulting system accurately enforces the security policy desired. This, however, is only the starting point, and it does not imply that you have to make a choice between confidentiality and data integrity, as both are important.

Confidentiality Models

Data confidentiality has generally been the chief concern of the military. For instance, the U.S. military encouraged the development of the **Bell-LaPadula security model** to address data confidentiality in computer operating systems. This model is especially useful in designing multilevel security systems that implement the military's hierarchical security scheme, which includes levels of classification such as *Unclassified, Confidential, Secret,* and *Top Secret.* Similar classification schemes can be used in industry, where classifications might include *Publicly Releasable, Proprietary,* and *Company Confidential.*

A second confidentiality model, the **Brewer-Nash security model**, is one defined by controlling read and write access based on conflict of interest rules. This model is also known as the Chinese Wall model, after the concept of separating groups through the use of an impenetrable wall.

Bell-LaPadula Model

The Bell-LaPadula security model employs both mandatory and discretionary access control mechanisms when implementing its two basic security principles. The first of these principles is called the **Simple Security Rule**, which states that no subject (such as a user or a program) can read information from an object (such as a file) with a security classification higher than that possessed by the subject itself. This means that the system must prevent a user with only a Secret clearance, for example, from reading a document labeled Top Secret. This rule is often referred to as the "no-read-up" rule.

The second security principle enforced by the Bell-LaPadula security model is known as the ***-property** (pronounced "star property"). This principle states that a subject can write to an object only if the target's security classification is greater than or equal to the object's security classification. This means that a user with a Secret clearance can write to a file with a Secret or Top Secret classification but cannot write to a file with only an Unclassified classification. This at first may appear to be a bit confusing, since this principle allows users to write to files that they are not allowed to view, thus enabling them to actually destroy files that they don't have the classification to see. This is true, but keep in mind that the Bell-LaPadula model is designed to enforce confidentiality, not integrity. Writing to a file that you don't have the clearance to view is not considered a confidentiality issue; it is an integrity issue.

 The Simple Security Rule is just that: the most basic of security rules. It essentially states that in order for you to see something, you have to be authorized to see it.

Whereas the *-property allows a user to write to a file of equal or greater security classification, it doesn't allow a user to write to a file with a lower security classification. This, too, may be confusing at first—after all, shouldn't a user with a Secret clearance, who can view a file marked Unclassified, be allowed to write to that file? The answer to this, from a security perspective, is "no." The reason again relates to wanting to avoid either accidental or deliberate security disclosures. The system is designed to make it impossible (hopefully) for data to be disclosed to those without the appropriate level to view it. As shown in Figure 2.5, if it were possible for a user with a Top Secret clearance to either deliberately or accidentally write Top Secret information and place it in a file marked Confidential, a user with only a Confidential security clearance could then access this file and view the Top Secret information. Thus, data would have been disclosed to an individual not authorized to view it. This is what the system should protect against and is the reason for what is known as the "no-write-down" rule.

Not all environments are more concerned with confidentiality than integrity. In a financial institution, for example, viewing somebody's bank balance is an issue, but a greater issue would be the ability to actually modify that balance. In environments where integrity is more important, a different model than the Bell-LaPadula security model is needed.

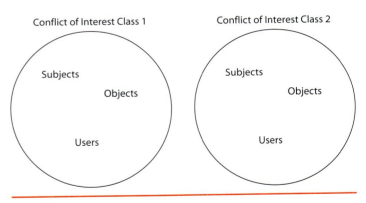

Unclassified users should not access Top Secret material (no read up)
Top Secret files should not be written to Confidential storage (no write down)

● **Figure 2.5**   Bell-LaPadula security model

Brewer-Nash Security Model

One of the tenets associated with access is *need to know*. Separate groups within an organization may have differing needs with respect to access to information. A security model that takes into account user conflict-of-interest aspects is the Brewer-Nash security model. In this model, information flows are modeled to prevent information from flowing between subjects and objects when a conflict of interest would occur. As previously noted, this model is also known as a Chinese Wall model, after the Great Wall of China, a structure designed to separate groups of people. As shown in Figure 2.6, separate groups are defined and access controls are designed to enforce the separation of the groups.

Conflict of Interest Class 1

Subjects

Objects

Users

Conflict of Interest Class 2

Subjects

Objects

Users

● **Figure 2.6**   Brewer-Nash security model

Integrity Models

The Bell-LaPadula model was developed in the early 1970s but was found to be insufficient for all environments. As an alternative, Kenneth Biba studied the integrity issue and developed what is called the **Biba security model** in the late 1970s. Additional work was performed in the 1980s that led to the Clark-Wilson security model, which also places its emphasis on integrity rather than confidentiality.

No write up
Prevent errors
From low integrity

No Read Down
Prevent reading
untrue material

Maintainers of reference truth should not read down, lest pollute the truth with errors.
Untrained Users should never write to a higher level, lest they promote errors

• **Figure 2.7** Bibb Security Model

The Biba Security Model

In the Biba model (see Figure 2.7), instead of security classifications, *integrity levels* are used. A principle of integrity levels is that data with a higher integrity level is believed to be more accurate or reliable than data with a lower integrity level. Integrity levels indicate the level of "trust" that can be placed in information at the different levels. Integrity levels differ from security levels in another way—they limit the modification of information as opposed to the flow of information.

An initial attempt at implementing an integrity-based model was captured in what is referred to as the **Low-Water-Mark policy**. This policy in many ways is the opposite of the *-property in that it prevents subjects from writing to objects of a higher integrity level. The policy also contains a second rule that states the integrity level of a subject will be lowered if it reads an object of a lower integrity level. The reason for this is that if the subject then uses data from that object, the highest the integrity level can be for a new object created from it is the same level of integrity of the original object. In other words, the level of trust you can place in data formed from data at a specific integrity level cannot be higher than the level of trust you have in the subject creating the new data object, and the level of trust you have in the subject can only be as high as the level of trust you had in the original data. The final rule contained in the Low-Water-Mark policy states that a subject can execute a program only if the program's integrity level is equal to or less than the integrity level of the subject. This ensures that data modified by a program only has the level of trust (integrity level) that can be placed in the individual who executed the program.

While the Low-Water-Mark policy certainly prevents unauthorized modification of data, it has the unfortunate side effect of eventually lowering the integrity levels of all subjects to the lowest level on the system (unless the subject always views files with the same level of integrity). This is because of the second rule, which lowers the integrity level of the subject after accessing an object of a lower integrity level. There is no way specified in the policy to ever raise the subject's integrity level back to its original value. A second policy, known as the **Ring policy**, addresses this issue by allowing any subject to read any object without regard to the object's level of integrity and without lowering the subject's integrity level. This, unfortunately, can lead to a situation where data created by a subject after reading data of a lower integrity level could end up having a higher level of trust placed upon it than it should.

The Biba security model implements a hybrid of the Ring and Low-Water-Mark policies. Biba's model in many respects is the opposite of the Bell-LaPadula model in that what it enforces are "no-read-down" and "no-write-up" policies. It also implements a third rule that prevents subjects from executing programs of a higher level. The Biba security model thus addresses the problems mentioned with both the Ring and Low-Water-Mark policies.

The Clark-Wilson Security Model

The **Clark-Wilson security model** takes an entirely different approach than the Biba and Bell-LaPadula models, using transactions as the basis for its rules. It defines two levels of integrity only: constrained data items (CDIs) and unconstrained data items (UDIs). CDI data is subject to integrity controls while UDI data is not. The model then defines two types of processes: integrity verification processes (IVPs), which ensure that CDI data meets integrity constraints (to ensure the system is in a valid state), and transformation processes (TPs), which change the state of data from one valid state to another. Data in this model cannot be modified directly by a user; it must be changed by trusted TPs, access to which can be restricted (thus restricting the ability of a user to perform certain activities).

It is useful to return to the prior example of the banking account balance to describe the need for integrity-based models. In the Clark-Wilson model, the account balance would be a CDI because its integrity is a critical function for the bank. A client's color preference for their checkbook is not a critical function and would be considered a UDI. Since the integrity of account balances is of extreme importance, changes to a person's balance must be accomplished through the use of a TP. Ensuring that the balance is correct would be the duty of an IVP. Only certain employees of the bank should have the ability to modify an individual's account, which can be controlled by limiting the number of individuals who have the authority to execute TPs that result in account modification. Certain very critical functions may actually be split into multiple TPs to enforce another important principle, *separation of duties* (introduced earlier in the chapter). This limits the authority any one individual has so that multiple individuals will be required to execute certain critical functions.

Chapter 2 Review

■ Chapter Summary

After reading this chapter and completing the exercises, you should understand the following regarding the basics of security, security terminology, and security models.

Define basic terms associated with computer and information security

- Information assurance and information security place the security focus on the information and not on the hardware or software used to process it.

- The original goal of computer and network security was to provide confidentiality, integrity, and availability—the "CIA" of security.

- Additional elements of security can include authentication, authorization, auditability, and nonrepudiation.

- The operational model of computer security tells us that protection is provided by prevention, detection, and response.

Identify the basic approaches to computer and information security

- Host security focuses on protecting each computer and device individually, whereas network security focuses on addressing protection of the network as a whole.

- For many organizations, a combination of host security and network security is needed to adequately address the wide range of possible security threats.

Identify the basic principles of computer and information security

- Principle of least privilege is to use the minimum privileges necessary to perform a task.

- Principle of separation of privilege states that critical items should require multiple parties.

- Principle of fail-safe default states that deny by default (implicit deny) and only grant access with explicit permission should be employed in access decisions.

- Principle of economy of mechanism states that protection mechanisms should be small and simple.

- Principle of complete mediation states that protection mechanisms should cover every access to every object and should never be bypassed.

- Principle of open design states that protection mechanisms should not depend upon secrecy of the mechanism itself.

- Principle of least common mechanism states that the protection mechanisms should be shared to the least degree possible among users.

- Principle of psychological acceptability states that protection mechanisms should not impact users, or if they do, the impact should be minimal.

- Principle of defense in depth, or layered security, is that multiple layers of differing, overlapping controls should be employed.

- Diversity of defense is a concept that complements the idea of various layers of security. It means to make the layers dissimilar so that if one layer is penetrated, the next layer can't also be penetrated using the same method.

Distinguish among various methods to implement access controls

- Access is the ability of a subject to interact with an object. Access controls are those devices and methods used to limit which subjects may interact with specific objects.

- An access control list (ACL) is a mechanism that is used to define whether a user has certain access privileges for a system. Other methods include discretionary access control (DAC), mandatory access control (MAC), role-based access control (RBAC), and rule-based access control.

Describe methods used to verify the identity and authenticity of an individual

- Authentication mechanisms ensure that only valid users are provided access to the computer system or network.

- The three general methods commonly used in authentication involve users providing either something they know, something they have, or something unique about them (something they are).

Recognize some of the basic models used to implement security in operating systems

- Security models enforce the chosen security policy.
- There are two basic categories of models: those that ensure confidentiality and those that ensure integrity.
- Bell-LaPadula is a confidentiality security model whose development was prompted by the demands of the U.S. military and its security clearance scheme.
- The Bell-LaPadula security model enforces "no-read-up" and "no-write-down" rules to avoid the deliberate or accidental disclosure of information to individuals not authorized to receive it.

- The Brewer-Nash security model (Chinese Wall model) is a confidentiality model that separates users based on conflicts of interest.
- The Biba security model is an integrity-based model that, in many respects, implements the opposite of what the Bell-LaPadula model does— that is, "no-read-down" and "no-write-up" rules.
- The Clark-Wilson security model is an integrity-based model designed to limit the processes an individual may perform as well as require that critical data be modified only through specific transformation processes.

Key Terms

*-property *(34)*
access control *(31)*
auditability *(20)*
authentication *(20)*
availability *(20)*
Bell-LaPadula security model *(34)*
Biba security model *(35)*
Brewer-Nash security model *(34)*
Clark-Wilson security model *(37)*
complete mediation *(27)*
confidentiality *(20)*
default deny *(26)*
defense in depth *(29)*
diversity of defense *(31)*
economy of mechanism *(27)*
fail-safe defaults *(26)*
hacking *(19)*
host security *(23)*

implicit deny *(26)*
integrity *(20)*
layered security *(29)*
least common mechanism *(28)*
least privilege *(24)*
Low-Water-Mark policy *(36)*
network security *(24)*
nonrepudiation *(20)*
open design *(27)*
operational model of computer security *(20)*
phreaking *(19)*
psychological acceptability *(29)*
Ring policy *(36)*
security through obscurity *(28)*
separation of duties *(25)*
separation of privilege *(25)*
Simple Security Rule *(34)*

Key Terms Quiz

Use terms from the Key Terms list to complete the sentences that follow. Don't use the same term more than once. Not all terms will be used.

1. _____ is a term used to describe the condition where a user cannot deny that an event has occurred.

2. The _____ is an integrity-based security model that bases its security on control of the processes that are allowed to modify critical data, referred to as constrained data items.

3. The security principle used in the Bell-LaPadula security model that states that no subject can read from an object with a higher security classification is called the _____.

4. The principle that states a subject has only the necessary rights and privileges to perform its task, with no additional permissions, is called _____.

5. _____ is the principle in security where protection mechanisms should be kept as simple and as small as possible.

6. _____ is the principle that protection mechanisms should minimize user-level impact.

7. _____ is the process used to ensure that an individual is who they claim to be.

8. The architecture in which multiple methods of security defense are applied to prevent realization of threat-based risks is called _____.

9. _____ is the process of combining seemingly unimportant information with other pieces of information to divulge potentially sensitive information.

10. Implicit deny is an operationalization of the principle of _____.

■ Multiple-Choice Quiz

1. Which of the following is not a principle of security?
   A. Principle of least privilege
   B. Principle of economy of mechanism
   C. Principle of efficient access
   D. Principle of open access

2. The CIA of security includes:
   A. Confidentiality, integrity, authentication
   B. Confidentiality, integrity, availability
   C. Certificates, integrity, availability
   D. Confidentiality, inspection, authentication

3. The security principle used in the Bell-LaPadula security model that states that no subject can read from an object with a higher security classification is the:
   A. Simple Security Rule
   B. Ring policy
   C. Mandatory access control
   D. *-property

4. Which of the following concepts requires users and system processes to use the minimal amount of permission necessary to function?
   A. Layer defense
   B. Diversified defense
   C. Simple Security Rule
   D. Least privilege

5. Which security model separates users based on conflict-of-interest issues?
   A. Bell-LaPadula
   B. Brewer-Nash
   C. Biba
   D. Clark-Wilson

6. The Bell-LaPadula security model is an example of a security model that is based on:
   A. The integrity of the data
   B. The availability of the data
   C. The confidentiality of the data
   D. The authenticity of the data

7. The term used to describe the requirement that different portions of a critical process must be performed by different people is:
   A. Least privilege
   B. Defense in depth
   C. Separation of duties
   D. Job rotation

8. Hiding information to prevent disclosure is an example of:
   A. Security through obscurity
   B. Certificate-based security
   C. Discretionary data security
   D. Defense in depth

9. The problem with the Low-Water-Mark policy is that it:

   A. Is aimed at ensuring confidentiality and not integrity

   B. Could ultimately result in all subjects having the integrity level of the least-trusted object on the system

   C. Could result in the unauthorized modification of data

   D. Does not adequately prevent users from viewing files they are not entitled to view

10. The concept of blocking an action unless it is specifically authorized is:

    A. Implicit deny

    B. Least privilege

    C. Simple Security Rule

    D. Hierarchical defense model

▪ Essay Quiz

1. Your company has decided to increase the authentication security by requiring remote employees to use a security token as well as a password to log onto the network. The employees are grumbling about the new requirements because they don't want to have to carry around the token with them and don't understand why it's necessary. Write a brief memo to the staff to educate them on the general ways that authentication can be performed. Then explain why your company has decided to use security tokens in addition to passwords.

2. The new CEO for your company just retired from the military and wants to use some of the same computer systems and security software she used while with the military. Explain to her the reasons that confidentiality-based security models are not adequate for all environments. Provide at least two examples of environments where a confidentiality-based security model is not sufficient.

3. Describe why the concept of "security through obscurity" is generally considered a bad principle to rely on. Provide some real-world examples of where you have seen this principle used.

4. Write a brief essay describing the principle of least privilege and how it can be employed to enhance security. Provide at least two examples of environments in which it can be used for security purposes.

Lab Projects

• Lab Project 2.1

In an environment familiar to you (your school or where you work, for example), determine whether the principle of diversity of defense has been employed and list the different layers of security that are employed. Discuss whether you think they are sufficient and whether the principle of diversity of defense has also been used.

• Lab Project 2.2

Pick an operating system that enforces some form of access control and determine how it is implemented in that system.

chapter 3

Operational and Organizational Security

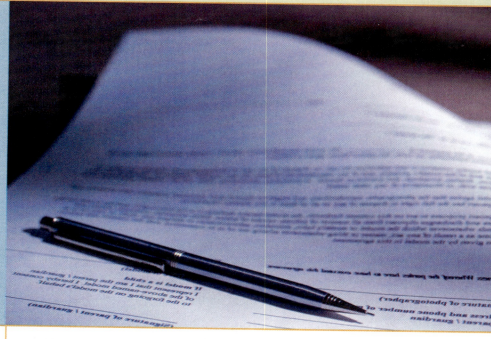

We will bankrupt ourselves in the vain search for absolute security.

—Dwight David Eisenhower

In this chapter, you will learn how to

- Identify various operational aspects to security in your organization
- Identify various policies and procedures in your organization
- Identify the security awareness and training needs of an organization
- Understand the different types of agreements employed in negotiating security requirements
- Describe the physical security components that can protect your computers and network
- Identify environmental factors that can affect security
- Identify factors that affect the security of the growing number of wireless technologies used for data transmission
- Prevent disclosure through electronic emanations

Organizations achieve operational security through policies and procedures that guide user's interactions with data and data processing systems. Developing and aligning these efforts with the goals of the business is a crucial part of developing a successful security program. One method of ensuring coverage is to align efforts with the operational security model described in the last chapter. This breaks efforts into groups; prevention, detection, and response elements.

Prevention technologies are designed to keep individuals from being able to gain access to systems or data they are not authorized to use. Originally, this was the sole approach to security. Eventually we learned that in an operational environment, prevention is extremely difficult and relying on prevention technologies alone is not sufficient. This led to the rise of technologies to detect and respond to events that occur when prevention fails. Together, the prevention technologies and the detection and response technologies form the operational model for computer security.

Policies, Procedures, Standards, and Guidelines

An important part of any organization's approach to implementing security are the policies, procedures, standards, and guidelines that are established to detail what users and administrators should be doing to maintain the security of the systems and network. Collectively, these documents provide the guidance needed to determine how security will be implemented in the organization. Given this guidance, the specific technology and security mechanisms required can be planned for.

Policies are high-level, broad statements of what the organization wants to accomplish. They are made by management when laying out the organization's position on some issue. **Procedures** are the step-by-step instructions on how to implement policies in the organization. They describe exactly how employees are expected to act in a given situation or to accomplish a specific task. **Standards** are mandatory elements regarding the implementation of a policy. They are accepted specifications that provide specific details on how a policy is to be enforced. Some standards are externally driven. Regulations for banking and financial institutions, for example, require certain security measures be taken by law. Other standards may be set by the organization to meet its own security goals. **Guidelines** are recommendations relating to a policy. The key term in this case is *recommendations*—guidelines are not mandatory steps.

Just as the network itself constantly changes, the policies, procedures, standards, and guidelines should be included in living documents that are periodically evaluated and changed as necessary. The constant monitoring of the network and the periodic review of the relevant documents are part of the process that is the operational model. When applied to policies, this process results in what is known as the *policy lifecycle*. This operational process and policy lifecycle roughly consist of four steps in relation to your security policies and solutions:

1. Plan (adjust) for security in your organization.
2. Implement the plans.
3. Monitor the implementation.
4. Evaluate the effectiveness.

In the first step, you develop the policies, procedures, and guidelines that will be implemented and design the security components that will protect your network. There are a variety of governing instruments, from standards to compliance rules that will provide boundaries for these documents. Once these documents are designed and developed, you can implement the plans. Part of the implementation of any policy, procedure, or guideline is an instruction period during which those who will be affected by the change or introduction of this new document learn about its contents. Next, you monitor to ensure that both the hardware and the software as well as the policies, procedures, and guidelines are effective in securing your systems. Finally, you evaluate the effectiveness of the security measures you have in place. This step may include a *vulnerability assessment* (an attempt to identify and prioritize the list of vulnerabilities within a system

These documents guide how security will be implemented in the organization:

Policies High-level, broad statements of what the organization wants to accomplish

Procedures Step-by-step instructions on how to implement the policies

Standards Mandatory elements regarding the implementation of a policy

Guidelines Recommendations relating to a policy

or network) and a *penetration test* (a method to check the security of a system by simulating an attack by a malicious individual) of your system to ensure the security is adequate. After evaluating your security posture, you begin again with step one, this time adjusting the security mechanisms you have in place, and then continue with this cyclical process.

Regarding security, every organization should have several common policies in place (in addition to those already discussed relative to access control methods). These include, but are not limited to, security policies regarding change management, classification of information, acceptable use, due care and due diligence, due process, need to know, disposal and destruction of data, service level agreements, human resources issues, codes of ethics, and policies governing incident response.

Security Policies

In keeping with the high-level nature of policies, the **security policy** is a high-level statement produced by senior management that outlines both what security means to the organization and the organization's goals for security. The main security policy can then be broken down into additional policies that cover specific topics. Statements such as "this organization will exercise the principle of least access in its handling of client information" would be an example of a security policy. The security policy can also describe how security is to be handled from an organizational point of view (such as describing which office and corporate officer or manager oversees the organization's security program).

In addition to policies related to access control, the organization's security policy should include the specific policies described in the next sections. All policies should be reviewed on a regular basis and updated as needed. Generally, policies should be updated less frequently than the procedures that implement them, since the high-level goals will not change as often as the environment in which they must be implemented. All policies should be reviewed by the organization's legal counsel, and a plan should be outlined that describes how the organization will ensure that employees will be made aware of the policies. Policies can also be made stronger by including references to the authority who made the policy (whether this policy comes from the CEO or is a department-level policy, for example) and references to any laws or regulations that are applicable to the specific policy and environment.

Change Management Policy

The purpose of *change management* is to ensure proper procedures are followed when modifications to the IT infrastructure are made. These modifications can be prompted by a number of different events, including new legislation, updated versions of software or hardware, implementation of new software or hardware, or improvements to the infrastructure. The term "management" implies that this process should be controlled in some systematic way, and that is indeed the purpose. Changes to the infrastructure might have a detrimental impact on operations. New versions of operating systems or application software might be incompatible with other software or hardware the organization is using. Without a process to manage the change, an organization might suddenly find itself unable to conduct business. A change management process should include various stages, including a method to request a change to the infrastructure, a review and approval process for the request, an examination of the consequences of the change, resolution (or mitigation) of any detrimental effects the change might incur, implementation of the change, and documentation of the process as it related to the change.

Data Policies

System integration with third parties frequently involves the sharing of data. Data can be shared for the purpose of processing or storage. Control over data is a significant issue in third-party relationships. There are numerous questions that need to be addressed. The question of who owns the data, both the data shared with third parties and subsequent data developed as part of the relationship, is an issue that needs to be established.

Data Ownership

Data requires a data owner. Data ownership roles for all data elements need to be defined in the business. Data ownership is a business function, where the requirements for security, privacy, retention, and other business functions must be established. Not all data requires the same handling restrictions, but all data requires these characteristics to be defined. This is the responsibility of the data owner.

Unauthorized Data Sharing

Unauthorized data sharing can be a significant issue, and in today's world, data has value and is frequently used for secondary purposes. Ensuring that all parties in the relationship understand the data-sharing requirements is an important prerequisite. Equally important is ensuring that all parties understand the security requirements of shared data.

Data Backups

Data ownership requirements include backup responsibilities. Data backup requirements include determining the level of backup, restore objectives, and level of protection requirements. These can be defined by the data owner and then executed by operational IT personnel. Determining the backup responsibilities and developing the necessary operational procedures to ensure that adequate backups occur are important security elements.

Classification of Information

A key component of IT security is the protection of the information processed and stored on the computer systems and network. Organizations deal with many different types of information, and they need to recognize that not all information is of equal importance or sensitivity. This requires classification of information into various categories, each with its own requirements for its handling. Factors that affect the classification of specific information include its value to the organization (what will be the impact to the organization if it loses this information?), its age, and laws or regulations that govern its protection. The most widely known system of classification of information is that implemented by the U.S. government (including the military), which classifies information into categories such as *Confidential, Secret,* and *Top Secret.* Businesses have similar desires to protect information and often use categories such as *Publicly Releasable, Proprietary, Company Confidential,* and *For Internal Use Only.* Each policy for the classification of information should describe how it should be protected, who may have access to it, who has the authority to release it and how, and how it should be destroyed. All employees of the organization should be trained in the procedures for handling the information that they are authorized to access. Discretionary and mandatory access control techniques use classifications as a method to identify who may have access to what resources.

Data Labeling, Handling, and Disposal

Effective data classification programs include data labeling, which enables personnel working with the data to know whether it is sensitive and to understand the levels of protection required. When the data is inside an information-processing system, the protections should be designed into the system. But when the data leaves this cocoon of protection, whether by printing, downloading, or copying, it becomes necessary to ensure continued protection by other means. This is where data labeling assists users in fulfilling their responsibilities. Training to ensure that labeling occurs and that it is used and followed is important for users whose roles can be impacted by this material.

Training plays an important role in ensuring proper data handling and disposal. Personnel are intimately involved in several specific tasks associated with data handling and data destruction/disposal and, if properly trained, can act as a security control. Untrained or inadequately trained personnel will not be a productive security control and, in fact, can be a source of potential compromise.

Need to Know

Another common security principle is that of *need to know,* which goes hand-in-hand with *least privilege.* The guiding factor here is that each individual in the organization is supplied with only the absolute minimum amount of information and privileges he or she needs to perform their work tasks. To obtain access to any piece of information, the individual must have a justified need to know. A policy spelling out these two principles as guiding philosophies for the organization should be created. The policy should also address who in the organization can grant access to information and who can assign privileges to employees.

Disposal and Destruction Policy

Many potential intruders have learned the value of dumpster diving. An organization must be concerned about not only paper trash and discarded objects, but also the information stored on discarded objects such as computers. Several government organizations have been embarrassed when old computers sold to salvagers proved to contain sensitive documents on their hard drives. It is critical for every organization to have a strong *disposal and destruction policy* and related procedures.

Important papers should be shredded, and *important* in this case means anything that might be useful to a potential intruder. It is amazing what intruders can do with what appear to be innocent pieces of information.

Before magnetic storage media (such as disks or tapes) is discarded in the trash or sold for salvage, it should have all files deleted, and should be overwritten at least three times with all 1's, all 0's, and then random characters. Commercial products are available to destroy files using this process. It is not sufficient simply to delete all files and leave it at that, since the deletion process affects only the pointers to where the files are stored and doesn't actually get rid of all the bits in the file. This is why it is possible to "undelete" files and recover them after they have been deleted.

A safer method for destroying files from a storage device is to destroy the data magnetically, using a strong magnetic field to *degauss* the media. This effectively destroys all data on the media. Several commercial degaussers are available for this purpose. Another method that can be used on hard drives is to use a file on them (the sort of file you'd find in a hardware store) and actually file off the magnetic material from the surface of the platter. Shredding floppy media is normally sufficient, but simply cutting a floppy disk into a few pieces is not enough—data has been successfully recovered from floppies that were cut into only a couple of pieces. CDs and DVDs also need to be disposed of appropriately. Many paper shredders now have the ability to shred these forms of storage media. In some highly secure environments, the only acceptable method of disposing of hard drives and other storage devices is the actual physical destruction of the devices. Matching the security action to the level of risk is important to recognize in this instance. Destroying hard drives that do not have sensitive information is wasteful; proper file scrubbing is probably appropriate. For drives with ultra-sensitive information, physical destruction makes sense. There is no single answer, but as in most things associated with information security, the best practice is to match the action to the level of risk.

Human Resources Policies

It has been said that the weakest links in the security chain are the humans. Consequently, it is important for organizations to have policies in place relative to their employees. Policies that relate to the hiring of individuals are primarily important. The organization needs to make sure that it hires individuals who can be trusted with the organization's data and that of its clients. Once employees are hired, they should be kept from slipping into the category of "disgruntled employee." Finally, policies must be developed to address the inevitable point in the future when an employee leaves the organization—either on his or her own or with the "encouragement" of the organization itself. Security issues must be considered at each of these points.

Many organizations overlook the security implications that decisions by Human Resources may have. Human Resources personnel and security personnel should have a close working relationship. Decisions on the hiring and firing of personnel have direct security implications for the organization. As a result, procedures should be in place that specify which actions must be taken when an employee is hired, is terminated, or retires.

Code of Ethics

Numerous professional organizations have established codes of ethics for their members. Each of these describes the expected behavior of their members from a high-level standpoint. Organizations can adopt this idea as well. For organizations, a code of ethics can set the tone for how employees will be expected to act and to conduct business. The code should demand honesty from employees and require that they perform all activities in a professional manner. The code could also address principles of privacy and confidentiality and state how employees should treat client and organizational data. Conflicts of interest can often cause problems, so this could also be covered in the code of ethics.

By outlining a code of ethics, the organization can encourage an environment that is conducive to integrity and high ethical standards. For additional ideas on possible codes of ethics, check professional organizations such as the Institute for Electrical and Electronics Engineers (IEEE), the Association for Computing Machinery (ACM), or the Information Systems Security Association (ISSA).

Job Rotation

An interesting approach to enhance security that is gaining increasing attention is *job rotation*. Organizations often discuss the benefits of rotating individuals through various jobs in an organization's IT department. By rotating through jobs, individuals gain a better perspective on how the various parts of IT can enhance (or hinder) the business. Since security is often a misunderstood aspect of IT, rotating individuals through security positions can result in a much wider understanding throughout the organization about potential security problems. It also can have the side benefit of a company not having to rely on any one individual too heavily for security expertise. If all security tasks are the domain of one employee, and that individual leaves suddenly, security at the organization could suffer. On the other hand, if security tasks are understood by many different individuals, the loss of any one individual has less of an impact on the organization.

Employee Hiring and Promotions

It is becoming common for organizations to run background checks on prospective employees and to check the references prospective employees supply. Frequently, organizations require drug testing, check for any past criminal activity, verify claimed educational credentials, and confirm reported work history. For highly sensitive environments, special security background investigations can also be required. Make sure that your organization hires the most capable and trustworthy employees, and that your policies are designed to ensure this.

After an individual has been hired, your organization needs to minimize the risk that the employee will ignore company rules and affect security. Periodic reviews by supervisory personnel, additional drug checks, and monitoring of activity during work may all be considered by the organization. If the organization chooses to implement any of these reviews, this must be specified in the organization's policies, and prospective employees should be made aware of these policies before being hired. What an organization can do in terms of monitoring and requiring drug tests, for example, can be severely restricted if not spelled out in advance as terms of employment. New hires should be made aware of all pertinent policies, especially those applying to security, and should be asked to sign documents indicating that they have read and understood them.

Occasionally an employee's status will change within the company. If the change can be construed as a negative personnel action (such as a demotion), supervisors should be alerted to watch for changes in behavior that

Tech Tip

Hiring Hackers

Hiring a skilled hacker may make sense from a technical skills point of view, but an organization also has to consider the broader ethical and business consequences and associated risks. Is the hacker completely reformed or not? How much time is needed to determine this? The real question is not "Would you hire a hacker?" but rather "Can you fire a hacker once he has had access to your systems?" Trust is an important issue with employees who have system administrator access, and the long-term ramifications need to be considered.

Tech Tip

Accounts of Former Employees

When conducting security assessments of organizations, security professionals frequently find active accounts for individuals who no longer work for the company. This is especially true for larger organizations, which may lack a clear process for the personnel office to communicate with the network administrators when an employee leaves the organization. These old accounts, however, are a weak point in the security perimeter for the organization and should be eliminated.

might indicate the employee is contemplating or conducting unauthorized activity. It is likely that the employee will be upset, and whether he acts on this to the detriment of the company is something that needs to be guarded against. In the case of a demotion, the individual may also lose certain privileges or access rights, and these changes should be made quickly so as to lessen the likelihood that the employee will destroy previously accessible data if he becomes disgruntled and decides to take revenge on the organization. On the other hand, if the employee is promoted, privileges may still change, but the need to make the change to access privileges may not be as urgent, though it should still be accomplished as quickly as possible. If the move is a lateral one, changes may also need to take place, and again they should be accomplished as quickly as possible.

Retirement, Separation, or Termination of an Employee

An employee leaving an organization can be either a positive or a negative action. Employees who are retiring by their own choice may announce their planned retirement weeks or even months in advance. Limiting their access to sensitive documents the moment they announce their intention may be the safest thing to do, but it might not be necessary. Each situation should be evaluated individually. If the situation is a forced retirement, the organization must determine the risk to its data if the employee becomes disgruntled as a result of the action. In this situation, the wisest choice might be to cut off the employee's access quickly and provide her with some additional vacation time. This might seem like an expensive proposition, but the danger to the company of having a disgruntled employee may justify it. Again, each case should be evaluated individually.

When an employee decides to leave a company, generally as a result of a new job offer, continued access to sensitive information should be carefully considered. If the employee is leaving as a result of hard feelings toward the company, it might be wise to quickly revoke her access privileges.

If the employee is leaving the organization because he is being terminated, you should assume that he is or will become disgruntled. While it may not seem the friendliest thing to do, an employee in this situation should immediately have his access privileges to sensitive information and facilities revoked.

Combinations should also be quickly changed once an employee has been informed of their termination. Access cards, keys, and badges should be collected; the employee should be escorted to her desk and watched as she packs personal belongings; and then she should be escorted from the building.

Mandatory Vacations

Organizations have provided vacation time to their employees for many years. Few, however, force employees to take this time if they don't want to. At some companies, employees are given the choice to either "use or lose" their vacation time; if they do not take all of their vacation time, they lose at least a portion of it. From a security standpoint, an employee who never takes time off might be involved in nefarious activity, such as fraud or embezzlement, and might be afraid that if he leaves on vacation, the organization will discover his illicit activities. As a result, requiring employees to use their vacation time through a policy of mandatory vacations can be

It is better to give a potentially disgruntled employee several weeks of paid vacation than to have him trash sensitive files to which he has access. Because employees typically know the pattern of management behavior with respect to termination, doing the right thing will pay dividends in the future for a firm.

Organizations commonly neglect to have a policy that mandates the removal of an individual's computer access upon termination. Not only should such a policy exist, but it should also include the procedures to reclaim and "clean" a terminated employee's computer system and accounts.

a security protection mechanism. Using mandatory vacations as a tool to detect fraud will require that somebody else also be trained in the functions of the employee who is on vacation. Having a second person familiar with security procedures is also a good policy in case something happens to the primary employee.

On-boarding/Off-boarding Business Partners

Just as it is important to manage the on- and off-boarding processes of company personnel, it is important to consider the same types of elements when making arrangements with third parties. Agreements with business partners tend to be fairly specific with respect to terms associated with mutual expectations associated with the process of the business. Considerations regarding the on-boarding and off-boarding processes are important, especially the off-boarding. When a contract arrangement with a third party comes to an end, issues as to data retention and destruction by the third party need to be addressed. These considerations need to be made prior to the establishment of the relationship, not added at the time that it is coming to an end.

On-boarding and off-boarding business procedures should be well documented to ensure compliance with legal requirements.

Social Media Networks

The rise of social media networks has changed many aspects of business. Whether used for marketing, communications, customer relations, or some other purpose, social media networks can be considered a form of third party. One of the challenges in working with social media networks and/or applications is their terms of use. While a relationship with a typical third party involves a negotiated set of agreements with respect to requirements, there is no negotiation with social media networks. The only option is to adopt their terms of service, so it is important to understand the implications of these terms with respect to the business use of the social network.

Acceptable Use Policy

An **acceptable use policy (AUP)** outlines what the organization considers to be the appropriate use of company resources, such as computer systems, e-mail, Internet access, and networks. Organizations should be concerned about personal use of organizational assets that does not benefit the company.

The goal of the AUP is to ensure employee productivity while limiting organizational liability through inappropriate use of the organization's assets. The AUP should clearly delineate what activities are not allowed. It should address issues such as the use of resources to conduct personal business, installation of hardware or software, remote access to systems and networks, the copying of company-owned software, and the responsibility of users to protect company assets, including data, software, and hardware. Statements regarding possible penalties for ignoring any of the policies (such as termination) should also be included.

Related to appropriate use of the organization's computer systems and networks by employees is the appropriate use by the organization. The most important of such issues is whether the organization considers it appropriate to monitor the employees' use of the systems and network.

If monitoring is considered appropriate, the organization should include a statement to this effect in the banner that appears at login. This repeatedly warns employees, and possible intruders, that their actions are subject to monitoring and that any misuse of the system will not be tolerated. Should the organization need to use in a civil or criminal case any information gathered during monitoring, the issue of whether the employee had an expectation of privacy, or whether it was even legal for the organization to be monitoring, is simplified if the organization can point to a statement that is always displayed that instructs users that use of the system constitutes consent to monitoring. Before any monitoring is conducted, or the actual wording on the warning message is created, the organization's legal counsel should be consulted to determine the appropriate way to address this issue in the particular jurisdiction.

In today's highly connected environment, every organization should have an AUP that spells out to all employees what the organization considers appropriate and inappropriate use of its computing and networks resources. Having this policy may be critical should the organization need to take disciplinary actions based on an abuse of its resources.

Internet Usage Policy

In today's highly connected environment, employee use of access to the Internet is of particular concern. The goal of the *Internet usage policy* is to ensure maximum employee productivity and to limit potential liability to the organization from inappropriate use of the Internet in a workplace. The Internet provides a tremendous temptation for employees to waste hours as they surf the Web for the scores of games from the previous night, conduct quick online stock transactions, or read the review of the latest blockbuster movie everyone is talking about. In addition, allowing employees to visit sites that may be considered offensive to others (such as pornographic or hate sites) can open the company to accusations of condoning a hostile work environment and result in legal liability.

The Internet usage policy needs to address what sites employees are allowed to visit and what sites they are not allowed to visit. If the company allows them to surf the Web during nonwork hours, the policy needs to clearly spell out the acceptable parameters, in terms of when they are allowed to do this and what sites they are still prohibited from visiting (such as potentially offensive sites). The policy should also describe under what circumstances an employee would be allowed to post something from the organization's network on the Web (on a blog, for example). A necessary addition to this policy would be the procedure for an employee to follow to obtain permission to post the object or message.

E-Mail Usage Policy

Related to the Internet usage policy is the *e-mail usage policy,* which deals with what the company will allow employees to send in, or as attachments to, e-mail messages. This policy should spell out whether nonwork e-mail traffic is allowed at all or is at least severely restricted. It needs to cover the type of message that would be considered inappropriate to send to other employees (for example, no offensive language, no sex-related or ethnic jokes, no harassment, and so on). The policy should also specify any disclaimers that must be attached to an employee's message sent to an individual outside the company. The policy should remind employees of the risks of clicking on links in e-mails, or opening attachments, as these can be social engineering attacks.

Clean Desk Policy

Preventing access to information is also important in the work area. Firms with sensitive information should have a "clean desk policy" specifying that sensitive information must not be left unsecured in the work area when the worker is not present to act as custodian. Even leaving the desk area and going to the bathroom can leave information exposed and subject to compromise. The clean desk policy should identify and prohibit things that are not obvious upon first glance, such as passwords on sticky notes under keyboards and mouse pads or in unsecured desk drawers. All of these elements that demonstrate the need for a clean desk are lost if employees do not make them personal. Training for clean desk activities needs to make the issue a personal one, where consequences are understood and the workplace reinforces the positive activity.

Bring Your Own Device (BYOD) Policy

Everyone seems to have a smartphone, a tablet, or other personal Internet device that they use in their personal lives. Bringing these to work is a natural extension of one's normal activities, but this raises the question of what policies are appropriate before a firm allows these devices to connect to the corporate network and access company data. Like all other policies, planning is needed to define the appropriate pathway to the company objectives. Personal devices offer cost savings and positive user acceptance, and in many cases these factors make allowing BYOD a sensible decision.

The primary purpose of a BYOD policy is to lower the risk associated with connecting a wide array of personal devices to a company's network and accessing sensitive data on them. This places security, in the form of risk management, as a center element of a BYOD policy. Devices need to be maintained in a current, up-to-date software posture, and with certain security features, such as screen locks and passwords enabled. Remote wipe and other features should be enabled, and highly sensitive data, especially in aggregate, should not be allowed on the devices. Users should have specific training as to what is allowed and what isn't and should be made aware of the increased responsibility associated with a mobile means of accessing corporate resources.

In some cases it may be necessary to define a policy associated with personally owned devices. This policy will describe the rules and regulations associated with use of personally owned devices with respect to corporate data, network connectivity, and security risks.

Privacy Policy

Customers place an enormous amount of trust in organizations to which they provide personal information. These customers expect their information to be kept secure so that unauthorized individuals will not gain access to it and so that authorized users will not use the information in unintended ways. Organizations should have a *privacy policy* that explains what their guiding principles will be in guarding personal data to which they are given access.

A special category of private information that is becoming increasingly important today is personally identifiable information (PII). This category of information includes any data that can be used to uniquely identify an individual. This would include an individual's name, address, driver's license number, and other details. An organization that collects PII on its employees and customers must make sure that it takes all necessary measures to protect the data from compromise.

Cross Check

Privacy

Privacy is an important consideration in today's computing environment. As such, it has been given its own chapter, Chapter 25. Additional details on privacy issues can be found there.

Due Care and Due Diligence

Due care and due diligence are terms used in the legal and business community to define reasonable behavior. Basically, the law recognizes the responsibility of an individual or organization to act reasonably relative to another party. If party A alleges that the actions of party B have caused it loss or injury, party A must prove that party B failed to exercise due care or due diligence and that this failure resulted in the loss or injury. These terms often are used synonymously, but **due care** generally refers to the standard of care a reasonable person is expected to exercise in all situations, whereas **due diligence** generally refers to the standard of care a business is expected to exercise in preparation for a business transaction. An organization must take reasonable precautions before entering a business transaction or it might be found to have acted irresponsibly. In terms of security, organizations are expected to take reasonable precautions to protect the information that they maintain on individuals. Should a person suffer a loss as a result of negligence on the part of an organization in terms of its security, that person typically can bring a legal suit against the organization.

The standard applied—reasonableness—is extremely subjective and often is determined by a jury. The organization will need to show that it had taken reasonable precautions to protect the information, and that, despite these precautions, an unforeseen security event occurred that caused the injury to the other party. Since this is so subjective, it is hard to describe what would be considered reasonable, but many sectors have a set of "security best practices" for their industry, which provides a basis for organizations in that sector to start from. If the organization decides not to follow any of the best practices accepted by the industry, it needs to be prepared to justify its reasons in court should an incident occur. If the sector the organization is in has regulatory requirements, justifying why the mandated security practices were not followed will be much more difficult (if not impossible).

Tech Tip

Prudent Person Principle

The concepts of due care and due diligence are connected. Due care addresses whether the organization has a minimal set of policies that provides reasonable assurance of success in maintaining security. Due diligence requires that management actually do something to ensure security, such as implement procedures for testing and review of audit records, internal security controls, and personnel behavior. The standard applied is one of a "prudent person"; would a prudent person find the actions appropriate and sincere? To apply this standard, all one has to do is ask the following question for the issue under consideration: "What would a prudent person do to protect and ensure that the security features and procedures are working or adequate?" Failure of a security feature or procedure doesn't necessarily mean the person acted imprudently.

Due diligence is the application of a specific standard of care. *Due care* is the degree of care that an ordinary person would exercise.

Due Process

Due process is concerned with guaranteeing fundamental fairness, justice, and liberty in relation to an individual's legal rights. In the United States, due process is concerned with the guarantee of an individual's rights as outlined by the Constitution and Bill of Rights. Procedural due process is based on the concept of what is "fair." Also of interest is the recognition by courts of a series of rights that are not explicitly specified by the Constitution but that the courts have decided are implicit in the concepts embodied by the Constitution. An example of this is an individual's right to privacy. From an organization's point of view, due process may come into play during an administrative action that adversely affects an employee. Before an employee is terminated, for example, were all of the employee's rights protected? An actual example pertains to the rights of privacy regarding employees' e-mail messages. As the number of cases involving employers examining employee e-mails grows, case law continues to be established and the courts eventually will settle on what rights an employee can expect. The best thing an employer can do if faced with this sort of situation is to work closely with HR staff to ensure that appropriate policies are followed and that those policies are in keeping with current laws and regulations.

Incident Response Policies and Procedures

No matter how careful an organization is, eventually a security incident of some sort will occur. When it happens, how effectively the organization responds to it will depend greatly on how prepared it is to handle incidents. An **incident response policy** and associated procedures should be developed to outline how the organization will prepare for security incidents and respond to them when they occur. Waiting until an incident happens is not the right time to establish your policies—they need to be designed in advance. The incident response policy should cover five phases: preparation, detection, containment and eradication, recovery, and follow-up actions.

Cross Check

Incident Response

Incident response is covered in detail in Chapter 22. This section serves only as an introduction to policy elements associated with the topic. For complete details on incident response, please examine Chapter 22.

■ Security Awareness and Training

Security awareness and training programs can enhance an organization's security posture in two direct ways. First, they teach personnel how to follow the correct set of actions to perform their duties in a secure manner. Second, they make personnel aware of the indicators and effects of social engineering attacks.

There are many tasks that employees perform that can have information security ramifications. Properly trained employees are able to perform their duties in a more effective manner, including their duties associated with information security. The extent of information security training will vary depending on the organization's environment and the level of threat, but initial employee security training at the time of being hired is important, as is periodic refresher training. A strong security education and awareness training program can go a long way toward reducing the chance that a social engineering attack will be successful. Security awareness programs and campaigns, which might include seminars, videos, posters, newsletters, and similar materials, are also fairly easy to implement and are not very costly.

Security Policy Training and Procedures

Personnel cannot be expected to perform complex tasks without training with respect to the tasks and expectations. This applies both to the security policy and to operational security details. If employees are going to be expected to comply with the organization's security policy, they must be properly trained in its purpose, meaning, and objectives. Training with respect to the information security policy, individual responsibilities, and expectations is something that requires periodic reinforcement through refresher training.

Because the security policy is a high-level directive that sets the overall support and executive direction with respect to security, it is important that the meaning of this message be translated and supported. Second-level policies such as password, access, information handling, and acceptable use policies also need to be covered. The collection of policies should paint a picture describing the desired security culture of the organization. The training should be designed to ensure that people see and understand the whole picture, not just the elements.

Role-based Training

For training to be effective, it needs to be targeted to the user with regard to their role in the subject of the training. While all employees may need general security awareness training, they also need specific training in areas where they have individual responsibilities. Role-based training with regard to information security responsibilities is an important part of information security training.

If a person has job responsibilities that may impact information security, then role-specific training is needed to ensure that the individual understands the responsibilities as they relate to information security. Some roles, such as system administrator or developer, have clearly defined information security responsibilities. The roles of others, such as project manager or purchasing manager, have information security impacts that are less obvious, but these roles require training as well. In fact, the less-obvious but wider-impact roles of middle management can have a large effect on the information security culture, and thus if a specific outcome is desired, it requires training.

As in all personnel-related training, two elements need attention. First, retraining over time is necessary to ensure that personnel keep proper levels of knowledge. Second, as people change jobs, a reassessment of the required training basis is needed, and additional training may be required. Maintaining accurate training records of personnel is the only way this can be managed in any significant enterprise.

Compliance with Laws, Best Practices, and Standards

There is a wide array of laws, regulations, contractual requirements, standards, and best practices associated with information security. Each places its own set of requirements upon an organization and its personnel. The only effective way for an organization to address these requirements is to build them into their own policies and procedures. Training to one's own policies and procedures would then translate into coverage of these external requirements.

It is important to note that many of these external requirements impart a specific training and awareness component upon the organization. Organizations subject to the requirements of the Payment Card Industry Data Security Standard (PCI DSS), Gramm Leach Bliley Act (GLBA), or Health Insurance Portability Accountability Act (HIPAA) are among the many that must maintain a specific information security training program. Other organizations should do so as a matter of best practice.

User Habits

Individual user responsibilities vary between organizations and the type of business each organization is involved in, but there are certain very basic responsibilities that all users should be instructed to adopt:

- Lock the door to your office or workspace, including drawers and cabinets.
- Do not leave sensitive information inside your car unprotected.
- Secure storage media containing sensitive information in a secure storage device.
- Shred paper containing organizational information before discarding it.
- Do not divulge sensitive information to individuals (including other employees) who do not have an authorized need to know it.
- Do not discuss sensitive information with family members. (The most common violation of this rule occurs in regard to HR information, as employees, especially supervisors, may complain to their spouse or friends about other employees or about problems that are occurring at work.)
- Protect laptops and other mobile devices that contain sensitive or important organization information wherever the device may be stored or left. (It's a good idea to ensure that sensitive information is encrypted on the laptop or mobile device so that, should the equipment be lost or stolen, the information remains safe.)
- Be aware of who is around you when discussing sensitive corporate information. Does everybody within earshot have the need to hear this information?

- Enforce corporate access control procedures. Be alert to, and do not allow, piggybacking, shoulder surfing, or access without the proper credentials.

- Be aware of the correct procedures to report suspected or actual violations of security policies.

- Follow procedures established to enforce good password security practices. Passwords are such a critical element that they are frequently the ultimate target of a social engineering attack. Though such password procedures may seem too oppressive or strict, they are often the best line of defense.

- **User habits** are a front-line security tool in engaging the workforce to improve the overall security posture of an organization.

> User responsibilities are easy training topics about which to ask questions on the CompTIA Security+ exam, so commit to memory your knowledge of the points listed here.

New Threats and Security Trends/Alerts

At the end of the day, information security practices are about managing risk, and it is well known that the risk environment is one marked by constant change. The ever-evolving threat environment frequently encounters new threats, new security issues, and new forms of defense. Training people to recognize the new threats necessitates continual awareness and training refresher events.

New Viruses

New forms of viruses, or malware, are being created every day. Some of these new forms can be highly destructive and costly, and it is incumbent upon all users to be on the lookout for and take actions to avoid exposure. Poor user practices are counted on by malware authors to assist in the spread of their attacks. One way of explaining proper actions to users is to use an analogy to cleanliness. Training users to practice good hygiene in their actions can go a long way toward assisting the enterprise in defending against these attack vectors.

Phishing Attacks

The best defense against phishing and other social engineering attacks is an educated and aware body of employees. Continual refresher training about the topic of social engineering and specifics about current attack trends are needed to keep employees aware of and prepared for new trends in social engineering attacks. Attackers rely upon an uneducated, complacent, or distracted workforce to enable their attack vector. Social engineering has become the gateway for many of the most damaging attacks in play today. Social engineering is covered extensively in Chapter 4.

Social Networking and P2P

With the rise in popularity of peer-to-peer (P2P) communications and social networking sites—notably Facebook, Twitter, and LinkedIn—many people have gotten into a habit of sharing too much information. Using a status of "Returning from sales call to XYZ company" reveals information to people who have no need to know this information. Confusing sharing with friends and sharing business information with those who don't need to know is a line people are crossing on a regular basis. Don't be the employee who mixes business and personal information and releases information to parties who should not have it, regardless of how innocuous it may seem.

Users need to understand the importance of not using common programs such as torrents and other file sharing in the workplace, as these programs can result in infection mechanisms and data-loss channels. The information security training and awareness program should cover these issues. If the issues are properly explained to employees, their motivation to comply won't simply be to avoid adverse personnel action for violating a policy; they will want to assist in the security of the organization and its mission.

Training Metrics and Compliance

Training and awareness programs can yield much in the way of an educated and knowledgeable workforce. Many laws, regulations, and best practices have requirements for maintaining a trained workforce. Having a record-keeping system to measure compliance with attendance and to measure the effectiveness of the training is a normal requirement. Simply conducting training is not sufficient. Following up and gathering training metrics to validate compliance and security posture is an important aspect of security training management.

A number of factors deserve attention when managing security training. Because of the diverse nature of role-based requirements, maintaining an active, up-to-date listing of individual training and retraining requirements is one challenge. Monitoring the effectiveness of the training is yet another challenge. Creating an effective training and awareness program when measured by actual impact on employee behavior is a challenging endeavor. Training needs to be current, relevant, and interesting to engage employee attention. Simple repetition of the same training material has not proven to be effective, so regularly updating the program is a requirement if it is to remain effective over time.

Tech Tip

Security Training Records

Requirements for both periodic training and retraining drive the need for good training records. Maintaining proper information security training records is a requirement of several laws and regulations and should be considered a best practice.

■ Interoperability Agreements

Many business operations involve actions between many different parties—some within an organization, and some in different organizations. These actions require communication between the parties, defining the responsibilities and expectations of the parties, the business objectives, and the environment within which the objectives will be pursued. To ensure an agreement is understood between the parties, written agreements are used. Numerous forms of legal agreements and contracts are used in business, but with respect to security, some of the most common ones are the service level agreement, business partnership agreement, memorandum of understanding, and interconnection security agreement.

Service Level Agreements

Service level agreements (SLAs) are contractual agreements between entities that describe specified levels of service that the servicing entity agrees to guarantee for the customer. SLAs essentially set the requisite level of performance of a given contractual service. SLAs are typically included as part of a service contract and set the level of technical expectations. An SLA can define specific services, the performance level associated with a service, issue management and resolution, and so on. SLAs are negotiated between customer and supplier and represent the agreed-upon terms. An organization contracting with a service provider should remember to include in the agreement a section describing the service provider's responsibility in terms of business continuity and disaster recovery. The provider's backup plans and processes for restoring lost data should also be clearly described.

Typically, a good SLA will satisfy two simple rules. First, it will describe the entire set of product or service functions in sufficient detail that their requirement will be unambiguous. Second, the SLA will provide a clear means of determining whether a specified function or service has been provided at the agreed-upon level of performance.

Business Partnership Agreement

A **business partnership agreement (BPA)** is a legal agreement between partners establishing the terms, conditions, and expectations of the relationship between the partners. These details can cover a wide range of issues, including typical items such as the sharing of profits and losses, the responsibilities of each partner, the addition or removal of partners, and any other issues. The Uniform Partnership Act (UPA), established by state law and convention, lays out a uniform set of rules associated with partnerships to resolve any partnership terms. The terms in a UPA are designed as "one size fits all" and are not typically in the best interest of any specific partnership. To avoid undesired outcomes that may result from UPA terms, it is best for partnerships to spell out specifics in a BPA.

Memorandum of Understanding

A **memorandum of understanding (MOU)** is a legal document used to describe a bilateral agreement between parties. It is a written agreement expressing a set of intended actions between the parties with respect to some common pursuit or goal. It is more formal and detailed than a simple handshake, but it generally lacks the binding powers of a contract. It is also common to find MOUs between different units within an organization to detail expectations associated with the common business interest.

Interconnection Security Agreement

Be sure you understand the differences between the interoperability agreements SLA, BPA, MOU, and ISA. The differences hinge upon the purpose for each document.

An **interconnection security agreement (ISA)** is a specialized agreement between organizations that have interconnected IT systems, the purpose of which is to document the security requirements associated with the interconnection. An ISA can be a part of an MOU detailing the specific technical security aspects of a data interconnection.

The Security Perimeter

The discussion to this point has not included any mention of the specific technology used to enforce operational and organizational security or a description of the various components that constitute the organization's security perimeter. If the average administrator were asked to draw a diagram depicting the various components of their network, the diagram would probably look something like Figure 3.1.

This diagram includes the major components typically found in a network. The connection to the Internet generally has some sort of protection attached to it such as a firewall. An intrusion detection system (IDS), also often part of the security perimeter for the organization, may be either on the inside or the outside of the firewall, or it may in fact be on both sides. The specific location depends on the company and what it is more concerned about preventing (that is, insider threats or external threats). The router can also be thought of as a security device, as it can be used to enhance security such as in the case of wireless routers that can be used to enforce encryption settings. Beyond this security perimeter is the corporate network. Figure 3.1 is obviously a very simple depiction—an actual network can have numerous subnets and extranets as well as wireless access points—but the basic components are present. Unfortunately, if this were the diagram provided by the administrator to show the organization's basic network structure, the administrator would have missed a very important component. A more astute administrator would provide a diagram more like Figure 3.2.

This diagram includes other possible access points into the network, including the public switched telephone network (PSTN) and wireless access points. The organization may or may not have any authorized modems or wireless networks, but the savvy administrator would realize that the potential exists for unauthorized versions of both.

When considering the policies, procedures, and guidelines needed to implement security for the organization, both networks need to be considered. Another development that has brought the telephone and computer networks together is the implementation of *voice over IP (VoIP)*, which eliminates the traditional land lines in an organization and replaces them with special telephones that connect to the IP data network.

While Figure 3.2 provides a more comprehensive view of the various components that need to be protected, it is still incomplete. Most experts will agree that the biggest danger to any organization does not come from external attacks but rather from the insider—a disgruntled employee or somebody else who has physical access to the facility. Given physical access to an office, the knowledgeable attacker will quickly find the information needed to gain access to the organization's computer systems

• **Figure 3.1**   Basic diagram of an organization's network

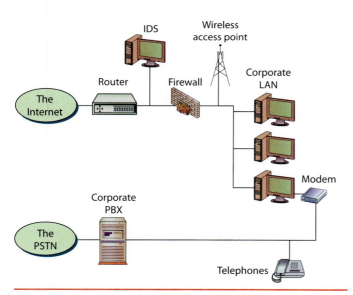

• **Figure 3.2**   A more complete diagram of an organization's network and network. Consequently, every organization also needs security policies, procedures, and guidelines that cover physical security, and every security administrator should be concerned with these as well. While physical security (which can include such things as locks, cameras, guards and entry points, alarm systems, and physical barriers) will probably not fall under the purview of the security administrator, the operational state of the organization's physical security measures is just as important as many of the other network-centric measures.

Physical Security

Physical security consists of all mechanisms used to ensure that physical access to the computer systems and networks is restricted to only authorized users. Additional physical security mechanisms may be used to provide increased security for especially sensitive systems such as servers and devices such as routers, firewalls, and intrusion detection systems. When considering physical security, access from all six sides should be considered—not only should the security of obvious points of entry be examined, such as doors and windows, but the walls themselves as well as the floor and ceiling should also be considered. Questions such as the following should be addressed:

- Is there a false ceiling with tiles that can be easily removed?
- Do the walls extend to the actual ceiling or only to a false ceiling?
- Is there a raised floor?
- Do the walls extend to the actual floor, or do they stop at a raised floor?
- How are important systems situated?
- Do the monitors face away from windows, or could the activity of somebody at a system be monitored?
- Who has access to the facility?
- What type of access control is there, and are there any guards?
- Who is allowed unsupervised access to the facility?
- Is there an alarm system or security camera that covers the area?
- What procedures govern the monitoring of the alarm system or security camera and the response should unauthorized activity be detected?

These are just some of the numerous questions that need to be asked when examining the physical security surrounding a system.

Physical Access Controls

The purpose of physical access controls is the same as that of computer and network access controls—you want to restrict access to only those who are authorized to have it. Physical access is restricted by requiring the individual to somehow authenticate that they have the right or authority to have

An increasing number of organizations are implementing VoIP solutions to bring the telephone and computer networks together. While there are some tremendous advantages to doing this in terms of both increased capabilities and potential monetary savings, bringing the two networks together may also introduce additional security concerns. Another common method to access organizational networks today is through wireless access points. These may be provided by the organization itself to enhance productivity, or they may be attached to the network by users without organizational approval. The impact of all of these additional methods that can be used to access a network is to increase the complexity of the security problem.

Tech Tip

Physical Security Is Also Important to Computer Security

Computer security professionals recognize that they cannot rely only on computer security mechanisms to keep their systems safe. Physical security must be maintained as well, because in many cases, if an attacker gains physical access, he can steal data and destroy the system.

the desired access. As in computer authentication, access in the physical world can be based on something the individual has, something they know, or something they are. Frequently, when dealing with the physical world, the terms "authentication" and "access control" are used interchangeably.

The most common physical access control device, which has been around in some form for centuries, is a lock. Combination locks represent an access control device that depends on something the individual knows (the combination). Locks with keys depend on something the individual has (the key). Each of these has certain advantages and disadvantages. Combinations don't require any extra hardware, but they must be remembered (which means individuals may write them down—a security vulnerability in itself) and are hard to control. Anybody who knows the combination may provide it to somebody else. Key locks are simple and easy to use, but the key may be lost, which means another key has to be made or the lock has to be rekeyed. Keys may also be copied, and their dissemination can be hard to control. Newer locks replace the traditional key with a card that must be passed through a reader or placed against it. The individual may also have to provide a personal access code, thus making this form of access both a something-you-know and something-you-have method.

In addition to locks on doors, other common physical security devices include video surveillance and even simple access control logs (sign-in logs). While sign-in logs don't provide an actual barrier, they do provide a record of access and, when used in conjunction with a guard who verifies an individual's identity, can dissuade potential adversaries from attempting to gain access to a facility. As mentioned, another common access control mechanism is a human security guard. Many organizations employ a guard to provide an extra level of examination of individuals who want to gain access to a facility. Other devices are limited to their designed function. A human guard can apply common sense to situations that might have been unexpected. Having security guards also addresses the common practice of piggybacking (aka tailgating), where an individual follows another person closely to avoid having to go through the access control procedures.

Biometrics

Access controls that utilize something you know (for example, combinations) or something you have (such as keys) are not the only methods to limit facility access to authorized individuals. A third approach is to utilize something unique about the individual—their fingerprints, for example—to identify them. Unlike the other two methods, the something-you-are method, known as **biometrics**, does not rely on the individual to either remember something or to have something in their possession. Biometrics is a more sophisticated access control approach and can be more expensive. Biometrics also suffer from false positives and false negatives, making them less than 100 percent effective. For this reason they are frequently used in conjunction with another form of authentication. The advantage is the user always has them (cannot leave at home or share) and they tend to have better entropy than passwords. Other methods to accomplish biometrics include handwriting analysis, retinal scans, iris scans, voiceprints, hand geometry, and facial geometry.

Tech Tip

Physical and Information Security Convergence

In high-security sites, physical access controls and electronic access controls to information are interlocked. This means that before data can be accessed from a particular machine, the physical access control system must agree with the finding that the authorized party is present.

There are many similarities between authentication and access controls in computers and in the physical world. Remember the three common techniques for verifying a person's identity and access privileges: something you know, something you have, and something about you.

Both access to computer systems and networks and physical access to restricted areas can be controlled with biometrics. However, biometric methods for controlling physical access are generally not the same as those employed for restricting access to computer systems and networks. Hand geometry, for example, requires a fairly large device. This can easily be placed outside of a door to control access to the room but would not be as convenient to control access to a computer system, since a reader would need to be placed with each computer or at least with groups of computers. In a mobile environment where laptops are being used, a device such as a hand geometry reader would be unrealistic.

Physical Barriers

An even more common security feature than locks is a physical barrier. Physical barriers help implement the physical-world equivalent of layered security. The outermost layer of physical security should contain the more publicly visible activities. A guard at a gate in a fence, for example, would be visible by all who happen to pass by. As you progress through the layers, the barriers and security mechanisms should become less publicly visible to make determining what mechanisms are in place more difficult for observers. Signs are also an important element in security, as they announce to the public which areas are public and which are private. A *man trap* can also be used in this layered approach. It generally consists of a small space that is large enough for only one person at a time, with two locking doors. An individual has to enter the first door, close the first door, then attempt to open the second door. If unsuccessful, perhaps because they do not have the proper access code, the person can be caught inside this small location until security personnel show up.

In addition to walls and fences, open space can also serve as a barrier. While this may at first seem to be an odd statement, consider the use of large areas of open space around a facility. For an intruder to cross this open space takes time—time in which they are vulnerable and their presence may be discovered. In today's environment in which terrorist attacks have become more common, additional precautions should be taken for areas that may be considered a possible target for terrorist activity. In addition to open space, which is necessary to lessen the effect of explosions, concrete barriers that stop vehicles from getting too close to facilities should also be used. It is not necessary for these to be unsightly concrete walls; many facilities have placed large, round concrete circles, filled them with dirt, and then planted flowers and other plants to construct a large, immovable planter.

■ Environmental Issues

Environmental issues may not at first seem to be related to security, but when considering the availability of a computer system or network, they must be taken into consideration. Environmental issues include items such as **heating, ventilation, and air conditioning (HVAC)** systems, electrical power, and the "environments of nature." HVAC systems are used to maintain the

Tech Tip

Biometric Devices
Once only seen in spy or science fiction movies, biometrics such as hand and fingerprint readers, eye-scanning technology, and voiceprint devices are now becoming more common in the real world. The accuracy of these devices has improved and the costs have dropped, making them realistic solutions to many access control situations.

Tech Tip

Signs
Signs can be an effective control, warning unauthorized personnel not to enter, locating critical elements for first responders, and providing paths to exits in emergencies. Proper signage is an important aspect of physical security controls.

comfort of an office environment. A few years back, they were also critical for the smooth operation of computer systems that had low tolerances for humidity and heat. Today's desktop systems are much more tolerant, and the limiting factor is now often the human user. The exception to this HVAC limitation is when large quantities of equipment are co-located, in server rooms and network equipment closets. In these heat-dense areas, HVAC is needed to keep equipment temperatures within reasonable ranges. Often certain security devices such as firewalls and intrusion detection systems are located in these same equipment closets and the loss of HVAC systems can cause these critical systems to fail. One interesting aspect of HVAC systems is that they themselves are often computer controlled and frequently provide remote access via telephone or network connections. These connections should be protected in a similar manner to computer modems, or else attackers may locate them and change the HVAC settings for an office or building.

Electrical power is obviously an essential requirement for computer systems and networks. Electrical power is subject to momentary surges and disruption. Surge protectors are needed to protect sensitive electronic equipment from fluctuations in voltage. An **uninterruptible power supply (UPS)** should be considered for critical systems so that a loss of power will not halt processing. The size of the batteries associated with a UPS will determine the amount of time that it can operate before it too loses power. Many sites ensure sufficient power to provide administrators the opportunity to cleanly bring the system or network down. For installations that require continuous operations, even in the event of a power outage, electric generators that automatically start when a loss of power is detected can be installed. These systems may take a few seconds to start before they reach full operation, so a UPS should also be considered to smooth the transition between normal and backup power.

Fire Suppression

Fires are a common disaster that can affect organizations and their computing equipment. Fire detection and fire suppression devices are two approaches to addressing this threat. Detectors can be useful because some may be able to detect a fire in its very early stages before a fire suppression system is activated, and they can potentially sound a warning. This warning could provide employees with the opportunity to deal with the fire before it becomes serious enough for the fire suppression equipment to kick in. Suppression systems come in several varieties, including sprinkler-based systems and gas-based systems. Standard sprinkler-based systems are not optimal for data centers because water will ruin large electrical infrastructures and most integrated circuit–based devices—such as computers. Gas-based systems are a good alternative, though they also carry special concerns. More extensive coverage of fire detection and suppression is provided in Chapter 8.

Wireless

When someone talks about wireless communication, they generally are referring to cellular telephones ("cell phones"). These devices have become ubiquitous in today's modern office environment. A cell phone network consists of the phones themselves, the cells with their accompanying base stations that they are used in, and the hardware and software that allow them to communicate. The base stations are made up of antennas, receivers, transmitters, and amplifiers. The base stations communicate with those cell phones that are currently in the geographical area that is serviced by that station. As a person travels across town, they may exit and enter multiple cells. The stations must conduct a handoff to ensure continuous operation for the cell phone. As the individual moves toward the edge of a cell, a mobile switching center notices the power of the signal beginning to drop, checks whether another cell has a stronger signal for the phone (cells frequently overlap), and, if so, switches operation to this new cell and base station. All of this is done without the user ever knowing that they have moved from one cell to another.

Wireless technology can also be used for networking. There are two main standards for wireless network technology. **Bluetooth** is designed as a short-range (approximately ten meters) personal area network (PAN) cable-replacement technology that can be built into a variety of devices, such as mobile phones, tablets, and laptop computers. The idea is to create low-cost wireless technology so that many different devices can communicate with each other. Bluetooth is also interesting because, unlike other wireless technology, it is designed so that devices can talk directly with each other without having to go through a central device (such as the base station described previously). This is known as *peer-to-peer communication.*

The other major wireless standard is the **IEEE 802.11** set of standards, which is well suited for the local area network (LAN) environment. 802.11 networks can operate either in an ad hoc peer-to-peer fashion or in infrastructure mode, which is more common. In infrastructure mode, computers with 802.11 network cards communicate with a wireless access point. This access point connects to the network so that the computers communicating with it are essentially also connected to the network.

While wireless networks are very useful in today's modern office (and home), they are not without their security problems. Access points are generally placed throughout a building so that all employees can access the corporate network. The transmission and reception areas covered by access points are not easily controlled. Consequently, many publicly accessible areas might fall into the range of one of the organization's access points, or its Bluetooth-enabled systems, and thus the corporate network may become vulnerable to attack. Wireless networks are designed to incorporate some security measures, but all too often the networks are set up without security enabled, and serious security flaws exist in the 802.11 design.

Tech Tip

Wireless Network Security Issues

Due to a number of advantages, such as the ability to take your laptop with you as you move around your building and still stay connected, wireless networks have grown in popularity. They also eliminate the need to string network cables all over the office. At the same time, however, they can be a security nightmare if not adequately protected. The signal for your network doesn't stop at your office door or wall just because it is there. It will continue propagating to areas that may be open to anybody. This provides the opportunity for others to access your network. To avoid this, you must take steps such as encrypting transmissions so that your wireless network doesn't become the weak link in your security chain.

■ Electromagnetic Eavesdropping

In 1985, a paper by Wim van Eck of the Netherlands described what became known as the van Eck phenomenon. In the paper van Eck described how eavesdropping on what was being displayed on monitors could be accomplished by picking up and then decoding the electromagnetic interference produced by the monitors. With the appropriate equipment, the exact image of what is being displayed can be re-created some distance away. While the original paper discussed emanations as they applied to video display units (monitors), the same phenomenon applies to other devices such as printers and computers.

This phenomenon had actually been known about for quite some time before van Eck published his paper. The U.S. Department of Defense used the term **TEMPEST** (referred to by some as the *Transient ElectroMagnetic Pulse Emanation STandard*) to describe both a program in the military to control these electronic emanations from electrical equipment and the actual process for controlling the emanations. There are three basic ways to prevent these emanations from being picked up by an attacker:

- Put the equipment beyond the point that the emanations can be picked up.
- Provide shielding for the equipment itself.
- Provide a shielded enclosure (such as a room) to put the equipment in.

One of the simplest ways to protect against equipment being monitored in this fashion is to put enough distance between the target and the attacker. The emanations can be picked up from only a limited distance. If the physical security for the facility is sufficient to put enough space between the equipment and publicly accessible areas that the signals cannot be picked up, then the organization doesn't have to take any additional measures to ensure security.

Distance is not the only way to protect against eavesdropping on electronic emanations. Devices can be shielded so their emanations are blocked. Acquiring enough property to provide the necessary distance needed to protect against an eavesdropper may be possible if the facility is in the country with lots of available land surrounding it. Indeed, for smaller organizations that occupy only a few offices or floors in a large office building, it would

Principles of Computer Security

be impossible to acquire enough space. In this case, the organization may resort to purchasing shielded equipment. A "TEMPEST approved" computer will cost significantly more than what a normal computer would cost. Shielding a room (in what is known as a *Faraday cage*) is also an extremely expensive endeavor.

A natural question to ask is, how prevalent is this form of attack? The equipment needed to perform electromagnetic eavesdropping is not readily available, but it would not cost an inordinate amount of money to produce it. The cost could certainly be afforded by any large corporation, and industrial espionage using such a device is a possibility. While there are no public records of this sort of activity being conducted, it is reasonable to assume that it does take place in large corporations and the government, especially in foreign countries.

Modern Eavesdropping

Not just electromagnetic information can be used to carry information out of a system to an adversary. Recent advances have demonstrated the feasibility of using the webcams and microphones on systems to spy on users, recording keystrokes and other activities. There are even devices built to intercept the wireless signals between wireless keyboards and mice and transmit them over another channel to an adversary. USB-based keyloggers can be placed in the back of machines, as in many cases the back of a machine is unguarded or facing the public (watch for this the next time you see a receptionist's machine).

One of the challenges in security is determining how much to spend on security without spending too much. Security spending should be based on likely threats to your systems and network. While electronic emanations can be monitored, the likelihood of this taking place in most situations is remote, which makes spending on items to protect against it at best a low priority.

Chapter 3 Review

■ Chapter Summary

After reading this chapter and completing the exercises, you should understand the following regarding operational and organizational security.

Identify various operational aspects to security in your organization

- Prevention technologies are designed to keep individuals from being able to gain access to systems or data they are not authorized to use.
- Previously in operational environments, prevention was extremely difficult and relying on prevention technologies alone was not sufficient. This led to the rise of technologies to detect and respond to events that occur when prevention fails.
- An important part of any organization's approach to implementing security is to establish policies, procedures, standards, and guidelines to detail what users and administrators should be doing to maintain the security of the systems and network.

Identify various policies and procedures in your organization

- Policies, procedures, standards, and guidelines are important in establishing a security program within an organization.
- The security policy and supporting policies play an important role in establishing and managing system risk.
- Policies and procedures associated with Human Resources functionality include job rotation, mandatory vacations, and hiring and termination policies.

Identify the security awareness and training needs of an organization

- Security training and awareness efforts are vital in engaging the workforce to act within the desired range of conduct with respect to security.
- Security awareness and training is important in achieving compliance objectives.
- Security awareness and training should be measured and managed as part of a comprehensive security program.

Understand the different types of agreements employed in negotiating security requirements

- The different interoperability agreements, including SLA, BPA, MOU and ISA, are used to establish security expectations between various parties.

Describe the physical security components that can protect your computers and network

- Physical security consists of all mechanisms used to ensure that physical access to the computer systems and networks is restricted to only authorized users.
- The purpose of physical access controls is the same as that of computer and network access controls—to restrict access to only those who are authorized to have it.
- The careful placement of equipment can provide security for known security problems exhibited by wireless devices and that arise due to electronic emanations.

Identify environmental factors that can affect security

- Environmental issues are important to security because they can affect the availability of a computer system or network.
- Loss of HVAC systems can lead to overheating problems that can affect electronic equipment, including security-related devices.
- The frequency of natural disasters is a contributing factor that must be considered when making contingency processing plans for an installation.
- Fires are a common problem for organizations. Two general approaches to addressing this problem are fire detection and fire suppression.

Identify factors that affect the security of the growing number of wireless technologies used for data transmission

- Wireless networks have many security issues, including the transmission and reception areas covered by access points, which are not easily controlled and can thus provide easy network access for intruders.

Prevent disclosure through electronic emanations

- With the appropriate equipment, the exact image of what is being displayed on a computer monitor can be re-created some distance away, allowing eavesdroppers to view what you are doing.

- Providing a lot of distance between the system you wish to protect and the closest place an eavesdropper could be is one way to protect against eavesdropping on electronic emanations. Devices can also be shielded so that their emanations are blocked.

Key Terms

acceptable use policy (AUP) *(50)*

biometrics *(62)*

Bluetooth *(65)*

business partnership agreement (BPA) *(59)*

due care *(53)*

due diligence *(53)*

guidelines *(43)*

heating, ventilation, and air conditioning (HVAC) *(63)*

IEEE 802.11 *(65)*

incident response policy *(54)*

interconnection security agreement (ISA) *(59)*

memorandum of understanding (MOU) *(59)*

physical security *(61)*

policies *(43)*

procedures *(43)*

security policy *(44)*

service level agreement (SLA) *(59)*

standards *(43)*

TEMPEST *(66)*

uninterruptible power supply (UPS) *(64)*

user habits *(57)*

Key Terms Quiz

Use terms from the Key Terms list to complete the sentences that follow. Don't use the same term more than once. Not all terms will be used.

1. _____ are high-level statements made by management that lay out the organization's position on some issue.

2. The collective term used to refer to the systems that are used to maintain the comfort of an office environment and that are often controlled by computer systems is _____.

3. A(n) _____ is a device designed to provide power to essential equipment for a period of time when normal power is lost.

4. _____ are a foundational security tool in engaging the workforce to improve the overall security posture of an organization.

5. _____ are accepted specifications providing specific details on how a policy is to be enforced.

6. _____ is a wireless technology designed as a short-range (approximately ten meters) personal area network (PAN) cable-replacement technology that may be built into a variety of devices such as mobile phones, tablets, and laptop computers.

7. A(n) _____ is a legal document used to describe a bilateral agreement between parties.

8. _____ are step-by-step instructions that describe exactly how employees are expected to act in a given situation or to accomplish a specific task.

9. The set of standards for wireless networks that is well suited for the LAN environment and whose normal mode is to have computers with network cards communicating with a wireless access point is _____.

10. A(n) _____ is a legal agreement between organizations establishing the terms, conditions, and expectations of the relationship between them.

■ Multiple-Choice Quiz

1. Which of the following is a physical security threat?

   A. Cleaning crews are allowed unsupervised access because they have a contract.

   B. Employees undergo background criminal checks before being hired.

   C. All data is encrypted before being backed up.

   D. All the above.

2. The benefit of fire detection equipment over fire suppression devices is:

   A. Fire detection equipment is regulated, whereas fire suppression equipment is not.

   B. Fire detection equipment will often catch fires at a much earlier stage, meaning that the fire can be addressed before significant damage can occur.

   C. Fire detection equipment is much more reliable than fire suppression equipment.

   D. There is no advantage of fire detection over fire suppression other than the cost of fire detection equipment is much less than the cost of fire suppression equipment.

3. Which of the following is a contractual agreement between entities that describes specified levels of service that the servicing entity agrees to guarantee for the customer?

   A. Service level agreement

   B. Support level agreement

   C. Memorandum of understanding

   D. Business service agreement

4. During which step of the policy lifecycle does training of users take place?

   A. Plan for security.

   B. Implement the plans.

   C. Monitor the implementation.

   D. Evaluate for effectiveness.

5. Biometric access controls are typically used in conjunction with another form of access control because:

   A. Biometrics are still expensive.

   B. Biometrics cannot be copied.

   C. Biometrics are not always convenient to use.

   D. Biometrics are not 100 percent accurate, having some level of misidentifications.

6. Procedures can be described as:

   A. High-level, broad statements of what the organization wants to accomplish

   B. Step-by-step instructions on how to implement the policies

   C. Mandatory elements regarding the implementation of a policy

   D. Recommendations relating to a policy

7. What technique can be used to protect against electromagnetic eavesdropping (known as the van Eck phenomenon)?

   A. Provide sufficient distance between the potential target and the nearest location an attacker could be.

   B. Put the equipment that you are trying to protect inside a shielded room.

   C. Purchase "TEMPEST approved" equipment.

   D. All of the above.

8. Key user habits that can improve security efforts include:

   A. Do not discuss business issues outside of the office.

   B. Never leave laptops or tablets inside your car unattended.

   C. Be alert of people violating physical access rules (piggybacking through doors).

   D. Items B and C.

9. When should a human security guard be used for physical access control?

   A. When other electronic access control mechanisms will not be accepted by employees

   B. When necessary to avoid issues such as piggybacking, which can occur with electronic access controls

   C. When other access controls are too expensive to implement

   D. When the organization wants to enhance its image

10. What device should be used by organizations to protect sensitive equipment from fluctuations in voltage?

    A. A surge protector

    B. An uninterruptible power supply

    C. A backup power generator

    D. A redundant array of inline batteries (RAIB)

■ Essay Quiz

1. Describe the difference between fire suppression and fire detection systems.

2. Discuss why physical security is also important to computer security professionals.

3. Why should we be concerned about HVAC systems when discussing security?

4. Outline the various components that make up (or should make up) an organization's security perimeter. Which of these can be found in your organization (or school)?

Lab Projects

● Lab Project 3.1

Take a tour of your building on campus or at work. What is secured at night when workers are absent? Record the location and type of physical access control devices. How do these access controls change at night when workers are absent? How well trained do guards and other employees appear to be? Do they allow "piggybacking" (somebody slipping into a facility behind an authorized individual without being challenged)? What are the policies for visitors and contractors? How does this all impact physical security?

● Lab Project 3.2

Describe the four steps of the policy lifecycle. Obtain a policy from your organization (such as an acceptable use policy or Internet usage policy). How are users informed of this policy? How often is it reviewed? How would changes to it be suggested and who would make decisions on whether the changes were accepted?

The Role of People in Security

chapter 4

In this chapter, you will learn how to

- Define basic terminology associated with social engineering
- Describe steps organizations can take to improve their security
- Describe common user actions that may put an organization's information at risk
- Recognize methods attackers may use to gain information about an organization
- Determine ways in which users can aid instead of detract from security
- Recognize the role training and awareness plays in assisting the people side of security

The operational model of computer security discussed in the previous chapter acknowledges that absolute protection of computer systems and networks is not possible and that we need to be prepared to detect and respond to attacks that are able to circumvent our security mechanisms. Another very basic fact that should be recognized is that technology alone will not solve the security problem. No matter how advanced the technology is, it will ultimately be deployed in an environment where humans exist. It is the human element that poses the biggest security challenge. It is hard to compensate for all of the possible ways that humans can deliberately or accidentally cause security problems or circumvent our security mechanisms. Despite all of the technology, despite all of the security procedures we have in place, and despite all of the security training we may provide, somebody will invariably fail to do what they are supposed to do, or do something they are not supposed to do, and create a vulnerability in the organization's security posture. This chapter discusses the human element and the role that people play in security—both the user practices that can aid in securing an organization and the vulnerabilities or holes in security that users can introduce.

■ People—A Security Problem

The operational model of computer security acknowledges that prevention technologies are not sufficient to protect our computer systems and networks. There are a number of explanations for why this is true, some of them technical, but one of the biggest reasons that prevention technologies are not sufficient is that every network and computer system has at least one human user, and humans are prone to make mistakes and are often easily misled or fooled.

Social Engineering

Social engineering, if you recall from Chapter 2, is the process of convincing an authorized individual to provide confidential information or access to an unauthorized individual. It is a technique in which the attacker uses various deceptive practices to convince the targeted person to divulge information they normally would not divulge or to convince the target of the attack to do something they normally wouldn't do. Social engineering is very successful for two general reasons. The first is the basic desire of most people to be helpful. When somebody asks a question for which we know the answer, our normal response is not to be suspicious but rather to answer the question. The problem with this is that seemingly innocuous information can be used either directly in an attack or indirectly to build a bigger picture that an attacker can use to create an aura of authenticity during an attack—the more information an individual has about an organization, the easier it will be to convince others that he is part of the organization and has a right to even sensitive information. An attacker who is attempting to exploit the natural tendency of people to be helpful may take one of several approaches:

- The attacker may simply ask a question, hoping to immediately obtain the desired information. For basic information that is not considered sensitive, this approach generally works. As an example, an attacker might call and ask who the IT manager is.

- The attacker may first attempt to engage the target in conversation and try to evoke sympathy so that the target feels sorry for the individual and is more prone to provide the information. For information that is even slightly sensitive in nature, the request of which could possibly arouse suspicion, this technique may be tried. As an example, an attacker might call and claim to be under some deadline from a supervisor who is upset for some reason. The target, feeling sorry for an alleged fellow worker, may give up the information, thinking they are helping them avoid trouble with the supervisor.

- The attacker may appeal to an individual's ego. As an example, an attacker might call the IT department, claiming to have some sort of problem, and praising them for work they supposedly did to help another worker. After being told how great they are and how much they helped somebody else, they will often be tempted to demonstrate that they can supply the same level of help to another individual. This technique may be used to obtain sensitive information, such as having the target's password reset.

Tech Tip

Social Engineering Works!

Skilled social engineers set up scenarios where the victim is boxed in by various social/work issues and then makes an exception that enables the social engineer to gain some form of access. The attacker can pretend to be an important party and intimidate a lower-level employee, or create a sense of emergency, scarcity, or urgency that moves the victim to act in a manner to reduce the conflict. The attacker can become a "victim," creating a sense of fellowship with the target, creating a false sense of familiarity, and then using that to drive an action. Social engineers can sell ice to Eskimos and make them proud of their purchase, so they are masters at psychological manipulation.

The second reason that social engineering is successful is that individuals normally seek to avoid confrontation and trouble. If the attacker attempts to intimidate the target, threatening to call the target's supervisor because of a lack of help, the target may give in and provide the information to avoid confrontation. This variation on the attack is often successful in organizations that have a strict hierarchical structure. In the military, for example, a lower-ranking individual may be coerced into providing information to an individual claiming to be of higher rank or to be working for another individual higher up in the chain of command.

Social engineering may also be accomplished using other means besides direct contact between the target and the attacker. For example, an attacker might send a forged e-mail with a link to a bogus web site that has been set up to obtain information from the target or convince the target to perform some action. Again, the goal in social engineering is to convince the target to provide information that they normally wouldn't divulge or to perform some act that they normally would not do. An example of a slightly different attack that is generally still considered a social engineering attack is one in which an attacker replaces the blank deposit slips in a bank's lobby with ones containing his or her own account number but no name. When an unsuspecting customer uses one of the slips, a teller who is not observant may end up crediting the attacker's account with the deposit.

Cross Check

Types of Social Engineering

Chapters 1 and 2 both discussed social engineering. Electronic versions of social engineering have become very common. What are the different types of social engineering (especially electronic versions) that we have discussed?

Obtaining Insider Information

An excellent example of social engineering occurred in 1978 when Stanley Mark Rifkin, from Carlsbad, California, stole $10.2 million from the Security Pacific Bank in Los Angeles. Details of the story vary, as Rifkin has never publicly detailed his actions, but a number of facts are known. At the time of the attack, Rifkin was working as a computer consultant for the bank. While working there, he learned details on how money could easily be transferred to accounts anywhere in the United States. The problem would be to actually obtain the money in the first place. In order to do this, he needed to have access to the electronic funds transfer (EFT) code used by the bank to transfer money to other banks. Using the excuse of checking on the computer equipment inside of the room from which the bank made its transfers, Rifkin was able to observe the code for that day. After leaving the room, he used this information to impersonate a bank officer and ordered the transfer of the $10.2 million. Since he had knowledge of the supposedly secret code, the transfer was made with little fanfare (this amount was well below any level that would trigger any suspicion). Earlier Rifkin had set up a bogus account in a New York bank, using a false name, and he deposited the money into that account. He later transferred the money again to another account in Switzerland under a different name. He then used the money to purchase millions of dollars in diamonds, which he then smuggled back into the United States. The crime might have gone undetected if he had not boasted of his exploits to an individual who was more than happy to turn him in. In 1979, Rifkin was sentenced to eight years in prison. At his trial he attempted to convince the judge that he should be released so he could teach others how to protect their systems against the type of activity he perpetrated. The judge denied this request. The diamonds were ultimately turned over to the bank, which tried to recover its loss by selling them.

Phishing

Phishing (pronounced "fishing") is a type of social engineering in which an attacker attempts to obtain sensitive information from a user by masquerading as a trusted entity in an e-mail or instant message sent to a large group of often random users. The attacker attempts to obtain information such as usernames, passwords, credit card numbers, and details about the user's bank accounts. The message sent often encourages the user to go to a web site that appears to be for a reputable entity such as PayPal or eBay, both of which have frequently been used in phishing attempts. The web site the user actually visits is not owned by the reputable organization, however, and asks the user to supply information that can be used in a later attack. Often the message sent to the user will state that the user's account has been compromised and will request, for security purposes, the user to enter their account information to verify the details.

In another very common example of phishing, the attacker sends a bulk e-mail, supposedly from a bank, telling the recipients that a security breach has occurred and instructing them to click a link to verify that their account has not been tampered with. If the individual actually clicks the link, they are taken to a site that appears to be owned by the bank but is actually controlled by the attacker. When they supply their account and password for "verification" purposes, they are actually giving it to the attacker.

The e-mails and web sites generated by the attackers often appear to be legitimate. A few clues, however, can tip off the user that the e-mail might not be what it claims to be. The e-mail may contain grammatical and typographical errors, for example. Organizations that are used in these phishing attempts (such as eBay and PayPal) are careful about their images and will not send a security-related e-mail to users containing obvious errors. In addition, almost unanimously, organizations tell their users that they will never ask for sensitive information (such as a password or account number) via an e-mail. The URL of the web site that the users are taken to may also provide a clue that the site is not what it appears to be. Despite the increasing media coverage concerning phishing attempts, some Internet users still fall for them, which results in attackers continuing to use this relatively cheap method to gain the information they are seeking.

A recent development has been the introduction of a modification to the original phishing attack. *Spear phishing* is the term that has been created to refer to the special targeting of groups with something in common when launching a phishing attack. By targeting specific groups, the ratio of successful attacks (that is, the number of responses received) to the total num-

Up to this point, social engineering has been discussed in the context of an outsider attempting to gain information about the organization. This does not have to be the case. Insiders may also attempt to gain information they are not authorized to have. In many cases, the insider may be much more successful since they will already have a certain level of information regarding the organization and can therefore better spin a story that may be believable to other employees.

Phishing is now the most common form of social engineering attack related to computer security. The target may be a computer system and access to the information found on it (such as is the case when the phishing attempt asks for a user ID and password) or the target may be personal information, generally financial, about an individual (in the case of phishing attempts that ask for an individual's banking information).

Another specialized version of phishing is closely related to spear phishing. Again, specific individuals are targeted, but in this case the individuals are important individuals high up in an organization such as the corporate officers. The goal is to go after these "bigger targets," and thus the term that is used to refer to this form of attack is *whaling*.

ber of e-mails or messages sent usually increases because a targeted attack will seem more plausible than a message sent to users randomly.

Pharming consists of misdirecting users to fake web sites made to look official. Using phishing, individuals are targeted one by one by sending out e-mails. To become a victim, the recipient must take an action (for example, respond by providing personal information). In pharming, the user will be directed to the fake web site as a result of activity such as DNS poisoning (an attack that changes URLs in a server's domain name table) or modification of local host files, which are used to convert URLs to the appropriate IP address. Once at the fake site, the user may supply personal information, believing that they are connected to the legitimate site.

Vishing

Vishing is a variation of phishing that uses voice communication technology to obtain the information the attacker is seeking. Vishing takes advantage of the trust that some people place in the telephone network. Users are unaware that attackers can spoof (simulate) calls from legitimate entities using Voice over IP (VoIP) technology. Voice messaging can also be compromised and used in these attempts. Generally, the attackers are hoping to obtain credit card numbers or other information that can be used in identity theft. The user may receive an e-mail asking him or her to call a number that is answered by a potentially compromised voice message system. Users may also receive a recorded message that appears to come from a legitimate entity. In both cases, the user will be encouraged to respond quickly and provide the sensitive information so that access to their account is not blocked. If a user ever receives a message that claims to be from a reputable entity and asks for sensitive information, the user should not provide it but instead should use the Internet or examine a legitimate account statement to find a phone number that can be used to contact the entity. The user can then verify that the message received was legitimate or report the vishing attempt.

SPAM

Though not generally considered a social engineering issue, nor a security issue for that matter, **SPAM** *can*, however, be a security concern. SPAM, as just about everybody knows, is bulk unsolicited e-mail. It can be legitimate in the sense that it has been sent by a company advertising a product or service, but it can also be malicious and could include an attachment that contains malicious software designed to harm your system, or a link to a malicious web site that may attempt to obtain personal information from you. Though not as well known, a variation on SPAM is *SPIM*, which is basically SPAM delivered via an instant messaging application such as Yahoo! Messenger or AIM. The purpose of hostile SPIM is the same as that of SPAM—the delivery of malicious content or links.

Shoulder Surfing

Shoulder surfing does not necessarily involve direct contact with the target, but instead involves the attacker directly observing the individual entering sensitive information on a form, keypad, or keyboard. The attacker may simply look over the shoulder of the user at work, for example, or may

Tech Tip

Beware of Vishing

Vishing (phishing conducted using voice systems) is generally successful because of the trust that individuals place in the telephone system. With caller ID, people believe they can identify who it is that is calling them. They do not understand that, just like many protocols in the TCP/IP protocol suite, caller ID can be spoofed.

set up a camera or use binoculars to view the user entering sensitive data. The attacker can attempt to obtain information such as a personal identification number (PIN) at an automated teller machine (ATM), an access control entry code at a secure gate or door, or a calling card or credit card number. Many locations now use a small shield to surround a keypad so that it is difficult to observe somebody entering information. More sophisticated systems can actually scramble the location of the numbers so that the top row at one time includes the numbers 1, 2, and 3 and the next time 4, 8, and 0. While this makes it a bit slower for the user to enter information, it thwarts an attacker's attempt to observe what numbers are pressed and enter the same buttons/pattern, since the location of the numbers constantly changes.

A related, somewhat obvious security precaution is that a person should not use the same PIN for all of their different accounts, gate codes, and so on, since an attacker who learns the PIN for one type of access could then use it for all of the other types of access.

Although methods such as adding shields to block the view or having the pad "scramble" the numbers can help make shoulder surfing more difficult, the best defense is for users to be aware of their surroundings and to not allow individuals to get into a position from which they can observe what the user is entering.

The attacker may attempt to increase the chance of successfully observing the target entering the data by starting a conversation with the target. This provides an excuse for the attacker to be physically closer to the target. Otherwise, the target may be suspicious if the attacker is standing too close. In this sense, shoulder surfing can be considered a social engineering attack.

Reverse Social Engineering

A slightly different approach to social engineering is called **reverse social engineering**. In this technique, the attacker hopes to convince the target to initiate the contact. This obviously differs from the traditional approach, where the target is the one that is contacted. The reason this attack may be successful is that, since the target is the one initiating the contact, attackers may not have to convince the target of their authenticity. The tricky part of this attack is, of course, convincing the target to make that initial contact. Possible methods to accomplish this might include sending out a spoofed e-mail (fake e-mail designed to appear authentic) that claims to be from a reputable source and provides another e-mail address or phone number to call for "tech support," or posting a notice or creating a bogus web site for a legitimate company that also claims to provide "tech support." This may be especially successful if timed to coincide with a company's deployment of a new software or hardware platform. Another potential time to target an organization with this sort of attack is when there is a significant change in the organization itself, such as when two companies merge or a smaller company is acquired by a larger one. During these times, employees are not familiar with the new organization or its procedures, and amidst the confusion, it is easy to conduct either a social engineering or reverse social engineering attack.

Tech Tip

Be Aware of Reverse Social Engineering
Reverse social engineering is not nearly as widely understood as social engineering and is a bit trickier to execute. If the attacker is successful in convincing an individual to make the initial contact, however, the process of convincing them of the authenticity of the attacker is generally much easier than in a social engineering attack.

Hoaxes

At first glance, it might seem that a hoax related to security would be considered a nuisance and not a real security issue. This might be the case for some hoaxes, especially those of the urban legend type, but the reality of the situation is that a hoax can be very damaging if it causes users to take some sort of action that weakens security. One real hoax, for example, described a new, highly destructive piece of malicious software. It instructed users to check for the existence of a certain file and to delete it if the file was found. In reality, the file mentioned was an important file used by the operating system, and deleting it caused problems the next time the system was booted. The damage caused by users modifying security settings can be serious. As with other forms of social engineering, *training and awareness* are the best and first line of defense for both users and administrators. Users should be trained to be suspicious of unusual e-mails and stories and should know who to contact in the organization to verify their validity if they are received. Hoaxes often also advise the user to send it to their friends so they know about the issue as well—and by doing so, they help spread the hoax. Users need to be suspicious of any e-mail telling them to "spread the word."

Poor Security Practices

A significant portion of human-created security problems results from poor security practices. These poor practices may be those of an individual user who is not following established security policies or processes, or they may be caused by a lack of security policies, procedures, or training within the user's organization.

Password Selection

For many years, computer intruders have relied on users' poor selection of passwords to help the intruders in their attempts to gain unauthorized access to a system or network. If attackers could obtain a list of the users' names, chances were good they could eventually access the system. Users tend to pick passwords that are easy for them to remember, and what easier password could there be than the same sequence of characters that they use for their user ID? If a system has an account with the username *jdoe*, an attacker's reasonable first guess of the account's password would be *jdoe*. If this doesn't work, the attacker would try variations on the same, such as *doej, johndoe, johnd,* and *eodj,* all of which would be reasonable possibilities.

If the attacker's attempt to use variations on the username does not yield the correct password, they might simply need more information. Users also frequently pick names of family members, pets, or favorite sports team. If the user lives in San Antonio, Texas, for example, a possible password might be *gospursgo* in honor of the city's professional basketball team. If these attempts don't work for the attacker, then the attacker might next try hobbies of the user, the name of the user's favorite make or model of car, or similar pieces of information. The key is that the user often picks something easy for them to remember, which means that the more the attacker knows about the user, the better the chance of discovering the user's password.

In an attempt to complicate the attacker's job, organizations have encouraged their users to mix upper- and lowercase characters and to include numbers and special characters in their password. While this does make the password harder to guess, the basic problem still remains: users will pick something that is easy for them to remember. Thus, our user in San Antonio may select the password *G0*Spurs*G0*, capitalizing three of the letters, inserting a special character twice, and substituting the number

Poor password selection is one of the most common of poor security practices, and one of the most dangerous. Numerous studies that have been conducted on password selection have found that, while overall more users are learning to select good passwords, a significant percentage of users still make poor choices. The problem with this, of course, is that a poor password choice can enable an attacker to compromise a computer system or network more easily. Even when users have good passwords, they often resort to another poor security practice—writing the password down in an easily located place, which can also lead to system compromise if an attacker gains physical access to the area.

zero for the letter *O*. This makes the password harder to crack, but there are a finite number of variations on the basic *gospursgo* password, so, while the attacker's job has been made more difficult, it is still possible to guess the password.

Organizations have also instituted additional policies and rules relating to password selection to further complicate an attacker's efforts. Organizations, for example, may require users to frequently change their password. This means that if an attacker is able to guess a password, it is only valid for a limited period of time before a new password is selected, after which the attacker is locked out. All is not lost for the attacker, however, since, again, users will select passwords they can remember. For example, password changes often result in a new password that simply incorporates a number at the end of the old one. Thus, our San Antonio user might select *G0*Spurs*G1* as the new password, in which case the benefit of forcing password changes on a periodic, or even frequent, basis has been totally lost. It is a good bet that the next password chosen will be *G0*Spurs*G2*, followed by *G0Spurs*G3*, and so forth.

Another policy or rule governing password selection often adopted by organizations is that passwords must not be written down. This, of course, is difficult to enforce, and thus users will frequently write them down, often as a result of what is referred to as the "password dilemma." The more difficult we make it for attackers to guess our passwords, and the more frequently we force password changes, the more difficult the passwords are for authorized users to remember and the more likely they are to write them down. Writing them down and putting them in a secure place is one thing, but all too often users will write them on a slip of paper and keep them in their calendar, wallet, or purse. Most security consultants generally agree that if they are given physical access to an office, they will be able to find a password somewhere—the top drawer of a desk, inside of a desk calendar, attached to the underside of the keyboard, or even simply on a yellow "sticky note" attached to the monitor.

With the proliferation of computers, networks, and users, the password dilemma has gotten worse. Today, the average Internet user probably has at least a half dozen different accounts and passwords to remember. Selecting a different password for each account, following the guidelines mentioned previously regarding character selection and frequency of changes, only aggravates the problem of remembering the passwords. This results in users all too frequently using the same password for all accounts. If a user does this, and then one of the accounts is broken, all other accounts are subsequently also vulnerable to attack.

The need for good password selection and the protection of passwords also applies to another common feature of today's electronic world, PINs. Most people have at least one PIN associated with things such as their ATM card or a security code to gain physical access to a room. Again, users will invariably select numbers that are easy to remember. Specific numbers, such as the individual's birth date, their spouse's birth date, or the date of some other significant event, are all common numbers to select. Other people will pick patterns that are easy to remember—2580, for example, uses all of the center numbers on a standard numeric pad on a telephone. Attackers know this, and guessing PINs follows the same sort of process that guessing a password does.

Tech Tip

Heartbleed Vulnerability

In 2014, a vulnerability in the OpenSSL cryptography was discovered and given the name Heartbleed because it originated in the heartbeat signal employed by the system. This vulnerability resulted in the potential loss of passwords and other sensitive data across multiple platforms and up to a million web servers and related systems. Heartbleed resulted in random data loss from servers, as 64K blocks of memory were exfiltrated from the system. Among the items that may be lost in Heartbleed attacks are user credentials, user IDs, and passwords. The discovery of this vulnerability prompted users to change a massive number of passwords across the Web, as users had no knowledge as to the status of their credentials. One of the common pieces of advice to users was to not reuse passwords between systems. This advice is universally good advice, not just for Heartbleed, but for all systems, all the time.

Know the rules for good password selection. Generally, these are to use eight or more characters in your password, include a combination of upper- and lowercase letters, include at least one number and one special character, do not use a common word, phrase, or name, and choose a password that you can remember so that you do not need to write it down.

Password selection is an individual activity, and ensuring that individuals are making good selections is the realm of the entity's password policy. To ensure users make appropriate choices, they need to be aware of the issue and their personal role in securing accounts. An effective password policy conveys both the user role and responsibility associated with password usage and does so in a simple enough manner that it can be conveyed via screen notes during mandated password change events.

Shoulder Surfing

As discussed earlier, *shoulder surfing* does not involve direct contact with the user, but instead involves the attacker directly observing the target entering sensitive information on a form, keypad, or keyboard. The attacker may simply look over the shoulder of the user at work, watching as a coworker enters their password. Although defensive methods can help make shoulder surfing more difficult, the best defense is for a user to be aware of their surroundings and to not allow individuals to get into a position from which they can observe what the user is entering. A related security comment can be made at this point: a person should not use the same PIN for all of their different accounts, gate codes, and so on, since an attacker who learns the PIN for one could then use it for all the others.

Piggybacking

People are often in a hurry and will frequently not follow good physical security practices and procedures. Attackers know this and may attempt to exploit this characteristic in human behavior. **Tailgating** or **piggybacking** is the simple tactic of following closely behind a person who has just used their own access card or PIN to gain physical access to a room or building. An attacker can thus gain access to the facility without having to know the access code or having to acquire an access card. It is similar to shoulder surfing in that it relies on the attacker taking advantage of an authorized user not following security procedures. Frequently the attacker may even start a conversation with the target before reaching the door so that the user may be more comfortable with allowing the individual in without challenging them. In this sense piggybacking is related to social engineering attacks. Both the piggybacking and shoulder surfing attack techniques can be easily countered by using simple procedures to ensure nobody follows you too closely or is in a position to observe your actions. Both techniques rely on the poor security practices of an authorized user to be successful. A more sophisticated countermeasure to piggybacking is a "man trap," which utilizes two doors to gain access to the facility. The second door does not open until the first one is closed and is spaced close enough to the first that an enclosure is formed that only allows one individual through at a time.

Dumpster Diving

As mentioned earlier, attackers need a certain amount of information before launching their attack. One common place to find this information, if the attacker is in the vicinity of the target, is the target's trash. The attacker might find little bits of information that could be useful for an attack. This process of going through a target's trash in hopes of finding valuable information that might be used in a penetration attempt is known in the computer community as **dumpster diving**. The tactic is not, however, unique to the computer community; it has been used for many years by others, such as identity thieves, private investigators, and law enforcement personnel, to obtain information about an individual or organization. If the attackers are very lucky, and the target's security procedures are very poor, they may actually find user IDs and passwords. As mentioned in the discussion on passwords, users sometimes write their password down. If, when the password is changed, they discard the paper the old password was written on without shredding it, the lucky dumpster diver can gain a valuable clue. Even if the attacker isn't lucky enough to obtain a password directly, he undoubtedly will find employee names, from which it's not hard to determine user IDs, as discussed earlier. Finally, the attacker may gather a variety of information that can be useful in a social engineering attack. In most locations, trash is no longer considered private property after it has been discarded (and even where dumpster diving is illegal, little enforcement occurs). An organization should have policies about discarding materials. Sensitive information should be shredded and the organization should consider securing the trash receptacle so that individuals can't forage through it. People should also consider shredding personal or sensitive information that they wish to discard in their own trash. A reasonable quality shredder is inexpensive and well worth the price when compared with the potential loss that could occur as a result of identity theft.

Try This!

Diving into Your Dumpster

The amount of useful information that users throw away in unsecured trash receptacles often amazes security professionals. Hackers know that they can often find manuals, network diagrams, and even user IDs and passwords by rummaging through dumpsters. After coordinating this with your security office, try seeing what you can find that individuals in your organization have discarded (assuming that there is no shredding policy) by either going through your organization's dumpsters or just through the office trash receptacles. What useful information did you find? Is there an obvious suggestion that you might make to enhance the security of your organization?

Installing Unauthorized Hardware and Software

Organizations should have a policy that restricts the ability of normal users to install software and new hardware on their systems. A common example is a user installing unauthorized communication software and a modem to allow them to connect to their machine at work via a modem from their home. Another common example is a user installing a wireless access point so that they can access the organization's network from many different areas. In these examples, the user has set up a backdoor into the network, circumventing all the other security mechanisms in place. The term "rogue

It has already been mentioned that gaining physical access to a computer system or network often guarantees an attacker success in penetrating the system or the network it is connected to. At the same time, there may be a number of individuals who have access to a facility but are not authorized to access the information the systems store and process. We become complacent to the access these individuals have because they often quietly go about their job so as to not draw attention to themselves and to minimize the impact on the operation of the organization. They may also be overlooked because their job does not impact the core function of the organization. A prime example of this is the custodial staff. Becoming complacent about these individuals and not paying attention to what they may have access to, however, could be a big mistake, and users should not believe that everybody who has physical access to the organization has the same level of concern for or interest in the welfare of the organization.

modem" or "rogue access point" may be used to describe these two cases. A **backdoor** is an avenue that can be used to access a system while circumventing normal security mechanisms and can often be used to install additional executable files that can lead to more ways to access the compromised system. Security professionals can use widely available tools to scan their own systems periodically for either of these rogue devices to ensure that users haven't created a backdoor.

Another common example of unauthorized software that users install on their systems is games. Unfortunately, not all games come in shrink-wrapped packages. Numerous small games can be downloaded from the Internet. The problem with this is that users don't always know where the software originally came from and what may be hidden inside it. Many individuals have unwittingly installed what seemed to be an innocuous game, only to have downloaded a piece of malicious code capable of many things, including opening a backdoor that allows attackers to connect to, and control, the system from across the Internet.

Because of these potential hazards, many organizations do not allow their users to load software or install new hardware without the knowledge and assistance of administrators. Many organizations also screen, and occasionally intercept, e-mail messages with links or attachments that are sent to users. This helps prevent users from, say, unwittingly executing a hostile program that was sent as part of a worm or virus. Consequently, many organizations have their mail servers strip off executable attachments to e-mail so that users can't accidentally cause a security problem.

Data Handling

Understanding the responsibilities of proper data handling associated with one's job is an important training topic. Information can be deceptive in that it is not directly tangible, and people tend to develop bad habits around other job measures … at the expense of security. Employees require training in how to recognize the data classification and handling requirements of the data they are using, and they need to learn how to follow the proper handling processes. If certain data elements require special handling because of contracts, laws, or regulations, there is typically a training clause associated with this requirement. Personnel assigned to these tasks should be specifically trained with regard to the security requirements. The spirit of the training clause is you get what you train, and if security over specific data types is a requirement, then it should be trained. This same principle holds for corporate data-handling responsibilities; you get the behaviors you train and reward.

Physical Access by Non-Employees

As has been mentioned, if an attacker can gain physical access to a facility, chances are very good that the attacker can obtain enough information to penetrate computer systems and networks. Many organizations require employees to wear identification badges when at work. This is an easy method to quickly spot who has permission to have physical access to the organization and who does not. While this method is easy to implement and can be a significant deterrent to unauthorized individuals, it also requires that employees actively challenge individuals who are not wearing the required identification badge. This is one area where organizations fail. Combine an attacker who slips in by piggybacking off of an authorized individual and an environment where employees have not been encouraged to challenge individuals without appropriate credentials and you have a situation where you might as well not have any badges in the first place. Organizations also frequently become complacent when faced with what appears to be a legitimate reason to access the facility, such as when an individual shows up with a warm pizza claiming it was ordered by an employee. It has often been stated by security consultants that it is amazing what you can obtain access to with a pizza box or a vase of flowers.

Another aspect that must be considered is personnel who have legitimate access to a facility but also have intent to steal intellectual property or otherwise exploit the organization. Physical access provides an easy opportunity for individuals to look for the occasional piece of critical information carelessly left out. With the proliferation of devices such as cell phones with built-in cameras, an individual could easily photograph information without it being obvious to employees. Contractors, consultants, and partners frequently not only have physical access to the facility but may also have network access. Other individuals who typically have unrestricted access to the facility when no one is around are nighttime custodial crewmembers and security guards. Such positions are often contracted out. As a result, hackers have been known to take temporary custodial jobs simply to gain access to facilities.

Preventing access to information is also important in the work area. Firms with sensitive information should have a "clean desk policy" specifying that sensitive information is not left unsecured in the work area when the worker is not present to act as custodian.

Clean Desk Policies

Preventing access to information is also important in the work area. Firms with sensitive information should have a "clean desk policy" specifying that sensitive information must not be left unsecured in the work area when the worker is not present to act as custodian. Even leaving the desk area and going to the bathroom can leave information exposed and subject to compromise. The clean desk policy should identify and prohibit things that are not obvious upon first glance, such as passwords on sticky notes under keyboards and mouse pads or in unsecured desk drawers.

■ People as a Security Tool

An interesting paradox when speaking of social engineering attacks is that people are not only the biggest problem and security risk but also the best tool in defending against a social engineering attack. The first step a company should take to fight potential social engineering attacks is to create the policies and procedures that establish the roles and responsibilities for not only security administrators but for all users. What is it that management expects, security-wise, from all employees? What is it that the organization is trying to protect, and what mechanisms are important for that protection?

Per the 2014 Verizon Data Breach Investigation Report, introduced in Chapter 1, hacks were discovered more often by internal employees than by outsiders. This means that trained users can be an important part of a security plan.

Security Awareness

Probably the single most effective method to counter potential social engineering attacks, after establishment of the organization's security goals and policies, is an active security awareness program. The extent of the training will vary depending on the organization's environment and the level of threat, but initial employee training on social engineering at the time a person is hired is important, as well as periodic refresher training.

An important element that should be stressed in training about social engineering is the type of information that the organization considers sensitive and which may be the target of a social engineering attack. There are undoubtedly signs that the organization could point to as indicative of an attacker attempting to gain access to sensitive corporate information. All employees should be aware of these indicators. The scope of information that an attacker may ask for is very large, and many questions attackers pose might also be legitimate in another context (asking for someone's phone number, for example). Employees should be taught to be cautious about revealing personal information and should especially be alert for questions regarding account information, personally identifiable information, or passwords.

 Try This!

Security Awareness Programs

A strong security education and awareness training program can go a long way toward reducing the chance that a social engineering attack will be successful. Awareness programs and campaigns, which might include seminars, videos, posters, newsletters, and similar materials, are also fairly easy to implement and not very costly. There is no reason for an organization to not have an awareness program in place. A lot of information and ideas are available on the Internet. See what you can find that might be usable for your organization that you can obtain at no charge from various organizations on the Internet. (Tip: Check organizations such as NIST and NSA, which have developed numerous security documents and guidelines.)

As a final note on user responsibilities, corporate security officers must cultivate an environment of trust in their office, as well as an understanding of the importance of security. If users feel that security personnel are only there to make their life difficult or to dredge up information that will result in an employee's termination, the atmosphere will quickly turn adversarial and be transformed into an "us versus them" situation. Security personnel need the help of all users and should strive to cultivate a team environment in which users, when faced with a questionable situation, will not hesitate to call the security office. In situations like this, security offices should remember the old adage of "don't shoot the messenger."

Security Policy Training and Procedures

People in an organization play a significant role in the security posture of the organization, As such, training is important as it can provide the basis for awareness of issues such as social engineering and desired employee security habits. These are detailed in Chapter 2.

Chapter 4 Review

■ Chapter Summary

After reading this chapter and completing the exercises, you should understand the following regarding the role people can play in security.

Define basic terminology associated with social engineering

- Social engineering is a technique in which the attacker uses various deceptive practices to convince the targeted person to divulge information they normally would not divulge, or to convince the target to do something they normally wouldn't do.
- In reverse social engineering, the attacker hopes to convince the target to initiate contact.

Describe steps organizations can take to improve their security

- Organizations should have a policy that restricts the ability of normal users to install new software and hardware on their systems.
- Contractors, consultants, and partners may frequently have not only physical access to the facility but also network access. Other groups that are given unrestricted, and unobserved, access to a facility are nighttime custodial crewmembers and security guards. Both are potential security problems and organizations should take steps to limit these individuals' access.
- The single most effective method to counter potential social engineering attacks, after establishing the organization's security goals and policies, is an active security awareness program.

Describe common user actions that may put an organization's information at risk

- No matter how advanced security technology is, it will ultimately be deployed in an environment where the human element may be its greatest weakness.

- Attackers know that employees are frequently very busy and don't stop to think about security. They may attempt to exploit this work characteristic through piggybacking or shoulder surfing.

Recognize methods attackers may use to gain information about an organization

- For many years computer intruders have relied on users' poor selection of passwords to help the intruders in their attempts to gain unauthorized access to a system or network.
- One common way to find useful information (if the attacker is in the vicinity of the target, such as a company office) is to go through the target's trash looking for bits of information that could be useful to a penetration attempt.

Determine ways in which users can aid instead of detract from security

- An interesting paradox of social engineering attacks is that people are not only the biggest problem and security risk but also the best line of defense against a social engineering attack.
- A significant portion of employee-created security problems arise from poor security practices.
- Users should always be on the watch for attempts by individuals to gain information about the organization and should report suspicious activity to their employer.

Recognize the role training and awareness plays in assisting the people side of security

- Individual users can enhance security of a system through proper execution of their individual actions and responsibilities.
- Training and awareness programs can reinforce user knowledge of desired actions.

Key Terms

backdoor *(82)*

dumpster diving *(81)*

phishing *(75)*

piggybacking *(80)*

reverse social engineering *(77)*

shoulder surfing *(76)*

social engineering *(73)*

SPAM *(76)*

tailgating *(80)*

vishing *(76)*

Key Terms Quiz

Use terms from the Key Terms list to complete the sentences that follow. Don't use the same term more than once. Not all terms will be used.

1. A _____ is an avenue that can be used to access a system while circumventing normal security mechanisms.

2. _____ is a procedure in which attackers position themselves in such a way as to be able to observe an authorized user entering the correct access code.

3. The process of going through a target's trash searching for information that can be used in an attack, or to gain knowledge about a system or network, is known as _____.

4. _____ is the simple tactic of following closely behind a person who has just used their access card or PIN to gain physical access to a room or building.

5. In _____, the attacker hopes to convince the target to initiate contact.

6. _____ is a variation of _____ that uses voice communication technology to obtain the information the attacker is seeking.

Multiple-Choice Quiz

1. Which of the following is considered a good practice for password security?

   A. Using a combination of upper- and lowercase characters, a number, and a special character in the password itself

   B. Not writing the password down

   C. Changing the password on a regular basis

   D. All of the above

2. The password dilemma refers to the fact that:

   A. Passwords that are easy for users to remember are also easy for attackers to guess.

   B. The more difficult we make it for attackers to guess our passwords, and the more frequently we force password changes, the more difficult the passwords are for authorized users to remember and the more likely they are to write them down.

   C. Users will invariably attempt to select passwords that are words they can remember. This means they may select things closely associated with them, such as their spouse's or child's name, a beloved sports team, or a favorite model of car.

   D. Passwords assigned by administrators are usually better and more secure, but are often harder for users to remember.

3. The simple tactic of following closely behind a person who has just used their own access card or PIN to gain physical access to a room or building is called:

   A. Shoulder surfing

   B. Tagging-along

   C. Piggybacking

   D. Access drafting

4. The process of going through a target's trash in hopes of finding valuable information that might be used in a penetration attempt is known as:

   A. Dumpster diving

   B. Trash trolling

   C. Garbage gathering

   D. Refuse rolling

5. Which of the following is a type of social engineering attack in which an attacker attempts to obtain sensitive information from a user by masquerading as a trusted entity in an e-mail?

   A. SPAM

   B. SPIM

   C. Phishing

   D. Vishing

6. Reverse social engineering involves:

   A. Contacting the target, eliciting some sensitive information, and convincing them that nothing out of the ordinary has occurred

   B. Contacting the target in an attempt to obtain information that can be used in a second attempt with a different individual

   C. An individual lower in the chain of command convincing somebody at a higher level to divulge information that the attacker is not authorized to have

   D. An attacker attempting to somehow convince the target to initiate contact in order to avoid questions about authenticity

7. The reason for not allowing users to install new hardware or software without the knowledge of security administrators is:

   A. They may not complete the installation correctly and the administrator will have to do more work, taking them away from more important security tasks.

B. They may inadvertently install more than just the hardware or software; they may accidentally install a backdoor into the network.

   C. They may not have paid for it and thus may be exposing the organization to civil penalties.

   D. Unauthorized hardware and software are usually for leisure purposes and will distract employees from the job they were hired to perform.

8. Once an organization's security policies have been established, the single most effective method of countering potential social engineering attacks is:

   A. An active security awareness program

   B. A separate physical access control mechanism for each department in the organization

   C. Frequent testing of both the organization's physical security procedures and employee telephone practices

   D. Implementing access control cards and the wearing of security identification badges

9. Which of the following types of attacks utilizes instant messaging services?

   A. SPAM

   B. SPIM

   C. Phishing

   D. Vishing

10. In what way are PINs similar to passwords?

   A. Users will normally pick a PIN that is easy to remember, such as a date or specific pattern.

   B. Attackers know common PINs and will try to use them or will attempt to learn more about the user in order to make an educated guess as to what their PIN might be.

   C. Users may write them down to remember them.

   D. All of the above are true.

Essay Quiz

1. Explain the difference between social engineering and reverse social engineering.

2. Discuss how a security-related hoax might become a security issue.

3. How might shoulder surfing be a threat in your school or work environment? What can be done to make this sort of activity more difficult?

4. For an environment familiar to you (such as work or school), describe the different non-employees who may have access to facilities that could contain sensitive information.

5. Describe some of the user security responsibilities that you feel are most important for users to remember.

Lab Projects

• Lab Project 4.1

If possible at either your place of employment or your school, attempt to determine how easy it would be to perform dumpster diving to gain access to information at the site. Are trash receptacles easy to gain access to? Are documents shredded before being discarded? Are areas where trash is stored easily accessible?

• Lab Project 4.2

Perform a search on the Web for articles and stories about social engineering attacks or reverse social engineering attacks. Choose and read five or six articles. How many of the attacks were successful? How many failed and why? How could those that may have initially succeeded been prevented?

• Lab Project 4.3

Similar to Lab Project 4.2, perform a search on the Web for articles and stories about phishing attacks. Choose and read five or six articles. How many of the attacks were successful? How many failed and why? How might the successful attacks have been mitigated or successfully accomplished?

Cryptography

If you are designing cryptosystems, you've got to think about long-term applications. You've got to try to figure out how to build something that is secure against technology in the next century that you cannot even imagine.

—WHITFIELD DIFFIE

In this chapter, you will learn how to

- Understand the fundamentals of cryptography
- Identify and describe the three types of cryptography
- List and describe current cryptographic algorithms
- Explain how cryptography is applied for security

Cryptography is the science of *encrypting,* or hiding, information—something people have sought to do since they began using language. Although language allowed people to communicate with one another, those in power attempted to hide information by controlling who was taught to read and write. Eventually, more complicated methods of concealing information by shifting letters around to make the text unreadable were developed. These complicated methods are cryptographic algorithms, also known as *ciphers.* The word cipher comes from the Arabic word *sifr,* meaning empty or zero.

When material, called *plaintext,* needs to be protected from unauthorized interception or alteration, it is encrypted into *ciphertext.* This is done using an algorithm and a key, and the rise of digital computers has provided a wide array of algorithms and increasingly complex keys. The choice of specific algorithm depends on several factors, and they will be examined in this chapter.

Cryptanalysis, the process of analyzing available information in an attempt to return the encrypted message to its original form, required advances in computer technology for complex encryption methods. The birth of the computer made it possible to easily execute the calculations required by more complex encryption algorithms. Today, the computer almost exclusively powers how encryption is performed. Computer technology has also aided cryptanalysis, allowing new methods to be developed, such as linear and differential cryptanalysis. **Differential cryptanalysis** is done by comparing the input plaintext to the output ciphertext to try and determine the key used to encrypt the information. **Linear cryptanalysis** is similar in that it uses both plaintext and ciphertext, but it puts the plaintext through a simplified cipher to try and deduce what the key is likely to be in the full version of the cipher.

Cryptography in Practice

While cryptography may be a science, it performs critical functions in the enabling of trust across computer networks in business and other functions. Before we dig deep into the technical nature of cryptographic practices, an overview of current capabilities is useful. Examining cryptography from a high level, there are several relevant points today.

Cryptography has been a long-running event of advances both on the side of cryptography and the side of breaking it via analysis. With the advent of digital cryptography, the advantage has clearly swung to the side of cryptography. Modern computers have also increased the need for, and lowered the cost of employing, cryptography to secure information. In the past, the effectiveness rested in the secrecy of the algorithm, but with modern digital cryptography, the strength is based on sheer complexity. The power of networks and modern algorithms has also been employed to manage automatic key management.

Cryptography has many uses besides just enabling confidentiality in communication channels. Cryptographic functions are used in a wide range of applications, including, but not limited to, hiding data, resisting forgery, resisting unauthorized change, resisting repudiation, policy enforcement, and key exchanges. In spite of the strengths of modern cryptography, it still fails due to other issues; known plaintext attacks, poorly protected keys, and repeated passphrases are examples of how strong cryptography is rendered weak via implementation mistakes.

Modern cryptographic algorithms are far stronger than needed given the state of cryptanalysis. The weaknesses in cryptosystems come from the system surrounding the algorithm, implementation, and operationalization details. Adi Shamir, the *S* in RSA, states it clearly: "Attackers do not break crypto; they bypass it."

Over time, weaknesses and errors, as well as shortcuts, are found in algorithms. When an algorithm is reported as broken, the term "broken" can have many meanings. This could mean that the algorithm is of no further use, or it could mean that it has weaknesses that may someday be employed to break it, or anything between these extremes. As all methods can be broken with brute force, one question is how much effort is required, at what cost, when compared to the value of the asset under protection.

Cryptography is much more than encryption. Cryptographic methods enable data protection, data hiding, integrity checks, nonrepudiation services, policy enforcement, key management and exchange, and many more elements used in modern computing. If you used the Web today, odds are you used cryptography without even knowing it.

When examining the strength of a cryptosystem, it is worth examining the following types of levels of protection:

1. The mechanism is no longer useful for any purpose.

2. The cost of recovering the clear text without benefit of the key has fallen to a low level.

3. The cost has fallen to equal to or less than the value of the data or the next least cost attack.

4. The cost has fallen to within several orders of magnitudes of the cost of encryption or the value of the data.

5. The elapsed time of attack has fallen to within magnitudes of the life of the data, regardless of the cost thereof.

6. The cost has fallen to less than the cost of a brute-force attack against the key.

7. Someone has recovered one key or one message.

This list of conditions is a descending list of risks/benefits. Conditions 6 and 7 are regular occurrences in cryptographic systems, and generally not worth worrying about at all. In fact, it is not until the fourth point that one has to have real concerns. With all this said, most organizations consider replacement between 5 and 6. If any of the first three are positive, the organization seriously needs to consider changing their cryptographic methods.

Fundamental Methods

Modern cryptographic operations are performed using both an algorithm and a key. The choice of algorithm depends on the type of cryptographic operation that is desired. The subsequent choice of key is then tied to the specific algorithm. Cryptographic operations include encryption (for the protection of confidentiality), hashing (for the protection of integrity), digital signatures (to manage nonrepudiation), and a bevy of specialty operations such as key exchanges.

The methods used to encrypt information are based on two separate operations, substitution and transposition. **Substitution** is the replacement of an item with a different item. **Transposition** is the changing of the order of items. Pig Latin, a child's cipher, employs both operations in simplistic form and is thus easy to decipher. These operations can be done on words, characters, and, in the digital world, bits. What makes a system secure is the complexity of the changes employed. To make a system reversible (so you can reliably decrypt it), there needs to be a basis for the pattern of changes. Historical ciphers used relatively simple patterns, and ones that required significant knowledge (at the time) to break.

Modern cryptography is built around complex mathematical functions. These functions have specific properties that make them resistant to reversing or solving by means other than the application of the algorithm and key.

While the mathematical specifics of these operations can be very complex and are beyond the scope of this level of material, the knowledge to properly employ them is not. Cryptographic operations are characterized by the quantity and type of data, as well as the level and type of protection

Assurance is a specific term in security that means that something is not only true but can be proven to be so to some specific level of certainty.

sought. Integrity protection operations are characterized by the level of assurance desired. Data can be characterized by its state: data in transit, data at rest, or data in use. It is also characterized in how it is used, either in block form or stream form.

Comparative Strengths and Performance of Algorithms

There are several factors that play a role in determining the strength of a cryptographic algorithm. First and most obvious is the size of the key and the resulting **keyspace**. The keyspace is defined as a set of every possible key value. One method of attack is to simply try all of the possible keys in a brute-force attack. The other factor is referred to as *work factor,* which is a subjective measurement of the time and effort needed to perform operations. If the work factor is low, then the rate at which keys can be tested is high, meaning that larger keyspaces are needed. Work factor also plays a role in protecting systems such as password hashes, where having a higher work factor can be part of the security mechanism.

A larger keyspace allows the use of keys of greater complexity, and therefore more security, assuming the algorithm is well designed. It is easy to see how key complexity affects an algorithm when you look at some of the encryption algorithms that have been broken. The Data Encryption Standard (DES) uses a 56-bit key, allowing 72,000,000,000,000,000 possible values, but it has been broken by modern computers. The modern implementation of DES, Triple DES (3DES), uses three 56-bit keys, for a total key length of 168 bits (although for technical reasons the effective key length is 112 bits), or 340,000,000,000,000,000,000,000,000,000,000,000,000 possible values.

When an algorithm lists a certain number of bits as a key, it is defining the keyspace. Some algorithms have key lengths of 8192 bits or more, resulting in very large keyspaces, even by digital computer standards.

Modern computers have also challenged work factor elements as algorithms can be rendered very quickly by specialized hardware such as high-end graphic chips. To defeat this, many algorithms have repeated cycles to add to the work and reduce the ability to parallelize operations inside processor chips. This is done to increase the inefficiency of a calculation, but in a manner that still results in suitable performance when given the key and still complicates matters when done in a brute-force manner with all keys.

Tech Tip

Keyspace Comparisons

Because the keyspace is a numeric value, it is very important to ensure that comparisons are done using similar key types. Comparing a key made of 1 bit (2 possible values) and a key made of 1 letter (26 possible values) would not yield accurate results. Fortunately, the widespread use of computers has made almost all algorithms state their keyspace values in terms of bits.

■ Historical Perspectives

Cryptography is as old as secrets. Humans have been designing secret communication systems for as long they've needed to keep communication private. The Spartans of ancient Greece would write on a ribbon wrapped around a cylinder with a specific diameter (called a *scytale*). When the ribbon was unwrapped, it revealed a strange string of letters. The message could be read only when the ribbon was wrapped around the same diameter cylinder. This is an example of a **transposition cipher**, where the same

• **Figure 5.1** Any shift cipher can easily be encoded and decoded on a wheel of two pieces of paper with the alphabet set as a ring; by moving one circle the specified number in the shift, you can translate the characters.

letters are used but the order is changed. In all these cipher systems, the unencrypted input text is known as **plaintext** and the encrypted output is known as **ciphertext**.

Substitution Ciphers

The Romans typically used a different method known as a **shift cipher**. In this case, one letter of the alphabet is shifted a set number of places in the alphabet for another letter. A common modern-day example of this is the ROT13 cipher, in which every letter is rotated 13 positions in the alphabet: *n* is written instead of *a*, *o* instead of *b*, and so on. These types of ciphers are commonly encoded on an alphabet wheel, as shown in Figure 5.1.

These ciphers were simple to use and also simple to break. Because hiding information was still important, more advanced transposition and substitution ciphers were required. As systems and technology became more complex, ciphers were frequently automated by some mechanical or electromechanical device. A famous example of a relatively modern encryption machine is the German Enigma machine from World War II (see Figure 5.2). This machine used a complex series of substitutions to perform encryption, and interestingly enough it gave rise to extensive research in computers.

Caesar's cipher uses an algorithm and a key: the algorithm specifies that you offset the alphabet either to the right (forward) or to the left (backward), and the key specifies how many letters the offset should be. For example, if the algorithm specifies offsetting the alphabet to the right, and the key is 3, the cipher substitutes an alphabetic letter three to the right for the real letter, so *d* is used to represent *a*, *f* represents *c*, and so on. In this example, both the algorithm and key are simple, allowing for easy cryptanalysis of the cipher and easy recovery of the plaintext message.

The ease with which shift ciphers were broken led to the development of *substitution ciphers,* which were popular in Elizabethan England (roughly the second half of the 16th century) and more complex than shift ciphers. Substitution ciphers work on the principle of substituting a different

• **Figure 5.2** One of the surviving German Enigma machines

letter for every letter: *a* becomes *g*, *b* becomes *d*, and so on. This system permits 26 possible values for every letter in the message, making the cipher many times more complex than a standard shift cipher. Simple analysis of the cipher could be performed to retrieve the key, however. By looking for common letters such as *e* and patterns found in words such as *ing*, you can determine which cipher letter corresponds to which plaintext letter. The examination of ciphertext for frequent letters is known as *frequency analysis*. Making educated guesses about words will eventually allow you to determine the system's key value (see Figure 5.3).

To correct this problem, more complexity had to be added to the system. The **Vigenère cipher** works as a *polyalphabetic substitution cipher* that depends on a password. This is done by setting up a substitution table like this one:

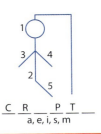

• **Figure 5.3** Making educated guesses is much like playing hangman—correct guesses can lead to more or all of the key being revealed.

```
A B C D E F G H I J K L M N O P Q R S T U V W X Y Z
B C D E F G H I J K L M N O P Q R S T U V W X Y Z A
C D E F G H I J K L M N O P Q R S T U V W X Y Z A B
D E F G H I J K L M N O P Q R S T U V W X Y Z A B C
E F G H I J K L M N O P Q R S T U V W X Y Z A B C D
F G H I J K L M N O P Q R S T U V W X Y Z A B C D E
G H I J K L M N O P Q R S T U V W X Y Z A B C D E F
H I J K L M N O P Q R S T U V W X Y Z A B C D E F G
I J K L M N O P Q R S T U V W X Y Z A B C D E F G H
J K L M N O P Q R S T U V W X Y Z A B C D E F G H I
K L M N O P Q R S T U V W X Y Z A B C D E F G H I J
L M N O P Q R S T U V W X Y Z A B C D E F G H I J K
M N O P Q R S T U V W X Y Z A B C D E F G H I J K L
N O P Q R S T U V W X Y Z A B C D E F G H I J K L M
O P Q R S T U V W X Y Z A B C D E F G H I J K L M N
P Q R S T U V W X Y Z A B C D E F G H I J K L M N O
Q R S T U V W X Y Z A B C D E F G H I J K L M N O P
R S T U V W X Y Z A B C D E F G H I J K L M N O P Q
S T U V W X Y Z A B C D E F G H I J K L M N O P Q R
T U V W X Y Z A B C D E F G H I J K L M N O P Q R S
U V W X Y Z A B C D E F G H I J K L M N O P Q R S T
V W X Y Z A B C D E F G H I J K L M N O P Q R S T U
W X Y Z A B C D E F G H I J K L M N O P Q R S T U V
X Y Z A B C D E F G H I J K L M N O P Q R S T U V W
Y Z A B C D E F G H I J K L M N O P Q R S T U V W X
Z A B C D E F G H I J K L M N O P Q R S T U V W X Y
```

Then the password is matched up to the text it is meant to encipher. If the password is not long enough, the password is repeated until one character of the password is matched up with each character of the plaintext. For example, if the plaintext is *Sample Message* and the password is *password*, the resulting match is

SAMPLEMESSAGE
PASSWORDPASSW

The cipher letter is determined by use of the grid, matching the plaintext character's row with the password character's column, resulting in a single ciphertext character where the two meet. Consider the first letters *S* and *P*: when plugged into the grid they output a ciphertext character of *H*. This process is repeated for every letter of the message. Once the rest of the letters are processed, the output is HAEHHSDHHSSYA.

In this example, the key in the encryption system is the password. The example also illustrates that an algorithm can be simple and still provide

One-time pads are examples of perfect ciphers from a mathematical point of view. But when put into practice, the implementation creates weaknesses that result in less than perfect security. This is an important reminder that perfect ciphers from a mathematical point of view do not create perfect security in practice because of the limitations associated with implementation.

strong security. If someone knows about the table, they can determine how the encryption was performed, but they still will not know the key to decrypting the message.

The more complex the key, the greater the security of the system. The Vigenère cipher system and systems like it make the algorithms rather simple but the key rather complex, with the best keys comprising very long and very random data. Key complexity is achieved by giving the key a large number of possible values.

One-time Pads

One-time pads are an interesting form of encryption in that they theoretically are perfect and unbreakable. The key is the same size or larger than the material being encrypted. The plaintext is XOR'ed against the key producing the ciphertext. What makes the one-time pad "perfect" is the size of the key. If you use a keyspace full of keys, you will decrypt every possible message of the same length as the original, with no way to discriminate which one is correct. This makes a one-time pad unable to be broken by even brute-force methods, provided that the key is not reused. This makes a one-time pad less than practical for any mass use.

■ Algorithms

Every current encryption scheme is based upon an **algorithm**, a step-by-step, recursive computational procedure for solving a problem in a finite number of steps. The cryptographic algorithm—what is commonly called the *encryption algorithm* or *cipher*—is made up of mathematical steps for encrypting and decrypting information. The following illustration shows a diagram of the encryption and decryption process and its parts. There are three types of encryption algorithms commonly used: hashing, symmetric, and asymmetric. Hashing is a very special type of encryption algorithm that takes an input and mathematically reduces it to a unique number known as a hash, which is not reversible. Symmetric algorithms are also known as shared secret algorithms, as the same key is used for encryption and decryption. Finally, asymmetric algorithms use a very different process employing two keys, a public key and a private key, making up what is known as a *key pair*.

The best algorithms are always public algorithms that have been published for peer review by other cryptographic and mathematical experts. Publication is important, as any flaws in the system can be revealed by others before actual use of the system. This process greatly encourages the use of proven technologies. Several proprietary algorithms have been reverse-engineered, exposing the confidential data the algorithms try to protect. Examples of this include the decryption of Nikon's proprietary RAW format, white-balance encryption, and the cracking of the ExxonMobil Speedpass RFID encryption. The use of a proprietary system can actually be less secure than using a published system. Whereas proprietary systems are not made available to be tested by potential crackers, public systems are made public for precisely this purpose.

A system that maintains its security after public testing can be reasonably trusted to be secure. A public algorithm can be more secure because good systems rely on the *encryption key* to provide security, not the algorithm itself. The actual steps for encrypting data can be published, because without the key, the protected information cannot be accessed (see Figure 5.4).

A **key** is a special piece of data used in both the encryption and decryption processes. The algorithms stay the same in every implementation, but a different key is used for each, which ensures that even if someone knows the algorithm you use to protect your data, he cannot break your security.

Comparing the strength of two different algorithms can be mathematically very challenging; fortunately for the layperson, there is a rough guide. Most current algorithms are listed with their key size in bits. Unless a specific algorithm has been shown to be flawed, in general, the greater number of bits will yield a more secure system. This works well for a given algorithm, but is meaningless to compare different algorithms. The good news is that most modern cryptography is more than strong enough for all but technical uses, and for those uses experts can determine appropriate algorithms and key lengths to provide the necessary protections.

 One of the most common cryptographic failures is the creation of your own encryption scheme. Rolling your own cryptography, whether in creating algorithms or implementation of existing algorithms yourself, is a recipe for failure. Always use approved algorithms and always use approved crypto libraries to implement.

Tech Tip

XOR

A popular function in cryptography is eXclusive OR (XOR), which is a bitwise function applied to data. When you apply a key to data using XOR, then a second application undoes the first operation. This makes for speedy encryption/decryption, but makes the system totally dependent upon the secrecy of the key. A hard-coded key in a program will be discovered, making this a weak security mechanism in most cases.

• **Figure 5.4** While everyone knows how to use a knob to open a door, without the key to unlock the knob, that knowledge is useless.

Tech Tip

Man-in-the-Middle Attack

A man-in-the-middle attack is designed to defeat proper key exchange by intercepting the remote party's key and replacing it with the attacker's key in both directions. If done properly, only the attacker knows that the encrypted traffic is not secure and the encrypted traffic can be read by the attacker.

Key Management

Because the security of the algorithms relies on the key, **key management** is of critical concern. Key management includes anything having to do with the exchange, storage, safeguarding, and revocation of keys. It is most commonly associated with asymmetric encryption, since asymmetric encryption uses both public and private keys. To be used properly for authentication, a key must be current and verified. If you have an old or compromised key, you need a way to check to see that the key has been revoked.

Key management is also important for symmetric encryption, because symmetric encryption relies on both parties having the same key for the algorithm to work. Since these parties are usually physically separate, key management is critical to ensure keys are shared and exchanged easily. They must also be securely stored to provide appropriate confidentiality of the encrypted information. There are many different approaches to secure storage of keys, such as putting them on a USB flash drive or smart card. While keys can be stored in many different ways, new PC hardware often includes the Trusted Platform Module (TPM), which provides a hardware-based key storage location that is used by many applications. (More specific information about the management of keys is provided later in this chapter and in Chapter 6.)

Random Numbers

Many digital cryptographic algorithms have a need for a random number to act as a seed and provide true randomness. One of the strengths of computers is that they can do a task over and over again in the exact same manner—no noise or randomness. This is great for most tasks, but in generating a random sequence of values, it presents challenges. Software libraries have pseudo-random generators, functions that produce a series of numbers that statistically appear random. But these random number generators are deterministic in that, given the sequence, you can calculate future values. This makes them inappropriate for use in cryptographic situations.

The level or amount of randomness is referred to as **entropy**. Entropy is the measure of uncertainty associated with a series of values. Perfect entropy equates to complete randomness, such that given any string of bits, there is no computation to improve guessing the next bit in the sequence. A simple "measure" of entropy is in bits, where the bits are the power of 2 that represents the number of choices. So if there are 2048 options, then this would represent 11 bits of entropy. In this fashion, one can calculate the entropy of passwords and measure how "hard they are to guess."

To resolve the problem of appropriate randomness, there are systems to create cryptographic random numbers. The level of complexity of the system is dependent upon the level of pure randomness needed. For some functions, such as master keys, the only true solution is a hardware-based random number generator that can use physical properties to derive entropy. In other, less demanding cases, a cryptographic library call can provide the necessary entropy. While the theoretical strength of the cryptosystem depends on the algorithm, the strength of the implementation in practice can depend on issues such as the key. This is a very important issue and mistakes made in implementation can invalidate even the strongest algorithms in practice.

Tech Tip

Randomness Issues

The importance of proper random number generation in cryptosystems cannot be underestimated. Recent reports by the Guardian *and the* New York Times *assert that the U.S. National Security Agency (NSA) has put a backdoor into the Cryptographically Secure Random Number Generator (CSPRNG) algorithms described in NIST SP 800-90A, particularly the Dual_EC_DRBG algorithm. Further allegations are that the NSA paid RSA $10 million to use the resulting standard in its product line.*

Hashing Functions

Hashing functions are commonly used encryption methods. A *hashing function* or *hash function* is a special mathematical function that performs a *one-way function*, which means that once the algorithm is processed, there is no feasible way to use the ciphertext to retrieve the plaintext that was used to generate it. Also, ideally, there is no feasible way to generate two different plaintexts that compute to the same **hash** value. The hash value is the output of the hashing algorithm for a specific input. The illustration shows the one-way nature of these functions.

Common uses of hashing algorithms are to store computer passwords and to ensure message integrity. The idea is that hashing can produce a unique value that corresponds to the data entered, but the hash value is also reproducible by anyone else running the same algorithm against the same data. So you could hash a message to get a message authentication code (MAC), and the computational number of the message would show that no intermediary has modified the message. This process works because hashing algorithms are typically public, and anyone can hash data using the specified algorithm. It is computationally simple to generate the hash, so it is simple to check the validity or integrity of something by matching the given hash to one that is locally generated. Several programs can compute hash values for an input file, as shown in Figure 5.5. Hash-based Message Authentication Code (HMAC) is a special subset of hashing technology. It is a hash algorithm applied to a message to make a MAC, but it is done with a previously shared secret. So the HMAC can provide integrity simultaneously with authentication. HMAC-MD5 is used in the NT LAN Manager version 2 challenge/response protocol.

A hash algorithm can be compromised with what is called a **collision attack**, in which an attacker finds two different messages that hash to the same value. This type of attack is very difficult and requires generating a separate algorithm that attempts to find a text that will hash to the same value of a known hash. This must occur faster than simply editing characters until you hash to the same value, which is a brute-force type attack. The consequence of a hash function that suffers from collisions is a loss of integrity. If an attacker can make two different inputs purposefully hash to the same value, she might trick people into running malicious code and cause other problems. Popular hash algorithms are the Secure Hash Algorithm (SHA) series, the RIPEMD algorithms, and the Message Digest (MD) hash of varying versions (MD2, MD4, MD5). Because of weaknesses, and collision attack vulnerabilities, many hash functions are now considered to be insecure, including MD2, MD4, MD5, and SHA-1 series.

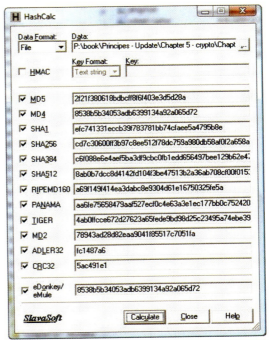

• **Figure 5.5** There are several programs available that will accept an input and produce a hash value, letting you independently verify the integrity of downloaded content.

Hashing functions are very common and play an important role in the way information, such as passwords, is stored securely, and the way in which messages can be signed. By computing a digest of the message, less data needs to be signed by the more complex asymmetric encryption, and this still maintains assurances about message integrity. This is the primary purpose for which the protocols were designed, and their success will allow greater trust in electronic protocols and digital signatures.

SHA

Secure Hash Algorithm (SHA) refers to a set of hash algorithms designed and published by the National Institute of Standards and Technology (NIST) and the National Security Agency (NSA). These algorithms are included in the SHA standard Federal Information Processing Standards (FIPS) 180-2 and 180-3. The individual standards are named SHA-1, SHA-224, SHA-256, SHA-384, and SHA-512. The latter three variants are occasionally referred to collectively as SHA-2. The newest version is known as SHA-3, which is specified in FIPS 202.

SHA-1

SHA-1, developed in 1993, was designed as the algorithm to be used for secure hashing in the U.S. Digital Signature Standard (DSS). It is modeled on the MD4 algorithm and implements fixes in that algorithm discovered by the NSA. It creates message digests 160 bits long that can be used by the Digital Signature Algorithm (DSA), which can then compute the signature of the message. This is computationally simpler, as the message digest is typically much smaller than the actual message—smaller message, less work.

SHA-1 works, as do all hashing functions, by applying a compression function to the data input. It accepts an input of up to 2^{64} bits or less and then compresses down to a hash of 160 bits. SHA-1 works in block mode, separating the data into words first, and then grouping the words into blocks. The words are 32-bit strings converted to hex; grouped together as 16 words, they make up a 512-bit block. If the data that is input to SHA-1 is not a multiple of 512, the message is padded with zeros and an integer describing the original length of the message. Once the message has been formatted for processing, the actual hash can be generated. The 512-bit blocks are taken in order until the entire message has been processed.

At one time, SHA-1 was one of the more secure hash functions, but it has been found to be vulnerable to a collision attack. This attack found a collision in 2^{69} computations, less than the brute-force method of 2^{80} computations. While this is not a tremendously practical attack, it does suggest a weakness. Thus, many security professionals are suggesting that implementations of SHA-1 be moved to one of the other SHA versions. These longer versions, SHA-256, SHA-384, and SHA-512, all have longer hash results, making them more difficult to attack successfully. The added security and resistance to attack in SHA-2 does require more processing power to compute the hash.

SHA-2

SHA-2 is a collective name for SHA-224, SHA-256, SHA-384, and SHA-512. SHA-256 is similar to SHA-1 in that it also accepts input of less than 2^{64} bits and reduces that input to a hash. This algorithm reduces to 256 bits instead of SHA-1's 160. Defined in FIPS 180-2 in 2002, SHA-256 is listed as an update to the original FIPS 180 that defined SHA. Similar to SHA-1, SHA-256 uses 32-bit words and 512-bit blocks. Padding is added until the entire message is a multiple of 512. SHA-256 uses sixty-four 32-bit words, eight working variables, and results in a hash value of eight 32-bit words, hence 256 bits. SHA-224 is a truncated version of the SHA-256 algorithm that results in a 224-bit hash value. There are no known collision attacks against SHA-256; however, an attack on reduced-round SHA-256 is possible.

SHA-512 is also similar to SHA-1, but it handles larger sets of data. SHA-512 accepts 2^{128} bits of input, which it pads until it has several blocks of data in 1024-bit blocks. SHA-512 also uses 64-bit words instead of SHA-1's 32-bit words. It uses eight 64-bit words to produce the 512-bit hash value. SHA-384 is a truncated version of SHA-512 that uses six 64-bit words to produce a 384-bit hash.

While SHA-2 is not as common as SHA-1, more applications are starting to utilize it after SHA-1 was shown to be potentially vulnerable to a collision attack.

SHA-3

SHA-3 is the name for the SHA-2 replacement. In 2012, the Keccak hash function won the NIST competition and was chosen as the basis for the SHA-3 method. Because the algorithm is completely different from the previous SHA series, it has proved to be more resistant to attacks that are successful against them. As the SHA-3 series is relatively new, it has not been widely adopted in many cipher suites yet.

The SHA-2 and SHA-3 series are currently approved for use. SHA-1 has been deprecated and its use discontinued in many strong cipher suites.

RIPEMD

RACE Integrity Primitives Evaluation Message Digest (RIPEMD) is a hashing function developed by the RACE Integrity Primitives Evaluation (RIPE) consortium. It originally provided a 128-bit hash and was later shown to have problems with collisions. RIPEMD was strengthened to a 160-bit hash known as RIPEMD-160 by Hans Dobbertin, Antoon Bosselaers, and Bart Preneel. There are also 256-and 320-bit versions of the algorithm known as RIPEMD-256 and RIPEMD-320.

RIPEMD-160

RIPEMD-160 is an algorithm based on MD4, but it uses two parallel channels with five rounds. The output consists of five 32-bit words to make a 160-bit hash. There are also larger output extensions of the RIPEMD-160 algorithm. These extensions, RIPEMD-256 and RIPEMD-320, offer outputs of 256 bits and 320 bits, respectively. While these offer larger output sizes, this does not make the hash function inherently stronger.

Message Digest

Message Digest (MD) is the generic version of one of several algorithms that are designed to create a message digest or hash from data input into the algorithm. MD algorithms work in the same manner as SHA in that they use a secure method to compress the file and generate a computed output of a specified number of bits. The MD algorithms were all developed by Ronald L. Rivest of MIT.

MD2

MD2 was developed in 1989 and is in some ways an early version of the later MD5 algorithm. It takes a data input of any length and produces a hash output of 128 bits. It is different from MD4 and MD5 in that MD2 is optimized for 8-bit machines, whereas the other two are optimized for 32-bit machines. After the function has been run for every 16 bytes of the message, the output result is a 128-bit digest. The only known attack that is successful against MD2 requires that the checksum not be appended to the message before the hash function is run. Without a checksum, the algorithm can be vulnerable to a collision attack. Some collision attacks are based upon the algorithm's initialization vector (IV).

MD4

MD4 was developed in 1990 and is optimized for 32-bit computers. It is a fast algorithm, but it is subject to more attacks than more secure algorithms such as MD5. An extended version of MD4 computes the message in parallel and produces two 128-bit outputs—effectively a 256-bit hash. Even though a longer hash is produced, security has not been improved because of basic flaws in the algorithm. A cryptographer, Hans Dobbertin, has shown how collisions in MD4 can be found in under a minute using just a PC. This vulnerability to collisions applies to 128-bit MD4 as well as 256-bit MD4. Because of weaknesses, people have moved away from MD4 to more robust hash functions.

MD5

MD5 was developed in 1991 and is structured after MD4 but with additional security to overcome the problems in MD4. Therefore, it is very similar to the MD4 algorithm, only slightly slower and more secure.

Recently, successful attacks on the algorithm have occurred. Cryptanalysis has displayed weaknesses in the compression function. However, this weakness does not lend itself to an attack on MD5 itself. Czech cryptographer Vlastimil Klíma published work showing that MD5 collisions can be computed in about eight hours on a standard home PC. In November 2007, researchers published results showing the ability to have two entirely different Win32 executables with different functionality but the same MD5 hash. This discovery has obvious implications for the development of malware. The combination of these problems with MD5 has pushed people to adopt a strong SHA version for security reasons.

Hashing Summary

Hashing functions are very common, and they play an important role in the way information, such as passwords, is stored securely and the way in which messages can be signed. By computing a digest of the message, less data needs to be signed by the more complex asymmetric encryption, and this still maintains assurances about message integrity. This is the primary purpose for which the protocols were designed, and their success will allow

MD5 creates a 128-bit hash of a message of any length.

Tech Tip

Rainbow Tables

Rainbow tables are precomputed hash tables that enable looking up small text entries via their hash values. This makes hashed passwords "reversible" by looking up the hash in a precomputed hash table. This works for small passwords (less than 10 characters) and is very fast. Salting passwords is one of the defenses against these tables.

greater trust in electronic protocols and digital signatures. The following illustration shows an MD5 hash calculation in Linux.

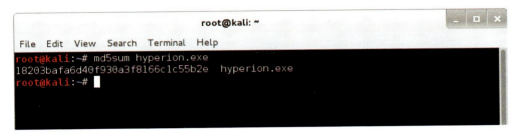

Symmetric Encryption

Symmetric encryption is the older and simpler method of encrypting information. The basis of symmetric encryption is that both the sender and the receiver of the message have previously obtained the same key. This is, in fact, the basis for even the oldest ciphers—the Spartans needed the exact same size cylinder, making the cylinder the "key" to the message, and in shift ciphers both parties need to know the direction and amount of shift being performed. All symmetric algorithms are based upon this **shared secret** principle, including the unbreakable one-time pad method.

Figure 5.6 is a simple diagram showing the process that a symmetric algorithm goes through to provide encryption from plaintext to ciphertext. This ciphertext message is, presumably, transmitted to the message recipient, who goes through the process to decrypt the message using the same key that was used to encrypt the message. Figure 5.6 shows the keys to the algorithm, which are the same value in the case of symmetric encryption.

• **Figure 5.6** Layout of a symmetric algorithm

Unlike with hash functions, a cryptographic key is involved in symmetric encryption, so there must be a mechanism for *key management* (discussed earlier in the chapter). Managing the cryptographic keys is critically important in symmetric algorithms because the key unlocks the data that is being protected. However, the key also needs to be known by, or transmitted to in a confidential way, the party to which you wish to communicate. A key must be managed at all stages, which requires securing it on the local computer, securing it on the remote one, protecting it from data corruption, protecting it from loss, and, probably the most important step, protecting it while it is transmitted between the two parties. Later in the chapter we will look at public key cryptography, which greatly eases the key management issue, but for symmetric algorithms the most important lesson is to store and send the key only by known secure means.

Some of the more popular symmetric encryption algorithms in use today are DES, 3DES, AES, and IDEA.

DES

DES, the Data Encryption Standard, was developed in response to the National Bureau of Standards (NBS), now known as the National Institute of Standards and Technology (NIST), issuing a request for proposals for a standard cryptographic algorithm in 1973. NBS received a promising response in an algorithm called Lucifer, originally developed by IBM. The NBS and the NSA worked together to analyze the algorithm's security, and eventually DES was adopted as a federal standard in 1976.

DES is what is known as a **block cipher**; it segments the input data into blocks of a specified size, typically padding the last block to make it a multiple of the block size required. This is in contrast to a *stream cipher*, which encrypts the data bit by bit. In the case of DES, the block size is 64 bits, which means DES takes a 64-bit input and outputs 64 bits of ciphertext. This process is repeated for all 64-bit blocks in the message. DES uses a key length of 56 bits, and all security rests within the key. The same algorithm and key are used for both encryption and decryption.

At the most basic level, DES performs a substitution and then a permutation (a form of transposition) on the input, based upon the key. This action is called a *round*, and DES performs this 16 times on every 64-bit block. The algorithm goes step by step, producing 64-bit blocks of ciphertext for each plaintext block. This is carried on until the entire message has been encrypted with DES. As mentioned, the same algorithm and key are used to decrypt and encrypt with DES. The only difference is that the sequence of key permutations is used in reverse order.

Over the years that DES has been a cryptographic standard, a lot of cryptanalysis has occurred, and while the algorithm has held up very well, some problems have been encountered. *Weak keys* are keys that are less secure than the majority of keys allowed in the keyspace of the algorithm. In the case of DES, because of the way the initial key is modified to get the subkey, certain keys are weak keys. The weak keys equate in binary to having all 1's or all 0's, like those shown in Figure 5.7, or to having half the key all 1's and the other half all 0's.

Semiweak keys, with which two keys will encrypt plaintext to identical ciphertext, also exist, meaning that either key will decrypt the ciphertext. The total number of possibly weak keys is 64, which is very small relative to the 2^{56} possible keys in DES.

With 16 rounds and not using a weak key, DES is reasonably secure and, amazingly, has been for more than two decades. In 1999, a distributed effort consisting of a supercomputer and 100,000 PCs over the Internet was made to break a 56-bit DES key. By attempting more than 240 billion keys per second, the effort was able to retrieve the key in less than a day. This demonstrates an incredible resistance to cracking a 20-year-old algorithm, but it also demonstrates that more stringent algorithms are needed to protect data today.

Key
0000000 0000000
0000000 FFFFFFF
FFFFFFF 0000000
FFFFFFF FFFFFFF

• **Figure 5.7**   Weak DES keys

3DES

Triple DES (3DES) is a variant of DES. Depending on the specific variant, it uses either two or three keys instead of the single key that DES uses. It also spins through the DES algorithm three times via what's called **multiple encryption**.

Multiple encryption can be performed in several different ways. The simplest method of multiple encryption is just to stack algorithms on top of each other—taking plaintext, encrypting it with DES, then encrypting the first ciphertext with a different key, and then encrypting the second ciphertext with a third key. In reality, this technique is less effective than the technique that 3DES uses. One of the modes of 3DES (EDE mode) is to encrypt with one key, then decrypt with a second, and then encrypt with a third, as shown in Figure 5.8.

This greatly increases the number of attempts needed to retrieve the key and is a significant enhancement of security. The additional security comes at a price, however. It can take up to three times longer to compute 3DES than to compute DES. However, the advances in memory and processing power in today's electronics should make this problem irrelevant in all devices except for very small low-power handhelds.

The only weaknesses of 3DES are those that already exist in DES. However, due to the use of different keys in the same algorithm, effecting a longer key length by adding the first keyspace to the second keyspace, and the greater resistance to brute-forcing, 3DES has less actual weakness. While 3DES continues to be popular and is still widely supported, AES has taken over as the symmetric encryption standard.

• **Figure 5.8**   Diagram of 3DES

AES

The current gold standard for symmetric encryption is the AES algorithm. Developed in response to a worldwide call in the late 1990s for a new symmetric cipher, a group of Dutch researchers submitted a method called *Rijndael* (pronounced "rain doll").

In the fall of 2000, NIST picked Rijndael to be the new AES. It was chosen for its overall security as well as its good performance on limited-capacity devices. Rijndael's design was influenced by Square, also written by Joan Daemen and Vincent Rijmen. Like Square, Rijndael is a block cipher that separates data input into 128-bit blocks. Rijndael can also be configured to use blocks of 192 or 256 bits, but AES has standardized on 128-bit blocks. AES can have key sizes of 128, 192, and 256 bits, with the size of the key affecting the number of rounds used in the algorithm. Longer key versions are known as AES-192 and AES-256, respectively.

The Rijndael/AES algorithm is well thought out and has a suitable key length to provide security for many years to come. While no efficient attacks currently exist against AES, more time and analysis will tell if this standard can last as long as DES has.

Tech Tip

AES in Depth
For a more in-depth description of AES, see the NIST document http://csrc.nist.gov/publications/ fips/fips197/fips-197.pdf.

CAST

CAST is an encryption algorithm that is similar to DES in its structure. It was designed by Carlisle Adams and Stafford Tavares. CAST uses a 64-bit block size for 64- and 128-bit key versions, and a 128-bit block size for the 256-bit key version. Like DES, it divides the plaintext block into a left half and a right half. The right half is then put through function *f* and then is XORed with the left half. This value becomes the new right half, and the original right half becomes the new left half. This is repeated for eight rounds for a 64-bit key, and the left and right output is concatenated to form the ciphertext block. The algorithm in CAST-256 form was submitted for the AES standard but was not chosen. CAST has undergone thorough analysis, with only minor weaknesses discovered that are dependent on low numbers of rounds. Currently, no better way is known to break high-round CAST than by brute-forcing the key, meaning that with sufficient key length, CAST should be placed with other trusted algorithms.

RC

RC is a general term for several ciphers all designed by Ron Rivest—RC officially stands for *Rivest Cipher*. RC1, RC2, RC3, RC4, RC5, and RC6 are all ciphers in the series. RC1 and RC3 never made it to release, but RC2, RC4, RC5, and RC6 are all working algorithms.

RC2

RC2 was designed as a DES replacement, and it is a variable-key-size block-mode cipher. The key size can be from 8 bits to 1024 bits, with the block size being fixed at 64 bits. RC2 breaks up the input blocks into four 16-bit words and then puts them through 18 rounds of either mix or mash operations, outputting 64 bits of ciphertext for 64 bits of plaintext.

According to RSA, RC2 is up to three times faster than DES. RSA maintained RC2 as a trade secret for a long time, with the source code eventually being illegally posted on the Internet. The ability of RC2 to accept different key lengths is one of the larger vulnerabilities in the algorithm. Any key length below 64 bits can be easily retrieved by modern computational power. Additionally, there is a related key attack that needs 234 chosen plaintexts to work. Considering these weaknesses, RC2 is not recommended as a strong cipher.

RC5

RC5 is a block cipher, written in 1994. It has multiple variable elements, numbers of rounds, key sizes, and block sizes. This algorithm is relatively new, but if configured to run enough rounds, RC5 seems to provide adequate security for current brute-forcing technology. Rivest recommends using at least 12 rounds. With 12 rounds in the algorithm, cryptanalysis in a linear fashion proves less effective than brute-force against RC5, and differential analysis fails for 15 or more rounds. A newer algorithm is RC6.

RC6

RC6 is based on the design of RC5. It uses a 128-bit block size, separated into four words of 32 bits each. It uses a round count of 20 to provide security, and it has three possible key sizes: 128, 192, and 256 bits. RC6 is a modern algorithm that runs well on 32-bit computers. With a sufficient number of rounds, the algorithm makes both linear and differential cryptanalysis infeasible. The available key lengths make brute-force attacks extremely time-consuming. RC6 should provide adequate security for some time to come.

RC4

RC4 was created before RC5 and RC6, but it differs in operation. RC4 is a **stream cipher**, whereas all the symmetric ciphers we have looked at so far have been block ciphers. A stream cipher works by enciphering the plaintext in a stream, usually bit by bit. This makes stream ciphers faster than block-mode ciphers. Stream ciphers accomplish this by performing a bitwise XOR with the plaintext stream and a generated keystream.

RC4 operates in this manner. It was developed in 1987 and remained a trade secret of RSA until it was posted to the Internet in 1994. RC4 can use a key length of 8 to 2048 bits, though the most common versions use 128-bit keys or, if subject to the old export restrictions, 40-bit keys. The key is used to initialize a 256-byte state table. This table is used to generate the pseudo-random stream that is XORed with the plaintext to generate the ciphertext. Alternatively, the stream is XORed with the ciphertext to produce the plaintext.

The algorithm is fast, sometimes ten times faster than DES. The most vulnerable point of the encryption is the possibility of weak keys. One key in 256 can generate bytes closely correlated with key bytes. Proper implementations of RC4 need to include weak key detection.

 RC4 is the most widely used stream cipher and is used in popular protocols such as Transport Layer Security (TLS) and WEP/WPA/WPA2.

Blowfish

Blowfish was designed in 1994 by Bruce Schneier. It is a block-mode cipher using 64-bit blocks and a variable key length from 32 to 448 bits. It was designed to run quickly on 32-bit microprocessors and is optimized for situations with few key changes. Encryption is done by separating the 64-bit input block into two 32-bit words, and then a function is executed every round. Blowfish has 16 rounds; once the rounds are completed, the two words are then recombined to form the 64-bit output ciphertext. The only successful cryptanalysis to date against Blowfish has been against variants that used a reduced number of rounds. There does not seem to be a weakness in the full 16-round version.

Twofish

Twofish was developed by Bruce Schneier, David Wagner, Chris Hall, Niels Ferguson, John Kelsey, and Doug Whiting. Twofish was one of the five finalists for the AES competition. Like other AES entrants, it is a block cipher, utilizing 128-bit blocks with a variable-length key of up to 256 bits. It uses 16 rounds and splits the key material into two sets, one to perform the actual encryption and the other to load into the algorithm's S-boxes. This algorithm is available for public use and has proven to be secure.

IDEA

IDEA (International Data Encryption Algorithm) started out as PES, or Proposed Encryption Cipher, in 1990, and it was modified to improve its resistance to differential cryptanalysis and its name was changed to IDEA in 1992. It is a block-mode cipher using a 64-bit block size and a 128-bit key. The input plaintext is split into four 16-bit segments, *A*, *B*, *C*, and *D*. The

> **Tech Tip**
>
> **S-Boxes**
>
> *S-boxes, or substitution boxes, are a method used to provide confusion, a separation of the relationship between the key bits and the ciphertext bits. Used in most symmetric schemes, they perform a form of substitution and can provide significant strengthening of an algorithm against certain forms of attack. They can be in the form of lookup tables, either static like DES, or dynamic (based on the key) in other forms such as Twofish.*

process uses eight rounds, with a final four-step process. The output of the last four steps is then concatenated to form the ciphertext.

All current cryptanalysis on full, eight-round IDEA shows that the most efficient attack would be to brute-force the key. The 128-bit key would prevent this attack being accomplished, given current computer technology. The only known issue is that IDEA is susceptible to a weak key—like a key that is made of all 0's. This weak key condition is easy to check for, and the weakness is simple to mitigate.

Block vs. Stream

When encryption operations are performed on data, there are two primary modes of operation, block and stream. Block operations are performed on blocks of data, enabling both transposition and substitution operations. This is possible when large pieces of data are present for the operations. Stream data has become more common with audio and video across the Web. The primary characteristic of stream data is that it is not available in large chunks, but either bit by bit or byte by byte, pieces too small for block operations. Stream ciphers operate using substitution only and therefore offer less robust protection than block ciphers. Table 5.1 compares and contrasts block and stream ciphers.

Table 5.1	Comparison of Block and Stream Ciphers
Block Ciphers	**Stream Ciphers**
Require more memory to process	Faster than block in operation
Stronger	More difficult to implement correctly
High diffusion	Low diffusion
Resistant to insertions/modifications	Susceptible to insertions and/or modifications
Susceptible to error propagation	Low error propagation
Can provide for authentication and integrity verification	Cannot provide integrity or authentication protections
Common algorithms: 3DES, AES	Common algorithms: A5, RC4

Symmetric Encryption Summary

Symmetric algorithms are important because they are comparatively fast and have few computational requirements. Their main weakness is that two geographically distant parties both need to have a key that matches the other key exactly (see Figure 5.9).

• **Figure 5.9** Symmetric keys must match exactly to encrypt and decrypt the message.

Asymmetric Encryption

Asymmetric encryption is more commonly known as *public key cryptography*. Asymmetric encryption is in many ways completely different from symmetric encryption. While both are used to keep data from being seen by unauthorized users, asymmetric cryptography uses two keys instead of one. It was invented by Whitfield Diffie and Martin Hellman in 1975. The system uses a pair of keys: a private key that is kept secret and a public key that can be sent to anyone. The system's security relies upon resistance to deducing one key, given the other, and thus retrieving the plaintext from the ciphertext.

Asymmetric encryption creates the possibility of digital signatures and also addresses the main weakness of symmetric cryptography. The ability to send messages securely without senders and receivers having had prior contact has become one of the basic concerns with secure communication. Digital signatures will enable faster and more efficient exchange of all kinds of documents, including legal documents. With strong algorithms and good key lengths, security can be assured.

Asymmetric encryption involves two separate but mathematically related keys. The keys are used in an opposing fashion. One key undoes the actions of the other and vice versa. So, as shown in Figure 5.10, if you encrypt a message with one key, the other key is used to decrypt the message. In the top example, Alice wishes to send a private message to Bob, so she uses Bob's public key to encrypt the message. Then, since only Bob's private key can decrypt the message, only Bob can read it. In the lower example, Bob wishes to send a message, with proof that it is from him. By encrypting it with his private key, anyone who decrypts it with his public key knows the message came from Bob.

• **Figure 5.10** Using an asymmetric algorithm

Asymmetric keys are distributed using certificates. A digital certificate contains information about the association of the public key to an entity, and additional information that can be used to verify the current validity of the certificate and the key. When keys are exchanged between machines, such as during an SSL/TLS handshake, the exchange is done by passing certificates.

Public key systems typically work by using hard math problems. One of the more common methods relies on the difficulty of factoring large numbers. These functions are often called **trapdoor functions**, as they are difficult to process without the key but easy to process when you have the key—the trapdoor through the function. For example, given a prime number, say 293, and another prime, such as 307, it is an easy function to multiply them together to get 89,951. Given 89,951, it is not simple to find the factors 293 and 307 unless you know one of them already. Computers can easily multiply very large primes with hundreds or thousands of digits but cannot easily factor the product.

The strength of these functions is very important: Because an attacker is likely to have access to the public key, he can run tests of known plaintext

Public key cryptography always involves two keys, a public key and a private key, which together are known as a *key pair*. The public key is made widely available to anyone who may need it, while the private key is closely safeguarded and shared with no one.

Asymmetric methods are significantly slower than symmetric methods and thus are typically not suitable for bulk encryption.

and produce ciphertext. This allows instant checking of guesses that are made about the keys of the algorithm. Public key systems, because of their design, also form the basis for *digital signatures,* a cryptographic method for securely identifying people. RSA, Diffie-Hellman, elliptic curve cryptography (ECC), and ElGamal are all popular asymmetric protocols. We will look at all of them and their suitability for different functions.

> ## ✓ Cross Check
>
> ### Digital Certificates
>
> In Chapter 6 you will learn more about digital certificates and how encryption is important to a public key infrastructure. Why is an asymmetric algorithm so important to digital signatures?

Diffie-Hellman

Diffie-Hellman (DH) was created in 1976 by Whitfield Diffie and Martin Hellman. This protocol is one of the most common encryption protocols in use today. It plays a role in the electronic key exchange method of the Secure Sockets Layer (SSL) protocol. It is also used by the Transport Layer Security (TLS), Secure Shell (SSH), and IP Security (IPsec) protocols. Diffie-Hellman is important because it enables the sharing of a secret key between two people who have not contacted each other before.

The protocol, like RSA, uses large prime numbers to work. Two users agree to two numbers, P and G, with P being a sufficiently large prime number and G being the generator. Both users pick a secret number, a and b. Then both users compute their public number:

User 1 $X = Ga \bmod P$, with X being the public number
User 2 $Y = Gb \bmod P$, with Y being the public number

The users then exchange public numbers. User 1 knows P, G, a, X, and Y.

User 1   Computes $Ka = Y^a \bmod P$
User 2   Computes $Kb = X^b \bmod P$

With $Ka = Kb = K$, now both users know the new shared secret K.

This is the basic algorithm, and although methods have been created to strengthen it, Diffie-Hellman is still in wide use. It remains very effective because of the nature of what it is protecting—a temporary, automatically generated secret key that is good only for a single communication session.

Variations of Diffie-Hellman include Ephemeral Diffie-Hellman (EDH), Elliptic Curve Diffie-Hellman (ECDH), and Elliptic Curve Diffie-Hellman Ephemeral (ECDHE). These are discussed in detail later in the chapter.

 Diffie-Hellman is the gold standard for key exchange, and for the CompTIA Security+ exam, you should understand the subtle differences between the different forms, DH, EDH, ECDH, and ECDHE.

RSA

RSA is one of the first public key cryptosystems ever invented. It can be used for both encryption and digital signatures. RSA is named after its inventors, Ron Rivest, Adi Shamir, and Leonard Adleman, and was first published in 1977.

This algorithm uses the product of two very large prime numbers and works on the principle of difficulty in factoring such large numbers. It's best to choose large prime numbers that are from 100 to 200 digits in length and are equal in length. These two primes will be P and Q. Randomly choose an encryption key, E, so that E is greater than 1, E is less than $P * Q$, and E must be odd. E must also be relatively prime to $(P - 1)$ and $(Q - 1)$. Then compute the decryption key D:

$$D = E^{-1} \bmod ((P - 1)(Q - 1))$$

Now that the encryption key and decryption key have been generated, the two prime numbers can be discarded, but they should not be revealed.

To encrypt a message, it should be divided into blocks less than the product of P and Q. Then,

$$C_i = M_i^E \bmod (P * Q)$$

C is the output block of ciphertext matching the block length of the input message, M. To decrypt a message, take ciphertext, C, and use this function:

$$M_i = C_i^D \bmod (P * Q)$$

The use of the second key retrieves the plaintext of the message.

This is a simple function, but its security has withstood the test of more than 20 years of analysis. Considering the effectiveness of RSA's security and the ability to have two keys, why are symmetric encryption algorithms needed at all? The answer is speed. RSA in software can be 100 times slower than DES, and in hardware it can be even slower.

RSA can be used to perform both regular encryption and digital signatures. Digital signatures try to duplicate the functionality of a physical signature on a document using encryption. Typically, RSA and the other public key systems are used in conjunction with symmetric key cryptography. Public key, the slower protocol, is used to exchange the symmetric key (or shared secret), and then the communication uses the faster symmetric key protocol. This process is known as *electronic key exchange.*

Since the security of RSA is based upon the supposed difficulty of factoring large numbers, the main weaknesses are in the implementations of the protocol. Until recently, RSA was a patented algorithm, but it was a de facto standard for many years.

ElGamal

ElGamal can be used for both encryption and digital signatures. Taher ElGamal designed the system in the early 1980s. This system was never patented and is free for use. It is used as the U.S. government standard for digital signatures.

The system is based upon the difficulty of calculating discrete logarithms in a finite field. Three numbers are needed to generate a key pair. User 1 chooses a prime, P, and two random numbers, F and D. F and D should both be less than P. Then user 1 can calculate the public key A:

$$A = D^F \bmod P$$

Then A, D, and P are shared with the second user, with F being the private key. To encrypt a message, M, a random key, k, is chosen that is relatively prime to $P - 1$. Then,

$$C_1 = D^k \bmod P$$
$$C_2 = A^k M \bmod P$$

C_1 and C_2 make up the ciphertext. Decryption is done by

$$M = C_2 / C_1^F \bmod P$$

ElGamal uses a different function for digital signatures. To sign a message, M, once again choose a random value k that is relatively prime to $P - 1$. Then,

$$C_1 = D^k \bmod P$$
$$C_2 = (M - C_1 * F)/k \ (\bmod \ P - 1)$$

C_1 concatenated to C_2 is the digital signature.

ElGamal is an effective algorithm and has been in use for some time. It is used primarily for digital signatures. Like all asymmetric cryptography, it is slower than symmetric cryptography.

ECC

Elliptic curve cryptography (ECC) works on the basis of elliptic curves. An elliptic curve is a simple function that is drawn as a gently looping curve on the X,Y plane. Elliptic curves are defined by this equation:

$$y^2 = x^3 + ax^2 + b$$

Elliptic curves work because they have a special property—you can add two points on the curve together and get a third point on the curve, as shown in the illustration.

For cryptography, the elliptic curve works as a public key algorithm. Users agree on an elliptic curve and a fixed curve point. This information is not a shared secret, and these points can be made public without compromising the security of the system. User 1 then chooses a secret random number, K_1, and computes a public key based upon a point on the curve:

$$P_1 = K_1 * F$$

User 2 performs the same function and generates P_2. Now user 1 can send user 2 a message by generating a shared secret:

$$S = K_1 * P_2$$

User 2 can generate the same shared secret independently:

$$S = K_2 * P_1$$

This is true because

$$K_1 * P_2 = K_1 * (K_2 * F) = (K_1 * K_2) * F = K_2 * (K_1 * F) = K_2 * P_1$$

The security of elliptic curve systems has been questioned, mostly because of lack of analysis. However, all public key systems rely on the difficulty of certain math problems. It would take a breakthrough in math for any of the mentioned systems to be weakened dramatically, but research has been done about the problems and has shown that the elliptic curve problem has been more resistant to incremental advances. Again, as with all cryptography algorithms, only time will tell how secure they really are. The big benefit to ECC systems is that they require less computing power for a given bit strength. This makes ECC ideal for use in low-power mobile devices. The surge in mobile connectivity has led to secure voice, e-mail, and text applications that use ECC and AES algorithms to protect a user's data.

Elliptic curve functions can be used as part of a Diffie-Hellman key exchange, and when used, the method is referred to as Elliptic Curve DIffie-Hellman (ECDH). This technique can provide the advantages of elliptic curve and the functionality of Diffie-Hellman.

Asymmetric Encryption Summary

Asymmetric encryption creates the possibility of digital signatures and also corrects the main weakness of symmetric cryptography. The ability to send messages securely without senders and receivers having had prior contact has become one of the basic concerns with secure communication. Digital signatures will enable faster and more efficient exchange of all kinds of documents, including legal documents. With strong algorithms and good key lengths, security can be assured.

Symmetric vs. Asymmetric

Both symmetric and asymmetric encryption methods have advantages and disadvantages. Symmetric encryption tends to be faster, is less computationally involved, and is better for bulk transfers. But it suffers from a key management problem in that keys must be protected from unauthorized parties. Asymmetric methods resolve the key secrecy issue with public keys, but add significant computational complexity that makes them less suited for bulk encryption.

Bulk encryption can be done using the best of both systems, by using asymmetric encryption to pass a symmetric key. By adding in ephemeral key exchange, you can achieve perfect forward secrecy, discussed later in the chapter. Digital signatures, a highly useful tool, are not practical without asymmetric methods.

■ Quantum Cryptography

Cryptography is traditionally a very conservative branch of information technology. It relies on proven technologies and does its best to resist change. A big new topic in recent years has been quantum cryptography. *Quantum cryptography* is based on quantum mechanics, principally superposition and entanglement. A discussion of quantum mechanics is beyond the scope of this text, but the principle we are most concerned with in regard to cryptography is that in quantum mechanics, the measuring of data disturbs the data. What this means to cryptographers is that it is easy to tell if a message has been eavesdropped on in transit, allowing people to exchange key data while knowing that the data was not intercepted in transit. This use of quantum cryptography is called *quantum key distribution.* This is currently the only commercial use of quantum cryptography, and although there are several methods for sending the key, they all adhere to the same principle. Key bits are sent and then checked at the remote end for interception, and then more key bits are sent using the same process. Once an entire key has been sent securely, symmetric encryption can then be used.

The other field of research involving quantum mechanics and cryptography is quantum cryptanalysis. A quantum computer is capable of factoring large primes exponentially faster than a normal computer, potentially making the RSA algorithm, and any system based upon factoring prime numbers, insecure. This has led to research in cryptosystems that are not vulnerable to quantum computations, a field known as post-quantum cryptography.

■ Steganography

Steganography, an offshoot of cryptography technology, gets its meaning from the Greek word *steganos,* meaning covered. Invisible ink placed on a document hidden by innocuous text is an example of a steganographic message. Another example is a tattoo placed on the top of a person's head, visible only when the person's hair is shaved off.

Hidden writing in the computer age relies on a program to hide data inside other data. The most common application is the concealing of a text message in a picture file. The Internet contains multiple billions of image files, allowing a hidden message to be located almost anywhere without being discovered. Because not all detection programs can detect every kind of steganography, trying to find the message in an Internet image is akin to attempting to find a needle in a haystack the size of the Pacific Ocean; even a Google search for steganography returns thousands of images.

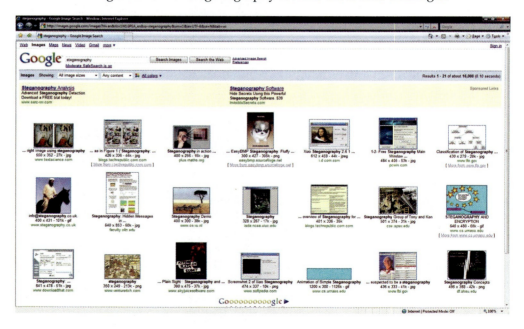

The nature of the image files also makes a hidden message difficult to detect. While it is most common to hide messages inside images, they can also be hidden in video and audio files.

The advantage to steganography over the use of encryption alone is that the messages do not attract attention, and this difficulty in detecting the hidden message provides an additional barrier to analysis. The data that is hidden in a steganographic message is frequently also encrypted, so that if it is discovered, the message will remain secure. Steganography has many uses but the most publicized uses are to hide illegal material, often pornography, or allegedly for covert communication by terrorist networks.

Steganographic encoding can be used in many ways and through many different media. Covering them all is beyond the scope for this book, but we will discuss one of the most common ways to encode into an image file, LSB encoding. LSB, Least Significant Bit, is a method of encoding information into an image while altering the actual visual image as little as possible. A computer image is made up of thousands or millions of pixels, all defined by 1's and 0's. If an image is composed of Red Green Blue (RGB) values, each pixel has an RGB value represented numerically from 0 to 255. For example, 0,0,0 is black, and 255,255,255 is white, which can also be represented as 00000000, 00000000, 00000000 for black and 11111111, 11111111, 11111111 for white. Given a white pixel, editing the least significant bit of the pixel to 11111110, 11111110, 11111110 changes the color. The change in color is undetectable to the human eye, but in an image with a million pixels, this creates a 125KB area in which to store a message.

Some popular steganography detection tools include Stegdetect, StegSecret, StegSpy, and the family of SARC tools. All of these tools use detection techniques based upon the same principle, pattern detection. By looking for known steganographic encoding schemes or artifacts, they can potentially detect embedded data. Additionally, steganography insertion tools can be used to attempt to decode images with suspected hidden messages. Invisible Ink is a small program for steganographic insertion of messages and then the extraction of those messages, as illustrated here.

■ Cryptography Algorithm Use

The use of cryptographic algorithms grows every day. More and more information becomes digitally encoded and placed online, and all of this data needs to be secured. The best way to do that with current technology is to use encryption. This section considers some of the tasks cryptographic algorithms accomplish and those for which they are best suited. Security is typically defined as a product of five components: confidentiality, integrity, availability, authentication, and nonrepudiation. Encryption addresses all of these components except availability. Key escrow will be one of the most important topics as information becomes universally encrypted; otherwise, everyone may be left with useless data. Digital rights management and intellectual property protection are also places where encryption algorithms are heavily used. Digital signatures combine several algorithms to provide reliable identification in a digital form.

Confidentiality

Confidentiality typically comes to mind when the term *security* is brought up. Confidentiality is the ability to keep some piece of data a secret. In the digital world, encryption excels at providing confidentiality. In most cases, symmetric encryption is favored because of its speed and because some asymmetric algorithms can significantly increase the size of the object being encrypted. Asymmetric cryptography also can be used to protect confidentiality, but its size and speed make it more efficient at protecting the confidentiality of small units for tasks such as electronic key exchange. In all cases, the strength of the algorithms and the length of the keys ensure the secrecy of the data in question.

Integrity

Integrity, better known as *message integrity,* is a crucial component of message security. When a message is sent, both the sender and recipient need to know that the message was not altered in transmission. This is especially important for legal contracts—recipients need to know that the contracts have not been altered. Signers also need a way to validate that a contract they sign will not be altered in the future.

Integrity is provided via one-way hash functions and digital signatures. The hash functions compute the message digests, and this guarantees the integrity of the message by allowing easy testing to determine whether any part of the message has been changed. The message now has a computed function (the hash value) to tell the users to resend the message if it was intercepted and interfered with. This hash value is combined with asymmetric cryptography by taking the message's hash value and encrypting it with the user's private key. This lets anyone with the user's public key decrypt the hash and compare it to the locally computed hash, not only ensuring the integrity of the message but positively identifying the sender.

Message integrity will become increasingly important as more commerce is conducted digitally. The ability to independently make sure that a document has not been tampered with is very important to commerce. More importantly, once the document is "signed" with a digital signature, it cannot be refuted that the person in question signed it.

Authentication

Authentication is the matching of a user to an account through previously shared credentials. This information must be protected and a combination of cryptographic methods are commonly employed. From hashing to key stretching to encryption and digital signatures, multiple techniques are used as part of the operations involved in authentication.

Nonrepudiation

An item of some confusion, the concept of nonrepudiation is actually fairly simple. Nonrepudiation means that the message sender cannot later deny that they sent the message. This is important in electronic exchanges of data, because of the lack of face-to-face meetings. Nonrepudiation is based upon public key cryptography and the principle of only you knowing your private key. The presence of a message signed by you, using your private key, which nobody else should know, is an example of nonrepudiation. When a third party can check your signature using your public key, that disproves any claim that you were not the one who actually sent the message. Nonrepudiation is tied to asymmetric cryptography and cannot be implemented with symmetric algorithms.

Try This!

Document Integrity

Download a hash calculator that works on your operating system, such as SlavaSoft HashCalc, available at www.slavasoft.com/hashcalc/index.htm. Then create a simple document file with any text that you prefer. Save it, and then use the hashing program to generate the hash and save the hash value. Now edit the file, even by simply inserting a single blank space, and resave it. Recalculate the hash and compare.

Cipher Suites

In many applications, the use of cryptography occurs as a collection of functions. Different algorithms can be used for authentication, encryption/decryption, digital signatures, and hashing. The term *cipher suite* refers to an arranged group of algorithms. For instance, TLS has a published TLS Cipher Suite Registry at www.iana.org/assignments/tls-parameters/tls-parameters.xhtml.

Tech Tip

HOTP

An HMAC-based One-Time Password (HOTP) algorithm is a key component of the Open Authentication Initiative (OATH). YubiKey is a hardware implementation of HOTP that has significant use.

Strong vs. Weak Ciphers

There is a wide range of ciphers, some old and some new, each with its own strengths and weaknesses. Over time, new methods and computational abilities change the viability of ciphers. The concept of strong versus weak ciphers is an acknowledgment that, over time, ciphers can become vulnerable to attacks. The application or selection of ciphers should take into consideration that not all ciphers are still strong. When selecting a cipher for use, it is important to make an appropriate choice.

Key Exchange

Cryptographic mechanisms use both an algorithm and a key, with the key requiring communication between parties. In symmetric encryption, the secrecy depends upon the secrecy of the key, so insecure transport of the key can lead to failure to protect the information encrypted using the key. *Key exchange* is the central foundational element of a secure symmetric encryption system. Maintaining the secrecy of the symmetric key is the basis of secret communications. In asymmetric systems, the key exchange problem is one of key publication. Because public keys are designed to be shared, the problem is reversed from one of secrecy to one of publicity.

Early key exchanges were performed by trusted couriers. People carried the keys from senders to receivers. One could consider this form of key exchange to be the ultimate in *out-of-band* communication. With the advent of digital methods and some mathematical algorithms, it is possible to pass keys in a secure fashion. This can occur even when all packets are subject to interception. The Diffie-Hellman key exchange is one example of this type of secure key exchange. The Diffie-Hellman key exchange depends upon two random numbers, each chosen by one of the parties, and kept secret. Diffie-Hellman key exchanges can be performed *in-band*, and even under external observation, as the secret random numbers are never exposed to outside parties.

Key Escrow

The impressive growth of the use of encryption technology has led to new methods for handling keys. Encryption is adept at hiding all kinds of information, and with privacy and identity protection becoming more of a concern, more information is encrypted. The loss of a key can happen for a multitude of reasons: it might simply be lost, the key holder might be incapacitated or dead, software or hardware might fail, and so on. In many cases, that information is locked up until the cryptography can be broken, and, as you have read, that could be millennia. This has raised the topic of **key escrow**, or keeping a copy of the encryption key with a trusted third party. Theoretically, this third party would only release your key to you or your official designate on the event of your being unable to get the key yourself. However, just as the old saying from Benjamin Franklin goes, "Three may keep a secret if two of them are dead." Anytime more than one copy of the key exists, the security of the system is broken. The extent of the insecurity of key escrow is a subject open to debate, and will be hotly contested in the years to come.

Additionally, with computer technology being miniaturized into smartphones and other relatively inexpensive devices, criminals and other ill-willed people have begun using cryptography to conceal communications and business dealings from law enforcement agencies. Because law enforcement agencies have not been able to break the encryption in many cases, government agencies have begun asking for mandatory key escrow legislation. In this sense, *key escrow* is a system by which your private key is kept both by you and by the government. This allows people with a court order to retrieve your private key to gain access to anything encrypted with your public key. The data is essentially encrypted by your key and the government key, giving the government access to your plaintext data. This process is similar to a search warrant of your home, but is used against your computer data. Whether or not this is how things should be is also open to debate, but it does raise the interesting possibility of encryption software that is incompatible with government key escrow being banned. The last major discussion for key escrow legislation was several years ago, but the prospect remains out there waiting for a high profile case to bring encryption into the spotlight. In 2015, many US Federal officials again called for forms of key escrow and back doors in the name of anti-terrorism and law enforcement. The result of this new round of argument will take years to decide the correct balance.

Key escrow can negatively impact the security provided by encryption, because the government requires a huge, complex infrastructure of systems

Tech Tip

Key Escrow Has Benefits and Hazards

Key escrow can solve many of the problems that result when a key is lost or becomes inaccessible, allowing access to data that otherwise would be impossible to access without key escrow, but it can open up private information to unauthorized access.

Principles of Computer Security

to hold every escrowed key, and the security of those systems is less effi-cient than the security of your memorizing the key. However, there are two sides to the key escrow coin. Without a practical way to recover a key if or when it is lost or the key holder dies, for example, some important informa-tion will be lost forever. Such issues will affect the design and security of encryption technologies for the foreseeable future.

Session Keys

A *session key* is a symmetric key used for encrypting messages during a com-munication session. It is generated from random seeds and is used for the duration of a communication session. When correctly generated and propa-gated during session setup, a session key provides significant levels of protec-tion during the communication session and also can afford perfect forward secrecy (described later in the chapter). Session keys offer the advantages of symmetric encryption, speed, strength, simplicity, and, with key exchanges possible via digital methods, significant levels of automated security.

Ephemeral Keys

Ephemeral keys are cryptographic keys that are used only once after they are generated. When an ephemeral key is used as part of the Diffie-Hellman scheme, it forms an Ephemeral Diffie-Hellman (EDH) key exchange. An EDH mechanism generates a temporary key for each connection, never using the same key twice. This provides for perfect forward secrecy. If the Diffie-Hellman involves the use of elliptic curves, it is called Elliptic Curve Diffie-Hellman Ephemeral (ECDHE).

Key Stretching

Key stretching is a mechanism that takes what would be weak keys and "stretches" them to make the system more secure against brute-force attacks. A typical methodology used for key stretching involves increasing the computational complexity by adding iterative rounds of computations. To extend a password to a longer length of key, you can run it through multiple rounds of variable-length hashing, each increasing the output by bits over time. This may take hundreds or thousands of rounds, but for single-use computations, the time is not significant. When one wants to use a brute-force attack, the increase in computational workload becomes sig-nificant when done billions of times, making this form of attack much more expensive.

The common forms of key stretching employed in use today include Password-Based Key Derivation Function 2 and Bcrypt.

PBKDF2

Password-Based Key Derivation Function 2 (PBKDF2) is a key derivation function designed to produce a key derived from a password. This func-tion uses a password or passphrase and a salt and applies an HMAC to the input thousands of times. The repetition makes brute-force attacks compu-tationally unfeasible.

Bcrypt

Bcrypt is a key-stretching mechanism that uses the Blowfish cipher and salting, and adds an adaptive function to increase the number of iterations. The result is the same as other key-stretching mechanisms (single use is computationally feasible), but when attempting to brute-force the function, the billions of attempts make it computationally unfeasible.

Secrecy Principles

There are several conditions and principles associated with secrecy. Two of these, confusion and diffusion, arise from Claude Shannon's seminal work in communication theory. The concept of entropy, presented earlier, is from the same source. While these are theoretical-centric ideas, there are implementation principles as well. Perfect forward secrecy is one of these as it applies to future message secrecy.

Confusion

Confusion is a principle to affect the randomness of an output. The concept is operationalized by ensuring that each character of ciphertext depends on several parts of the key. Confusion places a constraint on the relationship between the ciphertext and the key employed, forcing an effect that increases entropy.

Diffusion

Diffusion is a principle that the statistical analysis of plaintext and ciphertext results in a form of dispersion rendering one structurally independent of the other. In plain terms, a change in one character of plaintext should result in multiple changes in the ciphertext in a manner that changes in ciphertext do not reveal information as to the structure of the plaintext.

Perfect Forward Secrecy

Perfect forward secrecy is a property of a public key system in which a key derived from another key is not compromised even if the originating key is compromised in the future. This is especially important in session key generation, where the compromise of future communication sessions may become compromised; if perfect forward secrecy were not in place, then past messages that had been recorded could be decrypted.

Transport Encryption

Transport encryption is used to protect data that is in motion. When data is being transported across a network, it is at risk of interception. An examination of the OSI networking model shows a layer dedicated to transport, and this abstraction can be used to manage end-to-end cryptographic functions for a communication channel. When utilizing the TCP/IP protocol, TLS is the preferred method of managing the security at the transport level.

Digital Signatures

Digital signatures have been touted as the key to truly paperless document flow, and they do have promise for improving the system. Digital signatures are based on both hashing functions and asymmetric cryptography. Both encryption methods play an important role in signing digital documents. Unprotected digital documents are very easy for anyone to change. If a document is edited after an individual signs it, it is important that any modification can be detected. To protect against document editing, hashing functions are used to create a digest of the message that is unique and easily reproducible by both parties. This ensures that the message integrity is complete.

A *digital signature* is a cryptographic implementation designed to demonstrate authenticity and identity associated with a message. Using public key cryptography, a digital signature allows traceability to the person signing the message through the use of their private key. The addition of hash codes allows for the assurance of integrity of the message as well. The operation of a digital signature is a combination of cryptographic elements to achieve a desired outcome. The steps involved in digital signature generation and use are illustrated in Figure 5.11. The message to be signed is hashed, and the hash is encrypted using the sender's private key. Upon receipt, the recipient can decrypt the hash using the sender's public key. If a subsequent hashing of the message reveals an identical value, two things are known: First, the message has not been altered. Second, the sender possessed the private key of the named sender, so is presumably the sender him- or herself.

A digital signature does not by itself protect the contents of the message from interception. The message is still sent in the clear, so if confidentiality of the message is a requirement, additional steps must be taken to secure the message from eavesdropping. This can be done by encrypting the message itself, or by encrypting the channel over which it is transmitted.

> Digital signatures provide a means of verifying authenticity and integrity of a message: you know both who the sender is and that the message has not been altered. By itself, a digital signature does not protect the contents from unauthorized reading.

Digital Signature signing (send)

Digital Signature verification (receive)

If the digests match, message authenticity and integrity are assured.

• **Figure 5.11**   Digital signature operation

Digital Rights Management

Digital rights management (DRM) is the process for protecting intellectual property from unauthorized use. This is a broad area, but the most concentrated focus is on preventing piracy of software or digital content. Before easy access to computers, or the "digital revolution," the content we came in contact with was analog or print based. While it was possible to copy this content, it was difficult and time-consuming to do so, and usually resulted in a loss of quality. It was also much more difficult to send 1000 pages of a handwritten copy of a book to Europe, for example. Computers and the Internet have made such tasks trivial, and now it is very easy to copy a document, music, or video and quickly send it thousands of miles away.

Cryptography has entered the fray as a solution to protect digital rights, though it is currently better known for its failures than its successes. The DVD

Content Scramble System (CSS) was an attempt to make DVDs impossible to copy by computer. CSS used an encryption algorithm that was licensed to every DVD player; however, creative programmers were able to retrieve the key to this algorithm by disassembling a software-based DVD player. CSS has been replaced by the Advanced Access Content System (AACS), which is used on the next-generation Blu-ray discs. This system encrypts video content via the symmetric AES algorithm with one or more keys. Several decryption keys have been cracked and released to the Internet, allowing pirates to freely copy the protected content. The music and computer game industries have also attempted several different DRM applications, but nearly all of these have eventually been cracked, allowing piracy.

A common example of DRM that is mostly successful is the broadcast stream of digital satellite TV. Since the signal is beamed from space to every home in North America, the satellite TV provider must be able to protect the signal so that it can charge people to receive it. Smart cards are employed to securely hold the decryption keys that allow access to some or all of the content in the stream. This system has been cracked several times, allowing a subset of users free access to the content; however, the satellite TV providers learned from their early mistakes and upgraded new smart cards to correct the old problems.

DRM will also become very important in the industry of Software as a Service (SaaS). Similar to companies that provide satellite TV service, companies that provide SaaS rely on a subscription basis for profitability. If someone could pay for a single license and then distribute that to hundreds of employees, the provider would soon go out of business. Many systems in the past have been cracked because the key was housed inside the software. This has prompted some systems to use specific hardware to store and protect the key. These devices are commonly known as Hardware Security Modules, or HSMs. They are usually designed to protect the key in hardware so that even if the device is tampered with, it will not reveal key material. Smart cards are one example of this technology. Another example is hardware token USB keys that must be inserted into the machine for the software to decrypt and run. Placing the keys in hardware makes an attack to retrieve them much harder, a concept that is employed in the Trusted Platform Module; in fact, one of the primary complaints against the TPM is its inability to enforce DRM restrictions.

Cryptographic Applications

A few applications can be used to encrypt data conveniently on your personal computer. (This is by no means a complete list of every application.) *Pretty Good Privacy (PGP)* is mentioned in this book because it is a useful protocol suite. Created by Philip Zimmermann in 1991, it passed through several versions that were available for free under a noncommercial license. PGP is now an enterprise encryption product, acquired by the Symantec Corporation in 2010. PGP can be applied to popular e-mail programs to handle the majority of day-to-day encryption tasks using a combination of symmetric and asymmetric encryption protocols. One of the unique features of PGP is its ability to use both symmetric and asymmetric encryption methods, accessing the strengths of each method and avoiding the weaknesses of each as well. Symmetric keys are used for bulk encryption, taking advantage of the speed and efficiency of symmetric encryption. The symmetric keys are passed using asymmetric methods, capitalizing on the flexibility of this method. PGP-based technology is now sold as part of a commercial application, with home and corporate versions.

Cross Check

PGP

In Chapter 7 you will learn some additional details about PGP. Why is the ability to use asymmetric and symmetric encryption in the same program important?

GnuPG, or *Gnu Privacy Guard,* is an open source implementation of the OpenPGP standard. This command line–based tool is a public key encryption program designed to protect electronic communications such as e-mail. It operates similarly to PGP and includes a method for managing public/private keys.

File system encryption is becoming a standard means of protecting data while in storage. Even hard drives are available with built-in AES encryption. Microsoft expanded its Encrypting File System (EFS), available since the Windows 2000 operating system, with BitLocker, a boot-sector encryption method that protects data that was introduced with the Windows Vista operating system. BitLocker is also used in Windows Server 2008 and the Windows 7 and beyond operating systems. BitLocker utilizes AES encryption to encrypt every file on the hard drive automatically. All encryption occurs in the background, and decryption occurs seamlessly when data is requested. The decryption key can be stored in the TPM or on a USB key.

Database Encryption

Due partly to increased regulatory concerns and partly to more targeted attacks, databases have begun to offer native support for encryption. Protecting data at rest in the enterprise frequently involves data stored in databases. Building data protection mechanisms into the database systems is not new (it has been around for a long time), but enterprise adoption of this functionality has been slow. Symmetric encryption algorithms such as 3DES and AES are used to encrypt data internally in the database. Protection mechanisms that can be managed by row and by column are included in most major database applications; the challenge is in convincing organizations to use this proven protection methodology. It does add complexity to the system, but in today's environment of data breaches and corporate espionage, the complexity is easier to manage than the effects of a data loss.

Use of Proven Technologies

When setting up a cryptographic scheme, it is important to use proven technologies. Proven cryptographic libraries and proven cryptographically correct random number generators are the foundational elements associated with a solid program. Homegrown or custom elements in these areas can greatly increase risk associated with a broken system. Developing your own cryptographic algorithms is beyond the abilities of most groups. Algorithms are complex and difficult to create. Any algorithm that has not had public review can have weaknesses in the algorithm. Most good algorithms are approved for use only after a lengthy test and public review phase.

Chapter 5 Review

For More Information

- *Applied Cryptography, Second Edition*, Bruce Schneier (John Wiley & Sons)
- Cryptool: https://www.cryptool.org/en/
- Bruce Schneier Blog: https://www.schneier.com/cryptography.html

Lab Book Exercises

The following lab exercises from the companion lab manual, *Principles of Computer Security Lab Manual, Fourth Edition*, provide practical application of material covered in this chapter:

Lab 4.5l	Password Cracking
Lab 8.1m	Using GPG in Windows

Chapter Summary

After reading this chapter and completing the exercises, you should understand the following about cryptography.

Understand the fundamentals of cryptography

- Understand the fundamental methods.
- Understand how to compare strengths and performance of algorithms.
- Have an appreciation of the historical aspects of cryptography.

Identify and describe the three types of cryptography

- Symmetric cryptography is based upon the concept of a shared secret or key.
- Asymmetric cryptography is based upon a key that can be made openly available to the public, yet still provide security.
- One-way, or hashing, cryptography takes data and enciphers it. However, there is no way to decipher it and no key.
- Proper random number generation is essential for cryptographic use, as the strength of the implementation frequently depends upon it being truly random and unknown.

List and describe current cryptographic algorithms

- Hashing is the use of a one-way function to generate a message summary for data integrity.
- Hashing algorithms include SHA (Secure Hash Algorithm) and MD (Message Digest).

- Symmetric encryption is a shared secret form of encrypting data for confidentiality; it is fast and reliable, but needs secure key management.
- Symmetric algorithms include DES (Data Encryption Standard), 3DES, AES (Advanced Encryption Standard), CAST, Blowfish, IDEA, and RC (Rivest Cipher) variants.
- Asymmetric encryption is a public/private key-pair encryption used for authentication, nonrepudiation, and confidentiality.
- Asymmetric algorithms include RSA, Diffie-Hellman, ElGamal, and ECC.

Explain how cryptography is applied for security

- Confidentiality is gained because encryption is very good at scrambling information to make it look like random noise, when in fact a key can decipher the message and return it to its original state.
- Integrity is gained because hashing algorithms are specifically designed to check integrity. They can reduce a message to a mathematical value that can be independently calculated, guaranteeing that any message alteration would change the mathematical value.
- Nonrepudiation is the property of not being able to claim that you did not send the data. This property is gained because of the properties of private keys.

- Authentication, or being able to prove you are you, is achieved through the private keys involved in digital signatures.

- The use of key generation methods including ephemeral keys and key stretching are important tools in the implementation of strong cryptosystems.

- Digital signatures, combining multiple types of encryption, provide an authentication method verified by a third party, allowing you to use them as if you were actually signing the document with your regular signature.

- Digital rights management (DRM) uses some form of asymmetric encryption that allows an application to determine if you are an authorized user of the digital content you are trying to access. For example, things like DVDs and certain digital music formats such as AACS use DRM.

- The principle of perfect forward secrecy protects future messages from previous message key disclosures.

- Proven cryptographic technologies are important as most cryptographic systems fail and only a few stand the test of time. Homebrew systems are ripe for failure.

- Cipher suites provide information to assist developers in choosing the correct methods to achieve desired levels of protection.

■ Key Terms

algorithm *(96)*

block cipher *(104)*

ciphertext *(94)*

collision attack *(99)*

confusion *(120)*

cryptanalysis *(90)*

cryptography *(90)*

differential cryptanalysis *(91)*

diffusion *(120)*

digital rights management *(121)*

digital signature *(120)*

entropy *(98)*

ephemeral keys *(119)*

eXclusive OR (XOR) *(97)*

hash *(99)*

key *(97)*

key escrow *(118)*

key management *(98)*

keyspace *(93)*

key stretching *(119)*

linear cryptanalysis *(91)*

multiple encryption *(104)*

perfect forward secrecy *(120)*

plaintext *(94)*

shared secret *(103)*

shift cipher *(94)*

steganography *(114)*

stream cipher *(107)*

substitution *(92)*

transposition *(92)*

transposition cipher *(93)*

trapdoor function *(109)*

Vigenère cipher *(95)*

■ Key Terms Quiz

Use terms from the Key Terms list to complete the sentences that follow. Don't use the same term more than once. Not all terms will be used.

1. Making two inputs result in the exact same cryptographic hash is called a(n) _____.

2. A simple way to hide information, the _____ moves a letter a set number of places down the alphabet.

3. To provide for perfect forward security, one should use _____.

4. _____ is required for symmetric encryption.

5. _____ is the evaluation of a cryptosystem to test its security.

6. _____ refers to every possible value for a cryptographic key.

7. _____ is the function most commonly seen in cryptography, a "bitwise exclusive" or.

8. The measure of randomness in a data stream is called _____.

9. Processing through an algorithm more than once with different keys is called _____.

10. The basis for symmetric cryptography is the principle of a(n) _____.

■ Multiple-Choice Quiz

1. When a message is sent, no matter what its format, why do we care about its integrity?

    A. To ensure proper formatting

    B. To show that the encryption keys are undamaged

    C. To show that the message has not been edited in transit

    D. To show that no one has viewed the message

2. How is 3DES different from many other types of encryption described in this chapter?

    A. It only encrypts the hash.

    B. It hashes the message before encryption.

    C. It uses three keys and multiple encryption and/or decryption sets.

    D. It can display the key publicly.

3. If a message has a hash, how does the hash protect the message in transit?

    A. If the message is edited, the hash will no longer match.

    B. Hashing destroys the message so that it cannot be read by anyone.

    C. Hashing encrypts the message so that only the private key holder can read it.

    D. The hash makes the message uneditable.

4. What is the biggest drawback to symmetric encryption?

    A. It is too easily broken.

    B. It is too slow to be easily used on mobile devices.

    C. It requires a key to be securely shared.

    D. It is available only on UNIX.

5. What is Diffie-Hellman most commonly used for?

    A. Symmetric encryption key exchange

    B. Signing digital contracts

    C. Secure e-mail

    D. Storing encrypted passwords

6. What is public key cryptography a more common name for?

    A. Asymmetric encryption

    B. SHA

    C. Symmetric encryption

    D. Hashing

7. What algorithm can be used to provide for key stretching?

    A. PBKDF2

    B. SHA356

    C. RIPEMD

    D. 3DES

8. A good hash function is resistant to what?

    A. Brute-forcing

    B. Rainbow tables

    C. Interception

    D. Collisions

9. How is 3DES an improvement over normal DES?

    A. It uses public and private keys.

    B. It hashes the message before encryption.

    C. It uses three keys and multiple encryption and/or decryption sets.

    D. It is faster than DES.

10. What is the best kind of key to have?

    A. Easy to remember

    B. Long and random

    C. Long and predictable

    D. Short

■ Essay Quiz

1. Describe how polyalphabetic substitution works.

2. Explain why asymmetric encryption is called public key encryption.

3. Describe cryptanalysis.

Lab Projects

• Lab Project 5.1

Using a utility program, demonstrate how single character changes can make substantial changes to hash values.

• Lab Project 5.2

Create a keyset and use it to transfer a file securely.

chapter 6

Public Key Infrastructure

Without trust, there is nothing.

—Anonymous

In this chapter, you will learn how to

- Implement the basics of public key infrastructures
- Describe the role of registration authorities
- Use digital certificates
- Understand the lifecycle of certificates
- Explain the relationship between trust and certificate verification
- Describe the roles of certificate authorities and certificate repositories
- Identify centralized and decentralized infrastructures
- Describe public and in-house certificate authorities

Public key infrastructures (PKIs) are becoming a central security foundation for managing identity credentials in many companies. The technology manages the issue of binding public keys and identities across multiple applications. The other approach, without PKIs, is to implement many different security solutions and hope for interoperability and equal levels of protection.

PKIs comprise several components, including certificates, registration and certificate authorities, and a standard process for verification. PKIs are about managing the sharing of trust and using a third party to vouch for the trustworthiness of a claim of ownership over a credential document, called a **certificate**.

The Basics of Public Key Infrastructures

A **public key infrastructure (PKI)** provides all the components necessary for different types of users and entities to be able to communicate securely and in a predictable manner. A PKI is made up of hardware, applications, policies, services, programming interfaces, cryptographic algorithms, protocols, users, and utilities. These components work together to allow communication to take place using public key cryptography and symmetric keys for digital signatures, data encryption, and integrity.

Although many different applications and protocols can provide the same type of functionality, constructing and implementing a PKI boils down to establishing a level of trust. If, for example, John and Diane want to communicate securely, John can generate his own public/private key pair and send his public key to Diane, or he can place his public key in a directory that is available to everyone. If

> ### Cross Check
>
> #### PKIs and Encryption
>
> The technologies used in PKI include many cryptographic algorithms and mechanisms. Encryption technologies and public key principles were covered in Chapter 5. A basic understanding of public and private keys and their relationship to public key encryption is a prerequisite for this chapter. If needed, review that material before you attempt the details of PKI in this chapter.

Diane receives John's public key, either from him or from a public directory, how does she know the key really came from John? Maybe another individual, Katie, is masquerading as John and has replaced John's public key with her own, as shown in Figure 6.1 (referred to as a man-in-the-middle attack). If this took place, Diane would believe that her messages could be read only by John and that the replies were actually from him. However, she would actually be communicating with Katie. What is needed is a way to verify an individual's identity, to ensure that a person's public key is bound to their identity and thus ensure that the previous scenario (and others) cannot take place.

In PKI environments, entities called registration authorities (RAs) and certificate authorities (CAs) provide services similar to those of the Department of Motor Vehicles (DMV). When John goes to register for a driver's license, he has to prove his identity to the DMV by providing his passport, birth certificate, or other identification documentation. If the DMV is satisfied with the proof John provides (and John passes a driving test), the DMV will create a driver's license that can then be used by John to prove his identity. Whenever John needs to identify himself, he can show his driver's license. Although many people may not trust John to identify himself truthfully, they do trust the third party, the DMV.

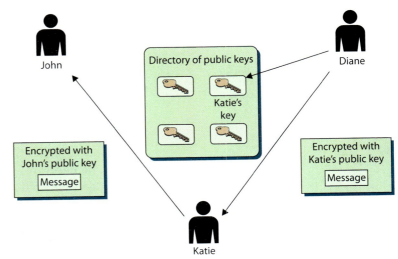

Man-in-the-Middle Attack

1. Katie replaces John's public key with her key in the publicly accessible directory.
2. Diane extracts what she thinks is John's key, but it is in fact Katie's key.
3. Katie can now read messages Diane encrypts and sends to John.
4. After Katie decrypts and reads Diane's message, she encrypts it with John's public key and sends it on to him so he will not be the wiser.

• **Figure 6.1** Without PKIs, individuals could spoof others' identities.

Exam Tip: PKIs are composed of several elements:

- Certificates (containing keys)
- Certificate authorities (CAs)
- Registration authorities (RAs)
- Certificate revocation lists (CRLs)
- Trust models

In the PKI context, while some variations exist in specific products, the RA will require proof of identity from the individual requesting a certificate and will validate this information. The RA will then advise the CA to generate a certificate, which is analogous to a driver's license. The CA will digitally sign the certificate using its private key. The use of the private key ensures to the recipient that the certificate came from the CA. When Diane receives John's certificate and verifies that it was actually digitally signed by a CA that she trusts, she will believe that the certificate is actually John's—not because she trusts John, but because she trusts the entity that is vouching for his identity (the CA).

This is commonly referred to as a *third-party trust model.* Public keys are components of digital certificates, so when Diane verifies the CA's digital signature, this verifies that the certificate is truly John's and that the public key the certificate contains is also John's. This is how John's identity is bound to his public key.

This process allows John to authenticate himself to Diane and others. Using the third-party certificate, John can communicate with Diane, using public key encryption, without prior communication or a preexisting relationship.

Once Diane is convinced of the legitimacy of John's public key, she can use it to encrypt messages between herself and John, as illustrated in Figure 6.2.

Numerous applications and protocols can generate public/private key pairs and provide functionality similar to what a PKI provides, but no trusted third party is available for both of the communicating parties. For each party to choose to communicate this way without a third party vouching for the other's identity, the two must choose to trust each other and the communication channel they are using. In many situations, it is impractical and dangerous to arbitrarily trust an individual you do not know, and this is when the components of a PKI must fall into place—to provide the necessary level of trust you cannot, or choose not to, provide on your own.

What does the "infrastructure" in "public key infrastructure" really mean? An infrastructure provides a sustaining groundwork upon which other things can be built. So an infrastructure works at a low level to provide a predictable and uniform environment that allows other, higher-level technologies to work together through uniform access points. The environment that the infrastructure provides allows these higher-level applications to communicate with each other and gives them the underlying tools to carry out their tasks.

Diane

John's certificate

John's public key

Encrypted message

1. Diane validates the certificate.
2. Diane extracts John's public key.
3. Diane uses John's public key for encryption purposes.

• **Figure 6.2** Public keys are components of digital certificates.

◼ Certificate Authorities

A **certificate authority (CA)** is a trusted authority that certifies individuals' identities and creates electronic documents indicating that individuals are who they say they are. The electronic document is referred to as a **digital certificate**, and it establishes an association between the subject's identity and a public key. The private key that is paired with the public key in the certificate is stored separately.

A CA is more than just a piece of software, however; it is actually made up of the software, hardware, procedures, policies, and people who are involved in validating individuals' identities and generating the certificates. This means that if one of these components is compromised, it can negatively affect the CA overall and can threaten the integrity of the certificates it produces.

 As noted in Chapter 5, it is important to safeguard the private key. Typically, it should never leave the machine or device where it was created.

 Cross Check

Certificates Stored on a Client PC

Certificates are stored on user PCs. Chapter 17 covers the use of the Internet and associated materials, including the use of certificates by web browsers. Take a moment to explore the certificates stored on your PC by your browser. To understand the details behind how certificates are stored and managed, the reader is directed to the details in Chapter 17.

Every CA should have a **certification practices statement (CPS)** that outlines how identities are verified; the steps the CA follows to generate, maintain, and transmit certificates; and why the CA can be trusted to fulfill its responsibilities.

The CPS describes how keys are secured, what data is placed within a digital certificate, and how revocations will be handled. If a company is going to use and depend on a public CA, the company's security officers, administrators, and legal department should review the CA's entire CPS to ensure that it will properly meet the company's needs, and to make sure that the level of security claimed by the CA is high enough for their use and environment. A critical aspect of a PKI is the trust between the users and the CA, so the CPS should be reviewed and understood to ensure that this level of trust is warranted.

The **certificate server** is the actual service that issues certificates based on the data provided during the initial registration process. The server constructs and populates the digital certificate with the necessary information and combines the user's public key with the resulting certificate. The certificate is then digitally signed with the CA's private key.

Registration Authorities

A **registration authority (RA)** is the PKI component that accepts a request for a digital certificate and performs the necessary steps of registering and authenticating the person requesting the certificate. The authentication requirements differ depending on the type of certificate being requested. Most CAs offer a series of classes of certificates with increasing trust by class. The specific classes are described in the upcoming Tech Tip sidebar, "Certificate Classes."

Each higher class of certificate can carry out more powerful and critical tasks than the one below it. This is why the different classes have different requirements for proof of identity. If you want to receive a Class 1 certificate, you may only be asked to provide your name, e-mail address, and

 Tech Tip

Trusting CAs

The question of whether a CA can be trusted is part of the continuing debate on how much security PKIs actually provide. Overall, people put a lot of faith in CAs. The companies that provide CA services understand this and also understand that their business is based on their reputation. If a CA was compromised or did not follow through on its various responsibilities, word would get out and it would quickly lose customers and business. CAs work diligently to ensure that the reputation of their products and services remains good by implementing very secure facilities, methods, procedures, and personnel. But it is up to the company or individual to determine what degree of trust can actually be given and what level of risk is acceptable.

131

physical address. For a Class 2 certification, you may need to provide the RA with more data, such as your driver's license, passport, and company information, that can be verified. To obtain a Class 3 certificate, you will be asked to provide even more information and most likely will need to go to the RA's office for a face-to-face meeting. Each CA will outline the certification classes it provides and the identification requirements that must be met to acquire each type of certificate.

In most situations, when a user requests a Class 1 certificate, the registration process will require the user to enter specific information into a web-based form. The web page will have a section that accepts the user's public key, or it will step the user through creating a public/private key pair, which will allow the user to choose the size of the keys to be created. Once these steps have been completed, the public key is attached to the certificate registration form and both are forwarded to the RA for processing. The RA is responsible only for the registration process and cannot actually generate a certificate. Once the RA is finished processing the request and verifying the individual's identity, the RA sends the request to the CA. The CA uses the RA-provided information to generate a digital certificate, integrates the necessary data into the certificate fields (user identification information, public key, validity dates, proper use for the key and certificate, and so on), and sends a copy of the certificate to the user. These steps are shown in Figure 6.3. The certificate may also be posted to a publicly accessible directory so that others can access it.

Note that a 1:1 correspondence does not necessarily exist between identities and certificates. An entity can have multiple key pairs, using separate public keys for separate purposes. Thus, an entity can have multiple certificates, each attesting to separate public key ownership. It is also possible to have different classes of certificates, again with different keys. This flexibility allows entities total discretion in how they manage their keys, and the PKI manages the complexity by using a unified process that allows key verification through a common interface.

If an application creates a key store that can be accessed by other applications, it will provide a standardized interface, called the *application programming interface (API)*. As an example, Figure 6.4 shows that application A went through the process of registering a certificate and generating a key pair. It created a key store that provides an interface to allow other applications to communicate with it and use the items held within the store.

The local key store is just one location where these items can be held. Often the digital certificate and public key are also stored in a certificate repository (as discussed in the "Certificate Repositories" section of this chapter) so that it is available to a subset of individuals.

Local Registration Authorities

A **local registration authority (LRA)** performs the same functions as an RA, but the LRA is closer to the end users. This component is usually implemented in companies that have their own internal PKIs and have distributed sites. Each site has users that need RA services, so instead of requiring them to communicate with one central RA, each site can have its own LRA.

1. The user registers for a digital certificate.
2. Some method is used to determine random values.
3. An algorithm generates a public/private key pair.
4. The key pair is stored in a key store on the workstation.
5. A copy of the public key and other identifying information is sent to the CA.
6. The CA generates a digital certificate containing the public key and other identifying information.
7. The new certificate is sent to the user.

• **Figure 6.3**   Steps for obtaining a digital certificate

This reduces the amount of traffic that would be created by several users making requests across wide area network (WAN) lines. The LRA performs identification, verification, and registration functions. It then sends the request, along with the user's public key, to a centralized CA so that the certificate can be generated. It acts as an interface between the users and the CA. LRAs simplify the RA/CA process for entities that desire certificates only for in-house use.

> **Tech Tip**
>
> **Sharing Key Stores**
> *Different applications from the same vendor may share key stores. Microsoft applications keep user keys and certificates in a Registry entry within that user's profile. The applications can then save and retrieve them from this single location or key store. Other applications could also use the same keys if they knew where they were stored by using Registry API calls.*

• **Figure 6.4**   Some key stores can be shared by different applications.

■ Digital Certificates

A digital certificate binds an individual's identity to a public key, and it contains all the information a receiver needs to be assured of the identity of the public key owner. After an RA verifies an individual's identity, the CA generates the digital certificate, but how does the CA know what type of data to insert into the certificate?

The certificates are created and formatted based on the X.509 standard, which outlines the necessary fields of a certificate and the possible values that can be inserted into the fields. As of this writing, X.509 version 3 is the most current version of the standard. X.509 is a standard of the International Telecommunication Union (www.itu.int). The IETF's Public Key Infrastructure (X.509), or PKIX, working group has adapted the X.509 standard to the more flexible organization of the Internet, as specified in RFC 5280, and is commonly referred to as PKIX for Public Key Infrastructure X.509.

Table 6.1 lists and describes the fields in an X.509 certificate.

Table 6.1	X.509 Certificate Fields
Field Name	**Field Description**
Certificate Version	X.509 version used for this certificate: Version 1 = 0 Version 2 = 1 Version 3 = 2
Serial Number	A nonnegative integer assigned by the certificate issuer that must be unique to the certificate.

Signature
  Algorithm
  Parameters (optional)
	The algorithm identifier for the algorithm used by the CA to sign the certificate. The optional Parameters field is used to provide the cryptographic algorithm parameters used in generating the signature.

Issuer	Identification for the entity that signed and issued the certificate. This must be a distinguished name within the hierarchy of CAs.

Validity
  Not valid before time
  Not valid after time
	Specifies a period of time during which the certificate is valid, using a "not valid before" time and a "not valid after" time (expressed in UTC or in a generalized time).

Subject	The name for the certificate owner.
Subject Public Key Info	An encryption algorithm identifier followed by a bit string for the public key.
Issuer Unique ID	Optional for versions 2 and 3—a unique bit-string identifier for the CA that issued the certificate.
Subject Unique ID	Optional for versions 2 and 3—a unique bit-string identifier for the subject of the certificate.

Extensions
  Extension ID
  Critical Extension
  Value
	Optional for version 3—the extensions area consists of a sequence of extension fields containing an extension identifier, a Boolean field indicating whether the extension is critical, and an octet string representing the value of the extension. Extensions can be defined in standards or defined and registered by organizations or communities.

Thumbprint Algorithm
  Algorithm
  Parameters (optional)
	Identifies the algorithm used by the CA to sign this certificate. This field must match the algorithm identified in the Signature Algorithm field.

Thumbprint	The signature is the bit-string hash value obtained when the CA signed the certificate. The signature certifies the contents of the certificate, binding the public key to the subject.

● **Figure 6.5** Fields within a digital certificate

Figure 6.5 shows the actual values of the different certificate fields for a particular certificate in Internet Explorer. The version of this certificate is V3 (X.509 v3) and the serial number is also listed—this number is unique for each certificate that is created by a specific CA. The CA used the MD5 hashing algorithm to create the message digest value and then signed it using the CA's private key using the RSA algorithm. The actual CA that issued the certificate is Root SGC Authority, and the valid dates indicate how long this certificate is valid. The subject is MS SGC Authority, which is the entity that registered this certificate and that is bound to the embedded public key. The actual public key is shown in the lower window and is represented in hexadecimal.

The subject of a certificate is commonly a person, but it does not have to be. The subject can also be a network device (router, web server, firewall, and so on), an application, a department, or a company. Each has its own identity that needs to be verified and proven to another entity before secure, trusted communication can be initiated. If a network device is using a certificate for authentication, the certificate may contain the identity of that device. This allows a user of the device to verify its authenticity based on the signed certificate and trust in the signing authority. This trust can be transferred to the identity of the device indicating authenticity.

Certificate Extensions

Certificate extensions allow for further information to be inserted within the certificate, which can be used to provide more functionality in a PKI implementation. Certificate extensions can be standard or private. *Standard certificate extensions* are implemented for every PKI implementation. *Private certificate extensions* are defined for specific organizations (or domains within one organization), and they allow companies to further define different, specific uses for digital certificates to best fit their business needs.

Several different extensions can be implemented, one being *key usage extensions*, which dictate how the public key that is held within the certificate can be used. Remember that public keys can be used for different functions: symmetric key encryption, data encryption, verifying digital signatures, and more.

Tech Tip

X.509 Digital Certificate Extensions

Following are some key examples of certificate extensions:

- **DigitalSignature** The key used to verify a digital signature

- **KeyEncipherment** The key used to encrypt other keys used for secure key distribution

- **DataEncipherment** The key used to encrypt data, which cannot be used to encrypt other keys

- **CRLSign** The key used to verify a CA signature on a CRL

- **KeyCertSign** The key used to verify CA signatures on certificates

- **NonRepudiation** The key used when a nonrepudiation service is being provided

A nonrepudiation service can be provided by a third-party notary. In this situation, the sender's digital signature is verified and then signed by the notary so that the sender cannot later deny signing and sending the message. This is basically the same function performed by a traditional notary using paper—validate the sender's identity and validate the time and date of an item being signed and sent. This is required when the receiver needs to be *really* sure of the sender's identity and wants to be legally protected against possible fraud or forgery.

If a company needs to be sure that accountable nonrepudiation services will be provided, a trusted time source needs to be used, which can be a trusted third party called a *time stamp authority (TSA)*. Using a trusted time source gives users a higher level of confidence as to *when* specific messages were digitally signed. For example, suppose Barry sends Ron a message and digitally signs it, and Ron later civilly sues Barry over a dispute. This digitally signed message may be submitted by Ron as evidence pertaining to an earlier agreement that Barry now is not fulfilling. If a trusted time source was not used in their PKI environment, Barry could claim that his private key had been compromised before that message was sent. If a trusted time source was implemented, then it could be shown that the message was signed *before* the date on which Barry claims his key was compromised. If a trusted time source is not used, no activity that was carried out within a PKI environment can be truly proven because it is so easy to change system and software time settings.

Critical and Noncritical Extensions

Certificate extensions are considered either *critical* or *noncritical*, which is indicated by a specific flag within the certificate itself. When this flag is set to critical, it means that the extension *must* be understood and processed by the receiver. If the receiver is not configured to understand a particular extension marked as critical, and thus cannot process it properly, the certificate cannot be used for its proposed purpose. If the flag does not indicate that the extension is critical, the certificate can be used for the intended purpose, even if the receiver does not process the appended extension.

Certificate Attributes

Four main types of certificates are used:

- End-entity certificates
- CA certificates
- Cross-certification certificates
- Policy certificates

End-entity certificates are issued by a CA to a specific subject, such as Joyce, the Accounting department, or a firewall, as illustrated in Figure 6.6. An end-entity certificate is the identity document provided by PKI implementations.

A **CA certificate** can be self-signed, in the case of a standalone or root CA, or it can be issued by a superior CA within a hierarchical model. In the model in Figure 6.6, the superior CA gives the authority and allows the subordinate CA to accept certificate requests and generate

Tech Tip

Critical Flag and Certificate Usage

When an extension is marked as critical, it means that the CA is certifying the key for only that specific purpose. If Joe receives a certificate with a DigitalSignature key usage extension and the critical flag is set, Joe can use the public key only within that certificate to validate digital signatures, and no more. If the extension was marked as noncritical, the key can be used for purposes outside of those listed in the extensions, so in this case it is up to Joe (and his applications) to decide how the key will be used.

the individual certificates itself. This may be necessary when a company needs to have multiple internal CAs, and different departments within an organization need to have their own CAs servicing their specific end-entities in their sections. In these situations, a representative from each department requiring a CA registers with the higher trusted CA and requests a Certificate Authority certificate. (Public and private CAs are discussed in the "Public Certificate Authorities" and "In-House Certificate Authorities" sections later in this chapter, as are the different trust models that are available for companies.)

A **cross-certification certificate**, or *cross-certificate*, is used when independent CAs establish peer-to-peer trust relationships. Simply put, cross-certificates are a mechanism through which one CA can issue a certificate allowing its users to trust another CA.

• **Figure 6.6**   End-entity and CA certificates

Within sophisticated CAs used for high-security applications, a mechanism is required to provide centrally controlled policy information to PKI clients. This is often done by placing the policy information in a **policy certificate**.

Certificate Lifecycles

Keys and certificates should have lifetime settings that force the user to register for a new certificate after a certain amount of time. Determining the proper length of these lifetimes is a trade-off: shorter lifetimes limit the ability of attackers to crack them, but longer lifetimes lower system overhead. More-sophisticated PKI implementations perform automated and often transparent key updates to avoid the time and expense of having users register for new certificates when old ones expire.

This means that the certificate and key pair has a lifecycle that must be managed. Certificate management involves administrating and managing each of these phases, including registration, certificate and key generation, renewal, and revocation. Additional management functions include CRL distribution, certificate suspension, and key destruction.

Setting certificate lifetimes way into the future and using them for long periods of time provides attackers with extended windows to attack the cryptography. As stated in Chapter 5, cryptography merely buys time against an attacker; it is never an absolute guarantee.

Registration and Generation

A key pair (public and private keys) can be generated locally by an application and stored in a local key store on the user's workstation. The key pair can also be created by a central key-generation server, which will require secure transmission of the keys to the user. The key pair that is created on the centralized server can be stored on the user's workstation or on the user's smart card, which will allow for more flexibility and mobility.

The act of verifying that an individual indeed has the corresponding private key for a given public key is referred to as *proof of possession*. Not all public/private key pairs can be used for digital signatures, so asking the individual to sign a message and return it to prove that she has the necessary private key will not always work. If a key pair is used for encryption, the RA can send a challenge value to the individual, who, in turn, can use her private key to encrypt that value and return it to the RA. If the RA can successfully decrypt this value with the public key that was provided earlier, the RA can be confident that the individual has the necessary private key and can continue through the rest of the registration phase.

Key regeneration and replacement is usually done to protect against these types of threats, although as the processing power of computers increases and our knowledge of cryptography and new possible cryptanalysis-based attacks expands, key lifetimes may drastically decrease. As with everything within the security field, it is better to be safe now than to be surprised later and sorry.

The PKI administrator usually configures the minimum required key size that users must use to have a key generated for the first time, and then for each renewal. In most applications, there is a drop-down list of possible algorithms to choose from, and possible key sizes. The key size should provide the necessary level of security for the current environment. The lifetime of the key should be long enough that continual renewal will not negatively affect productivity, but short enough to ensure that the key cannot be successfully compromised.

CSR

A **certificate signing request (CSR)** is the actual request to a CA containing a public key and the requisite information needed to generate a certificate. The CSR contains all of the identifying information that is to be bound to the key by the certificate generation process.

Renewal

The certificate itself has its own lifetime, which can be different from the key pair's lifetime. The certificate's lifetime is specified by the validity dates inserted into the digital certificate. These are beginning and ending dates indicating the time period during which the certificate is valid. The certificate cannot be used before the start date, and once the end date is met, the certificate is expired and a new certificate will need to be issued.

A renewal process is different from the registration phase in that the RA assumes that the individual has already successfully completed one registration round. If the certificate has not actually been revoked, the original keys and certificate can be used to provide the necessary authentication information and proof of identity for the renewal phase.

The certificate may or may not need to change during the renewal process; this usually depends on why the renewal is taking place. If the certificate just expired and the keys will still be used for the same purpose, a new certificate can be generated with new validity dates. If, however, the key pair functionality needs to be expanded or restricted, new attributes and extensions may need to be integrated into the new certificate. These new

Exam Tip: Good key management and proper key replacement intervals protect keys from being compromised through human error. Choosing a large key size makes a brute-force attack more difficult.

Tech Tip

Centralized vs. Local Key Generation

In most modern PKI implementations, users have two key pairs. One key pair is often generated by a central server and used for encryption and key transfers. This allows the corporate PKI to retain a copy of the encryption key pair for recovery, if necessary. The second key pair, a digital signature key pair, is usually generated by the user to make sure that she is the only one with a copy of the private key. Nonrepudiation can be challenged if there is any doubt about someone else obtaining a copy of an individual's signature private key. If the key pair was created on a centralized server, that could weaken the case that the individual was the only one who had a copy of her private key. If a copy of a user's signature private key is stored anywhere other than in her possession, or if there is a possibility of someone obtaining the user's key, then true nonrepudiation cannot be provided.

functionalities may require more information to be gathered from the individual renewing the certificate, especially if the class changes or the new key uses allow for more powerful abilities.

This renewal process is required when the certificate has fulfilled its lifetime and its end validity date has been met.

Suspension

When the owner of a certificate wishes to mark a certificate as no longer valid prior to its natural expiration, two choices exist: revocation and suspension. Revocation, discussed in the next section, is an action with a permanent outcome. Instead of being revoked, a certificate can be *suspended*, meaning it is temporarily put on hold. If, for example, Bob is taking an extended vacation and wants to ensure that his certificate will not be compromised or used during that time, he can make a suspension request to the CA. The CRL would list this certificate and its serial number, and in the field that describes why the certificate is revoked, it would instead indicate a hold state. Once Bob returns to work, he can make a request to the CA to remove his certificate from the list.

Another reason to suspend a certificate is if an administrator is suspicious that a private key might have been compromised. While the issue is under investigation, the certificate can be suspended to ensure that it cannot be used.

Exam Tip: A certificate suspension can be a useful process tool while investigating whether or not a certificate should be considered to be valid.

Relying on an expiration date on a certificate to "destroy" the utility of a key will not work. A new certificate can be issued with an "extended date." To end the use of a key set, an entry in a CRL is the only sure way to prevent reissuance and re-dating of a certificate.

Revocation

A certificate can be revoked when its validity needs to be ended before its actual expiration date is met, and this can occur for many reasons: for example, a user may have lost a laptop or a smart card that stored a private key; an improper software implementation may have been uncovered that directly affected the security of a private key; a user may have fallen victim to a social engineering attack and inadvertently given up a private key; data held within the certificate may no longer apply to the specified individual; or perhaps an employee left a company and should not be identified as a member of an in-house PKI any longer. In the last instance, the certificate, which was bound to the user's key pair, identified the user as an employee of the company, and the administrator would want to ensure that the key pair could not be used in the future to validate this person's affiliation with the company. Revoking the certificate does this.

If any of these things happens, a user's private key has been compromised or should no longer be mapped to the owner's identity. A different individual may have access to that user's private key and could use it to impersonate and authenticate as the original user. If the impersonator used the key to digitally sign a message, the receiver would verify the authenticity of the sender by verifying the signature by using the original user's public key, and the verification would go through perfectly—the receiver would believe it came from the proper sender and not the impersonator. If receivers could look at a list of certificates that had been revoked before verifying the digital signature, however, they would know not to trust the digital signatures on the list. Because of issues associated with the private key being compromised, revocation is permanent and final—once revoked,

Once revoked, a certificate cannot be reinstated. This is to prevent an unauthorized reinstatement by someone who has unauthorized access to the key(s). A key pair can be reinstated for use by issuing a new certificate if at a later time the keys are found to be secure. The old certificate would still be void, but the new one would be valid.

a certificate cannot be reinstated. If reinstatement was allowed and a user revoked his certificate, then the unauthorized holder of the private key could use it to restore the certificate validity.

Certificate Revocation List

The CA provides protection against impersonation and similar fraud by maintaining a **certificate revocation list (CRL)**, a list of serial numbers of certificates that have been revoked. The CRL also contains a statement indicating why the individual certificates were revoked and a date when the revocation took place. The list usually contains all certificates that have been revoked within the lifetime of the CA. Certificates that have expired are not the same as those that have been revoked. If a certificate has expired, it means that its end validity date was reached. The format of the CRL message is also defined by X.509. The list is signed, to prevent tampering, and contains information on certificates that have been revoked and the reasons for their revocation. These lists can grow quite long, and as such, there are provisions for date timestamping the list and for issuing delta lists, which show changes since the last list was issued.

Tech Tip

CRL Reason Codes

Per the X.509 v2 CRL standard, the following reasons for revocation are used:

Reason Code	Reason
0	Unspecified
1	All keys compromised; indicates compromise or suspected compromise
2	CA compromise; used only to revoke CA keys
3	Affiliation changed; indicates a change of affiliation on the certificate
4	Superseded; the certificate has been replaced by a more current one
5	Cessation; the certificate is no longer needed, but no reason exists to suspect it has been compromised
6	Certificate hold; indicates the certificate will not be issued at this point in time
7	Remove from CRL; used with delta CRL to indicate a CRL entry should be removed

The CA is the entity that is responsible for the status of the certificates it generates; it needs to be told of a revocation, and it must provide this information to others. The CA is responsible for maintaining the CRL and posting it in a publicly available directory.

We need to have some system in place to make sure people cannot arbitrarily have others' certificates revoked, whether for revenge or for malicious purposes. When a revocation request is submitted, the individual submitting the request must be authenticated. Otherwise, this could permit a type of denial-of-service attack, in which someone has another person's certificate revoked. The authentication can involve an agreed-upon password that was created during the registration process, but authentication should not be based on the individual proving that he has the corresponding private key, because it may have been stolen, and the CA would be authenticating an imposter.

The CRL's integrity needs to be protected to ensure that attackers cannot modify data pertaining to a revoked certification on the list. If this were allowed to take place, anyone who stole a private key could just delete that key from the CRL and continue to use the private key fraudulently. The integrity of the list also needs to be protected to ensure that bogus data is not added to it. Otherwise, anyone could add another person's certificate to the list and effectively revoke that person's certificate. The only entity that should be able to modify any information on the CRL is the CA.

The mechanism used to protect the integrity of a CRL is a *digital signature*. The CA's revocation service creates a digital signature for the CRL, as shown in Figure 6.7. To validate a certificate, the user accesses the directory where the CRL is posted, downloads the list, and verifies the CA's digital signature to ensure that the proper authority signed the list and to ensure that the list was not modified in an unauthorized manner. The user then looks through the list to determine whether the serial number of the certificate that he is trying to validate is listed. If the serial number is on the list, the private key should no longer be trusted, and the public key should no longer be used. This can be a cumbersome process, so it has been automated in several ways, which are described in the next section.

• **Figure 6.7**   The CA digitally signs the CRL to protect its integrity.

One concern is how up-to-date the CRL is—how often is it updated and does it actually reflect *all* the certificates currently revoked? The actual frequency with which the list is updated depends upon the CA and its certification practices statement (CPS). It is important that the list is updated in a timely manner so that anyone using the list has the most current information.

CRL Distribution

CRL files can be requested by individuals who need to verify and validate a newly received certificate, or the files can be periodically pushed down (sent) to all users participating within a specific PKI. This means the CRL can be pulled (downloaded) by individual users when needed or pushed down to all users within the PKI on a timed interval.

The actual CRL file can grow substantially, and transmitting this file and requiring PKI client software on each workstation to save and maintain it can use a lot of resources, so the smaller the CRL is, the better. It is also possible to first push down the full CRL and subsequently push down only *delta* CRLs, which contain only the changes to the original or base CRL. This can greatly reduce the amount of bandwidth consumed when updating CRLs.

In implementations where the CRLs are not pushed down to individual systems, the users' PKI software needs to know where to look for the posted CRL that relates to the certificate it is trying to validate. The certificate might have an extension that points the validating user to the necessary *CRL distribution point.* The network administrator sets up the distribution points, and one or more points can exist for a particular PKI. The distribution point holds one or more lists containing the serial numbers of revoked certificates, and the user's PKI software scans the list(s) for the serial number of the certificate the user is attempting to validate. If the serial number is not present, the user is assured that it has not been revoked. This approach helps point users to the right resource and also reduces the amount of information that needs to be scanned when checking that a certificate has not been revoked.

Online Certificate Status Protocol (OCSP)

One last option for checking distributed CRLs is an *online service.* When a client user needs to validate a certificate and ensure that it has not been revoked, he can communicate with an online service that will query the necessary CRLs available within the environment. This service can query the lists for the client instead of pushing down the full CRL to each and every system. So if Joe receives a certificate from Stacy, he can contact an online service and send to it the serial number listed in the certificate Stacy sent. The online service would query the necessary CRLs and respond to Joe, indicating whether or not that serial number was listed as being revoked.

One of the protocols used for online revocation services is the **Online Certificate Status Protocol (OCSP)**, a request and response protocol that obtains the serial number of the certificate that is being validated and reviews revocation lists for the client. The protocol has a responder service that reports the status of the certificate back to the client, indicating whether it has been revoked, is valid, or has an unknown status. This protocol and service saves the client from having to find, download, and process the right lists.

Key Destruction

Key pairs and certificates have set *lifetimes*, meaning that they will expire at some specified time. It is important that the certificates and keys are properly destroyed when that time comes, wherever the keys are stored (on users' workstations, centralized key servers, USB token devices, smart cards, and so on).

The goal is to make sure that no one can gain access to a key after its lifetime has ended and use that key for malicious purposes. An attacker might use the key to digitally sign or encrypt a message with the hopes of tricking someone else about his identity (this would be an example of a man-in-the middle attack). Also, if the attacker is performing some type of brute-force attack on your cryptosystem, trying to figure out specific keys that were used for encryption processes, obtaining an old key could give him more insight into how your cryptosystem generates keys. The less information you supply to potential hackers, the better.

■ Certificate Repositories

Once the requestor's identity has been proven, a certificate is registered with the public side of the key pair provided by the requestor. Public keys must be available to anybody who requires them to communicate within a PKI environment. These keys, and their corresponding certificates, are usually held in a publicly available repository. **Certificate repository** is a general term that describes a centralized directory that can be accessed by a subset of individuals. The directories are usually Lightweight Directory Access Protocol (LDAP)–compliant, meaning that they can be accessed and searched via an LDAP query from an LDAP client.

When an individual initializes communication with another, the sender can send her certificate and public key to the receiver, which will allow the receiver to communicate with the sender using encryption or digital signatures (or both) without needing to track down the necessary public key in a certificate repository. This is equivalent to the sender saying, "If you would like to encrypt any future messages you send to me, or if you would like the ability to verify my digital signature, here are the necessary components." But if a person wants to encrypt the first message sent to the receiver, the sender needs to find the receiver's public key in a certificate repository.

Cross Check

Certificates and Keys

Certificates are a standardized method of exchanging asymmetric key information. To understand the need for certificates, you should first be able to answer the questions:

- What do I need a public key for?
- How can I get someone's public key, and how do I know it is theirs?

For a refresher on how public and private keys come into play with encryption and digital signatures, refer to Chapter 5.

A certificate repository is a holding place for individuals' certificates and public keys that are participating in a particular PKI environment. The security requirements for repositories themselves are not as high as those needed for actual CAs and for the equipment and software used to carry out CA functions. Since each certificate is digitally signed by the CA, if a certificate stored in the certificate repository is modified, the recipient will be able to detect this change and know not to accept the certificate as valid.

■ Trust and Certificate Verification

We need to use a PKI if we do not automatically trust individuals we do not know. Security is about being suspicious and being safe, so we need a third party that we *do* trust to vouch for the other individual before confidence can be instilled and sensitive communication can take place. But what does it mean that we trust a CA, and how can we use this to our advantage?

Because certificates produce chains of trust, having an unnecessary certificate in your certificate store could lead to trust problems. Best practices indicate that you should understand the certificates in your store, and the need for each. When in doubt, remove it. If it is needed, you can add it back later.

When a user chooses to trust a CA, she will download that CA's digital certificate and public key, which will be stored on her local computer. Most browsers have a list of CAs configured to be trusted by default, so when a user installs a new web browser, several of the most well-known and most trusted CAs will be trusted without any change of settings. An example of this listing is shown in Figure 6.8.

In the Microsoft CAPI environment, the user can add and remove CAs from this list as needed. In production environments that require a higher degree of protection, this list will be pruned, and possibly the only CAs listed will be the company's *internal* CAs. This ensures that digitally signed software will be automatically installed only if it was signed by the company's CA. Other products, such as Entrust, use centrally controlled policies to determine which CAs are to be trusted, instead of expecting the user to make these critical decisions.

A number of steps are involved in checking the validity of a message. Suppose, for example, that Maynard receives a digitally signed message from Joyce, who he does not know or trust. Joyce has also included her digital certificate with her message, which has her public key embedded within it. Before Maynard can be sure of the authenticity of this message, he has some work to do. The steps are illustrated in Figure 6.9.

First, Maynard sees which CA signed Joyce's certificate and compares it to the list of CAs he has configured within his computer. He trusts the CAs in his list and no others. (If the certificate was signed by a CA that he does not have in the list, he would not accept the certificate as being valid, and thus he could not be sure that this message was actually sent from Joyce or that the attached key was actually her public key.)

• **Figure 6.8**   Browsers have a long list of CAs configured to be trusted by default.

Principles of Computer Security

Joyce

Message digest B

Joyce's digital certificate

Message

Maynard

Joyce's digital certificate

Encrypted with CA's private key

Message digest B

Message digest B

Hashing algorithm

Message

Message digest A

1. Joyce sends the message and digital certificate to Maynard.
2. Maynard extracts the certificate.
3. Maynard puts the certificate through a hashing algorithm.
4. The algorithm calculates a value of A.
5. Maynard extracts the encrypted message digest from the certificate.
6. Maynard decrypts the value with the CA's public key.
7. Maynard checks to see if the certificate was revoked.
7. Maynard compares values A and B.
8. The values are the same, so Maynard reads the message.

• **Figure 6.9**   Steps for verifying the authenticity and integrity of a certificate

Maynard sees that the CA that signed Joyce's certificate is indeed in his list of trusted CAs, so he now needs to verify that the certificate has not been altered. Using the CA's public key and the digest of the certificate, Maynard can verify the integrity of the certificate. Then Maynard can be assured that this CA did actually create the certificate, so he can now trust the origin of Joyce's certificate. The use of digital signatures allows certificates to be saved in public directories without the concern of them being accidentally or intentionally altered. If a user extracts a certificate from a repository and creates a message digest value that does not match the digital signature embedded within the certificate itself, that user will know that the certificate has been modified by someone other than the CA, and he will know not to accept the validity of the corresponding public key. Similarly, an attacker could not create a new message digest, encrypt it, and embed it within the certificate because he would not have access to the CA's private key.

But Maynard is not done yet. He needs to be sure that the issuing CA has not revoked this certificate. The certificate also has start and stop dates, indicating a time during which the certificate is valid. If the start date hasn't happened yet or the stop date has been passed, the certificate is not valid. Maynard reviews these dates to make sure the certificate is still deemed valid.

Another step Maynard may go through is to check whether this certificate has been revoked for any reason. To do so, he will refer to the *certificate revocation list (CRL)* to see if Joyce's certificate is listed. He could check the CRL directly with the CA that issued the certificate or via a specialized online service that supports the Online Certificate Status Protocol (OCSP). (Certificate revocation and list distribution were explained in the "Certificate Lifecycles" section, earlier in this chapter.)

Maynard now trusts that this certificate is legitimate and that it belongs to Joyce. Now what does he need to do? The certificate holds Joyce's public key, which he needs to validate the digital signature she appended to her message, so Maynard extracts Joyce's public key from her certificate, runs her message through a hashing algorithm, and calculates a message digest value of X. He then uses Joyce's public key to decrypt her digital signature (remember that a digital signature is just a message digest encrypted with a private key). This decryption process provides him with another message digest of value Y. Maynard compares values X and Y, and if they are the same, he is assured that the message has not been modified during transmission. Thus he has confidence in the integrity of the message. But how does Maynard know that the message actually came from Joyce? Because he can decrypt the digital signature using her public key, which indicates that only the associated private key could have been used. There is a miniscule risk that someone could create an identical key pair, but given the enormous keyspace for public keys, this is impractical. The public key can only decrypt something that was encrypted with the related private key, and only the owner of the private key is supposed to have access to it. Maynard can be sure that this message came from Joyce.

After all of this he reads her message, which says, "Hi. How are you?" All of that work just for this message? Maynard's blood pressure would surely go through the roof if he had to do all of this work only to end up with a short and not very useful message. Fortunately, all of this PKI work is performed without user intervention and happens behind the scenes. Maynard didn't have to exert any energy. He simply replies, "Fine. How are you?"

■ Centralized and Decentralized Infrastructures

Keys used for authentication and encryption within a PKI environment can be generated in a centralized or decentralized manner. In a *decentralized* approach, software on individual computers generates and stores cryptographic keys local to the systems themselves. In a *centralized* infrastructure, the keys are generated and stored on a central server, and the keys are transmitted to the individual systems as needed. You might choose one type over the other for several reasons.

If a company uses an asymmetric algorithm that is resource-intensive to generate the public/private key pair, and if large (and resource-intensive) key sizes are needed, then the individual computers may not have the necessary processing power to produce the keys in an acceptable fashion. In this situation, the company can choose a centralized approach in which a very high-end server with powerful processing abilities is used, probably along with a hardware-based random number generator.

Central key generation and storage offers other benefits as well. For example, it is much easier to back up the keys and implement key recovery procedures with central storage than with a decentralized approach. Implementing a key recovery procedure on each and every computer holding one or more key pairs is difficult, and many applications that generate their own key pairs do not usually interface well with a centralized archive system. This means that if a company chooses to allow its individual users to create and maintain their own key pairs on their separate workstations, no real key recovery procedure can be put in place. This puts the company at risk. If an employee leaves the organization or is unavailable for one reason or another, the company may not be able to access its own business information that was encrypted by that employee.

So a centralized approach seems like the best approach, right? Well, the centralized method has some drawbacks to consider, too. Secure key distribution is a tricky event. This can be more difficult than it sounds. A technology needs to be employed that will send the keys in an encrypted manner, ensure the keys' integrity, and make sure that only the intended user is receiving the key.

Also, the server that centrally stores the keys needs to be highly available and is a potential single point of failure, so some type of fault tolerance or redundancy mechanism may need to be put into place. If that one server goes down, users could not access their keys, which might prevent them from properly authenticating to the network, resources, and applications. Also, since all the keys are in one place, the server is a prime target for an attacker—if the central key server is compromised, the whole environment is compromised.

One other issue pertains to how the keys will actually be used. If a public/private key pair is being generated for digital signatures, and if the company wants to ensure that it can be used to provide *true* authenticity and nonrepudiation, the keys should not be generated at a centralized server. This would introduce doubt that only the one person had access to a specific private key. It is better to generate end-user keys on a local machine to eliminate doubt about who did the work and "owns" the keys.

If a company uses smart cards to hold users' private keys, each private key often has to be generated on the card itself and cannot be copied for archiving purposes. This is a disadvantage of the centralized approach. In addition, some types of applications have been developed to create their own public/private key pairs and do not allow other keys to be imported and used. This means the keys would have to be created locally by these applications, and keys from a central server could not be used. These are just some of the considerations that need to be evaluated before any decision is made and implementation begins.

Hardware Security Modules

PKIs can be constructed in software without special cryptographic hardware, and this is perfectly suitable for many environments. But software can be vulnerable to viruses, hackers, and hacking. If a company requires a higher level of protection than a purely software-based solution can provide, several hardware-based solutions are available. A **hardware security**

Tech Tip

Storing Critical Keys

HSMs take many different forms, including embedded cards, network-attached devices, and even USB flash drives. HSMs assist in the use of cryptographic keys across the lifecycle. They can provide dedicated support for centralized lifecycle management, from generation to distribution, storage, termination, archiving, and recordkeeping. HSMs can increase the efficiency of cryptographic operations and assist in compliance efforts. Common uses include use in PCI DSS solutions, DNSSEC, signing operations including certificates, code, documents, and e-mail, and large-scale data encryption efforts.

The security associated with the use of public key cryptography revolves around the security of the private key. Nonrepudiation depends upon the principle that the private key is only accessible to the holder of the key. If another person has access to the private key, they can impersonate the proper key holder.

module (HSM) is a physical device that safeguards cryptographic keys. HSMs enable a higher level of security for the use of keys, including generation and authentication.

In most situations, HSM solutions are used only for the most critical and sensitive keys, which are the root key and possibly the intermediate CA private keys. If those keys are compromised, the whole security of the PKI is gravely threatened. If a person obtained a root CA private key, she could digitally sign any certificate, and that certificate would be quickly accepted by all entities within the environment. Such an attacker might be able to create a certificate that has extremely high privileges, perhaps allowing her to modify bank account information in a financial institution, and no alerts or warnings would be initiated because the ultimate CA, the root CA, signed it.

Private Key Protection

Although a PKI implementation can be complex, with many different components and options, a critical concept common to all PKIs must be understood and enforced: the private key needs to stay private. A digital signature is created solely for the purpose of proving who sent a particular message by using a private key. This rests on the assumption that only one person has access to this private key. If an imposter obtains a user's private key, authenticity and nonrepudiation can no longer be claimed or proven.

When a private key is generated for the first time, it must be stored somewhere for future use. This storage area is referred to as a *key store,* and it is usually created by the application registering for a certificate, such as a web browser, smart card software, or other application. In most implementations, the application will prompt the user for a password, which will be used to create an encryption key that protects the key store. So, for example, if Cheryl used her web browser to register for a certificate, her private key would be generated and stored in the key store. Cheryl would then be prompted for a password, which the software would use to create a key that will encrypt the key store. When Cheryl needs to access this private key later that day, she will be prompted for the same password, which will decrypt the key store and allow her access to her private key.

Unfortunately, many applications do not require that a strong password be created to protect the key store, and in some implementations the user can choose not to provide a password at all. The user still has a private key available, and it is bound to the user's identity, so why is a password even necessary? If, for example, Cheryl decided not to use a password, and another person sat down at her computer, he could use her web browser and her private key and digitally sign a message that contains a nasty virus. If Cheryl's coworker Cliff received this message, he would think it came from Cheryl, open the message, and download the virus. The moral to this story is that users should be required to provide some type of authentication information (password, smart card, PIN, or the like) before being able to use private keys. Otherwise, the keys could be used by other individuals or imposters, and authentication and nonrepudiation would be of no use.

Because a private key is a crucial component of any PKI implementation, the key itself should contain the necessary characteristics and be protected at each stage of its life. The following list sums up the characteristics and requirements of proper private key use:

- The key size should provide the necessary level of protection for the environment.

- The lifetime of the key should correspond with how often it is used and the sensitivity of the data it is protecting.

- The key should be changed at the end of its lifetime and not used past its allowed lifetime.

- Where appropriate, the key should be properly destroyed at the end of its lifetime.

- The key should never be exposed in clear text.

- No copies of the private key should be made if it is being used for digital signatures.

- The key should not be shared.

- The key should be stored securely.

- Authentication should be required before the key can be used.

- The key should be transported securely.

- Software implementations that store and use the key should be evaluated to ensure they provide the necessary level of protection.

 The most sensitive and critical public/private key pairs are those used by CAs to digitally sign certificates. These need to be highly protected because if they were ever compromised, the trust relationship between the CA and all of the end-entities would be threatened. In high-security environments, these keys are often kept in a tamper-proof hardware encryption store, such as an HSM, and are accessible only to individuals with a need to know.

If digital signatures will be used for legal purposes, these points and others may need to be audited to ensure that true authenticity and nonrepudiation are provided.

Key Recovery

One individual could have one, two, or many key pairs that are tied to his or her identity. That is because users may have different needs and requirements for public/private key pairs. As mentioned earlier, certificates can have specific attributes and usage requirements dictating how their corresponding keys can and cannot be used. For example, David can have one key pair he uses to encrypt and transmit symmetric keys, another key pair that allows him to encrypt data, and yet another key pair to perform digital signatures. David can also have a digital signature key pair for his work-related activities and another key pair for personal activities, such as e-mailing his friends. These key pairs need to be used only for their intended purposes, and this is enforced through certificate attributes and usage values.

If a company is going to perform key recovery and maintain a key recovery system, it will generally back up only the key pair used to encrypt data, not the key pairs that are used to generate digital signatures. The reason that a company archives keys is to ensure that if a person leaves the company, falls off a cliff, or for some reason is unavailable to decrypt important company information, the company can still get to its company-owned data. This is just a matter of the organization protecting itself. A company would not need to be able to recover a key pair that is used for digital signatures, since those keys are to be used only to prove the authenticity of the individual who sent a message. A company would not benefit from having access to those keys and really should not have access to them, since they are tied to one individual for a specific purpose.

Two systems are important for backing up and restoring cryptographic keys: key archiving and key recovery. **Key archiving** is a way of backing up keys and securely storing them in a repository; **key recovery** is the process of restoring lost keys to the users or the company.

If keys are backed up and stored in a centralized computer, this system must be tightly controlled, because if it were compromised, an attacker would have access to all keys for the entire infrastructure. Also, it is usually unwise to authorize a single person to be able to recover all the keys within the environment, because that person could use this power for evil purposes instead of just recovering keys when they are needed for legitimate purposes. In security systems, it is best not to fully trust anyone.

Dual control can be used as part of a system to back up and archive data encryption keys. PKI systems can be configured to require multiple individuals to be involved in any key recovery process. When a key recovery is required, at least two people can be required to authenticate by the key recovery software before the recovery procedure is performed. This enforces *separation of duties*, which means that one person cannot complete a critical task by himself. Requiring two individuals to recover a lost key together is called **dual control**, which simply means that two people have to be present to carry out a specific task.

This approach to key recovery is referred to as the *m of n authentication*, where *n* number of people can be involved in the key recovery process, but at least *m* (which is a smaller number than *n*) *must* be involved before the task can be completed. The goal is to minimize fraudulent or improper use of access and permissions. A company would not require all possible individuals to be involved in the recovery process, because getting all the people together at the same time could be impossible considering meetings, vacations, sick time, and travel. At least some of all possible individuals must be available to participate, and this is the subset *m* of the number *n*. This form of secret splitting can increase security by requiring multiple people to perform a specific function. Requiring too many people for the *m* subset increases issues associated with availability, whereas requiring too few increases the risk of a small number of people colluding to compromise a secret.

All key recovery procedures should be highly audited. The audit logs should capture at least what keys were recovered, who was involved in the process, and the time and date. Keys are an integral piece of any encryption cryptosystem and are critical to a PKI environment, so you need to track who does what with them.

Key Escrow

Key recovery and key escrow are terms that are often used interchangeably, but they actually describe two different things. You should not use them interchangeably after you have read this section.

Key escrow is the process of giving keys to a third party so that they can decrypt and read sensitive information if the need arises. Key escrow almost always pertains to handing over encryption keys to the government, or to another higher authority, so that the keys can be used to collect evidence during investigations. A key pair used in a person's place of work may be required to be escrowed by the employer for two reasons. First, the keys are property of the enterprise, issued to the worker for use. Second, the firm may have need for them after an employee leaves the firm.

Several movements, supported by parts of the U.S. government, would require all or many people residing in the United States to hand over copies of the keys they use to encrypt communication channels. The movement in the late 1990s behind the Clipper chip is the most well-known effort to implement this requirement and procedure. It was suggested that all American-made communication devices should have a hardware encryption chip within them. The chip could be used to encrypt data going back and forth between two individuals, but if a government agency decided that it should be able to eavesdrop on this dialog, it would just need to obtain a court order. If the court order was approved, a law enforcement agent would take the order to two escrow agencies, each of which would have a piece of the key that was necessary to decrypt this communication information. The agent would obtain both pieces of the key and combine them, which would allow the agent to listen in on the encrypted communication outlined in the court order.

The Clipper chip standard never saw the light of day because it seemed too "Big Brother" to many American citizens. But the idea was that the encryption keys would be escrowed to two agencies, meaning that each agency would hold one piece of the key. One agency could not hold the whole key, because it could then use this key to wiretap people's conversations illegally. Splitting up the key is an example of separation of duties, put into place to try and prevent fraudulent activities. The current issue of governments demanding access to keys to decrypt information is covered in Chapter 24.

Exam Tip: Key escrow, allowing another trusted party to hold a copy of a key, has long been a controversial topic. This essential business process provides continuity should the authorized key-holding party leave an organization without disclosing keys. The security of the escrowed key is a concern, and it needs to be managed at the same security level as for the original key.

Public Certificate Authorities

An individual or company may decide to rely on a CA that is already established and being used by many other individuals and companies—a public CA. A company, on the other hand, may decide that it needs its own CA for internal use, which gives the company more control over the certificate registration and generation process and allows it to configure items specifically for its own needs. This second type of CA is referred to as a *private CA* (or *in-house CA*), discussed in the next section.

A public CA specializes in verifying individual identities and creating and maintaining their certificates. These companies issue certificates that are not bound to specific companies or intracompany departments. Instead, their services are to be used by a larger and more diversified group of people and organizations. If a company uses a public CA, the company will pay the CA organization for individual certificates and for the service of maintaining these certificates. Some examples of public CAs are VeriSign (including GeoTrust and Thawte), Entrust, and GoDaddy.

One advantage of using a public CA is that it is usually well known and easily accessible to many people. Most web browsers have a list of public CAs installed and configured by default, along with their corresponding root certificates. This means that if you install a web browser on your

Users can remove CAs from their browser list if they want to have more control over who their system trusts and who it doesn't. Unfortunately, system updates can restore them, requiring regular certificate store maintenance.

computer, it is already configured to trust certain CAs, even though you might have never heard of them before. So, if you receive a certificate from Bob, and his certificate was digitally signed by a CA listed in your browser, you automatically trust the CA and can easily walk through the process of verifying Bob's certificate. This has raised some eyebrows among security professionals, however, since trust is installed by default, but the industry has deemed this is a necessary approach that provides users with transparency and increased functionality.

Earlier in the chapter, the different certificate classes and their uses were explained. No global standard defines these classes, the exact requirements for obtaining these different certificates, or their uses. Standards are in place, usually for a particular country or industry, but this means that public CAs can define their own certificate classifications. This is not necessarily a good thing for companies that depend on public CAs, because it does not provide to the company enough control over how it should interpret certificate classifications and how they should be used.

This means another component needs to be carefully developed for companies that use and depend on public CAs, and this component is referred to as the *certificate policy (CP)*. This policy allows the company to decide what certification classes are acceptable and how they will be used within the organization. This is different from the CPS, which explains how the CA verifies entities, generates certificates, and maintains these certificates. The CP is generated and owned by an individual company that uses an external CA, and it allows the company to enforce *its* security decisions and control how certificates are used with its applications.

■ In-House Certificate Authorities

An *in-house CA* is implemented, maintained, and controlled by the company that implemented it. This type of CA can be used to create certificates for internal employees, devices, applications, partners, and customers. This approach gives the company complete control over how individuals are identified, what certification classifications are created, who can and cannot have access to the CA, and how the certifications can be used.

Choosing Between a Public CA and an In-House CA

When deciding between an in-house and public CA, various factors need to be identified and accounted for. Many companies have embarked upon implementing an in-house PKI environment with a rough estimate that would be implemented within x number of months and would cost approximately y amount in dollars. Without doing the proper homework, companies might not understand the current environment, might not completely hammer out the intended purpose of the PKI, and might not have enough skilled staff supporting the project; time estimates can double or triple and the required funds and resources can become unacceptable. Several companies have started on a PKI implementation, only to quit halfway through, resulting in wasted time and money, with nothing to show for it except heaps of frustration and many ulcers.

In some situations, it is better for a company to use a public CA, since public CAs already have the necessary equipment, skills, and technologies. In other situations, companies may decide it is a better business decision to take on these efforts themselves. This is not always a strictly monetary decision—a specific level of security might be required. Some companies do not believe that they can trust an outside authority to generate and maintain their users' and company's certificates. In this situation, the scale may tip toward an in-house CA.

Each company is unique, with various goals, security requirements, functionality needs, budgetary restraints, and ideologies. The decision of whether to use a private CA or an in-house CA depends on the expansiveness of the PKI within the organization, how integrated it will be with different business needs and goals, its interoperability with a company's current technologies, the number of individuals who will be participating, and how it will work with outside entities. This could be quite a large undertaking that ties up staff, resources, and funds, so a lot of strategic planning is required, and what will and won't be gained from a PKI should be fully understood before the first dollar is spent on the implementation.

 Certificate authorities come in many types: public, in-house, and outsourced. All of them perform the same functions, with the only difference being an organizational one. This can have a bearing on trust relationships, as one is more likely to trust in-house CAs over others for which there is arguably less control.

Outsourced Certificate Authorities

The last available option for using PKI components within a company is to outsource different parts of it to a specific service provider. Usually, the more complex parts are outsourced, such as the CA, RA, CRL, and key recovery mechanisms. This occurs if a company does not have the necessary skills to implement and carry out a full PKI environment.

Although outsourced services might be easier for your company to implement, you need to review several factors before making this type of commitment. You need to determine what level of trust the company is willing to give to the service provider and what level of risk it is willing to accept. Often a PKI and its components serve as large security components within a company's enterprise, and allowing a third party to maintain the PKI can introduce too many risks and liabilities that your company is not willing to undertake. The liabilities the service provider is willing to accept, the security precautions and procedures the outsourced CAs provide, and the surrounding legal issues need to be examined before this type of agreement is made.

Some large vertical markets have their own outsourced PKI environments set up because they share similar needs and usually have the same requirements for certification types and uses. This allows several companies within the same market to split the costs of the necessary equipment, and it allows for industry-specific standards to be drawn up and followed. For example, although many medical facilities work differently and have different environments, they have a lot of the same functionality and security needs. If several of them came together, purchased the necessary equipment to provide CA, RA, and CRL functionality, employed one person to maintain it, and then each connected its different sites to the centralized components, the medical facilities could save a lot of money and resources. In this case, not every facility would need to strategically plan its own full PKI, and each would not need to purchase redundant equipment or employ redundant staff members. Figure 6.10 illustrates how one outsourced service provider can offer different PKI components and services to different

Tech Tip

Outsourced CA vs. Public CA
An outsourced CA is different from a public CA in that it provides dedicated services, and possibly equipment, to an individual company. A public CA, in contrast, can be used by hundreds or thousands of companies—the CA doesn't maintain specific servers and infrastructures for individual companies.

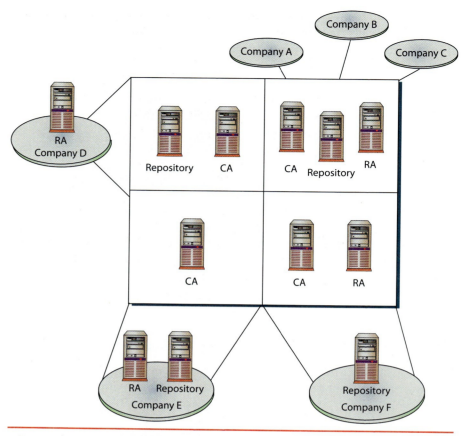

- **Figure 6.10** A PKI service provider (represented by the four boxes) can offer different PKI components to companies.

companies, and how companies within one vertical market can share the same resources.

A set of standards can be drawn up about how each different facility should integrate its own infrastructure and how it should integrate with the centralized PKI components. This also allows for less-complicated intercommunication to take place between the different medical facilities, which will ease information-sharing attempts.

Tying Different PKIs Together

In some cases, more than one CA may be needed for a specific PKI to work properly, and several requirements must be met for different PKIs to intercommunicate. Here are some examples:

- A company wants to be able to communicate seamlessly with its suppliers, customers, or business partners via a PKI.

- One department within a company has higher security requirements than all other departments and thus needs to configure and control its own CA.

- One department needs to have specially constructed certificates with unique fields and usages.

Principles of Computer Security

- Different parts of an organization want to control their own pieces of the network and the CA that is encompassed within it.

- The number of certificates that need to be generated and maintained would overwhelm one CA, so multiple CAs must be deployed.

- The political culture of a company inhibits one department from being able to control elements of another department.

- Enterprises are partitioned geographically, and different sites need their own local CA.

These situations can add much more complexity to the overall infrastructure, intercommunication capabilities, and procedures for certificate generation and validation. To control this complexity properly from the beginning, these requirements need to be understood, addressed, and planned for. Then the necessary trust model needs to be chosen and molded for the company to build upon. Selecting the right trust model will give the company a solid foundation from the beginning, instead of trying to add structure to an inaccurate and inadequate plan later on.

Trust Models

Potential scenarios exist other than just having more than one CA—each of the companies or each department of an enterprise can actually represent a trust domain itself. A *trust domain* is a construct of systems, personnel, applications, protocols, technologies, and policies that work together to provide a certain level of protection. All of these components can work together seamlessly within the same trust domain because they are known to the other components within the domain and are trusted to some degree. Different trust domains are usually managed by different groups of administrators, have different security policies, and restrict outsiders from privileged access.

Most trust domains (whether individual companies or departments) usually are not islands cut off from the world—they need to communicate with other, less-trusted domains. The trick is to figure out how much two different domains should trust each other, and how to implement and configure an infrastructure that would allow these two domains to communicate in a way that will not allow security compromises or breaches. This can be more difficult than it sounds.

In the nondigital world, it is difficult to figure out who to trust, how to carry out legitimate business functions, and how to ensure that one is not being taken advantage of or lied to. Jump into the digital world and add protocols, services, encryption, CAs, RAs, CRLs, and differing technologies and applications, and the business risks can become overwhelming and confusing. So start with a basic question: What criteria will we use to determine who we trust and to what degree?

One example of trust considered earlier in the chapter is the driver's license issued by the DMV. Suppose, for example, that Bob is buying a lamp from Carol and he wants to pay by check. Since Carol does not know Bob, she does not know if she can trust him or have much faith in his check. But if Bob shows Carol his driver's license, she can compare the name to what appears on the check, and she can choose to accept it. The *trust anchor* (the agreed-upon trusted third party) in this scenario is the DMV, since both Carol and Bob trust it more than they trust each other. Bob had to provide

Tech Tip

Trust Models
There are several forms of trust models associated with certificates. Hierarchical, peer-to-peer, and hybrid are the primary forms, with the web of trust being a form of hybrid. Each of these models has a useful place in the PKI architecture under different circumstances.

documentation to the DMV to prove his identity, that organization trusted him enough to generate a license, and Carol trusts the DMV, so she decides to trust Bob's check.

Consider another example of a trust anchor. If Joe and Stacy need to communicate through e-mail and would like to use encryption and digital signatures, they will not trust each other's certificate alone. But when each receives the other's certificate and sees that it has been digitally signed by an entity they both do trust—the CA—they have a deeper level of trust in each other. The trust anchor here is the CA. This is easy enough, but when we need to establish trust anchors between different CAs and PKI environments, it gets a little more complicated.

If two companies need to communicate using their individual PKIs, or if two departments within the same company use different CAs, two separate trust domains are involved. The users and devices from these different trust domains need to communicate with each other, and they need to exchange certificates and public keys, which means that trust anchors need to be identified and a communication channel must be constructed and maintained.

A trust relationship must be established between two issuing authorities (CAs). This happens when one or both of the CAs issue a certificate for the other CA's public key, as shown in Figure 6.11. This means that each CA registers for a certificate and public key from the other CA. Each CA validates the other CA's identification information and generates a certificate containing a public key for that CA to use. This establishes a trust path between the two entities that can then be used when users need to verify other users' certificates that fall within the different trust domains. The trust path can be unidirectional or bidirectional, so either the two CAs trust each other (bidirectional) or only one trusts the other (unidirectional).

As illustrated in Figure 6.11, all the users and devices in trust domain 1 trust their own CA, CA 1, which is their trust anchor. All users and devices in trust domain 2 have their own trust anchor, CA 2. The two CAs have

• **Figure 6.11**   A trust relationship can be built between two trust domains to set up a communication channel.

exchanged certificates and trust each other, but they do not have a common trust anchor between them.

The trust models describe and outline the trust relationships between the different CAs and different environments, which will indicate where the trust paths reside. The trust models and paths need to be thought out before implementation to restrict and control access properly and to ensure that as few trust paths as possible are used. Several different trust models can be used: the hierarchical, peer-to-peer, and hybrid models are discussed in the following sections.

Hierarchical Trust Model

The **hierarchical trust model** is a basic hierarchical structure that contains a root CA, intermediate CAs, leaf CAs, and end-entities. The configuration is that of an inverted tree, as shown in Figure 6.12. The root CA is the ultimate trust anchor for all other entities in this infrastructure, and it generates certificates for the intermediate CAs, which in turn generate certificates for the leaf CAs, and the leaf CAs generate certificates for the end-entities (users, network devices, and applications).

Intermediate CAs function to transfer trust between different CAs. These CAs are referred to as *subordinate CAs* because they are subordinate to the CA that they reference. The path of trust is walked up from the subordinate CA to the higher-level CA; in essence the subordinate CA is using the higher-level CA as a reference.

As shown in Figure 6.12, no bidirectional trusts exist—they are all unidirectional trusts, as indicated by the one-way arrows. Since no other entity can certify and generate certificates for the root CA, it creates a *self-signed certificate*. This means that the certificate's Issuer and Subject fields hold the same information, both representing the root CA, and the root CA's public key will be used to verify this certificate when that time comes. This root CA certificate and public key are distributed to all entities within this trust model.

Walking the Certificate Path

When a user in one trust domain needs to communicate with a user in another trust domain, one user will need to validate the other's certificate. This sounds simple enough, but what it really means is that each certificate for each CA, all the way up to a shared trusted anchor, also must be validated. If Debbie needs to validate Sam's certificate, as shown in Figure 6.12, she actually also needs to validate the Leaf D CA and Intermediate B CA certificates, as well as Sam's.

So in Figure 6.12, we have a user, Sam, who digitally signs a message and sends it and his certificate to Debbie. Debbie needs to validate this certificate before she can trust Sam's digital signature. Included in Sam's certificate is an Issuer field, which indicates that the certificate was issued by Leaf D CA. Debbie has to obtain Leaf D CA's digital certificate and public key to validate Sam's certificate. Remember that Debbie validates the certificate by verifying its digital signature. The digital signature was created by the certificate issuer using its private key, so Debbie needs to verify the signature using the issuer's public key.

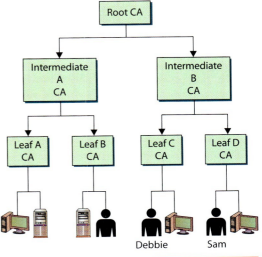

• **Figure 6.12**   The hierarchical trust model outlines trust paths.

Tech Tip

Root CA

If the root CA's private key were ever compromised, all entities within the hierarchical trust model would be drastically affected, because this is their sole trust anchor. The root CA usually has a small amount of interaction with the intermediate CAs and end-entities, and can therefore be taken offline much of the time. This provides a greater degree of protection for the root CA, because when it is offline it is basically inaccessible.

● **Figure 6.13** Verifying each certificate in a certificate path

Debbie tracks down Leaf D CA's certificate and public key, but she now needs to verify this CA's certificate, so she looks at the Issuer field, which indicates that Leaf D CA's certificate was issued by Intermediate B CA. Debbie now needs to get Intermediate B CA's certificate and public key.

Debbie's client software tracks this down and sees that the issuer for Intermediate B CA is the root CA, for which she already has a certificate and public key. So Debbie's client software had to follow the **certificate path**, meaning it had to continue to track down and collect certificates until it came upon a self-signed certificate. A self-signed certificate indicates that it was signed by a root CA, and Debbie's software has been configured to trust this entity as her trust anchor, so she can stop there. Figure 6.13 illustrates the steps Debbie's software had to carry out just to be able to verify Sam's certificate.

This type of simplistic trust model works well within an enterprise that easily follows a hierarchical organizational chart, but many companies cannot use this type of trust model because different departments or offices require their own trust anchors. These demands can be derived from direct business needs or from interorganizational politics. This hierarchical model might not be possible when two or more companies need to communicate with each other. Neither company will let the other's CA be the root CA, because each does not necessarily trust the other entity to that degree. In these situations, the CAs will need to work in a peer-to-peer relationship instead of in a hierarchical relationship.

Peer-to-Peer Model

In a **peer-to-peer trust model**, one CA is not subordinate to another CA, and no established trusted anchor between the CAs is involved. The end-entities will look to their issuing CA as their trusted anchor, but the different CAs will not have a common anchor.

Figure 6.14 illustrates this type of trust model. The two different CAs will certify the public key for each other, which creates a bidirectional trust. This is referred to as *cross-certification,* since the CAs are not receiving their certificates and public keys from a superior CA, but instead are creating them for each other.

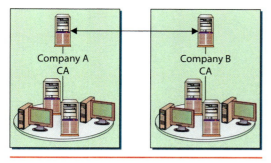

• **Figure 6.14** Cross-certification creates a peer-to-peer PKI model.

One of the main drawbacks to this model is scalability. Each CA must certify every other CA that is participating, and a bidirectional trust path must be implemented, as shown in Figure 6.15. If one root CA were certifying all the intermediate CAs, scalability would not be as much of an issue.

Figure 6.15 represents a fully connected *mesh architecture*, meaning that each CA is directly connected to and has a bidirectional trust relationship with every other CA. As you can see in this illustration, the complexity of this setup can become overwhelming.

In any network model, fully connected mesh architectures are wasteful and expensive. In trust transfer models, the extra level of redundancy is just that: redundant and unnecessary.

Hybrid Trust Model

A company can be internally complex, and when the need arises to communicate properly with outside partners, suppliers, and customers in an authorized and secured manner, this complexity can make sticking to either the hierarchical or peer-to-peer trust model difficult, if not impossible. In many implementations, the different model types have to be combined to provide the necessary communication lines and levels of trust. In a **hybrid trust model**, the two companies have their own internal hierarchical models and are connected through a peer-to-peer model using cross-certification.

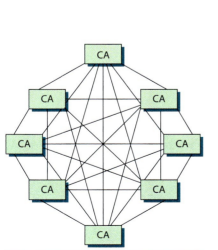

• **Figure 6.15** Scalability is a drawback in cross-certification models.

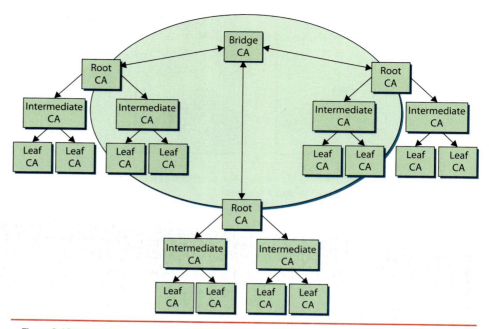

• Figure 6.16 A bridge CA can control the cross-certification procedures.

Exam Tip: Three trust models exist: hierarchical, peer-to-peer, and hybrid. Hierarchical trust is like an upside-down tree, peer-to-peer is a lateral series of references, and hybrid is a combination of hierarchical and peer-to-peer trust.

Another option in this hybrid configuration is to implement a *bridge CA*. Figure 6.16 illustrates the role that a bridge CA could play—it is responsible for issuing cross-certificates for all connected CAs and trust domains. The bridge is not considered a root or trust anchor, but merely the entity that generates and maintains the cross-certification for the connected environments.

Certificate-Based Threats

Although certificates bring much capability to security through practical management of trust, they also can present threats. Because much of the actual work is done behind the scenes, without direct user involvement, a false sense of security might ensue. End users might assume that if an HTTPS connection was made with a server, they are securely connected to the proper server. Spoofing, phishing, pharming, and a wide range of sophisticated attacks prey on this assumption. Today, industry has responded with a high-assurance certificate that is signed and recognized by browsers. Using this example, we can examine how an attacker might prey on a user's trust in software getting things correct.

If a hacker wishes to have something recognized as legitimate, he may have to obtain a certificate that proves this point to the end-user machine. One avenue would be to forge a false certificate, but this is challenging because of the public key signing of certificates by CAs. To overcome this problem, the hacker needs to install a false, self-signed root certificate on the end-user PC. This false key can then be used to validate malicious software as coming from a trusted source. This attack preys on the fact that end users do not know the contents of their root certificate store, nor do they have a means to validate changes. In an enterprise environment, this attack can be thwarted by locking down the certificate store and validating changes against a white list. This option really is not very practical for end users outside of an enterprise.

Stolen Certificates

Certificates act as a form of trusted ID and are typically handled without end-user intervention. To ensure the veracity of a certificate, a series of cryptographic controls is employed, including digital signatures to provide proof of authenticity. This statement aside, stolen certificates have been used in multiple cases of computer intrusions/system attacks. Specially crafted malware has been designed to steal both private keys and digital certificates from machines. One of the most infamous malware programs, the Zeus bot, has functionality to perform this task.

Stolen certificates have been implemented in a wide range of attacks. Malware designed to imitate antivirus software has been found dating back to 2009. The Stuxnet attack on the Iranian nuclear production facility used stolen certificates from third parties that were not involved in any way other than the unwitting contribution of a passkey in the form of a certificate. In less than a month after the Sony Pictures Entertainment attack became public in 2014, malware using Sony certificates appeared. Whether the certificates came from the break-in or one of the previous Sony hacks is unknown, but the result is the same.

 A stolen certificate and/ or private key can be used to bypass many security measures. Concern over stolen SSL/TLS credentials led to the creation of high-assurance certificates, which are discussed in Chapter 17.

Chapter 6 Review

Lab Book Exercise

The following lab exercise from the companion lab manual, *Principles of Computer Security Lab Manual,* *Fourth Edition,* provides practical application of material covered in this chapter:

Lab 8.5w   Using IPsec in Windows

Chapter Summary

After reading this chapter and completing the exercises, you should understand the following about public key infrastructures.

Implement the basics of public key infrastructures

- PKI solutions include certificate authorities (CAs) and registration authorities (RAs).
- PKIs form the central management functionality used to enable encryption technologies.
- The steps a user performs to obtain a certificate for use are listed in the text and are important to memorize.

Describe the role of registration authorities

- RAs verify identities to be used on certificates.
- RAs pass identity information to CAs for use in binding to a certificate.

Use digital certificates

- Certificates are handled via a certificate server and client software.
- There are three classes of certificates and they have the following typical uses:
  - **Class 1**   Personal e-mail use
  - **Class 2**   Software signing
  - **Class 3**   Setting up a CA

Understand the lifecycle of certificates

- Certificates are generated, registered, and historically verified by the originating CA.
- There are two main mechanisms to manage the revocation of a certificate: CRL and OCSP.
- Keys, and hence certificates, have a lifecycle; they are created, used for a defined period of time, and then destroyed.

Explain the relationship between trust and certificate verification

- Trust is based on an understanding of the needs of the user and what the item being trusted offers.
- Certificate verification provides assurance that the data in the certificate is valid, not whether it meets the needs of the user.

Describe the roles of certificate authorities and certificate repositories

- CAs create certificates for identified entities and maintain records of their issuance and revocation.
- CRLs provide a means of letting users know when certificates have been revoked before their end-of-life date.

Identify centralized and decentralized infrastructures

- There are three different architectures of CAs:
  - Hierarchical
  - Peer-to-peer
  - Hybrid
- Multiple CAs can be used together to create a web of trust.

Describe public and in-house certificate authorities

- Public CAs exist as a service that allows entities to obtain certificates from a trusted third party.
- In-house certificates provide certificates that allow a firm a means to use certificates within company borders.

Key Terms

authority revocation list (ARL) *(142)*
CA certificate *(136)*
certificate *(128)*
certificate authority (CA) *(130)*
certificate path *(158)*
certificate repository *(143)*
certificate revocation list (CRL) *(140)*
certificate server *(131)*
certificate signing request (CSR) *(138)*
certification practices statement (CPS) *(131)*
cross-certification certificate *(137)*
digital certificate *(130)*
dual control *(150)*

end-entity certificate *(136)*
hardware security module (HSM) *(147)*
hierarchical trust model *(157)*
hybrid trust model *(159)*
key archiving *(150)*
key escrow *(150)*
key recovery *(150)*
local registration authority (LRA) *(132)*
Online Certificate Status Protocol (OCSP) *(142)*
peer-to-peer trust model *(158)*
policy certificate *(137)*
public key infrastructure (PKI) *(129)*
registration authority (RA) *(131)*

Key Terms Quiz

Use terms from the Key Terms list to complete the sentences that follow. Don't use the same term more than once. Not all terms will be used.

1. The _____ is the trusted authority for certifying individuals' identities and creating an electronic document indicating that individuals are who they say they are.

2. A(n) _____ is the actual request to a CA containing a public key and the requisite information needed to generate a certificate.

3. The _____ is a method of determining whether a certificate has been revoked that does not require local machine storage of CRLs.

4. The _____ is the actual service that issues certificates based on the data provided during the initial registration process.

5. A physical device that safeguards cryptographic keys is called a(n) _____.

6. A(n) _____ is a holding place for individuals' certificates and public keys that are participating in a particular PKI environment.

7. A(n) _____ is used when independent CAs establish peer-to-peer trust relationships.

8. A(n) _____ is a structure that provides all of the necessary components for different types of users and entities to be able to communicate securely and in a predictable manner.

9. _____ is the process of giving keys to a third party so that they can decrypt and read sensitive information if the need arises.

10. In a(n) _____, one CA is not subordinate to another CA, and there is no established trust anchor between the CAs involved.

Multiple-Choice Quiz

1. When a user wants to participate in a PKI, what component does he or she need to obtain, and how does that happen?

    A. The user submits a certificate request to the CA.

    B. The user submits a key pair request to the CRL.

    C. The user submits a certificate request to the RA.

    D. The user submits proof of identification to the CA.

2. How does a user validate a digital certificate that is received from another user?

    A. The user first sees whether her system has been configured to trust the CA that digitally signed the other user's certificate and then validates that CA's digital signature.

    B. The user calculates a message digest and compares it to the one attached to the message.

C. The user first sees whether her system has been configured to trust the CA that digitally signed the certificate and then validates the public key that is embedded within the certificate.

D. The user validates the sender's digital signature on the message.

3. What is the purpose of a digital certificate?

A. It binds a CA to a user's identity.

B. It binds a CA's identity to the correct RA.

C. It binds an individual identity to an RA.

D. It binds an individual identity to a public key.

4. What steps does a user's software take to validate a CA's digital signature on a digital certificate?

A. The user's software creates a message digest for the digital certificate and decrypts the encrypted message digest included within the digital certificate. If the decryption performs properly and the message digest values are the same, the certificate is validated.

B. The user's software creates a message digest for the digital signature and encrypts the message digest included within the digital certificate. If the encryption performs properly and the message digest values are the same, the certificate is validated.

C. The user's software creates a message digest for the digital certificate and decrypts the encrypted message digest included within the digital certificate. If the user can encrypt the message digest properly with the CA's private key and the message digest values are the same, the certificate is validated.

D. The user's software creates a message digest for the digital signature and encrypts the message digest with its private key. If the decryption performs properly and the message digest values are the same, the certificate is validated.

5. Why would a company implement a key archiving and recovery system within the organization?

A. To make sure all data encryption keys are available for the company if and when it needs them

B. To make sure all digital signature keys are available for the company if and when it needs them

C. To create session keys for users to be able to access when they need to encrypt bulk data

D. To back up the RA's private key for retrieval purposes

6. Within a PKI environment, where does the majority of the trust actually lie?

A. All users and devices within an environment trust the RA, which allows them to indirectly trust each other.

B. All users and devices within an environment trust the CA, which allows them to indirectly trust each other.

C. All users and devices within an environment trust the CRL, which allows them to indirectly trust each other.

D. All users and devices within an environment trust the CPS, which allows them to indirectly trust each other.

7. Which of the following properly describes what a public key infrastructure (PKI) actually is?

A. A protocol written to work with a large subset of algorithms, applications, and protocols

B. An algorithm that creates public/private key pairs

C. A framework that outlines specific technologies and algorithms that must be used

D. A framework that does not specify any technologies but provides a foundation for confidentiality, integrity, and availability services

8. Once an individual validates another individual's certificate, what is the use of the public key that is extracted from this digital certificate?

A. The public key is now available to use to create digital signatures.

B. The user can now encrypt session keys and messages with this public key and can validate the sender's digital signatures.

C. The public key is now available to encrypt future digital certificates that need to be validated.

D. The user can now encrypt private keys that need to be transmitted securely.

9. Why would a digital certificate be added to a certificate revocation list (CRL)?

    A. If the public key had become compromised in a public repository

    B. If the private key had become compromised

    C. If a new employee joined the company and received a new certificate

    D. If the certificate expired

10. How can users have faith that the CRL was not modified to present incorrect information?

    A. The CRL is digitally signed by the CA.

    B. The CRL is encrypted by the CA.

    C. The CRL is open for anyone to post certificate information to.

    D. The CRL is accessible only to the CA.

Essay Quiz

1. Describe the pros and cons of establishing a key archiving system program for a small- to medium-sized business.

2. Why would a small- to medium-sized firm implement a PKI solution? What business benefits would ensue from such a course of action?

3. Describe the steps involved in verifying a certificate's validity.

4. Describe the steps in obtaining a certificate.

5. Compare and contrast the hierarchical trust model, peer-to-peer trust model, and hybrid trust model.

Lab Projects

• Lab Project 6.1

Investigate the process of obtaining a personal certificate or digital ID for e-mail usage. What information is needed, what are the costs, and what protection is afforded based on the vendor?

• Lab Project 6.2

Determine what certificates are registered with the browser instance on your computer.

PKI Standards and Protocols

The nice thing about standards is that you have so many to choose from.

—ANDREW S. TANENBAUM

```
<meta http
<meta http-equiv="con
<title>Document Title</ti
<link rev="made" href="ma
<link rev="start" href="
<style type="text/css" m
    @import "style/base.cs
/style>              ="text/javas
                     /javas
```

In this chapter, you will learn how to

- Identify the standards involved in establishing an interoperable Internet PKI

- Explain interoperability issues with PKI standards

- Describe how the common Internet protocols implement the PKI standards

None of the still steadily growing Internet commerce would be possible without the use of standards and protocols that provide a common, interoperable environment for exchanging information securely. Due to the wide distribution of Internet users and businesses, the most practical solution to date has been the commercial implementation of public key infrastructures (PKIs).

This chapter examines the standards and protocols involved in secure Internet transactions and e-business using a PKI. Although you may use only a portion of the related standards and protocols on a daily basis, you should understand how they interact to provide the services that are critical for security: confidentiality, integrity, availability, authentication, and nonrepudiation. This chapter will also include some related standards, such as FIPS and the Common Criteria.

Chapter 6 introduced the algorithms and techniques used to implement a public PKI, but, as you probably noticed, there is a lot of room for interpretation. Various organizations have developed and implemented standards and protocols that have been accepted as the basis for secure interaction in a PKI environment. These standards fall into three general categories:

- **Standards that define the PKI** These standards define the data and data structures exchanged and the means for managing that data to provide the functions of the PKI (certificate issuance, storage, revocation, registration, and management).

- **Standards that define the interface between applications and the underlying PKI** These standards use the PKI to establish the services required by applications (S/MIME, SSL, and TLS).

- **Other standards** These standards don't fit neatly in either of the other two categories. They provide bits and pieces that glue everything together; they not only can address the PKI structure and the methods and protocols for using it, but can also provide an overarching business process environment for PKI implementation (for example, ISO/IEC 27002, Common Criteria, and the Federal Information Processing Standards Publications [FIPS PUBS]).

Tech Tip

Revolutionary Technologies
The 1976 public disclosure of asymmetric key algorithms by Diffie, Hellman, Rivest, Shamir, and Adleman changed secure communications in a world-shattering way. It was a technology that met the need of another emerging technology; the development of the Internet during this same time led to the need for secure communications between anonymous parties— combined, a technologically revolutionary event.

Figure 7.1 shows the relationships between these standards and protocols and conveys the interdependence of the standards and protocols discussed in this chapter. The Internet **public key infrastructure (PKI)** relies on three main standards for establishing interoperable PKI services: PKI X.509 (PKIX), Public Key Cryptography Standards (PKCS), and X.509. Other protocols and standards help define the management and operation of the PKI and related services—Internet Security Association and Key Management Protocol (ISAKMP) and XML Key Management Specification (XKMS) are both key management protocols, while Certificate Management Protocol

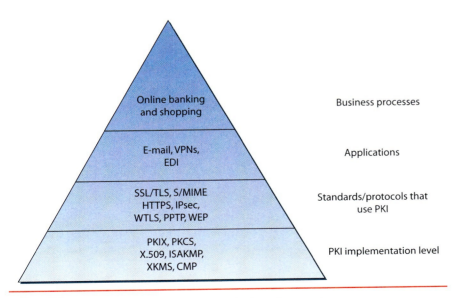

Figure 7.1   Relationships between PKI standards and protocols

(CMP) is used for managing certificates. Certificate Enrollment Protocol (CEP) is an alternative certificate issuance, distribution, and revocation mechanism. Finally, Pretty Good Privacy (PGP) provides an alternative method spanning the protocol and application levels.

This chapter examines each standard from the bottom up, starting with building an infrastructure through protocols and applications, and finishing with some of the inherent weaknesses of and potential attacks on a PKI.

■ PKIX and PKCS

Two main standards have evolved over time to implement PKIs on a practical level on the Internet. Both are based on the X.509 certificate standard (discussed shortly in the "X.509" section) and establish complementary standards for implementing PKIs. PKIX and PKCS intertwine to define the most commonly used set of standards.

PKIX was produced by the Internet Engineering Task Force (IETF) and defines standards for interactions and operations for four component types: the user (end-entity), certificate authority (CA), registration authority (RA), and the repository for certificates and certificate revocation lists (CRLs). PKCS defines many of the lower-level standards for message syntax, cryptographic algorithms, and the like. The PKCS set of standards is a product of RSA Security.

The PKIX working group was formed in 1995 to develop the standards necessary to support PKIs. At the time, the X.509 Public Key Certificate (PKC) format was proposed as the basis for a PKI. X.509 includes information regarding data formats and procedures used for CA-signed PKCs, but it doesn't specify values or formats for many of the fields within the PKC. PKIX provides standards for extending and using X.509 v3 certificates and for managing them, enabling interoperability between PKIs following the standards.

• Figure 7.2   The PKIX model

PKIX uses the model shown in Figure 7.2 for representing the components and users of a PKI. The user, called an *end-entity,* is not part of the PKI, but end-entities are either users of the PKI certificates, the subject of a certificate (an entity identified by it), or both. The **certificate authority (CA)** is responsible for issuing, storing, and revoking certificates—both PKCs and Attribute Certificates (ACs). The RA is responsible for management activities designated by the CA. The RA can, in fact, be a component of the CA rather than a separate component. The final component of the PKIX model is the repository, a system or group of distributed systems that provides certificates and CRLs to the end-entities. The **certificate revocation list (CRL)** is a digitally signed object that lists all of the current but revoked certificates issued by a CA.

PKIX Standards

Now that we have looked at how PKIX is organized, let's take a look at what PKIX does. Using X.509 v3, the PKIX working group addresses five major areas:

- *PKIX outlines certificate extensions and content not covered by X.509 v3 and the format of version 2 CRLs, thus providing compatibility standards for sharing certificates and CRLs between CAs and end-entities in different PKIs.* The PKIX profile of the X.509 v3 PKC describes the contents, required extensions, optional extensions, and extensions that need not be implemented. The PKIX profile suggests a range of values for many extensions. In addition, PKIX provides a profile for version 2 CRLs, allowing different PKIs to share revocation information.

- *PKIX provides certificate management message formats and protocols, defining the data structures, management messages, and management functions for PKIs.* The working group also addresses the assumptions and restrictions of their protocols. This standard identifies the protocols necessary to support online interactions between entities in the PKIX model. The management protocols support functions for entity registration, initialization of the certificate (possibly key-pair generation), issuance of the certificate, key-pair update, certificate revocation, cross-certification (between CAs), and key-pair recovery if available.

- *PKIX outlines certificate policies and certification practices statements (CPSs), establishing the relationship between policies and CPSs.* A policy is a set of rules that helps determine the applicability of a certificate to an end-entity. For example, a certificate for handling routine information would probably have a policy on creation, storage, and management of key pairs quite different from a policy for certificates used in financial transactions, due to the sensitivity of the financial information. A CPS explains the practices used by a CA to issue certificates. In other words, the CPS is the method used to get the certificate, while the policy defines some characteristics of the certificate and how it will be handled and used.

- *PKIX specifies operational protocols, defining the protocols for certificate handling.* In particular, protocol definitions are specified for using

File Transfer Protocol (FTP) and Hypertext Transfer Protocol (HTTP) to retrieve certificates from repositories. These are the most common protocols for applications to use when retrieving certificates.

■ *PKIX includes time-stamping and data certification and validation services, which are areas of interest to the PKIX working group, and which will probably grow in use over time.* A time stamp authority (TSA) certifies that a particular entity existed at a particular time. A Data Validation and Certification Server (DVCS) certifies the validity of signed documents, PKCs, and the possession or existence of data. These capabilities support nonrepudiation requirements and are considered building blocks for a nonrepudiation service.

PKCs are the most commonly used certificates, but the PKIX working group has been working on two other types of certificates: Attribute Certificates and Qualified Certificates. An Attribute Certificate (AC) is used to grant permissions using rule-based, role-based, and rank-based access controls. ACs are used to implement a privilege management infrastructure (PMI). In a PMI, an entity (user, program, system, and so on) is typically identified as a client to a server using a PKC. There are then two possibilities: either the identified client pushes an AC to the server, or the server can query a trusted repository to retrieve the attributes of the client. This situation is modeled in Figure 7.3.

The client push of the AC has the effect of improving performance, but no independent verification of the client's permissions is initiated by the server. The alternative is to have the server pull the information from an AC issuer or a repository. This method is preferable from a security standpoint, because the server or server's domain determines the client's access rights. The pull method has the added benefit of requiring no changes to the client software.

• **Figure 7.3**   The PKIX PMI model

The Qualified Certificate (QC) is based on the term used within the European Commission to identify certificates with specific legislative uses. This concept is generalized in the PKIX QC profile to indicate a certificate used to identify a specific individual (a single human rather than the *entity* of the PKC) with a high level of assurance in a nonrepudiation service.

There are dozens of IETF Requests for Comment (RFCs) that have been produced by the PKIX working group for each of these five areas.

For a complete list of current and pending documents associated with PKIX, see the Internet draft for the PKIX working group roadmap (https://www.ietf.org/archive/id/draft-ietf-pkix-roadmap-09.txt/).

PKCS

RSA Laboratories created the Public Key Cryptography Standards (PKCS) to fill some of the gaps in the standards that existed in PKI implementation. As they have with the PKIX standards, PKI developers have adopted many of these standards as a basis for achieving interoperability between different CAs. PKCS is composed of a set of (currently) 13 active standards, with 2 other standards that are no longer active. The standards are referred to as PKCS #1 through PKCS #15, as listed in Table 7.1. The standards combine to establish a common base for services required in a PKI.

Table 7.1	PKCS Standards
Standard	**Title and Description**
PKCS #1	RSA Cryptography Standard; definition of the RSA encryption standard.
PKCS #2	No longer active; it covered RSA encryption of message digests and was incorporated into PKCS #1.
PKCS #3	Diffie-Hellman Key Agreement Standard; definition of the Diffie-Hellman key-agreement protocol.
PKCS #4	No longer active; it covered RSA key syntax and was incorporated into PKCS #1.
PKCS #5	Password-Based Cryptography Standard; definition of a password-based encryption (PBE) method for generating a secret key.
PKCS #6	Extended-Certificate Syntax Standard; definition of an extended-certificate syntax that is made obsolete by X.509 v3.
PKCS #7	Cryptographic Message Syntax Standard; definition of the cryptographic message standard for encoded messages, regardless of encryption algorithm. Commonly replaced with PKIX Cryptographic Message Syntax.
PKCS #8	Private-Key Information Syntax Standard; definition of a private key information format, used to store private key information.
PKCS #9	Selected Attribute Types; definition of attribute types used in other PKCS standards.
PKCS #10	Certification Request Syntax Standard; definition of a syntax for certification requests.
PKCS #11	Cryptographic Token Interface Standard; definition of a technology-independent programming interface for cryptographic devices (such as smart cards).
PKCS #12	Personal Information Exchange Syntax Standard; definition of a format for storage and transport of a user's private keys, certificates, and other personal information.
PKCS #13	Is currently in development. Elliptic Curve Cryptography Standard; description of methods for encrypting and signing messages using elliptic curve cryptography.
PKCS #14	Is currently in development and covers pseudo-random number generation.
PKCS #15	Cryptographic Token Information Format Standard; definition of a format for storing cryptographic information in cryptographic tokens.

Though adopted early in the development of PKIs, some of these standards are being phased out. For example, PKCS #6 is being replaced by X.509 v3 (covered shortly in the "X.509" section) and PKCS #7 and PKCS #10 are being used less, as their PKIX counterparts are being adopted.

Why You Need to Know the PKIX and PKCS Standards

If your company is planning to use one of the existing certificate servers to support e-commerce, you may not need to know the specifics of these standards (except perhaps for the CompTIA Security+ exam). However, if you plan to implement a private PKI to support secure services within your organization, you need to understand what standards are out there and how the decision to use a particular PKI implementation (either home-grown or commercial) may lead to incompatibilities with other certificate-issuing entities. You must consider your business-to-business requirements when you're deciding how to implement a PKI within your organization.

Tech Tip

X.509 Essentials

X.509 specifies standard formats for public key certificates, certificate revocation lists, and Attribute Certificates.

X.509

What is a **certificate**? As explained in Chapter 6, a certificate is merely a data structure that binds a public key to subjects (unique names, DNS entries, or e-mails) and is used to authenticate that a public key indeed belongs to the subject. In the late 1980s, the X.500 OSI Directory Standard was defined by the International Organization for Standardization (ISO) and the International Telecommunication Union (ITU). It was developed for implementing a network directory system, and part of this directory standard was the concept of authentication of entities within the directory. **X.509** is the portion of the X.500 standard that addresses the structure of certificates used for authentication.

Several versions of the X.509 certificates have been created, with version 3 being the current version (as this is being written). Each version has extended the contents of the certificates to include additional information necessary to use certificates in a PKI. The original ITU X.509 definition was published in 1988, was formerly referred to as CCITT X.509, and is sometimes referred to as ISO/IEC/ITU 9594-8. Version 3 added additional optional extensions for more subject identification information, key attribute information, policy information, and certification path constraints. In addition, version 3 allows additional extensions to be defined in standards or to be defined and registered by organizations or communities.

Certificates are used to encapsulate the information needed to authenticate an entity. The X.509 specification defines a hierarchical certification structure that relies on a root CA that is *self-certifying* (meaning it issues its own certificate). All other certificates can be traced back to such a root through a *path*. A CA issues a certificate to a uniquely identifiable entity (person, corporation, computer, and so on)—issuing a certificate to "John Smith" would cause some real problems if that were all the information the CA had when issuing the certificate. We are saved somewhat by the requirement that the CA determines what identifier is unique (the distinguished name), but when certificates and trust are extended between CAs, the unique identification becomes critical.

Cross Check

Certificates

A detailed description of certificates and the supporting public key infrastructure is provided in Chapter 6.

■ SSL/TLS

Secure Sockets Layer (SSL) and **Transport Layer Security (TLS)** provide the most common means of interacting with a PKI and certificates. The older, SSL protocol was introduced by Netscape as a means of providing secure connections for web transfers using encryption. These two protocols provide secure connections between the client and server for exchanging information. They also provide server authentication (and optionally, client authentication) and confidentiality of information transfers. See Chapter 17 for a detailed explanation.

The IETF established the TLS working group in 1996 to develop a standard transport layer security protocol. The working group began with SSL version 3.0 as its basis and released RFC 2246, "The TLS Protocol Version 1.0," in 1999 as a proposed standard. The working group also published RFC 2712, "Addition of Kerberos Cipher Suites to Transport Layer Security (TLS)," as a proposed standard, and two RFCs on the use of TLS with HTTP. Like its predecessor, TLS is a protocol that ensures privacy between communicating applications and their users on the Internet. When a server and client communicate, TLS ensures that no third party can eavesdrop or tamper with any message.

TLS is composed of two parts: the TLS Record Protocol and the TLS Handshake Protocol. The TLS Record Protocol provides connection security by using supported encryption methods. The TLS Record Protocol can also be used without encryption. The TLS Handshake Protocol allows the server and client to authenticate each other and to negotiate a session encryption algorithm and cryptographic keys before data is exchanged.

Though TLS is based on SSL and is sometimes referred to as SSL, they are not interoperable. However, the TLS protocol does contain a mechanism that allows a TLS implementation to back down to SSL 3.0. The difference between the two is the way they perform key expansion and message authentication computations. The TLS Record Protocol is a layered protocol. At each layer, messages may include fields for length, description, and content. The Record Protocol takes messages to be transmitted, fragments the data into manageable blocks, optionally compresses the data, applies a message authentication code (HMAC) to the data, encrypts it, and transmits the result. Received data is decrypted, verified, decompressed, and reassembled, and then delivered to higher-level clients.

The TLS Handshake Protocol involves the following steps, which are summarized in Figure 7.4:

1. Exchange hello messages to agree on algorithms, exchange random values, and check for session resumption.

2. Exchange the necessary cryptographic parameters to allow the client and server to agree on a pre-master secret.

3. Exchange certificates and cryptographic information to allow the client and server to authenticate themselves.

Tech Tip

SSL/TLS Simplified

SSL and TLS are cryptographic protocols to provide data integrity and security over networks by encrypting network connections at the transport layer. In many cases people use the term SSL even when TLS is in fact the protocol being used.

⚠ SSL is deprecated. All versions of SSL, including v3, have exploitable vulnerabilities that make the protocol no longer considered secure. For all traffic where confidentiality is important, you should use TLS.

Server hello, server's random value, certificate, and optional certificate request

Client hello, random value, and algorithm list →

Server hello, server's random value, certificate, and optional certificate request ←

Client certificate (optional) →

Pre-master secret (encrypted) →

Client and server generate master secret

Change cipher spec (start using encryption) →

Client ——— Server

Server changes record layer security state — Server

Client finished →

Server finished ←

Exchange application data ↔

● Figure 7.4 TLS Handshake Protocol

4. Generate a master secret from the pre-master secret and exchange random values.

5. Provide security parameters to the record layer.

6. Allow the client and server to verify that their peer has calculated the same security parameters and that the handshake occurred without tampering by an attacker.

Though it has been designed to minimize this risk, TLS still has potential vulnerabilities to a man-in-the-middle attack. A highly skilled and well-placed attacker can force TLS to operate at lower security levels. Regardless, through the use of validated and trusted certificates, a secure cipher suite can be selected for the exchange of data.

Once established, a TLS session remains active as long as data is being exchanged. If sufficient inactive time has elapsed for the secure connection to time out, it can be reinitiated.

Tech Tip

Disabling SSL

Because all versions of SSL, including v3, have exploitable vulnerabilities that make the protocol no longer considered secure, users should not rely on it for security. Chrome no longer uses SSL. For Internet Explorer, you need to uncheck the SSL boxes under Internet Options.

Cipher Suites

In many applications, the use of cryptography occurs as a collection of functions. Different algorithms can be used for authentication, encryption/decryption, digital signatures, and hashing. The term *cipher suite* refers to an arranged group of algorithms. For instance, TLS has a published TLS Cipher Suite Registry at www.iana.org/assignments/tls-parameters/tls-parameters.xhtml.

There is a wide range of ciphers, some old and some new, each with its own strengths and weaknesses. Over time, new methods and computational abilities change the viability of ciphers. The concept of strong versus weak ciphers is an acknowledgment that, over time, ciphers can become vulnerable to attacks. The application or selection of ciphers should take into consideration that not all ciphers are still strong. When selecting a cipher for use, it is important to make an appropriate choice. For example, if a server offers SSL v3 and TLS, you should choose TLS only, as SSL v3 has been shown to be vulnerable.

ISAKMP

The **Internet Security Association and Key Management Protocol (ISAKMP)** provides a method for implementing a key exchange protocol and for negotiating a security policy. It defines procedures and packet formats to negotiate, establish, modify, and delete security associates. Because it is a framework, it doesn't define implementation-specific protocols, such as the key

Principles of Computer Security

exchange protocol or hash functions. Examples of ISAKMP are the Internet Key Exchange (IKE) protocol and IPsec, which are used widely throughout the industry.

An important definition for understanding ISAKMP is that of the term *security association*. A security association (SA) is a relationship in which two or more entities define how they will communicate securely. ISAKMP is intended to support SAs at all layers of the network stack. For this reason, ISAKMP can be implemented on the transport layer using TCP or User Datagram Protocol (UDP), or it can be implemented on IP directly.

Negotiation of an SA between servers occurs in two stages. First, the entities agree on how to secure negotiation messages (the ISAKMP SA). Once the entities have secured their negotiation traffic, they then determine the SAs for the protocols used for the remainder of their communications. Figure 7.5 shows the structure of the ISAKMP header. This header is used during both parts of the ISAKMP negotiation.

The Initiator Cookie is set by the entity requesting the SA, and the responder sets the Responder Cookie. The Payload byte indicates the type of the first payload to be encapsulated. Payload types include security associations, proposals, key transforms, key exchanges, vendor identities, and other things. The Major and Minor Revision fields refer to the major version number and minor version number for the ISAKMP. The Exchange Type helps determine the order of messages and payloads. The Flags bits indicate options for the ISAKMP exchange, including whether the payload is encrypted, whether the initiator and responder have "committed" to the SA, and whether the packet is to be authenticated only (and is not encrypted). The final fields of the ISAKMP header indicate the Message Identifier and a Message Length. Payloads encapsulated within ISAKMP use a generic header, and each payload has its own header format.

Once the ISAKMP SA is established, multiple protocol SAs can be established using the single ISAKMP SA. This feature is valuable due to the overhead associated with the two-stage negotiation. SAs are valid for specific periods of time, and once the time expires, the SA must be renegotiated. Many resources are also available for specific implementations of ISAKMP within the IPsec protocol.

Bit Position																															
0	1	2	3	4	5	6	7	8	9	10	11	12	13	14	15	16	17	18	19	20	21	22	23	24	25	26	27	28	29	30	31
Initiator Cookie (8 bytes)																															
Responder Cookie (8 bytes)																															
Payload (8 bits)								Major Rev. (4 bits)				Minor Rev. (4 bits)				Exchange Type (8 bits)								Flags (8 bits)							
Message Identifier (4 bytes)																															
Message Length (4 bytes)																															

• **Figure 7.5**   ISAKMP header format

■ CMP

The PKIX Certificate Management Protocol (CMP) is specified in RFC 4210. This protocol defines the messages and operations required to provide certificate management services within the PKIX model. Though part of the IETF PKIX effort, CMP provides a framework that works well with other standards, such as PKCS #7 and PKCS #10.

CMP provides for the following certificate operations:

- CA establishment, including creation of the initial CRL and export of the public key for the CA
- Certification of an end-entity, including the following:
  - Initial registration and certification of the end-entity (registration, certificate issuance, and placement of the certificate in a repository)
  - Updates to the key pair for end-entities, required periodically and when a key pair is compromised or keys cannot be recovered
  - End-entity certificate updates, required when a certificate expires
  - Periodic CA key-pair updates, similar to end-entity key-pair updates
  - Cross-certification requests, placed by other CAs
  - Certificate and CRL publication, performed under the appropriate conditions of certificate issuance and certificate revocation
  - Key-pair recovery, a service to restore key-pair information for an end-entity; for example, if a certificate password is lost or the certificate file is lost
  - Revocation requests, supporting requests by authorized entities to revoke a certificate

CMP also defines mechanisms for performing these operations, either online or offline using files, e-mail, tokens, or web operations.

■ XKMS

The XML Key Management Specification defines services to manage PKI operations within the Extensible Markup Language (XML) environment. These services are provided for handling PKI keys and certificates automatically. Developed by the World Wide Web Consortium (W3C), XKMS is intended to simplify integration of PKIs and management of certificates in applications. As well as responding to problems of authentication and verification of electronic signatures, XKMS also allows certificates to be managed, registered, or revoked.

XKMS services reside on a separate server that interacts with an established PKI. The services are accessible via a simple XML protocol. Developers can rely on the XKMS services, making it less complex to interface with the PKI. The services provide for retrieving key information (owner, key value, key issuer, and the like) and key management (such as key registration and revocation).

Retrieval operations rely on the XML signature for the necessary information. Three tiers of service are based on the client requests and application requirements. Tier 0 provides a means of retrieving key information by embedding references to the key within the XML signature. The signature contains an element called a *retrieval method* that indicates ways to resolve the key. In this case, the client sends a request, using the retrieval method, to obtain the desired key information. For example, if the verification key contains a long chain of X.509 v3 certificates, a retrieval method could be included to avoid sending the certificates with the document. The client would use the retrieval method to obtain the chain of certificates. For tier 0, the server indicated in the retrieval method responds directly to the request for the key, possibly bypassing the XKMS server. The tier 0 process is shown in Figure 7.6.

• **Figure 7.6**   XKMS tier 0 retrieval

With tier 1 operations, the client forwards the key-information portions of the XML signature to the XKMS server, relying on the server to perform the retrieval of the desired key information. The desired information can be local to the XKMS server, or it can reside on an external PKI system. The XKMS server provides no additional validation of the key information, such as checking whether the certificate has been revoked or is still valid. Just as in tier 0, the client performs final validation of the document. Tier 1 is called the *locate service* because it locates the appropriate key information for the client, as shown in Figure 7.7.

• **Figure 7.7**   XKMS tier 1 locate service

Tier 2 is called the *validate service* and is illustrated in Figure 7.8. In this case, just as in tier 1, the client relies on the XKMS service to retrieve the relevant key information from the external PKI. The XKMS server also performs data validation on a portion of the key information provided by the client for this purpose. This validation verifies the binding of the key information with the data indicated by the key information contained in the XML signature.

• **Figure 7.8**   XKMS tier 2 validate service

The primary difference between tier 1 and tier 2 is the level of involvement of the XKMS server. In tier 1, it can serve only as a relay or gateway between the client and the PKI. In tier 2, the XKMS server is actively involved in verifying the relation between the PKI information and the document containing the XML signature.

XKMS relies on the client or underlying communications mechanism to provide for the security of the communications with the XKMS server. The specification suggests using one of three methods for ensuring server authentication, response integrity, and relevance of the response to the request: digitally signed correspondence, a transport layer security protocol (such as SSL, TLS, or WTLS), or a packet layer security protocol (such as IPsec). Obviously, digitally signed correspondence introduces its own issues regarding validation of the signature, which is the purpose of XKMS.

It is possible to define other tiers of service. Tiers 3 and 4, an *assertion service* and an *assertion status service,* respectively, are mentioned in the defining XKMS specification, but they are not defined. The specification states they "could" be defined in other documents.

XKMS also provides services for key registration, key revocation, and key recovery. Authentication for these actions is based on a password or passphrase, which is provided when the keys are registered and when they must be recovered.

■ S/MIME

The **Secure/Multipurpose Internet Mail Extensions (S/MIME)** message specification is an extension to the MIME standard that provides a way to send and receive signed and encrypted MIME data. RSA Security created the first version of the S/MIME standard, using the RSA encryption algorithm and the PKCS series of standards. The second version dates from 1998 but had a number of serious restrictions, including the restriction to 40-bit Data Encryption Standard (DES). The current version of the IETF standard is dated July 2004 and requires the use of Advanced Encryption Standard (AES).

Cross Check

E-mail Encryption

Want to understand e-mail encryption? Flip ahead to Chapter 16 on e-mail and instant messaging for more details on e-mail encryption. Then answer these questions:

- Why is it important to encrypt e-mail?
- What impacts can malicious code have on a business?
- Why is instant messaging a higher risk than e-mail?

The changes in the S/MIME standard have been so frequent that the standard has become difficult to implement until v3. Far from having a stable standard for several years that product manufacturers could have time to gain experience with, there were many changes to the encryption algorithms being used. Just as importantly, and not immediately clear from the IETF documents, the standard places reliance upon more than one other standard for it to function. Key among these is the format of a public key certificate as expressed in the X.509 standard.

IETF S/MIME History

The S/MIME v2 specifications outline a basic strategy for providing security services for e-mail but lack many security features required by the Department of Defense (DoD) for use by the military. Shortly after the decision was made to revise the S/MIME v2 specifications, the DoD, its vendor community, and commercial industry met to begin development of the enhanced specifications. These new specifications would be known as S/MIME v3. Participants agreed that backward compatibility between S/MIME v3 and v2 should be preserved; otherwise, S/MIME v3–compatible applications would not be able to work with older S/MIME v2–compatible applications.

A minimum set of cryptographic algorithms was mandated so that different implementations of the new S/MIME v3 set of specifications could be interoperable. This minimum set must be implemented in an application for it to be considered S/MIME-compliant. Applications can implement additional cryptographic algorithms to meet their customers' needs, but the minimum set must also be present in the applications for interoperability with other S/MIME applications. Thus, users are not forced to use S/MIME-specified algorithms; they can choose their own, but if the application is to be considered S/MIME-compliant, the standard algorithms must also be present.

IETF S/MIME v3 Specifications

Building upon the original work by the IMC-organized group, the IETF has worked hard to enhance the S/MIME v3 specifications. The ultimate goal is to have the S/MIME v3 specifications receive recognition as an Internet standard. The current IETF S/MIME v3 set of specifications includes the following:

- Cryptographic Message Syntax (CMS)
- S/MIME v3 message specification
- S/MIME v3 certificate-handling specification
- Enhanced security services (ESS) for S/MIME

The CMS defines a standard syntax for transmitting cryptographic information about contents of a protected message. Originally based on the PKCS #7 version 1.5 specification, the CMS specification was enhanced by the IETF S/MIME working group to include optional security components. Just as the S/MIME v3 provides backward compatibility with v2, CMS provides backward compatibility with PKCS #7, so applications will be interoperable even if the new components are not implemented in a specific application.

Integrity, authentication, and nonrepudiation security features are provided by using digital signatures using the SignedData syntax described by the CMS. CMS also describes what is known as the EnvelopedData syntax to provide confidentiality of the message's content through the use of encryption. The PKCS #7 specification supports key encryption algorithms, such as RSA. Algorithm independence is promoted through the addition of several fields to the EnvelopedData syntax in CMS, which is the major difference between the PKCS #7 and CMS specifications. The goal was to be able to support specific algorithms such as Diffie-Hellman and the Key Exchange Algorithm (KEA), which is implemented on the Fortezza Crypto Card developed for the DoD. One final significant change to the original specifications is the ability to include X.509 Attribute Certificates in the SignedData and EnvelopedData syntaxes for CMS.

Tech Tip

S/MIME in a Nutshell
S/MIME provides two security services to e-mail: digital signatures and message encryption. Digital signatures verify sender identity, and encryption can keep contents private during transmission. These services can be used independently of each other, and provide the foundational basis for message security.

CMS Triple-Encapsulated Message

An interesting feature of CMS is the ability to nest security envelopes to provide a combination of security features. As an example, a CMS triple-encapsulated message can be created in which the original content and associated attributes are signed and encapsulated within the inner Signed-Data object. The inner SignedData object is in turn encrypted and encapsulated within an EnvelopedData object. The resulting EnvelopedData object is then also signed and finally encapsulated within a second SignedData object, the outer SignedData object. Usually the inner SignedData object is signed by the original user and the outer SignedData object is signed by another entity, such as a firewall or a mail list agent, providing an additional level of security.

This triple encapsulation is not required of every CMS object. All that is required is a single SignedData object created by the user to sign a message or an EnvelopedData object if the user desired to encrypt a message.

OpenPGP is a widely used e-mail encryption standard. A nonproprietary protocol for encrypting e-mail using public key cryptography, it is based on PGP as originally developed by Phil Zimmermann, and is defined by the OpenPGP working group of the IETF proposed standard RFC 4880.

PGP

Pretty Good Privacy (PGP) is a popular program that is used to encrypt and decrypt e-mail and files. It also provides the ability to digitally sign a message so the receiver can be certain of the sender's identity. Taken together, encrypting and signing a message allows the receiver to be assured of who sent the message and to know that it was not modified during transmission. Public-domain versions of PGP have been available for years, as have inexpensive commercial versions.

PGP was one of the most widely used programs and was frequently used by both individuals and businesses to ensure data and e-mail privacy. It was developed by Philip R. Zimmermann in 1991 and quickly became a de facto standard for e-mail security. The popularity of PGP lead to the OpenPGP Internet standard, RFC 4880, and open source solutions. GNU Privacy Guard (GPG) is a common alternative to PGP in use today.

How PGP Works

PGP uses a variation of the standard public key encryption process. In public key encryption, an individual (here called the *creator*) uses the encryption program to create a pair of keys. One key is known as the *public key* and is designed to be given freely to others. The other key is called the *private key* and is designed to be known only by the creator. Individuals who want to send a private message to the creator encrypt the message using the creator's public key. The algorithm is designed such that only the private key can decrypt the message, so only the creator will be able to decrypt it.

This method, known as *public key* or *asymmetric encryption,* is time consuming. *Symmetric encryption* uses only a single key and is generally faster. It is because of this that PGP is designed the way it is. PGP uses a symmetric encryption algorithm to encrypt the message to be sent. It then encrypts the symmetric key used to encrypt this message with the public

Tech Tip

A PGP Personal Note

After distributing PGP in 1991, including (indirectly) internationally, Zimmermann became a formal target of a criminal investigation by the U.S. government in 1993 for exporting munitions without a license, because cryptosystems using keys larger than 40 bits were considered "munitions" under U.S. export law. Zimmermann proceeded to publish the entire source code of PGP in a hardback book, which, unlike software, is protected from export laws by the First Amendment of the U.S. Constitution. The investigation of Zimmermann was dropped after several years.

key of the intended recipient. Both the encrypted key and message are then sent. The receiver's version of PGP first decrypts the symmetric key with the private key supplied by the recipient and then uses the resulting decrypted key to decrypt the rest of the message.

PGP can use two different public key algorithms: Rivest-Shamir-Adleman (RSA) and Diffie-Hellman. The RSA version uses the International Data Encryption Algorithm (IDEA) and a short symmetric key to encrypt the message and then uses RSA to encrypt the short IDEA key using the recipient's public key. The Diffie-Hellman version uses the Carlisle Adams and Stafford Tavares (CAST) algorithm to encrypt the message and the Diffie-Hellman algorithm to encrypt the CAST key. To decrypt the message, the reverse is performed. The recipient uses their private key to decrypt the IDEA or CAST key, and then uses that decrypted key to decrypt the message. These are both illustrated in Figure 7.9.

To generate a digital signature, PGP takes advantage of another property of public key encryption schemes. Normally, the sender encrypts using the receiver's public key and the message is decrypted at the other end using the receiver's private key. The process can be reversed so that the sender encrypts (signs) with his own private key. The receiver then decrypts the message with the sender's public key. Since the sender is the only individual who has a key that will correctly be decrypted with the sender's public key, the receiver knows that the message was created by the sender who claims to have sent it. The way PGP accomplishes this task is

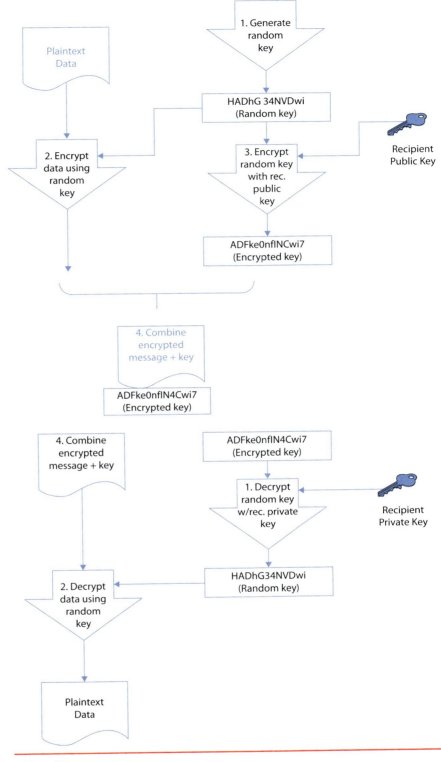

• **Figure 7.9** How PGP works for encryption

to generate a hash value from the user's name and other signature information. This hash value is then encrypted with the sender's private key known only by the sender. The receiver uses the sender's public key, which is available to everyone, to decrypt the hash value. If the decrypted hash value matches the hash value sent as the digital signature for the message, then the receiver is assured that the message was sent by the sender who claims to have sent it.

Typically, versions of PGP contain a user interface that works with common e-mail programs such as Microsoft Outlook. If you want others to be able to send you an encrypted message, you need to register your public key, generated by your PGP program, with a PGP public key server. Alternatively, you have to either send your public key to all those who want to send you an encrypted message or post your key to some location from which they can download it, such as your web page. Note that using a public key server is the better method, for all the reasons of trust described in the discussion of PKIs in Chapter 6.

HTTPS

Most web activity occurs using HTTP, but this protocol is prone to interception. HTTPS uses either SSL or TLS to secure the communication channel. Originally developed by Netscape Communications and implemented in its browser, HTTPS has since been incorporated into most common browsers. HTTPS uses the standard TCP port 443 for TCP/IP communications rather than the standard port 80 used for HTTP. As previously discussed, because of vulnerabilities in SSL, only TLS is recommended for HTTPS today.

IPsec

IPsec is a collection of IP security features designed to introduce security at the network or packet-processing layer in network communication. Other approaches have attempted to incorporate security at higher levels of the TCP/IP suite such as at the level where applications reside. IPsec is designed to provide secure IP communications over the Internet. In essence, IPsec provides a secure version of the IP by introducing authentication and encryption to protect Layer 4 protocols. IPsec is optional for IPv4 but is required for IPv6. Obviously, both ends of the communication need to use IPsec for the encryption/decryption process to occur.

IPsec provides two types of security service to ensure authentication and confidentiality for either the data alone (referred to as IPsec *transport mode*) or for both the data and header (referred to as *tunnel mode*). See Chapter 11 for more detail on tunneling and IPsec operation. IPsec introduces several new protocols, including the Authentication Header (AH), which basically provides authentication of the sender, and the Encapsulating Security Payload (ESP), which adds encryption of the data to ensure confidentiality.

IPsec also provides for payload compression before encryption using the IP Payload Compression Protocol (IPcomp). Frequently, encryption negatively impacts the ability of compression algorithms to fully compress data for transmission. By providing the ability to compress the data before encryption, IPsec addresses this issue.

■ CEP

Certificate Enrollment Protocol (CEP) was originally developed by VeriSign for Cisco Systems. It was designed to support certificate issuance, distribution, and revocation using existing technologies. Its use has grown in client and CA applications. The operations supported include CA and RA public key distribution, certificate enrollment, certificate revocation, certificate query, and CRL query.

One of the key goals of CEP was to use existing technology whenever possible. It uses both PKCS #7 (Cryptographic Message Syntax Standard) and PKCS #10 (Certification Request Syntax Standard) to define a common message syntax. It supports access to certificates and CRLs using either the Lightweight Directory Access Protocol (LDAP) or the CEP-defined certificate query.

■ Other Standards

There are many additional standards associated with information security that are not specifically or solely associated with PKI and/or cryptography. The remainder of the chapter will introduce these standards and protocols.

FIPS

The Federal Information Processing Standards Publications (FIPS PUBS or simply FIPS) describe various standards for data communication issues. These documents are issued by the U.S. government through the National Institute of Standards and Technology (NIST), which is tasked with their development. NIST creates these publications when a compelling government need requires a standard for use in areas such as security or system interoperability and no recognized industry standard exists. Three categories of FIPS PUBS are currently maintained by NIST:

- Hardware and software standards/guidelines
- Data standards/guidelines
- Computer security standards/guidelines

These documents require that products sold to the U.S. government comply with one (or more) of the FIPS standards. The standards can be obtained from www.nist.gov/itl/fips.cfm.

 FIPS 140-2 relates to specific cryptographic standards for the validation of components used in U.S. government systems. Systems can be accredited to the FIPS 140-2 standard to demonstrate levels of security from "approved algorithms" to higher levels that include additional protections up to and including physical security and tamperproof mechanisms.

Common Criteria

The Common Criteria for Information Technology Security (Common Criteria or CC) is the result of an effort to develop a joint set of security processes and standards that can be used by the international community. The major contributors to the CC are the governments of the United States, Canada, France, Germany, the Netherlands, and the United Kingdom. The CC also provides a listing of laboratories that apply the criteria in testing security products. Products that are evaluated by one of the approved laboratories receive an Evaluation Assurance Level of EAL1 through EAL7 (EAL7 is the highest level), with EAL4, for example, designed for environments requiring a moderate to high level of independently assured security, and EAL1 being designed for environments in which some confidence in the correct operation of the system is required but where the threats to the system are not considered serious. The CC also provides a listing of products by function that have performed at a specific EAL.

WTLS

The **Wireless Transport Layer Security (WTLS)** protocol is based on the TLS protocol. WTLS provides reliability and security for wireless communications using the **Wireless Application Protocol (WAP)**. WTLS is necessary due to the limited memory and processing abilities of WAP-enabled phones.

WTLS can be implemented in one of three classes: Class 1 is called *anonymous* authentication but is not designed for practical use. Class 2 is called *server* authentication and is the most common model. The clients and server may authenticate using different means. Class 3 is *server and client* authentication. In Class 3 authentication, the client's and server's WTLS certificates are authenticated. Class 3 is the strongest form of authentication and encryption.

ISO/IEC 27002 (Formerly ISO 17799)

ISO/IEC 27002 is a very popular and detailed standard for creating and implementing security policies. ISO/IEC 27002 was formerly ISO 17799, which was based on version 2 of the British Standard 7799 (BS7799) published in May 1999. With the increased emphasis placed on security in both the government and industry in recent years, many organizations are now training their audit personnel to evaluate their organizations against the ISO/IEC 27002 standard. The standard is divided into 12 sections, each containing more detailed statements describing what is involved for that topic:

- **Risk assessment**   Determine the impact of risks

- **Security policy**   Guidance and policy provided by management

- **Organization of information security**   Governance structure to implement security policy

- **Asset management**   Inventory and classification of assets

- **Human resources security**   Policies and procedures addressing security for employees including hires, changes, and departures

- **Physical and environmental security**   Protection of the computer facilities

- **Communications and operations management**   Management of technical security controls in systems and networks

- **Access control**   Restriction of access rights to networks, systems, applications, functions, and data

- **Information systems acquisition, development, and maintenance**   Building security into applications

- **Information security incident management**   Anticipating and responding appropriately to information security breaches

- **Business continuity management**   Protecting, maintaining, and recovering business-critical processes and systems

- **Compliance**   Ensuring conformance with information security policies, standards, laws, and regulations

SAML

Security Assertion Markup Language (SAML) is a single sign-on capability used for web applications to ensure user identities can be shared and are protected. It defines standards for exchanging authentication and authorization data between security domains. It is becoming increasingly important with cloud-based solutions and with Software-as-a-Service (SaaS) applications, because it ensures interoperability across identity providers.

SAML is an XML-based protocol that uses security tokens and assertions to pass information about a "principal" (typically an end user) with a SAML authority (an "identity provider" or IdP) and the service provider (SP). The principal requests a service from the SP which then requests and obtains an identity assertion from the IdP. The SP can then grant access or perform the requested service for the principal.

Chapter 7 Review

Chapter Summary

After reading this chapter and completing the exercises, you should understand the following about PKI standards and protocols.

Identify the standards involved in establishing an interoperable Internet PKI

- PKIX and PKCS define the most commonly used PKI standards.
- PKIX, PKCS, X.509, ISAKMP, XKMS, and CMP combine to implement PKI.
- SSL/TLS, S/MIME, HTTPS, and IPsec are protocols that use PKI.

Explain interoperability issues with PKI standards

- Standards and protocols are important because they define the basis for how communication will take place.
- The use of standards and protocols provides a common, interoperable environment for securely exchanging information.
- Without these standards and protocols, two entities may independently develop their own method to implement the various components for a PKI, and the two will not be compatible.
- On the Internet, not being compatible and not being able to communicate is not an option.

Describe how the common Internet protocols implement the PKI standards

- Three main standards have evolved over time to implement PKIs on the Internet.

- Two of the main standards are based on a third standard, the X.509 standard, and establish complementary standards for implementing PKIs. These two standards are Public Key Infrastructure X.509 (PKIX) and Public Key Cryptography Standards (PKCS).
- PKIX defines standards for interactions and operations for four component types: the user (end-entity), certificate authority (CA), registration authority (RA), and the repository for certificates and certificate revocation lists (CRLs).
- PKCS defines many of the lower-level standards for message syntax, cryptographic algorithms, and the like.
- There are other protocols and standards that help define the management and operation of the PKI and related services, such as ISAKMP, XKMS, and CMP.
- S/MIME is used to encrypt e-mail.
- SSL, TLS, and WTLS are used for secure packet transmission.
- IPsec is used to support virtual private networks.
- The Common Criteria establishes a series of criteria from which security products can be evaluated.
- The ISO/IEC 27002 standard provides a point from which security policies and practices can be developed in twelve areas.
- Various types of publications are available from NIST such as those found in the FIPS series.

Key Terms

certificate *(172)*
certificate authority (CA) *(169)*
certificate revocation list (CRL) *(169)*
Internet Security Association and Key Management Protocol (ISAKMP) *(174)*
IPsec *(182)*
Pretty Good Privacy (PGP) *(180)*
public key infrastructure (PKI) *(167)*

Secure/Multipurpose Internet Mail Extensions (S/MIME) *(178)*
Secure Sockets Layer (SSL) *(173)*
Security Assertion Markup Language (SAML) *(185)*
Transport Layer Security (TLS) *(173)*
Wireless Application Protocol (WAP) *(184)*
Wireless Transport Layer Security (WTLS) *(184)*
X.509 *(172)*

Key Terms Quiz

Use terms from the Key Terms list to complete the sentences that follow. Don't use the same term more than once. Not all terms will be used.

1. _____ is a protocol used to secure IP packets during transmission across a network. It offers authentication, integrity, and confidentiality services. It uses Authentication Headers (AHs) and Encapsulating Security Payload (ESP) to accomplish this functionality.

2. An encryption capability designed to encrypt above the transport layer, enabling secure sessions between hosts, is called _____.

3. A(n) _____ is an entity that is responsible for issuing and revoking certificates. This term is also applied to server software that provides these services.

4. A digitally signed object that lists all of the current but revoked certificates issued by a given certificate authority is called the _____. It allows users to verify whether a certificate is currently valid even if the expiration date hasn't passed.

5. _____ is a format that has been adopted to standardize digital certificates.

6. Infrastructure for binding a public key to a known user through a trusted intermediary, typically a certificate authority, is called the _____.

7. The _____ is a protocol framework that defines the mechanics of implementing a key exchange protocol and negotiation of a security policy.

8. The encryption protocol that is used on Wireless Application Protocol (WAP) networks is called _____.

9. A protocol for transmitting data to small handheld devices like cellular phones is the _____.

10. _____ is a popular encryption program that has the ability to encrypt and digitally sign e-mail and files.

Multiple-Choice Quiz

1. Which of the following is used to grant permissions using rule-based, role-based, and rank-based access controls?
   A. A Qualified Certificate
   B. A Control Certificate
   C. An Attribute Certificate
   D. An Optional Certificate

2. XKMS allows certificates to be all of the following except:
   A. Created
   B. Registered
   C. Managed
   D. Revoked

3. Transport Layer Security consists of which two protocols?
   A. The TLS Record Protocol and TLS Handshake Protocol
   B. The TLS Record Protocol and TLS Certificate Protocol
   C. The TLS Certificate Protocol and TLS Handshake Protocol
   D. The TLS Key Protocol and TLS Handshake Protocol

4. Which of the following provides a method for implementing a key exchange protocol?
   A. EISA
   B. ISAKMP
   C. ISA
   D. ISAKEY

5. Which of the following is a detailed standard for creating and implementing security policies?

   A. PKIX

   B. ISO/IEC 27002

   C. FIPS

   D. X.509

6. A relationship where two or more entities define how they will communicate securely is known as what?

   A. A three-way handshake

   B. A security association

   C. A three-way agreement

   D. A security agreement

7. What is the purpose of XKMS?

   A. Extends session associations over many transport protocols

   B. Encapsulates session associations over TCP/IP

   C. Defines services to manage heterogeneous PKI operations via XML

   D. Designed to replace SSL

8. Which of the following is a secure e-mail standard?

   A. POP3

   B. IMAP

   C. SMTP

   D. S/MIME

9. Which of the following is a joint set of security processes and standards used by approved laboratories to award an Evaluation Assurance Level (EAL) from EAL1 to EAL7?

   A. Common Criteria

   B. FIPS

   C. ISO 17700

   D. IEEE X.509

10. Transport Layer Security for HTTP uses what port to communicate?

    A. 53

    B. 80

    C. 143

    D. 443

■ Essay Quiz

1. You are the Information Security Officer at a medium-sized company (1500 employees). The CIO has asked you to explain why you recommend using commercial PKIs rather than implementing such a capability in-house with the software developers you already have. Write three succinct sentences that would get your point across and address three key issues.

2. Imagine you are a web developer for a small locally owned business. Explain when using HTTP would be satisfactory and why, and explain when you should use HTTPS and why.

3. Explain in your own words how, by applying both asymmetric and symmetric encryption, your browser uses TLS to protect the privacy of the information passing between your browser and a web server.

4. It is well understood that asymmetric encryption consumes more computing resources than symmetric encryption. Explain how PGP uses both asymmetric and symmetric encryption to be both secure and efficient.

Lab Projects

Note that for these lab projects, it would be best to have a partner so that you can each have your own pair of public/private keys to confirm the operation of PGP.

• Lab Project 7.1

Load either a trial version of PGP or Gnu Privacy Guard (GPG). Install it and create a public/private key pair for yourself. Create a document using a word processor and encrypt it using the receiver's public key. Send it to a partner (or yourself) and then decrypt it using the corresponding private key.

• Lab Project 7.2

Create another document different from the one used in Lab Project 7.1. This time use your private key to digitally sign the document and send it to a partner (or yourself) who can then use the public key to confirm that it really is from the indicated sender.

Physical Security

chapter 8

> *Baseball is 90 percent mental,*
> *the other half is physical.*
> —Yogi Berra

In this chapter, you will learn how to

- **Describe how physical security directly affects computer and network security**
- **Discuss steps that can be taken to help mitigate risks**
- **Identify the different types of fires and the various fire suppression systems designed to limit the damage caused by fires**
- **Explain electronic access controls and the principles of convergence**

For most homes, locks are the primary means of achieving physical security, and almost everyone locks the doors to his or her home upon leaving the residence. Some go even further and set up intrusion alarm systems in addition to locks. All these precautions are considered necessary because people believe they have something significant inside the house that needs to be protected, such as important possessions and important people.

Physical security is an important topic for businesses dealing with the security of networks and information systems. Businesses are responsible for securing their profitability, which requires securing a combination of assets: employees, product inventory, trade secrets, and strategy information. These and other important assets affect the profitability of a company and its future survival. Companies therefore perform many activities to attempt to provide physical security—locking doors, installing alarm systems, using safes, posting security guards, setting access controls, and more.

Most companies today have invested a large amount of time, money, and effort in both network security and information systems security. In this chapter, you will learn about how the strategies for securing the network and for securing information systems are linked, and you'll learn several methods by which companies can minimize their exposure to physical security events that can diminish their network security.

The Security Problem

The problem that faces professionals charged with securing a company's network can be stated rather simply: physical access negates all other security measures. No matter how impenetrable the firewall and intrusion detection system (IDS), if an attacker can find a way to walk up to and touch a server, he can break into it.

Consider that most network security measures are, from necessity, directed at protecting a company from Internet-based threats. Consequently, a lot of companies allow any kind of traffic on the local area network (LAN). So if an attacker attempts to gain access to a server over the Internet and fails, he may be able to gain physical access to the receptionist's machine and, by quickly compromising it, use it as a remotely controlled zombie to attack what he is really after. Figure 8.1 illustrates the use of a lower-privilege machine to obtain sensitive information. Physically securing information assets doesn't mean just the servers; it means protecting physical access to all the organization's computers and its entire network infrastructure.

Physical access to a corporation's systems can allow an attacker to perform a number of interesting activities, starting with simply plugging into an open Ethernet jack. The advent of handheld devices with the ability to run operating systems with full networking support has made this attack scenario even more feasible. Prior to handheld devices, the attacker would

• **Figure 8.1**   Using a lower-privilege machine to get at sensitive information

have to work in a secluded area with dedicated access to the Ethernet for a time. The attacker would sit down with a laptop and run a variety of tools against the network, and working internally typically put the attacker inside the firewall and IDS. Today's capable mobile devices can assist these efforts by allowing attackers to place the small device onto the network to act as a *wireless bridge,* as shown in Figure 8.2.

The attacker can then use a laptop to attack a network remotely via the bridge from outside the building. If power is available near the Ethernet jack, this type of attack can also be accomplished with an off-the-shelf access point. The attacker's only challenge is finding an Ethernet jack that isn't covered by furniture or some other obstruction.

Another simple attack that can be used when an attacker has physical access is called a **bootdisk**. Any media used to boot a computer into an operating system that is not the native OS on its hard drive could be classified as a bootdisk. These can be in the form of a floppy disk, CD, DVD, or a USB flash drive. Before bootable CDs or DVDs were available, a boot floppy was used to start the system and prepare the hard drives to load the operating system. A boot source can contain a number of programs, but the most typical ones would be NTFSDOS or a floppy-based Linux distribution that can be used to perform a number of tasks, including mounting the hard drives and performing at least read operations, all done via script. Once an attacker is able to read a hard drive, the password file can be copied off the machine for offline password-cracking attacks. If write access to the drive is obtained, the attacker could alter the password file or place a remote-control program to be executed automatically upon the next boot, guaranteeing continued access to the machine. Most new machines do not include floppy drives, so this attack is rapidly being replaced by the same concept with a USB device, CD, or DVD. The most obvious mitigation is to tell the BIOS not to boot from removable media, but this too has issues.

Attacker plugs a smartphone into an open Ethernet jack and uses 802.11 wireless to attack the network from outside the building.

• **Figure 8.2** A wireless bridge can allow remote access.

The bootable CD-ROMs and DVD-ROMs are actually more of a threat, because they are frequently used to carry a variety of software for updates and can utilize the much greater storage capacity of the CD or DVD media. This capacity can store an entire operating system and a complete tool set for a variety of tasks or malware, so when updating via CD/DVD, precautions must be taken to ensure the veracity of the media.

There are operating system distributions specifically designed to run the entire machine from an optical disc without using the hard drive. These are commonly referred to as LiveCDs. A **LiveCD** contains a bootable version of an entire operating system, typically a variant of Linux, complete with drivers for most devices. LiveCDs give an attacker a greater array of tools than could be loaded onto a floppy disk, such as scanners, sniffers, vulnerability exploits, forensic tools, drive imagers, password crackers, and so on. These sets of tools are too numerous to list here and are changing every day. The best resource is to search the Internet for popular LiveCD distributions like Kali/Backtrack, knoppix, and PHLAK. A sample collection of LiveCDs is shown in Figure 8.3.

• **Figure 8.3** A collection of sample LiveCDs

For example, with a LiveCD an attacker would likely have access to the hard disk and also to an operational network interface that would allow him to send the drive data over the Internet if properly connected. These bootable operating systems could also be custom built to contain any tool that runs under Linux, allowing an attacker to build a standard bootable attack image or a standard bootable foren-

 Try This!

Create a Bootdisk

Bootdisks allow you to boot a computer to the disk rather than the OS that is on the hard drive. Create a bootdisk for your own personal computer. The steps differ between different OSs and depending upon the media that you wish to make bootable. Perform a little research to determine the correct procedure for your OS and give it a try. Make a bootable CD/DVD or USB flash drive.

sic image, or something customized for the tools he likes to use. Bootable USB flash drives emulate the function of a CD-ROM and provide a device that is both physically smaller and logically larger. Cheap USB flash drives are now commonly available that provide greater than 32GB of storage, with more expensive versions stretching that capacity to 64, 128, and even 256GB. Electronic miniaturization has made these devices small enough to be unnoticed; a recent version extends only 5mm from the USB port. Made bootable, these devices can contain entire specialized operating systems, and unlike a bootable CD-ROM, these devices can also be written to, providing an offload point for collected data if an attacker chooses to leave the device and return later.

These types of devices have spawned a new kind of attack in which a CD, DVD, or flash drive is left in an opportunistic place where members of a target organization may pick up and use them. This CD/DVD or flash drive is typically loaded with malware and is referred to as a *road apple*. The attack relies on curious people to plug the device into their work computer to see what's on it. Occasionally the attacker may also try to tempt the passerby with enticing descriptions like "Employee Salaries" or even something as simple as "Confidential." Once a user loads the CD/DVD or flash drive, the malware will attempt to infect the machine. **Drive imaging** is the process of copying the entire contents of a hard drive to a single file on a different media. This process is often used by people who perform forensic investigations of computers. Typically, a bootable media is used to start the computer and load the drive imaging software. This software is designed to make a bit-by-bit copy of the hard drive in a file on another media, usually another hard drive or CD-R/DVD-R media. Drive imaging is used in investigations to make an exact copy that can be observed and taken apart, while keeping the original exactly as it was for evidence purposes.

From an attacker's perspective, drive imaging software is useful because it pulls *all* information from a computer's hard drive while still leaving the machine in its original state. The information contains every bit of data that is on the computer: any locally stored documents, locally stored e-mails, and every other piece of information that the hard drive contains. This data could be very valuable if the machine holds sensitive information about the company.

Physical access is the most common way of imaging a drive, and the biggest benefit for the attacker is that drive imaging leaves absolutely no trace of the crime. Besides physically securing access to your computers, you can do very little to prevent drive imaging, but you can minimize its impact. The use of encryption even for a few important files provides protection. Full encryption of the drive protects all files stored on it. Alternatively, placing files on a centralized file server keeps them from being imaged from an individual machine, but if an attacker is able to image the file server, the data will be copied.

Cross Check

Forensic Images

When taking a forensic-based image, it is important to follow proper forensic procedures to ensure the evidence is properly secured. Forensic processes and procedures are covered in detail in Chapter 23.

A denial-of-service (DoS) attack can also be performed with physical access. Physical access to the computers can be much more effective than a network-based DoS attack. Stealing a computer, using a bootdisk to erase all data on the drives, or simply unplugging computers are all effective DoS attacks. Depending on the company's quality and frequency of backing up critical systems, a DoS attack using these methods can have lasting effects.

Physical access can negate almost all the security that the network attempts to provide. Considering this, you must determine the level of physical access that attackers might obtain. Of special consideration are persons with authorized access to the building but who are not authorized users of the systems. Janitorial personnel and others have authorized access to many areas, but they do not have authorized system access. An attacker could pose as one of these individuals or attempt to gain access to the facilities through them.

Exam Tip: Drive imaging is a threat because all existing access controls to data can be bypassed and all the data stored on the drive can be read from the image.

Tech Tip

Encryption to TPM-Based Keys

Many computers now come with a security chip that follows the Trusted Platform Module standard. This TPM chip allows for the creation and storage of encryption keys. One of the strengths associated with this level of security is that if a copy of a drive, or even the drive itself, is stolen, the contents are unusable without the key. Having this key locked in hardware prevents hackers from stealing a copy of the key from a memory location.

■ Physical Security Safeguards

While it is difficult, if not impossible, to make an organization's computer systems totally secure, many steps can be taken to mitigate the risk to information systems from a physical threat. The following sections discuss access control methods and physical security policies and procedures that should be implemented.

Walls and Guards

The primary defense against a majority of physical attacks are the barriers between the assets and a potential attacker—walls, fences, gates, and doors. Some organizations also employ full- or part-time private security staff to attempt to protect their assets. These barriers provide the foundation upon which all other security initiatives are based, but the security must be designed carefully, as an attacker has to find only a single gap to gain access.

Walls may have been one of the first inventions of man. Once he learned to use natural obstacles such as mountains to separate him from his enemy, he next learned to build his *own* mountain for the same purpose. Hadrian's Wall in England, the Great Wall of China, and the Berlin Wall are all famous examples of such basic physical defenses. The walls of any building serve the same purpose, but on a smaller scale: they provide barriers to physical access to company assets. *Bollards* are small and round concrete pillars that are constructed and placed around a building to protect it from being damaged by someone driving a vehicle into the side of the building, or getting close and using a car bomb.

To protect the physical servers, you must look in all directions: Doors and windows should be safeguarded and a minimum number of each should be used in a server room. Less obvious entry points should also be considered: Is a drop ceiling used in the server room? Do the interior walls extend to the actual roof, raised floors, or crawlspaces? Access to the server room should be limited to the people who need access, not to all employees of the organization. If you are going to use a wall to protect an asset, make sure no obvious holes appear in that wall.

Fences

Outside of the building's walls, many organizations prefer to have a perimeter fence as a physical first layer of defense. Chain-link-type fencing is most commonly used, and it can be enhanced with barbed wire. Anti-scale fencing, which looks like very tall vertical poles placed close together to form a fence, is used for high-security implementations that require additional scale and tamper resistance.

To increase security against physical intrusion, higher fences can be employed. A fence that is three to four feet in height will deter casual or accidental trespassers. Six to seven feet will deter a general intruder. To deter more determined intruders, a minimum height of eight feet is recommended with the addition of barbed wire or razor wire on top for extreme levels of deterrence.

> **Exam Tip:** All entry points to server rooms and wiring closets should be closely controlled, and, if possible, access should be logged through an access control system.

> Another method of preventing surreptitious access is through the use of windows. Many high-security areas have a significant number of windows so that people's activities within the area can't be hidden. A closed server room with no windows makes for a quiet place for someone to achieve physical access to a device without worry of being seen. Windows remove this privacy element that many criminals depend upon to achieve their entry and illicit activities. Too many windows makes it easy to shoulder surf — balance is the key,

Guards

Guards provide an excellent security measure, because guards are a visible presence with direct responsibility for security. Other employees expect security guards to behave a certain way with regard to securing the facility. Guards typically monitor entrances and exits and can maintain access logs of who has entered and departed the building. In many organizations, everyone who passes through security as a visitor must sign the log, which can be useful in tracing who was at what location and why.

Security personnel are helpful in physically securing the machines on which information assets reside, but to get the most benefit from their presence, they must be trained to take a holistic approach to security. The value of data typically can be many times that of the machines on which the data is stored. Security guards typically are not computer security experts, so they need to be educated about the value of the data and be trained in network security as well as physical security involving users. They are the company's eyes and ears for suspicious activity, so the network security department needs to train them to notice suspicious network activity as well. Multiple extensions ringing in sequence during the night, computers rebooting all at once, or strange people parked in the parking lot with laptop computers are all indicators of a network attack that might be missed without proper training.

Many traditional physical security tools such as access controls and CCTV camera systems are transitioning from closed hardwired systems to Ethernet- and IP-based systems. This transition opens up the devices to network attacks traditionally performed on computers. With physical security systems being implemented using the IP network, everyone in physical security must become smarter about network security.

The bigger challenge associated with capturing surveillance activities or other attempted break-in efforts is their clandestine nature. These efforts are designed to be as low profile and nonobvious as possible to increase the chances of success. Training and awareness is necessary not just for security personnel but for all personnel. If an employee hears multiple extensions all start ringing in the middle of the night, do they know who to notify? If a security guard notes such activity, how does this information get reported to the correct team?

Physical Access Controls and Monitoring

Physical access control means control of doors and entry points. The design and construction of all types of access control systems, as well as the physical barriers to which they are most complementary, are fully discussed in other texts. Here, we explore a few important points to help you safeguard the information infrastructure, especially where it meets with the physical access control system. This section talks about physical locks, layered access systems, and electronic access control systems. It also discusses closed circuit television (CCTV) systems and the implications of different CCTV system types.

Locks

Locks have been discussed as a primary element of security. Although locks have been used for hundreds of years, their design has not changed much: a metal "token" is used to align pins in a mechanical device. As all mechanical devices have tolerances, it is possible to *sneak through* these tolerances by "picking" the lock. Most locks can be easily picked with simple tools, some of which are shown in Figure 8.4.

As we humans are always trying to build a better mousetrap, high-security locks have been designed to defeat attacks, such as the

• **Figure 8.4** Lockpicking tools

196

Principles of Computer Security

one shown in Figure 8.5; these locks are more sophisticated than a standard home deadbolt system. Typically found in commercial applications that require high security, these locks are made to resist picking and drilling, as well as other common attacks such as simply pounding the lock through the door. Another common feature of high-security locks is *key control*, which refers to the restrictions placed on making a copy of the key. For most residential locks, a trip to the hardware store will allow you to make a copy of the key. Key control locks use patented keyways that can only be copied at a locksmith, who will keep records on authorized users of a particular key.

High-end lock security is more important now that attacks such as "bump keys" are well known and widely available. A bump key is a key cut with all notches to the maximum depth, also known as "all nines." This key uses a technique that has been around a long time, but has recently gained a lot of popularity. The key is inserted into the lock and then sharply struck, bouncing the lock pins up above the shear line and allowing the lock to open. High-security locks attempt to prevent this type of attack through various mechanical means such as nontraditional pin layout, sidebars, and even magnetic keys.

Other physical locks include programmable or cipher locks; locks with a keypad that require a combination of keys to open the lock; and locks with a reader that require an access card to open the lock. These may have special options such as a hostage alarm (support a key combination to trigger an alarm). Master-keying (support key combinations to change the access code and configure the functions of the lock) and key-override functions (support key combinations to override the usual procedures) are also options on high-end programmable locks.

Device locks are used to lock a device to a physical restraint, preventing its removal. Another method of securing laptops and mobile devices is a cable trap, which allows a user to affix a cable lock to a secure structure.

Layered Access

Layered access is an important concept in security. It is often mentioned in conversations about network security perimeters, but in this chapter it relates to the concept of physical security perimeters. To help prevent an attacker from gaining access to important assets, these assets should be placed inside multiple perimeters. Servers should be placed in a separate secure area, ideally with a separate authentication mechanism. For example, if an organization has an electronic door control system using **contactless access cards** (such as the example shown in Figure 8.6) as well as a keypad, a combination of the card and a separate PIN code would be required to open the door to the server room.

Access to the server room should be limited to staff with a legitimate need to work on the servers. To layer the protection, the area surrounding the server room should also be limited to people who need to work in that area.

Electronic Access Control Systems

Many organizations use electronic access control systems to control the opening of doors. The use of proximity readers and contactless access cards provides user information to the control panel.

• **Figure 8.5** A high-security lock and its key

Exam Tip: Layered access is a form of defense in depth, a principle component of any strong security solution.

• **Figure 8.6** Contactless access cards act as modern keys to a building.

Doorways are electronically controlled via electronic door strikes and magnetic locks. These devices rely on an electronic signal from the control panel to release the mechanism that keeps the door closed. These devices are integrated into an access control system that controls and logs entry into all the doors connected to it, typically through the use of access tokens. Security is improved by having a centralized system that can instantly grant or refuse access based upon access lists and the reading of a token that is given to the user. This kind of system also logs user access, providing nonrepudiation of a specific user's presence in a controlled environment. The system will allow logging of personnel entry, auditing of personnel movements, and real-time monitoring of the access controls.

One caution about these kinds of systems is that they usually work with a software package that runs on a computer, and as such this computer should not be attached to the company network. While attaching it to the network can allow easy administration, the last thing you want is for an attacker to have control of the system that allows physical access to your facility. With this control, an attacker could input the ID of a badge that she owns, allowing full, legitimate access to an area the system controls. Another problem with such a system is that it logs only the person who initially used the card to open the door—so no logs exist for doors that are propped open to allow others access, or of people "tailgating" through a door opened with a card. The implementation of a **mantrap** is one way to combat tailgating. A mantrap comprises two doors closely spaced that require the user to card through one and then the other *sequentially*. Mantraps make it nearly impossible to trail through a doorway undetected—if you happen to catch the first door, you will be trapped in by the second door.

Doors

Doors to secured areas should have characteristics to make them less obvious. They should have similar appearance to the other doors to avoid catching the attention of intruders. Security doors should be self-closing and have no hold-open feature. They should trigger alarms if they are forcibly opened or have been held open for a long period.

Door systems, like many systems, have two design methodologies: fail-safe or fail-secure. While *fail-safe* is a common enough phrase to have entered the lexicon, think about what it really means—being safe when a system fails. In the case of these electronic door systems, fail-safe means that the door is unlocked should power fail. To *fail-secure* means that the system will lock the door when power is lost. This can also apply when door systems are manually bypassed. It is important to know how each door will react to a system failure, not only for security but also for fire code compliance, as fail-secure is not allowed for certain doors in a building.

Cameras

Closed circuit television (CCTV) cameras are similar to the door control systems—they can be very effective, but how they are implemented is an important consideration. The use of CCTV cameras for surveillance purposes dates back to at least 1961, when cameras were installed in the London Transport train station. The development of smaller and more sophisticated camera components and decreasing prices for the cameras have caused a boon in the CCTV industry since then.

CCTV cameras are used to monitor a workplace for security purposes. These systems are commonplace in banks and jewelry stores, places with high-value merchandise that is attractive to thieves. As the expense of these systems dropped, they became practical for many more industry segments. Traditional cameras are analog based and require a video multiplexer to combine all the signals and make multiple views appear on a monitor. IP-based cameras are changing that, as most of them are stand-alone units viewable through a web browser, such as the camera shown in Figure 8.7.

These IP-based systems add useful functionality, such as the ability to check on the building from the Internet. This network functionality, however, makes the cameras subject to normal IP-based network attacks. A DoS attack launched at the CCTV system just as a break-in is occurring is the last thing that anyone would want (other than the criminals). For this reason, IP-based CCTV cameras should be placed on their own separate network that can be accessed only by security personnel. The same physical separation applies to any IP-based camera infrastructure. Older time-lapse tape recorders are slowly being replaced with digital video recorders. While the advance in technology is significant, be careful if and when these devices become IP-enabled, since they will become a security issue, just like everything else that touches the network.

If you depend on the CCTV system to protect your organization's assets, carefully consider camera placement and the type of cameras used. Different iris types, focal lengths, and color or infrared capabilities are all options that make one camera superior to another in a specific location.

Alarms

There are several types of alarm systems. Local alarm systems ring only locally. A central station system is one where alarms (and CCTV) are monitored by a central station. Many alarms will have auxiliary or secondary reporting functions to local police or fire departments. Alarms work by alerting personnel to the triggering of specific monitoring controls. Typical controls include the following:

- Dry contact switches use metallic foil tape as a contact detector to detect whether a door or window is opened.

- Electro-mechanical detection systems detect a change or break in a circuit. They can be used as a contact detector to detect whether a door or window is opened.

- Vibration detection systems detect movement on walls, ceiling, floors, and so forth by vibration.

- Pressure mats detect whether someone is stepping on the mat.

- Photoelectric or photometric detection systems emit a beam of light and monitor the beam to detect for motion and break-in.

- Wave pattern motion detectors generate microwave or ultrasonic wave and monitor the emitted waves to detect for motion.

- Passive infrared detection systems detect changes of heat waves generated by an intruder.

Tech Tip

PTZ Cameras

Pan-tilt-zoom (PTZ) cameras *are cameras that have the functionality to enable camera movement in multiple axes, as well as the ability to zoom in on an item. These cameras provide additional capability, especially in situations where the video is monitored and the monitoring station can maneuver the camera.*

• **Figure 8.7**   IP-based cameras leverage existing IP networks instead of needing a proprietary CCTV cable.

- Audio or acoustical-seismic detection systems listen for changes in noise levels.
- Proximity detectors or capacitance detectors emit a magnetic field and monitor the field to detect any interruption.

Convergence

There is a trend to converge elements of physical and information security to improve identification of unauthorized activity on networks. If a access control system is asked to approve access to an insider using an outside address, yet the physical security system identifies them as being in the building, then an anomaly exists and should be investigated. This trend is called **convergence** and can significantly improve defenses against cloned credentials.

Policies and Procedures

A policy's effectiveness depends on the culture of an organization, so all of the policies mentioned here should be followed up by functional procedures that are designed to implement them. Physical security **policies and procedures** relate to two distinct areas: those that affect the computers themselves and those that affect users.

To mitigate the risk to computers, physical security needs to be extended to the computers themselves. To combat the threat of bootdisks, begin by removing or disabling the ability of a system to automatically play connected devices, such as USB flash drives. Other activities that typically require physical presence should be protected, such as access to a system's BIOS at bootup.

 Try This!

Exploring Your BIOS Settings

Next time you boot your PC, explore the BIOS settings. Usually, pressing the F2 key immediately on power-up will allow you to enter the BIOS setup screens. Most PCs will also have a brief time when they prompt for "Setup" and give a key to press, most commonly F2, or F12. Explore elements such as the boot order for devices, options for adding passwords, and other options. For safety, do not save changes unless you are absolutely certain that you want to make those changes and are aware of the consequences. To prevent an attacker from editing the boot order, you should set **BIOS passwords**.

BIOS

A safeguard that can be employed is the removal of removable media devices from the boot sequence in the computer's BIOS (basic input/output system). The specifics of this operation depend on the BIOS software of the individual machine. A related step that must be taken is to set a BIOS password. Nearly all BIOS software will support password protection that allows you to boot the machine but requires a password to edit any BIOS settings. While disabling the optical drive and setting a BIOS password are both good measures, do not depend on this strategy exclusively because, in some cases, BIOS manufacturers will have a default BIOS password that still works.

⚠️ Depending upon BIOS passwords is also not a guaranteed security measure. For many machines, it is trivial to remove and then replace the BIOS battery, which will reset the BIOS to the "no password" or default password state.

UEFI

Unified Extensible Firmware Interface (UEFI) is a standard firmware interface for PCs, designed to replace BIOS. Supported by Mac OS X, Linux (later versions), and Windows 8 and beyond, UEFI offers some significant security advantages. UEFI has a functionality known as secure boot, which

Principles of Computer Security

allows only digitally signed drivers and OS loaders to be used during the boot process, preventing bootkit attacks. As UEFI is replacing BIOS, and has additional characteristics, it is important to keep policies and procedures current with the advancement of technology.

USB

USB ports have greatly expanded users' ability to connect devices to their computers. USB ports automatically recognize a device being plugged into the system and usually work without the user needing to add drivers or configure software. This has spawned a legion of **USB devices**, from MP3 players to CD burners.

The most interesting of these, for security purposes, are the USB flash memory–based storage devices. USB drive keys, which are basically flash memory with a USB interface in a device typically about the size of your thumb, provide a way to move files easily from computer to computer. When plugged into a USB port, these devices automount and behave like any other drive attached to the computer. Their small size and relatively large capacity, coupled with instant read-write ability, present security problems. They can easily be used by an individual with malicious intent to conceal the removal of files or data from the building or to bring malicious files into the building and onto the company network.

In addition, well-intentioned users could accidentally introduce malicious code from USB devices by using them on an infected home machine and then bringing the infected device to the office, allowing the malware to bypass perimeter protections and possibly infect the organization. If USB devices are allowed, aggressive virus scanning should be implemented throughout the organization. The devices can be disallowed via Active Directory policy settings or with a Windows Registry key entry. USB can also be completely disabled, either through BIOS settings or by unloading and disabling the USB drivers from users' machines, either of which will stop all USB devices from working—however, doing this can create more trouble if users have USB keyboards and mice. There are two common ways to disable USB support in a Windows system. On older systems, editing the Registry key is probably the most effective solution for users who are not authorized to use these devices. On newer systems, the best way is through Group Policy in a domain or through the Local Security Policy MMC on a stand-alone box.

Autoplay

Another boot device to consider is the CD/DVD drive. This device can probably also be removed from or disabled on a number of machines. A DVD not only can be used as a boot device, but also can be exploited via the **autoplay** feature that some operating systems support. Autoplay was designed as a convenience for users, so that when a CD/DVD or USB containing an application is inserted, the computer instantly prompts for input versus requiring the user to explore the device filesystem and find the executable file. Unfortunately, since the autoplay functionality runs an executable, it can be programmed to do anything an attacker wants. If an autoplay executable is malicious, it could allow an attacker to gain remote control of the machine. Figure 8.8 illustrates an autoplay message prompt in Windows, giving a user at least minimal control over whether to run an item or not.

Exam Tip: USB devices can be used to inject malicious code onto any machine to which they are attached. They can be used to transport malicious code from machine to machine without using the network.

Laptops and tablets are popular targets for thieves and should be locked inside a desk when not in use, or secured with special computer lockdown cables. If desktop towers are used, use computer desks that provide a space in which to lock the computer. All of these measures can improve the physical security of the computers themselves, but most of them can be defeated by attackers if users are not knowledgeable about the security program and do not follow it.

• **Figure 8.8**   Autoplay on a Windows system

• **Figure 8.9** A LiveCD boots its own OS and bypasses any built-in security of the native operating system.

Since the optical drive can be used as a boot device, a DVD loaded with its own operating system (called a *LiveCD*, introduced earlier in the chapter) could be used to boot the computer with malicious system code (see Figure 8.9). This separate operating system will bypass any passwords on the host machine and can access locally stored files.

Tech Tip

Disabling the Autoplay Feature in Windows

Disabling the autoplay feature is an easy task using Local Group Policy Editor in Windows. Simply launch the Local Group Policy Editor (gpedit.msc) and navigate to this location:

Computer Configuration > Administrative Templates > Windows Components > AutoPlay Policies

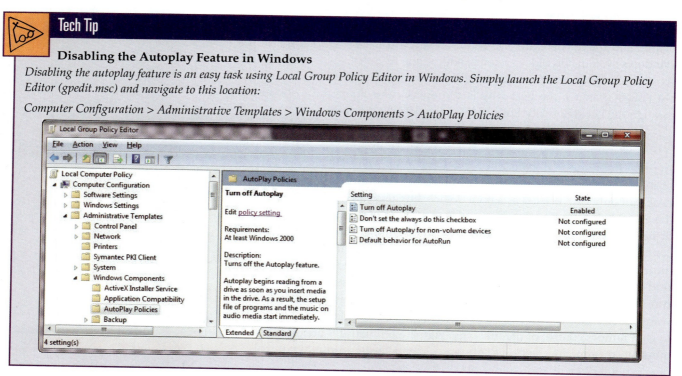

Principles of Computer Security

Device Theft

The outright theft of a computer is a simple physical attack. This attack can be mitigated in a number of ways, but the most effective method is to lock up equipment that contains important data. Insurance can cover the loss of the physical equipment, but this can do little to get a business up and running again quickly after a theft. Therefore, implementing special access controls for server rooms and simply locking the rack cabinets when maintenance is not being performed are good ways to secure an area. From a data standpoint, mission-critical or high-value information should be stored on a server only. This can mitigate the risk of a desktop or laptop being stolen for the data it contains. Loss of laptops has been a common cause of information breaches.

 Mobile device thefts from cars and other locations can occur in seconds. Thieves have been caught taking mobile devices from security screening areas at airports while the owner was distracted in screening. Snatch and grab attacks occur in restaurants, bars, and cafes. Tablets and smartphones have significant value and physical precautions should be taken at all times.

Cross Check

Mobile Device Security

Mobile device security is covered in depth in Chapter 14. For a more detailed analysis of safeguards unique to mobile devices, please refer to that section of the text.

Users can perform one of the most simple, yet important, information security tasks: lock a workstation immediately before they step away from it.

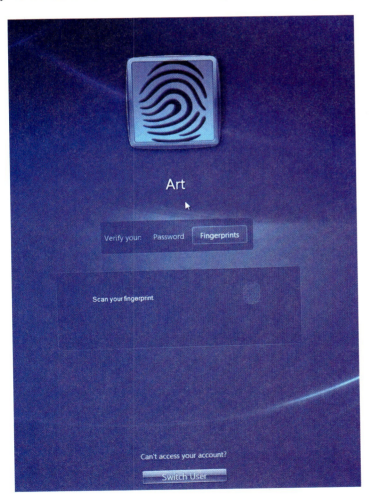

Although use of a self-locking screensaver is a good policy, setting it to lock at any point less than 10 to 15 minutes after becoming idle is often considered a nuisance and counterproductive to active use of the computer on the job as the computer will often lock while the employee is still actively using the computer. Thus, computers typically sit idle for at least 15 minutes before automatically locking under this type of policy. Users should manually lock their workstations, as an attacker only needs to be lucky enough to catch a machine that has been left alone for 5 minutes.

Environmental Controls

While the confidentiality of information is important, so is its availability. Sophisticated environmental controls are needed for current data centers. Servers can generate large levels of heat, and managing the heat is the job of the environmental control.

Controlling a data center's temperature and humidity is important to keeping servers running. Heating ventilating and air conditioning (HVAC) systems are critical for keeping data centers cool, because typical servers put out between 1000 and 2000 BTUs of heat. The temperature of a data center should be maintained between 70 and 74 degrees Fahrenheit (°F). If the temperature is too low, it may cause mechanisms to slow down. If the temperature is too high, it may cause equipment damage. The temperature-damaging points of different products are as follows:

- Magnetic media: 100°F
- Computer hardware: 175°F
- Paper products: 350°F

It should be noted that these are temperatures of the materials; the surrounding air is frequently cooler. Temperature measurements should be obtained on equipment itself to ensure appropriate protection.

Multiple servers in a confined area can create conditions too hot for the machines to continue to operate. This problem is made worse with the advent of blade-style computing systems and with many other devices shrinking in size. While physically smaller, they tend to still expel the same amount of heat. This is known as *increased data center density*—more servers and devices per rack, putting a greater load on the cooling systems. This encourages the use of a hot aisle/cold aisle layout. A data center that is arranged into hot and cold aisles dictates that all the intake fans on all equipment face the cold aisle, and the exhaust fans all face the opposite aisle. The HVAC system is then designed to push cool air underneath the raised floor and up through perforated tiles on the cold aisle. Hot air from the hot aisle is captured by return air ducts for the HVAC system. The use of this layout is designed to control airflow, with the purpose being never to mix the hot and cold air. This requires the use of blocking plates and side plates to close open rack slots. The benefits of this arrangement are that cooling is more efficient and can handle higher density. The failure of HVAC systems for any reason is cause for concern. Rising copper prices have made HVAC systems the targets for thieves, and general vandalism can result in costly downtime. Properly securing these systems is important in helping prevent an attacker from performing a physical DoS attack on your servers.

BTU stands for British Thermal Unit; a single BTU is defined as the amount of energy required to raise the temperature of one pound of liquid water one degree Fahrenheit.

Fire Suppression

According to the Fire Suppression Systems Association (www.fssa.net), 43 percent of businesses that close as a result of a significant fire never reopen. An additional 29 percent fail within three years of the event. The ability to respond to a fire quickly and effectively is thus critical to the long-term success of any organization. Addressing potential fire hazards and vulnerabilities has long been a concern of organizations in their risk analysis process. The goal obviously should be never to have a fire, but in the event that one does occur, it is important that mechanisms are in place to limit the damage the fire can cause.

Water-Based Fire Suppression Systems

Water-based fire suppression systems have long been, and still are today, the primary tool to address and control structural fires. Considering the amount of electrical equipment found in today's office environment and the fact that, for obvious reasons, this equipment does not react well to large applications of water, it is important to know what to do with equipment if it does become subjected to a water-based sprinkler system. The National Fire Protection Association's 2013 *NFPA 75: Standard for the Protection of Information Technology Equipment* outlines measures that can be taken to minimize the damage to electronic equipment exposed to water. This guidance includes these suggestions:

- Open cabinet doors, remove side panels and covers, and pull out chassis drawers to allow water to run out of equipment.

- Set up fans to move room-temperature air through the equipment for general drying. Move portable equipment to dry air-conditioned areas.

- Use compressed air at no higher than 50 psi to blow out trapped water.

- Use handheld dryers on lowest setting to dry connectors, backplane wirewraps, and printed circuit cards.

- Use cotton-tipped swabs for hard-to-reach places. Lightly dab the surfaces to remove residual moisture.

Even if these guidelines are followed, damage to the systems may have already occurred. Since water is so destructive to electronic equipment, not only because of the immediate problems of electronic shorts to the system but also because of longer-term corrosive damage water can cause, alternative fire suppression methods have been sought.

Halon-Based Fire Suppression Systems

A fire needs fuel, oxygen, and high temperatures for the chemical combustion to occur. If you remove any of these, the fire will not continue. Halon interferes with the chemical combustion present in a fire. Even though halon production was banned in 1994, a number of these systems still exist today. They were originally popular because halon will mix quickly with the air

Keep the dryers well away from components and wires. Overheating of electrical components can cause permanent damage.

in a room and will not cause harm to computer systems. Halon is, however, dangerous to humans, especially when subjected to extremely hot temperatures (such as might be found during a fire), when it can degrade into other toxic chemicals. As a result of these dangers, and also because halon has been linked with the issue of ozone depletion, halon is banned in new fire suppression systems. It is important to note that under the Environmental Protection Agency (EPA) rules that mandated no further production of halon, existing systems were not required to be destroyed. Replacing the halon in a discharged system, however, will be a problem, since only existing stockpiles of halon may be used and the cost is becoming prohibitive. For this reason, many organizations are switching to alternative solutions.

Clean-Agent Fire Suppression Systems

These alternatives are known as *clean-agent fire suppression systems,* since they not only provide fire suppression capabilities but also protect the contents of the room, including people, documents, and electronic equipment. Examples of clean agents include carbon dioxide, argon, Inergen, and FM-200 (heptafluoropropane). Carbon dioxide (CO_2) has been used as a fire suppression agent for a long time. The Bell Telephone Company used portable CO_2 extinguishers in the early part of the 20th century. Carbon dioxide extinguishers attack all three necessary elements for a fire to occur. CO_2 displaces oxygen so that the amount of oxygen remaining is insufficient to sustain the fire. It also provides some cooling in the fire zone and reduces the concentration of "gasified" fuel. Argon extinguishes fire by lowering the oxygen concentration below the 15 percent level required for combustible items to burn. Argon systems are designed to reduce the oxygen content to about 12.5 percent, which is below the 15 percent needed for the fire but is still above the 10 percent required by the EPA for human safety. Inergen, a product of Ansul Corporation, is composed of three gases: 52 percent nitrogen, 40 percent argon, and 8 percent carbon dioxide. In a manner similar to pure argon systems, Inergen systems reduce the level of oxygen to about 12.5 percent, which is sufficient for human safety but not sufficient to sustain a fire. Another chemical used in the phase-out of halon is FE-13, or trifluoromethane. This chemical was originally developed as a chemical refrigerant and works to suppress fires by inhibiting the combustion chain reaction. FE-13 is gaseous, leaves behind no residue that would harm equipment, and is considered safe to use in occupied areas. Other halocarbons are also approved for use in replacing halon systems, including FM-200 (heptafluoropropane), a chemical used as a propellant for asthma medication dispensers.

Handheld Fire Extinguishers

Automatic fire suppression systems designed to discharge when a fire is detected are not the only systems you should be aware of. If a fire can be caught and contained before the automatic systems discharge, it can mean significant savings to the organization in terms of both time and equipment costs (including the recharging of the automatic system). Handheld extinguishers are common in offices, but the correct use of them must be understood or disaster can occur. There are four different types of fire, as shown in Table 8.1. Each type of fire has its own fuel source and method for

Table 8.1	Types of Fire and Suppression Methods		
Class of Fire	Type of Fire	Examples of Combustible Materials	Example Suppression Method
A	Common combustibles	Wood, paper, cloth, plastics	Water or dry chemical
B	Combustible liquids	Petroleum products, organic solvents	CO_2 or dry chemical
C	Electrical	Electrical wiring and equipment, power tools	CO_2 or dry chemical
D	Flammable metals	Magnesium, titanium	Copper metal or sodium chloride

extinguishing it. Type A systems, for example, are designed to extinguish fires with normal combustible material as the fire's source. Water can be used in an extinguisher of this sort, since it is effective against fires of this type. Water, as we've discussed, is not appropriate for fires involving wiring or electrical equipment. Using a type A extinguisher against an electrical fire will not only be ineffective but can result in additional damage. Some extinguishers are designed to be effective against more than one type of fire, such as the common ABC fire extinguishers. This is probably the best type of system to have in a data processing facility. All fire extinguishers should be easily accessible and should be clearly marked. Before anybody uses an extinguisher, they should know what type of extinguisher it is and what the source of the fire is. When in doubt, evacuate and let the fire department handle the situation.

Exam Tip: The type of fire distinguishes the type of extinguisher that should be used to suppress it. Remember that the most common type is the ABC fire extinguisher, which is designed to handle all types of fires except flammable-metal fires, which are rare.

 Try This!

Handheld Fire Extinguishers

Computer security professionals typically do not have much influence over the type of fire suppression system that their office includes. It is, however, important that they are aware of what type has been installed, what they should do in case of an emergency, and what needs to be done to recover after the release of the system. One area that they can influence, however, is the type of handheld fire extinguisher that is located in their area. Check your facility to see what type of fire suppression system is installed. Also check to see where the fire extinguishers are in your office and what type of fires they are designed to handle.

Fire Detection Devices

An essential complement to fire suppression systems and devices are fire detection devices (fire detectors). Detectors may be able to detect a fire in its very early stages, before a fire suppression system is activated, and sound a warning that potentially enables employees to address the fire before it becomes serious enough for the fire suppression equipment to kick in.

There are several different types of fire detectors. One type, of which there are two varieties, is activated by smoke. The two varieties of smoke detector are ionization and photoelectric. A photoelectric detector is good for potentially providing advance warning of a smoldering fire. This type of device monitors an internal beam of light. If something degrades the

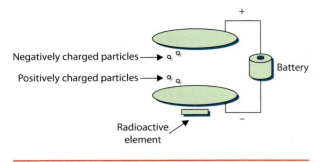

Negatively charged particles →

Positively charged particles →

Battery

Radioactive
element

• **Figure 8.10** An ionization chamber for an ionization type
of smoke detector

light, for example by obstructing it, the detector assumes it is something like smoke and the alarm sounds. An ionization style of detector uses an ionization chamber and a small radioactive source to detect fast-burning fires. Shown in Figure 8.10, the chamber consists of two plates, one with a positive charge and one with a negative charge. Oxygen and nitrogen particles in the air become "ionized" (an ion is freed from the molecule). The freed ion, which has a negative charge, is attracted to the positive plate, and the remaining part of the molecule, now with a positive charge, is attracted to the negative plate. This movement of particles creates a very small electric current that the device measures. Smoke inhibits this process, and the detector will detect the resulting drop in current and sound an alarm. Both of these devices are often referred to generically as smoke detectors, and combinations of both varieties are possible. For more information on smoke detectors, see http://home.howstuffworks.com/home-improvement/household-safety/fire/smoke2.htm.

Another type of fire detector is activated by heat. These devices also come in two varieties. Fixed-temperature or fixed-point devices activate if the temperature in the area ever exceeds some predefined level. Rate-of-rise or rate-of-increase temperature devices activate when there is a sudden increase in local temperature that may indicate the beginning stages of a fire. Rate-of-rise sensors can provide an earlier warning but are also responsible for more false warnings.

A third type of detector is flame activated. This type of device relies on the flames from the fire to provide a change in the infrared energy that can be detected. Flame-activated devices are generally more expensive than the other two types but can frequently detect a fire sooner.

Tech Tip

Testing Controls

Because of the importance of their protection, safety controls should be periodically tested for proper operation and alerting. This should be a system-level, not device-level, test to ensure the entire control system performs in the intended manner.

Tech Tip

UPS Attributes

UPS systems have several attributes to consider:

■ *The electrical load they can support (measured in kVA)*

■ *The length of time they can support the load*

■ *The speed of providing power when there is a power failure*

■ *The physical space they occupy*

■ Power Protection

Computer systems require clean electrical power, and for critical systems, uninterrupted power can be important as well. There are several elements used to manage the power to systems, including uninterruptible power supplies and backup power systems.

UPS

An uninterruptible power supply (UPS) is used to protect against short-duration power failures. There are two types of UPS, online and standby. An online UPS is in continuous use because the primary power source goes through it to the equipment. It uses AC line voltage to charge a bank of batteries. When the primary power source fails, an inverter in the UPS will change DC of the batteries into AC. A standby UPS has sensors to detect power failures. If there is a power failure, the load will be switched to the UPS. It stays inactive before a power failure, and takes more time than an online UPS to provide power when the primary source fails.

Backup Power and Cable Shielding

Backup power sources, such as a motor generator, another electrical substation, and so on, are used to protect against a long-duration power failure. A voltage regulator and line conditioner are used to protect against unstable power supply and spikes. Proper grounding is essential for all electrical devices to protect against short circuits and static electricity.

In more sensitive areas, cable shielding can be employed to avoid interference. Power line monitoring can be used to detect changes in frequency and voltage amplitude, warning of brownouts or spikes. An *emergency power off (EPO) switch* can be installed to allow for the quick shutdown of power when required. To prevent electromagnetic interference and voltage spikes, electrical cables should be placed away from powerful electrical motors and lighting. Another source of power-induced interference can be fluorescent lighting, which can cause radio frequency interference.

Electromagnetic Interference

Electromagnetic interference, or EMI, can plague any type of electronics, but the density of circuitry in the typical data center can make it a haven for EMI. *EMI* is defined as the disturbance on an electrical circuit caused by that circuit's reception of electromagnetic radiation. Magnetic radiation enters the circuit by induction, where magnetic waves create a charge on the circuit. The amount of sensitivity to this magnetic field depends on a number of factors, including the length of the circuit, which can act like an antenna. EMI is grouped into two general types: narrowband and broadband. Narrowband EMI is, by its nature, electromagnetic energy with a small frequency band and, therefore, typically sourced from a device that is purposefully transmitting in the specified band. Broadband EMI covers a wider array of frequencies and is typically caused by some type of general electrical power use such as power lines or electric motors.

In the United States, the Federal Communications Commission has responsibility for regulating products that produce EMI and has developed a program for equipment manufacturers to adhere to standards for EMI immunity. Modern circuitry is designed to resist EMI. Cabling is a good example; the twist in unshielded twisted pair, or Category 6/6a, cable is there to reduce EMI. EMI is also controlled by metal computer cases that are grounded; by providing an easy path to ground, the case acts as an EMI shield. A bigger example would be a Faraday cage or Faraday shield, which is an enclosure of conductive material that is grounded. These can be room sized or built into a building's construction; the critical element is that there is no significant gap in the enclosure material. These measures can help shield EMI, especially in high radio frequency environments.

While we have talked about the shielding necessary to keep EMI radiation out of your circuitry, there is also technology to try and help keep it in. Known by some as TEMPEST, it is also known as Van Eck emissions. A computer's monitor or LCD display produces electromagnetic radiation that can be remotely observed with the correct equipment. TEMPEST was the code word for an NSA program to secure equipment from this type of eavesdropping. While some of the information about TEMPEST is still classified, there are guides on the Internet that describe protective measures, such as shielding and electromagnetic-resistant enclosures. A company has even developed a commercial paint that offers radio frequency shielding.

■ Electronic Access Control Systems

Access tokens are defined as "something you have." An access token is a physical object that identifies specific access rights. Access tokens are frequently used for physical access solutions, just as your house key is a basic physical access token that allows you access into your home. Although keys have been used to unlock devices for centuries, they do have several limitations. Keys are paired exclusively with a lock or a set of locks, and they are not easily changed. It is easy to add an authorized user by giving the user a copy of the key, but it is far more difficult to give that user selective access unless that specified area is already set up as a separate key. It is also difficult to take access away from a single key or key holder, which usually requires a rekey of the whole system.

In many businesses, physical access authentication has moved to contactless radio frequency cards and proximity readers. When passed near a card reader, the card sends out a code using radio waves. The reader picks up this code and transmits it to the control panel. The control panel checks the code against the reader from which it is being read and the type of access the card has in its database. One of the advantages of this kind of token-based system is that any card can be deleted from the system without affecting any other card or the rest of the system. The RFID-based contactless entry card shown in Figure 8.11 is a common form of this token device employed for door controls and is frequently put behind an employee badge. In addition, all doors connected to the system can be segmented in any form or fashion to create multiple access areas, with different permissions for each one. The tokens themselves can also be grouped in multiple ways to provide different access levels to different groups of people. All of the access levels or segmentation of doors can be modified quickly and easily if building space is retasked. Newer technologies are adding capabilities to the standard token-based systems.

• **Figure 8.11** Smart cards have an internal chip as well as multiple external contacts for interfacing with a smart card reader.

The advent of **smart cards** (cards that contain integrated circuits capable of generating and storing cryptographic keys) has enabled cryptographic types of authentication. Smart card technology has proven reliable enough that it is now part of a governmental standard for physical and logical authentication. Known as *Personal Identity Verification, or PIV,* cards, they adhere to the FIPS 201 standard. This smart card includes a cryptographic chip and connector, as well as a contactless proximity card circuit. It also has standards for a printed photo and name printing on the front. Biometric data can be stored on the card, providing an additional authentication factor, and if the PIV standard is followed, several forms of identification are needed to get a card.

The primary drawback of token-based authentication is that only the token is being authenticated. Therefore, the theft of the token could grant anyone who possessed the token access to what the system protects. The risk of theft of the token can be offset by the use of multiple-factor authentication. One of the ways that people have tried to achieve multiple-factor authentication is to add a biometric factor to the system.

Access Tokens

Electronic access control systems were spawned from the need to have more logging and control than provided by the older method of metallic keys. Most electronic systems currently use a token-based card that if passed near a reader will unlock the door strike and let you pass into the area (assuming you have permission from the system). Newer technology attempts to make the authentication process easier and more secure.

The following sections discuss how tokens and biometrics are being used for authentication. It also looks into how multiple-factor authentication can be used for physical access.

Biometrics

Biometrics use the measurements of certain biological factors to identify one specific person from others. These factors are based on parts of the human body that are unique. The most well known of these unique biological factors is the fingerprint. Fingerprint readers have been available for several years in laptops. These come in a variety of form factors, such as the example shown in Figure 8.12, and as standalone USB devices.

• **Figure 8.12**   Newer laptop computers often include a fingerprint reader.

However, many other biological factors can be used, such as the retina or iris of the eye, the geometry of the hand, and the geometry of the face. When these are used for authentication, there is a two-part process: enrollment and then authentication. During enrollment, a computer takes the image of the biological factor and reduces it to a numeric value. When the user attempts to authenticate, their feature is scanned by the reader, and the computer compares the numeric value being read to the one stored in the database. If they match, access is allowed. Since these physical factors are unique, theoretically only the actual authorized person would be allowed access.

In the real world, however, the theory behind biometrics breaks down. Tokens that have a digital code work very well because everything remains in the digital realm. A computer checks your code, such as 123, against the database; if the computer finds 123 and that number has access, the computer opens the door. Biometrics, however, take an analog signal, such as a fingerprint or a face, and attempt to digitize it, and it is then matched against the digits in the database. The problem with an analog signal is that it might not encode the exact same way twice. For example, if you came to work with a bandage on your chin, would the face-based biometrics grant you access or deny it?

Engineers who designed these systems understood that if a system was set to exact checking, an encoded biometric might never grant access since it might never scan the biometric exactly the same way twice. Therefore, most systems have tried to allow a certain amount of error in the scan, while not allowing too much. This leads to the concepts of false positives and false negatives. A **false positive** occurs when a biometric is scanned and allows access to someone who is not authorized—for example, two people who have very similar fingerprints might be recognized as the same person by the computer, which grants access to the wrong person. A **false negative** occurs when the system denies access to someone who is actually authorized—for example, a user at the hand geometry scanner forgot to wear a ring he usually wears and the computer doesn't recognize his hand and denies him access. For biometric authentication to work properly, and also be trusted, it must minimize the existence of both false positives and false negatives. To do that, a balance between exacting and error must be created so that the machines allow a little physical variance—but not too much.

False Positives and False Negatives   When a decision is made on information and an associated range of probabilities, the conditions exist for a false decision. Figure 8.13 illustrates two overlapping probabilities; an item belongs

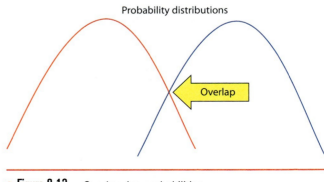

Probability distributions

Overlap

• **Figure 8.13**   Overlapping probabilities

Principles of Computer Security

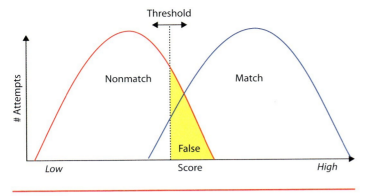

• **Figure 8.14** False positive

to either the red curve or the blue curve, but not both. The problem in deciding which curve an item belongs to occurs when the curves overlap.

When there is an overlapping area, it is typically referred to as the false positive and false negative rate. Note that in the accompanying figures, the size of overlap is greatly exaggerated to make it easy to see. Figure 8.14 illustrates a false positive detection. If the value observed is the dotted line, then it could be considered either a match or a non-match. If in fact it should not match, and the system tags it as a match, it is a false positive. In biometrics, a false positive would allow access to an unauthorized party.

Figure 8.15 illustrates a false negative detection. If the value observed is the dotted line, then it could be considered either a match or a non-match. If in fact it should match, and the system tags it as a non-match, it is a false negative. A false negative would prevent an authorized user from obtaining access.

To solve the false positive and false negative issue, the probabilistic engine must produce two sets of curves that do not overlap. This is equivalent to very low, <0.001%, false positive and false negative rates. Because

> **Exam Tip:** *False positive* and *false negative* are frequently confused. The true definitions revolve around the statistical term *null hypothesis*. For authentication, it is assumed that the person is not authorized. If the person is not authorized, and the test incorrectly rejects the null hypothesis and allows entry, this is a false positive—also called a *Type I error*. If the person is authorized, and the test fails to allow entry, then this is a false negative, or *Type II error*. The important element is the direction of the null hypothesis, which, for authentication, would be to deny entry.

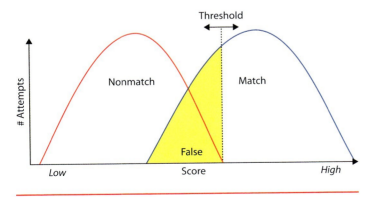

• **Figure 8.15** False negative

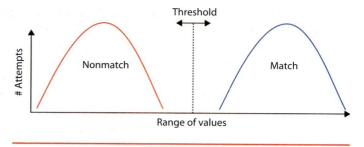

● **Figure 8.16**   Desired situation

the curves technically have tails that go forever, there will always be some false rates, but the numbers have to be exceedingly small to assure security. Figure 8.16 illustrates the desired, but typically impractical, separation of the curves.

A more realistic situation has the two curves crossing over at some point, and this point is known as the **crossover error rate (CER)**. The CER is the point where the false acceptance and false rejection rates are equal. While a system has the ability to adjust which of the two false rates to favor, the CER provides a means of comparing systems performance at discriminating signals. A system with a CER of 2 percent is more accurate (and has more separation) than one with a CER of 5 percent.

Another concern with biometrics is that if someone is able to steal the uniqueness factor that the machine scans—your fingerprint from a glass, for example—and is able to reproduce that factor in a substance that fools the scanner, that person now has your access privileges. This idea is compounded by the fact that it is impossible for you to change your fingerprint if it gets stolen. It is easy to replace a lost or stolen token and delete the missing one from the system, but it is far more difficult to replace a human hand. Another problem with biometrics is that parts of the human body can change. A human face can change, through scarring, weight loss or gain, or surgery. A fingerprint can be changed through damage to the fingers. Eye retinas can be affected by some types of diabetes or by pregnancy. All of these changes force the biometric system to allow a higher tolerance for variance in the biometric being read. This has led the way for high-security installations to move toward multiple-factor authentication.

Multiple-Factor Authentication

Multiple-factor authentication is simply the combination of two or more types of authentication. Three broad categories of authentication can be used: what you are (for example, biometrics), what you have (for instance, tokens), and what you know (passwords and other information). Two-factor authentication combines any two of these before granting access. An example would be a card reader that then turns on a fingerprint scanner—if your fingerprint matches the one on file for the card, you are granted access. Three-factor authentication would combine all three types, such as a smart card reader that asks for a PIN before enabling a retina scanner. If all three correspond to a valid user in the computer database, access is granted.

Principles of Computer Security

Multiple-factor authentication methods greatly enhance security by making it very difficult for an attacker to obtain all the correct materials for authentication. They also protect against the risk of stolen tokens, as the attacker must have the correct biometric, password, or both. More important, multiple-factor authentication enhances the security of biometric systems, by protecting against a stolen biometric. Changing the token makes the biometric useless unless the attacker can steal the new token. It also reduces false positives by trying to match the supplied biometric with the one that is associated with the supplied token. This prevents the computer from seeking a match using the entire database of biometrics. Using multiple factors is one of the best ways to ensure proper authentication and access control.

Exam Tip: Two-factor authentication combines any two methods of authentication, matching items such as a token with a biometric. Three-factor authentication combines any three, such as a passcode, biometric, and a token.

■ Chapter Summary

After reading this chapter and completing the exercises, you should understand the following facts about how physical security impacts network security.

Describe how physical security directly affects computer and network security

- Physical access defeats all network security protections.
- Bootdisks allow file system access.
- Drive imaging is simple to accomplish with physical access.
- Access to the internal network is simple with physical access.
- Theft of hardware can be an attack in and of itself.

Discuss steps that can be taken to help mitigate risks

- Removal of floppy drives and other media drives when they are unnecessary can help mitigate bootdisk attacks.
- Removal of CD-ROM devices also makes physical access attacks more difficult.
- BIOS passwords should be used to protect the boot sequence.

- USB devices are a threat and thus, if possible, USB drivers should be removed.
- All users need security training.
- Authentication systems should use multiple factors when feasible.

Identify the different types of fires and the various fire suppression systems designed to limit the damage caused by fires

- Fires can be caused by and can consume a number of different materials. It is important to recognize what type of fire is occurring, because the extinguisher to use depends on the type of fire.
- The ABC fire extinguisher is the most common type and is designed to handle most types of fires. The only type of fire it is not designed to address is one with combustible metals.

Explain electronic access controls and the principles of convergence

- Access controls should have layered areas and electronic access control systems.
- Electronic physical security systems need to be protected from network-based attacks.

■ Key Terms

access tokens *(210)*
autoplay *(201)*
biometrics *(211)*
BIOS passwords *(200)*
bootdisk *(192)*
closed circuit television (CCTV) *(198)*
contactless access cards *(197)*
convergence *(200)*
crossover error rate (CER) *(214)*
drive imaging *(194)*
false negative *(212)*

false positive *(212)*
layered access *(197)*
LiveCD *(193)*
mantrap *(198)*
multiple-factor authentication *(214)*
physical access control *(196)*
policies and procedures *(200)*
smart cards *(211)*
Unified Extensible Firmware Interface (UEFI) *(200)*
USB devices *(201)*

Key Terms Quiz

Use terms from the Key Terms list to complete the sentences that follow. Don't use the same term more than once. Not all terms will be used.

1. A door system designed to only allow a single person through is called a(n) _____.

2. _____ include MP3 players and flash drives.

3. A(n) _____ happens when an unauthorized user is allowed access.

4. Removable media from which a computer can be booted is called a(n) _____.

5. _____ forces a user to authenticate again when entering a more secure area.

6. Items carried by the user to allow them to be authenticated are called _____.

7. _____ is the measurement of unique biological properties, like the fingerprint.

8. _____ prevent an attacker from making the machine boot off the DVD drive.

9. _____ is a system where the camera and monitor are directly linked.

10. Using a token, fingerprint reader, and PIN keypad would be an example of _____.

Multiple-Choice Quiz

1. What is the most common example of an access token?

   A. Smart card

   B. Handwriting sample

   C. PDA

   D. Key

2. Which one is not commonly used as a biometric?

   A. Eye retina

   B. Hand geometry

   C. Shoulder-to-waist geometry

   D. Fingerprint

3. Probably the simplest physical attack on the computer system is:

   A. Accessing an Ethernet jack to attack the network

   B. Using an imitation to fool a biometric authenticator

   C. Installing a virus on the CCTV system

   D. Outright theft of the computers

4. What is a common threat to token-based access controls?

   A. The key

   B. Demagnetization of the strip

   C. A system crash

   D. Loss or theft of the token

5. Why can USB flash drives be a threat?

   A. They use too much power.

   B. They can bring malicious code past other security mechanisms.

   C. They can be stolen.

   D. They can be encrypted.

6. Why is HVAC important to computer security?

   A. Sabotage of the AC unit could take out the electrical power.

   B. Sabotage of the AC unit would make the computers overheat and shut down.

   C. The AC units could be connected to the network.

   D. HVAC is not important to security.

7. Why should security guards get cross-training in network security?

   A. They are the eyes and ears of the corporation when it comes to security.

   B. They are the only people in the building at night.

   C. They are more qualified to know what a security threat is.

   D. They have the authority to detain violators.

8. Why is enrollment important to biometrics?

   A. Fingerprints are unique.

   B. It adds another layer to the layered access model.

   C. If enrollment is not done carefully, false positives will increase.

   D. It completely prevents false positives.

9. Why is physical security so important to good network security?

   A. Because encryption is not involved

   B. Because physical access defeats nearly all network security measures

   C. Because an attacker can steal biometric identities

   D. Authentication

10. How does multiple-factor authentication improve security?

    A. By using biometrics, no other person can authenticate.

    B. It restricts users to smaller spaces.

    C. By using a combination of authentications, it is more difficult for someone to gain illegitimate access.

    D. It denies access to an intruder multiple times.

Essay Questions

1. You have been asked to report on the feasibility of installing an IP CCTV camera system at your organization. Detail the pros and cons of an IP CCTV system and how you would implement the system.

2. Write a memo justifying layered access for devices in an organization.

3. Write a memo justifying more user education about physical security.

4. Write a sample policy regarding the use of USB devices in an organization.

Lab Projects

• Lab Project 8.1

Load a LiveCD on your machine and examine the tools it provides. You will need the following materials:

- A computer with a version of Windows installed and a CD/DVD burner

- An empty CD or DVD

Then do the following:

1. Download a copy of Kali Linux. A good site from which to obtain this is www.kali.org/downloads/.

2. Burn the ISO file to the CD/DVD.

3. Reboot the machine, allowing the LiveCD to start the machine in Linux.

4. Once Kali Linux is running, open a terminal window and type wireshark.

5. With Wireshark open as a sniffing program, record the traffic to and from this computer.

   A. Open Capture | Options.

   B. Select Start on your Ethernet interface, usually eth0.

   C. Stop Capture by selecting Capture | Stop.

   D. Click any packet listed to view the analysis.

6. View the other tools on the CD under KDE | Kali.

• Lab Project 8.2

Disable autoplay on your system for several types of media. You will need the following materials:

- A computer with Windows
- A USB flash drive that is set to be bootable
- A CD/DVD with an autoplay file

Then do the following:

1. Insert the CD/DVD and verify that autoplay is on and working.

2. Follow this chapter's instructions on disabling autoplay.

3. Reinsert the CD/DVD and verify that autoplay is disabled—nothing should appear when the CD/DVD is inserted now.

4. Insert the USB flash drive and see if autoplay works for it; if it does, disable it using the same method.

Network Fundamentals

The value of a communications network is proportional to the square of the number of its users.

—Metcalfe's Law

In this chapter, you will learn how to

- Identify the basic network architectures
- Define the basic network protocols
- Explain routing and address translation
- Classify security zones

By the simplest definition in the data world, a **network** is a means to connect two or more computers together for the purposes of sharing information. The term "network" has different meanings depending on the context and usage. A network can be a group of friends and associates, a series of interconnected tunnels, or, from a computer-oriented perspective, a collection of interconnected devices. Network sizes and shapes vary drastically, ranging from two personal computers connected with a crossover cable or wireless router all the way up to the Internet, encircling the globe and linking together untold numbers of individual, distributed systems. Though data networks vary widely in size and scope, they are generally defined in terms of their architecture, topology, and protocols.

Network Architectures

Every network has an architecture—whether by design or by accident. Defining or describing a specific network's architecture involves identifying the network's physical configuration, logical operation, structure, procedures, data formats, protocols, and other components. For the sake of simplicity and categorization, people tend to divide network architectures into two main categories: LANs and WANs. A **local area network (LAN)** typically is smaller in terms of size and geographic coverage and consists of two or more connected devices. Home networks and most small office networks can be classified as LANs. A **wide area network (WAN)** tends to be larger, covering more geographic area, and consists of two or more systems in geographically separated areas connected by any of a variety of methods such as leased lines, radio waves, satellite relays, microwaves, or even dial-up connections. With the advent of wireless networking, optical, and cellular technology, the lines between LAN and WAN sometimes seem to merge seamlessly

• **Figure 9.1**   Corporate WAN connecting multiple offices

into a single network entity. For example, most corporations have multiple LANs within each office location that all connect to a WAN that provides intercompany connectivity. Figure 9.1 shows an example of a corporate network. Each office location will typically have one or more LANs, which are connected to the other offices and the company headquarters through a corporate WAN.

Over time, as networks have grown, diversified, and multiplied, the line between LAN and WAN has become blurred. To better describe emerging, specialized network structures, new terms have been coined to classify networks based on size and use:

> **Exam Tip:** A LAN is a local area network—an office building, home network, and so on. A WAN is a wide area network—a corporate network connecting offices in Dallas, New York, and San Jose, for example.

- **Campus area network (CAN)**   A network connecting any number of buildings in an office or university complex (also referred to as a campus wide area network).

- **Intranet**   A "private" network that is accessible only to authorized users. Many large corporations host an intranet to facilitate information sharing within their organization.

- **Internet**   The "global network" connecting hundreds of millions of systems and users.

- **Metropolitan area network (MAN)**   A network designed for a specific geographic locality such as a town or a city.

- **Storage area network (SAN)**   A high-speed network connecting a variety of storage devices such as tape systems, RAID arrays, optical drives, file servers, and others.

- **Virtual local area network (VLAN)**   A logical network allowing systems on different physical networks to interact as if they were connected to the same physical network.

- **Client/server**   A network in which powerful, dedicated systems called *servers* provide resources to individual workstations or *clients.*

- **Peer-to-peer**   A network in which every system is treated as an equal, such as a home network.

- **Figure 9.2**   Star topology

■ Network Topology

One major component of every network's architecture is the network's **topology**—how the network is physically or logically arranged. Terms to classify a network's topology have been developed, often reflecting the physical layout of the network. The main classes of network topologies are star, ring, bus, and mixed.

- **Star topology**   Network components are connected to a central point. (See Figure 9.2.)

- **Bus topology**   Network components are connected to the same cable, often called "the bus" or "the backbone." (See Figure 9.3.)

- **Ring topology**   Network components are connected to each other in a closed loop with each device directly connected to two other devices. (See Figure 9.4.)

- **Figure 9.3**   Bus topology

- **Figure 9.4**   Ring topology

Larger networks, such as those inside an office complex, may use more than one topology at the same time. For example, an office complex may have a large ring topology that interconnects all the buildings in the complex. Each building may have a large bus topology to interconnect star topologies located on each floor of the building. This is called a mixed topology or hybrid topology. (See Figure 9.5.)

• **Figure 9.5**   Mixed topology

With recent advances in technology, these topology definitions often break down. While a network consisting of five computers connected to the same coaxial cable is easily classified as a bus topology, what about those same computers connected to a switch using Cat-5 cables? With a switch, each computer is connected to a central node, much like a star topology, but the backplane of the switch is essentially a shared medium. With a switch, each computer has its own exclusive connection to the switch like a star topology, but has to share the switch's communications backbone with all the other computers, much like a bus topology. To avoid this type of confusion, many people use topology definitions only to identify the physical layout of the network, focusing on how the devices are connected to the network. If we apply this line of thinking to our example, the five-computer network becomes a star topology whether we use a hub or a switch.

Network Protocols

How do all these interconnected devices communicate? What makes a PC in China able to view web pages on a server in Brazil? When engineers first started to connect computers together via networks, they quickly realized they needed a commonly accepted method for communicating—a protocol.

Protocols

A **protocol** is an agreed-upon format for exchanging or transmitting data between systems. A protocol defines a number of agreed-upon parameters, such as the data compression method, the type of error checking to use, and mechanisms for systems to signal when they have finished either receiving or transmitting data. There is a wide variety of protocols, each designed with certain benefits and uses in mind. Some of the more common protocols

Wireless networks use radio waves as their medium to transmit packets, and those radio waves don't stop at the walls of your house or your organization. Anyone within range can "see" those radio waves and attempt to either sniff your traffic or connect to your network. Encryption, MAC address filtering, and suppression of beacon frames are all security mechanisms to consider when using wireless networks. Wireless networks, because of the signal propagation, can easily assume a mesh structure.

that have been used in networking are listed next. Today, most networks are dominated by Ethernet and Internet Protocol.

- **AppleTalk**   The communications protocol developed by Apple to connect Macintosh computers and printers.

- **Asynchronous Transfer Mode (ATM)**   A protocol based on transferring data in fixed-size packets. The fixed packet sizes help ensure that no single data type monopolizes the available bandwidth.

- **Ethernet**   The LAN protocol developed jointly by Xerox, DEC, and Intel—the most widely implemented LAN standard.

- **Fiber Distributed Data Interface (FDDI)**   The protocol for sending digital data over fiber-optic cabling.

- **Internet Protocols (IP)**   The protocols for managing and transmitting data between packet-switched computer networks, originally developed for the Department of Defense. Most users are familiar with Internet protocols such as e-mail, File Transfer Protocol (FTP), Telnet, and Hypertext Transfer Protocol (HTTP).

- **Internetwork Packet Exchange (IPX)**   The networking protocol created by Novell for use with Novell NetWare operating systems.

- **Signaling System 7 (SS7)**   The telecommunications protocol used between private branch exchanges (PBXs) to handle tasks such as call setup, routing, and teardown.

- **Systems Network Architecture (SNA)**   A set of network protocols developed by IBM, originally used to connect IBM's mainframe systems.

- **Token Ring**   A LAN protocol developed by IBM that requires systems to possess the network "token" before transmitting data.

- **Transmission Control Protocol/Internet Protocol (TCP/IP)**   The collection of communications protocols used to connect hosts on the Internet. TCP/IP is by far the most commonly used network protocol and is a combination of the TCP and IP protocols.

- **X.25A protocol**   Developed by the Comité Consultatif International Téléphonique et Télégraphique (CCITT) for use in packet-switched networks. The CCITT was a subgroup within the International Telecommunication Union (ITU) before the CCITT was disbanded in 1992.

A little history on the IP protocol from Wikipedia: "In May, 1974, the Institute of Electrical and Electronic Engineers (IEEE) published a paper entitled 'A Protocol for Packet Network Interconnection.' The paper's authors, Vint Cerf and Bob Kahn, described an internetworking protocol for sharing resources using packet-switching among the nodes."

In most cases, communications protocols were developed around the Open System Interconnection (OSI) model. The OSI model, or OSI Reference Model, is an International Organization for Standardization (ISO) standard for worldwide communications that defines a framework for implementing protocols and networking components in seven distinct layers. Within the OSI model, control is passed from one layer to another (top-down) before it exits one system and enters another system, where control is passed bottom-up to complete the communications cycle. It is important to note that most protocols only loosely follow the OSI model; several protocols combine one or more layers into a single function. The OSI model also provides a certain level of abstraction and isolation for each layer, which only needs to know how to interact with the layer above and below it. The application layer, for example, only needs to know how to communicate with the presentation layer—it does not need to talk directly to the physical layer. Figure 9.6 shows the different layers of the OSI model.

Packets

Networks are built to share information and resources, but like other forms of communication, networks and the protocols they use have limits and rules that must be followed for effective communication. For example, large chunks of data must typically be broken up into smaller, more manageable chunks before they are transmitted from one computer to another. Breaking the data up has advantages—you can more effectively share bandwidth with other systems and you don't have to retransmit the entire dataset if there is a problem in transmission. When data is broken up into smaller pieces for transmission, each of the smaller pieces is typically called a **packet**. Each protocol has its own definition of a packet—dictating how much data can be carried, what information is stored where, how the packet should be interpreted by another system, and so on.

A standard packet structure is a crucial element in a protocol definition. Without a standard packet structure, systems would not be able to interpret the information coming to them from other systems. Packet-based communication systems have other unique characteristics, such as size, which need to be addressed. This is done via a defined maximum and fragmenting packets that are too big, as shown in the next sections.

Maximum Transmission Unit

When transmitting packets across a network, there are many intervening protocols and pieces of equipment, each with its own set of limitations. One of the factors used to determine how many packets a message must be broken into is the Maximum Transmission Unit (MTU). The MTU is the largest packet that can be carried across a network channel. The value of the MTU is used by TCP to prevent packet fragmentation at intervening devices. *Packet fragmentation* is the splitting of a packet while in transit into two packets so that they fit past an MTU bottleneck.

Packet Fragmentation

Built into the Internet Protocol is a mechanism for handling of packets that are larger than allowed across a hop. Under ICMP v4, a router has two options when it encounters a packet that is too large for the next hop: break the packet into two fragments, sending each separately, or drop the packet and send an ICMP message back to the originator, indicating that the packet is too big. When a fragmented packet arrives at the receiving host, it must be reunited with the other packet fragments and reassembled. One of the problems with fragmentation is that it can cause excessive levels of packet retransmission as TCP must retransmit an entire packet for the loss of a single fragment. In IPv6, to avoid fragmentation, hosts are required to determine the minimal path MTU before transmission of packets to avoid fragmentation en route. Any fragmentation requirements in IPv6 are resolved at the origin, and if fragmentation is required, it occurs before sending.

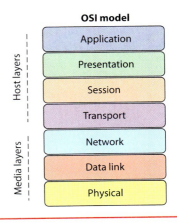

• **Figure 9.6**   The OSI Reference Model

The concept of breaking a message into pieces before sending it is as old as networking. The terms used to describe these pieces can vary from protocol to protocol. Frame Relay and Ethernet both use the term *frame*. ATM calls them *cells*. Many protocols use the generic term *packet*. In the OSI model, the term *datagram* is used. At the end of the day, regardless of what it is called, these pieces are protocol-defined, formatted structures used to carry information.

Tech Tip

IPv6 and Fragmentation
IPv6 systems calculate the MTU and then adhere to that from host to host. This prevents fragmentation en route; instead all fragmentation is done by the originating host to fit under the MTU limit.

IP fragmentation can be exploited in a variety of ways to bypass security measures. Packets can be purposefully constructed to split exploit code into multiple fragments to avoid IDS detection. Because the reassembly of fragments is dependent upon data in the fragments, it is possible to manipulate the fragments to result in datagrams that exceed the 64KB limit, resulting in denial of service.

Internet Protocol

The **Internet Protocol** is not a single protocol but a suite of protocols. The relationship between some of the IP suite and the OSI model is shown in Figure 9.7. As you can see, there are differences between the two versions of the protocol in use, v4 and v6. The protocol elements and their security implications are covered in the next sections of this chapter. One of these differences is the replacement of the Internet Group Management Protocol (IGMP) with the Internet Control Message Protocol (ICMP) and Multicast Listener Discovery (MLD) in IPv6.

• **Figure 9.7**   Internet Protocol suite components

IP Packets

To better understand packet structure, let's examine the packet structure defined by the IP protocol. An IP packet, often called a **datagram**, has two main sections: the header and the data section (sometimes called the payload). The header section contains all of the information needed to describe the packet (see Figure 9.8).

(a) IPv4

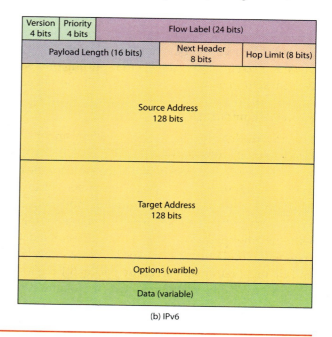

(b) IPv6

• **Figure 9.8**   Logical layout of an IP packet, (a) IPv4 (b) IPv6

In IPv4, there are common fields to describe the following options.

- What kind of packet it is (protocol version number)

- How large the header of the packet is (packet header length)

- How to process this packet (type of service telling the network whether or not to use options such as minimize delay, maximize throughput, maximize reliability, and minimize cost)

- How large the entire packet is (overall length of packet—since this is a 16-bit field, the maximum size of an IP packet is 65,535 bytes, but in practice most packets are around 1500 bytes)

- A unique identifier so that this packet can be distinguished from other packets

- Whether or not this packet is part of a longer data stream and should be handled relative to other packets

- Flags that indicate whether or not special handling of this packet is necessary

- A description of where this packet fits into the data stream as compared to other packets (the fragment offset)

- A "time to live" field that indicates the packet should be discarded if the value is zero

- A protocol field that describes the encapsulated protocol

- A checksum of the packet header (to minimize the potential for data corruption during transmission)

- Where the packet is from (source IP address, such as 10.10.10.5)

- Where the packet is going (destination IP address, such as 10.10.10.10)

- Option flags that govern security and handling restrictions, whether or not to record the route this packet has taken, whether or not to record time stamps, and so on

- The data this packet carries

In IPv6, the source and destination addresses take up much greater room, and for equipment and packet handling reasons, most of the informational options have been moved to the optional area after the addresses. This series of optional extension headers allows the efficient use of the header in processing the routing information during packet routing operations.

One of the most common options is the IPsec extension, which is used to establish IPsec connections. IPsec uses encryption to provide a variety of protections to packets. IPsec is fully covered in Chapter 11.

As you can see, this standard packet definition allows systems to communicate. Without this type of "common language," the global connectivity we enjoy today would be impossible—the IP protocol is the primary means for transmitting information across the Internet.

TCP vs. UDP

Protocols are typically developed to enable a certain type of communication or solve a specific problem. Over the years, this approach has led to the

Tech Tip

The Importance of Understanding TCP/IP Protocols

A security professional must understand how the various TCP/IP protocols operate. For example, if you're looking at a packet capture of a suspected port scan, you need to know how "normal" TCP and UDP traffic works so you will be able to spot "abnormal" traffic. This chapter provides a very basic overview of the most popular protocols: TCP, UDP, and ICMP.

development of many different protocols, each critical to the function or process it supports. However, there are two protocols that have grown so much in popularity and use that without them, the Internet as we know it would cease to exist. These two protocols, the **Transmission Control Protocol (TCP)** and **User Datagram Protocol (UDP)**, are protocols that run on top of the IP network protocol. As separate protocols, they each have their own packet definitions, capabilities, and advantages, but the most important difference between TCP and UDP is the concept of "guaranteed" reliability and delivery.

UDP is known as a "connectionless" protocol as it has very few error-recovery services and no guarantee of packet delivery. With UDP, packets are created and sent on their way. The sender has no idea whether the packets were successfully received or whether they were received in order. In that respect, UDP packets are much like postcards—you address them and drop them in the mailbox, not really knowing if, when, or how the postcards reach your intended audience. Even though packet loss and corruption are relatively rare on modern networks, UDP is considered to be an unreliable protocol and is often only used for network services that are not greatly affected by the occasional lost or dropped packet. Time synchronization requests, name lookups, and streaming audio are good examples of network services based on UDP. UDP also happens to be a fairly "efficient" protocol in terms of content delivery versus overhead. With UDP, more time and space is dedicated to content (data) delivery than with other protocols such as TCP. This makes UDP a good candidate for streaming protocols, as more of the available bandwidth and resources are used for data delivery than with other protocols.

TCP is a "connection-oriented" protocol and was specifically designed to provide a reliable connection between two hosts exchanging data. TCP was also designed to ensure that packets are processed in the same order in which they were sent. As part of TCP, each packet has a sequence number to show where that packet fits into the overall conversation. With the sequence numbers, packets can arrive in any order and at different times and the receiving system will still know the correct order for processing them. The sequence numbers also let the receiving system know if packets are missing—receiving packets 1, 2, 4, and 7 tells us that packets 3, 5, and 6 are missing and needed as part of this conversation. The receiving system can then request retransmission of packets from the sender to fill in any gaps.

The "guaranteed and reliable" aspect of TCP makes it very popular for many network applications and services such as HTTP, FTP, and Telnet. As part of the connection, TCP requires that systems follow a specific pattern when establishing communications. This pattern, often called the **three-way handshake** (shown in Figure 9.9), is a sequence of very specific steps:

1. The originating host (usually called the client) sends a SYN (synchronize) packet to the destination host (usually called the server). The SYN packet tells the server what port the client wants to connect to and the initial packet sequence number of the client.

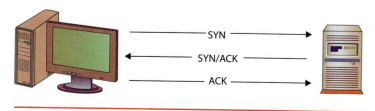

• **Figure 9.9**   TCP's three-way handshake

2. The server sends a SYN/ACK packet back to the client. This SYN/ACK (synchronize/acknowledge) tells the client "I received your request" and also contains the server's initial packet sequence number.

3. The client responds to the server with an ACK packet to complete the connection establishment process.

Think of the three-way handshake as being similar to a phone call. You place a call to your friend—that's the SYN. Your friend answers the phone and says "hello"—that's the SYN/ACK. Then you say "Hi, it's me"—that's the ACK. Your connection is established and you can start your conversation.

ICMP

While TCP and UDP are arguably the most common protocols, the **Internet Control Message Protocol (ICMP)** is probably the third most commonly used protocol. During the early development of large networks, it was quickly discovered that there needed to be some mechanism for managing the overall infrastructure—handling connection status, traffic flow, availability, and errors. This mechanism is ICMP. ICMP is a control and information protocol and is used by network devices to determine such things as a remote network's availability, the length of time to reach a remote network, and the best route for packets to take when traveling to that remote network (using ICMP redirect messages, for example). ICMP can also be used to handle the flow of traffic, telling other network devices to "slow down" transmission speeds if packets are coming in too fast.

ICMP, like UDP, is a connectionless protocol.

Tech Tip

TCP Packet Flags

TCP packets contain flags—dedicated fields that are used to help the TCP protocol control and manage the TCP session. There are eight different flags in a TCP packet, and when a flag is "set," it is set to a value of 1. The eight different flags are

- **CWR (Congestion Window Reduced)** *Set by a host to indicate that it received a packet with the ECE flag set and is taking action to help reduce congestion.*

- **ECE (ECN-Echo)** *Indicates that the TCP peer is ECN capable when used during the three-way handshake. During normal traffic, this flag means that a packet with a Congestion Experienced flag in its IP header was received by the host sending this packet.*

- **URG (Urgent)** *When set, the urgent pointer in the packets should be read as valid and followed for additional data.*

- **ACK (Acknowledgment)** *Indicates that the data in the ACK field should be processed.*

- **PSH (Push)** *Indicates that data delivery should start immediately rather than waiting for buffers to fill up first.*

- **RST (Reset)** *Resets the current connection—a start-over feature often used by IPS/IDS devices to interrupt sessions.*

- **SYN (Synchronize)** *Used to help synchronize sequence numbers.*

- **FIN (Finish)** *Indicates the sender is finished and has no more data to send.*

ICMP was designed to carry small messages quickly with minimal overhead or impact to bandwidth. ICMP packets are sent using the same header structure as IP packets, with the protocol field set to 1 to indicate that it is an ICMP packet. ICMP packets also have their own header, which follows the IP header and contains type, code, checksum, sequence number, identifier, and data fields. The "type" field indicates what type of ICMP message it is, and the "code" field tells us what the message really means. For example, an ICMP packet with a type of 3 and a code of 2 would tell us this is a "destination unreachable" message and, more specifically, a "host unreachable" message—usually indicating that we are unable to communicate with the intended destination. Because ICMP messages in IPv6 can use IPsec, ICMP v6 messages can have significant protections from alteration.

Unfortunately, ICMP has been greatly abused by attackers over the last few years to execute **denial-of-service (DoS)** attacks. Because ICMP packets

Tech Tip

ICMP Message Codes

With ICMP packets, the real message of the packet is contained in the "type and code" fields, not the data field. Following are some of the more commonly seen ICMP type codes. Note that ICMP v6 has broken the listing into two types: error messages (0–127) and informational messages (128–255, presented in the latter half of the table).

IPv6 introduces many new protocols, two of which will have significant implications: the Neighbor Discovery Protocol (NDP), which manages the interactions between neighboring IPv6 nodes, and Multicast Listener Discovery (MLD), which manages IPv6 multicast groups.

Type	ICMP v4	ICMP v6 (Error Messages, 0–127)
0	Echo reply	Reserved
1	Reserved	Destination unreachable
2	Reserved	Packet too big
3	Destination unreachable	Time Exceeded
4	Source quench (deprecated)	Parameter Problem
5	Redirect	Reserved
8	Echo request	Reserved
11	Time exceeded	Reserved
13	Timestamp	Reserved
30	Traceroute (deprecated)	Reserved

ICMP v6 Informational Messages (128–255)

Type		ICMP v6
128		Echo request
129		Echo reply
130		Multicast Listener Query
131		Multicast Listener Report
132		Multicast Listener Done
133		Router Solicitation (NDP)
134		Router Advertisement (NDP)
135		Neighbor Solicitation (NDP)
136		Neighbor Advertisement (NDP)
137		Redirect Message (NDP)
138		Router Renumbering
139		ICMP Node Information Query
140		ICMP Node Information Response
141		Inverse Neighbor Discovery Solicitation Message
142		Inverse Neighbor Discovery Advertisement Message
143		Multicast Listener Discovery (MLD v2) reports (RFC 3810)
144		Home Agent Address Discovery Request Message
145		Home Agent Address Discovery Reply Message
146		Mobile Prefix Solicitation
147		Mobile Prefix Advertisement
148		Certification Path Solicitation (SEND)
149		Certification Path Advertisement (SEND)
151		Multicast Router Advertisement (MRD)
152		Multicast Router Solicitation (MRD)
153		Multicast Router Termination (MRD)
155		RPL Control Message
255		Reserved for expansion of ICMP v6 informational messages

Many of the messages have associated code values that make the message more specific. For example, ICMP v4 messages with a type of 3 can have any of the following codes:

Code	Name
1	Net unreachable
2	Host unreachable
3	Protocol unreachable
4	Port unreachable
5	Fragmentation needed and DF bit set
6	Source route failed
7	Destination network unknown
8	Destination host unknown
9	Source host isolated
10	Communication with destination network is administratively prohibited
11	Communication with destination host is administratively prohibited
12	Destination network unreachable for TOS
13	Destination host unreachable for TOS

Cross Check

Ping Sweep

In Chapter 1 you learned about a "ping sweep." What is a ping sweep and what is it used for? What types of ICMP packets could you use to conduct a ping sweep? How does this differ between ICMP v4 and ICMP v6?

Tech Tip

Should You Block ICMP?

*ICMP is a protocol used for troubleshooting, error reporting, and a wide variety of associated functionality. This functionality expands in ICMP v6 into multicasting. ICMP got a bad name primarily because of issues associated with **ping** and **traceroute** commands, but these represent a tiny minority of the protocol functionality. There are numerous important uses associated with ICMP, and blocking it in its entirety is a bad practice. Blocking specific commands and specific sources makes sense; blanket blocking is a poor practice that will lead to network inefficiencies. Blocking ICMP v6 in its entirety will block a lot of IPv6 functionality because ICMP is now an integral part of the protocol suite.*

are very small and connectionless, thousands and thousands of ICMP packets can be generated by a single system in a very short period of time. Attackers have developed methods to trick many systems into generating thousands of ICMP packets with a common destination—the attacker's target. This creates a literal flood of traffic that the target, and in most cases the network the target sits on, is incapable of dealing with. The ICMP flood drowns out any other legitimate traffic and prevents the target from accomplishing its normal duties—denying access to the service the target normally provides. This has led to many organizations blocking all external ICMP traffic at the perimeter of their organization.

IPv4 vs. IPv6

The most common version of IP in use is IPv4, but the release of IPv6, spurred by the depletion of the IPv4 address space, has begun a typical logarithmic adoption curve. IPv6 has many similarities to the previous version, but it also has significant new enhancements, many of which have significant security implications.

Tech Tip

IPv6 Top Security Concerns

There are numerous IPv6 security concerns, some technical, some operational. Some of the top security concerns are

- *Lack of IPv6 security training/education.*

- *Security device bypass via IPv6.*

- *Poor IPv6 security policies.*

- *Address notation makes grepping through logs difficult if not impossible.*

- *IPv6 complexity increases operational challenges for correct deployment.*

Expanded Address Space

The expansion of the address space from 32 bits to 128 bits is a significant change. Where IPv4 did not have enough addresses for each person on earth, IPv6 has over 1500 addresses per square meter of the entire earth's surface. This has one immediate implication: where you could use a scanner to search all addresses for responses in IPv4, doing the same in IPv6 will take significantly longer. A one millisecond scan in IPv4 equates to a 2.5 billion year scan in IPv6. In theory, the 128 bits of IPv6 address space will express 3.4×10^{38} possible nodes. The IPv6 addressing protocol has been designed to allow for a hierarchal division of the address space into several layers of subnets, to assist in the maintaining of both efficient and logical address allocations. One example is the embedding of the IPv4 address space in the IPv6 space. This also has an intentional effect of simplifying the backbone routing infrastructures by reducing the routing table size.

Network Discovery

IPv6 introduces the Network Discovery (NDP) protocol, which is useful for auto-configuration of networks. NDP can enable a variety of interception and interruption threat modes. A malevolent router can attach itself to a network and reroute or interrupt traffic flows.

Benefits of IPv6

Change is always a difficult task, and when the change will touch virtually everything in your system, this makes it even more difficult. Changing from IPv4 to IPv6 is not a simple task, for it will have an effect on every networked resource. The good news is that this is not a sudden or surprise process; vendors have been making products IPv6 capable for almost a decade. By this point, virtually all the network equipment you rely upon will be dual-stack capable, meaning that they can operate in both IPv4 and IPv6 networks. This provides a method for an orderly transfer from IPv4 to IPv6.

IPv6 has many useful benefits and ultimately will be more secure because it has many security features built into the base protocol series. IPv6 has a simplified packet header and new addressing scheme. This can lead to more efficient routing through smaller routing tables and faster packet processing. IPv6 was designed to incorporate multicasting flows natively, which allows bandwidth-intensive multimedia streams to be sent simultaneously to multiple destinations. IPv6 has a host of new services, from auto-configuration to mobile device addressing, and service enhancements to improve the robustness of QoS and VoIP functions.

The security model of IPv6 is baked into the protocol, and is significantly enhanced from the nonexistent one in IPv4. IPv6 is designed to be secure from sender to receiver, with IPsec available natively across the protocol. This will significantly improve communication level security, but it has also drawn a lot of attention. The use of IPsec will change the way security functions are performed across the enterprise. Old IPv4 methods, such as NAT and packet inspection methods of IDS, will need to be adjusted to the new model. Security appliances will have to adapt to the new protocol and its enhanced nature.

Packet Delivery

Protocols are designed to help information get from one place to another, but in order to deliver a packet we have to know where it is going. Packet delivery can be divided into two sections: local and remote. Ethernet is common for local delivery, while IP works for remote delivery. Local packet delivery applies to packets being sent out on a local network, while remote packet delivery applies to packets being delivered to a remote system, such as across the Internet. Ultimately, packets may follow a local delivery–remote delivery–local delivery pattern before reaching their intended destination. The biggest difference in local versus remote delivery is how packets are addressed. Network systems have addresses, not unlike office numbers or street addresses, and before a packet can be successfully delivered, the sender needs to know the address of the destination system.

Tech Tip

MAC Addresses

Every network device should have a unique MAC address. Manufacturers of network cards and network chipsets have blocks of MAC addresses assigned to them, so you can often tell what type of equipment is sending packets by looking at the first three pairs of hexadecimal digits in a MAC address. For example "00-00-0C" would indicate the network device was built by Cisco Systems.

Ethernet

Ethernet is the most widely implemented Layer 2 protocol. Ethernet is standardized under IEEE 802.3. Ethernet works by forwarding packets on a hop-to-hop basis using MAC addresses. Layer 2 addressing can have numerous security implications. Layer 2 addresses can be poisoned, spanning tree algorithms can be attacked, VLANs can be hopped, and more. Because of its near ubiquity, Ethernet is a common attack vector. It has many elements that make it useful from a networking point of view, such as its broadcast nature and its ability to run over a wide range of media. But these can also act against security concerns. Wireless connections are frequently considered to be weak from a security point of view, but so should Ethernet, for unless you own the network, you should consider the network to be at risk.

Local Packet Delivery

Packets delivered on a network, such as an office LAN, are usually sent using the destination system's hardware address, or **Media Access Control (MAC) address**. Each network card or network device is supposed to have a unique hardware address so that it can be specifically addressed for network traffic. MAC addresses are assigned to a device or network card by the manufacturer, and each manufacturer is assigned a specific block of MAC addresses to prevent two devices from sharing the same MAC address. MAC addresses are usually expressed as six pairs of hexadecimal digits, such as 00:07:e9:7c:c8:aa. In order for a system to send data to another system on the network, it must first find out the destination system's MAC address.

Maintaining a list of every local system's MAC address is both costly and time consuming, and although a system may store MAC addresses temporarily for convenience, in many cases the

Try This!

Finding MAC Addresses on Windows Systems

Open a command prompt on a Windows system. Type the command **ipconfig /all** and find your system's MAC address. *Hint:* It should be listed under "Physical Address" on your network adapters. Now type the command **arp –a** and press ENTER. What information does this display? Can you find the MAC address of your default gateway?

MAC addresses can be "spoofed" or faked. Some operating systems allow users with administrator-level privileges to explicitly set the MAC address for their network card(s). For example, in Linux operating systems you can use the **ifconfig** command to change a network adapter's MAC address. The command **ifconfig eth0 hw ether 00:07:e9:7c:c8:aa** will set the MAC address of adapter eth0 to 00:07:e9:7c:c8:aa. There are also a number of software utilities that allow you to do this through a GUI, such as the GNU MAC Changer. GUI utilities to change MAC addresses on Windows systems are also available.

sender must find the destination MAC address before sending any packets. To find another system's MAC address, the **Address Resolution Protocol (ARP)** is used. Essentially, this is the computer's way of finding out "who owns the blue convertible with license number 123JAK." In most cases, systems know the IP address they wish to send to, but not the MAC address. Using an ARP request, the sending system will send out a query: Who is 10.1.1.140? This broadcast query is examined by every system on the local network, but only the system whose IP address is 10.1.1.140 will respond. That system will send back a response that says "I'm 10.1.1.140 and my MAC address is 00:07:e9:7c:c8:aa." The sending system will then format the packet for delivery and drop it on the network media, stamped with the MAC address of the destination workstation.

Cross Check

Mandatory Access Control vs. Media Access Control

In Chapter 2 you learned about a different MAC—mandatory access control. What is the difference between mandatory access control and Media Access Control? What is each used for? When using acronyms it can be critical to ensure all parties are aware of the context of their usage.

Tech Tip

Rogue Device Detection

There is always a risk of a rogue (unauthorized) device being inserted into the network. To detect when this happens, maintaining a list of all authorized MAC addresses can help detect these devices. Although MACs can be copied and spoofed, this would also set up a conflict if the original device was present. Monitoring for these conditions can detect the insertion of a rogue device.

ARP Attacks

ARP operates in a simplistic and efficient manner—a broadcast request followed by a unicast reply. This method leaves ARP open to attack, which in turn can result in losses of integrity, confidentiality, and availability. Because ARP serves to establish communication channels, failures at this level can lead to significant system compromises. There is a wide range of ARP-specific attacks, but one can classify them into types based on effect.

ARP can be a vector employed to achieve a man-in-the-middle attack. There are many specific ways to create false entries in a machine's ARP cache, but the effect is the same: communications will be routed to an attacker. This type of attack is called *ARP poisoning*. The attacker can use this method to inject himself into the middle of a communication, hijack a session, sniff traffic to obtain passwords or other sensitive items, or block the flow of data, creating a denial of service.

Although ARP is not secure, all is not lost with many ARP-based attacks. Higher-level packet protections such as IPsec can be employed so that the packets are unreadable by interlopers. This is one of the security gains associated with IPv6, because when security is employed at the IPsec level, packets are protected below the IP level, making Layer 2 attacks less successful.

Remote Packet Delivery

While packet delivery on a LAN is usually accomplished with MAC addresses, packet delivery to a distant system is usually accomplished using Internet Protocol (IP) addresses. IP addresses are 32-bit numbers that usually are expressed as a group of four numbers (such as 10.1.1.132). In order to send a packet to a specific system on the other side of the world, you have to know the remote system's IP address. Storing large numbers of IP addresses on every PC is far too costly, and most humans are not good at remembering collections of numbers. However, humans are good at remembering names, so the **Domain Name System (DNS)** protocol was created.

DNS

DNS translates names into IP addresses. When you enter the name of your favorite web site into the location bar of your web browser and press ENTER, the computer has to figure out what IP address belongs to that name. Your computer takes the entered name and sends a query to a local DNS server. Essentially, your computer asks the DNS server, "What IP address goes with www.myfavoritesite.com?" The DNS server, whose main purpose in life is to handle DNS queries, looks in its local records to see if it knows the answer. If it doesn't, the DNS server queries another, higher-level domain server. That server checks its records and queries the server above it, and so on until a match is found. That name-to–IP address matching is passed back down to your computer so it can create the web request, stamp it with the right destination IP address, and send it.

Before sending the packet, your system will first determine if the destination IP address is on a local or remote network. In most cases, it will be on a remote network and your system will not know how to reach that remote network. Again, it would not be practical for your system to know how to directly reach every other system on the Internet, so your system will forward the packet to a network gateway. Network gateways, usually called routers, are devices that are used to interconnect networks and move packets from one network to another. That process of moving packets from one network to another is called **routing** and is critical to the flow of information across the Internet. To accomplish this task, routers use forwarding tables to determine where a packet should go. When a packet reaches a router, the router looks at the destination address to determine where to send the packet. If the router's forwarding tables indicate where the packet should go, the router sends the packet out along the appropriate route. If the router does not know where the destination network is, it forwards the packet to its defined gateway, which repeats the same process. Eventually, after traversing various networks and being passed through various routers, your packet arrives at the router serving the network with the web site you are trying to reach. This router determines the appropriate MAC address of the destination system and forwards the packet accordingly.

DNSSEC

Because of the critical function DNS performs and the security implications of DNS, a cryptographically signed version of DNS was created. DNSSEC is an extension of the original DNS specification, making it trustworthy. DNS is one of the pillars of authority associated with the Internet—it provides the addresses used by machines for communications. Lack of trust in DNS and the inability to authenticate DNS messages drove the need for and creation of DNSSEC. The DNSSEC specification was formally published in 2005, but system-wide adoption has been slow. In 2008, Dan Kaminsky introduced a method of DNS cache poisoning, demonstrating the need for DNSSEC adoption. Although Kaminsky worked with virtually all major

The Domain Name System is critical to the operation of the Internet—if your computer can't translate www.espn.com into 68.71.212.159, then your web browser won't be able to access the latest scores. (As DNS is a dynamic system, the IP address may change for www.espn.com; you can check with the **tracert** command.)

vendors and was behind one of the most coordinated patch rollouts ever, the need for DNSSEC still remains and enterprises are slow to adopt the new methods. One of the reasons for slow adoption is complexity. Having DNS requests and replies digitally signed requires significantly more work and the increase in complexity goes against the stability desires of network engineers.

DNS was designed in the 1980s when the threat model was substantially different than today. The Internet today, and its use for all kinds of critical communications, needs a trustworthy addressing mechanism. DNSSEC is that mechanism, and as it rolls out, it will significantly increase the level of trust associated with addresses. Although certificate-based digital signatures are not perfect, the level of effort to compromise this type of protection mechanism changes the nature of the attack game, making it out of reach to all but the most resourced players. The coupled nature of the trust chains in DNS also serves to alert to any intervening attacks, making attacks much harder to hide.

IP Addresses and Subnetting

The last section mentioned that IPv4 addresses are 32-bit numbers. Those 32 bits are represented as four groups of 8 bits each (called *octets*). You will usually see IP addresses expressed as four sets of decimal numbers in dotted-decimal notation, 10.120.102.15 for example. Of those 32 bits in an IP address, some are used for the network portion of the address (the network ID), and some are used for the host portion of the address (the host ID). **Subnetting** is the process that is used to divide those 32 bits in an IP address and tell you how many of the 32 bits are being used for the network ID and how many are being used for the host ID. As you can guess, where and how you divide the 32 bits determines how many networks and how many host addresses you may have. To interpret the 32-bit space correctly, we must use a **subnet mask**, which tells us exactly how much of the space is the network portion and how much is the host portion. Let's look at an example using the IP address 10.10.10.101 with a subnet mask of 255.255.255.0.

First we must convert the address and subnet mask to their binary representations:

Subnet Mask: 11111111.11111111.11111111.00000000
IP Address: 00001010.00001010.00001010.01100101

Then, we perform a bitwise AND operation to get the network address. The bitwise AND operation examines each set of matching bits from the binary representation of the subnet mask and the binary representation of the IP address. For each set where both the mask and address bits are 1, the result of the AND operation is a 1. Otherwise, if either bit is a 0, the result is a 0. So, for our example we get

Network Address: 00001010.00001010.00001010.00000000

which in decimal is 10.10.10.0, the network ID of our IP network address (translate the binary representation to decimal).

The network ID and subnet mask together tell us that the first three octets of our address are network-related (10.10.10.), which means that the last octet of our address is the host portion (101 in this case). In our example, the network portion of the address is 10.10.10 and the host portion is 101.

Another shortcut in identifying which of the 32 bits is being used in the network ID is to look at the subnet mask after it's been converted to its binary representation. If there's a 1 in the subnet mask, then the corresponding bit in the binary representation of the IP address is being used as part of the network ID. In the preceding example, the subnet mask of 255.255.255.0 in binary representation is 11111111.11111111.11111111.00000000. We can see that there's a 1 in the first 24 spots, which means that the first 24 bits of the IP address are being used as the network ID (which is the first three octets of 255.255.255).

Network address spaces are usually divided into one of three classes:

- **Class A**   Supports 16,777,214 hosts on each network with a default subnet mask of 255.0.0.0
Subnets: 0.0.0.0 to 126.255.255.255 (127.0.0.0 to 127.255.255.255 is reserved for loopback)

- **Class B**   Supports 65,534 hosts on each network with a default subnet mask of 255.255.0.0
Subnets: 128.0.0.0 to 191.255.255.255

- **Class C**   Supports 253 hosts on each network with a default subnet mask of 255.255.255.0 (see Figure 9.10)
Subnets: 192.0.0.0 to 223.255.255.255

Everything above 224.0.0.0 is reserved for either multicasting or future use.

In addition, certain subnets are reserved for private use and are not routed across public networks such as the Internet:

- 10.0.0.0 to 10.255.255.255
- 172.16.0.0 to 172.31.255.255
- 192.168.0.0 to 192.168.255.255
- 169.254.0.0 to 169.254.255.255 (Automatic Private IP Addressing)

Finally, when determining the valid hosts that can be placed on a particular subnet, you have to keep in mind that the "all 0's" address of the host portion is reserved for the network address and the "all 1's" address of the host portion is reserved for the broadcast address of that particular subnet. Again from our earlier example:

Subnet Network Address:
10.10.10.**0**
00001010.00001010.00001010.**00000000**

Broadcast Address:
10.10.10.**255**
00001010.00001010.00001010.**11111111**

In their forwarding tables, routers maintain lists of networks and the accompanying subnet mask. With these two pieces, the router can examine the destination address of each packet and then forward the packet on to the appropriate destination.

As mentioned earlier, subnetting allows us to divide networks into smaller logical units, and we use subnet masks to do this. But how does this work? Remember that the subnet mask tells us how many bits are being used to describe the network ID—adjusting the subnet mask (and the number of bits used to describe the

Tech Tip

RFC 1918—Private Address Spaces
RFC 1918 is the technical specification for private address space. RFC stands for "Request for Comment" and there are RFCs for just about everything to do with the Internet—protocols, routing, how to handle e-mail, and so on. You can find RFCs at www.ietf.org/rfc.html.

• **Figure 9.10**   A subnet mask of 255.255.255.0 indicates this is a Class C address space.

Dynamic Host Configuration Protocol

When an administrator sets up a network, they usually assign IP addresses to systems in one of two ways: statically or through DHCP. A static IP address assignment is fairly simple; the administrator decides what IP address to assign to a server or PC, and that IP address stays assigned to that system until the administrator decides to change it. The other popular method is through the **Dynamic Host Configuration Protocol (DHCP)**. *Under DHCP, when a system boots up or is connected to the network, it sends out a query looking for a DHCP server. If a DHCP server is available on the network, it answers the new system and temporarily assigns to the new system an IP address from a pool of dedicated, available addresses. DHCP is an "as available" protocol—if the server has already allocated all the available IP addresses in the DHCP pool, the new system will not receive an IP address and will not be able to connect to the network. Another key feature of DHCP is the ability to limit how long a system may keep its DHCP-assigned IP address. DHCP addresses have a limited lifespan, and once that time period expires, the system using that IP address must either renew use of that address or request another address from the DHCP server. The requesting system either may end up with the same IP address or may be assigned a completely new address, depending on how the DHCP server is configured and on the current demand for available addresses. DHCP is very popular in large user environments where the cost of assigning and tracking IP addresses among hundreds or thousands of user systems is extremely high.*

Calculating Subnets and Hosts

Given a network ID of 192.168.10.X and a subnet mask of 255.255.255.224, you should be able to create eight networks with space for 30 hosts on each network. Calculate the network address, the first usable IP address in that subnet, and the last usable IP address in that subnet. *Hint:* The first network will be 192.168.10.0. The first usable IP address in that subnet is 192.168.10.1 and the last usable IP address in that subnet is 192.168.10.30.

network ID) allows us to divide an address space into multiple, smaller logical networks. Let's say you have a single address space of 192.168.45.0 that you need to divide into multiple networks. The default subnet mask is 255.255.255.0, which means you're using 24 bits as the network ID and 8 bits as the host ID. This gives you 254 different host addresses. But what if you need more networks and don't need as many host addresses? You can simply adjust your subnet mask to borrow some of the host bits and use them as network bits. If you use a subnet mask of 255.255.255.224, you are essentially "borrowing" the first 3 bits from the space you were using to describe host IDs and using them to describe the network ID. This gives you more space to create different networks but means that each network will now have fewer available host IDs. With a 255.255.255.224 subnet mask, you can create six different subnets, but each subnet can only have 30 unique host IDs. If you borrow 6 bits from the host ID portion and use a subnet mask of 255.255.255.252, you can create 62 different networks but each of them can only have two unique host IDs.

Network Address Translation

If you're thinking that a 32-bit address space that's chopped up and subnetted isn't enough to handle all the systems in the world, you're right. While IPv4 address blocks are assigned to organizations such as companies and universities, there usually aren't enough Internet-visible IP addresses to assign to every system on the planet a unique, Internet-routable IP address. To compensate for this lack of available IP address space, we use **Network Address Translation (NAT)**. NAT translates private (nonroutable) IP addresses into public (routable) IP addresses.

From our discussions earlier in this chapter, you may remember that certain IP address blocks are reserved for "private use," and you'd probably agree that not every system in an organization needs a direct, Internet-routable IP address. Actually, for security reasons, it's much better if most of an organization's systems are hidden from direct Internet access. Most organizations build their internal networks using the private IP address ranges (such as 10.1.1.X) to prevent outsiders from directly accessing those internal networks. However, in many cases those systems still need to be able to reach the Internet. This is accomplished by using a NAT device (typically a firewall or router) that translates the many internal IP addresses into one of a small number of public IP addresses.

For example, consider a fictitious company, ACME.com. ACME has several thousand internal systems using private IP addresses in the 10.X.X.X range. To allow those IPs to communicate with the outside world, ACME leases an Internet connection and a few public IP addresses, and deploys a NAT-capable device. ACME administrators configure all their internal hosts to use the NAT device as their default gateway. When internal hosts need to send packets outside the company, they send them to the NAT device. The NAT device removes the internal source IP address out of the outbound packets and replaces it with the NAT device's public, routable address and sends them on their way. When response packets are received from outside sources, the device performs NAT in reverse, stripping off the external, public IP address in the destination address field and replacing it with the correct internal, private IP address in the destination address field and replacing it with the correct internal, private IP address before sending it on into the private ACME.com network. Figure 9.11 illustrates this NAT process.

Tech Tip

Different Approaches for Implementing NAT

While the concept of NAT remains the same, there are actually several different approaches to implementing NAT. For example:

- **Static NAT**   *Maps an internal, private address to an external, public address. The same public address is always used for that private address. This technique is often used when hosting something you wish the public to be able to get to, such as a web server, behind a firewall.*

- **Dynamic NAT**   *Maps an internal, private IP address to a public IP address selected from a pool of registered (public) IP addresses. This technique is often used when translating addresses for end-user workstations and the NAT device must keep track of internal/external address mappings.*

- **Port Address Translation (PAT)**   *Allows many different internal, private addresses to share a single external IP address. Devices performing PAT replace the source IP address with the NAT IP address and replace the source port field with a port from an available connection pool. PAT devices keep a translation table to track which internal hosts are using which ports so that subsequent packets can be stamped with the same port number. When response packets are received, the PAT device reverses the process and forwards the packet to the correct internal host. PAT is a very popular NAT technique and in use at many organizations.*

In Figure 9.11, we see an example of NAT being performed. An internal workstation (10.10.10.12) wants to visit the ESPN web site at www.espn.com (68.71.212.159). When the packet reaches the NAT device, the device translates the 10.10.10.12 source address to the globally routable 63.69.110.110 address, the IP address of the device's externally visible interface. When the ESPN web site responds, it responds to the device's address just as if the NAT device had originally requested the information. The NAT device must then remember which internal workstation requested the information and route the packet to the appropriate destination.

Source: 10.10.12
Destination: 199.181.132.250

Source: 63.110.110
Destination: 199.181.132.250

Firewall performing NAT

ESPN.com

ACME internal network

Source: 199.181.132.250
Destination: 10.10.10.12

Source: 199.181.132.250
Destination: 63.69.110.110

• **Figure 9.11**   Logical depiction of NAT

■ Security Zones

The first aspect of security is a layered defense. Just as a castle has a moat, an outside wall, an inside wall, and even a keep, so, too, does a modern secure network have different layers of protection. Different zones are designed to provide layers of defense, with the outermost layers providing basic protection and the innermost layers providing the highest level of protection. A constant issue is that accessibility tends to be inversely related to level of protection, so it is more difficult to provide complete protection and unfettered access at the same time. Trade-offs between access and security are handled through zones, with successive zones guarded by firewalls enforcing ever-increasingly strict security policies. The outermost zone is the Internet, a free area, beyond any specific controls. Between the inner, secure corporate network and the Internet is an area where machines are considered at risk. This zone has come to be called the **DMZ**, after its military counterpart, the demilitarized zone, where neither side has any specific controls. Once inside the inner, secure network, separate branches are frequently carved out to provide specific functionality; under this heading, we will also discuss intranets, extranets, flat networks, enclaves, virtual LANs (VLANs), and zones and conduits.

DMZ

The DMZ is a military term for ground separating two opposing forces, by agreement and for the purpose of acting as a buffer between the two sides. A DMZ in a computer network is used in the same way; it acts as a buffer zone between the Internet, where no controls exist, and the inner, secure network, where an organization has security policies in place (see Figure 9.12). To demarcate the zones and enforce separation, a firewall is used on each side of the DMZ. The area between these firewalls is accessible from either the inner, secure network or the Internet. Figure 9.12 illustrates these zones as caused by firewall placement. The firewalls are specifically designed to prevent access across the DMZ directly, from the Internet to the inner, secure network. It is important to note that typically only filtered Internet traffic is allowed into the DMZ. For example, an organization hosting a web server and an FTP server in its DMZ may want the public to be able to "see" those services but nothing else. In that case the firewall may allow FTP, HTTP, and HTTPS traffic into the DMZ from the Internet and then filter out everything else.

Special attention should be paid to the security settings of network devices placed in the DMZ, and they should be considered at all times to be at risk for compromise by unauthorized use. A common industry term, *hardened operating system,* applies to machines whose functionality is locked down to preserve

• **Figure 9.12**   The DMZ and zones of trust

security—unnecessary services and software are removed or disabled, functions are limited, and so on. This approach needs to be applied to the machines in the DMZ, and although it means that their functionality is limited, such precautions ensure that the machines will work properly in a less-secure environment.

Many types of servers belong in this area, including web servers that are serving content to Internet users, as well as remote access servers and external e-mail servers. In general, any server directly accessed from the outside, untrusted Internet zone needs to be in the DMZ. Other servers should not be placed in the DMZ. Domain name servers for your inner, trusted network and database servers that house corporate databases should not be accessible from the outside. Application servers, file servers, print servers— all of the standard servers used in the trusted network—should be behind both firewalls and the routers and switches used to connect these machines.

The idea behind the use of the DMZ topology is to provide publicly visible services without allowing untrusted users access to your internal network. If the outside user makes a request for a resource from the trusted network, such as a data element from an internal database that is accessed via a publicly visible web page in the DMZ, then this request needs to follow this scenario:

1. A user from the untrusted network (the Internet) requests data via a web page from a web server in the DMZ.

2. The web server in the DMZ requests the data from the application server, which can be in the DMZ or in the inner, trusted network.

3. The application server requests the data from the database server in the trusted network.

4. The database server returns the data to the requesting application server.

5. The application server returns the data to the requesting web server.

6. The web server returns the data to the requesting user from the untrusted network.

> **Exam Tip:** DMZs act as a buffer zone between unprotected areas of a network (the Internet) and protected areas (sensitive company data stores), allowing for the monitoring and regulation of traffic between these two zones.

This separation accomplishes two specific, independent tasks. First, the user is separated from the request for data on a secure network. By having intermediaries do the requesting, this layered approach allows significant security levels to be enforced. Users do not have direct access or control over their requests, and this filtering process can put controls in place. Second, scalability is more easily realized. The multiple-server solution can be made to be very scalable, literally to millions of users, without slowing down any particular layer.

Internet

The Internet is a worldwide connection of networks and is used to transport e-mail, files, financial records, remote access—you name it—from one network to another. The Internet is not a single network, but a series of interconnected networks that allows protocols to operate and enable data to flow across it. This means that even if your network doesn't have direct contact with a resource, as long as a neighbor, or a neighbor's neighbor, and

There are over 3.2 billion users on the Internet, and English is the most used language.

so on, can get there, so can you. This large web allows users almost infinite ability to communicate between systems.

Because everything and everyone can access this interconnected web and it is outside of your control and ability to enforce security policies, the Internet should be considered an untrusted network. A firewall should exist at any connection between your trusted network and the Internet. This is not to imply that the Internet is a bad thing—it is a great resource for all networks and adds significant functionality to our computing environments.

The term World Wide Web (WWW) is frequently used synonymously to represent the Internet, but the WWW is actually just one set of services available via the Internet. WWW or "the Web" is more specifically the Hypertext Transfer Protocol (HTTP)–based services that are made available over the Internet. This can include a variety of actual services and content, including text files, pictures, streaming audio and video, and even viruses and worms.

Intranet

An **intranet** describes a network that has the same functionality as the Internet for users but lies completely inside the trusted area of a network and is under the security control of the system and network administrators. Typically referred to as *campus* or *corporate* networks, intranets are used every day in companies around the world. An intranet allows a developer and a user the full set of protocols—HTTP, FTP, instant messaging, and so on— that is offered on the Internet, but with the added advantage of trust from the network security. Content on intranet web servers is not available over the Internet to untrusted users. This layer of security offers a significant amount of control and regulation, allowing users to fulfill business functionality while ensuring security.

Two methods can be used to make information available to outside users: Duplication of information onto machines in the DMZ can make it available to other users. Proper security checks and controls should be made prior to duplicating the material to ensure security policies concerning specific data availability are being followed. Alternatively, *extranets* (discussed in the next section) can be used to publish material to trusted partners.

Should users inside the intranet require access to information from the Internet, a proxy server can be used to mask the requestor's location. This helps secure the intranet from outside mapping of its actual topology. All Internet requests go to the proxy server. If a request passes filtering requirements, the proxy server, assuming it is also a cache server, looks in its local cache of previously downloaded web pages. If it finds the page in its cache, it returns the page to the requestor without needing to send the request to the Internet. If the page is not in the cache, the proxy server, acting as a client on behalf of the user, uses one of its own IP addresses to request the page from the Internet. When the page is returned, the proxy server relates it to the original request and forwards it on to the user. This masks the user's IP address from the Internet. Proxy servers can perform several functions for a firm; for example, they can monitor traffic requests, eliminating improper requests such as inappropriate content for work. They can also act as a cache server, cutting down on outside network requests for the same object. Finally, proxy servers protect the identity of internal

Exam Tip: An intranet is a private, internal network that uses common network technologies (such as HTTP, FTP, and so on) to share information and provide resources to organizational users.

IP addresses using NAT, although this function can also be accomplished through a router or firewall using NAT as well.

Extranet

An **extranet** is an extension of a selected portion of a company's intranet to external partners. This allows a business to share information with customers, suppliers, partners, and other trusted groups while using a common set of Internet protocols to facilitate operations. Extranets can use public networks to extend their reach beyond a company's own internal network, and some form of security, typically VPN, is used to secure this channel. The use of the term *extranet* implies both privacy and security. Privacy is required for many communications, and security is needed to prevent unauthorized use and events from occurring. Both of these functions can be achieved through the use of technologies described in this chapter and other chapters in this book. Proper firewall management, remote access, encryption, authentication, and secure tunnels across public networks are all methods used to ensure privacy and security for extranets.

> **Exam Tip:** An extranet is a semiprivate network that uses common network technologies (such as HTTP, FTP, and so on) to share information and provide resources to business partners. Extranets can be accessed by more than one company, because they share information between organizations.

Flat Networks

As networks have become more complex, with multiple layers of tiers and interconnections, a problem can arise in connectivity . One of the limitations of the Spanning Tree Protocol (STP) is its inability to manage Layer 2 traffic efficiently across highly complex networks. STP was created to prevent loops in Layer 2 networks and has been improved to the current version of Rapid Spanning Tree Protocol (RSTP). RSTP creates a spanning tree within the network of Layer 2 switches, disabling links that are not part of the spanning tree. RSTP, IEEE 802.1w, provides a more rapid convergence to a new spanning tree solution after topology changes are detected. The problem with the spanning tree algorithms is that the network traffic is interrupted while the system recalculates and reconfigures. These disruptions can cause problems in network efficiencies and have led to a push for **flat network** designs, which avoid packet-looping issues through an architecture that does not have tiers.

One name associated with flat network topologies is *network fabric*, a term meant to describe a flat, depthless network. These are becoming increasingly popular in data centers, and other areas of high traffic density, as they can offer increased throughput and lower levels of network jitter and other disruptions. While this is good for efficiency of network operations, this "everyone can talk to everyone" idea is problematic with respect to security.

Enclaves

Modern networks, with their increasingly complex connections, result in systems where navigation can become complex between nodes. Just as a DMZ-based architecture allows for differing levels of trust, the isolation of specific pieces of the network using security rules can provide differing trust environments. The concept of breaking a network into **enclaves** can create areas of trust where special protections can be employed and traffic from outside the enclave is limited or properly screened before admission.

Enclaves are not diametrically opposed to the concept of a flat network structure; they are just carved-out areas, like gated neighborhoods, where one needs special credentials to enter. A variety of security mechanisms can be employed to create a secure enclave. Layer 2 addressing (subnetting) can be employed, making direct addressability an issue. Firewalls, routers, and application-level proxies can be employed to screen packets before entry or exit from the enclave. Even the people side of the system can be restricted through the use of a special set of sysadmins to manage the systems.

Enclaves are an important tool in modern secure network design. Figure 9.13 shows a network design with a standard two-firewall implementation of a DMZ. On the internal side of the network, multiple firewalls can be seen, carving off individual security enclaves, zones where the same security rules apply. Common enclaves include those for high-security databases, low-security users (call centers), public-facing kiosks, and the management interfaces to servers and network devices. Having each of these in its own zone provides for more security control. On the management layer, using a nonroutable IP address scheme for all of the interfaces prevents them from being directly accessed from the Internet.

VLANs

A LAN is a set of devices with similar functionality and similar communication needs, typically co-located and operated off a single switch. This is the lowest level of a network hierarchy and defines the domain for certain protocols at the data link layer for communication. A virtual LAN (VLAN) is a logical implementation of a LAN and allows computers connected to different physical networks to act and communicate as if they were on the same physical network. A VLAN has many of the same characteristic attributes of a LAN and behaves much like a physical LAN but is implemented

• **Figure 9.13**   Secure enclaves

using switches and software. This very powerful technique allows significant network flexibility, scalability, and performance and allows administrators to perform network reconfigurations without having to physically relocate or recable systems.

Trunking

Trunking is the process of spanning a single VLAN across multiple switches. A trunk-based connection between switches allows packets from a single VLAN to travel between switches, as shown in Figure 9.14. Two trunks are shown in the figure: VLAN 10 is implemented with one trunk and VLAN 20 is implemented with the other. Hosts on different VLANs cannot communicate using trunks and thus are switched across the switch network. Trunks enable network administrators to set up VLANs across multiple switches with minimal effort. With a combination of trunks and VLANs, network administrators can subnet a network by user functionality without regard to host location on the network or the need to recable machines.

Security Implications

VLANs are used to divide a single network into multiple subnets based on functionality. This permits accounting and marketing, for example, to share a switch because of proximity yet still have separate traffic domains. The physical placement of equipment and cables is logically and programmatically separated so that adjacent ports on a switch can reference separate subnets. This prevents unauthorized use of physically close devices through separate subnets that are on the same equipment. VLANs also allow a network administrator to define a VLAN that has no users and map all of the unused ports to this VLAN (some managed switches allow administrators to simply disable unused ports as well). Then, if an unauthorized user should gain access to the equipment, that user will be unable to use unused ports, as those ports will be securely defined to nothing. Both a purpose and a security strength of VLANs is that systems on separate VLANs cannot directly communicate with each other.

Exam Tip: A broadcast domain is a logical division of a computer network. Systems connected to a broadcast domain can communicate with each other as if they were connected to the same physical network even when they are not.

Trunks and VLANs have security implications that you need to heed so that firewalls and other segmentation devices are not breached through their use. You also need to understand how to use trunks and VLANs, to prevent an unauthorized user from reconfiguring them to gain undetected access to secure portions of a network.

● **Figure 9.14**   VLANs and trunks

Zones and Conduits

The terms *zones* and *conduits* have specialized meaning in control system networks. Control systems are the computers used to control physical processes, ranging from traffic lights to refineries, manufacturing plants, critical infrastructure, and more. These networks are now being attached to enterprise networks and this will result in the inclusion of control system network terminology into IT/network/security operations terminology. A term commonly used in control system networks is zone. A zone is a grouping of elements that share common security requirements. A conduit is defined as the path for the flow of data between zones.

Zones are similar to enclaves in that they have a defined set of common security requirements that differ from outside the zone. The zone is marked on a diagram, indicating the boundary between what is in and outside the zone. All data flows in or out of a zone must be by a defined conduit. The conduit allows a means to focus the security function on the data flows, ensuring the appropriate conditions are met before data enters or leaves a zone.

■ Tunneling

Tunneling is a method of packaging packets so that they can traverse a network in a secure, confidential manner. Tunneling involves encapsulating packets within packets, enabling dissimilar protocols to coexist in a single communication stream, as in IP traffic routed over an Asynchronous Transfer Mode (ATM) network. Tunneling also can provide significant measures of security and confidentiality through encryption and encapsulation methods. The best example of this is a VPN that is established over a public network through the use of a tunnel, as shown in Figure 9.15, connecting a firm's Boston office to its New York City (NYC) office.

Assume, for example, that a company has multiple locations and decides to use the public Internet to connect the networks at these locations. To make these connections secure from outside unauthorized use, the company can employ a VPN connection between the different networks. On each network, an edge device, usually a router or VPN concentrator, connects to another edge device on the other network. Then, using IPsec protocols, these routers establish a secure, encrypted path between them. This securely encrypted set of packets cannot be read by outside routers; only the addresses of the edge routers are visible. This arrangement acts as a tunnel across the public Internet and establishes a private connection, secure from outside snooping or use.

Boston offfice   IPsec enabled router   Tunnel — Internet   IPsec enabled router   NYC headquarters

● **Figure 9.15** Tunneling across a public network

Because of ease of use, low-cost hardware, and strong security, tunnels and the Internet are a combination that will see more use in the future. IPsec, VPN, and tunnels will become a major set of tools for users requiring secure network connections across public segments of networks. For more information on VPNs and remote access, refer to Chapter 11.

 A VPN concentrator is a specialized piece of hardware designed to handle the encryption and decryption required for remote, secure access to an organization's network.

Storage Area Networks

Storage area networks (SANs) are systems which provide remote storage of data across a network connection. The design of SAN protocols is such that the disk appears to actually be on the client machine as a local drive rather than as attached storage, as in network attached storage (NAS). This makes the disk visible in disk and volume management utilities and allows their functionality. Common SAN protocols include iSCSI and Fibre Channel.

iSCSI

The Internet Small Computer System Interface (iSCSI) is a protocol for IP-based storage. iSCSI can be used to send data over existing network infrastructures, enabling SANs. Positioned as a low-cost alternative to Fibre Channel storage, the only real limitation is one of network bandwidth.

Fibre Channel

Fibre Channel (FC) is a high-speed network technology (with throughput up to 16 Gbps) used to connect storage to computer systems. The FC protocol is a transport protocol similar to the TCP protocol in IP networks. Carried via special cables, one of the drawbacks of FC-based storage is cost.

FCoE

The Fibre Channel over Ethernet (FCoE) protocol encapsulates the FC frames, enabling FC communication over 10-Gigabit Ethernet networks.

Chapter 9 Review

For More Information

- **Networking**

  CompTIA Network+ Certification All-in-One Exam Guide, Premium Fifth Edition, McGraw-Hill, 2014

- **The Internet Engineering Task Force**

  www.ietf.org

- **Wikipedia articles:**

Routing   http://en.wikipedia.org/wiki/Routing

NAT   http://en.wikipedia.org/wiki/Network_address_translation

ICMP   http://en.wikipedia.org/wiki/Internet_Control_Message_Protocol

Subnetting   http://en.wikipedia.org/wiki/Subnetting

Lab Manual Exercises

The following lab exercises from the companion lab manual, *Principles of Computer Security Lab Manual, Fourth Edition,* provide practical application of material covered in this chapter:

Lab 1.2w	Name Resolution in Windows
Lab 1.3w	Windows IPv6 Basics (netsh/ping6)
Lab 2.1w	Network Communication Analysis in Windows
Lab 2.2l	Linux-Based Port Connection Status
Lab 2.2w	Windows-Based Port Connection Status
Lab 4.1w	Using Nmap in Windows

Chapter Summary

After reading this chapter and completing the exercises, you should understand the following about networks.

Identify the basic network architectures

- There are two broad categories of networks: LANs and WANs.

- The physical arrangement of a network is typically called the network's topology.

- There are four main types of network topologies: ring, bus, star, and mixed.

Define the basic network protocols

- Protocols, agreed-upon formats for exchanging or transmitting data between systems, enable computers to communicate.

- When data is transmitted over a network, it is usually broken up into smaller pieces called packets.

- Most protocols define the types and format for packets used in that protocol.

- TCP is connection oriented, requires the three-way handshake to initiate a connection, and provides guaranteed and reliable data delivery.

- UDP is connectionless, lightweight, and provides limited error checking and no delivery guarantee.

- Each network device has a unique hardware address known as a MAC address. The MAC address is used for packet delivery.

- Network devices are also typically assigned a 32-bit number known as an IP address.

- The Domain Name Service (DNS) translates names, like www.cnn.com, into IP addresses.

Explain routing and address translation

- The process of moving packets from one end device to another through different networks is called routing.

- Subnetting is the process of dividing a network address space into smaller networks.

- DHCP allows network devices to be automatically configured on a network and temporarily assigned an IP address.

- Network Address Translation (NAT) converts private, internal IP addresses to public, routable IP addresses and vice versa.

Classify security zones

- A DMZ is a buffer zone between networks with different trust levels. Companies often place public resources in a DMZ so that Internet users and internal users may access those resources without exposing the internal company network to the Internet.

- An intranet is a private, internal network that uses common network technologies (such as HTTP, FTP, and so on) to share information and provide resources to organizational users.

- An extranet is a semiprivate network that uses common network technologies (such as HTTP, FTP, and so on) to share information and provide resources to business partners.

- An enclave is a specialized security zone with common security requirements.

- A VLAN (or virtual LAN) is a group of ports on a switch that is configured to create a logical network of computer that appears to be connected to the same network even if they are located on different physical network segments. Systems on a VLAN can communicate with each other but cannot communicate directly with systems on other VLANs.

- Trunking is the process of spanning a single VLAN across multiple switches.

- Tunneling is a method of packaging packets so that they can traverse a network in a secure, confidential manner.

■ Key Terms

Address Resolution Protocol (ARP) *(234)*

bus topology *(222)*

datagram *(226)*

denial-of-service (DoS) *(229)*

Domain Name System (DNS) *(235)*

DMZ *(240)*

Dynamic Host Configuration Protocol (DHCP) *(238)*

enclave *(243)*

Ethernet *(233)*

extranet *(243)*

flat network *(243)*

Internet Control Message Protocol (ICMP) *(229)*

Internet Protocol (IP) *(226)*

intranet *(242)*

local area network (LAN) *(221)*

Media Access Control (MAC) address *(233)*

Network Address Translation (NAT) *(238)*

network *(220)*

packet *(225)*

protocol *(223)*

ring topology *(222)*

routing *(235)*

star topology *(222)*

storage area network (SAN) *(221)*

subnetting *(236)*

subnet mask *(236)*

three-way handshake *(228)*

topology *(222)*

Transmission Control Protocol (TCP) *(228)*

trunking *(245)*

tunneling *(246)*

User Datagram Protocol (UDP) *(228)*

virtual local area network (VLAN) *(222)*

wide area network (WAN) *(221)*

■ Key Terms Quiz

Use terms from the Key Terms list to complete the sentences that follow. Don't use the same term more than once. Not all terms will be used.

1. A(n) _____ is a group of two or more devices linked together to share data.

2. A packet in an IP network is sometimes called a(n) _____.

3. Moving packets from source to destination across multiple networks is called _____.

4. The _____ is the hardware address used to uniquely identify each device on a network.

5. A(n) _____ tells you what portion of a 32-bit IP address is being used as the network ID and what portion is being used as the host ID.

6. The shape or arrangement of a network, such as bus, star, ring, or mixed, is known as the _____ of the network.

7. A small, typically local network covering a relatively small area such as a single floor of an office building is called a(n) _____.

8. A(n) _____ is an agreed-upon format for exchanging information between systems.

9. The packet exchange sequence (SYN, SYN/ACK, ACK) that initiates a TCP connection is called the _____.

10. _____ is the protocol that allows the use of private, internal IP addresses for internal traffic and public IP addresses for external traffic.

■ Multiple-Choice Quiz

1. What is Layer 1 of the OSI model called?
   A. The physical layer
   B. The network layer
   C. The initial layer
   D. The presentation layer

2. The UDP protocol:
   A. Provides excellent error-checking algorithms
   B. Is a connectionless protocol
   C. Guarantees delivery of packets
   D. Requires a permanent connection between source and destination

3. The process that dynamically assigns an IP address to a network device is called:
   A. NAT
   B. DNS
   C. DHCP
   D. Routing

4. What is the three-way handshake sequence used to initiate TCP connections?
   A. ACK, SYN/ACK, ACK
   B. SYN, SYN/ACK, ACK
   C. SYN, SYN, ACK/ACK
   D. ACK, SYN/ACK, SYN

5. Which of the following is a control and information protocol used by network devices to determine such things as a remote network's availability and the length of time required to reach a remote network?
   A. UDP
   B. NAT
   C. TCP
   D. ICMP

6. What is the name of the protocol that translates names into IP addresses?
   A. TCP
   B. DNS
   C. ICMP
   D. DHCP

7. Dividing a network address space into smaller, separate networks is called what?
   A. Translating
   B. Network configuration
   C. Subnetting
   D. Address translation

8. Which protocol translates private (nonroutable) IP addresses into public (routable) IP addresses?

    A. NAT

    B. DHCP

    C. DNS

    D. ICMP

9. The TCP protocol:

    A. Is connectionless

    B. Provides no error checking

    C. Allows for packets to be processed in the order they were sent

    D. Has no overhead

10. Which of the following would be a valid MAC address?

    A. 00:07:e9

    B. 00:07:e9:7c:c8

    C. 00:07:e9:7c:c8:aa

    D. 00:07:e9:7c:c8:aa:ba

■ Essay Quiz

1. A developer in your company is building a new application and has asked you if it should use TCP- or UDP-based communications. Provide her with a brief discussion of the advantages and disadvantages of each protocol.

2. Your boss wants to know if DHCP is appropriate for both server and PC environments. Provide her with your opinion and be sure to include a discussion of how DHCP works.

3. Describe the three basic types of network topologies and provide a sample diagram of each type.

4. Describe the three-way handshake process used to initiate TCP connections.

5. Your boss wants to know how subnetting works. Provide her with a brief description and be sure to include an example to illustrate how subnetting works.

Lab Projects

• Lab Project 9.1

A client of yours only has five external, routable IP addresses but has over 50 systems that it wants to be able to reach the Internet for web surfing, e-mail, and so on. Design a network solution for the client that addresses their immediate needs but will still let them grow in the future.

• Lab Project 9.2

Your boss wants you to learn how to use the **arp** and **nslookup** commands. Find a Windows machine and open a command/DOS prompt. Type in **arp** and press ENTER to see the options for the **arp** command. Use the **arp** command to find the MAC address of your system and at least five other systems on your network. When you are finished with **arp**, type in **nslookup** and press ENTER. At the prompt, type in the name of your favorite web site, such as www.cnn.com. The **nslookup** command will return the IP addresses that match that domain name. Find the IP addresses of at least five different web sites.

Infrastructure Security

The higher your structure is to be, the deeper must be its foundation.
—SAINT AUGUSTINE

In this chapter, you will learn how to

- Construct networks using different types of network devices
- Enhance security using security devices
- Enhance security using NAC/NAP methodologies
- Identify the different types of media used to carry network signals
- Describe the different types of storage media used to store information
- Use basic terminology associated with network functions related to information security
- Describe the different types and uses of cloud computing

Infrastructure security begins with the design of the infrastructure itself. The proper use of components improves not only performance but security as well. Network components are not isolated from the computing environment and are an essential aspect of a total computing environment. From the routers, switches, and cables that connect the devices, to the firewalls and gateways that manage communication, from the network design, to the protocols that are employed—all these items play essential roles in both performance and security.

■ Devices

A complete network computer solution in today's business environment consists of more than just client computers and servers. *Devices* are needed to connect the clients and servers and to regulate the traffic between them. Devices are also needed to expand this network beyond simple client computers and servers to include yet other devices, such as wireless and handheld systems. Devices come in many forms and with many functions, from hubs and switches, to routers, wireless access points, and special-purpose devices such as virtual private network (VPN) devices. Each device has a specific network function and plays a role in maintaining network infrastructure security.

Cross Check

The Importance of Availability

In Chapter 2, we examined the *CIA* of security: confidentiality, integrity, and availability. Unfortunately, the availability component is often overlooked, even though availability is what has moved computing into the modern networked framework and plays a significant role in security.

Security failures can occur in two ways. First, a failure can allow unauthorized users access to resources and data they are not authorized to use, compromising information security. Second, a failure can prevent a user from accessing resources and data the user is authorized to use. This second failure is often overlooked, but it can be as serious as the first. The primary goal of network infrastructure security is to allow all authorized use and deny all unauthorized use of resources.

Workstations

Most users are familiar with the client computers used in the client/server model called *workstation* devices. The **workstation** is the machine that sits on the desktop and is used every day for sending and reading e-mail, creating spreadsheets, writing reports in a word processing program, and playing games. If a workstation is connected to a network, it is an important part of the security solution for the network. Many threats to information security can start at a workstation, but much can be done in a few simple steps to provide protection from many of these threats.

Cross Check

Workstations and Servers

Servers and workstations are key nodes on networks. The specifics for securing these devices ares covered in Chapter 14.

Servers

Servers are the computers in a network that host applications and data for everyone to share. Servers come in many sizes, from small single-CPU boxes that may be less powerful than a workstation, to multiple-CPU monsters, up to and including mainframes. The operating systems used by servers range from Windows Server, to UNIX, to Multiple Virtual Storage (MVS) and other mainframe operating systems. The OS on a server tends to be more robust than the OS on a workstation system and is designed to service multiple users over a network at the same time. Servers can host a variety of applications, including web servers, databases, e-mail servers, file servers, print servers, and application servers for middleware applications.

Virtualization

Virtualization technology is used to allow a computer to have more than one OS present and, in many cases, operating at the same time. **Virtualization** is an abstraction of the OS layer, creating the ability to host multiple OSs on a single piece of hardware. One of the major advantages of virtualization is the separation of the software and the hardware, creating a barrier that can improve many system functions, including security. The underlying hardware is referred to as the host machine, and on it is a host OS. Either the host OS has built-in hypervisor capability or an application is needed to provide the hypervisor function to manage the virtual machines (VMs). The virtual machines are typically referred to as the guest OSs.

Newer OSs are designed to natively incorporate virtualization hooks, enabling virtual machines to be employed with greater ease. There are several common virtualization solutions, including Microsoft Hyper-V, VMware, Oracle VM VirtualBox, Parallels, and Citrix Xen. It is important to distinguish between virtualization and boot loaders that allow different OSs to boot on hardware. Apple's Boot Camp allows you to boot into Microsoft Windows on Apple hardware. This is different from Parallels, a product with complete virtualization capability for Apple hardware.

Virtualization offers much in terms of host-based management of a system. From snapshots that allow easy rollback to previous states, faster system deployment via preconfigured images, ease of backup, and the ability to test systems, virtualization offers many advantages to system owners. The separation of the operational software layer from the hardware layer can offer many improvements in the management of systems.

Exam Tip: A hypervisor is the interface between a virtual machine and the host machine hardware. Hypervisors are the layer that enables virtualization.

Snapshots

A *snapshot* is a point-in-time saving of the state of a virtual machine. Snapshots have great utility because they are like a savepoint for an entire system. Snapshots can be used to roll a system back to a previous point in time, undo operations, or provide a quick means of recovery from a complex, system-altering change that has gone awry. Snapshots act as a form of backup and are typically much faster than normal system backup and recovery operations.

Patch Compatibility

Having an OS operate in a virtual environment does not change the need for security associated with the OS. Patches are still needed and should be applied, independent of the virtualization status. Because of the nature of a virtual environment, it should have no effect on the utility of patching, as the patch is for the guest OS.

Host Availability/Elasticity

When you set up a virtualization environment, protecting the host OS and hypervisor level is critical for system stability. The best practice is to avoid the installation of any applications on the host-level machine. All apps should be housed and run in a virtual environment. This aids in the stability by providing separation between the application and the host OS. The term *elasticity* refers to the ability of a system to expand/contract as system requirements dictate. One of the advantages of virtualization is that a virtual machine can be moved to larger or smaller environments based on needs. If a VM needs more processing power, then migrating the VM to a new hardware system with greater CPU capacity allows the system to expand without having to rebuild it.

Security Control Testing

When applying security controls to a system to manage security operations, it is important to test the controls to ensure that they are providing the desired results. Putting a system into a VM does not change this requirement. In fact, it may complicate it because of the nature of the guest OS to hypervisor relationship. It is essential to specifically test all security controls inside the virtual environment to ensure their behavior is still effective.

Sandboxing

Sandboxing refers to the quarantine or isolation of a system from its surroundings. Virtualization can be used as a form of sandboxing with respect to an entire system. You can build a VM, test something inside the VM, and, based on the results, make a decision with regard to stability or whatever concern was present.

Mobile Devices

Mobile devices such as laptops, tablets, and mobile phones are the latest devices to join the corporate network. Mobile devices can create a major security gap, as a user may access separate e-mail accounts, one personal, without antivirus protection, and the other corporate. Mobile devices are covered in detail in Chapter 12.

Device Security, Common Concerns

As more and more interactive devices (that is, devices you can interact with programmatically) are being designed, a new threat source has appeared. In an attempt to build security into devices, typically, a default account and password must be entered to enable the user to access and configure the device remotely. These default accounts and passwords are well known in the hacker community, so one of the first steps you must take to secure such devices is to change the default credentials. Anyone who has purchased a home office router knows the default configuration settings and can check to see if another user has changed theirs. If they have not, this is a huge security hole, allowing outsiders to "reconfigure" their network devices.

Tech Tip

Default Accounts

Always reconfigure all default accounts on all devices before exposing them to external traffic. This is to prevent others from reconfiguring your devices based on known access settings.

Network Attached Storage

Because of the speed of today's Ethernet networks, it is possible to manage data storage across the network. This has led to a type of storage known as **Network Attached Storage (NAS)**. The combination of inexpensive hard drives, fast networks, and simple application-based servers has made NAS devices in the terabyte range affordable for even home users. Because of the large size of video files, this has become popular for some users as a method of storing TV and video libraries. Because NAS is a network device, it is susceptible to various attacks, including sniffing of credentials and a variety of brute-force attacks to obtain access to the data.

Removable Storage

Because removable devices can move data outside of the corporate-controlled environment, their security needs must be addressed. Removable devices can bring unprotected or corrupted data into the corporate environment. All removable devices should be scanned by antivirus software upon connection to the corporate environment. Corporate policies should address the copying of data to removable devices. Many mobile devices can be connected via USB to a system and used to store data—and in some cases vast quantities of data. This capability can be used to avoid some implementations of data loss prevention mechanisms.

■ Networking

Networks are used to connect devices together. Networks are composed of components that perform networking functions to move data between devices. Networks begin with network interface cards, then continue in layers of switches and routers. Specialized networking devices are used for specific purposes, such as security and traffic management.

Network Interface Cards

To connect a server or workstation to a network, a device known as a **network interface card (NIC)** is used. A NIC is a card with a connector port for a particular type of network connection, either Ethernet or Token Ring. The most common network type in use for LANs is the Ethernet protocol, and the most common connector is the RJ-45 connector.

A NIC is the physical connection between a computer and the network. The purpose of a NIC is to provide lower-level protocol functionality from the OSI (Open System Interconnection) model. Because the NIC defines the type of physical layer connection, different NICs are used for different physical protocols. NICs come as single-port and multiport, and most workstations use only a single-port NIC, as only a single network connection is needed. Figure 10.1 shows a common form of a NIC. For servers, multiport NICs are used to increase the number of network connections, increasing the data throughput to and from the network.

Each NIC port is serialized with a unique code, 48 bits long, referred to as a Media Access Control address (MAC address). These are created by the manufacturer, with 24 bits representing the manufacturer and 24 bits being a serial number, guaranteeing uniqueness. MAC addresses are used in the addressing and delivery of network packets to the correct machine and in a variety of security situations.

• **Figure 10.1**   Linksys network interface card (NIC)

Unfortunately, these addresses can be changed, or "spoofed," rather easily. In fact, it is common for personal routers to clone a MAC address to allow users to use multiple devices over a network connection that expects a single MAC.

Hubs

A **hub** is networking equipment that connects devices that are using the same protocol at the physical layer of the OSI model. A hub allows multiple machines in an area to be connected together in a star configuration, with the hub as the center. This configuration can save significant amounts of cable and is an efficient method of configuring an Ethernet backbone. All connections on a hub share a single **collision domain**, a small cluster in a network where collisions occur. As network traffic increases, it can become limited by collisions. The collision issue has made hubs obsolete in newer, higher performance networks, with inexpensive switches and switched Ethernet keeping costs low and usable bandwidth high. Hubs also create a security weakness in that all connected devices see all traffic, enabling sniffing and eavesdropping to occur. In today's networks, hubs have all but disappeared, being replaced by low-cost switches.

Bridges

Bridges are networking equipment that connect devices using the same protocol at the data link layer of the OSI model. A **bridge** operates at the data link layer, filtering traffic based on MAC addresses. Bridges can reduce collisions by separating pieces of a network into two separate collision domains, but this only cuts the collision problem in half. Although bridges are useful, a better solution is to use switches for network connections.

Switches

A **switch** forms the basis for connections in most Ethernet-based LANs. Although hubs and bridges still exist, in today's high-performance network environment, switches have replaced both. A switch has separate collision domains for each port. This means that for each port, two collision domains exist: one from the port to the client on the downstream side, and one from the switch to the network upstream. When *full duplex* is employed, collisions are virtually eliminated from the two nodes, host and client. This also acts as a hub-based system, where a single sniffer can see all of the traffic to and from connected devices.

Switches operate at the data link layer, while routers act at the network layer. For intranets, switches have become what routers are on the Internet—the device of choice for connecting machines. As switches have become the primary network connectivity device, additional functionality has been added to them. A switch is usually a Layer 2 device, but Layer 3 switches incorporate routing functionality.

Hubs have been replaced by switches because switches perform a number of features that hubs cannot perform. For example, the switch improves network performance by filtering traffic. It filters traffic by only sending the data to the port on the switch that the destination system resides on. The switch knows what port each system is connected to and sends the data only to that port. The switch also provides security features, such as the option to disable a port so that it cannot be used without authorization. The switch also supports a feature called port security, which allows the administrator to control which systems can send data to each of the ports. The switch uses the MAC address of the systems to incorporate traffic filtering and port security features, which is why it is considered a Layer 2 device.

Port address security based on MAC addresses can determine whether a packet is allowed or blocked from a connection. This is the very function that a firewall uses for its determination, and this same functionality is what allows an 802.1X device to act as an "edge device."

One of the security concerns with switches is that, like routers, they are intelligent network devices and are therefore subject to hijacking by hackers. Should a hacker break into a switch and change its parameters, he might be able to eavesdrop on specific or all communications, virtually undetected. Switches are commonly administered using the Simple Network Management Protocol (SNMP) and Telnet protocol, both of which have a serious weakness in that they send passwords across the network in cleartext. A hacker armed with a sniffer that observes maintenance on a switch can capture the administrative password. This allows the hacker to come back to the switch later and configure it as an administrator. An additional problem is that switches are shipped with default passwords, and if these are not changed when the switch is set up, they offer an unlocked door to a hacker.

Switches are also subject to electronic attacks, such as ARP poisoning and MAC flooding. ARP poisoning is where a device spoofs the MAC address of another device, attempting to change the ARP tables through spoofed traffic and the ARP table-update mechanism. MAC flooding is where a switch is bombarded with packets from different MAC addresses, flooding the switch table and forcing the device to respond by opening all ports and acting as a hub. This enables devices on other segments to sniff traffic.

Loop Protection

Switches operate at Layer 2, at which there is no countdown mechanism to kill packets that get caught in loops or on paths that will never resolve. The Layer 2 space acts as a mesh, where potentially the addition of a new device can create loops in the existing device interconnections. To prevent loops, a technology called spanning trees is employed by virtually all switches. The Spanning Tree Protocol (STP) allows for multiple, redundant paths, while breaking loops to ensure a proper broadcast pattern. Loop protection is covered in detail in Chapter 9.

Routers

A **router** is a network traffic management device used to connect different network segments together. Routers operate at the network layer (Layer 3) of the OSI model, using the network address (typically an IP address) to route traffic and using routing protocols to determine optimal routing paths across a network. Routers form the backbone of the Internet, moving traffic from network to network, inspecting packets from every communication as they move traffic in optimal paths.

Routers operate by examining each packet, looking at the destination address, and using algorithms and tables to determine where to send the packet next. This process of examining the header to determine the next hop can be done in quick fashion.

Routers use access control lists (ACLs) as a method of deciding whether a packet is allowed to enter the network. With ACLs, it is also possible to examine the source address and determine whether or not to allow a packet to pass. This allows routers equipped with ACLs to drop packets according to rules built into the ACLs. This can be a cumbersome process to set up and maintain, and as the ACL grows in size, routing efficiency can be decreased. It is also possible to configure some routers to act as quasi–application gateways, performing stateful packet inspection and using contents as well as IP addresses to determine whether or not to permit a packet to pass. This can tremendously increase the time for a router to pass traffic and can significantly decrease router throughput. Configuring ACLs and other aspects of setting up routers for this type of use are beyond the scope of this book.

One serious security concern regarding router operation is limiting who has access to the router and control of its internal functions. Like a switch, a router can be accessed using SNMP and Telnet and programmed remotely. Because of the geographic separation of routers, this can become a necessity, for many routers in the world of the Internet can be hundreds of miles apart, in separate locked structures. Physical control over a router is absolutely necessary, for if any device, be it a server, switch, or router, is physically accessed by a hacker, it should be considered compromised. Thus, such access must be prevented. As with switches, it is important to ensure that the administrator password is never passed in the clear, that only secure mechanisms are used to access the router, and that all of the default passwords are reset to strong passwords.

As with switches, the most assured point of access for router management control is via the serial control interface port. This allows access to the control aspects of the router without having to deal with traffic-related issues. For internal company networks, where the geographic dispersion of routers may be limited, third-party solutions to allow out-of-band remote management exist. This allows complete control over the router in a secure fashion, even from a remote location, although additional hardware is required.

Routers are available from numerous vendors and come in sizes big and small. A typical small home office router for use with cable modem/DSL service is shown in Figure 10.2. Larger routers can handle traffic of up to tens of gigabytes per second per channel, using fiber-optic inputs and moving tens of thousands of concurrent Internet connections across the network. These routers, which can cost hundreds of thousands of dollars, form an essential part of e-commerce infrastructure, enabling large enterprises such as Amazon and eBay to serve many customers' use concurrently.

ACLs can require significant effort to establish and maintain. Creating them is a straightforward task, but their judicious use will yield security benefits with a limited amount of maintenance. Cisco routers have standard and extended ACLs; standard ACLs can filter traffic based only on the source IP address, whereas extended ACLs can filter traffic by source/destination IP address, protocol, and port. This can be very important in security zones such as a DMZ and at edge devices, blocking undesired outside contact while allowing known inside traffic.

• **Figure 10.2**   A small home office router for cable modem/DSL

Exam Tip: A firewall is a network device (hardware, software, or combination of the two) that enforces a security policy. All network traffic passing through the firewall is examined—traffic that does not meet the specified security criteria or violates the firewall policy is blocked.

Tech Tip

Firewall Rules

Firewalls are in reality policy enforcement devices. Each rule in a firewall should have a policy behind it, as this is the only manner of managing firewall rule sets over time. The steps for successful firewall management begin and end with maintaining a policy list by firewall of the traffic restrictions to be imposed. Managing this list via a configuration management process is important to prevent network instabilities from faulty rule sets or unknown "left-over" rules.

Orphan or left-over rules are rules that were created for a special purpose (testing, emergency, visitor or vendor, etc.) and then forgotten about and not removed after their use ended. These rules can clutter up a firewall and result in unintended challenges to the network security team.

Firewalls

A **firewall** is a network device—hardware, software, or a combination thereof—whose purpose is to enforce a security policy across its connections by allowing or denying traffic to pass into or out of the network. A firewall is a lot like a gate guard at a secure facility. The guard examines all the traffic trying to enter the facility—cars with the correct sticker or delivery trucks with the appropriate paperwork are allowed in; everyone else is turned away (see Figure 10.3).

The heart of a firewall is the set of security policies that it enforces. Management determines what is allowed in the form of network traffic between devices, and these policies are used to build rule sets for the firewall devices used to filter network traffic across the network.

Firewall security policies are a series of rules that defines what traffic is permissible and what traffic is to be blocked or denied. These are not universal rules, and there are many different sets of rules for a single company with multiple connections. A web server connected to the Internet may be configured only to allow traffic on port 80 for HTTP, and have all other ports blocked. An e-mail server may have only necessary ports for e-mail open, with others blocked. A key to security policies for firewalls is the same as has been seen for other security policies—the principle of least access. Only allow the necessary access for a function; block or deny all unneeded functionality. How an organization deploys its firewalls determines what is needed for security policies for each firewall. You may even have a small office–home office firewall at your house, such as the RVS4000 shown in Figure 10.4. This device from Linksys provides both routing and firewall functions.

The security topology determines what network devices are employed at what points in a network. At a minimum, the corporate connection to the Internet should pass through a firewall, as shown in Figure 10.5. This firewall should block all network traffic except that specifically authorized by the security policy. This is actually easy to do: blocking communications on a port is simply a matter of telling the firewall to close the port. The

• **Figure 10.3** How a firewall works

Principles of Computer Security

issue comes in deciding what services are needed and by whom, and thus which ports should be open and which should be closed. This is what makes a security policy useful but, in some cases, difficult to maintain.

The perfect firewall policy is one that the end user never sees and one that never allows even a single unauthorized packet to enter the network. As with any other perfect item, it will be rare to find the perfect security policy for a firewall.

To develop a complete and comprehensive security policy, it is first necessary to have a complete and comprehensive understanding of your network resources and their uses. Once you know what your network will be used for, you will have an idea of what to permit. Also, once you understand what you need to protect, you will have an idea of what to block. Firewalls are designed to block attacks before they get to a target machine. Common targets are web servers, e-mail servers, DNS servers, FTP services, and databases. Each of these has separate functionality, and each of these has separate vulnerabilities. Once you have decided who should receive what type of traffic and what types should be blocked, you can administer this through the firewall.

• **Figure 10.4**   Linksys RVS4000 SOHO firewall

• **Figure 10.5**   Logical depiction of a firewall protecting an organization from the Internet

How Do Firewalls Work?

Firewalls enforce the established security policies. They can do this through a variety of mechanisms, including:

- **Network Address Translation (NAT)**   As you may remember from Chapter 9, NAT translates private (nonroutable) IP addresses into public (routable) IP addresses.

- **Basic packet filtering**   Basic packet filtering looks at each packet entering or leaving the network and then either accepts the packet or rejects the packet based on user-defined rules. Each packet is examined separately.

- **Stateful packet filtering**   Stateful packet filtering also looks at each packet, but it can examine the packet in its relation to other packets. Stateful firewalls keep track of network connections and can apply slightly different rule sets based on whether the packet is part of an established session or not.

Routers help control the flow of traffic into and out of your network. Through the use of ACLs, routers can act as first-level firewalls and can help weed out malicious traffic.

NAT is the process of modifying network address information in datagram packet headers while in transit across a traffic routing device, such as a router or firewall, for the purpose of remapping a given address space into another. See Chapter 9 for a more detailed discussion on NAT.

- **Access control lists (ACLs)**   ACLs are simple rule sets that are applied to port numbers and IP addresses. They can be configured for inbound and outbound traffic and are most commonly used on routers and switches.

- **Application layer proxies**   An application layer proxy can examine the content of the traffic as well as the ports and IP addresses. For example, an application layer has the ability to look inside a user's web traffic, detect a malicious web site attempting to download malware to the user's system, and block the malware.

One of the most basic security functions provided by a firewall is NAT. This service allows you to mask significant amounts of information from outside of the network. This allows an outside entity to communicate with an entity inside the firewall without truly knowing its address.

Basic packet filtering, also known as stateless packet inspection, involves looking at packets, their protocols and destinations, and checking that information against the security policy. Telnet and FTP connections may be prohibited from being established to a mail or database server, but they may be allowed for the respective service servers. This is a fairly simple method of filtering based on information in each packet header, like IP addresses and TCP/UDP ports. This will not detect and catch all undesired packets, but it is fast and efficient.

To look at all packets, determining the need for each and its data, requires stateful packet filtering. Advanced firewalls employ stateful packet filtering to prevent several types of undesired communications. Should a packet come from outside the network, in an attempt to pretend that it is a response to a message from inside the network, the firewall will have no record of it being requested and can discard it, blocking access. As many communications will be transferred to high ports (above 1023), stateful monitoring will enable the system to determine which sets of high-port communications are permissible and which should be blocked. The disadvantage to stateful monitoring is that it takes significant resources and processing to do this type of monitoring, and this reduces efficiency and requires more robust and expensive hardware. However, this type of monitoring is essential in today's comprehensive networks, particularly given the variety of remotely accessible services.

As they are in routers, switches, servers, and other network devices, ACLs are a cornerstone of security in firewalls. Just as you must protect the device from physical access, ACLs do the same task for electronic access. Firewalls can extend the concept of ACLs by enforcing them at a packet level when packet-level stateful filtering is performed. This can add an extra layer of protection, making it more difficult for an outside hacker to breach a firewall.

Some high-security firewalls also employ application layer proxies. As the name implies, packets are not allowed to traverse the firewall, but data instead flows up to an application that in turn decides what to do with it. For example, an SMTP proxy may accept inbound mail from the Internet and forward it to the internal corporate mail server, as depicted in Figure 10.6. While proxies provide a high level of security by making it very difficult for an attacker to manipulate the actual packets arriving at the destination, and while they provide the opportunity for an application to interpret the data

---

Tech Tip

Firewalls and Access Control Lists

Many firewalls read firewall and ACL rules from top to bottom and apply the rules in sequential order to the packets they are inspecting. Typically they will stop processing rules when they find a rule that matches the packet they are examining. If the first line in your rule set reads "allow all traffic," then the firewall will pass any network traffic coming into or leaving the firewall—ignoring the rest of your rules below that line. Many firewalls have an implied "deny all" line as part of their rule sets. This means that any traffic that is not specifically allowed by a rule will get blocked by default.

Exam Tip: Many firewalls contain, by default, an *implicit deny* at the end of every ACL or firewall rule set. This simply means that any traffic not specifically permitted by a previous rule in the rule set is denied.

Internet

Firewall with SMTP proxy

Firewall examines
inbound mail

Invalid
e-mail is
deleted

Valid e-mail
goes to mail
server

• **Figure 10.6**   Firewall with SMTP application layer proxy

prior to forwarding it to the destination, they generally are not capable of the same throughput as stateful packet-inspection firewalls. The trade-off between performance and speed is a common one and must be evaluated with respect to security needs and performance requirements.

Firewalls can also act as network traffic regulators in that they can be configured to mitigate specific types of network-based attacks. In denial-of-service and distributed denial-of-service attacks, an attacker can attempt to flood a network with traffic. Firewalls can be tuned to detect these types of attacks and act as flood guards, mitigating the effect on the network.

Next-Generation Firewalls

Firewalls operate by inspecting packets and by using rules associated with IP addresses and ports. **Next-generation firewalls** have significantly more capability and are characterized by these features:

- Deep packet inspection

- Move beyond port/protocol inspection and blocking

- Add application-level inspection

- Add intrusion prevention

- Bring intelligence from outside the firewall

Next-generation firewalls are more than just a firewall and IDS coupled together; they offer a deeper look at what the network traffic represents. In a legacy firewall, with port 80 open, all web traffic is allowed to pass. Using a next-generation firewall, traffic over port 80 can be separated by web site, or even activity on a web site (for example, allow Facebook, but not games on Facebook). Because of the deeper packet inspection and the ability to create rules based on content, traffic can be managed based on content, not merely site or URL.

Web Application Firewalls vs. Network Firewalls

Increasingly, the term "firewall" is getting attached to any device or software package that is used to control the flow of packets or data into or out of an organization. For example, a *web application firewall* is the term given to any software package, appliance, or filter that applies a rule set to HTTP/HTTPS traffic. Web application firewalls shape web traffic and can be used to filter out SQL injection attacks, malware, cross-site scripting (XSS), and so on. By contrast, a network firewall is a hardware or software package that controls the flow of packets into and out of a network. Web application firewalls operate on traffic at a much higher level than network firewalls, as web application firewalls must be able to decode the web traffic to determine whether or not it is malicious. Network firewalls operate on much simpler aspects of network traffic such as source/destination port and source/destination address.

Concentrators

Network devices called **concentrators** act as traffic management devices, managing flows from multiple points into single streams. Concentrators typically act as endpoints for a particular protocol, such as SSL/TLS or VPN. The use of specialized hardware can enable hardware-based encryption and provide a higher level of specific service than a general-purpose server. This provides both architectural and functional efficiencies.

To prevent unauthorized wireless access to the network, configuration of remote access protocols to a wireless access point is common. Forcing authentication and verifying authorization is a seamless method of performing basic network security for connections in this fashion. These access protocols are covered in Chapter 11.

Wireless Devices

Wireless devices bring additional security concerns. There is, by definition, no physical connection to a wireless device; radio waves or infrared carry data, which allows anyone within range access to the data. This means that unless you take specific precautions, you have no control over who can see your data. Placing a wireless device behind a firewall does not do any good, because the firewall stops only physically connected traffic from reaching the device. Outside traffic can come literally from the parking lot directly to the wireless device and into the network.

The point of entry from a wireless device to a wired network is performed at a device called a **wireless access point**. Wireless access points can support multiple concurrent devices accessing network resources through the network node they create. A typical wireless access point is shown here.

Several mechanisms can be used to add wireless functionality to a machine. For PCs, this can be done via an expansion card. For notebooks, a PCMCIA adapter for wireless networks is available from several vendors. For both PCs and notebooks, vendors have introduced USB-based wireless connectors. The following illustration shows one vendor's card—note the extended length used as an antenna. Not all cards have the same configuration, although they all perform the same function: to enable a wireless network connection.

• A typical wireless access point

The numerous wireless protocols (802.11a, b, g, i, and n) are covered in Chapter 12. Wireless access points and cards must be matched by protocol for proper operation.

Modems

Modems were once a slow method of remote connection that was used to connect client workstations to remote services over standard telephone lines. **Modem** is a shortened form of *modulator/demodulator,* converting analog signals to digital and vice versa. Connecting a digital computer signal to the analog telephone line required one of these devices. Today, the use of the term has expanded to cover devices connected to special digital telephone lines—DSL modems—and to cable television lines—cable modems. Although these devices are not actually modems in the true sense of the word, the term has stuck through market-

• A typical PCMCIA wireless network card

ing efforts directed to consumers. DSL and cable modems offer broadband high-speed connections and the opportunity for continuous connections to the Internet. Along with these new desirable characteristics come some undesirable ones, however. Although they both provide the same type of service, cable and DSL modems have some differences. A DSL modem provides a direct connection between a subscriber's computer and an Internet connection at the local telephone company's switching station. This private connection offers a degree of security, as it does not involve others sharing the circuit. Cable modems are set up in shared arrangements that theoretically could allow a neighbor to sniff a user's cable modem traffic.

Cable modems were designed to share a party line in the terminal signal area, and the cable modem standard, Data Over Cable Service Interface Specification (DOCSIS), was designed to accommodate this concept. DOCSIS includes built-in support for security protocols, including authentication and packet filtering. Although this does not guarantee privacy, it prevents ordinary subscribers from seeing others' traffic without using specialized hardware.

Figure 10.7 is a modern cable modem. It has an imbedded wireless access point, a VoIP connection, a local router, and DHCP server. The size of the device is fairly large, but it has a built-in lead-acid battery to provide VoIP service when power is out.

Both cable and DSL services are designed for a continuous connection, which brings up the question of IP address life for a client. Although some services originally used a static IP arrangement, virtually all have now

• **Figure 10.7** Modern cable modem

adopted the Dynamic Host Configuration Protocol (DHCP) to manage their address space. A static IP address has an advantage of remaining the same and enabling convenient DNS connections for outside users. As cable and DSL services are primarily designed for client services as opposed to host services, this is not a relevant issue. A security issue of a static IP address is that it is a stationary target for hackers. The move to DHCP has not significantly lessened this threat, however, because the typical IP lease on a cable modem DHCP server is for days. This is still relatively stationary, and some form of firewall protection needs to be employed by the user.

Cable/DSL Security

The modem equipment provided by the subscription service converts the cable or DSL signal into a standard Ethernet signal that can then be connected to a NIC on the client device. This is still just a direct network connection, with no security device separating the two. The most common security device used in cable/DSL connections is a router that acts as a hardware firewall. The firewall/router needs to be installed between the cable/DSL modem and client computers.

Telephony

A **private branch exchange (PBX)** is an extension of the public telephone network into a business. Although typically considered separate entities from data systems, PBXs are frequently interconnected and have security requirements as part of this interconnection, as well as security requirements of their own. PBXs are computer-based switching equipment designed to connect telephones into the local phone system. Basically digital switching systems, they can be compromised from the outside and used by phone hackers (*phreakers*) to make phone calls at the business's expense. Although this type of hacking has decreased as the cost of long-distance calling has decreased, it has not gone away, and as several firms learn every year, voice mail boxes and PBXs can be compromised and the long-distance bills can get very high, very fast.

Another problem with PBXs arises when they are interconnected to the data systems, either by corporate connection or by rogue modems in the hands of users. In either case, a path exists for connection to outside data networks and the Internet. Just as a firewall is needed for security on data connections, one is needed for these connections as well. Telecommunications firewalls are a distinct type of firewall designed to protect both the PBX and the data connections. The functionality of a telecommunications firewall is the same as that of a data firewall: it is there to enforce security policies. Telecommunication security policies can be enforced even to cover hours of phone use, to prevent unauthorized long-distance usage through the implementation of access codes and/or restricted service hours.

VPN Concentrator

A virtual private network (VPN) is a construct used to provide a secure communication channel between users across public networks such as the Internet. The most common implementation of VPN is via IPsec, a protocol for IP security. IPsec is mandated in IPv6 and is optional in IPv4. IPsec

Tech Tip

Coexisting Communications

Data and voice communications have coexisted in enterprises for decades. Recent connections inside the enterprise of Voice over IP (VoIP) and traditional private branch exchange (PBX) solutions increase both functionality and security risks. Specific firewalls to protect against unauthorized traffic over telephony connections are available to counter the increased risk.

can be implemented in hardware, software, or a combination of both and is used to encrypt all IP traffic. In Chapter 11, a variety of techniques are described that can be employed to instantiate a VPN connection. The use of encryption technologies allows either the data in a packet to be encrypted or the entire packet to be encrypted. If the data is encrypted, the packet header can still be sniffed and observed between source and destination, but the encryption protects the contents of the packet from inspection. If the entire packet is encrypted, it is then placed into another packet and sent via tunnel across the public network. Tunneling can protect even the identity of the communicating parties.

> **Exam Tip:** A VPN concentrator is a hardware device designed to act as a VPN endpoint, managing VPN connections to an enterprise.

Security Devices

There are a range of security devices that can be employed at the network layer to instantiate security functionality in the network layer. Devices can be used for intrusion detection, network access control, and a wide range of other security functions. Each device has a specific network function and plays a role in maintaining network infrastructure security.

Intrusion Detection Systems

Intrusion detection systems (IDSs) are an important element of infrastructure security. IDSs are designed to detect, log, and respond to unauthorized network or host use, both in real time and after the fact. IDSs are available from a wide selection of vendors and are an essential part of a comprehensive network security program. These systems are implemented using software, but in large networks or systems with significant traffic levels, dedicated hardware is typically required as well. IDSs can be divided into two categories: network-based systems and host-based systems.

Cross Check

Intrusion Detection

From a network infrastructure point of view, network-based IDSs can be considered part of infrastructure, whereas host-based IDSs are typically considered part of a comprehensive security program and not necessarily infrastructure. Two primary methods of detection are used: signature-based and anomaly-based. IDSs are covered in detail in Chapter 13.

Network Access Control

Networks comprise connected workstations and servers. Managing security on a network involves managing a wide range of issues, from various connected hardware and the software operating these devices. Assuming that the network is secure, each additional connection involves risk. Managing the endpoints on a case-by-case basis as they connect is a security methodology known as **network access control**. Two main competing methodologies exist that deal with network access control: **Network Access Protection (NAP)** is a Microsoft technology for controlling network access of a computer host, and **Network Admission Control (NAC)** is Cisco's technology for controlling network admission.

Microsoft's NAP system is based on measuring the system health of the connecting machine, including patch levels of the OS, antivirus protection, and system policies. The objective behind NAP is to enforce policy and governance standards on network devices before they are allowed data-level access to a network. NAP was first utilized in Windows XP Service Pack 3, Windows Vista, and Windows Server 2008, and it requires additional infrastructure servers to implement the health checks. The system includes enforcement agents that interrogate clients and verify admission criteria. Admission criteria can include client machine ID, status of updates, and so forth. Using NAP, network administrators can define granular levels of network access based on multiple criteria; who a client is, what groups a client belongs to, and the degree to which that client is compliant with corporate client health requirements. These health requirements include OS updates, antivirus updates, and critical patches. Response options include rejection of the connection request or restriction of admission to a subnet. NAP also provides a mechanism for automatic remediation of client health requirements and restoration of normal access when healthy.

Cisco's NAC system is built around an appliance that enforces policies chosen by the network administrator. A series of third-party solutions can interface with the appliance, allowing the verification of many different options, including client policy settings, software updates, and client security posture. The use of third-party devices and software makes this an extensible system across a wide range of equipment.

Both Cisco NAC and Microsoft NAP are in their early stages of widespread implementation, with only large enterprises typically taking these steps. Although they have been available for over 5 years, they are not being embraced across most firms. The concept of automated admission checking based on client device characteristics is here to stay, as it provides timely control in the ever-changing network world of today's enterprises.

Network Monitoring/Diagnostic

A computer network itself can be considered a large computer system, with performance and operating issues. Just as a computer needs management, monitoring, and fault resolution, so do networks. SNMP was developed to perform this function across networks. The idea is to enable a central monitoring and control center to maintain, configure, and repair network devices, such as switches and routers, as well as other network services, such as firewalls, IDSs, and remote access servers. SNMP has some security limitations, and many vendors have developed software solutions that sit on top of SNMP to provide better security and better management tool suites.

The concept of a **network operations center (NOC)** comes from the old phone company network days, when central monitoring centers monitored the health of the telephone network and provided interfaces for maintenance and management. This same concept works well with computer networks, and companies with midsize and larger networks employ the same philosophy. The NOC allows operators to observe and interact with the network, using the self-reporting and, in some cases, self-healing nature of

SNMP, Simple Network Management Protocol, is a part of the Internet Protocol suite of protocols. It is an open standard, designed for transmission of management functions between devices. Do not confuse this with SMTP, Simple Mail Transfer Protocol, which is used to transfer mail between machines.

Principles of Computer Security

network devices to ensure efficient network operation. Although generally a boring operation under normal conditions, when things start to go wrong, as in the case of a virus or worm attack, the NOC can become a busy and stressful place as operators attempt to return the system to full efficiency while not interrupting existing traffic.

As networks can be spread out literally around the world, it is not feasible to have a person visit each device for control functions. Software enables controllers at NOCs to measure the actual performance of network devices and make changes to the configuration and operation of devices remotely. The ability to make remote connections with this level of functionality is both a blessing and a security issue. Although this allows efficient network operations management, it also provides an opportunity for unauthorized entry into a network. For this reason, a variety of security controls are used, from secondary networks to VPNs and advanced authentication methods with respect to network control connections.

Network monitoring is an ongoing concern for any significant network. In addition to monitoring traffic flow and efficiency, monitoring of security-related events is necessary. IDSs act merely as alarms, indicating the possibility of a breach associated with a specific set of activities. These indications still need to be investigated and an appropriate response needs to be initiated by security personnel. Simple items such as port scans may be ignored by policy, but an actual unauthorized entry into a network router, for instance, would require NOC personnel to take specific actions to limit the potential damage to the system. In any significant network, coordinating system changes, dynamic network traffic levels, potential security incidents, and maintenance activities is a daunting task requiring numerous personnel working together. Software has been developed to help manage the information flow required to support these tasks. Such software can enable remote administration of devices in a standard fashion, so that the control systems can be devised in a hardware vendor–neutral configuration.

SNMP is the main standard embraced by vendors to permit interoperability. Although SNMP has received a lot of security-related attention of late due to various security holes in its implementation, it is still an important part of a security solution associated with network infrastructure. Many useful tools have security issues; the key is to understand the limitations and to use the tools within correct boundaries to limit the risk associated with the vulnerabilities. Blind use of any technology will result in increased risk, and SNMP is no exception. Proper planning, setup, and deployment can limit exposure to vulnerabilities. Continuous auditing and maintenance of systems with the latest patches is a necessary part of operations and is essential to maintaining a secure posture.

Load Balancers

Certain systems, such as servers, are more critical to business operations and should therefore be the object of fault-tolerance measures. **Load balancers** are designed to distribute the processing load over two or more systems. They are used to help improve resource utilization and throughput but also have the added advantage of increasing the fault tolerance of the overall system since a critical process may be split across several systems. Should any one system fail, the others can pick up the processing it was handling.

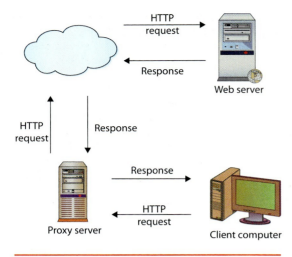

HTTP request

Response

HTTP request

Response

Web server

Response

HTTP request

Proxy server

Client computer

• **Figure 10.8** HTTP proxy handling client requests and web server responses

Proxies

Proxies serve to manage connections between systems, acting as relays for the traffic. Proxies can function at the circuit level, where they support multiple traffic types, or they can be application-level proxies, which are designed to relay specific application traffic. An HTTP proxy can manage an HTTP conversation as it understands the type and function of the content. Application-specific proxies can serve as security devices if they are programmed with specific rules designed to provide protection against undesired content.

Though not strictly a security tool, a **proxy server** (or simply *proxy*) can be used to filter out undesirable traffic and prevent employees from accessing potentially hostile web sites. A proxy server takes requests from a client system and forwards them to the destination server on behalf of the client, as shown in Figure 10.8. Proxy servers can be completely transparent (these are usually called *gateways* or *tunneling proxies*), or a proxy server can modify the client request before sending it on, or even serve the client's request without needing to contact the destination server. Several major categories of proxy servers are in use:

- **Anonymizing proxy**   An anonymizing proxy is designed to hide information about the requesting system and make a user's web browsing experience "anonymous." This type of proxy service is often used by individuals who are concerned about the amount of personal information being transferred across the Internet and the use of tracking cookies and other mechanisms to track browsing activity.

- **Caching proxy**   This type of proxy keeps local copies of popular client requests and is often used in large organizations to reduce bandwidth usage and increase performance. When a request is made, the proxy server first checks to see whether it has a current copy of the requested content in the cache; if it does, it services the client request immediately without having to contact the destination server. If the content is old or the caching proxy does not have a copy of the requested content, the request is forwarded to the destination server.

- **Content-filtering proxy**   Content-filtering proxies examine each client request and compare it to an established acceptable use policy (AUP). Requests can usually be filtered in a variety of ways, including by the requested URL, destination system, or domain name or by keywords in the content itself. Content-filtering proxies typically support user-level authentication, so access can be controlled and monitored and activity through the proxy can be logged and analyzed. This type of proxy is very popular in schools, corporate environments, and government networks.

- **Open proxy**   An open proxy is essentially a proxy that is available to any Internet user and often has some anonymizing capabilities as well. This type of proxy has been the subject of some controversy, with advocates for Internet privacy and freedom on one side of the argument, and law enforcement, corporations, and government entities on the other side. As open proxies are often used to circumvent corporate proxies, many corporations attempt to block the use of open proxies by their employees.

- **Reverse proxy**   A reverse proxy is typically installed on the server side of a network connection, often in front of a group of web servers. The reverse proxy intercepts all incoming web requests and can perform a number of functions, including traffic filtering and shaping, SSL decryption, serving of common static content such as graphics, and performing load balancing.

- **Web proxy**   A web proxy is solely designed to handle web traffic and is sometimes called a *web cache*. Most web proxies are essentially specialized caching proxies.

Exam Tip: A proxy server is a system or application that acts as a go-between for clients' requests for network services. The client tells the proxy server what it wants and, if the client is authorized to have it, the proxy server connects to the appropriate network service and gets the client what it asked for. Web proxies are the most commonly deployed type of proxy server.

Deploying a proxy solution within a network environment is usually done either by setting up the proxy and requiring all client systems to configure their browsers to use the proxy or by deploying an intercepting proxy that actively intercepts all requests without requiring client-side configuration.

From a security perspective, proxies are most useful in their ability to control and filter outbound requests. By limiting the types of content and web sites employees can access from corporate systems, many administrators hope to avoid loss of corporate data, hijacked systems, and infections from malicious web sites. Administrators also use proxies to enforce corporate AUPs and track use of corporate resources. Most proxies can be configured to either allow or require individual user authentication—this gives them the ability to log and control activity based on specific users or groups. For example, an organization might want to allow the human resources group to browse Facebook during business hours but not allow the rest of the organization to do so.

Web Security Gateways

Some security vendors combine proxy functions with content-filtering functions to create a product called a **web security gateway**. Web security gateways are intended to address the security threats and pitfalls unique to web-based traffic. Web security gateways typically provide the following capabilities:

- **Real-time malware protection (a.k.a. malware inspection)**   The ability to scan all outgoing and incoming web traffic to detect and block undesirable traffic such as malware, spyware, adware, malicious scripts, file-based attacks, and so on.

- **Content monitoring**   The ability to monitor the content of web traffic being examined to ensure that it complies with organizational policies.

- **Productivity monitoring**   The ability to measure types and quantities of web traffic that is being generated by specific users, groups of users, or the entire organization.

- **Data protection and compliance**   Scanning web traffic for sensitive or proprietary information being sent outside of the organization as well as the use of social network sites or inappropriate sites.

Internet Content Filters

With the dramatic proliferation of Internet traffic and the push to provide Internet access to every desktop, many corporations have implemented content-filtering systems, called an **Internet content filter**, to protect them from employees' viewing of inappropriate or illegal content at the workplace and the subsequent complications that occur when such viewing takes place. Internet content filtering is also popular in schools, libraries, homes, government offices, and any other environment where there is a need to limit or restrict access to undesirable content. In addition to filtering undesirable content, such as pornography, some content filters can also filter out malicious activity such as browser hijacking attempts or XSS attacks. In many cases, content filtering is performed with or as a part of a proxy solution as the content requests can be filtered and serviced by the same device. Content can be filtered in a variety of ways, including via the requested URL, the destination system, the domain name, by keywords in the content itself, and by type of file requested.

Content-filtering systems face many challenges, because the ever-changing Internet makes it difficult to maintain lists of undesirable sites (sometime called black lists); terms used on a medical site can also be used on a pornographic site, making keyword filtering challenging; and determined users are always seeking ways to bypass proxy filters. To help administrators, most commercial content-filtering solutions provide an update service, much like IDS or antivirus products that updates keywords and undesirable sites automatically.

> The term "Internet content filter" or "content filter" is applied to any device, application, or software package that examines network traffic (especially web traffic) for undesirable or restricted content. A content filter could be a software package loaded on a specific PC or a network appliance capable of filtering an entire organization's web traffic.

Data Loss Prevention

Data loss prevention (DLP) refers to technology employed to detect and prevent transfers of data across an enterprise. Employed at key locations, DLP technology can scan packets for specific data patterns. This technology can be tuned to detect account numbers, secrets, specific markers, or files. When specific data elements are detected, the system can block the transfer. The primary challenge in employing DLP technologies is the placement of the sensor. The DLP sensor needs to be able observe the data, so if the channel is encrypted, DLP technology can be thwarted.

Unified Threat Management

Many security vendors offer "all-in-one security appliances," which are devices that combine multiple functions into the same hardware appliance. Most commonly these functions are firewall, IDS/IPS, and antivirus, although all-in-one appliances can include VPN capabilities, antispam, malicious web traffic filtering, antispyware, content filtering, traffic shaping, and so on. All-in-one appliances are often sold as being cheaper, easier to manage, and more efficient than having separate solutions that accomplish each of the functions the all-in-one appliance is capable of performing. A common name for these all-in-one appliances is a **unified threat management (UTM)** appliance. Using a UTM solution simplifies the security activity as a single task, under a common software package for operations. This reduces the learning curve to a single tool rather than a collection of tools. A UTM solution can have better integration and efficiencies in handling network traffic and incidents than a collection of tools connected together.

Figure 10.9 illustrates the advantages of UTM processing. Rather than processing elements in a linear fashion, as shown in 10.9a, the packets are processed in a parallelized fashion (b). There is a need to coordinate between the elements and many modern solutions do this with parallelized hardware.

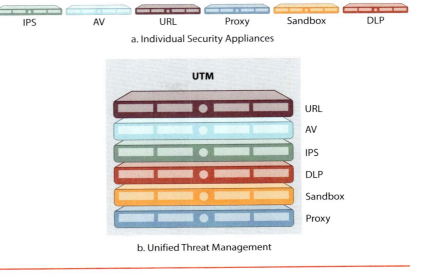

a. Individual Security Appliances

b. Unified Threat Management

• **Figure 10.9** Unified threat management architecture

URL Filtering

URL filters block connections to web sites that are in a prohibited list. The use of a UTM appliance, typically backed by a service to keep the list of prohibited web sites updated, provides an automated means to block access to sites deemed dangerous or inappropriate. Because of the highly volatile nature of web content, automated enterprise-level protection is needed to ensure a reasonable chance of blocking sources of inappropriate content, malware, and other malicious content.

Content Inspection

Instead of just relying on a URL to determine the acceptability of content, UTM appliances can also inspect the actual content being served. Content inspection is used to filter web requests that return content with specific components, such as names of body parts, music or video content, and other content that is inappropriate for the business environment.

Malware Inspection

Malware is another item that can be detected during network transmission, and UTM appliances can be tuned to detect malware. Network-based malware detection has the advantage of having to update only a single system as opposed to all machines.

■ Media

The base of communications between devices is the physical layer of the OSI model. This is the domain of the actual connection between devices, whether by wire, fiber, or radio frequency waves. The physical layer separates the definitions and protocols required to transmit the signal physically between boxes from higher-level protocols that deal with the details of the data itself. Four common methods are used to connect equipment at the physical layer:

- Coaxial cable
- Twisted-pair cable
- Fiber-optics
- Wireless

Coaxial Cable

Coaxial cable is familiar to many households as a method of connecting televisions to VCRs or to satellite or cable services. It is used because of its high bandwidth and shielding capabilities. Compared to standard twisted-pair lines such as telephone lines, **coaxial cable** ("coax") is much less prone to outside interference. It is also much more expensive to run, both from a cost-per-foot measure and from a cable-dimension measure. Coax costs much more per foot than standard twisted-pair wires and carries only a single circuit for a large wire diameter.

An original design specification for Ethernet connections, coax was used from machine to machine in early Ethernet implementations. The connectors were easy to use and ensured good connections, and the limited distance of most office LANs did not carry a large cost penalty. Today, almost all of this older Ethernet specification has been replaced by faster, cheaper twisted-pair alternatives, and the only place you're likely to see coax in a data network is from the cable box to the cable modem.

Because of its physical nature, it is possible to drill a hole through the outer part of a coax cable and connect to the center connector. This is called a "vampire tap" and is an easy method to get access to the signal and data being transmitted.

● A coax connector

● A typical 8-wire UTP line

UTP/STP

Twisted-pair wires have all but completely replaced coaxial cables in Ethernet networks. Twisted-pair wires use the same technology used by the phone company for the movement of electrical signals. Single pairs of twisted wires reduce electrical crosstalk and electromagnetic interference. Multiple groups of twisted pairs can then be bundled together in common groups and easily wired between devices.

● A typical 8-wire STP line

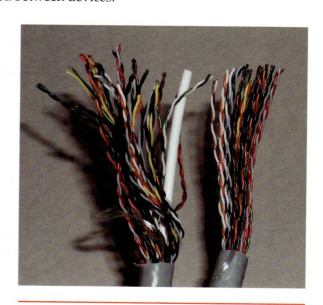

● A bundle of UTP wires

Twisted pairs come in two types, shielded and unshielded. **Shielded twisted-pair (STP)** has a foil shield around the pairs to provide extra shielding from electromagnetic interference. **Unshielded twisted-pair (UTP)** relies on the twist to eliminate interference. UTP has a cost advantage over STP and is usually sufficient for connections, except in very noisy electrical areas.

Twisted-pair lines are categorized by the level of data transmission they can support. Three current categories are in use:

- **Category 3 (Cat 3)**   Minimum for voice and 10-Mbps Ethernet.

- **Category 5 (Cat 5/Cat 5e)**   For 100-Mbps Fast Ethernet; Cat 5e is an enhanced version of the Cat 5 specification to address far-end crosstalk and is suitable for 1000 Mbps.

- **Category 6 (Cat 6/Cat 6a)**   For 10-Gigabit Ethernet over short distances; Cat 6a is used for longer, up to 100m, 10-Gbps cables.

The standard method for connecting twisted-pair cables is via an 8-pin connector, called an RJ-45 connector that looks like a standard phone jack connector but is slightly larger. One nice aspect of twisted-pair cabling is that it's easy to splice and change connectors. Many a network administrator has made Ethernet cables from stock Cat-5 wire, two connectors, and a crimping tool. This ease of connection is also a security issue; because twisted-pair cables are easy to splice into, rogue connections for sniffing could be made without detection in cable runs. Both coax and fiber are much more difficult to splice because each requires a tap to connect, and taps are easier to detect.

Fiber

Fiber-optic cable uses beams of laser light to connect devices over a thin glass wire. The biggest advantage to fiber is its bandwidth, with transmission capabilities into the terabits per second range. Fiber-optic cable is used to make high-speed connections between servers and is the backbone medium of the Internet and large networks. For all of its speed and bandwidth advantages, fiber has one major drawback—cost.

The cost of using fiber is a two-edged sword. When measured by bandwidth, using fiber is cheaper than using competing wired technologies. The length of runs of fiber can be much longer, and the data capacity of fiber is much higher. But connections to a fiber are difficult and expensive, and fiber is impossible to splice. Making the precise connection on the end of a fiber-optic line is a highly skilled job and is done by specially trained professionals who maintain a level of proficiency. Once the connector is fitted on

• A type of fiber terminator

• A typical fiber-optic fiber, terminator, and connector block

the end, several forms of connectors and blocks are used, as shown in the images above.

Splicing fiber is practically impossible; the solution is to add connectors and connect through a repeater. This adds to the security of fiber in that unauthorized connections are all but impossible to make. The high cost of connections to fiber and the higher cost of fiber per foot also make it less attractive for the final mile in public networks where users are connected to the public switching systems. For this reason, cable companies use coax and DSL providers use twisted-pair to handle the "last mile" scenario.

Unguided Media

Electromagnetic waves have been transmitted to convey signals literally since the inception of radio. *Unguided media* is a phrase used to cover all transmission media not guided by wire, fiber, or other constraints; it includes radio frequency, infrared, and microwave methods. Unguided media have one attribute in common: they are unguided and as such can travel to many machines simultaneously. Transmission patterns can be modulated by antennas, but the target machine can be one of many in a reception zone. As such, security principles are even more critical, as they must assume that unauthorized users have access to the signal.

Infrared

Infrared (IR) is a band of electromagnetic energy just beyond the red end of the visible color spectrum. IR has been used in remote-control devices for years. IR made its debut in computer networking as a wireless method to connect to printers. Now that wireless keyboards, wireless mice, and mobile devices exchange data via IR, it seems to be everywhere. IR can also be used to connect devices in a network configuration, but it is slow compared to other wireless technologies. IR cannot penetrate walls but instead bounces off them. Nor can it penetrate other solid objects, so if you stack a few items in front of the transceiver, the signal is lost.

RF/Microwave

The use of radio frequency (RF) waves to carry communication signals goes back to the beginning of the 20th century. RF waves are a common method of communicating in a wireless world. They use a variety of frequency bands, each with special characteristics. The term *microwave* is used to describe a specific portion of the RF spectrum that is used for communication and other tasks, such as cooking.

Point-to-point microwave links have been installed by many network providers to carry communications over long distances and rough terrain. Many different frequencies are used in the microwave bands for many different purposes. Today, home users can use wireless networking throughout their house and enable laptops to surf the Web while they're moved around the house. Corporate users are experiencing the same phenomenon, with wireless networking enabling corporate users to check e-mail on laptops while riding a shuttle bus on a business campus. These wireless solutions are covered in detail in Chapter 12.

One key feature of microwave communications is that microwave RF energy can penetrate reasonable amounts of building structure. This allows you to connect network devices in separate rooms, and it can remove the constraints on equipment location imposed by fixed wiring. Another key feature is broadcast capability. By its nature, RF energy is unguided and can be received by multiple users simultaneously. Microwaves allow multiple users access in a limited area, and microwave systems are seeing application as the last mile of the Internet in dense metropolitan areas. Point-to-multipoint microwave devices can deliver data communication to all the business users in a downtown metropolitan area through rooftop antennas, reducing the need for expensive building-to-building cables. Just as microwaves carry cell phone and other data communications, the same technologies offer a method to bridge the last-mile solution.

The "last mile" problem is the connection of individual consumers to a backbone, an expensive proposition because of the sheer number of connections and unshared line at this point in a network. Again, cost is an issue, as transceiver equipment is expensive, but in densely populated areas, such as apartments and office buildings in metropolitan areas, the user density can help defray individual costs. Speed on commercial microwave links can exceed 10 Gbps, so speed is not a problem for connecting multiple users or for high-bandwidth applications.

Tech Tip

Wireless Options
There are numerous radio-based alternatives for carrying network traffic. They vary in capacity, distance, and other features. Commonly found examples are WiFi, WiMAX, ZigBee, Bluetooth, 900 MHz, and NFC. Understanding the security requirements associated with each is important and is covered in more detail in Chapter 12.

■ Removable Media

One concept common to all computer users is data storage. Sometimes storage occurs on a file server and sometimes it occurs on movable media, allowing it to be transported between machines. Moving storage media represents a security risk from a couple of angles, the first being the potential loss of control over the data on the moving media. Second is the risk of introducing unwanted items, such as a virus or a worm, when the media are attached back to a network. Both of these issues can be remedied through policies and software. The key is to ensure that the policies are enforced and

Removable and transportable media make the physical security of the data a more difficult task. The only solution to this problem is encryption, which is covered in Chapter 5.

the software is effective. To describe media-specific issues, media can be divided into three categories: magnetic, optical, and electronic.

Magnetic Media

Magnetic media store data through the rearrangement of magnetic particles on a nonmagnetic substrate. Common forms include hard drives, floppy disks, zip disks, and magnetic tape. Although the specific format can differ, the basic concept is the same. All these devices share some common characteristics: Each has sensitivity to external magnetic fields. Attach a floppy disk to the refrigerator door with a magnet if you want to test the sensitivity. They are also affected by high temperatures, as in fires, and by exposure to water.

Hard Drives

Hard drives used to require large machines in mainframes. Now they are small enough to attach to mobile devices. The concepts remain the same among all of them: a spinning platter rotates the magnetic media beneath heads that read the patterns in the oxide coating. As drives have gotten smaller and rotation speeds have increased, the capacities have also grown. Today gigabytes of data can be stored in a device slightly larger than a bottle cap. Portable hard drives in the 1TB to 3TB range are now available and affordable.

One of the security controls available to help protect the confidentiality of the data is full drive encryption built into the drive hardware. Using a key that is controlled, through a Trusted Platform Module (TPM) interface for instance, this technology protects the data if the drive itself is lost or stolen. This may not be important if a thief takes the whole PC, but in larger storage environments, drives are placed in separate boxes and remotely accessed. In the specific case of notebook machines, this layer can be tied to smart card interfaces to provide more security. As this is built into the controller, encryption protocols such as Advanced Encryption Standard (AES) and Triple Data Encryption Standard (3DES) can be performed at full drive speed.

● 2TB USB hard drive

Diskettes

Floppy disks were the computer industry's first attempt at portable magnetic media. The movable medium was placed in a protective sleeve, and the drive remained in the machine. Capacities up to 1.4MB were achieved, but the fragility of the device as the size increased, as well as competing media, has rendered floppies almost obsolete. Diskettes are part of history now.

Tape

Magnetic tape has held a place in computer centers since the beginning of computing. Its primary use has been bulk offline storage and backup. Tape functions well in this role because of its low cost. The disadvantage of tape is its nature as a serial access medium, making it slow to work with for large quantities of data. Several types of magnetic tape are in use today, ranging from quarter inch to digital linear tape (DLT) and digital audio tape (DAT). These cartridges can hold upward of 60GB of compressed data.

Tapes are still a major concern from a security perspective, as they are used to back up many types of computer systems. The physical protection afforded the tapes is of concern, because if a tape is stolen, an unauthorized user could establish a network and recover your data on his system, because it's all stored on the tape. Offsite storage is needed for proper disaster recovery protection, but secure offsite storage and transport is what is really needed. This important issue is frequently overlooked in many facilities. The simple solution to maintain control over the data even when you can't control the tape is through encryption. Backup utilities can secure the backups with encryption, but this option is frequently not used, for a variety of reasons. Regardless of the rationale for not encrypting data, once a tape is lost, not using the encryption option becomes a lamented decision.

• A magnetic tape cartridge for backups

Optical Media

Optical media involve the use of a laser to read data stored on a physical device. Instead of having a magnetic head that picks up magnetic marks on a disk, a laser picks up deformities embedded in the media that contain the information. As with magnetic media, optical media can be read-write, although the read-only version is still more common.

CD-R/DVD

The compact disc (CD) took the music industry by storm, and then it took the computer industry by storm as well. A standard CD holds more than 640MB of data, in some cases up to 800MB. The digital video disc (DVD) can hold almost 5GB of data single sided, 8.5GB dual layer. These devices operate as optical storage, with little marks burned in them to represent 1's and 0's on a microscopic scale. The most common type of CD is the read-only version, in which the data is written to the disc once and only read afterward. This has become a popular method for distributing computer software, although higher-capacity DVDs have replaced CDs for program distribution.

A second-generation device, the recordable compact disc (CD-R), allows users to create their own CDs using a burner device in their PC and special software. Users can now back up data, make their own audio CDs, and use CDs as

• A DVD (left) and CD (right)

high-capacity storage. Their relatively low cost has made them economical to use. CDs have a thin layer of aluminum inside the plastic, upon which bumps are burned by the laser when recorded. CD-Rs use a reflective layer, such as gold, upon which a dye is placed that changes upon impact by the recording laser. A newer type, CD-RW, has a different dye that allows discs to be erased and reused. The cost of the media increases from CD, to CD-R, to CD-RW.

Blu-ray Discs

The latest version of optical disc is the Blu-ray disc. Using a smaller, violet-blue laser, this system can hold significantly more information than a DVD. Blu-ray discs can hold up to 128GB in four layers. The transfer speed of Blu-ray at > 48 Mbps is over four times greater than that of DVD systems. Designed for high-definition (HD) video, Blu-ray offers significant storage for data as well.

DVDs now occupy the same role that CDs have in the recent past, except that they hold more than seven times the data of a CD. This makes full-length movie recording possible on a single disc. The increased capacity comes from finer tolerances and the fact that DVDs can hold data on both sides. A wide range of formats for DVDs include DVD+R, DVD-R, dual layer, and now HD formats, HD-DVD and Blu-ray. This variety is due to competing "standards" and can result in confusion. DVD+R and -R are distinguishable only when recording, and most devices since 2004 should read both. Dual layers add additional space but require appropriate dual-layer–enabled drives.

Electronic Media

The latest form of removable media is electronic memory. Electronic circuits of static memory, which can retain data even without power, fill a niche where high density and small size are needed. Originally used in audio devices and digital cameras, these electronic media come in a variety of vendor-specific types, such as smart cards, SmartMedia, SD cards, flash cards, memory sticks, and CompactFlash devices. These memory devices range from small card-like devices, of which microSD cards are smaller than dimes and hold 2GB, to USB sticks that hold up to 64GB. These devices are becoming ubiquitous, with new PCs and netbooks containing built-in slots to read them like any other storage device.

Although they are used primarily for photos and music, these devices could be used to move any digital information from one machine to another. To a machine equipped with a connector port, these devices look like any other file storage location. They can be connected to a system through a special reader or directly via a USB port. In newer PC systems, a USB boot device has replaced the older floppy drive. These devices are small, can hold a significant amount of data—over 128GB at time of writing—and are easy to move from machine to machine. Another novel interface is a mouse that has a slot for a memory stick. This dual-purpose device conserves space, conserves USB ports, and is easy to use. The memory stick is placed in the mouse,

SD, microSD, and CompactFlash cards

• **Figure 10.10** 512GB solid-state half-height minicard

which can then be used normally. The stick is easily removable and transportable. The mouse works with or without the memory stick; it is just a convenient device to use for a portal.

The advent of large-capacity USB sticks has enabled users to build entire systems, OSs, and tools onto them to ensure security and veracity of the OS and tools. With the expanding use of virtualization, a user could carry an entire system on a USB stick and boot it using virtually any hardware. With USB 3.0 and its 640-Mbps speeds, this is a highly versatile form of memory that enables many new capabilities.

Solid-State Hard Drives

With the rise of solid-state memory technologies comes a solid-state "hard drive." **Solid-state drives (SSDs)** are moving into mobile devices, desktops, and even servers. Memory densities are significantly beyond physical drives, there are no moving parts to wear out or fail, and SSDs have vastly superior performance specifications. Figure 10.10 shows a 512GB SSD from a laptop, on a half-height minicard mSATA interface. The only factor that has slowed the spread of this technology has been cost, but recent cost reductions have made this form of memory a first choice in many systems.

• 128GB USB 3.0 memory stick

■ Security Concerns for Transmission Media

The primary security concern for a system administrator has to be preventing physical access to a server by an unauthorized individual. Such access will almost always spell disaster, for with direct access and the correct tools, any system can be infiltrated. One of the administrator's next major concerns should be preventing unfettered access to a network connection. Access to switches and routers is almost as bad as direct access to a server, and access to network connections would rank third in terms of worst-case scenarios. Preventing such access is costly, yet the cost of replacing a server because of theft is also costly.

Physical Security Concerns

A balanced approach is the most sensible approach when addressing physical security, and this applies to transmission media as well. Keeping network switch rooms secure and cable runs secure seems obvious, but cases of using janitorial closets for this vital business purpose abound. One of the keys to mounting a successful attack on a network is information. User-names, passwords, server locations—all of these can be obtained if someone has the ability to observe network traffic in a process called *sniffing*. A sniffer can record all the network traffic, and this data can be mined for accounts, passwords, and traffic content, all of which can be useful to an unauthorized user. One starting point for many intrusions is the insertion of an unauthorized sniffer into the network, with the fruits of its labors driving the remaining unauthorized activities. Many common scenarios exist when unauthorized entry to a network occurs, including these:

- Inserting a node and functionality that is not authorized on the network, such as a sniffer device or unauthorized wireless access point
- Modifying firewall security policies
- Modifying ACLs for firewalls, switches, or routers
- Modifying network devices to echo traffic to an external node

Network devices and transmission media become targets because they are dispersed throughout an organization, and physical security of many dispersed items can be difficult to manage. Although limiting physical access is difficult, it is essential. The least level of skill is still more than sufficient to accomplish unauthorized entry into a network if physical access to the network signals is allowed. This is one factor driving many organizations to use fiber-optics, for these cables are much more difficult to tap. Although many tricks can be employed with switches and VLANs to increase security, it is still essential that you prevent unauthorized contact with the network equipment.

Cross Check

Physical Infrastructure Security

The best first effort is to secure the actual network equipment to prevent this type of intrusion. As you should remember from Chapter 8, physical access to network infrastructure provides a myriad of issues, and most of them can be catastrophic with respect to security. Physically securing access to network components is one of the "must dos" of a comprehensive security effort.

Wireless networks make the intruder's task even easier, as they take the network to the users, authorized or not. A technique called *war-driving* involves using a laptop and software to find wireless networks from outside the premises. A typical use of war-driving is to locate a wireless network with poor (or no) security and obtain free Internet access, but other uses can be more devastating. A simple solution is to place a firewall between the wireless access point and the rest of the network and authenticate users before allowing entry. Business users use VPN technology to secure their connection to the Internet and other resources, and home users can do the same thing to prevent neighbors from "sharing" their Internet connections. To ensure that unauthorized traffic does not enter your network through a wireless access point, you must either use a firewall with an authentication system or establish a VPN.

Cloud Computing

Cloud computing is a common term used to describe computer services provided over a network. These computing services are computing, storage, applications, and services that are offered via the Internet Protocol. One of the characteristics of cloud computing is transparency to the end user. This improves usability of this form of service provisioning. Cloud computing offers much to the user: improvements in performance, scalability, flexibility, security, and reliability, among other items. These improvements are a direct result of the specific attributes associated with how cloud services are implemented.

Security is a particular challenge when data and computation are handled by a remote party, as in cloud computing. The specific challenge is how does one allow data outside their enterprise and yet remain in control over how the data is used, and the common answer is encryption. By properly encrypting data before it leaves the enterprise, external storage can still be performed securely.

Clouds can be created by many entities, internal and external to an organization. Commercial cloud services are already available and offered by a variety of firms, as large as Google and Amazon, to smaller, local providers. Internal services can replicate the advantages of cloud computing while improving the utility of limited resources. The promise of cloud computing is improved utility and, as such, is marketed under the concepts of Software as a Service, Platform as a Service, and Infrastructure as a Service.

Private

If your organization is highly sensitive to sharing resources, you may wish to consider the use of a private cloud. Private clouds are essentially reserved resources used only for your organization—your own little cloud within the cloud. This service will be considerably more expensive, but it should also carry less exposure and should enable your organization to better define the security, processing, and handling of data that occurs within your cloud.

Public

The term *public cloud* refers to when the cloud service is rendered over a system that is open for public use. In most cases, there is little operational difference between public and private cloud architectures, but the security ramifications can be substantial. Although public cloud services will separate users with security restrictions, the depth and level of these restrictions, by definition, will be significantly less in a public cloud.

Hybrid

A hybrid cloud structure is one where elements are combined from private, public, and community cloud structures. When examining a hybrid structure, you need to remain cognizant that operationally these differing environments may not actually be joined, but rather used together. Sensitive information can be stored in the private cloud and issue-related information can be stored in the community cloud, all of which information is accessed by an application. This makes the overall system a hybrid cloud system.

Community

A community cloud system is one where several organizations with a common interest share a cloud environment for the specific purposes of the shared endeavor. For example, local public entities and key local firms may share a community cloud dedicated to serving the interests of community initiatives. This can be an attractive cost-sharing mechanism for specific data-sharing initiatives.

Software as a Service

Software as a Service (SaaS) is the offering of software to end users from within the cloud. Rather than installing software on client machines, SaaS acts as software on demand where the software runs from the cloud. This has several advantages, as updates are often seamless to end users and integration between components is enhanced.

Platform as a Service

Platform as a Service (PaaS) is a marketing term used to describe the offering of a computing platform in the cloud. Multiple sets of software, working together to provide services, such as database services, can be delivered via the cloud as a platform.

Infrastructure as a Service

Infrastructure as a Service (IaaS) is a term used to describe cloud-based systems that are delivered as a virtual platform for computing. Rather than building data centers, IaaS allows firms to contract for utility computing as needed.

Lab Manual Exercise

The following lab exercise from the companion lab manual, *Principles of Computer Security Lab Manual, Fourth Edition,* provides practical application of material covered in this chapter:

Lab 7.3l   Configuring a Personal Firewall in Linux

Chapter Summary

After reading this chapter and completing the exercises, you should understand the following aspects of networking and secure infrastructures.

Construct networks using different types of network devices

- Understand the differences between basic network devices, such as hubs, bridges, switches, and routers.
- Understand the security implications of network devices and how to construct a secure network infrastructure.

Enhance security using security devices

- Understand the use of firewalls, next-generation firewalls, and intrusion detection systems.
- Understand the role of load balancers and proxy servers as part of a secure network solution.
- Understand the use of security appliances, such as web security gateways, data loss prevention, and unified threat management.

Enhance security using NAC/NAP methodologies

- The Cisco NAC protocol and the Microsoft NAP protocol provide security functionality when attaching devices to a network.
- NAC and NAP play a crucial role in the securing of infrastructure as devices enter and leave the network.
- NAC and NAP can be used together to take advantage of the strengths and investments in each technology to form a strong network admission methodology.

Identify the different types of media used to carry network signals

- Guided and unguided media can both carry network traffic.
- Wired technology from coax cable, through twisted-pair Ethernet, provides a cost-effective means of carrying network traffic.
- Fiber technology is used to carry higher bandwidth.
- Unguided media, including infrared and RF (including wireless and Bluetooth), provide short-range network connectivity.

Describe the different types of storage media used to store information

- There are a wide array of removable media types from memory sticks to optical discs to portable drives.
- Data storage on removable media, because of increased physical access, creates significant security implications.

Use basic terminology associated with network functions related to information security

- Understanding and using the correct vocabulary for device names and relationships to networking is important as a security professional.
- Security appliances add terminology, including specific items for IDS and firewalls.

Describe the different types and uses of cloud computing

- Understand the types of clouds in use.
- Understand the use of Software as a Service, Infrastructure as a Service, and Platform as a Service.

Key Terms

Key Terms Quiz

Use terms from the Key Terms list to complete the sentences that follow. Don't use the same term more than once. Not all terms will be used.

1. A(n) _____ routes packets based on IP addresses.

2. To offer software to end users from the cloud is a form of _____.

3. To connect a computer to a network, you use a(n) _____.

4. A(n) _____ or _____ distributes traffic based on MAC addresses.

5. To verify that a computer is properly configured to connect to a network, the network can use _____.

6. _____ is a name for the typical computer a user uses on a network.

7. A(n) _____ repeats all data traffic across all connected ports.

8. Cat 5 is an example of _____ cable.

9. Basic packet filtering occurs at the _____.

10. A(n) _____ is an extension of the telephone service into a firm's telecommunications network.

Multiple-Choice Quiz

1. Switches operate at which layer of the OSI model?

   A. Physical layer

   B. Network layer

   C. Data link layer

   D. Application layer

2. UTP cables are terminated for Ethernet using what type of connector?

   A. A BNC plug

   B. An Ethernet connector

   C. A standard phone jack connector

   D. An RJ-45 connector

Principles of Computer Security

3. Coaxial cable carries how many physical channels?

   A. Two

   B. Four

   C. One

   D. None of the above

4. Network access control is associated with which of the following?

   A. NAP

   B. IPsec

   C. IPv6

   D. NAT

5. The purpose of twisting the wires in twisted-pair circuits is to:

   A. Increase speed

   B. Increase bandwidth

   C. Reduce crosstalk

   D. Allow easier tracing

6. Microsoft NAP permits:

   A. Restriction of connections to a restricted subnet only

   B. Checking of a client OS patch level before a network connection is permitted

   C. Denial of a connection based on client policy settings

   D. All of the above

7. SNMP is a protocol used for which of the following functions?

   A. Secure e-mail

   B. Secure encryption of network packets

   C. Remote access to user workstations

   D. Remote access to network infrastructure

8. Firewalls can use which of the following in their operation?

   A. Stateful packet inspection

   B. Port blocking to deny specific services

   C. NAT to hide internal IP addresses

   D. All of the above

9. SMTP is a protocol used for which of the following functions?

   A. E-mail

   B. Secure encryption of network packets

   C. Remote access to user workstations

   D. None of the above

10. USB-based flash memory is characterized by:

   A. High cost

   B. Low capacity

   C. Slow access

   D. None of the above

■ Essay Quiz

1. Compare and contrast routers and switches by describing what the advantages and disadvantages are of each.

2. Describe the common threats to the transmission media in a network, by type of transmission media.

Lab Projects

• Lab Project 10.1

Using two PCs and a small home office–type router, configure them to communicate across the network with each other.

• Lab Project 10.2

Demonstrate network connectivity using Windows command-line tools.

chapter 11

Authentication and Remote Access

We should set a national goal of making computers and Internet access available for every American.
—William Jefferson Clinton

In this chapter, you will learn how to

- Identify the differences among user, group, and role management
- Implement password and domain password policies
- Describe methods of account management (SSO, time of day, logical token, account expiration)
- Describe methods of access management (MAC, DAC, and RBAC)
- Discuss the methods and protocols for remote access to networks
- Identify authentication, authorization, and accounting (AAA) protocols
- Explain authentication methods and the security implications in their use
- Implement virtual private networks (VPNs) and their security aspects
- Describe Internet Protocol Security (IPsec) and its use in securing communications

On single-user systems such as PCs, the individual user typically has access to most of the system's resources, processing capability, and stored data. On multiuser systems, such as servers and mainframes, an individual user typically has very limited access to the system and the data stored on that system. An administrator responsible for managing and maintaining the multiuser system has much greater access. So how does the computer system know which users should have access to what data? How does the operating system know what applications a user is allowed to use?

On early computer systems, anyone with physical access had fairly significant rights to the system and could typically access any file or execute any application. As computers became more popular and it became obvious that some way of separating and restricting users was needed, the concepts of users, groups, and privileges came into being (**privileges** mean you have the ability to "do something" on a computer system such as create a directory, delete a file, or run a program). These concepts continue to be developed and refined and are now part of what we call *privilege management*.

Privilege management is the process of restricting a user's ability to interact with the computer system. Essentially, everything a user can do to or with a computer system falls into the realm of privilege management. Privilege management occurs at many different points within an operating system or even within applications running on a particular operating system.

Remote access is another key issue for multiuser systems in today's world of connected computers. Isolated computers, not connected to networks or the Internet, are rare items these days. Except for some special-purpose machines, most computers need interconnectivity to fulfill their purpose. Remote access enables users outside a network to have network access and privileges as if they were inside the network. Being *outside* a network means that the user is working on a machine that is not physically connected to the network and must therefore establish a connection through a remote means, such as by dialing in, connecting via the Internet, or connecting through a wireless connection.

Authentication is the process of establishing a user's identity to enable the granting of permissions. To establish network connections, a variety of methods are used, the choice of which depends on network type, the hardware and software employed, and any security requirements.

■ User, Group, and Role Management

To manage the privileges of many different people effectively on the same system, a mechanism for separating people into distinct entities (*users*) is required, so you can control access on an individual level. At the same time, it's convenient and efficient to be able to lump users together when granting many different people (*groups*) access to a resource at the same time. At other times, it's useful to be able to grant or restrict access based on a person's job or function within the organization (*role*). While you can manage privileges on the basis of users alone, managing user, group, and role assignments together is far more convenient and efficient.

User

The term **user** generally applies to any person accessing a computer system. In privilege management, a user is a single individual, such as "John Forthright" or "Sally Jenkins." This is generally the lowest level addressed by privilege management and the most common area for addressing access, rights, and capabilities. When accessing a computer system, each user is generally given a **username**—a unique alphanumeric identifier he or she will use to identify himself or herself when logging into or accessing the system. When developing a scheme for selecting usernames, you should keep in mind that usernames must be unique to each user, but they must also be fairly easy for the user to remember and use.

Tech Tip

User ID vs. Username

The terms "user ID" and "username" are sometimes used interchangeably, but traditionally the term user ID is more often associated with UNIX operating systems. In UNIX operating systems, each user is identified by an unsigned integer called a user identifier, often shortened to user ID.

Exam Tip: A username is a unique alphanumeric identifier used to identify a user to a computer system. Permissions control what a user is allowed to do with objects on a computer system—what files they can open, what printers they can use, and so on. In Windows security models, permissions define the actions a user can perform on an object (open a file, delete a folder, and so on). **Rights** define the actions a user can perform on the system itself, such as change the time, adjust auditing levels, and so on. Rights are typically applied to operating system–level tasks.

With some notable exceptions, in general a user who wants to access a computer system must first have a username created for him on the system he wishes to use. This is usually done by a system administrator, security administrator, or other privileged user, and this is the first step in privilege management—a user should not be allowed to create their own account.

Once the account is created and a username is selected, the administrator can assign specific permissions to that user. **Permissions** control what the user is allowed to do with objects on the system—which files he may access, which programs he may execute, and so on. While PCs typically have only one or two user accounts, larger systems such as servers and mainframes can have hundreds of accounts on the same system. Figure 11.1 shows the Users management tab of the Computer Management utility on a Windows Server 2008 system. Note that several user accounts have been created on this system, each identified by a unique username.

A few "special" user accounts don't typically match up one-to-one with a real person. These accounts are reserved for special functions and typically have much more access and control over the computer system than the average user account. Two such accounts are the **administrator** account under Windows and the **root** account under UNIX. Each of these accounts is also known as the **superuser**—if something can be done on the system, the superuser has the power to do it. These accounts are not typically assigned to a specific individual and are restricted, accessed only when the full capabilities of that account are required.

Due to the power possessed by these accounts, and the few, if any, restrictions placed on them, they must be protected with strong passwords that are not easily guessed or obtained. These accounts are also the most common targets of attackers—if the attacker can gain root access or assume the privilege level associated with the root account, she can bypass most access controls and accomplish anything she wants on that system.

Another account that falls into the "special" category is the system account used by Windows operating systems. The system account has the same file privileges as the administrator account and is used by the operating system and by services that run under Windows. By default, the system account is granted full control to all files on an NTFS volume. Services

• **Figure 11.1** Users tab on a Windows Server 2008 system

and processes that need the capability to log on internally within Windows will use the system account—for example, the DNS Server and DHCP Server services in Windows Server 2008 use the Local System account.

Group

Under privilege management, a **group** is a collection of users with some common criteria, such as a need for access to a particular dataset or group of applications. A group can consist of one user or hundreds of users, and each user can belong to one or more groups. Figure 11.2 shows a common approach to grouping users—building groups based on job function.

Management

Engineering

Sales

• **Figure 11.2**   Logical representation of groups

By assigning membership in a specific group to a user, you make it much easier to control that user's access and privileges. For example, if every member of the engineering department needs access to product development documents, administrators can place all the users in the engineering department in a single group and allow that group to access the necessary documents. Once a group is assigned permissions to access a particular resource, adding a new user to that group will automatically allow that user to access that resource. In effect, the user "inherits" the permissions of the group as soon as she is placed in that group. As Figure 11.3 shows, a computer system can have many different groups, each with its own rights and permissions.

As you can see from the description for the Administrators group in Figure 11.3, this group has complete and unrestricted access to the system. This includes access to all files, applications, and datasets. Anyone who belongs to the Administrators group or is placed in this group will have a great deal of access and control over the system.

Some operating systems, such as Windows, have built-in groups— groups that are already defined within the operating system, such as Administrators, Power Users, and Everyone. The whole concept of groups revolves around making the tasks of assigning and managing permissions easier, and built-in groups certainly help to make these tasks easier.

• **Figure 11.3**   Groups tab on a Windows Server 2008 system

Chapter 11: Authentication and Remote Access

Individual users accounts can be added to built-in groups, allowing administrators to grant permission sets to users quickly and easily without having to specify permissions manually. For example, adding a user account named "bjones" to the Power Users group gives bjones all the permissions assigned to the built-in Power Users group, such as installing drivers, modifying settings, and installing software.

Role

Another common method of managing access and privileges is by roles. A **role** is usually synonymous with a job or set of functions. For example, the role of security admin in Microsoft SQL Server may be applied to someone who is responsible for creating and managing logins, reading error logs, and auditing the application. Security admins need to accomplish specific functions and need access to certain resources that other users do not—for example, they need to be able to create and delete logins, open and read error logs, and so on. In general, anyone serving in the role of security admin needs the same rights and privileges as every other security admin. For simplicity and efficiency, rights and privileges can be assigned to the role security admin, and anyone assigned to fulfill that role automatically has the correct rights and privileges to perform the required tasks.

■ Password Policies

The username/password combination is by far the most common means of controlling access to applications, web sites, and computer systems. The average user may have a dozen or more username and password combinations between school, work, and personal use. To help users select a good, difficult-to-guess password, most organizations implement and enforce a **password policy**, which typically has the following components:

- **Password construction**   How many characters a password should have; the use of capitalization, numbers, and special characters; not basing the password on a dictionary word or personal information; not making the password a slight modification of an existing password; and so on

- **Reuse restrictions**   Whether or not passwords can be reused, and, if so, with what frequency (how many different passwords must you use before you can use one you've used before)

- **Duration**   The minimum and maximum number of days a password can be used before it can be changed or must be changed

- **Protection of passwords**   Not writing down passwords where others can find them, not saving passwords and not allowing automated logins, not sharing passwords with other users, and so on

- **Consequences**   Consequences associated with violation of or noncompliance with the policy

The SANS Institute offers several examples of password policies (along with many other common information security policies) on its web site

Tech Tip

TOTP

A Time-based One-Time Password (TOTP) generator uses the current time as one of the seeds in a one-time password. This prevents replay attacks utilizing a captured password.

(www.sans.org—type **password policy** into the search box at the top of the SANS web site). The overall guidance established by the organization's security policy should be refined into specific guidance that administrators can enforce at the operating system level.

Domain Password Policy

A **domain password policy** is a password policy for a specific domain. As these policies are usually associated with the Windows operating system, a domain password policy is implemented and enforced on the **domain controller**, which is a computer that responds to security authentication requests, such as logging into a computer, for a Windows domain. The domain password policy usually falls under a **group policy object (GPO)** and has the following elements (see Figure 11.4):

- **Enforce password history**   Tells the system how many passwords to remember and does not allow a user to reuse an old password.

- **Maximum password age**   Specifies the maximum number of days a password may be used before it must be changed.

- **Minimum password age**   Specifies the minimum number of days a password must be used before it can be changed again.

- **Minimum password length**   Specifies the minimum number of characters that must be used in a password.

- **Password must meet complexity requirements**   Specifies that the password must meet the minimum length requirement and have characters from at least three of the following four groups: English uppercase characters (A through Z), English lowercase characters (a through z), numerals (0 through 9), and non-alphabetic characters (such as !, $, #, %).

- **Store passwords using reversible encryption**   Reversible encryption is a form of encryption that can easily be decrypted and is essentially the same as storing a plaintext version of the password (because

Exam Tip: A *password policy* is a set of rules designed to enhance computer security by requiring users to employ and maintain strong passwords. A *domain password policy* is a password policy that applies to a specific domain.

Not only is it essential to ensure every account has a strong password, but also it is essential to disable or delete unnecessary accounts. If your system does not need to support guest or anonymous accounts, then disable them. When user or administrator accounts are no longer needed, remove or disable them. As a best practice, all user accounts should be audited periodically to ensure there are no unnecessary, outdated, or unneeded accounts on your systems.

• **Figure 11.4**   Password policy options in Windows Local Security Policy

Calculating Unique Password Combinations

One of the primary reasons administrators require users to have longer passwords that use upper- and lowercase letters, numbers, and at least one "special" character is to help deter password-guessing attacks. One popular password-guessing technique, called a brute-force attack, *uses software to guess every possible password until one matches a user's password. Essentially, a brute force-attack tries* a, *then* aa, *then* aaa, *and so on until it runs out of combinations or gets a password match. Increasing both the pool of possible characters that can be used in the password and the number of characters required in the password can exponentially increase the number of "guesses" a brute-force program needs to perform before it runs out of possibilities. For example, if our password policy requires a three-character password that uses only lowercase letters, there are only 17,576 possible passwords (26 possible characters, 3 characters long is 26^3 combinations). Requiring a six-character password increases that number to 308,915,776 possible passwords (26^6). An eight-character password with upper- and lowercase, special symbol, and a number increases the possible passwords to 70^8 or over 576 trillion combinations.*

Precomputed hashes in rainbow tables can also be used to brute force past shorter passwords. As the length increases, so does the size of the rainbow table.

it's so easy to reverse the encryption and get the password). This should be used only when applications use protocols that require the user's password for authentication (such as Challenge-Handshake Authentication Protocol, or CHAP).

Domains are logical groups of computers that share a central directory database, known as the Active Directory database for the more recent Windows operating systems. The database contains information about the user accounts and security information for all resources identified within the domain. Each user within the domain is assigned his or her own unique account (that is, a domain is not a single account shared by multiple users), which is then assigned access to specific resources within the domain. In operating systems that provide domain capabilities, the password policy is set in the root container for the domain and applies to all users within that domain. Setting a password policy for a domain is similar to setting other password policies in that the same critical elements need to be considered (password length, complexity, life, and so on). If a change to one of these elements is desired for a group of users, a new domain needs to be created because the domain is considered a security boundary. In a Windows operating system that employs Active Directory, the domain password policy can be set in the Active Directory Users and Computers menu in the Administrative Tools section of the Control Panel.

■ Single Sign-On

To use a system, users must be able to access it, which they usually do by supplying their user IDs (or usernames) and corresponding passwords. As any security administrator knows, the more systems a particular user has access to, the more passwords that user must have and remember. The natural tendency for users is to select passwords that are easy to remember, or even the same password for use on the multiple systems they access. Wouldn't it be easier for the user simply to log in once and have to remember only a single, good password? This is made possible with a technology called single sign-on.

Single sign-on (SSO) is a form of authentication that involves the transferring of credentials between systems. As more and more systems are combined in daily use, users are forced to have multiple sets of credentials. A user may have to log into three, four, five, or even more systems every day just to do her job. Single sign-on allows a user to transfer her credentials, so that logging into one system acts to log her into all of them. Once the user has entered a user ID and password, the single sign-on system passes these credentials transparently to other systems so that repeated logons are not required. Put simply, you supply the right username and password once and you have access to all the applications and data you need, without having to log in multiple times and remember many different passwords. From a user standpoint, SSO means you need to remember only one username and one password. From an administration standpoint, SSO can be easier to manage and maintain. From a security standpoint, SSO can be even more secure, as users who need to remember only one password are less likely to

• **Figure 11.5**   Single sign-on process

choose something too simple or something so complex they need to write it down. Figure 11.5 shows a logical depiction of the SSO process:

1. The user signs in once, providing a username and password to the SSO server.

2. The SSO server provides authentication information to any resource the user accesses during that session. The server interfaces with the other applications and systems—the user does not need to log into each system individually.

In reality, SSO is usually a little more difficult to implement than vendors would lead you to believe. To be effective and useful, all your applications need to be able to access and use the authentication provided by the SSO process. The more diverse your network, the less likely this is to be the case. If your network, like most, contains different operating systems, custom applications, and a diverse user base, SSO may not even be a viable option.

Exam Tip: The CompTIA Security+ exam will very likely contain questions regarding single sign-on because it is such a prevalent topic and a very common approach to multisystem authentication.

Time of Day Restrictions

Some organizations need to tightly control certain users, groups, or even roles and limit access to certain resources to specific days and times. Most server-class operating systems enable administrators to implement time of day restrictions that limit when a user can log in, when certain resources can be accessed, and so on. Time of day restrictions are usually specified for individual accounts, as shown in Figure 11.6.

From a security perspective, time of day restrictions can be very useful. If a user normally accesses certain resources during normal business hours, an attempt

• **Figure 11.6**   Logon hours for Guest account

Chapter 11: Authentication and Remote Access

to access these resources outside this time period (either at night or on the weekend) might indicate an attacker has gained access to or is trying to gain access to that account. Specifying time of day restrictions can also serve as a mechanism to enforce internal controls of critical or sensitive resources. Obviously, a drawback to enforcing time of day restrictions is that it means that a user can't go to work outside of normal hours to "catch up" with work tasks. As with all security policies, usability and security must be balanced in this policy decision.

Tokens

While the username/password combination has been and continues to be the cheapest and most popular method of controlling access to resources, many organizations look for a more secure and tamper-resistant form of authentication. Usernames and passwords are "something you know" (which can be used by anyone else who knows or discovers the information). A more secure method of authentication is to combine the "something you know" with "something you have." A **token** is an authentication factor that typically takes the form of a physical or logical entity that the user must be in possession of to access their account or certain resources.

• **Figure 11.7** Token authenticator from Blizzard Entertainment

Most tokens are physical tokens that display a series of numbers that changes every 30 to 90 seconds, such as the token pictured in Figure 11.7 from Blizzard Entertainment. This sequence of numbers must be entered when the user is attempting to log in or access certain resources. The ever-changing sequence of numbers is synchronized to a remote server such that when the user enters the correct username, password, and matching sequence of numbers, he is allowed to log in. Even if an attacker obtains the username and password, the attacker cannot log in without the matching sequence of numbers. Other physical tokens include Common Access Cards (CACs), USB tokens, smart cards, and PC cards.

Tokens may also be implemented in software. Software tokens still provide two-factor authentication but don't require the user to have a physical device on hand. Some tokens require software clients that store a symmetric key (sometimes called a seed record) in a secured location on the user's device (laptop, desktop, tablet, and so on). Other software

Cross Check

Symmetric and Asymmetric Cryptography

You learned about symmetric and asymmetric cryptography in Chapter 5. What is the difference between the two methods? Which one uses public keys?

Principles of Computer Security

tokens use public key cryptography. Asymmetric cryptography solutions, such as public key cryptography, often associate a PIN with a specific user's token. To log in or access critical resources, the user must supply the correct PIN. The PIN is stored on a remote server and is used during the authentication process so that if a user presents the right token, but not the right PIN, the user's access can be denied. This helps prevent an attacker from gaining access if he gets a copy of or gains access to the software token.

Account and Password Expiration

Another common restriction that can be enforced in many access control mechanisms is either (or both) an account expiration or password expiration feature. This allows administrators to specify a period of time for which a password or an account will be active. For password expiration, when the expiration date is reached, the user generally is asked to create a new password. This means that if the password (and thus the account) has been compromised when the expiration date is reached and a new password is set, the attacker will again (hopefully) be locked out of the system. The attacker can't change the password himself, since the user would then be locked out and would contact an administrator to have the password reset, thus again locking out the attacker.

Another attack option would involve the attacker setting a new password on the compromised account and then attempting to reset the account back to the original, compromised password. If the attacker is successful, a new expiration time would be set for the account but the old password would still be used and the user would not be locked out of their account; in most cases, the user wouldn't notice anything had happened at all as their old password would continue to work. This is one reason why a *password history* mechanism should be used. The history is used to keep track of previously used passwords so that they cannot be reused.

■ Security Controls and Permissions

If multiple users share a computer system, the system administrator likely needs to control who is allowed to do what when it comes to viewing, using, or changing system resources. While operating systems vary in how they implement these types of controls, most operating systems use the concepts of permissions and rights to control and safeguard access to resources. As we discussed earlier, permissions control what a user is allowed to do with objects on a system and rights define the actions a user can perform on the system itself. Let's examine how the Windows operating systems implement this concept.

The Windows operating systems use the concepts of permissions and rights to control access to files, folders, and information resources. When using the NTFS file system, administrators can grant users and groups

Tech Tip

Best Practice: Password Expiration

One of the best practices an organization can implement is to attach an expiration date to user passwords. This helps ensure that if a password is compromised, the period that the account remains compromised is limited. In most environments and operating systems, this is expressed in terms of the number of days before the password expires and is no longer valid. For example, a maximum password age of 90 days means that a particular password will expire 90 days after that password was initially set to its current value.

Tech Tip

Heartbleed

In 2014 a vulnerability that could cause user credentials to be exposed was discovered in millions of systems. Called the Heartbleed incident, this resulted in numerous users being told to change their passwords because of potential compromise. Users were also warned of the dangers of reusing passwords across different accounts. Although this makes passwords easier to remember, it also improves guessing chances. What made this whole effort of protecting your passwords particularly challenging is that the breach was widespread—virtually all Linux systems—and the patching rate was uneven, so people could be suffering multiple exposures over time. After one year, an estimated 40% of all compromised systems remained unpatched. This highlights the importance of not reusing passwords across multiple accounts.

permission to perform certain tasks as they relate to files, folders, and Registry keys. The basic categories of NTFS permissions are as follows:

- **Full Control** A user/group can change permissions on the folder/file, take ownership if someone else owns the folder/file, delete subfolders and files, and perform actions permitted by all other NTFS folder permissions.

- **Modify** Users/groups can view and modify files/folders and their properties, can delete and add files/folders, and can delete or add properties to a file/folder.

- **Read & Execute** Users/groups can view the file/folder and can execute scripts and executables but cannot make any changes (files/folders are read-only).

- **List Folder Contents** A user/group can list only what is inside the folder (applies to folders only).

- **Read** Users/groups can view the contents of the file/folder and the file/folder properties.

- **Write** Users/groups can write to the file or folder.

• **Figure 11.8** Permissions for the Data folder

Figure 11.8 shows the permissions on a folder called Data from a Windows Server system. In the top half of the Permissions window are the users and groups that have permissions for this folder. In the bottom half of the window are the permissions assigned to the highlighted user or group.

The Windows operating system also uses user rights or privileges to determine what actions a user or group is allowed to perform or access. These user rights are typically assigned to groups, as it is easier to deal with a few groups than to assign rights to individual users, and they are usually defined in either a group or a local security policy. The list of user rights is quite extensive but a few examples of user rights are

- **Log on locally** Users/groups can attempt to log onto the local system itself.

- **Access this computer from the network** Users/groups can attempt to access this system through the network connection.

- **Manage auditing and security log** Users/groups can view, modify, and delete auditing and security log information.

Rights tend to be actions that deal with accessing the system itself, process control, logging, and so on. Figure 11.9 shows the user rights contained in the local security policy on a Windows system.

Folders and files are not the only things that can be safeguarded or controlled using permissions. Even access and use of peripherals, such as printers, can be controlled using permissions. Figure 11.10 shows the Security tab from a printer attached to a Windows system. Permissions can be assigned to control who can print to the printer, who can manage documents and

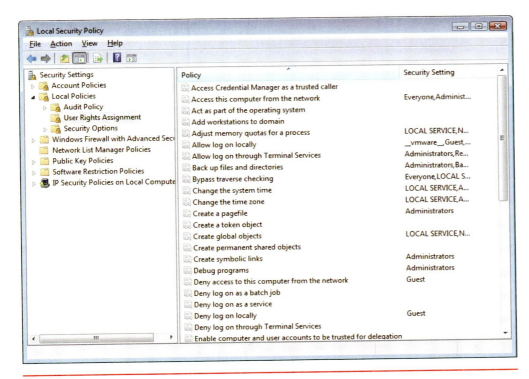

Figure 11.9   User Rights Assignment options from Windows Local Security Policy

print jobs sent to the printer, and who can manage the printer itself. With this type of granular control, administrators have a great deal of control over how system resources are used and who uses them.

A very important concept to consider when assigning rights and privileges to users is the concept of least privilege. Least privilege requires that

Exam Tip: Although it is very important to get security settings "right the first time," it is just as important to perform routine audits of security settings such as user accounts, group memberships, file permissions, and so on.

Figure 11.10   Security tab showing printer permissions in Windows

users be given the absolute minimum number of rights and privileges required to perform their authorized duties. For example, if a user does not need the ability to install software on their own desktop to perform their job, then don't give them that ability. This reduces the likelihood the user will load malware, insecure software, or unauthorized applications onto their system.

Access Control Lists

The term **access control list (ACL)** is used in more than one manner in the field of computer security. When discussing routers and firewalls, an ACL is a set of rules used to control traffic flow into or out of an interface or network. When discussing system resources, such as files and folders, an ACL lists permissions attached to an object—who is allowed to view, modify, move, or delete that object.

To illustrate this concept, consider an example. Figure 11.11 shows the access control list (permissions) for the Data folder. The user identified as Billy Williams has Read & Execute, List Folder Contents, and Read permissions, meaning this user can open the folder, see what's in the folder, and so on. Figure 11.12 shows the permissions for a user identified as Leah Jones, who has only Read permissions on the same folder.

In computer systems and networks, there are several ways that access controls can be implemented. An *access control matrix* provides the simplest

• **Figure 11.11** Permissions for Billy Williams on the Data folder

• **Figure 11.12** Permissions for Leah Jones on the Data folder

Principles of Computer Security

Table 11.1	An Access Control Matrix				
	Process 1	**Process 2**	**File 1**	**File 2**	**Printer**
Process 1	Read, write, execute		Read, write	Read	Write
Process 2	Execute	Read, write, execute	Read, write	Read, write	Write

framework for illustrating the process. An example of an access control matrix is provided in Table 11.1. In this matrix, the system is keeping track of two processes, two files, and one hardware device. Process 1 can read both File 1 and File 2 but can write only to File 1. Process 1 cannot access Process 2, but Process 2 can execute Process 1. Both processes have the ability to write to the printer.

While simple to understand, the access control matrix is seldom used in computer systems because it is extremely costly in terms of storage space and processing. Imagine the size of an access control matrix for a large network with hundreds of users and thousands of files.

Mandatory Access Control (MAC)

Mandatory access control (MAC) is the process of controlling access to information based on the sensitivity of that information and whether or not the user is operating at the appropriate sensitivity level and has the authority to access that information. Under a MAC system, each piece of information and every system resource (files, devices, networks, and so on) is labeled with its sensitivity level (such as Public, Engineering Private, Jones Secret). Users are assigned a clearance level that sets the upper boundary of the information and devices that they are allowed to access.

The access control and sensitivity labels are required in a MAC system. Labels are defined and then assigned to users and resources. Users must then operate within their assigned sensitivity and clearance levels—they don't have the option to modify their own sensitivity levels or the levels of the information resources they create. Due to the complexity involved, MAC is typically run only on systems where security is a top priority such as Trusted Solaris, OpenBSD, and SELinux.

Figure 11.13 illustrates MAC in operation. The information resource on the left has been labeled "Engineering Secret," meaning only users in the Engineering group operating at the Secret sensitivity level or above can access that resource. The top user is operating at the Secret level but is not a member of Engineering and is denied access to the resource. The middle user is a member of Engineering but is operating at a Public sensitivity level and is therefore denied access to the resource. The bottom user is a member of Engineering, is operating at a Secret sensitivity level, and is allowed to access the information resource.

Exam Tip: Mandatory access control restricts access based on the sensitivity of the information and whether or not the user has the authority to access that information.

Tech Tip

MAC Objective

Mandatory access controls are often mentioned in discussions of multilevel security. For multilevel security to be implemented, a mechanism must be present to identify the classification of all users and files. A file identified as Top Secret (has a label indicating that it is Top Secret) may be viewed only by individuals with a Top Secret clearance. For this control mechanism to work reliably, all files must be marked with appropriate controls and all user access must be checked. This is the primary goal of MAC.

• **Figure 11.13** Logical representation of mandatory access control

Exam Tip: Discretionary access control restricts access based on the user's identity or group membership.

Discretionary Access Control (DAC)

Discretionary access control (DAC) is the process of using file permissions and optional ACLs to restrict access to information based on a user's identity or group membership. DAC is the most common access control system and is commonly used in both UNIX and Windows operating systems. The "discretionary" part of DAC means that a file or resource owner has the ability to change the permissions on that file or resource.

Under UNIX operating systems, file permissions consist of three distinct parts:

- **Owner permissions (read, write, and execute)** The owner of the file

- **Group permissions (read, write, and execute)** The group to which the owner of the file belongs

- **World permissions (read, write, and execute)** Anyone else who is not the owner and does not belong to the group to which the owner of the file belongs

For example, suppose a file called *secretdata* has been created by the owner of the file, Luke, who is part of the Engineering group. The owner permissions on the file would reflect Luke's access to the file (as the owner). The group permissions would reflect the access granted to anyone who is part of the Engineering group. The world permissions would represent the access granted to anyone who is not Luke and is not part of the Engineering group.

• **Figure 11.14** Discretionary file permissions in the UNIX environment

In UNIX, a file's permissions are usually displayed as a series of nine characters, with the first three characters representing the owner's permissions, the second three characters representing the group permissions, and the last three characters representing the permissions for everyone else, or for the world. This concept is illustrated in Figure 11.14.

Suppose the file secretdata is owned by Luke with group permissions for Engineering (because Luke is part of the Engineering group), and the permissions on that file are rwx, rw-, and ---, as shown in Figure 11.14. This would mean that:

- Luke can read, write, and execute the file (rwx).

- Members of the Engineering group can read and write the file but not execute it (rw-).

- The world has no access to the file and can't read, write, or execute it (---).

Remember that under the DAC model, the file's owner, Luke, can change the file's permissions any time he wants.

Role-Based Access Control (RBAC)

Access control lists can be cumbersome and can take time to administer properly. **Role-based access control (RBAC)** is the process of managing access and privileges based on the user's assigned roles. RBAC is the access control model that most closely resembles an organization's structure. In this scheme, instead of each user being assigned specific access permissions for the objects associated with the computer system or network, that user is assigned a set of roles that the user may perform. The roles are in turn assigned the access permissions necessary to perform the tasks associated with the role. Users will thus be granted permissions to objects in terms of the specific duties they must perform—not just because of a security classification associated with individual objects.

Under RBAC, you must first determine the activities that must be performed and the resources that must be accessed by specific roles. For example, the role of "securityadmin" in Microsoft SQL Server must be able to create and manage logins, read error logs, and audit the application. Once all the roles are created and the rights and privileges associated with those roles are determined, users can then be assigned one or more roles based on their job functions. When a role is assigned to a specific user, the user gets all the rights and privileges assigned to that role.

Unfortunately, in reality, administrators often find themselves in a position of working in an organization where more than one user has multiple roles or even access to multiple accounts (a situation quite common in smaller organizations). Users with multiple accounts tend to select the same or similar passwords for those accounts, thereby increasing the chance one compromised account can lead to the compromise of other accounts accessed by that user. Where possible, administrators should first eliminate shared or additional accounts for users and then examine the possibility of combining roles or privileges to reduce the "account footprint" of individual users.

Rule-Based Access Control

Rule-based access control is yet another method of managing access and privileges (and unfortunately shares the same acronym as role-based access control). In this method, access is either allowed or denied based on a set of predefined rules. Each object has an associated ACL (much like DAC), and when a particular user or group attempts to access the object, the appropriate rule is applied.

A good example for rule-based access control is permitted logon hours. Many operating systems give administrators the ability to control the hours during which users can log in. For example, a bank may allow its employees to log in only between the hours of 8 A.M. and 6 P.M. Monday through Saturday. If a user attempts to log in outside of these hours, 3 A.M. on Sunday for example, then the rule will reject the login attempt whether or not the user supplies valid login credentials.

Attribute-Based Access Control (ABAC)

Attribute-based access control (ABAC) is a new access control schema based on the use of attributes associated with an identity. These can use any type

As defined by the "Orange Book," a Department of Defense document (in the "rainbow series") that at one time was the standard for describing what constituted a trusted computing system, a *discretionary access control (DAC)* is "a means of restricting access to objects based on the identity of subjects and/or groups to which they belong. The controls are discretionary in the sense that a subject with a certain access permission is capable of passing that permission (perhaps indirectly) on to any other subject (unless restrained by mandatory access control)."

Exam Tip: Role-based and rule-based access control can both be abbreviated as RBAC. Standard convention is for RBAC to be used to denote role-based access control. A seldom-seen acronym for rule-based access control is RB-RBAC. *Role*-based focuses on the user's role (administrator, backup operator, and so on). *Rule*-based focuses on predefined criteria such as time of day (users can only log in between 8 A.M. and 6 P.M.) or type of network traffic (web traffic is allowed to leave the organization).

Exam Tip: The CompTIA Security+ exam will very likely expect you to be able to differentiate between the four major forms of access control discussed here: mandatory access control, discretionary access control, role-based access control, and rule-based access control.

of attributes (user attributes, resource attributes, environment attributes, and so on), such as location, time, activity being requested, and user credentials. An example would be a doctor getting one set of access for a specific patient versus a different patient. ABAC can be represented via the **eXtensible Access Control Markup Language (XACML)**, a standard that implements attribute- and policy-based access control schemes.

Account Expiration

In addition to all the other methods of controlling and restricting access, most modern operating systems allow administrators to specify the length of time an account is valid and when it "expires" or is disabled. This is a great method for controlling temporary accounts, or accounts for contractors or contract employees. For these accounts, the administrator can specify an expiration date; when the date is reached, the account automatically becomes locked out and cannot be logged into without administrator intervention. A related action can be taken with accounts that never expire: they can automatically be marked "inactive" and locked out if they have been unused for a specified number of days. Account expiration is similar to password expiration, in that it limits the time window of potential compromise. When an account has expired, it cannot be used unless the expiration deadline is extended.

Similarly, organizations must define whether accounts are deleted or disabled when no longer needed. Deleting an account removes the account from the system permanently, whereas disabling an account leaves it in place but marks it as unusable. Many organizations disable accounts for a period of time after an employee departs (30 or more days) prior to deleting the account. This prevents anyone from using the account and allows administrators to reassign files, forward mail, and "clean up" before taking any permanent actions on the account.

■ Preventing Data Loss or Theft

Identity theft and commercial espionage have become very large and lucrative criminal enterprises over the past decade. Hackers are no longer merely content to compromise systems and deface web sites. In many attacks performed today, hackers are after intellectual property, business plans, competitive intelligence, personal information, credit card numbers, client records, or any other information that can be sold, traded, or manipulated for profit. This has created a whole industry of technical solutions labeled data loss prevention (DLP) solutions.

It can be assumed that a hacker has assumed the identity of an authorized user, and DLP solutions exist to prevent the exfiltration of data regardless of access control restrictions. DLP solutions come in many forms, and each of these solutions has strengths and weaknesses. The best solution is a combination of security elements, some to secure data in storage (encryption) and some in the form of monitoring (proxy devices to monitor data egress for sensitive data), and even NetFlow analytics to identify new bulk data transfer routes.

Principles of Computer Security

The Remote Access Process

The process of connecting by remote access involves two elements: a temporary network connection and a series of protocols to negotiate privileges and commands. The temporary network connection can occur via a dial-up service, the Internet, wireless access, or any other method of connecting to a network. Once the connection is made, the primary issue is authenticating the identity of the user and establishing proper privileges for that user. This is accomplished using a combination of protocols and the operating system on the host machine.

The three steps in the establishment of proper privileges are authentication, authorization, and accounting, commonly referred to simply as **AAA**. **Authentication** is the matching of user-supplied credentials to previously stored credentials on a host machine, and it usually involves an account username and password. Once the user is authenticated, the authorization step takes place. **Authorization** is the granting of specific permissions based on the privileges held by the account. Does the user have permission to use the network at this time, or is her use restricted? Does the user have access to specific applications, such as mail and FTP, or are some of these restricted? These checks are carried out as part of authorization, and in many cases this is a function of the operating system in conjunction with its established security policies. **Accounting** is the collection of billing and other detail records. Network access is often a billable function, and a log of how much time, bandwidth, file transfer space, or other resources were used needs to be maintained. Other accounting functions include keeping detailed security logs to maintain an audit trail of tasks being performed.

When a user connects to the Internet through an ISP, this is similarly a case of remote access—the user is establishing a connection to her ISP's network, and the same security issues apply. The issue of authentication, the matching of user-supplied credentials to previously stored credentials on a host machine, is usually done via a user account name and password. Once the user is authenticated, the authorization step takes place. Remote authentication usually takes the common form of an end user submitting his credentials via an established protocol to a **remote access server (RAS)**, which acts upon those credentials, either granting or denying access.

Access controls define what actions a user can perform or what objects a user is allowed to access. Access controls are built upon the foundation of elements designed to facilitate the matching of a user to a process. These elements are identification, authentication, and authorization. There are a myriad of details and choices associated with setting up remote access to a network, and to provide for the management of these options, it is important for an organization to have a series of remote access policies and procedures spelling out the details of what is permitted and what is not for a given network.

Identification

Identification is the process of ascribing a computer ID to a specific user, computer, network device, or computer process. The identification process is typically performed only once, when a user ID is issued to a particular

Tech Tip

Securing Remote Connections

By using encryption, remote access protocols can securely authenticate and authorize a user according to previously established privilege levels. The authorization phase can keep unauthorized users out, but after that, encryption of the communications channel becomes very important in preventing nonauthorized users from breaking in on an authorized session and hijacking an authorized user's credentials. As more and more networks rely on the Internet for connecting remote users, the need for and importance of secure remote access protocols and secure communication channels will continue to grow.

user. User identification enables authentication and authorization to form the basis for accountability. For accountability purposes, user IDs should not be shared, and for security purposes, they should not be descriptive of job function. This practice enables you to trace activities to individual users or computer processes so that they can be held responsible for their actions. Identification links the logon ID or user ID to credentials that have been submitted previously to either HR or the IT staff. A required characteristic of user IDs is that they must be unique so that they map back to the credentials presented when the account was established.

Authentication

Authentication is the process of binding a specific ID to a specific computer connection. Two items need to be presented to cause this binding to occur— the user ID, and some "secret" to prove that the user is the valid possessor of the credentials. Historically, three categories of secrets are used to authenticate the identity of a user: what users know, what users have, and what users are. Today an additional category is used: what users do.

These methods can be used individually or in combination. These controls assume that the identification process has been completed and the identity of the user has been verified. It is the job of authentication mechanisms to ensure that only valid users are admitted. Described another way, authentication is using some mechanism to prove that you are who you claimed to be when the identification process was completed.

The most common method of authentication is the use of a password. For greater security, you can add an element from a separate group, such as a smart card token—something a user has in her possession. Passwords are common because they are one of the simplest forms and use user memory as a prime component. Because of their simplicity, passwords have become ubiquitous across a wide range of authentication systems.

Another method to provide authentication involves the use of something that only valid users should have in their possession. A physical-world example of this would be a simple lock and key. Only those individuals with the correct key will be able to open the lock and thus gain admittance to a house, car, office, or whatever the lock was protecting. A similar method can be used to authenticate users for a computer system or network (though the key may be electronic and could reside on a smart card or similar device). The problem with this technology, however, is that people do lose their keys (or cards), which means not only that the user can't log into the system but that somebody else who finds the key may then be able to access the system, even though they are not authorized. To address this problem, a combination of the something-you-know and something-you-have methods is often used so that the individual with the key is also required to provide a password or passcode. The key is useless unless the user knows this code.

The third general method to provide authentication involves something that is unique about you. We are accustomed to this concept in our physical world, where our fingerprints or a sample of our DNA can be used to identify us. This same concept can be used to provide authentication in the computer world. The field of authentication that uses something about you or something that you are is known as *biometrics*. A number of different mechanisms can be used to accomplish this type of authentication, such as a fingerprint, iris, retinal, or hand geometry scan. All of these methods obviously require some additional hardware in order to operate. The inclusion of fingerprint readers on laptop computers is becoming common as the additional hardware is becoming cost effective.

A new method, based on how users perform an action, such as their gait when walking, or typing patterns has emerged as a source of a personal "signature". While not directly embedded into systems as yet, this is an option that will be coming in the future.

While the three main approaches to authentication appear to be easy to understand and in most cases easy to implement, authentication is not to be taken lightly, since it is such an important component of security. Potential attackers are constantly searching for ways to get past the system's authentication mechanism, and they have employed some fairly ingenious methods to do so. Consequently, security professionals are constantly devising new methods, building on these three basic approaches, to provide authentication mechanisms for computer systems and networks.

Basic Authentication

Basic authentication is the simplest technique used to manage access control across HTTP. Basic authentication operates by passing information encoded in Base64 form using standard HTTP headers. This is a plaintext method without any pretense of security. Figure 11.15 illustrates the operation of basic authentication.

Username and password encoded
using Base64 encoding and sent to server

• **Figure 11.15**   How basic authentication operates

Digest Authentication

Digest authentication is a method used to negotiate credentials across the Web. Digest authentication uses hash functions and a nonce to improve security over basic authentication. Digest authentication works as follows, as illustrated in Figure 11.16:

1. The client requests login.
2. The server responds with a challenge and provides a nonce.
3. The client hashes the password and nonce.
4. The client returns the hashed password to the server.
5. The server requests the password from a password store.
6. The server hashes the password and nonce.
7. If both hashes match, login is granted.

• **Figure 11.16**   How digest authentication operates

Exam Tip: The bottom line for both basic and digest authentication is that these are insecure methods and should not be relied upon for any level of security.

Exam Tip: Two tickets are used in Kerberos. The first is a ticket-granting ticket (TGT) obtained from the authentication server (AS). The TGT is presented to a ticket-granting server (TGS) when access to a server is requested and a client-to-server ticket is issued, granting access to the server. Typically both the AS and the TGS are logically separate parts of the key distribution center (KDC).

Digest authentication, although it improves security over basic authentication, does not provide any significant level of security. Passwords are not sent in the clear. Digest authentication is subject to man-in-the-middle attacks and potentially replay attacks.

Kerberos

Developed as part of MIT's project Athena, **Kerberos** is a network authentication protocol designed for a client/server environment. The current version is Kerberos 5 release 1.13.2 and is supported by all major operating systems. Kerberos securely passes a symmetric key over an insecure network using the Needham-Schroeder symmetric key protocol. Kerberos is built around the idea of a trusted third party, termed a **key distribution center (KDC)**, which consists of two logically separate parts: an **authentication server (AS)** and a **ticket-granting server (TGS)**. Kerberos communicates via "tickets" that serve to prove the identity of users.

Taking its name from the three-headed dog of Greek mythology, Kerberos is designed to work across the Internet, an inherently insecure environment. Kerberos uses strong encryption so that a client can prove its identity to a server and the server can in turn authenticate itself to the client. A complete Kerberos environment is referred to as a Kerberos *realm*. The Kerberos server contains user IDs and hashed passwords for all users that will have authorizations to realm services. The Kerberos server also has shared secret keys with every server to which it will grant access tickets.

The basis for authentication in a Kerberos environment is the ticket. Tickets are used in a two-step process with the client. The first ticket is a *ticket-granting ticket (TGT)* issued by the AS to a requesting client. The client can then present this ticket to the Kerberos server with a request for a ticket to access a specific server. This *client-to-server ticket* (also called a *service ticket*) is used to gain access to a server's service in the realm. Since the entire session can be encrypted, this eliminates the inherently insecure transmission of items such as a password that can be intercepted on the network. Tickets are time-stamped and have a lifetime, so attempting to reuse a ticket will not be successful. Figure 11.17 details Kerberos operations.

To illustrate how the Kerberos authentication service works, think about the common driver's license. You have received a license that you

Tech Tip

Kerberos Authentication

Kerberos is a third-party authentication service that uses a series of tickets as tokens for authenticating users. The six steps involved are protected using strong cryptography:

- *The user presents his credentials and requests a ticket from the key distribution center (KDC).*
- *The KDC verifies credentials and issues a ticket-granting ticket (TGT).*
- *The user presents a TGT and request for service to the KDC.*
- *The KDC verifies authorization and issues a client-to-server ticket (or service ticket).*
- *The user presents a request and a client-to-server ticket to the desired service.*
- *If the client-to-server ticket is valid, service is granted to the client.*

but the purpose is the same: determine whether a given user who has been identified has permissions for a particular object or resource being requested. This functionality is frequently part of the operating system and is transparent to users.

The separation of tasks, from identification to authentication to authorization, has several advantages. Many methods can be used to perform each task, and on many systems several methods are concurrently present for each task. Separation of these tasks into individual elements allows combinations of implementations to work together. Any system or resource, be it hardware (router or workstation) or a software component (database system), that requires authorization can use its own authorization method once authentication has occurred. This makes for efficient and consistent application of these principles.

Access Control

The term **access control** has been used to describe a variety of protection schemes. It sometimes refers to all security features used to prevent unauthorized access to a computer system or network—or even a network resource such as a printer. In this sense, it may be confused with authentication. More properly, *access* is the ability of a subject (such as an individual or a process running on a computer system) to interact with an object (such as a file or hardware device). Once the individual has verified their identity, access controls regulate what the individual can actually do on the system. Just because a person is granted entry to the system, that does not mean that they should have access to all data the system contains.

Tech Tip

Access Control vs. Authentication
It may seem that access control and authentication are two ways to describe the same protection mechanism. This, however, is not the case. Authentication provides a way to verify to the computer who the user is. Once the user has been authenticated, the access controls decide what operations the user can perform. The two go hand-in-hand but are not the same thing.

■ Remote Access Methods

When a user requires access to a remote system, the process of remote access is used to determine the appropriate controls. This is done through a series of protocols and processes described in the remainder of this chapter.

IEEE 802.1X

IEEE 802.1X is an authentication standard that supports port-based authentication services between a user and an authorization device, such as an edge router. IEEE 802.1X is used by all types of networks, including Ethernet, Token Ring, and wireless. This standard describes methods used to authenticate a user prior to granting access to a network and the authentication server, such as a RADIUS server. 802.1X acts through an intermediate device, such as an edge switch, enabling ports to carry normal traffic if the connection is properly authenticated. This prevents unauthorized clients from accessing the publicly available ports on a switch, keeping unauthorized users out of a LAN. Until a client has successfully authenticated itself to the device, only Extensible Authentication Protocol over LAN (EAPOL) traffic is passed by the switch.

EAPOL is an encapsulated method of passing EAP messages over 802.1 frames. EAP is a general protocol that can support multiple methods of

One security issue associated with 802.1X is that the authentication occurs only upon initial connection, and that another user can insert themselves into the connection by changing packets or using a hub. The secure solution is to pair 802.1X, which authenticates the initial connection, with a VPN or IPsec, which provides persistent security.

authentication, including one-time passwords, Kerberos, public keys, and security device methods such as smart cards. Once a client successfully authenticates itself to the 802.1X device, the switch opens ports for normal traffic. At this point, the client can communicate with the system's AAA method, such as a RADIUS server, and authenticate itself to the network.

Wireless Protocols

802.1X is commonly used on wireless access points as a port-based authentication service prior to admission to the wireless network. 802.1X over wireless uses either 802.11i or EAP-based protocols, such as EAP-TLS or PEAP-TLS.

Cross Check

Wireless Remote Access

Wireless is a common method of allowing remote access to a network, as it does not require physical cabling and allows mobile connections. Wireless security, including protocols such as 802.11i and EAP-based solutions, is covered in Chapter 12.

RADIUS

Remote Authentication Dial-In User Service (RADIUS) is an AAA protocol. It was submitted to the Internet Engineering Task Force (IETF) as a series of RFCs: RFC 2058 (RADIUS specification), RFC 2059 (RADIUS accounting standard), and updated RFCs 2865–2869, which are now standard protocols.

RADIUS is designed as a connectionless protocol that uses the User Datagram Protocol (UDP) as its transport layer protocol. Connection type issues, such as timeouts, are handled by the RADIUS application instead of the transport layer. RADIUS utilizes UDP port 1812 for authentication and authorization and UDP 1813 for accounting functions.

RADIUS is a client/server protocol. The RADIUS client is typically a network access server (NAS). Network access servers act as intermediaries, authenticating clients before allowing them access to a network. RADIUS, RRAS (Microsoft), RAS, and VPN servers can all act as network access servers. The RADIUS server is a process or daemon running on a UNIX or Windows Server machine. Communications between a RADIUS client and RADIUS server are encrypted using a shared secret that is manually configured into each entity and not shared over a connection. Hence, communications between a RADIUS client (typically a NAS) and a RADIUS server are secure, but the communications between a user (typically a PC) and the RADIUS client are subject to compromise. This is important to note, for if the user's machine (the PC) is not the RADIUS client (the NAS), then communications between the PC and the NAS are typically not encrypted and are passed in the clear.

RADIUS Authentication

The RADIUS protocol is designed to allow a RADIUS server to support a wide variety of methods to authenticate a user. When the server is given a username and password, it can support Point-to-Point Protocol (PPP), Password Authentication Protocol (PAP), Challenge-Handshake Authentication Protocol (CHAP), UNIX login, and other mechanisms, depending on what was established when the server was set up. A user login authentication consists of a query (Access-Request) from the RADIUS client and a corresponding response (Access-Accept, Access-Challenge, or Access-Reject) from the RADIUS server, as you can see in Figure 11.18. The Access-Challenge response is the initiation of a challenge/response handshake. If the client cannot support challenge/response, then it treats the Challenge message as an Access-Reject.

The Access-Request message contains the username, encrypted password, NAS IP address, and port. The message also contains information concerning the type of session the user wants to initiate. Once the RADIUS server receives this information, it searches its database for a match on the username. If a match is not found, either a default profile is loaded or an Access-Reject reply is sent to the user. If the entry is found or the default

1) User initiates PPP connection to NAS.

2) NAS prompts user for either
   • Username and password (PAP) or
   • Challenge (CHAP)

3) User replies to NAS with credentials.

4) RADIUS Client sends username and encrypted password to RADIUS server.

5) RADIUS server responds with either
   • Access-Accept,
   • Access-Reject, or
   • Access-Challenge

6) RADIUS client acts upon authentication, authorization, and accounting rules, allowing access to remote resources.

• **Figure 11.18**   RADIUS communication sequence

profile is used, the next phase involves authorization, for in RADIUS, these steps are performed in sequence. Figure 11.18 shows the interaction between a user and the RADIUS client and RADIUS server and the steps taken to make a connection.

RADIUS Authorization

In the RADIUS protocol, the authentication and authorization steps are performed together in response to a single Access-Request message, although they are sequential steps (see Figure 11.18). Once an identity has been established, either known or default, the authorization process determines what parameters are returned to the client. Typical authorization parameters include the service type allowed (shell or framed), the protocols allowed, the IP address to assign to the user (static or dynamic), and the access list to apply or static route to place in the NAS routing table.

These parameters are all defined in the configuration information on the RADIUS client and server during setup. Using this information, the RADIUS server returns an Access-Accept message with these parameters to the RADIUS client.

RADIUS Accounting

The RADIUS accounting function is performed independently of RADIUS authentication and authorization. The accounting function uses a separate UDP port, 1813 (see Table 11.2 in the "Connection Summary" section at the end of the chapter). The primary functionality of RADIUS accounting was established to support ISPs in their user accounting, and it supports typical accounting functions for time billing and security logging. The RADIUS accounting functions are designed to allow data to be transmitted at the beginning and end of a session, and they can indicate resource utilization, such as time, bandwidth, and so on.

Diameter

Diameter is the name of an AAA protocol suite, designated by the IETF to replace the aging RADIUS protocol. Diameter operates in much the same way as RADIUS in a client/server configuration, but it improves upon RADIUS, resolving discovered weaknesses. Diameter is a TCP-based service and has more extensive AAA capabilities. Diameter is also designed for all types of remote access, not just modem pools. As more and more users adopt broadband and other connection methods, these newer services require more options to determine permissible usage properly and to account for and log the usage. Diameter is designed with these needs in mind.

Diameter also has an improved method of encrypting message exchanges to prohibit replay and man-in-the-middle attacks. Taken all together, Diameter, with its enhanced functionality and security, is an improvement on the proven design of the old RADIUS standard.

TACACS+

The *Terminal Access Controller Access Control System+ (TACACS+)* protocol is the current generation of the TACACS family. Originally TACACS was developed by BBN Planet Corporation for MILNET, an early military network, but it has been enhanced by Cisco, which has expanded its functionality twice. The original BBN TACACS system provided a combination process of authentication and authorization. Cisco extended this to Extended Terminal Access Controller Access Control System (XTACACS), which provided for separate authentication, authorization, and accounting processes. The current generation, TACACS+, has extended attribute control and accounting processes.

One of the fundamental design aspects is the separation of authentication, authorization, and accounting in this protocol. Although there is a straightforward lineage of these protocols from the original TACACS, TACACS+ is a major revision and is not backward-compatible with previous versions of the protocol series.

TACACS+ uses TCP as its transport protocol, typically operating over TCP port 49. This port is used for the login process and is reserved in RFC 3232, "Assigned Numbers," manifested in a database from the Internet Assigned Numbers Authority (IANA). In the IANA specification, both UDP port 49 and TCP port 49 are reserved for the TACACS+ login host protocol (see Table 11.2 in the "Connection Summary" section at the end of the chapter).

TACACS+ is a client/server protocol, with the client typically being a NAS and the server being a daemon process on a UNIX, Linux, or Windows server. This is important to note, for if the user's machine (usually a PC) is not the client (usually a NAS), then communications between PC and NAS are typically not encrypted and are passed in the clear. Communications between a TACACS+ client and TACACS+ server are encrypted using a shared secret that is manually configured into each entity and is not shared over a connection. Hence, communications between a TACACS+ client (typically a NAS) and a TACACS+ server are secure, but the communications between a user (typically a PC) and the TACACS+ client are subject to compromise.

TACACS+ Authentication

TACACS+ allows for arbitrary length and content in the authentication exchange sequence, enabling many different authentication mechanisms to be used with TACACS+ clients. Authentication is optional and is determined as a site-configurable option. When authentication is used, common forms include PPP PAP, PPP CHAP, PPP EAP, token cards, and Kerberos. The authentication process is performed using three different packet types: START, CONTINUE, and REPLY. START and CONTINUE packets originate from the client and are directed to the TACACS+ server. The REPLY packet is used to communicate from the TACACS+ server to the client.

The authentication process is illustrated in Figure 11.19, and it begins with a START message from the client to the server. This message may be in response to an initiation from a PC connected to the TACACS+ client. The START message describes the type of authentication being requested (simple plaintext password, PAP, CHAP, and so on). This START message may also contain additional authentication data, such as a username and password. A START message is also sent as a response to a restart request from the server in a REPLY message. A START message always has its sequence number set to 1.

1) User initiates PPP connection to NAS.

2) NAS prompts user for either
   • Username and password (PAP) or
   • Challenge (CHAP)

3) User replies to NAS with credentials.

4) TACACS+ client START request.

5) TACACS+ server replies with either
   • Complete authentication or
   • Client sending CONTINUE and loop until complete

6) TACACS+ client and server authentication requests.

7) TACACS+ client acts upon authentication, authorization, and accounting rules to permit access to remote resources.

• **Figure 11.19** TACACS+ communication sequence

When a TACACS+ server receives a START message, it sends a REPLY message. This REPLY message indicates whether the authentication is complete or needs to be continued. If the process needs to be continued, the REPLY message also specifies what additional information is needed. The response from a client to a REPLY message requesting additional data is a CONTINUE message. This process continues until the server has all the information needed, and the authentication process concludes with a success or failure.

TACACS+ Authorization

Authorization is defined as the granting of specific permissions based on the privileges held by the account. This generally occurs after authentication, as shown in Figure 11.19, but this is not a firm requirement. A default state of "unknown user" exists before a user is authenticated, and permissions can be determined for an unknown user. As with authentication, authorization is an optional process and may or may not be part of a site-specific operation. When it is used in conjunction with authentication, the authorization process follows the authentication process and uses the confirmed user identity as input in the decision process.

The authorization process is performed using two message types: REQUEST and RESPONSE. The authorization process is performed using an authorization session consisting of a single pair of REQUEST and RESPONSE messages. The client issues an authorization REQUEST message containing a fixed set of fields enumerating the authenticity of the user or process requesting permission and a variable set of fields enumerating the services or options for which authorization is being requested.

The RESPONSE message in TACACS+ is not a simple yes or no; it can also include qualifying information, such as a user time limit or IP restrictions. These limitations have important uses, such as enforcing time limits on shell access or enforcing IP access list restrictions for specific user accounts.

TACACS+ Accounting

As with the two previous services, accounting is also an optional function of TACACS+. When utilized, it typically follows the other services. Accounting in TACACS+ is defined as the process of recording what a user or process has done. Accounting can serve two important purposes:

- It can be used to account for services being utilized, possibly for billing purposes.
- It can be used for generating security audit trails.

TACACS+ accounting records contain several pieces of information to support these tasks. The accounting process has the information revealed in the authorization and authentication processes, so it can record specific requests by user or process. To support this functionality, TACACS+ has three types of accounting records: START, STOP, and UPDATE. Note that these are record types, not message types as earlier discussed.

Authentication Protocols

Numerous authentication protocols have been developed, used, and discarded in the brief history of computing. Some have come and gone because they did not enjoy market share, others have had security issues, and yet others have been revised and improved in newer versions. Although it's impossible and impractical to cover them all, some of the common ones follow.

L2TP and PPTP

Layer 2 Tunneling Protocol (L2TP) and Point-to-Point Tunneling Protocol (PPTP) are both OSI Layer 2 tunneling protocols. *Tunneling* is the encapsulation of one packet within another, which allows you to hide the original packet from view or change the nature of the network transport. This can be done for both security and practical reasons.

From a practical perspective, assume that you are using TCP/IP to communicate between two machines. Your message may pass over various networks, such as an Asynchronous Transfer Mode (ATM) network, as it moves from source to destination. As the ATM protocol can neither read nor understand TCP/IP packets, something must be done to make them passable across the network. By encapsulating a packet as the payload in a separate protocol, so it can be carried across a section of a network, a mechanism called a *tunnel* is created. At each end of the tunnel, called the tunnel *endpoints,* the payload packet is read and understood. As it goes into the tunnel, you can envision your packet being placed in an envelope with the address of the appropriate tunnel endpoint on the envelope. When the envelope arrives at the tunnel endpoint, the original message (the tunnel packet's payload) is re-created, read, and sent to its appropriate next stop. The information being tunneled is understood only at the tunnel endpoints; it is not relevant to intermediate tunnel points because it is only a payload.

PPP

Point-to-Point Protocol (PPP) is an older, still widely used protocol for establishing dial-in connections over serial lines or Integrated Services Digital Network (ISDN) services. PPP has several authentication mechanisms, including PAP, CHAP, and the Extensible Authentication Protocol (EAP). These protocols are used to authenticate the peer device, not a user of the system. PPP is a standardized Internet encapsulation of IP traffic over point-to-point links, such as serial lines. The authentication process is performed only when the link is established.

PPTP

Microsoft led a consortium of networking companies to extend PPP to enable the creation of virtual private networks (VPNs). The result was the **Point-to-Point Tunneling (PPTP)**, a network protocol that enables the secure transfer of data from a remote PC to a server by creating a VPN across a TCP/IP network. This remote network connection can also span a public switched telephone network (PSTN) and is thus an economical way of connecting remote dial-in users to a corporate data network. The incorporation of PPTP into the Microsoft Windows product line provides a built-in secure method of remote connection using the operating system, and this has given PPTP a large marketplace footprint.

For most PPTP implementations, three computers are involved: the PPTP client, the NAS, and a PPTP server, as shown in Figure 11.20. The connection between the remote client and the network is established in stages,

• **Figure 11.20**   PPTP communication diagram

PPP
GRE
PPP
IP
Data

GRE
PPP
IP
Data

IP
Data

Valid Internet
addresses

Valid internal
network addresses

Encrypted

Plaintext

• **Figure 11.21**   PPTP message encapsulation during transmission

as illustrated in Figure 11.21. First the client makes a PPP connection to a NAS, typically an ISP. (In today's world of widely available broadband, if there is already an Internet connection, then there is no need to perform the PPP connection to the ISP.) Once the PPP connection is established, a second connection is made over the PPP connection to the PPTP server. This second connection creates the VPN connection between the remote client and the PPTP server. A typical VPN connection is one in which the user is in a hotel with a wireless Internet connection, connecting to a corporate network. This connection acts as a tunnel for future data transfers. Although these diagrams illustrate a telephone connection, this first link can be virtually any method. Common in hotels today are wired connections to the Internet. These wired connections typically are provided by a local ISP and offer the same services as a phone connection, albeit at a much higher data transfer rate.

PPTP establishes a tunnel from the remote PPTP client to the PPTP server and enables encryption within this tunnel. This provides a secure method of transport. To do this and still enable routing, an intermediate addressing scheme, Generic Routing Encapsulation (GRE), is used.

To establish the connection, PPTP uses communications across TCP port 1723 (see Table 11.2 in the "Connection Summary" section at the end of the chapter), so this port must remain open across the network firewalls for PPTP to be initiated. Although PPTP allows the use of any PPP authentication scheme, CHAP is used when encryption is specified, to provide an appropriate level of security. For the encryption methodology, Microsoft chose the RSA RC4 cipher, with either a 40- or 128-bit session key length, and this is OS driven. Microsoft Point-to-Point Encryption (MPPE) is an extension to PPP that enables VPNs to use PPTP as the tunneling protocol.

EAP

Extensible Authentication Protocol (EAP) is a universal authentication framework defined by RFC 3748 that is frequently used in wireless networks and point-to-point connections. Although EAP is not limited to wireless and can be used for wired authentication, it is most often used in wireless LANs. EAP is discussed in detail in Chapter 12.

CHAP

Challenge-Handshake Authentication Protocol (CHAP) is used to provide authentication across a point-to-point link using PPP. In this protocol, authentication after the link has been established is not mandatory. CHAP is designed to provide authentication periodically through the use of a challenge/response system that is sometimes described as a *three-way handshake,* as illustrated in Figure 11.22. The initial challenge (a randomly generated number) is sent to the client. The client uses a one-way hashing function to calculate what the response should be and then sends this back. The server compares the response to what it calculated the response should be. If they match, communication continues. If the two values don't match, then the connection is terminated. This mechanism relies on a shared secret between the two entities so that the correct values can be calculated.

• **Figure 11.22** The CHAP challenge/response sequence

Microsoft has created two versions of CHAP, modified to increase the usability of CHAP across Microsoft's product line. MSCHAP v1, defined in RFC 2433, has been deprecated and was dropped in Windows Vista. The current standard, version 2, defined in RFC 2759, was introduced with Windows 2000.

NTLM

NT LAN Manager (NTLM) is an authentication protocol designed by Microsoft, for use with the Server Message Block (SMB) protocol. SMB is an application-level network protocol primarily used for sharing of files and printers in Windows-based networks. NTLM was designed as a replacement for the LANMAN protocol. The current version is NTLM v2, which was introduced with Windows NT 4.0 SP4. Although Microsoft has adopted the Kerberos protocol for authentication, NTLM v2 is still used when

- Authenticating to a server using an IP address
- Authenticating to a server that belongs to a different Active Directory forest
- Authenticating to a server that doesn't belong to a domain
- No Active Directory domain exists ("workgroup" or "peer-to-peer" connection)

PAP

Password Authentication Protocol (PAP) involves a two-way handshake in which the username and password are sent across the link in cleartext. PAP authentication does not provide any protection against playback and line sniffing. PAP is now a deprecated standard.

L2TP

Layer 2 Tunneling Protocol (L2TP) is also an Internet standard and came from the Layer 2 Forwarding (L2F) protocol, a Cisco initiative designed to address issues with PPTP. Whereas PPTP is designed around PPP and IP networks, L2F, and hence L2TP, is designed for use across all kinds of networks, including ATM and Frame Relay. Additionally, whereas PPTP is designed to be implemented in software at the client device, L2TP was conceived as a hardware implementation using a router or a special-purpose appliance. L2TP can be configured in software and is in Microsoft's RRAS servers, which use L2TP to create a VPN.

L2TP works in much the same way as PPTP, but it opens up several items for expansion. For instance, in L2TP, routers can be enabled to concentrate VPN traffic over higher-bandwidth lines, creating hierarchical networks of VPN traffic that can be more efficiently managed across an enterprise. L2TP also has the ability to use IPsec and Data Encryption Standard (DES) as encryption protocols, providing a higher level of data security. L2TP is also designed to work with established AAA services such as RADIUS and TACACS+ to aid in user authentication, authorization, and accounting.

L2TP is established via UDP port 1701, so this is an essential port to leave open across firewalls supporting L2TP traffic. Microsoft supports L2TP in Windows 2000 and above, but because of the computing power required, most implementations will use specialized hardware (such as a Cisco router).

Telnet

One of the methods to grant remote access to a system is through Telnet. Telnet is the standard terminal-emulation protocol within the TCP/IP protocol series, and it is defined in RFC 854. Telnet allows users to log in remotely and access resources as if the user had a local terminal connection. Telnet is an old protocol and offers little security. Information, including account names and passwords, is passed in cleartext over the TCP/IP connection.

Telnet makes its connection using TCP port 23. As Telnet is implemented on most products using TCP/IP, it is important to control access to Telnet on machines and routers when setting them up. Failure to control access by using firewalls, access lists, and other security methods, or even by disabling the Telnet daemon, is equivalent to leaving an open door for unauthorized users on a system.

> **Exam Tip:** Telnet uses TCP port 23. Be sure to memorize the common ports used by common services for the exam.

SSH

Secure Shell (SSH) is a protocol series designed to facilitate secure network functions across an insecure network. SSH provides direct support for secure remote login, secure file transfer, and secure forwarding of TCP/IP and X Window System traffic. An SSH connection is an encrypted channel, providing for confidentiality and integrity protection.

SSH has its origins as a replacement for the insecure Telnet application from the UNIX operating system. An original component of UNIX, Telnet allowed users to connect between systems. Although Telnet is still used today, it has some drawbacks, as discussed in the preceding section. Some enterprising University of California, Berkeley, students subsequently developed the **r-** commands, such as **rlogin**, to permit access based on the user and source system, as opposed to passing passwords. This was not perfect either, however, because when a login was required, it was still passed in the clear. This led to the development of the SSH protocol series,

Exam Tip: SSH uses TCP port 22. SCP (secure copy) and SFTP (secure FTP) use SSH, so each also uses TCP port 22.

designed to eliminate all of the insecurities associated with Telnet, **r-** commands, and other means of remote access.

SSH opens a secure transport channel between machines by using an SSH daemon on each end. These daemons initiate contact over TCP port 22 and then communicate over higher ports in a secure mode. One of the strengths of SSH is its support for many different encryption protocols. SSH 1.0 started with RSA algorithms, but at the time they were still under patent, and this led to SSH 2.0 with extended support for Triple DES (3DES) and other encryption methods. Today, SSH can be used with a wide range of encryption protocols, including RSA, 3DES, Blowfish, International Data Encryption Algorithm (IDEA), CAST128, AES256, and others.

The SSH protocol has facilities to encrypt data automatically, provide authentication, and compress data in transit. It can support strong encryption, cryptographic host authentication, and integrity protection. The authentication services are host-based and not user-based. If user authentication is desired in a system, it must be set up separately at a higher level in the OSI model. The protocol is designed to be flexible and simple, and it is designed specifically to minimize the number of round-trips between systems. The key exchange, public key, symmetric key, message authentication, and hash algorithms are all negotiated at connection time. Individual data-packet integrity is assured through the use of a message authentication code that is computed from a shared secret, the contents of the packet, and the packet sequence number.

The SSH protocol consists of three major components:

- **Transport layer protocol** Provides server authentication, confidentiality, integrity, and compression
- **User authentication protocol** Authenticates the client to the server
- **Connection protocol** Provides multiplexing of the encrypted tunnel into several logical channels

SSH is very popular in the UNIX environment, and it is actively used as a method of establishing VPNs across public networks. Because all communications between the two machines are encrypted at the OSI application layer by the two SSH daemons, this leads to the ability to build very secure solutions and even solutions that defy the ability of outside services to monitor. As SSH is a standard protocol series with connection parameters established via TCP port 22, different vendors can build differing solutions that can still interoperate.

Although Windows Server implementations of SSH exist, this has not been a popular protocol in the Windows environment from a server perspective. The development of a wide array of commercial SSH clients for the Windows platform indicates the marketplace strength of interconnection from desktop PCs to UNIX-based servers utilizing this protocol.

FTP/FTPS/SFTP

One of the methods of transferring files between machines is through the use of the File Transfer Protocol (FTP). FTP is a plaintext protocol that operates by communicating over TCP between a client and a server. The client initiates a transfer with an FTP request to the server's TCP port 21. This is

Tech Tip

RDP

Remote Desktop Protocol (RDP) is a proprietary Microsoft protocol designed to provide a graphical connection to another computer. The computer requesting the connection has RDP client software (built into Windows), and the target uses an RDP server. This software has been available for many versions of Windows and was formerly called Terminal Services. Client and server versions also exist for Linux platforms. RDP uses TCP and UDP ports 3389, so if RDP is desired, these ports need to be open on the firewall.

322

the control connection, and this connection remains open over the duration of the file transfer. The actual data transfer occurs on a negotiated data transfer port, typically a high-order port number. FTP was not designed to be a secure method of transferring files. If a secure method is desired, then using FTPS or SFTP is best.

FTPS is the use of FTP over an SSL/TLS secured channel. This can be done either in explicit mode, where an **AUTH TLS** command is issued, or in implicit mode, where the transfer occurs over TCP port 990 for the control channel and TCP port 989 for the data channel. SFTP is not FTP per se, but rather a completely separate Secure File Transfer Protocol as defined by an IETF Draft, the latest of which, version 6, expired in July 2007, but has been incorporated into products in the marketplace.

It is also possible to run FTP over SSH, as later versions of SSH allow securing of channels such as the FTP control channel; this has also been referred to as Secure FTP. This leaves the data channel unencrypted, a problem that has been solved in version 3.0 of SSH, which supports FTP commands. The challenge of encrypting the FTP data communications is that the mutual port agreement must be opened on the firewall, and for security reasons, high-order ports that are not explicitly defined are typically secured. Because of this challenge, Secure Copy (SCP) is often a more desirable alternative to SFTP when using SSH.

> **Exam Tip:** FTP uses TCP port 21 as a control channel and TCP port 20 as a typical active mode data port, as some firewalls are set to block ports above 1024.

VPNs

A **virtual private network (VPN)** is a secure *virtual* network built on top of a *physical* network. The security of a VPN lies in the encryption of packet contents between the endpoints that define the VPN. The physical network upon which a VPN is built is typically a public network, such as the Internet. Because the packet contents between VPN endpoints are encrypted, to an outside observer on the public network, the communication is secure, and depending on how the VPN is set up, security can even extend to the two communicating parties' machines.

Virtual private networking is not a protocol per se, but rather a method of using protocols to achieve a specific objective—secure communications—as shown in Figure 11.23. A user who wants to have a secure communication channel with a server across a public network can set up two intermediary devices, VPN endpoints, to accomplish this task. The user can communicate

• **Figure 11.23**   VPN service over an Internet connection

with his endpoint, and the server can communicate with its endpoint. The two endpoints then communicate across the public network. VPN endpoints can be software solutions, routers, or specific servers set up for specific functionality. This implies that VPN services are set up in advance and are not something negotiated on-the-fly.

A typical use of VPN services is a user accessing a corporate data network from a home PC across the Internet. The employee installs VPN software from work on a home PC. This software is already configured to communicate with the corporate network's VPN endpoint; it knows the location, the protocols that will be used, and so on. When the home user wants to connect to the corporate network, she connects to the Internet and then starts the VPN software. The user can then log into the corporate network by using an appropriate authentication and authorization methodology. The sole purpose of the VPN connection is to provide a private connection between the machines, which encrypts any data sent between the home user's PC and the corporate network. Identification, authorization, and all other standard functions are accomplished with the standard mechanisms for the established system.

VPNs can use many different protocols to offer a secure method of communicating between endpoints. Common methods of encryption on VPNs include PPTP, IPsec, SSH, and L2TP, all of which are discussed in this chapter. The key is that both endpoints know the protocol and share a secret. All of this necessary information is established when the VPN is set up. At the time of use, the VPN only acts as a private tunnel between the two points and does not constitute a complete security solution.

IPsec

Internet Protocol Security (IPsec) is a set of protocols developed by the IETF to securely exchange packets at the network layer (Layer 3) of the OSI model (RFCs 2401–2412). Although these protocols work only in conjunction with IP networks, once an IPsec connection is established, it is possible to tunnel across other networks at lower levels of the OSI model. The set of security services provided by IPsec occurs at the network layer of the OSI model, so higher-layer protocols, such as TCP, UDP, Internet Control Message Protocol (ICMP), Border Gateway Protocol (BGP), and the like, are not functionally altered by the implementation of IPsec services.

The IPsec protocol series has a sweeping array of services it is designed to provide, including but not limited to access control, connectionless integrity, traffic-flow confidentiality, rejection of replayed packets, data security (encryption), and data-origin authentication. IPsec has two defined methods—transport and tunneling—that provide different levels of security. IPsec also has three modes of connection: host-to-server, server-to-server, and host-to-host.

The transport method encrypts only the data portion of a packet, thus enabling an outsider to see source and destination IP addresses. The transport method protects the higher-level protocols associated with a packet and protects the data being transmitted but allows knowledge of the transmission itself. Protection of the data portion of a packet is referred to as **content protection**.

Exam Tip: In transport mode (end-to-end), security of packet traffic is provided by the endpoint computers. In tunnel mode (portal-to-portal), security of packet traffic is provided between endpoint node machines in each network and not at the terminal host machines.

Tunneling provides encryption of source and destination IP addresses, as well as of the data itself. This provides the greatest security, but it can be done only between IPsec servers (or routers) because the final destination needs to be known for delivery. Protection of the header information is known as **context protection**.

It is possible to use both methods at the same time, such as using transport within one's own network to reach an IPsec server, which then tunnels to the target server's network, connecting to an IPsec server there, and then using the transport method from the target network's IPsec server to the target host.

Security Associations

A **security association (SA)** is a formal manner of describing the necessary and sufficient portions of the IPsec protocol series to achieve a specific level of protection. Because many options exist, both communicating parties must agree on the use of the protocols that are available, and this agreement is referred to as a security association. SAs exist both for integrity-protecting systems and confidentiality-protecting systems. In each IPsec implementation, a security association database (SAD) defines parameters associated with each SA. The SA is a one-way (simplex) association, and if two-way communication security is desired, two SAs are used—one for each direction.

> **Exam Tip:** A security association is a logical set of security parameters designed to facilitate the sharing of information between entities.

IPsec Configurations

Four basic configurations can be applied to machine-to-machine connections using IPsec. The simplest is a host-to-host connection between two machines, as shown in Figure 11.24. In this case, the Internet is not a part of the SA between the machines. If bidirectional security is desired, two SAs are used. The SAs are effective from host to host.

The second case places two security devices in the stream, relieving the hosts of the calculation and encapsulation duties. These two gateways have an SA between them. The network is assumed to be secure from each machine to its gateway, and no IPsec is performed across these hops. Figure 11.25 shows the two security gateways with a tunnel across the Internet, although either tunnel or transport mode could be used.

Case 1:
Two SAs from host to host for bidirectional secure communications

SA 1

SA 2

Internet

Host 1   Internet   Internet   Host 2
                server   server

• **Figure 11.24**   A host-to-host connection between two machines

Case 2:
IPsec between machines using gateway security devices

Tunnel

Host 1

Security gateway

Internet

Security gateway

Host 2

• **Figure 11.25**   Two security gateways with a tunnel across the Internet

The third case combines the first two. A separate SA exists between the gateway devices, but an SA also exists between hosts. This could be considered a tunnel inside a tunnel, as shown in Figure 11.26.

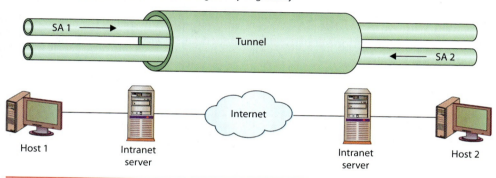
Case 3:
Separate IPsec tunnels, host to host and gateway to gateway

SA 1

Tunnel

SA 2

Host 1

Intranet server

Internet

Intranet server

Host 2

• **Figure 11.26**   A tunnel inside a tunnel

Remote users commonly connect through the Internet to an organization's network. The network has a security gateway through which it secures traffic to and from its servers and authorized users. In the last case, illustrated in Figure 11.27, the user establishes an SA with the security gateway and then a separate SA with the desired server, if required.

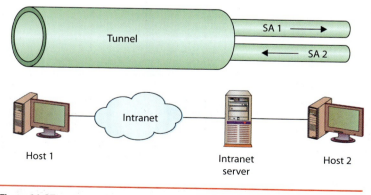
Case 4:
Tunnel from host to gateway
Optinal: Two SAs for bidirectional secure communications

Tunnel

SA 1

SA 2

Host 1

Intranet

Intranet server

Host 2

• **Figure 11.27**   Tunnel from host to gateway

This can be done using software on a remote laptop and hardware at the organization's network.

Windows can act as an IPsec server, as can routers and other servers. The primary issue is CPU usage and where the computing power should be implanted. This consideration has led to the rise of IPsec appliances, which are hardware devices that perform the IPsec function specifically for a series of communications. Depending on the number of connections, network bandwidth, and so on, these devices can be inexpensive for small office or home office use or quite expensive for large, enterprise-level implementations.

IPsec Security

IPsec uses two protocols to provide traffic security:

- **Authentication Header (AH)**   A header added to a packet for the purposes of integrity checking

- **Encapsulating Security Payload (ESP)**   A method of encrypting the data portion of a datagram to provide confidentiality

For key management and exchange, three protocols exist:

- **Internet Security Association and Key Management Protocol (ISAKMP)**

- **Oakley**

- **Secure Key Exchange Mechanism for Internet (SKEMI)**

These key management protocols can be collectively referred to as *Internet Key Management Protocol (IKMP)* or *Internet Key Exchange (IKE)*.

IPsec does not define specific security algorithms, nor does it require specific methods of implementation. IPsec is an open framework that allows vendors to implement existing industry-standard algorithms suited for specific tasks. This flexibility is key in IPsec's ability to offer a wide range of security functions. IPsec allows several security technologies to be combined into a comprehensive solution for network-based confidentiality, integrity, and authentication. IPsec uses the following:

> **Exam Tip:** IPsec AH protects integrity, but it does not provide privacy. IPsec ESP provides confidentiality, but it does not protect integrity of the packet. To cover both privacy and integrity, both headers can be used at the same time.

- Diffie-Hellman key exchange between peers on a public network

- Public key signing of Diffie-Hellman key exchanges to guarantee identity and avoid man-in-the-middle attacks

- Bulk encryption algorithms, such as IDEA and 3DES, for encrypting data

- Keyed hash algorithms, such as HMAC, and traditional hash algorithms, such as MD5 and SHA-1, for packet-level authentication

- Digital certificates to act as digital ID cards between parties

To provide traffic security, two header extensions have been defined for IP datagrams. The AH, when added to an IP datagram, ensures the integrity of the data and also the authenticity of the data's origin. By protecting the nonchanging elements in the IP header, the AH protects the IP address, which enables data-origin authentication. The ESP provides security services for the higher-level protocol portion of the packet only, not the IP header.

AH and ESP can be used separately or in combination, depending on the level and types of security desired. Both also work with the transport and tunnel modes of IPsec protocols. In transport mode, the two communication endpoints provide security primarily for the upper-layer protocols. The cryptographic endpoints, where encryption and decryption occur, are located at the source and destination of the communication channel. When AH is in transport mode, the original IP header is exposed, but its contents are protected via the AH block in the packet, as illustrated in Figure 11.28. When AH is employed in tunnel mode, portions of the outer IP header are given the same header protection that occurs in transport mode, with the entire inner packet receiving protection. This is illustrated in

Authentication header in transport mode

• **Figure 11.28**   IPsec use of AH in transport mode

Authentication header in tunnel mode

Before AH: | Original IP header | Original IP packet |

After AH: | New IP header | AH | Original IP header | Original IP packet |

Authenticated except for changeable portions of IP header

• **Figure 11.29**   IPsec use of AH in tunnel mode

Encapsulating security payload in transport mode

Before ESP: | Original IP header | TCP | Data |

After ESP: | Original IP header | ESP | TCP | Data | ESP trailer | ESP authentication |

Encrypted

Authenticated

• **Figure 11.30**   IPsec use of ESP in transport mode

Encapsulating security payload in tunnel mode

Before ESP: | Original IP header | TCP | Data |

After ESP: | Original IP header | Original IP header | TCP | Data | ESP trailer | MAC |

Encrypted

Authenticated

Message authentication code calculation

• **Figure 11.31**   IPsec use of ESP in tunnel mode

Figure 11.29. The use of tunnel mode allows easier crossing of firewalls, for without it, specific firewall rules would be needed to pass the modified transport packet header.

Tunneling is a means of encapsulating packets inside a protocol that is understood only at the entry and exit points of the tunnel. This provides security during transport in the tunnel, because outside observers cannot decipher packet contents or even the identities of the communicating parties. IPsec has a tunnel mode that can be used from server to server across a public network. Although the tunnel endpoints are referred to as *servers,* these devices can be routers, appliances, or servers. In tunnel mode, the tunnel endpoints merely encapsulate the entire packet with new IP headers to indicate the endpoints, and they encrypt the contents of this new packet. The true source and destination information is contained in the inner IP header, which is encrypted in the tunnel. The outer IP header contains the addresses of the endpoints of the tunnel.

ESP provides a means of encrypting the packet's contents, as shown in Figure 11.30. In this case, in transport mode, the datagram contents are encrypted and authenticated via the ESP header and footer/trailer that are inserted into the datagram. As mentioned, AH and ESP can be employed in tunnel mode. ESP affords the same encryption protection to the contents of the tunneled packet, which is the entire packet from the initial sender, as illustrated in Figure 11.31. Together, in tunnel mode, AH and ESP can provide complete protection across the packet, as shown in Figure 11.32. The specific combination of AH and ESP is referred to as a *security association* in IPsec.

AH packet

ESP packet

| New IP header | AH header | ESP header | Original IP header | TCP | Data | ESP trailer | MAC |

Encrypted

Authenticated

Message authentication code calculation

• **Figure 11.32**   IPsec ESP and AH packet construction in tunnel mode

In IP version 4 (IPv4), IPsec is an add-on, and its acceptance is vendor driven. It is not a part of the original IP—one of the short-sighted design flaws of the original IP. In IPv6, IPsec is integrated into IP and is native on all packets. Its use is still optional, but its inclusion in the protocol suite will guarantee interoperability across vendor solutions when they are compliant with IPv6 standards.

IPsec uses cryptographic keys in its security process and has both manual and automatic distribution of keys as part of the protocol series. Manual key distribution is included, but it is practical only in small, static environments and does not scale to enterprise-level implementations. The default method of key management, **Internet Key Exchange (IKE)**, is automated. IKE authenticates each peer involved in IPsec and negotiates the security policy, including the exchange of session keys. IKE creates a secure tunnel between peers and then negotiates the security association for IPsec across this channel. This is done in two phases: the first develops the channel, and the second develops the security association.

Figure 11.33 illustrates the different levels of protection offered by VPNs and IPsec. This shows the advantages of IPsec and its more comprehensive coverage.

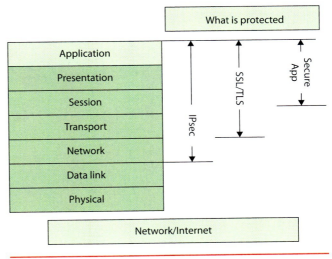

• **Figure 11.33**   Protection from different levels of encryption

Vulnerabilities of Remote Access Methods

The primary vulnerability associated with many of these methods of remote access is the passing of critical data in cleartext. Plaintext passing of passwords provides no security if the password is sniffed, and sniffers are easy to use on a network. Even plaintext passing of user IDs gives away information that can be correlated and possibly used by an attacker. Plaintext credential passing is one of the fundamental flaws with Telnet and is why SSH was developed. This is also one of the flaws with RADIUS and TACACS+, as they have a segment unprotected. There are methods for overcoming these limitations, although they require discipline and understanding in setting up a system.

The strength of the encryption algorithm is also a concern. Should a specific algorithm or method prove to be vulnerable, services that rely solely on it are also vulnerable. To get around this dependency, many of the protocols allow numerous encryption methods, so that should one prove vulnerable, a shift to another restores security.

As with any software implementation, there always exists the possibility that a bug could open the system to attack. Bugs have been corrected in most software packages to close holes that made systems vulnerable, and remote access functionality is no exception. This is not a Microsoft-only phenomenon, as one might believe from the popular press. Critical flaws have been found in almost every product, from open system implementations such as OpenSSH to proprietary systems such as Cisco IOS. The important issue is not the presence of software bugs, for as software continues to become more complex, this is an unavoidable issue. The true key is vendor responsiveness to fixing the bugs once they are discovered, and

Tech Tip

IPsec in a Nutshell

IPsec has two primary modes, transport mode and tunnel mode. Transport mode is simpler and adds fewer bytes to a packet, but can have issues transiting items such as firewalls. Tunneling mode resolves the firewall issue by total encapsulation. IPsec has two primary mechanisms, AH and ESP. AH provides for authentication of datagram contents, but no protection in the form of secrecy. ESP encrypts the datagram, providing secrecy, and when used with EH, ESP provides authentication as well.

329

the major players, such as Cisco and Microsoft, have been very responsive in this area.

■ Connection Summary

There are many protocols used for remote access and authentication and related purposes. These methods have their own assigned ports and these assignments are summarized in Table 11.2.

Table 11.2	Common TCP/UDP Remote Access Networking Port Assignments		
TCP Port Number	UDP Port Number	Keyword	Protocol
20		FTP-Data	File Transfer (Default Data)
21		FTP	File Transfer Control
22		SSH	Secure Shell Login
22		SCP	SCP uses SSH
22		SFTP	SFTP uses SSH
23		TELNET	Telnet
25		SMTP	Simple Mail Transfer
37	37	TIME	Time
49	49	TACACS+	TACACS+ login
53	53	DNS	Domain Name Server
65	65	TACACS+	TACACS+ database service
	69	TFTP	Trivial File Transfer Protocol
80		HTTP	Web
88	88	Kerberos	Kerberos
	137	NetBIOS	Name Service
	138	NetBIOS	Datagram Service
139		NetBIOS	NetBIOS
443		HTTPS	HTTPS
500	500	ISAKMP	ISAKMP protocol
512		rexec	
513		rlogin	UNIX rlogin
	513	rwho	UNIX Broadcast Naming Service
514		rsh	UNIX rsh and rep
	514	SYSLOG	UNIX system logs
614	614	SSHELL	SSL Shell
989		FTPS	FTPS (implicit mode) data channel
990		FTPS	FTPS (implicit mode) control channel
	1645	RADIUS	RADIUS: Historical
	1646	RADIUS	RADIUS: Historical
	1701	L2TP	L2TP
1723	1723	PPTP	PPTP
1812	1812	RADIUS	RADIUS authorization
1813	1813	RADIUS-actg	RADIUS accounting

Chapter 11 Review

For More Information

- **Microsoft's TechNet Group Policy page** http://technet.microsoft.com/en-us/windowsserver/grouppolicy/default.aspx

- **SANS Consensus Policy Resource Community – Password Policy** https://www.sans.org/security-resources/policies/general/pdf/password-protection-policy

Lab Manual Exercises

The following lab exercises from the companion lab manual, *Principles of Computer Security Lab Manual, Fourth Edition*, provide practical application of material covered in this chapter:

Chapter Summary

After reading this chapter and completing the exercises, you should understand the following about privilege management, authentication, and remote access protocols.

Identify the differences among user, group, and role management

- Privilege management is the process of restricting a user's ability to interact with the computer system.

- Privilege management can be based on an individual user basis, on membership in a specific group or groups, or on a function/role.

- Key concepts in privilege management are the ability to restrict and control access to information and information systems.

- One of the methods used to simplify privilege management is single sign-on, which requires a user to authenticate successfully once. The validated credentials and associated rights and privileges are then automatically carried forward when the user accesses other systems or applications.

Implement password and domain password policies

- Password policies are sets of rules that help users select, employ, and store strong passwords. Tokens combine "something you have" with "something you know," such as a password or PIN, and can be hardware or software based.

- Passwords should have a limited span and should expire on a scheduled basis.

Describe methods of account management (SSO, time of day, logical token, account expiration)

- Administrators have many different tools at their disposal to control access to computer resources including password and account expiration methods.

- User authentication methods can include several factors including tokens.

- Users can be limited in the hours during which they can access resources.

- Resources such as files, folders, and printers can be controlled through permissions or access control lists.

- Permissions can be assigned based on a user's identity or their membership in one or more groups.

Describe methods of access management (MAC, DAC, and RBAC)

- Mandatory access control is based on the sensitivity of the information or process itself.

- Discretionary access control uses file permissions and ACLs to restrict access based on a user's identity or group membership.

- Role-based access control restricts access based on the user's assigned role or roles.

- Rule-based access control restricts access based on a defined set of rules established by the administrator.

Discuss the methods and protocols for remote access to networks

- Remote access protocols provide a mechanism to remotely connect clients to networks.
- A wide range of remote access protocols has evolved to support various security and authentication mechanisms.
- Remote access is granted via remote access servers, such as RRAS or RADIUS.

Identify authentication, authorization, and accounting (AAA) protocols

- Authentication is a cornerstone element of security, connecting access to a previously approved user ID.
- Authorization is the process of determining whether an authenticated user has permission.
- Accounting protocols manage connection time and cost records.

Explain authentication methods and the security implications in their use

- Password-based authentication is still the most widely used because of cost and ubiquity.

- Ticket-based systems, such as Kerberos, form the basis for most modern authentication and credentialing systems.

Implement virtual private networks (VPNs) and their security aspects

- VPNs use protocols to establish a private network over a public network, shielding user communications from outside observation.
- VPNs can be invoked via many different protocol mechanisms and involve either a hardware or software client on each end of the communication channel.

Describe Internet Protocol Security (IPsec) and its use in securing communications

- IPsec is the native method of securing IP packets; it is optional in IPv4 and mandatory in IPv6.
- IPsec uses Authentication Headers (AH) to authenticate packets.
- IPsec uses Encapsulating Security Payload (ESP) to provide confidentiality service at the datagram level.

■ Key Terms

AAA *(305)*

access control *(311)*

access control list (ACL) *(300)*

accounting *(305)*

administrator *(290)*

attribute-based access control (ABAC) *(303)*

authentication *(305)*

Authentication Header (AH) *(41)*

authentication server (AS) *(308)*

authorization *(305)*

content protection *(324)*

context protection *(325)*

discretionary access control (DAC) *(302)*

domain controller *(293)*

domain password policy *(293)*

Encapsulating Security Payload (ESP) *(41)*

eXtensible Access Control Markup Language (XACML) *(304)*

group *(291)*

group policy object (GPO) *(293)*

identification *(305)*

Internet Key Exchange (IKE) *(329)*

Internet Protocol Security (IPsec) *(324)*

Internet Security Association and Key Management Protocol (ISAKMP) *(41)*

Kerberos *(308)*

key distribution center (KDC) *(308)*

Layer 2 Tunneling Protocol (L2TP) *(320)*

mandatory access control (MAC) *(301)*
Oakley *(41)*
password policy *(292)*
permissions *(290)*
Point-to-Point Tunneling Protocol (PPTP) *(317)*
privilege management *(288)*
privileges *(288)*
remote access server (RAS) *(305)*
rights *(289)*
role *(292)*
role-based access control (RBAC) *(303)*

root *(290)*
rule-based access control *(303)*
Secure Key Exchange Mechanism for
    Internet (SKEMI) *(41)*
security association (SA) *(325)*
single sign-on (SSO) *(294)*
superuser *(290)*
ticket-granting server (TGS) *(308)*
token *(296)*
user *(289)*
username *(289)*
virtual private network (VPN) *(323)*

■ Key Terms Quiz

Use terms from the Key Terms list to complete the sentences that follow. Don't use the same term more than once. Not all terms will be used.

1. _____ is an authentication model designed around the concept of using tickets for accessing objects.

2. _____ is designed around the type of tasks people perform.

3. A formal manner of describing the necessary and sufficient portions of the IPsec protocol series to achieve a specific level of protection is a(n) _____.

4. _____ describes a system where every resource has access rules set for it all of the time.

5. _____ is an authentication process where the user can enter their user ID

(or username) and password and then be able to move from application to application or resource to resource without having to supply further authentication information.

6. In IPsec, a security association is defined by a specific combination of _____ and _____.

7. The protection of the data portion of a packet is _____.

8. The protection of the header portion of a packet is _____.

9. _____ is a key management and exchange protocol used with IPsec.

10. The process of comparing credentials to those established during the identification process is referred to as _____.

■ Multiple-Choice Quiz

1. Authentication is typically based upon what?

   A. Something a user possesses

   B. Something a user knows

   C. Something measured on a user, such as a fingerprint

   D. All of the above

2. On a VPN, traffic is encrypted and decrypted at:

   A. Endpoints of the tunnel only

   B. Users' machines

   C. Each device at each hop

   D. The data link layer of access devices

3. A ticket-granting server is an important element in which of the following authentication models?

   A. L2TP

   B. RADIUS

   C. PPP

   D. Kerberos

4. What protocol is used for RADIUS?

   A. UDP

   B. NetBIOS

   C. TCP

   D. Proprietary

5. Under which access control system is each piece of information and every system resource (files, devices, networks, and so on) labeled with its sensitivity level?

   A. Discretionary access control

   B. Resource access control

   C. Mandatory access control

   D. Media access control

6. IPsec provides which options as security services?

   A. ESP and AH

   B. ESP and AP

   C. EA and AP

   D. EA and AH

7. Secure Shell uses which port to communicate?

   A. TCP port 80

   B. UDP port 22

   C. TCP port 22

   D. TCP port 110

8. Elements of Kerberos include which of the following?

   A. Tickets, ticket-granting server, ticket-authorizing agent

   B. Ticket-granting ticket, authentication server, ticket

   C. Services server, Kerberos realm, ticket authenticators

   D. Client-to-server ticket, authentication server ticket, ticket

9. To establish a PPTP connection across a firewall, you must do which of the following?

   A. Do nothing; PPTP does not need to cross firewalls by design.

   B. Do nothing; PPTP traffic is invisible and tunnels past firewalls.

   C. Open a UDP port of choice and assign it to PPTP.

   D. Open TCP port 1723.

10. To establish an L2TP connection across a firewall, you must do which of the following?

   A. Do nothing; L2TP does not cross firewalls by design.

   B. Do nothing; L2TP tunnels past firewalls.

   C. Open a UDP port of choice and assign it to L2TP.

   D. Open UDP port 1701.

■ Essay Quiz

1. A co-worker with a strong Windows background is having difficulty understanding UNIX file permissions. Describe UNIX file permissions for him. Compare UNIX file permissions to Windows file permissions.

2. How are authentication and authorization alike and how are they different. What is the relationship, if any, between the two?

3. What is a VPN and what technologies are used to create one?

Lab Projects

• **Lab Project 11.1**

Using two workstations and some routers, set up a simple VPN. Using Wireshark (a shareware network protocol analyzer, available at http://wireshark.com), observe traffic inside and outside the tunnel to demonstrate protection.

• **Lab Project 11.2**

Using freeSSHd and freeFTPd (both shareware programs, available at www.freesshd.com) and Wireshark, demonstrate the security features of SSH compared to Telnet and FTP.

Wireless Security and Mobile Devices

We must plan for freedom, and not only for security, if for no other reason than that only freedom can make security secure.

—KARL POPPER

In this chapter, you will learn how to

- Describe the different wireless systems in use today
- Detail WAP and its security implications
- Identify 802.11's security issues and possible solutions
- Examine the elements needed for enterprise wireless deployment
- Examine the security of mobile systems

Wireless is increasingly the way people access the Internet. Because wireless access is considered a consumer benefit, many businesses have added wireless access points to lure customers into their shops. With the rollout of fourth-generation (4G) high-speed cellular networks, people are also increasingly accessing the Internet from their mobile phones. The massive growth in popularity of nontraditional computers such as netbooks, e-readers, and tablets has also driven the popularity of wireless access.

As wireless use increases, the security of the wireless protocols has become a more important factor in the security of the entire network. As a security professional, you need to understand wireless network applications because of the risks inherent in broadcasting a network signal where anyone can intercept it. Sending unsecured information across public airwaves is tantamount to posting your company's passwords by the front door of the building. This chapter opens with looks at several current wireless protocols and their security features. The chapter finishes with an examination of mobile systems and their security concerns.

Introduction to Wireless Networking

Wireless networking is the transmission of packetized data by means of a physical topology that does not use direct physical links. This definition can be narrowed to apply to networks that use radio waves to carry the signals over either public or private bands, instead of using standard network cabling. Some proprietary applications like long-distance microwave links use point-to-point technology with narrowband radios and highly directional antennas. However, this technology is not common enough to produce any significant research into its vulnerabilities, and anything that was developed would have limited usefulness. So this chapter focuses on point-to-multipoint systems, the two most common of which are the family of cellular protocols and IEEE 802.11. IEEE 802.11 is a family of protocols instead of a single specification; this is a summary table of the 802.11 family.

Specification	Speed	Frequency Range
802.11a	54 Mbps	5.2 GHz
802.11b	11 Mbps	2.4 GHz
802.11g	11 Mbps/54 Mbps	2.4 GHz
802.11i	11 Mbps/54 Mbps	2.4 GHz
802.11n	124–248 Mbps	2.4 GHz/5 GHz
802.11ac	150 Mbps–2.6 Gbps	2.4 GHz/5 GHz

The **IEEE 802.11** protocol has been standardized by the IEEE for wireless local area networks (LANs). Three versions are currently in production—802.11g, 802.11a, and 802.11n. The latest standard is 802.11ac, but it provides backward compatibility with 802.11g hardware. Cellular phone technology has moved rapidly to embrace data transmission and the Internet. The Wireless Application Protocol (WAP) was one of the pioneers of mobile data applications, but it has been overtaken by a variety of protocols pushing us to fourth-generation (4G) mobile networks.

Bluetooth is a short-range wireless protocol typically used on small devices such as mobile phones. Early versions of these phones also had Bluetooth on and discoverable as a default, making the compromise of a nearby phone easy. Security research has focused on finding problems with these devices simply because the devices are so common.

The security world ignored wireless for a long time, and then within the space of a few months, it seemed like everyone was attempting to breach the security of wireless networks and transmissions. One reason wireless suddenly found itself to be such a target is that wireless networks are so abundant and so unsecured. The dramatic proliferation of these inexpensive products has made the security ramifications of the protocol astonishing.

No matter what the system, wireless security is a very important topic as more and more applications are designed to use wireless to send data. Wireless is particularly problematic from a security standpoint, because there is no control over the physical layer of the traffic. In most wired LANs, the administrators have physical control over the network and can control to some degree who can actually connect to the physical medium. This prevents large amounts of unauthorized traffic and makes snooping around and listening to the traffic difficult. Wireless does away with the physical

Tech Tip

Wireless Systems

There are several different wireless bands in common use today, the most common of which is the Wi-Fi series, referring to the 802.11 Wireless LAN standards certified by the Wi-Fi Alliance. Another set of bands is **WiMAX***, which refers to the set of 802.16 wireless network standards ratified by the WiMAX Forum. Lastly, there is* **ZigBee***, a low-power, personal area networking technology described by the IEEE 802.15.4 series.*

Building interior

● **Figure 12.1**   Wireless transmission extending beyond the facility's walls

limitations. If an attacker can get close enough to the signal's source as it is being broadcast, he can at the very least listen to the access point and clients talking to capture all the packets for examination, as depicted in Figure 12.1.

Attackers can also try to modify the traffic being sent or try to send their own traffic to disrupt the system. In this chapter, you will learn about the different types of attacks that wireless networks face.

■ Mobile Phones

When cellular phones first hit the market, security wasn't an issue—if you wanted to keep your phone safe, you'd simply keep it physically secure and not loan it to people you didn't want making calls. Its only function was that of a telephone.

● Early cell phones just allowed you to make calls.

The advance of digital circuitry has added amazing power in smaller and smaller devices, causing security to be an issue as the software becomes more and more complicated. Today's small and inexpensive products have made the wireless market grow by leaps and bounds, as traditional wireless devices such as cellular phones and pagers have been replaced by tablets and smartphones.

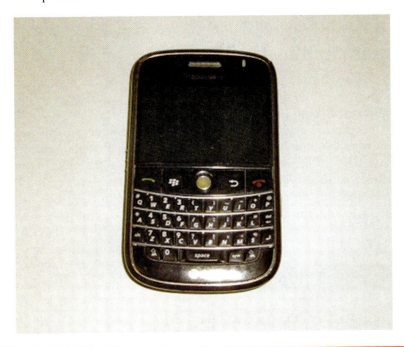

• Today's phones allow you to carry computers in your pocket.

Today's smartphones support multiple wireless data access methods, including 802.11, Bluetooth, and cellular. These mobile phones and tablet devices have caused consumers to demand access to the Internet anytime and anywhere. This has generated a demand for additional data services. The **Wireless Application Protocol (WAP)** attempted to satisfy the needs for more data on mobile devices, but it is falling by the wayside as the mobile networks' capabilities increase. The need for more and more bandwidth has pushed carriers to adopt a more IP-centric routing methodology with technologies such as High Speed Packet Access (HSPA) and Evolution Data Optimized (EVDO). Mobile phones have ruthlessly advanced with new technologies and services, causing phones and the carrier networks that support them to be described in generations—1G, 2G, 3G, and 4G. 1G refers to the original analog cellular standard, Advanced Mobile Phone System (AMPS). 2G refers to the digital network that superseded it. 3G is the system of mobile networks that followed, with many different implementations carrying data at up to 400 Kbps. 4G represents the current state of mobile phones with LTE being the primary method. 4G allows carriers to offer a wider array of services to the consumer, including broadband data service up to 14.4 Mbps and video calling. 4G is also a move to an entirely IP-based network for all services, running voice over IP (VoIP) on your mobile phone and speeds up to 1 Gbps.

All of these "gee-whiz" features are nice, but how secure are your bits and bytes going to be when they're traveling across a mobile carrier's network? All the protocols mentioned have their own security implementations—WAP applies its own Wireless Transport Layer Security (WTLS) to attempt to secure data transmissions, but WAP still has issues such as the "WAP gap" (as discussed next). 3G networks have attempted to push a large amount of security down the stack and rely on the encryption designed into the wireless protocol.

Wireless Application Protocol

WAP was introduced to compensate for the relatively low amount of computing power on handheld devices as well as the generally poor network throughput of cellular networks. It uses the **Wireless Transport Layer Security (WTLS)** encryption scheme, which encrypts the plaintext data and then sends it over the airwaves as ciphertext. The originator and the recipient both have keys to decrypt the data and reproduce the plaintext. This method of ensuring confidentiality is very common, and if the encryption is well designed and implemented, it is difficult for unauthorized users to take captured ciphertext and reproduce the plaintext that created it. As described in Chapter 5, **confidentiality** is the ability to keep protected data a secret.

WTLS uses a modified version of the Transport Layer Security (TLS) protocol, which is the replacement for Secure Sockets Layer (SSL). The WTLS protocol supports several popular bulk encryption algorithms, including Data Encryption Standard (DES), Triple DES (3DES), RC5, and International Data Encryption Algorithm (IDEA).

WTLS implements integrity through the use of *message authentication codes (MACs)*. A MAC algorithm generates a one-way hash of the compressed WTLS data. WTLS supports the MD5 and SHA MAC algorithms. The MAC algorithm is also decided during the WTLS handshake. The TLS protocol that WTLS is based on is designed around Internet-based computers, machines that have relatively high processing power, large amounts of memory, and sufficient bandwidth available for Internet applications. Devices that WTLS must accommodate are limited in all these respects. Thus, WTLS has to be able to cope with small amounts of memory and limited processor capacity, as well as long round-trip times that TLS could not handle well. These requirements are the primary reasons that WTLS has security issues.

As the protocol is designed around more capable servers than devices, the WTLS specification can allow connections with little to no security. Clients with low memory or CPU capabilities cannot support encryption, and choosing null or weak encryption greatly reduces confidentiality. Authentication is also optional in the protocol, and omitting authentication reduces security by leaving the connection vulnerable to a man-in-the-middle–type attack. In addition to the general flaws in the protocol's implementation, several known security vulnerabilities exist, including those to the chosen-plaintext attack, the PKCS #1 attack, and the alert message truncation attack.

The chosen-plaintext attack works on the principle of a predictable **initialization vector (IV)**. By the nature of the transport medium that it is using, WAP, WTLS needs to support unreliable transport. This forces the IV to be based on data already known to the client, and WTLS uses a linear IV computation. Because the IV is based on the sequence number of the packet, and several packets are sent unencrypted, entropy is severely decreased. This lack of entropy in the encrypted data reduces confidentiality.

Now consider the PKCS #1 attack. Public Key Cryptography Standards (PKCS), used in conjunction with RSA encryption, provide standards for formatting the padding used to generate a correctly formatted block size. When the client receives the block, it will reply to the sender as to the validity of the block. An attacker takes advantage of this by attempting to send multiple guesses at the padding to force a padding error. In vulnerable implementations, when RSA signatures and encryption are performed per PKCS #1, the RSA messages can be decrypted with approximately 2^{20} chosen ciphertext queries. Alert messages in WTLS are sometimes sent in plaintext and are not authenticated. This fact could allow an attacker to overwrite an encrypted packet from the actual sender with a plaintext alert message, leading to possible disruption of the connection through, for instance, a truncation attack.

Some concern over the so-called **WAP gap** involves confidentiality of information where the two different networks meet, the WAP gateway, as shown in Figure 12.2.

WTLS acts as the security protocol for the WAP network, and TLS is the standard for the Internet, so the WAP gateway has to perform translation from one encryption standard to the other. This translation forces all messages to be seen by the WAP gateway in plaintext. This is a weak point in the network design, but from an attacker's perspective, it's a much more difficult target than the WTLS protocol itself. Threats to the WAP gateway can be minimized through careful infrastructure design, such as selecting a secure physical location and allowing only outbound traffic from the gateway. A risk of compromise still exists, however, and an attacker would find a WAP gateway an especially appealing target, as plaintext messages are processed through it from all wireless devices, not just a single user. The solution for this is to have end-to-end security layered over anything underlying, in effect creating a VPN from the endpoint to the mobile device, or to standardize on a full implementation of TLS for end-to-end encryption and strong authentication. The limited nature of the devices hampers the ability of the security protocols to operate as intended, compromising any real security to be implemented on WAP networks.

Tech Tip

Weakness in WAP Aggregation
WAP is a point-to-multipoint protocol, but it can face disruptions or attacks because it aggregates at well-known points: the cellular antenna towers.

• **Figure 12.2**   The WAP gap shows an unencrypted space between two enciphered connections.

3G Mobile Networks

Our cell phones are one of the most visible indicators of advancing technology. Within recent memory, we were forced to switch from old analog phones to digital models. The networks have been upgraded to 3G, greatly enhancing speed and lowering latency. This has reduced the need for lightweight protocols to handle data transmission, and more standard protocols such as IP can be used. The increased power and memory of the handheld devices also reduce the need for lighter-weight encryption protocols. This has caused the protocols used for 3G mobile devices to build in their own encryption protocols. Security will rely on these lower-level protocols or standard application-level security protocols used in normal IP traffic.

Several competing data transmission standards exist for 3G networks, such as HSPA and EVDO. However, all the standards include transport layer encryption protocols to secure the voice traffic traveling across the wireless signal as well as the data sent by the device. The cryptographic standard proposed for 3G is known as *KASUMI*. This modified version of the MISTY1 algorithm uses 64-bit blocks and 128-bit keys. Multiple attacks have been launched against this cipher. While the attacks tend to be

---

3G, 4G, LTE...What's the Difference?

In today's mobile marketing campaigns, we hear of 3G, 4G, and LTE. What do these terms mean? 3G is the "old" network today, but it is still very capable for a variety of purposes. 4G phones are supposed to be even faster, but that's not always the case. A lot depends on what you use the phone for. There are several technologies called "4G," each with multiple implementations. This makes the term almost meaningless from a technical point of view. The International Telecommunication Union (ITU), a standards body, issued requirements that a network needed to meet to be called "4G," but those requirements were ignored by carriers. Now the move is to LTE, which stands for Long Term Evolution of the Universal Mobile Telecommunications System (UMTS). UMTS is the group of standards that defines 3G for GSM networks across the world, and now LTE. There are numerous technical implementations of LTE, but one of the key elements is the use of two different types of air interfaces (radio links), one for downlink (from tower to device) and one for uplink (from device to tower). This is one of the reasons LTE is much faster when uploading information from the phone to the Internet. LTE offers high speed (up to 30 Mbps) and low latency. But not all LTE is equal. Recent tests indicate as much as an order of magnitude difference in speeds between carriers.

As LTE expands, newer versions, each with its own set of characteristics picked from the overall "standard," are deployed by carriers. While the LTE-A standard has been approved, no carriers currently meet the entire standard. Each carrier has picked the elements of the standard they feel meet their needs.

Bottom line: 4G has become a marketing term, and the only guide one has is to use actual survey results in the area of your service to determine the best solution for your use requirements.

impractical, this shows that application layer security is needed for secure transmission of data on mobile devices. WAP and WTLS can be used over the lower-level protocols, but traditional TLS can also be used.

4G Mobile Networks

Just as the mobile network carriers were finishing the rollout of 3G services, 4G networks appeared on the horizon. The desire for anywhere, anytime Internet connectivity at speeds near that of a wired connection drives deployment of these next-generation services. 4G can support high-quality VoIP connections, video calls, and real-time video streaming. Just as 3G had some intermediaries that were considered 2.9G, LTE and WiMAX networks are sometimes referred to as 3.5G, 3.75G, or 3.9G. The carriers are marketing these new networks as 4G, although they do not adhere to the ITU standards for 4G speeds.

True 4G would require a firm to meet all of the technical standards issued by the ITU, including specifications that apply to the tower side of the system. Some of the 4G requirements are

- Be based on an all-IP packet switched network

- Offer high quality of service for next-generation multimedia support

- Smooth handovers across heterogeneous networks

- Peak data rates of up to approximately 100 Mbps for high mobility (mobile access)

- Peak data rates of up to approximately 1 Gbps for low mobility such as nomadic/local wireless access

- Dynamically share and use the network resources to support more simultaneous users per cell

- Use scalable channel bandwidths of 5–20 MHz, optionally up to 40 MHz

- Peak link spectral efficiency of 15-bps/Hz in the downlink, and 6.75-bps/Hz in the uplink

To achieve these and other technical elements requires specific tower-side equipment as well as handset specifications. Different carriers have chosen different sets of these to include in their offerings, each building upon their existing networks and existing technologies.

Most 4G deployments are continuations of technologies already deployed—just newer evolutions of standards. This is how LTE, LTE Advanced, WiMAX, and WiMAX 2 were born. LTE and WiMAX series come from separate roots, and are not interchangeable. Within the families, interoperability is possible and is dependent upon carrier implementation.

■ Bluetooth

Bluetooth was originally developed by Ericsson and known as multi-communicator link; in 1998, Nokia, IBM, Intel, and Toshiba joined Ericsson and adopted the Bluetooth name. This consortium became known as the Bluetooth Special Interest Group (SIG). The SIG now has more than 24,000

343

members and drives the development of the technology and controls the specification to ensure interoperability.

• Bluetooth icon

Most people are familiar with Bluetooth as it is part of many mobile phones and headsets, such as those shown in Figure 12.3. This short-range, low-power wireless protocol transmits in the **2.4 GHz band**, the same band used for 802.11. The concept for the short-range (approx. 32 feet) wireless protocol is to transmit data in personal area networks (PANs).

Bluetooth transmits and receives data from a variety of devices, the most common being mobile phones, laptops, printers, and audio devices. The mobile phone has driven a lot of Bluetooth growth and has even spread Bluetooth into new cars as a mobile phone hands-free kit.

Bluetooth has gone through a few releases. Version 1.1 was the first commercially successful version, with version 1.2 released in 2007 and correcting some of the problems found in 1.1. Version 1.2 allows speeds up to 721 Kbps and improves resistance to interference. Version 1.2 is backward-compatible with version 1.1. With the rate of advancement and the life of most tech items, Bluetooth 1 series is basically extinct. Bluetooth 2.0 introduced enhanced data rate (EDR), which allows the transmission of up to 3.0 Mbps. Bluetooth 3.0 has the capability to use an 802.11 channel to achieve speeds up to 24 Mbps. The current version is the Bluetooth 4.0 standard with support for three modes: classic, high speed, and low energy.

Bluetooth 4 introduces a new method to support collecting data from devices that generate data at a very low rate. Some devices, such as medical devices, may only collect and transmit data at low rates. This feature, called

• **Figure 12.3**   Headsets and cell phones are two of the most popular types of Bluetooth-capable devices.

Principles of Computer Security

Low Energy (LE), was designed to aggregate data from various sensors, like heart rate monitors, thermometers, and so forth, and carries the commercial name Bluetooth Smart.

As Bluetooth became popular, people started trying to find holes in it. Bluetooth features easy configuration of devices to allow communication, with no need for network addresses or ports. Bluetooth uses pairing to establish a trust relationship between devices. To establish that trust, the devices advertise capabilities and require a passkey. To help maintain security, most devices require the passkey to be entered into both devices; this prevents a default passkey–type attack. The Bluetooth's protocol advertisement of services and pairing properties is where some of the security issues start.

Bluetooth Attacks

As a wireless method of communication, Bluetooth is open to connection and attack from outside the intended sender and receiver. Several different attack modes have been discovered that can be used against Bluetooth systems.

Bluejacking is a term used for the sending of unauthorized messages to another Bluetooth device. This involves setting a message as a phonebook contact:

Then the attacker sends the message to the possible recipient via Bluetooth. Originally, this involved sending text messages, but more recent phones can send images or audio as well. A popular variant of this is the transmission of "shock" images, featuring disturbing or crude photos. As Bluetooth is a short-range protocol, the attack and victim must be within roughly 10 yards of each other. The victim's phone must also have Bluetooth enabled and must be in discoverable mode. On some early phones, this was the default configuration, and while it makes connecting external devices easier, it also allows attacks against the phone. If Bluetooth is turned off, or if the device is set to nondiscoverable, bluejacking can be avoided.

Bluesnarfing is similar to bluejacking in that it uses the same contact transmission protocol. The difference is that instead of sending an unsolicited message to the victim's phone, the attacker copies off the victim's information, which can include e-mails, contact lists, calendar, and anything else that exists on that device. More recent phones with media capabilities can be snarfed for private photos and videos. Bluesnarfing used to require a laptop with a Bluetooth adapter, making it relatively easy to identify a possible attacker, but bluesnarfing applications are now available for mobile devices. Bloover, a combination of Bluetooth and Hoover, is one such application that runs as a Java applet. The majority of Bluetooth phones need to be discoverable for the bluesnarf attack to work, but it does not necessarily need to be paired. In theory, an attacker can also brute-force the device's unique 48-bit name. A program called RedFang attempts to perform this brute-force attack by sending all possible names and seeing what gets a response. This approach was addressed in Bluetooth 1.2 with an anonymity mode.

Bluebugging is a far more serious attack than either bluejacking or bluesnarfing. In bluebugging, the attacker uses Bluetooth to establish a serial connection to the device. This allows access to the full AT command set—GSM phones use AT commands similar to Hayes-compatible modems.

This connection allows full control over the phone, including the placing of calls to any number without the phone owner's knowledge. Fortunately, this attack requires pairing of the devices to complete, and phones initially vulnerable to the attack have updated firmware to correct the problem. To accomplish the attack now, the phone owner would need to surrender her phone and allow an attacker to physically establish the connection.

Bluetooth DOS is the use of Bluetooth technology to perform a denial-of-service attack against another device. In this attack, an attacker repeatedly requests pairing with the victim device. This type of attack does not divulge information or permit access, but is a nuisance. And, more importantly, if done repeatedly it can drain a device's battery, or prevent other operations from occurring on the victim's device. As with all Bluetooth attacks, because of the short range involved, all one has to do is leave the area and the attack would cease.

Bluetooth technology is likely to grow due to the popularity of mobile phones. Software and protocol updates have helped to improve the security of the protocol. Almost all phones now keep Bluetooth turned off by default, and they allow you to make the phone discoverable for only a limited amount of time. User education about security risks is also a large factor in avoiding security breaches.

Near Field Communication

Near field communication (NFC) is a set of wireless technologies that enables smartphones and other devices to establish radio communication over a short proximity, typically a distance of 10 cm (3.9 in) or less. This technology did not see much use until recently when it started being employed to move data between cell phones and in mobile payment systems. NFC is likely to become a high use technology in the years to come as multiple uses exist for the technology, and the next generation of smartphones is surely to see this as a standard function.

IEEE 802.11 Series

The 802.11b protocol is an IEEE standard ratified in 1999. The standard launched a range of products (such as wireless routers, an example of which is shown in Figure 12.4) that would open the way to a whole new genre of possibilities for attackers and a new series of headaches for security administrators everywhere. 802.11 was a new standard for sending packetized data traffic over radio waves in the unlicensed 2.4 GHz band.

This group of IEEE standards is also called Wi-Fi, which is a certification owned by an industry group, the Wi-Fi Alliance. A device marked as Wi-Fi Certified adheres to the standards of the alliance. As the products matured and became easy to use and affordable, security experts began to deconstruct the limited security that had been built into the standard.

The 802.11b standard was the first to market, 802.11a followed, and 802.11g products currently are the most common ones being sold. These chipsets have also commonly been combined into devices that support

• Figure 12.4   A common wireless router

a/b/g standards. 802.11n is the latest standard. This table shows the standards with their frequency ranges.

Specification	Frequency	Base Data Rates (Mbps)
802.11a	5.180 GHz to 5.320 GHz divided into 8 channels	6, 9, 12, 18, 24, 36, 48, 54
802.11b	2.401 GHz to 2.473 GHz divided into 11 channels	1, 2, 5.5, 11
802.11g	2.401 GHz to 2.473 GHz divided into 11 channels	6, 9, 12, 18, 24, 36, 48, 54
802.11i	N/A	
802.11n	2.401 GHz to 2.473 GHz and the 5 GHz band	7.2–150
802.11ac	5 GHz	7.2–866
802.11ad	60 GHz	Up to 6.75 Gbps

802.11a is the wireless networking standard that supports traffic on the **5 GHz band**, allowing faster speeds over shorter ranges. Features of 802.11b and 802.11a were later joined to create 802.11g, an updated standard that allows the faster speeds of the 5 GHz specification on the 2.4 GHz band. Security problems were discovered in the implementations of these early wireless standards, principally involving the Wired Equivalent Privacy (WEP) protocol. These problems included an attacker's ability to break the cryptography and monitor other users' traffic. The security problems in WEP were a top concern until the adoption of 802.11i-compliant products enhanced the security with Wi-Fi Protected Access (WPA), discussed later in the chapter. 802.11ac is the latest standard; it focuses on achieving much higher speeds for wireless networks. **Direct-sequence spread spectrum (DSSS)** is a modulation type that spreads the traffic sent over the entire bandwidth. It does this by injecting a noise-like signal into the information stream and transmitting the normally narrowband information over the wider band available. The primary reason that spread-spectrum technology is used in 802.11 protocols is to avoid interference on the public 2.4 GHz and 5 GHz bands. **Orthogonal frequency division multiplexing (OFDM)** multiplexes, or separates, the data to be transmitted into smaller chunks and then transmits the chunks on several subchannels. This use of subchannels is what the "frequency division" portion of the name refers to. Both of these techniques, multiplexing and frequency division, are used to avoid interference. *Orthogonal* refers to the manner in which the subchannels are assigned, principally to avoid crosstalk, or interference with your own channels.

802.11: Individual Standards

The 802.11b protocol provides for multiple-rate Ethernet over 2.4 GHz spread-spectrum wireless. It provides transfer rates of 1 Mbps, 2 Mbps, 5.5 Mbps, and 11 Mbps and uses DSSS. The most common layout is a point-to-multipoint environment, with the available bandwidth being shared by all users. Typical range is roughly 100 yards indoors and 300 yards outdoors, line of sight. While the wireless transmissions of 802.11 can penetrate some walls and other objects, the best range is offered when both the access point and network client devices have an unobstructed view of each other.

802.11a uses a higher band and has higher bandwidth. It operates in the 5 GHz spectrum using OFDM. Supporting rates of up to 54 Mbps, it is the faster brother of 802.11b; however, the higher frequency used by 802.11a shortens the usable range of the devices and makes it incompatible with 802.11b. The chipsets tend to be more expensive for 802.11a, which has slowed adoption of the standard.

The 802.11g standard uses portions of both of the other standards: it uses the 2.4 GHz band for greater range but uses the OFDM transmission method to achieve the faster 54 Mbps data rates. As it uses the 2.4 GHz band, this standard interoperates with the older 802.11b standard. This allows an 802.11g access point (AP) to give access to both "G" and "B" clients.

The 802.11n version improves on the older standards by greatly increasing speed. It has a functional data rate of up to 600 Mbps, gained through the use of wider bands and multiple-input multiple-output (MIMO) processing. MIMO uses multiple antennas and can bond separate channels together to increase data throughput.

802.11ac is the latest in the 5 GHz band, with functional data rates up to a theoretical 6+ Gbps using multiple antennas. The 802.11ac standard was ratified in 2014, and chipsets have been available since late 2011. Designed for multimedia streaming and other high-bandwidth operations, the individual channels are twice the width of 802.11n channels, and as many as eight antennas can be deployed in a Mu-MIMO form.

802.11 proposals don't stop with "ac" though. There are several ideas that extend the 802.11 standard for new and interesting applications. For example, 802.11s is a proposed standard for wireless mesh networks where all nodes on the network are equal instead of using an access point and a client. 802.11p is another example; it defines an application where mobile vehicles can communicate with other vehicles or roadside stations for safety information or toll collection.

All these protocols operate in bands that are "unlicensed" by the FCC. This means that people operating this equipment do not have to be certified by the FCC, but it also means that the devices could possibly share the band with other devices, such as cordless phones, closed-circuit TV (CCTV) wireless transceivers, and other similar equipment. This other equipment can cause interference with the 802.11 equipment, possibly causing speed degradation.

The 802.11 protocol designers expected some security concerns and attempted to build provisions into the 802.11 protocol that would ensure adequate security. The 802.11 standard includes attempts at rudimentary authentication and confidentiality controls. Authentication is handled in its most basic form by the 802.11 AP, forcing the clients to perform a handshake when attempting to "associate" to the AP.

Association is the process required before the AP will allow the client to talk across the AP to the network. Association occurs only if the client has all the correct parameters needed in the handshake, among them the **service set identifier (SSID)**. This SSID setting should limit access only to the authorized users of the wireless network. The SSID is a phrase-based mechanism that helps ensure that you are connecting to the correct AP. This SSID phrase is transmitted in all the access point's **beacon frames**. The beacon frame is an 802.11 management frame for the network and contains several different fields, such as the timestamp and beacon interval, but most

The 2.4 GHz band is commonly used by many household devices that are constantly on, such as cordless phones. It is also the frequency used by microwave ovens to heat food. So if you are having intermittent interference on your Wi-Fi LAN, check to see if the microwave is on.

SSIDs can be set to anything by the person setting up an access point. So, while "FBI Surveillance Van #14" may seem humorous, what about SSIDs with the name of the airport you are in, Starbucks, or the hotel you are in? Can you trust them? Since anyone can use any name, the answer is no. So, if you need a secure connection, you should use some form of secure channel such as a VPN for communication security. For even more security, you can carry your own access point and create a wireless channel that you control.

importantly the SSID. This allows attackers to scan for the beacon frame and retrieve the SSID.

The designers of the 802.11 standard also attempted to maintain confidentiality by introducing **Wired Equivalent Privacy (WEP)**, which uses the **RC4 stream cipher** to encrypt the data as it is transmitted through the air. WEP has been shown to have an implementation problem that can be exploited to break security.

To understand all the 802.11 security problems, you must first look at some of the reasons it became such a prominent technology. Wireless networks came along in 2000 and became very popular. For the first time, it was possible to have almost full-speed network connections without having to be tied down to an Ethernet cable. The technology quickly took off, allowing prices to drop into the consumer range. Once the market shifted to focus on customers who were not necessarily technologists, the products also became very easy to install and operate. Default settings were designed to get the novice users up and running without having to alter anything substantial, and products were described as being able to just plug in and work. These developments further enlarged the market for the low-cost, easy-to-use wireless access points. Then attackers realized that instead of attacking machines over the Internet, they could drive around and seek out these APs.

Typically, access to actual Ethernet segments is protected by physical security measures. This structure allows security administrators to plan for only internal threats to the network and gives them a clear idea of the types and number of machines connected to it. Wireless networking takes the keys to the kingdom and tosses them out the window and into the parking lot. A typical wireless installation broadcasts the network right through the physical controls that are in place. An attacker can drive up and have the same access as if he plugged into an Ethernet jack inside the building—in fact, better access, because 802.11 is a shared medium, allowing sniffers to view all packets being sent to or from the AP and all clients. These APs are also typically behind any security measures the companies have in place, such as firewalls and intrusion detection systems (IDSs). This kind of access into the internal network has caused a large stir among computer security professionals and eventually the media. War-driving, war-flying, war-walking, war-chalking—all of these terms have been used in security article after security article to describe attacks on wireless networks.

 Cross Check

Intrusion Detection Systems

Chapter 13 has a lot more information about intrusion detection systems, whereas this chapter references methods of getting past the IDSs. When you learn more about the different IDSs, how would you design an IDS that can catch wireless attackers?

Attacking 802.11

Wireless is a popular target for several reasons: the access gained from wireless, the lack of default security, and the wide proliferation of devices.

However, other reasons also make it attackable. The first of these is *anonymity*: An attacker can probe your building for wireless access from the street. Then he can log packets to and from the AP without giving any indication that an attempted intrusion is taking place. The attacker will announce his presence only if he attempts to associate to the AP. Even then, an attempted association is recorded only by the MAC address of the wireless card associating to it, and most APs do not have alerting functionality to indicate when users associate to it. This fact gives administrators a very limited view of who is gaining access to the network, if they are even paying attention at all. It gives attackers the ability to seek out and compromise wireless networks with relative impunity.

The second reason is the low cost of the equipment needed. A single wireless access card costing less than $100 can give access to any unsecured AP within driving range. Finally, attacking a wireless network is relatively easy compared to attacking other target hosts. Windows-based tools for locating and sniffing wireless-based networks have turned anyone who can download files from the Internet and has a wireless card into a potential attacker.

Locating wireless networks was originally termed *war-driving,* an adaptation of the term *war-dialing.* War-dialing comes from the 1983 movie *WarGames*; it is the process of dialing a list of phone numbers looking for modem-connected computers. *War-drivers* drive around with a wireless locater program recording the number of networks found and their locations. This term has evolved along with *war-flying* and *war-walking,* which mean exactly what you expect. *War-chalking* started with people using chalk on sidewalks to mark some of the wireless networks they found.

The most common tools for an attacker to use are reception-based programs that listen to the beacon frames output by other wireless devices, and programs that promiscuously capture all traffic. The most widely used of these programs is called NetStumbler, created by Marius Milner and shown in Figure 12.5. This program listens for the beacon frames of APs that are within range of the card attached to the NetStumbler computer. When it receives the frames, it logs all available information about the AP for later analysis. Since it listens only to beacon frames, NetStumbler displays only networks that have the SSID broadcast turned on. If the computer has a

Anonymity also works in another way; once an attacker finds an unsecured AP with wireless access, they can use an essentially untraceable IP address to attempt attacks on other Internet hosts.

MAC	SSID	Name	Ch.	Vendor	Ty..	W..	SN..	Sign..	Noi..	SN..	Latitude	Longitude	First Se..	Last Se..	Sig..	Noi..	Fla..
00045AD82	linksys	Prism I	6	Linksys	AP			-86	-102	16	N29.4745..	W98.4658..	21:24:52	21:25:05			0001
0060B3665	WSR-5000	Prism I	1	Z-Com	AP			-85	-102	16	N29.4728..	W98.4647..	21:24:31	21:24:21			0001
00601DF24..	peruna	peruna	1	Agere..	AP			-73	-146	49	N29.4723..	W98.4604..	21:21:50	21:24:21			0001
00045A0E0..	YoungbloodHome		6	Linksys	AP			-91	-98	7	N29.4749..	W98.4435..	21:17:57	21:17:57			0005
004005DE..	default		6	D-Link	AP			-91	-99	8	N29.4749..	W98.4428..	21:17:53	21:17:59			0011
00045AD22..	linksys		6	Linksys	AP	Yes		-79	-102	20	N29.4749..	W98.4414..	21:17:36	21:17:45			0002
0200F2D8A..	wireless		6		Pe..			-84	-103	17	N29.4831..	W98.4311..	21:15:36	21:15:46			0011
0060B36F4..	ChasDawes		1	Z-Com	AP			-93	-100	7	N29.4911..	W98.4268..	21:14:07	21:14:07			0001
00045A0EF..	OEM		6	Linksys	AP			-90	-98	8	N29.5156..	W98.4357..	21:08:28	21:08:28			0011
005018071..	tetcostores		7	Advan..	AP	Yes		-88	-106	14	N29.5153..	W98.4363..	21:07:09	21:08:18			0001
0090D1015..	tetcowest		1	Addtron	AP			-93	-100	5	N29.5155..	W98.4362..	21:06:45	21:08:21			0031
00409634F..	NEISD Wireless		6	Cisco..	AP	Yes		-95	-99	4	N29.5107..	W98.4345..	21:06:42	21:06:42			0001
00045A0EE..	linksys		6	Linksys	AP			-78	-102	23	N29.5022..	W98.4532..	20:59:49	21:00:42			0001
00045ADB..	linksys	Prism I	6	Linksys	AP			-68	-106	33	N29.5022..	W98.4529..	20:59:30	21:00:33			0001
0004E20E7..	CROWAP		6		AP			-72	-102	28	N29.5023..	W98.4549..	20:58:26	20:59:33			0001
00022D20C..	Raymond Airnet		1	Agere..	AP			-91	-99	8	N29.5031..	W98.4575..	20:58:01	20:58:02			0001
00601DF05..	Apple Network 3b2cbc		1	Agere..	AP			-92	-100	8	N29.5001..	W98.4664..	20:54:15	20:54:17			0001
00045ADA..	LHAH	Prism I	6,9	Linksys	AP			-87	-145	43	N29.4980..	W98.4667..	20:52:31	20:53:54			0021
004096384..	TXA1		6	Cisco..	AP			-86	-104	15	N29.4919..	W98.4663..	20:46:55	20:50:01			0001
00045AD0..	linksys	Prism I	6	Linksys	AP			-85	-103	14	N29.4903..	W98.4663..	20:45:45	20:46:10			0001
00022D095..	Barcelona		1	Agere..	AP			-95	-97	2	N29.4912..	W98.4567..	20:44:10	20:44:10			0011
00045AD0..	decypher		6	Linksys	AP	Yes		-73	-102	26	N29.4914..	W98.4516..	20:42:40	20:42:52			0011
00022D115..	2WIRE749		6	Agere..	AP	Yes		-96	-101	5	N29.4827..	W98.4507..	20:38:15	20:38:16			0011
00022D046..	0462ea		1	Agere..	AP	Yes		-92	-101	8	N29.4809..	W98.4514..	20:37:36	20:37:37			0011
00022D1E4..	1e41d5		1	Agere..	AP	Yes		-87	-100	12	N29.4755..	W98.4512..	20:36:45	20:36:49			0001
00022D233..	2WIRE043		6	Agere..	AP	Yes		-90	-97	6	N29.4729..	W98.4535..	20:35:18	20:35:26			0001
00045AF99..	linksys		6	Linksys	AP			-78	-103	23	N29.4726..	W98.4579..	20:33:56	21:21:38			0001
00045AD1..	linksys	Prism I	6	Linksys	AP			-80	-104	19	N29.4723..	W98.4594..	20:33:37	21:22:35			0001
00601DF01..	pooh		1	Agere..	AP			-78	-102	22	N29.4712..	W98.4645..	20:32:15	20:32:25			0001
00045ADB..	linksys		6	Linksys	AP			-92	-99	7	N29.4748..	W98.4669..	20:31:21	20:31:24			0001
00032F011..	Pirate's Den		4	GST (..	AP			-73	-103	24	N29.4767..	W98.4693..	20:29:19	21:27:25			0001

• **Figure 12.5** NetStumbler on a Windows PC

Tech Tip

IV Attack

Because of the small length of the initialization vector (IV) in WEP, the protection is subject to attack over time by examining packets and determining when the IV + RC4 key repeats, enabling the defeat of the protection.

Tech Tip

Another Meaning of Rogue Access Point

A "rogue access point" can also refer to an attacker's access point, set up as a man in the middle to capture login information from unsuspecting users.

GPS unit attached to it, the program also logs the AP's coordinates. This information can be used to return to the AP or to plot maps of APs in a city.

Once an attacker has located a network, and assuming that he cannot directly connect and start active scanning and penetration of the network, he will use the best attack tool there is: a network sniffer. The network sniffer, when combined with a wireless network card it can support, is a powerful attack tool, as the shared medium of a wireless network exposes all packets to interception and logging. Popular wireless sniffers are Wireshark (formerly Ethereal) and Kismet. Regular sniffers used on wired Ethernet have also been updated to include support for wireless. Sniffers are also important because they allow you to retrieve the MAC addresses of the nodes of the network. APs can be configured to allow access only to prespecified MAC addresses, and an attacker spoofing the MAC can bypass this feature.

There are specialized sniffer tools designed with a single objective: to crack Wired Equivalent Privacy (WEP) keys. As described earlier, WEP is an encryption protocol that 802.11 uses to attempt to ensure confidentiality of wireless communications. Unfortunately, it has turned out to have several problems. WEP's weaknesses are specifically targeted for attack by the specialized sniffer programs. They work by exploiting weak initialization vectors in the encryption algorithm. To exploit this weakness, an attacker needs a certain number of ciphertext packets; once he has captured enough packets, however, the program can very quickly decipher the encryption key being used. WEPCrack was the first available program to use this flaw to crack WEP keys; however, WEPCrack depends on a dump of actual network packets from another sniffer program. AirSnort is a standalone program that captures its own packets; once it has captured enough ciphertext, it provides the WEP key of the network.

Local users of the network are susceptible to having their entire traffic decoded and analyzed. A proper site survey is an important step in securing a wireless network to avoid sending critical data beyond company walls. Recurring site surveys are important because wireless technology is cheap and typically comes unsecured in its default configuration. If anyone attaches a wireless AP to your network, you want to know about it immediately.

If unauthorized wireless is set up, it is known as a **rogue access point**. Rogue access points can be set up by well-meaning employees or hidden by an attacker with physical access. An attacker might set up a rogue access point if they have a limited amount of physical access to an organization, perhaps by sneaking into the building briefly. The attacker can then set up an AP on the network and, by placing it behind the external firewall or network IDS (NIDS) type of security measures, can attach to the wireless at a later date at their leisure. This approach reduces the risk of getting caught by physical security staff, and if the AP is found, it does not point directly back to any kind of traceable address.

Another type of 802.11 attack is known as the **evil twin** attack. This is the use of an access point owned by an attacker that usually has been enhanced with higher-power and higher-gain antennas to look like a better connection to the users and computers attaching to it. By getting users to connect through the evil access point, attackers can more easily analyze traffic and perform man-in-the-middle–type attacks. For simple denial of service, an attacker could use interference to jam the wireless signal, not allowing any computer to connect to the access point successfully.

802.11 networks have two features used primarily for security: one is designed solely for authentication, and the other is designed for authentication and confidentiality. Part of the authentication

Cross Check

Identifying Rogue Access Points

In Chapter 8 you learned about how physical security can impact information security, and how several different devices can act as a wireless bridge and be a rogue access point. Can you think of some physical security policies that can help reduce the risk of rogue access points? What about some information security policies?

function, introduced earlier, is known as the service set identifier (SSID). This unique 32-octet identifier is attached to the header of the packet. The SSID is broadcast by default as a network name, but broadcasting of this beacon frame can be disabled. Users can authenticate to a network regardless of whether the SSID is broadcast or not, but they do need to know the SSID to connect.

Many APs also use a default SSID; for Cisco APs, this default is *tsunami*, which may indicate an AP that has not been configured for any security. Renaming the SSID and disabling SSID broadcast are both good ideas; however, because the SSID is part of every frame, these measures should not be considered adequate to secure the network. As the SSID is, hopefully, a unique identifier, only people who know the identifier will be able to complete association to the AP. While the SSID is a good idea in theory, it is sent in plaintext in the packets, so in practice SSID offers little security significance—any sniffer can determine the SSID.

This weakness is magnified by most APs' default settings to transmit beacon frames. The beacon frame's purpose is to announce the wireless network's presence and capabilities so that WLAN cards can attempt to associate to it. This can be disabled in software for many APs, especially the more sophisticated ones. From a security perspective, the beacon frame is damaging because it contains the SSID, and this beacon frame is transmitted at a set interval (ten times per second by default). Since a default AP without any other traffic is sending out its SSID in plaintext ten times a second, you can see why the SSID does not provide true authentication. Scanning programs such as NetStumbler work by capturing the beacon frames and thereby the SSIDs of all APs.

Most APs also have the ability to lock access in only to known MAC addresses, providing a limited authentication capability. Given sniffers' capacity to grab all active MAC addresses on the network, this capability is not very effective. An attacker simply configures his wireless cards to a known good MAC address.

WEP encrypts the data traveling across the network with an RC4 stream cipher, attempting to ensure confidentiality. This synchronous method of encryption ensures some method of authentication. The system depends on the client and the AP having a shared secret key, ensuring that only authorized people with the proper key have access to the wireless network. WEP supports two key lengths, 40 and 104 bits, though these are more typically referred to as 64 and 128 bits, because 24 bits of the overall key length are used for the initialization vector (IV). In 802.11a and 802.11g, manufacturers have extended this to 152-bit WEP keys, again with 24 bits being used for the IV.

Exam Tip: MAC filtering can be employed on WAPs but can be bypassed by attackers observing allowed MAC addresses and spoofing the allowed MAC address for the wireless card.

Tech Tip

WEP Isn't Equivalent

WEP should not be trusted alone to provide confidentiality. If WEP is the only protocol supported by your AP, place it outside the corporate firewall and VPN to add more protection.

The IV is the primary reason for the weaknesses in WEP. The IV is sent in the plaintext part of the message, and because the total keyspace is approximately 16 million keys, the same key will be reused. Once the key has been repeated, an attacker has two ciphertexts encrypted with the same key stream. This allows the attacker to examine the ciphertext and retrieve the key. This attack can be improved by examining only packets that have weak IVs, reducing the number of packets needed to crack the key. Using only weak IV packets, the number of required captured packets is reduced to around four or five million, which can take only a few hours to capture on a fairly busy AP. For a point of reference, this means that equipment with an advertised WEP key of 128 bits can be cracked in less than a day, whereas to crack a normal 128-bit key would take roughly 2,000,000,000,000,000,000 years on a computer able to attempt one trillion keys a second. As mentioned, AirSnort is a modified sniffing program that takes advantage of this weakness to retrieve the WEP keys.

The biggest weakness of WEP is that the IV problem exists regardless of key length, because the IV always remains at 24 bits.

After the limited security functions of a wireless network are broken, the network behaves exactly like a regular Ethernet network and is subject to the exact same vulnerabilities. The host machines that are on or attached to the wireless network are as vulnerable as if they and the attacker were physically connected. Being on the network opens up all machines to vulnerability scanners, Trojan horse programs, virus and worm programs, and traffic interception via sniffer programs. Any unpatched vulnerability on any machine accessible from the wireless segment is now open to compromise.

Current Security Methods

WEP was designed to provide some measure of confidentiality on an 802.11 network similar to what is found on a wired network, but that has not been the case. Accordingly, the Wi-Fi Alliance developed Wi-Fi Protected Access (WPA) to improve upon WEP. The 802.11i standard is the IEEE standard for security in wireless networks, also known as Wi-Fi Protected Access 2 (WPA2). It uses 802.1X to provide authentication. WPA2 can use Advanced Encryption Standard (AES) as the encryption protocol. The 802.11i standard specifies the use of the Temporal Key Integrity Protocol (TKIP) and uses AES with the Counter Mode with CBC-MAC Protocol (in full, the Counter Mode with Cipher Block Chaining–Message Authentication Codes Protocol, or simply CCMP). These two protocols have different functions, but they both serve to enhance security.

TKIP works by using a shared secret combined with the card's MAC address to generate a new key, which is mixed with the IV to make per-packet keys that encrypt a single packet using the same RC4 cipher used by traditional WEP. This overcomes the WEP key weakness, as a key is used on only one packet. The other advantage to this method is that it can be retrofitted to current hardware with only a software change, unlike AES and 802.1X. CCMP is actually the mode in which the AES cipher is used to provide message integrity. Unlike TKIP, CCMP requires new hardware to perform the AES encryption. The advances of 802.11i have corrected the weaknesses of WEP.

WPA

The first standard to be used in the market to replace WEP was Wi-Fi Protected Access (WPA). This standard uses the flawed WEP algorithm with the Temporal Key Integrity Protocol (TKIP).

While WEP uses a 40-bit or 104-bit encryption key that must be manually entered on wireless access points and devices and does not change, TKIP employs a per-packet key, generating a new 128-bit key for each packet. This can generally be accomplished with only a firmware update, enabling a simple solution to the types of attacks that compromise WEP.

TKIP

Temporal Key Integrity Protocol (TKIP) was created as a stopgap security measure to replace the WEP protocol without requiring the replacement of legacy hardware. The breaking of WEP had left Wi-Fi networks without viable link-layer security, and a solution was required for already deployed hardware. TKIP works by mixing a secret root key with the IV before the RC4 encryption. WPA/TKIP uses the same underlying mechanism as WEP, and consequently is vulnerable to a number of similar attacks. TKIP is no longer considered secure and has been deprecated with the release of WPA2.

WPA2

IEEE 802.11i is the standard for security in wireless networks and is also known as **Wi-Fi Protected Access 2 (WPA2)**. It uses 802.1x to provide authentication and uses the Advanced Encryption Standard (AES) as the encryption protocol. WPA2 uses the AES block cipher, a significant improvement over WEP's and WPA's use of the RC4 stream cipher. The 802.11i standard specifies the use of the Counter Mode with CBC-MAC Protocol (in full, the Counter Mode with Cipher Block Chaining–Message Authentication Codes Protocol, or simply CCMP).

WPS

Wi-Fi Protected Setup (WPS) is a network security standard that was created to provide users with an easy method of configuring wireless networks. Designed for home networks and small business networks, this standard involves the use of an eight-digit PIN to configure wireless devices. WPS consists of a series of Extensible Authentication Protocol (EAP) messages and has been shown to be susceptible to a brute-force attack. A successful attack can reveal the PIN and subsequently the WPA/WPA2 passphrase and allow unauthorized parties to gain access to the network. Currently, the only effective mitigation is to disable WPS.

Setting Up WPA2

If WPS is not safe for use, how does one set up WPA2? To set up WPA2, you need to have several parameters. Figure 12.6 shows the screens for a WPA2 setup in Windows 7.

The first element is to choose a security framework. When configuring an adapter to connect to an existing network, you need to match the

• **Figure 12.6**   WPA2 setup options in Windows 7

choice of the network. When setting up your own network, you can choose whichever option you prefer. There are many selections, but for security purposes, you should choose WPA2-Personal or WPA2-Enterprise. Both of these require the choice of an encryption type, either TKIP or AES. TKIP has been deprecated, so choose AES. The last element is the choice of the network security key—the secret that is shared by all users. WPA2-Enterprise, which is designed to be used with an 802.1x authentication server that distributes different keys to each user, is typically used in business environments.

EAP

Extensible Authentication Protocol (EAP) is defined in RFC 2284 (obsoleted by 3748). EAP-TLS relies on Transport Layer Security (TLS), an attempt to standardize the SSL structure to pass credentials. EAP-TTLS (the acronym stands for EAP–Tunneled TLS protocol) is a variant of the EAP-TLS protocol. EAP-TTLS works much the same way as EAP-TLS, with the server authenticating to the client with a certificate, but the protocol tunnels the client side of the authentication, allowing the use of legacy authentication protocols such as Password Authentication Protocol (PAP), Challenge-Handshake Authentication Protocol (CHAP), MS-CHAP, or MS-CHAP-V2.

LEAP

Cisco designed a proprietary EAP known as Lightweight Extensible Authentication Protocol (LEAP); however, this is being phased out for newer protocols such as PEAP or EAP-TLS. Susceptible to offline password guessing, and with tools available that actively break LEAP security, this protocol has been deprecated in favor of stronger methods of EAP.

PEAP

PEAP, or Protected EAP, was developed to protect the EAP communication by encapsulating it with TLS. This is an open standard developed jointly by Cisco, Microsoft, and RSA. EAP was designed assuming a secure communication channel. PEAP provides that protection as part of the protocol via a TLS tunnel. PEAP is widely supported by vendors for use over wireless networks.

Implementing 802.1X

The **IEEE 802.1X** protocol can support a wide variety of authentication methods and also fits well into existing authentication systems such as RADIUS and LDAP. This allows 802.1X to interoperate well with other systems such as VPNs and dial-up RAS. Unlike other authentication methods, such as the Point-to-Point Protocol over Ethernet (PPPoE), 802.1X does not use encapsulation, so the network overhead is much lower. Unfortunately, the protocol is just a framework for providing implementation, so no specifics guarantee strong authentication or key management. Implementations of the protocol vary from vendor to vendor in method of implementation and strength of security, especially when it comes to the difficult test of wireless security.

Three common methods are used to implement 802.1X: EAP-TLS, EAP-TTLS, and EAP-MD5. EAP-TLS relies on TLS, an attempt to standardize the SSL structure to pass credentials. The standard, developed by Microsoft, uses X.509 certificates and offers dynamic WEP key generation. This means that the organization must have the ability to support the public key infrastructure (PKI) in the form of X.509 digital certificates. Also, per-user, per-session dynamically generated WEP keys help prevent anyone from cracking the WEP keys in use, as each user individually has her own WEP key. Even if a user were logged onto the AP and transmitted enough traffic to allow cracking of the WEP key, access would be gained only to that user's traffic. No other user's data would be compromised, and the attacker could not use the WEP key to connect to the AP. This standard authenticates the client to the AP, but it also authenticates the AP to the client, helping to avoid man-in-the-middle attacks. The main problem with the EAP-TLS protocol is that it is designed to work only with Microsoft's Active Directory and Certificate Services; it will not take certificates from other certificate issuers. Thus a mixed environment would have implementation problems.

As discussed earlier, EAP-TTLS works much the same way as EAP-TLS, with the server authenticating to the client with a certificate, but the protocol tunnels the client side of the authentication, allowing the use of legacy authentication protocols such as Password Authentication Protocol (PAP), Challenge-Handshake Authentication Protocol (CHAP), MS-CHAP, or MS-CHAP-V2. This makes the protocol more versatile while still supporting the enhanced security features such as dynamic WEP key assignment.

EAP-MD5, while it does improve the authentication of the client to the AP, does little else to improve the security of your AP. The protocol works by using the MD5 encryption protocol to hash a user's username and password. This protocol, unfortunately, provides no way for the AP to authenticate with the client, and it does not provide for dynamic WEP key assignment. In the wireless environment, without strong two-way authentication, it is very easy for an attacker to perform a man-in-the-middle attack. Normally, these types of attacks are difficult to perform, requiring a traffic redirect of some kind, but wireless changes all those rules. By setting up a rogue AP, an attacker can attempt to get clients to connect to it as if it were authorized and then simply authenticate to the real AP, a simple way to have access to the network and the client's credentials. The problem of not dynamically generating WEP keys is that it simply opens up the network to the same lack of confidentiality to which a normal AP is vulnerable. An attacker has to wait only for enough traffic to crack the WEP key, and he can then observe all traffic passing through the network.

Because the security of wireless LANs has been so problematic, many users have simply switched to a layered security approach—that is, they have moved their APs to untrustworthy portions of the network and have forced all clients to authenticate through the firewall to a third-party VPN system. The additional security comes at a price of putting more load on the firewall and VPN infrastructure and possibly adding cumbersome software to the users' devices. While wireless can be set up in a very secure manner in this fashion, it can also be set up poorly. Some systems lack strong authentication of both endpoints, leading to possibilities of a man-in-the-middle attack. Also, even though the data is tunneled through, IP addresses are still sent in the clear, giving an attacker information about what and where your VPN endpoint is.

Another phenomenon of wireless is borne out of its wide availability and low price. All the security measures of the wired and wireless network can be defeated by the rogue AP. This is the third possible type of rogue access point discussed in this chapter; they all share the same name as they all represent a security breach. However, since they are implemented with different motives and accordingly pose slightly different threats, we discuss them all separately. In this case, a well-intentioned employee who is trying to make the work environment more convenient purchases an AP at a local retailer and installs it. When installed, it works fine, but it typically will have no security installed. Since the IT department doesn't know about it, it is an uncontrolled entry point into the network.

No matter what kind of rogue AP we are dealing with, the rogue AP must be detected and controlled. The most common way to control rogue APs is some form of wireless scanning to ensure only legitimate wireless is in place at an organization. While complete wireless IDSs will detect APs, this can also be done with a laptop and free software.

> ### Try This!
> **Scanning for Rogue Wireless**
> Once you have completed Lab Project 12.1 and have NetStumbler or Kismet installed on the computer, take it to several locations around your workplace or school and attempt to scan for wireless access points that should not be there.

CCMP

As previously mentioned in the discussion of WPA2, CCMP stands for Counter Mode with Cipher Block Chaining–Message Authentication Codes Protocol (or Counter Mode with CBC-MAC Protocol). CCMP is a data encapsulation encryption mechanism designed for wireless use. CCMP is actually the mode in which the AES cipher is used to provide message integrity. Unlike WPA, CCMP requires new hardware to perform the AES encryption.

MAC Filtering

MAC filtering is the selective admission of packets based on a list of approved Media Access Control (MAC) addresses. Employed on switches, this method is used to provide a means of machine authentication. In wired networks, this enjoys the protection afforded by the wires, making interception of signals to determine their MAC addresses difficult. In wireless networks, this same mechanism suffers from the fact that an attacker can see the MAC addresses of all traffic to and from the access point, and then can spoof the MAC addresses that are permitted to communicate via the access point.

 Exam Tip: MAC filtering can be employed on wireless access points, but can be bypassed by attackers observing allowed MAC addresses and spoofing the allowed MAC address for the wireless card.

■ Wireless Systems Configuration

Wireless systems are more than just protocols. Putting up a functional wireless system in a house is as easy as plugging in a wireless access point and connecting. But in an enterprise, where multiple access points will be needed, the configuration takes significantly more work. Site surveys are needed to determine proper access point and antenna placement, as well as channels and power levels.

Antenna Types

The standard access point is equipped with an omnidirectional antenna. Omnidirectional antennas operate in all directions, making the relative orientation between devices less important. Omnidirectional antennas cover the greatest area per antenna. The weakness occurs in corners and hard-to-reach areas, as well as boundaries of a facility where directional antennas are needed to complete coverage. Figure 12.7 shows a sampling of common Wi-Fi antennas: (a) is a common home wireless router, (b) is a commercial indoor wireless access point, and (c) is an outdoor directional antenna. These can be visible as shown, or hidden above ceiling tiles.

Wireless networking problems caused by weak signal strength can sometimes be solved by installing upgraded Wi-Fi radio antennas on the access points. On business networks, the complexity of multiple access points typically requires a comprehensive site survey to map the Wi-Fi signal strength in and around office buildings. Additional wireless access points can then be strategically placed where needed to resolve dead spots in coverage. For small businesses and homes, where a single access point may be all that is needed, an antenna upgrade may be a simpler and more cost-effective option to fix Wi-Fi signal problems.

Two common forms of upgraded antennas are the Yagi antenna and the panel antenna. An example of a Yagi antenna is shown in Figure 12.7(c). Both Yagi and panel antennas are directional in nature, spreading the RF energy in a more limited field, increasing effective range in one direction while limiting it in others. Panel antennas can provide solid room performance while preventing signal bleed behind the antennas. This works well on the edge of a site, limiting the stray emissions that could be captured off-site. Yagi antennas act more like a rifle, funneling the energy along a beam. This allows much longer communication distances using standard power. This also enables eavesdroppers to capture signals from much greater distances because of the gain provided by the antenna itself.

Antenna Placement

Wi-Fi is by nature a radio-based method of communication, and as such uses antennas to transmit and receive the signals. The actual design and placement of the antennas can have a significant effect on the usability of the radio frequency (RF) medium for carrying the traffic. Antennas come in a variety of types, each with its own transmission pattern and gain factor. High-gain antennas can deal with weaker signals, but also have more-limited coverage. Wide-coverage, omnidirectional antennas can cover wider areas, but at lower levels of gain. The objective of antenna placement is to maximize the coverage over a physical area and reduce low-gain areas. This can be very complex in buildings with walls, electrical interference, and other sources of interference and frequently requires a site survey to determine proper placement.

Exam Tip: Because wireless antennas can transmit outside a facility, tuning and placement of antennas can be crucial for security. Adjusting radiated power through the power level controls will assist in keeping wireless signals from being broadcast outside areas under physical access control.

a   b   c

• **Figure 12.7**   Wireless access point antennas

Principles of Computer Security

MIMO

MIMO is a set of multiple-input and multiple-output antenna technologies where the available antennas are spread over a multitude of independent access points each having one or multiple antennas. This can enhance the usable bandwidth and data transmission capacity between the access point and user. There are a wide variety of MIMO methods, and this technology, once considered cutting edge or advanced, is becoming mainstream.

Power Level Controls

Wi-Fi power levels can be controlled by the hardware for a variety of reasons. The lower the power used, the less the opportunity for interference. But if the power levels are too low, then signal strength limits range. Access points can have the power level set either manually or via programmatic control. For most users, power level controls are not very useful, and leaving the unit in default mode is the best option. In complex enterprise setups, with site surveys and planned overlapping zones, this aspect of signal control can be used to increase capacity and control on the network.

Site Surveys

When developing a coverage map for a complex building site, you need to take into account a wide variety of factors, particularly walls, interfering sources, and floor plans. A **site survey** involves several steps: mapping the floor plan, testing for RF interference, testing for RF coverage, and analysis of material via software. The software can suggest placement of access points. After deploying the APs, the site is surveyed again, mapping the results versus the predicted, watching signal strength and signal-to-noise ratios. Figure 12.8 illustrates what a site survey looks like. The different

• **Figure 12.8**   Example site survey

shades indicate signal strength, showing where reception is strong and where it is weak. Site surveys can be used to ensure availability of wireless, especially when it's critical for users to have connections.

Captive Portals

Captive portal refers to a specific technique of using an HTTP client to handle authentication on a wireless network. Frequently employed in public hotspots, a captive portal opens a web browser to an authentication page. This occurs before the user is granted admission to the network. The access point uses this simple mechanism by intercepting all packets and returning the web page for login. The actual web server that serves up the authentication page can be in a walled-off section of the network, blocking access to the Internet until the user successfully authenticates.

Securing Public Wi-Fi

Public Wi-Fi is a common perk that some firms provide for their customers and visitors. When providing a Wi-Fi hotspot, even free open-to-the-public Wi-Fi, security should still be a concern. One of the issues associated with wireless transmissions is that they are subject to interception by anyone within range of the hotspot. This makes it possible for others to intercept and read traffic of anyone using the hotspot, unless encryption is used. For this reason, it has become common practice to use wireless security, even when the intent is to open the channel for everyone. Having a default password, even one that everyone knows, will make it so that people cannot observe other traffic.

There is an entire open wireless movement, designed around a sharing concept that promotes sharing of the Internet to all. For information, check out https://openwireless.org.

Although the data transmissions between many mobile devices are secured via carrier methods (GSM) and device methods (RIM Blackberry), voice transmissions have been intercepted and later used to embarrass the parties. Third-party voice encryption methods exist for smartphones, but are considered expensive and difficult to deploy by most people. They also suffer from the problem that both ends of a conversation need the device to have a secured communication. As more and more businesses find value in secured voice communications, this solution may become mainstream in the future.

■ Mobile Devices

This section will review a large number of topics specific to mobile devices. You'll likely find that the security principles you've already learned apply and just need to be adapted to mobile technologies. This is one of the fastest-changing areas of computer security because mobile technology is likely the fastest-changing technology.

Many mobile devices have significant storage capacity, allowing them to transfer files and data. Data must be protected, devices must be properly configured, and good user habits must be encouraged. This makes mobile devices no different from any other mobile media source, capable of carrying and delivering viruses, worms, and other forms of malware. They are also capable of removing data from within a network, in the case of an insider attack. Mobile devices are also commonly Bluetooth enabled, making various wireless attacks against the device a risk. One reason to attack the mobile device is to use it to relay the attack onto the internal network when the device is synced up. Bluetooth attacks are covered in Chapter 12.

Mobile Device Security

Security principles similar to those applicable to laptop computers must be followed when using mobile devices such as smartphones and tablet computing devices. Data must be protected, devices must be properly configured, and good user habits must be encouraged. This chapter will review a large number of topics specific to mobile devices. You'll likely find that the security principles you've already learned apply and just need to be adapted to mobile technologies. This is one of the fastest-changing areas of computer security because mobile technology is likely the fastest-changing technology.

Full Device Encryption

Just as laptop computers should be protected with whole disk encryption to protect the laptop in case of loss or theft, you may need to consider encryption for mobile devices used by your company's employees. Mobile devices are much more likely to be lost or stolen, so you should consider encrypting data on your devices. More and more, mobile devices are used when accessing and storing business-critical data or other sensitive information. Protecting the information on mobile devices is becoming a business imperative. This is an emerging technology, so you'll need to complete some rigorous market analysis to determine what commercial product meets your needs.

Remote Wiping

Today's mobile devices are almost innumerable and are very susceptible to loss and theft. Further, it is unlikely that a lost or stolen device will be recovered, thus making even encrypted data stored on a device more vulnerable to decryption. If the thief can have your device for a long time, he can take all the time he wants to try to decrypt your data. Therefore, many companies prefer to just remotely wipe a lost or stolen device. **Remote wiping** a mobile device typically removes data stored on the device and resets the device to factory settings. There is a dilemma in the use of BYOD (bring your own device) devices that store both personal and enterprise data. Wiping the device usually removes all data, both personal and enterprise. Therefore, if corporate policy requires wiping a lost device that may mean the device's user loses personal photos and data. The software controls for separate data containers, one for business and one for personal, are one of the reasons for enterprises to adopt mobile device management (MDM) solutions.

Lockout

A user likely will discover in a relatively short time that they've lost their device, so a quick way to protect their device is to remotely lock the device as soon as they recognize it has been lost or stolen. Several products are available on the market today to help enterprises manage their devices. Remote lockout is usually the first step taken in securing a mobile device.

Screen-locks

Most corporate policies regarding mobile devices require the use of the mobile device's **screen-locking** capability. This usually consists of entering a passcode or PIN to unlock the device. It is highly recommended that screen locks be enforced for all mobile devices. Your policy regarding the quality of the passcode should be consistent with your corporate password policy.

However, many companies merely enforce the use of screen-locking. Thus, users tend to use convenient or easy-to-remember passcodes. Some devices allow complex passcodes. As shown in Figure 12.9, the device screen on the left supports only a simple iOS passcode, limited to four numbers, while the device screen on the right supports a passcode of indeterminate length and can contain alphanumeric characters.

Some more advanced forms of screen-locks work in conjunction with device wiping. If the passcode is entered incorrectly a specified number of times, the device is automatically wiped. This is one of the security features of BlackBerry that has traditionally made it of interest to security-conscious users. Apple has made this an option on newer iOS devices. Apple also allows remote locking of a device from the user's iCloud account.

GPS

Most mobile devices are now capable of using the Global Positioning System (GPS) for tracking device location. Many apps rely heavily on GPS location, such as device-locating services, mapping apps, traffic monitoring apps, and apps that locate nearby businesses such as gas stations and restaurants. Such technology can be exploited to track movement location of the mobile device. This tracking can be used to assist in the recovery of lost devices.

Storage Segmentation

On mobile devices, it can be very difficult to keep personal data separate from corporate data. Some companies have developed capabilities to create separate virtual containers to keep personal data separate from corporate

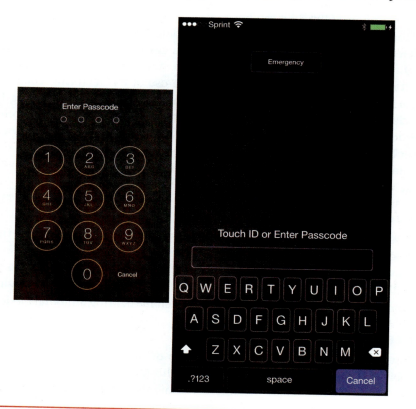

• **Figure 12.9** iOS lock screens

data and applications. For devices that are used to handle highly sensitive corporate data, this form of protection is highly recommended.

Asset Control

Because each user can have multiple devices connecting to the corporate network, it is important to implement a viable asset tracking and inventory control mechanism. For security and liability reasons, the company needs to know what devices are connecting to its systems and what access has been granted. Just as in IT systems, maintaining a list of approved devices is a critical control.

Mobile Device Management

Mobile device management (MDM) is one of the hottest topics in device security today. MDM began as a marketing term for a collective set of commonly employed protection elements associated with mobile devices. When viewed as a comprehensive set of security options for mobile devices, every corporation should have and enforce an MDM policy. The policy should require

- Device locking with a strong password
- Encryption of data on the device
- Device locking automatically after a certain period of inactivity
- The capability to remotely lock the device if it is lost or stolen
- The capability to wipe the device automatically after a certain number of failed login attempts
- The capability to remotely wipe the device if it is lost or stolen

Password policies should extend to mobile devices, including lockout and, if possible, the automatic wiping of data. Corporate policy for data encryption on mobile devices should be consistent with the policy for data encryption on laptop computers. In other words, if you don't require encryption of portable computers, then should you require it for mobile devices? There is not a uniform answer to this question; mobile devices are much more mobile in practice than laptops, and more prone to loss. This is ultimately a risk question that management must address: What is the risk and what are the costs of the options employed? This also raises a bigger question: Which devices should have encryption as a basic security protection mechanism? Is it by device type, or by user based on what data would be exposed to risk? Fortunately, MDM solutions exist to make the choices manageable.

> **Exam Tip:** Mobile device management (MDM) is a marketing term for a collective set of commonly employed protection elements associated with mobile devices.

Device Access Control

The principles of access control for mobile devices need to be managed just like access control from wired or wireless desktops and laptops. This will become more critical as storage in the cloud and Software as a Service (SaaS) become more prevalent. Emerging tablet/mobile device sharing intends to provide the user with a seamless data access experience across many devices. Data access capabilities will continue to evolve to meet this need. Rigorous data access principles need to be applied, and they become even more important with the inclusion of mobile devices as fully functional computing devices. When reviewing possible solutions, it is important to consider seeking proof of security and procedures rather than relying on marketing brochures.

Removable Storage

Because removable devices can move data outside of the corporate-controlled environment, their security needs must be addressed. Removable devices can bring unprotected or corrupted data into the corporate environment. All removable devices should be scanned by antivirus software upon connection to the corporate environment. Corporate policies should address the copying of data to removable devices. Many mobile devices can be connected via USB to a system and used to store data—and in some cases vast quantities of data. This capability can be used to avoid some implementations of data loss prevention mechanisms.

Disabling Unused Features

As with all computing devices, features that are not used or that present a security risk should be disabled. Bluetooth access is particularly problematic. It is best to make Bluetooth connections undiscoverable. But, users will need to enable it to pair with a new headset or car connection, for example. Requiring Bluetooth connections to be undiscoverable is very hard to enforce but should be encouraged as a best practice. Users should receive training as to the risks of Bluetooth—not so they avoid Bluetooth, but so they understand when they should turn it off. Having a mobile device with access to sensitive information carries with it a level of responsibility. Helping users understand this and act accordingly can go a long way toward securing mobile devices.

BYOD Concerns

Permitting employees to "bring your own device" (BYOD) has many advantages in business, and not just from the perspective of device cost. Users tend to prefer having a single device rather than carrying multiple devices. Users have less of a learning curve on devices they already have an interest in learning.

Data Ownership

BYOD blurs the lines of data ownership because it blurs the lines of device management. If a company owns a smartphone issued to an employee, the company can repossess the phone upon employee termination. This practice may protect company data by keeping the company-issued devices in the hands of employees only. However, a company cannot rely on a simple factory reset before reissuing a device, because factory resetting may not remove all the data on the device. If a device is reissued, it is possible that some of the previous owner's personal information, such as private contacts, still remains on the device. On the other hand, if the employee's device is a personal device that has been used for business purposes, upon termination of the employee, it is likely that some company data remains on the phone despite the company's best efforts to remove its data from the device. If that device is resold or recycled, the company's data may remain on the device and be passed on to the subsequent owner. Keeping business data in separate, MDM-managed containers is one method of dealing with this issue.

Storage Segmentation

On mobile devices, it can be very difficult to keep personal data separate from corporate data. Some companies have developed capabilities to create separate virtual containers to keep personal data separate from corporate data and applications. For devices that are used to handle highly sensitive corporate data, this form of protection is highly recommended.

Support Ownership

Support costs for mobile devices are an important consideration for corporations. Each device has its own implementation of various functions. While those functions typically are implemented against a specification, software implementations may not fully or properly implement the specification. This may result in increased support calls to your help desk or support organization. It is very difficult for a corporate help desk to be knowledgeable on all aspects of all possible devices that access a corporate network. For example, your support organization must be able to troubleshoot iPhones, Android devices, tablets, and so forth. These devices are updated frequently, new devices are released, and new capabilities are added on a regular basis. Your support organization will need viable knowledge base articles and job aids in order to provide sufficient support for the wide variety of ever-changing devices.

Patch Management

Just as your corporate policy should enforce the prompt update of desktop and laptop computers to help eliminate security vulnerabilities on those platforms, it should also require mobile devices to be kept current with respect to patches. Having the latest applications, operating system, and so on is an important best defense against viruses, malware, and other threats. It is important to recognize that "**jailbreaking**" or "rooting" your device may remove the manufacturer's security mechanisms and protection against malware and other threats. These devices may also no longer be able to update their applications or OS against known issues. Jailbreaking or rooting is also a method used to bypass security measures associated with the device manufacturer control, and in some locations, this can be illegal. Mobile devices that are jailbroken or rooted should not be trusted on your enterprise network or allowed to access sensitive data.

Antivirus Management

Just like desktop and laptop computers, smartphones, tablets, and other mobile devices need protection against viruses and malware. It is important that corporate policy and personal usage keep operating systems and applications current. Antivirus and malware protection should be employed as widely as possible and kept up-to-date against current threats.

Forensics

Mobile device forensics is a rapidly evolving and fast-changing field. Because devices are evolving so quickly and changing so fast, it is difficult to stay

Tech Tip

BYOD Concerns

There is a dilemma in the use of BYOD devices that store both personal and enterprise data. Wiping the device usually removes all data, both personal and enterprise. Therefore, if corporate policy requires wiping a lost device, that policy may mean the device's user loses personal photos and data. The software controls for separate data containers, one for business and one for personal, have been proposed but are not a mainstream option yet.

current in this field. Solid forensics principles should always be followed. Devices should be properly handled by using RF-shielded bags or containers. Because of the rapid changes in this area, it's best to engage the help of trained forensic specialists to ensure data isn't contaminated and the device state and memory are unaltered. If forensics are needed on a device that has both personal and business data, then policies need to be in place to cover the appropriate privacy protections on the personal side of the device.

Privacy

When an employee uses his personal device to perform his work for the company, he may have strong expectations that privacy will be protected by the company. The company policy needs to consider this and address it explicitly. On company-owned devices, it's quite acceptable for the company to reserve the right to access and wipe any company data on the device. The company can thus state that the user can have no expectation of privacy when using a company device. But when the device is a personal device, the user may feel stronger ownership. Expectations of privacy and data access on personal devices should be included in your company policy.

On-board Camera/Video

Many mobile devices include on-board cameras, and the photos/videos they take can divulge information. This information can be associated with anything the camera can image—whiteboards, documents, even the location of the device when the photo/video was taken via geo-tagging. Another challenge presented by mobile devices is the possibility that they will be used for illegal purposes. This can create liability for the company if it is a company-owned device. Despite all the potential legal concerns, possibly the greatest concern of mobile device users is that their personal photos will be lost during a device wipe originated by the company.

On-boarding/Off-boarding

Most companies and individuals find it relatively easy to connect mobile devices to the corporate network. Often there are not controls around connecting a device other than having a Microsoft Exchange account. When new employees join a company, the on-boarding processes need to include provisions for mobile device responsibilities. It is easy for new employees to bypass security measures if they are not part of the business process of on-boarding.

Employee termination needs to be modified to include termination of accounts on mobile devices. It's not uncommon to find terminated employees with accounts or even company devices still connecting to the corporate network months after being terminated. E-mail accounts should be removed promptly as part of the employee termination policy and process. Mobile devices supplied by the company should be collected upon termination. BYOD equipment should have its access to corporate resources terminated as part of the off-boarding process. Regular audits for old or unterminated accounts should be performed to ensure prompt deletion of accounts for terminated employees.

Adherence to Corporate Policies

Your corporate policies regarding BYOD devices should be consistent with your existing computer security policies. Your training programs should include instruction on mobile device security. Disciplinary actions should be consistent. Your monitoring programs should be enhanced to include monitoring and control of mobile devices.

User Acceptance

BYOD inherently creates a conflict between personal and corporate interests. An employee who uses her own device to conduct corporate business inherently feels strong ownership over the device and may resent corporate demands to control corporate information downloaded to the device. On the other hand, the corporation expects that corporate data be properly controlled and protected and thus desires to impose remote wiping or lockout requirements in order to protect corporate data. An individual who loses her personal photos from a special event will likely harbor ill feelings toward the corporation if it wipes her device, including those irreplaceable photos. Your corporate BYOD policy needs to be well defined, approved by the corporate legal department, and clearly communicated to all employees through training.

Architecture/Infrastructure Considerations

Mobile devices consume connections to your corporate IT infrastructure. It is not unusual now for a single individual to be connected to the corporate infrastructure with one or more smartphones, tablets, and laptop or desktop computers. Some infrastructure implementations in the past have not been efficient in their design, sometimes consuming multiple connections for a single device. This can reduce the number of available connections for other end users. It is recommended that load testing be performed to ensure that your design or existing infrastructure can support the potentially large number of connections from multiple devices.

Multiple connections can also create security issues when the system tracks user accounts against multiple connections. Users will need to be aware of this, so that they don't inadvertently create incident response situations or find themselves locked out by their own actions. This can be a tricky issue requiring a bit more intelligent design than the traditional philosophy of one userid equals one current connection.

Legal Concerns

It should be apparent from the various topics discussed in this chapter that there are many security challenges presented by mobile devices used for corporate business. Because the technology is rapidly changing, it's best to make sure you have solid legal review of policies. There are both legal and public relation concerns when it comes to mobile devices. Employees who use both company-owned and personal devices have responsibilities when company data is involved. Policies and procedures should be reviewed on a regular basis to stay current with technology.

Another challenge presented by mobile devices is the possibility that they will be used for illegal purposes. This can create liability for the company if it is a company-owned device.

Acceptable Use Policy

Similar to your acceptable use policies for laptops and desktops, your mobile device policies should address acceptable use of mobile or BYOD devices. Authorized usage of corporate devices for personal purposes should be addressed. Disciplinary actions for violation of mobile device policies should be defined. BYOD offers both the company and the user advantages; ramifications should be specifically spelled out, along with the specific user responsibilities.

Location Services

Mobile devices by their specific nature can move, and hence location of the device can have significant ramifications with respect to its use. Mobile devices can connect to multiple public Wi-Fi locations, and they can provide users with navigation and other location context-sensitive information, such as a local sale. To enable this functionality, location services are a set of functions to enable, yet control, the location information possessed by the device.

Geo-Tagging

Geo-tagging is the posting of location information into a data stream signifying where the device was when the stream was created. As many mobile devices include on-board cameras, and the photos/videos they take can divulge information, geo-tagging can make location part of any picture or video. This information can be associated with anything the camera can image—whiteboards, documents, even the location of the device when the photo/video was taken via **geo-tagging**.

Posting photos with geo-tags embedded in them has its use, but it can also unexpectedly publish information that users may not want to share. For example, if you use your smartphone to take a photo of your car in the driveway and then post the photo on the Internet in an attempt to sell your car, if geo-tagging was enabled on the smartphone, the location of where the photo was taken is embedded as metadata in the digital photo. Such a posting could inadvertently expose where your home is located. Some social media applications strip out the metadata on a photo before posting, but then they post where you posted it from in the posting itself. There has been much public discussion on this topic, and geo-tagging can be disabled on most mobile devices. It is recommended that it be disabled unless you have a specific reason for having the location information embedded in the photo.

Mobile Application Security

Devices are not the only concern in the mobile world. Applications that run on the devices also represent security threats to the information that is stored on and processed by the device. Applications are the software elements that can be used to violate security, even when the user is not aware. Many games and utilities offer value to the user, but at the same time they scrape information stores on the device for information.

Application Control

Most mobile device vendors provide some kind of app store for finding and purchasing apps for their mobile devices. The vendors do a reasonable job of making sure that offered apps are approved and don't create an overt security risk. Yet many apps request access to various information stores on the mobile device as part of their business model. Understanding what access is requested and approved upon installation of apps is an important security precaution. Your company may have to restrict the types of apps that can be downloaded and used on mobile devices. If you need very strong protection, your company can be very proactive and provide an enterprise app store where only company-approved apps are available, with a corresponding policy that apps cannot be obtained from any other source.

Key and Credential Management

The MDM marketplace is maturing quickly. Key and credential management services are being integrated into most MDM services to ensure that existing strong policies and procedures can be extended to mobile platforms securely. These services include protection of keys for digital signatures and S/MIME encryption and decryption. Keys and credentials are among the highest-value items that can be found on mobile devices, so ensuring protection for them is a key element in mobile device security. The keys and credentials stored on the device can be used by multiple applications. Providing protection of these keys while still maintaining usability of them is an essential element of modern mobile application security.

Authentication

When mobile devices are used to access business networks, authentication becomes an issue. There are several levels of authentication that can be an issue. Is the device allowed to access the network? Is the user of the device a network user? If so, how do you authenticate the user? Mobile devices have some advantages in that they can store certificates, which by their very nature are more secure than passwords. This moves the authentication problem to the endpoint, where it relies on passcodes, screen-locks, and other mobile device protections. These can be relatively weak unless structured together, including wiping after a limited number of failures. The risk in mobile authentication is that strong credentials stored in the device are protected by the less rigorous passcode and the end user. End users can share their mobile devices, and by proxy unwittingly share their strong corporate authentication codes.

Application Whitelisting

As discussed in the "Application Control" section earlier in the chapter, controlling what applications a device can access may be an important element of your company's mobile device policy. Application whitelisting and blacklisting enables you to control and block applications available on the mobile device. This is usually administered through some type of MDM capability. Application whitelisting can improve security by preventing unapproved applications from being installed and run on the device.

Encryption

Just as the device should be encrypted, thereby protecting all information on the device, applications should be encrypted as well. Just employing encryption for the data store is not sufficient. If the device is fully encrypted, then all apps would have to have access to the data, in essence bypassing the encryption from an app point of view. Apps with sensitive information should control access via their own set of protections. The only way to segregate data within the device is for apps to manage their own data stores through app-specific encryption. This will allow sensitive data to be protected from rogue applications that would leak data if uniform access was allowed.

Transitive Trust/Authentication

Security across multiple domains/platforms is provided through trust relationships. When trust relationships between domains or platforms exist, authentication for each domain trusts the authentication for all other trusted domains. Thus when an application is authenticated, its authentication is accepted by all other domains/platforms that trust the authenticating domain or platform. Trust relationships can be very complex in mobile devices, and often security aspects aren't properly implemented. Mobile devices tend to be used across numerous systems, including business, personal, public, and private. This greatly expands the risk profile and opportunity for transitive trust–based attacks. As with all other applications, mobile applications should be carefully reviewed to ensure that trust relationships are secure.

Chapter Summary

After reading this chapter and completing the exercises, you should understand the following about wireless security and mobile devices.

Describe the different wireless systems in use today

- Wireless Application Protocol (WAP) is used on small, handheld devices like cell phones for out-of-the-office connectivity.

- 802.11 is the IEEE standard for wireless local area networks. The standard includes several different specifications of 802.11 networks, such as 802.11b, 802.11a, 802.11g, and 802.11n.

Detail WAP and its security implications

- WAP is the data protocol used by many cellular phones to deliver e-mail and lightweight web services.

- Designers created WTLS as a method to ensure privacy of data being broadcast over WAP.

- WTLS has a number of inherent security problems, such as weak encryption necessitated by the low computing power of the devices and the network transition that must occur at the cellular provider's network, or the WAP gap.

Identify 802.11's security issues and possible solutions

- 802.11 does not allow physical control of the transport mechanism.

- Transmission of all network data wirelessly transmits frames to all wireless machines, not just a single client, similar to Ethernet hub devices.

- Poor authentication is caused by the SSID being broadcast to anyone listening.

- Flawed implementation of the RC4 encryption algorithm makes even encrypted traffic subject to interception and decryption.

Examine the elements needed for enterprise wireless deployment

- Wireless coverage can be a function of antenna type, placement, and power levels.

- Captive portals can be used to control access to wireless systems.

Examine the security of mobile systems

- Mobile devices have specific security concerns and specific controls to assist in securing them.

- BYOD has its own concerns and policies and procedures to manage mobile devices in the enterprise.

- Mobile applications require security, and the issues associated with mobile, apps, and security need to be addressed.

Key Terms

2.4 GHz band (344)
5 GHz band (348)
beacon frames (349)
bluebugging (346)
bluejacking (345)
bluesnarfing (346)
Bluetooth DOS (346)
captive portal (362)
confidentiality (340)
direct-sequence spread spectrum (DSSS) (348)
evil twin (352)
geo-tagging (370)
IEEE 802.1X (357)
IEEE 802.11 (337)
initialization vector (IV) (340)

jailbreaking (367)
MAC filtering (359)
MIMO (361)
mobile device management (MDM) (365)
near field communication (NFC) (347)
orthogonal frequency division multiplexing (OFDM) (348)
RC4 stream cipher (350)
remote wiping (363)
rogue access point (352)
screen locking (363)
service set identifier (SSID) (349)
site survey (361)
Temporal Key Integrity Protocol (TKIP) (355)
WAP gap (341)
Wi-Fi Protected Access 2 (WPA2) (355)

■ Key Terms Quiz

Use terms from the Key Terms list to complete the sentences that follow. Don't use the same term more than once. Not all terms will be used.

1. An AP uses _____ to advertise its existence to potential wireless clients.

2. The _____ is the part of the RC4 cipher that has a weak implementation in WEP.

3. Two common mobile device security measures are _____ and _____.

4. WAP uses the _____ protocol to attempt to ensure confidentiality of data.

5. The 32-character identifier attached to the header of a packet used for authentication to an 802.11 access point is the _____.

6. _____ is a feature that can disclose a user's position when sharing photos.

7. 802.11i updates the flawed security deployed in _____.

8. The standard for wireless local area networks is called _____.

9. The type of application used to control security across multiple mobile devices in an enterprise is called _____.

10. 802.11a uses frequencies in the _____.

■ Multiple-Choice Quiz

1. Bluebugging can give an attacker what?
   A. All of your contacts
   B. The ability to send "shock" photos
   C. Total control over a mobile phone
   D. A virus

2. How does 802.11n improve network speed?
   A. Wider bandwidth
   B. Higher frequency
   C. Multiple-input multiple-output (MIMO)
   D. Both A and C

3. WTLS ensures integrity through what device?
   A. Public key encryption
   B. Message authentication codes
   C. Source IP
   D. Digital signatures

4. WEP has used an implementation of which of the following encryption algorithms?
   A. SHA
   B. ElGamal
   C. RC4
   D. Triple-DES

5. What element does not belong in a mobile device security policy in an enterprise employing BYOD?
   A. Separation of personal and business-related information
   B. Remote wiping
   C. Passwords and screen-locking
   D. Mobile device carrier selection

6. What is bluejacking?
   A. Stealing a person's mobile phone
   B. Sending an unsolicited message via Bluetooth
   C. Breaking a WEP key
   D. Leaving your Bluetooth in discoverable mode

7. While the SSID provides some measure of authentication, why is it not very effective?
   A. It is dictated by the manufacturer of the access point.
   B. It is encrypted.
   C. It is broadcast in every beacon frame.
   D. SSID is not an authentication function.

8. The 802.1X protocol is a protocol for Ethernet:
   A. Authentication
   B. Speed

C. Wireless

D. Cabling

9. What is the best way to avoid problems with Bluetooth?

A. Keep personal info off your phone

B. Keep Bluetooth discoverability off

C. Buy a new phone often

D. Encryption

10. Why is attacking wireless networks so popular?

A. There are more wireless networks than wired.

B. They all run Windows.

C. It's easy.

D. It's more difficult and more prestigious than other network attacks.

▪ Essay Quiz

1. Produce a report on why sensitive information should not be sent over the Wireless Application Protocol.

2. When you want to start scanning for rogue wireless networks, your supervisor asks you to write a memo detailing the threats of rogue wireless access points. What information would you include in the memo?

3. Write a security policy for company-owned cell phones that use the Bluetooth protocol.

4. Write a memo recommending upgrading your organization's old 802.11b infrastructure to an 802.11i-compliant network, and detail the security enhancements.

Lab Projects

• Lab Project 12.1

Set up NetStumbler or Kismet on a computer, and then use it to find wireless access points. You will need the following:

- A laptop with Windows or Linux installed
- A compatible wireless 802.11 network adapter

Then do the following:

1. Download NetStumbler from www .netstumbler.com or Kismet from www .kismetwireless.net.

2. For NetStumbler, run the Windows Installer. For Kismet, untar the source file and then execute, in order, **./configure**, **make**, and **make install**.

3. Start the program and make sure that it sees your wireless adapter.

4. Take the laptop on your normal commute (or drive around your neighborhood) with NetStumbler/Kismet running.

5. Log any access points you detect.

• Lab Project 12.2

Attempt to scan the area for Bluetooth devices. You will need a cell phone with Bluetooth installed or a computer with a Bluetooth adapter. Then do the following:

1. If you're using a PC, download BlueScanner from SourceForge at http://sourceforge.net/ projects/bluescanner/.

2. Take your phone or computer to a place with many people, such as a café.

3. Start the program and make sure that it sees your Bluetooth adapter.

4. Attempt to scan for vulnerable Bluetooth devices.

5. If you're using your phone, tell it to scan for Bluetooth devices. Any devices that you find are running in "discoverable" mode and are potentially exploitable.

chapter 13

Intrusion Detection Systems and Network Security

One person's "paranoia" is another person's "engineering redundancy."

—MARCUS J. RANUM

In this chapter, you will learn how to

- Apply the appropriate network tools to facilitate network security
- Determine the appropriate use of tools to facilitate network security
- Apply host-based security applications

An **intrusion detection system (IDS)** is a security system that detects inappropriate or malicious activity on a computer or network. Most organizations use their own approaches to network security, choosing the layers that make sense for them after they weigh risks, potentials for loss, costs, and manpower requirements.

The foundation for a layered network security approach usually starts with a well-secured system, regardless of the system's function (whether it's a user PC or a corporate e-mail server). A well-secured system uses up-to-date application and operating system patches, requires well-chosen passwords, runs the minimum number of services necessary, and restricts access to available services. On top of that foundation, you can add layers of protective measures such as antivirus products, firewalls, sniffers, and IDSs.

Some of the more complicated and interesting types of network/data security devices are IDSs, which are to the network world what burglar alarms are to the physical world. The main purpose of an IDS is to identify suspicious or malicious activity, note activity that deviates from normal behavior, catalog and classify the activity, and, if possible, respond to the activity.

History of Intrusion Detection Systems

Like much of the network technology we see today, IDSs grew from a need to solve specific problems. Like the Internet itself, the IDS concept came from U.S. Department of Defense–sponsored research. In the early 1970s, the U.S. government and military became increasingly aware of the need to protect the electronic networks that were becoming critical to daily operations.

> **Early History of IDS**
>
> In 1972, James Anderson published a paper for the U.S. Air Force outlining the growing number of computer security problems and the immediate need to secure Air Force systems (James P. Anderson, "Computer Security Technology Planning Study Volume 2," October 1972, http://seclab.cs.ucdavis.edu/projects/history/papers/ande72.pdf). Anderson continued his research and in 1980 published a follow-up paper outlining methods to improve security auditing and surveillance methods ("Computer Security Threat Monitoring and Surveillance," April 15, 1980, http://csrc.nist.gov/publications/history/ande80.pdf). In this paper, Anderson pioneered the concept of using system audit files to detect unauthorized access and misuse. He also suggested the use of automated detection systems, which paved the way for misuse detection on mainframe systems in use at the time.
>
> While Anderson's work got the efforts started, the concept of a real-time, rule-based IDS didn't really exist until Dorothy Denning and Peter Neumann developed the first real-time IDS model, called "The Intrusion Detection Expert System (IDES)," from their research between 1984 and 1986. In 1987, Denning published "An Intrusion-Detection Model," a paper that laid out the model on which most modern IDSs are based (and which appears in *IEEE Transactions on Software Engineering*, Vol. SE-13, No. 2 [February 1987]: 222–232).

The U.S. government continued to fund research that led to projects such as Discovery, Haystack, Multics Intrusion Detection and Alerting System (MIDAS), and Network Audit Director and Intrusion Reporter (NADIR). Finally, in 1989, Haystack Labs released Stalker, the first commercial IDS. Stalker was host-based and worked by comparing audit data to known patterns of suspicious activity. While the military and government embraced the concept, the commercial world was very slow to adopt IDS products, and it was several years before other commercial products began to emerge.

In the early to mid-1990s, as computer systems continued to grow, companies started to realize the importance of IDSs; however, the solutions available were host-based and required a great deal of time and money to manage and operate effectively. Focus began to shift away from host-based systems, and network-based IDSs began to emerge. In 1995, WheelGroup was formed in San Antonio, Texas, to develop the first commercial

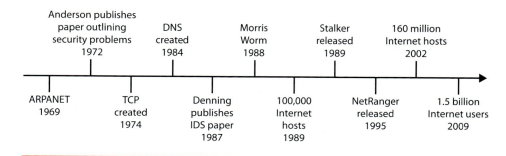

Figure 13.1 History of the Internet and IDS

network-based IDS product, called NetRanger. NetRanger was designed to monitor network links and the traffic moving across the links to identify misuse as well as suspicious and malicious activity. NetRanger's release was quickly followed by Internet Security Systems' RealSecure in 1996. Several other players followed suit and released their own IDS products, but it wasn't until the networking giant Cisco Systems acquired WheelGroup in February 1998 that IDSs were recognized as a vital part of any network security infrastructure. Figure 13.1 offers a timeline for these developments.

■ IDS Overview

Exam Tip: Know the differences between host-based and network-based IDSs. A host-based IDS runs on a specific system (server or workstation) and looks at all the activity on that host. A network-based IDS sniffs traffic from the network and sees only activity that occurs on the network.

As mentioned, an IDS is somewhat like a burglar alarm. It watches the activity going on around it and tries to identify undesirable activity. IDSs are typically divided into two main categories, depending on how they monitor activity:

- **Host-based IDS (HIDS)** Examines activity on an individual system, such as a mail server, web server, or individual PC. It is concerned only with an individual system and usually has no visibility into the activity on the network or systems around it.

- **Network-based IDS (NIDS)** Examines activity on the network itself. It has visibility only into the traffic crossing the network link it is monitoring and typically has no idea of what is happening on individual systems.

Whether it is network- or host-based, an IDS typically consists of several specialized components working together, as illustrated in Figure 13.2. These components are often logical and software-based rather than physical and will vary slightly from vendor to vendor and product to product. Typically, an IDS has the following logical components:

- **Traffic collector** (or sensor) Collects activity/events for the IDS to examine. On a HIDS, this could be log files, audit logs, or traffic coming to or leaving a specific system. On a NIDS, this is typically a mechanism for copying traffic off the network link—basically functioning as a sniffer. This component is often referred to as a sensor.

Figure 13.2 Logical depiction of IDS components

- **Analysis engine**   Examines the collected network traffic and compares it to known patterns of suspicious or malicious activity stored in the signature database. The analysis engine is the "brains" of the IDS.

- **Signature database**   A collection of patterns and definitions of known suspicious or malicious activity.

- **User interface and reporting**   Interfaces with the human element, providing alerts when appropriate and giving the user a means to interact with and operate the IDS.

Tech Tip

IDS Signatures
An IDS relies heavily on its signature database just like antivirus products rely on their virus definitions. If an attack is something completely new, an IDS may not recognize the traffic as malicious.

Let's look at an example to see how all these components work together. Imagine a network intruder is scanning your organization for systems running a web server. The intruder launches a series of network probes against every IP address in your organization. The traffic from the intruder comes into your network and passes through the traffic collector (sensor). The traffic collector forwards the traffic to the analysis engine. The analysis engine examines and categorizes the traffic—it identifies a large number of probes coming from the same outside IP address (the intruder). The analysis engine compares the observed behavior against the signature database and gets a match. The intruder's activity matches a TCP port scan. The intruder is sending probes to many different systems in a short period of time. The analysis engine generates an alarm that is passed off to the user interface and reporting mechanisms. The user interface generates a notification to the administrator (icon, log entry, and so on). The administrator sees the alert and can now decide what to do about the potentially malicious traffic. Alarm storage is simply a repository of alarms the IDS has recorded—most IDS products allow administrators to run customized reports that sift through the collected alarms for items the administrator is searching for, such as all the alarms generated by a specific IP address.

In addition to the network versus host distinction, some IDS vendors will further categorize an IDS based on how it performs the detection of suspicious or malicious traffic. The different models used are covered in the next section.

IDS Models

In addition to being divided along the host and network lines, IDSs are often classified according to the detection model they use: anomaly or misuse. For an IDS, a model is a method for examining behavior so that the IDS can determine whether that behavior is "not normal" or in violation of established policies.

An **anomaly detection model** is the more complicated of the two. In this model, the IDS must know what "normal" behavior on the host or network being protected really is. Once the "normal" behavior baseline is established, the IDS can then go to work identifying deviations from the norm, which are further scrutinized to determine whether or not that activity is malicious. Building the profile of normal activity is usually done by the IDS, with some input from security administrators, and can take days to months. The IDS must be flexible and capable enough to account for things such as new systems, new users, movement of information resources, and

Most IDSs can be tuned to fit a particular environment. Certain signatures can be turned off, telling the IDS not to look for certain types of traffic. For example, if you are operating in a pure UNIX environment, you may not wish to see Windows-based alarms, as they will not affect your systems. Additionally, the severity of the alarm levels can be adjusted depending on how concerned you are over certain types of traffic. Some IDSs also allow the user to exclude certain patterns of activity from specific hosts. In other words, you can tell the IDS to ignore the fact that some systems generate traffic that looks like malicious activity, because it really isn't.

other factors, but be sensitive enough to detect a single user illegally switching from one account to another at 3 A.M. on a Saturday.

Anomaly detection was developed to make the system capable of dealing with variations in traffic and better able to determine which activity patterns were malicious. A perfectly functioning anomaly-based system would be able to ignore patterns from legitimate hosts and users but still identify those patterns as suspicious should they come from a potential attacker. Unfortunately, most anomaly-based systems suffer from extremely high false positives, especially during the "break-in" period while the IDS is learning the network. On the other hand, an anomaly-based system is not restricted to a specific signature set and is far more likely to identify a new exploit or attack tool that would go unnoticed by a traditional IDS.

A **misuse detection model** is a little simpler to implement, and therefore it's the more popular of the two models. In a misuse detection model, the IDS looks for suspicious activity or activity that violates specific policies and then reacts as it has been programmed to do. This reaction can be an alarm, e-mail, router reconfiguration, or TCP reset message. Technically, misuse detection is the more efficient model, as it takes fewer resources to operate, does not need to learn what "normal" behavior is, and will generate an alarm whenever a pattern is successfully matched. However, the misuse model's greatest weakness is its reliance on a predefined signature base—any activity, malicious or otherwise, that the misuse-based IDS does not have a signature for will go undetected. Despite that drawback and because it is easier and cheaper to implement, most commercial IDS products are based on the misuse detection model.

Some analysts break IDS models down even further into four categories depending on how the IDS operates and detects malicious traffic (the same models can also be applied to intrusion prevention systems as well—both NIPS and HIPS):

- **Behavior-based** This model relies on a collected set of "normal behavior": what should happen on the network and is considered "normal" or "acceptable" traffic. Behavior that does not fit into the "normal" activity categories or patterns is considered suspicious or malicious. This model can potentially detect zero-day or unpublished attacks but carries a high false positive rate as any new traffic pattern can be labeled as "suspect."

- **Signature-based** This model relies on a predefined set of patterns (called *signatures*). The IDS has to know what behavior is considered "bad" ahead of time before it can identify and act upon suspicious or malicious traffic.

- **Anomaly-based** This model is essentially the same as behavior-based. The IDS is first taught what "normal" traffic looks like and then looks for deviations to those "normal" patterns.

- **Heuristic** This model uses artificial intelligence to detect intrusions and malicious traffic. A heuristic model is typically implemented through algorithms that help an IDS decide if a traffic pattern is malicious or not. For example, a URL containing 10 or more of the same repeating character may be considered "bad" traffic as a single signature. With a heuristic model, the IDS understands that if 10 repeating characters are bad, 11 are still bad, and 20 are even worse. This implementation of fuzzy logic allows this model to fall somewhere between signature-based and behavior-based models.

Signatures

As you have probably deduced from the discussion so far, one of the critical elements of any good IDS is the signature database—the set of patterns the IDS uses to determine whether or not activity is potentially hostile. Signatures can be very simple or remarkably complicated, depending on the activity they are trying to highlight. In general, signatures can be divided into two main groups, depending on what the signature is looking for: content-based and context-based.

Content-based signatures are generally the simplest. They are designed to examine the content of such things as network packets or log entries. Content-based signatures are typically easy to build and look for simple things, such as a certain string of characters or a certain flag set in a TCP packet. Here are some example content-based signatures:

- *Matching the characters /etc/passwd in a Telnet session.* On a UNIX system, the names of valid user accounts (and sometimes the passwords for those user accounts) are stored in a file called *passwd* located in the *etc* directory.

- *Matching the characters "to: decode" in the header of an e-mail message.* On certain older versions of sendmail, sending an e-mail message to "decode" would cause the system to execute the contents of the e-mail.

Context-based signatures are generally more complicated, as they are designed to match large patterns of activity and examine how certain types of activity fit into the other activities going on around them. Context signatures generally address the question: How does this event compare to other events that have already happened or might happen in the near future? Context-based signatures are more difficult to analyze and take more resources to match, as the IDS must be able to "remember" past events to match certain context signatures. Here are some example context-based signatures:

- *Match a potential intruder scanning for open web servers on a specific network.* A potential intruder may use a port scanner to look for any systems accepting connections on port 80. To match this signature, the IDS must analyze all attempted connections to port 80 and then be able to determine which connection attempts are coming from the same source but are going to multiple, different destinations.

- *Identify a Nessus scan.* Nessus is an open-source vulnerability scanner that allows security administrators (and potential attackers) to quickly examine systems for vulnerabilities. Depending on the tests chosen, Nessus typically performs the tests in a certain order, one after the other. To be able to determine the presence of a Nessus scan, the IDS must know which tests Nessus runs as well as the typical order in which the tests are run.

- *Identify a ping flood attack.* A single ICMP packet on its own is generally regarded as harmless, certainly not worthy of an IDS signature. Yet thousands of ICMP packets coming to a single system in a short period of time can have a devastating effect on the receiving system. By flooding a system with thousands of valid ICMP packets, an attacker can keep a target system so busy it doesn't have time to do anything else—a very effective denial-of-service attack. To identify a ping flood, the IDS must recognize each ICMP packet and keep track of how many ICMP packets different systems have received in the recent past.

To function, the IDS must have a decent signature base with examples of known, undesirable activity that it can use when analyzing traffic or events. Any time an IDS matches current events against a signature, the IDS could be considered successful, as it has correctly matched the current event against a known signature and reacted accordingly (usually with an alarm or alert of some type).

False Positives and False Negatives

Viewed in its simplest form, an IDS is really just looking at activity (be it host-based or network-based) and matching it against a predefined set of patterns. When it matches activity to a specific pattern, the IDS cannot know the true intent behind that activity—whether it is benign or hostile—and therefore it can react only as it has been programmed to do. In most cases, this means generating an alert that must then be analyzed by a human who tries to determine the intent of the traffic from whatever information is available. When an IDS matches a pattern and generates an alarm for benign traffic, meaning the traffic was not hostile and not a threat, this is called a **false positive**. In other words, the IDS matched a pattern and raised an alarm when it didn't really need to do so. Keep in mind that the IDS can only match patterns and has no ability to determine intent behind the activity, so in some ways this is an unfair label. Technically, the IDS is functioning correctly by matching the pattern, but from a human standpoint this is not information the analyst needed to see, as it does not constitute a threat and does not require intervention.

An IDS is also limited by its signature set—it can match only activity for which it has stored patterns. Hostile activity that does not match an IDS signature and therefore goes undetected is called a **false negative**. In this case, the IDS is not generating any alarms, even though it should be, giving a false sense of security.

■ Network-Based IDSs

Network-based IDSs (NIDSs) actually came along a few years after host-based systems. After running host-based systems for a while, many organizations grew tired of the time, energy, and expense involved with managing the first generation of these systems—the host-based systems were not centrally managed, there was no easy way to correlate alerts between systems, and false-positive rates were high. The desire for a "better way" grew along with the amount of interconnectivity between systems and, consequently, the amount of malicious activity coming across the networks themselves. This fueled development of a new breed of IDS designed to focus on the source for a great deal of the malicious traffic—the network itself.

The NIDS integrated very well into the concept of **perimeter security**. More and more companies began to operate their computer security like a castle or military base (see Figure 13.3), with attention and effort focused on securing and controlling the ways in and out—the idea being that if you could restrict and control access at the perimeter, you didn't have to worry as much about activity inside the organization. Even though the idea of a security perimeter is somewhat flawed (many security incidents originate inside the perimeter), it caught on very quickly, as it was easy to understand and devices such as firewalls, bastion hosts, and routers were available to define and secure that perimeter. The best way to secure the perimeter from outside attack is to reject all traffic from external entities, but this is impossible and impractical to do, so security personnel needed a way to let traffic in but still be able to determine whether or not the traffic was malicious. This is the problem that NIDS developers were trying to solve.

As its name suggests, a NIDS focuses on network traffic—the bits and bytes traveling along the cables and wires that interconnect the systems. A NIDS must examine the network traffic as it passes by and be able to analyze traffic according to protocol, type, amount, source, destination, content, traffic already seen, and other factors. This analysis must happen quickly, and the NIDS must be able to handle traffic at whatever speed the network operates to be effective.

NIDSs are typically deployed so that they can monitor traffic in and out of an organization's major links: connections to the Internet, remote offices, partners, and so on. Like host-based systems, NIDSs look for certain activities that typify hostile actions or misuse, such as the following:

- Denial-of-service attacks
- Port scans or sweeps
- Malicious content in the data payload of a packet or packets
- Vulnerability scanning
- Trojans, viruses, or worms
- Tunneling
- Brute-force attacks

In general, most NIDSs operate in a fairly similar fashion. Figure 13.4 shows the logical layout of a NIDS. By considering the function and activity of each component, you can gain some insight into how a NIDS operates.

In the simplest form, a NIDS has the same major components: traffic collector, analysis engine, reports, and a user interface.

In a NIDS, the *traffic collector* is specifically designed to pull traffic from the network. This component usually behaves in much the same way as a network traffic sniffer—it simply pulls every packet it can see off the network to which it is connected. In a NIDS, the traffic collector will logically attach itself to a network interface card (NIC) and instruct the NIC to accept

Tech Tip

Network Visibility

A network IDS has to be able to see traffic to find the malicious traffic. Encrypted traffic such as SSH or HTTPS sessions must be decrypted before a network IDS can examine them.

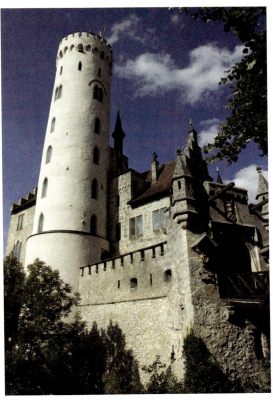

• **Figure 13.3**   Network perimeters are a little like castles—firewalls and NIDSs form the gates and guards to keep malicious traffic out.

• **Figure 13.4** Network IDS components

every packet it can. A NIC that accepts and processes every packet regardless of the packet's origin and destination is said to be in *promiscuous mode*.

The *analysis engine* in a NIDS serves the same function as its host-based counterpart, with some substantial differences. The network analysis engine must be able to collect packets and examine them individually or, if necessary, reassemble them into an entire traffic session. The patterns and signatures being matched are far more complicated than host-based signatures, so the analysis engine must be able to remember what traffic preceded the traffic currently being analyzed so that it can determine whether or not that traffic fits into a larger pattern of malicious activity. Additionally, the network-based analysis engine must be able to keep up with the flow of traffic on the network, rebuilding network sessions and matching patterns in real time.

☑ Cross Check

NIDS and Encrypted Traffic

You learned about encrypted traffic in Chapter 5, so check your memory with these questions. What is SSH? What is a one-time pad? Can you name at least three different algorithms?

The NIDS *signature database* is usually much larger than that of a host-based system. When examining network patterns, the NIDS must be able to recognize traffic targeted at many different applications and operating systems as well as traffic from a wide variety of threats (worms, assessment tools, attack tools, and so on). Some of the signatures themselves can be quite large, as the NIDS must look at network traffic occurring in a specific order over a period of time to match a particular malicious pattern.

Using the lessons learned from early host-based systems, NIDS developers modified the logical component design somewhat to distribute the user interface and reporting functions. As many companies had more than one network link, they would need an IDS capable of handling multiple links in many different locations. The early IDS vendors solved this dilemma by dividing the components and assigning them to separate entities. The traffic collector, analysis engine, and signature database were bundled into a single entity, usually called a *sensor* or *appliance.* The sensors would report to and be controlled by a central system or master console. This central system, shown in Figure 13.5, consolidated alarms and provided the user interface and reporting functions that allowed users in one location to manage, maintain, and monitor sensors deployed in a variety of remote locations.

By creating separate components designed to work together, the NIDS developers were able to build a more capable and flexible system. With encrypted communications, network sensors could be placed around both local and remote perimeters and still be monitored and managed securely from a central location. Placement of the sensors very quickly became an issue for most security personnel, as the sensors obviously had to have visibility of the network traffic in order to analyze it. Because most organizations with NIDSs also had firewalls, location of the NIDS relative to

• **Figure 13.5**   Distributed network IDS components

the firewall had to be considered as well. Placed before the firewall, as shown in Figure 13.6, the NIDS will see all traffic coming in from the Internet, including attacks against the firewall itself. This includes traffic that the firewall stops and does not permit into the corporate network. With this type of deployment, the NIDS sensor will generate a large number of alarms (including alarms for traffic that the firewall would stop). This tends to overwhelm the human operators managing the system.

Placed after the firewall, as shown in Figure 13.7, the NIDS sensor sees and analyzes the traffic that is being passed through the firewall and into the corporate network. While this does not allow the NIDS to see attacks against the firewall, it generally results in far fewer alarms and is the most popular placement for NIDS sensors.

• **Figure 13.6**   NIDS sensor placed in front of firewall

• **Figure 13.7**   NIDS sensor placed behind firewall

As you already know, NIDSs examine the network traffic for suspicious or malicious activity. Here are two examples of suspicious traffic to illustrate the operation of a NIDS:

- **Port scan** A port scan is a reconnaissance activity a potential attacker uses to find out information about the systems he wants to attack. Using any of a number of tools, the attacker attempts to connect to various services (web, FTP, SMTP, and so on) to see if they exist on the intended target. In normal network traffic, a single user might connect to the FTP service provided on a single system. During a port scan, an attacker may attempt to connect to the FTP service on every system. As the attacker's traffic passes by the IDS, the IDS will notice this pattern of attempting to connect to different services on different systems in a relatively short period of time. When the IDS compares the activity to its signature database, it will very likely match this traffic against the port scanning signature and generate an alarm.

- **Ping of death** Toward the end of 1996, it was discovered that certain operating systems, such as Windows, could be crashed by sending a very large Internet Control Message Protocol (ICMP) echo request packet to that system. This is a fairly simple traffic pattern for a NIDS to identify, as it simply has to look for ICMP packets over a certain size.

Port scanning activity is rampant on the Internet. Most organizations with NIDS see hundreds or thousands of port scan alarms every day from sources around the world. Some administrators reduce the alarm level of port scan alarms or ignore port scanning traffic because there is simply too much traffic to track down and respond to each alarm.

Advantages of a NIDS

A NIDS has certain advantages that make it a good choice for certain situations:

- *Providing IDS coverage requires fewer systems.* With a few well-placed NIDS sensors, you can monitor all the network traffic going in and out of your organization. Fewer sensors usually equates to less overhead and maintenance, meaning you can protect the same number of systems at a lower cost.

- *Deployment, maintenance, and upgrade costs are usually lower.* The fewer systems that have to be managed and maintained to provide IDS coverage, the lower the cost to operate the IDS. Upgrading and maintaining a few sensors is usually much cheaper than upgrading and maintaining hundreds of host-based processes.

- *A NIDS has visibility into all network traffic and can correlate attacks among multiple systems.* Well-placed NIDS sensors can see the "big picture" when it comes to network-based attacks. The network sensors can tell you whether attacks are widespread and unorganized or focused and concentrated on specific systems.

Disadvantages of a NIDS

A NIDS has certain disadvantages:

- *It is ineffective when traffic is encrypted.* When network traffic is encrypted from application to application or system to system, a NIDS sensor will not be able to examine that traffic. With the increasing popularity of encrypted traffic, this is becoming a bigger problem for effective IDS operations.

■ *It can't see traffic that does not cross it.* The IDS sensor can examine only traffic crossing the network link it is monitoring. With most IDS sensors being placed on perimeter links, traffic traversing the internal network is never seen.

■ *It must be able to handle high volumes of traffic.* As network speeds continue to increase, the network sensors must be able to keep pace and examine the traffic as quickly as it can pass the network. When NIDSs were introduced, 10-Mbps networks were the norm. Now 100-Mbps and even 1-Gbps networks are commonplace. This increase in traffic speeds means IDS sensors must be faster and more powerful than ever before.

■ *It doesn't know about activity on the hosts themselves.* NIDSs focus on network traffic. Activity that occurs on the hosts themselves will not be seen by a NIDS.

Active vs. Passive NIDSs

Most NIDSs can be distinguished by how they examine the traffic and whether or not they interact with that traffic. On a *passive* system, the NIDS simply watches the traffic, analyzes it, and generates alarms. It does not interact with the traffic itself in any way, and it does not modify the defensive posture of the system to react to the traffic. A passive NIDS is very similar to a simple motion sensor—it generates an alarm when it matches a pattern, much as the motion sensor generates an alarm when it sees movement. An *active* NIDS contains all the same components and capabilities of the passive NIDS with one critical addition—the active NIDS can *react* to the traffic it is analyzing. These reactions can range from something simple, such as sending a TCP reset message to interrupt a potential attack and disconnect a session, to something complex, such as dynamically modifying firewall rules to reject all traffic from specific source IP addresses for the next 24 hours.

NIDS Tools

There are numerous examples of NIDS tools in the marketplace, from open source projects to commercial entries. **Snort** has been the de facto standard IDS engine since its creation in 1998. It has a large user base and set the standard for many IDS element, including rule sets and formats. Snort rules are the list of activities that Snort will alert on and provide the flexible power behind the IDS platform. Snort rule sets are updated by a large active community as well as Sourcefire Vulnerability Research Team, the company behind Snort. Snort VRT rule sets are available to subscribers and provide such elements as same-day protection for items such as Microsoft patch Tuesday vulnerabilities. These rules are moved to the open community after 30 days.

A newer entrant to the IDS marketplace is **Suricata**. Suricata is an open source IDS, begun with grant money from the U.S. government and maintained by the Open Source Security Foundation (OSIF). Suricata has one

Tech Tip

TCP Reset

The most common defensive ability for an active NIDS is to send a TCP reset message. Within TCP, the reset message (RST) essentially tells both sides of the connection to drop the session and stop communicating immediately. While this mechanism was originally developed to cover situations such as systems accidentally receiving communications intended for other systems, the reset message works fairly well for NIDSs—with one serious drawback: a reset message affects only the current session. Nothing prevents the attacker from coming back and trying again and again. Despite the "temporariness" of this solution, sending a reset message is usually the only defensive measure implemented on NIDS deployments, as the fear of blocking legitimate traffic and disrupting business processes, even for a few moments, often outweighs the perceived benefit of discouraging potential intruders.

advantage over Snort: it supports multithreading, while Snort only supports single-threaded operation. Both of these systems are highly flexible and scalable, operating on both Windows and Linux platforms.

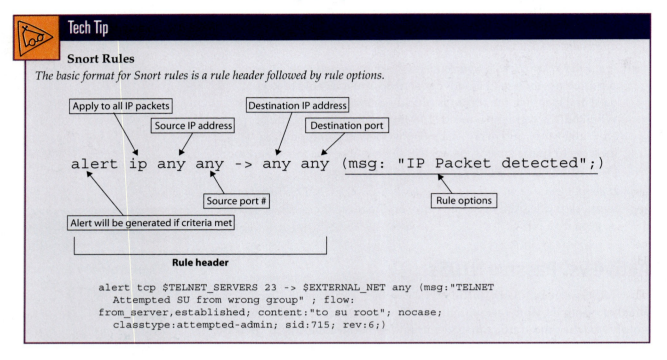

Host-Based IDSs

The very first IDSs were host-based and designed to examine activity only on a specific host. A host-based IDS (HIDS) examines log files, audit trails, and network traffic coming into or leaving a specific host. HIDSs can operate in *real time,* looking for activity as it occurs, or in *batch mode,* looking for activity on a periodic basis. Host-based systems are typically self-contained, but many of the newer commercial products have been designed to report to and be managed by a central system. Host-based systems also take local system resources to operate. In other words, a HIDS will use up some of the memory and CPU cycles of the system it is protecting. Early versions of HIDSs ran in batch mode, looking for suspicious activity on an hourly or daily basis, and typically looked only for specific events in the system's log files. As processor speeds increased, later versions of HIDSs looked through the log files in real time and even added the ability to examine the data traffic the host was generating and receiving.

Most HIDSs focus on the log files or audit trails generated by the local operating system. On UNIX systems, the examined logs usually include those created by syslog, such as messages, kernel logs, and error logs. On Windows systems, the examined logs are typically the three event logs: Application, System, and Security. Some HIDSs can cover specific applications, such as FTP or web services, by examining the logs produced by those specific applications or examining the traffic from the services themselves.

Within the log files, the HIDS is looking for certain activities that typify hostile actions or misuse, such as the following:

- Logins at odd hours
- Login authentication failures
- Additions of new user accounts
- Modification or access of critical system files
- Modification or removal of binary files (executables)
- Starting or stopping processes
- Privilege escalation
- Use of certain programs

In general, most HIDSs operate in a very similar fashion. (Figure 13.8 shows the logical layout of a HIDS.) By considering the function and activity of each component, you can gain some insight into how HIDSs operate.

As on any IDS, the *traffic collector* on a HIDS pulls in the information the other components, such as the analysis engine, need to examine. For most HIDSs, the traffic collector pulls data from information the local system has already generated, such as error messages, log files, and system files. The traffic collector is responsible for reading those files, selecting which items are of interest, and forwarding them to the analysis engine. On some HIDSs, the traffic collector also examines specific attributes of critical files, such as file size, date modified, or checksum.

The *analysis engine* is perhaps the most important component of the HIDS, as it must decide what activity is "okay" and what activity is "bad." The analysis engine is a sophisticated decision and pattern-matching mechanism—it looks at the information provided by the traffic collector and tries to match it against known patterns of activity stored in the signature database. If the activity matches a known pattern, the analysis engine can react, usually by issuing an alert or alarm. An analysis engine may also be capable of remembering how the activity it is looking at right now compares to traffic it has already seen or may see in the near future, so that it can match more complicated, multistep malicious activity patterns. An analysis engine must also be capable of examining traffic patterns as quickly as possible, as the longer it takes to match a malicious pattern, the less time the HIDS or human operator has to react to malicious traffic. Most HIDS vendors build a decision tree into their analysis engines to expedite pattern matching.

The *signature database* is a collection of predefined activity patterns that have already been identified and categorized—patterns that typically indicate suspicious or malicious activity. When the analysis engine has an activity or traffic pattern to examine, it compares that pattern to the appropriate signatures in the database. The signature database can contain anywhere from a few to a few thousand signatures, depending on the vendor, type of HIDS, space available on the system to store signatures, and other factors.

The user interface is the visible component of the HIDS—the part that humans interact with. The user interface varies widely depending on the product and vendor and could be anything from a detailed GUI to a simple command line. Regardless of the type and complexity, the interface is provided to allow the user to interact with the system: changing parameters, receiving alarms, tuning signatures and response patterns, and so on.

• **Figure 13.8** Host-based IDS components

 Critical files are those that are vital to the system's operation or overall functionality. They may be program (or binary) files, files containing user accounts and passwords, or even scripts to start or stop system processes. Any unexpected modifications to these files could mean the system has been compromised or modified by an attacker. By monitoring these files, the HIDS can warn users of potentially malicious activity.

Tech Tip

Decision Trees

In computer systems, a tree is a data structure, each element of which is attached to one or more structures directly beneath it (the connections are called branches). Structures on the end of a branch without any elements below them are called leaves. Trees are most often drawn inverted, with the root at the top and all subsequent elements branching down from the root. Trees in which each element has no more than two elements below it are called binary trees. In IDSs, a decision tree is used to help the analysis engine quickly examine traffic patterns and eliminate signatures that don't apply to the particular traffic or activity being examined, so that the fewest number of comparisons need to be made. For example, as shown in this illustration, the decision tree may contain a section that divides the activity into one of three subsections based upon the origin of the activity (a log entry for an event taken from the system logs, a file change for a modification to a critical file, or a user action for something a user has done):

When the analysis engine looks at the activity pattern and starts down the decision tree, it must decide which path to follow. If it is a log entry, the analysis engine can then concentrate on only the signatures that apply to log entries and it does not need to worry about signatures that apply to file changes or user actions. This type of decision tree allows the analysis engine to function much faster, as it does not have to compare activities to every signature in the database, just the signatures that apply to that particular type of activity. It is important to note that HIDSs can look at both activities occurring on the host itself and the network traffic coming into or leaving the host.

To better understand how a HIDS operates, take a look at the following examples from a UNIX system and a Windows system.

On a UNIX system, the HIDS is likely going to examine any of a number of system logs—basically, large text files containing entries about what is happening on the system. For this example, consider the following lines from the "messages" log on a Red Hat system:

```
Jan 5 18:20:39 jeep su(pam_unix)[32478]: session opened for
    user bob by (uid=0)
Jan 5 18:20:47 jeep su(pam_unix)[32516]: authentication
    failure; logname= uid=502 euid=0 tty= ruser=bob rhost=
    user=root
Jan 5 18:20:53 jeep su(pam_unix)[32517]: authentication
    failure; logname= id=502 euid=0 tty= ruser=bob
    rhost= user=root
Jan 5 18:21:06 jeep su(pam_unix)[32519]: authentication
    failure; logname= uid=502 euid=0 tty= ruser=bob
    rhost= user=root
```

In the first line beginning Jan 5, you see a session being opened by a user named *bob*. This usually indicates that whoever owns the account bob has logged into the system. On the next three lines beginning `Jan 5`, you see authentication failures as bob tries to become *root*—the superuser account that can do anything on the system. In this case, user bob tries three times to become root and fails on each try. This pattern of activity could mean a number of different things—bob could be an admin who has forgotten the password for the root account, bob could be an admin and someone changed the root password without telling him, bob could be a user attempting to guess the root password, or an attacker could have compromised bob's account and is now trying to compromise the root account on the system. In any case, our HIDS will work through its decision tree to determine whether an authentication failure in the message log is something it needs to examine. In this instance, when the HIDS examines these lines in the log, it will note the fact that three of the lines in the log match one of the patterns it has been told to look for (as determined by information from the decision tree and the signature database), and it will react accordingly, usually by generating an alarm or alert of some type that appears on the user interface or in an e-mail, page, or other form of message.

On a Windows system, the HIDS will likely examine the logs generated by the operating system. The three basic types of logs (Application, System, and Security) are similar to the logs on a UNIX system, though the Windows logs are not stored as text files and typically require a utility or application to read them. This example uses the Security log from a Windows Vista system:

```
Audit Failure 5/2/2009 6:47:29 PM Microsoft-Windows-
   Security-Auditing Logon 529
Audit Failure 5/2/2009 6:47:54 PM Microsoft-Windows-
   Security-Auditing Logon 542
Audit Failure 5/2/2009 6:48:22 PM Microsoft-Windows-
   Security-Auditing Logon 578
Audit Success 5/2/2009 6:49:14 PM Microsoft-Windows-
   Security-Auditing Logon 601
```

In the first three main lines of the Security log, you see an `Audit Failure` entry for the `Logon` process. This indicates someone has tried to log into the system three times and has failed each time (much like our UNIX example) and then succeeded on the fourth try. You won't see the name of the account until you expand the log entry within the Windows Event Viewer tool, but for this example, assume it was the administrator account—the Windows equivalent of the root account. Here again, you see three login failures—if the HIDS has been programmed to look for failed login attempts, it will generate alerts when it examines these log entries.

Advantages of HIDSs

HIDSs have certain advantages that make them a good choice for certain situations:

- *They can be very operating system–specific and have more detailed signatures.* A HIDS can be very specifically designed to run on a certain operating system or to protect certain applications. This narrow focus lets developers concentrate on the specific things that affect the specific environment they are trying to protect. With this

Tech Tip

Analyst-Driven Log Analysis
Log analysis is the art of translating computer-generated logs into meaningful data. For example, a computer can't always tell you if an administrator-level login at 3 A.M. on a Saturday is definitely a bad thing, but an analyst can. Human analysts can add value through the interpretation of information in context with other sources of information.

type of focus, the developers can avoid generic alarms and develop much more specific, detailed signatures to identify malicious traffic more accurately.

- *They can reduce false-positive rates.* When running on a specific system, the HIDS process is much more likely to be able to determine whether or not the activity being examined is malicious. By more accurately identifying which activity is "bad," the HIDS will generate fewer false positives (alarms generated when the traffic matches a pattern but is not actually malicious).

- *They can examine data after it has been decrypted.* With security concerns constantly on the rise, many developers are starting to encrypt their network communications. When designed and implemented in the right manner, a HIDS will be able to examine traffic that is unreadable to a network-based IDS. This particular ability is becoming more important each day as more and more web sites start to encrypt all of their traffic.

- *They can be very application specific.* On a host level, the IDS can be designed, modified, or tuned to work very well on specific applications without having to analyze or even hold signatures for other applications that are not running on that particular system. Signatures can be built for specific versions of web server software, FTP servers, mail servers, or any other application housed on that host.

- *They can determine whether or not an alarm may impact that specific system.* The ability to determine whether or not a particular activity or pattern will really affect the system being protected assists greatly in reducing the number of generated alarms. Because the HIDS resides on the system, it can verify things such as patch levels, presence of certain files, and system state when it analyzes traffic. By knowing what state the system is in, the HIDS can more accurately determine whether an activity is potentially harmful to the system.

Disadvantages of HIDSs

HIDSs also have certain disadvantages that must be weighed in making the decision of whether to deploy this type of technology:

- *The HIDS must have a process on every system you want to watch.* You must have a HIDS process or application installed on every host you want to watch. To watch 100 systems, then, you would need to deploy 100 HIDSs, or remote agents.

- *The HIDS can have a high cost of ownership and maintenance.* Depending on the specific vendor and application, a HIDS can be fairly costly in terms of time and manpower to maintain. Unless some type of central console is used that allows you to maintain remote processes, administrators must maintain each HIDS process individually. Even with a central console, with a HIDS, there will be a high number of processes to maintain, software to update, and parameters to tune.

- *The HIDS uses local system resources.* To function, the HIDS must use CPU cycles and memory from the system it is trying to protect. Whatever resources the HIDS uses are no longer available for the system to perform its other functions. This becomes extremely important on applications such as high-volume web servers, where fewer resources usually means fewer visitors served and the need for more systems to handle expected traffic.

- *The HIDS has a very focused view and cannot relate to activity around it.* The HIDS has a limited view of the world, as it can see activity only on the host it is protecting. It has little to no visibility into traffic around it on the network or events taking place on other hosts. Consequently, a HIDS can tell you only if the system it is running on is under attack.

- *The HIDS, if logging only locally, could be compromised or disabled.* When a HIDS generates alarms, it typically stores the alarm information in a file or database of some sort. If the HIDS stores its generated alarm traffic on the local system, an attacker that is successful in breaking into the system may be able to modify or delete those alarms. This makes it difficult for security personnel to discover the intruder and conduct any type of post-incident investigation. A capable intruder may even be able to turn off the HIDS process completely.

 A security best practice is to store or make a copy of log information, especially security-related log information, on a separate system. When a system is compromised, the attacker typically hides their tracks by clearing out any log files on the compromised system. If the log files are only stored locally on the compromised system, you'll know an attacker was present (due to the empty log files) but you won't know what they did or when they did it.

Active vs. Passive HIDSs

Most IDSs can be distinguished by how they examine the activity around them and whether or not they interact with that activity. This is certainly true for HIDSs. On a *passive* system, the HIDS is exactly that—it simply watches the activity, analyzes it, and generates alarms. It does not interact with the activity itself in any way, and it does not modify the defensive posture of the system to react to the traffic. A passive HIDS is similar to a simple motion sensor—it generates an alarm when it matches a pattern, much as the motion sensor generates an alarm when it sees movement.

An *active* IDS will contain all the same components and capabilities of the passive IDS with one critical exception—the active IDS can *react* to the activity it is analyzing. These reactions can range from something simple, such as running a script to turn a process on or off, to something as complex as modifying file permissions, terminating the offending processes, logging off specific users, and reconfiguring local capabilities to prevent specific users from logging in for the next 12 hours.

Resurgence and Advancement of HIDSs

The past few years have seen a strong resurgence in the use of HIDSs. With the great advances in processor power, the introduction of multicore processors, and the increased capacity of hard drives and memory systems, some of the traditional barriers to running a HIDS have been overcome. Combine those advances in technology with the widespread adoption of always-on broadband connections, the rise in the use of telecommuting, and a greater overall awareness of the need for computer security, and solutions such as HIDSs start to become an attractive and sometimes effective solution for business and home users alike.

The latest generation of HIDSs has introduced new capabilities designed to stop attacks by preventing them from ever executing or accessing protected files in the first place, rather than relying on a specific signature set that only matches known attacks. The more advanced host-based offerings, which most vendors refer to as host-based intrusion prevention systems (HIPSs), combine the following elements into a single package:

- **Integrated system firewall**   The firewall component checks all network traffic passing into and out of the host. Users can set rules for what types of traffic they want to allow into or out of their system.

- **Behavioral- and signature-based IDS**   This hybrid approach uses signatures to match well-known attacks and generic patterns for catching "zero-day" or unknown attacks for which no signatures exist.

- **Application control**   This allows administrators to control how applications are used on the system and whether or not new applications can be installed. Controlling the addition, deletion, or modification of existing software can be a good way to control a system's baseline and prevent malware from being installed.

- **Enterprise management**   Some host-based products are installed with an "agent" that allows them to be managed by and report back to a central server. This type of integrated remote management capability is essential in any large-scale deployment of host-based IDS/IPS.

- **Malware detection and prevention**   Some HIDSs/HIPSs include scanning and prevention capabilities that address spyware, malware, rootkits, and other malicious software.

Integrated security products can provide a great deal of security-related features in a single package. This is often cheaper and more convenient than purchasing a separate antivirus product, a firewall, and an IDS. However, integrated products are not without potential pitfalls—if one portion of the integrated product fails, the entire protective suite may fail. Symantec's Endpoint Protection and McAfee's Internet Security are examples of integrated, host-based protection products.

■ Intrusion Prevention Systems

An **intrusion prevention system (IPS)** monitors network traffic for malicious or unwanted behavior and can block, reject, or redirect that traffic in real time. Sound familiar? It should: while many vendors will argue that an IPS is a different animal from an IDS, the truth is that most IPSs are merely expansions of existing IDS capabilities. As a core function, an IPS must be able to monitor for and detect potentially malicious network traffic, which is essentially the same function as an IDS. However, an IPS does not stop at merely monitoring traffic—it must be able to block, reject, or redirect that traffic in real time to be considered a true IPS. It must be able to stop or prevent malicious traffic from having an impact. To qualify as an IDS, a system just needs to see and classify the traffic as malicious. To qualify as an IPS, a system must be able to do something about that traffic. In reality, most products that are called IDSs, including the first commercially available IDS, NetRanger, can interact with and stop malicious traffic, so the distinction between the two is often blurred.

The term *intrusion prevention system* was originally coined by Andrew Plato in marketing literature developed for NetworkICE, a company that was purchased by ISS and which is now part of IBM. The term IPS has effectively taken the place of the term "active IDS."

Like IDSs, most IPSs have an internal signature database to compare network traffic against known "bad" traffic patterns. IPSs can perform content-based inspections, looking inside network packets for unique packets, data values, or patterns that match known malicious patterns. Some IPSs can perform protocol inspection, in which the IPS decodes traffic and analyzes it as it would appear to the server receiving it. For example, many

IPSs can do HTTP protocol inspection, so they can examine incoming and outgoing HTTP traffic and process it as an HTTP server would. The advantage here is that the IPS can detect and defeat popular evasion techniques such as encoding URLs because the IPS "sees" the traffic in the same way the web server would when it receives and decodes it. The IPS can also detect activity that is abnormal or potentially malicious for that protocol, such as passing an extremely large value (over 10,000 characters) to a login field on a web page.

Unlike a traditional IDS, an IPS must sit inline (in the flow of traffic) to be able to interact effectively with the network traffic. Most IPSs can operate in "stealth mode" and do not require an IP address for the connections they are monitoring. When an IPS detects malicious traffic, it can drop the offending packets, reset incoming or established connections, generate alerts, quarantine traffic to/from specific IP addresses, or even block traffic from offending IP addresses on a temporary or permanent basis. As they are sitting inline, most IPSs can also offer *rate-based monitoring* to detect and mitigate denial-of-service attacks. With rate-based monitoring, the IPS can watch the amount of traffic traversing the network. If the IPS sees too much traffic coming into or going out from a specific system or set of systems, the IPS can intervene and throttle down the traffic to a lower and more acceptable level. Many IPSs perform this function by "learning" what are "normal" network traffic patterns with regard to number of connections per second, amount of packets per connection, packets coming from or going to specific ports, and so on, and comparing current traffic rates for network traffic (TCP, UDP, ARP, ICMP, and so on) to those established norms. When a traffic pattern reaches a threshold or varies dramatically from those norms, the IPS can react and intervene as needed.

Like a traditional IDS, the IPS has a potential weakness when dealing with encrypted traffic. Traffic that is encrypted will typically pass by the IPS untouched (provided it does not trigger any non-content–related alarms such as rate-based alarms). To counter this problem, some IPS vendors are including the ability to decrypt Secure Sockets Layer (SSL) sessions for further inspection. To do this, some IPS solutions store copies of any protected web servers' private keys on the sensor itself. When the IPS sees a session initiation request, it monitors the initial transactions between the server and the client. By using the server's stored private keys, the IPS will be able to determine the session keys negotiated during the SSL session initiation. With the session keys, the IPS can decrypt all future packets passed between server and client during that web session. This gives the IPS the ability to perform content inspection on SSL-encrypted traffic.

You will often see IPSs (and IDSs) advertised and marketed by the amount of traffic they can process without dropping packets or interrupting the flow of network traffic. In reality, a network will never reach its hypothetical maximum transmission rate, or wire speed, due to errors, collisions, retransmissions, and other factors; therefore, a 1-Gbps network is not actually capable of passing 1 Gbps of network traffic, even if all the components are rated to handle 1 Gbps. When used in a marketing sense, wire speed is the maximum throughput rate the networking or security device equipment can process without impacting that network traffic. For example, a 1-Gbps IPS should be able to process, analyze, and protect 1 Gbps of network traffic without impacting traffic flow. IPS vendors often quote

Exam Tip: An IDS is like a burglar alarm—it watches and alerts you when something bad happens. An IPS is like an armed security guard—it watches, stops the bad activity, and then lets you know what happened.

Tech Tip

Inline Network Devices

An "inline" network device is something that is positioned in the flow of traffic—network traffic must pass through it going into or out of the network. Any inline device has the potential to stop network traffic if that device fails. To allow network traffic to flow, many network devices will fail "open," meaning they simply pass traffic from one interface to another without inspecting it or interacting with it. Some administrators choose to have their firewalls and IPSs fail "closed," meaning that if the devices are not functioning correctly, all traffic is stopped until those devices can be repaired.

The term *wire speed* refers to the theoretical maximum transmission rate of a cable or other medium and is based on a number of factors, including the properties of the cable itself and the connection protocol in use (in other words, how much data can be pushed through under ideal conditions).

their products' capacity as the combined throughput possible through all available ports on the IPS sensor—a 10-Gbps sensor may have 12 Gigabit Ethernet ports but is capable of handling only 10 Gbps of network traffic.

Honeypots and Honeynets

As is often the case, one of the best tools for information security personnel has always been knowledge. To secure and defend a network and the information systems on that network properly, security personnel need to know what they are up against. What types of attacks are being used? What tools and techniques are popular at the moment? How effective is a certain technique? What sort of impact will this tool have on my network? Often this sort of information is passed through white papers, conferences, mailing lists, or even word of mouth. In some cases, the tool developers themselves provide much of the information in the interest of promoting better security for everyone.

Information is also gathered through examination and forensic analysis, often after a major incident has already occurred and information systems are already damaged. One of the most effective techniques for collecting this type of information is to observe activity firsthand—watching an attacker as he probes, navigates, and exploits his way through a network. To accomplish this without exposing critical information systems, security researchers often use something called a honeypot.

A **honeypot**, sometimes called a **digital sandbox**, is an artificial environment where attackers can be contained and observed without putting real systems at risk. A good honeypot appears to an attacker to be a real network consisting of application servers, user systems, network traffic, and so on, but in most cases it's actually made up of one or a few systems running specialized software to simulate the user and network traffic common to most targeted networks. Figure 13.9 illustrates a simple honeypot layout in which a single system is placed on the network to deliberately attract attention from potential attackers.

Figure 13.9 shows the security researcher's view of the honeypot, while Figure 13.10 shows the attacker's view. The security administrator knows that the honeypot, in this case, actually consists of a single system running

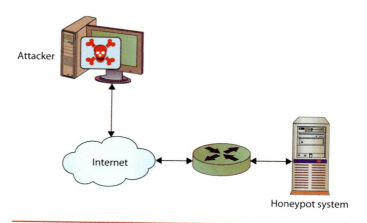

• **Figure 13.9** Logical depiction of a honeypot

Principles of Computer Security

software designed to react to probes, reconnaissance attempts, and exploits as if it were an entire network of systems. When the attacker connects to the honeypot, she is presented with an entire "virtual" network of servers and PCs running a variety of applications. In most cases, the honeypot will appear to be running versions of applications that are known to be vulnerable to specific exploits. All this is designed to provide the attacker with an enticing, hopefully irresistible, target.

Any time an attacker has been lured into probing or attacking the virtual network, the honeypot records the activity for later analysis: what the attacker does, which systems and applications she concentrates on, what tools are run, how long the attacker stays, and so on. All this information is collected and analyzed in the hopes that it will allow security personnel to better understand and protect against the threats to their systems.

There are many honeypots in use, specializing in everything from wireless to denial-of-service attacks; most are run by research, government, or law enforcement organizations. Why aren't more businesses running honeypots? Quite simply, the time and cost are prohibitive. Honeypots take a lot of time and effort to manage and maintain, and even more effort to sort, analyze, and classify the traffic the honeypot collects. Unless they are developing security tools, most companies focus their limited security efforts on preventing attacks, and in many cases, companies aren't even that concerned with detecting attacks as long as the attacks are blocked, are unsuccessful, and don't affect business operations. Even though honeypots can serve as a valuable resource by luring attackers away from production systems and allowing defenders to identify and thwart potential attackers before they cause any serious damage, the costs and efforts involved deter many companies from using honeypots.

A **honeynet** is a collection of two or more honeypots. Larger, very diverse network environments can deploy multiple honeypots (thus forming a honeynet) when a single honeypot device does not provide enough coverage. Honeynets are often integrated into an organization-wide IDS/IPS because the honeynet can provide relevant information about potential attackers.

> **Exam Tip:** A honeypot is a system designed to attract potential attackers by pretending to be one or more systems with open network services.

Virtual network created by the honeypot

• **Figure 13.10** Virtual network created by the honeypot

■ Tools

Tools are a vital part of any security professional's skill set. You may not be an "assessment professional" who spends most of his or her career examining networks looking for vulnerabilities, but you can use many of the same tools for internal assessment activities, tracking down infected systems, spotting inappropriate behavior, and so on. Knowing the right tool for the job can be critical to performing effectively.

Protocol Analyzer

A **protocol analyzer** (also known as a *packet sniffer, network analyzer,* or *network sniffer*) is a piece of software or an integrated software/hardware system that can capture and decode network traffic. Protocol analyzers have been popular with system administrators and security professionals for decades because they are such versatile and useful tools for a network environment. From a security perspective, protocol analyzers can be used for a number of activities, such as the following:

- Detecting intrusions or undesirable traffic (an IDS/IPS must have some type of capture and decode ability to be able to look for suspicious/malicious traffic)
- Capturing traffic during incident response or incident handling
- Looking for evidence of botnets, Trojans, and infected systems
- Looking for unusual traffic or traffic exceeding certain thresholds
- Testing encryption between systems or applications

From a network administration perspective, protocol analyzers can be used for activities such as these:

- Analyzing network problems
- Detecting misconfigured applications or misbehaving applications
- Gathering and reporting network usage and traffic statistics
- Debugging client/server communications

> **Exam Tip:** A sniffer must use a NIC placed in promiscuous (promisc) mode or it will not see all the network traffic coming into the NIC.

Regardless of the intended use, a protocol analyzer must be able to see network traffic in order to capture and decode it. A software-based protocol analyzer must be able to place the NIC it is going to use to monitor network traffic in *promiscuous mode* (sometimes called *promisc mode*). Promiscuous mode tells the NIC to process every network packet it sees regardless of the intended destination. Normally, a NIC processes only *broadcast* packets (which go to everyone on that subnet) and packets with the NIC's Media Access Control (MAC) address as the destination address inside the packet. As a sniffer, the analyzer must process every packet crossing the wire, so the ability to place a NIC into promiscuous mode is critical.

With older networking technologies, such as hubs, it was easier to operate a protocol analyzer, as the hub broadcasted every packet across every interface regardless of the destination. With switches now the standard for networking equipment, placing a protocol analyzer becomes more difficult as switches do not broadcast every packet across every port. While this may make it harder for administrators to sniff the traffic, it also makes it harder for eavesdroppers and potential attackers.

To accommodate protocol analyzers, IDS devices, and IPS devices, most switch manufacturers support **port mirroring** or a Switched Port Analyzer (SPAN) port (discussed in the next section). Depending on the manufacturer and the hardware, a mirrored port will see all the traffic passing through the switch or through a specific VLAN(s), or all the traffic passing through other specific switch ports. The network traffic is essentially copied (or mirrored) to a specific port, which can then support a protocol analyzer.

Another option for traffic capture is to use a **network tap**, a hardware device that can be placed inline on a network connection and that will copy traffic passing through the tap to a second set of interfaces on the tap. Network taps are often used to sniff traffic passing between devices at the network perimeter, such as the traffic passing between a router and a firewall.

Many common network taps work by bridging a network connection and passing incoming traffic out one tap port (A) and outgoing traffic out another tap port (B), as shown in Figure 13.11.

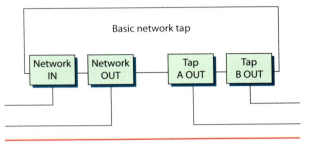

A popular, open source protocol analyzer is Wireshark (www.wireshark.org). Available for both UNIX and Windows operating systems, Wireshark is a GUI-based protocol analyzer that allows users to capture and decode network traffic on any available network interface in the system on which the software is running (including wireless interfaces), as demonstrated in Figure 13.12. Wireshark has some interesting features, including the ability to "follow the TCP stream," which allows the user to select a single TCP packet and then see all the other packets involved in that TCP conversation.

• **Figure 13.11** A basic network tap

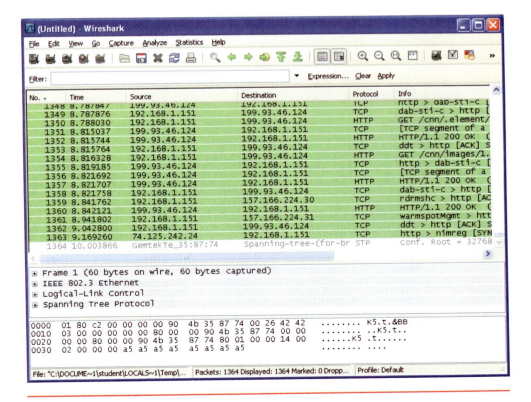

• **Figure 13.12** Wireshark—a popular, open source protocol analyzer

Chapter 13: Intrusion Detection Systems and Network Security

Switched Port Analyzer

The term **Switched Port Analyzer (SPAN)** is usually associated with Cisco switches—other vendors refer to the same capability as *port mirroring* or *port monitoring*. A SPAN has the ability to copy network traffic passing through one or more ports on a switch or one or more VLANs on a switch and forward that copied traffic to a port designated for traffic capture and analysis (as shown in Figure 13.13). A SPAN port or mirror port creates the collection point for traffic that will be fed into a protocol analyzer or IDS/IPS. SPAN or mirror ports can usually be configured to monitor traffic passing into interfaces, passing out of interfaces, or passing in both directions. When configuring port mirroring, you need to be aware of the capabilities of the switch you are working with. Can it handle the volume of traffic? Can it successfully mirror all the traffic, or will it end up dropping packets to the SPAN if traffic volume gets too high?

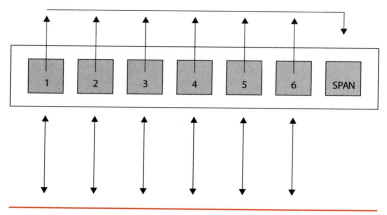

• **Figure 13.13**   A SPAN port collects traffic from other ports on a switch.

Port Scanner

A port scanner is a tool designed to probe a system or systems for open ports. Its job is to probe for open (or listening) ports and report back to the user which ports are closed, which are filtered, and which are open. Port scanners are available for virtually every operating system and almost every popular mobile computing platform—from tablets to smartphones. Having a good port-scanning tool in your toolset and knowing how to use it can be very beneficial. The good news/bad news about port scanners is that the "bad guys" use them for basically the same reasons the good guys use them. Port scanners can be used to do the following:

■   *Search for "live" hosts on a network.* Most port scanners enable you to perform a quick scan using ICMP, TCP, or UDP packets to search for active hosts on a given network or network segment. ICMP is still very popular for this task, but with the default blocking of ICMP v4 in many modern operating systems, such as Windows 7 and beyond, users are increasingly turning to TCP or UDP scans for these tasks.

■   *Search for any open ports on the network.* Port scanners are most often used to identify any open ports on a host, group of hosts, or network. By scanning a large number of ports over a large number of hosts, a port scanner can provide you (or an attacker) with a very good picture of what services are running on which hosts on your network. Scans can be done for the "default" set of popular ports, a large range of ports, or every possible port (from 1 to 65535).

- *Search for specific ports.* Only looking for web servers? Mail servers? Port scanners can also be configured to just look for specific services.

- *Identify services on ports.* Some port scanners can help identify the services running on open ports based on information returned by the service or the port/service assigned (if standards have been followed). For example, a service running on port 80 is likely to be a web server.

- *Look for TCP/UDP services.* Most port scanners can perform scans for both TCP and UDP services, although some tools do not allow you to scan for both protocols at the same time.

As a security professional, you'll use port scanners in much the same way an attacker would: to probe the systems in your network for open services. When you find open services, you'll need to determine if those services should be running at all, if they should be running on the system(s) you found them on, and if you can do anything to limit what connections are allowed to those services. For example, you may want to scan your network for any system accepting connections on TCP port 1433 (Microsoft SQL Server). If you find a system accepting connections on TCP port 1433 in your Sales group, chances are someone has installed something they shouldn't have (or someone installed something for them).

So how does a port scanner actually work? Much will depend on the options you select when configuring your scan, but for the sake of this example, assume you're running a standard TCP connect scan against 192.168.1.20 for ports 1–10000. The scanner will attempt to create a TCP connection to each port in the range 1–10000 on 192.168.1.20. When the scanner sends out that SYN packet, it waits for the responding SYN/ACK. If a SYN/ACK is received, the scanner will attempt to complete the three-way handshake and mark the port as "open." If the sent packet times out or an RST packet is received, the scanner will likely mark that port as "closed." If an "administratively prohibited" message or something similar comes back, the scanner may mark that port as "filtered." When the scan is complete, the scanner will present the results in a summary format—listing the ports that are open, closed, filtered, and so on. By examining the responses from each port, you can typically deduce a bit more information about the system(s) you are scanning, as detailed here:

- **Open** Open ports accept connections. If you can connect to these with a port scanner, the ports are not being filtered at the network level. However, there are instances where you may find a port that is marked as "open" by a port scanner that will immediately drop your connections if you attempt to connect to it in some other manner. For example, port 22 for SSH may appear "open" to a port scanner but will immediately drop your SSH connections. In such a case, the service is likely being filtered by a host-based firewall or a firewall capability within the service itself.

- **Closed**   You will typically see this response when the scanned target returns an RST packet.

- **Filtered**   You will typically see this response when an ICMP unreachable error is returned. This usually indicates that port is being filtered by a firewall or other device.

- **Additional types**   Some port scanners will attempt to further classify responses, such as dropped, blocked, denied, timeout, and so on. These are fairly tool specific, and you should refer to any documentation or help file that accompanies that port scanner for additional information.

In general, you will want to run your scanning efforts multiple times using different options to ensure you get a better picture. A SYN scan may return different results than a NULL scan or FIN scan. You'll want to run both TCP and UDP scans as well. You may need to alter your scanning approach to use multiple techniques at different times of the day/night to ensure complete coverage. The bad guys are doing this against your network right now, so you might as well use the same tools they do to see what they see. Port scanners can also be very useful for testing firewall configurations because the results of the port scans can show you exactly which ports are open, which ones you allow through, which ports are carrying services, and so on.

So how do you defend against port scans? Well, it's tough. Port scans are pretty much a part of the Internet traffic landscape now. Although you can block IP addresses that scan you, most organizations don't because you run the risk of an attacker spoofing source addresses as decoys for other scanning activity. The best defense is to carefully control what traffic you let in and out of your network, using firewalls, network filters, and host filters. Then carefully monitor any traffic that you do allow in.

Passive vs. Active Tools

Tools can be classified as active or passive. *Active tools* interact with a target system in a fashion where their use can be detected. Scanning a network with Nmap (Network Mapper) is an active act that can be detected. In the case of Nmap, the tool may not be specifically detectable, but its use, the sending of packets, can be detected. When you need to map out your network or look for open services on one or more hosts, a port scanner is probably the most efficient tool for the job. Figure 13.14 shows a screen shot of Zenmap, a cross-platform version of the very popular Nmap port scanner available from http://insecure.org.

Passive tools are those that do not interact with the system in a manner that would permit detection, as in sending packets or altering traffic. An example of a passive tool is Tripwire, which can detect changes to a file based on hash values. Another passive example is the OS mapping by

● **Figure 13.14**   Zenmap—a port scanner based on Nmap

analyzing TCP/IP traces with a tool such as Wireshark. Passive sensors can use existing traffic to provide data for analysis.

Banner Grabbing

Banner grabbing is a technique used to gather information from a service that publicizes information via a banner. Banners can be used for many things; for example, they can be used to identify services by type, version, and so forth, and they enable administrators to post information, including warnings, to users when they log in. Attackers can use banners to determine what services are running, and typically do for common banner-issuing services such as HTTP, FTP, SMTP, and Telnet. Figure 13.15 shows

Exam Tip: Passive tools receive traffic only and do nothing to the traffic flow that would permit others to know they are interacting with the network. Active tools modify or send traffic and are thus discoverable by their traffic patterns.

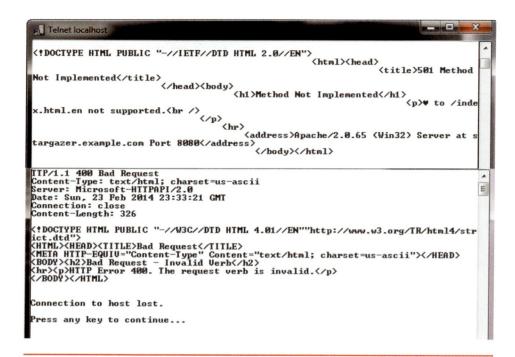

```
<!DOCTYPE HTML PUBLIC "-//IETF//DTD HTML 2.0//EN">
                                        <html><head>
                                        <title>501 Method
Not Implemented</title>
              </head><body>
                            <h1>Method Not Implemented</h1>
                                        <p>♥ to /inde
x.html.en not supported.<br />
                    </p>
                            <hr>
                            <address>Apache/2.0.65 (Win32) Server at s
targazer.example.com Port 8080</address>
                                        </body></html>

TTP/1.1 400 Bad Request
Content-Type: text/html; charset=us-ascii
Server: Microsoft-HTTPAPI/2.0
Date: Sun, 23 Feb 2014 23:33:21 GMT
Connection: close
Content-Length: 326

<!DOCTYPE HTML PUBLIC "-//W3C//DTD HTML 4.01//EN""http://www.w3.org/TR/html4/str
ict.dtd">
<HTML><HEAD><TITLE>Bad Request</TITLE>
<META HTTP-EQUIV="Content-Type" Content="text/html; charset=us-ascii"></HEAD>
<BODY><h2>Bad Request - Invalid Verb</h2>
<hr><p>HTTP Error 400. The request verb is invalid.</p>
</BODY></HTML>


Connection to host lost.

Press any key to continue...
```

• **Figure 13.15**   Banner grabbing using Telnet

a couple of banner grabs being performed from a Telnet client against a web server. In this example, Telnet sends information to two different web servers and displays the responses (the banners). The top response is from an Apache instance (Apache/2.0.65) and the bottom is from Microsoft IIS (Microsoft-HTTPAPI/2.0).

Chapter 13 Review

For More Information

- **SANS Intrusion Detection FAQ** www.sans.org/security-resources/idfaq/
- **SANS Reading Room—Firewalls & Perimeter Protection** www.sans.org/reading_room/whitepapers/firewalls/
- **The Honeynet Project** www.honeynet.org
- **Fight Spam on the Internet!** http://spam.abuse.net/

Lab Manual Exercises

The following lab exercises from the companion lab manual, *Principles of Computer Security Lab Manual, Fourth Edition,* provide practical application of material covered in this chapter:

Lab 9.2l   Using an Intrusion Detection System (Snort) in Linux

Lab 9.4w   Using Honeypots in Windows

Chapter Summary

After reading this chapter and completing the exercises, you should understand the following facts about intrusion detection systems and network security.

Apply the appropriate network tools to facilitate network security

- Intrusion detection is a mechanism for detecting unexpected or unauthorized activity on computer systems.
- IDSs can be host-based, examining only the activity applicable to a specific system, or network-based, examining network traffic for a large number of systems.
- Protocol analyzers, often called sniffers, are tools that capture and decode network traffic.
- Honeypots are specialized forms of intrusion detection that involve setting up simulated hosts and services for attackers to target.
- Honeypots are based on the concept of luring attackers away from legitimate systems by presenting more tempting or interesting systems that, in most cases, appear to be easy targets.

Determine the appropriate use of tools to facilitate network security

- IDSs match patterns known as signatures that can be content- or context-based. Some IDSs are

model-based and alert an administrator when activity does not match normal patterns (anomaly-based) or when it matches known suspicious or malicious patterns (misuse detection).

- Newer versions of IDSs include prevention capabilities that automatically block suspicious or malicious traffic before it reaches its intended destination. Most vendors call these intrusion prevention systems (IPSs).
- Analyzers must be able to see and capture network traffic to be effective, and many switch vendors support network analysis through the use of mirroring or SPAN ports.
- Network traffic can also be viewed using network taps, a device for replicating network traffic passing across a physical link.
- By monitoring activity within the honeypot, security personnel are better able to identify potential attackers along with their tools and capabilities.

Apply host-based security applications

- Host-based IDSs can apply specific context-sensitive rules because of the known host role.
- Host-based IPSs can provide better control over specific attacks as the scope of control is limited to a host.

Key Terms

analysis engine *(379)*

anomaly detection model *(379)*

banner grabbing *(403)*

content-based signature *(381)*

context-based signature *(381)*

digital sandbox *(396)*

false negative *(382)*

false positive *(382)*

honeynet *(397)*

honeypot *(396)*

host-based IDS (HIDS) *(378)*

intrusion detection system (IDS) *(376)*

intrusion prevention system (IPS) *(394)*

misuse detection model *(380)*

network tap *(399)*

network-based IDS (NIDS) *(378)*

perimeter security *(383)*

port mirroring *(399)*

protocol analyzer *(398)*

signature database *(379)*

Snort *(387)*

Suricata *(387)*

Switched Port Analyzer (SPAN) *(400)*

traffic collector *(378)*

user interface and reporting *(379)*

Key Terms Quiz

Use terms from the Key Terms list to complete the sentences that follow. Don't use the same term more than once. Not all terms will be used.

1. A(n) _____ is a piece of software or an integrated software/hardware system that can capture and decode network traffic.

2. When an IDS generates an alarm on "normal" traffic that is actually not malicious or suspicious, that alarm is called a(n) _____.

3. An attacker scanning a network full of inviting, seemingly vulnerable targets might actually be scanning a(n) _____ where the attacker's every move can be watched and monitored by security administrators.

4. A(n) _____ looks at a certain string of characters inside a TCP packet.

5. An IDS that looks for unusual or unexpected behavior is using a(n) _____.

6. _____ allows administrators to send all traffic passing through a network switch to a specific port on the switch.

7. Within an IDS, the _____ examines the collected network traffic and compares it to known patterns of suspicious or malicious activity stored in the signature database.

8. _____ is a technique where a host is queried and identified based on its response to a query.

9. _____ is a technique to match an element against a large set of patterns and use activity as a screening element.

10. _____ is a new entry in the IDS toolset as a replacement for Snort.

Multiple-Choice Quiz

1. What are the two main types of intrusion detection systems?

   A. Network-based and host-based

   B. Signature-based and event-based

   C. Active and reactive

   D. Intelligent and passive

2. What are the two main types of IDS signatures?

   A. Network-based and file-based

   B. Context-based and content-based

   C. Active and reactive

   D. None of the above

3. Which of the following describes a passive, host-based IDS?

   A. Runs on the local system

   B. Does not interact with the traffic around it

C. Can look at system event and error logs

D. All of the above

4. Which of the following is *not* a capability of network-based IDS?

   A. Can detect denial-of-service attacks

   B. Can decrypt and read encrypted traffic

   C. Can decode UDP and TCP packets

   D. Can be tuned to a particular network environment

5. An active IDS can:

   A. Respond to attacks with TCP resets

   B. Monitor for malicious activity

   C. A and B

   D. None of the above

6. Honeypots are used to:

   A. Attract attackers by simulating systems with open network services

   B. Monitor network usage by employees

   C. Process alarms from other IDSs

   D. Attract customers to e-commerce sites

7. Connecting to a server and sending a request over a known port in an attempt to identify the version of a service is an example of:

   A. Port sniffing

   B. Protocol analysis

   C. Banner grabbing

   D. TCP reset

8. Preventative intrusion detection systems:

   A. Are cheaper

   B. Are designed to stop malicious activity from occurring

   C. Can only monitor activity

   D. Were the first types of IDS

9. IPS stands for:

   A. Intrusion processing system

   B. Intrusion prevention sensor

   C. Intrusion prevention system

   D. Interactive protection system

10. A protocol analyzer can be used to:

    A. Troubleshoot network problems

    B. Collect network traffic statistics

    C. Monitor for suspicious traffic

    D. All of the above

Essay Quiz

1. Discuss the differences between an anomaly-based and a misuse-based detection model. Which would you use to protect a corporate network of 10,000 users? Why would you choose that model?

2. Pick three technologies discussed in this chapter and describe how you would deploy them to protect a small business network. Describe the protection each technology provides.

Lab Projects

• Lab Project 13.1

Design three content-based and three context-based signatures for use in an IDS. Name each signature and describe what the signature should look for, including traffic patterns or characters that need to be matched. Describe any activity that could generate a false positive for each signature.

• Lab Project 13.2

Use the Internet to research Snort (an open source IDS). With your instructor's permission, download Snort and install it on your classroom network. Examine the traffic and note any alarms that are generated. Research and note the sources of the alarm traffic. See if you can track down the sources of the alarm traffic and discover why they are generating those alarms on your IDS.

System Hardening and Baselines

chapter 14

People can have the Model T in any color—so long as it's black.
—HENRY FORD

In this chapter, you will learn how to

- Harden operating systems and network operating systems
- Implement host-level security
- Harden applications
- Establish group policies
- Secure alternative environments (SCADA, real-time, etc.)

The many uses for systems and operating systems require flexible components that allow users to design, configure, and implement the systems they need. Yet it is this very flexibility that causes some of the biggest weaknesses in computer systems. Computer and operating system developers often build and deliver systems in "default" modes that do little to secure the system from external attacks. From the view of the developer, this is the most efficient mode of delivery, as there is no way they can anticipate what every user in every situation will need. From the user's view, however, this means a good deal of effort must be put into protecting and securing the system before it is ever placed into service. The process of securing and preparing a system for the production environment is called **hardening**. Unfortunately, many users don't understand the steps necessary to secure their systems effectively, resulting in hundreds of compromised systems every day.

Hardening systems, servers, workstations, networks, and applications is a process of defining the required uses and needs and aligning security controls to limit a system's desired functionality. Once this is determined, you have a system baseline that you can compare changes to over the course of a system's lifecycle.

Overview of Baselines

To secure systems effectively and consistently, you must take a structured and logical approach. This starts with an examination of the system's intended functions and capabilities to determine what processes and applications will be housed on the system. As a best practice, anything that is not required for operations should be removed or disabled on the system; then, all the appropriate patches, hotfixes, and settings should be applied to protect and secure it.

This process of establishing a system's security state is called **baselining**, and the resulting product is a security **baseline** that allows the system to run safely and securely. Once the process has been completed for a particular hardware and software combination, any similar systems can be configured with the same baseline to achieve the same level and depth of security and protection. Uniform baselines are critical in large-scale operations, because maintaining separate configurations and security levels for hundreds or thousands of systems is far too costly.

After administrators have finished patching, securing, and preparing a system, they often create an initial baseline configuration. This represents a secure state for the system or network device and a reference point that can be used to help keep the system secure. If this initial baseline can be replicated, it can also be used as a template when deploying similar systems and network devices.

Constructing a baseline or hardened system is similar for servers, workstations, and network OSs. The specifics may vary, but the objects are the same.

Operating System and Network Operating System Hardening

The **operating system (OS)** of a computer is the basic software that handles things such as input, output, display, memory management, and all the other highly detailed tasks required to support the user environment and associated applications. Most users are familiar with the Microsoft family of desktop operating systems: Windows Vista, Windows 7, Windows 8, and Windows 10. Indeed, the vast majority of home and business PCs run some version of a Microsoft operating system. Other users may be familiar with Mac OS X, Solaris, or one of the many varieties of the UNIX/Linux operating system.

A **network operating system (NOS)** is an operating system that includes additional functions and capabilities to assist in connecting computers and devices, such as printers, to a local area network (LAN). Some of the more familiar network operating systems include Novell's NetWare and PC Micro's LANtastic. For most modern operating systems, including Windows 2008, Solaris, and Linux, the terms *operating system* and *network operating system* are used interchangeably as they perform all the basic functions and provide enhanced capabilities for connecting to LANs.

OS Security

The operating system itself is the foundation of system security. The operating system does this through the use of a security kernel. The **security kernel** is also called a **reference monitor** and is the component of the operating system that enforces the security policies of the operating system. The core of the OS is constructed so that all operations must pass through and be moderated by the security kernel, placing it in complete control over the enforcement of rules. Security kernels must exhibit some properties to be relied upon: they must offer complete mediation, as just discussed, and must be tamperproof and verifiable in operation. Because they are part of the OS and are in fact a piece of software, ensuring that security kernels are tamperproof and verifiable is a legitimate concern. To achieve assurance with respect to these attributes is a technical matter that is rooted in the actual construction of the OS and technically beyond the level of this book.

Protection Rings

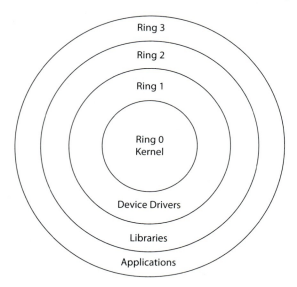

Protection rings were devised in the Multics operating system in the 1960s, to deal with security issues associated with time-sharing operations. Protection rings can be enforced by hardware, software, or a combination, and serve to act as a means of managing privilege in a hierarchical manner. Ring 0 is the level with the highest privilege and is the element that acts directly with the physical hardware (CPU and memory). Higher levels, with less privilege, must interact through adjoining rings through specific gates in a predefined manner. Use of rings separates elements such as applications from directly interfacing with the hardware without going through the OS and, specifically, the security kernel.

■ Host Security

Most environments are filled with different operating systems (Windows, Linux, OS X), different versions of those operating systems, and different types of installed applications. Also, today, host-based security for mobile device operating systems is an important security issue, which expands the operating system list to include iOS, Android, and BlackBerry. Each operating system has security configurations that differ from other systems, and different versions of the same operating system may in fact have variations between them. Ensuring that every computer is "locked down" to the same degree as every other system in the environment can be overwhelming and often results in an unsuccessful and frustrating effort.

Host security is important and should always be addressed. Security, however, should not stop there, as host security is a complementary process to be combined with network security. If individual host computers have vulnerabilities embodied within them, then network security can provide another layer of protection that will, hopefully, stop any intruders who have gotten that far into the environment.

Machine Hardening

The key management issue behind running a secure server setup is to identify the specific needs of a server for its proper operation and enable only items necessary for those functions. Keeping all other services and users off the system improves system throughput and increases security. Reducing the attack surface area associated with a server reduces the vulnerabilities now and in the future as updates are required.

Once a server has been built and is ready to be placed into operation, the recording of hash values on all of its crucial files will provide valuable information later in case of a question concerning possible system integrity after a detected intrusion. The use of hash values to detect changes was first developed by Gene Kim and Eugene Spafford at Purdue University in 1992. The concept became the product Tripwire, which is now available in commercial and open source forms. The same basic concept is used by many security packages to detect file-level changes.

The primary method of controlling the security impact of a system on a network is to reduce the available attack surface area. Turning off all services that are not needed or permitted by policy will reduce the number of vulnerabilities. Removing methods of connecting additional devices to a workstation to move data—such as optical drives and USB ports—assists in controlling the movement of data into and out of the device. User-level controls, such as limiting e-mail attachment options, screening all attachments at the e-mail server level, and reducing network shares to needed shares only, can be used to limit the excessive connectivity that can impact security.

Tech Tip

Server Hardening Tips

Specific security needs can vary depending on the server's specific use, but as a minimum, the following are beneficial:

- *Remove unnecessary protocols such as Telnet, NetBIOS, Internetwork Packet Exchange (IPX), and File Transfer Protocol (FTP).*
- *Remove unnecessary programs such as Internet Information Services (IIS).*
- *Remove all shares that are not necessary.*
- *Rename the administrator account, securing it with a strong password.*
- *Remove the Local Admin account in Windows.*
- *Disable unnecessary user accounts.*
- *Disable unnecessary ports and services.*
- *Keep the operating system (OS) patched and up to date.*
- *Keep all applications patched and up to date.*
- *Turn on event logging for determined security elements.*
- *Control physical access to servers.*

Securing a Workstation

Workstations are attractive targets for crackers because they are numerous and can serve as entry points into the network and the data that is commonly the target of an attack. Although security is a relative term, following these basic steps will increase workstation security immensely:

- *Remove unnecessary protocols such as Telnet, NetBIOS, and IPX.*
- *Remove unnecessary software.*
- *Remove modems unless needed and authorized.*
- *Remove all shares that are not necessary.*
- *Rename the administrator account, securing it with a strong password.*
- *Remove the Local Admin account in Windows.*
- *Disable unnecessary user accounts.*
- *Disable unnecessary ports and services.*
- *Install an antivirus program and keep abreast of updates.*
- *If the floppy drive is not needed, remove or disconnect it.*
- *Consider disabling USB ports via CMOS to restrict data movement to USB devices.*
- *If no corporate firewall exists between the machine and the Internet, install a firewall.*
- *Keep the operating system (OS) patched and up to date.*
- *Keep all applications patched and up to date.*
- *Turn on event logging for determined security elements.*

Operating System Security and Settings

Operating systems are complex programs designed to provide a platform for a wide variety of services to run. Some of these services are extensions of the OS itself, while others are standalone applications that use the OS as a mechanism to connect to other programs and hardware resources. It is up to the OS to manage the security aspects of the hardware being utilized. Things such as access control mechanisms are great in theory, but it is the practical implementation of these security elements in the OS that provides the actual security profile of a machine.

Early versions of home operating systems did not have separate named accounts for separate users. This was seen as a convenience mechanism; after all, who wants the hassle of signing into the machine? This led to the simple problem that all users could then see and modify and delete everyone else's content. Content could be separated by using access control mechanisms, but that required configuration of the OS to manage every user's identity. Early versions of many OSs came with literally every option turned on. Again, this was a convenience factor, but it led to systems running processes and services that they never used, and increasing the attack surface of the host unnecessarily.

Determining the correct settings and implementing them correctly is an important step in securing a host system. The following sections explore the multitude of controls and options that need to be employed properly to achieve a reasonable level of security on a host system.

OS Hardening

You must meet several key requirements to ensure that the system hardening processes described in this section achieve their security goals. These are OS independent and should be a normal part of all system maintenance operations:

Exam Tip: System hardening is the process of preparing and securing a system and involves the removal of all unnecessary software and services.

- The base installation of all OS and application software comes from a trusted source, and is verified as correct by using hash values.
- Machines are connected only to a completely trusted network during the installation, hardening, and update processes.
- The base installation includes all current service packs and updates for both the OS and applications.
- Current backup images are taken after hardening and updates to facilitate system restoration to a known state.

These steps ensure that you know what is on the machine, can verify its authenticity, and have an established backup version.

Hardening Microsoft Operating Systems

For this book, Windows Vista, Windows 7 and 8, as well as server products Windows Server 2008, 2008 R2, and 2012, are the focus of the discussion. Older Microsoft OSs, such as Windows 3.11, 95, 98, Me, and XP, are no longer supported by Microsoft and won't be covered in this chapter.

Hardening Windows

With the release of Windows Vista, Microsoft tried to make similar security improvements to its mainstream desktop OS as it did to its main server OS, Windows 2003. As a desktop OS, Windows has provided a range of security features for users to secure their systems. Most of these options can be employed via group policies in enterprise setups, making them easily deployable and maintainable across an enterprise.

Here are some of the security capabilities introduced with Vista and continued in later versions of Windows:

- *User Account Control allows users to operate the system without requiring administrative privileges.* If you've used Windows Vista and beyond, you've undoubtedly seen the "Windows needs your permission to continue" pop-ups. While annoying to many users (one of Apple's "I'm a Mac" commercials focused specifically on this feature), this feature does help prevent users from "accidentally" making changes to their system configuration. Figure 14.1 shows the User Account Control feature in Windows 7.

- *Windows Firewall includes an outbound filtering capability.* Windows allows filtering of traffic coming into and leaving the system, which is useful for controlling things like peer-to-peer applications.

- *BitLocker allows encryption of all data on a server, including any data volumes.* This capability is only available in the higher-end distributions of Windows.

- *Windows clients work with Network Access Protection.* See the discussion of NAP in the following "Hardening Windows Server 2008" section for more details.

- *Windows Defender is a built-in malware detection and removal tool.* Windows Defender detects many types of potentially suspicious software and can prompt the user before allowing applications to make potentially malicious changes.

Hardening Windows Server 2008

Microsoft touted Windows Server 2008 as its "most secure server" to date upon its release. Building on the changes it made to the Windows Server 2003 and Vista OSs, Microsoft attempted to add more defense-in-depth protections to Windows Server 2008. (Microsoft has a

Tech Tip

Vulnerability Scanning
One valuable method for helping administrators secure their systems is vulnerability scanning. Vulnerability scanning is the process of examining your systems and network devices for holes, weaknesses, and issues and finding them before a potential attacker does. Specialized tools called vulnerability scanners are designed to help administrators discover and address vulnerabilities. But there is much more to vulnerability scanning than simply running tools and examining the results—administrators must be able to analyze any discovered vulnerabilities and determine their severity and how to address those vulnerabilities if needed, and if any business processes will be affected by potential fixes. Vulnerability scanning can also help administrators identify common misconfigurations in account setup, patch levels, applications, and operating systems. Most organizations look at vulnerability scanning as an ongoing process, as it is not enough to scan systems once and assume they will be secure from that point on.

• **Figure 14.1**   Windows 7 User Account Control in action

free hardening guide for the Windows Server 2008 OS from its Download Center.) Here are some of the new security capabilities that were introduced in Windows Server 2008:

- *BitLocker allows encryption of all data on a server, including any data volumes.* This capability is also available in certain versions of Vista (and beyond).

- *Role-based installation of functions and capabilities minimizes the server's footprint.* For example, if a server is going to be a web server, it does not need DNS or SMTP software, and thus those features are no longer installed by default.

- *Network Access Protection (NAP) controls access to network resources based on a client computer's identity and compliance with corporate governance policy.* NAP allows network administrators to define granular levels of network access based on client identity, group membership, and the degree to which that client is compliant with corporate policies. NAP can also ensure that clients comply with corporate policies. Suppose, for example, that a sales manager connects her laptop to the corporate network. NAP can be used to examine the laptop and see if it is fully patched and running a company-approved antivirus product with updated signatures. If the laptop does not meet those standards, network access for that laptop can be restricted until the laptop is brought back into compliance with corporate standards.

- *Read-only domain controllers can be created and deployed in high-risk locations, but they can't be modified to add new users, change access levels, and so on.* This new ability to create and deploy "read-only" domain controllers can be very useful in high-threat environments.

- *More-granular password policies allow for different password policies on a group or user basis.* This allows administrators to assign different password policies and requirements for the sales group and the engineering group if that capability is needed.

- *Web sites or web applications can be administered within IIS 7.* This allows administrators quicker and more convenient administration capabilities, such as the ability to turn on or off specific modules through the IIS management interface. For example, removing CGI support from a web application is a quick and simple operation in IIS 7.

Figure 14.2 lists the initial configuration tasks for Windows 2008.

Hardening Windows Server 2012

With the release of Windows Server 2012, Microsoft added significant enhancements to its security baseline for its server line:

- Replaced the traditional ROM-BIOS with Unified Extensible Firmware Interface (UEFI). Microsoft is using the security-hardened 2.3.1 version, which prevents boot code updates without appropriate digital certificates and signatures.

- Extended the trustworthy and verified boot process to the entire Windows OS boot code with a feature known as Secure Boot. UEFI

• **Figure 14.2**   Windows 2008 Initial Configuration Tasks

and Secure Boot significantly reduce the risk of malicious code, such as rootkits and boot viruses.

■ Improved BitLocker functionality to allow administrator-less reboots.

■ Instituted Early Launch Anti-Malware (ELAM) to ensure that only known, digitally signed antimalware programs can load right after Secure Boot finishes (it does not require UEFI or Secure Boot). This permits legitimate antimalware programs to get into memory and start doing their job before fake antivirus programs or other malicious code can act.

■ Fully integrated DNSSEC.

■ Integrated Data Classification with Rights Management Service, so that you can control which users and groups can access which documents based upon content or marked classification.

■ Included Managed Service Accounts, introduced in Server 2008 R2, to allow for advanced self-maintaining features with extremely long passwords, which automatically reset every 30 days, all under Active Directory control in the enterprise.

Windows 2012 R2 continued the security feature set through refinements and improvements across many of the security features. Consistent with Microsoft's claim that Windows Server 2008 was its most secure server to date at the time of release, its subsequent track record shows that the company is committed to unrivaled security in enterprise server products. The tools available in each subsequent release of the server OS are designed to increase the difficulty factor for attackers, eliminating known methods of exploitation. The challenge is in administrating the security functions, although the integration of many of these via Active Directory makes this much more manageable than in the past.

Microsoft Security Compliance Manager

Microsoft provides a tool, Security Compliance Manager (SCM), to assist system and enterprise administrators with the configuration of security options across a wide range of Microsoft platforms. SCM allows administrators to use group policy objects (GPOs) to deploy security configurations across Internet Explorer, the desktop OSs, server OSs, and common applications such as Microsoft Office. Figure 14.3 illustrates some of the menu options available in SCM, currently version 3.0.

Microsoft Attack Surface Analyzer

One of the challenges in a modern enterprise is understanding the impact of system changes from the installation or upgrade of an application on a system. To help you overcome that challenge, Microsoft has released the Attack Surface Analyzer (ASA), a free tool that can be deployed on a system

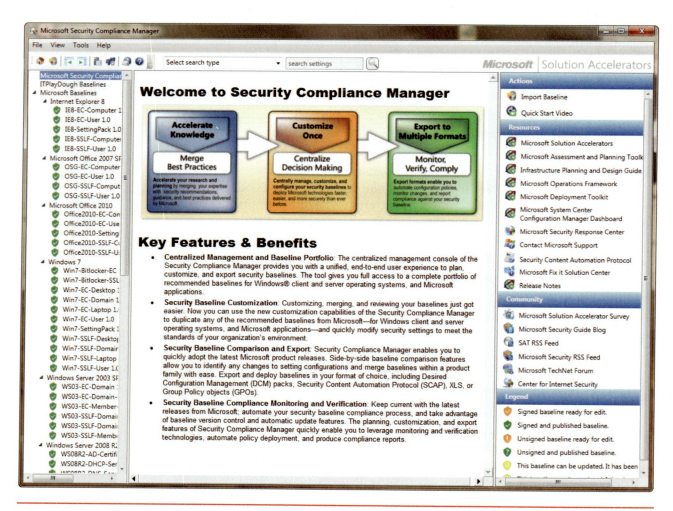

• **Figure 14.3** Microsoft Security Compliance Manager

before a change and again after a change to analyze the changes to various system properties as a result of the change.

Using ASA, developers can view changes in the attack surface resulting from the introduction of their code onto the Windows platform, and system administrators can assess the aggregate attack surface change by the installation of an application. Security auditors can use the tool to evaluate the risk of a particular piece of software installed on the Windows platform. And if ASA is deployed in a baseline mode before an incident, security incident responders can potentially use ASA to gain a better understanding of the state of a system's security during an investigation.

Hardening UNIX- or Linux-based Operating Systems

While you do not have the advantage of a single manufacturer for all UNIX operating systems (like you do with Windows operating systems), the concepts behind securing different UNIX- or Linux-based operating systems are similar whether the manufacturer is Red Hat or Sun Microsystems. Indeed, the overall tasks involved with hardening all operating systems are remarkably similar.

Establishing General UNIX Baselines

General UNIX baselining follows similar concepts as baselining for Windows OSs: disable unnecessary services, restrict permissions on files and directories, remove unnecessary software, apply patches, remove unnecessary users, and apply password guidelines. Some versions of UNIX provide GUI-based tools for these tasks, while others require administrators to edit configuration files manually. In most cases, anything that can be accomplished through a GUI can be accomplished from the command line or by manually editing configuration files.

Like Windows systems, UNIX systems are easiest to secure and baseline if they are providing a single service or performing a single function, such as acting as a Simple Mail Transfer Protocol (SMTP) server or web server. Prior to performing any software installations or baselining, the administrator should define the purpose of the system and identify all required capabilities and functions. One nice advantage of UNIX systems is that you typically have complete control over what does or does not get installed on the system. During the installation process, the administrator can select which services and applications are placed on the system, offering an opportunity to not install services and applications that will not be required. However, this assumes that the administrator knows and understands the purpose of this system, which is not always the case. In other cases, the function of the system itself may have changed.

Regardless of the installation decisions, the administrator may need to remove applications or components that are no longer needed. With UNIX systems, no "add/remove program" wizard is usually available, unlike Windows, but you will often encounter package managers that help you remove unneeded components and applications automatically. On some UNIX versions, though, you must manually delete the files associated with the applications or services you want to remove.

Tech Tip

Runlevels

Runlevels are used to describe the state of init (initialization) and what system services are operating in UNIX systems. For example, runlevel 0 is shutdown. Runlevel 1 is single-user mode (typically for administrative purposes). Runlevels 2 through 5 are user defined (that is, administrators can define what services are running at each level). Runlevel 6 is for reboot.

Services on a UNIX system (called *daemons*) can be controlled through a number of different mechanisms. As the root user, an administrator can start and stop services manually from the command line or through a GUI tool. The OS can also stop and start services automatically through configuration files (usually contained in the /etc directory). (Note that UNIX systems vary a good deal in this regard, as some use a super-server process, such as inetd, while others have individual configuration files for each network service.) Unlike Windows, UNIX systems can also have different **runlevels**, in which the system can be configured to bring up different services depending on the runlevel selected.

On a running UNIX system, you can see which processes, applications, and services are running by using the process status, or **ps**, command, as shown in Figure 14.3. To stop a running service, an administrator can identify the service by its unique **process identifier (PID)** and then use the **kill** command to stop the service. For example, if you wanted to stop the bluetooth-applet service in Figure 14.4, you would use the command **kill 2443**. To prevent this service from starting again when the system is rebooted, you would have to modify the appropriate runlevels to remove this service, as shown in Figure 14.5, or modify the configuration files that control this service.

Accounts on a UNIX system can also be controlled via GUIs in some cases and command-line interfaces in others. On most popular UNIX versions, the user information can be found in the passwd file located in the /etc directory. By manually editing this file, you can add, delete, or modify user accounts on the system. By examining this file, an administrator can see which user accounts exist on the system and then determine which accounts to remove or disable. On most UNIX systems, if you remove the user account from the passwd file, you must manually remove any files that belong to that user, including home directories. Most modern UNIX versions store the actual password associated with a user account in a **shadow file** located in the /etc directory. The shadow file contains

```
                        root@localhost:~
File   Edit   View   Terminal   Tabs   Help
student   2369      1   0 13:47 ?        00:00:00 /usr/libexec/trashapplet --oaf-a
student   2373      1   0 13:47 ?        00:00:00 /usr/libexec/gvfsd-burn --spawne
student   2375      1   0 13:47 ?        00:00:00 /usr/libexec/mixer_applet2 --oaf
student   2377      1   0 13:47 ?        00:00:00 /usr/libexec/clock-applet --oaf-
student   2379      1   0 13:47 ?        00:00:00 /usr/libexec/gdm-user-switch-app
student   2381      1   0 13:47 ?        00:00:00 /usr/libexec/notification-area-a
student   2383      1   3 13:47 ?        00:00:00 mono /usr/lib/tomboy/Tomboy.exe
student   2398      1   1 13:47 ?        00:00:00 gnome-terminal
student   2403   2398   0 13:47 ?        00:00:00 gnome-pty-helper
student   2404   2398   0 13:47 pts/0    00:00:00 bash
student   2433   2043   1 13:47 ?        00:00:00 python /usr/share/system-config-
student   2437   2043   0 13:47 ?        00:00:00 kerneloops-applet
root      2439   2404   0 13:47 pts/0    00:00:00 su -
student   2443   2043   0 13:47 ?        00:00:00 bluetooth-applet
student   2446   2043   0 13:47 ?        00:00:00 gpk-update-icon
student   2448   2043   0 13:47 ?        00:00:00 imsettings-applet --disable-xset
student   2449   2043   0 13:47 ?        00:00:00 nm-applet --sm-disable
student   2454      1   0 13:47 ?        00:00:00 gnome-power-manager
root      2469      1   0 13:47 ?        00:00:00 /usr/sbin/packagekitd
student   2472      1   2 13:47 ?        00:00:00 /usr/bin/python -E /usr/bin/seal
student   2474      1   1 13:47 ?        00:00:00 /usr/libexec/notification-daemon
root      2489   2439   0 13:47 pts/0    00:00:00 -bash
root      2527   2489   0 13:47 pts/0    00:00:00 ps -eaf
[root@localhost ~]#
```

• **Figure 14.4**   `ps` command run on a Fedora system

• **Figure 14.5**   Service Configuration utility from a Fedora system the actual password hashes for each user account and is readable only by the root user (or a process with root-level permissions).

How you patch a UNIX system depends a great deal on the UNIX version in use and the patch being applied. In some cases, a patch will consist of a series of manual steps requiring the administrator to replace files, change permissions, and alter directories. In other cases, the patches are executable scripts or utilities that perform the patch actions automatically. Some UNIX versions, such as Red Hat and Solaris, have built-in utilities that handle the patching process. In those cases, the administrator downloads a specifically formatted file that the patching utility then processes to perform any modifications or updates that need to be made.

To better illustrate UNIX baselines, we will examine two popular UNIX-based operating systems: Solaris and Red Hat Linux.

Hardening Linux

Linux is a rather unique operating system. It is UNIX-based, very powerful, open source, can be obtained for free, and is available in many different "versions" or distributions ("distros") from several vendors. Linux was initially conceived and written by Linus Torvalds in 1991. His concept of creating a lightweight, flexible, and free operating system gave rise to an entirely new operating system that is very popular and is installed on millions of computers around the world. Due to its open nature, the entire source-code base for the operating system is available to anyone who wants to examine it, modify it, or recompile it for their own specific uses. Linux is a favored operating system among many security professionals, system administrators, and other highly technical users who enjoy the flexibility and power that Linux provides.

While most versions of Linux can be obtained for free simply by downloading them from the Internet (including major commercial distributions), you can also purchase commercial versions of the Linux operating system from vendors, such as Red Hat, Slackware, SuSE, and Debian, who have built a business out of providing custom versions of Linux along with support and training. We will use Fedora, a popular (and free) Linux distribution, as the example for the rest of this section. Regardless of which Linux version you prefer, baselining a Linux system follows the same guidelines as any other UNIX system: disable unnecessary services, restrict permissions on files and directories, remove unnecessary software, apply patches, remove unnecessary users, and apply password guidelines.

Services under Linux are normally controlled by their own configuration files or by xinetd, the extended Internet services daemon. Instead of starting all Internet services, such as FTP servers, at system startup, some Linux distributions use xinetd to listen for incoming connections. Xinetd listens to all the appropriate ports (those that match the services in its configuration files), and when a connection request comes in, xinetd starts the appropriate server and hands over the connection request. This "master process" approach makes it fairly simple to disable unwanted services—all the configuration information for each server is located in /etc/xinetd.d, with a configuration file for each process.

Permissions under Linux are the same as for other UNIX-based operating systems. There are permissions for owner, group, and others (or world). Permissions are based on the same read-write-execute principle and can

Tech Tip

TCP Wrappers

*TCP wrappers can be a great additional layer of protection for UNIX systems. When creating a security baseline for UNIX systems, be sure to consider the use of **TCP wrappers**.*

Another method of examining a system for vulnerabilities is done through observation—monitoring network traffic from specific systems, for example. This is called *passive vulnerability scanning* as administrators are merely observing what the system does and how it behaves. For instance, if an administrator sees FTP traffic traveling to a dedicated mail server, then they know they need to examine and possibly disable that FTP service.

Pluggable Authentication Modules (PAM) are a mechanism for providing interoperation and secure access to a variety of services on different platforms. They provide a common authentication scheme that can be used with a wide variety of applications. PAM has an extensive documentation set with details about both using PAM and writing modules to integrate PAM with applications.

Many Linux distributions are "open source," meaning if you have the time, energy, and expertise, you can access and modify the code that comprises the operating system itself.

419

Tech Tip

Linux Variants

The original Linux code is open source, and from this code many diverse variants have been developed. While these are all very similar, there are difference in how developers approached some activities such as patching and source code repositories. The different distros of Linux and methods of applying them are related to the lineage of the Linux distro itself. For distros that derive from the Debian line (Debian, Ubuntu, Linux Mint) the file format .deb is used. For distros derived from Redhat (Redhat, RHEL, Fedora, CentOS, SUSE) the .rpm file structure is used.

The two formats, .deb and .rpm, are basically archive files with metadata to assist installers. The differences are noticeable when a user uses tools to apply the updates. The underlying tool for .deb is dpkg, and rpm for .rpm. But these are simple tools, not repository managers; for repository management and better functionality, apt-get is used with .deb and yum is used with rpm. Although each of these options is different in usage and each has its champions, at the end of the day, both paths provide the same services for administrators. The key takeaway is although similar, there are differences in versions of Linux that make administration less universal in process.

be adjusted using the **chmod** command. Individual and group ownership information can be changed using **chown** and **chgrp**, respectively. As with other baselining exercises, permissions should be as restrictive as functionally possible, giving read-only access when possible and write or execute access when necessary.

Adding and removing software under Linux is typically done through a package manager. In Fedora Core Linux, the package manager is called Red Hat Package Manager, or rpm for short. Using rpm, you can add, modify, update, or remove software packages from your system. Using the **rpm –qa** command will give you a list of all the software packages installed on your Red Hat system. You can remove any packages you do not wish to leave installed by using the **rpm -e** command. As with most things under Linux, there is a GUI-based utility to accomplish this same task. The GUI-based Add/Remove Software utility is shown in Figure 14.6.

Patching and keeping a Fedora Linux system up to date is a fairly simple exercise, as well. Fedora has provided an Update Agent that, once configured, will examine your system, obtain the list of available updates, and, if desired, install those updates on your system. Like any other operating system, it is important to maintain the patch level of your Fedora system. For more information on the Fedora Update Agent, see the "Updates (a.k.a. Hotfixes, Service Packs, and Patches)" section later in this chapter.

Managing and maintaining user accounts under Linux can be accomplished with either the command line or a GUI. Unlike certain other operating systems, there's really only one default account for Linux systems—the root, or superuser, account. The root account has complete and total control over the system and should therefore be protected with an exceptionally strong password. Many administrators will configure their systems to prevent anyone from logging in directly as root; instead they must log in with their own personal accounts and switch to the root account using the **su** command. Adding user accounts can be done with the **useradd** command, and unwanted user accounts can be removed using the **userdel** command. Additionally you can manually edit /etc/passwd to add or remove user accounts. User accounts can also be managed via a GUI, as shown in Figure 14.7.

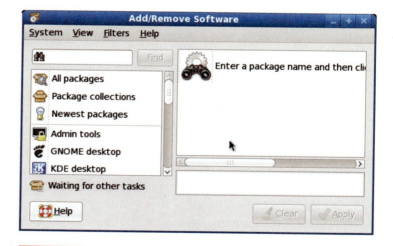

• **Figure 14.6**   Fedora Add/Remove Software utility

For increased local security, Fedora also provides a built-in firewall function that can be managed either via the command line or through a GUI, as shown in Figure 14.8. To protect network access to the local system, administrators can control which ports external users may connect to, such as mail, FTP, or web. Administrators may choose a security level, from high, medium, off, or a customized option that enables them to individually select which ports on which interfaces external users may connect to.

In addition to the built-in firewall functions, administrators may also use TCP wrappers like those discussed earlier in this chapter. By specifying host and port combinations in /etc/hosts.allow, administrators can allow certain hosts to connect on certain ports. The firewall function and hosts.allow must work together if both functions are used on the same system. The connection must be allowed by both utilities or it will be dropped.

• **Figure 14.7** Fedora User Manager

Hardening Mac OS X

Apple's operating system is essentially a new variant of the UNIX operating system. While this POSIX-compliant OS brings a new level of power, flexibility, and stability to Mac users everywhere, it also brings a new level of security concerns. Traditionally, the Mac operating system was largely ignored by the hacker community—the deployment was relatively small

• **Figure 14.8** Fedora Firewall Configuration GUI

and largely restricted to individual users or departments. With the migration to a UNIX-based OS and a rise in the number of Macs on the market, Mac users should anticipate a sharp increase in unwanted attention and scrutiny from potential attackers.

Because it is a UNIX-based OS, the same rough guidelines for all UNIX systems apply to Mac OS X. Apple has included some security-specific features to help protect its user base:

- **Mandatory access controls for access to system resources**   Only processes that are explicitly granted access are allowed to access system resources such as networking, file systems, process execution, and so on.

- **Tagged downloads**   Any file downloaded with Safari, iChat, or Mail is automatically tagged with metadata, including the source URL, date and time of download, and so on. If the download was an archive (such as a zip file), the same metadata is tagged to any file extracted from the archive. Users are prompted with this information the first time they try to run or open the downloaded file.

- **Execute disable**   Leopard (OS X 10.5) and beyond provides no-execute stack protection. Essentially this means that certain portions of the stack have been marked as "data only" and the OS will not execute any instructions in regions marked as data only. This helps protect against buffer-overflow attacks.

- **Library randomization**   In another attempt to help defeat buffer-overflow attacks, Leopard (OS X 10.5) and beyond loads system libraries into random locations, making it harder for attackers to reference static system library locations in their exploit code.

- **FileVault**   FileVault encrypts files with AES encryption. When this feature is enabled, everything in the user's home directory is automatically encrypted.

- **Application-aware firewall**   The Apple Application firewall allows users to restrict network access on both a per-application and a per-port basis.

- **Pre-emptive multitasking and memory protection**   These features provide a means for the system to ensure that multiple applications can be run simultaneously without interrupting or corrupting each other.

- **Gatekeeper**   The Gatekeeper application is employed to make it safer to download and deploy applications. The combination of the Gatekeeper application and the control Apple exerts over applications in its App store provides one of the safest sets of software distribution.

- **App Sandbox**   The App Sandbox in OS X provides a means of ensuring that apps are separated from the OS in ways to protect critical components from malicious software.

File permissions in OS X are nearly identical to those in any other UNIX variant and are based on separate read, write, and execute permissions for owner, group, and world. While these permissions can be adjusted manually from a command-line interface, with the standard **chown**, **chmod**, and **chgrp** commands, Apple again provides some nice interface capabilities for viewing and managing file and directory permissions. By selecting the properties of any given file or folder, the user can view and modify the permissions for that file or folder, as shown in Figure 14.9. Note that the GUI follows the same user-group-world pattern of permissions that other UNIX variants follow, though Apple uses the term *others* as opposed to *world*.

This GUI allows users to restrict access to sensitive files and directories quickly and effectively. By default, OS X limits a user's ability to access or modify certain areas of the file system, including those areas containing system binaries. However, these restrictions can be circumvented by a user with the appropriate permissions or by certain third-party applications.

Removing unwanted or unnecessary programs in OS X is usually done through the program's own uninstaller utility or by simply using the Finder to locate and then delete the folder containing the program and associated utilities. Like Windows, OS X maps certain file extensions to specific programs, so deleting a program that handles specific extension types may require that an administrator clear up associated extensions.

Like most UNIX-based OSs, OS X is a multiuser platform. As part of the baselining effort, the active user accounts should be examined to ensure they have the right level of access, permissions, group memberships, and so on. Mac OS X also permits administrators to lock accounts so that they can be modified only by users with administrative-level privileges.

• **Figure 14.9** Setting file permissions in Mac OS X

Updates (a.k.a. Hotfixes, Service Packs, and Patches)

Operating systems are large and complex mixes of interrelated software modules written by dozens or even thousands of separate individuals. With the push toward GUI-based functionality and enhanced capabilities that has occurred over the past several years, operating systems have continued to grow and expand. Windows Vista contains approximately 50 million lines of code, and though it may be one of the largest in that respect, other modern operating systems are not far behind. As operating systems continue to grow and introduce new functions, the potential for problems with the code grows as well. It is almost impossible for an operating system vendor to test its product on every possible platform under every possible circumstance, so functionality and security issues do arise after an operating system has been released. To the average user or system administrator, this means a fairly constant stream of updates designed to correct problems, replace sections of code, or even add new features to an installed operating system.

Vendors typically follow a hierarchy for software updates:

- **Hotfix** This is a term given to a (usually) small software update designed to address a specific problem, such as a buffer overflow in an application that exposes the system to attacks. Hotfixes are typically developed in reaction to a discovered problem and are produced and then released rather quickly. Hotfixes typically address critical, security-related issues and should be applied to the affected application or operating system as soon as possible.

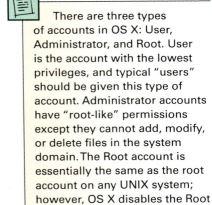

There are three types of accounts in OS X: User, Administrator, and Root. User is the account with the lowest privileges, and typical "users" should be given this type of account. Administrator accounts have "root-like" permissions except they cannot add, modify, or delete files in the system domain. The Root account is essentially the same as the root account on any UNIX system; however, OS X disables the Root account by default. You must enable the Root account if you want to use it on a Mac.

- **Patch** This term is usually applied to a more formal, larger software update that may address several or many software problems. Patches often contain enhancements or additional capabilities as well as fixes for known bugs. Patches are usually developed over a longer period of time.

- **Service pack** This term is usually given to a large collection of patches and hotfixes rolled into a single, rather large package. Service packs are designed to bring a system up to the latest known good level all at once, rather than requiring the user or system administrator to download dozens or hundreds of updates separately.

Every operating system, from Linux to Solaris to Windows, requires software updates, and each operating system has different methods of assisting users in keeping their systems up to date. Microsoft, for example, typically makes updates available for download from its web site. While most administrators or technically proficient users may prefer to identify and download updates individually, Microsoft recognizes that nontechnical users prefer a simpler approach, which Microsoft has built into its operating systems. Beginning with Windows Vista, and Server 2003, Microsoft provides an automated update functionality that will, once configured, locate any required updates, download them to your system, and even install the updates if that is your preference. Figure 14.10 shows the Automatic

• **Figure 14.10** Automatic Updates settings in Windows 7

Principles of Computer Security

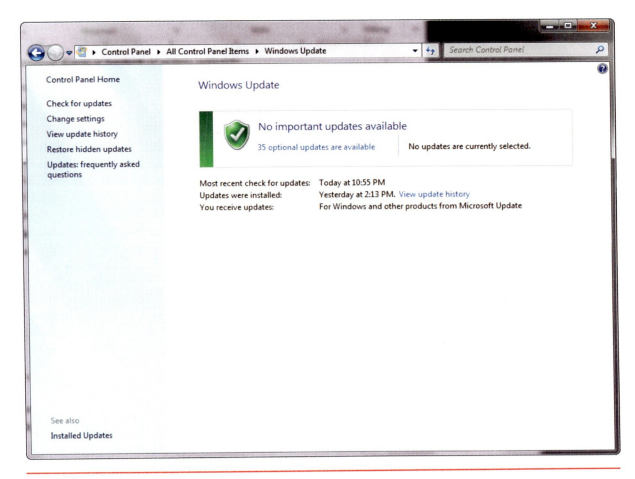

• **Figure 14.11**   Windows Update utility in Windows 7

Updates window, which can be found in the Control Panel. Note that both the web-based updates and Automatic Updates require active Internet connections to retrieve information and updates from Microsoft.

The Windows Update utility (see Figure 14.11) can perform an on-demand search for updates or be configured to scan for, download, and even install updates automatically—essentially the same functions as Automatic Updates with a new look. An especially nice feature of Windows Update is the ability to scan for and download patches for other Microsoft software, such as Office, as well as updates and patches for the operating system itself.

Microsoft is not alone in providing utilities to assist users in keeping their systems up to date and secure. Fedora Linux contains a utility called the Package Updater, shown in Figure 14.12, which does essentially the same thing. Running the utility will show you which updates are available and allow you to select which updates to download and apply. As with most operating systems, you can configure Fedora to automatically download and apply available updates.

Regardless of the method you use to update the operating system, it is critically important to keep systems up to date.

• **Figure 14.12**   Fedora software package update utility

New security advisories come out every day, and while a buffer overflow may be a "potential" problem today, it will almost certainly become a "definite" problem in the near future. Much like the steps taken to baseline and initially secure an operating system, keeping every system patched and up to date is critical to protecting the system and the information it contains.

Operating System Patching

Every OS, from Linux to Windows, requires software updates, and each OS has different methods of assisting users in keeping their systems up to date. Microsoft, for example, typically makes updates available for download from its web site. While most administrators or technically proficient users may prefer to identify and download updates individually, Microsoft recognizes that nontechnical users prefer a simpler approach, which Microsoft has built into its operating systems. In Windows 7 and 8 and Windows Server 2012, Microsoft provides an automated update functionality that will, once configured, locate any required updates, download them to your system, and even install the updates if that is your preference. In Microsoft Windows, the Windows Update utility (see Figure 14.11) can perform an on-demand search for updates or be configured to scan for, download, and even install updates automatically—essentially the same functions as Automatic Updates with a new look. An especially nice feature of Windows Update is the ability to scan for and download patches for other Microsoft software, such as Office, as well as updates and patches for the OS itself.

How you patch a Linux system depends a great deal on the specific version in use and the patch being applied. In some cases, a patch will consist of a series of manual steps requiring the administrator to replace files, change permissions, and alter directories. In other cases, the patches are executable scripts or utilities that perform the patch actions automatically. Some Linux versions, such as Red Hat, have built-in utilities that handle the patching process. In those cases, the administrator downloads a specifically formatted file that the patching utility then processes to perform any modifications or updates that need to be made.

Regardless of the method you use to update the OS, it is critically important to keep systems up to date. New security advisories come out every day, and while a buffer overflow may be a "potential" problem today, it will almost certainly become a "definite" problem in the near future. Much like the steps taken to baseline and initially secure an OS, keeping every system patched and up to date is critical to protecting the system and the information it contains.

Application Updates

Just as operating systems need patches, so do applications. Managing the wide variety of applications and the required updates from numerous different software vendors can be a daunting challenge. This has created a niche market for patch-management software. In most enterprises, some form of automated patch management solution is used, both to reduce labor and to ensure updates are applied appropriately across the enterprise.

Antimalware

In the early days of PC use, threats were limited: most home users were not connected to the Internet 24/7 through broadband connections, and the most common threat was a virus passed from computer to computer via an infected floppy disk (much like the medical definition, a computer virus is something that can infect the host and replicate itself). But things have changed dramatically since those early days, and current threats pose a much greater risk than ever before. According to SANS Internet Storm Center, the average survival time of an unpatched Windows PC on the Internet is less than 60 minutes (http://isc.sans.org/survivaltime.html). This is the estimated time before an automated probe finds the system, penetrates it, and compromises it. Automated probes from botnets and worms are not the only threats roaming the Internet—there are viruses and malware spread by e-mail, phishing, infected web sites that execute code on your system when you visit them, adware, spyware, and so on. Fortunately, as the threats increase in complexity and capability, so do the products designed to stop them.

Cross Check

Malware

Malware comes in many forms and is covered specifically in Chapter 15. Antivirus solutions and proper workstation configurations are part of a defensive posture against various forms of malware. Additional steps include policy and procedure actions, prohibiting file sharing via USB or external media, and prohibiting access to certain web sites.

Antivirus

Antivirus (AV) products attempt to identify, neutralize, or remove malicious programs, macros, and files. These products were initially designed to detect and remove computer viruses, though many of the antivirus products are now bundled with additional security products and features.

Although antivirus products have had over two decades to refine their capabilities, the purpose of the antivirus products remains the same: to detect and eliminate computer viruses and malware. Most antivirus products combine the following approaches when scanning for viruses:

- **Signature-based scanning**   Much like an intrusion detection system (IDS), the antivirus products scan programs, files, macros, e-mails, and other data for known worms, viruses, and malware. The antivirus product contains a virus dictionary with thousands of known virus signatures that must be frequently updated, as new viruses are discovered daily. This approach will catch known viruses but is limited by the virus dictionary—what it does not know about it cannot catch.

- **Heuristic scanning (or analysis)**   Heuristic scanning does not rely on a virus dictionary. Instead, it looks for suspicious behavior— anything that does not fit into a "normal" pattern of behavior for the OS and applications running on the system being protected.

As signature-based scanning is a familiar concept, let's examine heuristic scanning in more detail. **Heuristic scanning** typically looks for commands or instructions that are not normally found in application programs, such

Most current antivirus software packages provide protection against a wide range of threats, including viruses, worms, Trojans, and other malware. Use of an up-to-date antivirus package is essential in the current threat environment.

Exam Tip: Heuristic scanning is a method of detecting potentially malicious or "virus-like" behavior by examining what a program or section of code does. Anything that is "suspicious" or potentially "malicious" is closely examined to determine whether or not it is a threat to the system. Using heuristic scanning, an antivirus product attempts to identify new viruses or heavily modified versions of existing viruses before they can damage your system.

427

Computer virus writers' intentions have changed over the years, from simply spreading a virus and wanting to be noticed, to today's stealthy botnet-creating criminals. One method of remaining hidden is to produce viruses that can morph to lower their detection rates by standard antivirus programs. The number of variants for some viruses has increased from less than 10 to greater than 10,000. This explosion in signatures has created two issues. One, users must constantly (sometimes more than daily) update their signature file. And, more importantly, detection methods are having to change as the number of signatures become too large to scan quickly. For end users, the bottom line is simple: update signatures automatically, and at least daily.

as attempts to access a reserved memory register. Most antivirus products use either a weight-based system or a rule-based system in their heuristic scanning (more effective products use a combination of both techniques). A *weight-based system* rates every suspicious behavior based on the degree of threat associated with that behavior. If the set threshold is passed based on a single behavior or a combination of behaviors, the antivirus product will treat the process, application, macro, and so on that is performing the behavior(s) as a threat to the system. A *rule-based system* compares activity to a set of rules meant to detect and identify malicious software. If part of the software matches a rule, or if a process, application, macro, and so on performs a behavior that matches a rule, the antivirus software will treat that as a threat to the local system.

Some heuristic products are very advanced and contain capabilities for examining memory usage and addressing, a parser for examining executable code, a logic flow analyzer, and a disassembler/emulator so they can "guess" what the code is designed to do and whether or not it is malicious.

As with IDS/IPS products, encryption and obfuscation pose a problem for antivirus products: anything that cannot be read cannot be matched against current virus dictionaries or activity patterns. To combat the use of encryption in malware and viruses, many heuristic scanners look for encryption and decryption loops. As malware is usually designed to run alone and unattended, if it uses encryption, it must contain all the instructions to encrypt and decrypt itself as needed. Heuristic scanners look for instructions such as the initialization of a pointer with a valid memory address, manipulation of a counter, or a branch condition based on a counter value. While these actions don't always indicate the presence of an encryption/decryption loop, if the heuristic engine can find a loop, it might be able to decrypt the software in a protected memory space, such as an emulator, and evaluate the software in more detail. Many viruses share common encryption/decryption routines that help antivirus developers.

Current antivirus products are highly configurable and most offerings will have the following capabilities:

- **Automated updates** Perhaps the most important feature of a good antivirus solution is its ability to keep itself up to date by automatically downloading the latest virus signatures on a frequent basis. This usually requires that the system be connected to the Internet in some fashion and that updates be performed on a daily (or more frequent) basis.

- **Automated scanning** Most antivirus products allow for the scheduling of automated scans so that you can designate when the antivirus product will examine the local system for infected files. These automated scans can typically be scheduled for specific days and times, and the scanning parameters can be configured to specify what drives, directories, and types of files are scanned.

- **Media scanning** Removable media is still a common method for virus and malware propagation, and most antivirus products can be configured to automatically scan optical media, USB drives, memory sticks, or any other type of removable media as soon as they are connected to or accessed by the local system.

- **Manual scanning**   Many antivirus products allow the user to scan drives, files, or directories (folders) "on demand."

- **E-mail scanning**   E-mail is still a major method of virus and malware propagation. Many antivirus products give users the ability to scan both incoming and outgoing messages as well as any attachments.

- **Resolution**   When the antivirus product detects an infected file or application, it can typically perform one of several actions. The antivirus product may quarantine the file, making it inaccessible; it may try to repair the file by removing the infection or offending code; or it may delete the infected file. Most antivirus products allow the user to specify the desired action, and some allow for an escalation in actions such as cleaning the infected file if possible and quarantining the file if it cannot be cleaned.

Antivirus solutions are typically installed on individual systems (desktops, servers, and even mobile devices), but network-based antivirus capabilities are also available in many commercial gateway products. These gateway products often combine firewall, IDS/IPS, and antivirus capabilities into a single integrated platform. Most organizations will also employ antivirus solutions on e-mail servers, as that continues to be a very popular propagation method for viruses.

While the installation of a good antivirus product is still considered a necessary best practice, there is growing concern about the effectiveness of antivirus products against developing threats. Early viruses often exhibited destructive behaviors; were poorly written, modified files; and were less concerned with hiding their presence than they were with propagation. We are seeing an emergence of viruses and malware created by professionals, sometimes financed by criminal organizations or governments, which go to great lengths to hide their presence. These viruses and malware are often used to steal sensitive information or turn the infected PC into part of a larger botnet for use in spamming or attack operations.

> **Exam Tip:** Antivirus is an essential security application on all platforms. There are compliance schemes that mandate antivirus deployment, such as PCI DSS and NERC CIP.

Antivirus Software for Servers

The need for antivirus protection on servers depends a great deal on the use of the server. Some types of servers, such as e-mail servers, require extensive antivirus protection because of the services they provide. Other servers (domain controllers and remote access servers, for example) may not require any antivirus software, as they do not allow users to place files on them. File servers need protection, as do certain types of application servers. There is no general rule, so each server and its role in the network will need to be examined to determine whether it needs antivirus software.

Antivirus Software for Workstations

Antivirus packages are available from a wide range of vendors. Running a network of computers without this basic level of protection will be an exercise in futility. Even though the number of widespread, indiscriminate broadcast virus attacks has decreased because of the effectiveness of antivirus software, it is still necessary to use antivirus software; the time and money you would spend cleaning up after a virus attack more than equals the cost of antivirus protection. The majority of viruses today exist to create zombie machines for botnets that enable others to control resources on your PC. Even more important, once connected by networks, computers can spread a virus from machine to machine with an ease that's even greater than simple USB flash drive transfer. One unprotected machine can lead to problems throughout a network as other machines have to use their antivirus software to attempt to clean up a spreading infection.

Apple Mac computers were once considered by many users to be immune because very few examples of malicious software targeting Macs existed. This was not due to anything other than a low market share, and hence the devices were ignored by the malware community as a whole. As Mac has increased in market share, so has its exposure, and today a variety of Mac OS X malware steals files and passwords and is even used to take users' pictures with the computer's built-in webcam. All user machines need to install antivirus software in today's environment, because any computer can become a target.

Antispam

If you have an e-mail account, you've likely received *spam*, that endless stream of unsolicited, electronic junk mail advertising get-rich-quick schemes, asking you to validate your bank account's password, or inviting you to visit one web site or another. Despite federal legislation (such as the CAN-SPAM Act of 2003) and promises from IT industry giants like Bill Gates ("Two years from now, spam will be solved"—2004), spam is alive and well and filling up your inbox as you read this. Industry experts have been fighting the spam battle for years, and while significant progress has been made in the development of antispam products, unfortunately the spammers have proven to be very creative and very dedicated in their quest to fill your inbox.

Antispam products attempt to filter out that endless stream of junk e-mail so you don't have to. Some antispam products operate at the corporate level, filtering messages as they enter or leave designated mail servers. Other products operate at the host level, filtering messages as they come into your personal inbox. Most antispam products use similar techniques and approaches for filtering out spam:

- **Black listing** Several organizations maintain lists of servers or domains that generate or have generated spam. Most gateway- or server-level products can reference these black lists and automatically reject any mail coming from servers or domains on the black lists.

- **Header filtering** The antispam products look at the message headers to see if they are forged. E-mail headers typically contain information such as sender, receiver, servers used to transmit the message, and so on. Spammers often forge information in message headers in an attempt to hide where the message is really coming from.

- **Content filtering** The content of the message is examined for certain key words or phrases that are common to spam but rarely seen in legitimate e-mails ("get rich now" for example). Unfortunately, content filtering does occasionally flag legitimate messages as spam.

- **Language filtering** Some spam products allow you to filter out e-mails written in certain languages.

Spam is not a new problem. It's reported that the first spam message was sent on May 1, 1978 by a Digital Equipment Corporation sales representative. This sales representative attempted to send a message to all ARPANET users on the West Coast.

Principles of Computer Security

- **User-defined filtering**   Most antispam products allow end users to develop their own filters, such as always allowing e-mail from a specific source even if it would normally be blocked by a content filter.

- **Trapping**   Some products will monitor unpublished e-mail addresses for incoming spam—anything sent to an unpublished and otherwise unused account is likely to be spam.

- **Enforcing the specifications of the protocol**   Some spam-generation tools don't properly follow the SMTP protocol. By enforcing the technical requirements of SMTP, some spam can be rejected as delivery is attempted.

- **Egress filtering**   This technique scans mail as it leaves an organization to catch spam before it is sent to other organizations.

Cross Check

Spam

The topic of spam and all the interesting details of undesired e-mail is presented in Chapter 16. Spam is listed here as it is considered a client threat, but the main methods of combating spam are covered in Chapter 16.

Antispyware

Most antivirus products will include antispyware capabilities as well. While antivirus programs were designed to watch for the writing of files to the file system, many current forms of malware avoid the file system to avoid this form of detection. Newer antivirus products are adapting and scanning memory as well as watching file system access in an attempt to detect advanced malware. *Spyware* is the term used to define malware that is designed to steal information from the system, such as keystrokes, passwords, PINs, and keys. Antispyware helps protect your systems from the ever-increasing flood of malware that seeks to watch your keystrokes, steal your passwords, and report sensitive information back to attackers. Many of these attack vectors work in system memory to avoid easy detection.

Windows Defender

As part of its ongoing efforts to help secure its PC operating systems, Microsoft released a free utility called Windows Defender in February 2006. The stated purpose of Windows Defender is to protect your computer from spyware and other unwanted software (http://windows.microsoft.com/en-us/windows/using-defender#1TC=windows-7). Windows Defender is standard with all versions of the Vista and Windows 7 operating systems and is available via free download in both 32- and 64-bit versions. It has the following capabilities:

- **Spyware detection and removal**   Windows Defender is designed to find and remove spyware and other unwanted programs that display pop-ups, modify browser or Internet settings, or steal personal information from your PC.

- **Scheduled scanning**   You can schedule when you want your system to be scanned or you can run scans on demand.

- **Automatic updates**   Updates to the product can be automatically downloaded and installed without user interaction.

- **Real-time protection**   Processes are monitored in real time to stop spyware and malware when they first launch, attempt to install themselves, or attempt to access your PC.

- **Software Explorer**   One of the more interesting capabilities within Windows Defender is the ability to examine the various programs running on your computer. Windows Defender allows you to look at programs that run automatically on startup, are currently running on your PC, or are accessing network connections on your PC. Windows Defender provides you with details such as the publisher of the software, when it was installed on your PC, whether or not the software is "good" or considered to be known malware, the file size, publication date, and other information.

- **Configurable responses**   Windows Defender lets you choose what actions you want to take in response to detected threats (see Figure 14.13); you can automatically disable the software, quarantine it, attempt to uninstall it, and perform other tasks.

Pop-up Blockers

One of the most annoying nuisances associated with web browsing is the pop-up ad. Pop-up ads are online advertisements designed to attract web

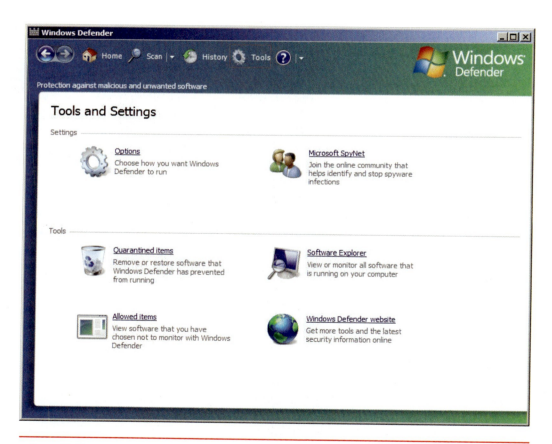

• **Figure 14.13**   Windows Defender configuration options

Principles of Computer Security

traffic to specific web sites, capture e-mail addresses, advertise a product, and perform other tasks. If you've spent more than an hour surfing the Web, you've undoubtedly seen them. They're created when the web site you are visiting opens a new web browser window for the sole purpose of displaying an advertisement. Pop-up ads typically appear in front of your current browser window to catch your attention (and disrupt your browsing). Pop-up ads can range from mildly annoying, generating one or two pop-ups, to system crippling if a malicious web site attempts to open thousands of pop-up windows on your system.

Similar to the pop-up ad is the pop-under ad that opens up behind your current browser window. You won't see these ads until your current window is closed, and they are considered by some to be less annoying than pop-ups. Another form of pop-up is the hover ad that uses Dynamic HTML to appear as a floating window superimposed over your browser window. To some users, pop-up ads are as undesirable as spam, and many web browsers now allow users to restrict or prevent pop-ups with functionality either built into the web browser or available as an add-on. Internet Explorer contains a built-in **Pop-up Blocker** (shown in Figure 14.14 and available from the Tools menu in Internet Explorer 11).

Firefox also contains a built-in pop-up blocker (available by choosing Tools | Options and then selecting the Content tab). Popular add-ons such as the Google and Yahoo! toolbars also contain pop-up blockers. If these freely available options are not enough for your needs, many commercial security suites from McAfee, Symantec, and Check Point contain pop-up blocking capabilities as well. Users must be careful when selecting a pop-up blocker, as some unscrupulous developers have created adware products disguised as free pop-up blockers or other security tools.

Pop-ups ads can be generated in a number of ways, including JavaScript and Adobe Flash, and an effective pop-up blocker must be able to deal with the many methods used to create pop-ups. When a pop-up is created, users typically can click a close or cancel button inside the pop-up or close the new window using a method available through the OS, such as closing the window from the taskbar in Windows. With the advanced features available to them in a web development environment, some unscrupulous developers program the close or cancel button in their pop-ups to launch new pop-ups, redirect the user, run commands on the local system, or even load software.

Pop-ups should not be confused with adware. Pop-ups are ads that appear as you visit web pages. Adware is advertising-supported software. Adware automatically downloads and displays ads on your computer after the adware has been installed, and these ads are typically shown while the software is being used. Adware is often touted as "free" software, as the user pays nothing for the software but must agree to allow ads to be downloaded and displayed before using the software. This approach is very popular on smartphones and mobile devices.

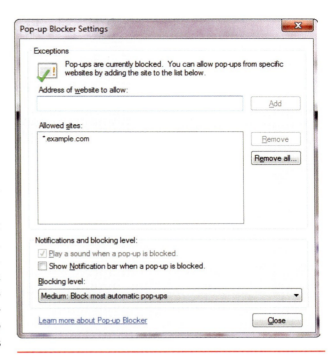

• **Figure 14.14** Pop-up Blocker in IE 11

Exam Tip: Pop-up blockers are used to prevent web sites from opening additional web browser windows or tabs without specific user consent.

White Listing vs. Black Listing Applications

Applications can be controlled at the OS at the time of start via black listing or white listing. **Black listing** is essentially noting which applications should not be allowed to run on the machine. This is basically a permanent "ignore" or "call block" type capability. **White listing** is the exact opposite: it consists of a list of allowed applications. Each of these approaches has advantages and disadvantages. Black listing is difficult to use against dynamic threats, as the identification of a specific application can easily be avoided through minor changes. White listing is easier to employ from the aspect of the identification of applications that are allowed to run—hash values can be used to ensure the executables are not corrupted. The challenge in white listing is the number of potential applications that are run on a typical machine. For a single-purpose machine, such as a database server, white listing can be relatively easy to employ. For multipurpose machines, it can be more complicated.

Microsoft has two mechanisms that are part of the OS to control which users can use which applications:

- **Software restrictive policies** Employed via group policies and allow significant control over applications, scripts, and executable files. The primary mode is by machine and not by user account.

- **User account level control** Enforced via AppLocker, a service that allows granular control over which users can execute which programs. Through the use of rules, an enterprise can exert significant control over who can access and use installed software.

On a Linux platform, similar capabilities are offered from third-party vendor applications.

AppLocker

AppLocker is a component of Windows 7 and later that enables administrators to enforce which applications are allowed to run via a set of predefined rules. AppLocker is an adjunct to Software Restriction Policies (SRP). SRP required significant administration on a machine-by-machine basis and was difficult to administer across an enterprise. AppLocker was designed so the rules can be distributed and enforced by GPO. They both act to prevent the running of both unauthorized software and malware on a machine, but AppLocker is significantly easier to administer. Figure 14.15 shows the AppLocker interface in Windows 7. Some of the features that are enabled via AppLocker are restrictions by user and the ability to run in an audit mode, where results are logged but not enforced, allowing settings to be tested before use.

Trusted OS

A **Trusted Operating System** is one that is designed to allow multilevel security in its operation. This is further defined by its ability to meet a series of criteria required by the U.S. government. Trusted OSs are expensive to create and maintain because any change must typically undergo a recertification process. The most common criteria used to define a Trusted OS is the Common Criteria for Information Technology Security Evaluation

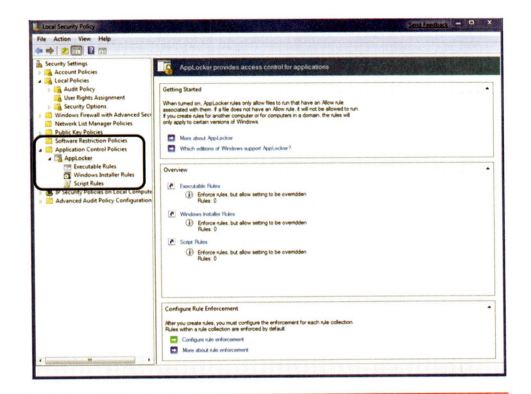

• Figure 14.15   AppLocker in Windows 7

(abbreviated as Common Criteria, or CC), a harmonized security criteria recognized by many nations, including the United States, Canada, Great Britain, and most of the EU countries, as well as others. Versions of Windows, Linux, mainframe OSs, and specialty OSs have been qualified to various Common Criteria levels.

Exam Tip: The term *Trusted Operating System* is used to refer to a system that has met a set of criteria and demonstrated correctness to meet requirements of multilevel security. The Common Criteria is one example of a standard used by government bodies to determine compliance to a level of security need.

Host-based Firewalls

Personal firewalls are host-based protective mechanisms that monitor and control traffic passing into and out of a single system. Designed for the end user, software firewalls often have a configurable security policy that allows the user to determine which traffic is "good" and is allowed to pass and which traffic is "bad" and is blocked. Software firewalls are extremely commonplace—so much so that most modern OSs come with some type of personal firewall included.

Linux-based OSs have had built-in software-based firewalls (see Figure 14.16) for a number of years, including TCP Wrappers, ipchains, and iptables.

TCP Wrappers is a simple program that limits inbound network connections based on port number, domain, or IP address and is managed with two text files called hosts.allow and hosts.deny. If the inbound connection is coming from a trusted IP address and destined for a port to which it is allowed to connect, then the connection is allowed.

• Figure 14.16   Linux firewall

Ipchains is a more advanced, rule-based software firewall that allows for traffic filtering, Network Address Translation (NAT), and redirection. Three configurable "chains" are used for handling network traffic: input, output, and forward. The input chain contains rules for traffic that is coming into the local system. The output chain contains rules for traffic that is leaving the local system. The forward chain contains rules for traffic that was received by the local system but is not destined for the local system. Iptables is the latest evolution of ipchains. Iptables uses the same three chains for policy rules and traffic handling as ipchains, but with iptables each packet is processed only by the appropriate chain. Under ipchains, each packet passes through all three chains for processing. With iptables, incoming packets are processed only by the input chain and packets leaving the system are processed only by the output chain. This allows for more granular control of network traffic and enhances performance.

In addition to the "free" firewalls that come bundled with OSs, many commercial personal firewall packages are available. Programs such as ZoneAlarm from Check Point Software Technologies provide or bundle additional capabilities not found in some bundled software firewalls. Many commercial software firewalls limit inbound and outbound network traffic, block pop-ups, detect adware, block cookies, block malicious processes, and scan instant messenger traffic. While you can still purchase or even download a free software-based personal firewall, most commercial vendors are bundling the firewall functionality with additional capabilities such as antivirus and antispyware.

Microsoft Windows has had a personal software firewall since Windows XP SP2. Windows Firewall (see Figure 14.17) is enabled by default and has warnings when disabled. Windows Firewall is fairly configurable; it can be set up to block all traffic, make exceptions for traffic you want to allow, and log rejected traffic for later analysis.

With the introduction of the Vista operating system, Microsoft modified Windows Firewall to make it more capable and configurable. More options were added to allow for more granular control of network traffic as well as the ability to detect when certain components are not behaving as expected. For example, if your MS Outlook client suddenly attempts to connect to a remote web server, Windows Firewall can detect this as a deviation from normal behavior and block the unwanted traffic.

Hardware Security

Hardware, in the form of servers, workstations, and even mobile devices, can represent a weakness or vulnerability in the security system associated with an enterprise. While hardware can be easily replaced if lost or stolen, the information that is contained by the devices complicates the security picture. Data or information can be safeguarded from loss by backups, but this does little in the way of protecting it from disclosure to an unauthorized party. There are software measures that can assist in the

• **Figure 14.17** Windows Firewall is enabled by default in XP SP2, Vista, and Windows 7.

form of encryption, but these also have drawbacks in the form of scalability and key distribution.

There are some hardware protection mechanisms that should be employed to safeguard information in servers, workstations, and mobile devices. Cable locks can be employed on mobile devices to prevent their theft. Locking cabinets and safes can be used to secure portable media, USB drives, and CDs/DVDs. Physical security is covered in more detail in Chapter 8.

Host Software Baselining

To secure the software on a system effectively and consistently, you must take a structured and logical approach. This starts with an examination of the system's intended functions and capabilities to determine what processes and applications will be housed on the system. As a best practice, anything that is not required for operations should be removed or disabled on the system; then, all the appropriate patches, hotfixes, and settings should be applied to protect and secure it.

This process of establishing software's base security state is called *baselining*, and the resulting product is a security baseline that allows the software to run safely and securely. Software and hardware can be tied intimately when it comes to security, so they must be considered together. Once the process has been completed for a particular hardware and software combination, any similar systems can be configured with the same baseline to achieve the same level and depth of security and protection. Uniform software baselines are critical in large-scale operations, because maintaining separate configurations and security levels for hundreds or thousands of systems is far too costly.

After administrators have finished patching, securing, and preparing a system, they often create an initial baseline configuration. This represents a secure state for the system or network device and a reference point of the software and its configuration. This information establishes a reference that can be used to help keep the system secure by establishing a known safe configuration. If this initial baseline can be replicated, it can also be used as a template when deploying similar systems and network devices.

■ Host-based Security Controls

Security controls can be implemented on a host machine for the express purpose of providing data protection on the host. This section explores methods to implement the appropriate controls to ensure data security.

Hardware-based Encryption Devices

Hardware-based encryption devices are designed to assist in the encryption/decryption actions via hardware rather than software on a system. Integration of encryption functionality via hardware offers both performance and security advantages for these solutions.

TPM

The **Trusted Platform Module (TPM)** is a hardware solution on the motherboard, one that assists with key generation and storage as well as random number generation. When the encryption keys are stored in the TPM, they are not accessible via normal software channels and are physically separated from the hard drive or other encrypted data locations. This makes the TPM a more secure solution than storing the keys on the machine's normal storage.

HSM

A **hardware security module (HSM)** is a device used to manage or store encryption keys. It can also assist in cryptographic operations such as encryption, hashing, or the application of digital signatures. HSMs are typically peripheral devices, connected via USB or a network connection. HSMs have tamper protection mechanisms to prevent physical access to the secrets they protect. Because of their dedicated design, they can offer significant performance advantages over general-purpose computers when it comes to cryptographic operations. When an enterprise has significant levels of cryptographic operations, HSMs can provide throughput efficiencies.

USB Encryption

Universal Serial Bus (USB) offers an easy connection mechanism to connect devices to a computer. This acts as the mechanism of transport between the computer and an external device. When data traverses the USB connection, it typically ends up on a portable device and thus requires an appropriate level of security. Many mechanisms exist, from encryption on the USB device itself, to OS-enabled encryption, to independent encryption before moving the data. Each of these mechanisms has advantages and disadvantages, and it is ultimately up to the user to choose the best method based on the sensitivity of the data.

Hard Drive

As hard drives exist to store information, having the drive itself offer encryption services can provide flexibility in terms of performance and security. It is possible to buy hard drives today with integrated AES encryption, so that the drive content is secured and the keys can be stored separately in a TPM. This offers significant performance and security enhancements over other, software-based solutions.

Data Encryption

Data encryption continues to be the best solution for data security. Properly encrypted, the data is not readable by an unauthorized party. There are numerous ways to enact this level of protection on a host machine.

Full Disk

Full disk encryption refers to the act of encrypting an entire partition in one operation. Then as specific elements are needed, those particular sectors can be decrypted for use. This offers a simple convenience factor and ensures that all of the data is protected. It does come at a performance cost, as the act of decrypting and encrypting takes time. For some high-performance data stores, especially those with latency issues, this performance hit may be critical. Although better performance can be achieved with specialized hardware, as with all security controls there needs to be an evaluation of the risk involved versus the costs.

Database

Major database engines have built-in encryption capabilities. The advantage to these encryption schemes is that they can be tailored to the data structure, protecting the essential columns while not impacting columns that are not sensitive. Properly employing database encryption requires that the data schema and its security requirements be designed into the database implementation. The advantage is in better protection against any database compromise, and the performance hit is typically negligible with respect to other alternatives.

Individual Files

Individual files can be encrypted as well in a system. This can be done either at the OS level or via a third-party application. Managing individual file encryption can be tricky, as the problem moves to an encryption key security problem. When using built-in encryption methods with an OS, the key issue is resolved by the OS itself, with a single key being employed and stored with the user credentials. One of the advantages of individual file encryption comes when transferring data to another user. Transporting a single file via an unprotected channel such as e-mail can be done securely with single-file encryption.

Removable Media

Removable media, by its very nature, can be moved to another location, making the securing of the data stored on the device essential. Again, encryption becomes the tool of choice, and a wide range of encryption methods and applications support the protection of removable media. Microsoft BitLocker, built in to current editions of its Enterprise, Ultimate, and Pro OSs, offers the ability to protect data stored on removable media.

Mobile Devices

Mobile device security, covered in detail in Chapter 12, is also essential when critical or sensitive data is transmitted to mobile devices. The protection of mobile devices goes beyond simple encryption of the data, as the device can act as an authorized endpoint for the system, opening up avenues of attack.

Data Security

Data or information is the most important element to protect in the enterprise. Equipment can be purchased, replaced, and shared without consequence; it is the information that is being processed that has the value. *Data security* refers to the actions taken in the enterprise to secure data, wherever it resides: in transit, at rest, or in use.

Data in Transit

Data has value in the enterprise, but for the enterprise to fully realize the value, data elements need to be shared and moved between systems. Whenever data is *in transit*, being moved from one system to another, it needs to be protected. The most common method of this protection is via encryption. What is important is to ensure that data is always protected in proportion to the degree of risk associated with a data security failure.

Data at Rest

Data at rest refers to data being stored. Data is stored in a variety of formats: in files, in databases, and as structured elements. Whether in ASCII, XML, JavaScript Object Notation (JSON), or a database, and regardless of on what media it is stored, data at rest still requires protection commensurate with its value. Again, as with data in transit, encryption is the best means of protection against unauthorized access or alteration.

Data in Use

Data is processed in applications, is used for various functions, and can be at risk when in system memory or even in the act of processing. Protecting data while in use is a much trickier proposition than protecting it in transit or in storage. While encryption can be used in these other situations, it is not practical to perform operations on encrypted data. This means that other means need to be taken to protect the data. Protected memory schemes and address space layout randomization are two tools that can be used to prevent data security failures during processing. Secure coding principles, including the definitive wiping of critical data elements once they are no longer needed, can assist in protecting data in use.

Handling Big Data

Big data is the industry buzzword for very large data sets being used in many enterprises. Data sets in the petabyte, exabyte, and even zettabyte range are now being explored in some applications. Data sets of these sizes require special hardware and software to handle them, but this does not alleviate the need for security. Planning for security on this scale requires enterprise-level thinking, but it is worth noting that eventually some subset of the information makes its way to a host machine for use. It is at this point that the data is vulnerable, because whatever protection scheme is in place on the large storage system, the data is outside that realm now. This means that local protection mechanisms, such as provided by Kerberos-based authentication, can be critical in managing this type of protection scheme.

Cloud Storage

Cloud computing is the use of online resources for storage, processing, or both. When storing data in the cloud, encryption can be used to protect the data, so that what is actually stored is encrypted data. This reduces the risk of data disclosure both in transit to the cloud and back as well as while in storage.

Storage Area Network

A storage area network (SAN) is a means of storing data across a secondary dedicated network. SANs operate to connect data storage devices as if they were local storage, yet they are separate and can be collections of disks, tapes, and other storage devices. Because the dedicated network is separate from the normal IP network, accessing the SAN requires going through one of the attached machines. This makes SANs a bit more secure than other forms of storage, although loss through a compromised client machine is still a risk.

Permissions/ACL

Access control lists (ACLs) form one of the foundational bases for security on a machine. ACLs can be used by the operating system to make determinations as to whether or not a user can access a resource. This level of permission restriction offers significant protection of resources and transfers the management of the access control problem to the management of ACLs, a smaller and more manageable problem.

■ Network Hardening

While considering the baseline security of systems, you must consider the role the network connection plays in the overall security profile. The tremendous growth of the Internet and the affordability of multiple PCs and Ethernet networking have resulted in almost every computer being attached to some kind of network, and once computers are attached to a network, they are open to access from any other user on that network. Proper controls over network access must be established on computers by controlling the services that are running and the ports that are opened for network access. In addition to servers and workstations, however, network devices must also be examined: routers, switches, and modems, as well as various other components.

These network devices should be configured with very strict parameters to maintain network security. Like normal computer OSs that need to be patched and updated, the software that runs network infrastructure components needs to be updated regularly. Finally, an outer layer of security should be added by implementing appropriate firewall rules and router ACLs.

Cross Check

Network Devices, NAT, and Security

Chapter 9 discussed NAT (Network Address Translation). How do network devices that perform NAT services help secure private networks from Internet-based attacks?

Software Updates

Maintaining current vendor patch levels for your software is one of the most important things you can do to maintain security. This is also true for the infrastructure that runs the network. While some equipment is unmanaged and typically has no network presence and few security risks, any managed equipment that is responding on network ports will have some software or firmware controlling it. This software or firmware needs to be updated on a regular basis.

The most common device that connects people to the Internet is the network router. Dozens of brands of routers are available on the market, but Cisco Systems products dominate. The popular Cisco Internetwork Operating System (IOS) runs on more than 70 of Cisco's devices and is installed countless times at countless locations. Its popularity has fueled research into vulnerabilities in the code, and over the past few years quite a few vulnerabilities have been reported. These vulnerabilities can take many forms because routers send and receive several different kinds of traffic, from the standard Telnet remote terminal, to routing information in the form of Routing Information Protocol (RIP) or Open Shortest Path First (OSPF) packets, to Simple Network Management Protocol (SNMP) packets. This highlights the need to update the Cisco IOS software on a regular basis.

Cisco IOS also runs on many of its Ethernet switching products. Like routers, these have capabilities for receiving and processing protocols such as Telnet and SNMP. Smaller network components do not usually run large software suites and typically have smaller software loaded on internal non-volatile RAM (NVRAM). While the update process for this kind of software is typically called a **firmware update**, this does not change the security implications of keeping it up to date. In the case of a corporate network with several devices, someone must take ownership of updating the devices, and updates must be performed regularly according to security and administration policies.

While we focus on Cisco in our discussion, it's important to note that every network device, regardless of the manufacturer, needs to be maintained and patched to remain secure.

Device Configuration

As important as it is to keep software up to date, properly configuring network devices is equally, if not more, important. Many network devices, such as routers and switches, now have advanced remote management capabilities, with multiple open ports accepting network connections. Proper configuration is necessary to keep these devices secure. Choosing a good password is very important in maintaining external and internal security, and closing or limiting access to any open ports is also a good step for securing the devices. On the more advanced devices, you must carefully consider what services the device is running, just as with a computer. Here are some general steps to take when securing networking devices:

- **Limit access to only those who need it** If your networking device allows management via a web interface, SSH, or any other method, limit who can connect to those services. Many networking devices allow you to specify which IP addresses are allowed to connect to those management services.

- **Choose good passwords** Always change default passwords and follow good password selection guidelines. If the device supports encryption, ensure passwords are stored in encrypted format on the device.

- **Password-protect console and remote access** If the device supports password protection, ensure that all local and remote access capabilities are password protected.

- **Turn off unnecessary services** If your networking equipment supports Telnet but your organization doesn't need it, turn that service off. It's always a good idea to disable or remove unused services. Your device may also support the use of ACLs to limit access to services such as Telnet or SSH on the device itself.

- **Change SNMP community strings** SNMP is widely used to manage networking equipment and typically allows a "public" string, which can typically only read information from a device, and a "private" string, which can often read and write to a device's configuration. Some manufacturers use default or well-known strings (such as "public" for the public string)—always change both the public and private strings if you are using SNMP.

 Exam Tip: The use of the word "public" as an SNMP community string is an extremely well-known vulnerability. Any system using an SNMP community string of "public" should be changed immediately.

Securing Management Interfaces

Some network security devices will have "management interfaces" that allow for remote management of the devices themselves. Often seen on firewalls, routers, and switches, a management interface allows connections to the device's management application, an SSH service, or even a web-based configuration GUI, which are not allowed on any other interface. Due to this high level of access, management interfaces and management applications must be secured against unauthorized access. They should not be connected to public network connections (the Internet) and DMZ connections. Where possible, access to management interfaces and applications should be restricted within an organization so employees without the proper access rights and privileges cannot even connect to those interfaces and applications.

VLAN Management

A *virtual LAN*, or VLAN, is a group of hosts that communicate as if they were on the same broadcast domain. A VLAN is a logical construct that can be used to help control broadcast domains, manage traffic flow, and restrict traffic between organizations, divisions, and so on. Layer 2 switches, by definition, will not bridge IP traffic across VLANs, which gives administrators the ability to segment traffic quite effectively. For example, if multiple departments are connected to the same physical switch, VLANs can be used to segment the traffic such that one department does not see the broadcast traffic from the other departments. By controlling the members of a VLAN, administrators can logically separate network traffic throughout the organization.

IPv4 vs. IPv6

IPv4 (Internet Protocol version 4) is the de facto communication standard in use on almost every network around the planet. Unfortunately, IPv4 contains some inherent shortcomings and vulnerabilities. In an effort to address these issues, the Internet Engineering Task Force (IETF) launched an effort to update or replace IPv4; the result is IPv6. Using a new packet format and much larger address space, IPv6 is designed to speed up packet processing by routers and supply 3.4×10^{38} possible addresses (IPv4 uses only 32 bits for addressing; IPv6 uses 128 bits). Additionally, IPv6 has security "built in" with mandatory support for network layer security. Although widely adopted under IPv4, IPsec support is mandatory in IPv6. The issue now is one of conversion. IPv4 and IPv6 networks cannot talk directly to each other and must rely on some type of gateway. Many operating systems and devices currently support dual IP stacks and can run both IPv4 and IPv6. While adoption of IPv6 is proceeding, it is moving slowly and has yet to gain a significant foothold.

Exam Tip: A "hotfix" is designed to address/fix a specific problem—a buffer overflow in a specific application, for example. A patch is usually a collection of one or more fixes.

Some application "patches" contain new or enhanced functions and some change user-defined settings back to defaults during installation of the patch. If you are deploying an application patch across a large group of users, it is important to understand exactly what that application patch really does. Patches should first be tested in a nonproduction environment before deployment to determine exactly how they affect the system and the network it is connected to.

Application Hardening

Perhaps as important as OS and network hardening is **application hardening**—securing an application against local and Internet-based attacks. Hardening applications is fairly similar to hardening operating systems—you remove the functions or components you don't need, restrict access where you can, and make sure the application is kept up to date with patches. In most cases, the last step in that list is the most important for maintaining application security. After all, applications must be accessible to users or they serve no purpose. As most problems with applications tend to be buffer overflows in legitimate user input fields, patching the application is often the only way to secure it from attack.

Application Configuration Baseline

As with operating systems, applications (particularly those providing public services such as web servers and mail servers) will have recommended security and functionality settings. In some cases, vendors will provide those recommend settings, and, in other cases, an outside organization such as NSA, ISSA, or SANS will provide recommended configurations for popular applications. Many large organizations will develop their own *application configuration baseline*—that list of settings, tweaks, and modifications that creates a functional and hopefully secure application for use within the organization. Developing an application baseline and using it anytime that application is deployed within the organization helps to ensure a consistent (and hopefully secure) configuration across the organization.

Application Patches

As obvious as this seems, application patches are most likely going to come from the vendor that sells the application. After all, who else has access to the source code? In some cases, such as with Microsoft's IIS, this is the same company that sold the OS that the application runs on. In other cases, such as Apache, the vendor is OS independent and provides an application with versions for many different OSs.

Tech Tip

Port Scanners

To find out what services are open on a given host or network devices, many administrators will use a tool called a port scanner. A port scanner is a tool designed to probe remote systems for open TCP and UDP services. Nmap is a very popular (and free) port scanner (see http://nmap.org).

Application patches are likely to come in three varieties: hotfixes, patches, and upgrades. As described for OSs earlier in the chapter, hotfixes are usually small sections of code designed to fix a specific problem. For example, a hotfix may address a buffer overflow in the login routine for an application. Patches are usually collections of fixes, tend to be much larger, and are usually released on a periodic basis or whenever enough problems have been addressed to warrant a patch release. Upgrades are another popular method of patching applications, and they tend to be presented with a more positive spin than patches. Even the term *upgrade* has a positive connotation—you are moving up to a better, more functional, and more secure application. For this reason, many vendors release "upgrades" that consist mainly of fixes rather than new or enhanced functionality.

Exam Tip: Patch management is the process of planning, testing, and deploying patches in a controlled manner.

Patch Management

In the early days of network computing, things were easy—fewer applications existed, vendor patches came out annually or quarterly, and access was restricted to authorized individuals. Updates were few and easy to handle. Now application and OS updates are pushed constantly as vendors struggle to provide new capabilities, fix problems, and address vulnerabilities. Microsoft created "Patch Tuesday" in an effort to condense the update cycle and reduce the effort required to maintain its products, and has now gone to continuous patching of its newest OS. As the number of patches continues to rise, many organizations struggle to keep up with patches—which patches should be applied immediately, which are compatible with the current configuration, which will not affect current business operations, and so on. To help cope with this flood of patches, many organizations have adopted **patch management**, the process of planning, testing, and deploying patches in a controlled manner.

Patch management is a disciplined approach to the acquisition, testing, and implementation of OS and application patches and requires a fair amount of resources to implement properly. To implement patch management effectively, you must first have a good inventory of the software used in your environment, including all OSs and applications. Then you must set up a process to monitor for updates to those software packages. Many vendors provide the ability to update their products automatically or to automatically check for updates and inform the user when updates are available.

Keeping track of patch availability is merely the first step; in many environments, patches must be analyzed and tested. Does the patch apply to the software you are running? Does the patch address a vulnerability or critical issue that must be addressed immediately? What is the impact of applying that patch or group of patches? Will it break something else if you apply this patch? To address these issues, it is recommended that you use development or test platforms, where you can carefully analyze and test patches before placing them into a production environment. While patches are generally "good," they are not always exhaustively tested; some have been known to "break" other products or functions within the product being patched; and some have introduced new vulnerabilities while attempting to address an existing vulnerability. The extent of analysis and testing

Tech Tip

Patch-Management Solutions

Keeping track of current patch levels in a system or group of systems can be a daunting job. There are a variety of software solutions to assist administrators in this task. One of these programs is Secunia Personal Software Inspector (PSI), http:// secunia.com. This program, which is free for personal use, will track updates for applications installed on a machine.

• Secunia Personal Software Inspector results screen

varies widely from organization to organization. Testing and analysis will also vary depending on the application or OS and the extent of the patch.

Once a patch has been analyzed and tested, administrators have to determine when to apply the patch. As many patches require a restart of applications or services or even a reboot of the entire system, most operational environments apply patches only at specific times, to reduce downtime and possible impact and to ensure administrators are available if something goes wrong. Many organizations will also have a rollback plan that allows them to recover the systems back to a known good configuration prior to the patch, in case the patch has unexpected or undesirable effects. Some organizations require extensive coordination and approval of patches prior to implementation, and some institute "lockout" dates where no patching or system changes (with few exceptions) can be made, to ensure business operations are not disrupted. For example, an e-commerce site might have a lockout between the Thanksgiving and Christmas holidays to ensure the site is always available to holiday shoppers.

With any environment, but especially with larger environments, it can be a challenge to track the update status of every desktop and server in the organization. Documenting and maintaining patch status can be a challenge. However, with a disciplined approach, training, policies, and procedures, even the largest environments can be managed. To assist in their patch-management efforts, many organizations use a patch-management product that automates many of the mundane and manpower-intensive

Tech Tip

Production Patching

Patching of production systems brings risk in the change process. This risk should be mitigated via a change management process. Change management is covered in detail in Chapter 21. Patching of production systems should follow the enterprise change management process.

tasks associated with patch management. For example, many patch-management products provide the following:

- Ability to inventory applications and operating systems in use
- Notification of patches that apply to your environment
- Periodic or continual scanning of systems to validate patch status and identify missing patches
- Ability to select which patches to apply and to which systems to apply them
- Ability to push patches to systems on an on-demand or scheduled basis
- Ability to report patch success or failure
- Ability to report patch status on any or all systems in the environment

Patch-management solutions can also be useful to satisfy audit or compliance requirements, as they can show a structured approach to patch management, show when and how systems are patched, and provide a detailed accounting of patch status within the organization.

Microsoft provides a free patch-management product called Windows Server Update Services (WSUS), shown in Figure 14.18. Using the WSUS product, administrators can manage updates for any compatible Windows-based system in their organization. The WSUS product can be configured to download patches automatically from Microsoft based on a variety of factors (such as OS, product family, criticality, and so on). When updates are

• Figure 14.18   Windows Server Update Services

downloaded, the administrator can determine whether or not to push out the patches and when to apply them to the systems in their environment. The WSUS product can also help administrators track patch status on their systems, which is a useful and necessary feature.

Host Software Baselining

To secure, configure, and patch software, administrators must first know what software is installed and running on systems. Maintaining an accurate picture of what operating systems and applications are running inside an organization can be a very labor-intensive task for administrators—especially if individual users have the ability to load software onto their own servers and workstations. To address this issue, many organizations develop *software baselines* for hosts and servers. Sometimes called "default," "gold," or "standard" configurations, a software baseline contains all the approved software that should appear on a desktop or server within the organization. While software baselines can differ slightly due to disparate needs between groups of users, the more "standard" a software baseline becomes, the easier it will be for administrators to secure, patch, and maintain systems within the organization.

Vulnerability Scanner

A vulnerability scanner is a program designed to probe hosts for weaknesses, misconfigurations, old versions of software, and so on. There are essentially three main categories of vulnerability scanners: network, host, and application.

A **network vulnerability scanner** probes a host or hosts for issues across their network connections. Typically a network scanner will either contain or use a port scanner to perform an initial assessment of the network to determine which hosts are alive and which services are open on those hosts. Each system and service is then probed. Network scanners are very broad tools that can run potentially thousands of checks, depending on the OS and services being examined. This makes them a very good "broad sweep" for network-visible vulnerabilities.

Network scanners are essentially the equivalent of a Swiss army knife for assessments. They do lots of tasks and are extremely useful to have around—they may not be as good as a tool dedicated to examining one specific type of service, but if you can only run a single tool to examine your network for vulnerabilities, you'll want that tool to be a network vulnerability scanner. Figure 14.19 shows a screenshot of Nessus from Tenable Network Security, a very popular network vulnerability scanner.

Bottom line: If you need to perform a broad sweep for vulnerabilities on one or more hosts across the network, a network vulnerability scanner is the right tool for the job.

Host vulnerability scanners are designed to run on a specific host and look for vulnerabilities and misconfigurations on that host. Host scanners tend to be more specialized because they're looking for issues associated with a specific operating system or set of operating systems. A good example of a host scanner is the Microsoft Baseline Security Analyzer (MBSA), shown in Figure 14.20. MBSA is designed to examine the security state of a Windows host and offer guidance to address any vulnerabilities, misconfigurations, or

Due to the number of checks they can perform, network scanners can generate a great deal of traffic and a large number of connections to the systems being examined, so care should be taken to minimize the impact on production systems and production networks.

• **Figure 14.19** Nessus—a network vulnerability scanner

missing patches. Although MBSA can be run against remote systems across the network, it is typically run on the host being examined and requires you to have access to that local host (at the Administrator level). The primary thing to remember about host scanners is that they are typically looking for vulnerabilities on the system they are running on.

Selecting the right type of vulnerability scanner isn't that difficult. Just focus on what types of vulnerabilities you need to scan for and how you will be accessing the host/services/applications being scanned. It's also worth noting that to do a thorough job, you will likely need both network-based and host-based scanners—particularly for critical assets. Host- and network-based scanners perform different tests and provide visibility into different types of vulnerabilities. If you want to ensure the best coverage, you'll need to run both.

Application vulnerability scanners are designed to look for vulnerabilities in applications or certain types of applications. Application scanners are some of the most specialized scanners—even though they contain hundreds or even thousands of checks, they only look for misconfigurations or vulnerabilities in a specific type of application. Arguably the most popular type of application scanners are designed to test for weaknesses and vulnerabilities in web-based applications. Web applications are designed to be visible, interact with users, and accept and process user input—all things that make them attractive targets for attackers. More details on application vulnerability scanners can be found in Chapter 18.

Exam Tip: If you want to scan a specific host for vulnerabilities, weak password policies, or unchanged passwords, and you have direct access to the host, a host vulnerability scanner might be just the tool to use.

Exam Tip: If you want to examine a specific application or multiple instances of the same type of application (such as a web site), an application scanner is the tool of choice.

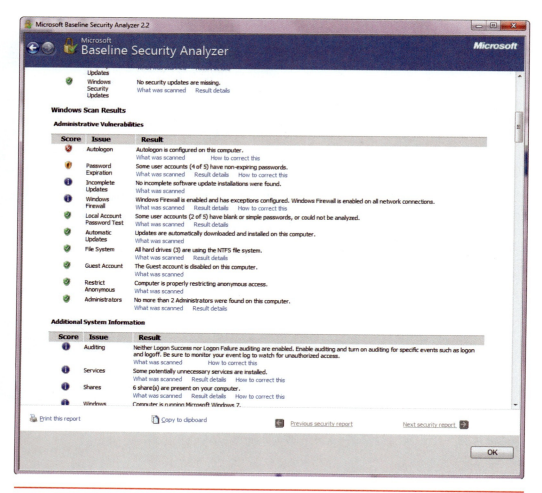

• **Figure 14.20**   Microsoft Baseline Security Analyzer

■ Group Policies

Microsoft defines a **group policy** as "an infrastructure used to deliver and apply one or more desired configurations or policy settings to a set of targeted users and computers within an Active Directory environment. This infrastructure consists of a Group Policy engine and multiple client-side extensions (CSEs) responsible for writing specific policy settings on target client computers." Introduced with the Windows 2000 operating system, group policies are a great way to manage and configure systems centrally in an Active Directory environment (Windows NT had policies—but technically not "group policies"). Group policies can also be used to manage users, making these policies valuable tools in any large environment.

Within the Windows environment, group policies can be used to refine, set, or modify a system's Registry settings, auditing and security policies, user environments, logon/logoff scripts, and so on. Policy settings are stored in a **group policy object (GPO)** and are referenced internally by the OS using a **globally unique identifier (GUID)**. A single policy can be linked to a single user, a group of users, a group of machines, or an entire organizational unit (OU), which makes updating common settings on large groups of users or systems much easier. Users and systems can have more than one GPO assigned and active, which can create conflicts between policies that must then be resolved at an attribute level. Group policies can also overwrite local policy settings. Group policies should not be confused with local policies. *Local* policies are created and applied to a specific system (locally), are not user specific (you can't have local policy X for user A and local policy Y for user B), and are overwritten by GPOs. Further confusing some administrators and users, policies can be applied at the local, site, domain, and OU level. Policies are applied in hierarchical order—local, then site, then domain, and so on. This means settings in a local policy can be overridden or reversed by settings in the domain policy if there is a conflict between the two policies. If there is no conflict, the policy settings are aggregated.

Try This!

Windows Local Security Policies

Open a command prompt as either administrator or a user with administrator privileges on a Windows system. Type the command **secpol** and press ENTER (this should bring up the Local Security Policy utility). Expand Account Policies on the left side of the Local Security Policy window (which should have a + next to it). Click Password Policy. Look in the right side of the Local Security Policy window. What is the minimum password length? What is the maximum password age in days? Now explore some of the policy settings—but be careful! Changes made to the local security policy can affect the functionality or usability of your system.

Creating GPOs is usually done through either the Group Policy Object Editor, shown in Figure 14.21, or the Group Policy Management Console (GPMC). The GPMC is a more powerful GUI-based tool that can summarize GPO settings; simplify security filtering settings; backup, clone, restore, and edit GPOs; and perform other tasks. After creating a GPO, administrators will associate it with the desired targets. After association, group policies operate on a *pull model*. At a semi-random interval, the Group Policy client will collect and apply any policies associated to the system and the currently logged-on user.

Microsoft group policies can provide many useful options including:

- **Network location awareness** Systems are now "aware" of which network they are connected to and can apply different GPOs as needed. For example, a system can have a very restrictive GPO when connected to a public network and a less restrictive GPO when connected to an internal, trusted network.

- **Ability to process without ICMP** Older group policy processes would occasionally time out or fail completely if the targeted system did not respond to ICMP packets. Current implementations in Windows Vista and Windows 7 do not rely on ICMP during the GPO update process.

- **VPN compatibility** As a side benefit of network location awareness, mobile users who connect through VPNs can receive a GPO update in the background after connecting to the corporate network via VPN.

- **Power management** Starting with Windows Vista, power management settings can be configured using GPOs.

- **Device access blocking** Under Windows Vista and Windows 7, policy settings have been added that allow administrators to restrict

● **Figure 14.21** Group Policy Object Editor

In Windows, policies are applied in hierarchical order. Local policies get applied first, then site policies, then domain policies, and finally OU policies. If a setting from a later policy conflicts with a setting from an earlier policy, the setting from the later policy "wins" and is applied. Keep this in mind when building group policies.

Exam Tip: A security template is a collection of security settings that can be applied to a system. Microsoft security template files have an .inf extension and are usually stored in C:\WINDOWS\security\templates.

user access to USB drives, CD-RW drives, DVD-RW drives, and other removable media.

- **Location-based printing** Users can be assigned to various printers based on their location. As mobile users move, their printer locations can be updated to the closest local printer.

■ Security Templates

A **security template** is simply a collection of security settings that can be applied to a system. Within the Windows OSs, security templates can contain hundreds of settings that control or modify system settings such as password length, auditing of user actions, or restrictions on network access. Security templates can be standalone files that are applied manually to each system, but they can also be part of a group policy, allowing common security settings to be applied to systems on a much wider scale.

As an administrator, when you are creating a security template, all settings are initially "not configured," which means the template will make no changes to whatever settings are already in place. By selecting the settings you want to modify, you can fine-tune the template to create a more (or less) secure system. Security templates typically configure settings in the following areas:

- **Account policies**   Settings for user accounts, such as password length, complexity requirements, account lockouts, and so on.

- **Event log settings**   Settings that apply to the three main audit logs within Windows (Application, System, and Security), such as log file size, retention of older entries, and so on.

- **File permissions**   Settings that apply to files and folders, such as permission inheritance, locking permissions, and so on.

- **Registry permissions**   Settings that control who can access the Registry and how it can be accessed.

- **Restricted groups**   Settings that control who should be allowed to join or be part of certain groups. If the user is not already a member of a group as defined in the policy, you will not be able to add that user to the corresponding group on the local system.

- **System services**   Settings for services that run on the system, such as startup mode, whether or not users can stop/start the service, and so on.

- **User rights**   Settings that control what a user can and cannot do on the system.

Tech Tip

A Good Administrator's Work Is Never Done
Once a system or network device is baselined, an administrator's work is far from over. Continuous security monitoring is the never-ending process of collecting data points and metrics, analyzing them, and using the collected data to adjust security postures as needed. When the security monitoring uncovers an issue or vulnerability, the process of remediation begins. Remediation is the process of addressing a security flaw, vulnerability, or similar issue. You might say that a good administrator's work is never done.

You can create and/or modify security templates on your local system through the Microsoft Management Console (if you have the Security Templates snap-in installed). Microsoft includes a series of predefined security templates (usually stored in \WINDOWS\security\templates) that will appear under Security Templates in your MMC window. These templates range from minimal to maximal security and can all be applied as-is or modified as needed. You can also create a completely new security template and then customize each of the settings to your specifications. Figure 14.22 shows the MMC with the Security Templates snap-in enabled.

• **Figure 14.22**   MMC with Security Templates snap-in

■ Alternative Environments

Alternative environments are those that are not traditional computer systems in a common IT environment. This is not to say that these environments are rare; in fact, there are millions of systems, composed of hundreds of millions of devices, all across society. Computers exist in many systems where they perform critical functions specifically tied to a particular system. These alternative systems are frequently static in nature; that is, their software is unchanging over the course of its function. Updates and revisions are few and far between. While this may seem to be counter to current security practices, it isn't: because these alternative systems are constrained to a limited, defined set of functionality, the risk from vulnerabilities is limited. Examples of these alternative environments include embedded systems, SCADA systems, mobile devices, mainframes, game consoles, and in-vehicle computers.

SCADA

SCADA is an acronym for *supervisory control and data acquisition*, a system designed to control automated systems in cyber-physical environments. SCADA systems control manufacturing plants, traffic lights, refineries, energy networks, water plants, building automation and environmental controls, and a host of other systems. SCADA is also known by names such as distributed control systems (DCS) and industrial control systems (ICS), the variations depending on the industry and the configuration. Where computers control a physical process directly, a SCADA system likely is involved.

Most SCADA systems involve multiple components networked together to achieve a set of functional objectives. These systems frequently include a human machine interface (HMI), where an operator can exert a form of directive control over the operation of the system under control. SCADA systems historically have been isolated from other systems, but the isolation is decreasing as these systems are being connected across traditional networks to improve business functionality. Many older SCADA systems were air gapped from the corporate network; that is, they shared no direct network connections. This meant that data flows in and out were handled manually and took time to accomplish. Modern systems wished to remove this constraint and added direct network connections between the SCADA networks and the enterprise IT network. These connections increase the attack surface and the risk to the system, and the more they resemble an IT networked system, the greater the need for security functions.

SCADA systems have been drawn into the security spotlight with the Stuxnet attack on Iranian nuclear facilities, initially reported in 2010. Stuxnet is malware designed to specifically attack a specific SCADA system and cause failures resulting in plant equipment damage. This attack was complex and well designed, crippling nuclear fuel processing in Iran for a significant period of time. This attack raised awareness of the risks associated with SCADA systems, whether connected to the Internet or not (Stuxnet crossed an air gap to hit its target).

Embedded Systems

Embedded system is the name given to a computer that is included as an integral part of a larger system. From computer peripherals like printers, to household devices like smart TVs and thermostats, to the car you drive, embedded systems are everywhere. Embedded systems can be as simple as a microcontroller with fully integrated interfaces (a system on a chip) or as complex as the tens of interconnected embedded systems in a modern automobile. Embedded systems are designed with a single control purpose in mind and have virtually no additional functionality, but this does not mean that they are free of risk or security concerns. The vast majority of security exploits involve getting a device or system to do something it is capable of doing, and technically designed to do, even if the resulting functionality was never an intended use of the device or system.

The designers of embedded systems typically are focused on minimizing costs, with security seldom seriously considered as part of either the design or the implementation. Because most embedded systems operate as isolated systems, the risks have not been significant. However, as capabilities have increased, and these devices have become networked together, the risks have increased significantly. For example, smart printers have been hacked as a way into enterprises, and as a way to hide from defenders. And when next-generation automobiles begin to talk to each other, passing traffic and other information between them, and begin to have navigation and other inputs being beamed into systems, the risks will increase and security will become an issue. This has already been seen in the airline industry, where the separation of in-flight Wi-Fi, in-flight entertainment, and cockpit digital flight control networks has become a security issue.

> **Exam Tip:** Understand static environments, systems in which the hardware, OS, applications, and networks are configured for a specific function or purpose. These systems are designed to remain unaltered through their lifecycle, rarely requiring updates.

Building-automation systems, climate control systems, HVAC systems, elevator control systems, and alarm systems are just some of the examples of systems that are managed by embedded systems. Although these systems used to be independent and standalone systems, the rise of hyperconnectivity has shown value in integrating them. Having a "smart building" that reduces building resources in accordance with the number and distribution of people inside increases efficiency and reduces costs. Interconnecting these systems and adding in Internet-based central control mechanisms does increase the risk profile from outside attacks.

Phones and Mobile Devices

Mobile devices may seem to be a static environment, one where the OS rarely changes or is rarely updated, but as these devices become more and more ubiquitous in capability, this is not turning out to be the case. Mobile devices have regular software updates to the OS, and users add applications, making most mobile devices a complete security challenge. Mobile devices frequently come with Bluetooth connectivity mechanisms. Protection of the devices from attacks against the Bluetooth connection, such as bluejacking and bluesnarfing, is an important mitigation. To protect against unauthorized connections, a Bluetooth device should always have discoverable mode turned off unless the user is deliberately pairing the device.

There are many different operating systems used in mobile devices, the most common of these by market share being Android and iOS from Apple.

Android is by far the largest footprint, followed distantly by Apple's iOS. Microsoft and Blackberry have their own OSs, but neither has major numbers of users.

Android

Android is a generic name associated with the mobile OS that is based on Linux. Google acquired the Android platform, made it open source, and began shipping devices in 2008. Android has undergone several updates since, and most systems have some degree of customization added for specific mobile carriers. Android has had numerous security issues over the years, ranging from vulnerabilities that allow attackers access to the OS, to malware-infected applications. The Android platform continues to evolve as the code is cleaned up and the number of vulnerabilities is reduced. The issue of malware-infected applications is much tougher to resolve, as the ability to create content and add it to the app store (Google Play) is considerably less regulated than in the Apple and Microsoft ecosystems.

The use of mobile device management (MDM) systems is advised in enterprise deployments, especially when BYOD occurs. This and other security aspects specific to mobile devices are covered in Chapter 12.

iOS

iOS is the name of Apple's proprietary operating system for its mobile platforms. Because Apple does not license the software for use other than on its own devices, Apple retains full and complete control over the OS and any specific capabilities. Apple has also exerted significant control over its application store, which has dramatically limited the incidence of malware in the Apple ecosystem.

Jailbreaking

A common hack associated with iOS devices is the jailbreak. *Jailbreaking* is a process by which the user escalates their privilege level, bypassing the operating system's controls and limitations. The user still has the complete functionality of the device, but also has additional capabilities, bypassing the OS-imposed user restrictions. There are several schools of thought concerning the utility of jailbreaking, but the important issue from a security point of view is that running any device with enhanced privileges can result in errors that cause more damage, because normal security controls are typically bypassed.

Mainframe

Mainframes represent the history of computing, and although many people think they have disappeared, they are still very much alive in enterprise computing. Mainframes are high-performance machines that offer large quantities of memory, computing power, and storage. Mainframes have been used for decades for high-volume transaction systems as well as high-performance computing. The security associated with mainframe systems tends to be built into the operating system on specific-purpose mainframes. Mainframe environments tend to have very strong configuration control mechanisms, and very high levels of stability.

Mainframes have become a cost-effective solution for many high-volume applications because many instances of virtual machines can run on the mainframe hardware. This opens the door for many new security vulnerabilities—not on the mainframe hardware per se, but rather through vulnerabilities in the guest OS in the virtual environment.

Game Consoles

Computer-based game consoles can be considered a type of embedded system designed for entertainment. The OS in a game console is not there for the user, but rather there to support the specific applications or game. There typically is no user interface to the OS on a game console for a user to interact with; rather, the OS is designed for a sole purpose. With the rise of multifunction entertainment consoles, the attack surface of a gaming console can be fairly large, but it is still constrained by the closed nature of the gaming ecosystem. Updates for the firmware and OS-level software are provided by the console manufacturer. This closed environment offers a reasonable level of risk associated with the security of the systems that are connected. As game consoles become more general in purpose and include features such as web browsing, the risks increase to levels commensurate with any other general computing platform.

In-vehicle Computing Systems

Motor vehicles have had embedded computers in them for years, regulating engine functions, environmental controls, and dashboard displays. Recently the functionality has expanded to onscreen entertainment and navigation systems. As the functionality of the systems is expanding, with the addition of networking capability, the same security risks associated with other networked systems emerge. As the in-vehicle computing systems continue to integrate with mobile electronics, and with the coming vehicle-to-vehicle and vehicle-to-roadway communications, security risks will increase and become a pressing issue.

Alternative Environment Methods

Many of the alternative environments can be considered static systems. Static systems are those that have a defined scope and purpose and do not regularly change in a dynamic manner, unlike most PC environments. Static systems tend to have closed ecosystems, with complete control over all functionality by a single vendor. A wide range of security techniques can be employed in the management of alternative systems. Network segmentation, security layers, wrappers, and firewalls assist in the securing of the network connections between these systems. Manual updates, firmware control, and control redundancy assist in the security of the device operation.

Network Segmentation

Network segmentation is the use of the network architecture to limit communication between devices. A variety of networking mechanisms can be used to limit access to devices at the network level. Logical network segmentation can be done via VLANs, MAC and IP address restrictions at routers and switches, firewall filtering, and access control mechanisms. One of the challenges with alternative systems is that the devices themselves may not have typical security controls such as access controls or encryption included in their function sets. This makes external controls such as network segmentation even more critical as part of a security solution.

Security Layers

The use of different layers to perform different functions has been a staple of computer science for decades. Employing layers to enforce security aspects has also been a long-standing concept. Not all layers have the same information or processing capability, and using each layer to achieve a part of the security solution leads to more robust security solutions. While a network can manage traffic based on networking information, this is not a complete security solution. Adding additional layers, such as application layer firewalls and authentication services, adds additional security functions that further reduce the risk associated with the system.

Application Firewalls

Application firewalls are policy-enforcement mechanisms that operate at the application layer to enforce a set of communication rules. While a network firewall examines network traffic and enforces rules based on addresses, an application firewall adds significantly greater ability to control an application's communications across the network.

Manual Updates

All systems eventually require updates to fix issues, patch vulnerabilities, and even change functionality. In alternative environments, these changes are in many cases done in a manual manner. Manual updates can be used to restrict the access to the system, preventing unauthorized changes to a system. In some cases, because of scale, an automated system may be used to push out the updates, but the principle of tightly controlling access to system update functionality needs to be preserved.

Firmware Version Control

Firmware is present in virtually every system, but in many embedded systems it plays an even more critical role, as it may also contain the OS and application. Maintaining strict control measures over the changing of firmware is essential to ensuring the authenticity of the software on a system. Firmware updates require extreme quality measures to ensure that errors are not introduced as part of an update process. Updating firmware, although only occasionally necessary, is a very sensitive event, for failure can lead to system malfunction. If an unauthorized party is able to change the firmware of a system, as demonstrated in an attack against ATMs, an adversary can gain complete functional control over a system.

Wrappers

TCP wrappers are structures used to enclose or contain some other system. Wrappers have been used in a variety of ways, including to obscure or hide functionality. A Trojan horse is a form of wrapper. Wrappers also can be used to encapsulate information, such as in tunneling or VPN solutions. Wrappers can act as a form of channel control, including integrity and authentication information that a normal signal cannot carry. It is common to see wrappers used in alternative environments to prepare communications for IP transmission.

Control Redundancy and Diversity

Defense in depth is one of the underlying security fundamentals, and this is especially needed in alternative environments. Many alternative environments are not equipped with on-board encryption, access control, or authentication services. This makes the controls that surround the device even more critical in ensuring secure operation.

Designing overlapping controls such that each assists the others but does not duplicate them adds significant strength to a security solution. The objective is to raise barriers to entry, preventing unauthorized parties from reaching vulnerabilities, and to mitigate those vulnerabilities they can reach such that the attacker cannot proceed further. There is no such thing as perfect security, but a series of overlapping controls can make exploitation nearly impossible.

When the system is in an alternative environment, whether static or not, the principles of security still apply. In fact, in many cases, they are even more critical because the devices themselves have little to no security functionality and thus depend on the supporting environment to be secure. A diversity of controls in redundant, overlapping structures is the best method of providing this level of mitigation.

Exam Tip: Understand static environment security methods. Static systems require security and techniques such as network segmentation, security layers, firewalls, wrappers, and other security controls.

Chapter 14 Review

■ For More Information

- **Microsoft's Safety & Security Center** www .microsoft.com/security/default.mspx

- **SANS Reading Room: Application and Database Security** www.sans.org/reading_room/ whitepapers/application/

■ Lab Manual Exercises

The following lab exercises from the companion lab manual, *Principles of Computer Security Lab Manual, Fourth Edition,* provide practical application of material covered in this chapter:

Lab 1.1l   Linux Client Configuration

■ Chapter Summary

After reading this chapter and completing the exercises, you should understand the following about hardening systems and baselines.

Harden operating systems and network operating systems

- Security baselines are critical to protecting information systems, particularly those allowing connections from external users.

- The process of establishing a system's security state is called baselining, and the resulting product is a security baseline that allows the system to run safely and securely.

- Hardening is the process by which operating systems, network resources, and applications are secured against possible attacks.

- Securing operating systems consists of removing or disabling unnecessary services, restricting permissions on files and directories, removing unnecessary software (or not installing it in the first place), applying the latest patches, removing unnecessary user accounts, and ensuring strong password guidelines are in place.

- Securing network resources consists of disabling unnecessary functions, restricting access to ports and services, ensuring strong passwords are used, and ensuring the code on the network devices is patched and up to date.

- Securing applications depends heavily on the application involved but typically consists of removing samples and default materials, preventing reconnaissance attempts, and ensuring the software is patched and up to date.

Implement host-level security

- Anti-malware/spyware/virus protections are needed on host machines to prevent malicious code attacks.

- White listing can provide strong protections against malware on key systems.

- Host-based firewalls can provide specific protections from some attacks.

Harden applications

- Patch management is a disciplined approach to the acquisition, testing, and implementation of OS and application patches.

- A hotfix is a single package designed to address a specific, typically security-related, problem in an operating system or application.

- A patch is a fix or collection of fixes that addresses vulnerabilities or errors in operating systems or applications.

- A service pack is a large collection of fixes, corrections, and enhancements for an operating system, application, or group of applications.

Establish group policies

- Group policies are a method for managing the settings and configurations of many different users and systems in an Active Directory environment.

- Group policies can be used to refine, set, or modify a system's Registry settings, auditing and security policies, user environments, logon/logoff scripts, and so on.

- Security templates are collections of security settings that can be applied to a system. Security templates can contain hundreds of settings that control or modify settings on a system, such as password length, auditing of user actions, or restrictions on network access.

Secure alternative environments

- Alternative environments include process control (SCADA) networks, embedded systems, mobile devices, mainframes, game consoles, transportation systems, and more.

- Alternative environments require security, but are not universally equivalent to IT systems, so the specifics can vary tremendously from system to system.

Key Terms

antispam *(430)*
antivirus (AV) *(427)*
application hardening *(444)*
application vulnerability scanner *(449)*
baseline *(409)*
baselining *(409)*
black listing *(434)*
firmware update *(442)*
globally unique identifier (GUID) *(450)*
group policy *(450)*
group policy object (GPO) *(450)*
hardening *(408)*
hardware security module (HSM) *(438)*
heuristic scanning *(427)*
host vulnerability scanner *(448)*
hotfix *(423)*
network operating system (NOS) *(410)*
network segmentation *(457)*

network vulnerability scanner *(448)*
operating system (OS) *(409)*
patch *(424)*
patch management *(445)*
Pluggable Authentication Modules (PAM) *(419)*
pop-up blocker *(433)*
process identifier (PID) *(418)*
reference monitor *(410)*
runlevels *(418)*
security kernel *(410)*
security template *(452)*
service pack *(424)*
shadow file *(418)*
TCP wrappers *(419)*
Trusted Operating System *(434)*
Trusted Platform Module (TPM) *(438)*
white listing *(434)*

Key Terms Quiz

Use terms from the Key Terms list to complete the sentences that follow. Don't use the same term more than once. Not all terms will be used.

1. _____ is the process of establishing a system's security state.

2. Securing and preparing a system for the production environment is called _____.

3. A(n) _____ is a small software update designed to address a specific, often urgent, problem.

4. The basic software on a computer that handles input and output is called the _____.

5. _____ is the use of the network architecture to limit communication between devices.

6. A(n) _____ is a bundled set of software updates, fixes, and additional functions contained in a self-installing package.

7. In most UNIX operating systems, each running program is given a unique number called a(n) _____.

8. When a user or process supplies more data than was expected, a(n) _____ may occur.

9. _____ are used to describe the state of init and what system services are operating in UNIX systems.

10. A(n) _____ is a collection of security settings that can be applied to a system.

Multiple-Choice Quiz

1. A small software update designed to address an urgent or specific problem is called a:
    A. Hotfix
    B. Service pack
    C. Patch
    D. None of the above

2. In a UNIX operating system, which runlevel describes single-user mode?
    A. 0
    B. 6
    C. 4
    D. 1

3. TCP wrappers do what?
    A. Help secure the system by restricting network connections
    B. Help prioritize network traffic for optimal throughput
    C. Encrypt outgoing network traffic
    D. Strip out excess input to defeat buffer overflow attacks

4. File permissions under UNIX consist of what three types?
    A. Modify, read, and execute
    B. Read, write, and execute
    C. Full control, read-only, and run
    D. Write, read, and open

5. The mechanism that allows for centralized management and configuration of computers and remote users in an Active Directory environment is called:
    A. Baseline
    B. Group policies
    C. Simple Network Management Protocol
    D. Security templates

6. What feature in Windows Server 2008 controls access to network resources based on a client computer's identity and compliance with corporate governance policy?
    A. BitLocker
    B. Network Access Protection
    C. inetd
    D. Process identifiers

7. To stop a particular service or program running on a UNIX operating system, you might use the _____ command.
    A. netstat
    B. ps
    C. kill
    D. inetd

8. Updating the software loaded on nonvolatile RAM is called:
    A. A buffer overflow
    B. A firmware update
    C. A hotfix
    D. A service pack

9. The shadow file on a UNIX system contains:
    A. The password associated with a user account
    B. Group policy information
    C. File permissions for system files
    D. Network services started when the system is booted

10. On a UNIX system, if a file has the permissions **rwx r-x rw-**, what permissions does the owner of the file have?
    A. Read only
    B. Read and write
    C. Read, write, and execute
    D. None

■ Essay Quiz

1. Explain the difference between a "hotfix" and a "service pack" and describe why both are so important.

2. A new administrator needs some help creating a security baseline. Create a checklist/template that covers the basic steps in creating a security baseline to assist them, and explain why each step is important.

Lab Projects

• Lab Project 14.1

Use a lab system running Linux with at least one open service such as FTP, Telnet, or SMTP. From another lab system, connect to the Linux system and observe your results. Configure TCP wrappers on the Linux system to reject all connection attempts from the other lab system. Now try to reconnect, and observe your results. Document your steps and explain how TCP wrappers work.

• Lab Project 14.2

Using a system running Windows, experiment with the Password Policy settings under the Local Security Policy (Settings | Control Panel | Administrative Tools | Local Security Policy). Find the setting for Passwords Must Meet Complexity Requirements and make sure it is disabled. Set the password on the account you are using to **bob**.

Now enable the Passwords Must Meet Complexity Requirements settings and attempt to change your password to **jane**. Were you able to change it to "jane"? Explain why or why not. Set your password to something the system will allow and explain how you selected that password and how it meets the complexity requirements.

chapter 15

Types of Attacks and Malicious Software

If you know the enemy and know yourself you need not fear the results of a hundred battles.

—Sun Tzu

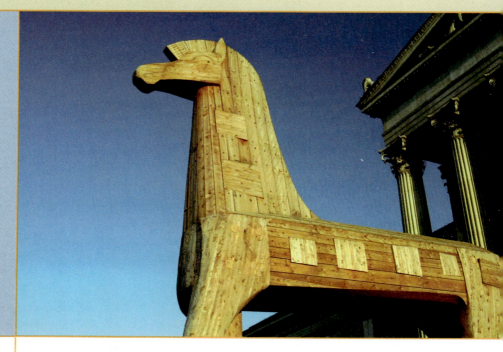

In this chapter, you will learn how to

- Describe the various types of computer and network attacks, including denial-of-service, spoofing, hijacking, and password guessing

- Identify the different types of malicious software that exist, including viruses, worms, Trojan horses, logic bombs, time bombs, and rootkits

- Explain how social engineering can be used as a means to gain access to computers and networks

- Describe the importance of auditing and what should be audited

Attacks can be made against virtually any layer or level of software, from network protocols to applications. When an attacker finds a vulnerability in a system, he exploits the weakness to attack the system. The effect of an attack depends on the attacker's intent and can result in a wide range of effects, from minor to severe. An attack on one system might not be visible on the user's system because the attack is actually occurring on a different system, and the data the attacker will manipulate on the second system is obtained by attacking the first system.

■ Avenues of Attack

A computer system is attacked for one of two general reasons: it is specifically targeted by an attacker, or it is a target of opportunity. In the first case, the attacker has chosen the target not because of the hardware or software the organization is running but for another reason, such as a political reason. For example, an individual in one country might attack a government system in another country to gather secret information. Or the attacker might target an organization as part of a "hacktivist" attack—the attacker could deface the web site of a company that sells fur coats because the attacker believes using animals in this way is unethical, for example. Perpetrating some sort of electronic fraud is another reason a specific system might be targeted for attack. Whatever the reason, the attacker usually begins an attack of this nature before he knows which hardware and software the organization uses.

The second type of attack, an attack against a target of opportunity, is launched against a site that has hardware or software that is vulnerable to a specific exploit. The attacker, in this case, is not targeting the organization; he has instead learned of a specific vulnerability and is simply looking for an organization with this vulnerability that he can exploit. This is not to say that an attacker might not be targeting a given sector and looking for a target of opportunity in that sector. For example, an attacker who wants to obtain credit card or other personal information may search for any exploitable company that stores credit card information on its system to accomplish the attack.

Targeted attacks are more difficult and take more time and effort than attacks on a target of opportunity. The latter type of attack simply relies on the fact that, with any piece of widely distributed software, somebody in the organization will not have patched the system as they should have.

> **Tech Tip**
>
> **Defense Begins with Eliminating Vulnerabilities**
> *Defense against attacks begins with elimination of vulnerabilities. Vulnerabilities are exploited by attackers to gain access to a system. Minimization of vulnerabilities is one of the foundational elements of defense.*

> ✓ **Cross Check**
>
> **Anatomy of an Attack**
>
> Hackers use a process when attacking, and this is covered in detail in Chapter 22.

Minimizing Possible Avenues of Attack

By understanding the steps an attacker can take, you can limit the exposure of your system and minimize the possible avenues an attacker can exploit. Your first step to minimize possible attacks is to ensure that all patches for the operating system and applications are installed. Many security problems, such as viruses and worms, exploit known vulnerabilities for which patches actually exist. These attacks are successful only because administrators have not taken the appropriate actions to protect their systems.

The next step is to limit the services that are running on the system. As mentioned in earlier chapters, limiting the number of services to those that are absolutely necessary provides two safeguards: it limits the possible avenues of attack (the possible services for which a vulnerability may exist and be exploited), and it reduces the number of services the administrator has to worry about patching in the first place.

Cross Check

Baseline Analysis and Patching of Systems

Keeping a system patched and up to date for the operating system and applications is the best defense against exposed vulnerabilities. How up to date is the system you are currently using? How do you know? Chapter 14 covers the baselining and patching of systems to understand and remove vulnerabilities. Refer to that chapter for more in-depth information on how to perform these activities.

Another step is to limit public disclosure of private information about your organization and its computing resources. Since the attacker is after this information, don't make it easy to obtain.

■ Malicious Code

Malicious code, or **malware**, refers to software that has been designed for some nefarious purpose. Such software can be designed to cause damage to a system, such as by deleting all files, or it can be designed to create a backdoor in the system to grant access to unauthorized individuals. Most malware instances attack vulnerabilities in programs or operating systems. This is why patching of vulnerabilities is so important, for it closes the point of entry for most malware. Generally the installation of malicious code is done in such a way that it is not obvious to the authorized users. Several different types of malicious software can be used, such as viruses, Trojan horses, logic bombs, spyware, and worms, and they differ in the ways they are installed and their purposes.

Malware can be fairly complex in its construction, with specific features designed to assist malware in avoiding detection. Modern malware can be multipart in construction, where several pieces work together to achieve a desired effect. When malware has multiple different objects that it specifically attacks, it is called *multipartite*. Many types of malware can include a changing encryption layer to resist pattern-matching detection. These are called *polymorphic*. If the malware actually changes the code at time of infection, this property is called *metamorphic*.

Viruses

The best-known type of malicious code is the **virus**. Much has been written about viruses as a result of several high-profile security events that involved them. A virus is a piece of malicious code that replicates by attaching itself to another piece of executable code. When the other executable code is run, the virus also executes and has the opportunity to infect other files and perform any other nefarious actions it was designed to do. The specific way that a virus infects other files, and the type of files it infects, depends on the type of virus. The first viruses created were of two types—boot sector viruses and program viruses.

Boot Sector Virus

A boot sector virus infects the boot sector portion of either a floppy disk or a hard drive (years ago, not all computers had hard drives, and many booted from a floppy). When a computer is first turned on, a small portion of the operating system is initially loaded from hardware. This small operating system then attempts to load the rest of the operating system from a specific location (sector) on either the floppy or the hard drive. A boot sector virus infects this portion of the drive.

An example of this type of virus was the Stoned virus, which moved the true Master Boot Record (MBR) from the first to the seventh sector of the first cylinder and replaced the original MBR with the virus code. When the system was turned on, the virus was first executed, which had a one-in-seven chance of displaying a message stating the computer was "stoned"; otherwise, it would not announce itself and would instead attempt to infect other boot sectors. This virus was rather tame in comparison to other viruses of its time, which were often designed to delete the entire hard drive after a period of time in which they would attempt to spread.

Program Virus

A second type of virus is the program virus, which attaches itself to executable files—typically files ending in .exe or .com on Windows-based systems. The virus is attached in such a way that it is executed before the program executes. Most program viruses also hide a nefarious purpose, such as deleting the hard drive data, which is triggered by a specific event, such as a date or after a certain number of other files are infected. Like other types of viruses, program viruses are often not detected until after they execute their malicious payload. One method that has been used to detect this sort of virus before it has an opportunity to damage a system is to calculate checksums for commonly used programs or utilities. Should the checksum for an executable ever change, it is quite likely that it is due to a virus infection.

Macro Virus

In the late 1990s, another type of virus appeared that now accounts for the majority of viruses. As systems and operating systems became more powerful, the boot sector virus, which once accounted for most reported infections, became less common. Systems no longer commonly booted from floppies, which were the main method for boot sector viruses to spread. Instead, the proliferation of software that included macro-programming languages resulted in a new breed of virus—the macro virus.

The Concept virus was the first known example of this new breed. It appeared to be created to demonstrate the possibility of attaching a virus to a document file, something that had been thought to be impossible before the introduction of software that included powerful macro language capabilities. By this time, however, Microsoft Word documents could include segments of code written in a derivative of Visual Basic. Further development of other applications that allowed macro capability, and enhanced versions of the original macro language, had the side effect of allowing the proliferation of viruses that took advantage of this capability.

Tech Tip

Modern Virus and Worm Threats

Early virus and worm attacks would cause damage to PCs, but they were generally visible to users. Many modern viruses and worms are used to deliver payloads that lead to machines becoming zombies in a botnet, controlled by an attacker. This type of attack is typically invisible to the end user, so as not to alert them to the malware.

This type of virus is so common today that it is considered a security best practice to advise users never to open a document attached to an e-mail if it seems at all suspicious. Many organizations now routinely have their mail servers eliminate any attachments containing Visual Basic macros.

Avoiding Virus Infection

Always being cautious about executing programs or opening documents sent to you is a good security practice. "If you don't know where it came from or where it has been, don't open or run it" should be the basic mantra for all computer users. Another security best practice for protecting against virus infection is to install and run an antivirus program. Since these programs are designed to protect against known viruses, it is also important to maintain an up-to-date listing of virus signatures for your antivirus software. Antivirus software vendors provide this information, and administrators should stay on top of the latest updates to the list of known viruses.

Two advances in virus writing have made it more difficult for antivirus software to detect viruses. These advances are the introduction of *stealth virus* techniques and *polymorphic viruses*. A stealthy virus employs techniques to help evade being detected by antivirus software that uses checksums or other techniques. Polymorphic viruses also attempt to evade detection, but they do so by changing the virus itself (the virus "evolves"). Because the virus changes, signatures for that virus may no longer be valid, and the virus may escape detection by antivirus software.

Modern viruses have a whole host of defenses from detection and analysis. Polymorphic viruses change their appearance, making signature matches difficult. Armored viruses resist being reverse-engineered to determine how they operate. Viruses are designed to be quiet, avoid detection, avoid analysis, and still work—they are significant threats.

Armored Virus

When a new form of malware/virus is discovered, antivirus companies and security researchers will decompile the program in an attempt to reverse-engineer its functionality. Much can be determined from reverse engineering, such as where the malware came from, how it works, how it communicates, how it spreads, and so forth. Armoring malware can make the process of determining this information much more difficult, if not impossible. Some malware, such as Zeus, comes encrypted in ways to prevent criminals from stealing the intellectual property of the very malware that they use.

Virus Hoaxes

Viruses have caused so much damage to systems that many Internet users become extremely cautious anytime they hear a rumor of a new virus. Many users will not connect to the Internet when they hear about a virus outbreak, just to be sure their machines don't get infected. This has given rise to virus hoaxes, in which word is spread about a new virus and the extreme danger it poses. It may warn users to not read certain files or connect to the Internet.

Hoaxes can actually be even more destructive than just wasting time and bandwidth. Some hoaxes warning of a dangerous virus have included instructions to delete certain files if they're found on the user's system. Unfortunately for those who follow the advice, the files may actually be part of the operating system, and deleting them could keep the system from booting properly. This suggests another good piece of security advice: make sure of the authenticity and accuracy of any virus report before following somebody's advice. Antivirus software vendors are a good source of factual data for this sort of threat as well.

Worms

It was once easy to distinguish between a worm and a virus. Recently, with the introduction of new breeds of sophisticated malicious code, the distinction has blurred. **Worms** are pieces of code that attempt to penetrate networks and computer systems. Once a penetration occurs, the worm will create a new copy of itself on the penetrated system. Reproduction of a worm thus does not rely on the attachment of the virus to another piece of code or to a file, which is the definition of a virus.

Viruses were generally thought of as a system-based problem, and worms were network-based. If the malicious code is sent throughout a network, it may subsequently be called a worm. The important distinction, however, is whether the code has to attach itself to something else (a virus) or if it can "survive" on its own (a worm).

Some examples of worms that have had high profiles include the Sobig worm of 2003, the SQL Slammer worm of 2003, the 2001 attacks of Code Red and Nimba, and the 2005 Zotob worm, which took down CNN Live. Nimba was particularly impressive in that it used five different methods to spread: via e-mail, via open network shares, from browsing infected web sites, using the directory-traversal vulnerability of Microsoft IIS 4.0/5.0, and, most impressively, through the use of backdoors left by Code Red II and sadmind worms. The Conficker worm, discovered in 2008, spawned such a response that it earned its own working group. Many modern malware items, such as Gameover Zeus, were spread as viruses.

Protection Against Worms

How you protect your system against worms depends on the type of worm. Those attached and propagated through e-mail can be avoided by following the same guidelines about not opening files and not running attachments unless you are absolutely sure of their origin and integrity. Protecting against worms involves securing systems and networks against penetration in the same way you would protect your systems against human attackers: install patches, eliminate unused and unnecessary services, enforce good password security, and use firewalls and intrusion detection systems. More sophisticated attacks, such as the Samy worm, are almost impossible to avoid.

Polymorphic Malware

The detection of malware by antimalware programs is primarily done through the use of a signature. Files are scanned for sections of code in the executable that act as markers, unique patterns of code that enable detection. Just as the human body creates antigens that match marker proteins, antimalware programs detect malware through unique markers present in the code of the malware.

Malware writers are aware of this functionality and have adapted methods to defeat it. One of the primary means of avoiding detection by sensors is the use of *polymorphic code,* which is code that changes on a regular basis. These changes or mutations are designed not to affect the functionality of the code, but rather to mask any signature from detection. Polymorphic programs can change their coding after each use, making each replicant different from a detection point of view.

Tech Tip

Social Media Worms

In 2005, a clever MySpace user looking to expand his friends list created the first self-propagating cross-site scripting (XSS) worm. In less than a day, the worm, now known as the Samy worm (or MySpace worm), had gone viral and user Samy had amassed more than 1 million friends on the popular online community. MySpace was taken down because the worm replicated too efficiently, eventually surpassing several thousand replications per second.

In 2008, Koobface appeared, and it spread via Facebook, Skype, and other social media platforms. Koobface gives an attacker access to your personal information, such as your banking information, passwords, or other personal details. It then makes the computer part of a botnet.

In one high-profile case, Sony BMG Corporation used rootkit technology to provide copy protection technology on some of the company's CDs. Two major issues led to this being a complete debacle for Sony: first, the software modified systems without the user's approval; and second, the software opened a security hole on Windows-based systems, creating an exploitable vulnerability at the rootkit level. This led the Sony case to be labeled as malware, which is the most common use of rootkits.

Exam Tip: Five types of rootkits exist:

- *Firmware* Attacks firmware on a system

- *Virtual* Attacks at the virtual machine level

- *Kernel* Attacks the kernel of the OS

- *Library* Attacks libraries used on a system

- *Application level* Attacks specific applications

Trojan Horses

A Trojan horse, or simply **Trojan**, is a piece of software that appears to do one thing (and may, in fact, actually do that thing) but hides some other functionality. The analogy to the famous story of antiquity is very accurate. In the original case, the object appeared to be a large wooden horse, and in fact it was. At the same time, it hid something much more sinister and dangerous to the occupants of the city of Troy. As long as the horse was left outside the city walls, it could cause no damage to the inhabitants. It had to be taken in by the inhabitants, and it was inside that the hidden purpose was activated. A computer Trojan works in much the same way. Unlike a virus, which reproduces by attaching itself to other files or programs, a Trojan is a standalone program that must be copied and installed by the user—it must be "brought inside" the system by an authorized user. The challenge for the attacker is enticing the user to copy and run the program. This generally means that the program must be disguised as something that the user would want to run—a special utility or game, for example. Once it has been copied and is inside the system, the Trojan will perform its hidden purpose, with the user often still unaware of its true nature.

The single best method to prevent the introduction of a Trojan to your system is never to run software if you are unsure of its origin, security, and integrity. A virus-checking program may also be useful in detecting and preventing the installation of known Trojans.

Rootkits

A **rootkit** is a form of malware that is specifically designed to modify the operation of the operating system in some fashion to facilitate nonstandard functionality. The history of rootkits goes back to the beginning of the UNIX operating system, where they were sets of modified administrative tools. Originally designed to allow a program to take greater control over operating system function when it fails or becomes unresponsive, the technique has evolved and is used in a variety of ways.

A rootkit can do many things—in fact, it can do virtually anything that the operating system does. Rootkits modify the operating system kernel and supporting functions, changing the nature of the system's operation. Rootkits are designed to avoid, either by subversion or evasion, the security functions of the operating system to avoid detection. Rootkits act as a form of malware that can change thread priorities to boost an application's performance, perform keylogging, act as a sniffer, hide other files from other applications, or create backdoors in the authentication system. The use of rootkit functionality to hide other processes and files enables an attacker to use a portion of a computer without the user or other applications knowing what is happening. This hides exploit code from antivirus and antispyware programs, acting as a cloak of invisibility.

Rootkits can load before the operating system loads, acting as a virtualization layer, as in SubVirt and Blue Pill. Rootkits can exist in firmware, and these have been demonstrated in both video cards and PCI expansion cards. Rootkits can exist as loadable library modules, effectively changing portions of the operating system outside the kernel. Further information on specific rootkits in the wild can be found at www.antirootkit.com.

Once a rootkit is detected, it needs to be removed and cleaned up. Because of rootkits' invasive nature, and the fact that many aspects of rootkits are not easily detectable, most system administrators don't even attempt to clean up or remove a rootkit. It is far easier to use a previously captured clean system image and reimage the machine than to attempt to determine the depth and breadth of the damage and fix individual files.

Logic Bombs

Logic bombs, unlike viruses and Trojans, are a type of malicious software that is deliberately installed, generally by an authorized user. A logic bomb is a piece of code that sits dormant for a period of time until some event invokes its malicious payload. An example of a logic bomb might be a program that is set to load and run automatically, and that periodically checks an organization's payroll or personnel database for a specific employee. If the employee is not found, the malicious payload executes, deleting vital corporate files.

Logic bombs are difficult to detect because they are often installed by authorized users and, in particular, by administrators who are also often responsible for security. This demonstrates the need for a separation of duties and a periodic review of all programs and services that are running on a system. It also illustrates the need to maintain an active backup program so that if your organization loses critical files to this sort of malicious code, it loses only transactions that occurred since the most recent backup and no permanent loss of data results.

Spyware

Spyware is software that "spies" on users, recording and reporting on their activities. Typically installed without user knowledge, spyware can do a wide range of activities. It can record keystrokes (commonly called *keylogging*) when the user logs into specific web sites. It can monitor how a user uses a specific piece of software (for example, monitor attempts to cheat at games).

Many uses of spyware seem innocuous at first, but the unauthorized monitoring of a system can be abused very easily. In other cases, the spyware is specifically designed to steal information. Many states have passed legislation banning the unapproved installation of software, but many cases of spyware circumvent this issue through complex and confusing end-user license agreements.

Adware

The business of software distribution requires a form of revenue stream to support the cost of development and distribution. One form of revenue stream is advertising. Software that is supported by advertising is called

If the event invoking the logic bomb is a specific date or time, the program will often be referred to as a *time bomb*. In one famous example of a time bomb, a disgruntled employee left a time bomb in place just prior to being fired from his job. Two weeks later, thousands of client records were deleted. Police were eventually able to track the malicious code to the disgruntled ex-employee, who was prosecuted for his actions. He had hoped that the two weeks that had passed since his dismissal would have caused investigators to assume he could not have been the individual who had caused the deletion of the records.

Keylogging is one of the holy grails for attackers, for if they can get a keylogger on a machine, the capturing of user-typed credentials is a quick win for the attacker.

adware. Adware comes in many different forms. With legitimate adware, the user is aware of the advertising and agrees to the arrangement in return for free use of the software. This type of adware often offers an alternative, ad-free version for a fee. Adware can also refer to a form of malware, which is characterized by software that presents unwanted ads. These ads are sometimes an irritant, and at other times represent an actual security threat. Frequently these ads are in the form of pop-up browser windows, and in some cases they cascade upon any user action.

Botnets

Malware can have a wide range of consequences on a machine, from relatively benign to extremely serious. One form of malware that is seemingly benign to a user is a botnet zombie. Hackers create armies of machines by installing malware agents on the machines, which then are called zombies. These collections of machines are called **botnets**. These zombies machines are used to conduct other attacks and to spread spam and other malware. Botnets have grown into networks of over a million nodes and are responsible for tens of millions of spam messages daily.

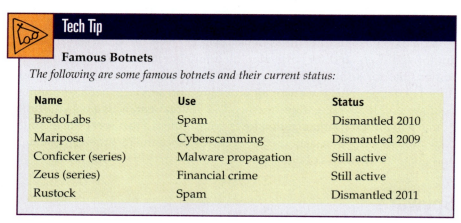

Tech Tip

Famous Botnets

The following are some famous botnets and their current status:

Name	Use	Status
BredoLabs	Spam	Dismantled 2010
Mariposa	Cyberscamming	Dismantled 2009
Conficker (series)	Malware propagation	Still active
Zeus (series)	Financial crime	Still active
Rustock	Spam	Dismantled 2011

Sometime before 2007, the FBI began an anti-botnet operation dubbed Bot Roast. The operation dismantled several botnets and led to several convictions of botnet operators. Other successful anti-botnet operations include the McColo takedown, which decimated Rustock, and coordinated efforts by industry, academia, and law enforcement that have led to the dismantling of BredoLabs, Mariposa, and significant inroads against Conficker and Zeus.

Backdoors and Trapdoors

Backdoors were originally (and sometimes still are) nothing more than methods used by software developers to ensure that they could gain access to an application even if something were to happen in the future to prevent normal access methods. An example would be a hard-coded password that could be used to gain access to the program in the event that administrators forgot their own system password. The obvious problem with this sort of backdoor (also sometimes referred to as a *trapdoor*) is that, since it is hard-coded, it cannot be removed. Should an attacker learn of the backdoor, all systems running that software would be vulnerable to attack.

The term *backdoor* is also, and more commonly, used to refer to programs that attackers install after gaining unauthorized access to a system to ensure that they can continue to have unrestricted access to the system, even if their initial access method is discovered and blocked. Backdoors can also be installed by authorized individuals inadvertently, should they run software that contains a Trojan horse (introduced earlier). A variation on the backdoor is the rootkit, discussed in the previous section, which is established not to gain root access but rather to ensure continued root access.

Ransomware

Ransomware is a form of malware that performs some action and extracts ransom from a user. The most common form of ransomware is one that encrypts a key file or set of files, rendering a system unusable, or dataset unavailable. The attacker releases the information after being paid, typically in a nontraceable means such as bitcoin.

Malware Defenses

Malware in all forms—virus, worm, spyware, botnet, and so on—can be defended against in a couple of simple steps:

- **Use an antivirus program**   Most major-vendor antivirus suites are designed to catch most widespread forms of malware. In some markets, the antivirus software is being referred to as anti-*x* software, indicating that it covers more than viruses. But because the threat environment changes literally daily, the signature files for the software need regular updates, which most antivirus programs offer to perform automatically.

- **Keep your software up to date**   Many forms of malware achieve their objectives through exploitation of vulnerabilities in software, both in the operating system and applications. Although operating system vulnerabilities were the main source of problems, today application-level vulnerabilities pose the greatest risk. Unfortunately, while operating system vendors are becoming more and more responsive to patching, most application vendors are not, and some, like Adobe, have very large footprints across most machines.

One of the challenges in keeping a system up to date is keeping track of the software that is on the system, and keeping track of all vendor updates. There are software products, such as Secunia's Personal Software Inspector (PSI) program, that can scan your machine to enumerate all the software installed and verify the vendor status of each product. For standalone machines, such as the one in your home, this type of program is a great time-saving item. In even small enterprises, these tools are essential to manage the complexity of patches needed across the machines.

Application-Level Attacks

Attacks against a system can occur at the network level, at the operating system level, at the application level, or at the user level (social engineering). Early attack patterns were against the network, but most of today's attacks are aimed at the applications. This is primarily because this is where the objective of most attacks resides; in the infamous words of bank robber Willie Sutton, "because that's where the money is." In fact, many of

 Common backdoors include Zeus, NetBus, and Back Orifice. Any of these, if running on your system, can allow an attacker remote access to your system—access that allows them to perform any function on your system.

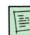 A current ransomware threat, appearing in 2013, is CryptoLocker. CryptoLocker is a Trojan horse that will encrypt certain files using RSA public key encryption. When the user attempts to get the files, they are provided with a message instructing them how to purchase the decryption key. Because CryptoLocker uses 2048-bit RSA encryption, brute-force decryption is out of the realm of recovery options. The system is highly automated and users have a short time window to get the private key. Failure to get the key will result in the loss of the data.

Tech Tip

Malware Defenses
There are two primary defense mechanisms against malware: backups and updates. Malware acts against vulnerabilities, which are patched via keeping software up to date. One of the primary sources of loss is from inability to recover, something covered by backups.

today's attacks on systems are combinations of using vulnerabilities in networks, operating systems, and applications, all means to an end to obtain the desired objective of an attack, which is usually some form of data.

Application-level attacks take advantage of several facts associated with computer applications. First, most applications are large programs written by groups of programmers and, by their nature, have errors in design and coding that create vulnerabilities. For a list of typical vulnerabilities, see the Common Vulnerability and Exposures (CVE) list maintained by Mitre, http://cve.mitre.org. Second, even when vulnerabilities are discovered and patched by software vendors, end users are slow to apply patches, as evidenced by the SQL Slammer incident in January 2003. The vulnerability exploited was a buffer overflow, and the vendor supplied a patch six months prior to the outbreak, yet the worm still spread quickly due to the multitude of unpatched systems.

Cross Check

Application Vulnerabilities

Applications are a common target of attacks, as attackers have shifted to easier targets as the network and OS have become more hardened. What applications are not up to date on the PC you use every day? How would you know? How would you update them? A more complete examination of common application vulnerabilities is presented in Chapter 18.

■ Attacking Computer Systems and Networks

From a high-level standpoint, attacks on computer systems and networks can be grouped into two broad categories: attacks on specific software (such as an application or the operating system) and attacks on a specific protocol or service. Attacks on a specific application or operating system are generally possible because of an oversight in the code (and possibly in the testing of that code) or because of a flaw, or bug, in the code (again indicating a lack of thorough testing). Attacks on specific protocols or services are attempts either to take advantage of a specific feature of the protocol or service or to use the protocol or service in a manner for which it was not intended. This section discusses various forms of attacks of which security professionals need to be aware.

Denial-of-Service Attacks

A **denial-of-service (DoS) attack** is an attack designed to prevent a system or service from functioning normally. A DoS attack can exploit a known vulnerability in a specific application or operating system, or it can attack features (or weaknesses) in specific protocols or services. In a DoS attack, the attacker attempts to deny authorized users access either to specific information or to the computer system or network itself. This can be accomplished by crashing the system—taking it offline—or by sending so many requests that the machine is overwhelmed.

The purpose of a DoS attack can be simply to prevent access to the target system, or the attack can be used in conjunction with other actions to gain unauthorized access to a computer or network. For example, a **SYN flood** attack can be used to prevent service to a system temporarily in order to take advantage of a trusted relationship that exists between that system and another.

SYN flooding is an example of a DoS attack that takes advantage of the way TCP/IP networks were designed to function, and it can be used to illustrate the basic principles of any DoS attack. SYN flooding uses the TCP three-way handshake that establishes a connection between two systems. Under normal circumstances, the first system sends a SYN packet

to the system with which it wants to communicate. The second system responds with a SYN/ACK if it is able to accept the request. When the initial system receives the SYN/ACK from the second system, it responds with an ACK packet, and communication can then proceed. This process is shown in Figure 15.1.

• **Figure 15.1**   The TCP three-way handshake

In a SYN flooding attack, the attacker sends fake communication requests to the targeted system. Each of these requests will be answered by the target system, which then waits for the third part of the handshake. Since the requests are fake (a nonexistent IP address is used in the requests, so the target system is responding to a system that doesn't exist), the target will wait for responses that never come, as shown in Figure 15.2. The target system will drop these connections after a specific time-out period, but if the attacker sends requests faster than the time-out period eliminates them, the system will quickly be filled with requests. The number of connections a system can support is finite, so when more requests come in than can be processed, the system will soon be reserving all its connections for fake requests. At this point, any further requests are simply dropped (ignored), and legitimate users who want to connect to the target system will not be able to do so, because use of the system has been denied to them.

A SYN/ACK is actually the SYN packet sent to the first system combined with an ACK packet acknowledging the first system's SYN packet.

Another simple DoS attack is the infamous *ping of death (POD)*, and it illustrates the other type of attack—one targeted at a specific application or operating system, as opposed to SYN flooding, which targets a protocol. In the POD attack, the attacker sends an Internet Control Message Protocol (ICMP) ping packet equal to, or exceeding, 64KB. Certain older systems are not able to handle this size of packet, and the system will hang or crash.

• **Figure 15.2**   A SYN flooding–based DoS attack

Distributed Denial-of-Service

DoS attacks are conducted using a single attacking system. A DoS attack employing multiple attacking systems is known as a **distributed denial-of-service (DDoS) attack**. The goal of a DDoS attack is also to deny the use of or access to a specific service or system. DDoS attacks were made famous in 2000 with the highly publicized attacks on eBay, CNN, Amazon, and Yahoo!.

In a DDoS attack, service is denied by overwhelming the target with traffic from many different systems. A network of attack agents (sometimes called *zombies*) is created by the attacker, and upon receiving the attack command from the attacker, the attack agents commence sending a specific type of traffic against the target. If the attack network is large enough, even ordinary web traffic can quickly overwhelm the largest of sites.

Creating a DDoS attack network is not a simple task. The attack agents are not willing agents—they are systems that have been compromised and on which the DDoS attack software has been installed. To compromise these agents, the attacker has to have gained unauthorized access to the system or tricked authorized users to run a program that installed the attack software. The creation of the attack network may in fact be a multistep process in which the attacker first compromises a few systems and then uses those systems as *handlers* or *masters*, which in turn compromise other systems. Once the network has been created, the agents wait for an attack message, which will include data on the specific target, before launching the attack. One important aspect of a DDoS attack is that with just a few messages to the agents, the attacker can have a flood of messages sent against the targeted system. Figure 15.3 illustrates a DDoS network with agents and handlers.

• **Figure 15.3**   DDoS attack

A final option you should consider that will address several forms of DoS and DDoS attacks is to block ICMP packets at your border, since many attacks rely on ICMP. Blocking ICMP packets at the border devices prevents external ICMP packets from entering your network, and while this may block some functionality, it will leave internal ICMP functionality intact. It is also possible to block specific forms of ICMP; blocking Type 8, for instance, will block ICMP-based ping sweeps. It is worth noting that not all pings occur via ICMP; some tools, such as hping2, use TCP and UDP to carry ping messages.

Smurf Attack

In a specific DoS attack known as a *smurf attack*, the attacker sends a spoofed packet to the broadcast address for a network, which distributes the packet to all systems on that network. Further details are listed in the IP Address Spoofing section.

Defending Against DOS-Type Attacks

How can you stop or mitigate the effects of a DoS or DDoS attack? One important precaution is to ensure that you have applied the latest patches

Principles of Computer Security

and upgrades to your systems and the applications running on them. Once a specific vulnerability is discovered, it does not take long before multiple exploits are written to take advantage of it. Generally you will have a small window of opportunity in which to patch your system between the time the vulnerability is discovered and the time exploits become widely available. A vulnerability can also be discovered by hackers, and exploits provide the first clues that a system has been compromised. Attackers can also reverse-engineer patches to learn what vulnerabilities have been patched, allowing them to attack unpatched systems.

Another approach involves changing the time-out option for TCP connections so that attacks such as the SYN flooding attack are more difficult to perform, because unused connections are dropped more quickly.

For DDoS attacks, much has been written about distributing your own workload across several systems so that any attack against your system would have to target several hosts to be completely successful. While this is effective against some DDoS attacks, if large enough DDoS networks are created (with tens of thousands of zombies, for example), any network, no matter how much the load is distributed, can be successfully attacked. Such an approach also involves additional costs to your organization to establish this distributed environment. Addressing the problem in this manner is actually an attempt to mitigate the effect of the attack, rather than preventing or stopping an attack.

To prevent a DDoS attack, you must either be able to intercept or block the attack messages or keep the DDoS network from being established in the first place. Tools have been developed that will scan your systems, searching for sleeping zombies waiting for an attack signal. Many of the current antivirus/spyware security suite tools will detect known zombie-type infections. The problem with this type of prevention approach, however, is that it is not something you can do to prevent an attack on your network—it is something you can do to keep your network from being used to attack other networks or systems. You have to rely on the community of network administrators to test their own systems to prevent attacks on yours.

War-Dialing and War-Driving

War-dialing is the term used to describe an attacker's attempt to discover unprotected modem connections to computer systems and networks. The term's origin is the 1983 movie *WarGames*, in which the star has his machine systematically call a sequence of phone numbers in an attempt to find a computer connected to a modem. In the case of the movie, the intent was to find a machine with games the attacker could play, though obviously an attacker could have other purposes once access is obtained.

War-dialing was surprisingly successful, mostly because of *rogue modems*—unauthorized modems attached to computers on a network by authorized users. Generally the reason for attaching the modem is not malicious—an individual may simply want to be able to go home and then connect to the organization's network to continue working. This has become history with the rise of remote desktop technology and ubiquitous Internet connectivity.

Another avenue of attack on computer systems and networks has seen a tremendous increase over the last few years because of the increase in the use of wireless networks. *War-driving* is the unauthorized scanning for and connecting to wireless access points, frequently done while driving near a facility. Wireless networks have some obvious advantages—they free employees from the cable connection to a port on their wall, allowing them to move throughout the building with their laptops and still be connected.

Cross Check

Wireless Vulnerabilities

Wireless systems have their own vulnerabilities unique to the wireless protocols. Wireless systems are becoming very common. If your machine is wireless capable, how many wireless access points can you see from your current location? Securing wireless systems from unauthorized access is an essential element of a comprehensive security program. This material is covered in depth in Chapter 12.

Social Engineering

Social engineering relies on lies and misrepresentation, which an attacker uses to trick an authorized user into providing information or access the attacker would not normally be entitled to. The attacker might, for example, contact a system administrator and pretend to be an authorized user, asking to have a password reset. Another common ploy is to pose as a representative from a vendor who needs temporary access to perform some emergency maintenance. Social engineering also applies to physical access. Simple techniques include impersonating pizza or flower delivery personnel to gain physical access to a facility.

Attackers know that, due to poor security practices, if they can gain physical access to an office, the chances are good that, given a little unsupervised time, a user ID and password pair might be found on a notepad or sticky note. Unsupervised access might not even be required, depending on the quality of the security practices of the organization. One of the authors of this book was once considering opening an account at a bank near his home. As he sat down at the desk across from the bank employee taking his information, the author noticed one of the infamous little yellow notes attached to the computer monitor the employee was using. The note read "password for June is junejune." It probably isn't too hard to guess what July's password might be. Unfortunately, this is all too often the state of security practices in most organizations. With that in mind, it is easy to see how social engineering might work and might provide all the information an attacker needs to gain unauthorized access to a system or network.

Null Sessions

Microsoft Windows systems prior to XP and Server 2003 exhibited a vulnerability in their Server Message Block (SMB) system that allowed users to establish null sessions. A **null session** is a connection to a Windows interprocess communications share (IPC$). The good news is that Windows XP, Server 2003, and beyond are not susceptible to this vulnerability by default.

Sniffing

The group of protocols that makes up the TCP/IP suite was designed to work in a friendly environment in which everybody who connected to the network used the protocols as they were designed. The abuse of this friendly assumption is illustrated by network-traffic sniffing programs, sometimes referred to as *sniffers*. **Sniffing** is when someone examines all the network traffic that passes their NIC, whether addressed for them or not.

A network sniffer is a software or hardware device that is used to observe traffic as it passes through a network on shared broadcast media. The device can be used to view all traffic, or it can target a specific protocol, service, or even string of characters (looking for logins, for example). Normally, the network device that connects a computer to a network is designed to ignore all traffic that is not destined for that computer. Network sniffers ignore this friendly agreement and observe all traffic on the network, whether destined for that computer or others, as shown in Figure 15.4. Some network sniffers are designed not just to observe all traffic but to modify traffic as well. Network sniffing is more difficult in switched network environments due to the way collision domains are eliminated in full-duplex switching, but certain techniques can be used (spanning ports, ARP poisoning, and attacks forcing a switch to fail and act as a hub) to circumvent this.

Network sniffers can be used by network administrators to monitor network performance. They can be used to perform traffic analysis, for example, to determine what type of traffic is most commonly carried on the network and to determine which segments are most active. They can also be used for network bandwidth analysis and to troubleshoot certain problems (such as duplicate MAC addresses).

Network sniffers can also be used by attackers to gather information that can be used in penetration attempts. Information such as an authorized username and password can be viewed and recorded for later use. The contents of e-mail messages can also be viewed as the messages travel across

the network. It should be obvious that administrators and security professionals will not want unauthorized network sniffers on their networks because of the security and privacy concerns they introduce. Fortunately, for network sniffers to be most effective, they need to be on the internal network, which generally means that the chances for outsiders to use them against you are extremely limited. This is another reason that physical security is an important part of information security in today's environment.

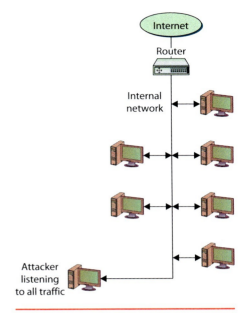

• Figure 15.4   Network sniffers listen to all network traffic.

Exam Tip: A network interface card (NIC) that is listening to all network traffic and not just its own is said to be in "promiscuous mode."

Cross Check

Physical Access and Security

One of the challenges in a modern network is getting a connection to a point in the network where your sniffing will result in the discovery of interesting information. Getting access to an open port, or to an equipment room where routers and switches are maintained, is a failure of physical security. Physical security is an important component of a comprehensive information security program. At this point ask yourself—where can I connect into my company network? Can I get connections near high-value targets such as database servers? Details on physical security measures are covered in Chapter 8.

Tech Tip

What Is Spoofing?

Spoofing *is when you assemble packets with false header information to deceive the receiver as to the true address of the sender. This can be done to manipulate return packets in the case of ping sweeps, or to provide anonymity for e-mails.*

Spoofing

Spoofing is nothing more than making data look like it has come from a different source. This is possible in TCP/IP because of the friendly assumptions behind the protocols. When the protocols were developed, it was assumed that individuals who had access to the network layer would be privileged users who could be trusted.

When a packet is sent from one system to another, it includes not only the destination IP address and port but the source IP address as well. You are supposed to fill in the source with your own address, but nothing stops you from filling in another system's address. This is one of the several forms of spoofing.

Spoofing E-Mail

In e-mail spoofing, a message is sent with a From address that differs from that of the sending system. This can be easily accomplished in several different ways using several programs. To demonstrate how simple it is to spoof an e-mail address, you can Telnet to port 25 (the port associated with e-mail) on a mail server. From there, you can fill in any address for the From and To sections of the message, whether or not the addresses are yours or even actually exist.

You can use several methods to determine whether an e-mail message was sent by the source it claims to have been sent from, but most users do not question their e-mail and will accept as authentic where it appears to have originated. A variation on e-mail spoofing, though not technically spoofing, is for the attacker to acquire a URL similar to the URL they want to spoof so that e-mail sent from their system appears to have come from the official site—until you read the address carefully. For example, if attackers want to spoof XYZ Corporation, which owns XYZ.com, the attackers might gain access to the URL XYZ.Corp.com. An individual receiving a message from the spoofed corporation site would not normally suspect it to be a spoof but would take it to be official. This same method can be, and has been, used to spoof web sites. If, however, the attackers made their spoofed site appear similar to the official one, they could easily convince many potential viewers that they were at the official site. Today, many .com and other domains of common sites, as well as common typos of URLs, are purchased and directed to the legitimate site.

Cross Check

E-mail Spoofing

E-mail was created in an era with a different security environment, one where attribution was not even an afterthought. This has led to issues associated with trust regarding e-mails. Full details of securing e-mails is covered in Chapter 16.

IP Address Spoofing

IP is designed to work so that the originators of any IP packet include their own IP address in the From portion of the packet. While this is the intent, nothing prevents a system from inserting a different address in the From portion of the packet. This is known as *IP address spoofing*. An IP address can be spoofed for several reasons. In a specific DoS attack known as a **smurf attack**, the attacker sends a spoofed packet to the broadcast address for a network, which distributes the packet to all systems on that network.

In the smurf attack, the packet sent by the attacker to the broadcast address is an echo request with the From address forged so that it appears that another system (the target system) has made the echo request. The normal response of a system to an echo request is an echo reply, and it is used in the ping utility to let a user know whether a remote system is reachable and is responding. In the smurf attack, the request is sent to all systems on the network, so all will respond with an echo reply to the target system, as shown in Figure 15.5. The attacker has sent one packet and has been able to generate as many as 254 responses aimed at the target. Should the attacker send several of these spoofed requests, or send them to several different networks, the target can quickly become overwhelmed with the volume of echo replies it receives.

• **Figure 15.5**   Smurfing used in a smurf DOS attack

Spoofing and Trusted Relationships

Spoofing can also take advantage of a *trusted relationship* between two systems. If two systems are configured to accept the authentication accomplished by each other, an individual logged onto one system might not be forced to go through an authentication process again to access the other system. An attacker can take advantage of this arrangement by sending a packet to one system that appears to have come from a trusted system. Since the trusted relationship is in place, the targeted system may perform the requested task without authentication.

Since a reply will often be sent once a packet is received, the system that is being impersonated could interfere with the attack, since it would receive an acknowledgment for a request it never made. The attacker will often initially launch a DoS attack (such as a SYN flooding attack) to temporarily take out the spoofed system for the period of time that the attacker is exploiting the trusted relationship. Once the attack is completed, the DoS attack on the spoofed system would be terminated, and the system administrators, apart from having a temporarily nonresponsive system, might never notice that the attack occurred. Figure 15.6 illustrates a spoofing attack that includes a SYN flooding attack.

Because of this type of attack, administrators are encouraged to strictly limit any trusted relationships between hosts. Firewalls should also be configured to discard any packets from outside of the firewall that have From addresses indicating they originated from inside the network (a situation that should not occur normally and that indicates spoofing is being attempted).

Exam Tip: A smurf attack allows an attacker to use a network structure to send large volumes of packets to a victim. By sending ICMP requests to a broadcast IP address, with the victim as the source address, the multitudes of replies will flood the victim system.

• **Figure 15.6**   Spoofing to take advantage of a trusted relationship

Spoofing and Sequence Numbers

How complicated the spoofing is depends heavily on several factors, including whether the traffic is encrypted and where the attacker is located relative to the target. Spoofing attacks from inside a network, for example, are much easier to perform than attacks from outside of the network, because the inside attacker can observe the traffic to and from the target and can do a better job of formulating the necessary packets.

Formulating the packets is more complicated for external attackers because a sequence number is associated with TCP packets. A **sequence number** is a 32-bit number established by the host that is incremented for each packet sent. Packets are not guaranteed to be received in order, and the sequence number can be used to help reorder packets as they are received and to refer to packets that may have been lost in transmission.

In the TCP three-way handshake, two sets of sequence numbers are created, as shown in Figure 15.7. The first system chooses a sequence number to send with the original SYN packet. The system receiving this SYN packet acknowledges with a SYN/ACK. It sends an acknowledgment number back, which is based on the first sequence number plus one (that is, it increments the sequence number sent to it by one). It then also creates its own sequence number and sends that along with it. The original system receives the SYN/ACK with the new sequence number. It increments the sequence number by one and uses it as the acknowledgment number in the ACK packet with which it responds.

• **Figure 15.7** Three-way handshake with sequence numbers

The difference in the difficulty of attempting a spoofing attack from inside a network and from outside involves determining the sequence number. If the attacker is inside of the network and can observe the traffic with which the target host responds, the attacker can easily see the sequence number the system creates and can respond with the correct sequence number. If the attacker is external to the network and the sequence number the target system generates is not observed, it is next to impossible for the attacker to provide the final ACK with the correct sequence number. So the attacker has to guess what the sequence number might be.

Sequence numbers are somewhat predictable, based on the operating systems in question. Sequence numbers for each session are not started from the same number, so that different packets from different concurrent connections will not have the same sequence numbers. Instead, the sequence number for each new connection is incremented by some large number to keep the numbers from being the same. The sequence number may also be incremented by some large number every second (or some other time period). An external attacker has to determine what values are used for these increments. The attacker can do this by attempting connections at various time intervals to observe how the sequence numbers are incremented. Once the pattern is determined, the attacker can attempt a legitimate connection to determine the current value, and then immediately attempt the spoofed connection. The spoofed connection sequence number should be the legitimate connection incremented by the determined value or values.

Sequence numbers are also important in session hijacking, which is discussed in the following section. When an attacker spoofs addresses and imposes his packets in the middle of an existing connection, this is the man-in-the-middle attack.

TCP/IP Hijacking

TCP/IP hijacking and *session hijacking* are terms used to refer to the process of taking control of an already existing session between a client and a server. The advantage to an attacker of hijacking over attempting to penetrate a computer system or network is that the attacker doesn't have to circumvent any authentication mechanisms, since the user has already authenticated and established the session. Once the user has completed the authentication sequence, the attacker can then usurp the session and carry on as if the attacker, and not the user, had authenticated with the system. To prevent the user from noticing anything unusual, the attacker can decide to attack the user's system and perform a DoS attack on it, taking it down so that the user, and the system, will not notice the extra traffic that is taking place.

Hijack attacks generally are used against web and Telnet sessions. Sequence numbers as they apply to spoofing also apply to session hijacking, since the hijacker will need to provide the correct sequence number to continue the appropriated sessions.

Man-in-the-Middle Attacks

A **man-in-the-middle attack**, as the name implies, generally occurs when attackers are able to place themselves in the middle of two other hosts that are communicating. Ideally, this is done by ensuring that all communication going to or from the target host is routed through the attacker's host (which can be accomplished if the attacker can compromise the router for the target host). The attacker can then observe all traffic before relaying it and can actually modify or block traffic. To the target host, it appears that communication is occurring normally, since all expected replies are received. Figure 15.8 illustrates this type of attack.

• **Figure 15.8**   A man-in-the-middle attack

There are numerous methods of instantiating a man-in-the-middle attack; one of the common methods is via session hijacking. Session hijacking can occur when information such as a cookie is stolen, allowing the attacker to impersonate the legitimate session. This attack can be as a result of a cross-site scripting attack, which tricks a user into executing code resulting in cookie theft. The amount of information that can be obtained in a man-in-the-middle attack will obviously be limited if the communication is encrypted. Even in this case, however, sensitive information can still be obtained, since knowing what communication is being conducted, and between which individuals, may, in fact, provide information that is valuable in certain circumstances.

Man-in-the-Middle Attacks on Encrypted Traffic

The term "man-in-the-middle attack" is sometimes used to refer to a more specific type of attack—one in which the encrypted traffic issue is addressed. If you wanted to communicate securely with your friend Bob, you might ask him for his public key so you could encrypt your messages to him. You, in turn, would supply Bob with your public key. An attacker can conduct a man-in-the-middle attack by intercepting your request for Bob's public key and the sending of your public key to him. The attacker would replace your public key with their public key, and she would send this on to Bob. The attacker's public key would also be sent to you by the attacker instead of Bob's public key. Now when either you or Bob encrypts a message, it will be encrypted using the attacker's public key, enabling the attacker to intercept it, decrypt it, and then send it on by re-encrypting it with the appropriate key for either you or Bob. Each of you thinks you are transmitting messages securely, but in reality your communication has been compromised. Well-designed cryptographic products use techniques such as mutual authentication to avoid this problem.

Cross Check

Encryption

Cryptography and encryption are tools that can solve many of our secrecy problems. The challenges solved through encryption and the new problems associated with the use of encryption require an understanding of the technical details. Public key encryption, discussed in detail in Chapters 5 and 6, uses two keys: a public key, which anybody can use to encrypt or "lock" your message, and a private key, which only you know and which is used to "unlock" or decrypt a message locked with your public key. One of the key challenges associated with the use of public keys and corresponding private keys is determining who has what key values. Do you have your own key pair? If so, do you know the public key value that you need to share with others?

Replay Attacks

A **replay attack** occurs when the attacker captures a portion of a communication between two parties and retransmits it at a later time. For example, an attacker might replay a series of commands and codes used in a financial transaction to cause the transaction to be conducted multiple times. Generally replay attacks are associated with attempts to circumvent authentication mechanisms, such as the capturing and reuse of a certificate or ticket.

The best way to prevent replay attacks is with encryption, cryptographic authentication, and time stamps. If a portion of the certificate or ticket includes a date/time stamp or an expiration date/time, and this portion is also encrypted as part of the ticket or certificate, replaying it at a later time will prove useless, since it will be rejected as having expired.

Exam Tip: The best method for defending against replay attacks is through the use of encryption and short time frames for legal transactions. Encryption can protect the contents from being understood, and a short time frame for a transaction prevents subsequent use.

Transitive Access

Transitive access is a means of attacking a system by violating the trust relationship between machines. A simple example is when servers are well protected and clients are not, and the servers trust the clients. In this case, attacking a client can provide transitive access to the servers.

Exam Tip: Trust is an essential part of security. If B trusts A and C trusts B, then C trusts A. A transitive attack takes advantage of this trust chain by obtaining trust from one element in the chain (for example, through spoofing) and then using that to gain transitive access to another trusted system via the chain of trust.

Spam

Though not generally considered a social engineering issue, nor a security issue for that matter, spam can, however, be a security concern. *Spam*, as just about everybody knows, is bulk unsolicited e-mail. It can be legitimate in the sense that it has been sent by a company advertising a product or service, but it can also be malicious and could include an attachment that contains malicious software designed to harm your system, or a link to a malicious web site that may attempt to obtain personal information from you.

Spim

Though not as well known, a variation on spam is *spim*, which is basically spam delivered via an instant messaging application such as Yahoo! Messenger or AOL Instant Messenger (AIM). The purpose of hostile spim is the same as that of spam—the delivery of malicious content or links.

Phishing

Phishing is the use of fraudulent e-mails or instant messages that appear to be genuine but are designed to trick users. The goal of a phishing attack is to obtain from the user information that can be used in an attack, such as login credentials or other critical information.

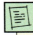 The Anti-Phishing Working Group (APWG) is "an industry association focused on eliminating the identity theft and fraud that result from the growing problem of phishing and email spoofing." APWG is located at www.antiphishing .org.

Spear Phishing

Spear phishing is the term that has been created to refer to a phishing attack that targets a specific group with something in common. By targeting a specific group, the ratio of successful attacks (that is, the number of responses received) to the total number of e-mails or messages sent usually increases because a targeted attack will seem more plausible than a message sent to users randomly.

Vishing

Vishing is a variation of phishing that uses voice communication technology to obtain the information the attacker is seeking. Vishing takes advantage of the trust that some people place in the telephone network. Users are unaware that attackers can spoof (simulate) calls from legitimate entities using voice over IP (VoIP) technology. Voice messaging can also be compromised and used in these attempts. Generally, the attackers are hoping to obtain credit card numbers or other information that can be used in identity theft. The user may receive an e-mail asking him or her to call a number that is answered by a potentially compromised voice message system. Users may also receive a recorded message that appears to come from a legitimate entity. In both cases, the user will be encouraged to respond quickly and provide the sensitive information so that access to their account is not blocked. If a user ever receives a message that claims to be from a reputable entity and asks for sensitive information, the user should not provide it but instead should use the Internet or examine a legitimate account statement to find a phone number that can be used to contact the entity. The user can then verify that the message received was legitimate or report the vishing attempt.

Pharming

Pharming consists of misdirecting users to fake web sites that have been made to look official. Using phishing, individuals are targeted one by one by e-mails. To become a victim, the recipient must take an action (for example, respond by providing personal information). In pharming, the user

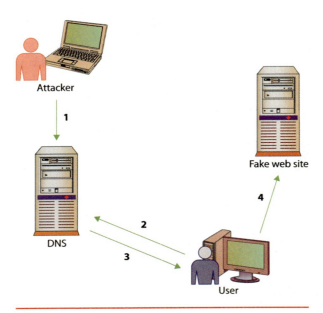

• **Figure 15.9**   How pharming works

will be directed to the fake web site as a result of activity such as DNS poisoning (an attack that changes URLs in a server's domain name table) or modification of local host files, which are used to convert URLs to the appropriate IP addresses. Once at the fake web site, the user may supply personal information, believing that they are connected to the legitimate site. Figure 15.9 illustrates how pharming operates. The first step is an attacker poisons the DNS system, so when the user queries it (step 2) they get a false address (step 3). This results in the user being directed to the fake web site (step 4).

Scanning Attacks

Scanners can be used to send specifically crafted packets in an attempt to determine TCP/UDP port status. An XMAS scan, named because the alternating bits in the TCP header look like Christmas lights, uses the URG, PSH, and FIN flags to determine TCP port availability. If the port is closed, an RST is returned. If the port is open, there is typically no return. An XMAS scan can help determine OS type and version, based upon TCP/IP stack responses, and can also help determine firewall rules. These attacks can also be used to consume system resources, resulting in DoS.

Simple stateless firewalls check for the SYN flag set to prevent SYN floods, and Christmas packets are designed not to have SYN set, so they pass right by these devices. Newer security devices such as advanced firewalls can detect these packets, alerting people to the scanning activities.

Attacks on Encryption

Encryption is the process of transforming *plaintext* into an unreadable format known as *ciphertext* using a specific technique or algorithm. Most encryption techniques use some form of key in the encryption process. The key is used in a mathematical process to scramble the original message to arrive at the unreadable ciphertext. Another key (sometimes the same one and sometimes a different one) is used to decrypt or unscramble the ciphertext to re-create the original plaintext. The length of the key often directly relates to the strength of the encryption.

Cryptanalysis is the process of attempting to break a cryptographic system—it is an attack on the specific method used to encrypt the plaintext. Cryptographic systems can be compromised in various ways.

Weak Keys

Certain encryption algorithms may have specific keys that yield poor, or easily decrypted, ciphertext. Imagine an encryption algorithm that consists solely of a single XOR function (an exclusive OR function where two bits are compared and a 1 is returned if either of the original bits, but not both, is a 1), where the key is repeatedly used to XOR with the plaintext. A key where all bits are 0's, for example, would result in ciphertext that is the same as

Tech Tip

XMAS Attack

The XMAS attack or Christmas attack comes from a specific set of protocol options. A Christmas tree packet is a packet that has all of its options turned on. The name comes from the observation that these packets are lit up like a Christmas tree. When sent as a scan, a Christmas tree packet has the FIN, URG, and PSH options set. Many OSs implement their compliance with the RFC governing IP packets, RFC 791, in slightly different manners. Their response to the packet can tell the scanner what type of OS is present. Another option is in the case of a DoS attack, where Christmas packets can take up significantly greater processing on a router, consuming resources.

the original plaintext. This would obviously be a weak key for this encryption algorithm. In fact, any key with long strings of 0's would yield portions of the ciphertext that were the same as the plaintext. In this simple example, many keys could be considered weak.

Cross Check

Cryptography and Encryption

Understanding the basics of cryptography is important to understanding various defenses from malware. If you are not familiar with encryption, decryption, hashes, and signatures, it would be wise to review them now. The various elements of cryptography and encryption are discussed in detail in Chapter 5.

Encryption algorithms used in computer systems and networks are much more complicated than a simple, single XOR function, but some algorithms have still been found to have weak keys that make cryptanalysis easier.

Exhaustive Search of Key Space

Even if the specific algorithm used to encrypt a message is complicated and has not been shown to have weak keys, the key length will still play a significant role in how easy it is to attack the method of encryption. Generally speaking, the longer a key, the harder it will be to attack. Thus, a 40-bit encryption scheme will be easier to attack using a brute-force technique (which tests all possible keys, one by one) than a 256-bit based scheme. This is easily demonstrated by imagining a scheme that employs a 2-bit key. Even if the resulting ciphertext were completely unreadable, performing a brute-force attack until one key is found that can decrypt the ciphertext would not take long, since only four keys are possible. Every bit that is added to the length of a key doubles the number of keys that have to be tested in a brute-force attack on the encryption. It is easy to understand why a scheme utilizing a 40-bit key would be much easier to attack than a scheme that utilizes a 256-bit key.

The bottom line is simple: an exhaustive search of the keyspace will decrypt the message. The strength of the encryption method is related to the sheer size of the keyspace, which with modern algorithms is large enough to provide significant time constraints when using this method to break an encrypted message. Algorithmic complexity is also an issue with respect to brute force, and you cannot immediately compare different key lengths from different algorithms and assume relative strength.

Indirect Attacks

One of the most common ways of attacking an encryption system is to find weaknesses in mechanisms surrounding the cryptography. Examples include poor random-number generators, unprotected key exchanges, keys stored on hard drives without sufficient protection, and other general programmatic errors, such as buffer overflows. In attacks that target these types of weaknesses, it is not the cryptographic algorithm itself that is being attacked, but rather the implementation of that algorithm in the real world.

Address System Attacks

Many aspects of a computer system are controlled by the use of addresses. IP addresses can be manipulated as shown earlier, and the other address schemes can be manipulated as well. In the summer of 2008, much was made of a serious Domain Name System (DNS) vulnerability that required the simultaneous patching of systems by over 80 vendors. This coordinated effort was to close a technical loophole in the domain name resolution infrastructure that would allow the hijacking and man-in-the-middle attack on the DNS system worldwide.

The DNS system has been the target of other attacks. One attack, **DNS kiting**, is an economic attack against the terms of using a new DNS entry. New DNS purchases are allowed a five-day "test period" during which the name can be relinquished for no fee. Creative users learned to register a name, use it for less than five days, relinquish the name, and then get the name and begin all over, repeating this cycle many times to use a name without paying for it. Typical registration versus permanent entry ratios of 15:1 occur, and in February 2007 GoDaddy reported that out of 55.1 million requests only 3.6 million were not canceled.

Another twist on this scheme is the concept of domain name front running, where a registrar places a name on a five-day hold after someone searches for it, and then offers it for sale at a higher price. In January 2008, Network Solutions was accused of violating the trust as a registrar by forcing people to purchase names from them after they engaged in domain name testing.

Cache Poisoning

Many network activities rely upon various addressing schemes to function properly. When you point your web browser at your bank, by typing the bank's URL, your browser consults the system's DNS system to turn the words into a numerical address. When a packet is being switched to your machine by the network, a series of address caches is involved. Whether the cache is for the DNS system or the ARP system, it exists for the same reason: efficiency. These caches prevent repeated redundant lookups, saving time for the system. But they can also be poisoned, sending incorrect information to the end user's application, redirecting traffic, and changing system behaviors.

DNS Poisoning

The DNS system is used to convert a name into an IP address. There is not a single DNS system, but rather a hierarchy of DNS servers, from root servers on the backbone of the Internet, to copies at your ISP, your home router, and your local machine, each in the form of a DNS cache. To examine a DNS query for a specific address, you can use the **nslookup** command. Figure 15.10 shows a series of DNS queries executed on a Windows machine. In the first request, the DNS server was with an ISP, while on the second request, the DNS server was from a VPN connection. Between the two requests, the network connections were changed, resulting in different DNS lookups. This is a form of DNS poisoning attack.

At times, **nslookup** will return a nonauthoritative answer, as shown in Figure 15.11. This typically means the result is from a cache as opposed to a server that has an authoritative (that is, known to be current) answer.

There are other commands you can use to examine and manipulate the DNS cache on a system. In Windows, the **ipconfig/displaydns** command will show the current DNS cache on a machine. Figure 15.12 shows a small DNS cache. This cache was recently emptied using the **ipconfig/flushdns** command to make it fit on the screen.

Looking at DNS as a complete system shows that there are hierarchical levels from the top (root server) down to the cache in an individual machine. DNS poisoning can occur at any of these levels, with the effect of the poisoning growing wider the higher up it occurs. In 2010, a DNS poisoning event resulted in the "Great Firewall of China" censoring inbound Internet traffic into China from the United States until caches were resolved. Today, after further examination, the attack was shown to be much more complex. The effort of the Chinese government actively seeks to strictly control all aspects of Internet traffic in China.

DNS poisoning is a variant of a larger attack class referred to as *DNS spoofing,* in which an attacker changes a DNS record through any of a multitude of means. There are many ways to perform DNS spoofing, a few of which include compromising a DNS server, the use of the Kaminsky attack, and the use of a false network node advertising a false DNS address. An attacker can even use DNS cache poisoning to result in DNS spoofing. By poisoning

• **Figure 15.10**   nslookup of a DNS query

• **Figure 15.11**   Cache response to a DNS query

• **Figure 15.12**   Cache response to a DNS table query

an upstream DNS cache, all of the downstream users will get spoofed DNS records.

Because of the importance of integrity on DNS requests and responses, a project has begun to secure the DNS infrastructure using digital signing of DNS records. This project, initiated by the U.S. government and called Domain Name System Security Extensions (DNSSEC), works by digitally signing records. This is done by adding records to the DNS system, a key and a signature attesting to the validity of the key. With this information, requestors can be assured that the information they receive is correct. It will take a substantial amount of time (years) for this new system to propagate through the entire DNS infrastructure, but in the end, the system will have much greater assurance.

ARP Poisoning

In moving packets between machines, a device sometimes needs to know where to send a packet using the MAC or Layer 2 address. Address Resolution Protocol (ARP) handles this problem through four basic message types:

- **ARP request**   "Who has this IP address?"
- **ARP reply**   "I have that IP address; my MAC address is..."
- **Reverse ARP request (RARP)**   "Who has this MAC address?"
- **RARP reply**   "I have that MAC address; my IP address is..."

These messages are used in conjunction with a device's ARP table, where a form of short-term memory associated with these data elements resides. The commands are used as a simple form of lookup. When a machine sends an ARP request to the network, the reply is received and entered into all devices that hear the reply. This facilitates efficient address lookups, but also makes the system subject to attack.

When the ARP table gets a reply, it automatically trusts the reply and updates the table. Some operating systems will even accept ARP reply data if they never heard the original request. There is no mechanism to verify the veracity of the data received. An attacker can send messages, corrupt the ARP table, and cause packets to be misrouted. This form of attack is called *ARP poisoning* and results in malicious address redirection, This can allow a mechanism whereby an attacker can inject themselves into the middle of a conversation between two machines, a man-in-the-middle attack.

Local MAC addresses can also be poisoned in the same manner, although it is called ARP poisoning. This can cause miscommunications locally. Poisoning attacks can be used to steal information, establish man-in-the-middle attacks, and even create DoS opportunities.

Exam Tip: ARP poisoning is the altering of the ARP cache on the local system.

Password Guessing

The most common form of authentication is the user ID and password combination. While it is not inherently a poor mechanism for authentication, the combination can be attacked in several ways. All too often, these attacks yield favorable results for the attacker not as a result of a weakness in the scheme but usually due to the user not following good password procedures.

Poor Password Choices

The least technical of the various password-attack techniques consists of the attacker simply attempting to guess the password of an authorized user of the system or network. It is surprising how often this simple method works, and the reason it does is because people are notorious for picking poor passwords. Users need to select a password that they can remember, so they create simple passwords, such as their birthday, their mother's maiden name, the name of their spouse or one of their children, or even simply their user ID itself. All it takes is for the attacker to obtain a valid user ID (often a simple matter, because organizations tend to use an individual's names in some combination—first letter of their first name combined with their last name, for example) and a little bit of information about the user before guessing can begin.

Dictionary Attack

Another method of determining passwords is to use a password-cracking program that uses a list of dictionary words to try to guess the password. The dictionary words can be used by themselves, or two or more smaller words can be combined to form a single possible password. A number of commercial and public-domain password-cracking programs employ a variety of methods to crack passwords, including using variations on the user ID.

Rules can also be defined so that the cracking program will substitute special characters for other characters or combine words. The ability of the attacker to crack passwords is directly related to the method the user employs to create the password in the first place, as well as the dictionary and rules used.

Brute-Force Attack

If the user has selected a password that is not found in a dictionary, even if simply by substituting various numbers or special characters for letters, the only way the password can be cracked is for an attacker to attempt a brute-force attack, in which the password-cracking program attempts all possible character combinations.

The length of the password and the size of the set of possible characters in the password will greatly affect the time a brute-force attack will take. A few years ago, this method of attack was very time consuming, since it took considerable time to generate all possible combinations. With the increase in computer speed, however, generating password combinations is much faster, making it more feasible to launch brute-force attacks against certain computer systems and networks.

 Modern multicore processors and large on-chip cache memories have significantly improved the speed of password-cracking programs, making brute-force methods practical in many cases.

A brute-force attack on a password can take place at two levels: The attacker can use a password-cracking program to attempt to guess the password directly at a login prompt, or the attacker can first steal a password file, use a password-cracking program to compile a list of possible passwords based on the list of password hashes contained in the password file (offline), and then use that narrower list to attempt to guess the password at the login prompt. The first attack can be made more difficult if the account locks after a few failed login attempts. The second attack can be thwarted if the password file is securely maintained so that others cannot obtain a copy of it.

Hybrid Attack

A hybrid password attack is an attack that combines the preceding dictionary and brute-force methods. Most cracking tools have this option built in, first attempting a dictionary attack, and then moving to brute-force methods.

The programs often permit the attacker to create various rules that tell the program how to combine words to form new possible passwords. Users commonly substitute certain numbers for specific letters. If the user wanted to use the word *secret* as a base for a password, for example, she could replace the letter *e* with the number *3*, yielding *s3cr3t*. This password will not be found in the dictionary, so a pure dictionary attack would not crack it, but the password is still easy for the user to remember. If the attacker created a rule that instructed the program to try all words in the dictionary and then try the same words substituting the number *3* for the letter *e*, however, the password would be cracked.

Birthday Attack

The **birthday attack** is a special type of brute-force attack that gets its name from something known as the *birthday paradox*, which states that in a group of at least 23 people, the chance that two individuals will have the same birthday is greater than 50 percent. Mathematically, the equation is $1.25 \times k^{1/2}$, where k equals the size of the set of possible values, which in the birthday paradox is 365 (the number of possible birthdays). This same phenomenon applies to passwords, with k (number of passwords) being quite a bit larger.

Pass-the-Hash Attacks

Pass the hash is a hacking technique where the attacker captures the hash used to authenticate a process. They can then use this hash, by injecting it into a process in place of the password. This is a highly technical attack, targeting the Windows authentication process, injecting a copy of the password hash directly into the system. The attacker does not need to know the password, but instead can use a captured hash and inject it directly, which will verify correctly, granting access. As this is a very technically specific hack, tools have been developed to facilitate its operation.

Software Exploitation

An attack that takes advantage of bugs or weaknesses in software is referred to as *software exploitation*. These bugs and weaknesses can be the result of poor design, poor testing, or poor coding practices. They can also result from what are sometimes called "features." An example of this might be a debugging feature, which when used during debugging might allow unauthenticated individuals to execute programs on a system. If this feature remains in the program when the final version of the software is shipped, it creates a weakness that is just waiting to be exploited.

Software exploitation is a preventable problem. Through the use of a secure development lifecycle process, coupled with tools such as threat modeling, bug tracking, fuzzing, and automated code analysis, many of exploitable elements can be identified and corrected before release. *Fuzzing* is the automated process of applying large sets of inputs to a system and analyzing the output to determine exploitable weaknesses. This technique has been used by hackers to determine exploitable issues and is being adopted by savvy test teams. Identification of potential vulnerabilities by the testing team is the best defense against zero-day attacks, which are attacks against currently unknown vulnerabilities.

Another element that can be exploited is the error messages from an application. Good programming practice includes proper error and exception handling. Proper error handling with respect to the testing team includes the return of significant diagnostic information to enable troubleshooting. Once the code goes to production, the diagnostic information is not as important as it does not help end users, and any potential information that can assist an attacker should be blocked from being presented to the end user. A prime example of this is in SQL injection attacks, where, through cleverly crafted injects, a database can be mapped and the data can even be returned to an attacker.

Buffer-Overflow Attack

A common weakness that has often been exploited is a **buffer overflow**, which occurs when a program is provided more data for input than it was designed to handle. For example, what would happen if a program that asks for a 7- to 10-character phone number instead receives a string of 150 characters? Many programs will provide some error checking to ensure that this will not cause a problem. Some programs, however, cannot handle this error, and the extra characters continue to fill memory, overwriting other portions of the program. This can result in a number of problems, including causing the program to abort or the system to crash. Under certain circumstances, the program can execute a command supplied by the attacker. Buffer overflows typically inherit the level of privilege enjoyed by the program being exploited. This is why programs that use root-level access are so dangerous when exploited with a buffer overflow, as the code that will execute does so at root-level access.

> **Exam Tip:** Buffer overflows were one of the most common vulnerabilities over the past ten years, although awareness and efforts to eradicate them over the past couple of years has been very successful in new code.

Integer Overflow

An **integer overflow** is a programming error condition that occurs when a program attempts to store a numeric value, an integer, in a variable that is too small to hold it. The results vary by language and numeric type. In some cases, the value saturates the variable, assuming the maximum value for the defined type and no more. In other cases, especially with signed integers, it can roll over into a negative value, as the most significant bit is usually reserved for the sign of the number. This can create significant logic errors in a program.

Integer overflows are easily tested for, and static code analyzers can point out where they are likely to occur. Given this, there are not any good excuses for having these errors end up in production code.

Client-Side Attacks

The web browser has become the major application for users to engage resources across the Web. The popularity and the utility of this interface has made it a prime target for attackers to gain access and control over a system. A wide variety of attacks can occur via a browser, typically resulting from a failure to validate input properly before use. Unvalidated input can result in a series of injection attacks, header manipulation, and other forms of attack.

Injection Attacks

When user input is used without input validation, this gives an attacker the opportunity to craft input to create specific events to occur when the input is parsed and used by an application. SQL injection attacks involve the manipulation of input, resulting in a SQL statement that is different than intended by the designer. XML and LDAP injections are done in the same fashion. As SQL, XML, and LDAP are used to store data, these types of injection attacks can give an attacker access to data against business rules. Command injection attacks can occur when input is used in a fashion that allows command-line manipulation, giving an attacker command-line access at the same privilege level as the application.

Header Manipulations

When HTTP is being dynamically generated through the use of user inputs, unvalidated inputs can give attackers an opportunity to change HTTP elements. When user-supplied information is used in a header, it is possible to deploy a variety of attacks, including cache poisoning, cross-site scripting, cross-user defacement, page hijacking, cookie manipulation, and open redirect.

Typo Squatting/URL Hijacking

Typo squatting is an attack form that involves capitalizing upon common typo errors. If a user mistypes a URL, then the result should be a 404 error, or "resource not found." But if an attacker has registered the mistyped URL, then you would land on the attacker's page. This attack pattern is also referred to as *URL hijacking, fake URL,* or *brandjacking* if the objective is to deceive based on branding.

There are several reasons that an attacker will pursue this avenue of attack. The most obvious is one of a phishing attack. The fake site collects credentials, passing them on to the real site, and then steps out of the conversation to avoid detection once the credentials are obtained. It can also be used to plant drive-by malware on the victim machine. It can move the packets through an affiliate network, earning click-through revenue based on the typos. There are numerous other forms of attacks that can be perpetrated using a fake URL as a starting point.

Drive-by Download Attacks

Browsers are used to navigate the Internet, using HTTP and other protocols to bring files to users' computers. Some of these files are images, some are scripts, and some are text based, and together they form the web pages that we see. Users don't ask for each component—it is the job of the browser to identify the needed files and fetch them. A new type of attack takes advantage of this mechanism by initiating downloads of malware, whether a user clicks it or not. This automated download of materials is referred to as a **drive-by download attack**.

Watering Hole Attack

The most commonly recognized attack vectors are those that are direct to a target. Because of their incoming and direct nature, defenses are crafted to detect and defend against them. But what if the user "asked" for the attack by visiting a web site? Just as a hunter waits near a watering hole for animals to come drink, attackers can plant malware at sites where users are likely to frequent. First identified by RSA, watering hole attacks involve the infecting of a target web site with malware. In some of the cases detected, the infection was constrained to a specific geographical area. These are not simple attacks, yet they can be very effective at delivering malware to specific groups of end users. Watering hole attacks are complex to achieve and appear to be backed by nation-states and other high-resource attackers. In light of the stakes, the typical attack vector will be a zero-day attack to further avoid detection.

Tech Tip

Watering Hole Attacks

Watering hole attacks can occur from even innocent web sites. Brian Krebs gives a strong analysis of watering hole attacks on his blog, Krebs on Security: http://krebsonsecurity. com/2012/09/espionage-hackers-target-watering-hole-sites.

■ Advanced Persistent Threat

The advanced persistent threat (APT) is a method of attack that primarily focuses on stealth and continuous presence on a system. APT is a very advanced method, requiring a team to maintain access and typically involves high-value targets. APT typically involves specially crafted attack vectors, coupled with phishing or spear phishing for the initial entry. Then techniques are employed to develop backdoors and multiple account access routes. The skill level of the attackers is typically exceedingly high and their aim is to completely own a system without being detected.

Once the attackers have completely penetrated a system, including elements like the ability to read e-mails to watch for reports of detection, they can accomplish their goal of stealing materials. Their long-term objectives are to remain hidden and undetected, while harvesting information over months and years. APTs are the attack method of choice for nation-states and industrial espionage.

Tech Tip

Signs of APT Attack

The following are indications of an APT attack:

- ■ ***Off-hours activity*** *If logs demonstrate "normal" activity at times when your workers are at home, this is a sign of compromised accounts. Look for large numbers of occurrences, as APT attackers tend to use multiple accounts.*

- ■ ***Finding multiple backdoor Trojans/remote access Trojans*** *When security scans begin to find a lot of malware, this can be a sign of APTs.*

- ■ ***Finding unknown files*** *APTs tend to bundle exfiltration data and keep it in encrypted form before slowly siphoning it out. Discovery of large files of unknown origin can be these bundles.*

- ■ ***Finding spear phishing e-mails and pass-the-hash tools*** *These advanced attack methods are indications of an advanced adversary.*

- ■ ***Strange data flows*** *This is the most telltale sign. Finding unusual data flows, movement of data not in the normal course of business, indicates leakage.*

Remote Access Trojans

Remote access Trojans (RATs) are malware designed to enable remote access to a machine. This functionality is similar to remote desktop administration, but rather than being visible to a user, it is hidden in the system. RATs enable attackers to have a way back into a system. The principal use of a RAT is to enable re-entry to a system and/or collect data on a system. Common data collection functions performed by RATs include capture of webcam images, keystrokes and mouse movements, and image capture of the screen. When these data elements are combined they can defeat image-based password systems. Complete shell access to the OS is typical, enabling the attacker full access to the system and processes.

A key function of a RAT is to provide a periodic beacon out, so even if firewalls and other security devices block unrequested packets, the beacon function makes them requested, bypassing many security checks. RATs have existed for years, and more recently, custom RATs, which avoid AV detection, are being used in APT-style attacks.

■ Tools

There are a variety of toolsets used by security professionals that could also be used for malicious purposes. These toolsets are used by penetration testers when testing the security posture of a system. The same tools in the hands of an adversary can be used for malicious purposes.

Metasploit

Metasploit is a framework that enables attackers to exploit systems (bypass controls) and inject payloads (attack code) into a system. Metasploit is widely distributed, powerful, and one of the most popular tools used by attackers. When new vulnerabilities are discovered in systems, Metasploit exploit modules are quickly created in the community, making this tool the go-to tool for most professionals.

BackTrack/Kali

BackTrack is a Linux distribution that is preloaded with many security tools. The current version is called Kali Linux. It includes a whole host of preconfigured, preloaded tools, including Metasploit, Social-Engineering Toolkit, and others.

Social-Engineering Toolkit

The Social-Engineering Toolkit (SET) is a set of tools that can be used to target attacks toward the people using systems. It has applets that can be used to create phishing e-mails, Java attack code, and other social engineering–type attacks. The SET is included in BackTrack/Kali and other distributions.

Cobalt Strike

Cobalt Strike is a powerful application that can replicate advanced threats and assist in the execution of targeted attacks on systems. Cobalt Strike expands the Armitage tool's capabilities, adding advanced attack methods.

Core Impact

Core Impact is an expensive commercial suite of penetration test tools. It has a wide spectrum of tools and proven attack abilities across an enterprise. Although expensive, the level of automation and integration makes this a powerful suite of tools.

Burp Suite

Burp Suite began as a port scanner tool with limited additional functionality in the arena of intercepting proxies, web application scanning, and web-based content. Burp Suite is a commercial tool, but it is reasonably priced and well liked and utilized in the pen-testing marketplace.

■ Auditing

Auditing, in the financial community, is done to verify the accuracy and integrity of financial records. Many standards have been established in the financial community about how to record and report a company's financial status correctly. In the computer security world, auditing serves a similar function. It is a process of assessing the security state of an organization compared against an established standard.

The important elements here are the standards. Organizations from different communities may have widely different standards, and any audit will need to consider the appropriate elements for the specific community. Audits differ from security or vulnerability assessments in that assessments measure the security posture of the organization but may do so without any mandated standards against which to compare them. In a security assessment, general security "best practices" can be used, but they may lack the regulatory teeth that standards often provide. Penetration tests can also be encountered—these tests are conducted against an organization to determine whether any holes in the organization's security can be found. The goal of the penetration test is to penetrate the security rather than measure it against some standard. Penetration tests are often viewed as *white-hat hacking* in that the methods used often mirror those that attackers (often called *black hats*) might use.

You should conduct some form of security audit or assessment on a regular basis. Your organization might spend quite a bit on security, and it is important to measure how effective the efforts have been. In certain communities, audits can be regulated on a periodic basis with very specific standards that must be measured against. Even if your organization is not part of such a community, periodic assessments are important.

One of the key management principles involves the measurement of a process. When referring to security, until it is measured, one should take answers with a grain of salt. Logging information is only good if you examine the logs and analyze them. Security controls work, but auditing their use provides assurance of their protection.

Many particulars can be evaluated during an assessment, but at a minimum, the security perimeter (with all of its components, including host-based security) should be examined, as well as the organization's policies, procedures, and guidelines governing security. Employee training is another aspect that should be studied, since employees are the targets of social-engineering and password-guessing attacks.

Security audits, assessments, and penetration tests are a big business, and a number of organizations can perform them for you. The costs of these vary widely depending on the extent of the tests you want, the background of the company you are contracting with, and the size of the organization to be tested.

A powerful mechanism for detecting security incidents is the use of security logs. For logs to be effective, however, they require monitoring. Monitoring of event logs can provide information concerning the events that have been logged. This requires making decisions in advance about the items to be logged. Logging too many items uses a lot of space and increases the workload for personnel who are assigned the task of reading those logs. The same is true for security, access, audit, and application-specific logs. The bottom line is that, although logs are valuable, preparation is needed to determine the correct items to log and the mechanisms by which logs are reviewed. Security Information Event Management (SIEM) software can assist in log file analysis.

Perform Routine Audits

As part of any good security program, administrators must perform periodic audits to ensure things "are as they should be" with regard to users, systems, policies, and procedures. Installing and configuring security mechanisms is important, but they must be reviewed on a regularly scheduled basis to ensure they are effective, up to date, and serving their intended function. Here are some examples, but by no means a complete list, of items that should be audited on a regular basis:

- **User access**   Administrators should review which users are accessing the systems, when they are doing so, what resources they are using, and so on. Administrators should look closely for users accessing resources improperly or accessing legitimate resources at unusual times.

- **User rights**   When a user changes jobs or responsibilities, she will likely need to be assigned different access permissions; she may gain access to new resources and lose access to others. To ensure that users have access only to the resources and capabilities they need for their current positions, all user rights should be audited periodically.

- **Storage**   Many organizations have policies governing what can be stored on "company" resources and how much space can be used by a given user or group. Periodic audits help to ensure that no undesirable or illegal materials exist on organizational resources.

- **Retention**   In some organizations, how long a particular document or record is stored can be as important as what is being stored. A records retention policy helps to define what is stored, how it is stored, how long it is stored, and how it is disposed of when the time comes. Periodic audits help to ensure that records or documents are removed when they are no longer needed.

- **Firewall rules**   Periodic audits of firewall rules are important to ensure the firewall is filtering traffic as desired and to help ensure that "temporary" rules do not end up as permanent additions to the rule set.

Chapter 15 Review

Lab Manual Exercises

The following lab exercises from the companion lab manual, *Principles of Computer Security Lab Manual, Fourth Edition*, provide practical application of material covered in this chapter:

Lab 4.4l	Using the Metasploit Framework		Lab 6.1w	Using the Dark Comet Trojan
Lab 4.6l	Using Cobalt Strike		Lab 6.2m	Man-in-the-Middle Attack
Lab 5.11i	Web SQL Injection in Linux		Lab 6.3w	Steganography in Windows

Chapter Summary

After reading this chapter and completing the exercises, you should understand the following aspects of attacks and malware.

Describe the various types of computer and network attacks, including denial-of-service, spoofing, hijacking, and password guessing

- Understand how denial-of-service (DoS) and distributed denial-of-service (DDoS) attacks are performed and the defenses against them.

- Both packet headers and e-mail headers can be spoofed to take advantage of the trust users place in these data elements, even when they are not protected from change.

- Understand how session hijacking and man-in-the-middle attacks are performed and what the defenses are against these attacks.

- Password systems can have numerous vulnerabilities, some based on the system and some on the choice of password itself.

Identify the different types of malicious software that exist, including viruses, worms, Trojan horses, logic bombs, time bombs, and rootkits

- Viruses are pieces of malware that require a file to infect a system.

- Worms are pieces of malware that can exist without infecting a file.

- Trojan horses are pieces of malware disguised as something else, something the user wants or finds useful.

- Logic bombs trigger when specific events occur in code, allowing an attack to be timed against an event.

- Time bombs are delayed malware designed to occur after a set period of time or on a specific date.

- Rootkits are pieces of malware designed to alter the lower-level functions of a system in a manner to escape detection.

Explain how social engineering can be used as a means to gain access to computers and networks

- Social engineering attacks are attacks against the operators and users of a system.

- Training and awareness is the best defensive measure against social engineering.

Describe the importance of auditing and what should be audited

- Logging is important because logs can provide information associated with attacks.

- Auditing is an essential component of a comprehensive security system.

■ Key Terms

auditing *(497)*
backdoor *(472)*
birthday attack *(492)*
botnet *(472)*
buffer overflow *(493)*
denial-of-service (DoS) attack *(474)*
distributed denial-of-service (DDoS) attack *(476)*
DNS kiting *(488)*
drive-by download attack *(494)*
integer overflow *(493)*
logic bomb *(471)*
malware *(466)*
man-in-the-middle attack *(483)*
null session *(478)*
pharming *(485)*
phishing *(485)*

ransomware *(473)*
replay attack *(484)*
rootkit *(470)*
sequence number *(482)*
smurf attack *(480)*
sniffing *(479)*
spear phishing *(485)*
spoofing *(480)*
spyware *(471)*
SYN flood *(475)*
TCP/IP hijacking *(483)*
Trojan *(470)*
typo squatting *(494)*
virus *(466)*
worm *(469)*
zombie *(476)*

■ Key Terms Quiz

Use terms from the Key Terms list to complete the sentences that follow. Don't use the same term more than once. Not all terms will be used.

1. Changing a source IP address for malicious purpose is an example of _____.

2. A(n) _____ is a way back into a machine via an unauthorized channel of access.

3. A malicious proxy could create a(n) _____ attack.

4. Abusing the TCP handshake in an effort to overuse server resources can be done using a(n) _____.

5. The main TCP/IP defense against a man-in-the-middle attack is the use of a(n) _____.

6. Holding a DNS name without paying is called _____.

7. When a keylogger is installed as malware, it is referred to as _____.

8. Rendering a resource useless is called a(n) _____.

9. An attack designed to match any user's password as opposed to a specific user's password is an example of a(n) _____.

10. A NIC can be set in promiscuous mode to enable _____.

■ Multiple-Choice Quiz

1. A SYN flood is an example of what type of attack?
   - **A.** Malicious code
   - **B.** Denial-of-service
   - **C.** Man-in-the-middle
   - **D.** Spoofing

2. An attack in which the attacker simply listens for all traffic being transmitted across a network, in the hope of viewing something such as a user ID and password combination, is known as:
   - **A.** A man-in-the-middle attack
   - **B.** A denial-of-service attack

C. A sniffing attack

D. A backdoor attack

3. Which attack takes advantage of a trusted relationship that exists between two systems?

   A. Spoofing

   B. Password guessing

   C. Sniffing

   D. Brute-force

4. In what type of attack does an attacker resend the series of commands and codes used in a financial transaction to cause the transaction to be conducted multiple times?

   A. Spoofing

   B. Man-in-the-middle

   C. Replay

   D. Backdoor

5. Rootkits are challenging security problems because:

   A. They can be invisible to the operating system and end user.

   B. Their true functionality can be cloaked, preventing analysis.

   C. They can do virtually anything an operating system can do.

   D. All of the above.

6. An attack in which an attacker attempts to lie and misrepresent himself in order to gain access to information that can be useful in an attack is known as:

   A. Social science

   B. White-hat hacking

   C. Social engineering

   D. Social manipulation

7. The first step in an attack on a computer system consists of:

   A. Gathering as much information about the target system as possible

   B. Obtaining as much information about the organization in which the target lies as possible

   C. Searching for possible exploits that can be used against known vulnerabilities

   D. Searching for specific vulnerabilities that may exist in the target's operating system or software applications

8. The best way to minimize possible avenues of attack for your system is to:

   A. Install a firewall and check the logs daily.

   B. Monitor your intrusion detection system for possible attacks.

   C. Limit the information that can be obtained on your organization and the services that are run by your Internet-visible systems.

   D. Ensure that all patches have been applied for the services that are offered by your system.

9. A war-driving attack is an attempt to exploit what technology?

   A. Fiber-optic networks, whose cables often run along roads and bridges

   B. Cellular telephones

   C. The public switched telephone network (PSTN)

   D. Wireless networks

10. Malicious code that is set to execute its payload on a specific date or at a specific time is known as:

   A. A logic bomb

   B. A Trojan horse

   C. A virus

   D. A time bomb

■ Essay Quiz

1. Compare and contrast port scanning and ping sweeps.

2. What is the best practice to employ to mitigate malware effects on a machine?

Lab Projects

• Lab Project 15.1

Using the Internet, research password-cracking tools. Then, using a tool of choice, examine how easy it is to crack passwords on Windows- and UNIX-based systems. Create a series of accounts with different complexities of passwords and see how well they fare.

• Lab Project 15.2

Obtain a copy of the nmap scanning tool. Explore the various command-line options to scan networks, fingerprint operating systems, and perform other network-mapping functions.

Note: Students should try these options, but only in a lab environment, not across the Internet from their home ISP.

E-Mail and Instant Messaging

The "free" distribution of unwelcome or misleading messages to thousands of people is an annoying and sometimes destructive use of the Internet's unprecedented efficiency.

—Bill Gates, *New York Times*, 1998

In this chapter, you will learn how to

- **Describe security issues associated with e-mail**
- **Implement security practices for e-mail**
- **Detail the security issues of instant messaging protocols**

E-mail is the most popular application on company networks. With over 2.6 billion e-mail users, 4.3 billion e-mail accounts and more than 200 billion e-mails per year, the usage numbers are staggering. The split between business and personal email is 55/45 percent, respectively. The total amount of spam is unknown, but even after extensive filtering, spam averages nearly 10 percent of inbox traffic.

How E-Mail Works

E-mail started with mailbox programs on early time-sharing machines, allowing researchers to leave messages for others using the same machine. The first intermachine e-mail was sent in 1972, and a new era in person-to-person communication was launched. E-mail proliferated, but it remained unsecured, only partly because most e-mail is sent in plaintext, providing no privacy in its default form. Current e-mail in its use is not different from its earlier versions; it's still a simple way to send a relatively short text message to another user. Users' dependence on e-mail has grown with the number of people accessing the Internet.

Internet e-mail depends on three primary protocols, SMTP, POP3, and IMAP. **Simple Mail Transfer Protocol (SMTP)** is the method by which mail is sent to the server as well as from server to server. SMTP by default uses TCP port 25. POP3 stands for Post Office Protocol version 3, which by default uses TCP port 110. POP3 is a method by which a client computer may connect to a server and download new messages. POP3 has been partly replaced by IMAP, or Internet Message Access Protocol, which uses port TCP 143 by default. IMAP is similar to POP3 in that it allows the client to retrieve messages from the server, but IMAP typically works in greater synchronization; for example, e-mails are left on the server until the client deletes them in the client, at which time IMAP instructs the server to delete them. As e-mail services became more standardized, the methods of transmission became easier to attack as they were not strange proprietary protocols. Also, as the world became more connected, there were many more available targets for the malware and commercial e-mails.

Secure versions of the common communication protocols exist via the STARTTLS method. STARTTLS is a means of using Transport Layer Security (TLS) to secure a communication channel for text-based communication protocols. Table 16.1 shows the port assignments associated with STARTTLS.

E-mail appears to be a client-to-client communication, between sender and receiver. In reality, a lot of steps are involved, as shown in Figure 16.1 and described here:

1. A user composes and sends an e-mail from the user's client machine.

2. The e-mail is sent to the client's e-mail server. In an Internet service provider (ISP) environment, this could be via the ISP. In the case of web mail, it is the mail service (Gmail, Hotmail/Live, etc.). In a corporate environment it is the corporate mail server.

3. a. The receiving e-mail server scans the e-mail for viruses, malware, and other threats.

   b. The mail server uses DNS to obtain the recipient e-mail server address via an MX record.

Tech Tip

E-mail and Firewalls

For e-mail applications to work with e-mail servers, they need to communicate across specific channels. To ensure communication, TCP ports 25, 110, and 143 need to be open on clients that need to connect to mail servers. This is for SMTP, POP3, and IMAP, respectively.

Table 16.1	STARTTLS Port Assignments			
Protocol	**Purpose**	**Normal Port**	**TLS Variant**	**TLS Port**
SMTP	Send e-mail	25/587	SMTPS	465 (legacy)
POP3	Retrieve e-mail	110	POP3S	995
IMAP	Read e-mail	143	IMAPS	993

How E-mail *Appears* to Work

Sender's out-box

Recipient's in-box

How E-mail Really *Does* Work

① Sender's out-box

②

③

④

⑤

⑥

⑦ Recipient's in-box

● **Figure 16.1**   How e-mail works

4. The mail server prepares the e-mail for transit across the Internet to the recipient's mail server.

5. The e-mail is routed across the Internet.

6. The receiving e-mail server scans the e-mail for viruses, malware, and other threats.

7. The e-mail is passed to the recipient's in-box, where it can be read.

This list of steps leaves out a lot of details, but it provides the main steps in e-mail transference. The steps are remarkably similar for instant messaging applications as well. Rather than in-boxes and e-mail as a medium, the instant messaging apps deliver the text messages directly to the screen of the app.

In technical terms, the application on the sender's machine is referred to as a **mail user agent (MUA)**, and the mail server is a **mail transfer agent (MTA)**. The recipient's mail server is referred to as a **mail delivery agent (MDA)**. These terms are used when discussing mail transfers to provide accuracy in the conversation. For communication from the MUA to the MTA, SMTP (port 25) is used, and communication from MTA to MTA is also SMTP. The protocol used for communication from the MDA to the MUA on the recipient machine is typically POP/IMAP.

E-Mail Structure

E-mail is structured in two elements, a header and the body. The entire message is sent via plain ASCII text, with attachments included using Base64 encoding. The e-mail header provides information for the handling of the e-mail between MUAs, MTAs, and MDAs. The following is a sample e-mail header:

```
Received: from smtp4.cc.uh.edu (129.7.234.211) by xFENode3B.mail.example.
net (129.7.40.150) with Microsoft SMTP Server id 8.2.255.0; Sat, 11 Apr 2015
18:54:42 -0500
Received: from smtp4.cc.uh.edu (smtp4.example.net [127.0.0.1]) by localhost
(Postfix) with SMTP id BC4DA1E004A for <waconklin@example.com>; Sat, 11 Apr
2015 18:53:55 -0500 (CDT)
Received: from nm22.bullet.mail.ne1.yahoo.com (nm22.bullet.mail.ne1.yahoo.com

 [98.138.90.85]) by smtp4.example.net (Postfix) with ESMTP id  538C31E0034 for
<waconklin@example.com>; Sat, 11 Apr 2015
 18:53:55 -0500 (CDT)
DKIM-Signature: v=1; a=rsa-sha256; c=relaxed/relaxed;
d=yahoo.com; s=s2048;
 t=1428796434; bh=esKcEn6Pe1DHaDx/5lqarnNbc5vZAFO5+z93Xt/06S0=;
h=Date:From:Reply-To:To:In-Reply-To:References:Subject:From:Subject;
b=OQTvNETmW6KKGn/cWXsQd43khwTbwsGpRFhpwB0iCopROLVxabwPryOB/6RpSb37JC5IYTxYrDj
rs
lDhaSBj1381Y8ior9CS83YyV3JnRzk6F+YrDQDUXAuG5vbhDo9lKUX0pNa/R4rdvK47T6uO92k-
7wf1+
+egSLATDeId5ccUFUZLBQpxBJx6WtLJbI6eValGPQLgLCNdhedkgGBEugp+Yfc0xDr975euYFsxwL
DS
36pi88etIkMso0FDbQLsGfk3SneIkm+o5wSDq7lAsWk3NX4p+yFjW16V7OjQSg2Xf6KnNt9gUh9v9
8U
+WW/Crwlq110xUHL1FjiP6oNsGkw==
Received: from [98.138.100.112] by nm22.bullet.mail.ne1.yahoo.com
with NNFMP;
 11 Apr 2015 23:53:54 -0000
Received: from [98.138.89.173] by tm103.bullet.mail.ne1.yahoo.com
with NNFMP;
 11 Apr 2015 23:53:53 -0000

Received: from [127.0.0.1] by omp1029.mail.ne1.yahoo.com with NNFMP;
11 Apr
 2015 23:53:53 -0000
X-Yahoo-Newman-Property: ymail-5
X-Yahoo-Newman-Id: 880223.99814.bm@omp1029.mail.ne1.yahoo.com
X-YMail-OSG: NKvYQJkVM1kWuLmyDvNnFXECaMumy9LBgfZhcKRiubzkoq9_NVdEUqlT7hMlkOv
 loWFqcbcyiJwpOTgEmUZIsGX2ZpKSfNrUUzmQ3.ksRewbg9xRVVDqnQbdJksIfeePVCUGNJ26elD
 Ts4mEjfkzWPGKiXkxmy8iNhDzszw0RmJpDOrRDymsdTE3ObnKA83ZXSj9w0CwXnkJ_UtmVSWtyl0
 NLDv8KRSPl0IaW8APZeaAmmTKPO06z.8jJg.GOGWAZbonqsm_zXvMjcfmmQ8wd8PBOh2pFqzvwvn
 cfwHL3.iDmOzcNBYrF5mNfbmdaoHAztYxA8edB2kFqN3vje3VJPkoPOCiOhq_c_wFIs8E6W02VjK
 0gCJRLAPEwyo30kyz_QDyGgfpfv4GAXrz9bQet8sy_e2ztRyVnj9GDu.DHSYnU5TaTLzvRhMQO3p
 082zOb2Qm_4Miilk36RzypHRAEWh_GlTxr3sRloz1RhsioTgMYqksk0E_7P2bBJOJb3HsTyG2o_i
 swOuz7CIt8U67Fe1IlDoPsU5hJj8DXHlSK_pGUl3j
Received: by 98.138.105.206; Sat, 11 Apr 2015 23:53:53 +0000
Date: Sat, 11 Apr 2015 23:53:52 +0000
From: Sender Name SenderName@yahoo.com
eply-To: Sender Name SenderName@yahoo.com
To: "Conklin, Wm. Arthur" waconklin@example.com
Message-ID: 517184424.1041513.1428796432644.JavaMail.yahoo@mail.yahoo.com
In-Reply-To: 9AF24FE2BE34BC42A10F1DE75C05D8871652896780@EXSERVER3.example.com
References: 9AF24FE2BE34BC42A10F1DE75C05D8871652896780@EXSERVER3.example.com
Subject: Re: Homework Lab 2
MIME-Version: 1.0
Content-Type: multipart/mixed;
        boundary="-----=_Part_1041512_683422731.1428796432643"
X-PMX-Version: 6.0.3.2322014, Antispam-Engine: 2.7.2.2107409, Antispam-Data:
2015.4.11.234523
X-PerlMx-Spam: Gauge=IIIIIIII, Probability=8%, Report='
HTML_50_70 0.1, HTML_NO_HTTP 0.1, BODYTEXTH_SIZE_10000_LESS 0,
BODYTEXTP_SIZE_3000_LESS 0, BODY_SIZE_10000_PLUS 0, DKIM_SIGNATURE 0,
ECARD_KNOWN_DOMAINS 0, REFERENCES 0, WEBMAIL_SOURCE 0, __ANY_URI 0,
__BOUNCE_CHALLENGE_SUBJ 0, __BOUNCE_NDR_SUBJ_EXEMPT 0, __C230066_P1_5 0, __CT
0, __CTYPE_HAS_BOUNDARY 0, __CTYPE_MULTIPART 0, __CTYPE_MULTIPART_MIXED 0,
__DQ_NEG_HEUR 0, __DQ_NEG_IP 0, __FORWARDED_MSG 0, __FRAUD_BODY_WEBMAIL 0,
__FRAUD_WEBMAIL 0, __FRAUD_WEBMAIL_FROM 0, __FRAUD_WEBMAIL_REPLYTO 0,
```

```
__FROM_YAHOO 0, __HAS_FROM 0, __HAS_HTML 0, __HAS_MSGID 0, __HAS_REPLYTO 0,
__HELO_YAHOO 0, __IN_REP_TO 0, __MIME_HTML 0, __MIME_VERSION 0, __RDNS_YAHOO
0, __REFERENCES 0, __REPLYTO_SAMEAS_FROM 0, __REPLYTO_SAMEAS_FROM_ACC 0,

__REPLYTO_SAMEAS_FROM_ADDY 0, __REPLYTO_SAMEAS_FROM_DOMAIN 0, __SANE_MSGID 0,
__SUBJ_ALPHA_NEGATE 0, __TAG_EXISTS_HTML 0, __TO_MALFORMED_2 0, __URI_NO_PATH
0,
__URI_NO_WWW 0, __URI_NS '
```

Return-Path: SenderName@yahoo.com

The specific elements shown in this header will be examined throughout this chapter. What is important to note is that the format of the message and its attachments are in plaintext.

MIME

When a message has an attachment, the protocol used to deliver the message is **Multipurpose Internet Mail Extensions (MIME)**. This protocol allows the exchange of different kinds of data across text-based e-mail systems. When MIME is used, it is marked in the header of the e-mail, along with supporting elements to facilitate decoding. The following is an excerpt from a header that has MIME elements:

```
Content-Type: multipart/alternative;
 boundary="------------04090503000604040406008"
This is a multi-part message in MIME format.
--------------04090503000604040406008
Content-Type: text/plain; charset=UTF-8; format=flowed
Content-Transfer-Encoding: 7bit

**Poster found in a Texas Gun Shop: ****

--------------04090503000604040406008
Content-Type: multipart/related;
 boundary="------------09050203060703030308090400"

--------------09050203060703030308090400
Content-Type: text/html; charset=UTF-8
Content-Transfer-Encoding: 8bit

<!DOCTYPE html PUBLIC "-//W3C//DTD HTML 4.01 Transitional//EN">
<html>
<head>
</head>
<body bgcolor="#ffffff" text="#000000">
<HTML E-MAIL message goes here>
</body>
</html>

--------------09050203060703030308090400
Content-Type: image/jpeg
Content-Transfer-Encoding: base64
Content-ID: <part1.00060501.01000908@example.com>
```

```
/9j/4AAQSkZJRgABAQAAAQABAAD/2wBDAAUDBAQEAwUEBAQEBAQFBQUGBwwIBwcHBw8LCwkMEQ8S
EhEPERETFhwXExEaFRERGCEYGh0dHx8fExciJCIeJBweHx7/2wBDAQUFBQcGBw4ICA4eFBEUHh4
Hh4eHh4eHh4eHh4eHh4eHh4eHh4eHh4eHh4eHh4eHh4eHh4eHh7/wAAR
CAJYAaQDASIAAhEBAxEB/8QAHwAAAQUBAQEBAQEAAAAAAAAAAECAwQFBgcICQoL/8QAtRAA
AgEDAwIEAwUFBAQAAAF9AQIDAAQRBRIhMUEGE1FhByJxFDKBkaEII0KxwRVS0fAkM2JyggkK
FhcYGRolJicoKSo0NTY3ODk6Q0RFRkdISUpTVFVWV1hZWmNkZWZnaGlqc3R1dnd4eXqDhIWG
h4iJipKTlJWWl5iZmqKjpKWmp6ipqrKztLW2t7i5usLDxMXGx8jJytLT1NXW19jZ2uHi4+Tl
5ufo6erx8vP09fb3+Pn6/8QAHwEAAwEBAQEBAQEBAQAAAAAAAAECAwQFBgcICQoL/8QAtREA
```
```
```

AgECBAQDBAcFBAQAAQJ3AAECAxEEBSExBhJBUQdhcRMiMoEIFEKRobHBCSMzUvAVYnLRChYk
NOEl8RcYGRomJygpKjU2Nzg5OkNERUZHSElKU1RVVldYWVpjZGVmZ2hpanN0dXZ3eHl6goOE
hYaHiImKkpOUlZaXmJmaoqOkpaanqKmqsrO0tba3uLm6wsPExcbHyMnK0tPU1dbX2Nna4uPk
5ebn6Onq8vP09fb3+Pn6/9oADAMBAAIRAxEAPwD46nml8+T96/3j/EfWo/Om/wCesn/fRpZ/
+PiT/fP86ioAk86b/nrJ/wB9Gjzpv+esn/fRqOigCTzpv+esn/fRo86b/nrJ/wB9Go6KAJPO
m/56yf8AfRo86b/nrJ/30ajooAk86b/nrJ/30aPOm/56yf99Go6KAJPOm/56yf99Go6KAJ9
56yf99Go6KAJPOm/56yf99GgCTzp

The e-mail text has been replaced with <HTML E-MAIL message goes here> and the JPEG image is truncated, but the structure of the sample shows how content can be encoded and included in an e-mail.

Security of E-Mail

E-mail can be used to move a variety of threats across the network. From spam, to viruses, to advanced malware in spear-phishing attacks, e-mail can act as a transmission medium. Spam is the most common attack but is now just a nuisance; the majority is now mostly cleaned up by mail server filters and software.

The **e-mail hoax** has become another regular occurrence; Internet-based urban legends are spread through e-mail, with users forwarding them in seemingly endless loops around the globe. And, of course, people still haven't found a good way to block ubiquitous spam e-mails (a sampling of which is shown in Figure 16.2), despite the remarkable advance of every other technology.

E-mail security is ultimately the responsibility of users themselves, because they are the ones who will actually be sending and receiving the messages. However, security administrators can give users the tools they need to fight malware, spam, and hoaxes. Secure/Multipurpose Internet

• **Figure 16.2** A typical list of spam e-mails

Mail Extensions (S/MIME) and Pretty Good Privacy (PGP) are two popular methods used for encrypting e-mail, as discussed later in the chapter. Server-based and desktop-based virus protection can help against malicious code, and spam filters attempt to block all unsolicited commercial e-mail. E-mail users need to be educated about security as well, however, because the popularity and functionality of e-mail is only going to increase with time.

Instant messaging (IM), while not part of the e-mail system, is similar to e-mail in many respects, particularly in the sense that it is commonly plaintext and can transmit files. IM's handling of files opens the application to virus exploitation just like e-mail. IM has experienced a boom in popularity in the last few years, so we will look at some popular IM programs later in this chapter, such as AOL Instant Messenger, shown in Figure 16.3.

Malicious Code

Viruses and worms are popular programs because they make themselves popular. When viruses were constrained to only one computer, they attempted to spread by attaching themselves to every executable program that they could find. This worked out very well for the viruses, because they could piggyback onto a floppy disk with a program that was being transferred to another computer. The virus would then infect the next computer, and the next computer after that. While often successful, virus propagation was slow, and floppies could be scanned for viruses.

The advent of computer networks was a computer virus writer's dream, allowing viruses to attempt to infect every network share to which the computer was attached. This extended the virus's reach from a set of machines that might share a floppy disk to every machine on the network. Because the e-mail protocol permits users to attach files to e-mail messages (see Figure 16.4), viruses can travel by e-mail from one local network to another, anywhere on

Exam Tip: Viruses and worms both can carry malicious payloads and cause damage. The difference is in how they are transmitted: viruses require a file to infect, whereas worms can exist independently of a file.

• **Figure 16.3** AOL Instant Messenger is a popular instant messaging program.

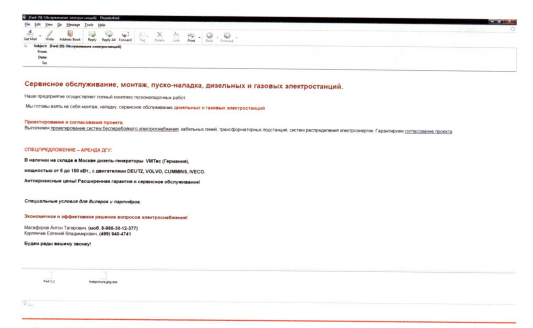

• **Figure 16.4**   Viruses commonly spread through e-mail attachments.

the Internet. This changed the nature of virus programs, since they once were localized but now could spread virtually everywhere. E-mail gave the virus a global reach.

When active content was designed for the Web, in the form of Java and ActiveX scripts, these scripts were interpreted and run by the web browser. E-mail programs also would run these scripts, and that's when the trouble began. Some e-mail programs, most notably Microsoft Outlook, use a preview pane, which allows users to read e-mails without opening them in the full screen (see Figure 16.5).

• **Figure 16.5**   The preview pane on the right can execute code in e-mails without opening them.

Unfortunately, this preview still activates all the content in the e-mail message, and because Outlook supports Visual Basic scripting, it is vulnerable to e-mail worms. A user doesn't need to run the program or even open the e-mail to activate the worm—simply previewing the e-mail in the preview pane can launch the malicious content. This form of automatic execution was the primary reason for the spread of the ILOVEYOU worm.

All malware is a security threat, with the several different types having different countermeasures. The antivirus systems that we have used for years have progressed to try and stop all forms of malicious software, but they are not a panacea. Worm prevention also relies on patch management of the operating system and applications. Viruses are user-launched, and since one of the most common transfer methods for viruses is through e-mail, the people using the e-mail system create the front line of defense against viruses. In addition to antivirus scanning of the user's system, and possibly an e-mail virus filter, users need to be educated about the dangers of viruses.

Although the great majority of users are now aware of viruses and the damage they can cause, more education may be needed to instruct them on the specific things that need to be addressed when a virus is received via e-mail. These can vary from organization to organization and from e-mail software to e-mail software; however, some useful examples of good practices involve examining all e-mails for a known source as well as a known destination, especially if the e-mails have attachments. Strange files or unexpected attachments should always be checked with an antivirus program before execution. Users also need to know that some viruses can be executed simply by opening the e-mail or viewing it in the preview pane. Education and proper administration is also useful in configuring the e-mail software to be as virus resistant as possible—turning off scripting support and the preview pane are good examples. Many organizations outline specific user responsibilities for e-mail, similar to network acceptable use policies. Some examples include using e-mail resources responsibly, avoiding the installation of untrusted programs, and using localized antivirus scanning programs, such as AVG.

Another protection is to carefully create virus-scanning procedures. If possible, perform virus scans on every e-mail as it comes into the company's e-mail server. This is actually the one place that spam may prove useful. The explosion in spam mail has driven the adoption of e-mail filtering gateways designed to greatly reduce spam messages. These specialized e-mail servers have evolved to attempt to protect against virus threats as well as spam. Some users will also attempt to retrieve e-mail offsite from a normal ISP account, which can bypass the server-based virus protection, so every machine should also be protected with a host-based virus protection program that scans all files on a regular basis and performs checks of files upon their execution. While these steps will not eliminate the security risks of malicious code in e-mail, they will limit infection and help to keep the problem to manageable levels.

Hoax E-Mails

E-mail hoaxes are mostly a nuisance, but they do cost everyone, not only in the time wasted by receiving and reading the e-mails, but also in the Internet bandwidth and server processing time they take up. E-mail hoaxes are global urban legends, perpetually traveling from one e-mail account to the next, and most have a common theme of some story you must tell ten other people about right away for good luck or some virus that will harm your friends unless you tell them immediately. Hoaxes are similar to chain letters, but instead of promising a reward, the story in the e-mail is typically what produces the action.

Hoaxes have been circling the Internet for many years, and many web sites are dedicated to debunking them, such as Snopes.com (see Figure 16.6).

> ⚠️ Forwarding hoax e-mails and other jokes, funny movies, and non-work-related e-mails at work can be a violation of your company's acceptable use policy and result in disciplinary actions.

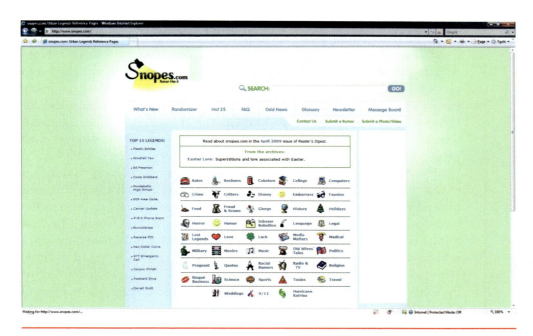

• **Figure 16.6**   Snopes is an online reference for urban legends common in hoax e-mails.

The most important thing to do in this case is educate e-mail users: they should be familiar with a hoax or two before they go online, and they should know how to search the Internet for hoax information. Users need to apply the same common sense on the Internet that they would in real life: If it sounds too outlandish to be true, it probably is a fabrication. The goal of education about hoaxes should be to change user behavior to delete the hoax e-mail and not send it on.

Unsolicited Commercial E-Mail (Spam)

Every e-mail user has received spam, and usually does on a daily basis. Spam refers to **unsolicited commercial e-mail** whose purpose is the same as the junk mail you get in your physical mailbox—it tries to persuade you to buy something. The term **spam** comes from a skit on *Monty Python's Flying Circus,* where two people are in a restaurant that serves only the potted meat product. This concept of the repetition of unwanted things is the key to e-mail spam.

The first spam e-mail was sent in 1978 by a DEC employee. However, the first spam that really captured everyone's attention was in 1994, when two lawyers posted a commercial message to every Usenet newsgroup. This was the origin of using the Internet to send one message to as many recipients as possible via an automated program. Commercial e-mail programs have taken over, resulting in the variety of spam that most users receive in their in-boxes every day. **Botnet** researchers have reported that a million–plus infected machines send more than 100 billion spam e-mails every day. According to the Symantec monthly State of Spam report in July 2009, over 90 percent of e-mail sent worldwide is spam.

The appeal to the people generating the spam is the extremely low cost per advertising impression. The senders of spam e-mail can generally send the messages for less than a cent apiece. This is much less expensive than more traditional direct mail or print advertisements, and this low cost will ensure the continued growth of spam e-mail unless something is done about it. The amount of spam being transmitted eventually spurred federal authorities into action. In late 2003 the Controlling the Assault of Non-Solicited Pornography and Marketing Act (CAN-SPAM) was signed into law. This law gave the Federal Trade Commission (FTC) authority to define the standards of spam e-mail and enforce the other provisions of the act. While several spammers have been caught and prosecuted under this act, it has not been restrictive enough to severely limit spam. This has forced most people to seek out technical solutions to the spam problem.

The front line of the war against spam e-mail is filtering. Almost all e-mail providers filter spam at some level; however, bandwidth is still used to send the spam, and the recipient e-mail server still has to process the message. To reduce spam, it must be fought on several fronts. The first thing to do is educate users about spam. A good way for users to fight spam is to be cautious about where on the Internet they post their e-mail address. However, you can't keep e-mail addresses secret just to avoid spam. One of the steps that the majority of system administrators running Internet e-mail servers have taken to reduce spam, and which is also a good e-mail security principle, is to shut down mail relaying. Port scanning occurs across all hosts all the time, typically with a single host scanning large subnets for a single port, and some of these people could be attempting to send spam

Exam Tip: Unsolicited commercial e-mail is referred to as spam.

Tech Tip

Controlling Port 25 on Mail Servers

SMTP authentication forces the users who use your server to obtain permission to send mail by first supplying a username and password. This helps to prevent open relay and abuse of your server and is highly recommended when your mail server has a routed IP address. This ensures that only known accounts can use your server's SMTP to send e-mail.

The number of connections to an SMTP server should be limited based on the specifications of the server hardware (memory, NIC bandwidth, CPU, etc.) and its nominal load per day. Limiting connections is useful to mitigate spam floods and DoS attacks that target your network infrastructure.

e-mail. When they scan for TCP port 25, they are looking for SMTP servers, and once they find a host that is an **open relay** (a mail server that will accept mail from anyone), they can use that host to send as many commercial e-mails as possible. The reason that they look for an open relay is that spammers typically do not want the e-mails traced back to them. **Mail relaying** is similar to dropping a letter off at a post office instead of letting the postal carrier pick it up at your mailbox. On the Internet, that consists of sending e-mail from a separate IP address, making it more difficult for the mail to be traced back to you. SMTP server software is typically configured to accept mail only from specific hosts or domains. All SMTP software can and should be configured to accept only mail from known hosts, or to known mailboxes; this closes down mail relaying and helps to reduce spam.

Since it may not be possible to close all mail relays, and because some spammers will mail from their own mail servers, software must be used to combat spam at the recipient's end. Spam can be filtered at two places: at the host itself or at the server. Filtering spam at the host level is done by the e-mail client software and usually employs basic pattern matching, focusing on the sender, subject, or text of the e-mail. This fairly effective system uses an inordinate amount of bandwidth and processing power on the host computer, however. These problems can be solved by filtering spam at the mail server level. Many companies offer a dedicated appliance designed as a specialty e-mail server with the primary task of filtering spam. This server typically uses a combination of techniques listed here. It also implements an internal database to allow more granular filtering based upon spam the appliance has already seen.

Tech Tip

Open Relays

Configure mail relay options carefully to avoid being an open relay. All mail servers have an option where you can specify which domains or IP addresses your mail server will relay mail for. It's very important to configure your mail relay parameter to be very restrictive so that your server does not become a gateway for spamming others, possibly resulting in your server getting blacklisted.

Try This!

Testing Your Mail Server for Open Relay

Make note of your e-mail server settings, and then try to send regular SMTP mail when you are on a different network, such as the Wi-Fi network at a coffee shop or other similar open access Internet connection. You should get an error refusing relaying. If the mail goes through, that server might have a misconfiguration.

The server-based approach can be beneficial because other methods of filtering spam can be used at the server: pattern matching is still used, but SMTP software can also use a process called Domain Name Service (DNS) blacklisting, or DNSBL. The **Real-time Blackhole List (RBL)** was the first list to utilize the concept of using DNS records to filter, or "blackhole," spam-sending IP addresses and domains. Started in 1997, this list was and is maintained in real time specifically for blocking spam e-mail. While the RBL was the first DNSBL, there are now many blackhole lists. The DNSBL service is so popular that many programs, such as sendmail, Postfix, and Eudora Internet Mail Server, include support for it by default.

In addition to the RBL, multiple other DNS-based blacklist services can assist filtering based upon DNS sources of mail. Commercial packages can block spam at the server level using both methods mentioned, maintaining their own blacklists and pattern-matching algorithms.

Many additional techniques exist for server-based spam filtering—enough to fill an entire book on the subject. One technique is to use a

Tech Tip

DNSBL Reference

The DNSBL process is detailed more thoroughly at www.dnsbl.com.

challenge/response system: once an e-mail is received by a "new" contact, a challenge is sent back to the originating address to confirm the contact. Since spammers send e-mails in bulk, the response mechanism is too cumbersome and they will not respond.

Another technique is known as *greylisting*. When an e-mail is received, it is bounced as a temporary rejection. SMTP servers that are RFC 5321–compliant will wait a configurable amount of time and attempt retransmission of the message. Obviously, spammers will not retry sending of any messages, so spam is reduced.

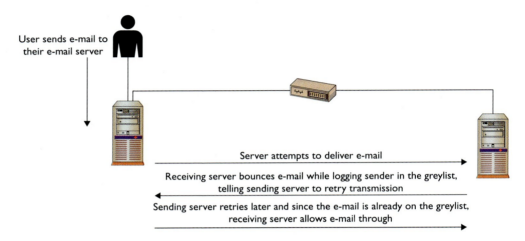

User sends e-mail to their e-mail server

Server attempts to deliver e-mail

Receiving server bounces e-mail while logging sender in the greylist, telling sending server to retry transmission

Sending server retries later and since the e-mail is already on the greylist, receiving server allows e-mail through

All these techniques have advantages and disadvantages, and most people will run some combination of techniques to attempt to filter as much spam as possible while not rejecting legitimate messages.

A side benefit of filtering spam at the receiving server is reduced e-mail. In enterprises, performing backups of information is a significant task. Backups are size dependent, both in cost and time, and reducing e-mail by eliminating spam can have significant impacts on e-mail backups. Spam reduction will also have a significant impact on the e-discovery process, as it reduces the quantity of material that needs to be searched. *E-discovery* is a term for electronic discovery, the electronic component of a legal discovery process. The discovery process is court mandated and, when applied to a corporate environment, can cause the shutdown of corporate operations until the process is complete. For this reason, anything that makes the process easier or faster will benefit the corporation.

Spam URI Real-time Block Lists

Spam URI Real-time Block Lists (SURBL) detects unwanted e-mail based on invalid or malicious links within a message. Using a SURBL filter is a valuable tool to protect users from malware and phishing attacks. Not all mail servers support SURBL, but this technology shows promise in the fight against malware and phishing.

Sender ID Framework

Microsoft offers another server-based solution to spam, called the **Sender ID Framework (SIDF)**. SIDF attempts to authenticate messages by checking the sender's domain name against a list of IP addresses authorized to send e-mail

Tech Tip

Activate Reverse DNS to Block Bogus Senders
Messaging systems use DNS lookups to verify the existence of e-mail domains before accepting a message. A reverse DNS lookup is an option for fighting off bogus mail senders, as it verifies the sender's address before accepting the e-mail. Reverse DNS lookup acts by having SMTP verify that the sender's IP address matches both the host and domain names that were submitted by the SMTP client in the EHLO/HELO command. This works by blocking messages that fail the address-matching test, suggesting that they did not come from where they say they came from.

by the domain name listed. This list is maintained in a text (TXT) record published by the DNS, called a **Sender Policy Framework (SPF)** record. So when a mail server receives an e-mail, it will check the sender's domain name in the DNS; if the outbound server's IP matches, the message gets a "pass" rating by SIDF. This is similar to the idea that routers should drop any outbound port 25 traffic that does not come from known e-mail servers on the subnet managed by the router. However, the SIDF system handles the authentication of the e-mail server when it is received, not when it is sent. This system still allows wasted bandwidth from the sender of the message to the receiver, and since bandwidth is increasingly a metered service, this means the cost of spam is still paid by the recipient. The SPF check ensures that the sending MTA is allowed to send mail on behalf of the sender's domain name. When SPF is activated on your server, the sending server's MX record (the DNS Mail Exchange record) is validated before message transmission takes place.

These methods can take care of up to 90 percent of the junk mail clogging our networks, but they cannot stop it entirely. Better control of port 25 traffic is required to slow the tide of spam hitting our in-boxes. This would stop spammers using remote open relays and, hopefully, prevent many users from running unauthorized e-mail servers of their own. Because of the low cost of generating spam, until serious action is taken, or spam is somehow made unprofitable, it will remain with us.

DomainKeys Identified Mail

DomainKeys Identified Mail (DKIM) is an e-mail validation system employed to detect e-mail spoofing. DKIM operates by providing a mechanism to allow receiving MTAs to check that incoming mail is authorized and that the e-mail (including attachments) has not been modified during transport. It does this through a digital signature included with the message that can be validated by the recipient using the signer's public key published in the DNS. DKIM is the result of the merging of two previous methods, Domain-Keys and Identified Internet Mail. DKIM is the basis for a series of IETF standards-track specifications and is used by AOL, Gmail, and Yahoo mail. Any mail from these organizations should carry a DKIM signature

The following is an example of the DKIM information that is in an e-mail header:

```
DKIM-Signature: v=1; a=rsa-sha256; d=example.net; s=brisbane;
     c=relaxed/simple; q=dns/txt; l=1234; t=1117574938;
x=1118006938;
     h=from:to:subject:date:keywords:keywords;
     bh=MTIzNDU2Nzg5MDEyMzQ1Njc4OTAxMjM0NTY3ODkwMTI=;
     b=dzdVyOfAKCdLXdJOc9G2q8LoXSlEniSbav+yuU4zGeeruD00lszZV
oG4ZHRNiYzR
```

The two signatures, b and bh, are for the message itself, header and body, and the header only.

■ Mail Encryption

The e-mail concerns discussed so far in this chapter are all global issues involving security, but e-mail suffers from a more important security problem—the lack of confidentiality, or, as it is sometimes referred to, privacy. As with many Internet applications, e-mail has always been a plaintext protocol. When many people first got onto the Internet, they heard a standard lecture about not sending anything through e-mail that they wouldn't want posted on a public bulletin board. Part of the reason for this was that e-mail is sent with the clear text of the message exposed to anyone who is sniffing the network. Any attacker at a choke point in the network could read all e-mail passing through that network segment.

Some tools can be used to solve this problem by using **encryption** on the e-mail's content. The first method is S/MIME and the second is PGP.

S/MIME

Secure/Multipurpose Internet Mail Extensions (S/MIME) is a *secure* implementation of the MIME protocol specification. MIME was created to allow Internet e-mail to support new and more creative features. The original e-mail RFC specified only text e-mail, so any nontext data had to be handled by a new specification—MIME. MIME handles audio files, images, applications, and multipart e-mails. MIME allows e-mail to handle multiple types of content in a message, including file transfers. Every time you send a file as an e-mail attachment, you are using MIME. S/MIME takes this content and specifies a framework for encrypting the message as a MIME attachment.

Cross Check

X.509 Certificates

In Chapter 7 you learned about X.509 certificate standards. Why is it important to have a standardized certificate format?

S/MIME was developed by RSA Data Security and uses the X.509 format for certificates. The specification supports both 40-bit RC2 and 3DES for symmetric encryption. The protocol can affect the message in one of two ways: the host mail program can encode the message with S/MIME, or the server can act as the processing agent, encrypting all messages between servers.

The host-based operation starts when the user clicks Send; the mail agent then encodes the message using the generated symmetric key. Then the symmetric key is encoded with the remote user's public key for confidentiality or signed with the local user's private key for authentication/nonrepudiation. This enables the remote user to decode the symmetric key and then decrypt the actual content of the message. Of course, all of this is handled by the user's mail program, requiring the user simply to tell the program to decode the message. If the message is signed by the sender, it will be signed with the sender's public key, guaranteeing the source of the message. The reason that both symmetric and asymmetric encryption are used in the mail is to increase the speed of encryption and decryption. As encryption is based on difficult mathematical problems, it takes time to encrypt and decrypt. To speed this up, the more difficult process, asymmetric encryption, is used only to encrypt a relatively small amount of data, the symmetric key. The symmetric key is then used to encrypt the rest of the message.

The S/MIME process of encrypting e-mails provides integrity, privacy, and, if the message is signed, authentication. Several popular e-mail programs support S/MIME, including the popular Microsoft products Outlook and Windows Mail. They both manage S/MIME keys and functions through the E-mail Security screen, shown in Figure 16.7. This figure shows the different settings that can be used to encrypt messages and use X.509 digital certificates. This allows interoperability with web certificates, and trusted authorities are available to issue the certificates. Trusted authorities are needed to ensure the senders are who they claim to be, an important part of authentication. In Windows Mail, the window is simpler (see Figure 16.8), but the same functions of key management and secure e-mail operation are available.

<table>
<tr><td>✓</td><td>**Cross Check**</td></tr>
</table>

Symmetric Encryption

In Chapter 5 you learned about symmetric encryption, including RC2 and the 3DES algorithms supported by S/MIME. What part of the CIA of security does symmetric encryption attempt to provide in this instance?

While S/MIME is a good and versatile protocol for securing e-mail, its implementation can be problematic. S/MIME allows the user to select low-strength (40-bit) encryption, which means a user can send a message

• **Figure 16.7**   S/MIME options in Outlook

• **Figure 16.8** S/MIME options in Windows Mail

that is thought to be secure but that can be more easily decoded than messages sent with 3DES encryption. Also, as with any protocol, bugs can exist in the software itself. Just because an application is designed for security does not mean that it, itself, is secure. Despite its potential flaws, however, S/MIME is a tremendous leap in security over regular e-mail.

PGP

Pretty Good Privacy (PGP) implements e-mail security in a similar fashion to S/MIME, but PGP uses completely different protocols. The basic framework is the same: The user sends the e-mail, and the mail agent applies encryption as specified in the mail program's programming. The content is encrypted with the generated symmetric key, and that key is encrypted with the public key of the recipient of the e-mail for confidentiality. The sender can also choose to sign the mail with a private key, allowing the recipient to authenticate the sender. Currently, PGP supports public key infrastructure (PKI) provided by multiple vendors, including X.509 certificates and Lightweight Directory Access Protocol (LDAP) key sources such as Microsoft's Active Directory.

In Figure 16.9, you can see how PGP manages keys locally in its own software. This is where a user stores not only local keys, but also any keys that were received from other users. A free key server is available for storing PGP public keys. PGP can generate its own keys using either Diffie-Hellman or RSA, and it can then transmit the public keys to the PGP LDAP server so other PGP users can search for and locate your public key to communicate with you. This key server is convenient, as each person using PGP for communications does not have to implement a server to handle key management. For the actual encryption of the e-mail content itself, PGP supports International Data Encryption Algorithm (IDEA), 3DES, and Carlisle Adams and Stafford Tavares (CAST) for symmetric encryption. PGP provides pretty good security against brute-force attacks by using a 3DES key length of 168 bits, an IDEA key length of 128 bits, and a CAST key

• **Figure 16.9** PGP key management

length of 128 bits. All of these algorithms are difficult to brute-force with existing hardware, requiring well over a million years to break the code. While this is not a promise of future security against brute-force attacks, the security is reasonable today.

PGP has plug-ins for many popular e-mail programs, including Outlook and Mozilla's Thunderbird. These plug-ins handle the encryption and decryption behind the scenes, and all that the user must do is enter the encryption key's passphrase to ensure that they are the owner of the key. In Figure 16.10, you can see the string of encrypted text that makes up the MIME

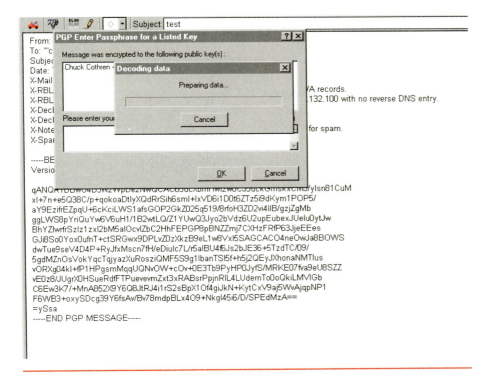

qANQR1DDwO4DSWZWpBeZNWQCACbJULXbmT1WIZwOCJJUCKGmskxCMJ/ylsn81CuM
xl+7n+e5Q38C/p+qokoaDtlyXQdRrSih6sml+lxVD6i1D0t6ZTz5i9dKym1POP5/
aY9EzifrEZpqU+6cKciLWS1afsGOP2GkZD25q519/8rfoH3ZD2vi4llB/gzjZgMb
ggLWS8pYriQuYw6V6uH1/1B2wtLQ/Z1YUwQ3Jyo2bVdz6U2upEubexJUeluOytJw
BhYZlwrfrSzlz1zxI2bM5alOcvlZbC2HhFEPGP8pBNZZmj7CXHzFRfP63JjeEEes
GJi8So0YoxOufnT+ctSRGwx9DPLvZDzXkzB9eL1w8VxI5SAGCACO4neOwJa8BOWS
dwTue9seV4D4P+RyJfxMscn7fH/eDiulc7L/r5alBU4f6Js2bJE36+5TzdTC/09/
5gdMZnOsVokYqcTqjyazXuRosziQMF5S9g1lbanTSl5f+h5j2QEyJXhonaNMTlus
vORXg04kI+fP1HPgsmMqqUQNvOW+cOv+0E3Tb9PyHP0JyfS/MRKE07fva9eU8SZZ
vE0z8/JUgrX0HSueRdfFTPuevevmZxt3xRABsrPpjnRIL4LUdemTo0oQkiLMVIGb
C6Ew3K7/+MnA852X9Y6Q8JtRJ4i1rS2sBpX1Of4giJkN+KytCxV9aj5WvAjqpNP1
F6WB3+oxySDcg39Y6fsAw/Bv78mdpBLx4O9+Nkgl45i6/D/SPEdMzA==
=ySsa
-----END PGP MESSAGE-----

• **Figure 16.10**   Decoding a PGP-encoded message

attachment. This text includes the encrypted content of the message and the encrypted symmetric key. You can also see that the program does not decrypt the message upon receipt; it waits until instructed to decrypt it. PGP also stores encrypted messages in the encrypted format, as does S/MIME. This is important, since it provides end-to-end security for the message.

Like S/MIME, PGP is not problem-free. You must be diligent about keeping the software up to date and fully patched, because vulnerabilities are occasionally found. For example, a buffer overflow was found in the way PGP was handled in Outlook, causing the overwriting of heap memory and leading to possible malicious code execution. There is also a lot of discussion about the way PGP handles key recovery, or key escrow. PGP uses what's called an *Additional Decryption Key (ADK)*, which is basically an additional public key stacked upon the original public key. An ADK, in theory, would give the proper organization a private key that would be used to retrieve the secret messages. In practice, the ADK is not always controlled by a properly authorized organization, and the danger exists for someone to add an ADK and then distribute it to the world. This creates a situation in which other users will be sending messages that they believe can be read only by the first party, but that can actually be read by the third party who modified the key. These are just examples of the current vulnerabilities in the product, showing that PGP is just a tool, not the ultimate answer to security.

■ Instant Messaging

Instant messaging (IM) is another technology that has seen widespread acceptance in recent years. With the growth of the Internet pulling customers away from AOL, one of the largest dial-up providers in the United States, the company had to look at new ways of providing content. It started **AOL Instant Messenger (AIM)**, which was conceived as a way to find people of like interests online, and it was modeled after earlier chat programs. With GUI features and enhanced ease of use, it quickly became popular enough for AOL to release to regular users of the Internet. Along with several competing programs, AIM was feeding the tremendous growth of the instant messaging segment.

The programs had to appeal to a wide variety of users, so ease of use was paramount, and security was not a priority. Now that people are accustomed to IM applications, they see the benefit of using them not only for personal chatting on the Internet, but also for legitimate business use. When people install these applications, they unwittingly expose the corporate network to security breaches through many of the same malicious software problems as e-mail. Instant messages traverse the Internet in plaintext and also cross third-party servers—be it Yahoo, Skype, Google, or AOL.

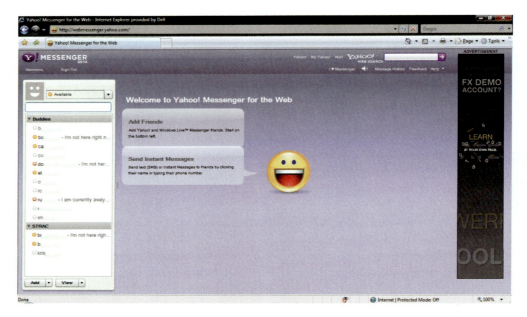

IM programs are designed to attach to a server, or a network of servers, and allow you to talk with other people on the same network of servers in near real time. The nature of this type of communication opens several holes in a system's security. First, the program has to attach to a server, typically announcing the IP address of the originating client. This is not a problem in most applications, but IM identifies a specific user associated with the IP address, making attacks more likely. Also associated with this fact is that for other users to be able to send you messages, the program is forced to announce your presence on the server. So now a user is displaying that his or her computer is on and is possibly broadcasting the source IP address to anyone who is looking. This problem is compounded by the tendency for people to run these programs in the background so that they don't miss any messages.

Popular IM clients were not implemented with security in mind. All support sending files as attachments, few currently support encryption, and currently none have a virus scanner built into the file-sharing utility.

File sharing in any form must be a carefully handled application to prevent the spread of viruses and other malicious code. Chat programs produce security risks, because the sharing is done ad hoc between end users, administrators have no control over the quality of the files being sent, and there is no monitoring of the original sources of those files. The only authentication for the files is the human interaction between the two users in question. This kind of vulnerability coupled with a social engineering attack can produce dramatic enough results that the CERT Coordination Center (CERT/CC) was compelled to issue an incident note (CERT Incident Note IN-2002-03: Social Engineering Attacks via IRC and Instant Messaging). This personal type of authentication was abused, tricking people into downloading and executing backdoor or Trojan horse programs.

A user can also be persuaded autonomously to download and run a file via IM. Several worms exist that attempt, via IM, to get users to download and run the payload. W32.pipeline uses AIM to install a rootkit. Goner, running via ICQ, another IM program, asks users to download a screen saver. Choke, spreading via MSN/Windows Live Messenger, attempts to get users to download a game; if the game is downloaded, the worm attempts to spread to any user the infected user chats with. These worms and others all depend on user interaction to run the payload. This file-sharing mechanism bypasses all the server-side virus protection that is part of most organizations' e-mail infrastructure. This pushes more of the responsibility for malware protection onto the local users' antivirus system. This can be problematic for users who do not regularly update their systems or who fail to perform regular antivirus scans.

One of the largest problems with IM programs is the lack of support for encryption. AIM, ICQ, Skype, and Yahoo Messenger all currently do not natively support encryption of the text messages traveling between users.

Tech Tip

Trillian

An IM client that supports encryption as well as all the popular networks like AIM, Yahoo, and Skype is Trillian. Trillian is available at www .trillian.im.

However, some third-party programs will add encryption as a plug-in. The lack of encryption was not a significant concern while these IM programs were still used primarily for personal communication, but with businesses moving to adopt the systems, people are not aware of the infrastructure difference between IM and e-mail. Intracompany e-mail never leaves the company's network, but an intracompany instant message typically will do so unless the organization purchases a product and operates an internal IM server. This can and does expose large amounts of confidential business information to anyone who is physically in a spot to monitor and has the desire to capture the traffic.

If you think about how often client information is sent via e-mail between two people at a company, you start to see the danger that sending it via IM creates. IM is an application that is typically installed by the end user, without the knowledge of the administrator. These types of rogue applications have always been a danger to a network's security, but administrators have typically been able to control them by eliminating the applications' ports through the firewall.

The protocols used for these chat applications have default TCP ports—AIM uses 5190, Jabber uses 5222 and 5269, Yahoo Messenger uses 5050, and MSN/Windows Live Messenger uses 1863. Some IM applications have been programmed for use as *rogue apps.* In the event that they can't reach a server on the default ports, they begin to scan all ports looking for one that is allowed out of the firewall. As these applications can connect on any port, including common ones such as Telnet port 23 and HTTP port 80, they are very hard to control. These types of security risks go above and beyond the routine security holes generated in IM software that arise as in any other piece of software, through coding errors.

Tech Tip

Securing IM

Tips to help secure corporate IM:

- *Run a corporate IM server*
- *Avoid file transfers*
- *Use encryption*

Modern Instant Messaging Systems

Instant messaging is an application that can increase productivity by saving communication time, but it's not without risks. The protocol sends messages in plaintext and thus fails to preserve their confidentiality. It also allows for sharing of files between clients, allowing a backdoor access method for files. There are some methods to minimize security risks, but more development efforts are required before IM is ready to be implemented in a secure fashion. The best ways in which to protect yourself on an IM network are similar to those for almost all Internet applications: avoid communication with unknown persons, avoid running any program you are unsure of, and do not write anything you wouldn't want posted with your name on it.

Instant messaging also plays a role in today's social media–driven world. There are many very popular "messaging systems" that are in popular use today, including Snapchat, Instagram, Jabber, Tumblr, WhatsApp, and more. These are instant sharing systems that allow user bases to share files, pictures, and videos between users. Each of these systems has large numbers of users and literally billions of transferred items every year. As the social aspect of the Web grows, so do the instant sharing systems connecting users in social webs. Apple has its own messaging service, as does Android, and apps exist for a wide range of different "messaging" systems.

Any list of messaging apps is one that will become outdated rather rapidly, but at the time this book goes to press the list would include the following:

- LINE
- Viber
- WhatsApp (now part of Facebook)
- Facebook Messenger
- Snapchat
- Kik
- Tango
- WeChat
- Instagram
- Jabber
- Tumblr

The main security threat on most of these is information disclosure. As they can be used from mobile devices outside of an enterprise network, there is the possibility for information to be captured and released across these platforms. For this reason, one of the security policies of high-security facilities is to not allow personal devices.

Chapter 16 Review

Lab Manual Exercises

The following lab exercises from the companion lab manual, *Principles of Computer Security Lab Manual, Fourth Edition,* provide practical application of material covered in this chapter:

Lab 3.2l   Linux E-mail: SMTP and POP3

Lab 3.2m   Windows E-mail: SMTP and POP3

Lab 5.3m   Exploiting E-mail Vulnerabilities in Windows

Chapter Summary

After reading this chapter and completing the exercises, you should understand the following about e-mail and IM security.

Describe security issues associated with e-mail

- Malicious code is code that performs something harmful to the computer it runs on. Malicious code is often sent through e-mail.

- Viruses are pieces of malicious code that require user action to spread.

- Trojan programs deceive the user into thinking that a program is something innocuous, when it is actually a piece of malicious code.

- Worms are pieces of malicious code that use automated methods to spread.

- Spam, or unsolicited commercial e-mail, is e-mail that is sent to you without your requesting it, attempting to sell you something. It is the electronic equivalent of a telemarketing call.

- Hoax e-mails are e-mails that travel from user to user because of the compelling story contained in them.

Implement security practices for e-mail

- Protecting your e-mail system from virus code requires several measures:

  - Don't execute any attachment from an unknown source.

  - Use antivirus programs that run on the server to filter all e-mails.

  - Use client-side antivirus programs to catch any viruses that might come from web-based e-mail accounts.

- Keeping all software up to date helps to prevent worm propagation.

- Server-side filtering software and the application of spam blackhole lists help limit the amount of unsolicited e-mail.

- E-mail encryption is a great way to protect the privacy of communication since e-mail is a cleartext medium.

- PGP, or Pretty Good Privacy, is a good specific application for e-mail encryption.

- S/MIME, or Secure/Multipurpose Internet Mail Extension, is the e-mail protocol that allows encryption applications to work.

- Antivirus software is important to protect against malware.

Detail the security issues of instant messaging protocols

- AOL Instant Messenger, ICQ, and Skype are all different versions of instant messaging programs.

- The most popular IM programs all send messages in the clear, without a native encryption built into the default clients.

- All the IM clients need to attach to a server to communicate. Therefore, when attached to the server, they announce the source IP of a particular user.

- Instant messaging can also transfer files. This activity typically bypasses any security built into the network, especially mail server virus protections.

Key Terms

AOL Instant Messenger (AIM) *(522)*
botnet *(514)*
DomainKeys Identified Mail (DKIM) *(517)*
e-mail *(505)*
e-mail hoax *(509)*
encryption *(518)*
instant messaging (IM) *(510)*
mail delivery agent (MDA) *(506)*
mail relaying *(515)*
mail transfer agent (MTA) *(506)*
mail user agent (MUA) *(506)*

Multipurpose Internet Mail Extensions (MIME) *(508)*
open relay *(515)*
Pretty Good Privacy (PGP) *(520)*
Real-time Blackhole List (RBL) *(515)*
Secure/Multipurpose Internet Mail Extensions (S/MIME) *(518)*
Sender ID Framework (SIDF) *(516)*
Sender Policy Framework (SPF) *(517)*
Simple Mail Transfer Protocol (SMTP) *(505)*
spam *(514)*
unsolicited commercial e-mail *(514)*

Key Terms Quiz

Use terms from the Key Terms list to complete the sentences that follow. Don't use the same term more than once. Not all terms will be used.

1. Spam is the popular term for _____.

2. _____ is a method to detect e-mail spoofing.

3. A large source of spam is zombie computers that are part of a(n) _____.

4. _____ is the protocol used to attach attachments to an email.

5. A(n) _____ is a compilation of servers that are blocked because they have been known to send spam.

6. _____ is one of the most popular chat programs.

7. _____ is a protocol for verifying e-mail addresses against IP addresses to reduce spa,.

8. A(n) _____ is a false e-mail that tells a compelling story, and typically prompts the user to forward it to other users.

9. _____ can have the same virus risks as e-mail.

10. The most prevalent protocol that e-mail is sent by is _____.

Multiple-Choice Quiz

1. What is one of the biggest reasons spam is prevalent today?
   A. Criminals use zombie botnets.
   B. Regular mail is too slow.
   C. Spam is popular among recipients.
   D. Spam is sent from the government.

2. What is spam?
   A. Unsolicited commercial e-mail
   B. A Usenet archive
   C. A computer virus
   D. An encryption algorithm

3. Why is an open e-mail relay bad?

   A. It allows anyone to remotely control the server.

   B. It makes the e-mail server reboot once a day.

   C. No e-mail will go through.

   D. It will allow anyone to send spam through the server.

4. What makes e-mail hoaxes popular enough to keep the same story floating around for years?

   A. They are written by award-winning authors.

   B. The story prompts action on the reader's part.

   C. The story will grant the user good luck only if he or she forwards it on.

   D. The hoax e-mail forwards itself.

5. What is greylisting?

   A. E-mail messages are temporarily rejected so that the sender is forced to resend.

   B. E-mail messages are run through a strong set of filters before delivery.

   C. E-mail messages are sent through special secure servers.

   D. E-mail is sent directly from the local host to the remote host, bypassing servers entirely.

6. Why are instant messaging protocols dangerous for file transfer?

   A. They bypass server-based virus protections.

   B. File sharing is never dangerous.

   C. They allow everyone you chat with to view all your files.

   D. You'll end up receiving many spam files.

7. Why do PGP and S/MIME need public key cryptography?

   A. Public keys are necessary to determine whether the e-mail is encrypted.

   B. The public key is necessary to encrypt the symmetric key.

   C. The public key unlocks the password to the e-mail.

   D. The public key is useless and gives a false sense of privacy.

8. Why is HTML e-mail dangerous?

   A. It can't be read by some e-mail clients.

   B. It sends the content of your e-mails to web pages.

   C. It can allow launching of malicious code from the preview pane.

   D. It is the only way spam can be sent.

9. If they are both text protocols, why is instant messaging traffic riskier than e-mail?

   A. More viruses are coded for IM.

   B. IM has no business purpose.

   C. IM traffic has to travel outside of the organization to a server.

   D. Emoticons.

10. What makes spam so popular as an advertising medium?

   A. Its low cost per impression

   B. Its high rate of return

   C. Its ability to canvass multiple countries

   D. Its quality of workmanship

Essay Quiz

1. How would you implement a successful spam-filtering policy?

2. Draft a memo describing malware risks to the common user and what the user can do to avoid infection.

Lab Projects

• Lab Project 16.1

Show that instant messaging is an insecure protocol. You will need a lab computer with Windows installed, an IM program, and a sniffer. Then do the following:

1. If you need to install an IM program, download AIM from www.aim.com.
2. Run the Installer program.
3. Generate a username and password and log in.
4. Start the sniffer program and set it to capture all traffic.
5. Start a chat session with a partner in the class.
6. Decode the sniff trace to view the cleartext messages of the chat.

• Lab Project 16.2

Find at least ten pieces of spam mail from any account, whether it be home, work, school, or something else. Using the e-mail headers, and any web site that might provide information, attempt to trace the spam mail back to its original source.
You will need the following materials:

1. Collect the e-mails and view the e-mail header information in your e-mail program.
2. Find the "Received:" field in the headers and write down as many DNS names or IP addresses as you can. Also look for common details in the header elements of the different messages, such as the same e-mail servers and spammers.
3. Using the Internet, research the physical locations of the IP addresses.
4. Report the different locations from which your spam e-mail originated. What did you learn about tracing e-mail and spam?

Web Components

chapter 17

Understanding the security risks associated with a web application is of critical importance to improving the security of the Web.

—AARON C. NEWMAN

In this chapter, you will learn how to

- **Describe the functioning of the SSL/TLS protocol suite**
- **Explain web applications, plug-ins, and associated security issues**
- **Describe secure file transfer options**
- **Explain directory usage for data retrieval**
- **Explain scripting and other Internet functions that present security concerns**
- **Use cookies to maintain parameters between web pages**
- **Examine web-based application security issues**

The World Wide Web was invented by Tim Berners-Lee to give physicists a convenient method of exchanging information. What began in 1990 as a physics tool in the European Laboratory for Particle Physics (CERN, the acronym for the original French name) has grown into a complex system that is used by millions of computer users for tasks from e-commerce, to e-mail, chatting, games, and even the original intended use—file and information sharing. Before the Web, plenty of methods were used to perform these tasks, and they were already widespread in use. File Transfer Protocol (FTP) was used to move files, and Telnet allowed users access to other machines. What was missing was the common architecture brought by Berners-Lee: first, a common addressing scheme, built around the concept of a **Uniform Resource Locator (URL)**; second, the concept of linking documents to other documents by URLs through the **Hypertext Markup Language (HTML)**.

Although these elements might seem minor, they formed a base that spread like wildfire. Berners-Lee developed two programs to demonstrate the usefulness of his vision: a web server to serve documents to users, and a web browser to retrieve documents for users. Both of these key elements contributed to the spread of this new technological innovation. The success

of these components led to network after network being connected together in a "network of networks" known today as the Internet. Much of this interconnection was developed and funded through grants from the U.S. government to further technological and economic growth.

Current Web Components and Concerns

The usefulness of the Web is due not just to browsers, but also to web components that enable services for end users through their browser interfaces. These components use a wide range of protocols and services to deliver the desired content. From a security perspective, they offer users an easy-to-use, secure method of conducting data transfers over the Internet. Many protocols have been developed to deliver this content, although for most users, the browser handles the details.

From a systems point of view, many security concerns have arisen, but they can be grouped into three main tasks:

- Securing a server that delivers content to users over the Web
- Securing the transport of information between users and servers over the Web
- Securing the user's computer from attack over a web connection

This chapter presents the components used on the Web to request and deliver information securely over the Internet.

Web Protocols

When two people communicate, several things must happen for the communication to be effective: they must use a language that both parties understand, and they must correctly use the language—that is, structure and syntax—to express their thoughts. The mode of communication is a separate entity entirely, for the previous statements are important in both spoken and written forms of communication. The same requirements are present with respect to computer communications, and they are addressed through *protocols*, agreed-upon sets of rules that allow different vendors to produce hardware and software that can interoperate with hardware and software developed by other vendors. Because of the worldwide nature of the Internet, protocols are very important and form the basis by which all the separate parts can work together. The specific instantiation of protocols is done through hardware and software components. The majority of this chapter concentrates on protocols related to the Internet as instantiated by software components.

 Exam Tip: Know the ports! HTTPS (HTTP over SSL) uses TCP port 443. FTPS (FTP over SSL) uses TCP port 990 (control) and TCP port 989 (data in active mode). Hypertext Transfer Protocol (HTTP) uses TCP port 80, and File Transfer Protocol (FTP) uses TCP port 21 (control) and TCP port 20 (data in active mode).

Encryption (SSL and TLS)

Secure Sockets Layer (SSL) is a general-purpose protocol developed by Netscape for managing the encryption of information being transmitted over

> All versions of SSL have been shown to be vulnerable to breach. This means the entire SSL suite is now no longer considered secure. SSL v3 fell to the POODLE attack in 2014, leaving only TLS as a secure method. It is important that both clients and web servers as well as other applications be updated to only use TLS in the future.

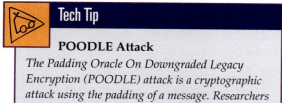

Tech Tip

POODLE Attack

The Padding Oracle On Downgraded Legacy Encryption (POODLE) attack is a cryptographic attack using the padding of a message. Researchers at Google have discovered how to perform such an attack on TLS and SSL. The best method of preventing the attack on clients is through the disabling of SSL v3. Google and Mozilla have both removed SSL support from Chrome and Firefox, respectively. The POODLE attack on TLS involves an implementation error on the server side and can be corrected via patching.

the Internet. It began as a competitive feature to drive sales of Netscape's web server product, which could then send information securely to end users. This early vision of securing the transmission channel between the web server and the browser became an Internet standard. Today, SSL is almost ubiquitous with respect to e-commerce—all browsers support it as do web servers, and virtually all e-commerce web sites use this method to protect sensitive financial information in transit between web servers and browsers.

The **Internet Engineering Task Force (IETF)** embraced SSL in 1996 through a series of RFCs and named the group of RFCs **Transport Layer Security (TLS)**. Starting with SSL 3.0, in 1999, the IETF issued RFC 2246, "TLS Protocol Version 1.0," followed by RFC 2712, which added Kerberos authentication, and then RFCs 2817 and 2818, which extended TLS to HTTP version 1.1 (HTTP/1.1). Although SSL has been through several versions, TLS begins with an equivalency to SSL 3.0, so today SSL and TLS are essentially the same, although not interchangeable. Recent attacks have left SSL vulnerable, and the consensus is that SSL is dead and TLS is the path forward, although everyone calls it SSL.

SSL/TLS is a series of functions that exists in the OSI (Open System Interconnection) model between the application layer and the transport and network layers. The goal of TCP is to send an unauthenticated, error-free stream of information between two computers. SSL/TLS adds message integrity and authentication functionality to TCP through the use of cryptographic methods. Because cryptographic methods are an ever-evolving field, and because both parties must agree on an implementation method, SSL/TLS has embraced an open, extensible, and adaptable method to allow flexibility and strength. When two programs initiate an SSL/TLS connection, one of their first tasks is to compare available protocols and agree on an appropriate common cryptographic protocol for use in this particular communication. As SSL/TLS can use separate algorithms and methods for encryption, authentication, and data integrity, each of these is negotiated and determined depending upon need at the beginning of a communication.

Browsers from Mozilla (Firefox) and Microsoft (Internet Explorer 11) allow fairly extensive SSL/TLS setup options (see Figure 17.1).

How SSL/TLS Works

SSL/TLS uses a wide range of cryptographic protocols. As of 2014, SSL is no longer considered secure, with SSLv3 falling victim to the POODLE (Padding Oracle On Downgraded Legacy Encryption) attack. Throughout the book, all references to SSL should be considered to be for TLS only. It will take a generation or longer for the term SSL to fade in favor of TLS, if ever.

The questions asked and answered are which protocol and which cryptographic algorithm will be used. For the client and server to communicate, both sides must agree on a commonly held protocol (SSL v1, v2, v3, or TLS v1, v1.1, v1.2). Commonly available cryptographic algorithms include Diffie-Hellman and RSA. The next step is to exchange certificates and keys as necessary to enable authentication.

Once authentication is established, the channel is secured with symmetric key cryptographic methods and hashes, typically RC4 or 3DES for symmetric key and MD5 or SHA-1 for the hash functions.

At this point, the authenticity of the server and possibly the client has been established, and the channel is protected by encryption against eavesdropping. Each packet is encrypted using the symmetric key before transfer across the network, and then decrypted by the receiver. All of this work requires CPU time; hence, SSL/TLS connections require significantly more overhead than unprotected connections. Establishing connections is particularly time consuming, so even stateless web connections are held in a stateful fashion when secured via SSL/TLS, to avoid repeating the handshake process for each request. This makes some web server functionality more difficult, such as implementing web farms, and requires that either an SSL/TLS appliance be used before the web server to maintain state or the SSL/TLS state information be maintained in a directory-type service accessible by all of the web farm servers. Either method requires additional infrastructure and equipment. However, to enable secure e-commerce and other private data transactions over the Internet, this is a cost-effective method to establish a specific level of necessary security.

The use of certificates could present a lot of data and complication to a user. Fortunately, browsers have incorporated much of this desired functionality into a seamless operation. Once you have decided always to accept code from XYZ Corporation, subsequent certificate checks are handled by the browser. The ability to manipulate certificate settings is under the Options menus in both Internet Explorer (Figures 17.2 and 17.3) and Mozilla Firefox (Figures 17.4 and 17.5).

Once a communication is in the SSL/TLS channel, it is very difficult to defeat the SSL protocol. Before data enters the secured channel, however, defeat is possible. A Trojan program that copies keystrokes and echoes them to another TCP/IP address in parallel with the intended communication can defeat SSL/TLS, for example, provided that the Trojan program copies the data prior to SSL/TLS encapsulation. This type of attack has occurred and

● **Figure 17.2**   Internet Explorer certificate management options

• **Figure 17.3**   Internet Explorer certificate store

• **Figure 17.4**   Firefox certificate options

• **Figure 17.5**   Firefox certificate store

has been used to steal passwords and other sensitive material from users, performing the theft as the user actually types in the data.

SSL/TLS Proxy Attack

SSL/TLS-based security is not foolproof. It can be defeated, as in the case of a proxy-based attack. Examining the handshake, the following steps could occur, as shown in this illustration:

• SSL/TLS man-in-the-middle attack

1. *The client (C) initiates a TLS session with their bank server (S) through a proxy (P).*

2. *P acts by echoing the information sent to it by C (step 1a) to S (step 1b), imitating C to S, and establishing a secure channel between P and S (TLS #1).*

3. *P creates a second secure channel to C (TLS #2), using information received from S, pretending to be S.*

4. *The user assumes that the dotted lines occur—a secure channel to the bank directly—when the client actually has only a secure channel to the proxy. In fact, the proxy has the secure channel to the bank, and as far as the bank is concerned, the proxy is the client and using the client's credentials. For a proxy that is not completely trusted, this could be a nightmare for the client.*

The advent of high-assurance certificates prevents the proxy from imitating the bank, as it cannot give the correct set of credentials back to the client to complete the high-assurance handshake. Mutual authentication is also designed to prevent this, as the proxy cannot simultaneously imitate both sides of the handshake. Mutual authentication is rarely used, as there is the issue of maintaining client certificates that are trusted to a server—a challenge for broad-reach sites like financial institutions and e-commerce sites.

• Figure 17.6   High-assurance notification in Internet Explorer

The Web (HTTP and HTTPS)

HTTP is used for the transfer of hyperlinked data over the Internet, from web servers to browsers. When a user types a URL such as http://www .example.com into a browser, the http:// portion indicates that the desired method of data transfer is HTTP. Although it was initially created just for HTML pages, today many protocols deliver content over this connection protocol. HTTP traffic takes place over TCP port 80 by default, and this port is typically left open on firewalls because of the extensive use of HTTP.

One of the primary drivers behind the development of SSL/TLS was the desire to hide the complexities of cryptography from end users. When using an SSL/TLS-enabled browser, this can be done simply by requesting a secure connection from a web server instead of a nonsecure connection. With respect to HTTP connections, this is as simple as using https:// in place of http://.

The entry of an SSL/TLS-based protocol will cause a browser to perform the necessary negotiations with the web server to establish the required level of security. Once these negotiations have been completed and the session is secured by a session key, a closed padlock icon is displayed in the lower right of the screen to indicate that the session is secure. If the protocol is *https:*, your connection is secure; if it is *http:*, then the connection is carried by plaintext for anyone to see. Figure 17.6 shows a secure connection in Internet Explorer, and Figure 17.7 shows the equivalent in Firefox. As of Internet Explorer 7, Microsoft places the padlock icon in an obvious position, next to the URL, instead of in the lower-right corner of the screen, where users could more easily miss it. To combat a variety of attacks, in 2006 the SSL/TLS landscape changed with the advent of extended validation certificates and high security browsers. These changes provide visual cues to the user when high assurance certificates are being used as part of a secure SSL/TLS connection. These improvements were in response to

• Figure 17.7   High-assurance notification in Firefox

Table 17.1	SSL/TLS-Protected Services	
Protocol	**TCP Port**	**Use**
HTTPS	443	SSL/TSL-secured HTTP traffic
SSMTP	465	SSL/TLS-secured SMTP for mail sending
SPOP3 (SecurePOP3	995	SSL/TLS-secured POP3 for mail receiving
sNEWS	563	SSL/TLS-secured Usenet news
SSL = LDAP	636	SSL/TLS-secured LDAP services

phishing sites and online fraud, and although they require additional costs and registration on the part of the vendors, this is a modest up-front cost to help reduce fraud and provide confidence to customers.

The objective of enabling cryptographic methods in this fashion is to make it easy for end users to use these protocols. SSL/TLS is designed to be *protocol agnostic*. Although designed to run on top of TCP/IP, it can operate on top of other, lower-level protocols, such as X.25. SSL/TLS requires a reliable lower-level protocol, so it is not designed and cannot properly function on top of a nonreliable protocol such as the User Datagram Protocol (UDP). Even with this limitation, SSL/TLS has been used to secure many common TCP/IP-based services, as shown in Table 17.1.

HTTPS Everywhere

When websites were first deployed, providing HTTPS was a resource cost issue, because it took processor cycles to encrypt all the connections. Today, with a variety of encryption technologies available, managing the resources for HTTPS connections is much easier, and a case has been made by many in security that all web connections should be HTTPS. This has resulted in the HTTPS Everywhere movement (https://www.eff.org/https-everywhere/), spearheaded by the Electronic Frontier Foundation (EFF).

If web sites everywhere would turn off HTTP in favor of using only HTTPS (with TLS in light of SSL vulnerabilities), this would not solve all the security problems, but it would raise the bar substantially for many attacks. HTTPS Everywhere would go a long way for privacy, because it would prevent data snooping. It would also prevent many man-in-the-middle attacks, such as SSL stripping.

Because not all sites are HTTPS yet, the EFF has developed a plug-in for browsers called HTTPS Everywhere. This plug-in helps the browser maintain an HTTPS connection and warns when it is not present.

HTTP Strict Transport Security

HTTP Strict Transport Security (HSTS) is an IETF standard and a mechanism to enforce rules to prevent browsers from downgrading security when accessing a site. The policy states that when a web server provides an HTTP response header field named "Strict-Transport-Security," then the user agent shall comply by not issuing insecure requests. The header field has a time period associated with it, set in the header, during which the policy is in effect.

HSTS was created in response to a series of attack profiles, the most critical being the SSL stripping man-in-the-middle attacks, first publicly introduced by Moxie Marlinspike. The **SSL stripping attack** works on both SSL and TLS by transparently converting the secure HTTPS connection into a plain HTTP connection, removing the transport layer encryption protections. Although an observant user might notice the drop in security, by then the damage may have been done, and this relies upon users knowing whether a page should be secure or not. No warnings are presented to the user during the downgrade process, which makes the attack fairly subtle to all but the most vigilant. Marlinspike's sslstrip tool fully automates the attack and is available on the Web.

Try This!

Sniff Your Own Connections!

Determining what level of protection you have when surfing the Web is easy. Use a packet-sniffing tool like Wireshark to record your own communications. Because HTTPS ends at your browser, the packet capture mechanism should reflect the same experience an outsider will see if sniffing your traffic. By examining the packets, you can see if traffic is encrypted, which traffic is encrypted, and what is visible to outsiders.

Directory Services (DAP and LDAP)

A *directory* is a data storage mechanism similar to a database, but it has several distinct differences designed to provide efficient data retrieval services compared to standard database mechanisms. A directory is designed and optimized for reading data, offering very fast search and retrieval operations. The types of information stored in a directory tend to be descriptive attribute data. A directory offers a static view of data that can be changed without a complex update transaction. The data is hierarchically described in a treelike structure, and a network interface for reading is typical.

> As directories are optimized for read operations, they are frequently employed where data retrieval is desired. Common uses of directories include e-mail address lists, domain server data, and resource maps of network resources.

To enable interoperability, the **X.500** standard was created as a standard for directory services. The primary method for accessing an X.500 directory is through the Directory Access Protocol (DAP), a heavyweight protocol that is difficult to implement completely, especially on PCs and more constrained platforms. This led to the **Lightweight Directory Access Protocol (LDAP)**, which contains the most commonly used functionality. LDAP can interface with X.500 services, and, most importantly, LDAP can be used over TCP with significantly less computing resources than a full X.500 implementation. LDAP offers all of the functionality most directories need and is easier and more economical to implement; hence LDAP has become the Internet standard for directory services.

> LDAP over TCP is a plaintext protocol, meaning data is passed in the clear and is susceptible to eavesdropping. Encryption can be used to remedy this problem, and the application of SSL/TLS-based services will protect directory queries and replies from eavesdroppers.

SSL/TLS LDAP

SSL/TLS provides several important functions to LDAP services. It can establish the identity of a data source through the use of certificates, and it can also provide for the integrity and confidentiality of the data being presented from an LDAP source. As LDAP and SSL/TLS are two separate independent protocols, interoperability is more a function of correct setup than anything else. To achieve LDAP over SSL/TLS, the typical setup is to establish an SSL/TLS connection and then open an LDAP connection over the protected channel. To do this requires that both the client and the server be enabled for SSL/TLS. In the case of the client, most browsers are already enabled. In the case of an LDAP server, this specific function must be enabled by a system administrator. As this setup initially is complicated, it's definitely a task for a competent system administrator.

Once an LDAP server is set up to function over an SSL/TLS connection, it operates as it always has. The LDAP server responds to specific queries with the data returned from a node in the search. The SSL/TLS functionality is transparent to the data flow from the user's perspective. From the outside, SSL/TLS prevents observation of the data request and response, ensuring confidentiality.

File Transfer (FTP and SFTP)

One of the original intended uses of the Internet was to transfer files from one machine to another in a simple, secure, and reliable fashion, which was needed by scientific researchers. Today, file transfers represent downloads of music content, reports, and other data sets from other computer systems to a PC-based client. Until 1995, the majority of Internet traffic was file transfers. With all of this need, a protocol was necessary so that two computers could agree on how to send and receive data. As such, FTP is one of the older protocols.

FTP

File Transfer Protocol (FTP) is an application-level protocol that operates over a wide range of lower-level protocols. FTP is embedded in most operating systems and provides a method of transferring files from a sender to a receiver. Most FTP implementations are designed to operate both ways, sending and receiving, and can enable remote file operations over a TCP/IP connection. FTP clients are used to initiate transactions, and FTP servers are used to respond to transaction requests. The actual request can be either to upload (send data from client to server) or to download (send data from server to client).

Clients for FTP on a PC can range from an application program, to the command-line FTP program in Windows/DOS, to most browsers. To open an FTP data store in a browser, you can enter **ftp://url** in the browser's address field to indicate that you want to see the data associated with the URL via an FTP session—the browser handles the details.

Blind FTP (Anonymous FTP)

To access resources on a computer, an account must be used to allow the operating system–level authorization function to work. In the case of an FTP server, you may not wish to control who gets the information, so a standard account called *anonymous* exists. This allows unlimited public access to the files and is commonly used when you want to have unlimited distribution. On a server, access permissions can be established to allow only downloading or only uploading or both, depending on the system's function.

As FTP servers can present a security risk, they are typically not permitted on workstations and are disabled on servers without need for this functionality.

SFTP

FTP operates in a plaintext mode, so an eavesdropper can observe the data being passed. If confidential transfer is required, Secure FTP (SFTP) combines both the Secure Shell (SSH) protocol and FTP to accomplish this task.

As FTP can be used to allow anyone access to upload files to a server, it is considered a security risk and is commonly implemented on specialized servers isolated from other critical functions.

SFTP operates as an application program that encodes both the commands and the data being passed and requires SFTP to be on both the client and the server. SFTP is not interoperable with standard FTP—the encrypted commands cannot be read by the standard FTP server program. To establish SFTP data transfers, the server must be enabled with the SFTP program, and then clients can access the server, provided they have the correct credentials. One of the first SFTP operations is the same as that of FTP: an identification function that uses a username and an authorization function that uses a password. There is no anonymous SFTP account by definition, so access is established and controlled from the server using standard access control lists (ACLs), IDs, and passwords.

Vulnerabilities

Modern encryption technology can provide significant levels of privacy, up to military-grade secrecy. The use of protocols such as TLS provides a convenient method for end users to use cryptography without having to understand how it works. This can result in complacency—the impression that once TLS is enabled, the user is safe, but this is not necessarily the case. If a Trojan program is recording keystrokes and sending the information to another unauthorized user, for example, TLS cannot prevent the security breach. If the user is connecting to an untrustworthy site, the mere fact that the connection is secure does not prevent the other site from running a scam.

Using TLS and other encryption methods will not guard against your credit card information being "lost" by a company with which you do business, as in the Egghead.com credit card hack of 2000. In December 2000, Egghead.com's credit card database was hacked, and as many as 3.7 million credit card numbers were exposed. This resulted eventually in the loss of the firm, which is now known as NewEgg. The year 2014 was a year filled with data breaches, losses of customer information—including credit card numbers—from many high-profile merchants such as Target. In these cases, the security failure was internal to the data storage in the company, not during transfer to the firm. So even with secure web controls, data can be lost after being stored in a company database.

The key to understanding what is protected and where it is protected is to understand what these protocols can and cannot do. The TLS suite can protect data in transit, but not on either end in storage. It can authenticate users and servers, provided that the certificate mechanisms are established and used by both parties. Properly set up and used, TLS can provide a very secure method of authentication, followed by confidentiality in data transfers and data integrity checking. But again, all of this occurs during transit, and the protection ends once the data is stored.

> TLS is not a guarantee of security. All TLS can do is secure the transport link between the computer and the server. There are still a number of vulnerabilities that can affect the security of the system. A keylogger on the client can copy the secrets before they go to the TLS-protected link. Malware on either end of the secure communication can copy and/or alter transmissions outside the secure link.

■ Code-Based Vulnerabilities

The ability to connect many machines together to transfer data is what makes the Internet so functional for so many users. Browsers enable much of this functionality, and as the types of data have grown on the Internet, browser functionality has grown as well. But not all functions can be anticipated or included in each browser release, so the idea of extending browser functions through plug-ins became a standard. Browsers can perform many types of data transfer, and in some cases, additional helper programs, or plug-ins, can increase functionality for specific types of data transfers. In other cases, separate application programs may be called by a browser to handle the data being transferred. Common examples of these plug-ins and programs include Shockwave and Flash plug-ins, Windows Media Player, and Adobe Acrobat (both plug-in and standalone). The richness that enables the desired functionality of the Internet has also spawned some additional types of interfaces in the form of ActiveX components and Java applets.

In essence, all of these are pieces of code that can be written by third parties, distributed via the Internet, and run on your PC. If the code does what the user wants, the user is happy. But the opportunity exists for these applications or plug-ins to include malicious code that performs actions not desired by the end user. Malicious code designed to operate within a web browser environment is a major tool for computer crackers to use to obtain unauthorized access to computer systems. Whether delivered by HTML-based e-mail, by getting a user to visit a web site, or even delivery via an ad server, the result is the same: malware performs malicious tasks in the browser environment.

Buffer Overflows

One of the most common exploits used to hack into software is the **buffer overflow**. The buffer overflow vulnerability is a result of poor coding practices on the part of software programmers—when any program reads input into a buffer (an area of memory) and does not validate the input for correct length, the potential for a buffer overflow exists. The buffer-overflow vulnerability occurs when an application can accept more input than it has assigned storage space and the input data overwrites other program areas. The exploit concept is simple: An attacker develops an executable program that performs some action on the target machine and appends this code to a legitimate response to a program on the target machine. When the target machine reads through the too-long response, a buffer-overflow condition causes the original program to fail. The extra malicious code fragment is now in the machine's memory, awaiting execution. If the attacker executed it correctly, the program will skip into the attacker's code, running it instead of crashing.

Cross Check

Dangers of Software Vulnerabilities

Errors in software lead to vulnerabilities associated with the code being run. These vulnerabilities are exploited by hackers to perform malicious activity on a machine. These errors are frequently related to web-enabled programs, as the Internet provides a useful conduit for hackers to achieve access to a system. The problem of code vulnerabilities, from buffer overflows, to arithmetic overflows, to cross-site request forgeries, cross-site scripting, and injection attacks, is a serious issue that has many faces. It is noted in this chapter because web components are involved, but full details on the severity of and steps to mitigate this issue are in Chapter 18. The next time you provide input to a web-based application, think of what malicious activity you could perform on the server in question.

Java

Java is a computer language invented by Sun Microsystems as an alternative to Microsoft's development languages. Designed to be platform-independent and based on C, Java offered a low learning curve and a way of implementing

542

programs across an enterprise, independent of platform. Although platform independence never fully materialized, and the pace of Java language development was slowed by Sun, Java has found itself to be a leader in object-oriented programming languages.

Java operates through an interpreter called a Java Virtual Machine (JVM) on each platform that interprets the Java code, and this JVM enables the program's functionality for the specific platform. Java's reliance on an interpretive step has led to performance issues, and Java is still plagued by poor performance when compared to most other languages. Security was one of the touted advantages of Java, but in reality, security is not a built-in function but an afterthought and is implemented independently of the language core. This all being said, properly coded Java can operate at reasonable rates, and when properly designed can act in a secure fashion. These facts have led to the wide dependence on Java for much of the server-side coding for e-commerce and other web-enabled functionality. Servers can add CPUs to address speed concerns, and the low learning curve has proven cost efficient for enterprises.

Java was initially designed to be used in trusted environments, and when it moved to the Internet for general use, safety became one of its much-hyped benefits. Java has many safety features, such as type checking and garbage collection, that actually improve a program's ability to run safely on a machine and not cause operating system–level failures. This isolates the user from many common forms of operating system faults that can end in the "blue screen of death" in a Windows environment, where the operating system crashes and forces a reboot of the system. Safety is not security, however, and although safe, a malicious Java program can still cause significant damage to a system.

The primary mode of a computer program is to interact with the operating system and perform functional tasks for a user, such as getting and displaying data, manipulating data, storing data, and so on. Although these functions can seem benign, when enabled across the Web they can have some unintended consequences. The ability to read data from a hard drive and display it on the screen is essential for many programs, but when the program is downloaded and run from the Internet and the data is, without the knowledge of the user, sent across the Internet to an unauthorized user, this enables a program to spy on a user and steal data. Writing data to the hard drive can also cause deletions if the program doesn't write the data where the user expects. Sun recognized these dangers and envisioned three different security policies for Java that would be implemented via the browser and JVM, providing different levels of security. The first policy is not to run Java programs at all. The second restricts Java program functionality when the program is not run directly from the system's hard drive—programs being directly executed from the Internet have severe restrictions that block disk access and force other security-related functions to be performed. The last policy runs any and all Java programs as presented.

Most browsers adopted the second security policy, restricting Java functionality on a client unless the program was loaded directly from the client's hard drive. Although this solved many problems initially, it also severely limited functionality. Today, browsers allow much more specific granularity on security for Java, based on security zones and user settings.

> Java is designed for safety, reducing the opportunity for system crashes. Java can still perform malicious activities, and the fact that many users falsely believe it is safe increases its usefulness to attackers.

> Java and JavaScript are completely separate entities. JavaScript does not create applets or stand-alone applications. JavaScript resides inside HTML documents, and can provide levels of interactivity to web pages that are not achievable with simple HTML. Java is used to create applications that run in a virtual machine or browser. JavaScript code is run on a browser only. JavaScript is not part of the Java environment.

● Figure 17.8 Java configuration settings in Internet Explorer

JavaScript

JavaScript is a scripting language developed by Netscape and designed to be operated within a browser instance. JavaScript works through the browser environment. The primary purpose of JavaScript is to enable features such as validation of forms before they are submitted to the server. Enterprising programmers found many other uses for JavaScript, such as manipulating the browser history files, now prohibited by design. JavaScript actually runs within the browser, and the code is executed by the browser itself. This has led to compatibility problems, and not just between vendors, such as Microsoft and Mozilla, but between browser versions. Security settings in Internet Explorer are done by a series of zones, allowing differing levels of control over .NET functionality, ActiveX functionality, and Java functionality (see Figure 17.8). Unfortunately, these settings can be changed by a Trojan program, altering the browser (without alerting the user) and lowering the security settings. In Firefox, using the NoScript plug-in is a solution to this, but the reduced functionality leads to other issues, as shown in Figure 17.9, and requires more diligent user intervention.

Although JavaScript was designed not to be able to access files or network resources directly, except through the browser functions, it has not proven to be as secure as desired. This fault traces back to a similar fault in the Java language, where security was added on, without the benefit of a comprehensive security model. So, although designers put thought and common sense into the design of JavaScript, the lack of a comprehensive security model left some security holes. For instance, a form could submit itself via e-mail to an undisclosed recipient, either eavesdropping, spamming, or causing other problems—imagine your machine sending death threat e-mails to high-level government officials from a rogue JavaScript implementation.

Further, most browsers do not have a mechanism to halt a running script, short of aborting the browser instance, and even this may not be possible if the browser has stopped responding to commands. Malicious JavaScripts can do many things, including opening two new windows every time

● Figure 17.9 Security setting functionality issues

Principles of Computer Security

you close one, each with the code to open two more. There is no way out of this one, short of killing the browser process from the operating system.

JavaScripts can also trick users into thinking they are communicating with one entity when in fact they are communicating with another. For example, a window may open asking whether you want to download and execute the new update from "http://www.microsoft.com..../update.exe," and what is covered by the ellipsis (...) is actually "www.microsoft.com. attacker.org/"—the user assumes this is a Microsoft address that is cut short by space restrictions on the display.

As a browser scripting language, JavaScript is here to stay. Its widespread popularity for developing applets such as animated clocks, mortgage calculators, and simple games will overcome its buggy nature and poor level of security.

ActiveX

ActiveX is the name given to a broad collection of application programming interfaces (APIs), protocols, and programs developed by Microsoft to download and execute code automatically over an Internet-based channel. The code is bundled together into an ActiveX control with an .ocx extension. These controls are referenced in HTML using the **<object>** tag. ActiveX is a tool for the Windows environment and can be extremely powerful. It can do simple things, such as enable a browser to display a custom type of information in a particular way, and it can also perform complex tasks, such as update the operating system and application programs. This range of abilities gives ActiveX a lot of power, but this power can be abused as well as used for good purposes. Internet Explorer has several options to control the execution of ActiveX controls, as illustrated in Figure 17.10.

To enable security and consumer confidence in downloaded programs such as ActiveX controls, Microsoft developed **Authenticode**, a system that uses digital signatures and allows Windows users to determine who produced a specific piece of code and whether or not the code has been altered. As in the case of Java, safety and security are different things, and Authenticode promotes neither in reality. Authenticode provides limited accountability at the time of download and provides reasonable assurance that the code has not been changed since the time of signing. Authenticode does

Many web sites may have behaviors that users deem less than desirable, such as popping open additional windows, either on top (pop-up) or underneath (pop-under). To prevent these behaviors, a class of applet referred to as a pop-up blocker may be employed. Although they may block some desired pop-ups, most pop-up blockers have settings to allow pop-ups on selected sites. The use of a pop-up blocker assists in retaining strict control over browser behavior and enhances security for the user.

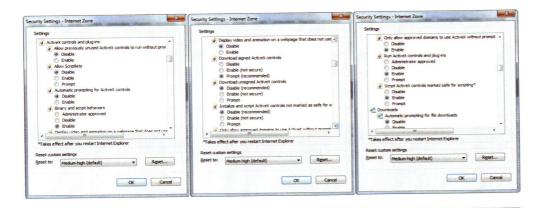

• **Figure 17.10**   ActiveX security settings in Internet Explorer

Exam Tip: ActiveX technology can be used to create complex application logic that is then embedded into other container objects such as a web browser. ActiveX components have very significant capabilities and thus malicious ActiveX objects can be very dangerous. Authenticode is a means of signing an ActiveX control so that a user can judge trust based on the control's creator.

not identify whether a piece of code will cause damage to a system, nor does it regulate how code is used, so a perfectly safe ActiveX control under one set of circumstances may be malicious if used improperly. As with a notary's signature, recourse is very limited—if code is signed by a terrorist organization and the code ruins your machine, all Authenticode did was make it seem legitimate. It is still incumbent upon the users to know from whom they are getting code and to determine whether or not they trust that organization.

Critics of Authenticode and other code-signing techniques are not against code signing, for this is a universally recognized good thing. What the critics argue is that code signing is not a panacea for security issues and that marketing it as doing more than it really does is irresponsible. Understanding the nuances of security is important in today's highly technical world, and leaving the explanations to marketing departments is not the ideal solution.

Securing the Browser

A great deal of debate concerns the relative security issue of browser extensions versus the rich user interaction that they provide. There is no doubt that the richness of the environment offered by ActiveX adds to the user experience. But as is the case in most coding situations, added features means weaker security, all other things being constant. If nothing else, a development team must spend some portion of its time on secure development practices, time that some developers and marketers would prefer to spend on new features. Although no browser is 100 percent safe, the use of Firefox coupled with the NoScript plug-in comes the closest to fitting the bill. Firefox will not execute ActiveX, so that threat vector is removed. The NoScript plug-in allows the user to determine from which domains to trust scripts. The use of NoScript puts the onus back on the user as to which domain scripts they choose to trust, and although it's not perfect from a security perspective, this at least allows a measure of control over what code you want to run on your machine.

CGI

The **Common Gateway Interface (CGI)** was the original method for having a web server execute a program outside the web server process, yet on the same server. CGI offered many advantages to web-based programs. The programs can be written in a number of languages, although Perl is a favorite. These scripted programs embrace the full functionality of a server, allowing access to databases, UNIX commands, other programs, and so on. This provides a wide range of functionality to the web environment. With this unrestrained capability, however, come security issues. Poorly written scripts can cause unintended consequences at runtime. The problem with poorly written scripts is that their defects are not always obvious. Sometimes scripts appear to be fine, but unexpected user inputs can have unintended consequences.

CGI is an outdated, and for the most part retired, technology. It has been replaced by newer scripting methods.

Server-Side Scripts

CGI has been replaced in many web sites through newer **server-side scripting** technologies such as Java, **Active Server Pages (ASP)**, **ASP.NET**, and **PHP**. All these technologies operate in much the same fashion as CGI: they allow programs to be run outside the web server and to return data to the web server to be served to end users via a web page. The term *server-side script* is actually a misnomer, as these are actually executable programs that are either interpreted or run in virtual machines. Each of these newer technologies has advantages and disadvantages, but all of them have stronger security models than CGI. With these security models come reduced functionality and, as each is based on a different language, a steeper learning curve. Still, the need for adherence to programming fundamentals exists in these technologies— code must be well designed and well written to avoid the same vulnerabilities that exist in all forms of code. Buffer overflows are still an issue. Changing languages or technologies does not eliminate the basic security problems associated with incorporating open-ended user input into code. Understanding and qualifying user responses before blindly using them programmatically is essential to the security of a system.

Cookies

Cookies are small chunks of ASCII text passed within an HTTP stream to store data temporarily in a web browser instance. Invented by Netscape, cookies pass back and forth between web server and browser and act as a mechanism to maintain state in a stateless world. *State* is a term that describes the dependence on previous actions. By definition, HTTP traffic served by a web server is *stateless*—each request is completely independent of all previous requests, and the server has no memory of previous requests. This dramatically simplifies the function of a web server, but it also significantly complicates the task of providing anything but the most basic functionality in a site. Cookies were developed to bridge this gap. Cookies are passed along with HTTP data through a Set-Cookie message in the header portion of an HTTP message.

> Cookies come in two types, session and persistent. Session cookies last only during a web browsing session with a web site. Persistent cookies are stored on the user's hard drive and last until an expiration date.

A cookie is actually a series of name-value pairs that is stored in memory during a browser instance. The specification for cookies established several specific name-value pairs for defined purposes. Additional name-value pairs may be defined at will by a developer. The specified set of name-value pairs includes the following:

- **Expires**   This field specifies when the cookie expires. If no value exists, the cookie is good only during the current browser session and will not be persisted to the user's hard drive. Should a value be given, the cookie will be written to the user's machine and persisted until this datetime value occurs.

- **Domain**   Specifies the domain where the cookie is used. Cookies were designed as memory-resident objects, but as the user or data can cause a browser to move between domains—say, from comedy.net to jokes.org—some mechanism needs to tell the browser which cookies belong to which domains.

- **Path** This name-value pair further resolves the applicability of the cookie into a specific path within a domain. If path = /directory, the cookie will be sent only for requests within /directory on the given domain. This allows a level of granular control over the information being passed between the browser and server, and it limits unnecessary data exchanges.

- **Secure** The presence of the keyword **[secure]** in a cookie indicates that it is to be used only when connected in an SSL/TLS session. This does not indicate any other form of security, as cookies are stored in plaintext on the client machine. Cookie management on a browser is normally an invisible process, but most browsers have methods for users to examine and manipulate cookies on the client side. Chrome users can examine, delete, and block individual cookies through the interface shown in Figure 17.11. Internet Explorer has a similar interface, with just a Delete option in the browser under Browsing History (see Figure 17.12). Additional cookie manipulation can be done through the file processing system, because cookies are stored as individual files, as shown in Figure 17.13. This combination allows easier bulk manipulation, which is a useful option, as cookies can become quite numerous in short order.

So what good are cookies? Disable cookies in your browser and go to some common sites that you visit, and you'll quickly learn the usefulness of cookies. Cookies store a variety of information, from customer IDs to

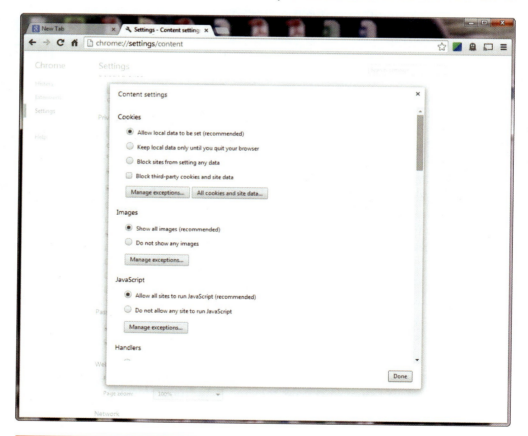

• **Figure 17.11** Chrome cookie management

Principles of Computer Security

• **Figure 17.12** Internet Explorer cookie management

data about previous visits. Because cookies are stored on a user's machine in a form that will allow simple manipulation, they must always be considered suspect and are not suitable for use as a security mechanism. They can, however, allow the browser to provide crucial pieces of information to a web server. Advertisers can use them to control which ads you are shown, based on previous ads you have viewed and regardless of ad location by site. Specific sites can use cookies to pass state information between pages, enabling functionality at the user's desired levels. Cookies can also

• **Figure 17.13** Internet Explorer cookie store

remember your ZIP code for a weather site, your ID for a stock tracker site, the items in your shopping cart—these are all typical cookie uses. In the final analysis, cookies are a part of the daily web experience, here to stay and useful if not used improperly (such as to store security data and to provide ID and authentication).

Disabling Cookies

If the user disables cookies in a browser, this type of information will not be available for the web server to use. IETF RFC 2109 describes the HTTP state-management system (cookies) and specifies several specific cookie functions to be enabled in browsers, specifically:

- The ability to turn on and off cookie usage
- An indicator as to whether cookies are in use
- A means of specifying cookie domain values and lifetimes

Several of these functions have already been discussed, but to surf cookie-free requires more than a simple step. Telling a browser to stop accepting cookies is a setup option available through an Options menu, but this has no effect on cookies already received and stored on the system. To prevent the browser from sending cookies already received, the user must delete the cookies from the system. This bulk operation is easily performed, and then the browser can run cookie-free. Several third-party tools enable even a finer granularity of cookie control.

Browser Plug-ins

The addition of browser scripting and ActiveX components allows a browser to change how it handles data, tremendously increasing its functionality as a user interface. But all data types and all desired functionality cannot be offered through these programming technologies. Plug-ins are used to fill these gaps.

Plug-ins are small application programs that increase a browser's ability to handle new data types and add new functionality. Sometimes these plug-ins are in the form of ActiveX components, which is the form Microsoft chose for its Office plug-in, which enables a browser to manipulate various Office files, such as pivot tables from Excel, over the Web. Adobe has developed Acrobat Reader, a plug-in that enables a browser to read and display Portable Document Format (PDF) files directly in a browser. PDF files offer platform independence for printed documents and are usable across a wide array of platforms—they are a compact way to provide printed information. Figure 17.14 illustrates the various plug-ins and browser helper objects (discussed in the next section) enabled in Internet Explorer.

The combination of a development environment for developers and plug-in–enabled browsers that can display the content has caused these technologies to see widespread use. The result is a tremendous increase in visual richness in web communications, and this, in turn, has made the Web more popular and has increased usage in various demographic segments.

Until recently, these plug-ins have had a remarkable safety record. As Flash-based content has grown more popular, crackers have examined the Flash plug-ins and software, determined vulnerabilities, and developed exploit code to use against the Flash protocol. Adobe has patched the issue, but as Apple has decided not to use Flash on its iPhones or iPads, the death of Flash is on the horizon.

Malicious Add-ons

Add-ons are pieces of code that are distributed to allow additional functionality to be added to an existing program. An example of these are browser helper objects (BHOs), which provide a means of creating a plug-in module that is loaded with Internet Explorer and provide a means of adding capability to the browser. The functionality can be significant, as in the case of the Adobe Acrobat BHO that allows PDFs to be rendered in the browser. A BHO has unrestricted access to the Internet Explorer event model and can do things such as capture keystrokes.

Other programs can have add-ons that utilize the permissions given the master program. You should only use add-ons from trusted sources, and you need to understand the level of interaction risk they pose. ActiveX is a technology implemented by Microsoft to enhance web-enabled systems through significant additions to user controls. For example, unless signed by a trusted authority using Authenticode, ActiveX content should not be allowed in browsers, as the nature of the code changes can present significant risk.

• **Figure 17.14**   Add-ons for Internet Explorer

Signed Applets

Code signing was an attempt to bring the security of shrink-wrapped software to software downloaded from the Internet. Code signing works by adding a digital signature and a digital certificate to a program file to demonstrate file integrity and authenticity. The certificate identifies the author, and the digital signature contains a hash value that covers code, certificate, and signature to prove integrity, and this establishes the integrity of the code and publisher via a standard browser certificate check. The purpose of a company signing the code is to state that it considers the code it created to be safe, and it is stating that the code will not do any harm to the system (to the company's knowledge). The digital signature also tells the user that the stated company is, indeed, the creator of the code.

The ability to use a certificate to sign an applet or a control allows the identity of the author of a control or applet to be established. This has many benefits. For instance, if a user trusts content from a particular vendor, such as Sun Microsystems, the user can trust controls that are signed by Sun Microsystems. This signing of a piece of code does not do anything other than identify the code's manufacturer and guarantee that the code has not been modified since it was signed.

A signed applet can be hijacked as easily as a graphic or any other file. The two ways an attacker could hijack a signed control are by inline access or by copying the file in its entirety and republishing it. **Inlining** is using an embedded control from another site with or without the other site's permission. Republishing a signed control is done much like stealing a GIF or JPEG image—a copy of the file is maintained on the unauthorized site and served from there instead of from the original location. If a signed control cannot be modified, why be concerned with these thefts, apart from the issue of intellectual property? The primary security concern comes from how the control is used. A cracker may be able to use a control in an unintended fashion, resulting in file loss or buffer overflow—conditions that weaken a system and can allow exploitation of other vulnerabilities. A common programming activity is cleaning up installation files from a computer's hard drive after successfully installing a software package. If a signed control is used for this task and permission has already been granted, then improperly using the control could result in the wrong set of files being deleted. The control will still function as designed, but the issue becomes who it is used by and how. These are concerns not addressed simply by signing a control or applet.

■ Application-Based Weaknesses

Web browsers are not the only aspect of software being abused by crackers. The application software written to run on servers and serve up the content for users is also a target. Web application security is a fairly hot topic in security, as it has become a prime target for professional crackers. Criminal hackers typically are after some form of financial reward, whether from stolen data, stolen identity, or some form of extortion. Attacking web-based applications has proven to be a lucrative venture for several reasons. First, the target is a rich environment, as company after company has developed a customer-facing web presence, often including custom-coded functionality that permits customer access to back-end systems for legitimate business purposes. Second, building these custom applications to high levels of security is a difficult if not impossible feat, especially given the corporate pressure on delivery time and cost.

 Cross Check

Common Application Vulnerabilities

There are some common application vulnerabilities that hackers use to attack web sites, including injection attacks, cross-site request forgeries, cross-site scripting attacks, and numeric attacks. These are attacks that use the browser's ability to submit input to a back-end server program, and they take advantage of coding errors on the back-end system, enabling behavior outside the desired program response. These errors are covered in more detail in Chapter 18, as they are fundamentally programming errors on the server side.

Principles of Computer Security

The same programmatic errors that plague operating systems, such as buffer overflows, can cause havoc with web-based systems. But web-based systems have a new history of rich customer interactions, including the collection of information from the customer and dynamically using customer-supplied information to modify the user experience. This makes the customer a part of the application, and when proper controls are not in place, errors such as the MySpace-based Samy worm can occur. Different types of errors are commonly observed in the deployment of web applications, and these have been categorized into six logical groupings of vulnerabilities: authentication, authorization, logical attacks, information disclosure, command execution, and client-side attacks. A total of 24 different types of vulnerabilities have been classified by the Web Application Security Consortium (WASC), an international organization that establishes best practices for web application security.

The changing nature of the web-based vulnerabilities is demonstrated by the changing of the OWASP Top Ten list of web application vulnerabilities maintained by The Open Web Application Security Project. OWASP is a worldwide free and open community focused on improving the security of application software and has published a series of Top Ten vulnerability lists highlighting the current state of the art and threat environment facing web application developers. OWASP maintains a web site (www.owasp.org) with significant resources to help firms build better software and eliminate these common and pervasive problems. The true challenge in this area is not just about coding, but also about developing an understanding of the nature of web applications and the difficulty of using user-supplied inputs for crucial aspects in a rich, user experience–based web application. The errors included in the OWASP Top Ten list have plagued some of the largest sites and those with arguably the best talent, including Amazon, eBay, MySpace, and Google.

Session Hijacking

When communicating across the Web, it is common to create a session to control communication flows. Sessions can be established and controlled using a variety of methods, including SSL/TLS and cookies. It is important to securely implement the setup and teardown of a session, for if one party ends the communication without properly tearing down the communication session, an interloper can take over the session, continue after one of the parties has left, and impersonate that party. If you log into your bank to conduct transactions, but allow a session hijacker in, then the hijacker can continue banking after you leave, using your account. This is one of the reasons it is so important to log off of banking and financial sites, rather than just closing the browser.

There are numerous methods of session hijacking, from man-in-the-middle attacks to side-jacking and browser takeovers. *Side-jacking* is the use of packet sniffing to steal a session cookie. Securing only the logon process and then switching back to standard HTTP can enable this attack methodology.

The best defenses are to use encryption correctly (TLS, not SSL) and to log out of and close applications when done. When using multitabbed browsers, it is best to close the entire browser instance, not just the tab.

Client-Side Attacks

The web browser has become the major application for users to engage resources across the Web. The popularity and the utility of this interface have made the web browser a prime target for attackers to gain access and control over a system. A wide variety of attacks can occur via a browser, typically resulting from a failure to properly validate input before use. Unvalidated input can result in a series of injection attacks, header manipulation, and other forms of attack.

Cross-Site Scripting

A cross-site scripting attack is a code injection attack in which an attacker sends code in response to an input request. This code is then rendered by the web server, resulting in the execution of the code by the web server. Cross-site scripting attacks take advantage of a few common elements in web-based systems. Cross-site scripting is covered in detail in Chapter 18.

Header Manipulations

When HTTP is being dynamically generated through the use of user inputs, unvalidated inputs can give attackers an opportunity to change HTTP elements. When user-supplied information is used in a header, it is possible to create a variety of attacks, including cache poisoning, cross-site scripting, cross-user defacement, page hijacking, cookie manipulation, and open redirect.

Exam Tip: A wide variety of attack vectors can be used against a client machine, including cache poisoning, cross-site scripting, cross-user defacement, page hijacking, cookie manipulation, and open redirect. All attacks should be known for the exam.

Web 2.0 and Security

A relatively new phenomenon has swept the Internet, Web 2.0, a collection of technologies that is designed to make web sites more useful for users. From new languages and protocols, such as AJAX, to user-provided content, to social networking sites and user-created mash-ups, the Internet has changed dramatically from its static HTML roots. There is a wide range of security issues associated with this new level of deployed functionality.

The new languages and protocols add significant layers of complexity to a web site's design, and errors can have significant consequences. Early efforts by Google to add Web 2.0 functionality to its applications created holes that allowed hackers access to a logged-in user's Gmail account and password. Google has fixed these errors, but they illustrate the dangers of rushing into new functionality without adequate testing. The fine details of Web 2.0 security concerns are far too numerous to detail here—in fact, they could comprise their own book. The important thing to remember is that the foundations of security apply the same way in Web 2.0 as they do elsewhere. In fact, with more capability and greater complexity comes a greater need for strong foundational security efforts, and Web 2.0 is no exception.

Chapter 17 Review

Lab Manual Exercise

The following lab exercises from the companion lab manual, *Principles of Computer Security Lab Manual, Fourth Edition*, provides practical application of material covered in this chapter:

Lab 5.2m   Web Browser Exploits

Chapter Summary

After reading this chapter and completing the exercises, you should understand the following about web components.

Describe the functioning of the SSL/TLS protocol suite

- SSL and TLS use a combination of symmetric and asymmetric cryptographic methods to secure traffic.
- Before an SSL session can be secured, a handshake occurs to exchange cryptographic information and keys.

Explain web applications, plug-ins, and associated security issues

- Web browsers have mechanisms to enable plug-in programs to manage applications such as Flash objects and videos.
- Firefox has a NoScript helper that blocks scripts from functioning.
- Plug-ins that block pop-up windows and phishing sites can improve end-user security by permitting greater control over browser functionality.

Describe secure file transfer options

- FTP operations occur in plaintext, allowing anyone who sees the traffic to read it.
- SFTP combines the file transfer application with the Secure Shell (SSH) application to provide for a means of confidential FTP operations.

Explain directory usage for data retrieval

- LDAP is a protocol describing interaction with directory services.

- Directory services are data structures optimized for retrieval and are commonly used where data is read many times more than written, such as ACLs.

Explain scripting and other Internet functions that present security concerns

- Scripts are pieces of code that can execute within the browser environment.
- ActiveX is a robust programming language that acts like a script in Microsoft Internet Explorer browsers to provide a rich programming environment.
- Some scripts or code elements can be called from the server side, creating the web environment of ASP.NET and PHP.

Use cookies to maintain parameters between web pages

- Cookies are small text files used to maintain state between web pages.
- Cookies can be set for persistent (last for a defined time period) or session (expire when the session is closed).

Examine web-based application security issues

- As more applications move to a browser environment to ease programmatic deployment, it makes it easier for users to work with a familiar user environment.
- Browsers have become powerful programming environments that perform many actions behind the scenes for a user, and malicious programmers can exploit this hidden functionality to perform actions on a user's PC without the user's obvious consent.

Key Terms

Active Server Pages (ASP) *(547)*
ActiveX *(545)*
ASP.NET *(547)*
Authenticode *(545)*
buffer overflow *(542)*
code signing *(551)*
Common Gateway Interface (CGI) *(546)*
cookie *(547)*
File Transfer Protocol (FTP) *(540)*
Hypertext Markup Language (HTML) *(530)*
inlining *(552)*
Internet Engineering Task Force (IETF) *(532)*

Java *(542)*
JavaScript *(544)*
Lightweight Directory Access Protocol (LDAP) *(539)*
PHP *(547)*
plug-in *(550)*
Secure Sockets Layer (SSL) *(531)*
server-side scripting *(547)*
SSL stripping attack *(538)*
Transport Layer Security (TLS) *(532)*
Uniform Resource Locator (URL) *(530)*
X.500 *(539)*

Key Terms Quiz

Use terms from the Key Terms list to complete the sentences that follow. Don't use the same term more than once. Not all terms will be used.

1. The use of _____ can validate input responses from clients and prevent certain attack methodologies.

2. A(n) _____ is a small text file used to enhance web surfing by creating a link between pages visited on a web site.

3. _____ or _____ is a technology used to support confidentiality across the Internet for web sites.

4. A(n) _____ is a small application program that increases a browser's ability to handle new data types and add new functionality.

5. An application-level protocol that operates over a wide range of lower-level protocols and is used to transfer files is _____.

6. _____ files have the .ocx extension to identify them.

7. _____ is the standard for directory services.

8. Adding a digital signature and a digital certificate to a program file to demonstrate file integrity and authenticity is _____.

9. A(n) _____ is a descriptor where content is located on the Internet.

10. _____ is a system that uses digital signatures and allows Windows users to determine who produced a specific piece of code and whether or not the code has been altered.

Multiple-Choice Quiz

1. What is a cookie?
   A. A piece of data in a database that enhances web browser capability
   B. A small text file used in some HTTP exchanges
   C. A segment of script to enhance a web page
   D. A program that runs when you visit a web site so it remembers you

2. The use of certificates in SSL/TLS is similar to:
   A. A receipt proving purchase
   B. Having a notary notarize a signature

   C. A historical record of a program's lineage
   D. None of the above

3. Security for JavaScript is established by whom?
   A. The developer at the time of code development.
   B. The user at the time of code usage.
   C. The user through browser preferences.
   D. Security for JavaScript is not necessary—the Java language is secure by design.

4. ActiveX can be used for which of the following purposes?

    A. Add functionality to a browser

    B. Update the operating system

    C. Both A and B

    D. Neither A nor B

5. The keyword [secure] in a cookie:

    A. Causes the system to encrypt its contents

    B. Prevents the cookie from passing over HTTP connections

    C. Tells the browser that the cookie is a security upgrade

    D. None of the above

6. Code signing is used to:

    A. Allow authors to take artistic credit for their hard work

    B. Provide a method to demonstrate code integrity

    C. Guarantee code functionality

    D. Prevent copyright infringement by code copying

7. SSL provides which of the following functionality?

    A. Data integrity services

    B. Authentication services

    C. Data confidentiality services

    D. All of the above

8. High-security browsers can use what to validate SSL credentials for a user?

    A. AES encrypted links to a root server

    B. An extended-validation SSL certificate

    C. MD5 hashing to ensure integrity

    D. SSL v3.0

9. To establish an SSL connection for e-mail and HTTP across a firewall, you must:

    A. Open TCP ports 80, 25, 443, and 223.

    B. Open TCP ports 443, 465, and 995.

    C. Open a TCP port of choice and assign it to all SSL traffic.

    D. Do nothing; SSL tunnels past firewalls.

10. To prevent the use of cookies in a browser, a user must:

    A. Tell the browser to disable cookies via a setup option.

    B. Delete all existing cookies.

    C. Both A and B.

    D. The user need do nothing; by design, cookies are necessary and cannot be totally disabled.

■ Essay Quiz

1. Much has been made of the new Web 2.0 phenomenon, including social networking sites and user-created mash-ups. How does Web 2.0 change security for the Internet?

Lab Project

• Lab Project 17.1

Cookies and scripts can both enhance web browsing experiences. They can also represent a risk, and as such the option exists to turn them off. Using Firefox with the NoScript plug-in to disable scripts, compare the browsing experience at the following sites with and without cookies, and with and without scripts:

- E-commerce site like Amazon
- A bank
- An information site like Wikipedia
- A news site

Secure Software Development

chapter 18

Security Features != Secure Features

—MICHAEL HOWARD, MICROSOFT CORPORATION

In this chapter, you will learn how to

- Describe how secure coding can be incorporated into the software development process
- List the major types of coding errors and their root causes
- Describe good software development practices and explain how they impact application security
- Describe how using a software development process enforces security inclusion in a project
- Learn about application hardening techniques

Software engineering is the systematic development of software to fulfill a variety of functions, such as business, recreational, scientific, and educational functions, which are just a few of the many areas where software comes in handy. Regardless of the type of software, there is a universal requirement that the software work properly, perform the desired functions, and perform them in the correct fashion. The functionality of software ranges from spreadsheets that accurately add figures, to pacemakers that stimulate the heart. Developers know that functional specifications must be met for the software to be satisfactory. Software engineering, then, fits as many requirements as possible into the project management schedule timeline. But with analysts and developers working overtime to get as many functional elements correct as possible, the issue of nonfunctional requirements often gets pushed to the back burner, or neglected entirely.

Security has been described as a nonfunctional requirement. This places it into a category of secondary importance for many developers. Their view is that if timelines, schedules, and budgets are all in the green, then maybe there will be time to devote to security programming. As we depend more and more on computers driven by software, we will need systems to do the same—to not only function now, but to be protected from malfunction in the future.

The Software Engineering Process

Software does not build itself. This is good news for software designers, analysts, programmers, and the like, for the complexity of designing and building software enables them to engage in well-paying careers. To achieve continued success in this difficult work environment, software engineering processes have been developed. Rather than just sitting down and starting to write code at the onset of a project, software engineers use a complete development process. There are several major categories of software engineering processes. The waterfall model, the spiral model, and the evolutionary model are major examples. Within each of these major categories, there are numerous variations, and each group then personalizes the process to their project requirements and team capabilities.

Traditionally, security is an add-on item that is incorporated into a system after the functional requirements have been met. It is not an integral part of the software development lifecycle process. This places it at odds with both functional and lifecycle process requirements. The resolution to all of these issues is relatively simple: incorporate security into the process model and build it into the product along with each functional requirement. The challenge is in how to accomplish this goal. There are two separate and required elements needed to achieve this objective. First, the inclusion of security requirements and measures in the specific process model being used. Second, the use of secure coding methods to prevent opportunities to introduce security failures into the software's design.

> ⚠️ This chapter contains many details of how to test for exploitable vulnerabilities in software. Do not perform or attempt these steps outside of systems for which you either are, or have explicit permission from, the owner. Otherwise, you may find yourself being accused of hacking and possibly even facing legal charges.

Process Models

There are several major software engineering process models, each with slightly different steps and sequences, yet they all have many similar items. The **waterfall model** is characterized by a multistep process in which steps follow each other in a linear, one-way fashion, like water over a waterfall. The **spiral model** has steps in phases that execute in a spiral fashion, repeating at different levels with each revolution of the model. The **agile model** is characterized by iterative development, where requirements and solutions evolve through an ongoing collaboration between self-organizing cross-functional teams. The **evolutionary model** is an iterative model designed to enable the construction of increasingly complex versions of a project. There are numerous other models and derivations in use today. The details of these process models are outside the scope of this book, and most of the detail is not significantly relevant to the issue of security. From a secure coding perspective, a **secure development lifecycle (SDL) model** is essential to success. From requirements to system architecture to coding to testing, security is an embedded property in all aspects of the process. There are several specific items of significance with respect to security. Four primary items of interest, regardless of the particular model or methodology employed in software creation, are requirements, design, coding, and testing phases. These phases are described in the following section.

Secure Development Lifecycle

There may be as many different software engineering methods as there are software engineering groups. But an analysis of these methods indicates that most share common elements from which an understanding of a universal methodology can be obtained. For decades, secure coding—that is, creating code that does what it is supposed to do, and only what it is supposed to do—has not been high on the radar for most organizations. The past decade of explosive connectivity and the rise of malware and hackers have raised awareness of this issue significantly. A recent alliance of several major software firms concerned with secure coding principles revealed several interesting patterns. First, they were all attacking the problem using different methodologies, but yet in surprisingly similar fashions. Second, they found a series of principles that appears to be related to success in this endeavor.

First and foremost, recognition of the need to include secure coding principles into the development process is a common element among all firms. Microsoft has been very open and vocal about its implementation of its Security Development Lifecycle (SDL) and has published significant volumes of information surrounding its genesis and evolution (https://www.microsoft.com/en-us/sdl/default.aspx).

The Software Assurance Forum for Excellence in Code (SAFECode) is an organization formed by some of the leading software development firms with the objective of advancing software assurance through better development methods. SAFECode (www.safecode.org) members include EMC, Microsoft, and Intel. An examination of SAFECode members' processes reveals an assertion that secure coding must be treated as an issue that exists throughout the development process and cannot be effectively treated at a few checkpoints with checklists. Regardless of the software development process used, the first step down the path to secure coding is to infuse the process with secure coding principles.

Threat Modeling and Attack Surface Area Minimization

Two important tools have come from the secure coding revolution: threat modeling and attack surface area minimization. Attack surface area minimization is a strategy to reduce the places where code can be attacked.

The second major design effort is one built around *threat modeling,* the process of analyzing threats and their potential effects on software in a very finely detailed fashion. The output of the threat model process is a compilation of threats and how they interact with the software. This information is communicated across the design and coding team, so that potential weaknesses can be mitigated before the software is released.

Threat Modeling Steps

Follow the steps used to conduct threat modeling.

Step 1   *Define scope.* Communicate what is in scope and out of scope with respect to the threat modeling effort. This includes both attacks and software components.

Step 2   *Enumerate assets.* List all of the component parts of the software being examined.

Step 3   *Decompose assets.* Break apart the software into small subsystems composed of inputs and outputs. This is to simplify data flow analysis and to capture internal entry points.

Step 4   *Enumerate threats.* List all the threats to the software.

Step 5   *Classify threats.* Classify the threats by their mode of operation.

Step 6   *Associate threats to assets.* Connect specific threats and modes to specific software subsystems.

Step 7   *Score and rank threats.* Score each specific threat–asset pair and then rank them from most dangerous to least dangerous.

Step 8   *Create threat trees.* Create a graphical representation of the required elements for an attack vector.

Step 9   *Determine and score mitigation.* Score the mitigation efforts associated with each attack vector.

For more details on threat modeling, see http://msdn.microsoft.com/en-us/security/aa570411.aspx.

Requirements Phase

The **requirements phase** should define the specific security requirements if there is any expectation of them being designed into the project. Regardless of the methodology employed, the process is all about completing the requirements. Secure coding does not refer to adding security functionality into a piece of software. Security functionality is a standalone requirement. The objective of the secure coding process is to properly implement this and all other requirements, so that the resultant software performs as desired and only as desired.

The requirements process is a key component of security in software development. Security-related items enumerated during the requirements process are visible throughout the rest of the software development process. They can be architected into the systems and subsystems, addressed during coding, and tested. For the subsequent steps to be effective, the security requirements need to be both specific and positive. Requirements such as "make secure code" or "no insecure code" are nonspecific and not helpful in the overall process. Specific requirements such as "prevent unhandled buffer overflows and unhandled input exceptions" can be specifically coded for in each piece of code.

During the requirements activity, it is essential that the project/program manager and any business leaders who set schedules and allocate resources are aware of the need and requirements of the secure development process. The cost of adding security at a later time rises exponentially, with the most expensive form being the common release-and-patch process used by many firms. The development of both functional and nonfunctional security requirements occurs in tandem with other requirements through the development of use cases, analysis of customer inputs, implementation of company policies, and compliance with industry best practices. Depending on the nature of a particular module, special attention may be focused on sensitive issues such as personally identifiable information (PII), sensitive data, or intellectual property data.

One of the outputs of the requirements phase is a security document that helps guide the remaining aspects of the development process, ensuring that secure code requirements are being addressed. These requirements can be infused into design, coding, and testing, ensuring they are addressed throughout the development process.

Design Phase

Coding without designing first is like building a house without using plans. This might work fine on small projects, but as the scope grows, so do complexity and the opportunity for failure. Designing a software project is a multifaceted process. Just as there are many ways to build a house, there are many ways to build a program. Design is a process involving trade-offs and choices, and the criteria used during the design decisions can have lasting impacts on program construction. There are two secure coding principles that can be applied during the design phase that can have a large influence on the code quality. The first of these is the concept of *minimizing attack surface area*. Reducing the avenues of attack available to a hacker can have obvious benefits. Minimizing attack surface area is a concept that tends to run counter to the way software has been designed—most designs come as a result of incremental accumulation, adding features and functions without regard to maintainability.

Coding Phase

The point at which the design is implemented is the coding step in the software development process. The act of instantiating an idea into code is a point where an error can enter the process. These errors are of two types: the failure to include desired functionality, and the inclusion of undesired behavior in the code. Testing for the first type of error is relatively easy if the requirements are enumerated in a previous phase of the process.

Testing for the inclusion of undesired behavior is significantly more difficult. Testing for an *unknown* is a virtually impossible task. What makes this possible at all is the concept of testing for categories of previously determined errors. Several classes of common errors have been observed. Enumerations of known software weaknesses and vulnerabilities have been compiled and published as the **Common Weakness Enumeration (CWE)** and **Common Vulnerabilities and Exposures (CVE)** by the MITRE Corporation, a government-funded research group (www.mitre.org). These enumerations have enabled significant advancement in the development of methods to reduce code vulnerabilities. The CVE and CWE are vendor- and language-neutral methods of describing errors. These enumerations allow a common vocabulary for communication about weaknesses and vulnerabilities. This common vocabulary has also led to the development of automated tools to manage the tracking of these issues.

There are many common coding errors, but some of the primary and most damaging are least privilege violations and cryptographic failures. Language-specific failures are another common source of vulnerabilities.

There are several ways to go about searching for coding errors that lead to vulnerabilities in software. One method is by manual code inspection. Developers can be trained to "not make mistakes," but this approach has not proven successful. This has led to the development of a class of tools designed to analyze code for potential defects.

Static code-analysis tools are a type of tool that can be used to analyze software for coding errors that can lead to known types of vulnerabilities and weaknesses. Sophisticated static code analyzers can examine codebases to find function calls of unsafe libraries, potential buffer-overflow conditions, and numerous other conditions. Currently, the CWE describes more than 750 different weaknesses, far too many for developer memory and direct knowledge. In light of this, and due to the fact that some weaknesses are more prevalent than others, MITRE has collaborated with SANS to develop the **CWE/SANS Top 25 Most Dangerous Software Errors** list. One of the ideas behind the **Top 25 list** is that it can be updated periodically as the threat landscape changes. Explore the current listing at http://cwe.mitre.org/top25/.

There are two main enumerations of common software errors: the Top 25 list maintained by MITRE and the OWASP Top Ten list for web applications. Depending on the type of application being evaluated, these lists provide a solid starting point for security analysis of known error types. MITRE is the repository of the industry standard list for standard programs, and OWASP is for web applications. As the causes of common errors do not change quickly, these lists are not updated every year.

Least Privilege   One of the central paradigms of security is the notion of running a process with the least required privilege. **Least privilege** requires that the developer understand what privileges are needed specifically for an application to execute and access all its necessary resources. Obviously, from a developer point of view, it would be easier to use administrative-level permission for all tasks, which removes access controls from the equation, but this also removes the very protections that access-level controls are designed to provide. The other end of the spectrum is software designed for operating systems without any built-in security, such as early versions of Windows and some mainframe OSs, where security comes in the form of an application package. When migrating these applications to platforms, the issue of access controls arises.

As developers increasingly are tasked with incorporating security into their work, the natural tendency is to code around this "new" security requirement, developing in the same fashion as before, as if security is not

2011 CWE/SANS Top 25 Most Dangerous Software Errors

SQL Injection

OS Command Injection

Buffer Overflow

Cross-Site Scripting (XSS)

Missing Authentication for Critical Function

Missing Authorization

Use of Hard-coded Credentials

Missing Encryption of Sensitive Data

Unrestricted Upload of File with Dangerous Type

Reliance on Untrusted Inputs in a Security Decision

Execution with Unnecessary Privileges

Cross-Site Request Forgery (CSRF)

Improper Limitation of a Pathname to a Restricted Directory ('Path Traversal')

Download of Code Without Integrity Check

Incorrect Authorization

Inclusion of Functionality from Untrusted Control Sphere

Incorrect Permission Assignment for Critical Resource

Use of Potentially Dangerous Function

Use of a Broken or Risky Cryptographic Algorithm

Incorrect Calculation of Buffer Size

Improper Restriction of Excessive Authentication Attempts

URL Redirection to Untrusted Site ('Open Redirect')

Uncontrolled Format String

Integer Overflow or Wraparound

Use of a One-Way Hash without a Salt

Developers who do development and testing on an integrated environment on their own PC—that is, they have a web server and/or database engine on their PC—can produce code that works fine on their machine, where unified account permissions exist (and are frequently administrator). When this code is transitioned to a distributed environment, permissions can become an issue. The proper method is to manage permissions appropriately on the developer box from the beginning.

an issue. This is commonly manifested as a program that runs only under an administrative-level account, or runs as a service utilizing the SYSTEM account for permissions in Windows. Both of these practices are bad practices that reduce security, introduce hard-to-fix errors, and produce code that is harder to maintain and extend.

The key principle in designing and coding software with respect to access-level controls is to plan and understand the nature of the software's interaction with the operating system and system resources. Whenever the software accesses a file, a system component, or another program, the issue of appropriate access control needs to be addressed. And although the simple practice of just giving everything root or administrative access may solve this immediate problem, it creates much bigger security issues that will be much less apparent in the future. An example is when a program runs correctly when initiated from an administrator account but fails when run under normal user privileges. The actual failure may stem from a privilege issue, but the actual point of failure in the code may be many procedures away, and diagnosing these types of failures is a difficult and time-consuming operation.

The bottom line is actually simple. Determine what needs to be accessed and what the appropriate level of permission is, then use that level in design and implementation. Repeat this for every item accessed. In the end, it is rare that administrative access is needed for many functions. Once the application is designed, the whole process will need to be repeated with the installation procedure, because frequently, installing software will need a higher level of access than needed for executing the software. Design and implementation details must be determined with respect to required permission levels, not to a higher level such as administrative root access just for convenience.

The cost of failure to heed the principle of least privilege can be twofold. First, you have expensive, time-consuming access-violation errors that are hard to track down and correct. The second problem is when an exploit is found that allows some other program to use portions of your code in an unauthorized fashion. A prime example is the sendmail exploit in the UNIX environment. Because sendmail requires root-level access for some functions, the sendmail exploit inserts foreign code into the process stream, thereupon executing its code at root-level access because the sendmail process thread itself has root-level access. In this case, sendmail needs the root-level access, but this exploit illustrates that the risk is real and will be exploited once found. Proper design can, in many cases, eliminate the need for such high access privilege levels.

Cryptographic Failures Hailed as a solution for all problems, cryptography has as much chance of being the ultimate cure-all as did the tonics sold by traveling salesmen of a different era. There is no such thing as a universal solution, yet there are some very versatile tools that provide a wide range of protections. Cryptography falls into this "very useful tool" category. Proper use of cryptography can provide a wealth of programmatic functionality, from authentication and confidentiality to integrity and nonrepudiation. These are valuable tools, and many programs rely on proper cryptographic function for important functionality. The need for this functionality in an application tempts programmers to roll their own cryptographic functions. This is a task fraught with opportunity for catastrophic error.

Cryptographic errors come from several common causes. One typical mistake is choosing to develop your own cryptographic algorithm. Development of a secure cryptographic algorithm is far from an easy task, and even when done by experts, weaknesses can occur that make them unusable. Cryptographic algorithms become trusted after years of scrutiny and attacks, and any new algorithms would take years to join the trusted set. If you instead decide to rest on secrecy, be warned that secret or proprietary algorithms have never provided the desired level of protection. One of the axioms of cryptography is that there is no security through obscurity.

Deciding to use a trusted algorithm is a proper start, but there still are several major errors that can occur. The first is an error in instantiating the algorithm. An easy way to avoid this type of error is to use a library function that has already been properly tested. Sources of these library functions

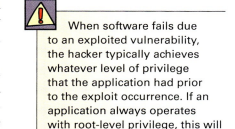
When software fails due to an exploited vulnerability, the hacker typically achieves whatever level of privilege that the application had prior to the exploit occurrence. If an application always operates with root-level privilege, this will pass on to the hacker as well.

Tech Tip

Only Use Approved Cryptographic Functions
Always use vetted and approved libraries for all cryptographic work. Never create your own cryptographic functions, even when using known algorithms. For example, the .NET Framework has a number of cryptography classes that developers can call upon to perform encryption services.

abound, and they provide an economical solution to this functionality's needs. Once you have an algorithm, and have chosen a particular instantiation, the next item needed is the random number to generate a random key. Cryptographic functions use an algorithm and a key, the latter being a digital number.

The generation of a real random number is not a trivial task. Computers are machines that are renowned for reproducing the same output when given the same input, so generating a pure, nonreproducible random number is a challenge. There are functions for producing random numbers built into the libraries of most programming languages, but these are pseudorandom number generators, and although the distribution of output numbers appears random, it generates a reproducible sequence. Given the same input, a second run of the function will produce the same sequence of "random" numbers. Determining the seed and random sequence and using this knowledge to "break" a cryptographic function has been used more than once to bypass the security. This method was used to subvert an early version of Netscape's SSL implementation. Using a number that is **cryptographically random**—suitable for an encryption function—resolves this problem, and again the use of trusted library functions designed and tested for generating such numbers is the proper methodology.

Now you have a good algorithm and a good random number—so where can you go wrong? Well, storing private keys in areas where they can be recovered by an unauthorized person is the next worry. Poor key management has failed many a cryptographic implementation. A famous exploit of getting cryptographic keys from an executable and using them to break a cryptographic scheme is the case of hackers using this exploit to break DVD encryption and develop the DeCSS program. Tools have been developed that can search code for "random" keys and extract the key from the code or running process. The bottom line is simple: do not hard-code secret keys in your code. They can, and will, be discovered. Keys should be generated, and then passed by reference, minimizing the travel of copies across a network or application. Storing them in memory in a noncontiguous fashion is also important, to prevent external detection. Again, trusted cryptographic library functions come to the rescue.

You might have deduced by this point that the term "library function" has become synonymous with this section. This is not an accident. In fact, this is probably one of the best pieces of advice from this chapter: use commercially proven functions for cryptographic functionality.

Language-Specific Failures Modern programming languages are built around libraries that permit reuse and speed the development process. The development of many library calls and functions was done without regard to secure coding implications, and this has led to issues related to specific library functions. As mentioned previously, **strcpy()** has had its fair share of involvement in buffer overflows and should be avoided. Developing and maintaining a series of **deprecated functions** and prohibiting their use in new code, while removing them from old code when possible, is a proven path toward more secure code.

Banned functions are easily handled via automated code reviews during the check-in process. The challenge is in garnering the developer awareness as to the potential dangers and the value of safer coding practices.

Exam Tip: Never hard-code secrets into code bases. Hackers can use disassemblers and various code differential tools to dissect your code and find static information.

Tech Tip

Microsoft Recommended Deprecated C Functions

Function families to deprecate/ remove:

- *strcpy() and strncpy()*
- *strcat() and strncat()*
- *scanf()*
- *sprint()*
- *gets()*
- *memcpy(), CopyMemory(), and RtlCopyMemory()*

Testing Phase

If the requirements phase marks the beginning of the generation of security in code, then the **testing phase** marks the other boundary. Although there are additional functions after testing, no one wants a user to validate errors in code. And errors discovered after the code has shipped are the most expensive to fix, regardless of the severity. Employing **use cases** to compare program responses to known inputs and then comparing the output to the desired output is a proven method of testing software. The design of use cases to test specific functional requirements occurs based on the requirements determined in the requirements phase. Providing additional security-related use cases is the process-driven way of ensuring that security specifics are also tested.

The testing phase is the last opportunity to determine that the software performs properly before the end user experiences problems. Errors found in testing are late in the development process, but at least they are still learned about internally, before the end customer suffers. Testing can occur at each level of development: module, subsystem, system, and completed application. The sooner errors are discovered and corrected, the lower the cost and the lesser the impact will be to project schedules. This makes testing an essential step in the process of developing good programs.

Testing for security requires a much broader series of tests than functional testing does. Misuse cases can be formulated to verify that vulnerabilities cannot be exploited. Fuzz testing (also known as *fuzzing*) uses random inputs to check for exploitable buffer overflows. Code reviews by design and development teams are used to verify that security elements such as input and output validation are functional, as these are the best defenses against a wide range of attacks, including cross-site scripting and cross-site request forgeries. Code walkthroughs begin with design reviews, architecture examinations, unit testing, subsystem testing, and, ultimately, complete system testing.

Testing includes **white-box testing**, where the test team has access to the design and coding elements; **black-box testing**, where the team does not have access; and **grey-box testing**, where the test team has more information than in black-box testing but not as much as in white-box testing. These modes of testing are used for different objectives; for example, fuzz testing works perfectly fine regardless of the type of testing, whereas certain types of penetration tests are better in a white-box testing environment. Testing is also performed on the production code to verify that error handling and exception reporting, which may provide detailed diagnostic information during development, are squelched to prevent information release during error conditions.

Final code can be subjected to *penetration tests,* designed specifically to test configuration, security controls, and common defenses such as input and output validation and error handling. Penetration testing can explore the functionality and whether or not specific security controls can be bypassed. Using the attack surface analysis information, penetration testers can emulate adversaries and attempt a wide range of known attack vectors in order to verify that the known methods of attack are all mitigated.

One of the most powerful tools that can be used in testing is **fuzzing**, the systematic application of a series of malformed inputs to test how the program responds. Fuzzing has been used by hackers for years to find potentially exploitable buffer overflows, without any specific knowledge of the coding. A tester can use a fuzzing framework to automate numerous input sequences. In examining whether a function can fall prey to a buffer overflow, numerous inputs can be run, testing lengths and ultimate payload-delivery options. If a particular input string results in a crash that can be exploited, this input would then be examined in detail. Fuzzing is new to the development scene but is rapidly maturing and will soon be on nearly equal footing with other automated code-checking tools.

Secure Coding Concepts

Application security begins with code that is secure and free of vulnerabilities. Unfortunately, all code has weaknesses and vulnerabilities, so instantiating the code in a manner that has effective defenses preventing the exploitation of vulnerabilities can maintain a desired level of security. Proper handling of configurations, errors and exceptions, and inputs can assist in the creation of a secure application. Testing of the application throughout the system life-cycle can be used to determine the actual security risk profile of a system.

There are numerous individual elements in the secure development lifecycle (SDL) that can assist a team in developing secure code. Correct SDL processes, such as input validation, proper error and exception handling, and cross-site scripting and cross-site request forgery mitigations, can improve the security of code. Process elements such as security testing, fuzzing, and patch management also help to ensure applications meet a desired risk profile.

Error and Exception Handling

Every application will encounter errors and exceptions, and these need to be handled in a secure manner. One attack methodology includes forcing errors to move an application from normal operation to exception handling. During an exception, it is common practice to record/report the condition, including supporting information such as the data that resulted in the error. This information can be invaluable in diagnosing the cause of the error condition. The challenge is in where this information is captured. The best method is to capture it in a log file, where it can be secured by an ACL. The worst case is when it is echoed to the user. Echoing error condition details to users can provide valuable information to attackers when they cause errors on purpose.

Improper exception handling can lead to a wide range of disclosures. Errors associated with SQL statements can disclose data structures and data elements. Remote procedure call (RPC) errors can give up sensitive information such as filenames, paths, and server names. Programmatic errors can give up line numbers that an exception occurred on, the method that was invoked, and information such as stack elements.

Exam Tip: All errors/ exceptions should be trapped and handled in the generating routine.

Input and Output Validation

With the move to web-based applications, the errors have shifted from buffer overflows to input-handling issues. Users have the ability to manipulate input, so it is up to the developer to handle the input appropriately to prevent malicious entries from having an effect. Buffer overflows could be considered a class of improper input, but newer attacks include canonicalization attacks and arithmetic attacks. Probably the most important defensive mechanism that can be employed is input validation. Considering all inputs to be hostile until properly validated can mitigate many attacks based on common vulnerabilities. This is a challenge, as the validation efforts need to occur after all parsers have completed manipulating input streams, a common function in web-based applications using Unicode and other international character sets.

Input validation is especially well suited for the following vulnerabilities: buffer overflow, reliance on untrusted inputs in a security decision, cross-site scripting, cross-site request forgery, path traversal, and incorrect calculation of buffer size. Input validation may seem suitable for various injection attacks, but given the complexity of the input and the ramifications from legal but improper input streams, this method falls short for most injection attacks. What can work is a form of recognition and whitelisting approach, where the input is validated and then parsed into a standard structure that is then executed. This restricts the attack surface to not only legal inputs but also expected inputs.

In today's computing environment, a wide range of character sets is used. Unicode allows multilanguage support. Character codesets allow multilanguage capability. Various encoding schemes, such as hex encoding, are supported to allow diverse inputs. The net result of all these input methods is that there are numerous ways to create the same input to a program. *Canonicalization* is the process by which application programs manipulate strings to a base form, creating a foundational representation of the input. **Canonicalization errors** arise from the fact that inputs to a web application may be processed by multiple applications, such as the web server, application server, and database server, each with its own parsers to resolve appropriate canonicalization issues. Where this is an issue relates to the form of the input string at the time of error checking. If the error-checking routine occurs prior to resolution to canonical form, then issues may be missed. The string representing /../, used in directory traversal attacks, can be obscured by encoding and hence missed by a character string match before an application parser manipulates it to canonical form.

The first line of defense is to write solid code. Regardless of the language used, or the source of outside input, prudent programming practice is to treat all input from outside a function as hostile. Validate all inputs as if they were hostile and an attempt to force a buffer overflow. Accept the notion that although during development everyone may be on the same team, be conscientious, and be compliant with design rules, future maintainers may not be as robust.

A second, and equally important, line of defense is proper string handling. String handling is a common event in programs, and string-handling functions are the source of a large number of known buffer-overflow vulnerabilities. Using **strncpy()** in place of **strcpy()** is a possible method of improving security because **strncpy()** requires an input length for the number of characters to be copied. This simple function call replacement can ultimately fail, however, because Unicode and other encoding methods can make character counts meaningless. To resolve this issue requires new library calls, and much closer attention to how input strings, and subsequently output strings, can be abused. Proper use of functions to achieve program objectives is essential to prevent unintended effects such as buffer

A Rose Is a Rose Is a r%6fse

Canonical form refers to simplest form, *and, due to the many encoding schemes in use, can be a complex issue. Characters can be encoded in ASCII, Unicode, hex, UTF-8, or even combinations of these. So, if the attacker desires to obfuscate his response, then several things can happen.*

By URL encoding URL strings, it may be possible to circumvent filter security systems and IDS:

```
http://www.myweb.com/cgi?file=/etc/passwd
```

can become

```
http://www.myweb.com/cgi?file=/
%2F%65%74%63%2F%70%61%73%73%77%64
```

Double encoding can complicate the matter even further. Round 1 decoding

```
scripts/..%255c../winnt
```

becomes

```
scripts/..%5c../winnt
(%25 = "%" Character)
```

Round 2 decoding

```
scripts/..%5c../winnt
```

becomes

```
scripts/..\../winnt
```

The bottom line is simple: Know that encoding can be used, and plan for it when designing input verification mechanisms. Expect encoded transmissions to be used to attempt to bypass security mechanisms.

overflows. Use of the **gets()** function can probably never be totally safe since it reads from the *stdin* stream until a linefeed or carriage return. In most cases, there is no way to predetermine whether the input is going to overflow the buffer. A better solution is to use a C++ stream object or the **fgets()** function. The function **fgets()** requires an input buffer length, and hence avoids the overflow. Simply replace

```
{
    char buf[512];
    gets( buf );  ← if buf is > 512 bytes, overflow will
occur
/*      The rest of your code ... */
}
```

with

```
{
    char buf[512];
    fgets( buf, sizeof(buf), stdin );
    /* ... the rest of your code ... */
}
```

Output validation is just as important in many cases as input validation. If querying a database for a username and password match, the expected forms of the output of the match function should be either one match or none. If using record count to indicate the level of match, which is a common practice, then a value other than 0 or 1 would be an error. Defensive coding using output validation would not act on values >1, as these are clearly an error and should be treated as a failure.

Fuzzing

One of the most powerful tools that can be used in testing is *fuzzing* (a.k.a. fuzz testing), which is the systematic application of a series of malformed inputs to test how the program responds. Fuzzing has been used by hackers for years to find potentially exploitable buffer overflows, without any specific knowledge of the coding. Fuzz testing works perfectly fine regardless of the type of testing, white box or black box. Fuzzing serves as a best practice for finding unexpected input validation errors.

A tester can use a fuzzing framework to automate numerous input sequences. In examining whether a function can fall prey to a buffer overflow, a tester can run numerous inputs, testing lengths and ultimate payload-delivery options. If a particular input string results in a crash that can be exploited, the tester would then examine this input in detail. Fuzzing is still relatively new to the development scene but is rapidly maturing and will soon be on nearly equal footing with other automated code-checking tools.

Bug Tracking

Bug tracking is a foundational element in secure development. All bugs are enumerated, classified, and tracked. If the classification of a bug exceeds a set level, then it must be resolved before the code advances to the next level of development. Bugs are classified based on the risk the vulnerability exposes. Microsoft uses four levels:

Critical A security vulnerability having the highest potential for damage

Important A security vulnerability having significant potential for damage, but less than Critical

Moderate A security vulnerability having moderate potential for damage, but less than Important

Low A security vulnerability having low potential for damage

Examples of Critical vulnerabilities include those that without warning to the user can result in remote exploit involving elevation of privilege. Critical is really reserved for the most important risks. As an example of the distinction between Critical and Important, a vulnerability that would lead to a machine failure requiring reinstallation of software would only score Important. The key difference is that the user would know of this penetration and risk, whereas for a Critical vulnerability, the user may never know that it occurred.

The tracking of errors serves several purposes. First, from a management perspective, what is measured is managed, both by management and by those involved. Over time, fewer errors will occur if the workforce knows they are being tracked, taken seriously, and represent an issue with the product. Second, since not all errors are immediately correctable, this enables future correction when a module is rewritten. Zero defects in code is like zero defects in quality: not an achievable objective. But this does not mean that constant improvement of the process cannot dramatically reduce the error rates. Evidence from firms involved in SAFECode support this, as they are reaping the benefits of lower error rates and reduced development costs from lower levels of corrective work.

■ Application Attacks

Attacks against a system can occur at the network level, at the operating system level, at the application level, or at the user level (social engineering). Early attack patterns were against the network, but most of today's attacks are aimed at the applications, primarily because that is where the objective of most attacks resides—in the infamous words of bank robber Willie Sutton, "because that's where the money is." In fact, many of today's attacks on systems use combinations of vulnerabilities in networks, operating systems, and applications, all means to an end to obtain the desired objective of an attack, which is usually some form of data.

Application-level attacks take advantage of several facts associated with computer applications. First, most applications are large programs written by groups of programmers, and by their nature have errors in design and coding that create vulnerabilities. For a list of typical vulnerabilities, see the Common Vulnerabilities and Exposures (CVE) list maintained by MITRE (http://cve.mitre.org). Second, even when vulnerabilities are discovered and patched by software vendors, end users are slow to apply patches, as evidenced by the SQL Slammer incident in January 2003. The vulnerability exploited was a buffer overflow, and the vendor supplied a patch six months prior to the outbreak, yet the worm still spread quickly due to the multitude of unpatched systems.

Cross-Site Scripting

Cross-site scripting (XSS) is one of the most common web attack methodologies.

A cross-site scripting attack is a code injection attack in which an attacker sends code in response to an input request. This code is then rendered by the web server, resulting in the execution of the code by the web server. Cross-site scripting attacks take advantage of a few common elements in web-based systems. First is the common failure to perform complete input validation. XSS sends script in response to an input request, even when script is not the expected or authorized input type. Second is the nature of web-based systems to dynamically self-create output. Web-based systems are frequently collections of images, text, scripts, and more, which are presented by a web server to a browser that interprets and renders. XSS attacks can exploit the dynamically self-created output by executing a script in the client browser that receives the altered output.

Cross-site scripting is abbreviated XSS to distinguish it from Cascading Style Sheets (CSS).

The cause of the vulnerability is weak user input validation. If input is not validated properly, an attacker can include a script in their input and have it rendered as part of the web process. There are several different types of XSS attacks, which are distinguished by the effect of the script:

- **Nonpersistent XSS attack**   The injected script is not persisted or stored, but rather is immediately executed and passed back via the web server.

- **Persistent XSS attack**   The script is permanently stored on the web server or some back-end storage. This allows the script to be used against others who log into the system.

- **DOM-based XSS attack**   The script is executed in the browser via the Document Object Model (DOM) process as opposed to the web server.

Cross-site scripting attacks can result in a wide range of consequences, and in some cases, the list can be anything that a clever scripter can devise. Common uses that have been seen in the wild include the following:

- Theft of authentication information from a web application
- Session hijacking
- Deploying hostile content
- Changing user settings, including future users
- Impersonating a user
- Phishing or stealing sensitive information

Controls to defend against XSS attacks include the use of anti-XSS libraries to strip scripts from the input sequences. Various other ways to mitigate XSS attacks include limiting types of uploads and screening the size of uploads, whitelisting inputs, and so on, but attempting to remove scripts from inputs can be a tricky task. Well-designed anti-XSS input library functions have proven to be the best defense. Cross-site scripting vulnerabilities are easily tested for and should be a part of the test plan for every application. Testing a variety of encoded and unencoded inputs for scripting vulnerability is an essential test element.

Injections

Use of input to a function without validation has already been shown to be risky behavior. Another issue with unvalidated input is the case of **code injection**. Rather than the input being appropriate for the function, this code injection changes the function in an unintended way. A **SQL injection** attack is a form of code injection aimed at any Structured Query Language (SQL)–based database, regardless of vendor.

The primary method of defense against this type of vulnerability is similar to that for buffer overflows: validate all inputs. But rather than validating toward just length, you need to validate inputs for content. Imagine a web page that asks for user input, and then uses that input in the building of a subsequent page. Now imagine that the user puts the text for a JavaScript function in the middle of their input sequence, along with a call to the script. Now, the generated web page has an added JavaScript function that is called when displayed. Passing the user input through an **HTMLencode** function before use can prevent such attacks.

Again, good programming practice goes a long way toward preventing these types of vulnerabilities. This places the burden not just on the programmers, but also on the process of training programmers, the software engineering process that reviews code, and the testing process to catch programming errors. This is much more than a single-person responsibility; everyone involved in the software development process needs to be aware of the types and causes of these errors, and safeguards need to be in place to prevent their propagation.

SQL Injection

A SQL injection attack is a form of code injection aimed at any Structured Query Language (SQL)–based database, regardless of vendor. An example of this type of attack is where the function takes the user-provided inputs for username and password and substitutes them into a *where* clause of a SQL statement with the express purpose of changing the *where* clause into one that gives a false answer to the query.

Assume the desired SQL statement is

```
select count(*) from users_table where username = 'JDoe' and
password = 'newpass'
```

The values JDoe and newpass are provided from the user and are simply inserted into the string sequence. Though seemingly safe functionally, this can be easily corrupted by using the sequence

```
' or 1=1 —
```

since this changes the *where* clause to one that returns all records:

```
select count(*) from users_table where username = 'JDoe' and
password = '' or 1=1 —'
```

The addition of the *or* clause, with an always true statement and the beginning of a comment line to block the trailing single quote, alters the SQL statement to one in which the *where* clause is rendered inoperable.

LDAP Injection

LDAP-based systems are also subject to injection attacks. When an application constructs an LDAP request based on user input, a failure to validate the input can lead to bad LDAP requests. Just as the SQL injection can be used to execute arbitrary commands in a database, the LDAP injection can do the same in a directory system. Something as simple as a wildcard character (*) in a search box can return results that would normally be beyond the scope of a query. Proper input validation is important before passing the request to an LDAP engine.

XML Injection

XML can be tampered with via injection as well. XML injections can be used to manipulate an XML-based system. As XML is nearly ubiquitous in the web application world, this form of attack has a wide range of targets.

Defense Against Injection Attacks

The primary method of defense against injection attacks is similar to that for buffer overflows: validate all inputs. But rather than validating toward just length, you need to validate inputs for content. Imagine a web page that asks for user input, and then uses that input in the building of a subsequent page. Also imagine that the user puts the text for a JavaScript function in the middle of their input sequence, along with a call to the script. Now, the generated web page has an added JavaScript function that is called when displayed. Passing the user input through an **HtmlEncode** function before use can prevent such attacks.

> **Exam Tip:** For the exam, you should understand injection-type attacks and how they manipulate the systems they are injecting, SQL, LDAP, and XML.

Directory Traversal/Command Injection

A directory traversal attack is when an attacker uses special inputs to circumvent the directory tree structure of the file system. Adding encoded symbols for "../.." in an unvalidated input box can result in the parser resolving the encoding to the traversal code, bypassing many detection elements, and passing the input to the file system and resulting in the program executing commands in a different location than designed. When combined with a command injection, the input can result in execution of code in an unauthorized manner. Classified as input validation errors, these can be difficult to detect without doing code walkthroughs and specifically looking for them. This illustrates the usefulness of the Top 25 Most Dangerous Software Errors checklist during code reviews, as it would alert developers to this issue during development.

Directory traversals can be masked by using encoding of input streams. If the security check is done before the string is decoded by the system parser, then recognition of the attack form may be impaired. There are many ways to represent a particular input form, the simplest of which is the canonical form (introduced earlier in the "A Rose Is a Rose Is a r%6fse" Tech Tip). Parsers are used to render the canonical form for the OS, but these embedded parsers may act after input validation, making it more difficult to detect certain attacks from just matching a string.

Buffer Overflow

If there's one item that could be labeled as the "Most Wanted" in coding security, it would be the **buffer overflow**. The CERT/CC at Carnegie Mellon University estimates that nearly half of all exploits of computer programs stem historically from some form of buffer overflow. Finding a vaccine to buffer overflows would stamp out half of these security-related incidents, by type, and probably 90 percent by volume. The Morris finger worm in 1988 was an exploit of an overflow, as were more recent big-name events such as Code Red and Slammer. The generic classification of buffer overflows includes many variants, such as static buffer overruns, indexing errors, format string bugs, Unicode and ANSI buffer size mismatches, and heap overruns.

The concept behind these vulnerabilities is relatively simple. The input buffer that is used to hold program input is overwritten with data that is larger than the buffer can hold. The root cause of this vulnerability is a mixture of two things: poor programming practice and programming language weaknesses. For example, what would happen if a program that asks for a 7- to 10-character phone number instead receives a string of 150 characters? Many programs will provide some error checking to ensure that this will not cause a problem. Some programs, however, cannot handle this error, and the extra characters continue to fill memory, overwriting other portions of the program. This can result in a number of problems, including causing the program to abort or the system to crash. Under certain circumstances, the program can execute a command supplied by the attacker. Buffer overflows typically inherit the level of privilege enjoyed by the program being exploited. This is why programs that use root-level access are so dangerous when exploited with a buffer overflow, as the code that will execute does so at root-level access.

Programming languages such as C were designed for space and performance constraints. Many functions in C, like **gets()**, are unsafe in that they will permit unsafe operations, such as unbounded string manipulation into fixed buffer locations. The C language also permits direct memory access via pointers, a functionality that provides a lot of programming power but carries with it the burden of proper safeguards being provided by the programmer.

Buffer overflows are input validation attacks, designed to take advantage of input routines that do not validate the length of inputs. Surprisingly simple to resolve, all that is required is the validation of all input lengths prior to writing to memory. This can be done in a variety of manners, including the use of safe library functions for inputs. This is one of the vulnerabilities that has been shown to be solvable, and in fact the prevalence is declining substantially among major security-conscious software firms.

Integer Overflow

An *integer overflow* is a programming error condition that occurs when a program attempts to store a numeric value, an integer, in a variable that is too small to hold it. The results vary by language and numeric type. In some cases, the value saturates the variable, assuming the maximum value for the defined type and no more. In other cases, especially with signed integers, it can roll over into a negative value, as the most significant bit is usually reserved for the sign of the number. This can create significant logic errors in a program.

Integer overflows are easily tested for, and static code analyzers can point out where they are likely to occur. Given this, there are not any good excuses for having these errors end up in production code.

Cross-Site Request Forgery

Cross-site request forgery (XSRF) attacks utilize unintended behaviors that are proper in defined use but are performed under circumstances outside the authorized use. This is an example of a "confused deputy" problem, a class of problems where one entity mistakenly performs an action on behalf of another. An XSRF attack relies upon several conditions to be effective. It is performed against sites that have an authenticated user and exploits the site's trust in a previous authentication event.

Then, by tricking a user's browser to send an HTTP request to the target site, the trust is exploited. Assume your bank allows you to log in and perform financial transactions, but does not validate the authentication for each subsequent transaction. If a user is logged in and has not closed their browser, then an action in another browser tab could send a hidden request to the bank, resulting in a transaction that appears to be authorized but in fact was not done by the user.

There are many different mitigation techniques that can be employed, from limiting authentication times, to cookie expiration, to managing some specific elements of a web page like header checking. The strongest method is the use of random XSRF tokens in form submissions. Subsequent requests cannot work, as the token was not set in advance. Testing for XSRF takes a bit more planning than for other injection-type attacks, but this, too, can be accomplished as part of the design process.

Zero-Day

Zero-day is a term used to define vulnerabilities that are newly discovered and not yet addressed by a patch. Most vulnerabilities exist in an unknown state until discovered by a researcher or the developer. If a researcher or developer discovers a vulnerability but does not share the information, then this vulnerability can be exploited without a vendor's ability to fix it, because for all practical knowledge the issue is unknown, except to the person who found it. From the time of discovery until a fix or patch is made available, the vulnerability goes by the name zero-day, indicating that it has not been addressed yet. The most frightening thing about zero-days is the unknown factor—their capability and effect on risk are unknown.

Attachments

Attachments can also be used as an attack vector. If a user inputs a graphics file (for instance, a JPEG file), and that file is altered to contain executable code such as Java, then when the image is rendered, the code is executed. This can enable a wide range of attacks.

Locally Shared Objects

Locally shared objects (LSOs) are pieces of data that are stored on a user's machine to save information from an application, such as a game. Frequently these are cookies used by Adobe Flash, called Flash Cookies, and can store information such as user preferences. As these can be manipulated outside of the application, they can represent a security or privacy threat.

Client-Side Attacks

The web browser has become the major application for users to engage resources across the Web. Web-based attacks are covered in detail in Chapter 17.

 Exam Tip: A wide variety of attack vectors can be used against a client machine, including cache poisoning, cross-site scripting, cross-user defacement, page hijacking, cookie manipulation, and open redirect. All attacks should be known for the exam.

Arbitrary/Remote Code Execution

One of the risks involved in taking user input and using it to create a command to be executed on a system is arbitrary or remote code execution. This attack involves an attacker preparing an input statement that changes the form or function of a prepared statement. A form of command injection, this attack can allow a user to insert arbitrary code and then remotely execute it on a system. This is a form of input validation failure, as users should not have the ability to change the way a program interacts with the host OS outside of a set of defined and approved methods.

CVE provides security personnel with a common language to use when discussing vulnerabilities. If one is discussing a specific vulnerability in the Flash object that allows an arbitrary execution of code, then using the nomenclature CVE-2005-2628 records the specifics of the vulnerability and ensures everyone is discussing the same problem.

Open Vulnerability and Assessment Language

The MITRE Corporation has done extensive research into software vulnerabilities. To enable collaboration between the many different parties involved in software development and maintenance, MITRE has developed a taxonomy of vulnerabilities, the *Common Vulnerabilities and Exposures (CVE)*. This is just one of the many related enumerations that MITRE has developed, in an effort to make machine-readable data exchanges to facilitate system management across large enterprises. The CVE led to efforts such as the development of the Open Vulnerability and Assessment Language (OVAL). OVAL comprises two main elements: an XML-based machine-readable language for describing vulnerabilities, and a repository; see http://oval.mitre.org.

In addition to the CVE and OVAL efforts, MITRE has developed a wide range of enumerations and standards designed to ease the automation of security management at the lowest levels across an enterprise. Additional efforts include the following:

- Common Attack Pattern Enumeration and Classification (CAPEC)
- Extensible Configuration Checklist Description Format (XCCDF)
- Security Content Automation Protocol (SCAP)
- Common Configuration Enumeration (CCE)
- Common Platform Enumeration (CPE)
- Common Weakness Enumeration (CWE)
- Common Event Expression (CEE)
- Common Result Format (CRF)

The *Common Weakness Enumeration (CWE)* is important for secure development in that it enumerates common patterns of development that lead to weakness and potential vulnerabilities. Additional information can be obtained from the MITRE Making Security Measurable web site, http://measurablesecurity.mitre.org.

■ Application Hardening

Application hardening works in the same fashion as system hardening (discussed in Chapter 14). The first step is the removal of unnecessary components or options. The second step is the proper configuration of the system as it is implemented. Every update or patch can lead to changes to these conditions, and they should be confirmed after every update.

The primary tools used to ensure a hardened system are a secure application configuration baseline and a patch management process. When properly employed, these tools can lead to the most secure system.

Application Configuration Baseline

A *baseline* is the set of proper settings for a computer system. An *application configuration baseline* outlines the proper settings and configurations for an application or set of applications. These settings include many elements, from application settings to security settings. Protection of the settings is crucial, and the most common mechanisms used to protect them include access control lists and protected directories. The documentation of the desired settings is an important security document, assisting administrators in ensuring that proper configurations are maintained across updates.

Application Patch Management

Application patch management is a fundamental component of application and system hardening. The objective is to be running the most secure version of an application, and, with very few exceptions, that would be the most current version of software, including patches. Most updates and patches include fixing security issues and closing vulnerabilities. Current patching is a requirement of many compliance schemes as well.

Patching does not always go as planned, and some patches may result in problems in production systems. A formal system of patch management is needed to test and implement patches in a change-controlled manner.

 Exam Tip: Patch management might be referred to as *update management*, *configuration management*, or *change management*. Although these terms are not strictly synonyms, they might be used interchangeably on the exam.

NoSQL Databases vs. SQL Databases

Current programming trends include topics such as whether to use SQL databases or NoSQL databases. SQL databases are those that use Structured Query Language to manipulate items that are referenced in a relational manner in the form of tables. *NoSQL* refers to data stores that employ neither SQL nor relational table structures. Each system has its strengths and weaknesses, and both can be used for a wide range of data storage needs.

SQL databases are by far the most common, with implementations by IBM, Microsoft, and Oracle being the major players. NoSQL databases tend to be custom-built using low-level languages and lack many of the standards of existing databases. This has not stopped the growth of NoSQL databases in large-scale, well-resourced environments.

The important factor in accessing data in a secure fashion is in the correct employment of programming structures and frameworks to abstract the access process. Methods such as inline SQL generation coupled with input validation errors is a recipe for disaster in the form of SQL injection attacks.

Server-Side vs. Client-Side Validation

In a modern client/server environment, data can be checked for compliance with input/output requirements either on the server or on the client. There

Exam Tip: All input validation should be performed on the server side of the client–server relationship, where it is free from outside influence and change.

are advantages to verifying data elements on a client before sending to the server—namely, efficiency. Doing checks on the client saves a round-trip, and its delays, before a user can be alerted to a problem. This can improve usability of software interfaces.

The client is not a suitable place to perform any critical value checks or security checks. The reasons for this are twofold. First, the client can change anything after the check. And second, the data can be altered while in transit or at an intermediary proxy. For all checks that are essential, either for business reasons or security, the verification steps should be performed on the server side, where the data is free from unauthorized alterations. Input validation checks can be safely performed only on the server side.

Chapter 18 Review

For More Information

- **SAFECode** www.safecode.org
- **DHS Build Security In** https://buildsecurityin.us-cert.gov
- **Microsoft SDL** www.microsoft.com/sdl
- **CVE** http://cve.mitre.org
- **CWE** http://cwe.mitre.org
- **CWE/SANS Top 25** http://cwe.mitre.org/top25/index.html

Chapter Summary

After reading this chapter and completing the exercises, you should understand the following about security issues related to software development.

Describe how secure coding can be incorporated into the software development process

- The requirements phase is the most important part of the software engineering process since it outlines the project's future requirements, thus defining its scope and limitations.
- The use of an enhanced lifecycle development process to include security elements will build security into the product.

List the major types of coding errors and their root causes

- The commonest coding error is a buffer-overflow condition.
- Code injection errors can result in undesired code execution as defined by the end user.
- Input validation is the best method of insuring against buffer overflows and code injection errors.

Describe good software development practices and explain how they impact application security

- Early testing helps resolve errors at an earlier stage and results in cleaner code.
- Security-related use cases can be used to test for specific security requirements.
- Fuzz testing can find a wide range of errors.

Describe how using a software development process enforces security inclusion in a project

- Security is built into the software by including security concerns and reviews throughout the software development process.
- Regardless of the specific software engineering process model used, security can be included in the normal process by being input as requirements.

Learn about application hardening techniques

- The first step in application hardening is determining the application configuration baseline.
- Applications require patching as well as the OS, and proper enterprise application patch management is important.
- All validations of client-to-server data need to be done on the server side, for this is the security controllable side of the communication.

Key Terms

agile model *(559)*

black-box testing *(567)*

buffer overflow *(575)*

canonicalization error *(569)*

code injection *(573)*

Common Vulnerabilities and Exposures (CVE) *(563)*

Common Weakness Enumeration (CWE) *(563)*

cryptographically random *(566)*

CWE/SANS Top 25 Most Dangerous Software Errors *(563)*

deprecated function *(566)*

evolutionary model *(559)*

fuzzing *(567)*

grey-box testing *(567)*

least privilege *(563)*

requirements phase *(561)*

secure development lifecycle (SDL) model *(559)*

spiral model *(559)*

SQL injection *(573)*

■ Key Terms Quiz

Use terms from the Key Terms list to complete the sentences that follow. Don't use the same term more than once. Not all terms will be used.

1. The _____ is a linear software engineering model with no repeating steps.

2. A(n) _____ causes an application to malfunction due to a misrepresented name for a resource.

3. CWE-20: Improper Input Validation refers to a(n) _____.

4. Using a series of malformed input to test for conditions such as buffer overflows is called _____.

5. Modifying a SQL statement through false input to a function is an example of _____.

6. Using an administrator-level account for all functions is a violation of the principle of _____.

7. The _____ is the first opportunity to address security functionality during a project.

8. The banning of _____ helps improve code quality by using safer library calls.

9. A(n) _____ is a vulnerability that has been discovered by hackers, but not by the developers of the software.

10. A number that is suitable for an encryption function is called _____.

■ Multiple-Choice Quiz

1. Which of the following is not related to a buffer overflow?

   A. Static buffer overflow

   B. Index error

   C. Canonicalization error

   D. Heap overflow

2. Which of the following is not involved with a code injection error?

   A. SQL statement building

   B. Input validation

   C. JavaScript

   D. A pointer in the C language

3. Input validation is important to prevent what?

   A. Buffer overflow

   B. Index sequence error

   C. Operator overload error

   D. Unhandled exception

4. It's most important to define security requirements during:

   A. Testing

   B. Use case development

   C. Code walkthroughs

   D. The requirements phase of the project

5. The largest class of errors in software engineering can be attributed to:

   A. Poor testing

   B. Privilege violations

   C. Improper input validation

   D. Canonicalization errors

6. Least privilege applies to:

   A. Only the application code

   B. Only to calls to operating system objects

   C. All resource requests from applications to other entities

   D. Applications under named user accounts

7. Common cryptographic failures include which of the following?

   A. Use of cryptographically random numbers

   B. Cryptographic sequence failures

   C. Poor encryption protocols

   D. Canonicalization errors

8. When is testing best accomplished?

   A. After all code is finished

   B. As early as possible in the process

   C. Using cryptographically random elements

   D. Using third-party testing software

9. Code review by a second party is helpful to do what?

   A. Increase creativity of the junior programmer

   B. Reduce cost—making for a better, cheaper method of testing

   C. Catch errors early in the programming process

   D. Ensure all modules work together

10. One of the most fundamental rules to good coding practice is:

   A. Code once, test twice.

   B. Validate all inputs.

   C. Don't use pointers.

   D. Use obscure coding practices so viruses cannot live in the code.

■ Essay Quiz

1. Describe the relationship of the requirements phase, testing phase, and use cases with respect to software engineering development and secure code.

2. Develop a list of five security-related issues to be put into a requirements document as part of a secure coding initiative.

3. Choose two requirements from the previous question and describe use cases that would validate them in the testing phase.

4. You have been asked by your manager to develop a worksheet for code walkthroughs, another name for structured code reviews. This worksheet should include a list of common errors to look for during the examination, acting as a memory aid. You want to leave a lasting impression on the team as a new college grad. Outline what you would include on the worksheet related to security.

Lab Projects

• Lab Project 18.1

Learn the specific software engineering process model used at a local firm (or you may be able to research a company online or find one in a software engineering textbook at a library).

Examine where security is built, or could be built, into the model. Provide an overview of the strengths and opportunities of the model with respect to designing secure code.

• Lab Project 18.2

Develop an example of a SQL injection statement for a web page inquiry. List the web page inputs, what the projected back-end SQL is, and how it can be changed.

chapter
19

Business Continuity and Disaster Recovery, and Organizational Policies

The superior man, when resting in safety, does not forget that danger may come. When in a state of security he does not forget the possibility of ruin. When all is orderly, he does not forget disorder may come. Thus his person is not endangered and his States and all their clans are preserved.

—CONFUCIUS

In this chapter, you will learn how to

- **Describe the various components of a business continuity plan**
- **Describe the elements of disaster recovery plans**
- **Describe the various ways backups are conducted and stored**
- **Explain different strategies for alternative site processing**

Much of this book focuses on avoiding the loss of confidentiality or integrity due to a security breach. The issue of availability is also discussed in terms of specific events, such as denial-of-service and distributed DoS attacks. In reality, however, there are many things that can disrupt the operations of your organization. From the standpoint of your clients and employees, whether your organization's web site is unavailable because of a storm or because of an intruder makes little difference—the site is still unavailable. In this chapter, we'll discuss what do to when a situation arises that results in the disruption of services. This discussion includes both disaster recovery and business continuity.

Business Continuity

Keeping an organization running when an event occurs that disrupts operations is not accomplished spontaneously but requires advance planning and periodically exercising those plans to ensure they will work. A term that is often used when discussing the issue of continued organizational operations is **business continuity (BC)**.

There are many risk management best practices associated with business continuity. The topics of planning, business impact analysis, identification of critical systems and components, single points of failure, and more are detailed in the following sections.

Exam Tip: The terms DR and BC are often used synonymously and sometimes together as in BC/DR, but there are subtle differences between them. Study this section carefully to ensure that you can discriminate between the two terms.

Business Continuity Plans

As in most operational issues, planning is a foundational element to success. This is true in business continuity, and the *business continuity plan (BCP)* represents the planning and advance policy decisions to ensure the business continuity objectives are achieved during a time of obvious turmoil. You might wonder what the difference is between a disaster recovery plan and a business continuity plan—after all, isn't the purpose of disaster recovery the continued operation of the organization or business during a period of disruption? Many times, these two terms are sometimes used synonymously, and for many organizations there may be no major difference in the two. There are, however, real differences between a BCP and a DRP, one of which is the *focus*.

The focus of a BCP is the continued operation of the essential elements business or organization. Business continuity is not about operations as normal, but rather about trimmed-down, essential operations only. Like life-support, good for a period to buy time to recover, but not a leaner way of running the operation. The focus of a DRP is on the recovery and rebuilding of the organization after a disaster has occurred. And this recovery is all the way back to a complete operation of all elements of the business. The DRP is part of the larger picture, while the BCP is a tactical necessity until operations can be restored. A major focus of the DRP is the protection of human life. Evacuation plans and system shutdown procedures should be addressed. The safety of employees should be a theme throughout a DRP. In a BCP, you will see a more significant emphasis placed on the limited number of critical systems the organization needs to operate. The BCP will describe the functions that are most critical, based on a previously conducted business impact analysis, and will describe the order in which functions should be returned to operation. The BCP describes what is needed in order for the business to continue to operate in the short term, even if all requirements are not met and risk profiles are changed.

Business Impact Analysis

Business impact analysis (BIA) is the term used to describe the document that details the specific impact of elements on a business operation (this may also be referred to as a *business impact assessment*). A BIA outlines what the loss of any of your critical functions will mean to the organization. The BIA is a foundational document used to establish a wide range of priorities, including system backups and restoration, which are needed in maintaining continuity of operation, and more. While each person may consider their individual tasks to be important, the BIA is a business-level analysis of the criticality of all elements with respect to the business as a whole. The BIA will take into account the increased risk from minimal operations, and is designed to determine and justify what is essentially critical for a business to survive versus what someone may state or wish.

Conducting a BIA is a critical part of developing your DRP. This assessment will allow you to focus on the most critical elements of your organization. These critical elements are the ones that you want to ensure are recovered first, and this priority should be reflected in your DRP.

Identification of Critical Systems and Components

A foundational element of a security plan is an understanding of the criticality of systems, the data, and the components. Identifying the critical systems and components is one of the first steps an organization needs to undertake in designing the set of security controls. As the systems evolve and change, the continued identification of the critical systems needs to occur, keeping the information up-to-date and current.

Removing Single Points of Failure

A key security methodology is to attempt to avoid a single point of failure in critical functions within an organization. When developing your BCP, you should be on the lookout for areas in which a critical function relies on a single item (such as switches, routers, firewalls, power supplies, software, or data) that if lost would stop this critical function. When these points are identified, think about how each of these possible single points of failure can be eliminated (or mitigated).

In addition to the internal resources you need to consider when evaluating your business functions, there are many resources external to your organization that can impact the operation of your business. You must look beyond hardware, software, and data to consider how the loss of various critical infrastructures can also impact business operations.

Risk Assessment

The principles of risk assessment can be applied to business continuity planning. Determining the sources and magnitudes of risks is necessary in all business operations, including business continuity planning.

Succession Planning

Business continuity planning is more than just ensuring that hardware is available and operational. The people who operate and maintain the system are also important, and in the event of a disruptive event, the availability of key personnel is as important as hardware for successful business continuity operations. The development of a succession plan that identifies key personnel and develops qualified personnel for key functions is a critical part of a successful BCP.

Continuity of Operations

The continuity of operations is imperative, as it has been shown that businesses that cannot quickly recover from a disruption have a real chance of never recovering, and they may go out of business. The overall goal of business continuity planning is to determine which subset of normal operations needs to be continued during periods of disruption.

Exam Tip: Business continuity is not only about hardware; plans need to include people as well. Succession planning is a proactive plan for personnel substitutions in the event that the primary person is not available to fulfill their assigned duties.

■ Disaster Recovery

Many types of disasters, whether natural or caused by people, can disrupt your organization's operations for some length of time. Such disasters are unlike threats that intentionally target your computer systems and networks, such as industrial espionage, hacking, attacks from disgruntled employees, and insider threats, because the events that cause the disruption are not specifically aimed at your organization. Although both disasters and intentional threats must be considered important in planning for disaster recovery, the purpose of this section is to focus on recovering from disasters.

How long your organization's operations are disrupted depends in part on how prepared it is for a disaster and what plans are in place to mitigate the effects of a disaster. Any of the following events could cause a disruption in operations:

fire	flood	tornado	hurricane
electrical storm	earthquake	political unrest/riot	blizzard
gas leak/explosion	chemical spill	terrorism	war
sabotage	network outage	human error	malware

Fortunately, these types of events do not happen frequently in any one location. It is more likely that business operations will be interrupted due to employee error (such as accidental corruption of a database or unplugging a system to plug in a vacuum cleaner—an event that has occurred at more than one organization). A good disaster recovery plan will prepare your organization for any type of organizational disruption.

Disaster Recovery Plans/Process

No matter what event you are worried about—whether natural or not, targeted at your organization or not—you can make preparations to lessen the impact on your organization and the length of time that your organization will be out of operation. A **disaster recovery plan (DRP)** is critical for effective

Disasters can be caused by nature (such as fires, earthquakes, and floods) or can be the result of some manmade event (such as war or a terrorist attack). The plans an organization develops to address a disaster need to recognize both of these possibilities. While many of the elements in a disaster recovery plan will be similar for both natural and manmade events, some differences might exist. For example, recovering data from backup tapes after a natural disaster can use the most recent backup available. If, on the other hand, the event was a loss of all data as a result of a computer virus that wiped your system, restoring from the most recent backup tapes might result in the reinfection of your system if the virus had been dormant for a planned period of time. In this case recovery might entail restoring some files from earlier backups.

Table 19.1	DRP Considerations	
Category	Level of the Function's Need	How Long Can the Organization Last Without the Function?
Critical	Absolutely essential for operations. Without the function, the basic mission of the organization cannot occur.	The function is needed immediately. The organization cannot function without it.
Necessary for normal processing	Required for normal processing, but the organization can live without it for a short period of time.	Can live without it for at most 30 days before your organization is severely impacted.
Desirable	Not needed for normal processing but enhances the organization's ability to conduct its mission efficiently.	Can live without the function for more than 30 days, but it is a function that will eventually need to be accomplished when normal operations are restored.
Optional	Nice to have but does not affect the operation of the organization.	Not essential, and no subsequent processing will be required to restore this function.
Consider eliminating	No discernible purpose for the function.	No impact to the organization; the function is not needed for any organizational purpose.

The difference between a DRP and BCP is that the BCP will be used to ensure that your operations continue in the face of whatever event has occurred that has caused a disruption in operations. If a disaster has occurred and has destroyed all or part of your facility, the DRP portion of the BCP will address the building or acquisition of a new facility. The DRP can also include details related to the long-term recovery of the organization.

However you view these two plans, an organization that is not able to quickly restore business functions after an operational interruption is an organization that will most likely suffer an unrecoverable loss and may cease to exist.

IT Contingency Planning

Important parts of any organization today are the information technology (IT) processes and assets. Without computers and networks, most organizations could not operate. As a result, it is imperative that a BCP includes IT contingency planning. Due to the nature of the Internet and the threats that come from it, an organization's IT assets will likely face some level of disruption before the organization suffers from a disruption due to a natural disaster. Events such as viruses, worms, computer intruders, and denial-of-service attacks could result in an organization losing part or all of its computing resources without warning. Consequently, the IT contingency plans are more likely to be needed than the other aspects of a BCP. These plans should account for disruptions caused by any of the security threats discussed throughout this book as well as disasters or simple system failures.

Test, Exercise, and Rehearse

An organization should practice its DRP periodically. The time to find out whether it has flaws is not when an actual event occurs and the recovery of data and information means the continued existence of the organization. The DRP should be tested to ensure that it is sufficient and that all key

Tech Tip

DRP vs. BCP

Although the terms DRP and BCP may be used synonymously in small firms, in large firms, there is a difference in focus between the two plans. The focus of the BCP is on continued operation of a business, albeit at a reduced level or through different means during some period of time. The DRP is focused specifically on recovering from a disaster. In many cases, both of these functions happen at the same time, and hence they are frequently combined in small firms and in many discussions. In large, complex entities, they are separate plans used to provide management options for a range of situations.

individuals know their role in the specific plan. The security plan determines if the organization's plan and the individuals involved perform as they should during a simulated security incident.

A test implies a "grade" will be applied to the outcome. Did the organization's plan and the individuals involved perform as they should? Was the organization able to recover and continue to operate within the predefined tolerances set by management? If the answer is no, then during the follow-up evaluation of the exercise, the failures should be identified and addressed. Was it simply a matter of untrained or uninformed individuals, or was there a technological failure that necessitates a change in hardware, software, and procedures?

Whereas a test implies a "grade," an exercise can be conducted without the stigma of a pass/fail grade being attached. *Security exercises* are conducted to provide the opportunity for all parties to practice the procedures that have been established to respond to a security incident. It is important to perform as many of the recovery functions as possible, without impacting ongoing operations, to ensure that the procedures and technology will work in a real incident. You may want to periodically rehearse portions of the recovery plan, particularly those aspects that either are potentially more disruptive to actual operations or require more frequent practice because of their importance or degree of difficulty.

Additionally, there are different formats for exercises with varying degrees of impact on the organization. The most basic is a checklist walk-through in which individuals go through a recovery checklist to ensure that they understand what to do should the plan be invoked and confirm that all necessary equipment (hardware and software) is available. This type of exercise normally does not reveal "holes" in a plan but will show where discrepancies exist in the preparation for the plan. To examine the completeness of a plan, a different type of exercise needs to be conducted. The simplest is a tabletop exercise in which participants sit around a table with a facilitator who supplies information related to the "incident" and the processes that are being examined. Another type of exercise is a functional test in which certain aspects of a plan are tested to see how well they work (and how well prepared personnel are). At the most extreme are full operational exercises designed to actually interrupt services in order to verify that all aspects of a plan are in place and sufficient to respond to the type of incident that is being simulated.

Tabletop Exercises

Exercising operational plans is an effort that can take on many different forms. For senior decision makers, the point of action is more typically a desk or a conference room, with their method being meetings and decisions. A common form of exercising operational plans for senior management is the tabletop exercise. The senior management team, or elements of it, are gathered together and presented a scenario. They can walk through their decision-making steps, communicate with others, and go through the motions of the exercise in the pattern in which they would likely be involved. The scenario is presented at a level to test the responsiveness of their decisions and decision-making process. Because the event is frequently run in a conference room, around a table, the name *tabletop exercise* has come to define this form of exercise.

Exercises are an often overlooked aspect of security. Many organizations do not believe that they have the time to spend on such events, but the question to ask is whether they can afford to *not* conduct these exercises, as they ensure the organization has a viable plan to recover from disasters and that operations can continue. Make sure you understand what is involved in these critical tests of your organization's plans.

Principles of Computer Security

Recovery Time Objective and Recovery Point Objective

The term **recovery time objective (RTO)** is used to describe the target time that is set for a resumption of operations after an incident. This is a period of time that is defined by the business, based on the needs of the enterprise. A shorter RTO results in higher costs because it requires greater coordination and resources. This term is commonly used in business continuity and disaster recovery operations.

Recovery point objective (RPO), a totally different concept from RTO, is the time period representing the maximum period of acceptable data loss. The RPO determines the frequency of backup operations necessary to prevent unacceptable levels of data loss. A simple example of establishing RPO is to answer the following questions: How much data can you afford to lose? How much rework is tolerable?

RTP and RPO are seemingly related but in actuality measure different things entirely. The RTO serves the purpose of defining the requirements for business continuity, while the RPO deals with backup frequency. It is possible to have an RTO of 1 day and an RPO of 1 hour, or an RTO of 1 hour and an RPO of 1 day. The determining factors are the needs of the business.

> Although recovery time objective and recovery point objective seem to be the same or similar, they are very different. The RTO serves the purpose of defining the requirements for business continuity, while the RPO deals with backup frequency.

Backups

A key element in any BC/DR plan is the availability of backups. This is true not only because of the possibility of a disaster, but also because hardware and storage media will periodically fail, resulting in loss or corruption of critical data. An organization might also find backups critical when security measures have failed and an individual has gained access to important information that may have become corrupted or at the very least can't be trusted. Data backup is thus a critical element in these plans, as well as in normal operation. There are several factors to consider in an organization's data backup strategy:

- How frequently should backups be conducted?
- How extensive do the backups need to be?
- What is the process for conducting backups?
- Who is responsible for ensuring backups are created?
- Where will the backups be stored?
- How long will backups be kept?
- How many copies will be maintained?

Keep in mind that the purpose of a backup is to provide valid, uncorrupted data in the event of corruption or loss of the original file or the media where the data was stored. Depending on the type of organization, legal requirements for maintaining backups can also affect how it is accomplished.

Tech Tip

Backups Are a Key Responsibility for Administrators
One of the most important tools a security administrator has is a backup. While backups will not prevent a security event (or natural disaster) from occurring, they often can save an organization from a catastrophe by allowing it to quickly return to full operation after an event occurs. Conducting frequent backups and having a viable backup and recovery plan are two of the most important responsibilities of a security administrator.

What Needs to Be Backed Up

Backups commonly comprise the data that an organization relies on to conduct its daily operations. While this is certainly essential, a good backup plan will consider more than just the data; it will include any application programs needed to process the data and the operating system and utilities that the hardware platform requires to run the applications. Obviously, the application programs and operating system will change much less frequently than the data itself, so the frequency with which these items need to be backed up is considerably different. This should be reflected in the organization's backup plan and strategy.

The BC/DR plan should also address other items related to backups. Personnel, equipment, and electrical power must also be part of the plan. Somebody needs to understand the operation of the critical hardware and software used by the organization. If the disaster that destroyed the original copy of the data and the original systems also results in the loss of the only personnel who know how to process the data, having backup data will not be enough to restore normal operations for the organization. Similarly, if the data requires specific software to be run on a very specific hardware platform, then having the data without the application program or required hardware will also not be sufficient.

Strategies for Backups

The process for creating a backup copy of data and software requires more thought than simply stating "copy all required files." The size of the resulting backup must be considered, as well as the time required to conduct the backup. Both of these will affect details such as how frequently the backup will occur and the type of storage medium that will be used for the backup. Other considerations include who will be responsible for conducting the backup, where the backups will be stored, and how long they should be maintained. Short-term storage for accidentally deleted files that users need to have restored should probably be close at hand. Longer-term storage for backups that may be several months or even years old should occur in a different facility. It should be evident by now that even something that sounds as simple as maintaining backup copies of essential data requires careful consideration and planning.

Types of Backups The amount of data that will be backed up, and the time it takes to accomplish this, has a direct bearing on the type of backup that should be performed. Table 19.2 outlines the four basic types of backups that can be conducted, the amount of space required for each, and the ease of restoration using each strategy.

The values for each of the strategies in Table 19.2 are highly variable depending on your specific environment. The more frequently files are changed between backups, the more these strategies will look alike. What each strategy entails bears further explanation.

The easiest type of backup to understand is the **full backup**. In a full backup, all files and software are copied onto the storage media. Restoration from a full backup is similarly straightforward—you must copy all the

Table 19.2	Backup Types and Characteristics			
	Full	**Differential**	**Incremental**	**Delta**
Amount of Space	Large	Medium	Medium	Small
Restoration	Simple	Simple	Involved	Complex

individuals know their role in the specific plan. The security plan determines if the organization's plan and the individuals involved perform as they should during a simulated security incident.

A test implies a "grade" will be applied to the outcome. Did the organization's plan and the individuals involved perform as they should? Was the organization able to recover and continue to operate within the predefined tolerances set by management? If the answer is no, then during the follow-up evaluation of the exercise, the failures should be identified and addressed. Was it simply a matter of untrained or uninformed individuals, or was there a technological failure that necessitates a change in hardware, software, and procedures?

Whereas a test implies a "grade," an exercise can be conducted without the stigma of a pass/fail grade being attached. *Security exercises* are conducted to provide the opportunity for all parties to practice the procedures that have been established to respond to a security incident. It is important to perform as many of the recovery functions as possible, without impacting ongoing operations, to ensure that the procedures and technology will work in a real incident. You may want to periodically rehearse portions of the recovery plan, particularly those aspects that either are potentially more disruptive to actual operations or require more frequent practice because of their importance or degree of difficulty.

Additionally, there are different formats for exercises with varying degrees of impact on the organization. The most basic is a checklist walk-through in which individuals go through a recovery checklist to ensure that they understand what to do should the plan be invoked and confirm that all necessary equipment (hardware and software) is available. This type of exercise normally does not reveal "holes" in a plan but will show where discrepancies exist in the preparation for the plan. To examine the completeness of a plan, a different type of exercise needs to be conducted. The simplest is a tabletop exercise in which participants sit around a table with a facilitator who supplies information related to the "incident" and the processes that are being examined. Another type of exercise is a functional test in which certain aspects of a plan are tested to see how well they work (and how well prepared personnel are). At the most extreme are full operational exercises designed to actually interrupt services in order to verify that all aspects of a plan are in place and sufficient to respond to the type of incident that is being simulated.

Exercises are an often overlooked aspect of security. Many organizations do not believe that they have the time to spend on such events, but the question to ask is whether they can afford to *not* conduct these exercises, as they ensure the organization has a viable plan to recover from disasters and that operations can continue. Make sure you understand what is involved in these critical tests of your organization's plans.

Tabletop Exercises

Exercising operational plans is an effort that can take on many different forms. For senior decision makers, the point of action is more typically a desk or a conference room, with their method being meetings and decisions. A common form of exercising operational plans for senior management is the tabletop exercise. The senior management team, or elements of it, are gathered together and presented a scenario. They can walk through their decision-making steps, communicate with others, and go through the motions of the exercise in the pattern in which they would likely be involved. The scenario is presented at a level to test the responsiveness of their decisions and decision-making process. Because the event is frequently run in a conference room, around a table, the name *tabletop exercise* has come to define this form of exercise.

files back onto the system. This process can take a considerable amount of time. Consider the size of even the average home PC today, for which storage is measured in tens and hundreds of gigabytes. Copying this amount of data takes time. In a full backup, the archive bit is cleared.

In a **differential backup**, only the files and software that have changed since the last full backup was completed are backed up. This also implies that periodically a full backup needs to be accomplished. The frequency of the full backup versus the interim differential backups depends on your organization and needs to be part of your defined strategy. Restoration from a differential backup requires two steps: the last full backup first needs to be loaded, and then the last differential backup performed can be applied to update the files that have been changed since the full backup was conducted. Again, this is not a difficult process, but it does take some time. The amount of time to accomplish the periodic differential backup, however, is much less than that for a full backup, and this is one of the advantages of this method. Obviously, if a lot of time has passed between differential backups, or if most files in your environment change frequently, then the differential backup does not differ much from a full backup. It should also be obvious that to accomplish the differential backup, the system has to have a method to determine which files have been changed since some given point in time. The archive bit is not cleared in a differential backup since the key for a differential is to back up all files that have changed since the last full backup.

With incremental backups, even less information will be stored in each backup. The **incremental backup** is a variation on a differential backup, with the difference being that instead of copying all files that have changed since the last full backup, the incremental backup backs up only files that have changed since the last full *or* incremental backup occurred, thus requiring fewer files to be backed up. Just as in the case of the differential backup, the incremental backup relies on the occasional full backup being accomplished. After that, you back up only files that have changed since the last backup of any sort was conducted. To restore a system using this type of backup method requires quite a bit more work. You first need to go back to the last full backup and reload the system with this data. Then you have to update the system with every incremental backup that has occurred since the full backup. The advantage of this type of backup is that it requires less storage and time to accomplish. The disadvantage is that the restoration process is more involved. Assuming that you don't frequently have to conduct a complete restoration of your system, however, the incremental backup is a valid technique. An incremental backup will clear the archive bit.

Finally, the goal of the **delta backup** is to back up as little information as possible each time you perform a backup. As with the other strategies, an occasional full backup must be accomplished. After that, when a delta backup is conducted at specific intervals, only the portions of the files that have been changed will be stored. The advantage of this is easy to illustrate. If your organization maintains a large database with thousands of records comprising several hundred megabytes of data, the entire database would be copied in the previous backup types even if only one record has changed. For a delta backup, only the actual record that changed would be stored. The disadvantage of this method is that restoration is a complex process, because it requires more than just loading a file (or several files).

It requires that application software be run to update the records in the files that have been changed.

There are some newer backup methods that are similar to delta backups in that they minimize what is backed up. There are real-time or near-real-time backup strategies, such as journaling, transactional backups, and electronic vaulting, that can provide protection against loss in real-time environments. Implementing these methods into an overall backup strategy can increase options and flexibility during times of recovery.

Each type of backup has advantages and disadvantages. Which type is best for your organization depends on the amount of data you routinely process and store, how frequently the data changes, how often you expect to have to restore from a backup, and a number of other factors. The type you select will shape your overall backup strategy and processes.

Backup Frequency and Retention

The type of backup strategy an organization employs is often affected by how frequently the organization conducts the backup activity. The usefulness of a backup is directly related to how many changes have occurred since the backup was created, and this is obviously affected by how often backups are created. The longer it has been since the backup was created, the more changes that likely will have occurred. There is no easy answer, however, to how frequently an organization should perform backups. Every organization should consider how long it can survive without current data from which to operate. It can then determine how long it will take to restore from backups, using various methods, and decide how frequently backups need to occur. This sounds simple, but it is a serious, complex decision to make.

Related to the frequency question is the issue of how long backups should be maintained. Is it sufficient to simply maintain a single backup from which to restore data? Security professionals will tell you no; multiple backups should be maintained, for a variety of reasons. If the reason for restoring from the backup is the discovery of an intruder in the system, it is important to restore the system to its pre-intrusion state. If the intruder has been in the system for several months before being discovered, and backups are taken weekly, it will not be possible to restore to a pre-intrusion state if only one backup is maintained. This would mean that all data and system files would be suspect and may not be reliable. If multiple backups were maintained, at various intervals, then it is easier to return to a point before the intrusion (or before the security or operational event that is necessitating the restoration) occurred.

There are several strategies or approaches to backup retention. One common and easy-to-remember strategy is the "rule of three," in which the three most recent backups are kept. When a new backup is created, the oldest backup is overwritten. Another strategy is to keep the most recent copy of backups for various time intervals. For example, you might keep the latest daily, weekly, monthly, quarterly, and yearly backups. Note that in certain environments, regulatory issues may prescribe a specific frequency and retention period, so it is important to know your organization's requirements when determining how often you will create a backup and how long you will keep it.

If you are not in an environment for which regulatory issues dictate the frequency and retention for backups, your goal will be to optimize the frequency. In determining the optimal backup frequency, two major costs need to be considered: the cost of the backup strategy you choose and the cost of recovery if you do not implement this backup strategy (that is, if no backups were created). You must also factor into this equation the probability that the backup will be needed on any given day. The two figures to consider then are these:

> *Alternative 1: (probability the backup is needed) × (cost of restoring with no backup)*

> *Alternative 2: (probability the backup isn't needed) × (cost of the backup strategy)*

The first of these two figures, alternative 1, can be considered the probable loss you can expect if your organization has no backup. The second figure, alternative 2, can be considered the amount you are willing to spend to ensure that you can restore, should a problem occur (think of this as backup insurance—the cost of an insurance policy that may never be used but that you are willing to pay for, just in case). For example, if the probability of a backup being needed is 10 percent, and the cost of restoring with no backup is $100,000, then the first equation would yield a figure of $10,000. This can be compared with the alternative, which would be a 90 percent chance the backup is not needed multiplied by the cost of implementing your backup strategy (of taking and maintaining the backups), which is, say, $10,000 annually. The second equation yields a figure of $9000. In this example, the cost of maintaining the backup is less than the cost of not having backups, so the former would be the better choice. While conceptually this is an easy trade-off to understand, in reality it is often difficult to accurately determine the probability of a backup being needed.

Fortunately, the figures for the potential loss if there is no backup are generally so much greater than the cost of maintaining a backup that a mistake in judging the probability will not matter—it just makes too much sense to maintain backups. This example also uses a straight comparison based solely on the cost of the process of restoring with and without a backup strategy. What needs to be included in the cost of both of these is the loss that occurs while the asset is not available as it is being restored—in essence, a measurement of the value of the asset itself.

To optimize your backup strategy, you need to determine the correct balance between these two figures. Obviously, you do not want to spend more in your backup strategy than you face losing should you not have a backup plan at all. When working with these two calculations, you have to remember that this is a cost-avoidance exercise. The organization is not going to increase revenues with its backup strategy. The goal is to minimize the potential loss due to some catastrophic event by creating a backup strategy that will address your organization's needs.

When you're calculating the cost of the backup strategy, consider the following:

- The cost of the backup media required for a single backup
- The storage costs for the backup media based on the retention policy
- The labor costs associated with performing a single backup
- The frequency with which backups are created

All of these considerations can be used to arrive at an annual cost for implementing your chosen backup strategy, and this figure can then be used as previously described.

Storage of Backups

An important element to factor into the cost of the backup strategy is the expense of storing the backups. A simple strategy might be to store all your backups together for quick and easy recovery actions. This is not, however, a good idea. Suppose the catastrophic event that necessitated the restoration of backed-up data was a fire that destroyed the computer system the data was processed on. In this case, any backups that were stored in the same facility might also be lost in the same fire.

The solution is to keep copies of backups in separate locations. The most recent copy can be stored locally, as it is the most likely to be needed, while other copies can be kept at other locations. Depending on the level of security your organization desires, the storage facility itself could be reinforced against possible threats in your area (such as tornados or floods). A more recent advance is online backup services. A number of third-party companies offer high-speed connections for storing data in a separate facility. Transmitting the backup data via network connections alleviates some other issues with physical movement of more traditional storage media, such as care during transportation (tapes do not fare well in direct sunlight, for example) or the time that it takes to transport the tapes.

Issues with Long-Term Storage of Backups

Depending on the media used for an organization's backups, degradation of the media is a distinct possibility and needs to be considered. Magnetic media degrades over time (measured in years). In addition, tapes can be used a limited number of times before the surface begins to flake off. Magnetic media should thus be rotated and tested to ensure that it is still usable.

Another consideration is advances in technology. The media you used to store your data two years ago may now be considered obsolete (5.25-inch floppy disks, for example). Software applications also evolve, and the media may be present but may not be compatible with current versions of the software. This may mean that you need to maintain backup copies of both hardware and software in order to recover from older backup media.

Another issue is security related. If the file you stored was encrypted for security purposes, does anybody in the company remember the password to decrypt the file to restore the data? More than one employee in the company should know the key to decrypt the files, and this information should be passed along to another person when a critical employee with that information leaves, is terminated, or dies.

Alternative Sites

An issue related to the location of backup storage is where the restoration services will be conducted. Determination of when or if an alternative site is needed should be included in recovery and continuity plans. If the organization has suffered physical damage to a facility, having offsite storage of data is only part of the solution. This data will need to be processed somewhere, which means that computing facilities similar to those used in normal operations are required. There are a number of ways to approach this problem, including hot sites, warm sites, cold sites, and mobile backup sites.

A **hot site** is a fully configured environment that is similar to the normal operating environment and that can be operational immediately or within a few hours, depending on its configuration and the needs of the organization. A **warm site** is partially configured, usually having the peripherals and software but perhaps not the more expensive main processing computer. It is designed to be operational within a few days. A **cold site** has the basic environmental controls necessary to operate but has few of the computing components necessary for processing. Getting a cold site operational may take weeks. A mobile backup site generally is a trailer with the required computers and electrical power that can be driven to a location within hours of a disaster and set up to commence processing immediately.

Shared alternate sites may also be considered. These sites can be designed to handle the needs of different organizations in the event of an emergency. The hope is that the disaster will affect only one organization at a time. The benefit of this method is that the cost of the site can be shared among organizations. Two similar organizations located close to each should not share the same alternate site as there is a greater chance that they would both need it at the same time.

Exam Tip: Understanding the differences between hot, warm, and cold sites is fundamental to understanding different business continuity strategies. Make sure that you understand the simple differences between these sites, the primary of which is how soon the alternative site can begin processing your organization's work.

Try This!

Research Alternative Processing Sites

There is an industry built upon providing alternative processing sites in case of a disaster of some sort. Using the Internet or other resources, determine what resources are available in your area for hot, warm, and cold sites. Do you live in an area in which a lot of these services are offered? Do other areas of the country have more alternative processing sites available? What makes where you live a better or worse place for alternative sites?

All of these options can come with a considerable price tag, which makes another option, mutual aid agreements, a possible alternative. With a **mutual aid agreement**, similar organizations agree to assume the processing for the other party in the event a disaster occurs. This is sometimes referred to as a *reciprocal site.* The obvious assumption here is that both organizations will not be hit by the same disaster and that both have similar processing environments. If these two assumptions are correct, then a mutual aid agreement should be considered. Such an arrangement may not be legally enforceable, even if it is in writing, and organizations must consider this when developing their disaster plans. In addition, if the organization that the mutual aid agreement is made with also is hit by the same disaster, then both organizations will be in trouble. Additional contingencies need to be planned for even if a mutual aid agreement is made with another organization. There are also the obvious security concerns that must be considered when having another organization assume your organization's processing.

Utilities

The interruption of power is a common issue during a disaster. Computers and networks obviously require power to operate, so emergency power must be available in the event of any disruption of operations. For short-term interruptions, such as what might occur as the result of an electrical storm, uninterruptible power supplies (UPSs) may suffice. These devices contain a battery that provides steady power for short periods of time—enough to keep a system running should power only be lost for a few minutes, enough time to allow administrators to gracefully halt the system or network. For continued operations that extend beyond a few minutes, another source of power will be required. Generally this is provided by a backup emergency generator.

While backup generators are frequently used to provide power during an emergency, they are not a simple, maintenance-free solution. Generators need to be tested on a regular basis, and they can easily become strained if they are required to power too much equipment. If your organization is going to rely on an emergency generator for backup power, you must ensure that the system has reserve capacity beyond the anticipated load for the unanticipated loads that will undoubtedly be placed on it.

Generators also take time to start up, so power to your organization will most likely be lost, even if only briefly, until the generators kick in. This means that you should also use a UPS to allow for a smooth transition to backup power. Generators are also expensive and require fuel—when looking for a place to locate your generator, don't forget the need to deliver fuel to it or you may find yourself hauling cans of fuel up a number of stairs.

When determining the need for backup power, don't forget to factor in environmental conditions. Running computer systems in a room with no air conditioning in the middle of the summer can result in an extremely uncomfortable environment for all to work in. Mobile backup sites, generally using trailers, often rely on generators for their power but also factor in the requirement for environmental controls.

Power is not the only essential utility for operations. Depending on the type of disaster that has occurred, telephone and Internet communication may also be lost, and wireless services may not be available. Planning for redundant means of communication (such as using both land lines and wireless) can help with most outages, but for large disasters, your backup plans should include the option to continue operations from a completely different location while waiting for communications in your area to be restored. Telecommunication carriers have their own emergency equipment and are fairly efficient at restoring communications, but it may take a few days.

Secure Recovery

Several companies offer recovery services, including power, communications, and technical support that your organization may need if its operations are disrupted. These companies advertise secure recovery sites or offices from which your organization can again begin to operate in a secure environment. Secure recovery is also advertised by other organizations that provide services that can remotely (over the Internet, for example) provide restoration services for critical files and data.

In both cases—the actual physical suites and the remote service—security is an important element. During a disaster, your data does not become any less important, and you will want to make sure that you maintain the security (in terms of confidentiality and integrity, for example) of your data.

As in other aspects of security, the decision to employ these services should be made based on a calculation of the benefits weighed against the potential loss if alternative means are used.

Cloud Computing

One of the newer innovations coming to computing via the Internet is the concept of cloud computing. Instead of owning and operating a dedicated set of servers for common business functions such as database services, file storage, e-mail services, and so forth, an organization can contract with third parties to provide these services over the Internet from their server farms. This is commonly referred to as Infrastructure as a Service (IaaS). The concept is that operations and maintenance is an activity that has become a commodity, and the Internet provides a reliable mechanism to access this more economical form of operational computing.

Pushing computing into the cloud may make good business sense from a cost perspective, but doing so does not change the fact that your organization is still responsible for ensuring that all the appropriate security measures are properly in place. How are backups being performed? What plan is in place for disaster recovery? How frequently are systems patched? What is the service level agreement (SLA) associated with the systems? It is easy to ignore the details when outsourcing these critical yet costly elements, but when something bad occurs, you must have confidence that the appropriate level of protections has been applied. These are the serious questions and difficult issues to resolve when moving computing into the cloud—location may change, but responsibility and technical issues are still there and form the risk of the solution.

High Availability and Fault Tolerance

Some other terms that may be used in discussions of continuity of operations in the face of a disruption of some sort are high availability and fault tolerance.

One of the objectives of security is the availability of data and processing power when an authorized user desires it. **High availability** refers to the ability to maintain availability of data and operational processing despite a disrupting event. Generally this requires redundant systems, in terms of both power and processing, so that should one system fail, the other can take over operations without any break in service. High availability is more than data redundancy; it requires that both data and services be available.

Fault tolerance basically has the same goal as high availability—the uninterrupted access to data and services—and is accomplished by the mirroring of data and systems. Should a "fault" occur, causing disruption in a device such as a disk controller, the mirrored system provides the requested data with no apparent interruption in service to the user. High availability clustering is another method used to provide redundancy in critical situations. These clusters consist of additional computers upon which a critical process can be started if the cluster detects that there has been a hardware or software problem on the main system.

Certain systems, such as servers, are more critical to business operations and should, therefore, be the object of fault-tolerance measures. A common

Exam Tip: Fault tolerance and high availability are similar in their goals, yet they are separate in application. *High availability* refers to maintaining both data and services in an operational state even when a disrupting event occurs. *Fault tolerance* is a design objective to achieve high availability should a fault occur.

technique used in fault tolerance is load balancing. Another closely related technique is clustering. Both techniques are discussed in the following sections.

Obviously, providing redundant systems and equipment comes with a price, and the need to provide this level of continuous, uninterrupted operation needs to be carefully evaluated.

Clustering

Clustering links a group of systems to have them work together, functioning as a single system. In many respects, a cluster of computers working together can be considered a single larger computer, with the advantage of costing less than a single comparably powerful computer. A cluster also has the fault-tolerant advantage of not being reliant on any single computer system for overall system performance.

Load Balancing

Load balancing is designed to distribute the processing load over two or more systems. It is used to help improve resource utilization and throughput but also has the added advantage of increasing the fault tolerance of the overall system, because a critical process may be split across several systems. Should any one system fail, the others can pick up the processing it was handling. While there may be an impact to overall throughput, the operation does not go down entirely. Load balancing is often utilized for systems that handle web sites and high-bandwidth file transfers.

Single Point of Failure

Related to the topic of high availability is the concept of a *single point of failure*. A single point of failure is a critical operation in the organization upon which many other operations rely and which itself relies on a single item that, if lost, would halt this critical operation. A single point of failure can be a special piece of hardware, a process, a specific piece of data, or even an essential utility. Single points of failure need to be identified if high availability is required because they are potentially the "weak links" in the chain that can cause disruption of the organization's operations. Generally, the solution to a single point of failure is to modify the critical operation so that it does not rely on this single element or to build redundant components into the critical operation to take over the process should one of these points fail.

In addition to the internal resources you need to consider when evaluating your business functions, there are many external resources that can impact the operation of your business. You must look beyond hardware, software, and data to consider how the loss of various critical infrastructures can also impact business operations. The type of infrastructures you should consider in your BCP is the subject of the next section.

Failure and Recovery Timing

Several important concepts are involved in the issue of fault tolerance and system recovery. The first is *mean time to failure* (or *mean time between failures*). This term refers to the predicted average time that will elapse before failure (or between failures) of a system (generally referring to hardware components). Knowing what this time is for hardware components of various critical systems can help an organization plan for maintenance and equipment replacement.

A second important concept to understand is *mean time to restore* (or *mean time to recovery*). This term refers to the average time that it will take to restore a system to operational status (to recover from any failure). Knowing what this time is for critical systems and processes is important to developing effective, and realistic, recovery plans, including DRP, BCP, and backup plans.

The last two concepts are closely tied. As previously described, the *recovery time objective* is the goal an organization sets for the time within which it wants to have a critical service restored after a disruption in service occurs. It is based on the calculation of the maximum amount of time that can occur before unacceptable losses take place. Also covered was the *recovery point objective,* which is based on a determination of how much data loss an organization can withstand.

Taken together, these four concepts are important considerations for an organization developing its various contingency plans. Having RTO and RPO that are shorter than the MTTR can result in losses. And attempting to lower the mean time between failures or the recovery time objectives below what is required by the organization wastes money that could be better spent elsewhere. The key is in understanding these figures and balancing them.

Backout Planning

An issue related to backups is the issue of returning to an earlier release of a software application in the event that a new release causes either a partial or complete failure. Planning for such an event is referred to as **backout planning**. These plans should address both a partial or full return to previous releases of software. Sadly, this sort of event is more frequent than most would suspect. The reason for this is the interdependence of various aspects of a system. It is not uncommon for one piece of software to take advantage of some feature of another. Should this feature change in a new release, another critical operation may be impacted.

RAID

One popular approach to increasing reliability in disk storage is **Redundant Array of Independent Disks (RAID)** (previously known as *Redundant Array of Inexpensive Disks*). RAID takes data that is normally stored on a single disk and spreads it out among several others. If any single disk is lost, the data can be recovered from the other disks where the data also resides. With the price of disk storage decreasing, this approach has become increasingly popular to the point that many individual users even have RAID arrays for their home systems. RAID can also increase the speed of data recovery, as multiple drives can be busy retrieving requested data at the same time instead of relying on just one disk to do the work.

Several different RAID approaches can be considered:

- **RAID 0** (striped disks) simply spreads the data that would be kept on the one disk across several disks. This decreases the time it takes to retrieve data, because the data is read from multiple drives at the same time, but it does not improve reliability, because the loss of any single drive will result in the loss of all the data (since portions

Tech Tip

Load Balancing, Clusters, Farms

A cluster is a group of servers deployed to achieve a common objective. Clustered servers are aware of one another and have a mechanism to exchange their states, so each server's state is replicated to the other clustered servers. Load balancing is a mechanism where traffic is directed to identical servers based on availability. In load balancing, the servers are not aware of the state of other servers. For purposes of load, it is not uncommon to have a load balancer distribute requests to clustered servers.

Database servers are typically clustered, as the integrity of the data structure requires all copies to be identical. Web servers and other content distribution mechanisms can use load balancing alone whenever maintaining state changes is not necessary across the environment. A server farm is a group of related servers in one location serving an enterprise. It can be either clustered, load balanced, or both.

of files are spread out among the different disks). With RAID 0, the data is split across all the drives with no redundancy offered.

- **RAID 1** (mirrored disks) is the opposite of RAID 0. RAID 1 copies the data from one disk onto two or more disks. If any single disk is lost, the data is not lost since it is also copied onto the other disk(s). This method can be used to improve reliability and retrieval speed, but it is relatively expensive when compared to other RAID techniques.

- **RAID 2** (bit-level error-correcting code) is not typically used, as it stripes data across the drives at the bit level as opposed to the block level. It is designed to be able to recover the loss of any single disk through the use of error-correcting techniques.

- **RAID 3** (byte-striped with error check) spreads the data across multiple disks at the byte level with one disk dedicated to parity bits. This technique is not commonly implemented, because input/output operations can't be overlapped due to the need for all to access the same disk (the disk with the parity bits).

- **RAID 4** (dedicated parity drive) stripes data across several disks but in larger stripes than in RAID 3, and it uses a single drive for parity-based error checking. RAID 4 has the disadvantage of not improving data retrieval speeds, since all retrievals still need to access the single parity drive.

- **RAID 5** (block-striped with error check) is a commonly used method that stripes the data at the block level and spreads the parity data across the drives. This provides both reliability and increased speed performance. This form requires a minimum of three drives.

RAID 0 through 5 are the original techniques, with RAID 5 being the most common method used, as it provides both the reliability and speed improvements. Additional methods have been implemented, such as duplicating the parity data across the disks (RAID 6) and a stripe of mirrors (RAID 10).

Spare Parts and Redundancy

RAID increases reliability through the use of *redundancy*. When developing plans for ensuring that an organization has what it needs to keep operating, even if hardware or software fails or if security is breached, you should consider other measures involving redundancy and spare parts. Some common applications of redundancy include the use of redundant servers, redundant connections, and redundant ISPs. The need for redundant servers and connections may be fairly obvious, but the need for redundant ISPs may not be so, at least initially. Many ISPs already have multiple accesses to the Internet on their own, but by having additional ISP connections, an organization can reduce the chance that an interruption of one ISP will negatively impact the organization. Ensuring uninterrupted access to the Internet by employees or access to the organization's e-commerce site for customers is becoming increasingly important.

Many organizations don't see the need for maintaining a supply of spare parts. After all, with the price of storage dropping and the speed of processors increasing, why replace a broken part with older technology? However,

Exam Tip: Knowledge of the basic RAID structures by number designation is a testable element and should be memorized for the exam.

An interesting historical note is that RAID originally stood for Redundant Array of Inexpensive Disks but the name was changed to the currently accepted Redundant Array of *Independent* Disks as a result of industry influence.

Principles of Computer Security

a ready supply of spare parts can ease the process of bringing the system back online. Replacing hardware and software with newer versions can sometimes lead to problems with compatibility. An older version of some piece of critical software may not work with newer hardware, which may be more capable in a variety of ways. Having critical hardware (or software) spares for critical functions in the organization can greatly facilitate maintaining business continuity in the event of software or hardware failures.

Chapter 19 Review

■ Chapter Summary

After reading this chapter and completing the exercises, you should understand the following regarding disaster recovery and business continuity.

Describe the various components of a business continuity plan

- A business continuity plan should contemplate the many types of disasters that can cause a disruption to an organization.

- A business impact assessment (BIA) can be conducted to identify the most critical functions for an organization.

- A business continuity plan is created to outline the order in which business functions will be restored so that the most critical functions are restored first.

- One of the most critical elements of any disaster recovery plan is the availability of system backups.

Describe the elements of disaster recovery plans

- Critical elements of disaster recovery plans include business continuity plans and contingency planning.

- A disaster recovery plan outlines an organization's plans to recover in the event a disaster strikes.

Describe the various ways backups are conducted and stored

- Backups should include not only the organization's critical data but critical software as well.

- Backups may be conducted by backing up all files (full backup), only the files that have changed since the last full backup (differential backup), only the files that have changed since the last full or differential backup (incremental backup), or only the portion of the files that has changed since the last delta or full backup (delta backup).

- Backups should be stored both onsite for quick access if needed as well as offsite in case a disaster destroys the primary facility, its processing equipment, and the backups that are stored onsite.

Explain different strategies for alternative site processing

- Plans should be created to continue operations at an alternative site if a disaster damages or destroys a facility.

- Possibilities for an alternative site include hot, warm, and cold sites.

- Developing a mutual aid agreement with a similar organization that could host your operations for a brief period of time after a disaster is another alternative.

■ Key Terms

backout planning *(601)*
business continuity plan (BCP) *(585)*
business impact analysis (BIA) *(586)*
cold site *(597)*
delta backup *(593)*
differential backup *(593)*
disaster recovery plan (DRP) *(587)*
fault tolerance *(599)*
full backup *(592)*

high availability *(599)*
hot site *(597)*
incremental backup *(593)*
mutual aid agreement *(597)*
recovery point objective (RPO) *(591)*
recovery time objective (RTO) *(591)*
Redundant Array of Independent Disks (RAID) *(601)*
warm site *(597)*

Key Terms Quiz

Use terms from the Key Terms list to complete the sentences that follow. Don't use the same term more than once. Not all terms will be used.

1. _____ is the maximum period of time in terms of data loss that is acceptable during an outage.

2. A(n) _____ is a partially configured backup processing facility that usually has the peripherals and software but perhaps not the more expensive main processing computer.

3. A backup that includes only the files that have changed since the last full backup was completed is called a(n) _____.

4. A(n) _____ is an evaluation of the impact that a loss of critical functions will have on the organization.

5. Linking multiple systems together to appear as one large system in terms of capacity is called _____.

6. A _____ is performed to identify critical business functions needed during times of disaster or other reduced capability.

7. An agreement in which similar organizations agree to assume the processing for the other in the event a disaster occurs is known as a(n) _____.

8. The average time that it will take to restore a system to operational status is called _____.

9. A(n) _____ is a fully configured backup environment that is similar to the normal operating environment and that can be operational within a few hours.

10. _____ is a method to ensure high availability that is accomplished by the mirroring of data and systems. Should an event occur that causes disruption in a device, the mirrored system provides the requested data, with no apparent interruption in service.

Multiple-Choice Quiz

1. Why is it important that security exercises be conducted?

   A. To provide the opportunity for all parties to practice the procedures that have been established to respond to a security incident.

   B. To determine if the organization's plan and the individuals involved perform as they should during a simulated security incident.

   C. To determine if processes developed to handle security incidents are sufficient for the organization.

   D. All of the above.

2. A good backup plan will include which of the following?

   A. The critical data needed for the organization to operate

   B. Any software that is required to process the organization's data

   C. Specific hardware to run the software or to process the data

   D. All of the above

3. In which backup strategy are only those portions of the files and software that have changed since the last backup backed up?

   A. Full

   B. Differential

   C. Incremental

   D. Delta

4. Which of the following is a consideration in calculating the cost of a backup strategy?

   A. The cost of the backup media

   B. The storage costs for the backup media

   C. The frequency with which backups are created

   D. All of the above

5. Which of the following is the name for a partially configured environment that has the peripherals and software that the normal processing facility contains and that can be operational within a few days?

   A. Hot site

   B. Warm site

C. Online storage system

D. Backup storage facility

6. Which of the following is considered an issue with long-term storage of magnetic media, as discussed in the chapter?

   A. Tape media can be used a limited number of times before it degrades.

   B. Software and hardware evolve, and the media stored may no longer be compatible with current technology.

   C. Both A and B.

   D. None of the above.

7. What common utility or infrastructure is important to consider when developing your recovery plans?

   A. Transportation

   B. Oil and gas

   C. Communications

   D. Television/cable

8. For organizations that draw a distinction between a BCP and a DRP, which of the following is true?

   A. The BCP details the functions that are most critical and outlines the order in which critical functions should be returned to service to maintain business operations.

   B. The BCP is a subset of the DRP.

   C. The DRP outlines the minimum set of business functions required for the organization to continue functioning.

   D. The DRP is always developed first and the BCP normally is an attachment to this document.

9. A business impact assessment (BIA) is conducted to:

   A. Outline the order in which critical functions should be returned to service to maintain business operations

   B. Identify the most critical functions for an organization

   C. Identify the critical employees who must be onsite to implement the BCP

   D. Establish the policies governing the organization's backup policy

10. To ensure that critical systems is not lost during a failure, it is important that which of the following be true?

    A. MTTF < MTTR.

    B. MTTR < RTO.

    C. RPO < MTTF.

    D. RTO = RPO.

Essay Quiz

1. Write a paragraph outlining the differences between a disaster recovery plan and a business continuity plan. Is one more important than the other?

2. Write a brief description of the different backup strategies. Include a discussion of which of these strategies requires the greatest amount of storage space to conduct and which of the strategies involves the most complicated restoration scheme.

3. Your boss recently attended a seminar in which the importance of creating and maintaining a backup of critical data was discussed. He suggested to you that you immediately make a tape backup of all data, place it in a metal box, lock it, and keep it at home. You don't agree with this specific method, but you need to develop a plan that he will understand and find persuasive. Write a proposal describing your recommendations, making sure to include the issues involved with the long-term storage of backups.

Lab Project

• Lab Project 19.1

The Windows operating system considers backups to be an essential task and will send system maintenance reminders via the Action Center. Determine the backup condition of your PC using the Action Center and demonstrate how it changes when backed up.

Risk Management

chapter 20

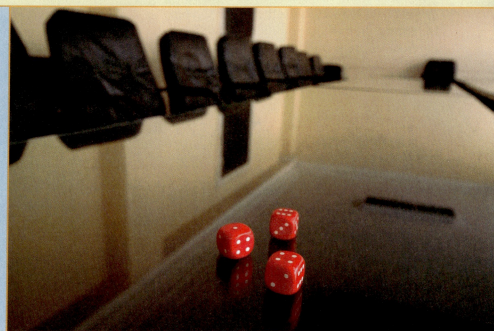

The revolutionary idea that defines the boundary between modern times and the past is the mastery of risk: the notion that the future is more than a whim of the gods and that men and women are not passive before nature. Until human beings discovered a way across that boundary, the future was the mirror of the past or the murky domain of oracles and soothsayers who held a monopoly over knowledge of anticipated events.

—Peter Bernstein

In this chapter, you will learn how to

- Use risk management tools and principles to manage risk effectively
- Explore risk mitigation strategies
- Describe risk models
- Explain the differences between qualitative and quantitative risk assessment
- Use risk management tools
- Examine risk management best practices

Risk management can best be described as a decision-making process. In the simplest terms, when you manage risk, you determine what could happen to your business, you assess the impact if it were to happen, and you decide what you could do to control that impact as much as you or your management deems necessary. You then decide to act or not to act, and, finally, you evaluate the results of your decision. The process may be iterative, as industry best practices clearly indicate that an important aspect of effectively managing risk is to consider it an ongoing process.

Cross Check

Change Management and Risk Management Are Critical Management Tools

Risk management is one of the reasons behind change management. Change management is a process designed to enable management efforts to understand implications of changes prior to incorporation in production systems. When someone requests a change to production, do they have answers to questions such as these:

1. What are the security implications of this change?
2. What is the backout plan in the event the change causes unintentional problems?

For more detail, refer to Chapter 21, which explains details of change management as a critical management tool.

■ An Overview of Risk Management

Risk management is an essential element of management from the enterprise level down to the individual project. Risk management encompasses all the actions taken to reduce complexity, increase objectivity, and identify important decision factors. There has been, and will continue to be, discussion about the complexity of risk management and whether or not it is worth the effort. Businesses must take risks to retain their competitive edge, however, and as a result, risk management must occur as part of managing any business, program, or project.

Risk management is both a skill and a task that is performed by all managers, either deliberately or intuitively. It can be simple or complex, depending on the size of the project or business and the amount of risk inherent in an activity. Every manager, at all levels, must learn to manage risk. The required skills can be learned.

Risk management is about making a business profitable— not about buying insurance.

Example of Risk Management at the International Banking Level

The Basel Committee on Banking Supervision comprises government central-bank governors from around the world. This body created a basic, global risk management framework for market and credit risk. It implemented internationally a flat 8 percent capital charge to banks to manage bank risks. In layman's terms, this means that for every $100 a bank makes in loans, it must possess $8 in reserve to be used in the event of financial difficulties. However, if banks can show they have very strong risk mitigation procedures and controls in place, that capital charge can be reduced to as low as $0.37 (0.37 percent). If a bank has poor procedures and controls, that capital charge can be as high as $45 (45 percent) for every $100 the bank loans out. See www.bis .org/bcbs/ for source documentation regarding the Basel Committee.

Exam Tip: This chapter contains several bulleted lists. These are designed for easy memorization in preparation for taking the CompTIA Security+ exam.

This example shows that risk management can be and is used at very high levels—the remainder of this chapter focuses on smaller implementations and demonstrates that risk management is used in many aspects of business conduct.

Risk Management Vocabulary

You need to understand a number of key terms to manage risk successfully. Some of these terms are defined here because they are used throughout the chapter. This list is somewhat ordered according to the organization of this chapter. More comprehensive definitions and other pertinent terms are listed alphabetically in the glossary at the end of this book.

Risk   **Risk** is the possibility of suffering harm or loss.

Risk management   **Risk management** is the overall decision-making process of identifying threats and vulnerabilities and their potential impacts, determining the costs to mitigate such events, and deciding what actions are cost effective for controlling these risks.

Risk assessment   **Risk assessment** is the process of analyzing an environment to identify the risks (threats and vulnerabilities) and mitigating actions to determine (either quantitatively or qualitatively) the impact of an event that would affect a project, program, or business. Also referred to as **risk analysis**.

Asset   An **asset** is any resource or information an organization needs to conduct its business.

Threat   A **threat** is any circumstance or event with the potential to cause harm to an asset. For example, a malicious hacker might choose to hack your system by using readily available hacking tools.

Threat actor   A **threat actor** (agent) is the entity behind a threat.

Threat vector   A **threat vector** is a method used to effect a threat—for example, malware (threat) that is delivered via a watering-hole attack (vector).

Vulnerability   A **vulnerability** is any characteristic of an asset that can be exploited by a threat to cause harm. A vulnerability can also be the result of a lack of security controls, or weaknesses in controls. Your system has a security vulnerability, for example, if you have not installed patches to fix a cross-site scripting (XSS) error on your web site.

Impact   **Impact** is the loss (or harm) resulting when a threat exploits a vulnerability. A malicious hacker (threat agent) uses an XSS tool (threat vector) to hack your unpatched web site (the vulnerability), stealing credit card information (threat) that is then used fraudulently. The credit card company pursues legal recourse against your company to recover the losses from the credit card fraud (the impact).

Control   A **control** is a measure taken to detect, prevent, or mitigate the risk associated with a threat. Also called **countermeasure** or **safeguard**.

Tech Tip

Types of Controls

Controls can be classified based on the types of actions they perform. Three classes of controls exist:

- *Management or Administrative*
- *Technical*
- *Operational or Physical*

For each of these classes, there are six types of controls:

- *Deterrent (to discourage occurrences)*
- *Preventative (to avoid occurrence)*
- *Detective (to detect or identify occurrence)*
- *Corrective (to correct or restore controls)*
- *Recovery (to restore resources, capabilities, or losses)*
- *Compensating (to mitigate when direct control is not possible)*

Principles of Computer Security

Qualitative risk assessment   Qualitative risk assessment is the process of subjectively determining the impact of an event that affects a project, program, or business. Completing the assessment usually involves the use of expert judgment, experience, or group consensus.

Quantitative risk assessment   Quantitative risk assessment is the process of objectively determining the impact of an event that affects a project, program, or business. Completing the assessment usually involves the use of metrics and models.

Mitigate   The term mitigate refers to taking action to reduce the likelihood of a threat occurring, and to reduce the impact if a threat does occur.

Single loss expectancy (SLE)   The single loss expectancy (SLE) is the monetary loss or impact of each occurrence of a threat exploiting a vulnerability.

Exposure factor   Exposure factor is a measure of the magnitude of loss of an asset. Used in the calculation of single loss expectancy.

Annualized rate of occurrence (ARO)   Annualized rate of occurrence (ARO) is the frequency with which an event is expected to occur on an annualized basis.

Annualized loss expectancy (ALE)   Annualized loss expectancy (ALE) is how much an event is expected to cost per year.

Systematic Risk   Systematic risk is the chance of loss that is predictable under relatively stable circumstances. Examples such as fire, wind, or flood produce losses that, in the aggregate over time, can be accurately predicted despite short-term fluctuations. Systematic risk can be diversified away, which gives managers a level of control that can be employed.

Unsystematic Risk   Unsystematic risk is the chance of loss that is unpredictable in the aggregate because it results from forces difficult to predict. Examples include, but are not limited to, recession, unemployment, epidemics, war-related events, and so forth. Unsystematic risk cannot be mitigated via diversification, limiting management responses.

Hazard   A hazard is a circumstance that increases the likelihood or probable severity of a loss. For example, running systems without antivirus is a hazard because it increases the probability of loss due to malware.

The distinction between qualitative and quantitative risk assessment will be more apparent as you read the section "Qualitative vs. Quantitative Risk Assessment," later in the chapter.

Exam Tip: These terms are important, and you should completely memorize their meanings before taking the CompTIA Security+ exam.

What Is Risk Management?

Three definitions relating to risk management reveal why it is sometimes considered difficult to understand:

- The dictionary defines *risk* as the possibility of suffering harm or loss.

- Carnegie Mellon University's Software Engineering Institute (SEI) defines *continuous risk management* as "processes, methods, and tools for managing risks in a project. It provides a disciplined environment for proactive decision-making to 1) assess continuously what could go wrong (risks); 2) determine which risks are important

Tech Tip

Risk Management Applies to All Business Processes

Even Human Resource Management relies on risk management. For example, risk management theory used to posit that older workers were more likely to create liabilities. Recent studies have shown that as the workforce ages, it has become apparent that older workers have lower absenteeism, are more productive, and have higher levels of job satisfaction. Their greatest risk is longer recovery time from accidents—companies are finding ways to prevent accidents to manage that risk.

to deal with; and 3) implement strategies to deal with those risks" (SEI, *Continuous Risk Management Guidebook* [Pittsburgh, PA: Carnegie Mellon University, 1996], 22).

■ The Information Systems Audit and Control Association (ISACA) says, "In modern business terms, risk management is the process of identifying vulnerabilities and threats to an organization's resources and assets and deciding what countermeasures, if any, to take to reduce the level of risk to an acceptable level based on the value of the asset to the organization" (ISACA, *Certified Information Systems Auditor (CISA) Review Manual, 2002* [Rolling Meadows, IL: ISACA, 2002], 344).

These three definitions show that risk management is based on what can go wrong and what action should be taken, if any. Figure 20.1 provides a macro-level view of how to manage risk.

Risk Management Culture

Organizations have a culture associated with their operation. Frequently, this culture is set and driven by the activities of senior management personnel. The risk management culture of an organization can have an effect upon actions being taken by others. Table 20.1 illustrates the symptoms and results associated with risk management culture.

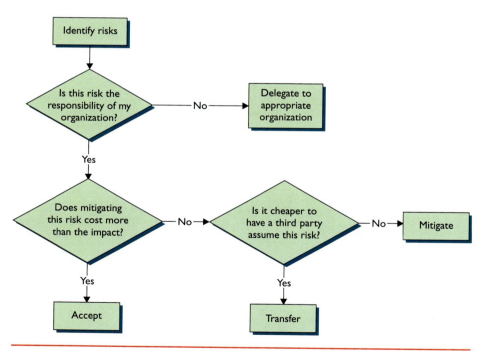

• Figure 20.1   A planning decision flowchart for risk management

Table 20.1	Characteristics of Risk Management Culture		
	Management Styles		
	Pathological	**Bureaucratic**	**Enlightened**
Situational awareness	Don't want to know	May not find out	Actively seek
Communication style	Messengers shot	Heard if it arrives	Messengers rewarded
Responsibility	Shirked or blamed	Compartmentalized	Shared
Failures are	Punished	Local repairs only	Source of reforms
Ideas/solutions	Discouraged	Beget problems	Welcomed

Business Risks

No comprehensive identification of all risks in a business environment is possible. In today's technology-dependent business environment, risk is often simplistically divided into two areas: business risk and, a major subset, technology risk.

Examples of Business Risks

Following are some of the most common business risks:

- **Treasury management** Management of company holdings in bonds, futures, currencies, and so on

- **Revenue management** Management of consumer behavior and the generation of revenue

- **Contract management** Management of contracts with customers, vendors, partners, and so on

- **Fraud** Deliberate deception made for personal gain, to obtain property or services, and so on

- **Environmental risk management** Management of risks associated with factors that affect the environment

- **Regulatory risk management** Management of risks arising from new or existing regulations

- **Business continuity management** Management of risks associated with recovering and restoring business functions after a disaster or major disruption occurs

- **Technology** Management of risks associated with technology in its many forms

Examples of Technology Risks

Following are some of the most common technology risks:

- **Security and privacy** The risks associated with protecting personal, private, or confidential information

Tech Tip

Transferring Risk
One possible action to manage risk is to transfer that risk. The most common method of transferring risk is to purchase insurance. Insurance allows some level of risk to be transferred to a third party that manages specific types of risk for multiple parties, thus reducing the individual cost. Note that transferring risk usually applies to financial aspects of risk; it normally does not apply to legal accountability, or responsibility.

It is important that you understand that technology, itself, is a business risk. Hence, it must be managed along with other risks. Today, technology risks are so important they should be considered separately.

- **Information technology operations**   The risks associated with the day-to-day operation of information technology systems

- **Business systems control and effectiveness**   The risks associated with manual and automated controls that safeguard company assets and resources

- **Business continuity management**   The risks associated with the technology and processes to be used in the event of a disaster or major disruption

- **Information systems testing**   The risks associated with testing processes and procedures of information systems

- **Reliability and performance management**   The risks associated with meeting reliability and performance agreements and measures

- **Information technology asset management**   The risks associated with safeguarding information technology physical assets

- **Project risk management**   The risks associated with managing information technology projects

- **Change management**   The risks associated with managing configurations and changes (see Chapter 21)

■ Risk Mitigation Strategies

Risk mitigation strategies are the action plans developed after a thorough evaluation of the possible threats, hazards, and risks associated with business operations. These strategies are employed to lessen the risks associated with operations. The focus of risk mitigation strategies is to reduce the effects of threats and hazards. Common mitigation strategies include change management, incident management, user rights and permission reviews, audits, and technology controls.

Change Management

Change management has its roots in system engineering and takes the overall view of systems components and processes. Configuration management specifically applies to a lower level of detail, the actual configuration of components, such as hosts, devices, and so forth. Configuration management might be considered a subset of change management, but they are not the same thing. Most of today's software and hardware change management practices derive from long-standing system engineering configuration management practices. Computer hardware and software development have also evolved to the point that proper management structure and controls must exist to ensure the products operate as planned. It is normal for an enterprise to have a Change Control Board to approve all production changes and ensure the change management procedures are followed before changes are introduced to a system.

Configuration control is the process of controlling changes to items that have been baselined. Configuration control ensures that only approved changes to a baseline are allowed to be implemented. It is easy to understand why a software system, such as a web-based order-entry system, should not be changed without proper testing and control—otherwise, the system might stop functioning at a critical time. Configuration control is a key step that provides valuable insight to managers. If a system is being changed, and configuration control is being observed, managers and others concerned will be better informed. This ensures proper use of assets and avoids unnecessary downtime due to the installation of unapproved changes.

> **Exam Tip:** Change management ensures proper procedures are followed when modifying the IT infrastructure.

Incident Management

When an incident occurs, having an incident response management methodology is a key risk mitigation strategy. Incident response and incident management are essential security functions and are covered in detail in Chapter 22.

User Rights and Permissions Reviews

User rights and permissions reviews are one of the more powerful security controls. But the strength of this control depends upon it being kept up to date and properly maintained. Ensuring that the list of users and associated rights is complete and up to date is a challenging task in anything bigger than the smallest enterprises. A compensating control that can assist in keeping user rights lists current is a set of periodic audits of the user base and associated permissions.

Data Loss or Theft

Data is the primary target of most attackers. The value of the data can vary, making some data more valuable and hence more at risk of theft. Data can also be lost through a variety of mechanisms, with hardware failure, operator error, and system errors being common causes. Regardless of the cause of loss, an organization can take various actions to mitigate the effects of the loss. Backups lead the list of actions, for backups can provide the ultimate in protection against loss.

To prevent theft, a variety of controls can be employed. Some are risk mitigation steps, such as data minimization, which is the act of not storing what isn't needed. If it must be stored and has value, then technologies such as data loss prevention can be used to provide a means of protection. Simple security controls such as firewalls and network segmentation can also act to make data theft more difficult.

> **Exam Tip:** When taking the exam, understand the policies and procedures to prevent data loss or theft.

■ Risk Management Models

Risk management concepts are fundamentally the same despite their definitions, and they require similar skills, tools, and methodologies. Several models can be used for managing risk through its various phases. Two models are presented here: the first can be applied to managing risks in general, and the second is tailored for managing risk in software projects.

General Risk Management Model

The following five steps can be used in virtually any risk management process. Following these steps will lead to an orderly process of analyzing and mitigating risks.

Step 1. Asset Identification

Identify and classify the assets, systems, and processes that need protection because they are vulnerable to threats. Use a classification that fits your business. This classification leads to the ability to prioritize assets, systems, and processes and to evaluate the costs of addressing the associated risks. Assets can include the following:

- Inventory
- Buildings
- Cash
- Information and data
- Hardware
- Software

- Services
- Documents
- Personnel
- Brand recognition
- Organization reputation
- Goodwill

Step 2: Threat Assessment

After identifying the assets, you identify both the possible threats and the possible vulnerabilities associated with each asset and the likelihood of their occurrence. Threats can be defined as any circumstance or event with the potential to cause harm to an asset. Common classes of threats include (with examples):

- **Natural disasters**   Hurricane, earthquake, lightning, and so on.

- **Man-made disasters**   Earthen dam failure, such as the 1976 Teton Dam failure in Idaho; car accident that destroys a municipal power distribution transformer; the 1973 explosion of a railcar containing propane gas in Kingman, Arizona.

- **Terrorism**   The 2001 destruction of the World Trade Center, the 1995 gas attack on the Shinjuku train station in Tokyo.

- **Errors**   Employee not following safety or configuration management procedures.

- **Malicious damage or attacks**   A disgruntled employee purposely corrupting data files.

- **Fraud**   An employee falsifying travel expenses or vendor invoices and payments.

- **Theft**   An employee stealing from the loading dock a laptop computer after it has been inventoried but not properly secured.

- **Equipment or software failure**   An error in the calculation of a company-wide bonus overpaying employees.

Vulnerabilities are characteristics of resources that can be exploited by a threat to cause harm. Common classes of vulnerabilities include (with examples):

- **Unprotected facilities**   Company offices with no security officer present or no card-entry system.

- **Unprotected computer systems**   A server temporarily connected to the network before being properly configured/secured.

- **Unprotected data**   Not installing critical security patches to eliminate application security vulnerabilities.

- **Insufficient procedures and controls**   Allowing an accounts payable clerk to create vendors in the accounting system, enter invoices, and authorize check payments.

- **Insufficient or unqualified personnel**   A junior employee not sufficiently securing a server due to a lack of training.

Step 3: Impact Determination and Quantification

An impact is the loss created when a threat exploits a vulnerability. When a threat is realized, it turns risk into impact. Impacts can be either tangible or intangible. A **tangible impact** results in financial loss or physical damage. For an **intangible impact**, assigning a financial value of the impact can be difficult. For example, in a manufacturing facility, storing and using flammable chemicals creates a risk of fire to the facility. The vulnerability is that flammable chemicals are stored there. The threat would be that a person could cause a fire by mishandling the chemicals (either intentionally or unintentionally). A tangible impact would be the loss incurred (say, $500,000) if a person ignites the chemicals and fire then destroys part of the facility. An example of an intangible impact would be the loss of goodwill or brand damage caused by the impression that the company doesn't safely protect its employees or the surrounding geographic area.

Tangible impacts include

- Direct loss of money
- Endangerment of staff or customers
- Loss of business opportunity
- Reduction in operational efficiency or performance
- Interruption of a business activity

Intangible impacts include

- Breach of legislation or regulatory requirements
- Loss of reputation or goodwill (brand damage)
- Breach of confidence

Tech Tip

Business Dependencies

An area often overlooked in risk assessment is the need to address business dependencies—each organization must assess risks caused by other organizations with which it interacts. This occurs when the organization is either a consumer of or a supplier to other organizations (or both). For example, if a company is dependent on products produced by a laboratory, then the company must determine the impact of the laboratory not delivering the product when needed. Likewise, an organization must assess risks that can occur when it is the supplier to some other company dependent on its products.

Step 4: Control Design and Evaluation

In this step, you determine which controls to put in place to mitigate the risks. Controls (also called countermeasures or safeguards) are designed to control risk by reducing vulnerabilities to an acceptable level. (For use in this text, the terms *control*, countermeasure, and safeguard are considered synonymous and are used interchangeably.)

Controls can be actions, devices, or procedures. They can be preventive or detective. *Preventive controls* are designed to prevent the vulnerability from causing an impact. *Detective controls* are those that detect a vulnerability that has been exploited so that action can be taken.

Exam Tip: The steps in the general risk management model should allow you to identify the steps in any risk management process.

617

Step 5: Residual Risk Management

Understand that risk cannot be completely eliminated. A risk that remains after implementing controls is termed a **residual risk**. In this step, you further evaluate residual risks to identify where additional controls are required to reduce risk even more. This leads us to the earlier statement that the risk management process is iterative.

Software Engineering Institute Model

In an approach tailored for managing risk in software projects, SEI uses the following paradigm (SEI, *Continuous Risk Management Guidebook* [Pittsburgh, PA: Carnegie Mellon University, 1996], 23). Although the terminology varies slightly from the previous model, the relationships are apparent, and either model can be applied wherever risk management is used.

1. **Identify**—Look for risks before they become problems.

2. **Analyze**—Convert the data gathered into information that can be used to make decisions. Evaluate the impact, probability, and timeframe of the risks. Classify and prioritize each of the risks.

3. **Plan**—Review and evaluate the risks and decide what actions to take to mitigate them. Implement those mitigating actions.

4. **Track**—Monitor the risks and the mitigation plans. Trends may provide information to activate plans and contingencies. Review periodically to measure progress and identify new risks.

5. **Control**—Make corrections for deviations from the risk mitigation plans. Correct products and processes as required. Changes in business procedures may require adjustments in plans or actions, as do faulty plans and risks that become problems.

NIST Risk Models

NIST has several informative risk models that can be applied to an enterprise. NIST has published several Special Publications (SPs) associated with risk management. SP 800-39, *Managing Information Security Risk: Organization, Mission, and Information System View,* presents several key insights:

- Establish a relationship between aggregated risk from information systems and mission/business success

- Encourage senior leaders to recognize the importance of managing information security risk within the organization

- Help those with system-level security responsibilities understand how system-level issues affect the organization/mission as a whole

SP 800-39 does this through the use of a model, illustrated in Figure 20.2. This model has two distinct levels of analysis, which work together as one in describing risk management actions.

The first level of analysis is represented by four elements: Frame, Assess, Respond, and Monitor. The second level is related to the tiers

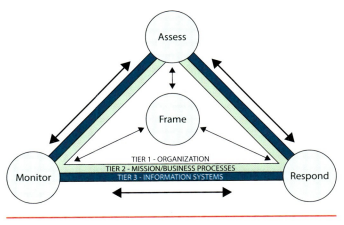

● **Figure 20.2**   NIST risk management process applied across the tiers

represented in the hierarchical triangles: Organization, Mission/Business Processes, and Information Systems.

The Frame element represents the organization's risk framing that establishes the context and provides a common perspective on how the organization manages risk. Risk framing is central to the model, as illustrated by the arrows to the other elements. Its principal output is a risk management strategy that addresses how the organization assesses risk, responds to risk, and monitors risk. The three tiers represent the different distinct layers in an organization that are associated with risk. Tier 1, representing the executive function, is where the risk framing occurs. At Tier 2, the mission and business process layer, the risk management functions of assess, respond, and monitor occur. Tier 3 is the information system layer where activities of risk management are manifested in the systems of the organization.

Model Application

The three model examples define steps that can be used in any general or software risk management process. These risk management principles can be applied to any project, program, or business activity, no matter how simple or complex. Figure 20.3 shows how risk management can be applied across the continuum and that the complexity of risk management generally increases with the size of the project, program, or business to be managed.

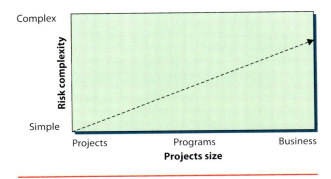

● **Figure 20.3**   Risk complexity versus project size

■ Qualitatively Assessing Risk

Qualitative risk analysis allows expert judgment and experience to assume a prominent role. To assess risk qualitatively, you compare the impact of the threat with the probability of occurrence and assign an impact level and probability level to the risk. For example, if a threat has a high impact and a high probability of occurring, the risk exposure is high and probably requires some action to reduce this threat (pale green box in Figure 20.4). Conversely, if the impact is low with a low probability, the risk exposure is low and no action may be required to reduce the likelihood of the occurrence or impact of this threat (white box in Figure 20.4). Figure 20.4 shows an example of a *binary assessment*, where only two outcomes are possible each for impact and probability. Either it will have an impact or it will not (or it will have a low or high impact), and it will occur or it won't (or it will have a high probability of occurring or a low probability of occurring).

Impact		
High impact/Low probability	High impact/High probability
Low impact/Low probability	Low impact/High probability

Probability

• **Figure 20.4**   Binary assessment

Impact					
High	Low	High	Medium	High	High
Medium	Low	Medium	Medium	Medium	High
Low	Low	Low	Medium	Low	High

Probability

• **Figure 20.5**   Three levels of analysis

Impact					
Very high	Low	Very high	Medium	Very high	High
High	Low	High	Medium	High	High
Medium	Low	Medium	Medium	Medium	High
Low	Low	Low	Medium	Low	High
Very low	Low	Very low	Medium	Very low	High

Probability

• **Figure 20.6**   A 3-by-5 level analysis

In reality, a few threats can usually be identified as presenting high-risk exposure and a few threats present low-risk exposure. The threats that fall somewhere between (pale blue boxes in Figure 20.4) will have to be evaluated by judgment and management experience.

If the analysis is more complex, requiring three levels of analysis, such as low-medium-high or green-yellow-red nine combinations are possible, as shown in Figure 20.5. Again, the pale green boxes probably require action, the white boxes may or may not require action, and the pale blue boxes require judgment. (Note that for brevity, in Figure 20.5 the first term in each box refers to the magnitude of the impact, and the second term refers to the probability of the threat occurring.)

Other levels of complexity are possible. With five levels of analysis, 25 values of risk exposure are possible. In this case, the possible values of impact and probability could take on the values very low, low, medium, high, or very high. Also, note that the matrix does not have to be symmetrical. For example, if the probability is assessed with three values (low, medium, high) and the impact has five values (very low, low, medium, high, very high), the analysis would be as shown in Figure 20.6. (Again, note that the first term in each box refers to the impact, and the second term in each box refers to the probability of occurrence.)

So far, the examples have focused on assessing likelihood versus impact. Qualitative risk assessment can be adapted to a variety of attributes and situations in combination with each other. For example, Figure 20.7 shows the comparison of some specific risks that have been identified during a security assessment. The assessment identified the risk areas listed in the first

Qualitative Assessment of Findings

Legend
- 🔴 High
- 🟡 Medium
- 🟢 Low

	Business impact	Probability of attack	Cost to fix	Difficulty to fix	Risk
Weak intranet security	🔴	🔴	🔴	🔴	🔴
High number of modems	🔴	🔴	🟡	🟢	🔴
Internet attack vulnerabilities	🔴	🔴	🟢	🟡	🟡
Weak incident detection/ response mechanism	🟡	🔴	🟡	🔴	🟡

• **Figure 20.7** Example of a combination assessment

column (weak intranet security, high number of modems, Internet attack vulnerabilities, and weak incident detection and response mechanism). The assessment also identified various potential impacts, listed across the top (business impact, probability of attack, cost to fix, and difficulty to fix). Each of the impacts has been assessed as low, medium, or high—depicted using green, yellow, and red, respectively. Each of the risk areas has been assessed with respect to each of the potential impacts, and an overall risk assessment has been determined in the last column.

Quantitatively Assessing Risk

Whereas qualitative risk assessment relies on judgment and experience, quantitative risk assessment applies historical information and trends to attempt to predict future performance. This type of risk assessment is highly dependent on historical data, and gathering such data can be difficult. Quantitative risk assessment can also rely heavily on models that provide decision-making information in the form of quantitative metrics, which attempt to measure risk levels across a common scale.

It is important to understand that key assumptions underlie any model, and different models will produce different results even when given the same input data. Although significant research and development have been invested in improving and refining the various risk analysis models, expert judgment and experience must still be considered an essential part of any risk assessment process. Models can never replace judgment and experience, but they can significantly enhance the decision-making process.

Adding Objectivity to a Qualitative Assessment

It is possible to move a qualitative assessment toward being more quantitative. Making a qualitative assessment more objective can be as simple as

Table 20.2	Adding Weights and Definitions to the Potential Impacts	
Impact	**Explanation**	**Weight**
Business impact	If exploited, what is the business impact?	4
Probability of attack	How likely is a potential attacker to try this technique or attack?	3
Cost to fix	How much will it cost in dollars and resources to correct this vulnerability?	2
Difficulty to fix	How hard is this to fix from a technical standpoint?	1

assigning numeric values to one of the tables shown in Figures 20.4 through 20.7. For example, the impacts listed in Figure 20.7 can be prioritized from highest to lowest and then weighted, as shown in Table 20.2, with business impact weighted the most and difficulty to fix weighted least.

Next, values can be assigned to reflect how each risk was assessed. Figure 20.7 can thus be made more objective by assigning a value to each color that represents an assessment. For example, a red assessment indicates many critical, unresolved issues, and this will be given an assessment value of 3. Green means few issues are unresolved, so it is given a value of 1. Table 20.3 shows values that can be assigned for an assessment using red, yellow, and green.

The last step is to calculate an overall risk value for each risk area (each row in Figure 20.7) by multiplying the weights depicted in Table 20.2 times the assessed values from Table 20.3 and summing the products:

$$\text{Risk} = W_1 * V_1 + W_2 * V_2 + \ldots W_4 * V_4$$

The risk calculation and final risk value for each risk area listed in Figure 20.7 have been incorporated into Figure 20.8. The assessed areas can then be ordered from highest to lowest based on the calculated risk value to aid management in focusing on the risk areas with the greatest potential impact.

Risk Calculation

More complex models permit a variety of analyses based on statistical and mathematical models. A common method is the calculation of the annualized loss expectancy (ALE). Calculating the ALE creates a monetary value of the impact. This calculation begins by calculating a single loss expectancy (SLE).

Table 20.3	Adding Values to Assessments	
Assessment	**Explanation**	**Value**
Red	Many critical, unresolved issues	3
Yellow	Some critical, unresolved issues	2
Green	Few unresolved issues	1

Quantitative Assessment of Findings

	Business impact (4)		Probability of attack (3)		Cost to fix (2)		Difficulty to fix (1)		Risk
Weak intranet security	🔴		🔴		🔴		🔴		🔴
	4*3	+	3*3	+	2*3	+	1*3	=	30
High number of modems	🔴		🔴		🟡		🟢		🔴
	4*3	+	3*3	+	2*2	+	1*1	=	26
Internet attack vulnerabilities	🔴		🔴		🟢		🟡		🟡
	4*3	+	3*3	+	2*1	+	1*2	=	25
Weak incident detection/ response mechanism	🟡		🔴		🟡		🔴		🟡
	4*2	+	3*3	+	2*2	+	1*3	=	24

Legend: 🔴 High 🟡 Medium 🟢 Low

• **Figure 20.8**   Final quantitative assessment of the findings

SLE

The single loss expectancy is calculated using the following formula:

SLE = asset value (AV) × exposure factor (EF)

Exposure factor is a measure of the magnitude of loss of an asset.

For example, to calculate the exposure factor, assume the asset value of a small office building and its contents is $2 million. Also assume that this building houses the call center for a business, and the complete loss of the center would take away about half of the capability of the company. Therefore, the exposure factor is 50 percent. The SLE is

$2 million × 0.5 = $1 million

ALE

The ALE is then calculated simply by multiplying the SLE by the likelihood or number of times the event is expected to occur in a year, which is called the annualized rate of occurrence (ARO):

ALE = SLE × ARO

ARO

The annualized rate of occurrence (ARO) is a representation of the frequency of the event, measured in a standard year. If the event is expected to occur once in 20 years, then the ARO is 1/20. Typically the ARO is defined by historical data, either from a company's own experience or from industry surveys. Continuing our example, assume that a fire at this business's location is expected to occur about once in 20 years. Given this information, the ALE is

$1 million × 1/20 = $50,000

The ALE determines a threshold for evaluating the cost/benefit ratio of a given countermeasure. Therefore, a countermeasure to protect this business adequately should cost no more than the calculated ALE of $50,000 per year.

The examples in this chapter have been simplistic, but they demonstrate the concepts of both qualitative and quantitative risk analysis. More complex algorithms and software packages are available for accomplishing risk analyses, but these examples suffice for the purposes of this text.

Exam Tip: It is always advisable to memorize these fundamental equations for certifications such as CompTIA Security+:

SLE = AV × EF
ALE = SLE × ARO

Impact

The impact of an event is a measure of the actual loss when a threat exploits a vulnerability. Federal Information Processing Standards (FIPS) 199 defines three levels of impact using the terms high, moderate, and low. The impact needs to be defined in terms of the context of each organization, as what is high for some firms may be low for much larger firms. The common method is to define the impact levels in terms of important business criteria. Impacts can be in terms of cost (dollars), performance (service level agreement [SLA] or other requirements), schedule (deliverables), or any other important item. Impact can also be categorized in terms of the information security attribute that is relevant to the problem: confidentiality, integrity, or availability.

MTTR

Mean time to repair (MTTR) is a common measure of how long it takes to repair a given failure. This is the average time, and may or may not include the time needed to obtain parts.

MTBF

Mean time between failures (MTBF) is a common measure of reliability of a system and is an expression of the average time between system failures. The time between failures is measured from the time a system returns to service until the next failure. The MTBF is an arithmetic mean of a set of system failures:

MTBF = σ (start of downtime – start of uptime) / number of failures

MTTF

Mean time to failure (MTTF) is a variation of MTBF, one that is commonly used instead of MTBF when the system is replaced in lieu of being repaired. Other than the semantic difference, the calculations are the same, and the meaning is essentially the same.

> **Measurement of Availability**
>
> **Availability** is a measure of the amount of time a system performs its intended function. Reliability is a measure of the frequency of system failures. Availability is related to, but different than, reliability and is typically expressed as a percentage of time the system is in its operational state. To calculate availability, both the MTTF and the MTTR are needed:
>
> Availability = MTTF / (MTTF + MTTR)
>
> Assuming a system has an MTTF of 6 months and the repair takes 30 minutes, the availability would be
>
> Availability = 6 months / (6 months + 30 minutes) = 99.9884%

■ Qualitative vs. Quantitative Risk Assessment

It is recognized throughout industry that it is *impossible* to conduct risk management that is purely *quantitative*. Usually risk management includes both qualitative and quantitative elements, requiring both analysis and judgment or experience. In contrast to quantitative assessment, it is *possible* to accomplish *purely qualitative* risk management. It is easy to see that it is impossible to define and quantitatively measure all factors that exist in a given risk assessment. It is also easy to see that a risk assessment that measures no factors quantitatively but measures them all qualitatively is possible.

The decision of whether to use qualitative versus quantitative risk management depends on the criticality of the project, the resources available, and the management style. The decision will be influenced by the degree to which the fundamental risk management metrics, such as asset value, exposure factor, and threat frequency, can be quantitatively defined.

■ Tools

Many tools can be used to enhance the risk management process. The following tools can be used during the various phases of risk assessment to add objectivity and structure to the process. Understanding the details of each of these tools is not necessary for the CompTIA Security+ exam, but understanding what they can be used for is important. More information on these tools can be found in any good project-management text.

- ■ **Affinity grouping** A method of identifying items that are related and then identifying the principle that ties them together.

Tech Tip

Accepting Risk

In addition to mitigating risk or transferring risk, a manager, knowing the potential cost of a given risk and its associated probability, may accept responsibility for the risk if it does happen. For example, a manager may choose to allow a programmer to make "emergency" changes to a production system (in violation of good segregation of duties) because the system cannot go down during a given period of time. The manager accepts the risk that the programmer could possibly make unauthorized changes because of the high availability requirement of that system. However, there should always be some additional controls such as a management review or a standardized approval process to ensure the assumed risk is adequately managed.

- **Baseline identification and analysis** The process of establishing a baseline set of risks. It produces a "snapshot" of all the identified risks at a given point in time.

- **Cause and effect analysis** Identifying relationships between a risk and the factors that can cause it. This is usually accomplished using *fishbone diagrams* developed by Dr. Kaoru Ishikawa, former professor of engineering at the Science University of Tokyo.

- **Cost/benefit analysis** A straightforward method for comparing cost estimates with the benefits of a mitigation strategy.

- **Gantt charts** A management tool for diagramming schedules, events, and activity duration.

- **Interrelationship digraphs** A method for identifying cause-and-effect relationships by clearly defining the problem to be solved, identifying the key elements of the problem, and then describing the relationships between each of the key elements.

- **Pareto charts** A histogram that ranks the categories in a chart from most frequent to least frequent, thus facilitating risk prioritization.

- **PERT (program evaluation and review technique) charts** A diagram depicting interdependencies between project activities, showing the sequence and duration of each activity. When complete, the chart shows the time necessary to complete the project and the activities that determine that time (the critical path).

- **Risk management plan** A comprehensive plan documenting how risks will be managed on a given project. It contains processes, activities, milestones, organizations, responsibilities, and details of each major risk management activity and how it is to be accomplished. It is an integral part of the project management plan.

Cost-Effectiveness Modeling

Cost-effectiveness modeling assumes you are incurring a cost and focuses on the question of what the value of that cost is. This is a rational means of economic analysis used to determine the utility of a specific strategy. It is a nearly foregone conclusion you will be spending resources on security; this just reframes the question to one of utility and outcome from the activity.

A related term, total cost of ownership (TCO), is the set of all costs, everything from capital costs to operational and exception-handling costs, that is associated with a technology. There are a lot of arguments over how to calculate TCO, typically to favor one solution over another, but that is not important in this instance. It is important to note the differences between normal operational costs and exception handling. Exception handling is always more expensive.

The objective in risk management is to have a set of overlapping controls such that the TCO is minimized. This means that the solution has a measured effectiveness across the risk spectrum and that exceptions are minimalized. This is where the compliance versus security debate becomes interesting. We establish compliance rules for a variety of reasons, but once established, their future effectiveness depends upon the assumption that

Tech Tip

Risks Really Don't Change, but They Can Be Mitigated

One final thought to keep in mind is that the risk itself doesn't really change, no matter what actions are taken to mitigate that risk. A high risk will always be a high risk. However, actions can be taken to reduce the likelihood of the risk, and the impact of that risk if it occurs.

the same risk environment exists as when they were created. Should the risk, the value, or the impact change over time, the cost effectiveness of the compliance-directed control can shift, frequently in a negative fashion.

Risk Management Best Practices

Best practices are the best defenses that an organization can employ in any activity. One manner of examining best practices is to ensure that the business has the set of best practices to cover its operational responsibilities. At a deeper level, the details of these practices need to themselves be best practices if one is to get the best level of protection. At a minimum, risk mitigation best practices include business continuity, high availability, fault tolerance, and disaster recovery concepts.

None of these operate in isolation. In fact, they are all interconnected, sharing elements as they all work together to achieve a common purpose: the security of the data in the enterprise, which is measured in terms of risk exposure. Key elements of best practices include understanding of vulnerabilities, understanding the threat vectors and likelihoods of occurrence, and the use of mitigation techniques to reduce residual risk to manageable levels.

System Vulnerabilities

Vulnerabilities are characteristics of an asset that can be exploited by a threat to cause harm. All systems have bugs or errors. Not all errors or bugs are vulnerabilities. For an error or bug to be classified as a vulnerability, it must be exploitable, meaning an attacker must be able to use the bug to cause a desired result. There are three elements needed for a vulnerability to occur:

- The system must have a flaw.
- The flaw must be accessible by an attacker.
- The attacker must possess the ability to exploit the flaw.

Vulnerabilities can exist in many levels and from many causes. From design errors, coding errors, or unintended (and untested) combinations in complex systems, there are numerous forms of vulnerabilities. Vulnerabilities can exist in software, hardware, and procedures. Whether in the underlying system, in a security control designed to protect the system, or in the procedures employed in the operational use of the system, the result is the same: a vulnerability represents an exploitable weakness that increases the level of risk associated with the system.

Exam Tip: Vulnerabilities can be fixed, removed, and mitigated. They are part of any system and represent weaknesses that may be exploited.

Threat Vectors

A threat is any circumstance or event with the potential to cause harm to an asset. For example, a malicious hacker might choose to hack your system by using readily available hacking tools. Threats can be classified in groups, with the term *threat vector* describing the elements of these groups. A threat vector is the path or tool used by an attacker to attack a target.

There are a wide range of threat vectors that a security professional needs to understand:

- The Web (fake sites, session hijacking, malware, watering hole attacks)
- Wireless unsecured hotspots
- Mobile devices (iOS/Android)
- USB (removable) media
- E-mail (links, attachments, malware)
- Social engineering (deceptions, hoaxes, scams, and fraud)

This listing is merely a sample of threat vectors. From a defensive point of view, it is important not to become fixated on specific threats, but rather to pay attention to the threat vectors. If a user visits a web site that has malicious code, then the nature of the code, although important from a technical view in one respect, is not the primary concern. The primary issue is the malicious site, as this is the threat vector.

Probability/Threat Likelihood

The probability or likelihood of an event is a measure of how often it is expected to occur. From a qualitative assessment using terms such as frequent, occasionally, and rare, to the quantitative measure ARO, the purpose is to allow scaling based on frequency of an event. Determining the specific probabilities of security events with any accuracy is a nearly impossible feat. What is important in the use of probabilities and likelihoods is the relationship it has with respect to determining relative risk. Just as an insurance company cannot tell you when you will have an accident, no one can predict when a security event will occur. What can be determined is that over some course of time—say, the next year—a significant number of users will click malicious links in e-mails. The threat likelihood of different types of attacks will change over time. Years ago, web defacements were all the rage. Today, spear phishing is more prevalent.

When examining risk, the probability or threat likelihood plays a significant role in the determination of risk and mitigation options. In many cases, the likelihood is treated as certain, and for repeat attacks, this may be appropriate, but it certainly is not universally true.

Risk-Avoidance, Transference, Acceptance, Mitigation, Deterrence

Risks are absolutes—they cannot be removed or eliminated. Actions can be taken to change the effects that a risk poses to a system, but the risk itself doesn't really change, no matter what actions are taken to mitigate that risk. A high risk will always be a high risk. However, actions can be taken to reduce the impact of that risk if it occurs. A limited number of strategies can be used to manage risk. The risk can be avoided, transferred, mitigated, or accepted.

Avoiding the risk can be accomplished in many ways. Although threats cannot be removed from the environment, one's exposure can be altered. Not deploying a module that increases risk is one manner of risk avoidance.

The use of insurance-type actuarial models for risk determination is useful when risks are independent, such as in auto accidents. But controls need to be added when a factor becomes less independent, such as a bad driver. In cybersecurity, once an attack is successful, it is repeatedly employed against a victim, breaking any form of independence and making the probability = 1. This lessens the true usefulness of the insurance-type actuarial models in cybersecurity practice.

Another possible action to manage risk is to transfer that risk. A common method of transferring risk is to purchase insurance. Insurance allows risk to be transferred to a third party that manages specific types of risk for multiple parties, thus reducing the individual cost. Another common example of risk transfer is the protection against fraud that consumers have on their credit cards. The risk is transferred to another party, so people can use the card in confidence.

Risk can also be mitigated through the application of controls that reduce the impact of an attack. Controls can alert operators so that the level of exposure is reduced through process intervention. When an action occurs that is outside the accepted risk profile, a second set of rules can be applied, such as calling the customer for verification before committing a transaction. Controls such as these can act to reduce the risk associated with potential high-risk operations.

Accepting risk is always an option; in fact, if risks are not addressed, then this action occurs as a default. Understand that risk cannot be completely eliminated. A risk that remains after implementing controls is termed a *residual risk*. In this step, you further evaluate residual risks to identify where additional controls are required to reduce risk even more. This leads us to the earlier statement, in the chapter introduction, that the risk management process is iterative.

Risks Associated with Cloud Computing and Virtualization

When examining a complex system such as a cloud or virtual computing environment from a risk perspective, several basic considerations always need to be observed. First, the fact that a system is either in the cloud or virtualized does not change how risk works. Risk is everywhere, and changing a system to a new environment does not change the fact that there are risks. Second, complexity can increase risk exposure.

There are specific risks associated with both virtualization and cloud environments. Having data and computing occur in environments that are not under the direct control of the data owner adds both a layer of complexity and a degree of risk. The potential for issues with confidentiality, integrity, and availability increases with the loss of direct control over the environment. The virtualization and cloud layers also present new avenues of attack into a system.

Security is a particular challenge when data and computation are handled by a remote party, as in cloud computing. The specific challenge is how to allow data outside your enterprise and yet remain in control over the use of the data. The common answer is encryption. Through the proper use of encryption of data before it leaves the enterprise, external storage can still be performed securely by properly employing cryptographic elements. The security requirements associated with confidentiality, integrity, and availability remain the responsibility of the data owner, and measures must be taken to ensure that these requirements are met, regardless of the location or usage associated with the data. Another level of protections is through the use of service level agreements (SLAs) with the cloud vendor, although these frequently cannot offer much remedy in the event of data loss.

Chapter 20 Review

■ Chapter Summary

After reading this chapter and completing the exercises, you should understand the following about risk management.

Use risk management tools and principles to manage risk effectively

- Risk management is a key management process that must be used at every level, whether managing a project, a program, or an enterprise.

- Risk management is also a strategic tool to more effectively manage increasingly sophisticated, diverse, and geographically expansive business opportunities.

- Common business risks include fraud and management of treasury, revenue, contracts, environment, regulatory issues, business continuity, and technology.

- Technology risks include security and privacy, information technology operations, business systems control and effectiveness, information systems testing, and management of business continuity, reliability and performance, information technology assets, project risk, and change.

Explore risk mitigation strategies

- Many business processes can be used to mitigate specific forms of risk. These tools include change and incident management, user rights and permission reviews, routine system audits, and the use of technological controls to prevent or alert on data loss.

Describe risk models

- A general model for managing risk includes asset identification, threat assessment, impact determination and quantification, control design and evaluation, and residual risk management.

- The SEI model for managing risk includes these steps: identify, analyze, plan, track, and control.

Explain the differences between qualitative and quantitative risk assessment

- Both qualitative and quantitative risk assessment approaches must be used to manage risk

effectively, and a number of approaches were presented in this chapter.

- Qualitative risk assessment relies on expert judgment and experience by comparing the impact of a threat with the probability of it occurring.

- Qualitative risk assessment can be a simple binary assessment weighing high or low impact against high or low probability. Additional levels can be used to increase the comprehensiveness of the analysis. The well-known red-yellow-green stoplight mechanism is qualitative in nature and is easily understood.

- Quantitative risk assessment applies historical information and trends to assess risk. Models are often used to provide information to decision-makers.

- A common quantitative approach calculates the annualized loss expectancy from the single loss expectancy and the annualized rate of occurrence (ALE = SLE × ARO).

- It is important to understand that it is impossible to conduct a purely quantitative risk assessment, but it is possible to conduct a purely qualitative risk assessment.

Use risk management tools

- Numerous tools can be used to add credibility and rigor to the risk assessment process.

- Risk assessment tools help identify relationships, causes, and effects. They assist in prioritizing decisions and facilitate effective management of the risk management process.

Examine risk management best practices

- Explore business continuity concepts.

- Explore the relationships between vulnerabilities, threat vectors, probabilities, and threat likelihoods as they apply to risk management.

- Understand the differences between risk avoidance, transference, acceptance, mitigation, and deterrence.

Key Terms

annualized loss expectancy (ALE) *(611)*
annualized rate of occurrence (ARO) *(611)*
asset *(610)*
availability *(625)*
control *(610)*
countermeasure *(611)*
exposure factor *(611)*
hazard *(611)*
impact *(610)*
intangible impact *(617)*
mean time between failures (MTBF) *(624)*
mean time to failure (MTTF) *(625)*
mean time to repair (MTTR) *(624)*
mitigate *(611)*
qualitative risk assessment *(611)*

quantitative risk assessment *(611)*
residual risk *(618)*
risk *(610)*
risk analysis *(610)*
risk assessment *(610)*
risk management *(610)*
safeguard *(610)*
single loss expectancy (SLE) *(611)*
systematic risk *(611)*
tangible impact *(617)*
threat *(610)*
threat actor *(610)*
threat vector *(610)*
unsystematic risk *(611)*
vulnerability *(610)*

Key Terms Quiz

Use terms from the Key Terms list to complete the sentences that follow. Don't use the same term more than once. Not all terms will be used.

1. Asset value × exposure factor = _____.

2. A control may also be called a(n) _____ or a(n) _____.

3. When a threat exploits a vulnerability, you experience a(n) _____.

4. Single loss expectancy × annualized rate of occurrence = _____.

5. If you reduce the likelihood of a threat occurring, you _____ a risk.

6. The _____ measures the magnitude of the loss of an asset.

7. Risk analysis is synonymous with _____.

8. Any circumstance or event with the potential to cause harm to an asset is a(n) _____.

9. A characteristic of an asset that can be exploited by a threat to cause harm is its _____.

10. _____ is a circumstance that increases the likelihood or probable severity of a loss.

Multiple-Choice Quiz

1. Which of the following correctly defines qualitative risk management?

   A. The process of objectively determining the impact of an event that affects a project, program, or business

   B. The process of subjectively determining the impact of an event that affects a project, program, or business

   C. The loss that results when a vulnerability is exploited by a threat

   D. To reduce the likelihood of a threat occurring

2. Which of the following correctly defines risk?

   A. The risk still remaining after an iteration of risk management

   B. The loss that results when a vulnerability is exploited by a threat

   C. Any circumstance or event with the potential to cause harm to an asset

   D. The possibility of suffering harm or loss

3. Single loss expectancy (SLE) can best be defined by which of the following equations?

   A. SLE = annualized loss expectancy × annualized rate of occurrence

   B. SLE = asset value × exposure factor

   C. SLE = asset value × annualized rate of occurrence

   D. SLE = annualized loss expectancy × exposure factor

4. Which of the following correctly defines annualized rate of occurrence?

   A. How much an event is expected to cost per year

   B. A measure of the magnitude of loss of an asset

   C. On an annualized basis, the frequency with which an event is expected to occur

   D. The resources or information an organization needs to conduct its business

For questions 5 and 6, assume the following: The asset value of a small distribution warehouse is $5 million, and this warehouse serves as a backup facility. Its complete destruction by a disaster would take away about 1/5 of the capability of the business. Also assume that this sort of disaster is expected to occur about once every 50 years.

5. Which of the following is the calculated single loss expectancy (SLE)?

   A. SLE = $25 million

   B. SLE = $1 million

   C. SLE = $2.5 million

   D. SLE = $5 million

6. Which of the following is the calculated annualized loss expectancy (ALE)?

   A. ALE = $50,000

   B. ALE = $1 million

   C. ALE = $20,000

   D. ALE = $50 million

7. When discussing qualitative risk assessment versus quantitative risk assessment, which of the following is true?

   A. It is impossible to conduct a purely quantitative risk assessment, and it is impossible to conduct a purely qualitative risk assessment.

   B. It is possible to conduct a purely quantitative risk assessment, but it is impossible to conduct a purely qualitative risk assessment.

   C. It is impossible to conduct a purely quantitative risk assessment, but it is possible to conduct a purely qualitative risk assessment.

   D. It is possible to conduct a purely quantitative risk assessment, and it is possible to conduct a purely qualitative risk assessment.

8. Which of the following correctly defines residual risk?

   A. The risk still remaining after an iteration of risk management

   B. The possibility of suffering a loss

   C. The result of a vulnerability being exploited by a threat that results in a loss

   D. Characteristics of an asset that can be exploited by a threat to cause harm

9. Which of the following statements about risk is true?

   A. A manager can accept the risk, which will reduce the risk.

   B. The risk itself doesn't really change. However, actions can be taken to reduce the impact of the risk.

   C. A manager can transfer the risk, which will reduce the risk.

   D. A manager can take steps to increase the risk.

10. Fill in the blanks. Availability is calculated using the formula
    Availability = A / (B + C)
    A = _____
    B = _____
    C = _____

Essay Quiz

1. You are drafting an e-mail to your risk management team members to explain the difference between tangible assets and intangible assets. Relate potential threats and risk to tangible and intangible impacts. Write a short paragraph that explains the difference and include two examples of each.

2. You have been tasked to initiate a risk management program for your company. The CEO has just asked you to succinctly explain the relationship between impact, threat, and vulnerability. Think quick on your feet and give a single sentence that explains the relationship.

3. Your CEO now says, "You mentioned that risks always exist. If I take enough measures, can't I eliminate the risk?" Explain why risks always exist.

4. You are explaining your risk management plan to a new team member just brought on as part of a college internship program. The intern asks, "With respect to impact, what does a threat do to a risk?" How would you answer?

5. The intern mentioned in Question 4 now asks you to compare and contrast accepting risk, transferring risk, and mitigating risk. What's your response?

Lab Projects

• Lab Project 20.1

The asset value of a distribution center (located in the midwestern United States) and its inventory is $10 million. It is one of two identical facilities (the other is in the southwestern United States). Its complete destruction by a disaster would thus take away half of the capability of the business. Also assume that this sort of disaster is expected to occur about once every 100 years. From this, calculate the annualized loss expectancy.

• Lab Project 20.2

You have just completed a qualitative threat assessment of the computer security of your organization, with the impacts and probabilities of occurrence listed in the table that follows. Properly place the threats in a 3-by-3 table similar to that in Figure 20.5. Which of the threats should you take action on, which should you monitor, and which ones may not need your immediate attention?

Threat	Impact	Probability of Occurrence
Virus attacks	High	High
Internet hacks	Medium	High
Disgruntled employee hacks	High	Medium
Weak incidence response mechanisms	Medium	Medium
Theft of information by a trusted third-party contractor	Low	Medium
Competitor hacks	High	Low
Inadvertent release of noncritical information	Low	Low

chapter

21

Change Management

It is not the strongest of the species that survive, nor the most intelligent, but the one most responsive to change.

—Charles Darwin

In this chapter, you will learn how to

■ Use change management as an important enterprise management tool

■ Institute the key concept of separation of duties

■ Identify the essential elements of change management

■ Implement change management

■ Use the concepts of the Capability Maturity Model Integration

It is well recognized that today's computer systems are extremely complex, and it is obvious that inventory management systems for large international enterprises such as Wal-Mart and Home Depot are probably as complex as an aircraft or skyscraper. Prominent operating systems such as Windows and UNIX are also very complex, as are computer processors on a chip. Many of today's web-based applications are extremely complex as well. For example, today's web-based applications typically consist of flash content on web sites interacting with remote databases through a variety of services or service-oriented architectures hosted on web servers located anywhere in the world.

You wouldn't think of constructing an aircraft, large building, computer chip, or automobile in the informal manner sometimes used to develop and operate computer systems of equal complexity. Computer systems have grown to be so complex and mission-critical that enterprises cannot afford to develop and maintain them in an ad hoc manner.

Change management procedures can add structure and control to the development and management of large software systems as they move from development to implementation and during operation. In this chapter, change management refers to a standard methodology for performing and recording changes during software development and system operation. The methodology defines steps that ensure that system changes are required by the organization and are properly authorized, documented, tested, and approved by management. In many conversations, the term **configuration management** is considered synonymous with change management and, in a more limited manner, version control or release control.

The term change management is often applied to the management of changes in the business environment, typically as a result of business process reengineering or quality enhancement efforts. The term change management as used in this chapter is directly related to managing and controlling software development, maintenance, and system operation. Configuration management is the application of change management principles to configuration of both software and hardware.

Why Change Management?

To manage the system development and maintenance processes effectively, you need discipline and structure to help conserve resources and enhance effectiveness. Change management, like risk management, is often considered expensive, nonproductive, unnecessary, and confusing—an impediment to progress. However, like risk management, change management can be scaled to control and manage the development and maintenance of systems effectively.

Cross Check

Risk Management and Change Management Are Essential Business Processes

Chapter 20 presented risk management as an essential decision-making process. In much the same way, change management is an essential practice for managing a system during its entire lifecycle, from development through deployment and operation, until it is taken out of service. What security-specific risk-based questions should be asked during change management reviews?

Change management should be used in all phases of a system's life: development, testing, quality assurance (QA), and production. Short development cycles have not changed the need for an appropriate amount of management control over software development, maintenance, and operation. In fact, short turnaround times make change management more necessary, because once a system goes active in today's services-based environments, it often cannot be taken offline to correct errors—it must stay up and online or business will be lost and brand recognition damaged. In today's volatile stock market, for example, even small indicators of lagging performance can have dramatic impacts on a company's stock value.

The following scenarios exemplify the need for appropriate change management policy and for procedures over software, hardware, and data:

- *The developers can't find the latest version of the production source code.* Change management practices support versioning of software changes.

- *A bug corrected a few months ago mysteriously reappears.* Proper change management ensures developers always use the most recently changed source code.

- *Fielded software was working fine yesterday but does not work properly today.* Good change management controls access to previously modified modules so that previously corrected errors aren't reintroduced into the system.

- *Development team members overwrote each other's changes.* Today's change management tools support collaborative development.

- *A programmer spent several hours changing the wrong version of the software.* Change management tools support viable management of previous software versions.

- *New tax rates stored in a table have been overwritten with last year's tax rates.* Change control prevents inadvertent overwriting of critical reference data.

- *A network administrator inadvertently brings down a server as he incorrectly punched down the wrong wires.* Just like a blueprint shows key electrical paths, data center connection paths can be version-controlled.

- *A newly installed server is hacked soon after installation because it is improperly configured.* Network and system administrators use change management to ensure configurations consistently meet security standards.

Try This!

Scope of Change Management

See if you can explain why each of the following should be placed under an appropriate change management process:

- Web pages
- Service packs
- Security patches
- Third-party software releases
- Test data and test scripts
- Parameter files
- Scripts, stored procedures, or job control language–type programs
- Customized vendor code
- Source code of any kind
- Applications

Just about anyone with more than a year's experience in software development or system operations can relate to at least one of the preceding scenarios. However, each of these scenarios can be controlled, and impacts mitigated, through proper change management procedures.

The Sarbanes-Oxley Act of 2002, officially entitled the Public Company Accounting Reform and Investor Protection Act of 2002, was enacted July 30, 2002, to help ensure management establishes viable governance environments and control structures to ensure accuracy of financial reporting. Section 404 outlines the requirements most applicable to information technology. Change management is an essential part of creating a viable governance and control structure and critical to compliance with the Sarbanes-Oxley Act.

■ The Key Concept: Separation of Duties

A foundation for change management is the recognition that involving more than one individual in a process can reduce risk. Good business control practices require that duties be assigned to individuals in such a way that no one individual can control all phases of a process or the processing and recording of a transaction. This is called **separation of duties** (also called *segregation of duties*). It is an important means by which errors and fraudulent or malicious acts can be discouraged and prevented. Separation of duties can be applied in many organizational scenarios because it establishes a basis for accountability and control. Proper separation of duties can safeguard enterprise assets and protect against risks. They should be documented, monitored, and enforced.

A well-understood business example of separation of duties is in the management and payment of vendor invoices. If a person can create a vendor in the finance system, enter invoices for payment, and then authorize a payment check to be written, it is apparent that fraud could be perpetrated because the person could write a check to himself for services never performed. Separating duties by requiring one person to create the vendors and another person to enter invoices and write checks makes it more difficult for someone to defraud an employer.

Information technology (IT) organizations should design, implement, monitor, and enforce appropriate separation of duties for the enterprise's information systems and processes. Today's computer systems are rapidly evolving into an increasingly decentralized and networked computer infrastructure. In the absence of adequate IT controls, such rapid growth may allow exploitation of large amounts of enterprise information in a short time. Further, the knowledge of computer operations held by IT staff is significantly greater than that of an average user, and this knowledge could be abused for malicious purposes.

Some of the best practices for ensuring proper separation of duties in an IT organization are as follows:

- Separation of duties between development, testing, QA, and production should be documented in written procedures and implemented by software or manual processes.

- Program developers' and program testers' activities should be conducted on "test" data only. They should be restricted from accessing "live" production data. This will assist in ensuring an independent and objective testing environment without jeopardizing the confidentiality and integrity of production data.

- End users or computer operations personnel should not have direct access to program source code. This control helps lessen the opportunity of exploiting software weaknesses or introducing malicious code (or code that has not been properly tested) into the production environment either intentionally or unintentionally.

- Functions of creating, installing, and administrating software programs should be assigned to different individuals. For example, since developers create and enhance programs, they should not be able to install it on the production system. Likewise, database administrators should not be program developers on database systems they administer.

- All accesses and privileges to systems, software, or data should be granted based on the principle of least privilege, which gives users no more privileges than are necessary to perform their jobs. Access privileges should be reviewed regularly to ensure that individuals who no longer require access have had their access removed.

- Formal change management policy and procedures should be enforced throughout the enterprise. Any changes in hardware and software components (including emergency changes) that are implemented after the system has been placed into production must go through the approved formal change management mechanism.

Tech Tip

Steps to Implement Separation of Duties

1. *Identify an indispensable function that is potentially subject to abuse.*

2. *Divide the function into separate steps, each containing a small part of the power that enables the function to be abused.*

3. *Assign each step to a different person or organization.*

Managers at all levels should review existing and planned processes and systems to ensure proper separation of duties. Smaller business entities may not have the resources to implement all of the preceding practices fully, but other control mechanisms, including hiring qualified personnel, bonding contractors, and using training, monitoring, and evaluation practices, can reduce any organization's exposure to risk. The establishment of such practices can ensure that enterprise assets are properly safeguarded and can also greatly reduce error and the potential for fraudulent or malicious activities.

Change management practices implement and enforce separation of duties by adding structure and management oversight to the software development and system operation processes. Change management techniques can ensure that only correct and authorized changes, as approved by management or other authorities, are allowed to be made, following a defined process.

■ Elements of Change Management

Change management has its roots in system engineering, where it is commonly referred to as *configuration management*. Most of today's software and hardware change management practices derive from long-standing system engineering configuration management practices. Computer hardware and software development have evolved to the point that proper management structure and controls must exist to ensure the products operate as planned. Issues such as the Heartbleed and Shellshock incidents illustrate the need to understand configurations and change.

Change management and configuration management use different terms for their various phases, but they all fit into the four general phases defined under configuration management:

- Configuration identification
- Configuration control
- Configuration status accounting
- Configuration auditing

Configuration identification is the process of identifying which assets need to be managed and controlled. These assets could be software modules, test cases or scripts, table or parameter values, servers, major subsystems, or entire systems. The idea is that, depending on the size and complexity of the system, an appropriate set of data and software (or other assets) must be identified and properly managed. These identified assets are called **configuration items** or **computer software configuration items**.

Related to configuration identification, and the result of it, is the definition of a baseline. A **baseline** serves as a foundation for comparison or measurement. It provides the necessary visibility to control change. For example, a software baseline defines the software system as it is built and running at a point in time. As another example, network security best practices clearly state that any large organization should build its servers to a standard build configuration to enhance overall network security. The servers are the configuration items, and the standard build is the server baseline.

> **Tech Tip**
>
> **Change Management**
> *The* ITIL v3 Glossary *defines change management as* "The process responsible for controlling the lifecycle of all changes. The primary objective of change management is to enable beneficial changes to be made, with minimum disruption to IT services." *See https://www.axelos .com/glossaries-of-terms.*

Large enterprise application systems require viable change management systems. For example, SAP has its own change management system called the Transport Management System (TMS). Third-party software such as Phire Architect (www.phire-soft .com) and Stat for PeopleSoft (http://software.dell.com/ products/stat-peoplesoft/) provide change management applications for Oracle's PeopleSoft or E-Business Suite.

It is important that you understand that even though all servers may be initially configured to the same baseline, individual applications might require a system-specific configuration to run properly. Change management actually facilitates system-specific configuration in that all exceptions from the standard configuration are documented. All people involved in managing and operating these systems will have documentation to help them quickly understand why a particular system is configured in a unique way.

Configuration control is the process of controlling changes to items that have been baselined. Configuration control ensures that only approved changes to a baseline are allowed to be implemented. It is easy to understand why a software system, such as a web-based order entry system, should not be changed without proper testing and control—otherwise, the system might stop functioning at a critical time. Configuration control is a key step that provides valuable insight to managers. If a system is being changed, and configuration control is being observed, managers and others concerned will be better informed. This ensures proper use of assets and avoids unnecessary downtime due to the installation of unapproved changes.

Configuration status accounting consists of the procedures for tracking and maintaining data relative to each configuration item in the baseline. It is closely related to configuration control. Status accounting involves gathering and maintaining information relative to each configuration item. For example, it documents what changes have been requested; what changes have been made, when, and for what reason; who authorized the change; who performed the change; and what other configuration items or systems were affected by the change.

Returning to our example of servers being baselined, if the operating system of those servers is found to have a security flaw, then the baseline can be consulted to determine which servers are vulnerable to this particular security flaw. Those systems with this weakness can be updated (and only those that need to be updated). Configuration control and configuration status accounting help ensure that systems are more consistently managed and, ultimately in this case, the organization's network security is maintained. It is easy to imagine the state of an organization that has not built all servers to a common baseline and has not properly controlled its systems' configurations. It would be very difficult to know the configuration of individual servers, and security could quickly become weak.

Configuration auditing is the process of verifying that the configuration items are built and maintained according to the requirements, standards, or contractual agreements. It is similar to how audits in the financial world are used to ensure that generally accepted accounting principles and practices are adhered to and that financial statements properly reflect the financial status of the enterprise. Configuration audits ensure that policies and procedures are being followed, that all configuration items (including hardware and software) are being properly maintained, and that existing documentation accurately reflects the status of the systems in operation.

Configuration auditing takes on two forms: functional and physical. A *functional configuration audit* verifies that the configuration item performs as defined by the documentation of the system requirements. A *physical configuration audit* confirms that all configuration items to be included in a release, install, change, or upgrade are actually included, and that no additional items are included—no more, no less.

■ Implementing Change Management

Change management requires some structure and discipline in order to be effective. The change management function is scalable from small to enterprise-level projects. Figure 21.1 illustrates a sample software change

Developer checks out source code, modifies it, checks it back into the code-control tool, and notifies the buildmaster

Buildmaster incorporates modified code, compiles code into new build, and notifies sysadmin that it is ready for Test/QA

Sysadmin moves executables to Test/QA system; Test/QA completes tests and notifies manager

Manager approves change and sysadmin moves executables to production

• **Figure 21.1**   Software change control workflow

management flow appropriate for medium to large projects. It can be adapted to small organizations by having the developer perform work only on her workstation (never on the production system) and having the system administrator serve in the buildmaster function. The buildmaster is usually an independent person responsible for compiling and incorporating changed software into an executable image.

Figure 21.1 shows that developers never have access to the production system or data. It also demonstrates proper separation of duties between developers, QA and test personnel, and production. It implies that a distinct separation exists between development, testing and QA, and production environments. This workflow is for changes that have a major impact on production or the customer's business process. For minor changes that have minimal risk or impact on business processes, some of the steps may be omitted.

The change management workflow proceeds as follows:

1. The developer checks out source code from the code-control tool archive to the development system.

2. The developer modifies the code and conducts unit testing of the changed modules.

3. The developer checks the modified code into the code-control tool archive.

4. The developer notifies the buildmaster that changes are ready for a new build and testing/QA.

5. The buildmaster creates a build incorporating the modified code and compiles the code.

6. The buildmaster notifies the system administrator that the executable image is ready for testing/QA.

7. The system administrator moves the executables to the test/QA system.

Tech Tip

Release Management
The ITIL v3 Glossary *defines release management as "The process responsible for planning, scheduling and controlling the movement of releases to test and live environments. The primary objective of release management is to ensure that the integrity of the live environment is protected and that the correct components are released." See https://www.axelos .com/glossaries-of-terms.*

8. QA tests the new executables. If the tests are passed, test/QA notifies the manager. If tests fail, the process starts over.

9. Upon manager approval, the system administrator moves the executable to the production system.

Backout Plan

One of the key elements of a change plan is a comprehensive backout plan. If in the course of a planned change activity in production a problem occurs that prevents going forward, it is essential to have a backout plan to restore the system to its previous operating condition. A common element in many operating system updates is the inability to go back to a previous version. This is fine provided that the update goes perfectly, but if for some reason it fails, what then? For a personal device, there may be some inconvenience. For a server in production, this can have significant business implications. The ultimate in backout plans is the restoration of a complete backup of the system. Backups can be time consuming and difficult in some environments, but the spread of virtualization into the enterprise provides many more options in configuration management and backout plans.

■ The Purpose of a Change Control Board

To oversee the change management process, most organizations establish a **change control board (CCB)**. In practice, a CCB not only facilitates adequate management oversight, but also facilitates better coordination between projects. The CCB convenes on a regular basis, usually weekly or monthly, and can be convened on an emergency or as-needed basis as well. Figure 21.2 shows the process for implementing and properly controlling hardware or software during changes.

The CCB's membership should consist of development project managers, network administrators, system administrators, test/QA managers, an information security manager, an operations center manager, and a help desk manager. Others can be added as necessary, depending on the size and complexity of the organization.

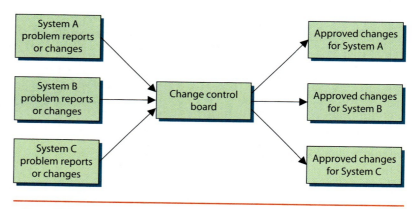

• **Figure 21.2** Change control board process

A **system problem report (SPR)** is used to track changes through the CCB. The SPR documents changes or corrections to a system. It reflects who requested the change and why, what analysis must be done and by whom, and how the change was corrected or implemented. Figure 21.3 shows a sample SPR. Most large enterprises cannot rely on a paper-based SPR process and instead use one of the many software systems available to perform change management functions. While this example shows a paper-based SPR, it contains all the elements of change management: it describes the problem and who reported it, it outlines resolution of the problem, and it documents approval of the change.

Figure 21.4 shows the entire change management process and its relationship to incident management and release management.

Code Integrity

One key benefit of adequate change management is the assurance of code consistency and integrity. Whenever a modified program is moved to

SYSTEM PROBLEM REPORT (SPR)

❑ Error   SPR Number: _____

❑ Improvement   Originator: _____

-------------------------- **Problem** --------------------------------

System Affected: _____

Related Systems: _____

Classification: Problem Description: _____

❑ Software   _____

❑ Hardware   _____

❑ Documentation   _____

❑ Comment   _____

Analysis Assigned to: _____

-------------------------- **Analysis** -------------------------------

(Prepared by responsible software design organization)   Date Received: _____

Classification: Explanation:

❑ Design   _____

❑ Coding   _____

❑ Documentation   _____

❑ Environment   _____

Signatures

Analyst: _____ Date: _____ Originator: _____ Date: _____

-------------------------- **Correction** -----------------------------

Brief Description of Work and List of Modules Changed:

_____

_____

Documentation Changed:

_____

_____

Signatures

Developer: _____ Date: _____ Manager: _____ Date: _____

• **Figure 21.3**   Sample system problem report

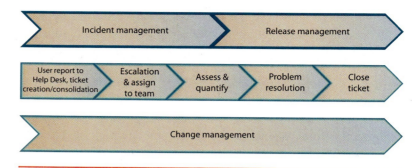

• **Figure 21.4** Change, incident, and release management

the production source-code library, the executable version should also be moved to the production system. Automated change management systems greatly simplify this process and are therefore better controls for ensuring executable and source-code integrity. Remember that at no time should the user or application developer have access to production source and executable code libraries in the production environment.

Finally, in today's networked environment, the integrity of the executable code is critical. A common hacking technique is to replace key system executable code with modified code that contains backdoors, allowing unauthorized access or functions to be performed. Executable code integrity can be verified using host-based intrusion detection systems. These systems create and maintain a database of the size and content of executable modules. Conceptually, this is usually done by performing some kind of hashing or sophisticated checksum operation on the executable modules and storing the results in a database. The operation is performed on a regular schedule against the executable modules, and the results are compared to the database to identify any unauthorized changes that may have occurred to the executable modules.

■ The Capability Maturity Model Integration

An important set of process models are the **Capability Maturity Model Integration (CMMI)** series developed at Carnegie Mellon University's Software Engineering Institute (SEI). SEI has created three capability maturity model integrations that replace the older Capability Maturity Model (CMM): the Capability Maturity Model Integration for Acquisition (CMMI-ACQ), the Capability Maturity Model Integration for Development (CMMI-DEV), and the Capability Maturity Model Integration for Services (CMMI-SVC). CMMI-DEV is representative of the three models. One of the fundamental concepts of CMMI-DEV is configuration or change management, which provides organizations with the ability to improve their software and other processes by providing an evolutionary path from ad hoc processes to disciplined management processes.

The CMMI-DEV defines five maturity levels:

- **Level 1: Initial** At maturity level 1, processes are generally ad hoc and chaotic. The organization does not provide a stable environment to support processes.

- **Level 2: Managed** At maturity level 2, processes are planned and executed in accordance with policy. The projects employ skilled people who have adequate resources to produce controlled outputs; involve relevant stakeholders; are monitored, controlled, and reviewed; and are evaluated for adherence to their process descriptions.

- **Level 3: Defined** At maturity level 3, processes are well characterized and understood, and are described in standards, procedures, tools, and methods. These standard processes are used to establish consistency across the organization.

- **Level 4: Quantitatively Managed** At maturity level 4, the organization establishes quantitative objectives for quality and process performance and uses them as criteria in managing projects. Quantitative objectives are based on the needs of the customer, end users, organization, and process implementers. Quality and process performance is understood in statistical terms and is managed throughout the life of projects.

- **Level 5: Optimizing** At maturity level 5, an organization continually improves its processes based on a quantitative understanding of its business objectives and performance needs. The organization uses a quantitative approach to understanding the variation inherent in the process and the causes of process outcomes.

Exam Tip: To complete your preparations for the CompTIA Security+ exam, it is recommended that you consult SEI's web site (www.sei.cmu.edu) for specific CMMI definitions. Be sure that you understand the differences between capability levels and maturity levels as defined in CMMI.

Change management is a key process to implementing the CMMI-DEV in an organization. For example, if an organization is at CMMI-DEV level 1, it probably has minimal formal change management processes in place. At level 3, an organization has a defined change management process that is followed consistently. At level 5, the change management process is a routine, quantitatively evaluated part of improving software products and implementing innovative ideas across the organization. For an organization to manage software development, operation, and maintenance, it should have effective change management processes in place.

Change management is an essential management tool and control mechanism. The concept of segregation of duties ensures that no single individual or organization possesses too much control in a process, helping to prevent errors and fraudulent or malicious acts. The elements of change management—configuration identification, configuration control, configuration status accounting, and configuration auditing—coupled with a defined process and a change control board, will provide management with proper oversight of the software lifecycle. Once such a process and management oversight exists, the company can use CMMI-DEV to move from ad hoc activities to a disciplined software management process.

Chapter 21 Review

■ Chapter Summary

After reading this chapter and completing the exercises, you should understand the following about change management.

Use change management as an important enterprise management tool

- Change management should be used in all phases of the software lifecycle.
- Change management can be scaled to effectively control and manage software development and maintenance.
- Change management can prevent some of the most common software development and maintenance problems.

Institute the key concept of separation of duties

- Separation of duties ensures that no single individual or organization possesses too much control in a process.
- Separation of duties helps prevent errors and fraudulent or malicious acts.
- Separation of duties establishes a basis for accountability and control.
- Separation of duties can help safeguard enterprise assets and protect against risks.

Identify the essential elements of change management

- Configuration identification identifies assets that need to be controlled.

- Configuration control keeps track of changes to configuration items that have been baselined.
- Configuration status accounting tracks each configuration item in the baseline.
- Configuration auditing verifies the configuration items are built and maintained appropriately.

Implement change management

- A standardized process and a change control board provide management with proper oversight and control of the software development lifecycle.
- A good change management process will exhibit good separation of duties and have clearly defined roles, responsibilities, and approvals.
- An effective change control board facilitates good management oversight and coordination between projects.

Use the concepts of the Capability Maturity Model Integration

- Once proper management oversight exists, the company will be able to use CMMI to help the organization move from ad hoc activities to a disciplined software management process.
- CMMI relies heavily on change management to provide organizations with the capability to improve their software processes.

■ Key Terms

baseline *(639)*
Capability Maturity Model Integration (CMMI) *(644)*
change control board (CCB) *(642)*
change management *(635)*
computer software configuration items *(639)*
configuration auditing *(640)*
configuration control *(640)*

configuration identification *(639)*
configuration items *(639)*
configuration management *(635)*
configuration status accounting *(640)*
separation of duties *(637)*
system problem report (SPR) *(643)*

Key Terms Quiz

Use terms from the Key Terms list to complete the sentences that follow. Don't use the same term more than once. Not all terms will be used.

1. The _____ is the body that provides oversight to the change management process.

2. _____ is a standard methodology for performing and recording changes during software development and operation.

3. _____ is the process of assigning responsibilities to different individuals such that no single individual can commit fraudulent or malicious actions.

4. Procedures for tracking and maintaining data relative to each configuration item in the baseline are _____.

5. A _____ describes a system as it is built and functioning at a point in time.

6. A structured methodology that provides an evolutionary path from ad hoc processes to disciplined software management is the _____.

7. The process of verifying that configuration items are built and maintained according to requirements, standards, or contractual agreements is _____.

8. The document used by the change control board to track changes to software is called a _____.

9. When you identify which assets need to be managed and controlled, you are performing _____.

10. _____ is the process of controlling changes to items that have been baselined.

Multiple-Choice Quiz

1. Why should developers and testers avoid using "live" production data to perform various testing activities?

   A. The use of "live" production data ensures a full and realistic test database.

   B. The use of "live" production data can jeopardize the confidentiality and integrity of the production data.

   C. The use of "live" production data ensures an independent and objective test environment.

   D. Developers and testers should be allowed to use "live" production data for reasons of efficiency.

2. Software change management procedures are established to:

   A. Ensure continuity of business operations in the event of a natural disaster

   B. Add structure and control to the development of software systems

   C. Ensure changes in business operations caused by a management restructuring are properly controlled

   D. Identify threats, vulnerabilities, and mitigating actions that could impact an enterprise

3. Which of the following correctly defines the principle of least privilege?

   A. Access privileges are reviewed regularly to ensure that individuals who no longer require access have had their privileges removed.

   B. Authorization of a subject's access to an object depends on sensitivity labels.

   C. The administrator determines which subjects can have access to certain objects based on organizational security policy.

   D. Users have no more privileges than are necessary to perform their jobs.

4. Which of the following does *not* adhere to the principles of separation of duties?

   A. Software development, testing, quality assurance, and production should be assigned to the same individuals.

   B. Software developers should not have access to production data and source-code files.

   C. Software developers and testers should be restricted from accessing "live" production data.

D. The functions of creating, installing, and administrating software programs should be assigned to different individuals.

5. Configuration auditing is:

   A. The process of controlling changes to items that have been baselined

   B. The process of identifying which assets need to be managed and controlled

   C. The process of verifying that the configuration items are built and maintained properly

   D. The procedures for tracking and maintaining data relative to each configuration item in the baseline

6. Why should end users not be given access to program source codes?

   A. It could allow an end user to identify weaknesses or errors in the source code.

   B. It ensures that testing and quality assurance perform their proper functions.

   C. It assists in ensuring an independent and objective testing environment.

   D. It could allow an end user to execute the source code.

7. Configuration control is:

   A. The process of controlling changes to items that have been baselined

   B. The process of identifying which assets need to be managed and controlled

   C. The process of verifying that the configuration items are built and maintained properly

   D. The procedures for tracking and maintaining data relative to each configuration item in the baseline

8. Configuration identification is:

   A. The process of verifying that the configuration items are built and maintained properly

   B. The procedures for tracking and maintaining data relative to each configuration item in the baseline

   C. The process of controlling changes to items that have been baselined

   D. The process of identifying which assets need to be managed and controlled

9. Which position is responsible for approving the movement of executable code to the production system?

   A. System administrator

   B. Developer

   C. Manager

   D. Quality assurance

10. The purpose of a change control board (CCB) is to:

    A. Facilitate management oversight and better project coordination

    B. Identify which assets need to be managed and controlled

    C. Establish software processes that are structured enough that success with one project can be repeated for another similar project

    D. Track and maintain data relative to each configuration item in the baseline

■ Essay Quiz

1. You are the project manager for a new web-based online shopping system. Due to market competition, your management has directed you to go live with your systems one week earlier than originally scheduled. One member of your development team is a sharp, smart programmer with less than one year of experience. He asks you why your team is required to follow what he calls cumbersome, out-of-date change management procedures. What would you tell him?

2. Explain why the change management principles discussed in this chapter should be used when managing operating system patches.

3. Explain why a database administrator (DBA) should not be allowed to develop programs on the systems they administer.

4. Your company has just decided to follow the Capability Maturity Model Integration. You manage a development shop of 15 programmers

with four team leaders. You and your team have determined that you are currently at CMMI-DEV level 1, Initial. Describe the actions you might take to move your shop to level 3, the Defined maturity level.

5. You have just been made Director of E-commerce Applications, responsible for over 30 programmers and ten major software projects. Your projects include multiple web pages on ten different production servers, system security for those servers, three development servers, three test/QA servers, and some third-party software. Which of those resources would you place under change management practices and why?

Lab Projects

• Lab Project 21.1

Using a typical IT organization from a medium-sized company (100 developers, managers, and support personnel), describe the purpose, organization, and responsibilities of a change control board appropriate for this organization.

• Lab Project 21.2

You are the IT staff auditor for the company mentioned in the first lab project. You have reviewed the change control board processes and found they have instituted the following change management process. Describe two major control weaknesses in this particular change management process. What would you do to correct these control weaknesses?

Incident Response

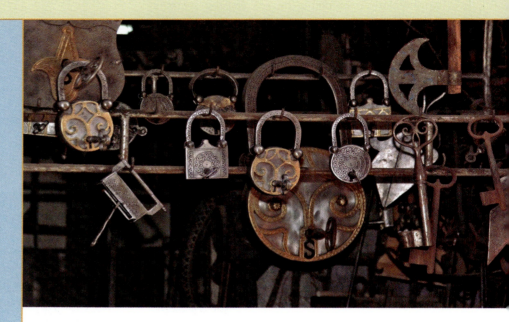

Bad guys will follow the rules of your network to accomplish their mission.

—RON SCHAFFER, SANS INCIDENT DETECTION SUMMIT

In this chapter, you will learn how to

- **Understand the foundations of incident response processes**
- **Implement the detailed steps of an incident response process**
- **Describe standards and best practices that are involved in incident response**

Incident response is becoming the new norm in security operations. The new reality is that keeping adversaries off your network and preventing unauthorized activity is not going to provide the level of security the enterprise requires. This means that the system needs to be able to operate in a state of compromise, yet still achieve the desired security objectives. The mindset has to change from preventing intrusion and attack to preventing loss.

This chapter explores the use of an incident response function to achieve the goals of minimizing loss under all operating conditions. This will mean a shift in focus, and a change in priorities as well as security strategy. These efforts can only succeed on top of a solid foundation of security fundamentals as presented earlier in the book, so this is not a starting place, but rather the next step in the evolution of defense.

Foundations of Incident Response

An **incident** is any event in an information system or network where the results are different than normal. Incident response is not just an information security operation. Incident response is an effort that involves the entire business. The security team may form a nucleus of the effort, but the key tasks are performed by many parts of the business.

Incident response is a term used to describe the steps an organization performs in response to any situation determined to be abnormal in the operation of a computer system. The causes of incidents are many, from the environment (storms), to errors on the part of users, to unauthorized actions by unauthorized users, to name a few. Although the causes may be many, the results can be classified into classes. A low-impact incident may not result in any significant risk exposure, so no action other than repairing the broken system is needed. A moderate-risk incident will require greater scrutiny and response efforts, and a high-level risk exposure incident will require the greatest scrutiny. To manage incidents when they occur, a table of guidelines for the incident response team needs to be created to assist in determining the level of response.

Two major elements play a role in determining the level of response. Information criticality is the primary determinant, and this comes from the data classification and the quantity of data involved. **Information criticality** is defined as the relative importance of specific information to the business. Information criticality is a key measure used in the prioritization of actions throughout the incident response process. The loss of one administrator password is less serious than the loss of all of them. The second major element involves a business decision on how this incident plays into current business operations. A series of breaches, whether minor or not, indicates a pattern that can have public relations and regulatory issues.

Once an incident happens, it is time to react, and proper reaction requires a game plan. Contrary to what many want to believe, there are no magic silver bullets to kill the security demons. What is required is a solid, well-rehearsed incident response plan. This plan is custom-tailored to the information criticalities, the actual hardware and software architectures, and the people. Like all large, complex projects, the challenges rapidly become organizational in nature—budget, manpower, resources, and commitment.

Incident Management

Having an incident response management methodology is a key risk mitigation strategy. One of the steps that should be taken to establish a plan to handle business interruptions as a result of a cyber event of some sort is the establishment of a **Computer Incident Response Team (CIRT)** or a **Computer Emergency Response Team (CERT)**.

The organization's CIRT will conduct the investigation into the incident and make the recommendations on how to proceed. The CIRT should consist of not only permanent members but also ad hoc members who may be called upon to address special needs depending on the nature of the incident. In addition to individuals with a technical background, the CIRT should include nontechnical personnel to provide guidance on ways to handle media attention, legal issues that may arise, and management issues

A successful incident response effort requires two components, knowledge of one's own systems and knowledge of the adversary. The ancient warrior/philosopher Sun Tzu explains it well in *The Art of War:* "If you know the enemy and know yourself, you need not fear the result of a hundred battles. If you know yourself but not the enemy, for every victory gained you will also suffer a defeat. If you know neither the enemy nor yourself, you will succumb in every battle".

CERT is a trademark of Carnegie Mellon, and is frequently used in some situations, such as the US-CERT.

regarding the continued operation of the organization. The CIRT should be created and team members should be identified before an incident occurs. Policies and procedures for conducting an investigation should also be worked out in advance of an incident occurring. It is also advisable to have the team periodically meet to review these procedures.

Anatomy of an Attack

Attackers have a method by which they attack a system. Although the specifics may differ from event to event, there are some common steps that are commonly employed. There are numerous types of attacks, from old-school hacking to the new advanced persistent threat (APT) attack. The differences are subtle and are related to the objectives of each form of attack.

Old School

Attacks are not a new phenomenon in enterprise security, and a historical examination of large numbers of attacks show some common methods. These are the traditional steps:

1. Footprinting
2. Scanning
3. Enumeration
4. Gain access
5. Escalate privilege
6. Pilfer
7. Create backdoors
8. Cover tracks
9. Denial of service (DOS)

Footprinting is the determination of the boundaries of a target space. There are numerous sources of information, including web sites, DNS records, and IP address registrations. Understanding the boundaries assists an attacker in knowing what is in their target range and what isn't. Scanning is the examination of machines to determine what operating systems, services, and vulnerabilities exist. The enumeration step is a listing of the systems and vulnerabilities to build an attack game plan. The first actual incursion is the gaining of access to an account on the system, almost always an ordinary user, as higher-privilege accounts are harder to target.

The next step is to gain access to a higher-privilege account. From a higher-privilege account, the range of accessible activities is greater, including pilfering files, creating back doors so you can return, and covering you tracks by erasing logs. The detail associated with each step may vary from hack to hack, but in most cases, these steps were employed in this manner to achieve an objective.

Tech Tip

Using nmap to Fingerprint an Operating System

*To use **nmap** to fingerprint an operating system, use the –O option:*

```
nmap -O -v
scanme.nmap.org
```

This command performs a scan of interesting ports on the target (scanme.nmap.org) and attempts to identify the operating system. The –v option indicates that you want verbose output.

Principles of Computer Security

Advanced Persistent Threat

A relatively new attack phenomenon has been labeled the advanced persistent threat. An **advanced persistent threat (APT)** is an attack that always maintains a primary focus on remaining in the network, operating undetected, and having multiple ways in and out. APTs began with nation-state attackers, but the utility of the long-term attack has proven valuable, and many sophisticated attacks have moved to this route. Most APTs begin via a phishing or spear phishing attack, which establishes a foothold in the system under attack. From this foothold, the attack methodology is similar to the traditional attack method described in the previous section, but additional emphasis is placed on the steps needed to maintain a presence on a network:

1. Define target
2. Research target
3. Select tools
4. Test for detection
5. Initial intrusion
6. Establish outbound connection
7. Obtain credentials
8. Expand access
9. Strengthen foothold
10. Cover tracks
11. Exfiltrate data

The initial intrusion is usually performed via social engineering (spear phishing), over e-mail, using zero-day-based custom malware. Another popular infection method is the use of a watering hole attack, planting the malware on a web site that the victim employees will likely visit. The use of custom malware makes detection of the attack by antivirus/malware programs a near impossibility. After the attackers gain access, they attempt to expand access and strengthen the foothold. This is done by planting **remote administration Trojan (RAT)** software in the victim's network, creating network backdoors and tunnels allowing stealth access to its infrastructure.

The next step, obtaining credentials and escalating privileges, is performed through the use of exploits and password cracking. The true objective is to acquire administrator privileges over a victim's computer and ultimately expand it to Windows domain administrator accounts. One of the hallmarks of an APT attack is the emphasis on maintaining a presence on the system to ensure continued control over access channels and credentials acquired in previous steps. A common technique used is lateral movement across a network. Moving laterally allows an attacker to expand control to other workstations, servers, and infrastructure elements and perform data harvesting on them. Attackers also perform internal reconnaissance, collecting information on surrounding infrastructure, trust relationships, and information concerning the Windows domain structure.

Goals of Incident Response

The goals of an incident response process are multidimensional in nature:

- Confirm or dispel incident
- Promote accurate information accumulation
- Establish controls for evidence
- Protect privacy rights
- Minimize disruption to operations
- Allow for legal/civil recourse
- Provide accurate reports/recommendations

Incident response depends upon accurate information. Without it, the chance of following data in the wrong direction is a possibility, as is missing crucial information and only finding dead ends. The preceding goals are essential for the viability of an incident response process and the desired outcomes.

■ Incident Response Process

Incident response is the set of actions security personnel perform in response to a wide range of triggering events. These actions are vast and varied because they have to deal with a wide range of causes and consequences. Through the use of a structured framework, coupled with properly prepared processes, incident response becomes a manageable task. Without proper preparation, this task can quickly become impossible or intractably expensive.

Incident response is the new business cultural norm in information security. The key is to design the procedures to include appropriate business personnel, not keep it as a pure information security endeavor. The challenges are many, including the aspect of timing as the activities quickly become a case of one group of professionals pursuing another.

Incident response is a multistep process with several component elements. The first is organization preparation, followed by system preparation. An initial detection is followed by initial response, then isolation, investigation, recovery, and reporting. There are additional process steps of follow-up and lessons learned, each of which is presented in following sections. Incident response is a key element of a security posture and must involve many different aspects of the business to properly respond. This is best built upon the foundation of a comprehensive **incident response policy** that details the roles and responsibilities of the organizational elements with respect to the process elements detailed in this chapter.

Tech Tip

Incident Response Defined

NIST Special Publication 800-61 defines an incident as the act of violating an explicit or implied security policy. This violation can be intentional, incidental, or accidental, with causes being wide and varied in nature. These include but are not limited to the following:

- *Attempts (either failed or successful) to gain unauthorized access to a system or its data*
- *Unwanted disruption or denial of service*
- *The unauthorized use of a system for the processing or storage of data*
- *Changes to system hardware, firmware, or software characteristics without the owner's knowledge, instruction, or consent*
- *Environmental changes that result in data loss or destruction*
- *Accidental actions that result in data loss or destruction*

Preparation

Incident response efforts begin before an incident occurs—that is, before "something goes wrong." Preparing for an incident is the first phase. The organization needs to establish the steps to be taken when an incident is discovered (or suspected); determine points of contact; train all employees and security professionals so they understand the steps to take and who to call; establish an incident response team; acquire the equipment necessary to detect, contain, and recover from an incident; establish the procedures and guidelines for the use of the equipment obtained; and train those who will use the equipment. During this phase, general user training in areas such as social engineering should be accomplished, as well as any additional specialized training in areas such as computer forensics that is determined to be necessary.

The old adage that "those who fail to prepare, prepare to fail" certainly applies to incident response. Without advance preparation, an organization's response to a security incident will be haphazard and ineffective. Establishing the processes and procedures to follow in advance of an event is critical.

Organization Preparation

Preparing an organization requires a plan, both for the initial effort and for maintenance of that effort. Over time, the organization shifts based on business objectives, personnel change, business efforts and focus change, new programs, new capabilities; virtually any change can necessitate shifts in the incident response activities. At a minimum, the following items should be addressed and periodically reviewed in terms of incident response preparation:

- Develop and maintain comprehensive incident response policies and procedures
- Establish and maintain an Incident Response Team

- Obtain top-level management support
  - Agree to ground rules/rules of engagement
  - Develop scenarios and responses
- Develop and maintain an incident response toolkit
  - System plans and diagrams
  - Network architectures
  - Critical asset lists
- Practice response procedures
  - Fire drills
  - Scenarios ("Who do you call?")

System Preparation

Systems require preparation for effective incident response efforts. Incident responders are dependent upon documentation for understanding hardware, software, and network layouts. Understanding how access control is employed, including specifics across all systems, is key when determining who can do what—a common incident response question. Understanding the logging methodology and architecture will make incident response data retrieval easier. All of these questions should be addressed in planning of diagrams, access control, and logging, to ensure that these critical security elements are capturing the correct information before an incident.

Having lists of critical files and their hash values, all stored offline, can make system investigation a more efficient process. In the end, when architecting a system, taking the time to plan for incident response processes will be crucial to a successful response once an incident occurs. Preparing systems for incident response is similar to preparing them for maintainability, so these efforts can yield regular dividends to the system owners. Determining the steps to isolate specific machines and services can be a complex endeavor, and is one best accomplished before an incident, through the preparation phase.

Researching Vulnerabilities

After the hacker has a list of software running on the systems, he will start researching the Internet for vulnerabilities associated with that software. Numerous web sites provide information on vulnerabilities in specific application programs and operating systems. Understanding how hackers navigate systems is important, for system administrators and security personnel can use the same steps to research potential vulnerabilities before a hacker strikes. This information is valuable to administrators who need to know what problems exist and how to patch them.

Incident Response Team

Establishing an incident response team is an essential step in the preparation phase. Although the initial response to an incident may be handled by an individual, such as a system administrator, the complete handling of an incident typically takes an entire team. An incident response team is a group of people that prepares for and responds to any emergency incident, such as a natural disaster or an interruption of business operations. A computer security incident response team in an organization typically

Tech Tip

Preparing for Incident Detection

To ensure that discovering incidents is not an ad hoc, hit-or-miss proposition, the organization needs to establish procedures that describe the process administrators must follow to monitor for possible security events. The tools for accomplishing this task are identified during the preparation phase, as well as any required training. The procedures governing the monitoring tools used should be established as part of the specific guidelines governing the use of the tools but should include references to the incident response policy.

includes key skilled members who bring a wide range of skills to bear in the response effort. Incident response teams are common in corporations as well as in public service organizations.

Incident response team members ideally are trained and prepared to fulfill the roles required by the specific situation (for example, to serve as incident commander in the event of a large-scale public emergency). Incident response teams are frequently dynamically sized to the scale and nature of an incident, and as the size of an incident grows and as more resources are drawn into the event, the command of the situation may shift through several phases. In a small-scale event, or in the case of a small firm, usually only a volunteer or ad hoc team may exist to respond. In cases where the incident spreads beyond the local control of the incident response team, higher-level resources through industry groups and government groups exist to assist in the incident. Advanced preparation in the form of contacting and establishing working relations with higher-level groups is an important preparation step.

The incident response team is a critical part of the incident response plan. Team membership will vary depending on the type of incident or suspected incident, but may include the following members:

- Team lead
- Network/security analyst
- Internal and external subject matter experts
- Legal counsel
- Public affairs officer
- Security office contact

In determining the specific makeup of the team for a specific incident, there are some general points to think about. The team needs a leader, preferably a higher-level manager who has the ability to obtain cooperation from employees as needed. It also needs a computer or network security analyst, since the assumption is that the team will be responding to a computer security incident. Specialists may be added to the team for specific hardware or software platforms as needed. The organization's legal counsel should be part of the team on at least a part-time or as-needed basis. The public affairs office should also be available on an as-needed basis, because it is responsible for formulating the public response should a security incident become public. The organization's security office should also be kept informed. It should designate a point of contact for the team in case criminal activity is suspected. In this case, care must be taken to preserve evidence should the organization decide to push for prosecution of the individual(s).

This is by no means a complete list, as each organization is different and needs to evaluate what the best mixture is for its own response team. Whatever the decision, the composition of the team, and how and when it will be formed needs to be clearly addressed in the preparation phase of the incident response policy.

To function in a timely and efficient manner, ideally a team has already defined a protocol or set of actions to perform to mitigate the negative effects of most common forms of an incident. One key and often overlooked member of the incident response team is the business. It may be an

Tech Tip

Incident Response Team Questions
Well-executed plans are often well tested; when and how often do you test your response plans? How will your team operate undetected in an environment owned by the adversary? Do you have a backup, separate e-mail system that is external to the enterprise solution? Is it encrypted?

IT system being investigated, but the data, processes, and value all belong to the business, and the business is the element that understands the risk and value of what is under attack. Having key, knowledgeable business members on the incident response team is a necessity to ensure that the security actions remain aligned with the business goals and objectives of the organization.

Security Measure Implementation

All data that is stored is subject to breach or compromise. Given this assumption, the question becomes, what is the best mitigation strategy to reduce the risk associated with breach or compromise? Data requires protection in each of the three states of the data lifecycle: in storage, in transit, and during processing. The level of risk in each state differs due to several factors:

- **Time** Data tends to spend more time in storage, and hence is subject to breach or compromise over longer time periods.

- **Quantity** Data in storage tends to offer a greater quantity to breach or compromise than data in transit, and data in processing offers even less. If records are being compromised while being processed, then only records being processed are subjected to risk.

- **Access** Different protection mechanisms exist in each of the domains, and this has a direct effect on the risk associated with breach or compromise. Operating systems tend to have very tight controls to prevent cross-process data issues such as error and contamination.

The next aspect of risk during processing is within process access to the data, and a variety of attack techniques address this channel specifically. Data in transit is subject to breach or compromise from a variety of network-level attacks and vulnerabilities. Some of these are under the control of the enterprise, and some are not.

One primary mitigation step is **data minimization**. Data minimization efforts can play a key role in both operational efficiency and security. One of the first rules associated with data is this: Don't keep what you don't need. A simple example of this is the case of spam remediation. If spam is separated from e-mail before it hits a mailbox, one can assert that it is not mail and not subject to storage, backup, or data retention issues. As spam can comprise greater than 50 percent of incoming mail, spam remediation can dramatically improve operational efficiency in terms of both speed and cost.

This same principle holds true for other forms of information. When processing credit card transactions, certain data elements are required for the actual transaction, but once the transaction is approved, they have no further business value. Storing of this information provides no business value, yet it does represent a risk in the case of a data breach. Data storage should be governed not by what you can store, but by the business need to store. What is not stored is not subject to breach, and minimizing storage to only what is supported by business need reduces risk and cost to the enterprise.

Minimization efforts begin before data even hits a system, let alone a breach. During system design, the appropriate security controls are determined and deployed, with periodic audits to ensure compliance. These controls are based on the sensitivity of the information being protected. One tool that can be used to assist in the selection of controls is a data classification scheme. Not all data is equally important, nor is it equally damaging in the event of loss. Developing and deploying a data classification scheme can assist in preventative planning efforts when designing security for data elements.

Exam Tip: Data breaches may not be preventable, but they can be mitigated through minimization and encryption efforts.

Incident Identification/Detection

An *incident* is defined as a situation that departs from normal, routine operations. Whether an incident is important or not is the first determination to be made as part of an incident response process. A single failed login is technically an incident, but if it is followed by a correct login, then it is not of any consequence. In fact, this could even be considered as normal. But 10,000 failed attempts on a system, or failures across a large number of accounts, are distinctly different and may be worthy of further investigation.

A key first step is in the processing of information and the determination of whether or not to invoke incident response processes. Incident information can come from a wide range of sources, including logs, employees, help desk calls, system monitoring, security devices, and more. The challenge is to detect that something other than simple common, routine errors is occurring. When evidence accumulates, or in some cases when specific items such as security device logs indicate a potential incident, the next step is to escalate the situation to the incident response team.

Detection

Of course, an incident response team can't begin an investigation until a suspected incident has been detected. At that point, the detection phase of the incident response policy kicks in. One of the first jobs of the incident response team is to determine whether an actual security incident has occurred. Many things can be misinterpreted as a possible security incident. For example, a software bug in an application may cause a user to lose a file, and the user may blame this on a virus or similar malicious software. The incident response team must investigate each reported incident and treat it as a potential security incident until it can determine whether it is or isn't. This means that your organization will want to respond initially with a limited response team before wasting a lot of time having the full team respond. This is the initial step to take when a report is received that a possible incident has been detected.

Security incidents can take a variety of forms, and who discovers the incident will vary as well. One of the groups most likely to discover an incident is the team of network and security administrators who run devices such as the organization's firewalls and intrusion detection systems.

Another common incident is a virus. Several packages are available that can help an organization detect potential virus activity or other malicious code. Administrators will often be the ones to notice something is amiss, but so might an average user who has been hit by the virus.

Social engineering is a common technique used by potential intruders to acquire information that may be useful in gaining access to computer systems, networks, or the physical facilities that house them. Anybody in the organization can be the target of a social engineering attack, so all employees need to know what to be looking for regarding this type of attack. In fact, the target might not even be one of your organization's employees—it could be a contractor, such as somebody on the custodial staff or nighttime security staff. Whatever the type of security incident suspected, and no matter who suspects it, a reporting procedure needs to be in place for the employees to use when an incident is detected. Everybody needs to know who to call should they suspect something, and everybody needs to know what to do. A common technique is to develop a reporting template that can be supplied to an individual who suspects an incident, so that the necessary information is gathered in a timely manner.

Initial Response

Although there is no such thing as a typical incident, for any incident there is a series of questions that can be answered to form a proper initial response. Regardless of the source, the following items are important to determine during an initial response:

- Current time and date
- Who/what is reporting the incident
- Nature of the incident
- When the incident occurred
- Hardware/software involved
- Point of contact for involved personnel

The purpose of an initial response is to begin the incident response action and place it on a proper pathway toward success. The initial response must support the goals of the information security program. If something is very critical, treating it as routine would be a mistake, so triage with respect to information criticality is important. The initial response must also be aligned with the business practices and objectives. Triage with respect to current business imperatives and conditions is important. The initial response actions need to be designed to comply with administrative and legal policies as well as to support decisions with regard to civil, administrative, or criminal investigations/actions. For these purposes, maintaining a forensically sound process from the beginning is important. It is also important that the information is delivered accurately and expeditiously to the appropriate decision-makers so that future actions can be timely. One of the greatest tools to achieve all of these goals is a simple and efficient process, so establishing fewer steps that are clear and clean is preferred. Complexity in the initial response process only leads to issues later because of delays, confusion, and incomplete information.

First Responder

A cyber first responder must do as much as possible to control damage or loss of evidence. Obviously, as time passes, evidence can be tampered with or destroyed. Look around on the desk, on the Rolodex, under the keyboard, in desktop storage areas, and on cubicle bulletin boards for any information that might be relevant. Secure floppy disks, optical discs, flash memory cards, USB drives, tapes, and other removable media. Request copies of logs as soon as possible. Most ISPs will protect logs that could be subpoenaed. Take photos (some localities require use of Polaroid photos, as they are more difficult to modify without obvious tampering) or video. Include photos of operating computer screens and hardware components from multiple angles. Be sure to photograph internal components before removing them for analysis. The first responder can do much to prevent damage, or can cause significant loss by digitally altering evidence, even inadvertently. Collecting data should be done in a forensically sound nature (see Chapter 23 for details), and be sure to pay attention to recording time values so time offsets can be calculated.

Incident Isolation

Once an incident is discovered and characterized, the most important step in the incident response process involves the isolation of the problem. Many incidents can spread to other machines and expand the damage footprint if not contained by the incident response team. When a particular machine or service becomes compromised, the team can invoke the preplanned steps to isolate the infected unit from others. This may have an impact on performance, but it will still be less than if the compromise is allowed to spread and more machines become compromised.

Containment and Eradication

Once the incident response team has determined that an incident most likely has occurred, it must attempt to quickly contain the problem. At this point, or very soon after containment begins, depending on the severity of the incident, management needs to decide whether the organization intends to prosecute the individual who has caused the incident (in which case collection and preservation of evidence is necessary), or simply wants to restore operations as quickly as possible without regard to possibly destroying evidence. In certain circumstances, management might not have a choice, such as if specific regulations or laws require it to report particular incidents. If management makes the decision to prosecute, specific procedures need to be followed in handling potential evidence. Individuals trained in forensics should be used in this case.

The incident response team must decide how to address containment as soon as it has determined that an actual incident has occurred. If an intruder is still connected to the organization's system, one response is to disconnect from the Internet until the system can be restored and vulnerabilities can be patched. This, however, means that your organization is not accessible to customers over the Internet during that time, which may result in lost revenue. Another response might be to stay connected and attempt to determine the origin of the intruder. A decision will need to be made as to which is more important for your organization. Your incident response policy should identify who is authorized to make this decision.

Other possible containment activities might include adding filtering rules or modifying existing rules on firewalls, routers, and intrusion detection systems, updating antivirus software, and removing specific pieces of hardware or halting specific software applications. If an intruder has gained access through a specific account, disabling or removing that account may also be necessary.

> **Tech Tip**
>
> **Common Technical Errors**
>
> *Common technical mistakes during initial response include:*
>
> - *Altering time/date stamps on evidence systems*
> - *"Killing" rogue processes*
> - *Patching the system*
> - *Not recording the steps taken on the system*
> - *Not acting passively*

> **Qakbot Worm Isolation**
>
> The following are summary notes made by a firm that was hit by the Qakbot worm. Consider how your incident response process would respond to this scenario.
>
> - Laptop infected while off network
> - When rejoined company network
>   - Spread to open network drives within minutes
>   - Spread to a group of computers within 60 minutes using a common administrator credential
> - Infection identified by server antivirus detecting dropped files
> - Malware analysis identified command and control connections
> - Identified additional infected systems from network logs
> - Could not immediately take infected computers out of service because they were being used in a critical function
> - Computers were also geographically dispersed
> - Had to isolate a portion of the network (while still allowing critical data flows) while remediating one computer at a time during a maintenance window

Once the immediate problems have been contained, the incident response team needs to address the cause of the incident. If the incident is the result of a vulnerability that was not patched, the patch must be obtained, tested, and applied. Accounts may need to be disabled or passwords may need to be changed. Complete reloading of the operating system might be necessary if the intruder has been in the system for an unknown length of time or has modified system files. Determining when an intruder first gained access to your system or network is critical in determining how far back to go in restoring the system or network.

Quarantine

One method of isolating a machine is through a quarantine process. **Quarantine** is a process of isolating an object from its surroundings, preventing normal access methods. The machine may be allowed to run, but its connection to other machines is broken in a manner to prevent the spread of infection. Quarantine can be accomplished through a variety of mechanisms, including the erection of firewalls restricting communication between machines. This can be a fairly complex process, but if properly configured in advance, the limitations of the quarantine operation can allow the machine to continue to run for diagnostic purposes, even if it no longer processes a workload.

Device Removal

A more extreme response is device removal. In the event that a machine becomes compromised, it is simply removed from production and replaced. When device removal entails the physical change of hardware, this is a resource-intensive operation. The reimaging of a machine can be a time-consuming and difficult endeavor. The advent of virtual machines changes this entirely, as the provisioning of virtual images on hardware can be accomplished in a much quicker fashion.

Escalation and Notification

One key decision point in initial response is that of escalation. When a threshold of information becomes known to an operator and the operator decides to escalate the situation, the incident response process moves to a notification and escalation phase. Not all incidents are of the same risk profile, and incident response efforts should map to the actual risk level associated with the incident. When the incident response team is notified of a potential incident, its first steps are to confirm the existence, scope, and magnitude of the event and then respond accordingly. This is typically done through a two-step escalation process, where a minimal quick-response team begins and then adds members as necessitated by the issue.

Making an assessment of the risk associated with an incident is an important first step. If the characteristics of an incident include a large number of packets destined for different services on a machine (an attack commonly referred to as a *port scan*), then the actions needed are different than those needed to respond to a large number of packets destined to a single machine service. Port scans are common, and to a degree relatively harmless, while port flooding can result in denial of service. Making a determination of the specific downstream risks is important in prioritizing response actions.

Strategy Formulation

The response to an incident will be highly dependent upon the particular circumstances of the intrusion. There are many paths one can take in the steps associated with an incident; the challenge is in choosing the best steps in each case. During the preparation stage, a wide range of scenarios can be examined, allowing time to formulate strategies. Even after an incident response team has planned a series of strategies to respond to various scenarios, determining how to employ those preplanned strategies to proper effect still depends on the circumstances of a particular incident. A variety of factors should be considered in the planning and deployment of strategies, including, but not limited to, the following:

- How critical are the impacted systems?
- How sensitive is the data?
- What is the potential overall dollar loss involved/rate of loss?
- How much downtime can be tolerated?
- Who are the perpetrators?
- What is the skill level of the attacker?
- Does the incident have adverse publicity potential?

These pieces of information provide boundaries for the upcoming investigations. There are still numerous issues that need to be determined with respect to the upcoming investigation. Addressing these issues helps provide focal points during the investigation:

- Restore normal operations
  - Offline recovery?
  - Online recovery?
- Determine public relations play
- "To spin or not to spin?"
- Determine probable attacker
  - Internal: handle internally or prosecute?
  - External: prosecute?
  - Involve law enforcement?
- Determine type of attack
  - DoS, theft, vandalism, policy violation?
  - Ongoing intrusion?
  - Pivoting?
- Classify victim system
  - Critical server/application?
  - Number of users?
  - What other systems are affected?

Using the answers to these questions helps the team determine the necessary steps in the upcoming investigation phase. Although it is impossible to account for all circumstances, this level of strategy can greatly assist in scoping the work ahead during the investigation phase.

Investigation

The true investigation phase of an incident is a multistep, multiparty event. With the exception of very simple events, most incidents will involve multiple machines and potentially impact the business in multiple ways.

The primary objective of the investigative phase is to make the following determinations:

- What happened
- What systems are affected
- What was compromised
- What was the vulnerability
- Who did it (if possible to determine)
- What are the recovery/remediation options

Looking at the list, it is daunting, but this is where the real work of incident response occurs. It will take a team effort, partly because of workload, partly because of specialized skills, and partly because the entire effort is being performed in a race against time.

Duplication

Duplication of drives is a common forensics process. It is important to have accurate copies and proper hash values so that any analysis is performed under proper conditions. Proper disk duplication is necessary to ensure all data, including metadata, is properly captured and analyzed as part of the overall process.

Network Monitoring

To monitor network flow data, including who is talking to whom, one source of information is NetFlow data. NetFlow is a protocol/standard for the collection of network metadata on the flows of network traffic. NetFlow is now an IETF standard, and allows for unidirectional captures of communication metadata. NetFlow can identify both common and unique data flows, and in the case of incident response, typically the new and unique NetFlow patterns are of most interest to incident responders.

Tech Tip

NetFlow Data

A flow is unidirectional, so bidirectional flow would be recorded as two separate flows. NetFlow data is defined by seven unique keys:

1. *Source IP address*
2. *Destination IP address*
3. *Source port*
4. *Destination port*
5. *Layer 3 protocol*
6. *TOS byte (DSCP)*
7. *Input interface (ifIndex)*

Recovery/Reconstitution Procedures

Recovery is an important step in all incidents. One of the first rules is to not trust a system that has been compromised, and this includes all aspects of an operating system. Whether there is known destruction or not, the safe path is one where the recovery step includes reconstruction of affected machines. Recovery efforts from an incident involve several specific elements. First, the cause of the incident needs to be determined and resolved. This is done through an incident response mechanism. Attempting to recover before the cause is known and corrected will commonly result in a continuation of the problem. Second, the data, if sensitive and subject to misuse, needs to be examined in the context of how it was lost, who would have access, and what business measures need to be taken to mitigate specific business damage as a result of the release. This may involve the changing of business plans if the release makes them suspect or subject to adverse impacts.

A key aspect in many incidents is that of external communications. Having a communications expert who is familiar with dealing with the press and has the language nuances necessary to convey the correct information and not inflame the situation is essential to the success of any communication plan. Many firms attempt to use their legal counsel for this, but generally speaking, the legally precise language used by an attorney is not useful from a PR standpoint, and a more nuanced communicator may provide a better image. In many cases of crisis management, it is not the crisis that determines the final costs, but the reaction to and communication of details after the initial crisis.

Recovery can be a two-step process. First, the essential business functions can be recovered, enabling business operations to resume. The second step is the complete restoration of all services and operations. Because of the difficulty and uncertainty involved in repairing systems, most best practices today involve reconstituting the underlying system and then transferring the operational data. Staging the recovery operations in a prioritized fashion allows a graceful return to an operating condition.

Restoration can be done in a wide variety of ways. For many systems, the reconstitution of a clean operating system can restore a system. This type of restoration requires a significant amount of preparation. Having a clean version of each of your assets provides for this type of restoration effort. Recovery sounds simple, but in large-scale incidents, the number of machines can be significant. Add to this the chance of reinfection as machines are restored. This means that simply replacing the machine with a clean machine is not sufficient, but rather the replacement needs protection against reinfection.

The other challenge in large-scale recovery events is the sequencing of the effort. When there are many machines to be restored, and the restoration process takes time and resources, scheduling is essential. Setting up a prioritized schedule is one of the steps that needs to be considered in the planning process. The time to do this type of planning is before the hectic pace of an incident occurs.

Reporting

After the system has been restored, the incident response team creates a report of the incident. Detailing what was discovered, how it was discovered, what was done, and the results, this report acts as a corporate memory and can be used for future incidents. Having a knowledge base of previous incidents and the actions used is a valuable resource because it is in the context of the particular enterprise. These reports also allow a mechanism to close the loop with management over the incident and, most importantly, provide a roadmap of the actions that can be used in the future to prevent events of identical or similar nature.

Part of the report will be recommendations, if appropriate, to change existing policies and procedures, including disaster recovery and business continuity. The similarity in objectives makes a natural overlap, and the cross-pollination between these operations is important to make all processes as efficient as possible.

Follow-up/Lessons Learned

Once the excitement of the incident is over and operations have been restored to their pre-incident state, it is time to take care of a few last items. Senior-level management must be informed about what occurred and what was done to address it. An after-action report should be created to outline what happened and how it was addressed. Recommendations for improving processes and policies should be incorporated so that a repeat incident will not occur. If prosecution of the individual responsible is desired, additional time will be spent helping law enforcement agencies and possibly testifying in court. Training material may also need to be developed or modified as part of the new, modified policies and procedures.

In the reporting process, a critical assessment of what went right, what went wrong, what can be improved, and what should be continued is prepared as a form of lessons learned. This is a critical part of self-improvement, and is not meant to place blame, but rather to assist in future prevention. Having things go wrong in a complex environment is part of normal operations; having repeat failures that are preventable is not. The key to the lessons learned section of the report is to make the necessary changes so that a repeat event will not occur. Because many incidents are a result of attackers using known methods, once the attack patterns are known in an enterprise and methods exist to mitigate them, then it is the task of the entire enterprise to take the necessary actions to mitigate future events.

■ Standards and Best Practices

There are many options available to a team when planning and performing processes and procedures. To assist the team in choosing a path, there are both standards and best practices to consult in the proper development of processes. From government sources to industry sources, there are many opportunities to gather ideas and methods, even from fellow firms.

State of Compromise

The new standard of information security involves living in a state of compromise, where one should always expect that adversaries are active in their networks. It is unrealistic to expect that you can keep attackers out of your network. Operating in a state of compromise does not mean that one must suffer significant losses. A working assumption when planning for, responding to, and managing the overall incident response process is that the systems are compromised and that prevention cannot be the only means of defense.

NIST

The National Institutes of Standards and Technology, a U.S. governmental entity under the Department of Commerce, produces a wide range of Special Publications (SPs) in the area of computer security. Grouped in several different categories, the most relevant SPs for incident response come from the Special Publications 800 series:

- *Computer Security Incident Handling Guide,* SP 800-61 Rev. 2

- *NIST Security Content Automation Protocol (SCAP),* SP 800-126 Rev 2

- *Information Security Continuous Monitoring for Federal Information Systems and Organizations,* SP 800-137

- *Guide to Selecting Information Technology Security Products,* NIST SP 800-36

- *Guide to Enterprise Patch Management Technologies,* NIST SP 800-40 Version 3

- *Guide to Using Vulnerability Naming Schemes* [CVE/CCE], NIST SP 800-51, Rev. 1

Department of Justice

In April 2015, the U.S. Department of Justice's Cybersecurity Unit released a best practices document, *Best Practices for Victim Response and Reporting of Cyber Incidents.* This document identifies steps to take before a cyber

Tech Tip

What *Not* to Do as Part of Incident Response

The U.S. Department of Justice has two specific recommended steps that you should not take as part of an incident response action.

- *Do not use the compromised system to communicate.*

- *Do not hack into or damage another network or system.*

The victim organization should always assume that any communications across affected machines will be compromised. This eavesdropping action is standard hacker behavior, and if you tip off your actions, they can be countered before you regain control of your system. Hacking, even retaliatory hacking, is illegal, and given the difficulty in attribution, attempts to respond by hacking the hacker may accidentally result in hacking an innocent third-party machine.

incident, the steps to take during an incident response action, a list of actions to not take, and what to do after the incident. The URL for the document is in the "For More Information" section at the end of the chapter.

Indicators of Compromise

Indicators of Compromise (IOCs) are artifacts left behind from computer intrusion activity. Detection of IOCs is a quick way to jumpstart a response element. Originated by the security firm Mandiant, IOCs have spread in usage to a wide range of firms. IOCs act as a tripwire for responders. An IOC can be tied to a specific observable event, which then can be traced to related events, and to stateful events such as Registry keys. One of the biggest challenges in incident response is getting on the trail of an attacker, and IOCs provide a means of getting on the trail.

Tech Tip

Common Indicators of Compromise

- *Unusual outbound traffic*   This probably is the clearest indicator that data is going where it shouldn't.
- *Geographical irregularities*   Communications going to countries in which no business ties exist is another key indicator that data is going where it shouldn't.
- *Unusual login activity*   Failed logins, login failures to nonexistent accounts, and so forth, indicate compromise.
- *Anomalous usage patterns for privileged accounts*   Changes in patterns of when administrators typically operate and what they typically access indicate compromise.
- *Changes in database access patterns*   This indicates hackers are searching for data, or reading it to collect large quantities.
- *Automated web traffic*   Timing can show some requests are scripts, not humans.
- *Change in HTML response sizes*   SQL injection can result in large HTML response sizes.
- *Large numbers of requests for specific files*   Numerous requests for specific files, such as join.php, may indicate automated attack patterns.
- *Mismatched port to application traffic*   Common method of attempting to hide activity.
- *Unusual DNS requests*   Command and control server traffic.
- *Unusual Registry changes*   Indications of changes to a system state.
- *Unexpected patching*   Some hackers/malware will patch to prevent other hackers from entering a target.
- *Bundles of data/files in wrong place*   Large aggregations of data, frequently encrypted, may be files being prepared for exfiltration.
- *Changes to mobile device profiles*   Mobile is the new perimeter, and changes may indicate malware.
- *DDoS/DoS attacks*   Denial of service is used as a tool to provide smokescreen or distraction.

There are several standards associated with IOCs, but the three main ones are Cyber Observable eXpression (CybOX), a method of information sharing developed by MITRE; OpenIOC, an open source initiative established by Mandiant that is designed to facilitate rapid communication of specific threat information associated with known threats; and the Incident Object Description Exchange Format (IODEF), an XML format specified in RFC 5070 for conveying incident information between response teams, both internally and externally with respect to organizations. The "For More Information" section at the end of the chapter provides URLs for all three standards.

Cyber Kill Chain

A modern cyberattack is a complex, multistage process. The concept of a kill chain is the targeting of specific steps of a multistep process with the goal of disrupting the overall process. The term **cyber kill chain** is the application of this philosophy to a cyber incident, with the expressed purpose of disrupting the attack.

Taking the information already presented, we know the steps that hackers take and we have indicators that can clue us in to the current status of an attack. Using this information, we can plan specific interventions to each step of the attacker's process. The kill chain process has received a lot of press since it was introduced by Lockheed Martin, some positive and some negative. In most cases, the negative press is related to what many would call a misapplication of the model. As with all security models and defensive strategies, it is important to customize and adapt how it interacts with the specific processes it is meant to protect.

Making Security Measurable

MITRE, working together with partners from government, industry, and academia, has created a set of techniques (called Making Security Measurable) to improve the measurability of security. This is a comprehensive effort, including registries of specific baseline data, standardized languages for the accurate communication of security information, and formats and standardized processes to facilitate accurate and timely communications.

The entirety of the project is beyond the scope of this text, but Table 22.1 lists some of the common items by category, a few of which are described next in a bit more detail.

STIX and TAXII

MITRE has continued its efforts in the process of making security measurable and adding automation to the mix. **Structured Threat Information eXpression (STIX)** is a structured language for cyberthreat intelligence information. MITRE created **Trusted Automated eXchange of Indicator Information (TAXII)** as the main transport mechanism for cyberthreat information represented by STIX. TAXII services allow organizations to share cyberthreat information in a secure and automated manner.

CybOX

Cyber Observable eXpression (CybOX) is a standardized schema for the communication of observed data from the operational domain. Designed to

Table 22.1	Sample Elements of Making Security Measurable	
Language/Format	**Registry**	**Standardized Processes**
Open Vulnerability and Assessment Language (OVAL)	Common Vulnerabilities and Exposures list (CVE)	NIST Security Content Automation Protocol (SCAP)
Malware Attribute Enumeration and Characterization (MAEC)	Common Weakness Enumeration (CWE)	*Information Security Continuous Monitoring for Federal Information Systems and Organizations* (SP 800-137)
Cyber Observable Expression (CybOX)	Open Vulnerability and Assessment Language (OVAL) Repository	*Guide to Selecting Information Technology Security Products* (NIST SP 800-36)
Structured Threat Information eXpression (STIX)	Common Attack Pattern Enumeration and Classification (CAPEC)	*Guide to Enterprise Patch Management Technologies,* (NIST SP 800-40 Rev. 3)
Trusted Automated eXchange of Indicator Information (TAXII)		*Guide to Using Vulnerability Naming Schemes* (CVE/CCE) (NIST SP 800-51, Rev. 1)

streamline communications associated with incidents, CybOX provides a means of communicating key elements, including event management, incident management, and more, in an effort to improve interoperability, consistency, and efficiency.

■ For More Information

- **CybOX** https://cybox.mitre.org/
- **DOJ** *Best Practices for Victim Response and Reporting of Cyber Incidents* www.justice.gov/sites/default/files/criminal-ccips/legacy/2015/04/30/04272015reporting-cyber-incidents-final.pdf

- **Incident Object Description Exchange Format (IODEF)** https://tools.ietf.org/html/rfc5070
- **Making Security Measurable** http://makingsecuritymeasurable.mitre.org/
- **Open IOC Framework** www.openioc.org/

■ Chapter Summary

After reading this chapter and completing the exercises, you should understand the following about incident response.

Understand the foundations of incident response processes

- The role of incident management is the control of a coordinated and comprehensive response to an incident.
- Learn the anatomy of an attack, both old versions and newer APT-style attacks.
- The goals of incident response in an organization are to restore systems to functioning order and prevent future risk.

Implement the detailed steps of an incident response process

- The major steps in the incident response process are preparation, incident identification, initial response, incident isolation, strategy formulation, investigation, recovery, reporting, and follow-up.

- Develop a detailed understanding of the components of each of the steps.
- Understand the linkages and interconnections between key process steps.

Describe standards and best practices that are involved in incident response

- Modern systems should expect to exist in a state of compromise and have policies and processes designed to operate under these conditions.
- The U.S. government, including NIST and the Department of Justice, have published useful guidance.
- Indicators of compromise provide early-warning triggers for incident response investigators.
- Taking actions against an incident in progress can be planned using a cyber kill chain philosophy.
- The Making Security Measurable material from MITRE can assist in the incident response process.

■ Key Terms

advanced persistent threat (APT) *(653)*
Computer Emergency Response Team (CERT) *(651)*
Computer Incident Response Team (CIRT) *(651)*
cyber kill chain *(669)*
Cyber Observable eXpression (CybOX) *(669)*
data minimization *(658)*
footprinting *(652)*
incident *(651)*
incident response *(651)*

incident response policy *(655)*
Indicator of Compromise (IOC) *(668)*
information criticality *(651)*
quarantine *(662)*
remote administration Trojan (RAT) *(653)*
Structured Threat Information eXpression (STIX) *(669)*
Trusted Automated eXchange of Indicator Information (TAXII) *(669)*

Key Terms Quiz

Use terms from the Key Terms list to complete the sentences that follow. Don't use the same term more than once. Not all terms will be used.

1. A(n) _____ is any event in an information system or network where the results are different than normal.

2. When the attackers are focused on maintaining a presence during an incident, the type of attack is typically called a(n) _____.

3. The determination of boundaries during an attack is a process called _____.

4. The steps an organization performs in response to any situation determined to be abnormal in the operation of a computer system are called _____.

5. One methodology for planning incident response defenses is known as _____.

6. A(n) _____ is an artifact that can be used to detect the presence of an attack.

7. To remove an item from normal operation and use is a process referred to as _____.

8. A(n) _____ is a team-based approach to incident response in an organization.

9. A key measure used to prioritize incident response actions is _____.

10. _____ and _____ are used to communicate cyberthreat information between organizations.

Multiple-Choice Quiz

1. Which of the following is not an Indicator of Compromise (IOC)?

   A. Unusual outbound traffic

   B. Increase in traffic over port 80

   C. Traffic to unusual foreign IP addresses

   D. Discovery of large encrypted data blocks that you don't know the purpose of

2. A sysadmin thinks a machine is under attack, so he logs in as root and attempts to see what is happening on the machine. Which common technical mistake is most likely to occur?

   A. The alteration of date/time stamps on files and objects in the system

   B. Failure to recognize the attacker by process ID

   C. Erasure of logs associated with an attack

   D. The cutting of a network connection between an attacker and the current machine

3. What is the last step of the incident response process?

   A. Reconstitution

   B. Recovery

   C. Follow-up

   D. Lessons learned

4. Which of the following are critical elements in an incident response toolkit? (Choose all that apply.)

   A. Accurate network diagram

   B. Findings of last penetration test report

   C. List of critical data/systems

   D. Phone list of people on-call by area

5. Your organization experienced an APT hack in the past and is very interested in preventing a reoccurrence. What step of the attack path is the best step at which to combat APT-style attacks?

   A. Escalate privilege

   B. Establish foothold

   C. Lateral movement

   D. Initial compromise

6. The goals of an incident response process include all of the following except:

   A. Confirm or dispel an incident occurrence

   B. Minimize security expenditures

   C. Protect privacy rights

   D. Minimize system disruption

7. During an initial response to an incident, which of the following is most important?

   A. Who or what is reporting the incident

   B. The time of the report

C. Who takes the initial report

D. Accurate information

8. When determining the level of risk of exposure for data in storage, in transit, or during processing, which of the following is not a factor?

   A. Time

   B. Quantity

   C. Data type

   D. Access

9. While working on an investigation, a colleague hands you a list of file creation and access times taken from a compromised workstation. To match the times with file access and creation times from other systems, what do you need to account for?

   A. Record time offsets

   B. Network Time Protocol

   C. Created, modified, and accessed times

   D. Operating system offsets

10. Which of the following activities should you *not* do during an incident response investigation associated with an APT?

    A. Use the corporate e-mail system to communicate

    B. Determine system time offsets

    C. Use only qualified and trusted tools

    D. Create an off-network site for data collection

■ Essay Quiz

1. The Chief Financial Officer (CFO) sees you in the lunch room. Knowing that you are leading the company's incident response initiative, she comes over to your table and asks if you have time to answer a question. You are surprised, but say yes. Her question is simple and to the point: "Can you explain this incident response thing to me, in nontechnical terms, so I can respond appropriately at the next board meeting in the discussion?" In response, you offer to prepare a written outline for the CFO. In one page, outline the major points that need to be addressed and give examples in language suitable for the audience.

2. Explain the relationship between the anatomy of a hack and Indicators of Compromise.

Computer Forensics

"How often have I said to you that when you have eliminated the impossible, whatever remains, however improbable, must be the truth?"

—Sir Arthur Conan Doyle

01000100
010110010101
0110011001100110
0011010000110100
110110111101
01101110

In this chapter, you will learn how to

- **Explore the basics of digital forensics**
- **Identify the rules and types of evidence**
- **Collect evidence**
- **Preserve evidence**
- **Maintain a viable chain of custody**
- **Investigate a computer crime or policy violation**
- **Examine system artifacts**
- **Develop forensic policies and procedures**
- **Examine the policies and procedures associated with e-discovery**

Computer forensics is certainly a popular buzzword in computer security. This chapter addresses the key aspects of computer forensics in preparation for the CompTIA Security+ certification exam. It is not intended to be a treatise on the topic or a legal tutorial regarding the presentation of evidence in a court of law. This material is only an introduction to the topic, and before one enters into forensic work or practice, much additional study is necessary. The principles presented in this chapter are of value in conducting any investigative processes, including internal or external audit procedures, but many nuances of handling legal cases are far beyond the scope of this text.

The term **forensics** relates to the application of scientific knowledge to legal problems. Specifically, computer forensics involves the preservation, identification, documentation, and interpretation of computer data. In today's practice, computer forensics can be performed for three purposes:

- Investigating and analyzing computer systems as related to a violation of law

- Investigating and analyzing computer systems for compliance with an organization's policies

- Responding to a request for digital evidence (e-discovery)

Forensics is often associated with incident response, the procedures used to respond to an abnormal condition in a system. There is subtle difference, however: incident response is about corrective action—returning the system to a normal operational state—whereas forensics is about figuring out what happened.

Cross Check

Incident Response

Incident response and associated policies and procedures are covered in Chapter 22.

If an unauthorized person accesses a system, that person likely has violated the law. However, a company employee who performs similar acts (accessing data remotely) may or may not violate laws, the determination of which depends on many factors, including specific authorizations and job duties. One can violate corporate policies while acting lawfully with respect to computer laws. It is worth noting that knowingly exceeding one's authorizations with respect to system access is a violation of the law.

Any of these situations could ultimately result in legal action and may require legal disclosure. Therefore, it is important to note that computer forensic actions may, at some point in time, deal with legal violations, and investigations could go to court proceedings. As a potential first responder, you should always seek legal counsel. Also seek legal counsel ahead of time as you develop and implement corporate policies and procedures. It is extremely important to understand that even minor procedural missteps can have significant legal consequences. The rule to follow is simple: always assume that the material will be used in a court of law and thus must be handled in a perfectly proper manner at all times. This further means that when dealing with forensics, you must ensure that all steps are performed by qualified forensic examiners.

■ Evidence

Evidence consists of the documents, verbal statements, and material objects that are admissible in a court of law. Evidence is critical to convincing management, juries, judges, or other authorities that some kind of violation has occurred. The submission of evidence is challenging, but it is even more challenging when computers are used because the people involved may not be technically educated and thus may not fully understand what's happened.

Computer evidence presents yet more challenges because the data itself cannot be experienced with the physical senses—that is, you can see printed characters, but you can't see the bits where that data is stored. Bits of data are merely magnetic pulses on a disk or some other storage technology. Therefore, data must always be evaluated through some kind of "filter" rather than sensed directly. This is often of concern to auditors, because good auditing techniques recommend accessing the original data or a version that is as close as possible to the original data.

The digital forensic process is a technically demanding one, with no room for errors. The most common cause of evidence from an investigation being excluded from court proceedings is *spoliation*, the unauthorized alteration of digital evidence. If the forensic process is less than perfect, spoliation is assumed. The best guidance is 1) always perform forensics as if you are going to court with the evidence, and 2) if you do not have qualified digital forensic investigators in-house, do nothing to the device/media—let a professional handle it.

Types of Evidence

All evidence is not created equal. Some evidence is stronger and better than other evidence. Several types of evidence can be germane:

- **Direct evidence**   Oral testimony that proves a specific fact (such as an eyewitness's statement). The knowledge of the facts is obtained through the five senses of the witness, with no inferences or presumptions.

- **Real evidence**   Also known as associative or physical evidence, this includes tangible objects that prove or disprove a fact. Physical evidence links the suspect to the scene of a crime.

- **Documentary evidence**   Evidence in the form of business records, printouts, manuals, and the like. Much of the evidence relating to computer crimes is documentary evidence.

- **Demonstrative evidence**   Used to aid the jury and can be in the form of a model, experiment, chart, and so on, offered to prove that an event occurred.

Standards for Evidence

Evidence in U.S. federal court cases is governed by a series of legal precedents, the most notable of which is the Daubert standard. Three U.S. Supreme Court cases articulate the Daubert standard and shape how materials are entered into evidence. Four specific elements are associated with the admission of scientific expert testimony. This is important with respect to digital forensics because the form of the evidence means that it can rarely speak for itself; rather, it must be interpreted by an expert and presented to the court.

The first element is that the Judge is the gatekeeper. Materials are not considered evidence until declared so by the judge. This is to ensure that experts are determined to be experts before the court relies upon their judgment. A second element is reliability and relevance. The trial judge is to determine that the expert's testimony is relevant to the proceedings at hand, and that the expert's methods are reliable with respect to the material being attested to. The third element is that expert knowledge should be based on science, specifically science that is based on the scientific method with a replicable methodology. The final element relates to this scientific methodology, stating that it must be based on proven science, subjected to peer review, with a known error rate or potential error rate and consensus among the scientific community that the methodology is generally accepted. After these elements are satisfied, the judge can admit the expert's testimony as evidence.

These factors all relate to a U.S. federal court decision and therefore are only binding in the U.S. federal judiciary, but the test is recognized and applied in similar form at many levels of jurisdiction. The bottom line is simple: the data can't speak for itself, and experts who can interpret the data operate under strict guidelines with respect to conduct, qualifications, principles, and methods.

To be credible, especially if evidence will be used in court proceedings or in corporate disciplinary actions that could be challenged legally, evidence must meet three standards:

- **Sufficient evidence**   It must be convincing or measure up without question.

- **Competent evidence**   It must be legally qualified and reliable.

- **Relevant evidence**   It must be material to the case or have a bearing on the matter at hand.

Three Rules Regarding Evidence

An item can become evidence when it is admitted by a judge in a case. Three rules guide the use of evidence with regard to its use in court proceedings:

- **Best evidence rule**   Courts prefer original evidence rather than a copy to ensure that no alteration of the evidence (whether intentional or unintentional) has occurred. In some instances, an evidence duplicate can be accepted, such as when the original is lost or destroyed by acts of God or in the normal course of business. A duplicate is also acceptable when a third party beyond the court's subpoena power possesses the original.

- **Exclusionary rule**   The Fourth Amendment to the U.S. Constitution precludes illegal search and seizure. Therefore, any evidence collected in violation of the Fourth Amendment is not admissible as evidence. Additionally, if evidence is collected in violation of the Electronic Communications Privacy Act (ECPA) or other related provisions of the U.S. Code, it may not be admissible to a court. For example, if no policy exists regarding the company's intent to monitor network traffic or systems electronically, and the employee has not acknowledged this policy by signing an agreement, sniffing the employee's network traffic could be a violation of the ECPA.

- **Hearsay rule**   Hearsay is secondhand evidence—evidence offered by the witness that is not based on the personal knowledge of the witness but is being offered to prove the truth of the matter asserted. Typically, computer-generated evidence is considered hearsay evidence, as the maker of the evidence (the computer) cannot be interrogated. There are exceptions being made where items such as logs and headers (computer-generated materials) are being accepted in court. There are exceptions, but they rarely apply to digital evidence.

■ Forensic Process

Forensics is the use of scientific methods in the analysis of matters in connection with crime or other legal matters. Because of the connection to law, it is an exacting process, with no room for error. In digital forensics, the issue of

Tech Tip

Evidence Control Mental Checklist
Keep these points in mind as you collect evidence:

- *Who collected the evidence?*
- *How was it collected?*
- *Where was it collected?*
- *Who has had possession of the evidence?*
- *How was it protected and stored?*
- *When was it removed from storage? Why? Who took possession?*

The laws mentioned here are U.S. laws. Other countries and jurisdictions may have similar laws that would need to be considered in a similar manner.

alteration becomes paramount, because changing 1's to 0's does not leave a trace in many situations. Because of the issue of contamination or spoliation of evidence, detailed processes are used in the processing of information.

From a high-level point of view, multiple steps are employed in a digital forensic investigation:

1. **Identification**   Recognize an incident from indicators and determine its type and scope. This is not explicitly within the field of forensics but is significant because it impacts other steps. What tools were used? How many systems are involved? How much data is to be copied? These questions all have ramifications on the successful outcome of a forensic process.

2. **Preparation**   Prepare tools, techniques, and search warrants and monitor authorizations and management support.

3. **Approach/strategy**   Dynamically formulate an approach based on potential impact on bystanders and the specific technology in question. The goal of the strategy should be to maximize the collection of untainted evidence while minimizing impact to the victim or owner.

4. **Preservation**   Isolate, secure, and preserve the state of physical and digital evidence. This includes preventing people from using the digital device or allowing other electromagnetic devices to be used within a certain proximity. Proper preservation is essential to prevent alteration of the source.

5. **Collection**   Record the physical scene and duplicate digital evidence using standardized and accepted procedures. This is where a digital camera and microphone are vital tools for capturing details—serial numbers, layouts, and so forth—quickly and definitively.

6. **Examination**   In-depth, systematic search of evidence relating to the suspected crime. This step occurs later, in a lab, and focuses on identifying and locating potential specific evidence elements, possibly within unconventional locations. It is important to construct detailed documentation for analysis, documenting the metadata and data values that may be relevant to the issues at hand in the investigation.

7. **Analysis**   Determine significance, reconstruct fragments of data, and draw conclusions based on the elements of evidence found. The data itself cannot tell a story, and in this step the investigator weaves the elements into a picture, hopefully the only one that can be supported. Although the intuition is to prove guilt, the skilled and seasoned investigator focuses on painting the picture that the data describes, regardless of outcome, and making it comprehensive and complete so that it will stand up to challenge. Multiple people with different skill sets may be needed to complete the picture.

8. **Presentation**   Summarize and provide an explanation of the conclusions. The results should be written in layperson's terms using abstracted terminology. If you cannot explain the information to a nontechnical layperson, then you do not understand it well enough to complete this aspect. All abstracted terminology should reference the specific details of the case.

9. **Returning evidence** Ensure physical and digital property is returned to its proper owner and determine how and what criminal evidence must be removed. (For example, hardware may be returned, but images of child pornography would be removed.) This is not an explicit step of forensic investigation, and most models that address how to seize evidence rarely address this aspect. But at the end of the day, the job is not done until all aspects are finished, and this includes this level of clean-up activity.

When information or objects are presented to management or admitted to court to support a claim, that information or those objects can be considered as evidence or documentation supporting your investigative efforts. Senior management will always ask a lot of questions—second- and third-order questions that you need to be able to answer quickly. Likewise, in a court, credibility is critical. Therefore, evidence must be properly acquired, identified, protected against tampering, transported, and stored.

Exam Tip: A digital camera is great for recording a scene and information. Screenshots of active monitor images may be obtained as well. Pictures can detail elements such as serial number plates, machines, drives, cable connections, and more. Photographs are truly worth a thousand words.

Acquiring Evidence

When an incident occurs, you will need to collect data and information to facilitate your investigation. If someone is committing a crime or intentionally violating a company policy, she will likely try to hide her tracks. Therefore, you should collect as much information as soon as you can. In today's highly networked world, evidence can be found not only on the workstation or laptop computer, but also on company-owned file servers, security appliances, and servers located with the Internet service provider (ISP).

Tech Tip

Data Volatility

From the most volatile to the most persistent:

1. *CPU storage (registers/cache)*
2. *System storage (RAM)*
3. *Kernel tables*
4. *Fixed media*
5. *Removable media*
6. *Output/hardcopy*

Microsoft produced a forensic tool for law enforcement called COFEE (Computer Online Forensics Evidence Extractor) that can be used to collect a wide range of data from a suspect machine. Restricted by license to law enforcement, it is out of reach for most investigators. An examination of how it functions provides useful information, and many of its functions can be readily copied by investigators. COFEE is a wrapper for a whole host of utilities—think Sysinternals and more—all integrated by script. This automated process can be re-created by any competent forensic investigator. Automated scripts and tools reduce errors and increase effectiveness.

A first responder must do as much as possible to control damage or loss of evidence. Obviously, as time passes, evidence can be tampered with or destroyed. Look around on the desk, on the Rolodex, under the keyboard, in desktop storage areas, and on cubicle bulletin boards for any information that might be relevant. Secure floppy disks, optical discs, flash memory cards, USB drives, tapes, and other removable media. Request copies of logs as soon as possible. Most ISPs protect logs that could be subpoenaed. Take photos (some localities require use of Polaroid photos, as they are more difficult to modify without obvious tampering) or video. Include photos of operating computer screens and hardware components from multiple angles. Be sure to photograph internal components before removing them for analysis.

When an incident occurs and the computer being used is going to be secured, you must consider two questions: Should it be turned off, and should it be disconnected from the network? Forensic professionals debate the reasons for turning a computer on or turning it off. Some state that the plug should be pulled in order to freeze the current state of the computer. However, this results in the loss of any data associated with an attack in progress from the machine. Any data in RAM will also be lost. Further, it may corrupt the computer's file system and could call into question the validity of your findings.

Imaging or dumping the physical memory of a computer system can help identify evidence that is not available on a hard drive. This is especially appropriate for rootkits, for which evidence on the hard drive is hard to find. Once the memory is imaged, you can use a hex editor to analyze the image offline on another system. (Memory-dumping tools and hex editors are available on the Internet.) Note that dumping memory is more applicable for investigative work where court proceedings will not be pursued. If a case is likely to end up in court, do not dump memory without first seeking legal advice to confirm that live analysis of the memory is acceptable; otherwise, the defendant will easily be able to dispute the claim that evidence was not tampered with.

On the other hand, it is possible for the computer criminal to leave behind a software bomb that you don't know about, and any commands you execute, including shutting down or restarting the system, could destroy or modify files, information, or evidence. The criminal may have anticipated such an investigation and altered some of the system's binary files.

While teaching at the University of Texas, Austin, Dr. Larry Leibrock led a research project to quantify how many files are changed when turning off and on a Windows workstation. The research documents that approximately 0.6 percent of the operating system files are changed each time a Windows XP system is shut down and restarted. An administrator looking at a machine at the behest of management can completely obfuscate any data that could be recovered, a process called *spoliation*. This cannot be undone and renders the data unusable in legal proceedings, whether court or human resources.

Further, if the computer being analyzed is a server, it is unlikely management will support taking it offline and shutting it down for investigation. So, from an investigative perspective, either course may be correct or incorrect, depending on the circumstances surrounding the incident. What is most important is that you are deliberate in your work, you document your actions, and you can explain why you took the actions you performed.

Many investigative methods are used. Figure 23.1 shows the continuum of investigative methods from simple to more rigorous.

Examine suspect system using its software without verification	Verify software on suspect system and use that software for investigation	Examine suspect system using external media with verified software	Build a new system that completely images suspect system	Boot suspect system with verified external OS, kernel, and tools	Use dedicated forensics workstation

Simple ◄————————————————————————————————————► Rigorous

• **Figure 23.1** Investigative method rigor

Figure 23.2 shows the relationship between the complexity of your investigation and both the reliability of your forensic data and the difficulty of investigation.

• **Figure 23.2** Required rigor of the investigative method versus both data reliability and the difficulty of investigation

Identifying Evidence

Evidence must be properly marked as it is collected so that it can be identified as a particular piece of evidence gathered at the scene. Properly label and store evidence, and make sure the labels can't be easily removed. Keep an evidence control log book identifying each piece of evidence (in case the label is removed); the persons who discovered it; the case number; the date, time, and location of the discovery; and the reason for collection. Keep a log of all staff hours and expenses. This information should be specific enough for recollection later in court. It is important to log other identifying marks, such as device make, model, serial number, cable configuration or type, and so on. Note any type of damage to the piece of evidence.

Being methodical is extremely important when identifying evidence. Do not collect evidence by yourself—have a second person who can serve as a witness to your actions. Keep logs of your actions during both seizure and during analysis and storage. A sample log, providing the minimum contents of an evidence control log book entry, is shown here:

Item Description	Investigator	Case #	Date	Time	Location	Reason
Dell Latitude laptop computer, D630, serial number 6RKC1G0	Smith	C-25	30 Jan 2014	1325 MST	Room 312 safe	Safekeeping

Protecting Evidence

Protect evidence from electromagnetic or mechanical damage. Ensure that evidence is not tampered with, damaged, or compromised by the procedures used during the investigation. This helps avoid potential liability problems later. Protect evidence from extremes in heat and cold, humidity, water, magnetic fields, and vibration. Use static-free evidence-protection gloves as opposed to standard latex gloves. Seal the evidence in a proper container with evidence tape, and mark it with your initials, date, and case number. For example, if a mobile phone with advanced capabilities is seized, it should be properly secured in a hard container designed to prevent accidentally pressing the keys during transit and storage. If the phone is to remain turned on for analysis, radio frequency isolation bags that attenuate the device's radio signal should be used. This will prevent remote wiping, locking, or disabling of the device.

You should never examine a system with the utilities provided by that system. You should always use utilities that have been verified as correct and uncorrupted. Even better, use a *forensic workstation*, a computer system specifically designed to perform computer forensic activities. Do not open any files or start any applications. If possible, document the current memory and swap files, running processes, and open files. Disconnect the system from the network and immediately contact senior management. Unless you have appropriate forensic training and experience, consider calling in a professional.

Third-party investigators are commonly used in civil matters. When doing digital forensics for a civil litigation–based case, it is important to consult with the retaining counsel concerning the level of detail and records desired. In civil litigation, anything written will be requested to be disclosed during pretrial discovery. This can provide strategy disclosure beyond what is desired by counsel. The alternative is to keep minimal required records as determined by counsel.

681

Exam Tip: Never analyze the seized system directly. Always make multiple images of the device and analyze a copy.

Transporting Evidence

Properly log all evidence in and out of controlled storage. Use proper packing techniques, such as placing components in static-free bags, using foam packing material, and using cardboard boxes. Be especially cautious during transport of evidence to ensure custody of evidence is maintained and the evidence isn't damaged or tampered with.

Storing Evidence

Store the evidence in an evidence room that has low traffic, restricted access, camera monitoring, and entry-logging capabilities. Store components in static-free bags, foam packing material, and cardboard boxes, and inside metal tamper-resistant cabinets or safes whenever possible. Many of today's electronics are sensitive to environmental factors. It is important for storage areas to have environmental controls to protect devices from temperature and humidity changes. It is also prudent to have environmental-monitoring devices to ensure that temperature and humidity remain within safe ranges for electronic devices.

Conducting the Investigation

When analyzing computer storage components, you must use extreme caution. A copy of the system should be analyzed—never the original system, as that will have to serve as evidence. A system specially designed for forensic examination, known as a forensic workstation, can be used. Forensic workstations typically contain hard drive bays, write blockers, analysis software, and other devices to safely image and protect computer forensic data. Analysis should be done in a controlled environment with physical security and controlled access.

Tech Tip

Tools of the Trade

- ■ *Disk wipe utilities*   Tools to completely delete files and overwrite contents
- ■ *File viewers*   Text and image viewers
- ■ *Forensic programs*   Tools to analyze disk space, file content, system configuration, and so on
- ■ *Forensic workstations*   Specialized workstations containing hardware, software, and component interface capabilities to perform computer forensic activities
- ■ *Hard drive tools*   Partition-viewing utilities, bootable CDs
- ■ *Unerase tools*   Tools to reverse file deletions

Remember that witness credibility is extremely important. It is easy to imagine how quickly credibility can be damaged if the witness is asked, "Did you lock the file system?" and can't answer affirmatively. Or, when asked, "When you imaged this disk drive, did you use a new system?" the witness can't answer that the destination disk was new or had been completely formatted using a low-level format before data was copied to it.

One of the key elements to preserving the chain of custody, protecting evidence, and having copies of data for analysis is the concept of digital forensic duplication of data. A digital forensic copy is a carefully controlled copy that has every bit the same as the original. Not just files, but all data structures associated with the device, including unused space, are copied in a digital forensic image copy, every bit, bit by bit. Making this type of copy is not something done with normal file utilities; specialty programs are required.

It is also important not to interface with the digital media using the host system, as all file systems both read and write to the storage media as part of their normal operation, altering the media. This type of alteration changes information, potentially damaging the trace evidence needed in the investigation. For this reason, a **write blocker** is commonly used to connect the media to the investigator's computer. Figure 23.3 shows a kit that contains both write blockers and a forensic duplicator.

It is common for forensic duplicator devices to have additional features to assist an investigator, such as making multiple copies at once and calculating hash values for the device and the duplicate. Capturing the hash values for all items is an essential first step in handling any digital evidence.

When conducting a digital forensic investigation, consider local laws. Many states require that independent investigators be licensed private investigators. If you are working as an analyst on in-house systems, the laws may have differing levels of applicability. Before consulting, it is best to investigate the need of a license.

• **Figure 23.3** (a) Write blocker devices and (b) forensic duplicator device

Tech Tip

Forensics-Based Drive Imaging

When a forensic investigation on a series of computers is needed to determine facts in a computer investigation, a variety of methods can be used to discover and recover the evidence. For example, if a developer group is being investigated, the investigator could look at each machine and find the specific evidence that is being sought. The problem with this approach is that in the process of doing the investigation, the other developers in the area become aware and have a chance to destroy critical evidence. For this reason, and to minimize disruption to a team, many times the investigation begins with a large-scale forensic duplication effort. The steps are remarkably simple and well practiced by many investigative firms:

1. *Document the scope of the machines being investigated, noting the number of drives and sizes.*

2. *Send in a team after hours to do the duplication.*

3. *Open each machine, disconnect the hard drives, and attach external cables.*

4. *Duplicate each drive using a forensic duplication procedure that makes a complete image of the hard drive on a separate media source.*

5. *Reassemble the machines, leaving no evidence that the duplication was performed.*

The forensic images are then examined one by one at a later time, away from inquisitive and prying eyes.

The number of files stored on today's hard drives can be very large, literally hundreds of thousands of files. Obviously this is far too many for the investigator to directly analyze. However, by matching the message digests for files installed by the most popular software products to the message digests of files on the drive being analyzed, the investigator can avoid analyzing approximately 90 percent of the files because he can assume they are unmodified. The National Software Reference Library (NSRL) collects software from various sources and incorporates file profiles into a Reference Data Set available for download as a service. See www.nsrl.nist.gov.

The CAINE Computer Forensics Linux Live Distro and SANS Investigative Forensic Toolkit (SIFT) are just two examples of the many tools you can use to perform computer forensic activities.

Tech Tip

Cleanup: Possible Remediation Actions After an Attack

These are things you'll need to do to restore your system after you've responded to an incident and completed your initial investigation:

- *Place the system behind a firewall.*
- *Reload the OS.*
- *Run scanners.*
- *Install security software.*
- *Remove unneeded services and applications.*
- *Apply patches.*
- *Restore the system from backup.*

■ Analysis

After successfully imaging the drives to be analyzed and calculating and storing the message digests, the investigator can begin the analysis. The details of the investigation will depend on the particulars of the incident being investigated. However, in general, the following steps will be involved:

1. Check the Recycle Bin for deleted files.
2. Check the web browser history files and address bar histories.
3. Check the web browser cookie files. Different web browsers store cookies in different places.
4. Check the Temporary Internet Files folders.
5. Search files for suspect character strings. To conserve valuable time, be wise in the choice of words you search for, choosing "confidential," "sensitive," "sex," or other explicit words and phrases related to your investigation.
6. Search the slack and free space for suspect character strings as described previously.

■ Chain of Custody

Evidence, once collected, must be properly controlled to prevent tampering. The chain of custody accounts for all persons who handled or had access to the evidence. The chain of custody shows who obtained the evidence, when and where it was obtained, where it was stored, and who had control or possession of the evidence for the entire time since the evidence was obtained.

The following shows critical steps in a chain of custody:

1. Record each item collected as evidence.
2. Record who collected the evidence, along with the date and time it was collected or recorded.
3. Write a description of the evidence in the documentation.
4. Put the evidence in containers and tag the containers with the case number, the name of the person who collected it, and the date and time it was collected or put in the container.
5. Record all message digest (hash) values in the documentation.
6. Securely transport the evidence to a protected storage facility.
7. Obtain a signature from the person who accepts the evidence at this storage facility.
8. Provide controls to prevent access to and compromise of the evidence while it is being stored.
9. Securely transport the evidence to court for proceedings.

■ Message Digest and Hash

If files, logs, and other information are going to be captured and used for evidence, you need to ensure that the data isn't modified. In most cases, a tool that implements a hashing algorithm to create message digests is used.

The mathematics behind hashing algorithms has been researched extensively, and although it is possible that two different data streams could produce the same message digest, it is very improbable. Most forensic tools still report MD5 hashes, although the industry is shifting to SHA-2 and SHA-3 series and the tools are catching up. Hashing is covered in detail in Chapter 5.

> ### ✓ Cross Check
>
> #### Hash Algorithms and Forensics
>
> Hash algorithms offer digital forensics the ability to "bag and tag" evidence. Although it does not protect the evidence from tampering, it provides clear proof of whether or not data has been changed. This is a very important issue to resolve, given how easy it is to change digital data and the fact that typically no trace is left of the change. A complete review of hashing algorithms is found in Chapter 5. The important question regarding hashes and forensics is this: How and where do you record hash values to protect their integrity as part of the investigative process?

A *hashing algorithm* performs a function similar to the familiar parity bits, checksum, or cyclical redundancy check (CRC). It applies mathematical operations to a data stream (or file) to calculate some number that is unique based on the information contained in the data stream (or file). If a subsequent hash created on the same data stream results in a different hash value, it usually means that the data stream was changed.

The hash tool is applied to each file or log, and the message digest value is noted in the investigation documentation. It is a good practice to write the logs to a write-once media such as CD-ROM. When the case actually goes to trial, the investigator may need to run the tool on the files or logs again to show that they have not been altered in any way since being obtained.

■ Host Forensics

Host forensics refers to the analysis of a specific system. Host forensics includes a wide range of elements, including the analysis of file systems and artifacts of the operating system. These elements often are specific to individual systems and operating systems, such as Linux or Windows.

File Systems

When a user deletes a file, the file is not actually deleted. Instead, a pointer in a file allocation table is deleted. This pointer was used by the operating system to track down the file when it was referenced, and the act of "deleting" the file merely removes the pointer and marks the cluster(s) holding the file as available for the operating system to use. The actual data originally stored on the disk remains on the disk (until that space is used again); it just isn't recognized as a coherent file by the operating system.

Partitions

Physical memory storage devices can be divided into a series of containers called partitions. A **partition** is a logical storage unit that is subsequently used by an operation system. Systems can have multiple partitions for a wide variety of reasons, ranging from hosting multiple operating systems to performance-maximizing efforts to protection efforts. The broad issue of partition operation and management is outside the scope of this chapter, but this is a critical topic to understand and examine when looking at a system forensically.

Free Space

Since a deleted file is not actually completely erased or overwritten, it sits on the hard disk until the operating system needs to use that space for another file or application. Sometimes the second file that is saved in the same area does not occupy as many clusters as the first file, so a fragment of the original file is left over.

The cluster that holds the fragment of the original file is referred to as **free space** because the operating system has marked it as usable when needed. As soon as the operating system stores something else in this cluster, it is considered *allocated*. The unallocated clusters still contain the original data until the operating system overwrites them. Looking at the free space might reveal information left over from files the user thought were deleted from the drive.

Slack Space

Another place that should be reviewed is **slack space**, which is different from free space. When a file is saved to a hard drive or other storage medium, the operating system allocates space in blocks of a predefined size, called *clusters*. Even if your file contains only ten characters, the operating system will allocate a full cluster—with space left over in the cluster. This is slack space.

It is possible for a user to hide malicious code, tools, or clues in slack space, as well as in the free space. You may also find information in slack space from files that previously occupied that same cluster. Therefore, an investigator should review slack space using utilities that can display the information stored in these areas.

Hidden Files

There are numerous ways to hide data on a system. One method is to hide files by setting the hidden attribute, which limits the listing of them by standard file utilities. Devised so that system files that should not be directly manipulated are hidden from easy view, this concept raises a broader question with respect to forensics. How can a user hide information from easy accessibility?

There is a wide range of methods of hiding files, and any attempt to list them would be long and subject to continual change. The major ones typically encountered include changing a file extension, encryption, streams, and storage on other partitions. We have already covered partitions—it is obvious that a forensic investigation should find, enumerate, and explore all partitions. Streams will be covered in the next section. Encrypted data, by its very nature, is hidden from view. Without the key, modern encryption methods resist any brute-force attempts to determine the contents. It is important to find encrypted data stores and document the locations for later use by legal counsel.

Changing a file's extension does not actually alter the contents or usability of a file. It merely breaks the automated runtime association manager that determines what executable is associated with the file type to properly handle it. The challenge of how to handle file types goes back to the early days of computers, when the magic number method was created. The term **magic number** describes a series of digits near the beginning of the file that provides information about the file format. In some cases the magic number can be read by humans, as GIF87a or GIF89a indicates both Graphics Interchange Format and the specification. Other file types are less obvious, such as a TIFF file on an Intel platform, which is II followed by 42 as a two-byte integer (49 49 2A 00).

Most integrated forensic tool suites handle file identification via magic number and are thus able to find hidden videos, pictures, and other items. The other thing these tools can do is complete searches across the entire storage structure for strings, and this can find many "hidden" items.

Streams

Streams is a short name for Alternate Data Streams, a specific data structure associated with NTFS in Windows. The normal location for data in an NTFS-based system is in the data stream, a location identified by a record in the Master File Table (MFT) called $DATA:, which is technically an unnamed data stream. Alternate data streams have names and are identified by $DATA:*StreamName*, where *StreamName* is the name of the stream being used. Streams can be used to hide information; although the information is still present, most of the normal file utilities do not deal with streams, so it will not be seen. Forensic tool suites have tools that can search for, report on, and analyze stream data on Windows systems.

Windows Metadata

Microsoft Windows–based systems have a wide range of artifacts with forensic value. Before we examine some of these artifacts, it is important to understand why they exist. The vast majority of artifacts exist for the purpose of improving the user experience. Tracking what users do and have done and making that information available to the operating system to improve future use is one of the primary reasons for the information; its forensic value is secondary.

Registry Analysis

The first and foremost Windows artifact is the system Registry, which acts a database repository of a whole host of information and provides a one-stop shop for a wide range of Windows forensic artifacts—what applications have been installed, user activity, activity associated with external devices, and more. Although the specific artifacts needed in an investigation differ based on the scope of the investigation, it is safe to assume that metadata recorded by the Windows operating system will serve a useful purpose in the investigation, especially since the Registry is stored by user and therefore the activity recorded in the Registry is attributable to a user.

The list of artifacts stored by the Registry is extremely long, but some of the major ones include event logs of a wide range of system and security information. There is also a wide range of file activity artifacts that can be analyzed, including analysis of shellbags, which provides evidence of folder opening. LNK files and most recently used (MRU) elements can point to file system activity. A wide range of date/time stamps on files, even deleted files, can be present for examination. There are specific toolsets designed to forensically explore the Registry and retrieve the desired artifacts from this voluminous store.

As mentioned before and will be mentioned again, Windows forensic analysis is no different from any other forensic analysis with respect to forensic procedures. Skill and proficiency in forensic procedures is the most important issue when analyzing a system, because damage may make use of the information impossible.

Linux Metadata

Linux systems have their own sets of artifacts. From a forensics perspective, Linux systems differ from Windows systems in three main ways:

- **No registry**   Program data is stored in scattered locations.
- **Different file system**   A multitude of different file systems are used, each with different attributes.
- **Plaintext abounds**   Files and data tend to be in plaintext, which impacts searching.

The lack of a registry to hold system and program information does not mean that the information is not there; it just means that it is distributed. The same is true of file systems. Rather than offering only two file system structures (NTFS and FAT), Linux comes with a whole host of different forms. Each of these has quirks, such as no file creation dates in many of them, and the zeroing of metadata when files are deleted results in forensic challenges.

When it comes to performing forensics on a Linux system, the value of a good sysadmin cannot be understated. Many of the artifacts of activity on a Linux system are scattered to various local locations, and a good sysadmin can assist in locating and recovering the essential elements for analysis. This is not a license for a sysadmin to begin performing forensic activities! The same rules and procedural requirements listed earlier still apply, and in most cases this necessitates the use of forensically trained professionals.

■ Device Forensics

Device forensics is the application of digital forensic principles to devices—mobile phones, tablets, the endless list of devices that comprise the "Internet of Things," and more. The fact that it is a device does not change the principles pertaining to the collection and handling of evidence. All of the forensic principles still apply and are just as important. What does change are the tools and processes employed to retrieve and analyze the data. This is because the file systems, data structures, operating systems, and artifacts are different than those in the world of servers and PCs.

■ Network Forensics

Network forensics is the capture, recording, and analysis of network events in order to discover the source of network problems or security incidents. Examining networks in a forensic fashion introduces several challenges. First is scale. The scale of a network is related to the number of nodes and the speed of traffic. Second is the issue of volume. Packet capture is not technically difficult, but it can necessitate large quantities of storage. And although storage is relatively cheap, large numbers of packets can be difficult to sort through and analyze. Because of these issues,—network forensics becomes an issue of specificity; if you know what target and what protocols you are looking for, you can selectively capture and analyze the traffic for those segments and have data that is useful. But therein lies the other challenge. Network data is temporal. It exists while the packet is in transit and then it is gone, forever. Metadata such as NetFlow data can provide some information, but it does not contain any content of the data being transmitted.

As a general-purpose tool, network forensics is nearly impossible because of the scale issues. But in specific situations, such as in front of high-value targets that have limited data movement, it can prove to be valuable. It can also be valuable in troubleshooting ongoing incidents and problems in the network.

The same rules apply to network forensics as apply to all other forensic collection efforts. Preserving the integrity of the data is paramount, and maintaining control over the data is always a challenge. Forensic rules (admissibility, chain of custody, etc.) do not change because the source of data has changed.

■ E-Discovery

Electronic discovery, or e-discovery, is the term used for the document and data production requirements as part of legal discovery in civil litigation. When a civil lawsuit is filed, under court approval, a firm can be compelled to turn over specific data from systems pursuant to the legal issue at hand. Electronic information is considered to be the same as paper documents in some respects and completely different in others. The evidentiary value can be identical. The fragility can be substantial—electronic records can be changed without leaving a trace. Electronic documents can also have metadata associated with the documents, such as who edited the document, previous version information, and more.

One of the pressing challenges in today's enterprise record store is the maintenance of the volumes of electronic information. Keeping track of the information stores based on a wide range of search terms is essential to comply with e-discovery requests. It is common for systems to use forensic processes and tools to perform e-discovery searches.

Reference Model

EDRM, a coalition of consumers and providers focused on improving e-discovery and information governance, has created a reference model for e-discovery. The Electronic Discovery Reference Model, shown in Figure 23.4, provides a framework for organizations to prepare for e-discovery. The major steps of

Electronic Discovery Reference Model

Electronic Discovery Reference Model / © 2014 / v3.0 / edrm.net

● **Figure 23.4**   Electronic Discovery Reference Model (courtesy of EDRM, EDRM.net)

the framework are thoroughly described on the EMDR web site (http://edrm.net). Additional resources available from EDRM include XML schemas, glossaries, metric, and more.

Big Data

It may seem that big data is all the rage in business today, but in reality it is simply a description of the times. We have created large data stores in most enterprises, a byproduct of cheap storage and the ubiquity of the Internet. Big data is an issue in e-discovery as well. The cataloging, storage, and maintenance of corporate records often becomes a big data issue. This facilitates the use of big data methods in many cases. This is an area of rapid development, both for forensics and e-discovery, as data volumes continue to grow exponentially.

Cloud

The cloud has become a resource for enterprise IT systems, and as such it is intimately involved in both e-discovery and forensics. Having data that may or may not be directly accessed by the tools of e-discovery and forensics can complicate the needed processes. An additional complication is the legal issues associated with the contracts between the organization and the cloud provider. As both forensics and e-discovery are secondary processes from a business perspective, they may or may not be addressed in a standard cloud agreement. Because these processes can become important—and if they do, it may be too late to contractually address them—it behooves an organization to prepare by addressing them in cloud agreements with third parties.

Principles of Computer Security

Chapter 23 Review

Lab Manual Exercises

The following lab exercises from the companion lab manual, *Principles of Computer Security Lab Manual, Fourth Edition,* provide practical application of material covered in this chapter:

Lab 9.1l   Log Analysis in Linux

Lab 9.1w   Log Analysis in Windows

Lab 10.1w   Live Analysis: Incident Determination in Windows

Lab 10.2w   Acquiring the Data in Windows

Lab 10.3w   Forensic Analysis in CAINE

Lab 10.4w   Remote Forensic Image Capture Over a Network

Chapter Summary

After reading this chapter and completing the exercises, you should understand the following about incident response and forensics.

Explore the basics of digital forensics

- Digital forensics is the collection of processes and procedures used to prepare digital information for use in legal or administrative proceedings.

- Because of the importance of veracity and the fragility of digital data to integrity violations that cannot be detected, it is imperative that processes be complete and comprehensive.

Identify the rules and types of evidence

- Evidence must meet the three standards of being sufficient, competent, and relevant if it is to be used in legal proceedings.

- There are four different types of evidence: direct, real, documentary, and demonstrative.

- There are three rules regarding evidence: the best evidence rule, the exclusionary rule, and the hearsay rule.

Collect evidence

- Evidence must be properly collected, protected, and controlled to be of value during court or disciplinary activities.

- When acquiring evidence, one must be deliberate to ensure evidence is not damaged and operations are not negatively impacted.

Preserve evidence

- Evidence must be properly marked so that it can be readily identified as that particular piece of evidence gathered at the scene.

- Evidence must be protected so that it is not tampered with, damaged, or compromised.

- Evidence should be transported cautiously to ensure custody of the evidence is maintained and the evidence itself is not tampered with or damaged.

- Evidence should be stored in properly controlled areas and conditions.

- When conducting an investigation on computer components, one must be deliberate and cautious to ensure evidence is not damaged.

Maintain a viable chain of custody

- A chain of custody that accounts for all persons who handled or have access to the evidence must be maintained to prevent evidence tampering or damage.

Investigate a computer crime or policy violation

- Information can be recorded and possibly hidden in various ways on a computer. Sometimes information will be hidden in either the free space or the slack space of the computer's disk drive.

- Free space is the space (clusters) on a storage medium that is available for the operating system to use.

- Slack space is the unused space on a disk drive created when a file is smaller than the allocated unit of storage, such as a cluster.

- The use of a message digest or hashing algorithm is essential to ensure that information stored on a computer's disk drives has not been changed.

- If the information in the data stream or file is changed, a different message digest will result, indicating the file has been tampered with.

- Forensic analysis of data stored on a hard drive can begin once the drive has been imaged and message digests of important files have been calculated and stored.

- Analysis typically involves investigating the Recycle Bin, web browser and address bar history files, cookie files, temporary Internet file folders, suspect files, and free space and slack space.

- Experience and knowledge are your most valuable tools available when performing computer forensic activities.

Examine System artifacts

- Different systems can have different artifacts based on the operating system and equipment employed.

- Windows and Linux systems have many similar artifacts, although they are located in different areas and preserved in different ways.

Develop Forensic policies and procedures

- The overarching principle for all digital forensic investigations is proper procedures. Any deviation from proper procedures can permanently alter evidence and render information unusable in follow-on procedures, whether criminal, civil, or administrative. Ensuring proper procedures by trained professionals is essential from the first aspect of an investigation.

Examine the policies and procedures associated with e-discovery

- E-discovery, is the term used for the document and data production requirements as part of legal discovery in civil litigation

- The Electronic Discovery Reference Model, provides a framework for organizations to prepare for e-discovery.

■ Key Terms

best evidence rule *(677)*

competent evidence *(677)*

demonstrative evidence *(676)*

device forensics *(688)*

direct evidence *(676)*

documentary evidence *(676)*

evidence *(675)*

exclusionary rule *(677)*

forensics *(675)*

free space *(686)*

hearsay rule *(677)*

magic number *(687)*

network forensics *(689)*

partition *(686)*

real evidence *(676)*

relevant evidence *(677)*

slack space *(686)*

stream *(687)*

sufficient evidence *(677)*

write blocker *(683)*

■ Key Terms Quiz

Use terms from the Key Terms list to complete the sentences that follow. Don't use the same term more than once. Not all terms will be used.

1. Evidence collected in violation of the Fourth Amendment of the U.S. Constitution, the Electronic Communications Privacy Act (ECPA), or other aspects of the U.S. Code may not be admissible to a court under the terms of the _____.

2. Evidence that is legally qualified and reliable is _____.

3. Documents, verbal statements, and material objects admissible in a court of law are called _____.

4. The rule whereby courts prefer original evidence rather than a copy to ensure that no alteration of the evidence (whether intentional or unintentional) has occurred is termed the _____.

5. Evidence that is convincing or measures up without question is _____.

6. _____ is the preservation, identification, documentation, and interpretation of computer data to be used in legal proceedings.

7. _____ is evidence that is material to the case or has a bearing on the matter at hand.

8. _____ is the unused space on a disk drive when a file is smaller than the allocated unit of storage.

9. _____ is oral testimony or other evidence that proves a specific fact (such as an eyewitness's statement, fingerprint, photo, and so on). The knowledge of the facts is obtained through the five senses of the witness. There are no inferences or presumptions.

10. _____ is the remaining sectors of a previously allocated file that are available for the operating system to use.

■ Multiple-Choice Quiz

1. Which of the following correctly defines evidence as being competent?

   A. The evidence is material to the case or has a bearing on the matter at hand.

   B. The evidence is presented in the form of business records, printouts, or other items.

   C. The evidence is convincing or measures up without question.

   D. The evidence is legally qualified and reliable.

2. Which of the following correctly defines evidence as being relevant?

   A. The evidence is material to the case or has a bearing on the matter at hand.

   B. The evidence is presented in the form of business records, printouts, or other items.

   C. The evidence is convincing or measures up without question.

   D. The evidence is legally qualified and reliable.

3. Which of the following correctly defines documentary evidence?

   A. The evidence is presented in the form of business records, printouts, manuals, and other items.

   B. The knowledge of the facts is obtained through the five senses of the witness.

   C. The evidence is used to aid the jury and may be in the form of a model, experiment, chart, or other item and be offered to prove an event occurred.

   D. Physical evidence that links the suspect to the scene of a crime.

4. Which of the following correctly defines real evidence?

   A. The evidence is convincing or measures up without question.

   B. The evidence is material to the case or has a bearing on the matter at hand.

   C. The evidence is used to aid the jury and may be in the form of a model, experiment, chart, or other item and be offered to prove an event occurred.

   D. Tangible objects that prove or disprove a fact.

5. Which of the following is the least rigorous investigative method?

   A. Using a dedicated forensic workstation

   B. Verifying software on a suspect system and using that software for the investigation

   C. Examining the suspect system using its software without verification

   D. Booting the suspect system with a verified floppy or CD, kernel, and tools

6. Which of the following correctly defines slack space?

   A. The space on a disk drive that is occupied by the boot sector

   B. The space located at the beginning of a partition

C. The remaining sectors of a previously allocated file that are available for the operating system to use

D. The unused space on a disk drive when a file is smaller than the allocated unit of storage

7. Which of the following correctly describes the minimum contents of an evidence control log book?

   A. Description, Investigator, Case #, Date, Time, Location, Reason

   B. Description, Investigator, Case #, Date, Location, Reason

   C. Description, Case #, Date, Time, Location, Reason

   D. Description, Coroner, Case #, Date, Time, Location, Reason

8. Which of the following correctly describes the chain of custody for evidence?

   A. The evidence is convincing or measures up without question.

   B. Accounts for all persons who handled or had access to a specific item of evidence.

   C. Description, Investigator, Case #, Date, Time, Location, Reason.

   D. The evidence is legally qualified and reliable.

9. Which of the following correctly defines the exclusionary rule?

   A. Any evidence collected in violation of the Fourth Amendment is not admissible as evidence.

   B. The evidence consists of tangible objects that prove or disprove a fact.

   C. The knowledge of the facts is obtained through the five senses of the witness.

   D. The evidence is used to aid the jury and may be in the form of a model, experiment, chart, or the like, offered to prove an event occurred.

10. Which of the following correctly defines free space?

    A. The unused space on a disk drive when a file is smaller than the allocated unit of storage (such as a sector)

    B. The space on a disk drive that is occupied by the boot sector

    C. The space located at the beginning of a partition

    D. The remaining sectors of a previously allocated file that are available for the operating system to use

■ Essay Quiz

1. A supervisor has brought to your office a confiscated computer that was allegedly used to view inappropriate material. He has asked you to look for evidence to support this allegation. Because you work for a small company, you do not have an extra computer you can dedicate to your analysis. How would you boot the system and begin forensic analysis? Provide a reason for your method.

2. Explain why you should always search the free space and slack space if you suspect a person has deliberately deleted files or information on a workstation that you are analyzing.

3. You have been asked by management to secure the laptop computer of an individual who was just dismissed from the company under unfavorable circumstances. Pretend that your own computer is the laptop that has been secured. Make the first entry in your log book and describe how you would start this incident off correctly by properly protecting and securing the evidence.

Lab Projects

• Lab Project 23.1

Use an MD5 or SHA-1 algorithm to obtain the hash value for a file of your choice. Record the hash value. Change the file with a word processor or text editor. Obtain the hash value for the modified file. Compare the result.

• Lab Project 23.2

To understand what information is stored on your computer, examine the contents of the Temporary Internet Files folders on your own computer. Review the filenames and examine the contents of a few of the files. Describe how this information could be used as evidence of a crime.

chapter 24

Legal Issues and Ethics

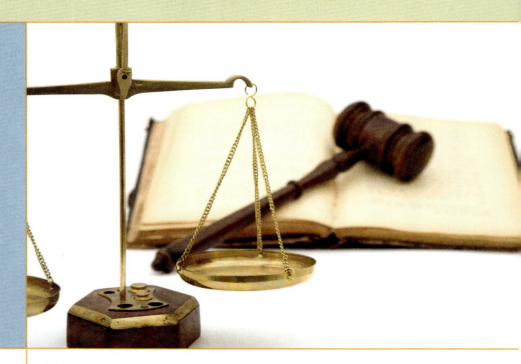

If you have ten thousand regulations you destroy all respect for the law.

—WINSTON CHURCHILL

In this chapter, you will learn how to

- Explain the laws and rules concerning importing and exporting encryption software
- Identify the laws that govern computer access and trespass
- Identify the laws that govern encryption and digital rights management
- Describe the laws that govern digital signatures
- Explore ethical issues associated with information security

Computer security is no different from any other subject in our society; as technological changes result in conflicts, laws are enacted to enable desired behaviors and prohibit undesired behaviors. The one substantial difference between this aspect of our society and others is that the speed of advancement in the information systems world as driven by business, computer network connectivity, and the Internet is much greater than in the legal system of compromise and lawmaking. In some cases, laws have been overly restrictive, limiting business options, such as in the area of importing and exporting encryption technology. In other cases, legislation has been slow in coming, and this fact has stymied business initiatives, such as in digital signatures. And in some areas, legislation has been both too fast and too slow, as in the case of privacy laws. One thing is certain: you will never satisfy everyone with a law, but it does delineate the rules of the game.

The cyber-law environment has not been fully defined by the courts. Laws have been enacted, but until they have been fully tested and explored by cases in court, the exact limits are somewhat unknown. This makes some aspects of interpretation more challenging, but the vast majority of the legal environment is known well enough that effective policies can be enacted to navigate this environment properly. Policies and procedures are tools you use to ensure understanding and compliance with laws and regulations affecting cyberspace.

Cybercrime

One of the many ways to examine cybercrime is to study how the computer is involved in the criminal act. Three types of computer crimes commonly occur: computer-assisted crime, computer-targeted crime, and computer-incidental crime. The differentiating factor is in how the computer is specifically involved from the criminal's point of view. Just as crime is not a new phenomenon, neither is the use of computers, and cybercrime has a history of several decades.

What is new is how computers are involved in criminal activities. The days of simple teenage hacking activities from a bedroom have been replaced by organized crime–controlled botnets (groups of computers commandeered by a malicious hacker) and acts designed to attack specific targets. The legal system has been slow to react, and law enforcement has been hampered by their own challenges in responding to the new threats posed by high-tech crime.

What comes to mind when most people think about cybercrime is a computer that is targeted and attacked by an intruder. The criminal attempts to benefit from some form of unauthorized activity associated with a computer. In the 1980s and '90s, cybercrime was mainly virus and worm attacks, each exacting some form of damage, yet the gain for the criminal was usually negligible. Enter the 21st century, with new forms of malware, rootkits, and targeted attacks; criminals can now target individual users and their bank accounts. In the current environment it is easy to predict where this form of attack will occur—if money is involved, a criminal will attempt to obtain a cut. A common method of criminal activity is computer-based fraud. Advertising on the Internet is big business, and hence the "new" crime of **click fraud** is now a concern. Click fraud involves a piece of malware that defrauds the advertising revenue counter engine through fraudulent user clicks.

The leader in the Internet auction space, eBay, and its subsidiary, PayPal, are frequent targets of fraud. Whether the fraud occurs by fraudulent listing, fraudulent bidding, or outright stealing of merchandise, the results are the same: a crime is committed. As users move toward online banking and stock trading, so moves the criminal element. Malware designed to install a keystroke logger and then watch for bank/brokerage logins is common on the Internet. Once the attacker finds the targets, he can begin looting accounts. His risk of getting caught and prosecuted is exceedingly low. Walk into a bank in the United States and rob it, and the odds are better than 95 percent that you will be doing time in federal prison after the FBI hunts you down and slaps the cuffs on your wrists. Do the same crime via a computer, and the odds are even better for the opposite: less than 1 percent of these attackers are caught and prosecuted.

The low risk of being caught is one of the reasons that criminals are turning to computer crime. Just as computers have become easy for ordinary people

Exam Tip: There are three forms of computer involvement in criminal activity:

- The computer as a tool of the crime
- The computer as a victim of a crime
- The computer that is incidental to a crime

to use, the trend continues for the criminal element. Today's cyber criminals use computers as tools to steal intellectual property or other valuable data and then subsequently market these materials through underground online forums. Using the computer to physically isolate the criminal from the direct event of the crime has made the investigation and prosecution of these crimes much more challenging for authorities.

The last way computers are involved with criminal activities is through incidental involvement. Back in 1931, the U.S. government used accounting records and tax laws to convict Al Capone of tax evasion. Today, similar records are kept on computers. Computers are also used to traffic child pornography and engage in other illicit activities—these computers act more as storage devices than as actual tools to enable the crime. Because child pornography existed before computers made its distribution easier, the computer is actually incidental to the crime itself.

With the three forms of computer involvement in criminal activities, multiplied by the myriad of ways a criminal can use a computer to steal or defraud, added to the indirect connection mediated by the computer and the Internet, computer crime of the 21st century is a complex problem indeed. Technical issues are associated with all the protocols and architectures. A major legal issue is the education of the entire legal system as to the serious nature of computer crimes. All these factors are further complicated by the use of the Internet to separate the criminal and his victim geographically. Imagine this defense: "Your honor, as shown by my client's electronic monitoring bracelet, he was in his apartment in California when this crime occurred. The victim claims that the money was removed from his local bank in New York City. Now, last time I checked, New York City was a long way from Los Angeles, so how could my client have robbed the bank?"

Common Internet Crime Schemes

To find crime, just follow the money. In the United States, the FBI and the National White Collar Crime Center (NW3C) have joined forces in developing the Internet Crime Complaint Center (IC3), an online clearinghouse that communicates issues associated with cybercrime. One of the items provided to the online community is a list of common Internet crime schemes and explanations of each (www.ic3.gov/crimeschemes.aspx). A separate list offers advice on how to prevent these crimes through individual actions (www.ic3.gov/preventiontips.aspx).

Sources of Laws

In the United States, three primary sources of laws and regulations affect our lives and govern our actions. A **statutory law** is passed by a legislative branch of government, be it the U.S. Congress or a local city council. Another source of laws and regulations is administrative bodies given power by other legislation. The power of government-sponsored agencies, such as the Environmental Protection Agency (EPA), the Federal Aviation Administration (FAA), the Federal Communication Commission (FCC), and others, lies in this powerful ability to enforce behaviors through administrative rule making, or **administrative law**. The last source of law in the United States is **common law**, or **case law**, which is based on previous events or precedent. This source of law comes from the judicial branch of government: judges decide on the applicability of laws and regulations.

All three sources have an involvement in computer security. Specific statutory laws, such as the Computer Fraud and Abuse Act (CFAA), govern behavior. The CFAA is designed to deal with cases of interstate computer fraud and cases of accessing national security information. The law has been amended several times to keep pace with technology. The primary charge from CFAA is typically one of accessing without authority, or exceeding authority on, a system involved with interstate commerce or national security. Administratively, the FCC and Federal Trade Commission (FTC) have made their presence felt in the Internet arena with respect to issues such as intellectual property theft and fraud. Common law cases are now working their ways through the judicial system, cementing the issues of computers and crimes into the system of precedents and constitutional basis of laws.

Exam Tip: Three types of laws are commonly associated with cybercrime: statutory law, administrative law, and common law (also called case law).

Computer Trespass

With the advent of global network connections and the rise of the Internet as a method of connecting computers between homes, businesses, and governments across the globe, a new type of criminal trespass can now be committed. Computer trespass is the unauthorized entry into a computer system via any means, including remote network connections. These crimes have introduced a new area of law that has both national and international consequences. For crimes that are committed within a country's borders, national laws apply. For cross-border crimes, international laws and international treaties are the norm. Computer-based trespass can occur even if countries do not share a physical border.

Computer trespass is treated as a crime in many countries. National laws against compute trespass exist in many countries, including Canada, the United States, and the member states of the European Union (EU). These laws vary by country, but they all have similar provisions defining the unauthorized entry into and use of computer resources for criminal activities. Whether called *computer mischief* as in Canada or *computer trespass* as in the United States, unauthorized entry and use of computer resources is treated as a crime with significant punishments. With the globalization of the computer network infrastructure, or Internet, issues that cross national boundaries have arisen and will continue to grow in prominence. Some of these issues are dealt with through the application of national laws upon request of another government. In the future, an international treaty may pave the way for closer cooperation.

Computer trespass is a convenient catchall law that can be used to prosecute cyber criminals when evidence of other criminal behavior, such as online fraud, identity theft, and so forth, is too weak to achieve a conviction.

Convention on Cybercrime

The Convention on Cybercrime is the first international treaty on crimes committed via the Internet and other computer networks. The convention is the product of four years of work by the Council of Europe (CoE), but also by the United States, Canada, Japan, and other non-CoE countries. The convention has been ratified and came into force in July 2004, and by September 2006, 15 member nations had also ratified it. The United States ratified it in the summer of 2006, with it entering into force in the United States in January 2007.

One of the main objectives of the Convention, set out in the preamble, is "to pursue, as a matter of priority, a common criminal policy aimed at the protection of society against cybercrime, *inter alia*, by adopting appropriate legislation and fostering international cooperation." This has become an important issue with the globalization of network communication. The ability to create a virus anywhere in the world and escape prosecution because of the lack of local laws has become a global concern.

The convention deals particularly with infringements of copyright, computer-related fraud, child pornography, and violations of network security. It also contains a series of powers and procedures covering, for instance, searches of computer networks and data interception. It has been supplemented by an additional protocol making any publication of racist and xenophobic propaganda via computer networks a criminal offense. This supplemental addition is in the process of separate ratification.

One of the challenges of enacting elements such as this convention is the varying legal and constitutional structures from country to country. Simple statements such as a ban on child pornography, although clearly desirable, can run into complicating issues, such as constitutional protections of free speech in the United States. Because of such issues, this well-intended joint agreement will have variations across the political boundaries of the world.

Significant U.S. Laws

The United States has been a leader in the development and use of computer technology. As such, it has a longer history associated with computers, and with cybercrime. Because legal systems tend to be reactive and move slowly, this leadership position has translated into a leadership position from a legal perspective as well. The one advantage of this legal leadership position is the concept that once an item is identified and handled by the legal system in one jurisdiction, subsequent adoption in other jurisdictions is typically quicker.

Electronic Communications Privacy Act (ECPA)

The **Electronic Communications Privacy Act (ECPA)** of 1986 was passed by Congress and signed by President Reagan to address a myriad of legal privacy issues that resulted from the increasing use of computers and other technology specific to telecommunications. Sections of this law address e-mail, cellular communications, workplace privacy, and a host of other issues related to communicating electronically. Section I was designed to modify federal wiretap statutes to include electronic communications. Section II, known as the **Stored Communications Act (SCA)**, was designed to establish criminal sanctions for unauthorized access to stored electronic records and communications. Section III covers pen registers and tap and trace issues. Tap and trace information is related to who is communicating with whom and when. Pen register data is the conversation information.

A major provision of ECPA was the prohibition against an employer's monitoring an employee's computer usage, including e-mail, unless consent is obtained (for example, clicking Yes on a warning banner is considered consent). Other legal provisions protect electronic communications from wiretap and outside eavesdropping, as users are assumed to have a reasonable expectation of privacy and afforded protection under the Fourth Amendment to the Constitution.

Cross Check

Cybercrime and Privacy

Cybercrime and privacy are concepts that are frequently interconnected. Identity theft is one of the fastest-rising crimes. How does using your personal computer to access the Internet increase your risk in today's world? Can you list a dozen specific risks you are personally exposed to? Privacy issues, being a significant topic in their own right, are covered in Chapter 25.

A common practice with respect to computer access today is the use of a warning banner. These banners are typically displayed whenever a network connection occurs and serve four main purposes. First, from a legal standpoint, they establish the level of expected privacy (usually none on a business system). Second, they serve notice to end users of the intent to conduct real-time monitoring from a business standpoint. Real-time monitoring can be conducted for security reasons, business reasons, or technical network performance reasons. Third, they obtain the user's consent to monitoring. The key is that the banner tells users that their connection to the network signals their consent to monitoring. Consent can also be obtained to look at files and records. In the case of government systems, consent is needed to prevent direct application of the Fourth Amendment. And the last reason is that the warning banner can establish the system or network administrator's common authority to consent to a law enforcement search.

Computer Fraud and Abuse Act (1986)

The **Computer Fraud and Abuse Act (CFAA)** of 1986, amended in 1994, 1996, in 2001 by the USA Patriot Act, and in 2008 by the Identity Theft Enforcement and Restitution Act, serves as the current foundation for criminalizing unauthorized access to computer systems. CFAA makes it a crime to knowingly access a computer that is either considered a government computer or used in interstate commerce, or to use a computer in a crime that is interstate in nature, which in today's Internet-connected age can be almost any machine. The act sets financial thresholds for defining a criminal act, which were lowered by the Patriot Act, but in light of today's investigation costs, these are easily met. The act also makes it a crime to knowingly transmit a program, code, or command that results in damage. Trafficking in passwords or similar access information is also criminalized. This is a wide-sweeping act, but the challenge of proving a case still exists.

Controlling the Assault of Non-Solicited Pornography And Marketing Act of 2003 (CAN-SPAM)

The CAN-SPAM Act was an attempt by the U.S. government to regulate commercial e-mail by establishing national guidelines and giving the FTC enforcement powers. The objective of the legislation was to curb unsolicited commercial e-mail, or *spam*. The act has applicability to mobile phones as well. Heralded as action to curb the rise of spam, since its enactment, the act has a very poor record.

Tech Tip

Header Manipulation
Falsifying header information is a serious violation of the CAN-SPAM Act. This can be considered an indicator of criminal or malicious intent and can bring the attention of other law enforcement agencies besides the FTC.

CAN-SPAM allows unsolicited commercial e-mail as long as it adheres to three rules of compliance:

- **Unsubscribe** It must include an obvious opt-out provision to allow users to unsubscribe, with these requests being honored within ten days.

- **Content** The content must be clear and not deceptive. Adult content must be clearly labeled, and subject lines must be clear and accurate.

- **Sending behavior** The sender must not use harvested e-mail addresses, falsify headers, or use open relays.

CAN-SPAM makes specific exemptions for e-mail pertaining to religious messages, political messages, and national security messages. The law also blocks people who receive spam from suing spammers and restricts states from enacting and enforcing stronger antispam statutes. The law does permit ISPs to sue spammers, and this has been used by some major ISPs to pursue cases against large-scale spam operations. Major firms such as AOL have considered the law useful in their battle against spam. Regarded largely as ineffective, statistics have shown that very few prosecutions have been pursued by the FTC. The act permits both criminal charges against individuals and civil charges against entities involved in suspected spamming operations.

USA Patriot Act

The USA Patriot Act of 2001, passed in response to the September 11 terrorist attacks on the World Trade Center in New York City and the Pentagon building in Arlington, Virginia, substantially changed the levels of checks and balances in laws related to privacy in the United States. This law extends the tap and trace provisions of existing wiretap statutes to the Internet and mandates certain technological modifications at ISPs to facilitate electronic wiretaps on the Internet and for ISPs to cooperate with the government to aid monitoring. The act also permits the Justice Department to proceed with its rollout of the Carnivore program, an eavesdropping program for the Internet. Much controversy exists over Carnivore, but until it's changed, the Patriot Act mandates that ISPs cooperate and facilitate monitoring. In recent actions, the name Carnivore has been retired, but the right of the government to eavesdrop and monitor communications continues to be a hot topic and one where actions continue. The Patriot Act also permits federal law enforcement personnel to investigate computer trespass (intrusions) and enacts civil penalties for trespassers.

Gramm-Leach-Bliley Act (GLBA)

In November 1999, President Clinton signed the **Gramm-Leach-Bliley Act (GLBA)**, a major piece of legislation affecting the financial industry that includes significant privacy provisions for individuals. The key privacy tenets enacted in GLBA include the establishment of an opt-out method for individuals to maintain some control over the use of the information provided in a business transaction with a member of the financial community. GLBA is enacted through a series of rules governed by state law, federal law, securities law, and federal rules. These rules cover a wider range of

---

Tech Tip

Computer Misuse

Two major laws, ECPA and CFAA (as amended), provide wide-sweeping tools for law enforcement to convict people who hack into computers or use them to steal information. Both laws have been strengthened and provide significant federal penalties. These laws are commonly used to convict criminals of computer misuse, even when other charges may have applied.

financial institutions, from banks and thrifts, to insurance companies, to securities dealers. Some internal information sharing is required under the Fair Credit Reporting Act (FCRA) between affiliated companies, but GLBA ended sharing to external third-party firms.

Sarbanes-Oxley Act (SOX)

In the wake of several high-profile corporate accounting/financial scandals in the United States, the federal government in 2002 passed sweeping legislation, the **Sarbanes-Oxley Act (SOX)**, overhauling the financial accounting standards for publicly traded firms in the United States. These changes were comprehensive, touching most aspects of business in one way or another. With respect to information security, one of the most prominent changes was the provision of **Section 404** controls, which specify that all processes associated with the financial reporting of a firm must be controlled and audited on a regular basis. Since the majority of firms use computerized systems, this places internal auditors into the IT shops, verifying that the systems have adequate controls to ensure the integrity and accuracy of financial reporting. These controls have resulted in controversy over the cost of maintaining them versus the risk of not using them.

Section 404 requires firms to establish a control-based framework designed to detect or prevent fraud that would result in misstatement of financials. In simple terms, these controls should detect insider activity that would defraud the firm. This has significant impacts on the internal security controls, because a system administrator with root-level access could perform many if not all tasks associated with fraud and would have the ability to alter logs and cover his tracks. Likewise, certain levels of power users of financial accounting programs would also have significant capability to alter records.

Privacy Laws

There is a wide range of privacy laws that are relevant to computers. There are laws for healthcare (HIPAA) and education records (FERPA), as well as other types of records including video rental records. These laws are described in detail in Chapter 25.

Payment Card Industry Data Security Standard (PCI DSS)

The payment card industry, including the powerhouses of MasterCard and Visa, through its PCI Security Standards Council designed a private-sector initiative to protect payment card information between banks and merchants. The **Payment Card Industry Data Security Standard (PCI DSS)** is a set of contractual rules governing how credit card data is to be protected (see the Tech Tip sidebar "PCI DSS Objectives and Requirements"). The current version is 3.1, which was released in April 2015. This is a voluntary, private-sector initiative that is proscriptive in its security guidance. Merchants and vendors can choose not to adopt these measures, but the standard has a steep price for noncompliance; the transaction fee for noncompliant vendors can be significantly higher, fines up to $500,000 can be levied, and in extreme cases the ability to process credit cards can be revoked.

Tech Tip

PCI DSS Objectives and Requirements

PCI DSS v3 includes six control objectives containing a total of 12 requirements:

1. *Build and Maintain a Secure Network*

   Requirement 1 *Install and maintain a firewall configuration to protect cardholder data*

   Requirement 2 *Do not use vendor-supplied defaults for system passwords and other security parameters*

2. *Protect Cardholder Data*

   Requirement 3 *Protect stored cardholder data*

   Requirement 4 *Encrypt transmission of cardholder data across open, public networks*

3. *Maintain a Vulnerability Management Program*

   Requirement 5 *Protect all systems against malware and regularly update antivirus software or programs*

   Requirement 6 *Develop and maintain secure systems and applications*

4. *Implement Strong Access Control Measures*

   Requirement 7 *Restrict access to cardholder data by business need-to-know*

   Requirement 8 *Identify and authenticate access to system components*

   Requirement 9 *Restrict physical access to cardholder data*

5. *Regularly Monitor and Test Networks*

   Requirement 10 *Track and monitor all access to network resources and cardholder data*

   Requirement 11 *Regularly test security systems and processes*

6. *Maintain an Information Security Policy*

   Requirement 12 *Maintain a policy that addresses information security for all personnel*

PCI DSS has two defined types of information, cardholder data and sensitive authentication data. The protection requirements established for these elements are detailed in Table 24.1.

Table 24.1	PCI DSS Data Retention Guidelines			
		Data Element	**Storage Permitted**	**Render Stored Data Unreadable**
Account Data	**Cardholder Data**	Primary Account Number (PAN)	Yes	Yes
		Cardholder Name	Yes	No
		Service Code	Yes	No
		Expiration Date	Yes	No
	Sensitive Authentication Data	Full Track Data	No	Cannot store per Requirement 3.2
		CAV2 / CVC2 / CVV2 / CID	No	Cannot store per Requirement 3.2
		PIN / PIN Block	No	Cannot store per Requirement 3.2

Import/Export Encryption Restrictions

Encryption technology has been controlled by governments for a variety of reasons. The level of control varies from outright banning to little or no regulation. The reasons behind the control vary as well, and control over import and export is a vital method of maintaining a level of control over encryption technology in general. The majority of the laws and restrictions are centered on the use of cryptography, which was until recently used mainly for military purposes. The advent of commercial transactions and network communications over public networks such as the Internet has expanded the use of cryptographic methods to include securing of network communications. As is the case in most rapidly changing technologies, the practice moves faster than law. Many countries still have laws that are outmoded in terms of e-commerce and the Internet. Over time, these laws will be changed to serve these new uses in a way consistent with each country's needs.

U.S. Law

Export controls on commercial encryption products are administered by the Bureau of Industry and Security (BIS) in the U.S. Department of Commerce. The responsibility for export control and jurisdiction was transferred from the State Department to the Commerce Department in 1996 and updated on June 6, 2002. Rules governing exports of encryption are found in the Export Administration Regulations (EAR), 15 C.F.R. Parts 730–774. Sections 740.13, 740.17, and 742.15 are the principal references for the export of encryption items.

Violation of encryption export regulations is a serious matter and is not an issue to take lightly. Until recently, encryption protection was accorded the same level of attention as the export of weapons for war. With the rise of the Internet, widespread personal computing, and the need for secure connections for e-commerce, this position has relaxed somewhat.

The U.S. encryption export control policy continues to rest on three principles: review of encryption products prior to sale, streamlined post-export reporting, and license review of certain exports of strong encryption to foreign government end users. The current set of U.S. rules requires notification to the BIS for export in all cases, but the restrictions are significantly lessened for mass-market products, as defined by all of the following:

- They are generally available to the public by being sold, without restriction, from stock at retail selling points by any of these means:
  - Over-the-counter transactions
  - Mail-order transactions
  - Electronic transactions
  - Telephone call transactions
- The cryptographic functionality cannot easily be changed by the user.
- They are designed for installation by the user without further substantial support by the supplier.
- When necessary, details of the items are accessible and will be provided, upon request, to the appropriate authority in the exporter's country in order to ascertain compliance with export regulations.

Tech Tip

Wassenaar Arrangement

The United States updated its encryption export regulations to provide treatment consistent with regulations adopted by the European Union, easing export and re-export restrictions among the EU member states and Argentina, Australia, Canada, Croatia, Japan, New Zealand, Norway, Republic of Korea, Russia, South Africa, Switzerland, Turkey, Ukraine, and the United States. The member nations of the Wassenaar Arrangement agreed to remove key-length restrictions on encryption hardware and software that is subject to certain reasonable levels of encryption strength. This action effectively removed "mass-market" encryption products from the list of dual-use items controlled by the Wassenaar Arrangement.

Mass-market commodities and software employing a key length greater than 64 bits for the symmetric algorithm must be reviewed in accordance with BIS regulations. Restrictions on exports by U.S. persons to terrorist-supporting states, as determined by the U.S. Department of State (currently Iran, Sudan, and Syria), their nationals, and other sanctioned entities are not changed by this rule.

705

As you can see, this is a very technical area, with significant rules and significant penalties for infractions. The best rule is that whenever you are faced with a situation involving the export of encryption-containing software, first consult an expert and get the appropriate permission or a statement that permission is not required. This is one case where it is better to be safe than sorry.

Non-U.S. Laws

Export control rules for encryption technologies fall under the Wassenaar Arrangement, an international arrangement on export controls for conventional arms and dual-use goods and technologies (see the Tech Tip sidebar, "Wassenaar Arrangement"). The Wassenaar Arrangement was established to contribute to regional and international security and stability by promoting transparency and greater responsibility in transfers of conventional arms and dual-use goods and technologies, thus preventing destabilizing accumulations. Participating states, of which the United States is one of 41, will seek, through their own national policies and laws, to ensure that transfers of these items do not contribute to the development or enhancement of military capabilities that undermine these goals, and are not diverted to support such capabilities.

Many nations have more restrictive policies than those agreed upon as part of the Wassenaar Arrangement. Australia, New Zealand, United States, France, and Russia go further than is required under Wassenaar and restrict general-purpose cryptographic software as dual-use goods through national laws. The Wassenaar Arrangement has had a significant impact on cryptography export controls, and there seems little doubt that some of the nations represented will seek to use the next round to move toward a more repressive cryptography export control regime based on their own national laws. There are ongoing campaigns to attempt to influence other members of the agreement toward less restrictive rules or, in some cases, no rules. These lobbying efforts are based on e-commerce and privacy arguments.

Digital rights management, secure USB solutions, digital signatures, and Secure Sockets Layer (SSL)–secured connections are examples of common behind-the-scenes use of cryptographic technologies. In 2007, the United Kingdom passed a new law mandating that when requested by UK authorities, either police or military, encryption keys must be provided to permit decryption of information associated with terror or criminal investigation. Failure to deliver either the keys or decrypted data can result in an automatic prison sentence of two to five years. Although this seems reasonable, it has been argued that such actions will drive certain financial entities offshore, as the rule applies only to data housed in the United Kingdom. As for deterrence, the two-year sentence may be lighter than a conviction for trafficking in child pornography; hence the law seems not to be as useful as it seems at first glance.

Digital Signature Laws

Whether a ring and wax seal, a stamp, or a scrawl indicating a name, signatures have been used to affix a sign of one's approval for centuries. As communications have moved into the digital realm, signatures need to evolve with the new medium, and hence digital signatures were invented. Using elements of cryptography to establish integrity and nonrepudiation, digital signature schemes can actually offer more functionality than their predecessors in the paper-based world.

U.S. Digital Signature Laws

On October 1, 2000, the Electronic Signatures in Global and National Commerce Act (commonly called the E-Sign law) went into effect in the United States. This law implements a simple principle: a signature, contract, or other record may not be denied legal effect, validity, or enforceability solely because it is in electronic form. Another source of law on digital signatures is the Uniform Electronic Transactions Act (UETA), which was developed by the National Conference of Commissioners on Uniform State Laws (NCCUSL) and has been adopted in all but four states—Georgia, Illinois, New York, and Washington—which have adopted a non-uniform version of UETA. The precise relationship between the federal E-Sign law and UETA has yet to be resolved and will most likely be worked out through litigation in the courts over complex technical issues.

Many states have adopted digital signature laws, the first being Utah in 1995. The Utah law, which has been used as a model by several other states, confirms the legal status of digital signatures as valid signatures, provides for use of state-licensed certification authorities, endorses the use of public key encryption technology, and authorizes online databases called repositories, where public keys would be available. The Utah act specifies a negligence standard regarding private encryption keys and places no limit on liability. Thus, if a criminal uses a consumer's private key to commit fraud, the consumer is financially responsible for that fraud, unless the consumer can prove that he or she used reasonable care in safeguarding the private key. Consumers assume a duty of care when they adopt the use of digital signatures for their transactions, not unlike the care required for PINs on debit cards.

From a practical standpoint, the existence of the E-Sign law and UETA has enabled e-commerce transactions to proceed, and the resolution of the technical details via court actions will probably have little effect on consumers beyond the need to exercise reasonable care over their signature keys. For the most part, software will handle these issues for the typical user.

> **Try This!**
>
> ### Digital Signature Agreements
>
> Digital signatures are becoming more common in everyday use. When a person signs up with a bank for electronic banking services, or with a brokerage account for online trading, that person typically agrees to electronic signatures. Using your bank or brokerage account—or if you don't have one, there are free online financial service firms you can sign up for—review the online agreement for electronic signature provisions.

UN Digital Signature Laws

The United Nations has a mandate to further harmonize international trade. With this in mind, the UN General Assembly adopted in 1996 the United Nations Commission on International Trade Law (UNCITRAL) Model Law on Electronic Commerce. To implement specific technical aspects of this model law, more work on electronic signatures was needed. The General Assembly then adopted in 2001 the UNCITRAL Model Law on Electronic

Signatures. These model laws have become the basis for many national and international efforts in this area.

Canadian Digital Signature Laws

Canada was an early leader in the use of digital signatures. Singapore, Canada, and the U.S. state of Pennsylvania were the first governments to have digitally signed an interstate contract. This contract, digitally signed in 1998, concerned the establishment of a Global Learning Consortium between the three governments (source: *Krypto-Digest* Vol. 1, No. 749, June 11, 1998). Canada went on to adopt a national model bill for electronic signatures to promote e-commerce. This bill, the Uniform Electronic Commerce Act (UECA), allows the use of electronic signatures in communications with the government. The law contains general provisions for the equivalence between traditional and electronic signatures (source: *BNA ECLR*, May 27, 1998, p. 700) and is modeled after the UNCITRAL Model Law on E-Commerce (source: *BNA ECLR*, September 13, 2000, p. 918). The UECA is similar to Bill C-54, Personal Information Protection and Electronic Documents Act (PIPEDA), in authorizing governments to use electronic technology to deliver services and communicate with citizens.

Individual Canadian provinces have passed similar legislation defining digital signature provisions for e-commerce and government use. These laws are modeled after the UNCITRAL Model Law on E-Commerce to enable widespread use of e-commerce transactions. These laws have also modified the methods of interactions between the citizens and the government, enabling electronic communication in addition to previous forms.

European Laws

The European Commission adopted a Communication on Digital Signatures and Encryption: "Ensuring Security and Trust in Electronic Communication—Towards a European Framework for Digital Signatures and Encryption." This communication states that a common framework at the EU level is urgently needed to stimulate "the free circulation of digital signature related products and services within the Internal market" and "the development of new economic activities linked to electronic commerce" as well as "to facilitate the use of digital signatures across national borders." Community legislation should address common legal requirements for certificate authorities, legal recognition of digital signatures, and international cooperation. This communication was debated, and a common position was presented to the member nations for incorporation into national laws.

On May 4, 2000, the European Parliament and Council approved the common position adopted by the council. In June 2000, the final version, the Electronic Commerce Directive (2000/31/EC), was adopted. The directive has been implemented by member states. To implement the articles contained in the directive, member states had to remove barriers, such as legal form requirements, to electronic contracting, leading to uniform digital signature laws across the EU.

Digital Rights Management

The ability to make flawless copies of digital media has led to another "new" legal issue. For years, the music and video industry has relied on technology to protect its rights with respect to intellectual property. It has been illegal for decades to copy information, such as music and videos, protected by copyright. Even with the law, people have for years made copies of music and videos to share, violating the law. Until the advent of digital copies (see Tech Tip sidebar "Digital Copies and Copyright"), this did not represent a significant economic impact in the eyes of the industry, as the copies were of lesser quality and people would pay for original quality in sufficient numbers to keep the economics of the industry healthy. As such, legal action against piracy was typically limited to large-scale duplication and sale efforts, commonly performed overseas and subsequently shipped to the United States as counterfeit items.

The primary statute enacted in the United States to bring copyright legal concerns up to date with the digital world is the **Digital Millennium Copyright Act (DMCA)**. The DMCA states its purpose as follows: "To amend title 17, United States Code, to implement the World Intellectual Property Organization Copyright Treaty and Performances and Phonograms Treaty, and for other purposes." The majority of this law was well crafted, but one section has drawn considerable comment and criticism. A section of the law makes it illegal to develop, produce, and trade any device or mechanism designed to circumvent technological controls used in copy protection.

Although, on the surface, this seems a reasonable requirement, the methods used in most cases are cryptographic in nature, and this provision had the ability to eliminate and/or severely limit research into encryption and the strengths and weaknesses of specific methods. A DMCA provision, Section 1201(g), was included to provide for specific relief and allow exemptions for legitimate research (see the Tech Tip sidebar "DMCA Research Exemption Requirements"). With this section, the law garnered industry support from several organizations, such as the Software & Information Industry Association (SIIA), Recording Industry Association of America (RIAA), and Motion Picture Association of America (MPAA). Based on these inputs, the U.S. Copyright Office issued a report supporting the DMCA in a required report to the U.S. Congress. This seemed to settle the issues until the RIAA threatened to sue an academic research team headed by Professor Edward Felten from Princeton University. The issue behind the suit was the potential publication of results demonstrating that several copy protection methods were flawed in their application. This research came in response to an industry-sponsored challenge to break the methods. After breaking the methods developed and published by the industry, Felten and his team prepared to publish their findings. The RIAA objected and threatened a suit under provisions of the DMCA. After several years of litigation and support of Felten by the Electronic Frontier Foundation (EFF), the case was eventually resolved in the academic team's favor, although no case law to prevent further industry-led threats was developed.

One of the controversial issues associated with DMCA is the issue of takedown notices. Carriers such as YouTube are granted protection from content violation, provided they remove the content when requested with a takedown order. The publishing industry uses scanners and automated systems to issue takedown notices, and these sometimes go awry (see the sidebar on the Mars Rover mishap). The issue of fair use is one that is not delineated by bright-line regulations, making the system one that sides with the takedown requestor unless the content poster takes them to court.

Tech Tip

Digital Copies and Copyright

The ability of anyone with a PC to make a perfect copy of digital media led to industry fears that individual piracy actions could cause major economic issues in the recording industry. To protect the rights of the recording artists and the economic health of the industry as a whole, the music and video recording industry lobbied the U.S. Congress for protection, which was granted under the Digital Millennium Copyright Act (DMCA) on October 20, 1998.

Tech Tip

DMCA Research Exemption Requirements

The DMCA has specific exemptions for research, provided four elements are satisfied:

- *The person lawfully obtained the encrypted copy, phonorecord, performance, or display of the published work.*

- *Such act is necessary to conduct such encryption research.*

- *The person made a good faith effort to obtain authorization before the circumvention.*

- *Such act does not constitute infringement under this title or a violation of applicable law other than this section, including section 1030 of title 18 and those provisions of title 18 amended by the Computer Fraud and Abuse Act of 1986.*

> **Mars Rover Crashed by DMCA**
>
> NASA maintains a YouTube channel where it posts videos of space events, such as the landing of the rover *Curiosity* on the surface of Mars. The content was developed by NASA with U.S. taxpayer money, yet it was served a takedown notice by Scripps News Service. The issue was remedied, but taxpayers lost early coverage and had to pay the legal bills to fight for their own content. This happens on a regular basis to the NASA channel, and although the law has provisions for prosecuting false takedowns, they are rarely used.

Exemptions are scattered throughout the DMCA, although many were created during various deliberations on the act and do not make sense when the act is viewed in whole. The effect of these exemptions upon people in the software and technology industry is not clear, and until restrained by case law, the DMCA gives large firms with deep legal pockets a potent weapon to use against parties who disclose flaws in encryption technologies used in various products. Actions have already been initiated against individuals and organizations who have reported security holes in products. This will be an active area of legal contention, as the real issues behind digital rights management have yet to be truly resolved.

■ Ethics

Ethics has been a subject of study by philosophers for centuries. It might be surprising to note that ethics associated with computer systems has a history dating back to the beginning of the computing age. The first examination of cybercrime occurred in the late 1960s, when the professional conduct of computer professionals was examined with respect to their activities in the workplace. If we consider ethical behavior to be consistent with that of existing social norms, it can be fairly easy to see what is considered right and wrong. But with the globalization of commerce, and the globalization of communications via the Internet, questions are raised on what is the *appropriate* social norm. Cultural issues can have wide-ranging effects on this, and although the idea of an appropriate code of conduct for the world is appealing, it is as yet an unachieved objective.

The issue of globalization has significant local effects. If a user wishes to express free speech via the Internet, is this protected behavior or criminal behavior? Different locales have different sets of laws to deal with items such as free speech, with some recognizing the right, and others prohibiting it. With the globalization of business, what are the appropriate controls for intellectual property when some regions support this right, while others do not even recognize intellectual property as something of value, but rather something owned by the collective of society? The challenge in today's business environment is to establish and communicate a code of ethics so that everyone associated with an enterprise can understand the standards of expected performance.

A great source of background information on all things associated with computer security, the SANS Institute published a set of IT ethical guidelines ("IT Code of Ethics") in April 2004: see www.sans.org/security-resources/ethics.php.

IT Code of Ethics

SANS Institute IT Code of Ethics,[1] Version 1.0, April 24, 2004:

I will strive to know myself and be honest about my capability.

- *I will strive for technical excellence in the IT profession by maintaining and enhancing my own knowledge and skills. I acknowledge that there are many free resources available on the Internet and affordable books and that the lack of my employer's training budget is not an excuse nor limits my ability to stay current in IT.*

- *When possible I will demonstrate my performance capability with my skills via projects, leadership, and/or accredited educational programs and will encourage others to do so as well.*

- *I will not hesitate to seek assistance or guidance when faced with a task beyond my abilities or experience. I will embrace other professionals' advice and learn from their experiences and mistakes. I will treat this as an opportunity to learn new techniques and approaches. When the situation arises that my assistance is called upon, I will respond willingly to share my knowledge with others.*

- *I will strive to convey any knowledge (specialist or otherwise) that I have gained to others so everyone gains the benefit of each other's knowledge.*

- *I will teach the willing and empower others with Industry Best Practices (IBP). I will offer my knowledge to show others how to become security professionals in their own right. I will strive to be perceived as and be an honest and trustworthy employee.*

- *I will not advance private interests at the expense of end users, colleagues, or my employer.*

- *I will not abuse my power. I will use my technical knowledge, user rights, and permissions only to fulfill my responsibilities to my employer.*

- *I will avoid and be alert to any circumstances or actions that might lead to conflicts of interest or the perception of conflicts of interest. If such circumstance occurs, I will notify my employer or business partners.*

- *I will not steal property, time or resources.*

- *I will reject bribery or kickbacks and will report such illegal activity.*

- *I will report on the illegal activities of myself and others without respect to the punishments involved. I will not tolerate those who lie, steal, or cheat as a means of success in IT.*

I will conduct my business in a manner that assures the IT profession is considered one of integrity and professionalism.

- *I will not injure others, their property, reputation, or employment by false or malicious action.*

- *I will not use availability and access to information for personal gains through corporate espionage.*

- *I distinguish between advocacy and engineering. I will not present analysis and opinion as fact.*

- *I will adhere to Industry Best Practices (IBP) for system design, rollout, hardening and testing.*

(Continued)

- I am obligated to report all system vulnerabilities that might result in significant damage.

- I respect intellectual property and will be careful to give credit for other's work. I will never steal or misuse copyrighted, patented material, trade secrets or any other intangible asset.

- I will accurately document my setup procedures and any modifications I have done to equipment. This will ensure that others will be informed of procedures and changes I've made.

I respect privacy and confidentiality.

- I respect the privacy of my co-workers' information. I will not peruse or examine their information including data, files, records, or network traffic except as defined by the appointed roles, the organization's acceptable use policy, as approved by Human Resources, and without the permission of the end user.

- I will obtain permission before probing systems on a network for vulnerabilities.

- I respect the right to confidentiality with my employers, clients, and users except as dictated by applicable law. I respect human dignity.

- I treasure and will defend equality, justice and respect for others.

- I will not participate in any form of discrimination, whether due to race, color, national origin, ancestry, sex, sexual orientation, gender/sexual identity or expression, marital status, creed, religion, age, disability, veteran's status, or political ideology.

[1]© 2000–2015 The SANS™ Institute. Reprinted with permission.

Principles of Computer Security

Chapter Summary

After reading this chapter and completing the exercises, you should understand the following regarding the basics of legal and ethical considerations associated with information security.

Explain the laws and rules concerning importing and exporting encryption software

- Import and export of high-strength cryptographic software is controlled in many countries, including the United States.
- Possession of encryption programs or encrypted data can be a crime in many countries.
- The Wassenaar Arrangement is an international agreement between countries concerning the import/export of cryptographic software and has enabled mass-marketed products to generally flow across borders.

Identify the laws that govern computer access and trespass

- Gaining unauthorized access, by whatever means, including using someone else's credentials, is computer trespass.
- Exceeding granted authority is also computer trespass.

- Many nations have versions of computer trespass or misuse statutes, although the terminology varies greatly among countries.

Identify the laws that govern encryption and digital rights management

- Encryption technology is used to protect digital rights management and prevent unauthorized use.
- Circumventing technological controls used to protect intellectual property is a violation of the DMCA.
- In some countries, carrying encrypted data can result in authorities demanding the keys or threatening prosecution for failure to disclose the keys.

Describe the laws that govern digital signatures

- Digital signatures have the same legal status as written signatures.
- Digital signatures use PINs or other "secrets" that require end-user safeguarding to be protected from fraud.

Explore ethical issues associated with information security

- Ethics is the social–moral environment in which a person makes decisions.
- Ethics can vary by socio-cultural factors and groups.

Key Terms

administrative law *(698)*

case law *(698)*

click fraud *(697)*

common law *(698)*

Computer Fraud and Abuse Act (CFAA) *(701)*

computer trespass *(699)*

Digital Millennium Copyright Act (DMCA) *(709)*

Electronic Communications Privacy Act (ECPA) *(700)*

Gramm-Leach-Bliley Act (GLBA) *(702)*

Payment Card Industry Data Security Standard (PCI DSS) *(703)*

Sarbanes-Oxley Act (SOX) *(703)*

Section 404 *(703)*

statutory law *(698)*

Stored Communications Act (SCA) *(700)*

Wassenaar Arrangement *(705)*

■ Key Terms Quiz

Use terms from the Key Terms list to complete the sentences that follow. Don't use the same term more than once. Not all terms will be used.

1. IT controls were mandated in public companies by _____, part of the Sarbanes-Oxley Act.

2. The contractual set of rules governing credit card security is the _____.

3. A catchall law to prosecute hackers is the statute on _____.

4. The _____ is the primary U.S. federal law on computer intrusion and misuse.

5. The power of government-sponsored agencies lies in _____.

6. A(n) _____ is passed by a legislative branch of government.

7. _____ comes from the judicial branch of government.

■ Multiple-Choice Quiz

1. Your Social Security number and other associated facts kept by your bank are protected by what law against disclosure?

   A. The Social Security Act of 1934

   B. The USA Patriot Act of 2001

   C. The Gramm-Leach-Bliley Act

   D. HIPAA

2. Breaking into another computer system in the United States, even if you do not cause any damage, is regulated by what law?

   A. State law, as the damage is minimal

   B. Federal law under the Identity Theft and Assumption Deterrence Act

   C. Federal law under the Electronic Communications Privacy Act (ECPA) of 1986

   D. Federal law under the USA Patriot Act of 2001

3. Export of encryption programs is regulated by which entity?

   A. U.S. State Department

   B. U.S. Commerce Department

   C. U.S. Department of Defense

   D. National Security Agency

4. For the FBI to install and operate Carnivore on an ISP's network, what is required?

   A. A court order specifying specific items being searched for

   B. An official request from the FBI

   C. An impact statement to assess recoverable costs to the ISP

   D. A written request from an ISP to investigate a computer trespass incident

5. True or false: A sysadmin who is reading employee e-mail to look for evidence of someone stealing company passwords is protected by the company-owned equipment exemption on eavesdropping.

   A. False, there is no "company-owned exemption."

   B. True, provided he or she has his or her manager's approval.

   C. True, provided he or she has senior management permission in writing.

   D. True, if it is in his or her job description.

6. True or false: Writing viruses and releasing them across the Internet is a violation of law.

   A. Always true. All countries have reciprocal agreements under international law.

   B. Partially true. Depends on the laws in the country of origin.

   C. False. Computer security laws do not cross international boundaries.

   D. Partially true. Depends on the specific countries involved, both of the virus author and the recipient.

7. Publication of flaws in encryption used for copy protection is a potential violation of:

   A. HIPAA

   B. U.S. Commerce Department regulations

   C. DMCA

   D. National Security Agency regulations

8. Circumventing technological controls to prevent reverse-engineering is a violation of:

    A. HIPAA

    B. DMCA

    C. ECPA

    D. All of the above

9. Logging in as your boss to fix your time records is:

    A. OK, if you are accurately reporting your time

    B. One of the obscure elements of DMCA

    C. A violation of the Separation of Duties Law

    D. A form of computer trespass

10. You are arrested as a result of your hacking activities and investigators find you have been breaking password files and sharing them across the Internet. Which law have you violated?

    A. CFAA

    B. ECPA

    C. DMCA

    D. HIPAA

■ Essay Quiz

1. You are being hired as the director of IT for a small firm that does retail trade business, and you will be the source of knowledge for all things IT, including security and legal regulations. Outline the legal elements you would want to have policy covering, and include how you would disseminate this information.

2. You have just been hired as a system administrator for a small college. The college's servers are used for database storage and a website that serves the college community. Describe the laws that will potentially impact your job with respect to computer security. What actions will you take to ensure compliance with laws and regulations?

Privacy

chapter 25

They who would give up an essential liberty for temporary security, deserve neither liberty or security.

—BENJAMIN FRANKLIN

In this chapter, you will learn how to

- Define privacy
- Identify privacy laws relative to computer security in various industries
- Describe issues associated with technology and privacy
- Explain the concept of personally identifiable information (PII)
- Craft a privacy policy for online records
- Recognize web-related privacy issues

The advent of interconnected computer systems has enabled businesses and governments to share and integrate information. This has led to a resurgence in the importance of privacy laws worldwide. Governments in Europe and the United States have taken different approaches in attempts to control privacy via legislation. As a new generation grows up in a digital world, its view of information sharing services, such as social networking sites, has created a shift in how people view privacy. Many social and philosophical differences have led to the differing views on privacy, but as the world becomes interconnected, understanding and resolving them will be important.

Privacy can be defined as the power to control what others know about you and what they can do with that information. In the computer age, personal information forms the basis for many decisions, from credit card transactions to purchase goods to the ability to buy an airplane ticket and fly. Although it is theoretically possible to live an almost anonymous existence today, the price for doing so is high—from higher prices at the grocery store (no frequent shopper discount), to higher credit costs, to challenges with air travel, opening bank accounts, and seeking employment.

Information is an important item in today's society. From instant credit, to digital access to a wide range of information via the Internet, to electronic service portals such as e-commerce sites, e-government sites, and so on, our daily lives have become intertwined with privacy issues. Information has become a valuable entity, for it is an enabler of many functions. A few hundred years ago, if someone wanted to procure ownership of an item, he would typically trade something of tangible value (for example, coins) with the current owner of the item, and an exchange would take place. The two parties, buyer and seller, would have to meet in space and time and conduct a transaction. Or, in some cases, they would employ a third-party agent to act as a proxy and do the transaction for them. Today, one would go online, search for the best deal (information-centric), conduct business via e-commerce (use computer programs as agents), pay for the item via bankcard transaction (information exchange concerning funds availability and transfer), and, in some cases, receive delivery digitally (in the case of software, books, videos, and so forth). The creation of an information-centric economy is as dramatic a revolution as the adoption of money to act as an economic utility, simplifying bartering. This revolution and reliance on information imbues information with value, creating the need to protect it.

 Privacy is the right to control information about you and what others can do with that information.

■ Personally Identifiable Information (PII)

When information is about a person, failure to protect it can have specific consequences. Business secrets are protected through trade secret laws, government information is protected through laws concerning national security, and privacy laws protect information associated with people. A set of elements that can lead to the specific identity of a person is referred to as **personally identifiable information (PII)**. By definition, PII can be used to identify a specific individual, even if an entire set is not disclosed.

 As little information as the ZIP code, gender, and date of birth can resolve to a single person.

PII is an essential element of many online transactions, but it can also be misused if disclosed to unauthorized parties. For this reason, it should be protected at all times, by all parties that possess it.

Tech Tip

Collecting PII

PII is by nature sensitive to end users. Loss or compromise of end-user PII can result in financial and other impacts borne by the end user. For this reason, collection of PII should be minimized to what is actually needed. Three great questions to ask when determining whether to collect PII are these:

- *Do I need each specific data element?*

- *What is my business purpose for each specific element?*

- *Will my customers/end users agree with my rationale for collecting each specific element?*

TRUSTe (www.truste.com), an independent trust authority, defines personally identifiable information as *any information… (i) that identifies or can be used to identify, contact, or locate the person to whom such information pertains, or (ii) from which identification or contact information of an individual person can be derived. Personally Identifiable Information includes, but is not limited to: name, address, phone number, fax number, e-mail address, financial profiles, medical profile, social security number, and credit card information.*

The concept of PII is used to identify which data elements require a specific level of protection. When records are used individually (not in aggregate form), then PII is the concept of connecting a set of data elements to a specific purpose. If this can be accomplished, then the information is PII and needs specific protections. The U.S. Federal Trade Commission (FTC) has repeatedly ruled that if a firm collects PII, it is responsible for it through the entire lifecycle, from initial collection through use, retirement, and destruction. Only after the PII is destroyed in all forms and locations is the company's liability for its compromise abated.

Sensitive PII

Some PII is so sensitive to disclosure and resulting misuse that it requires special handling to ensure protection. Data elements such as credit card data, bank account numbers, and government identifiers (social security number, driver's license number, and so on) require extra levels of protection to prevent harm from misuse. Should these elements be lost or compromised, direct, personal financial damage may occur to the person identified by the data. These elements need special attention when planning data stores and executing business processes associated with PII data, including collection, storage, and destruction.

Try This!

Search for Your Own PII

Modern Internet search engines have the ability to catalog tremendous quantities of information and make wide-area searches for specific elements easy. Using your own elements of PII, try searching the Internet and see what is returned on your name, address, phone number, social security number, date of birth, and so forth. For security reasons, be sure to be anonymous when doing this—that is, log out of Google applications before using Google Search, Microsoft/Live applications before using Bing, or Yahoo applications before using Yahoo Search. This step may seem minor, but with search records being stored, the last thing you want to do is provide records that can cross-correlate data about yourself. If you find data on yourself, analyze the source and whether or not the data should be publicly accessible.

If the accidental disclosure of user data could cause the user harm, such as discrimination (political, racial, health related, or lifestyle), then the best course of action is to treat the information as sensitive PII.

Notice, Choice, and Consent

As privacy is defined as the power to control what others know about you and what they can do with this information, and PII represents the core items that should be controlled, communication with the end user concerning privacy is paramount. Privacy policies are presented later in the chapter, but with respect to PII, three words can govern good citizenry when collecting PII. **Notice** refers to informing the customer that PII will be collected and used and/or stored. **Choice** refers to the opportunity for the end user to consent to the data collection or to opt out. **Consent** refers to the positive affirmation by a customer that she read the notice, understands her choices, and agrees to release her PII for the purposes explained to her.

U.S. Privacy Laws

Identity privacy and the establishment of identity theft crimes is governed by the Identity Theft and Assumption Deterrence Act, which makes it a violation of federal law to knowingly use another's identity. The collection of information necessary to do this is also governed by the Gramm-Leach-Bliley Act (GLBA), which makes it illegal for someone to gather identity information on another person under false pretenses. In the education area, privacy laws have existed for years (see "Family Education Records and Privacy Act (FERPA)," later in the chapter).

Tech Tip

Major Elements of the Privacy Act

The Privacy Act has numerous required elements and definitions. Among other things, the major elements require federal agencies to

- *Publish in the Federal Register a notice of each system of records that it maintains, including information about the type of records maintained, the purposes for which they are used, and the categories of individuals on whom they are maintained.*

- *Maintain only such information about an individual as required by law, or is needed to perform a statutory duty.*

- *Maintain information in a timely, accurate, relevant, secure, and complete form.*

- *Inform individuals about access to PII upon inquiry.*

- *Notify individuals from whom it requests information what authorizes it to request the information; whether disclosure is mandatory or voluntary; the purpose for which the information may be used; and penalties for not providing the requested information.*

- *Establish appropriate physical, technical, and administrative safeguards for the information that is collected and used.*

Additional elements can be found by examining provisions of the act itself, although it is drafted in legislative form and requires extensive cross-referencing and interpretation.

A task force from the Department of Health, Education, and Welfare (HEW), developed the Code of Fair Information Practices, consisting of five clauses: openness, disclosure, secondary use, correction, and security. These main subjects continue today as the core of many privacy practices. Two major privacy initiatives followed from the U.S. government, the Privacy Act of 1974 and the Freedom of Information Act of 1996.

Privacy Act of 1974

The **Privacy Act of 1974** was an omnibus act designed to affect the entire federal information landscape. This act has many provisions that apply across the entire federal government, with only minor exceptions for national security (classified information), law enforcement, and investigative provisions. This act has been amended numerous times, and you can find current, detailed information at the Electronic Privacy Information Center (EPIC) web site, http://epic.org/privacy/laws/privacy_act.html.

Freedom of Information Act (FOIA)

The **Freedom of Information Act (FOIA)** of 1996 is one of the most widely used privacy acts in the United States, so much so that its acronym, FOIA (pronounced "foya"), has reached common use. FOIA was designed to enable public access to U.S. government records, and "public" includes the press, which purportedly acts on the public's behalf and widely uses FOIA to obtain information. FOIA carries a presumption of disclosure; the burden is on the government, not the requesting party, to substantiate why information cannot be released. Upon receiving a written request, agencies of the U.S. government are required to disclose those records, unless they can be lawfully withheld from disclosure under one of nine specific exemptions in FOIA. The right of access is ultimately enforceable through the federal court system. The nine specific exemptions, listed in Section 552 of U.S. Code Title 5, fall within the following general categories:

1. National security and foreign policy information
2. Internal personnel rules and practices of an agency
3. Information specifically exempted by statute
4. Confidential business information
5. Inter- or intra-agency communication that is subject to deliberative process, litigation, and other privileges
6. Information that, if disclosed, would constitute a clearly unwarranted invasion of personal privacy
7. Law enforcement records that implicate one of a set of enumerated concerns
8. Agency information from financial institutions
9. Geological and geophysical information concerning wells

Record availability under FOIA is less of an issue than is the backlog of requests.

FOIA is frequently used and generates a tremendous amount of work for many federal agencies, resulting in delays to requests. This in itself is a testament to its effectiveness.

To defray some of the costs associated with record requests, and to prevent numerous trivial requests, agencies are allowed to charge for research time and duplication costs. These costs vary by agency, but are typically nominal, in the range of $8.00 to $45.00 per hour for search/review fees and $.10 to $.35 per page for duplication. Agencies are not allowed to demand a requester to make an advance payment unless the agency estimates that the fee is likely to exceed $250 or the requester previously failed to pay proper fees. For many uses, the first 100 pages are free, and under some circumstances the fees can be waived.

Family Education Records and Privacy Act (FERPA)

Student records have significant protections under the Family Education Records and Privacy Act of 1974, which includes significant restrictions on information sharing. FERPA operates on an opt-in basis, as the student must approve the disclosure of information prior to the actual disclosure. FERPA was designed to provide limited control to students over their education records. The law allows students to have access to their education records, an opportunity to seek to have the records amended, and some control over the disclosure of information from the records to third parties. For example, if the parent of a student who is 18 or older inquires about the student's schedule, grades, or other academic issues, the student has to give permission before the school can communicate with the parent, even if the parent is paying for the education.

FERPA is designed to protect privacy of student information. At the K–12 school level, students are typically too young to have legal standing associated with exercising their rights, so FERPA recognizes the parents as part of the protected party. FERPA provides parents with the right to inspect and review their children's education records, the right to seek to amend information in the records they believe to be inaccurate, misleading, or an invasion of privacy, and the right to consent to the disclosure of PII from their children's education records. When a student turns 18 years old or enters a postsecondary institution at any age, these rights under FERPA transfer from the student's parents to the student.

U.S. Computer Fraud and Abuse Act (CFAA)

The U.S. Computer Fraud and Abuse Act (as amended in 1994, 1996, 2001, and 2008) and privacy laws such as the EU Data Protection Directive have several specific objectives, but one of the main ones is to prevent unauthorized parties access to information they should not have access to. Fraudulent access, or even exceeding one's authorized access, is defined as a crime and can be punished. Although the CFAA is intended for broader purposes, it can be used to protect privacy related to computer records through its enforcement of violations of authorized access.

Cross Check

CFAA and Data Protection Directives and Privacy Issues

The primary purpose of these sweeping acts is to provide a simple tool for law enforcement to prosecute criminals who attempt to access systems to gain access to data and information. When this results in a privacy violation, the original computer trespass violation still exists and is prosecutable. What evidence would a sysadmin need to produce to demonstrate a violation associated with computer trespass? Additional information on these laws is in Chapter 24.

U.S. Children's Online Privacy Protection Act (COPPA)

Children lack the mental capacity to make responsible decisions concerning the release of PII. The U.S. Children's Online Privacy Protection Act of 1998 (COPPA) specifically addresses this privacy issue with respect to children accessing and potentially releasing information on the Internet. Any web site that collects information from children (ages 13 and under), even simple web forms to allow follow-up communications and so forth, is covered by this law. Before information can be collected and used, parental permission needs to be obtained. This act requires that sites obtain parental permission, post a privacy policy detailing specifics concerning information collected from children, and describe how the children's information will be used.

Video Privacy Protection Act (VPPA)

Considered by many privacy advocates to be the strongest U.S. privacy law, the Video Privacy Protection Act of 1988 provides civil remedies against unauthorized disclosure of personal information concerning video tape rentals and, by extension, DVDs and games as well. This is a federal statute, crafted in response to media searches of rental records associated with Judge Bork when he was nominated to the U.S. Supreme Court. Congress, upset with the liberal release of information, reacted with legislation, drafted by Senator Leahy, who noted during the floor debate that new privacy protections are necessary in "an era of interactive television cables, the growth of computer checking and check-out counters, of security systems and telephones, all lodged together in computers...." (S. Rep. No. 100-599, 100th Cong., 2d Sess. at 6 (1988)).

This statute, civil in nature, provides for civil penalties of up to $2500 per occurrence, as well as other civil remedies. The statute provides the protections by default, thus requiring a video rental company to obtain the renter's consent to opt out of the protections if the company wants to disclose personal information about rentals. Exemptions exist for issues associated with the normal course of business for the video rental company as well as for responding to warrants, subpoenas, and other legal requests. This law does not supersede state laws, of which there are several.

Principles of Computer Security

Many states have enacted laws providing both wider and greater protections than the federal VPPA statute. For example, Connecticut and Maryland laws brand video rental records as confidential, and therefore not subject to sale, while California, Delaware, Iowa, Louisiana, New York, and Rhode Island have adopted state statutes providing protection of privacy with respect to video rental records. Michigan's video privacy law is as sweeping as its broad super-DMCA state statute. This state law specifically protects records of book purchases, rentals, and borrowing as well as video rentals.

Health Insurance Portability & Accountability Act (HIPAA)

Medical and health information also has privacy implications, which is why the U.S. Congress enacted the **Health Insurance Portability and Accountability Act (HIPAA)** of 1996. HIPAA calls for sweeping changes in the way health and medical data is stored, exchanged, and used. From a privacy perspective, significant restrictions of data transfers to ensure privacy are included in HIPAA, including security standards and electronic signature provisions. HIPAA security standards mandate a uniform level of protections regarding all health information that pertains to an individual and is housed or transmitted electronically. The standards mandate safeguards for physical storage, maintenance, transmission, and access to individuals' health information. HIPAA mandates that organizations that use electronic signatures have to meet standards ensuring information integrity, signer authentication, and nonrepudiation. These standards leave to industry the task of specifying the technical solutions and mandate compliance only to significant levels of protection as provided by the rules being released by industry.

HIPAA's language is built upon the concepts of *Protected Health Information (PHI)* and **Notice of Privacy Practices (NPP)**. HIPAA describes "covered entities" including medical facilities, billing facilities, and insurance (third-party payer) facilities. Patients are to have access to their PHI and an expectation of appropriate privacy and security associated with medical records. HIPAA mandates a series of administrative, technical, and physical security safeguards for information, including elements such as staff training and awareness, and specific levels of safeguards for PHI when in use, stored, or in transit between facilities.

> **Tech Tip**
>
> **Protected Health Information (PHI)**
>
> *HIPAA regulations define* **Protected Health Information (PHI)** *as "any information, whether oral or recorded in any form or medium" that*
>
> *"[i]s created or received by a health care provider, health plan, public health authority, employer, life insurer, school or university, or health care clearinghouse"; and*
>
> *"[r]elates to the past, present, or future physical or mental health or condition of an individual; the provision of health care to an individual; or the past, present, or future payment for the provision of health care to an individual."*

> **Try This!**
>
> **Notice of Privacy Practices**
>
> Visit your local doctor's office, hospital, or clinic and ask for their Notice of Privacy Practices (NPP). This notice to patients details what information will be collected and the uses and safeguards that are applied. These can be fairly lengthy and detailed documents, and in many cases are in a booklet form.

In 2009, as part of the American Recovery and Reinvestment Act of 2009, the Health Information Technology for Economic and Clinical Health Act (HITECH Act) was passed into law. Although the primary purpose of the HITECH Act was to provide stimulus money for the adoption of electronic

Tech Tip

HIPAA Penalties

HIPAA civil penalties for willful neglect are increased under the HITECH Act. These penalties can extend up to $250,000, and repeat/uncorrected violations can extend up to $1.5 million. Under HIPAA and the HITECH Act an individual cannot bring a cause of action against a provider. The laws specify that a state attorney general can bring an action on behalf of state residents.

---

medical records (EMR) systems at all levels of the healthcare system, it also contained new security and privacy provisions to add teeth to those already in HIPAA. HIPAA protections were confined to the direct medical profession, and did not cover entities such as health information exchanges and other "business associates" engaged in the collection and use of PHI. Under HITECH, business associates will be required to implement the same security safeguards and restrictions on uses and disclosures, to protect individually identifiable health information, as covered entities under HIPAA. It also subjects business associates to the same potential civil and criminal liability for breaches as covered entities. HITECH also specifies that U.S. Department of Health & Human Services (HHS) is now required to conduct periodic audits of covered entities and business associates.

Gramm-Leach-Bliley Act (GLBA)

In the financial arena, GLBA introduced the U.S. consumer to privacy notices, requiring firms to disclose what they collect, how they protect the information, and with whom they will share it. Annual notices are required as well as the option for consumers to opt out of the data sharing. The primary concept behind U.S. privacy laws in the financial arena is that consumers be allowed to opt out. This was strengthened in GLBA to include specific wording and notifications as well as requiring firms to appointment a privacy officer. Most U.S. consumers have witnessed the results of GLBA, every year receiving privacy notices from their banks and credit card companies. These notices are one of the visible effects of GLBA on changing the role of privacy associated with financial information.

California Senate Bill 1386 (SB 1386)

California Senate Bill 1386 (SB 1386) was a landmark law concerning information disclosures. It mandates that Californians be notified whenever PII is lost or disclosed. Since the passage of SB 1386, numerous other states have modeled legislation on this bill, and although national legislation has been blocked by political procedural moves, it will eventually be passed. The current list of U.S. states and territories that require disclosure notices is up to 49, with only Alabama, New Mexico, and South Dakota without bills. Each of these disclosure notice laws is different, making the case for a unifying federal statute compelling, but currently it is low on the priority lists of most politicians.

U.S. Banking Rules and Regulations

Banking has always had an element of PII associated with it, from who has deposits to who has loans. As the scale of operations increased, both in numbers of customers and products, the importance of information for processing grew. Checks became a utility instrument to convey information associated with funds transfer between parties. As a check was basically a promise to pay, in the form of directions to a bank, occasionally the check was not honored and a merchant had to track down the party to demand payment. Thus, it became industry practice to write additional information on a check to assist a firm in later tracking down the drafting party. This information included items such as address, work phone number, a credit card number, and so on. This led to the co-location of information about an individual, and this information was used at times to perform a crime of **identity theft**. To combat this and prevent the gathering of this type of information, a series of banking and financial regulations were issued by the U.S. government to prohibit this form of information collection. Other regulations addressed items such as credit card numbers being printed on receipts, mandating only the last five digits be exposed.

Payment Card Industry Data Security Standard (PCI DSS)

As described in Chapter 24, the major credit card firms, such as MasterCard, Visa, American Express, and Discover, designed a private-sector initiative to deal with privacy issues associated with credit card transaction information. PCI DSS is a standard that provides guidance on what elements of a credit card transaction need protection and the level of expected protection. PCI DSS is not a law, but rather a contractual regulation, enforced through a series of fines and fees associated with performing business in this space. PCI DSS was a reaction to two phenomena, data disclosures and identity theft.

Fair Credit Reporting Act (FCRA)

The Fair Credit Reporting Act of 1999 brought significant privacy protections to the consumer credit reporting agencies (CRAs). This act requires that the agencies provide consumers notice of their rights and responsibilities. The agencies are required to perform timely investigations on inaccuracies reported by consumers. The agencies are also required to notify the other CRAs when consumers close accounts. The act also has technical issues associated with data integrity, data destruction, data retention, and consumer and third-party access to data. The details of FCRA proved to be insufficient with respect to several aspects of identity theft, and in 2003, the Fair and Accurate Credit Transactions Act was passed, modifying and expanding on the privacy and security provisions of FCRA.

Fair and Accurate Credit Transactions Act (FACTA)

The Fair and Accurate Credit Transactions Act of 2003 was passed to enact stronger protections for consumer information from identity theft, errors, and omissions. FACTA amended portions of FCRA to improve the accuracy of customer records in consumer reporting agencies, to improve timely resolution of consumer complaints concerning inaccuracies, and to make businesses take reasonable steps to protect information that can lead to identity theft.

FACTA also had other "disposal rules" associated with consumer information. FACTA mandates that information that is no longer needed must be properly disposed of, either by burning, pulverizing, or shredding. Any electronic information must be irreversibly destroyed or erased. Should third-party firms be used for disposal, the rules still pertain to the original contracting party, so third parties should be selected with care and monitored for compliance.

Tech Tip

FACTA and Credit Card Receipts

One of the provisions of FACTA compels businesses to protect credit card information on receipts. Before FACTA, it was common for receipts to have entire credit card numbers, as well as additional information. Today, receipts can display only the last five digits of the card number and cannot include the card expiration date. These rules went into effect in 2005 and merchants had one year to comply.

Tech Tip

FTC Disposal Rule

*The FTC's **Disposal Rule** applies to consumer reporting agencies as well as to any individuals and businesses that use consumer reports, such as lenders, insurers, employers, and landlords.*

Tech Tip

Red Flag Rules

*The FTC has adopted a set of **red flag rules** that are invoked to assist entities in determining when extra precautions must be taken concerning PII records. The following are some examples of **red flags** that should prompt an organization to initiate additional, specific data-handling steps to protect data:*

- *Change of address request. This is a common tool for identity thieves, and as such, firms should provide protection steps to verify change of address requests.*

- *Sudden use of an account that has been inactive for a long time, or radical changes in use of any account.*

- *A suspicious address or phone number. Many fraudulent addresses and numbers are known, and repeated applications should be quickly noted and stopped.*

- *Request for credit on a consumer account that has a credit freeze on a credit reporting record.*

Additional information is available from the FTC at www.ftc.gov/tips-advice/ business-center/guidance/fighting-identity-theft-red-flags-rule-how-guide-business.
Whenever a red flag issue occurs, the business must have special procedures in place to ensure that the event is not fraudulent. Calling the customer and verifying information before taking action is one example of this type of additional action.

Non-Federal Privacy Concerns in the United States

Despite the wide assortment of federal statutes associated with privacy, a significant gap remains in privacy protection in the United States. Government information about its citizens is not limited to just the federal government. State and local governments also have significant information holdings associated with individuals. In fact, it is not uncommon for the quantity and detail of information to increase as proximity to individuals increases. Local governments have significant quantities of government-compiled personal information (such as property ownership, court records, voter registration, fictitious business names, vital records, and so forth). Only about half the states have similar privacy acts concerning state government agencies' handling of personal information. In California, this statute is the Information Practices Act. Each state that has such protection provisions does so under its own set of rules and regulations, creating a patchwork approach to this topic. In only a handful of states does the state's "privacy act" extend to local government, where, as already noted, exists the lion's share of information. This lack of unified treatment has placed the United States behind many other nations with respect to this issue and has created safe harbor issues that regularly require time and effort to address at the highest levels of government, with a differing set of officials involved depending upon the source of the information. Safe harbor rules are a series of agreements to privacy handling across international boundaries. For example, if privacy concerns arise from travel issues, the Department of Homeland Security would respond; for financial transaction privacy issues, it would be the Treasury Department; and for export and import, it would be the Commerce Department. This channel-dependent responsibility complicates negotiations over issues as the U.S. government agency responsible for privacy is always changing as the source of the privacy issue changes.

International Privacy Laws

Privacy is not a U.S.-centric phenomenon, but it does have strong cultural biases. Legal protections for privacy tend to follow the socio-cultural norms by geography; hence, there are different policies in European nations than in the United States. In the United States, the primary path to privacy is via **opt-out**, whereas in Europe and other countries, it is via **opt-in**. What this means is that the fundamental nature of control shifts. In the U.S., a consumer must notify a firm that they wish to block the sharing of personal information; otherwise the firm has permission by default. In the EU, sharing is blocked unless the customer specifically opts in to allow it. The Far East has significantly different cultural norms with respect to individualism vs. collectivism, and this is seen in their privacy laws as well. Even in countries with common borders, distinct differences exist, such as the United States and Canada; Canadian laws and customs have strong roots to their UK history, and in many cases follow European ideals as opposed to U.S. ones. One of the primary sources of intellectual and political thought on privacy has been the Organization for Economic Co-operation and Development (OECD). This multinational entity has for decades conducted multilateral discussions and policy formation on a wide range of topics, including privacy.

OECD Fair Information Practices

OECD Fair Information Practices are the foundational element for many worldwide privacy practices. Dating to 1980, Fair Information Practices are a set of principles and practices that set out how an information-based society may approach information handling, storage, management, and flows with a view toward maintaining fairness, privacy, and security. Members of the OECD recognized that information was a critical resource in a rapidly evolving global technology environment, and that proper handling of this resource was critical for long-term sustainability of growth.

Tech Tip

OECD's Privacy Code

OECD's privacy code was developed to help "harmonise national privacy legislation and, while upholding such human rights, [to] at the same time prevent interruptions in international flows of data. [The Guidelines] represent a consensus on basic principles which can be built into existing national legislation, or serve as a basis for legislation in those countries which do not yet have it." (Source: "OECD Guidelines on the Protection of Privacy and Transborder Flows of Personal Data," www.oecd.org/sti/ieconomy/ oecdguidelinesontheprotectionofprivacyandtransborderflowsofpersonaldata.htm.)

European Laws

The EU has developed a comprehensive concept of privacy, which is administered via a set of statutes known as **data protection**. These privacy statutes cover all personal data, whether collected and used by government or by private firms. These laws are administered by state and national data protection agencies in each country. With the advent of the EU, this common comprehensiveness stands in distinct contrast to the patchwork of laws in the United States.

Privacy laws in Europe are built around the concept that privacy is a fundamental human right that demands protection through government administration. When the EU was formed, many laws were harmonized across the original 15 member nations, and data privacy was among those standardized. One important aspect of this harmonization is the Data Protection Directive, adopted by EU members, which has a provision allowing the European Commission to block transfers of personal data to any country outside the EU that has been determined to lack adequate data protection policies. The impetus for the EU directive is to establish the regulatory framework to enable the movement of personal data from one country to another, while at the same time ensuring that privacy protection is "adequate" in the country to which the data is sent. This can be seen as a direct result of early HEW task force (see "U.S. Privacy Laws," earlier in the chapter) and OECD directions. If the recipient country has not established a minimum standard of data protection, it is expected that the transfer of data will be prohibited.

Tech Tip

Safe Harbor Principles

Safe Harbor is built upon seven principles:

- **Notice**   *A firm must give notice of what is being collected, how it will be used, and with whom it will be shared.*

- **Choice**   *A firm must allow the option to opt out of transfer of PII to third parties.*

- **Onward Transfer**   *All disclosures of PII must be consistent with the previous principles of Notice and Choice.*

- **Security**   *PII must be secured at all times.*

- **Data Integrity**   *PII must be maintained accurately and, if incorrect, the customer has the right to correct it.*

- **Access**   *Individuals must have appropriate and reasonable access to PII for the purposes of verification and correction.*

- **Enforcement**   *Issues with privacy and PII must have appropriate enforcement provisions to remain effective.*

See www.export.gov/safeharbor/eg_main_018236.asp for more information.

The differences in approach between the U.S. and the EU with respect to data protection led the EU to issue expressions of concern about the adequacy of data protection in the United States, a move that could have paved the way to the blocking of data transfers. After negotiation, it was determined that U.S. organizations that voluntarily joined an arrangement known as **Safe Harbor** would be considered adequate in terms of data protection. Safe Harbor is a mechanism for self-regulation that can be enforced through trade practice law via the FTC. A business joining the Safe Harbor Consortium must make commitments to abide by specific guidelines concerning privacy. Safe Harbor members also agree to be governed by certain self-enforced regulatory mechanisms, backed ultimately by FTC action.

Another major difference between U.S. and European regulation lies in where the right of control is exercised. In European directives, the right of control over privacy is balanced in such a way as to favor consumers. Rather than having to pay to opt out, as with unlisted phone numbers in the United States, consumers have such services for free. Rather than having to opt out at all, the default privacy setting is deemed to be the highest level of data privacy, and users have to opt in to share information. This default setting is a cornerstone of the European Union's Directive on Protection of Personal Data and is enforced through national laws in all member nations.

Canadian Laws

Like many European countries, Canada has a centralized form of privacy legislation that applies to every organization that collects, uses, or discloses personal information, including information about employees. These regulations stem from the **Personal Information Protection and Electronic Data Act (PIPEDA)**, which requires that personal information be collected and used only for appropriate purposes. Individuals must be notified as to why the information is requested and how it will be used. The act has safeguards associated with storage, use, reuse, and retention.

To ensure leadership in the field of privacy issues, Canada has a national-level privacy commissioner and each province has a province-level privacy commissioner. These commissioners act as advocates on behalf of individuals and have used legal actions to enforce the privacy provisions associated with PIPEDA to protect personal information.

Asian Laws

Japan has a Personal Information Protection Law that requires protection of personal information used by the Japanese government, third parties, and the public sector. The Japanese law has provisions where the government entity must specify the purpose for which information is being collected, specify the safeguards applied, and, when permitted, discontinue use of the information upon request.

Hong Kong has an office of the Privacy Commissioner for Personal Data (PCPD), a statutory body entrusted with the task of protecting personal data privacy of individuals and to ensure compliances with the Personal Data (Privacy) Ordinance in Hong Kong. One main task of the Commissioner is public education, creating greater awareness of privacy issues and the need to comply with the Personal Data Ordinance.

China has had a long reputation of poor privacy practices. Some of this comes from the cultural bias toward collectivism, and some comes from the long-standing government tradition of surveillance. Recent news of the Chinese government eavesdropping on Skype and other Internet-related

Tech Tip

Encryption and Privacy

Encryption has long been held by governments to be a technology associated with the military. As such, different governments have regulated it in different manners. The U.S. government has greatly reduced controls over encryption in the past decade. Other countries, such as Great Britain, have enacted statutes that compel users to turn over encryption keys when asked by authorities. Countries such as France, Malaysia, and China still tightly control and license end-user use of encryption technologies. The primary driver for Phil Zimmerman to create Pretty Good Privacy (PGP) was the need for privacy in countries where the government was considered a threat to civil liberties.

communications has heightened this concern. China's constitution has provisions for privacy protections for the citizens. Even so, issues have come in the area of enforcement and penalties, and privacy items that have been far from uniform in their judicial history.

Privacy-Enhancing Technologies

One principal connection between information security and privacy is that without information security, you cannot have privacy. If privacy is defined as the ability to control information about oneself, then the aspects of confidentiality, integrity, and availability from information security become critical elements of privacy. Just as technology has enabled many privacy-impacting issues, technology also offers the means in many cases to protect privacy. An application or tool that assists in such protection is called a **privacy-enhancing technology (PET)**.

Encryption is at the top of the list of PETs for protecting privacy and anonymity. As noted earlier, one of the driving factors behind Phil Zimmerman's invention of PGP was the desire to enable people living in repressive cultures to communicate safely and freely. Encryption can keep secrets secret, and is a prime choice for protecting information at any stage in its lifecycle. The development of Tor routing to permit anonymous communications coupled with high-assurance, low-cost cryptography has made many web interactions securable and safe from eavesdropping.

Other PETs include small application programs, called **cookie cutters**, that are designed to prevent the transfer of cookies between browsers and web servers. Some cookie cutters block all cookies, while others can be configured to selectively block certain cookies. Some cookie cutters also block the sending of HTTP headers that may reveal personal information but may not be necessary to access a web site, and some block banner ads, pop-up windows, animated graphics, or other unwanted web elements. Some related PET tools are designed specifically to look for invisible images that set cookies (called web beacons or web bugs). Other PETs are available to PC users, including encryption programs that allow users to encrypt and protect their own data, even on USB keys.

Tech Tip

Privacy Compliance Steps

To ensure that an organization complies with the numerous privacy requirements and regulations, a structured approach to privacy planning and policies is recommended:

1. *Identify the role in the organization that will be responsible for compliance and oversight.*
2. *Document all applicable laws and regulations, industry standards, and contract requirements.*
3. *Identify any industry best practices.*
4. *Perform a privacy impact assessment (PIA) and a risk assessment.*
5. *Map the identified risks to compliance requirements.*
6. *Create a unified risk mitigation plan.*

Privacy Policies

One of the direct outcomes of the legal statutes associated with privacy has been the development of a need for corporate privacy policies associated with data collection. With a myriad of government agencies involved, each with a specific mandate to "assist" in the protection effort associated with PII, one can ask, what is the best path for an industry member? If your organization needs PII to perform its tasks, obtaining and using it is fine in most cases, but you must ensure that everyone in the organization complies with the acts, rules, and regulations associated with these government agencies. Policies and procedures are the best way to ensure uniform compliance across an organization. The development of a **privacy policy** is an essential foundational element of a company's privacy stance.

Privacy Impact Assessment

A **privacy impact assessment (PIA)** is a structured approach to determining the gap between desired privacy performance and actual privacy performance. A PIA is an analysis of how PII is handled through business processes and an assessment of risks to the PII during storage, use, and communication. A PIA provides a means to assess the effectiveness of a process relative to compliance requirements and identify issues that need to be addressed. A PIA is structured with a series of defined steps to ensure a comprehensive review of privacy provisions.

The following steps comprise a high-level methodology and approach for conducting a PIA:

1. *Establish PIA scope.* Determine the departments involved and the appropriate representatives. Determine which applications and business processes need to be assessed. Determine applicable laws and regulations associated with the business and privacy concerns.

2. *Identify key stakeholders.* Identify all business units that use PII. Examine staff functions such as HR, Legal, IT, Purchasing, and Quality Control.

3. *Document all contact with PII:*
   - PII collection, access, use, sharing, disposal
   - Processes and procedures, policies, safeguards, data-flow diagrams, and any other risk assessment data
   - Web site policies, contracts, HR, and administrative for other PII

4. *Review legal and regulatory requirements, including any upstream contracts.* The sources are many, but some commonly overlooked issues are agreements with suppliers and customers over information sharing rights.

5. *Document gaps and potential issues between requirements and practices.* All gaps and issues should be mapped against where the issue was discovered and the basis (requirement or regulation) that the gap maps to.

6. *Review findings with key stakeholders to determine accuracy and clarify any issues.* Before the final report is written, any issues or possible miscommunications should be clarified with the appropriate stakeholders to ensure a fair and accurate report.

7. *Create final report for management.*

■ Web Privacy Issues

The Internet acts as a large information-sharing domain, and as such can be a conduit for the transference of information among many parties. The Web offers much in the form of communication between machines, people, and systems, and this same exchange of information can be associated with privacy based on the content of the information and the reason for the exchange.

Cookies

Cookies are small bits of text that are stored on a user's machine and sent to specific web sites when the user visits. Cookies can store many different things, from tokens that provide a reference to a database server behind the web server to assist in maintaining state through an application, to the contents of a shopping cart. Cookies can also hold data directly, in which case there are possible privacy implications. When a cookie holds a token number that is meaningless to outsiders but meaningful to a back-end server, then the loss of the cookie represents no loss at all. When the cookie text contains meaningful information, then the loss can result in privacy issues. For instance, when a cookie contains a long number that has no meaning except to the database server, then the number has no PII. But if the cookie contains text, such as a ship-to address for an order, this can represent PII and can result in a privacy violation. It is common to encode the data in cookies, but Base64 encoding is not encryption and can be decoded by anyone, thus providing no confidentiality.

Cookies provide a useful service of allowing state to be maintained in a stateless process, web serving (see "Cookies" in Chapter 17). But because of the potential for PII leakage, many users have sworn off cookies. This leads to issues on numerous web sites, for when properly implemented, they pose no privacy danger and can greatly enhance web site usefulness.

The bottom line for cookies is fairly easy—done correctly, they do not represent a security or privacy issue. Done incorrectly, they can be a disaster. A simple rule solves most problems with cookies: never store data directly on a cookie; instead, store a reference to another web application that permits the correct actions to occur based on the key value.

■ Privacy in Practice

With privacy being defined as the power to control what others know about you and what they can do with that information, there remains the question of what you can do to exercise that control. Information is needed to obtain services, and in many cases the information is reused, often for additional and secondary purposes. Users agree to these uses through acceptance of a firm's privacy policy.

Shared information still requires control, and in this case the control function has shifted to the party that obtained the information. They may store it for future use, for record purposes, or for other uses. If they fail to adequately protect the information from loss or disclosure, then the owner no longer has authorized the uses it may be employed in. Data disclosures and information thefts both result in unauthorized use of information. Users can take actions to both protect their information and to mitigate risk from unauthorized sharing and use of their information.

User Actions

Users have to share information for a variety of legitimate purposes. Information has value, both to the authorized user and to those who would steal the information and use it for unauthorized purposes. If users are going to control their information, they have to take certain precautions. This is where security and privacy intersect at an operational level. Security functionality enables control and thus enables privacy functionality.

One aspect of maintaining control over information is in the proper security precautions presented throughout the book, so they will not be repeated here. A second level of actions can be employed by users to maintain knowledge over their information uses. The value of information is in its use, and in many cases, this use can be tracked. The two main types of information that have immediate value are financial and medical. Financial information, such as credit card information, identity information, and banking information, can be used by criminals to steal from others. Many times the use of identity or financial information will show up on the systems of record associated with the information. This is why it is important to actually read bank statements and verify charges.

In the same vein, one should periodically examine their credit report, looking for unauthorized credit requests or accounts. Periodic checks of healthcare insurance accounts and reports is essential for the same reason. Just because you have paid all your copays, you shouldn't shred unopened envelopes from the insurance company. If someone else is using your information, you may be authorizing their use of your stolen information by not alerting the insurance company to the misuse.

Users should periodically, as in annually, request copies of their credit bureau reports and examine them for unauthorized activity. Likewise, users should periodically verify with their healthcare insurers, looking for unauthorized activity there as well. These checks do not take much time and provide a means to prevent long-term penetration of identities.

Data Breaches

When a company loses data that it has stored on its network, the term is a data breach. Data breaches have become an almost daily news item, with people actually becoming desensitized to their occurrence. Data breaches act as means of notification that security efforts have failed. Verizon regularly publishes a data breach investigation report, examining the root causes behind hundreds of breach events. In the 2014 report, Verizon found that nine out of ten breaches can be described by the following nine distinct patterns:

- Point-of-sale (POS) intrusions
- Web app attacks
- Insider and privilege misuse
- Physical theft and loss
- Miscellaneous errors (misdelivery, misconfiguration, user errors)
- Crimeware
- Payment card skimmers
- Denial of service
- Cyber espionage

In 2014, over 63,000 security incidents were analyzed, with 1367 confirmed data breaches across 95 countries.

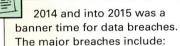

2014 and into 2015 was a banner time for data breaches. The major breaches include:

Anthem Healthcare	80,000,000 records
Home Depot	56,000,000 records
JP Morgan Chase	76,000,000 records
eBay	145,000,000 records
Target	70,000,000 records
Ashley Madison	37,000,000 records

Other major incidents include the Korean Credit Bureau breach, involving 20 million records in a country of 50 million people. Possibly the biggest news was the third breach of Sony, this time not just the PlayStation network, but virtually all corporate records associated with Sony Pictures Entertainment, the film studio subsidiary. Embarrassing e-mails, PII for employees, scripts...the content released was widespread, including that on contractor machines.

Chapter 25 Review

■ For More Information

Rebecca Herold, Privacy Professor

- **Monthly Privacy Professor Tips** www .privacyguidance.com/eTips.html
- **Blog** www.privacyguidance.com/blog/
- **Videos** www.privacyguidance.com/ eMy_Videos.html

Data Breaches

- **Information is Beautiful (visualizations)** www.informationisbeautiful.net/visualizations/ worlds-biggest-data-breaches-hacks/
- **Verizon Data Breach Investigations Report** www.verizonenterprise.com/DBIR

■ Chapter Summary

After reading this chapter and completing the exercises, you should understand the following aspects of privacy.

Define privacy

- Privacy is the power to control what others know about you and what they can do with that information.
- The concept of privacy does not translate directly to information about a business as it is not about a person.

Identify privacy laws relative to computer security in various industries

- Numerous U.S. federal statutes have privacy provisions, including FERPA, VPPA, GLBA, HIPAA, and so on.
- The number of state and local laws that address privacy issues is limited.
- A wide array of international laws address privacy issues, including those of the EU, Canada, and other nations.

Describe issues associated with technology and privacy

- A direct relationship exists between information security and privacy—one cannot have privacy without security.

- Privacy-enhancing technologies (PETs) are used in the technological battle to preserve anonymity and privacy.

Explain the concept of personally identifiable information (PII)

- Specific constituent elements of PII need to be protected.
- Corporate responsibilities associated with PII include the need to protect PII appropriately when in storage, use, or transmission.

Craft a privacy policy for online records

- Policies drive corporate actions, and privacy policies are required by several statutes and are essential to ensure compliance with the myriad of mandated actions.

Recognize web-related privacy issues

- Cookies represent a useful tool to maintain state when surfing the Web, but if used incorrectly, they can represent a security and privacy risk.

■ Key Terms

choice *(719)*
consent *(719)*
cookie cutters *(730)*
cookies *(732)*

data protection *(728)*
Disposal Rule *(725)*
Freedom of Information Act (FOIA) *(720)*
Health Insurance Portability and Accountability Act (HIPAA) *(723)*

identity theft *(725)*
notice *(719)*
Notice of Privacy Practices (NPP) *(723)*
opt-in *(727)*
opt-out *(727)*
Personal Information Protection and Electronic
   Data Act (PIPEDA) *(729)*
personally identifiable information (PII) *(717)*
privacy *(716)*

Privacy Act of 1974 *(720)*
privacy-enhancing technology (PET) *(730)*
privacy impact assessment (PIA) *(731)*
privacy policy *(730)*
Protected Health Information (PHI) *(723)*
red flag *(726)*
red flag rules *(726)*
Safe Harbor *(729)*

■ Key Terms Quiz

Use terms from the Key Terms list to complete the sentences that follow. Don't use the same term more than once. Not all terms will be used.

1. In the United States, the standard methodology for consumers with respect to privacy is to _____, whereas in the EU it is to _____.

2. _____ is the right to control information about oneself.

3. The FTC mandates firms' use of _____ procedures to identify instances where additional privacy measures are warranted.

4. Differences between privacy rules and regulations in the United States and the EU are resolved through _____ conventions.

5. Data that can be used to identify a specific individual is referred to as _____.

6. Programs used to control the use of _____ when web browsing are referred to as _____.

7. The major U.S. privacy statutes are _____ and _____.

8. Medical information in the United States is protected via the _____.

9. Many privacy regulations have specified that firms provide an annual _____ to customers.

10. To evaluate the privacy risks in a firm, a(n) _____ can be performed.

■ Multiple-Choice Quiz

1. HIPAA requires the following controls for medical records:

   A. Encryption of all data

   B. Technical safeguards

   C. Physical controls

   D. Administrative, technical, and physical controls

2. Which of the following is not PII?

   A. Customer name

   B. Customer ID number

   C. Customer social security number or taxpayer identification number

   D. Customer birth date

3. A privacy impact assessment:

  A. Determines the gap between a company's privacy practices and required actions

  B. Determines the damage caused by a breach of privacy

  C. Determines what companies hold information on a specific person

  D. Is a corporate procedure to safeguard PII

4. Which of the following should trigger a response under the Red Flag Rule?

  A. All credit requests for people under 25 or over 75

  B. Any new customer credit request, except for name changes due to marriage

  C. Request for credit from a customer who has a history of late payments and poor credit

  D. Request for credit from a customer with a credit freeze on his credit reporting record

5. Which of the following is an acceptable PII disposal procedure?

  A. Shredding

  B. Burning

  C. Electronic destruction per military data destruction standards

  D. All of the above

6. Safe Harbor principles include:

  A. Notice, Choice, Privacy Policy, Data Restrictions

  B. Notice, Choice, Security, Privacy, Integrity

  C. Notice, Physical Safeguards, Choice, Security, Data Integrity

  D. Notice, Choice, Onward Transfer, Enforcement, Security, Data Integrity

7. European privacy laws are built upon:

  A. EU Data Protection Directive

  B. Personal Information Protection and Electronic Data Act (PIPEDA)

  C. Safe Harbor principles

  D. Common law practices

8. In the United States, company responses to data disclosures of PII are regulated by:

  A. Federal law, the Privacy Act

  B. A series of state statutes

  C. Contractual agreements with banks and credit card processors

  D. The Gramm-Leach-Bliley Act (GLBA)

9. The primary factor(s) behind data-sharing compliance between U.S. and European companies is/are?

  A. Safe Harbor Provision

  B. European data privacy laws

  C. U.S. FTC enforcement actions

  D. All of the above

10. Privacy is defined as:

  A. One's ability to control information about himself or herself

  B. Being able to keep your information secret

  C. Making data-sharing illegal without consumer consent

  D. Something that is outmoded in the Internet age

■ Essay Quiz

1. Privacy and technology often clash, especially when technology allows data collection that can have secondary uses. In the case of automotive technology, black boxes to collect operational data are being installed in new cars in the United States. What are the privacy implications, and what protections exist?

2. Privacy policies are found all over the Web. Pick three web sites with privacy policies and compare and contrast them. What do they include and what is missing?

Lab Project

• Lab Project 25.1

Privacy-enhancing technologies can do much to protect a user's information and/or maintain anonymity when using the Web. Research onion routing and the Tor project. What do these things do? How do they work?

CompTIA Security+ Exam Objectives: SYO-401

Objective	Ch. No.
1.0 Network Security	
1.1 Implement security configuration parameters on network devices and other technologies.	
Firewalls	10
Routers	10
Switches	10
Load Balancers	10
Proxies	10
Web security gateways	10
VPN concentrators	10
NIDS and NIPS	13
Behavior based	13
Signature based	13
Anomaly based	13
Heuristic	13
Protocol analyzers	10
Spam filter	10
UTM security appliances	13
URL filter	13
Content inspection	13
Malware inspection	13
Web application firewall vs. network firewall	13
Application aware devices	10
Firewalls	10
IPS	10, 13
IDS	10, 13
Proxies	10
1.2 Given a scenario, use secure network administration principles.	
Rule-based management	9
Firewall rules	9
VLAN management	9
Secure router configuration	9

Objective	Ch. No.
Access control lists	2, 9
Port Security	11
802.1X	11, 12
Flood guards	11
Loop protection	11
Implicit deny	2
Network separation	11
Log analysis	13
Unified Threat Management	13
1.3 Explain network design elements and components.	
DMZ	9
Subnetting	9
VLAN	9
NAT	9
Remote Access	11
Telephony	11
NAC	9
Virtualization	10
Cloud Computing	10
Platform as a Service	10
Software as a Service	10
Infrastructure as a Service	10
Private	10
Public	10
Hybrid	10
Community	10
Layered security / Defense in depth	10
1.4 Given a scenario, implement common protocols and services.	
Protocols	11
IPSec	11
SNMP	11
SSH	11
DNS	11
TLS	11
SSL	11
TCP/IP	11
FTPS	11
HTTPS	11
SCP	11
ICMP	11

Objective	Ch. No.
2.6 Explain the importance of security related awareness and training.	
Security policy training and procedures	19
Role-based training	19
Personally identifiable information	19
Information classification	19
High	19
Medium	19
Low	19
Confidential	19
Private	19
Public	19
Data labeling, handling and disposal	19
Compliance with laws, best practices and standards	19
User habits	19
Password behaviors	19
Data handling	19
Clean desk policies	19
Prevent tailgating	19
Personally owned devices	19
New threats and new security trends/alerts	19
New viruses	19
Phishing attacks	19
Zero-day exploits	19
Use of social networking and P2P	19
Follow up and gather training metrics to validate compliance and security posture	19
2.7 Compare and contrast physical security and environmental controls.	
Environmental controls	8
HVAC	8
Fire suppression	8
EMI shielding	8
Hot and cold aisles	8
Environmental monitoring	8
Temperature and humidity controls	8
Physical security	8
Hardware locks	8
Mantraps	8
Video Surveillance	8
Fencing	8
Proximity readers	8
Access list	8

Objective	Ch. No.
2.9 Given a scenario, select the appropriate control to meet the goals of security.	
Confidentiality	2
Encryption	2
Access controls	2
Steganography	2
Integrity	2
Hashing	2
Digital signatures	2
Certificates	2
Non-repudiation	2
Availability	2
Redundancy	10
Fault tolerance	10
Patching	1, 10
Safety	8
Fencing	8
Lighting	8
Locks	8
CCTV	8
Escape plans	8
Drills	8
Escape routes	8
Testing controls	8
3.0 Threats and Vulnerabilities	
3.1 Explain types of malware.	
Adware	15
Virus	15
Spyware	15
Trojan	15
Rootkits	15
Backdoors	15
Logic bomb	15
Botnets	15
Ransomware	15
Polymorphic malware	15
Armored virus	15
3.2 Summarize various types of attacks.	
Man-in-the-middle	15
DDoS	15
DoS	15

Objective	Ch. No.
3.4 *Explain types of wireless attacks.*	
Rogue access points	12
Jamming/Interference	12
Evil twin	12
War driving	12
Bluejacking	12
Bluesnarfing	12
War chalking	12
IV attack	12
Packet sniffing	12
Near field communication	12
Replay attacks	12
WEP/WPA attacks	12
WPS attacks	12
3.5 *Explain types of application attacks.*	
Cross-site scripting	18
SQL injection	18
LDAP injection	18
XML injection	18
Directory traversal/command injection	18
Buffer overflow	18
Integer overflow	18
Zero-day	18
Cookies and attachments	18
LSO (Locally Shared Objects)	18
Flash Cookies	18
Malicious add-ons	18
Session hijacking	18
Header manipulation	18
Arbitrary code execution / remote code execution	18
3.6 *Analyze a scenario and select the appropriate type of mitigation and deterrent techniques.*	
Monitoring system logs	14
Event logs	14
Audit logs	14
Security logs	14
Access logs	14
Hardening	14
Disabling unnecessary services	14
Protecting management interfaces and applications	14
Password protection	14
Disabling unnecessary accounts	14

Objective	Ch. No.
Single sign-on	11
Access control	11
Implicit deny	11
Trusted OS	11
Authentication factors	11
Something you are	11
Something you have	11
Something you know	11
Somewhere you are	11
Something you do	11
Identification	11
Biometrics	11
Personal identification verification card	11
Username	11
Federation	11
Transitive trust/authentication	11
5.3 Install and configure security controls when performing account management, based on best practices.	
Mitigate issues associated with users with multiple account/roles and/or shared accounts	11
Account policy enforcement	11
Credential management	11
Group policy	11
Password complexity	11
Expiration	11
Recovery	11
Disablement	11
Lockout	11
Password history	11
Password reuse	11
Password length	11
Generic account prohibition	11
Group based privileges	11
User assigned privileges	11
User access reviews	11
Continuous monitoring	11
6.0 Cryptography	
6.1 Given a scenario, utilize general cryptography concepts.	
Symmetric vs. asymmetric	5
Session keys	5
In-band vs. out-of-band key exchange	5
Fundamental differences and encryption methods	5

Objective	Ch. No.
Block vs. stream	5
Transport encryption	5
Non-repudiation	5
Hashing	5
Key escrow	5
Steganography	5
Digital signatures	5
Use of proven technologies	5
Elliptic curve and quantum cryptography	5
Ephemeral key	5
Perfect forward secrecy	5
6.2 Given a scenario, use appropriate cryptographic methods.	
WEP vs. WPA/WPA2 and preshared key	5
MD5	5
SHA	5
RIPEMD	5
AES	5
DES	5
3DES	5
HMAC	5
RSA	5
Diffie-Hellman	5
RC4	5
One-time pads	5
NTLM	5
NTLMv2	5
Blowfish	5
PGP/GPG	5
TwoFish	5
DHE	5
ECDHE	5
CHAP	5
PAP	5
Comparative strengths and performance of algorithms	5
Use of algorithms/protocols with transport encryption	5
SSL	5
TLS	5
IPSec	5
SSH	5

Objective	Ch. No.
HTTPS	5
Cipher suites	5
Strong vs. weak ciphers	5
Key stretching	5
PBKDF2	5
Bcrypt	5
6.3 Given a scenario, use appropriate PKI, certificate management and associated components.	
Certificate authorities and digital certificates	6
CA	6
CRLs	6
OCSP	6
CSR	6
PKI	6
Recovery agent	6
Public key	6
Private key	6
Registration	6
Key escrow	6
Trust models	6

About the CD-ROM

The CD-ROM included with this book comes complete with Total Tester customizable practice exam software and a PDF copy of the book.

■ System Requirements

The Total Tester software requires Windows XP or higher and 30MB of hard disk space for full installation, in addition to a current or prior major release of Chrome, Firefox, Internet Explorer, or Safari. To run, the screen resolution must be set to 1024 × 768 or higher. The PDF copy of the book requires Adobe Acrobat, Adobe Reader, or Adobe Digital Editions.

■ Total Tester Premium Practice Exam Software

Total Tester provides you with a simulation of the actual exam. You can also create custom exams from selected certification objectives or chapters. You can further customize the number of questions and time allowed.

Total Tester does not provide simulations of the exam's performance-based question type. For further discussion on this question type, please see the book's Introduction.

The exams can be taken in either Practice Mode or Exam Mode. Practice Mode provides an assistance window with hints, references to the book, explanations of the correct and incorrect answers, and the option to check your answer as you take the test. Exam Mode provides a simulation of the actual exam. The number of questions, the types of questions, and the time allowed are intended to be an accurate representation of the exam environment. Both Practice Mode and Exam Mode provide an overall grade and a grade broken down by certification objective.

To take a test, launch Total Tester and select the exam suite from the Installed Question Packs list. You can then select Practice Mode, Exam Mode, or Custom Mode. After making your selection, click Start Exam to begin.

Installing and Running Total Tester Premium Practice Exam Software

From the CD-ROM's main screen you may install Total Tester by clicking the Install Total Tester Practice Exams link. This will begin the installation process and place an icon on your desktop and in your Start menu. To run Total Tester, navigate to Start | (All) Programs | Total Seminars, or double-click the icon on your desktop.

To uninstall the Total Tester software, go to Start | Settings | Control Panel | Add/Remove Programs (XP) or Programs And Features (Vista/7/8), and then select the Total Tester program. Select Remove, and Windows will completely uninstall the software.

PDF Copy of the Book

The entire contents of the book are provided in PDF on the CD-ROM. This file is viewable on your computer and many portable devices. Adobe Acrobat, Adobe Reader, or Adobe Digital Editions is required to view the file on your computer. A link to Adobe's web site, where you can download and install Adobe Reader, has been included on the CD-ROM.

To view the PDF copy of the book on a portable device, copy the PDF file to your computer from the CD-ROM, and then copy the file to your portable device using a USB or other connection. Adobe offers a mobile version of Adobe Reader, the Adobe Reader mobile app, which currently supports iOS and Android. For customers using Adobe Digital Editions and an iPad, you may have to download and install a separate reader program on your device. The Adobe web site has a list of recommended applications, and McGraw-Hill Education recommends the Bluefire Reader.

> For more information on Adobe Reader and to check for the most recent version of the software, visit Adobe's web site at www.adobe.com and search for the free Adobe Reader or look for Adobe Reader on the product page. Adobe Digital Editions can also be downloaded from the Adobe web site.

Technical Support

Technical Support information is provided in the following sections by feature.

Total Seminars Technical Support

For questions regarding the Total Tester software or operation of the CD-ROM, visit www.totalsem.com or e-mail support@totalsem.com.

McGraw-Hill Education Content Support

For questions regarding the PDF copy of the book, e-mail techsolutions@mhedu.com or visit http://mhp.softwareassist.com.

For questions regarding book content, e-mail customer.service@mheducation.com. For customers outside the United States, e-mail international_cs@mheducation.com.

GLOSSARY

*-property Pronounced "star property," this aspect of the Bell–La Padula security model is commonly referred to as the "no-write-down" rule because it doesn't allow a user to write to a file with a lower security classification, thus preserving confidentiality.

3DES Triple DES encryption—three rounds of DES encryption used to improve security.

802.11 *See* IEEE 802.11.

802.1X *See* IEEE 802.1X.

AAA *See* authentication, authorization, and accounting.

acceptable use policy (AUP) A policy that communicates to users what specific uses of computer resources are permitted.

access A subject's ability to perform specific operations on an object, such as a file. Typical access levels include read, write, execute, and delete.

access control list (ACL) A list associated with an object (such as a file) that identifies what level of access each subject (such as a user) has—what they can do to the object (such as read, write, or execute).

access controls Mechanisms or methods used to determine what access permissions subjects (such as users) have for specific objects (such as files).

access point Shorthand for *wireless access point*, the device that allows devices to connect to a wireless network.

access tokens A token device used for access control, an example of something you have.

Active Directory The directory service portion of the Windows operating system that stores information about network-based entities (such as applications, files, printers, and people) and provides a structured, consistent way to name, describe, locate, access, and manage these resources.

Active Server Pages (ASP) Microsoft's server-side script technology for dynamically generated web pages.

ActiveX A Microsoft technology that facilitates rich Internet applications, and therefore extends and enhances the functionality of Microsoft Internet Explorer. Like Java, ActiveX enables the development of interactive content. When an ActiveX-aware browser encounters a web page that includes an unsupported feature, it can automatically install the appropriate application so the feature can be used.

Address Resolution Protocol (ARP) A protocol in the TCP/IP suite specification used to map an IP address to a Media Access Control (MAC) address.

Advanced Encryption Standard (AES) The current U.S. government standard for symmetric encryption, widely used in all sectors.

Advanced Encryption Standard 256-bit (AES256) An implementation of AES using a 256-bit key.

advanced persistent threat (APT) A type of advanced threat where the actors desire long-term persistence in a system over short-term gain.

adware Advertising-supported software that automatically plays, displays, or downloads advertisements after the software is installed or while the application is being used.

agile model A software development mode built around the idea of many small iterations that continually yield a "finished" product at the completion of each iteration.

air gap The forced separation of networks, resulting in an air gap between systems. Communications across an air gap require a manual effort to move data from one network to another as no network connection exists between the two networks.

algorithm A step-by-step procedure—typically an established computation for solving a problem within a set number of steps.

annualized loss expectancy (ALE) How much an event is expected to cost the business per year, given the dollar cost of the loss and how often it is likely to occur. ALE = single loss expectancy × annualized rate of occurrence.

annualized rate of occurrence (ARO) The frequency with which an event is expected to occur on an annualized basis.

anomaly Something that does not fit into an expected pattern.

antispam Technology used to combat unsolicited junk e-mail, or spam.

antivirus (AV) Technology employed to screen for and block the execution of viruses and other malware.

application A program or group of programs designed to provide specific user functions, such as a word processor or web server.

application hardening The steps taken to harden an application, mitigating vulnerabilities and reducing the exploitable surface.

application programming interface (API) A set of instructions as to how to interface with a computer program so that developers can access defined interfaces in a program.

application service provider (ASP) A company that offers entities access over the Internet to applications and services.

application vulnerability scanner Technology used to scan applications for potential vulnerabilities and weaknesses.

ARP *See* Address Resolution Protocol.

ARP backscatter The use of ARP scanning against a gateway device to detect the presence of a device behind the gateway or router.

ARP poisoning An attack characterized by changing entries in an ARP table to cause misdirected traffic.

asset Resources and information an organization needs to conduct its business.

asymmetric encryption Also called public key cryptography, this is a system for encrypting data that uses two mathematically derived keys to encrypt and decrypt a message—a public key, available to everyone, and a private key, available only to the owner of the key.

attribute-based access control (ABAC) An access control model built around a set of rules built upon specific attributes.

auditability The property of an item that makes it available for verification upon inspection.

audit trail A set of records or events, generally organized chronologically, that records what activity has occurred on a system. These records (often computer files) are often used in an attempt to re-create what took place when a security incident occurred, and they can also be used to detect possible intruders.

auditing Actions or processes used to verify the assigned privileges and rights of a user, or any capabilities used to create and maintain a record showing who accessed a particular system and what actions they performed.

authentication The process by which a subject's (such as a user's) identity is verified.

authentication, authorization, and accounting (AAA) Three common functions performed upon system login. Authentication and authorization almost always occur, with accounting being somewhat less common.

Authentication Header (AH) A portion of the IPsec security protocol that provides authentication services and replay-detection ability. AH can be used either by itself or with Encapsulating Security Payload (ESP). Refer to RFC 2402.

authentication server (AS) A server used to perform authentication tasks.

Authenticode Microsoft code-signing technology used to provide integrity and attribution on software.

authority revocation list (ARL) A list of authorities that have had their certificates revoked.

authorization The function of determining what is permitted for an authorized user.

autoplay Technology employed to launch appropriate applications and play or display content on removable media when the media is mounted.

availability Part of the "CIA" of security. Availability applies to hardware, software, and data, specifically meaning that each of these should be present and accessible when the subject (the user) wants to access or use them.

backdoor A hidden method used to gain access to a computer system, network, or application. Often used by software developers to ensure unrestricted access to the systems they create. Synonymous with *trapdoor*.

backout planning   The part of a configuration change plan where steps are devised to undo a change, even when not complete, to restore a system back to the previous operating condition.

backup   Refers to copying and storing data in a secondary location, separate from the original, to preserve the data in the event that the original is lost, corrupted, or destroyed.

baseline   A system or software as it is built and functioning at a specific point in time. Serves as a foundation for comparison or measurement, providing the necessary visibility to control change.

Basic Input/Output System (BIOS)   A firmware element of a computer system that provides the interface between hardware and system software with respect to devices and peripherals. BIOS is being replaced by Extensible Firmware Interface (EFI), a more complex and capable system.

beacon frames   A series of frames used in WiFi (802.11) to establish the presence of a wireless network device.

Bell–La Padula security model   A computer security model built around the property of confidentiality and characterized by no-read-up and no-write-down rules.

best evidence rule   A legal principle that supports a true copy as equivalent to the original.

BGP   *See* Border Gateway Protocol.

Biba security model   An information security model built around the property of integrity and characterized by no-write-up and no-read-down rules.

biometrics   Used to verify an individual's identity to the system or network using something unique about the individual, such as a fingerprint, for the verification process. Examples include fingerprints, retinal scans, hand and facial geometry, and voice analysis.

BIOS   *See* Basic Input/Output System.

birthday attack   A form of attack in which the attack needs to match not a specific item but just one of a set of items.

black listing   The term used to describe the exclusion of items based on their being on a list (black list).

black-box testing   A form of testing where the tester has no knowledge of the inner workings of a mechanism.

block cipher   A cipher that operates on blocks of data.

Blowfish   A free implementation of a symmetric block cipher developed by Bruce Schneier as a drop-in replacement for DES and IDEA. It has a variable bit-length scheme from 32 to 448 bits, resulting in varying levels of security.

bluebugging   The use of a Bluetooth-enabled device to eavesdrop on another person's conversation using that person's Bluetooth phone as a transmitter. The bluebug application silently causes a Bluetooth device to make a phone call to another device, causing the phone to act as a transmitter and allowing the listener to eavesdrop on the victim's conversation in real time.

bluejacking   The sending of unsolicited messages over Bluetooth to Bluetooth-enabled devices such as mobile phones, tablets, or laptop computers.

bluesnarfing   The unauthorized access of information from a Bluetooth-enabled device through a Bluetooth connection, often between phones, desktops, laptops, and tablets.

Bluetooth   An RF technology used for short-range networking,

Border Gateway Protocol (BGP)   The interdomain routing protocol implemented in Internet Protocol (IP) networks to enable routing between autonomous systems.

botnet   A term for a collection of software robots, or bots, that runs autonomously and automatically and commonly invisibly in the background. The term is most often associated with malicious software, but it can also refer to the network of computers using distributed computing software.

Brewer-Nash security model   A security model defined by controlling read and write access based on conflict of interest rules. This model is also known as the Chinese-Wall model, after the concept of separating groups through the use of an impenetrable wall.

bridge   A network device that separates traffic into separate collision domains at the data layer of the OSI model.

bring your own device (BYOD)   A term used to describe an environment where users bring their personally owned devices into the enterprise and integrate them into business systems.

buffer overflow   A specific type of software coding error that enables user input to overflow the allocated storage area and corrupt a running program.

Bureau of Industry and Security (BIS) In the U.S. Department of Commerce, the department responsible for export administration regulations that cover encryption technology in the United States.

bus topology A network layout in which a common line (the bus) connects devices.

business continuity plan (BCP) The plans a business develops to continue critical operations in the event of a major disruption.

business impact analysis (BIA) An analysis of the impact to the business of a specific event.

business partnership agreement (BPA) A written agreement defining the terms and conditions of a business partnership.

BYOD *See* bring your own device.

CA certificate A digital certificate identifying the keys used by a certificate authority.

cache The temporary storage of information before use, typically used to speed up systems. In an Internet context, refers to the storage of commonly accessed web pages, graphic files, and other content locally on a user's PC or a web server. The cache helps to minimize download time and preserve bandwidth for frequently accessed web sites, and it helps reduce the load on a web server.

Capability Maturity Model (CMM) A structured methodology helping organizations improve the maturity of their software processes by providing an evolutionary path from ad hoc processes to disciplined software management processes. Developed at Carnegie Mellon University's Software Engineering Institute (SEI).

Capability Maturity Model Integration (CMMI) A trademarked process improvement methodology for software engineering. Developed at Carnegie Mellon University's Software Engineering Institute (SEI).

captive portal A website used to validate credentials before allowing access to a network connection.

centralized management A type of privilege management that brings the authority and responsibility for managing and maintaining rights and privileges into a single group, location, or area.

CERT *See* Computer Emergency Response Team.

certificate A cryptographically signed object that contains an identity and a public key associated with

this identity. The certificate can be used to establish identity, analogous to a notarized written document.

certificate authority (CA) An entity responsible for issuing and revoking certificates. CAs are typically not associated with the company requiring the certificate, although they exist for internal company use as well (such as Microsoft). This term also applies to server software that provides these services. The term *certificate authority* is used interchangeably with *certification authority*.

Certificate Enrollment Protocol (CEP) Originally developed by VeriSign for Cisco Systems to support certificate issuance, distribution, and revocation using existing technologies.

certificate path An enumeration of the chain of trust from one certificate to another tracing back to a trusted root.

certificate repository A storage location for certificates on a system so that they can be reused.

certificate revocation list (CRL) A digitally signed object that lists all of the current but revoked certificates issued by a given certification authority. This allows users to verify whether a certificate is currently valid even if it has not expired. A CRL is analogous to a list of stolen charge card numbers that allows stores to reject bad credit cards.

certificate server A server—part of a PKI system—that handles digital certificates.

certificate signing request (CSR) A structured message sent to a certificate authority requesting a digital certificate.

certification practices statement (CPS) A document that describes the policy for issuing digital certificates from a CA.

chain of custody Rules for documenting, handling, and safeguarding evidence to ensure no unanticipated changes are made to the evidence.

Challenge-Handshake Authentication Protocol (CHAP) Used to provide authentication across point-to-point links using the Point-to-Point Protocol (PPP).

change (configuration) management A standard methodology for performing and recording changes during software development and operation.

change control board (CCB) A body that oversees the change management process and enables management to oversee and coordinate projects.

CHAP *See* Challenge-Handshake Authentication Protocol.

CIA of security Refers to confidentiality, integrity, and authorization, the basic functions of any security system.

cipher A cryptographic system that accepts plaintext input and then outputs ciphertext according to its internal algorithm and key.

ciphertext Used to denote the output of an encryption algorithm. Ciphertext is the encrypted data.

CIRT *See* Computer Emergency Response Team.

Clark-Wilson security model A security model that uses transactions and a differentiation of constrained data items (CDI) and unconstrained data items (UDI).

closed circuit television (CCTV) A private television system usually hardwired in security applications to record visual information.

cloud computing The automatic provisioning of on-demand computational resources across a network.

coaxial cable A network cable that consists of a solid center core conductor and a physical spacer to the outer conductor which is wrapped around it. Commonly used in video systems.

code injection An attack where unauthorized executable code is injected via an interface in an attempt to get it to run on a system.

code signing The application of digital signature technology to software for purposes of integrity and authentication control.

cold site An inexpensive form of backup site that does not include a current set of data at all times. A cold site takes longer to get your operational system back up, but it is considerably less expensive than a warm or hot site.

collision attack An attack on a hash function in which a specific input is generated to produce a hash function output that matches another input.

collision domain An area of shared traffic in a network where packets from different conversations can collide.

collisions Used in the analysis of hashing cryptography, it is the property by which an algorithm will produce the same hash from two different sets of data.

Common Access Card (CAC) A smart card used to access federal computer systems, and to also act as an ID card.

Common Gateway Interface (CGI) An older, outdated technology used for server-side execution of programs on web sites.

Common Vulnerabilities and Exposures (CVE) A structured language (XML) schema used to describe known vulnerabilities in software.

Common Weakness Enumeration (CWE) A structured language (XML) schema used to describe known weakness patterns in software that can result in vulnerabilities.

complete mediation The principle that protection mechanisms should cover every access to every object.

Computer Emergency Response Team (CERT) Also known as a Computer Incident Response Team (CIRT), this group is responsible for investigating and responding to security breaches, viruses, and other potentially catastrophic incidents.

computer security In general terms, the methods, techniques, and tools used to ensure that a computer system is secure.

computer software configuration item *See* configuration item.

concentrator A device used to manage multiple similar networking operations, such as provide a VPN endpoint for multiple VPNs.

confidentiality Part of the CIA of security. Refers to the security principle that states that information should not be disclosed to unauthorized individuals.

configuration auditing The process of verifying that configuration items are built and maintained according to requirements, standards, or contractual agreements.

configuration control The process of controlling changes to items that have been baselined.

configuration identification The process of identifying which assets need to be managed and controlled.

configuration item Data or software (or other asset) that is identified and managed as part of the software change management process. Also known as computer software configuration item.

configuration status accounting Procedures for tracking and maintaining data relative to each configuration item in the baseline.

confusion A principle that, when employed, makes each character of ciphertext dependent on several parts of the key.

content protection The protection of the header and data portion of a user datagram.

context protection The protection of the header of a user datagram.

contingency planning (CP) The act of creating processes and procedures that are used under special conditions (contingencies).

Continuity of Operations Planning (COOP) The creation of plans related to continuing essential business operations.

control A measure taken to detect, prevent, or mitigate the risk associated with a threat.

Controller Area Network A bus standard for use in vehicles to connect microcontrollers.

cookie Information stored on a user's computer by a web server to maintain the state of the connection to the web server. Used primarily so preferences or previously used information can be recalled on future requests to the server.

COOP *See* Continuity of Operations Planning.

Counter Mode with Cipher Block Chaining Message Authentication Code Protocol (CCMP) An enhanced data cryptographic encapsulation mechanism based on the counter mode with CBC-MAC from AES and designed for use over wireless LANs.

countermeasure *See* control.

cracking A term used by some to refer to malicious hacking, in which an individual attempts to gain unauthorized access to computer systems or networks. *See also* hacking.

critical infrastructure Infrastructure whose loss or impairment would have severe repercussions on society.

CRC *See* cyclic redundancy check.

CRL *See* certificate revocation list.

cross-certification certificate A certificate used to establish trust between separate PKI's.

crossover error rate (CER) The point at which the false rejection rate and false acceptance rate are equal in a system.

cross-site request forgery (CSRF or XSRF) A method of attacking a system by sending malicious input to the system and relying upon the parsers and execution elements to perform the requested actions, thus instantiating the attack. XSRF exploits the trust a site has in the user's browser.

cross-site scripting (XSS) A method of attacking a system by sending script commands to the system input and relying upon the parsers and execution elements to perform the requested scripted actions, thus instantiating the attack. XSS exploits the trust a user has for the site.

cryptanalysis The process of attempting to break a cryptographic system.

cryptographically random A random number that is derived from a nondeterministic source, thus knowing one random number provides no insight into the next.

cryptography The art of secret writing that enables an individual to hide the contents of a message or file from all but the intended recipient.

Cyber Observable eXpression (CybOX) A structured (XML) language for describing cyber security events at a granular level.

cyclic redundancy check (CRC) An error detection technique that uses a series of two 8-bit block check characters to represent an entire block of data. These block check characters are incorporated into the transmission frame and then checked at the receiving end.

DAC *See* discretionary access control.

data aggregation A methodology of collecting information through the aggregation of separate pieces and analyzing the effect of their collection.

Data Encryption Standard (DES) A private key encryption algorithm adopted by the government as a standard for the protection of sensitive but unclassified information. Commonly used in Triple DES (3DES), where three rounds are applied to provide greater security.

Data Execution Prevention (DEP) A security feature of an OS that can be driven by software, hardware, or both, designed to prevent the execution of code from blocks of data in memory.

data loss prevention (DLP) Technology, processes, and procedures designed to detect when unauthorized removal of data from a system occurs. DLP is typically active, preventing the loss of data, either by blocking the transfer or dropping the connection.

datagram A packet of data that can be transmitted over a packet-switched system in a connectionless mode.

decision tree A data structure in which each element in the structure is attached to one or more structures directly beneath it.

default deny The use of an overarching rule that if not explicitly permitted, permission will be denied.

delta backup A type of backup that preserves only the blocks that have changed since the last full backup.

demilitarized zone (DMZ) A network segment that exists in a semi-protected zone between the Internet and the inner, secure trusted network.

denial-of-service (DoS) attack An attack in which actions are taken to deprive authorized individuals from accessing a system, its resources, the data it stores or processes, or the network to which it is connected.

DES *See* Data Encryption Standard.

DHCP *See* Dynamic Host Configuration Protocol.

Diameter The base protocol that is intended to provide an authentication, authorization, and accounting (AAA) framework for applications such as network access or IP mobility. Diameter is a draft IETF proposal.

differential backup A type of backup that preserves only changes since the last full backup.

differential cryptanalysis A form of cryptanalysis that uses different inputs to study how outputs change in a structured manner.

Diffie-Hellman A cryptographic method of establishing a shared key over an insecure medium in a secure fashion.

Diffie-Hellman Ephemeral (DHE) A cryptographic method of establishing a shared key over an insecure medium in a secure fashion using a temporary key to enable perfect forward secrecy (PFS).

diffusion A principle that the statistical analysis of plaintext and ciphertext results in a form of dispersion rendering one structurally independent of the other. In plain terms, a change in one character of plaintext should result in multiple changes in the ciphertext in a manner that changes in ciphertext do not reveal information as to the structure of the plaintext.

digital certificate *See* certificate.

digital rights management The control of user activities associated with a digital object via technological means.

digital sandbox The isolation of a program and its supporting elements from common operating system functions.

digital signature A cryptography-based artifact that is a key component of a public key infrastructure (PKI) implementation. A digital signature can be used to prove identity because it is created with the private key portion of a public/private key pair. A recipient can decrypt the signature and, by doing so, receive the assurance that the data must have come from the sender and that the data has not changed.

digital signature algorithm (DSA) A U.S. government standard for implementing digital signatures.

direct-sequence spread spectrum (DSSS) A method of distributing a communication over multiple frequencies to avoid interference and detection.

disaster recovery plan (DRP) A written plan developed to address how an organization will react to a natural or manmade disaster in order to ensure business continuity. Related to the concept of a business continuity plan (BCP).

discretionary access control (DAC) An access control mechanism in which the owner of an object (such as a file) can decide which other subjects (such as other users) may have access to the object, and what access (read, write, execute) these objects can have.

distributed denial-of-service (DDoS) attack A special type of DoS attack in which the attacker elicits the generally unwilling support of other systems to launch a many-against-one attack.

diversity of defense The approach of creating dissimilar security layers so that an intruder who is able to breach one layer will be faced with an entirely different set of defenses at the next layer.

DNS kiting The use of a DNS record during the payment grace period without paying.

DomainKeys Identified Mail (DKIM) An authentication system for e-mail designed to detect spoofing of e-mail addresses.

Domain Name System (DNS) The service that translates Internet domain names (such as www.mcgrawhill.com) into IP addresses.

DMZ *See* demilitarized zone.

drive-by download attack An attack on an innocent victim machine where content is downloaded without the user's knowledge.

DRP *See* disaster recovery plan.

DSSS *See* direct-sequence spread spectrum.

due care The degree of care that a reasonable person would exercise under similar circumstances.

due diligence The reasonable steps a person or entity would take in order to satisfy legal or contractual requirements—commonly used when buying or selling something of significant value.

dumpster diving The practice of searching through trash to discover sensitive material that has been thrown away but not destroyed or shredded.

Dynamic Host Configuration Protocol (DHCP) An Internet Engineering Task Force (IETF) Internet Protocol (IP) specification for automatically allocating IP addresses and other configuration information based on network adapter addresses. It enables address pooling and allocation and simplifies TCP/IP installation and administration.

dynamic link library (DLL) A shared library function used in the Microsoft Windows environment.

EAP *See* Extensible Authentication Protocol.

economy of mechanism The principle that designs should be small and simple.

electromagnetic interference (EMI) The disruption or interference of electronics due to an electromagnetic field.

elite hacker A hacker who has the skill level necessary to discover and exploit new vulnerabilities.

elliptic curve cryptography (ECC) A method of public-key cryptography based on the algebraic structure of elliptic curves over finite fields.

elliptic curve Diffie-Hellman Ephemeral (ECDHE) A cryptographic method using ECC to establish a shared key over an insecure medium in a secure fashion using a temporary key to enable perfect forward secrecy (PFS).

Encapsulating Security Payload (ESP) A portion of the IPsec implementation that provides for data confidentiality with optional authentication and replay detection services. ESP completely encapsulates user data in the datagram and can be used either by itself or in conjunction with Authentication Headers for varying degrees of IPsec services.

enclave A section of a network that serves a specific purpose and is isolated by protocols from other parts of a network.

encryption The reversible process of rendering data unreadable through the use of an algorithm and a key.

Encrypting File System (EFS) A security feature of Windows, from Windows 2000 onward, that enables the transparent encryption/decryption of files on the system.

entropy The measure of uncertainty associated with a series of values. Perfect entropy equates to complete randomness, such that given any string of bits, there is no computation to improve guessing the next bit in the sequence.

ephemeral keys Cryptographic keys that are used only once after they are generated.

escalation auditing The process of looking for an increase in privileges, such as when an ordinary user obtains administrator-level privileges.

Ethernet The common name for the IEEE 802.3 standard method of packet communication between two nodes at layer 2.

evidence The documents, verbal statements, and material objects admissible in a court of law.

evil twin A wireless attack performed using a second, rogue wireless access point designed to mimic a real access point.

eXclusive OR (XOR) Bitwise function commonly used in cryptography.

exposure factor A measure of the magnitude of loss of an asset. Used in the calculation of single loss expectancy (SLE).

eXtensible Access Control Markup Language (XACML)   An open standard XML-based language used to describe access control.

Extensible Authentication Protocol (EAP)   A universal authentication framework used in wireless networks and point-to-point connections. It is defined in RFC 3748 and has been updated by RFC 5247.

Extensible Markup Language (XML)   A text-based, human-readable data markup language.

fail-safe defaults   The principle that when a system fails, the default failure state will be a safe state by design.

false negative   Term used when a system makes an error and misses reporting the existence of an item that should have been detected.

false positive   Term used when a security system makes an error and incorrectly reports the existence of a searched-for object. Examples include an intrusion detection system that misidentifies benign traffic as hostile, an antivirus program that reports the existence of a virus in software that actually is not infected, or a biometric system that allows access to a system to an unauthorized individual.

fault tolerance   The characteristics of a system that permit it to operate even when sub-components of the overall system fail.

FHSS   *See* frequency-hopping spread spectrum.

file system access control list (FACL)   The implementation of access controls as part of a file system.

File Transfer Protocol (FTP)   An application-level protocol used to transfer files over a network connection.

File Transfer Protocol Secure (FTPS)   An application-level protocol used to transfer files over a network connection that uses FTP over an SSL or TLS connection.

firewall   A network device used to segregate traffic based on rules.

flood guard   A network device that blocks flooding-type DoS/DDoS attacks, frequently part of an IDS/IPS.

footprinting   The steps a tester uses to determine the range and scope of a system.

forensics (or computer forensics)   The preservation, identification, documentation, and interpretation of computer data for use in legal proceedings.

free space   Sectors on a storage medium that are available for the operating system to use.

frequency-hopping spread spectrum (FHSS)   A method of distributing a communication over multiple frequencies over time to avoid interference and detection.

full backup   A complete backup of all files and structures of a system to another location.

full disk encryption (FDE)   The application of encryption to an entire disk, protecting all of the contents in one container.

fuzzing   The use of large quantities of data to test an interface against security vulnerabilities. (Also known as fuzz testing.)

Generic Routing Encapsulation (GRE)   A tunneling protocol designed to encapsulate a wide variety of network layer packets inside IP tunneling packets.

geo-tagging   The metadata that contains location-specific information that is attached to other data elements.

Globally Unique Identifier (GUID)   A unique reference number used as an identifier of an item in a system.

Gnu Privacy Guard (GPG)   An application program that follows the openPGP standard for encryption.

grey box testing   A form of testing where the tester has limited or partial knowledge of the inner working of a system.

group policy   The mechanism that allows for centralized management and configuration of computers and remote users in a Microsoft Active Directory environment.

group policy object (GPO)   Stores the group policy settings in a Microsoft Active Directory environment.

hacker   A person who performs hacking activities.

hacking   The term used by the media to refer to the process of gaining unauthorized access to computer systems and networks. The term has also been used to refer to the process of delving deep into the code and protocols used in computer systems and networks. *See also* cracking.

hactivist   A hacker who uses his or her skills for political purposes.

hard disk drive (HDD)   A mechanical device used for the storing of digital data in magnetic form.

hardening   The process of strengthening a host level of security by performing specific system preparations.

hardware security module (HSM)   A physical device used to protect but still allow use of cryptographic keys. It is separate from the host machine.

hash   Form of encryption that creates a digest of the data put into the algorithm. These algorithms are referred to as one-way algorithms because there is no feasible way to decrypt what has been encrypted.

hashed message authentication code (HMAC)   The use of a cryptographic hash function and a message authentication code to ensure the integrity and authenticity of a message.

hash value   *See* message digest.

hazard   A hazard is a situation that increases risk.

HDD   *See* hard disk drive.

heating, ventilation, air conditioning (HVAC)   The systems used to heat and cool air in a building or structure.

HIDS   *See* host-based intrusion detection system.

hierarchical trust model   A trust model that has levels or tiers of an ascending nature.

highly structured threat   A threat that is backed by the time and resources to allow virtually any form of attack.

HIPS   *See* host-based intrusion prevention system.

honeynet   A network version of a honeypot, or a set of honeypots networked together.

honeypot   A computer system or portion of a network that has been set up to attract potential intruders, in the hope that they will leave the other systems alone. Since there are no legitimate users of this system, any attempt to access it is an indication of unauthorized activity and provides an easy mechanism to spot attacks.

host-based intrusion detection system (HIDS)   A system that looks for computer intrusions by monitoring activity on one or more individual PCs or servers.

host-based intrusion prevention system (HIPS)   A system that automatically responds to computer intrusions by monitoring activity on one or more individual PCs or servers and with the response being based on a rule set.

host security   Security functionality that is present on a host system.

hotfix   A set of updates designed to fix a specific problem.

hot site   A backup site that is fully configured with equipment and data and is ready to immediately accept transfer of operational processing in the event of failure of the operational system.

HSM   *See* hardware security module.

hub   A network device used to connect devices at the physical layer of the OSI model.

hybrid trust model   A combination of trust models including mesh, hierarchical, and network.

Hypertext Markup Language (HTML)   A protocol used to mark up text for use across HTTP.

Hypertext Transfer Protocol (HTTP)   A protocol for transfer of material across the Internet that contains links to additional material.

Hypertext Transfer Protocol over SSL/TLS (HTTPS)   A protocol for transfer of material across the Internet that contains links to additional material that is carried over a secure tunnel via SSL or TLS.

ICMP   *See* Internet Control Message Protocol.

IDEA   *See* International Data Encryption Algorithm.

identification   The process of determining identity as part of identity management and access control. Usually performed only once, when the user ID is assigned.

IEEE   *See* Institute for Electrical and Electronics Engineers.

IEEE 802.11   A family of standards that describe network protocols for wireless devices.

IEEE 802.1X   An IEEE standard for performing authentication over networks.

IETF   *See* Internet Engineering Task Force.

IKE   *See* Internet Key Exchange.

impact   The result of a vulnerability being exploited by a threat, resulting in a loss.

implicit deny   A philosophy that all actions are prohibited unless specifically authorized.

incident   A situation that is different than normal for a specific circumstance.

incident response   The process of responding to, containing, analyzing, and recovering from a computer-related incident.

incremental backup   A backup model where files that have changed since last full or incremental backup are backed up.

Indicator of Compromise (IOC)   A set of conditions or evidence that indicates a system may have been compromised.

information criticality   An assessment of the value of specific elements of information and the systems that handle it.

information security   Often used synonymously with computer security but places the emphasis on the protection of the information that the system processes and stores, instead of on the hardware and software that constitute the system.

information warfare   The use of information security techniques, both offensive and defensive, when combating an opponent.

Infrastructure as a Service (IaaS)   The automatic, on-demand provisioning of infrastructure elements, operating as a service; a common element of cloud computing.

initialization vector (IV)   A data value used to seed a cryptographic algorithm, providing for a measure of randomness.

instant messaging (IM)   A text-based method of communicating over the Internet.

Institute for Electrical and Electronics Engineers (IEEE)   A nonprofit, technical, professional institute associated with computer research, standards, and conferences.

intangible asset   An asset for which a monetary equivalent is difficult or impossible to determine. Examples are brand recognition and goodwill.

integer overflow   An error condition caused by the mismatch between a variable assigned storage size and the size of the value being manipulated.

integrity   Part of the CIA of security, the security principle that requires that information is not modified except by individuals authorized to do so.

interconnection security agreement (ISA)   An agreement between parties to establish procedures for mutual cooperation and coordination between them with respect to security requirements associated with their joint project.

International Data Encryption Algorithm (IDEA)   A symmetric encryption algorithm used in a variety of systems for bulk encryption services.

Internet Assigned Numbers Authority (IANA)   The central coordinator for the assignment of unique parameter values for Internet protocols. The IANA is chartered by the Internet Society (ISOC) to act as the clearinghouse to assign and coordinate the use of numerous Internet protocol parameters.

Internet Control Message Protocol (ICMP)   One of the core protocols of the TCP/IP protocol suite, used for error reporting and status messages.

Internet Engineering Task Force (IETF)   A large international community of network designers, operators, vendors, and researchers, open to any interested individual concerned with the evolution of the Internet architecture and the smooth operation of the Internet. The actual technical work of the IETF is done in its working groups, which are organized by topic into several areas (such as routing, transport, and security). Much of the work is handled via mailing lists, with meetings held three times per year.

Internet Key Exchange (IKE)   The protocol formerly known as ISAKMP/Oakley, defined in RFC 2409. A hybrid protocol that uses part of the Oakley and part of the Secure Key Exchange Mechanism for Internet (SKEMI) protocol suites inside the Internet Security Association and Key Management Protocol (ISAKMP) framework. IKE is used to establish a shared security policy and authenticated keys for services that require keys (such as IPsec).

Internet Message Access Protocol Version 4 (IMAP4)   One of two common Internet standard protocols for e-mail retrieval.

Internet Protocol (IP)   The network layer protocol used by the Internet for routing packets across a network.

Internet Protocol Security (IPsec)   A protocol used to secure IP packets during transmission across a network. IPsec offers authentication, integrity, and confidentiality services and uses Authentication Headers (AH) and Encapsulating Security Payload (ESP) to accomplish this functionality.

Internet Security Association and Key Management Protocol (ISAKMP)   A protocol framework that defines the mechanics of implementing a key exchange protocol and negotiation of a security policy.

Internet service provider (ISP)   A telecommunications firm that provides access to the Internet.

intrusion detection system (IDS)   A system to identify suspicious, malicious, or undesirable activity that indicates a breach in computer security.

intrusion prevention system (IPS)   A system to identify suspicious, malicious, or undesirable activity that indicates a breach in computer security and respond automatically without specific human interaction.

IPsec   *See* Internet Protocol Security.

ISA   *See* interconnection security agreement.

ISAKMP/Oakley   *See* Internet Key Exchange.

jailbreaking   The process of breaking OS security features designed to limit interactions with the OS itself. Commonly performed on mobile phones to unlock features or break locks to carriers.

Kerberos   A network authentication protocol designed by MIT for use in client/server environments.

key   In cryptography, a sequence of characters or bits used by an algorithm to encrypt or decrypt a message.

key archiving   The processes and procedures to make a secure backup of cryptographic keys.

key distribution center (KDC)   A portion of the Kerberos authentication system.

key escrow   The process of placing a copy of cryptographic keys with a trusted third party for backup purposes.

key recovery   A process by where lost keys can be recovered from a stored secret.

keyspace   The entire set of all possible keys for a specific encryption algorithm.

key stretching   A mechanism that takes what would be weak keys and "stretches" them to make the system more secure against brute-force attacks.

Layer 2 Tunneling Protocol (L2TP)   A Cisco switching protocol that operates at the data link layer.

layered security   The arrangement of multiple layers of defense, a form of defense in depth.

LDAP   *See* Lightweight Directory Access Protocol.

least common mechanism   The principle where protection mechanisms should be shared to the least degree possible among users.

least privilege   A security principle in which a user is provided with the minimum set of rights and privileges that he or she needs to perform required functions. The goal is to limit the potential damage that any user can cause.

Lightweight Directory Access Protocol (LDAP)   An application protocol used to access directory services across a TCP/IP network.

Lightweight Extensible Authentication Protocol (LEAP)   A version of EAP developed by Cisco prior to 802.11i to push 802.1X and WEP adoption.

linear cryptanalysis   The use of linear functions to approximate a cryptographic function as a means of analysis.

load balancer   A network device that distributes computing across multiple computers.

local area network (LAN)   A grouping of computers in a network structure confined to a limited area and using specific protocols, such as Ethernet for OSI Layer 2 traffic addressing.

local registration authority   A Registration Authority (RA) that is part of a local unit or enterprise. It is typically only useful within the enterprise, but in many cases this can be sufficient.

logic bomb   A form of malicious code or software that is triggered by a specific event or condition. *See also* time bomb.

loop protection   The requirement to prevent bridge loops at the Layer 2 level, which is typically resolved using the Spanning Tree algorithm on switch devices.

Low-Water-Mark policy   An integrity-based information security model derived from the Bell–La Padula model.

MAC   *See* mandatory access control or Media Access Control.

MAC filtering   The use of layer 2 MAC addresses to filter traffic to only authorized NIC cards.

malware   A class of software that is designed to cause harm.

mandatory access control (MAC) An access control mechanism in which the security mechanism controls access to all objects (files), and individual subjects (processes or users) cannot change that access.

man-in-the-middle attack Any attack that attempts to use a network node as the intermediary between two other nodes. Each of the endpoint nodes thinks it is talking directly to the other, but each is actually talking to the intermediary.

master boot record (MBR) A strip of data on a hard drive in Windows systems, meant to result in specific initial functions or identification.

maximum transmission unit (MTU) A measure of the largest payload that a particular protocol can carry in a single packet in a specific instance.

MD5 Message Digest 5, a hashing algorithm and a specific method of producing a message digest.

mean time between failure (MTBF) The statistically determined period of time between failures of the system.

mean time to failure (MTTF) The statistically determined time to the next failure.

mean time to repair (MTTR) A common measure of how long it takes to repair a given failure. This is the average time, and may or may not include the time needed to obtain parts.

Media Access Control (MAC) address The data link layer address for local network addressing.

memorandum of understanding (MOU) A document executed between two parties that defines some form of agreement.

message authentication code (MAC) A short piece of data used to authenticate a message. *See* hashed message authentication code.

message digest The result of applying a hash function to data. Sometimes also called a hash value. *See* hash.

metropolitan area network (MAN) A collection of networks interconnected in a metropolitan area and usually connected to the Internet.

Microsoft Challenge-Handshake Authentication Protocol (MSCHAP) A Microsoft-developed variant of the Challenge-Handshake Authentication Protocol (CHAP).

mitigate Action taken to reduce the likelihood of a threat occurring.

modem A modulator/demodulator that is designed to connect machines via telephone-based circuits.

Monitoring as a Service (MaaS) The use of a third party to provide security monitoring services.

MSCHAP *See* Microsoft Challenge-Handshake Authentication Protocol.

MTBF *See* mean time between failure.

MTTF *See* mean time to failure.

MTTR *See* mean time to repair.

multiple encryption The use of multiple layers of encryption to improve encryption strength.

multiple-factor authentication The use of more than one factor as proof in the authentication process.

Multipurpose Internet Mail Extensions (MIME) A standard that describes how to encode and attach non-textual elements in an e-mail.

NAC *See* network access control or Network Admission Control.

NAP *See* Network Access Protection.

NAT *See* Network Address Translation.

National Institute of Standards and Technology (NIST) A U.S. government agency responsible for standards and technology.

NDA *See* non-disclosure agreement.

near field communication (NFC) A set of standards and protocols for establishing a communication link over very short distances. Used in mobile devices.

network access control (NAC) An approach to endpoint security that involves monitoring and remediating endpoint security issues before allowing an object to connect to a network.

Network Access Protection (NAP) A Microsoft approach to network access control.

Network Address Translation (NAT) A method of read-dressing packets in a network at a gateway point to enable the use of local nonroutable IP addresses over a public network such as the Internet.

Network Admission Control (NAC) The Cisco technology approach for generic network access control.

Network Attached Storage (NAS)   The connection of storage to a system via a network connection.

network-based intrusion detection system (NIDS)   A system for examining network traffic to identify suspicious, malicious, or undesirable behavior.

network-based intrusion prevention system (NIPS)   A system that examines network traffic and automatically responds to computer intrusions.

Network Basic Input/Output System (NetBIOS)   A system that provides communication services across a local area network.

network forensics   The application of digital forensics processes to network traffic.

network interface card (NIC)   A piece of hardware designed to connect machines at the physical layer of the OSI model.

network operating system (NOS)   An operating system that includes additional functions and capabilities to assist in connecting computers and devices, such as printers, to a local area network.

network operations center (NOC)   A control point from where network performance can be monitored and managed.

network segmentation   The separation of a network into separate addressable segments to limit network traffic traversal to areas of limited scope.

network tap   A connection to a network that allows sampling, duplication, and collection of traffic.

Network Time Protocol (NTP)   A protocol for the transmission of time synchronization packets over a network.

network vulnerability scanner   The application of vulnerability scanning to network devices to search for vulnerabilities at the network level.

New Technology File System (NTFS)   A proprietary file system developed by Microsoft, introduced in 1993, that supports a wide variety of file operations on servers, PCs, and media.

New Technology LANMAN (NTLM)   A deprecated security suite from Microsoft that provides authentication, integrity, and confidentiality for users. Because it does not support current cryptographic methods, it is no longer recommended for use.

next-generation firewall   Firewall technology based on packet contents as opposed to simple address and port information.

NFC   *See* near field communication.

NIC   *See* network interface card.

NIST   *See* National Institute of Standards and Technology.

non-disclosure agreement (NDA)   A legal contract between parties detailing the restrictions and requirements borne by each party with respect to confidentiality issues pertaining to information to be shared.

nonrepudiation   The ability to verify that an operation has been performed by a particular person or account. This is a system property that prevents the parties to a transaction from subsequently denying involvement in the transaction.

null session   The way in which Microsoft Windows represents an unauthenticated connection.

Oakley protocol   A key exchange protocol that defines how to acquire authenticated keying material based on the Diffie-Hellman key exchange algorithm.

object reuse   Assignment of a previously used medium to a subject. The security implication is that before it is provided to the subject, any data present from a previous user must be cleared.

one-time pad   An unbreakable encryption scheme in which a series of nonrepeating, random bits is used once as a key to encrypt a message. Since each pad is used only once, no pattern can be established and traditional cryptanalysis techniques are not effective.

Online Certificate Status Protocol (OSCP)   A protocol used to request the revocation status of a digital certificate. This is an alternative to certificate revocation lists.

open design   The principle that protection mechanisms should not depend upon secrecy of design for security.

open relay   A mail server that receives and forwards mail from outside sources.

Open Vulnerability and Assessment Language (OVAL)   An XML-based standard for the communication of security information between tools and services.

operating system (OS)   The basic software that handles input, output, display, memory management, and all the other highly detailed tasks required to support the user environment and associated applications.

operational model of computer security Structuring activities into prevention, detection, and response.

opt in The primary privacy standard in the EU, where a party must opt in to sharing, otherwise the default option is not to share the information or give permission for other use.

opt out The primary privacy standard in the US, where a party must opt out of sharing; otherwise, the default option is to share the information and give permission for other use.

Orange Book The name commonly used to refer to the now outdated Department of Defense Trusted Computer Security Evaluation Criteria (TCSEC).

OVAL *See* Open Vulnerability and Assessment Language.

P2P *See* peer-to-peer.

PAC *See* Proxy Auto Configuration.

Packet Capture (PCAP) The methods and files associated with the capture of network traffic, in the form of text files.

PAM *See* Pluggable Authentication Modules.

pan-tilt-zoom (PTZ) A term used to describe a video camera that supports remote directional and zoom control.

PAP *See* Password Authentication Protocol.

password A string of characters used to prove an individual's identity to a system or object. Used in conjunction with a user ID, it is the most common method of authentication. The password should be kept secret by the individual who owns it.

Password Authentication Protocol (PAP) A simple protocol used to authenticate a user to a network access server.

Password-Based Key Derivation Function 2 (PBKDF2) A key derivation function that is part of the RSA Laboratories Public Key Cryptography Standards, published as IETF RFC 2898.

patch A replacement set of code designed to correct problems or vulnerabilities in existing software.

PBX *See* private branch exchange.

peer-to-peer (P2P) A network connection methodology involving direct connection from peer to peer.

peer-to-peer trust model A trust model built upon actual peer-to-peer connection and communication to establish trust.

penetration testing A security test in which an attempt is made to circumvent security controls in order to discover vulnerabilities and weaknesses. Also called a pen test.

permissions Authorized actions a subject can perform on an object. *See also* access controls.

personal electronic device (PED) A term used to describe an electronic device, owned by the user and brought into the enterprise, that uses enterprise data. This includes laptops, tablets, and mobile phones, to name a few.

Personal Identity Verification (PIV) Policies, procedures, hardware, and software used to securely identify federal workers.

personally identifiable information (PII) Information that can be used to identify a single person.

pharming The use of a fake web site to socially engineer someone out of credentials.

phishing The use of social engineering to trick a user into responding to something such as an e-mail to instantiate a malware-based attack.

phreaking Used in the media to refer to the hacking of computer systems and networks associated with the phone company. *See also* cracking.

physical security The policies, procedures, and actions taken to regulate actual physical access to and the environment of computing equipment.

PID *See* process identifier.

piggybacking A social engineering technique that involves following a credentialed person through a checkpoint to prevent having to present credentials—i.e., following someone through a door you need a badge to open, effectively using their badge for entry.

PII *See* personally identifiable information.

ping sweep The use of a series of ICMP ping messages to map out a network.

Plain Old Telephone Service (POTS) The term used to describe the old analog phone service and later the "landline" digital phone service.

plaintext In cryptography, a piece of data that is not encrypted. It can also mean the data input into an encryption algorithm that would output ciphertext.

Platform as a Service (PaaS) The concept of having provisionable operational platforms that can be obtained via a service.

Pluggable Authentication Modules (PAM) A mechanism used in Linux systems to integrate low-level authentication methods into an API.

Point-to-Point Protocol (PPP) The Internet standard for transmission of IP packets over a serial line, as in a dial-up connection to an ISP.

Point-to-Point Protocol Extensible Authentication Protocol (PPP EAP) A standard method for transporting multi-protocol datagrams over point-to-point links.

Point-to-Point Protocol Password Authentication Protocol (PPP PAP) PAP is a PPP extension that provides support for password authentication methods over PPP.

Point-to-Point Tunneling Protocol (PPTP) The use of generic routing encapsulation over PPP to create a methodology used for virtual private networking.

Port Address Translation (PAT) The manipulation of port information in an IP datagram at a point in the network to map ports in a fashion similar to Network Address Translation's change of network address.

port scan The examination of TCP and UDP ports to determine which are open and what services are running.

pre-shared key (PSK) A shared secret that has been previously shared between parties and is used to establish a secure channel.

Pretty Good Privacy (PGP) A popular encryption program that has the ability to encrypt and digitally sign e-mail and files.

preventative intrusion detection A system that detects hostile actions or network activity and prevents them from impacting information systems.

privacy Protecting an individual's personal information from those not authorized to see it.

privacy-enhancing technology Cryptographic protection mechanisms employed to ensure privacy of information.

privacy impact assessment (PIA) The process and procedure of determining the privacy impact and subsequent risk of data elements and their use in the enterprise.

private branch exchange (PBX) A telephone exchange that serves a specific business or entity.

privilege auditing The process of checking the rights and privileges assigned to a specific account or group of accounts.

privilege management The process of restricting a user's ability to interact with the computer system.

process identifier (PID) A unique identifier for a process thread in the operating system kernel.

Protected Extensible Authentication Protocol (PEAP) A protected version of EAP developed by Cisco, Microsoft, and RSA Security that functions by encapsulating the EAP frames in a TLS tunnel.

Protected Health Information (PHI) Information that can disclose health-related items for an individual that must be protected in the system. Similar to PII but health related in nature.

protocol analyzer A tool used by network personnel to identify packets and header information during network transit. The primary use is in troubleshooting network communication issues.

Proxy Auto Configuration (PAC) A method of automating the connection of web browsers to appropriate proxy services to retrieve a specific URL.

proxy server A server that acts as a proxy for individual requests and is used for performance and security purposes in a scalable fashion.

PSK *See* pre-shared key.

psychological acceptability The principle that protection mechanisms should not impact users, or if they do, the impact should be minimal.

PTZ *See* pan-tilt-zoom.

public key cryptography *See* asymmetric encryption.

public key infrastructure (PKI) Infrastructure for binding a public key to a known user through a trusted intermediary, typically a certificate authority.

qualitative risk assessment The process of subjectively determining the impact of an event that affects a project, program, or business. It involves the use of expert judgment, experience, or group consensus to complete the assessment.

quantitative risk assessment The process of objectively determining the impact of an event that affects a project, program, or business. It usually involves the use of metrics and models to complete the assessment.

RADIUS Remote Authentication Dial-In User Service, a standard protocol for providing authentication services. It is commonly used in dial-up, wireless, and PPP environments.

RAID *See* Redundant Array of Independent Disks.

ransomware Malware that encrypts sensitive files and offers their return for a ransom.

rapid application development (RAD) A software development methodology that favors the use of rapid prototypes and changes as opposed to extensive advanced planning.

RAS *See* Remote Access Service/Server.

RBAC *See* rule-based access control or role-based access control.

RC4 stream cipher A stream cipher used in TLS and WEP.

Real-time Blackhole List (RBL) A system that uses DNS information to detect and dump spam e-mails.

Real-time Transport Protocol (RTP) A protocol for a standardized packet format used to carry audio and video traffic over IP networks.

Recovery Agent (RA) In Microsoft Windows environments, the entity authorized by the system to use a public key recovery certificate to decrypt other users' files using a special private key function associated with the Encrypting File System (EFS).

recovery point objective (RPO) The amount of data that a business is willing to place at risk. It is determined by the amount of time a business has to restore a process before an unacceptable amount of data loss results from a disruption.

recovery time objective (RTO) The amount of time a business has to restore a process before unacceptable outcomes result from a disruption.

Redundant Array of Independent Disks (RAID) The use of an array of disks arranged in a single unit of storage for increasing storage capacity, redundancy, and performance characteristics. Formerly known as Redundant Array of Inexpensive disks.

reference monitor A non-bypassable element of the kernel that processes and enforces all security interactions including subject object accesses.

registration authority (RA) The party in the PKI process that establishes identity for the Certificate Authority to issue a certificate.

Remote Access Server/Service (RAS) A combination of hardware and software used to enable remote access to a network.

Remote Access Trojan (RAT) A form of malware designed to enable remote access to a system by an unauthorized party.

replay attack An attack where data is replayed through a system to reproduce a series of transactions.

repudiation The act of denying that a message was either sent or received.

reverse social engineering A social engineering attack pattern where the attacker prepositions themselves to be the person you call when you think you are attacked. Because you call them, your level of trust is lower.

residual risk Risks remaining after an iteration of risk management.

Ring policy Part of the Biba security model, a policy that allows any subject to read any object without regard to the object's level of integrity and without lowering the subject's integrity level.

RIPEMD A hash function developed in Belgium. The acronym expands to RACE Integrity Primitives Evaluation Message Digest, but this name is rarely used. The current version is RIPEMD-160.

risk The possibility of suffering a loss.

risk assessment or risk analysis The process of analyzing an environment to identify the threats, vulnerabilities, and mitigating actions to determine (either quantitatively or qualitatively) the impact of an event affecting a project, program, or business.

risk management Overall decision-making process of identifying threats and vulnerabilities and their potential impacts, determining the costs to mitigate such events, and deciding what actions are cost effective to take to control these risks.

Rivest, Shamir, Adleman (RSA) The names of the three men who developed a public key cryptographic system and the company they founded to commercialize the system.

rogue access point An unauthorized access point inserted into a network allowing unauthorized wireless access.

role-based access control (RBAC) An access control mechanism in which, instead of the users being assigned specific access permissions for the objects associated with the computer system or network, a set of roles that the user may perform is assigned to each user.

rootkit A form of malware that modifies the OS in a system to change the behavior of the system.

router A network device that operates at the network layer of the OSI model.

RTP *See* Real-time Transport Protocol.

rule-based access control (RBAC) An access control mechanism based on rules.

runlevels In UNIX and Linux systems, runlevels indicate the type of state the system is in, from 0 (halted) to 6 (rebooting). Lower runlevels indicate maintenance conditions with fewer services running, higher runlevels are normal operating conditions. Each UNIX variant employs the concept in the same manner, but the specifics for each runlevel can differ.

safeguard *See* control.

Safe Harbor A series of provisions to manage the different privacy policies between the US and EU when it comes to data sharing.

SAN *See* storage area network.

sandboxing The concept of isolating a system and specific processes form the OS in order to provide specific levels of security.

SCADA *See* supervisory control and data acquisition.

SCEP *See* Simple Certificate Enrollment Protocol.

script kiddie A hacker with little true technical skill and hence who uses only scripts that someone else developed.

Secure Copy Protocol (SCP) A network protocol that supports secure file transfers.

Secure Development Lifecycle (SDL) model A process model to include security function consideration as part of the build process of software in an effort to reduce attack surfaces and vulnerabilities.

Secure FTP A method of secure file transfer that involves the tunneling of FTP through an SSH connection. This is different than SFTP. *See* Secure Shell File Transfer Protocol.

Secure Hash Algorithm (SHA) A hash algorithm used to hash block data. The first version is SHA1, with subsequent versions detailing hash digest length: SHA256, SHA384, and SHA512.

Secure Hypertext Transfer Protocol (SHTTP) An alternative to HTTPS, in which only the transmitted pages and POST fields are encrypted. Rendered moot, by and large, by widespread adoption of HTTPS.

Secure Key Exchange Mechanism for Internet (SKEMI) A protocol and standard for the key exchange across the Internet.

Secure/Multipurpose Internet Mail Extensions (S/MIME) An encrypted implementation of the MIME (Multipurpose Internet Mail Extensions) protocol specification.

Secure Shell (SSH) A set of protocols for establishing a secure remote connection to a computer. This protocol requires a client on each end of the connection and can use a variety of encryption protocols.

Secure Shell File Transfer Protocol (SFTP) A secure file transfer subsystem associated with the Secure Shell (SSH) protocol.

Secure Sockets Layer (SSL) An encrypting layer between the session and transport layers of the OSI model designed to encrypt above the transport layer, enabling secure sessions between hosts.

Security Assertion Markup Language (SAML) An XML-based standard for exchanging authentication and authorization data.

security association (SA) An instance of security policy and keying material applied to a specific data flow. Both IKE and IPsec use SAs, although these SAs are independent of one another. IPsec SAs are unidirectional and are unique in each security protocol, whereas IKE SAs are bidirectional. A set of SAs is needed for a protected data pipe, one SA per direction per protocol. SAs are uniquely identified by destination (IPsec endpoint) address, security protocol (AH or ESP), and security parameter index (SPI).

security baseline The end result of the process of establishing an information system's security state. It is a known good configuration resistant to attacks and information theft.

Security Content Automation Protocol (SCAP) A method of using specific protocols and data exchanges to automate the determination of vulnerability management, measurement, and policy compliance across a system or set of systems.

security controls A group of technical, management, or operational policies and procedures designed to implement specific security functionality. Access controls are an example of a security control.

security information event management (SIEM) The name used for a broad range of technological solutions to the collection and analysis of security-related information across the enterprise.

security kernel *See* reference monitor.

security through obscurity An approach to security using the mechanism of hiding information to protect it.

separation (or segregation) of duties A basic control that prevents or detects errors and irregularities by assigning responsibilities to different individuals so that no single individual can commit fraudulent or malicious actions.

Sender Policy Framework (SPF) An e-mail verification system designed to detect spoofed e-mail addresses.

sequence number A number within a TCP packet to maintain TCP connections and conversation integrity.

server-side scripting The processing of scripts on the server side of an Internet connection to prevent client tampering with the process.

service level agreement (SLA) An agreement between parties concerning the expected or contracted uptime associated with a system.

service set identifier (SSID) Identifies a specific 802.11 wireless network. It transmits information about the access point to which the wireless client is connecting.

shadow file The file that stores the encrypted password in a system.

shielded twisted-pair (STP) A physical network connection consisting of two wires twisted and covered with a shield to prevent interference.

shift cipher A cipher that operates by substitution, the replacement of one character for another.

Short Message Service (SMS) A form of text messaging over phone and mobile phone circuits that allows up to 160-character messages to be carried over signaling channels.

shoulder surfing A technique from social engineering where you observe another's action, such as a password entry.

signature database A collection of activity patterns that have already been identified and categorized and that typically indicate suspicious or malicious activity.

Simple Certificate Enrollment Protocol (SCEP) A protocol used in public key infrastructure (PKI) for enrollment and other services.

Simple Mail Transfer Protocol (SMTP) The standard Internet protocol used to transfer e-mail between hosts.

Simple Network Management Protocol (SNMP) A standard protocol used to manage network devices across a network remotely.

Simple Object Access Protocol (SOAP) An XML-based specification for exchanging information associated with web services.

Simple Security Rule The principle that states complexity makes security more difficult and hence values simplicity.

single loss expectancy (SLE) Monetary loss or impact of each occurrence of a threat. SLE = asset value × exposure factor.

single sign-on (SSO) An authentication process by which the user can enter a single user ID and password and then move from application to application or resource to resource without having to supply further authentication information.

slack space Unused space on a disk drive created when a file is smaller than the allocated unit of storage (such as a sector).

smart cards A token with a chip to store cryptographic tokens. Because of the nature of smart cards, they are nearly impossible to copy or counterfeit.

SMS *See* Short Message Service.

smurf attack A method of generating significant numbers of packets for a DoS attack.

sniffer A software or hardware device used to observe network traffic as it passes through a network on a shared broadcast media.

sniffing The use of a software or hardware device (sniffer) to observe network traffic as it passes through a network on a shared broadcast media.

social engineering The art of deceiving another person so that he or she reveals confidential information. This is often accomplished by posing as an individual who should be entitled to have access to the information.

Software as a Service (SaaS) The provisioning of software as a service, commonly known as on-demand software.

software development lifecycle model (SDLC) The processes and procedures employed to develop software. Sometimes also called secure development lifecycle model when security is part of the development process.

solid-state drive (SSD) A mass storage device, such as a hard drive, that is composed of electronic memory as opposed to a physical device of spinning platters.

SONET *See* Synchronous Optical Network Technologies.

spam E-mail that is not requested by the recipient and is typically of a commercial nature. Also known as unsolicited commercial e-mail (UCE).

spam filter A security appliance designed to remove spam at the network layer before it enters e-mail servers.

spear phishing A form of targeted phishing where specific information is included to convince the recipient that the communication is genuine.

spim Spam sent over an instant messaging channel.

spoofing Making data appear to have originated from another source so as to hide the true origin from the recipient.

spyware Malware designed to spy on a use, typically recording information such as keystrokes for passwords.

SQL injection An attack against a SQL engine parser designed to perform unauthorized database activities.

SSD *See* solid-state drive.

SSL stripping attack A specific type of man-in-the-middle attack against SSL.

steganography The use of cryptography to hide communications.

storage area network (SAN) A technology-based storage solution consisting of network attached storage.

STP *See* shielded twisted-pair.

stream cipher An encryption process used against a stream of information, even bit by bit, as opposed to operations performed on blocks.

Structured Exception Handler (SEH) The process used to handle exceptions in the Windows OS core functions.

Structured Query Language (SQL) A language used in relational database queries.

structured threat A threat that has reasonable financial backing and can last for a few days or more. The organizational elements allow for greater time to penetrate and attack a system.

Structured Threat Information eXpression (STIX) A standard XML schema for describing and exchanging threat information.

subnet mask The information that tells a device how to interpret the network and host portions of an IP address.

subnetting The creation of a network within a network by manipulating how an IP address is split into network and host portions.

Subscriber Identity Module (SIM) An integrated circuit or hardware element that securely stores the International Mobile Subscriber Identity (IMSI) and the related key used to identify and authenticate subscribers on mobile telephones.

substitution The switching of one value for another in cryptography.

supervisory control and data acquisition (SCADA) A generic term used to describe the industrial control system networks used to interconnect infrastructure elements (such as manufacturing plants, oil and gas pipelines, power generation and distribution systems, and so on) and computer systems.

switch   A network device that operates at the data layer of the OSI model.

switched port analyzer (SPAN)   A technology employed that can duplicate individual channels crossing a switch to another circuit.

symmetric encryption   Encryption that needs all parties to have a copy of the key, sometimes called a shared secret. The single key is used for both encryption and decryption.

SYN flood   A method of performing DoS by exhausting TCP connection resources through partially opening connections and letting them time-out.

Synchronous Optical Network Technologies (SONET)   A set of standards used for data transfers over optical networks.

systematic risk   A form of risk that can be managed by diversification.

tangible asset   An asset for which a monetary equivalent can be determined. Examples are inventory, buildings, cash, hardware, software, and so on.

TCP wrappers   A host-based networking ACL system, used in some Linux systems to filter network access to Internet Protocol servers.

TCP/IP hijacking   An attack where the attacker intercepts and hijacks an established TCP connection.

Telnet   A network protocol used to provide cleartext bidirectional communication over TCP.

TEMPEST   The U.S. military's name for the field associated with electromagnetic eavesdropping on signals emitted by electronic equipment. *See also* Van Eck phenomenon.

Temporal Key Integrity Protocol (TKIP)   A security protocol used in 802.11 wireless networks.

Terminal Access Controller Access Control System+ (TACACS+)   A remote authentication system that uses the TACACS+ protocol, defined in RFC 1492, and TCP port 49.

threat   Any circumstance or event with the potential to cause harm to an asset.

threat actor   The party behind a threat, although it may be a non-person as in an environmental issue.

threat vector   The method by which a threat actor introduces a specific threat.

three-way handshake   A means of ensuring information transference through a three-step data exchange. Used to initiate a TCP connection.

ticket-granting server (TGS)   A portion of the Kerberos authentication system.

ticket-granting ticket (TGT)   A part of the Kerberos authentication system that is used to prove identity when requesting service tickets.

Time-based One-Time Password (TOTP)   A password that is used once and is only valid during a specific time period.

time bomb   A form of logic bomb in which the triggering event is a date or specific time. *See also* logic bomb.

TKIP   *See* Temporal Key Integrity Protocol.

token   A hardware device that can be used in a challenge-response authentication process.

Transaction Signature (TSIG)   A protocol used as a means of authenticating dynamic DNS records during DNS updates.

Transmission Control Protocol (TCP)   The connection-oriented transport layer protocol for use on the Internet that allows packet-level tracking of a conversation.

Transport Layer Security (TLS)   A newer form of SSL that is now an Internet standard.

transposition   The rearrangement of characters by position as part of cryptographic operations.

trapdoor   *See* backdoor.

Trivial File Transfer Protocol (TFTP)   A simplified version of FTP used for low-overhead file transfers using UDP port 69.

Trojan   A form of malicious code that appears to provide one service (and may indeed provide that service) but that also hides another purpose. This hidden purpose often has a malicious intent. This code may also be referred to as a Trojan horse.

trunking   The process of spanning a single VLAN across multiple switches.

Trusted Automated eXchange of Indicator Information (TAXII) An XML schema for the automated exchange of cyber indicators between trusted parties.

Trusted OS An OS that can provide appropriate levels of security and has mechanisms to provide assurance of security function.

Trusted Platform Module (TPM) A hardware chip to enable trusted computing platform operations.

tunneling The process of packaging packets so that they can traverse a network in a secure, confidential manner.

Unified Extensible Firmware Interface (UEFI) A specification that defines the interface between an OS and the hardware firmware. This is a replacement to BIOS.

unified threat management (UTM) The aggregation of multiple network security products into a single appliance for efficiency purposes.

Uniform Resource Identifier (URI) A set of characters used to identify the name of a resource in a computer system. A URL is a form of URI.

Uniform Resource Locator (URL) A specific character string used to point to a specific item across the Internet.

uninterruptible power supply (UPS) A source of power (generally a battery) designed to provide uninterrupted power to a computer system in the event of a temporary loss of power.

Universal Serial Bus (USB) An industry-standard protocol for communication over a cable to peripherals via a standard set of connectors.

unshielded twisted-pair (UTP) A form of network cabling in which pairs of wires are twisted to reduce crosstalk. Commonly used in LANs.

unstructured threat A threat that has no significant resources or ability—typically an individual with limited skill.

unsystematic risk Risk that cannot be mitigated by diversification. Unsystematic risks can result in loss across all types of risk controls.

usage auditing The process of recording who did what and when on an information system.

user acceptance testing (UAT) The application of acceptance-testing criteria to determine fitness for use according to end-user requirements.

User Datagram Protocol (UDP) A protocol in the TCP/IP protocol suite for the transport layer that does not sequence packets—it is "fire and forget" in nature.

user ID A unique alphanumeric identifier that identifies individuals when logging into or accessing a system.

UTP *See* unshielded twisted-pair.

vampire tap A tap that connects to a network line without cutting the connection.

Van Eck phenomenon Electromagnetic eavesdropping through the interception of electronic signals emitted by electrical equipment. *See also* Tempest.

video teleconferencing (VTC) A business process of using video signals to carry audio and visual signals between separate locations, thus allowing participants to meet via a virtual meeting instead of traveling to a physical location. Modern videoconferencing equipment can provide very realistic connectivity when lighting and backgrounds are controlled.

Vigenère cipher A polyalphabetic substitution cipher that depends on a password.

virtual local area network (VLAN) A broadcast domain inside a switched system.

virtual private network (VPN) An encrypted network connection across another network, offering a private communication channel across a public medium.

virtualization desktop infrastructure (VDI) The use of servers to host virtual desktops by moving the processing to the server and using the desktop machine as merely a display terminal. VDI offers operating efficiencies as well as cost and security benefits.

virus A form of malicious code or software that attaches itself to other pieces of code in order to replicate. Viruses may contain a payload, which is a portion of the code that is designed to execute when a certain condition is met (such as on a certain date). This payload is often malicious in nature.

vishing Phishing over voice circuits, specifically voice over IP (VoIP).

voice over IP (VoIP) The packetized transmission of voice signals (telephony) over Internet Protocol.

vulnerability A weakness in an asset that can be exploited by a threat to cause harm.

WAP *See* Wireless Application Protocol.

war-dialing An attacker's attempt to gain unauthorized access to a computer system or network by discovering unprotected connections to the system through the telephone system and modems.

war-driving The attempt by an attacker to discover unprotected wireless networks by wandering (or driving) around with a wireless device, looking for available wireless access points.

warm site A backup site, off premises, that has hardware but is not configured with data and will take some time to switch over to.

Wassenaar Arrangement A set of rules and regulations concerning dual-use technologies, including cryptography. These rules are related to arms trading and similar national security concerns and impact some cyber security elements.

web application firewall (WAF) A firewall that operates at the application level, specifically designed to protect web applications by examining requests at the application stack level.

WEP *See* Wired Equivalent Privacy.

whaling The targeting of high-value individuals.

white box testing A form of testing where the tester has knowledge of the inner workings of a system.

white listing A listing of items to be allowed by specific inclusion. The opposite of black listing.

wide area network (WAN) A network that spans a large geographic region.

Wi-Fi Protected Access (WPA/WPA2) A protocol to secure wireless communications using a subset of the 802.11i standard.

Wi-Fi Protected Setup (WPS) A network security standard that allows easy setup of a wireless home network.

Wired Equivalent Privacy (WEP) The encryption scheme used to attempt to provide confidentiality and data integrity on 802.11 networks.

wireless access point (WAP) A network access device that facilitates the connection of wireless devices to a network.

Wireless Application Protocol (WAP) A protocol for transmitting data to small handheld devices such as cellular phones.

wireless intrusion detection system (WIDS) An intrusion detection system established to cover a wireless network.

wireless intrusion prevention system (WIPS) An intrusion prevention system established to cover a wireless network.

Wireless Transport Layer Security (WTLS) The encryption protocol used on WAP networks.

worm An independent piece of malicious code or software that self-replicates. Unlike a virus, it does not need to be attached to another piece of code. A worm replicates by breaking into another system and making a copy of itself on this new system. A worm can contain a destructive payload but does not have to.

write blocker A specific interface for a storage media that does not permit writing to occur to the device. This allows copies to be made without altering the device.

X.500 The standard format for directory services including LDAP.

X.509 The standard format for digital certificates.

XML *See* Extensible Markup Language.

XSRF See cross-site request forgery.

XSS See cross-site scripting.

zero-day A name given to a vulnerability whose existence is known, but not to the developer of the software, hence it can be exploited before patches are developed and released.

zombie A machine that is at least partially under the control of a botnet.

Automatic Updates, Windows 7, 424–426
autoplay, 201–202
AV (antivirus) products. *See* antivirus (AV) products
availability
in CIA, 20
hosts and, 254–255
importance of, 253
measuring in risk calculation, 625

hardening (Cont.)
    system hardening. See system hardening
hardware
    encryption devices, 437–438
    installing unauthorized, 81–82
    securing, 436–437
hardware security modules (HSMs)
    hardware encryption devices, 438
    safeguarding cryptographic keys, 147–148
hash values
    in detecting intrusion, 411
    hashing functions and, 99
hashing algorithms
    ensuring forensic data is not modified, 685
    integrity and, 116
    IPsec using, 327
    MD (Message Digest), 101–102
    overview of, 99–100
    RIPEMD (RACE Integrity Primitives Evaluation Message Digest), 101
    SHA (Secure Hash Algorithm), 100–101
    summary, 102–103
    types of encryption algorithms, 96
Haystack, 377
hazards, 611
HD (high-definition) optical media, 280
header manipulation
    client-side attacks, 494
    violating CAN-SPAM act, 701
headers
    client-side attacks, 554
    in e-mail structure, 506–508
    spam filtering and, 430
Health Information Technology for Economic and Clinical Health Act (HITECH), 723–724
Health Insurance Portability and Accountability Act (HIPAA), 723–724
hearsay rule, rules of evidence, 677
Heartbleed vulnerability
    in OpenSSL cryptography, 79
    passworwwds and, 297
heating, ventilation, and air conditioning. See HVAC (heating, ventilation, and air conditioning)
Hellman, Martin, 109–110
heuristic scanning, antivirus products, 427–428

hex characters, 570
hidden files, system forensics and, 686
HIDSs (host-based IDSs)
    active and passive, 393
    advanced capabilities, 393–394
    advantages/disadvantages, 391–393
    defined, 378
    overview of, 388–391
    security devices, 267
hierarchical trust model, 155–157
high availability, 599–600
High Speed Packet Access (HSPA)
    3G mobile networks, 342
    demand for data services and, 339
highly structured threats, information warfare as, 11
hijacking attacks. See TCP/IP hijacking
HIPAA (Health Insurance Portability and Accountability Act), 723–724
HITECH (Health Information Technology for Economic and Clinical Health Act), 723–724
HMAC, IPsec using, 327
HMAC-based One-Time Password (HOTP), 117
hoaxes
    e-mail, 513–514
    security of e-mail and, 509
    social engineering attacks, 77–78
    viruses, 468
honeynets, 397
honeypots, 396–397
host-based IDSs. See HIDSs (host-based IDSs)
host forensics
    file systems, 685–687
    Linux metadata, 688
    overview of, 685
    Windows metadata, 687–688
host hardening, 427–430
    antimalware, 426–427
    antispam, 430–431
    antispyware, 431–432
    AppLocker, 434
    hardening Mac OS X, 421–423
    hardening UNIX/Linux OSs, 417–421
    hardening Windows OSs, 413–417
    hardware security, 436–437
    host-based firewalls, 435–436

host-based security controls, 437–440
    hotfixes, service packs, and patches, 423–426
    machine hardening, 411
    operating system security and, 412
    overview of, 410–411
    pop-up blockers, 432–433
    software baselining, 437
    Trusted OSs, 434–435
    whitelisting and blacklisting applications, 434
    Windows Defender, 431–432
hosts
    calculating, 238
    CompTIA Security+ Exam Objectives, 749–752
    security approaches, 23
    virtualization providing availability and elasticity, 254–255
    vulnerability scanners, 448–449
hot sites, alternative backup sites, 597
hotfixes, host hardening, 423–426
HOTP (HMAC-based One-Time Password), 117
HSMs (hardware security modules)
    hardware encryption devices, 438
    safeguarding cryptographic keys, 147–148
HSPA (High Speed Packet Access)
    3G mobile networks, 342
    demand for data services and, 339
HSTS (HTTP Strict Transport Security), 538–539
HTML (Hypertext Markup Language), 530
HTTP (Hypertext Transfer Protocol)
    for data transfer over web, 537–539
    header manipulation, 554
    Internet services, 242
    retrieving certificates from repositories, 170
    web application firewalls and, 264
HTTP Strict Transport Security (HSTS), 538–539
HTTPS Everywhere, 538
HTTPS (HTTPSecure)
    for data transfer over web, 537–539
    SSL and/or TLS used with, 182
    web application firewalls and, 264

monitoring
 CCTV (closed circuit TV) for, 198–199
 content, 271
 networks, 268–269, 665
 ports, 400
Morris worm
 buffer-overflow attacks, 575
 historical security incidents, 2
MOUs (memorandum of understanding), interoperability agreements, 59
MTA (mail transfer agent), e-mail agents, 506
MTBF (mean time between failures), 624
MTTF (mean time to failure), 625
MTTR (mean time to repair), 624
MTU (Maximum Transmission Unit), packets, 225
MUA (mail user agent), e-mail agents, 506
Multicast Listener Discovery (MLD), in IPv6, 226
Multics Intrusion Detection and Alerting System (MIDAS), 377
multifactor authentication, 310
multiple encryption, 3DES as example of, 104
multiple-factor authentication, 214–215
multiple-input multiple output (MIMO)
 antenna placement and, 361
 features in IEEE 802.11, 348–349
Multipurpose Internet Mail Extensions (MIME) protocol and, 508–509
multitasking, hardening Mac OS X, 422
multpartite nature, of malware, 466
mutual aid agreements, alternative backup sites, 597
mutual authentication, 310

N

NAC (Network Admission Control), 268
NADIR (Network Audit Director and Intrusion Repair), 377
NAP (Network Access Protection)
 controlling access to networks, 267
 hardening Windows OSs, 413–414
NAS (network access server), 312
NAS (Network Attached Storage), 255–256

NAT (Network Address Translation), 238–240, 261
nation-states
 current threat environment, 5–7
 types of threats, 10–11
National Institute of Science and Technology. See NIST (National Institute of Science and Technology)
National White Collar Crime Center (NW3C), 698
NDP (Network Discovery Protocol), 232
near field communication (NFC), 347
need to know principle
 Brewer-Nash model, 35
 in security, 46
Nessus, network vulnerability scanner, 448–449
NetFlow
 collecting network data, 665
 in network forensics, 689
NetRanger, monitoring network links, 378
NetStumbler, attacks on IEEE 802.11, 351–352
network access control, 267–268
Network Access Protection (NAP)
 controlling access to networks, 267
 hardening Windows OSs, 413–414
network access server (NAS), 312
Network Address Translation (NAT), 238–240, 261
Network Admission Control (NAC), 268
network analyzers. See sniffers/sniffing
Network Attached Storage (NAS), 255–256
Network Audit Director and Intrusion Repair (NADIR), 377
network-based IDSs. See NIDSs (network-based IDSs)
network-based intrusion detection, 267
Network Discovery Protocol (NDP), 232
network fabric, flat networks, 243
network hardening
 device configuration, 442–443
 IPv4 vs. IPv6, 443–444
 overview of, 441
 securing management interfaces, 443
 software updates, 442
 VLAN management, 443

network interface cards (NICs)
 overview of, 256–257
 promiscuous mode, 383–384, 398
network layer (layer 3), OSI model, routers operating at, 258
network operating systems (NOSs), 410
network operations center (NOC), 268–269
network segmentation, limiting communication between devices, 457–458
networks/networking
 access control, 267–268
 architectures, 221–222
 CompTIA Security+ Exam Objectives, 738–740
 concentrators, 264
 content and malware inspection, 273
 content filters, 272
 datagrams, 226–227
 DLP (data loss prevention), 272
 DMZ (demilitarized zone), 240–241
 enclaves, 243–244
 extranet, 242–243
 firewalls, 260–264
 flat networks, 243
 forensics, 689
 hubs, bridges, and switches, 257–258
 ICMP (Internet Control Message Protocol), 229–231
 IDSs (intrusion detection systems), 267
 Internet, 241–242
 intranet, 242–243
 IP addresses and subnetting, 236–238
 IP (Internet Protocol), 226
 IPv4 vs. IPv6, 231–232
 load balancers, 269
 modems, 265–266
 monitoring and diagnostics, 268–269, 665
 NAT (Network Address Translation), 238–240
 network taps by protocol analyzers, 399
 NICs (network interface cards), 256–257
 overview of, 220, 256
 packet delivery, 233–236
 packets, 225–226
 PBX (private branch exchange), 266

privilege management infrastructure (PMI), 170
privileges
    defined, 288
    escalation, 652
    jailbreaking, 456
    least privilege, 24–25
    managing, 288–289
    separation of privilege, 25–26
    using low-privilege machine to access sensitive information, 191
    Windows OSs, 298–300
procedures, 55
    defined, 43
    developing, 43–44
    incident response, 54
    physical security, 200
process ID (PID), hardening UNIX OSs, 418
process models, for software development, 559–560
production systems, patching, 446
productivity, web security gateways monitoring, 271
program evaluation and review technique (PERT) charts, 626
programs. See applications
promiscuous mode, NICs and, 383–384, 398
promotions, human resources policies, 48
proof of possession, public keys, 138
Protected EAP (PEAP)
    current security methods, 357
    PEAP-TLS, 312
Protected Health Information (PHI), 723
protection, in operational model of computer security, 20
protection rings, OS security and, 410
protocol analyzers. See also sniffers/sniffing, 398–399
protocols, network, 223–225
proxies
    application layer, 262–263
    proxy attacks, 270–271
    proxy servers, 270
    SSL/TLS, 535
prudent person principle, 53
ps command, viewing running services on UNIX OSs, 418
PSTN (public switched telephone network), 60
psychological acceptability, Saltzer and Schroeder's eight principles of security design, 29
PTZ (pan, tilt, zoom) cameras, 199

public CAs
    choosing between public and in-house CAs, 152–153
    outsourced CAs compared with, 153
    overview of, 151–152
public clouds, 284
Public Key Certificates (PKCs), 168, 169
public key cryptography. See asymmetric encryption
Public Key Cryptography Standards. See PKCS (Public Key Cryptography Standards)
public key infrastructure. See PKI (public key infrastructure)
public keys
    certificate repositories, 143
    CSR (certificate signing request), 138
    how PGP works, 180
    man-in-the-middle attacks, 129
    private keys compared with, 130
    proof of possession, 138
public switched telephone network (PSTN), 60
public Wi-Fi, securing, 362

■ Q

QA (quality assurance), change management and, 635
Qakbot worm, isolating, 662
QCs (Qualified Certificates), 170
qualitative risk assessment
    adding objectivity to, 621–622
    comparing with quantitative assessment, 625
    defined, 611
    overview of, 620–621
quality assurance (QA), change management and, 635
quantitative risk assessment
    defined, 611
    overview of, 621
quantum cryptanalysis, 114
quantum cryptography, 113–114
quantum mechanics, 113–114
quarantine, isolating incidents, 661

■ R

RACE Integrity Primitives Evaluation Message Digest (RIPEMD), 101
radio frequency. See RF (radio frequency)

RADIUS (Remote Authentication Dial-In User Service)
    accounting, 314
    authentication, 312–314
    authorization, 314
    overview of, 312
    remote access vulnerabilities, 329–330
RAID (Redundant Array of Independent Disks), 601–602
rainbow tables, 102
random numbers
    cryptography and, 566
    use with encryption algorithms, 98
ransomware, 473
Rapid Spanning Tree Protocol (RSTP), 243
RAs (registration authorities)
    local, 132–133
    overview of, 131–132
    PKIX standard and, 168
    services provided by, 129
RAS (remote access server), 305
RATs (remote access trojans), 496, 653
RBAC (role-based access control), 303
RBL (Real-time Blackhole List), 515
RC (Rivest Cipher)
    IEEE 802.11 attacks on RC4, 353
    RC4 used for confidentiality in WEP, 350
    RC4 used for SSL/TLS encryption, 533
    RC5 supported by WTLS, 340
    versions of, 106–107
RDP (Remote Desktop Protocol), 322
real (associative or physical) evidence, 676
Real-time Blackhole List (RBL), 515
real time, HIDSs operating in, 388
reciprocal sites, alternative backup sites, 597
records, security training and, 58
recovery agent, 150
recovery point objectives (RPOs)
    disaster recovery, 591
    failure and recovery timing, 601
recovery/reconstitution procedures, incident response, 665–666
recovery time objectives (RTO), disaster recovery, 591
red flag rules, FTC, 726
redundancy
    RAID (Redundant Array of Independent Disks), 601–602
    of spare parts, 602–603

smart cards, 280
smartphones, 339
SMTP (Simple Mail Transfer Protocol)
    controlling port 25 on mail
      servers, 514
    e-mail protocols, 505
    UNIX baselines and, 417
smurf attacks, 480–481
SNA (Systems Network
    Architecture), 224
snapshots, virtual machines, 254
sniffers/sniffing
    checking own connections, 539
    observing network traffic for
      unauthorized access, 282
    overview of, 479
    use for attacks on IEEE 802.11, 352
SNMP (Simple Network Management
    Protocol)
    changing community strings, 443
    interoperability and, 269
    managing routers, 259
    managing switches, 258
    software updates and, 442
Snort, NIDS tools, 387–388
social engineering
    hoaxes, 77–78
    obtaining insider information,
      74–75
    overview of, 73–74
    phishing attacks, 57, 75–76
    reverse social engineering, 77
    shoulder surfing, 76–77
    spam, 76
    types of attacks, 478
    vishing attacks, 76
Social-Engineering Toolkit (SET), 496
social media/social networking
    alerts regarding new threats and
      security trends, 57
    human resources policies, 49
    worms and, 469
software. *See also* applications
    baselines of host software, 437,
      448–449
    change control workflow, 641
    change management and, 636
    exploits, 492–493
    host-based firewalls, 435–436
    installing unauthorized, 81–82
    patches, 4, 13, 426
    updates, 425, 442, 473
    versions and change
      management, 636
    whitelisting and blacklisting, 434

Software as a Service (SaaS)
    cloud computing and, 284
    DRM (digital rights
      management) and, 122
Software Assurance Forum for
    Excellence in Code (SAFECode), 560
software development, 558
    application attacks, 572
    application configuration
      baseline, 579
    application hardening, 578–579
    application patch
      management, 579
    arbitrary/remote code
      execution, 578
    attachments as attack vector, 577
    buffer-overflow attacks, 575–576
    bug tracking, 571–572
    client-side attacks, 577
    coding phase, 562–566
    design phase, 562
    error/exception handling, 568
    fuzzing, 571
    injections, 573–575
    input/output validation, 568–571
    integer overflow attacks, 576
    LSOs (locally shared objects), 577
    NoSQL database vs. SQL
      database, 579
    OVAL (Open Vulnerability and
      Assessment Language), 578
    process models for, 559–560
    requirements phase, 561–562
    review and Q&A, 581–583
    secure coding concepts, 568
    securing development
      lifecycle, 560
    server-side vs. client-side
      validation, 579–580
    software engineering
      process, 559
    testing phase, 567–568
    threat modeling and attack
      surface area minimization,
      560–561
    XSRF (cross-site request
      forgery), 576–577
    XSS (cross-site scripting) attacks,
      572–573
    zero-day vulnerabilities, 577
Software Engineering Institute. *See* SEI
    (Software Engineering Institute)
software engineering process, 559
Software Restrictive Policies
    (SRP), 434

solid state drives (SSDs)
    forensics and, 688
    overview of, 281
Sony hack, 6–7
SOX (Sarbanes-Oxley Act),
    637, 703
spam
    antispam products, 430–431
    e-mail and, 514–516
    overview of, 484
    SIDF (Sender ID Framework)
      blocking, 516–517
    social engineering attacks, 76
Spam URI Real-time Block Lists
    (SURBL), in blocking spam, 516
SPAN (Switched Port Analyzer)
    IDSs supporting, 399
    overview of, 400
Spanning Tree Protocol (STP),
    243, 258
spare parts, redundancy of, 602–603
spear phishing attacks, 75, 485
SPF (Sender Policy Framework)
    record, in blocking spam, 517
spim attacks, 76, 485
spiral model, software development, 559
spoliation, altering digital evidence,
    676, 680
spoofing attacks
    DKIM (DomainKeys Identified
      Mail) detecting e-mail
      spoofing, 517
    e-mail spoofing, 480
    IP address spoofing, 480–481
    overview of, 480
    sequence numbers and,
      481–482
    trusted relationships and, 481
SPR (system problem report), 643
spyware
    antispyware products, 431–432
    overview of, 471
SQL database, 579
SQL injection attacks, 573–574
SQL Slammer, 572
SRP (Software Restrictive Policies), 434
SS7 (Signaling System 7), 224
SSDs (solid state drives)
    forensics and, 688
    overview of, 281
SSH (Secure Shell)
    DH protocol used by, 110
    securing network functions,
      321–322
    STFP using, 540

■ X